ACKNOWLEDGEMENTS

We are very grateful to many people for the work and expertise that contributed to this book. We owe a particular debt to Suzanne, Hannah, Emily, Charlotte, Jane and Michael for their patience and support while we researched, read and wrote.

We greatly benefited from the encouragement and the unstinting dedication to the project of Sonny Leong at Cavendish. We are very grateful to Jo Jacomb and Katherine Haw, to Marilyn Lannigan for her conscientious research, and to Denis Lanser, Dr Michael Watson, MA Ramjohn, Ruth Hayward, and Ann Holmes for their excellent contributions on criminal law, trusts, and negligence and employment law. We owe great thanks to Richard Hough for his dedicated and expert work on criminal justice and criminal procedure, and we benefited substantially from Vicki Scoble's outstanding professionalism in civil process and civil law. We are indebted to Professor Hazel Genn, Liz Rodgers, Michael Fealy, Jon Lloyd Steve Greenfield, Carolyn Bracknell, David Stott, Miceál Barden and Dr Janice Richardson who made very valuable comments on draft chapters. We thank Natalie Lexton for her computer skills. We are indebted to Vidhya Jayaprakash, Sheena Joseph and M. Ganapathi, for their tireless professional assiduity in the production of the text, and meticulous analysis of the manuscript.

Many others have given encouragement, observations and assistance, or have stimulated our thinking in a helpful way. Thanks are thus due to Doreen and Ivor Slapper, Clifford, Maxine, Pav, Anish, the late Raie Schwartz, David and Julie Whight, Professor Robert Reiner, Hugh McLaughlan, Ben Fitzpatrick, Professor Jeffrey Jowell, Professor Ian Dennis, Professor Tony Lentin, Frances Thomas, Dr Matthew Weait, Alison Morris, Patrick Whight, Frances Gibb at *The Times* and The Rt Hon The Lord Woolf.

PREFACE

It is difficult to dissent from the sentiment at the opening of chapter seven of *A Series of Unfortunate Events – The Bad Beginning* by Lemony Snicket:

"There are many, many types of books in the world, which makes good sense, because there are many, many types of people, and everybody wants to read something different."

So far, so good. It is harder, however, to agree with how the text goes on in the following passage:

"But one type of book that practically no one likes to read is a book about the law. Books about the law are notorious for being very long, very dull, and very difficult to read."

We are aware that, certainly, there have been dull law books published over the centuries. However, we hope it is not true that all long books about law are necessarily dull.

We have aimed in this text to provide the reader with a clear and accurate explanation of how the English legal system currently works, and the actual content of English law in all of its key areas of operation. Where we have deemed it appropriate, we have aimed to put a legal rule or principle in its social, historical or economic context. We have also put several areas of law into some legal theory settings. Given a little depth in another dimension, a plain legal rule will often be not just easier to understand but also more interesting.

English law probably exercises more influence, for better or worse, over people's lives across the world than any other set of legal principles and procedures. This is certainly so in most of the 53 members of the Commonwealth, including the considerable jurisdictions of places such as Canada, Pakistan, India and Australia. The population of the Commonwealth is 1.8 billion – that is almost a third of the people on the earth. It is also worthy of note that the original law and legal systems in North America were largely based on the principles of English law.

Few people go through life without, at various stages, developing strong opinions about the desirability or otherwise of some aspect of law. Moreover, lawyers constitute about one fifth of members in the House of Commons in the British Parliament, and it is clear that many debates about law are very important because the way the debates are resolved ultimately has a substantial effect upon the way we live.

We have, therefore, in this text allowed a critical element into our explanations and discussions. We have thought it helpful to present the legal theory underlying policies and law in many of the chapters of this book. At the end of the last century, a great many major changes were made to the English legal system and several areas of English law.

Since the first edition of this book in 2000, there have been myriad changes to the English legal system, and to substantive parts of English law. Many parts of civil process, and the criminal justice system have been legislatively changed. Legislation has also affected much of the law related to business and employment. The common law has developed very substantial parts of criminal law, contract law, the civil law of negligence, and of human rights jurisprudence. All parts of the book have been updated and revised.

This book is supported by website that provides access to periodic updates as they occur.

The book has been written to cover, comprehensively, all the main subjects of English law, and we have endeavoured to ensure that the text is legally up to date as at January, 2006.

Gary Slapper

David Kelly

April, 2006

CONTENTS

6   THE LAW OF CONTRACT   251

8 THE TORT OF NEGLIGENCE 405

14 THE CRIMINAL PROCESS: (2) THE PROSECUTION   845

TABLE OF CASES

Table of Cases

Table of Cases

TABLE OF STATUES

TABLE OF STATUTORY INSTRUMENTS

TABLE OF EC LEGISLATION

TABLE OF ABBREVIATIONS

ABWOR	Assistance By Way Of Representation
AC	Appeal Cases
ACAS	Advisory, Conciliation and Arbitration Service
ACLEC	Advisory Committee on Legal Education and Conduct
ACSA	Anti-Terrorism, Crime and Security Act
ADR	Alternative Dispute Resolution
AGM	Annual General Meeting
AJA	Administration of Justice Act
All ER	All England Law Reports
AOE	Attachments of Earnings orders
APR	Annual Percentage Rate
BA	Bail Act
BCS	British Crime Survey
BIS	Bail Information Schemes
BNA	Business Names Act
C(AICE)A	Companies (Audit, Investigations and Community Enterprise) Act
CA	Children Act
CAA	Criminal Appeal Act
CAFCASS	Children And Family Court Advisory and Support Service
CC	Competition Commission
CCA	Consumer Credit Act
CCPs	Chief Crown Prosecutors
CCRC	Criminal Cases Review Commission
CCS	Consumer Complaints Service
CDA	Crime and Disorder Act
CDDA	Company Directors Disqualification Act
CDS	Criminal Defence Service
CEDR	Centre for Effective Dispute Resolution
Ch D	Chancery Division
CHCC	Criminal High Cost Case
CIB	Companies Investigations Branch
Civil PRC	Civil Procedure Rule Committee
CJA	Criminal Justice Act
CJPA	Criminal Justice and Police Act
CJPOA	Criminal Justice and Public Order Act
CJR	Civil Justice Review
CLA	Criminal Law Act
CLCs	Citizens' Law Centres
CLS	Community Legal Service
CLSA	Courts and Legal Services Act
CLSPs	Community Legal Service Partnerships
CPIA	Criminal Procedure and Investigations Act

CPR	Civil Procedure Rules
CPS	Crown Prosecution Service
Crim PRC	Criminal Procedure Rule Committee
CSA	Child Support Agency
CSOs	Community Support Officers
DBE	Dames of the British Empire
DCA	Department for Constitutional Affairs
DCOA	Deregulation and Contracting Out Act
DFB	Deductions From Benefits
DMC	Donatio Mortis Causa
DPMCA	Domestic Proceedings and Magistrates' Courts Act
DPP	Director of Public Prosecutions
DTI	Department of Trade and Industry
EAT	Employment Appeal Tribunal
EC	European Community
ECHR	European Convention on Human Rights
ECJ	European Court of Justice
ECR	European Court Reports
ECtHR	European Court of Human Rights
EEC	European Economic Community
EGM	Extraordinary General Meeting
ERA	Employment Rights Act
EU	European Union
FAINS	Family Advice and Information Networks Pilot Project
FCT	First County Trust
FIFO	'First In First Out'
FRRP	Financial Reporting Review Panel
FSA	Financial Services Authority
GAD	Government Actuary's Department
GAR	Guaranteed Annuity Rate
GPSR	General Product Safety Regulations
HMCS	Her Majesty's Courts Service
HRA	Human Rights Act
IA	Insolvency Act
ILEX	Institute of Legal Executives
IRA	Infants' Relief Act
JA	Juries Act
JdA	Judicature Act
JP	Justice of the Peace
JPA	Justices of the Peace Act
JSB	Judicial Studies Board
KB/QB	King's/Queen's Bench

LCD	Lord Chancellor's Department
LECG	Law and Economics Consulting Group
LLP	Limited Liability Partnership
LLPA	Limited Liability Partnership Act
LLPR	Limited Liability Partnership Regulations
LPC	Legal Practice Course
LSC	Legal Services Commission
LSO	Legal Services Ombudsman
MA	Misrepresentation Act
MCA	Magistrates' Courts Act
MCCs	Magistrates' Courts Committees
MDPs	Multi-Disciplinary Partnerships
MNPs	Multi-National Partnerships
MP	Member of Parliament
MPS	Metropolitan Police Service
NAO	National Audit Office
NSPs	Non-Solicitor Partners
OFT	Office of Fair Trading
OSS	Office for the Supervision of Solicitors
PA	Partnership Act
PACE	Police and Criminal Evidence Act
PAPs	Pre-Action Protocols
PC	Practising Certificate
PCA	Parliamentary Commissioner for Administration
PCC(S)A	Powers of the Criminal Courts (Sentencing) Act
PDS	Public Defender Service
PNC	Police National Computer
POA	Prosecution of Offences Act
PSU	Practice Standards Unit
QBD	Queen's Bench Division
QCs	Queen's Counsel
RDCO	Recovery of Defence Costs Order
SCA	Supreme Court Act
SEA	Single European Act
SFO	Serious Fraud Office
SGSA	Supply of Goods and Services Act
SIA	Security Industry Authority
SJ	Solicitors Journal
SoGA	Sale of Goods Act
SSGA	Sale and Supply of Goods Act
TDA	Trade Descriptions Act
TLATA	Trusts of Land and Appointment of Trustees Act

TULR(C)A	Trade Union Labour Relations (Consolidation) Act
TURERA	Trade Union Reform and Employment Rights Act
UCTA	Unfair Contract Terms Act
VAT	Value Added Tax
VW	Volkswagen
WLR	Weekly Law Reports
YJCEA	Youth Justice and Criminal Evidence Act

CHAPTER 1

INTRODUCTION TO LAW

1.1 The Nature of Law

One of the most obvious and most central characteristics of all societies is that they must possess some degree of order to permit the members to interact over a sustained period of time. Different societies, however, have different forms of order. Some societies are highly regimented with strictly enforced social rules whereas others continue to function in what outsiders might consider a very unstructured manner with apparently few strict rules being enforced.

Order is therefore necessary, but the form through which order is maintained is certainly not universal as many anthropological studies have shown (see Mansell and Meteyard, *A Critical Introduction to Law*, 1999).

In our society, law plays an important part in the creation and maintenance of social order. We must be aware, however, that law, as we know it, is not the only means of creating order. Even in our society, order is not solely dependent on law, but also involves questions of a more general moral and political character. This book is not concerned with providing a general explanation of the form of order. It is concerned, more particularly, with describing and explaining the key institutional aspects of that particular form of order that is legal order.

The most obvious way in which law contributes to the maintenance of social order is the way in which it deals with disorder or conflict. This book, therefore, is particularly concerned with the institutions and procedures, both civil and criminal, through which law operates to ensure a particular form of social order by dealing with various conflicts when they arise.

Law is a formal mechanism of social control and as such it is essential that the student of law be fully aware of the nature of that formal structure. There are, however, other aspects to law that are less immediately apparent, but of no less importance, such as the inescapable political nature of law. Some textbooks focus more on this particular aspect of law than others and these differences become evident in the particular approach adopted by the authors. The approach favoured by the authors of this book is to recognise that studying English law is not just about learning legal rules but is also about considering a social institution of fundamental importance.

1.2 Categories of Law

There are various ways of categorising law which initially tend to confuse the non-lawyer and the new student of law. What follows will set out these categorisations in their usual dual form whilst at the same time trying to overcome the confusion inherent in such duality. It is impossible to avoid the confusing repetition of the same terms to mean different things and, indeed, the purpose of this section is to make sure that students are aware of the fact that the same words can have different meanings depending upon the context in which they are used.

1.2.1 Common law and civil law

In this particular juxtaposition, these terms are used to distinguish two distinct legal systems and approaches to law. The use of the term 'common law' in this context refers to all those legal systems which have adopted the historic English legal system. Foremost amongst these is, of course, the United States, but many other Commonwealth and former Commonwealth countries retain a common law system. The term 'civil law' refers to those other jurisdictions which have adopted the European continental system of law derived essentially from ancient Roman law, but owing much to the Germanic tradition.

The usual distinction to be made between the two systems is that the common law system tends to be case centred and hence judge centred, allowing scope for a discretionary, *ad hoc*, pragmatic approach to the particular problems that appear before the courts, whereas the civil law system tends to be a codified body of general abstract principles which control the exercise of judicial discretion. In reality, both these views are extremes, with the former over-emphasising the extent to which the common law judge can impose his discretion and the latter under-estimating the extent to which continental judges have the power to exercise judicial discretion. It is perhaps worth mentioning at this point that the European Court of Justice (ECJ), established, in theory, on civil law principles, is in practice increasingly recognising the benefits of establishing a body of case law.

It has to be recognised, and indeed the English courts do so, that, although the ECJ is not bound by the operation of the doctrine of *stare decisis* (see 2.4.1 below), it still does not decide individual cases on an *ad hoc* basis and, therefore, in the light of a perfectly clear decision of the European Court, national courts will be reluctant to refer similar cases to its jurisdiction. Thus, after the ECJ decided in *Grant v South West Trains Ltd* (1998) that Community law did not cover discrimination on grounds of sexual orientation, the High Court withdrew a similar reference in *R v Secretary of State for Defence ex p Perkins (No 2)* (1998).

1.2.2 Common law and equity

In this particular juxtaposition, the terms refer to a particular division within the English legal system.

The common law has been romantically and inaccurately described as the law of the common people of England. In fact, the common law emerged as the product of a particular struggle for political power. Prior to the Norman Conquest of England in 1066, there was no unitary, national legal system. The emergence of the common law represents the imposition of such a unitary system under the auspices and control of a centralised power in the form of a sovereign king; in that respect, it represented the assertion and affirmation of that central sovereign power.

Traditionally, much play is made about the circuit of judges travelling round the country establishing the 'King's peace' and, in so doing, selecting the best local customs and making them the basis of the law of England in a piecemeal but totally altruistic procedure. The reality of this process was that the judges were asserting the authority of the central State and its legal forms and institutions over the disparate and fragmented State and legal forms of the earlier feudal period. Thus, the common law was common *to* all in application, but certainly was not common *from* all. (The contemporary meaning and relevance and operation of the common law will be considered in more detail later in this chapter and in Chapter 2.)

By the end of the 13th century, the central authority had established its precedence at least partly through the establishment of the common law. Originally, courts had been no more than an adjunct of the King's Council, the *Curia Regis*, but gradually the common law courts began to take on a distinct institutional existence in the form of the Courts of Exchequer, Common Pleas and King's Bench. With this institutional autonomy, however, there developed an institutional sclerosis, typified by a reluctance to deal with matters that were not or could not be processed in the proper *form of action*. Such a refusal to deal with substantive injustices because they did not fall within the particular parameters of procedural and formal constraints by necessity led to injustice and the need to remedy the perceived weaknesses in the common law system. The response was the development of *equity*.

Plaintiffs unable to gain access to the three common law courts might directly appeal to the sovereign, and such pleas would be passed for consideration and decision to the Lord Chancellor, who acted as the king's conscience. As the common law courts became more formalistic and more inaccessible, pleas to the Chancellor correspondingly increased and eventually this resulted in the emergence of a specific court constituted to deliver 'equitable' or 'fair' decisions in cases which the common law courts declined to deal with. As had happened with the common law, the decisions of the Courts of Equity established principles which were used to decide later cases, so it should not be thought that the use of equity meant that judges had discretion to decide cases on the basis of their personal idea of what was just in each case.

The division between the common law courts and the Courts of Equity continued until they were eventually combined by the Judicature Acts (JdA) 1873–75. Prior to this legislation, it was essential for a party to raise an action in the appropriate court – for example, the courts of law would not implement equitable principles; the Acts, however, provided that every court had the power and the duty to decide cases in line with common law and equity, with the latter being paramount in the final analysis.

Some would say that, as equity was never anything other than a gloss on common law, it is perhaps appropriate, if not ironic, that now both systems have been effectively subsumed under the one term: common law.

Common law remedies are available as of right. Remedies in equity are discretionary, in other words they are awarded at the will of the court and depend on the behaviour and situation of the party claiming such remedies. This means that, in effect, the court does not have to award an equitable remedy where it considers that the conduct of the party seeking such an award has been such that the party does not deserve it (*D & C Builders v Rees* (1965)).

1.2.3 Common law and statute law

This particular conjunction follows on from the immediately preceding section, in that the common law here refers to the substantive law and procedural rules that have been created by the judiciary through the decisions in the cases they have heard. Statute law, on the other hand, refers to law that has been created by Parliament in the form of legislation. Although there has been a significant increase in statute law in the 20th and 21st centuries, the courts still have an important role to play in creating and operating law generally and in determining the operation of legislation in particular. The relationship of this pair of concepts is of central importance and is considered in more detail in Chapters 2 and 5.

1.2.4 Private law and public law

There are two different ways of understanding the division between private and public law.

At one level, the division relates specifically to actions of the State and its functionaries vis à vis the individual citizen, and the legal manner in which, and form of law through which, such relationships are regulated: public law. In the 19th century, it was at least possible to claim, as AV Dicey did, that there was no such thing as public law in this distinct administrative sense and that the powers of the State with regard to individuals were governed by the ordinary law of the land, operating through the normal courts. Whether such a claim was accurate or not when it was made – and it is unlikely – there certainly can be no doubt now that public law constitutes a distinct and growing area of law in its own right. The growth of public law in this sense has mirrored the growth and increased activity of the contemporary State, and has seen its role as seeking to regulate such activity. The crucial role of judicial review in relation to public law will be considered in some detail in Chapter 6, and the content and impact of the Human Rights Act 1998 will be considered later in this chapter.

There is, however, a second aspect to the division between private and public law. One corollary of the divide is that matters located within the private sphere are seen as purely a matter for individuals themselves to regulate, without the interference of the State, whose role is limited to the provision of the forum for deciding contentious issues and mechanisms for the enforcement of such decisions. Matters within the public sphere, however, are seen as issues relating to the interest of the State and general public, and as such are to be protected and prosecuted by the State. It can be seen, therefore, that the category to which any dispute is allocated is of crucial importance to how it is dealt with. Contract may be thought of as the classic example of private law, but the extent to which this purely private legal area has been subjected to the regulation of public law, in such areas as consumer protection, should not be under-estimated.

Equally, the most obvious example of public law in this context would be criminal law. Feminists have argued, however, that the allocation of domestic matters to the sphere of private law has led to a denial of a general interest in the treatment and protection of women. By defining domestic matters as private, the State and its functionaries have denied women access to its power to protect themselves from abuse. In doing so, it is suggested that, in fact, such categorisation has reflected and maintained the social domination of men over women.

1.2.5 Civil law and criminal law

Civil law is a form of private law and involves the relationships between individual citizens. It is the legal mechanism through which individuals can assert claims against others and have those rights adjudicated and enforced. The purpose of civil law is to settle disputes between individuals and to provide remedies; it is not concerned with punishment as such. The role of the State in relation to civil law is to establish the general framework of legal rules and to provide the legal institutions to operate those rights, but the activation of the civil law is strictly a matter for the individuals concerned. Contract, tort and property law are generally aspects of civil law.

Criminal law, on the other hand, is an aspect of public law and relates to conduct which the State considers with disapproval and which it seeks to control and/or eradicate. Criminal law involves the *enforcement* of particular forms of behaviour, and the State, as the representative of society, acts positively to ensure compliance. Thus, criminal cases are brought by the State in the name of the Crown and cases are reported in the form of *Regina v ...* (*Regina* is simply Latin for 'queen' and case references are usually abbreviated to *R v ...*), whereas civil cases are referred to by the names of the parties involved in the dispute, for example, *Smith v Jones*. In criminal law, a prosecutor prosecutes a defendant (or 'the accused'). In civil law, a claimant sues (or 'brings a claim against') a defendant.

In distinguishing between criminal and civil actions, it has to be remembered that the same event may give rise to both. For example, where the driver of a car injures someone through their reckless driving, they will be liable to be prosecuted under the Road Traffic legislation, but at the same time, they will also be responsible to the injured party in the civil law relating to the tort of negligence.

A crucial distinction between criminal and civil law is the level of proof required in the different types of cases. In the criminal case, the prosecution is required to prove that the defendant is guilty beyond reasonable doubt, whereas in a civil case, the degree of proof is much lower and has only to be on the balance of probabilities. This difference in the level of proof raises the possibility of someone being able to succeed in a civil case, although there may not be sufficient evidence for a criminal prosecution. Indeed, this strategy has been used successfully in a number of cases against the police where the Crown Prosecution Service (CPS) has considered there to be insufficient evidence to support a criminal conviction for assault. A successful civil action may even put pressure on the CPS to reconsider its previous decision not to prosecute (see further Chapter 14 below for an examination of the CPS).

In February 2004, the then Home Secretary, David Blunkett, caused no little consternation when, during a visit to India, he expressed the view that the standard of proof in criminal cases relating to terrorism should be reduced from the present criminal level to that of the civil law. That proposal was not included in a subsequent discussion paper issued by the Home Office in February of that year, although it did canvas the possibility of 'pre-emptive' trials for suspected terrorists to be held before special courts and the use of the civil standard of proof in relation to those suspected of being on the periphery of terrorist organisations.

It is essential not to confuse the standard of proof with the burden of proof. The latter refers to the need for the person making an allegation, be it the prosecution in a criminal case or the claimant in a civil case, to prove the facts of the case. In certain circumstances, once the prosecution/claimant has demonstrated certain facts, the burden of proof may shift to the defendant/respondent to provide evidence to prove their lack of culpability. The reverse burden of proof may be either *legal* or *evidential*, which in practice indicates the degree of evidence they have to provide in order to meet the burden they are under.

It should also be noted that the distinction between civil and criminal responsibility is further blurred in cases involving what may be described as hybrid offences. These are situations where a court awards a civil order against an individual, on the balance of probabilities, but with the attached sanction that any breach of the order will be subject to punishment as a criminal offence. As examples of this procedure may be cited the Protection from Harassment Act 1997 and the provision for the making of Anti Social Behaviour Orders available under s 1(1) of the Crime and Disorder Act 1998. Both of these provisions are of considerable interest and deserve some attention in their own right. The Protection from Harassment Act was introduced as a measure to deal with 'stalking', the harassment of individuals by people continuously following them, and allowed the victim of harassment to get a court order to prevent the stalking. Whereas stalking may have been the high profile source of the Act, it is possible, however, that its most useful provision, if it is used appropriately, may actually lie in providing more protection for women who are subject to assault and harassment from their partners than is available under alternative criminal or civil law procedures. In March 2001, the Act was used successfully against *The Sun* newspaper in an action by a black clerk in a City of London police station. The newspaper had published three articles about the woman after she had reported four police officers in her station for making racist comments about a Somali asylum seeker and as a consequence had received hate mail. The paper admitted that the articles were 'strident, aggressive and inflammatory' and the judge held that they were also racist. In his view, the Protection from Harassment Act gave the claimant 'a right to protection from harassment by all the world including the press'. The Court of Appeal subsequently refused an application by the newspaper to strike out the action (*Thomas v News Group Newspapers* (2002)) and consequently it can be concluded that the Act potentially offers significant protection to the ordinary members of the public who have been the object of what many see as press harassment. Such protection is, of course, additional to any other protection provided under the Human Rights Act 1998. Anti Social Behaviour Orders, available against individuals aged 10 or over on the application of the police or local authority, may be made in situations where there has been intimidation through threats, violence and a mixture of unpleasant actions – persistent unruly behaviour by a small group on an estate; families who resort to abuse when complaints are made to them; vandalism; serious and persistent organised bullying of children; persistent racial or homophobic harassment; and persistent anti-social behaviour as a result of drug or alcohol abuse. The role of anti-social orders was significantly extended under the Anti-social Behaviour Act 2003.

Whereas these Acts may seem initially to offer a welcome additional protection to the innocent individual, it has to be recognised that such advantage is achieved in effect by criminalising what was, and remains, in other circumstances non-criminal behaviour, and deciding its applicability on the basis of the lower civil law burden of proof. A further example of the relationship between criminal law and civil law may be seen in the courts' power to make an order for the confiscation of a person's property under the Proceeds of Crime Act 2002.

It should not be forgotten that although prosecution of criminal offences is usually the prerogative of the State, it remains open to the private individual to initiate a private prosecution in relation to a criminal offence. It has to be remembered, however, that even in the private prosecution, the test of the burden of proof remains the criminal one requiring the facts to be proved beyond reasonable doubt. An example of the problems inherent in such private actions can be seen in the case of Stephen Lawrence, the young black man who was gratuitously stabbed to death by a gang of white racists whilst standing at a bus stop in London. Although there was strong suspicion, and indeed evidence, against particular individuals, the CPS declined to press the charges against them on the basis of insufficiency of evidence. When the lawyers of the Lawrence family mounted a private prosecution against the suspects, the action failed for want of sufficient evidence to convict. As a consequence of the failure of the private prosecution, the rule against double jeopardy meant that the accused could not be re-tried for the same offence at any time in the future, even if the police subsequently acquired sufficient new evidence to support a conviction. The report of the Macpherson Inquiry into the manner in which the Metropolitan Police dealt with the Stephen Lawrence case gained much publicity for its finding of 'institutional racism' within the service, but it also made a clear recommendation that the removal of the rule against double jeopardy be considered. Subsequently, a Law Commission report recommended the removal of the double jeopardy rule and provision to remove it, under particular circumstances and subject to strict regulation, was contained in ss 75–79 of the Criminal Justice Act 2003.

In December 2000, the Lawrence family were reported to have accepted £320,000 in settlement of any claims against the Metropolitan Police Service, but, as yet, they have not initiated any civil action against the alleged perpetrators of their son's murder as they had been reported to be considering doing.

In considering the relationship between civil law and criminal law, it is sometimes thought that criminal law is the more important in maintaining social order, but it is at least arguable that, in reality, the reverse is the case. For the most part, people come into contact with the criminal law infrequently, whereas everyone is continuously involved with civil law, even if it is only the use of contract law to make some purchase. The criminal law of theft, for example, may be seen as simply the cutting edge of the wider and more fundamental rights established by general property law. In any case, there remains the fact that civil and criminal law each has its own distinct legal system. The nature of these systems will be considered in detail in later chapters. The structures of the civil courts and criminal courts are considered in Chapter 3.

1.3   The Separation of Powers

Although the idea of the separation of powers can be traced back to ancient Greek philosophy, it was advocated in early modern times by the English philosopher Locke and the later French philosopher Montesquieu, and found its practical expression in the constitution of the United States. The idea of the separation of powers is posited on the existence of three distinct functions of government (the legislative, executive and judicial functions) and the conviction that these functions should be kept apart in order to prevent the centralisation of too much power. Establishing the appropriate relationship between the actions of the State and the legal control over those actions crucially involves a consideration of whether there is any absolute limit on the authority of the government of the day. Answering that question inevitably involves an examination of the general constitutional structure of the UK and, in particular, the inter-relationship of two doctrines: parliamentary sovereignty and judicial independence. It also requires an understanding of the role of judicial review and the effect of the Human Rights Act 1998, and has caused no little friction between the judiciary and the executive, especially in the form of the Home Secretary.

1.3.1   Parliamentary sovereignty

As a consequence of the victory of the parliamentary forces in the English revolutionary struggles of the 17th century, Parliament became the sovereign power in the land. The independence of the judiciary was secured, however, in the Act of Settlement 1701. The centrality of the independence of the judges and the legal system from direct control or interference from the State in the newly established constitution was emphasised in the writing of John Locke, who saw it as one of the essential reasons for, and justifications of, the social contract on which the social structure was assumed to be based. It is generally accepted that the inspiration for Montesquieu's *Spirit of Law (De L'Esprit des Lois)* was the English constitution, but if that is truly the case, then his doctrine of the separation of powers was based on a misunderstanding of that constitution, as it failed to take account of the express *superiority of Parliament* in all matters, including its relationship with the judiciary and the legal system.

It is interesting that some Conservative thinkers have recently suggested that the whole notion of parliamentary sovereignty is itself a product of the self-denying ordinance of the common law. Consequently, they have suggested that it is open to a subsequent, more robust, judiciary, confident in its own position and powers within the developing constitution, to re-assert its equality with the other two elements. When, however, it is recalled that when the Conservative Party was in power, it was to no little extent embarrassed by, and not too understanding of, the actions of recalcitrant judges, it is at least a moot point whether such a proposition reflects a real commitment to judicial equality with the executive, or merely represents the gall of a defeated executive, hoping to enlist the judges in their oppositional role. It does not require an uncritical commitment to the role of the judiciary to recognise that powerful executives, which exercise effective control over acquiescent legislatures, do not take too well to the interference of an active judiciary, as may be seen in the fulminations against the courts by the former Home Secretary, David Blunkett. At least somewhat paradoxically, the Conservative Party argued against the enactment of the Human Rights Act by the Labour government in 1998 on the grounds that it diminished the power of Parliament and gave too much power to the unelected judiciary.

Given the existence of the doctrine of parliamentary sovereignty, which effectively means that Parliament, as the ultimate source of law, can make such law as it determines, the exact extent to which the doctrine of the separation of powers operates in the UK is a matter of some debate. For example, the current position of the Lord Chancellor, who is at the same time a member of the government and the most senior judge in the land with control over judicial appointments, is not unproblematic. The present government announced, in June 2003, that amongst its constitutional reforms it intended abolishing the position of Lord Chancellor. That proposal was introduced in the Constitutional Reform Bill, which was published in February 2004. There is, however, high judicial authority for claiming that the separation of powers is an essential element in the constitution of the UK (see *R v Hinds* (1979), in which Lord Diplock, whilst considering the nature of different Commonwealth constitutions in a Privy Council case, stated that 'It is taken for granted that the basic principle of the separation of powers will apply ...' at p 212). In any case, the point of considering the doctrine at this juncture is simply to highlight the distinction and relationship between the executive and the judiciary and to indicate the possibility of conflict between the two elements of the constitution. This relationship assumes crucial importance if one accepts, as some have suggested, that it is no longer possible to distinguish the executive from the legislature as, through its control of its majority in the House of Commons, the executive (that is, the government) can legislate as it wishes and, in so doing, can provide the most arbitrary of party political decisions with the form of legality. The question to be considered here is to what extent the judiciary can legitimately oppose the wishes of the government expressed in the form of legislation, or to what extent they can interfere with the pursuit of those wishes. As will be seen below, the power of the judiciary in relation to legislative provisions has been greatly enhanced by the passage of the Human Rights Act 1998.

1.3.2 Judicial independence

The exact meaning of 'judicial independence' became a matter of debate when some members and ex-members of the senior judiciary suggested that the last Conservative

Lord Chancellor, Lord Mackay of Clashfern, had adopted a too restrictive interpretation of the term which had reduced it to the mere absence of interference by the executive in the trial of individual cases. They asserted the right of the legal system to operate independently, as an autonomous system apart from the general control of the State, with the judiciary controlling its operation, or at least being free from the dictates and strictures of central control.

According to Lord Mackay, in the first of his series of Hamlyn lectures entitled 'The Administration of Justice' (1994):

> The fact that the executive and judiciary meet in the person of the Lord Chancellor should symbolise what I believe is necessary for the administration of justice in a country like ours, namely, a realisation that both the judiciary and the executive are parts of the total government of the country with functions that are distinct but which must work together in a proper relationship if the country is to be properly governed ... It seems more likely that the interests of the judiciary in matters within the concerns covered by the Treasury are more likely to be advanced if they can be pursued within government by a person with a lifetime of work in law and an understanding of the needs and concerns of the judiciary and who has responsibility as Head of the Judiciary, than if they were to be left within government as the responsibility of a minister with no such connection with the judiciary.

The tension inherent in the relationship between the courts and the executive government took on a more fundamental constitutional aspect with the passing of the Human Rights Act 1998. By means of that Act, the courts were given the right to subject the actions and operations of the executive and, indeed, all public authorities to the gaze and control of the law, in such a way as to prevent the executive from abusing its power. If the Human Rights Act represented a shift in constitutional power towards the judiciary, the Act was nonetheless sensitive to maintain the doctrine of parliamentary sovereignty. In the United States, with its written constitution, the judiciary in the form of the Supreme Court has the power to declare the Acts of the legislature unconstitutional and consequently invalid. No such power was extended to the UK courts under the Human Rights Act, although some commentators saw the Human Rights Act as eventually leading to a similar outcome in the UK. Such tension was further heightened when, in June 2003, the government announced its intentions to radically alter the constitution, and the judges' role within it, at an apparent single stroke by the expedient of removing the role of Lord Chancellor.

Given the judiciary's suspicion of Lord Mackay as Lord Chancellor, it is not a little ironic that the government's announcement of its intention to abolish the position of Lord Chancellor was met by strong judicial reaction, in language very similar to that used by that former holder of that office. The judges, supported by many parliamentarians and commentators, made it absolutely clear that they thought that their independence would best be protected by a strong, legally qualified, champion within the cabinet. Such a role had been performed by the Lord Chancellor; consequently, the judiciary generally regretted, not to say resisted, the abolition of the office as originally provided for in the Constitutional Reform Bill 2003. However, although such resistance succeeded in retaining the office of the Lord Chancellor, its functions were greatly reduced and s 2 of the Constitutional Reform Act of 2005 provides that the holder of the office should be 'qualified by experience', which need not include legal experience. Neither will the holder of the office necessarily sit in the House of Lords. In recognition of the sensitivities of the judiciary, s 3 of the Act, for the first time places a legal duty on government ministers to uphold the independence of the judiciary and specifically bars them from trying to influence judicial decisions through any special access to judges. S 1, also for the first time, recognises the centrality of the principle of the rule of law to the constitution of the United Kingdom.

1.4   The Rule of Law

The Rule of Law represents a symbolic ideal against which proponents of widely divergent political persuasions measure and criticise the shortcomings of contemporary State practice. This varied recourse to the Rule of Law is, of course, only possible because of the lack of precision in the actual meaning of the concept; its meaning tending to change over time and, as will be seen below, to change in direct correspondence with the beliefs of those who claim its support and claim, in turn, to support it. It is undeniable that the form and content of law and legal procedure have changed substantially in the course of the 20th century. It is usual to explain such changes as being a consequence of the way in which, and the increased extent to which, the modern State intervenes in everyday life, be it economic or social. As the State increasingly took over the regulation of many areas of social activity, it delegated wide ranging discretionary powers to various people and bodies in an attempt to ensure the successful implementation of its policies. The assumption and delegation of such power on the part of the State brought it into potential conflict with previous understandings of the Rule of Law which had entailed a strictly limited ambit of State activity.

1.4.1   Human rights discourse and the Rule of Law

In an article published in the *London Review of Books* and *The Guardian*, in May 1995, the High Court judge, as he then was, Sir Stephen Sedley, made explicit the links and tensions between the doctrine of the Rule of Law and the relationship of the courts and the executive, and the implications for the use of judicial review as a means of controlling the exercise of executive power. In his view:

> Our agenda for the 21st century is not necessarily confined to choice between a rights instrument interpreted by a judiciary with a long record of illiberal adjudication, and rejection of any rights instrument in favour of Parliamentary government. The better government becomes, the less scope there will be for judicial review of it.

> But, for the foreseeable future, we have a problem: how to ensure that as a society we are governed within a law which has internalised the notion of fundamental human rights. Although this means adopting the Rule of Law, like democracy, as a higher-order principle, we do have the social consensus which alone can accord it that primacy. And, if in our own society the Rule of Law is to mean much, it must at least mean that it is

the obligation of the courts to articulate and uphold the ground rules of ethical social existence which we dignify as fundamental human rights. There is a potential tension between the principle of democratic government and the principle of equality before the law ... The notion that the prime function of human rights and indeed the Rule of Law is to protect the weak against the strong is not mere sentimentality. It is the child of an era of history in which equality of treatment and opportunity has become perceived ... as an unqualified good, and of a significant recognition that you do not achieve equality merely by proclaiming it fundamental human rights to be real, have to steer towards outcomes which invert those inequalities of power that mock the principle of equality before the law.

Such talk of fundamental human rights denies the absolute sovereignty of Parliament in its recognition of areas that are beyond the legitimate exercise of State power. It also recognises, however, that notions of the Rule of Law cannot be satisfied by the provision of merely formal equality as Dicey and Friedrich von Hayek would have it and previous legal safeguards would have provided. For Sedley, the Rule of Law clearly imports, and is based on, ideas of substantive equality, that market systems and legal formalism cannot provide and, in fact, undermine. His version of the Rule of Law clearly involves a reconsideration of the relationship of the executive and the judiciary and involve the latter in a further reconsideration of their own previous beliefs and functions.

1.5   The Human Rights Act 1998

The UK was one of the initial signatories to the European Convention on Human Rights (ECHR) in 1950, which was set up in post-War Europe as a means of establishing and enforcing essential human rights. In 1966, it recognised the power of the European Commission on Human Rights to hear complaints from individual UK citizens and, at the same time, recognised the authority of the European Court of Human Rights (ECtHR) to adjudicate on such matters. It did not, however, at that time incorporate the European Convention into UK law.

The consequence of non-incorporation was that the Convention could not be directly enforced in English courts (*R v Secretary of State for the Home Department ex p Brind* (1991)). That situation has been remedied, however, by the passing of the Human Rights Act 1998 (HRA), which came into force in England and Wales in October 2000 and was by then already in effect in Scotland. The HRA incorporates the ECHR into UK law. The Articles incorporated into UK law and listed in Sched 1 to the Act cover the following matters:

- The right to life. Article 2 states that 'everyone's right to life shall be protected by law'.

- Prohibition of torture. Article 3 actually provides that 'no one shall be subjected to torture or inhuman or degrading treatment or punishment'.

- Prohibition of slavery and forced labour (Art 4).

- The right to liberty and security. After stating the general right, Art 5 is mainly concerned with the conditions under which individuals can lawfully be deprived of their liberty.

- The right to a fair trial. Article 6 provides that 'everyone is entitled to a fair and public hearing within a reasonable time by an independent and impartial tribunal established by law'.

- The general prohibition of the enactment of retrospective criminal offences. Article 7 does, however, recognise the *post hoc* criminalisation of previous behaviour where it is 'criminal according to the general principles of law recognised by civilised nations'.

- The right to respect for private and family life. Article 8 extends this right to cover a person's home and their correspondence.

- Freedom of thought, conscience and religion (Art 9).

- Freedom of expression. Article 10 extends the right to include 'freedom … to receive and impart information and ideas without interference by public authority and regardless of frontiers'.

- Freedom of assembly and association. Article 11 specifically includes the right to form and join trade unions.

- The right to marry (Art 12).

- Prohibition of discrimination (Art 14).

- The right to peaceful enjoyment of possessions and protection of property (Art 1 of Protocol 1).

- The right to education (subject to a UK reservation) (Art 2 of Protocol 1).

- The right to free elections (Art 3 of Protocol 1).

- The right not to be subjected to the death penalty (Arts 1 and 2 of Protocol 6).

The rights listed can be relied on by any person, non-governmental organisation, or group of individuals. Importantly, they also apply, where appropriate, to companies, which are incorporated entities and hence legal persons. However, they cannot be relied on by governmental organisations, such as local authorities.

The rights listed above are not all seen in the same way. Some are absolute and inalienable and cannot be interfered with by the State. Others are merely contingent and are subject to derogation, that is, signatory States can opt out of them in particular circumstances. The absolute rights are those provided for in Arts 2, 3, 4, 7 and 14. All of the others are subject to potential limitations; in particular, the rights provided for under Arts 8, 9, 10 and 11 are subject to legal restrictions, such as are:

> … necessary in a democratic society in the interests of national security or public safety, for the prevention of crime, for the protection of health or morals or the protection of the rights and freedoms of others. [Art 11(2)]

In deciding the legality of any derogation, courts are required not just to be convinced that there is a need for the derogation, but they must also be sure that the State's action has been proportionate to that need. In other words, the State must not overreact to a perceived problem by removing more rights than is necessary to effect the solution. The UK entered such a derogation in relation to the extended detention of terrorist suspects without charge under the Prevention of Terrorism (Temporary Provisions) Act 1989, subsequently replaced and extended by the Terrorism Act 2000. Those powers had been held to be contrary to Art 5 of the Convention by the ECtHR in *Brogan v United Kingdom* (1989). The UK also entered a derogation with regard to the Anti-Terrorism, Crime and Security Act 2001, which was enacted in response to the attack on the World Trade Center in New York on 11 September that year. The Act allows for the detention without trial of foreign citizens suspected of being involved in terrorist activity.

With further regard to the possibility of derogation, s 19 of the 1998 Act requires a minister, responsible for the passage of any Bill through Parliament, either to make a written declaration that it is compatible with the Convention or, alternatively, to declare that although it may not be compatible, it is still the Government's wish to proceed with it.

1.5.1   The structure of the Human Rights Act 1998

The HRA has profound implications for the operation of the English legal system. However, to understand the structure of the HRA, it is essential to be to aware of the nature of the changes introduced by the Act, especially in the apparent passing of fundamental powers to the judiciary. Under the doctrine of parliamentary sovereignty, the legislature could pass such laws at it saw fit, even to the extent of removing the rights of its citizens. The 1998 Act reflects a move towards the entrenchment of rights recognised under the ECHR but, given the sensitivity of the relationship between the elected Parliament and the unelected judiciary, it has been thought expedient to minimise the change in the constitutional relationship of Parliament and the judiciary.

Section 2 of the Act requires future courts to take into account any previous decision of the ECtHR. This provision impacts on the operation of the doctrine of precedent within the English legal system, as it effectively sanctions the overruling of any previous English authority that was in conflict with a decision of the ECtHR.

In *Price v Leeds City Council*, the Court of Appeal held that, where there were contradictory rulings from the House of Lords and the European Court of Human Rights, English courts should follow the ruling of the House of Lords. That approach was confirmed by the House of Lords in March 2006, which held that only in exceptional circumstances could the Court of Appeal favour a ECtHR decision.

Section 3 requires all legislation to be read, so far as possible, to give effect to the rights provided under the ECHR. As will be seen, this section provides the courts with new and extended powers of interpretation. It also has the potential to invalidate previously accepted interpretations of statutes which were made, by necessity, without recourse to the ECHR (see *Ghaidan v Godin-Mendoza* (2004).

Section 4 empowers the courts to issue a declaration of incompatibility where any piece of primary legislation is found to conflict with the rights provided under the ECHR. This has the effect that the courts cannot invalidate primary legislation, essentially Acts of Parliament but also Orders in Council, which is found to be incompatible; they can only make a declaration of such incompatibility, and leave it to the legislature to remedy the situation through new legislation. Section 10 provides for the provision of remedial legislation through a fast track procedure, which gives a minister of the Crown the power to alter such primary legislation by way of statutory instrument.

Section 5 requires the Crown to be given notice where a court considers issuing a declaration of incompatibility, and the appropriate government minister is entitled to be made a party to the case.

Section 6 declares it unlawful for any public authority to act in a way which is incompatible with the ECHR, and s 7 allows the 'victim of the unlawful act' to bring proceedings against the public authority in breach. Section 8 empowers the court to grant such relief or remedy against the public authority in breach of the Act as it considers just and appropriate.

Where a public authority is acting under the instructions of some primary legislation which is itself incompatible with the ECHR, the public authority will not be liable under s 6.

Section 19 of the Act requires that the minister responsible for the passage of any Bill through Parliament must make a written statement that the provisions of the Bill are compatible with ECHR rights. Alternatively, the minister may make a statement that the Bill does not comply with ECHR rights but that the Government nonetheless intends to proceed with it.

Reactions to the introduction of the HRA have been broadly welcoming, but some important criticisms have been raised. First, the ECHR is a rather old document and does not address some of the issues that contemporary citizens might consider as equally fundamental to those rights actually contained in the document. For example, it is silent on the rights to substantive equality relating to such issues as welfare and access to resources. Also, the actual provisions of the ECHR are uncertain in the extent of their application, or perhaps more crucially in the area where they can be derogated from, and at least to a degree they are contradictory. The most obvious difficulty arises from the need to reconcile Art 8's right to respect for private and family life with Art 10's freedom of expression. Newspaper editors have expressed their concern in relation to this particular issue, and fear the development, at the hands of the court, of an overly limiting law of privacy which would prevent investigative journalism. This leads to a further difficulty: the potential politicisation, together with a significant enhancement in the power, of the judiciary. Consideration of this issue will be postponed until some cases involving the HRA have been examined.

Perhaps the most serious criticism of the HRA was the fact that the Government did not see fit to establish a Human Rights Commission to publicise and facilitate the operation of its procedures. Many saw the setting up of such a body as a necessary step in raising human rights awareness and assisting individuals, who might otherwise be unable to use the Act, to enforce their rights. However, in October 2003, following new provisions against discrimination in relation to religion, belief or sexual orientation, to be followed by similar measures in relation to age, to come into effect in October 2006, the Government announced its intention to establish a new Commission for Equality and Human Rights. The new commission will bring together and replace the existing Commission for Racial Equality, the Equal Opportunities Commission and the Disability Rights Commission, with the remit of promoting 'an inclusive agenda, underlining the importance of equality for all in society as well as working to combat discrimination affecting specific groups'.

1.5.2 Cases decided under the Human Rights Act 1998

1.5.2.1 Proportionality

The way in which States can interfere with rights, so long as they do so in a way that is proportionate to the attainment of a legitimate end, can be seen in *Brown v Advocate General for Scotland* (2001). Brown had been arrested at a supermarket in relation to the theft of a bottle of gin. When the police officers noticed that she smelled of alcohol, they asked her how she had travelled to the superstore. Brown replied that she had driven and pointed out her car in the supermarket car park. Later, at the police station, the police used their powers under s 172(2)(a) of the Road Traffic Act 1988 to require her to say who had been driving her car at about 2.30 am; that is, at the time when she would have travelled in it to the supermarket. Brown admitted that she had been driving. After a positive breath test, Brown was charged with drunk driving, but appealed to the Scottish High Court of Justiciary for a declaration that the case could not go ahead on the grounds that her admission, as required under s 172, was contrary to the right to a fair trial under Art 6 of the ECHR.

The High Court of Justiciary supported her claim on the basis that the right to silence and the right not to incriminate oneself at trial would be worthless if an accused person did not enjoy a right of silence in the course of the criminal investigation leading to the court proceedings. If this were not the case, then the police could require an accused person to provide an incriminating answer which subsequently could be used in evidence against them at their trial. Consequently, the use of evidence obtained under s 172 of the Road Traffic Act 1988 infringed Brown's rights under Art 6(1).

However, on 5 December 2000, the Privy Council reversed the judgment of the Scottish appeal court. The Privy Council reached its decision on the grounds that the rights contained in Art 6 of the ECHR were not themselves absolute and could be restricted in certain limited conditions. Consequently, it was possible for individual States to introduce limited qualification of those rights so long as they were aimed at 'a clear public objective' and were 'proportionate to the situation' under consideration. The ECHR had to be read as balancing community rights with individual rights. With specific regard to the Road Traffic Act 1998, the objective to be attained was the prevention of injury and death from the misuse of cars, and s 172 was not a disproportionate response to that objective.

Section 3: duty to interpret legislation in line with the ECHR

It has long been a matter of concern that, in cases where rape has been alleged, the common defence strategy employed by lawyers has been to attempt to attack the credibility of the woman making the accusation. Judges had the discretion to allow questioning of the woman as to her sexual history where this was felt to be relevant, and in all too many cases this discretion was exercised in a way that allowed defence counsel to abuse and humiliate women accusers. Section 41 of the Youth Justice and Criminal Evidence Act 1999 (YJCEA) placed the court under a restriction that seriously limited evidence that could be raised in cross-examination of a sexual relationship between a complainant and an accused. Under s 41(3) of the 1999 Act, such evidence was limited to sexual behaviour 'at or about the same time' as the event giving rise to the charge that was 'so similar' in nature that it could not be explained as a coincidence.

In *R v A* (2000), the defendant in a case of alleged rape claimed that the provisions of the YJCEA were contrary to Art 6 of the ECHR to the extent that they prevented him from putting forward a full and complete defence. In reaching its decision, the House of Lords emphasised the need to protect women from humiliating cross-examination and prejudicial but valueless evidence in respect of their previous sex lives. It nonetheless held that the restrictions in s 41 of the 1999 Act were *prima facie* capable of preventing an accused from putting forward relevant evidence that could be crucial to his defence.

However, rather than make a declaration of incompatibility, the House of Lords preferred to make use of s 3 of the HRA to allow s 41 of the YJCEA to be read as permitting the admission of evidence or questioning relating to a relevant issue in the case where it was considered necessary by the trial judge to make the trial fair. The test of admissibility of evidence of previous sexual relations between an accused and a complainant under s 41(3) of the 1999 Act was whether the evidence was so relevant to the issue of consent that to exclude it would be to endanger the fairness of the trial under Art 6 of the Convention. Where the line is to be drawn is left to the judgment of trial judges. In reaching its decision, the House of Lords was well aware that its interpretation of s 41 did a violence to its actual meaning, but it nonetheless felt it within its power so to do.

In *Re S* (2002), the Court of Appeal used s 3 of the HRA in such a way as to create new guidelines for the operation of the Children Act 1989, which increased the courts' powers to intervene in the interests of children taken into care under the Act. This extension of the courts' powers in the pursuit of the improved treatment of such children was achieved by reading the Act in such a way as to allow the courts increased discretion to make interim rather than final care orders, and to establish what were referred to as 'starred milestones' within a child's care plan. If such starred milestones were not achieved within a reasonable time, then the courts could be approached to deliver fresh directions. In effect, what the Court of Appeal was doing was setting up a new and more active regime of court supervision in care cases.

The House of Lords, however, although sympathetic to the aims of the Court of Appeal, felt that it had exceeded its powers of interpretation under s 3 of the HRA and, in its exercise of judicial creativity, it had usurped the function of Parliament.

Lord Nicholls explained the operation of s 3:

> The Human Rights Act reserves the amendment of primary legislation to Parliament. By this means the Act seeks to preserve parliamentary sovereignty. The Act maintains the constitutional boundary. Interpretation of statutes is a matter for the courts; the enactment of statutes, are matters for Parliament ... [but that any interpretation which] departs substantially from a fundamental feature of an Act of Parliament is likely to have crossed the boundary between interpretation and amendment.

Unfortunately, the Court of Appeal had overstepped that boundary.

In *Ghaidan v Godin-Mendoza*, the Court of Appeal used s 3 to extend the rights of same-sex partners to inherit a statutory tenancy under the Rent Act 1977. In *Fitzpatrick v Sterling Housing Association Ltd* (1999), the House of Lords had extended the rights of such individuals to inherit the lesser assured tenancy by including them within the deceased person's family. It declined to allow them to inherit statutory tenancies, however, on the grounds that they could not be considered to be the wife or husband of the deceased as the Act required. In *Ghaidan v Godin-Mendoza*, the Court of Appeal held that the Rent Act 1977, as it had been construed by the House of Lords in *Fitzpatrick*, was incompatible with Art 14 of the ECHR on the grounds of its discriminatory treatment of surviving same-sex partners. The court, however, decided that the failing could be remedied by reading the words 'as his or her wife or husband' in the Act as meaning 'as if they were his or her wife or husband'. The Court of Appeal's decision and reasoning were subsequently confirmed by the House in 2004 in *Ghaidan v Godin-Mendoza*. *Mendoza* is of particular interest in the fact that it shows how the HRA can permit lower courts to avoid previous and otherwise binding decisions of the House of Lords. It also clearly shows the extent to which s 3 increases the powers of the judiciary in relation to statutory interpretation. In spite of this potential increased power, the House of Lords found itself unable to use s 3 in *Bellinger v Bellinger* (2003). The case related to the rights of transsexuals and the court found itself unable, or at least unwilling, to interpret s 11(c) of the Matrimonial Causes Act 1973 in such a way as to allow a male to female transsexual to be treated in law as a female. Nonetheless, the court did issue a declaration of incompatibility (see below for explanation).

1.5.2.2 *Declarations of incompatibility*

Where a court cannot interpret a piece of primary legislation in such a way as to make it compatible with the ECHR, it cannot declare the legislation invalid, but it can make a declaration that the legislation in question is not compatible with the rights provided by the Convention. The first declaration of incompatibility was issued in *R v (1) Mental Health Review Tribunal, North & East London Region (2) Secretary Of State For Health ex p H* in March 2001. In that case, the Court of Appeal held that ss 72 and 73 of the Mental Health Act 1983 were incompatible with Art 5(1) and (4) of the ECHR, inasmuch as they reversed the normal burden of proof by requiring the detained person to show that they should not be detained, rather than placing the burden on the authorities to show that they should be detained.

Wilson v First County Trust (2000) was, however, the first case in which a court indicated its likelihood of its making a declaration of incompatibility under s 4 of the HRA. The legislation in question was the Consumer Credit Act (CCA) 1974 and in particular s 127(3) of that Act, which proscribed the enforcement of any consumer credit agreement which did not comply with the requirements of the 1974 Act. Wilson had borrowed £5,000 from First County Trust (FCT) and had pledged her car as security for the loan. Wilson was to be charged a fee of £250 for drawing up the loan documentation but asked FCT to add it to the loan, which they agreed to do. The effect of this was that the loan document stated that the amount of the loan was £5,250. This, however, was inaccurate, as in reality the extra £250 was not part of the loan as such; rather, it was part of the charge for the loan. The loan document had therefore been drawn up improperly and did not comply with the requirement of s 61 of the CCA 1974.

When Wilson subsequently failed to pay the loan at the end of the agreed period, FCT stated their intention of selling the car unless she paid £7,000. Wilson brought proceedings: (a) for a declaration that the agreement was unenforceable by reason of s 127(3) of the 1974 Act because of the misstatement of the amount of the loan; and (b) for the agreement to be reopened on the basis that it was an extortionate credit bargain. The judge rejected Wilson's first claim but reopened the agreement and substituted a lower rate of interest, and Wilson subsequently redeemed her car on payment of £6,900. However, she then successfully appealed against the judge's decision as to the enforceability of the agreement, the Court of Appeal holding that s 127(3) clearly and undoubtedly had the effect of preventing the enforcement of the original agreement and Wilson was entitled to the repayment of the money she had paid to redeem her car. Consequently, Wilson not only got her car back but also retrieved the money she paid to FCT, who lost their money completely. In reaching its decision, however, the Court of Appeal expressed the opinion that it was at least arguable that s 127(3) was incompatible with Art 6(1) and/or Protocol 1 of Art 1 of the ECHR. First, the absolute prohibition of enforcement of the agreement appeared to be a disproportionate restriction on the right of the lender to have the enforceability of its loan determined by the court contrary to Art 6(1); and secondly, to deprive FCT of its property – that is, the money which it had lent to Wilson – appeared to be contrary to Protocol 1 of Art 1.

The Court of Appeal's final decision to issue a declaration of incompatibility was taken on appeal to the House of Lords, which overturned the earlier declaration of incompatibility. In reaching its decision, the House of Lords held that the Court of Appeal had wrongly used its powers retrospectively to cover an agreement that had been entered into before the HRA itself had come into force. This ground in itself was enough to overturn the immediate decision of the Court of Appeal. Nonetheless, the House of Lords went on to consider the compatibility question, and once again it disagreed with the lower court's decision. In the view of the House of Lords, the provision of the CCA 1974 was extremely severe in its consequences for the lender, to the extent that its provisions might even appear unreasonable on occasion. However, once again the court recognised a powerful social interest in the need to protect unsophisticated borrowers from potentially unscrupulous lenders. In seeking to protect this interest, the legislature could not be said to have acted in a disproportionate manner. Consequently, s 127(3) and (4) of the CCA 1974 was not incompatible with Art 1 of the First Protocol to the ECHR.

1.5.2.3   *A & Ors v Secretary of State for the Home Department (2004)*

This case, which considered the situation of individuals aliens suspected by the Home Secretary of being potential terrorists and consequently detained indefinitely, without charge, under the Anti-terrorism Crime and Security Act 2001, revealed the potential conflict between the judiciary and the executive in the strongest light yet. The House of Lords, by a majority of eight to one, held that the detention powers under section 23 of the Anti-terrorism Crime and Security Act 2001 were not compatible with the rights provided under the European Convention of Human Rights. Some of the speeches delivered by the judges in the case were extremely critical of the action taken by the government in introducing the Act. The 2001Act was subsequently replaced by the Prevention of Terrorism Act 2005, which introduced domestic control orders in the place of prison detention.

INTRODUCTION TO LAW

The Nature of Law

Legal systems are particular ways of establishing and maintaining social order. Law is a formal mechanism of social control. Studying the English legal system involves considering a fundamental institution in our society.

Categories of Law

Law can be categorised in a number of ways, although the various categories are not mutually exclusive.

Common law and civil law relate to distinct legal systems. The English legal system is a common law one as opposed to continental systems which are based on civil law.

Common law and equity distinguish the two historical sources and systems of English law. Common law emerged in the process of establishing a single legal system throughout the country. Equity was developed later to soften the formal rigour of the common law. The two systems are now united but in the final analysis equity should prevail.

Common law and statute relate to the source of law. Common law is judge made: statute law is produced by Parliament.

Private law and public law relate to whom the law is addressed. Private law relates to individual citizens whereas public law relates to institutions of government.

Civil law and criminal law distinguish between law whose purpose it is to facilitate the interaction of individuals and law that is aimed at enforcing particular standards of behaviour.

Separation of Powers

The judges and the executive in the separation of powers have distinct but interrelated roles in the constitution. The question arises as to the extent to which the courts can act to control the activities of the executive through the operation of judicial review. The position of the present Lord Chancellor as judge and member of the government has been questioned by some.

The Rule of Law

The Rule of Law represents a symbolic ideal against which proponents of widely divergent political persuasions measure and criticise the shortcomings of contemporary State practice.

The Human Rights Act 1998

The Human Rights Act 1998 incorporates the European Convention on Human Rights into domestic UK law. The Articles of the Convention cover the following matters:

- the right to life (Art 1);

- the prohibition of torture (Art 3);

- the prohibition of slavery and forced labour (Art 4);

- the right to liberty and security (Art 5);

- the right to a fair trial (Art 6);

- the general prohibition of the enactment of retrospective criminal offences (Art 7);

- the right to respect for private and family life (Art 8);

- freedom of thought, conscience and religion (Art 9);

- freedom of expression (Art 10);

- freedom of assembly and association (Art 11);

- the right to marry (Art 12);

- the prohibition of discrimination (Art 14);

- freedom from restrictions on the political activity of aliens (Art 16).

The incorporation of the Convention into UK law means that UK courts can decide cases in line with the above Articles. This has the potential to create friction between the judiciary and the executive/legislature.

CHAPTER 2

SOURCES OF LAW

2.1 European Community

Ever since the UK joined the European Economic Community (EEC), now the European Union (EU) (or European Community (EC) in some legal contexts), it has progressively but effectively passed the power to create laws which have effect in this country to the wider European institutions. In effect, the UK's legislative, executive and judicial powers are now controlled by, and can only be operated within, the framework of EC law. It is essential, therefore, that the contemporary law student is aware of the operation of the legislative and judicial powers of the EC.

The general aim of the EU is set out in Art 2 of the EC Treaty, as amended by the Treaty on European Union 1992 (the Maastricht Treaty), as follows:

> The Community shall have as its task, by establishing a common market and an economic and monetary union and by implementing the common policies or activities referred to in Art 3, to promote throughout the Community a harmonious and balanced development of economic activities, sustainable and non-inflationary growth respecting the environment, a high degree of convergence of economic performance, a high level of employment and of social protection, the raising of the standard of living and quality of life, and economic and social cohesion and solidarity among Member States.

Amongst the policies originally detailed in Art 3 were:

- the elimination, between Member States, of custom duties and of quantitative restrictions on the import and export of goods;

- the establishment of a common customs tariff and a common commercial policy towards third countries;

- the abolition, between Member States, of obstacles to the freedom of movement for persons, services and capital;

- the adoption of a common agricultural policy;

- the adoption of a common transport policy;

- the harmonisation of laws of Member States to the extent required to facilitate the proper functioning of the single market; and

- the creation of a European Social Fund, in order to improve the employment opportunities of workers in the EC and to improve their standard of living.

Article 3 has subsequently been extended to cover more social, as opposed to purely economic, matters and now incorporates policies relating to education, health, consumer protection, the environment, and culture generally. Before the UK joined the

EU, its law was just as foreign as law made under any other jurisdiction. On joining the EU, however, the UK and its citizens accepted and became subject to EC law. This subjection to European law remains the case even where the parties to any transaction are themselves both UK subjects. In other words, in areas where it is applicable, EU law supersedes any existing UK law to the contrary.

An example of EC law invalidating the operation of UK legislation can be found in the first *Factortame* case (*Factortame Ltd v Secretary of State for Transport (No 1)* (1989)).

The common fishing policy, established by the EEC, had placed limits on the amount of fish that any member country's fishing fleet was permitted to catch. In order to gain access to British fish stocks and quotas, Spanish fishing boat owners formed British companies and re-registered their boats as British. In order to prevent what it saw as an abuse and an encroachment on the rights of indigenous fishermen, the UK Government introduced the Merchant Shipping Act 1988, which provided that any fishing company seeking to register as British must have its principal place of business in the UK and at least 75% of its shareholders must be British nationals. This effectively debarred the Spanish boats from taking up any of the British fishing quota. Some 95 Spanish boat owners applied to the British courts for judicial review of the Merchant Shipping Act 1988 on the basis that it was contrary to EC law.

The High Court decided to refer the question of the legality of the legislation to the ECJ under Art 234 (formerly Art 177), but in the meantime granted interim relief, in the form of an injunction disapplying the operation of the legislation, to the fishermen. On appeal, the Court of Appeal removed the injunction, a decision confirmed by the House of Lords. However, the House of Lords referred the question of the relationship of Community law and contrary domestic law to the ECJ. Effectively, they were asking whether the domestic courts should follow the domestic law or Community law. The ECJ ruled that the Treaty of Rome requires domestic courts to give effect to the directly enforceable provisions of Community law and, in doing so, such courts are required to ignore any national law that runs counter to Community law. The House of Lords then renewed the interim injunction. The ECJ later ruled that, in relation to the original referral from the High Court, the Merchant Shipping Act 1988 was contrary to Community law and therefore the Spanish fishing companies should be able to sue for compensation in the UK courts. The subsequent claims also went all the way to the House of Lords before it was finally settled in October 2000 that the UK was liable to pay compensation, which has been estimated at between £50 million and £100 million.

2.1.1 Sources of EC law

Community law, depending on its nature and source, may have direct effect on the domestic laws of its various members; that is, it may be open to individuals to rely on it, without the need for their particular State to have enacted the law within its own legal system (see *Factortame (No 1)* (1989)).

There are two types of direct effect. Vertical direct effect means that the individual can rely on EC law in any action in relation to their government, but cannot use it against other individuals. Horizontal direct effect allows the individual to use an EC provision in an action against other individuals. Other EC provisions take effect only when they have been specifically enacted within the various legal systems within the EC.

The sources of EC law are fourfold:

- internal treaties and protocols;

- international agreements;

- secondary legislation; and

- decisions of the ECJ.

2.1.1.1   Internal treaties

Internal treaties govern the Member States of the EU and anything contained therein supersedes domestic legal provisions. The primary treaty is the EC Treaty (formerly called the Treaty of Rome), as amended by such legislation as the Single European Act (SEA) 1986, the Maastricht Treaty 1992, the Amsterdam Treaty 1997 and the Treaty of Nice 2000. Upon the UK joining the EC, the Treaty of Rome was incorporated into UK law by the European Communities Act 1972.

As long as Treaties are of a mandatory nature and are stated with sufficient clarity and precision, they have both vertical and horizontal effect (*Van Gend en Loos v Nederlandse Administratie der Belastingen* (1963)).

2.1.1.2   International treaties

International treaties are negotiated with other nations by the European Commission on behalf of the EU as a whole and are binding on the individual Members of the EU.

2.1.1.3   Secondary legislation

Three types of legislation may be introduced by the European Council and Commission. These are as follows:

- *Regulations* apply to, and within, Member States generally, without the need for those States to pass their own legislation. They are binding and enforceable from the time of their creation, and individual States do not have to pass any legislation to give effect to regulations. Thus, in *Macarthys Ltd v Smith* (1979), on a referral from the Court of Appeal to the ECJ, it was held that Art 141 (formerly Art 119) entitled the claimant to assert rights that were not available to her under national legislation (the Equal Pay Act 1970) which had been enacted before the UK had joined the EEC. Whereas the national legislation clearly did not include a comparison between former and present employees, Art 141's reference to 'equal pay for equal work' did encompass such a situation. Smith was consequently entitled to receive a similar level of remuneration to that of the former male employee who had done her job previously.

Regulations must be published in the Official Journal of the EU. The decision as to whether or not a law should be enacted in the form of a regulation is usually left to the Commission, but there are areas where the EC Treaty requires that the regulation form must be used. These areas relate to: the rights of workers to remain in Member States of which they are not nationals; the provision of State aid to particular indigenous undertakings or industries; the regulation of EU accounts; and budgetary procedures.

- *Directives*, on the other hand, state general goals and leave the precise implementation in the appropriate form to the individual Member States. Directives, however, tend to state the means as well as the ends to which they are aimed and the ECJ will give direct effect to directives which are sufficiently clear and complete (see *Van Duyn v Home Office* (1974)). Directives usually provide Member States with a time limit within which they are required to implement the provision within their own national laws. If they fail to do so, or implement the directive incompletely, then individuals may be able to cite and rely on the directive in their dealings with the State in question. Further, *Francovich v Italy* (1991) established that individuals who have suffered as a consequence of a Member State's failure to implement EC law may seek damages against that State.

  In contract law, the provisions in the Unfair Terms in Consumer Contracts Regulations 1994 (SI 1994/3159), repealed and replaced by the Unfair Terms in Consumer Contracts Regulations 1999 (SI 1999/2083), are an example of UK law being introduced in response to EU directives, and company law is continuously subject to the process of European harmonisation through directives.

- *Decisions* on the operation of European laws and policies are not intended to have general effect but are aimed at particular States or individuals. They have the force of law under Art 249 (formerly Art 189) of the EC Treaty.

- Additionally, Art 211 (formerly Art 155) provides for the Commission to issue recommendations and opinions in relation to the operation of Community law. These have no binding force, although they may be taken into account in trying to clarify any ambiguities in domestic law.

2.1.1.4 *Judgments of the ECJ*

The ECJ is the judicial arm of the EU and, in the field of Community law, its judgments overrule those of national courts. Under Art 234 (formerly Art 177) of the EC Treaty, national courts have the right to apply to the ECJ for a preliminary ruling on a point of Community law before deciding a case.

The mechanism through which Community law becomes immediately and directly effective in the UK is provided by s 2(1) of the European Communities Act 1972. Section 2(2) gives power to designated ministers or departments to introduce Orders in Council to give effect to other non-directly effective Community law.

2.1.2 The institutions of the EU

The major institutions of the EU are: the Council of Ministers; the European Parliament; the European Commission; and the ECJ.

2.1.2.1 *The Council of Ministers*

The Council is made up of ministerial representatives of each of the 25 Member States of the EU. The actual composition of the Council varies, depending on the nature of the matter to be considered: when considering economic matters, the various States will be represented by their finance ministers; if the matter before the Council relates to agriculture, the various agriculture ministers will attend. The Council of Ministers is the supreme decision-making body of the EU and, as such, has the final say in deciding upon EU legislation. Although it acts on recommendations and proposals made to it by the Commission, it does have the power to instruct the Commission to undertake particular investigations and to submit detailed proposals for its consideration.

Council decisions are taken on a mixture of voting procedures. Some measures only require a simple majority; in others, a procedure of qualified majority voting is used; in yet others, unanimity is required. Qualified majority voting is the procedure in which the votes of the 25 Member countries are weighted in proportion to their population from 29 down to three votes each: there is a total of 345 votes to be cast. Under the provisions of the Treaty of Nice, the qualifying majority is set at 258 and the blocking majority 88. This latter figure appears to require more than three of the four largest countries to defeat a proposal; however, the inclusion of a further blocking minority on the basis of population, that is, 62%, ensures that Germany and any of the two other largest countries can defeat any proposal.

2.1.2.2 *The European Parliament*

The European Parliament is the directly elected European institution and, to that extent, it can be seen as the body which exercises democratic control over the operation of the EU. As in national Parliaments, members are elected to represent constituencies, the elections being held every five years. There are a total of 732 members, divided amongst the 25 Member States in approximate proportion to the size of their various populations. Members of the European Parliament do not sit in national groups but operate within political groupings.

The increase in membership approved at Nice required changes in the level of representation in the Parliament. The new total was 732, but as the number of countries increased by 10 as from 1 May 2004, this overall increase actually requires a reduction in the number of members returned by all of the present Member countries except Germany. In recognition that it has by far the largest population, it kept the right to send 99 members to the Parliament. The UK, France and Italy went down to 72. At the lowest end of representation, Malta has five members, and Luxembourg, Estonia and Cyprus have six each.

The European Parliament's General Secretariat is based in Luxembourg and, although the Parliament sits in plenary session in Strasbourg for one week in each month, its detailed and preparatory work is carried out through 18 permanent committees, which usually meet in Brussels. These permanent committees consider proposals from the Commission and provide the full Parliament with reports of such proposals for discussion.

The Parliament is not a legislative institution and, in that respect, plays a subsidiary role to the Council of Ministers. Originally, its powers were merely advisory and supervisory and, since 1980, the Council has been required to wait for the Parliament's opinion before adopting any law. In its supervisory role, the Parliament scrutinises the activities of the Commission and has the power to remove the Commission by passing a motion of censure against it by a two-thirds majority.

The Parliament, together with the Council of Ministers, is the budgetary authority of the EU. The budget is drawn up by the Commission and is presented to both the Council and the Parliament. As regards what is known as obligatory expenditure, the Council has the final say but, in relation to non-obligatory expenditure, the Parliament has the final decision as to whether to approve the budget or not.

2.1.2.3 The European Commission

The European Commission is the executive of the EU and, in that role, is responsible for the administration of EU policies. There are 20 Commissioners, chosen from the various Member States to serve for renewable terms of four years. Commissioners are appointed to head departments with specific responsibility for furthering particular areas of EU policy. Once appointed, Commissioners are expected to act in the general interest of the EU as a whole, rather than in the partial interest of their own home country.

As a result of the Nice summit, the five largest countries, which previously each appointed two Commissioners, agreed to give up one of their appointees in 2005, and a system of rotation was implemented for the benefit of the smaller Member countries, whilst preventing an increase in the number of Commissioners to match the new membership.

In pursuit of EU policy, the Commission is responsible for ensuring that Treaty obligations between the Member States are met and that Community laws relating to individuals are enforced. In order to fulfil these functions, the Commission has been provided with extensive powers in relation to both the investigation of potential breaches of Community law and the subsequent punishment of offenders. The classic area in which these powers can be seen in operation is in the area of competition law. Under Arts 81 and 82 (formerly Arts 85 and 86) of the EC Treaty, the Commission has substantial powers to investigate and control potential monopolies and anticompetitive behaviour. It has used these powers to levy what, in the case of private individuals, would amount to huge fines where breaches of Community competition law have been discovered. In February 1993, the Commission imposed fines totalling more than £80 million on 17 steel producers for what was described as a very serious, illegal price fixing cartel. British Steel suffered the greatest individual imposition of £26.4 million.

In December 2000, the Staffordshire company JCB, the world's fifth largest producer of earthmoving equipment, was fined £22 million by the Commission. It had found that the company had engaged in what was described as 'a serious violation of EU competition law', in that JCB had created artificial barriers within the single market and had even at times fixed prices. It was stated that the company had entered into illegal agreements with its network of distributors that limited their ability to sell outside of their own territories, and prevented purchasers from enjoying any price differentials that existed within the EU.

In addition to these executive functions, the Commission also has a vital part to play in the EU's legislative process. The Council can only act on proposals put before it by the Commission. The Commission, therefore, has a duty to propose to the Council measures that will advance the achievement of the EU's general policies.

2.1.2.4 The ECJ

The ECJ is the judicial arm of the EU and, in the field of Community law, its judgments overrule those of national courts. It consists of 15 judges, assisted by nine Advocates General, and sits in Luxembourg. The role of the Advocate General is to investigate the matter submitted to the ECJ and to produce a report, together with a recommendation for the consideration of the Court. The ECJ is free to accept the report or not, as it sees fit.

The SEA 1986 provided for a new Court of First Instance to be attached to the existing ECJ. The jurisdiction of the Court of First Instance is limited mainly to internal claims by employees of the EC and to claims against fines made by the Commission under Community competition law. The aim is to reduce the burden of work on the ECJ, but there is a right of appeal, on points of law only, to the full Court of Justice. In July 2000, an appeal against a fine imposed by the Commission in 1998 against Europe's biggest car producer, Volkswagen (VW), was successful to the extent that the ECJ reduced the amount of the fine by £7.5 million. Unfortunately for VW, it upheld the essential finding of the Commission and imposed a fine of £57 million on it, a record for any individual company. VW was found guilty of 'an infringement which was particularly serious, the seriousness being magnified by the size of the Volkswagen group'. What the company had done was to prevent customers, essentially those in Germany and Austria, from benefiting from the weakness of the Italian lire between 1993 and 1996 by instructing the Italian dealers not to sell to foreign customers on the false basis that different specifications and warranty terms prevented cross-border sales. Not only had VW instructed that this should happen, but it threatened that Italian dealers would lose their franchises if they failed to comply.

The ECJ performs two key functions, as follows:

- It decides whether any measures adopted, or rights denied, by the Commission, Council or any national government are compatible with Treaty obligations. In October 2000, the ECJ annulled EC Directive 98/43, which required Member States to impose a ban on advertising and sponsorship relating to tobacco products, because it had been adopted on the basis of the wrong provisions of the EC Treaty.

The Directive had been adopted on the basis of the provisions relating to the elimination of obstacles to the completion of the internal market, but the Court decided that, under the circumstances, it was difficult to see how a ban on tobacco advertising or sponsorship could facilitate the trade in tobacco products.

Although a partial prohibition on particular types of advertising or sponsorship might legitimately come within the internal market provisions of the Treaty, the Directive was clearly aimed at protecting public health, and it was therefore improper to base its adoption on freedom to provide services (*Germany v European Parliament and EU Council* (Case C-376/98)).

A Member State may fail to comply with its Treaty obligations in a number of ways. It might fail, or indeed, refuse, to comply with a provision of the Treaty or a regulation; alternatively, it might refuse to implement a directive within the allotted time provided for. Under such circumstances, the State in question will be brought before the ECJ, either by the Commission or by another Member State or, indeed, by individuals within the State concerned.

In 1996, following the outbreak of 'mad cow disease' (BSE) in the UK, the European Commission imposed a ban on the export of UK beef. The ban was partially lifted in 1998 and, subject to conditions relating to the documentation of an animal's history prior to slaughter, from 1 August 1999 exports satisfying those conditions were authorised for despatch within the Community. When the French Food Standards Agency continued to raise concerns about the safety of British beef, the Commission issued a protocol agreement which declared that all meat and meat products from the UK would be distinctively marked as such. However, France continued in its refusal to lift the ban. Subsequently, the Commission applied to the ECJ for a declaration that France was in breach of Community law for failing to lift the prohibition on the sale of correctly labelled British beef in French territory. In December 2001, in *Commission of the European Communities v France*, the ECJ held that the French Government had failed to put forward a ground of defence capable of justifying the failure to implement the relevant Decisions and was therefore in breach of Community law.

- It provides authoritative rulings at the request of national courts under Art 234 (formerly Art 177) of the EC Treaty on the interpretation of points of Community law. When an application is made under Art 234, the national proceedings are suspended until such time as the determination of the point in question is delivered by the ECJ. Whilst the case is being decided by the ECJ, the national court is expected to provide appropriate interim relief, even if this involves going against a domestic legal provision (as in the *Factortame* case).

The question of the extent of the ECJ's authority arose in *Arsenal Football Club plc v Reed* (2003), which dealt with the sale of football souvenirs and memorabilia bearing the name of the football club and consequently infringing its registered trademarks. On first hearing, the Chancery Division of the High Court referred the question of the interpretation of the Trade Marks Directive (89/104) in relation to the issue of trademark infringement to the ECJ. After the ECJ had made its decision, the case came before Laddie J for application, who declined to follow its decision. The ground for so doing was that the ambit of the ECJ's powers was clearly set out in Art 234. Consequently, where, as in this case, the ECJ makes a finding of fact which reverses the finding of a national court on those facts, it exceeds its jurisdiction, and it follows that its decisions are not binding on the national court.

The Court of Appeal later reversed Laddie J's decision on the ground that the ECJ had not disregarded the conclusions of fact made at the original trial and, therefore, he should have followed its ruling and decided the case in the favour of Arsenal. Nonetheless, Laddie J's general point as to the ECJ's authority remains valid.

2.2   The European Court of Human Rights

This Court (the ECtHR) is the supreme court of the Council of Europe, that is, those States within Europe which have accepted to be bound by the European Convention on Human Rights. It has to be established, and emphasised, from the outset that the substance of this section has absolutely nothing to do with the EU as such; the Council of Europe is a completely distinct organisation and, although membership of the two organisations overlap, they are not the same. The Council of Europe is concerned not with economic matters but with the protection of civil rights and freedoms.

It is gratifying, at least to a degree, to recognise that the Convention and its Court are no longer a matter of mysterious external control, the Human Rights Act (HRA) 1998 having incorporated the Convention into UK law and having rendered the ECtHR the supreme court in matters related to its jurisdiction. Much attention was paid to the Convention and the HRA 1998 in Chapter 1 (see above, 1.5), so it only remains to consider the structure and operation of the ECtHR.

The Convention originally established two institutions:

- The European Commission of Human Rights: this body was charged with the task of examining and, if need be, investigating the circumstances of petitions submitted to it. If the Commission was unable to reach a negotiated solution between the parties concerned, it referred the matter to the ECtHR.

- The ECtHR: the European Convention on Human Rights provides that the judgment of the Court shall be final and that parties to it will abide by the decisions of the Court. This body, sitting in Strasbourg, was, and remains, responsible for all matters relating to the interpretation and application of the current Convention.

However, in the 1980s, as the Convention and its Court became more popular and widely known as a forum for asserting human rights, so its workload increased. This pressure was exacerbated by the break up of the old Communist Eastern Bloc and the fact that the newly independent countries, in both senses of the words, became signatories to the Convention. The statistics support the view of the incipient sclerosis of the original structure:

Applications registered with the Commission

Year	Number of applications registered
1981	404
1993	2,037
1997	4,750

Cases referred to the ECtHR

Year	Number of cases referred
1981	7
1993	52
1997	119

As a consequence of such pressure, it became necessary to streamline the procedure by amalgamating the two previous institutions into one Court. In pursuit of this aim, Protocol 11 of the Convention was introduced in 1994. The new ECtHR came into operation on 1 November 1998, although the Commission continued to deal with cases which had already been declared admissible for a further year. Following the reconstruction, however, applications to the new court continued to rise as follows:

1998	5,981
1999	8,396
2000	10,486
2001	13,858
2002	28,257

The ECtHR consists of 41 judges, representing the number of signatories to the Convention, although they do not have to be chosen from each State and, in any case, they sit as individuals rather than representatives of their State. Judges are generally elected, by the Parliamentary Assembly of the Council of Europe, for six years, but arrangements have been put in place so that one half of the membership of the judicial panel will be required to seek renewal every three years.

2.2.1 Structure of the Court

The Plenary Court elects its President, two Vice-Presidents and two Presidents of Section for a period of three years. The Court is divided into four Sections, whose composition, fixed for three years, is geographically and gender balanced, and takes account of the different legal systems of the Contracting States. Each Section is presided over by a President, two of the Section Presidents being at the same time

Vice-Presidents of the Court. Committees of three judges within each Section deal with preliminary issues, and to that extent they do the filtering formerly done by the Commission. Cases are actually heard by Chambers of seven members, who are chosen on the basis of rotation. Additionally, there is a Grand Chamber of 17 judges, made up of the President, Vice-Presidents and Section Presidents and other judges by rotation. The Grand Chamber deals with the most important cases that require a reconsideration of the accepted interpretations of the Convention.

2.2.2 Judgments

Chambers decide by a majority vote and, usually, reports give a single decision. However, any judge in the case is entitled to append a separate opinion, either concurring or dissenting.

Within three months of delivery of the judgment of a Chamber, any party may request that a case be referred to the Grand Chamber if it raises a serious question of interpretation or application, or a serious issue of general importance. Consequently, the Chamber's judgment only becomes final at the expiry of a three month period, or earlier if the parties state that they do not intend to request a referral. If the case is referred to the Grand Chamber, its decision, taken on a majority vote, is final. All final judgments of the Court are binding on the respondent States concerned. Responsibility for supervising the execution of judgments lies with the Committee of Ministers of the Council of Europe, which is required to verify that States have taken adequate remedial measures in respect of any violation of the Convention.

2.2.3 Margin of appreciation and derogation

This refers to the fact that the court recognises that there may well be a range of responses to particular crises or social situations within individual States which might well involve some legitimate limitation on the rights established under the Convention. The Court recognises that in such areas, the response should be decided at the local level rather than being imposed centrally. The most obvious, but by no means the only, situations that involve the recognition of the margin of appreciation are the fields of morality and State security. Thus, *Wingrove v United Kingdom* (1996) concerned the refusal of the British Board of Film Classification to give a certificate of classification to the video-film *Visions of Ecstasy* on the ground that it was blasphemous, thus effectively banning it. The applicant, the director of the film, claimed that the refusal to grant a certificate of classification to the film amounted to a breach of his rights to free speech under Art 10 of the Convention. The Court rejected his claim, holding that the offence of blasphemy, by its very nature, did not lend itself to precise legal definition. Consequently, national authorities 'must be afforded a degree of flexibility in assessing whether the facts of a particular case fall within the accepted definition of the offence'.

In *Civil Service Union v United Kingdom* (1987), it was held that national security interests were of such paramount concern that they outweighed individual rights of freedom of association. Hence, the unions had no response under the Convention to the removal of their members' rights to join and be members of a trade union.

It should also be borne in mind that States can enter a derogation from particular provisions of the Convention, or the way in which they operate in particular areas or circumstances. The UK has entered such derogation in relation to the extended detention of terrorist suspects without charge under the Terrorism Act 2000 and the Anti-Terrorism, Crime and Security Act 2001.

Even where States avail themselves of the margin of appreciation, they are not at liberty to interfere with rights to any degree beyond what is required as a minimum to deal with the perceived problem within the context of a democratic society. In other words, the doctrine of proportionality requires that there must be a relationship of necessity between the end desired and the means used to achieve it.

An example of the way in which the system operates may be seen in the case of *R v Saunders* (1996). Earnest Saunders was one of the original defendants in the Guinness fraud trial of 1990. Prior to his trial, Saunders had been interviewed by Department of Trade and Industry (DTI) inspectors and was required, under the provisions of the companies legislation, to answer questions without the right to silence. It was claimed that interviews under such conditions, and their subsequent use at the trial leading to his conviction, were in breach of the Convention on Human Rights. In October 1994, the Commission decided in Saunders' favour and the ECtHR confirmed that decision in 1996, although Saunders was not awarded damages. As a result, the Government has recognised that the powers given to DTI inspectors breach the Convention, and has declared an intention to alter them, but not in a retrospective way that would benefit Mr Saunders.

The ECtHR subsequently followed its *Saunders* ruling in the case of three others found guilty in the Guinness fraud trials: *IJL, GMR and AKP v United Kingdom* (2000).

2.3 Legislation

If the institutions of the EC are sovereign within its boundaries then, within the more limited boundaries of the UK, the sovereign power to make law lies with Parliament. Under UK constitutional law, it is recognised that Parliament has the power to enact, revoke or alter such, and any, law as it sees fit. Coupled to this wide power is the convention that no one Parliament can bind its successors in such a way as to limit their absolute legislative powers. Although we still refer to our legal system as a common law system, and although the courts still have an important role to play in the interpretation of statutes, it has to be recognised that legislation is the predominant method of law making in contemporary society. It is necessary, therefore, to have a knowledge of the workings of the legislative procedure through which law is made.

2.3.1   The legislative process

As an outcome of various historical political struggles, Parliament, and in particular the House of Commons, has asserted its authority as the ultimate source of law making in the UK. Parliament's prerogative to make law is encapsulated in the notion of the supremacy of Parliament.

Parliament consists of three distinct elements: the House of Commons, the House of Lords and the Monarch. Before any legislative proposal, known at that stage as a Bill, can become an Act of Parliament, it must proceed through and be approved by both Houses of Parliament and must receive the royal assent.

Before the formal law making procedure is started, the Government of the day, which in practice decides and controls what actually becomes law, may enter into a process of consultation with concerned individuals or organisations.

Green Papers are consultation documents issued by the Government which set out and invite comments from interested parties on particular proposals for legislation. After considering any response, the Government may publish a second document in the form of a White Paper, in which it sets out its firm proposals for legislation.

A Bill must be given three readings in both the House of Commons and the House of Lords before it can be presented for the royal assent. It is possible to commence the procedure in either House, although money Bills must be placed before the Commons in the first instance.

Before it can become law, any Bill introduced in the Commons must go through five distinct procedures:

- *First reading*

  This is a purely formal procedure, in which the Bill's title is read and a date is set for its second reading.

- *Second reading*

  At this stage, the general principles of the Bill are subject to extensive debate. The second reading is the critical point in the process of a Bill. At the end, a vote may be taken on its merits and, if it is approved, it is likely that it will eventually find a place in the statute book.

- *Committee stage*

  After its second reading, the Bill is passed to a standing committee, whose job is to consider the provisions of the Bill in detail, clause by clause. The committee has the power to amend it in such a way as to ensure that it conforms with the general approval given by the House at its second reading.

- *Report stage*

  At this point, the standing committee reports the Bill back to the House for consideration of any amendments made during the committee stage.

- *Third reading*

  Further debate may take place during this stage, but it is restricted solely to matters relating to the content of the Bill; questions relating to the general principles of the Bill cannot be raised.

When a Bill has passed all of these stages, it is passed to the House of Lords for consideration. After this, the Bill is passed back to the Commons, which must then consider any amendments to the Bill that might have been introduced by the Lords. Where one House refuses to agree to the amendments made by the other, Bills can be repeatedly passed between them; since Bills must complete their process within the life of a particular parliamentary session, however a failure to reach agreement within that period might lead to the total failure of the Bill.

Since the Parliament Acts of 1911 and 1949, the blocking power of the House of Lords has been restricted as follows:

- a 'Money Bill', that is, one containing only financial provisions, can be enacted without the approval of the House of Lords after a delay of one month;

- any other Bill can be delayed by one year by the House of Lords.

The royal assent is required before any Bill can become law. The procedural nature of the royal assent was highlighted by the Royal Assent Act 1967, which reduced the process of acquiring royal assent to a formal reading out of the short titles of any Act in both Houses of Parliament.

An Act of Parliament comes into effect on the date that royal assent is given, unless there is any provision to the contrary in the Act itself.

2.3.2 Types of legislation

Legislation can be categorised in a number of ways. For example, distinctions can be drawn between:

- *public Acts*, which relate to matters affecting the general public. These can be further sub-divided into either government Bills or Private Members' Bills;

- *private Acts*, which relate to the powers and interests of particular individuals or institutions, although the provision of statutory powers to particular institutions can have a major effect on the general public. For example, companies may be given the power to appropriate private property through compulsory purchase orders; and

- *enabling legislation*, which gives power to a particular person or body to oversee the production of the specific details required for the implementation of the general purposes stated in the parent Act. These specifics are achieved through the enactment of statutory instruments. (See below, for a consideration of delegated legislation.)

Acts of Parliament can also be distinguished on the basis of the function that they are designed to carry out. Some are unprecedented and cover new areas of activity previously not governed by legal rules, but other Acts are aimed at rationalising or amending existing legislative provisions:

- *Consolidating legislation* is designed to bring together provisions previously contained in a number of different Acts, without actually altering them. The Companies Act 1985 is an example of a consolidation Act. It brought together provisions contained in numerous amending Acts which had been introduced since the previous Consolidation Act 1948.

- *Codifying legislation* seeks not just to bring existing statutory provisions under one Act, but also looks to give statutory expression to common law rules. The classic examples of such legislation are the Partnership Act 1890 and the Sale of Goods Act 1893, now 1979.

- *Amending legislation* is designed to alter some existing legal provision. Amendment of an existing legislative provision can take one of two forms:
    - *textual amendments*, where the new provision substitutes new words for existing ones in a legislative text or introduces completely new words into that text. Altering legislation by means of textual amendment has one major drawback, in that the new provisions make very little sense on their own without the contextual reference of the original provision that it is designed to alter; or
    - *non-textual amendments* do not alter the actual wording of the existing text, but alter the operation or effect of those words. Non-textual amendments may have more immediate meaning than textual alterations, but they too suffer from the problem that, because they do not alter the original provisions, the two provisions have to be read together to establish the legislative intention.

Neither method of amendment is completely satisfactory, but the Renton Committee on the Preparation of Legislation (1975, Cmnd 6053) favoured textual amendments over non-textual amendments.

2.3.3 Delegated legislation

In contemporary practice, the full scale procedure detailed above is usually only undergone in relation to enabling Acts. These Acts set out general principles and establish a framework within which certain individuals or organisations are given power to make particular rules designed to give practical effect to the enabling Act. The law produced through this procedure is referred to as 'delegated legislation'.

As has been stated, delegated legislation is law made by some person or body to whom Parliament has delegated its general law making power. A validly enacted piece of delegated legislation has the same legal force and effect as the Act of Parliament under which it is enacted; equally, however, it only has effect to the extent that its enabling Act authorises it. Any action taken in excess of the powers granted is said to be *ultra vires* and the legality of such legislation can be challenged in the courts, as considered below.

The Deregulation and Contracting Out Act (DCOA) 1994 is an example of the wide-ranging power that enabling legislation can extend to ministers. The Act gives ministers the authority to amend legislation by means of statutory instruments, where they consider such legislation to impose unnecessary burdens on any trade, business, or profession. Although the DCOA 1994 imposes the requirement that ministers should consult with interested parties to any proposed alteration, it nonetheless gives them extremely wide powers to alter primary legislation without the necessity of following the same procedure as was required to enact that legislation in the first place. An example of the effect of the DCOA 1994 may be seen in the Deregulation (Resolutions of Private Companies) Order 1996 (SI 1996/1471), which simplifies the procedures that private companies have to comply with in passing resolutions. The effect of this statutory instrument was to introduce new sections into the Companies Act 1985 which relax the previous provisions in the area in question. A second example is the Deregulation (Model Appeal Provisions) Order 1996 (SI 1996/1678), which sets out a model structure for appeals against enforcement actions in business disputes.

The powers under the DCOA 1994 were extended in the Regulatory Reform Act 2001. It should also be remembered that s 10 of the HRA allows ministers to amend primary legislation by way of statutory instrument where a court has issued a declaration of incompatibility (see 1.5 above).

The output of delegated legislation in any year greatly exceeds the output of Acts of Parliament. For example, in 2003, Parliament passed just 45 general public Acts, in comparison to 3,300 statutory instruments. In statistical terms, therefore, it is at least arguable that delegated legislation is actually more significant than primary Acts of Parliament.

There are various types of delegated legislation, as follows:

- *Orders in Council* permit the Government, through the Privy Council, to make law. The Privy Council is nominally a non-party political body of eminent parliamentarians, but in effect it is simply a means through which the Government, in the form of a committee of ministers, can introduce legislation without the need to go through the full parliamentary process. Although it is usual to cite situations of State emergency as exemplifying occasions when the Government will resort to the use of Orders in Council, in actual fact a great number of Acts are brought into operation through Orders in Council. Perhaps the widest scope for Orders in Council is to be found in relation to EC law, for, under s 2(2) of the European Communities Act 1972, ministers can give effect to provisions of Community law which do not have direct effect.

- *Statutory instruments* are the means through which government ministers introduce particular regulations under powers delegated to them by Parliament in enabling legislation. Examples have already been considered in relation to the DCOA 1994.

- *Bylaws* are the means through which local authorities and other public bodies can make legally binding rules. Bylaws may be made by local authorities under such enabling legislation as the Local Government Act 1972, and public corporations are empowered to make regulations relating to their specific sphere of operation.

- *Court rule committees* are empowered to make the rules which govern procedure in the particular courts over which they have delegated authority under such acts as the Supreme Court Act 1981, the County Courts Act 1984 and the Magistrates' Courts Act 1980.

- *Professional regulations* governing particular occupations may be given the force of law under provisions delegating legislative authority to certain professional bodies which are empowered to regulate the conduct of their members. An example is the power given to The Law Society, under the Solicitors Act 1974, to control the conduct of practising solicitors.

2.3.4 Advantages of the use of delegated legislation

The advantages of using delegated legislation are as follows:

- *Timesaving*

  Delegated legislation can be introduced quickly where necessary in particular cases and permits rules to be changed in response to emergencies or unforeseen problems.

  The use of delegated legislation, however, also saves parliamentary time generally. Given the pressure on debating time in Parliament and the highly detailed nature of typical delegated legislation, not to mention its sheer volume, Parliament would not have time to consider each individual piece of law that is enacted in the form of delegated legislation.

- *Access to particular expertise*

  Related to the first advantage is the fact that the majority of Members of Parliament (MPs) simply do not have sufficient expertise to consider such provisions effectively. Given the highly specialised and extremely technical nature of many of the regulations that are introduced through delegated legislation, it is necessary that those who are authorised to introduce the legislation should have access to the external expertise required to formulate such regulations. With regard to bylaws, it practically goes without saying that local and specialist knowledge should give rise to more appropriate rules than reliance on the general enactments of Parliament.

- *Flexibility*

  The use of delegated legislation permits ministers to respond on an *ad hoc* basis to particular problems as and when they arise, and provides greater flexibility in the regulation of activity which is subject to the ministers' overview.

2.3.5 Disadvantages in the prevalence of delegated legislation

Disadvantages in the prevalence of delegated legislation are as follows:

- *Accountability*

  A key issue in the use of delegated legislation concerns the question of accountability and the erosion of the constitutional role of Parliament. Parliament is presumed to be the source of legislation but, with respect to delegated legislation, individual MPs are not the source of the law. Certain people, notably government ministers and the civil servants who work under them to produce the detailed provisions of delegated legislation, are the real source of such regulations. Even allowing for the fact that they are in effect operating on powers delegated to them from Parliament, it is not beyond questioning whether this procedure does not give them more power than might be thought appropriate or, indeed, constitutionally correct.

- *Scrutiny*

  The question of general accountability raises the need for effective scrutiny, but the very form of delegated legislation makes it extremely difficult for ordinary MPs to fully understand what is being enacted and, therefore, to effectively monitor it. This difficulty arises in part from the tendency for such regulations to be highly specific, detailed and technical. This problem of comprehension and control is compounded by the fact that regulations appear outside the context of their enabling legislation but only have any real meaning in that context.

- *Bulk*

  The problems faced by ordinary MPs in effectively keeping abreast of delegated legislation are further increased by the sheer mass of such legislation, and if parliamentarians cannot keep up with the flow of delegated legislation, the question has to be asked as to how the general public can be expected to do so.

2.3.6 Control over delegated legislation

The foregoing difficulties and potential shortcomings in the use of delegated legislation are, at least to a degree, mitigated by the fact that specific controls have been established to oversee the use of delegated legislation. These controls take two forms:

- *Parliamentary control over delegated legislation*

  Power to make delegated legislation is ultimately dependent upon the authority of Parliament, and Parliament retains general control over the procedure for enacting such law.

  New regulations, in the form of delegated legislation, are required to be laid before Parliament. This procedure takes one of two forms, depending on the provision of the enabling legislation. Some regulations require a positive resolution of one or both of the Houses of Parliament before they become law. Most Acts, however, simply require that regulations made under their auspices be placed before Parliament. They automatically become law after a period of 40 days, unless a resolution to annul them is passed.

Since 1973, there has been a Joint Select Committee on Statutory Instruments, whose function it is to consider statutory instruments. This committee scrutinises statutory instruments from a technical point of view as regards drafting and has no power to question the substantive content or the policy implications of the regulation. Its effectiveness as a general control is, therefore, limited. EC legislation is overseen by a specific committee and local authority bylaws are usually subject to the approval of the Department of the Deputy Prime Minister.

- *Judicial control of delegated legislation*

  It is possible for delegated legislation to be challenged through the procedure of judicial review, on the basis that the person or body to whom Parliament has delegated its authority has acted in a way that exceeds the limited powers delegated to them. Any provision which does not have this authority is *ultra vires* and void. Additionally, there is a presumption that any power delegated by Parliament is to be used in a reasonable manner and the courts may, on occasion, hold particular delegated legislation to be void on the basis that it is unreasonable.

  The power of the courts to scrutinise and control delegated legislation has been greatly increased by the introduction of the HRA. As has been noted previously, that Act does not give courts the power to strike down primary legislation as being incompatible with the rights contained in the ECHR. However, as – by definition – delegated legislation is not primary legislation, it follows that the courts now do have the power to declare invalid any such legislation which conflicts with the ECHR.

2.4 Case Law

The foregoing has highlighted the increased importance of legislation in today's society but, even allowing for this and the fact that case law can be overturned by legislation, the UK is still a common law system, and the importance and effectiveness of judicial creativity and common law principles and practices cannot be discounted. 'Case law' is the name given to the creation and refinement of law in the course of judicial decisions.

2.4.1 The meaning of precedent

The doctrine of binding precedent, or *stare decisis* (Latin for "to stand by decided matters"), lies at the heart of the English common law system. It refers to the fact that, within the hierarchical structure of the English courts, a decision of a higher court will be binding on any court which is lower than it in that hierarchy. In general terms, this means that, when judges try cases, they will check to see whether a similar situation has already come before a court. If the precedent was set by a court of equal or higher status to the court deciding the new case, then the judge in that case should follow the rule of law established in the earlier case. Where the precedent is set by a court lower in the hierarchy, the judge in the new case does not have to follow it, but he will certainly consider it and will not overrule it without due consideration.

The operation of the doctrine of binding precedent depends on the existence of an extensive reporting service to provide access to previous judicial decisions. The earliest summaries of cases appeared in the Year Books but, since 1865, cases have been reported by the Council of Law Reporting, which produces the authoritative reports of cases. Modern technology has resulted in the establishment of Lexis, a computer-based store of cases.

For reference purposes, the most commonly referenced law reports are cited as follows:

- *Law reports*

  Appeal Cases (AC)

  Chancery Division (Ch D)

  Family Division (Fam)

  King's/Queen's Bench (KB/QB)

- *Other general series of reports*

  All England Law Reports (All ER)

  Weekly Law Reports (WLR)

  Solicitors Journal (SJ)

  European Court Reports (ECR)

- *CD-ROMs and Internet facilities*

  As in most other fields, the growth of information technology has revolutionised law reporting and law finding. Many of the law reports mentioned above are both available on CD-ROM and on the Internet. See, for example, Justis, Lawtel, Lexis-Nexis and Westlaw UK, amongst others. Indeed, members of the public can now access law reports directly from their sources in the courts, both domestically and in Europe. The first major electronic cases database was the Lexis system, which gave immediate access to a huge range of case authorities, some unreported elsewhere. The problem for the courts was that lawyers with access to the system could simply cite lists of cases from the database without the courts having access to paper copies of the decisions. The courts soon expressed their displeasure at this indiscriminate citation of unreported cases trawled from the Lexis database (see *Stanley v International Harvester Co of Great Britain Ltd* (1983)).

In line with the ongoing modernisation of the whole legal system, the way in which cases are to be cited has been changed. Thus, from January 2001, following *Practice*

Direction (Judgments: Form and Citation) [2001] 1 WLR 194, a new neutral system was introduced; it was extended in a further Practice Direction in April 2002. Cases in the various courts are now cited as follows:

House of Lords	[year]	UKHL case no
Court of Appeal (Civil Division)	[year]	EWCA Civ case no
Court of Appeal (Criminal Division)	[year]	EWCA Crim case no
High Court		
Queen's Bench Division	[year]	EWHC case no (QB)
Chancery Division	[year]	EWHC case no (Ch)
Patents Court	[year]	EWHC case no (Pat)
Administrative Court	[year]	EWHC case no (Admin)
Commercial Court	[year]	EWHC case no (Comm)
Admiralty Court	[year]	EWHC case no (Admlty)
Technology & Construction Court	[year]	EWHC case no (TCC)
Family Division	[year]	EWHC case no (Fam)

Within the individual case, the paragraphs of each judgment are numbered consecutively and, where there is more than one judgment, the numbering of the paragraphs carries on sequentially. Thus, for example, the neutral citation for *International Transport Roth GmbH v Secretary of State for the Home Department* is [2002] EWCA Civ 158 and the citation for the quotation from Simon Brown LJ from the case is at para [53]. The specific law report series within which the case is reported is cited after the neutral citation: thus, the *International Transport Roth* decision may be found at [2002] 3 WLR 344.

2.4.2 The hierarchy of the courts and the setting of precedent

2.4.2.1 *House of Lords*

The House of Lords stands at the summit of the English court structure and its decisions are binding on all courts below it in the hierarchy. It must be recalled, however, that the ECJ is superior to the House of Lords in matters relating to EC law. As regards its own previous decisions, until 1966 the House of Lords regarded itself as bound by such decisions. In a *Practice Statement* (1966), Lord Gardiner indicated that the House of Lords would in future regard itself as being free to depart from its previous decisions where it appeared to be right to do so. Given the potentially destabilising effect on existing legal practice based on previous decisions of the House of Lords, this is not a discretion that the court exercises lightly. There have, however, been a number of cases in which the House of Lords has overruled or amended its own earlier decisions, for example: *Conway v Rimmer* (1968); *Herrington v BRB* (1972); *Miliangos v George Frank (Textiles) Ltd* (1976); and *R v Shivpuri* (1986). In *Herrington v BRB*, the House of Lords overturned the previous rule, established in *Addie v Dumbreck* (1929), that an occupier was only responsible for injury sustained to a trespassing child if the injury was caused either intentionally or recklessly by the occupier. In the modern context, the court preferred to establish responsibility on the basis of whether the occupier had done everything that a humane person should have done to protect the trespasser. Further, in *Miliangos v George Frank (Textiles) Ltd*, the House of Lords decided that, in the light of changed foreign exchange conditions, the previous rule that damages in English courts could only be paid in sterling no longer applied. They allowed payment in the foreign currency as specified in the contract and, in so doing, overruled *Re United Railways of the Havana & Regla Warehouses Ltd* (1961).

2.4.2.2 Court of Appeal

In civil cases, the Court of Appeal is generally bound by previous decisions of the House of Lords.

The Court of Appeal is also bound by its own previous decisions in civil cases. There are, however, a number of exceptions to this general rule. Lord Greene MR listed these exceptions in *Young v Bristol Aeroplane Co Ltd* (1944). They arise where:

- there is a conflict between two previous decisions of the Court of Appeal. In this situation, the later court must decide which decision to follow and, as a corollary, which decision to overrule (*Tiverton Estates Ltd v Wearwell Ltd* (1974));

- a previous decision of the Court of Appeal has been overruled, either expressly or impliedly, by the House of Lords. In this situation, the Court of Appeal is required to follow the decision of the House of Lords (*Family Housing Association v Jones* (1990)); or

- the previous decision was given *per incuriam*, in other words, that previous decision was taken in ignorance of some authority, either statutory or judge made, that would have led to a different conclusion. In this situation, the later court can ignore the previous decision in question (*Williams v Fawcett* (1985)).

There is also the possibility that, as a consequence of s 3 of the European Communities Act 1972, the Court of Appeal can ignore a previous decision of its own which is inconsistent with EC law or with a later decision of the ECJ.

The Court of Appeal may also make use of ss 2 and 3 of the HRA to overrule precedents no longer compatible with the rights provided under that Act (see 1.5 above). As has been seen in *Ghaidan v Godin-Mendoza* (2004), it extended the rights of same-sex partners to inherit tenancies under the Rent Act 1977 in a way that the House of Lords had not felt able to do in *Fitzpatrick v Sterling Housing Association Ltd* (1999), a case decided before the HRA had come into force. Doubtless the Court of Appeal would use the same powers to overrule its own previous decisions made without regard to rights provided by the 1998 Act.

Although, on the basis of *R v Spencer* (1985), it would appear that there is no difference, in principle, in the operation of the doctrine of *stare decisis* between the Criminal and Civil Divisions of the Court of Appeal, it is generally accepted that, in practice, precedent is not followed as strictly in the former as it is in the latter. Courts in the Criminal Division are not bound to follow their own previous decisions which they subsequently consider to have been based on either a misunderstanding or a misapplication of the law. The reason for this is that the criminal courts deal with matters which involve individual liberty and which, therefore, require greater discretion to prevent injustice.

2.4.2.3   High Court

The Divisional Courts, each located within the three divisions of the High Court, hear appeals from courts and tribunals below them in the hierarchy. They are bound by the doctrine of *stare decisis* in the normal way and must follow decisions of the House of Lords and the Court of Appeal. Each Divisional Court is usually also bound by its own previous decisions, although in civil cases it may make use of the exceptions open to the Court of Appeal in *Young v Bristol Aeroplane Co Ltd* (1944) and, in criminal appeal cases, the Queen's Bench Divisional Court may refuse to follow its own earlier decisions where it considers the earlier decision to have been made wrongly.

The High Court is also bound by the decisions of superior courts. Decisions by individual High Court judges are binding on courts which are inferior in the hierarchy, but such decisions are not binding on other High Court judges, although they are of strong persuasive authority and tend to be followed in practice.

Crown Courts cannot create precedent and their decisions can never amount to more than persuasive authority.

County courts and magistrates' courts do not create precedents.

2.4.3   The nature of precedent

Previous cases establish legal precedents which later courts must either follow or, if the decision was made by a court lower in the hierarchy, at least consider. It is essential to realise, however, that not every part of the case as reported in the law reports is part of the precedent. In theory, it is possible to divide cases into two parts: the *ratio decidendi* and *obiter dicta*:

- *Ratio decidendi*

  The *ratio decidendi* (Latin for "the reason for deciding") of a case may be understood as the statement of the law applied in deciding the legal problem raised by the concrete facts of the case. It is essential to establish that it is not the actual decision in a case that sets the precedent – it is the rule of law on which that decision is founded that does this. This rule, which is an abstraction from the facts of the case, is known as the *ratio decidendi* of the case.

- *Obiter dicta*

  Any statement of law that is not an essential part of the *ratio decidendi* is, strictly speaking, superfluous, and any such statement is referred to as *obiter dictum (obiter dicta* in the plural), that is, 'said by the way'. Although *obiter dicta* statements do not form part of the binding precedent, they are of persuasive authority and can be taken into consideration in later cases.

The division of cases into these two distinct parts is a theoretical procedure. It is the general misfortune of all those who study law that judges do not actually separate their judgments into the two clearly defined categories. It is the particular misfortune of a student of business law, however, that they tend to be led to believe that case reports are divided into two distinct parts: the *ratio*, in which the judge states what he takes to be the law; and *obiter* statements, in which the judge muses on alternative possibilities. Such is not the case: there is no such clear division and, in reality, it is actually later courts which effectively determine the *ratio* in any particular case. Indeed, later courts may declare *obiter* what was previously felt to be part of the *ratio*. One should never overestimate the objective, scientific nature of the legal process.

Students should always read cases fully; although it is tempting to rely on the headnote at the start of the case report, it should be remembered that this is a summary provided by the case reporter and merely reflects what he or she thinks the *ratio* is. It is not unknown for headnotes to miss an essential point in a case.

2.4.4 Evaluation

The foregoing has set out the doctrine of binding precedent as it operates, in theory, to control the ambit of judicial discretion. It has to be recognised, however, that the doctrine does not operate as stringently as it appears to at first sight, and there are particular shortcomings in the system that must be addressed in weighing up the undoubted advantages with the equally undoubted disadvantages.

2.4.5 Advantages of case law

There are numerous perceived advantages of the doctrine of *stare decisis*, amongst which are the following:

- *Consistency*

  This refers to the fact that like cases are decided on a like basis and are not apparently subject to the whim of the individual judge deciding the case in question. This aspect of formal justice is important in justifying the decisions taken in particular cases.

- *Certainty*

  This follows from, and indeed is presupposed by, the previous item. Lawyers and their clients are able to predict the likely outcome of a particular legal question in the light of previous judicial decisions. Also, once the legal rule has been established in one case, individuals can orient their behaviour with regard to that rule relatively secure in the knowledge that it will not be changed by some later court.

- *Efficiency*

This particular advantage follows from the preceding one. As the judiciary are bound by precedent, lawyers and their clients can be reasonably certain as to the likely outcome of any particular case on the basis of established precedent. As a consequence, most disputes do not have to be re-argued before the courts. With regard to potential litigants, it saves them money in court expenses because they can apply to their solicitor/barrister for guidance as to how their particular case is likely to be decided in the light of previous cases on the same or similar points.

- *Flexibility*

This refers to the fact that various mechanisms enable the judges to manipulate the common law in such a way as to provide them with an opportunity to develop law in particular areas without waiting for Parliament to enact legislation. It should be recognised that judges do have a considerable degree of discretion in electing whether or not to be bound by a particular authority.

Flexibility is achieved through the possibility of previous decisions being either overruled or distinguished, or the possibility of a later court extending or modifying the effective ambit of a precedent. The main mechanisms through which judges alter or avoid precedents are overruling and distinguishing:

○ *Overruling*

This is the procedure whereby a court which is higher in the hierarchy sets aside a legal ruling established in a previous case.

It is somewhat anomalous that, within the system of *stare decisis*, precedents gain increased authority with the passage of time. As a consequence, courts tend to be reluctant to overrule long standing authorities, even though they may no longer accurately reflect contemporary practices. In addition to the wish to maintain a high degree of certainty in the law, the main reason for the judicial reluctance to overrule old decisions would appear to be the fact that overruling operates retrospectively and the principle of law being overruled is held never to have been law. Overruling a precedent, therefore, might have the consequence of disturbing important financial arrangements made in line with what were thought to be settled rules of law. It might even, in certain circumstances, lead to the imposition of criminal liability on previously lawful behaviour. It has to be emphasised, however, that the courts will not shrink from overruling authorities where they see them as no longer representing an appropriate statement of law. The decision in *R v R* (1992) to recognise the possibility of rape within marriage may be seen as an example of this, although, even here, the House of Lords felt constrained to state that it was not actually altering the law but was merely removing a misconception as to the true meaning and effect of the law. As this demonstrates, the courts are rarely ready to challenge the legislative prerogative of Parliament in an overt way.

Overruling should not be confused with reversing, which is the procedure whereby a court higher in the hierarchy reverses the decision of a lower court in the same case.

○ *Distinguishing*

The main device for avoiding binding precedents is distinguishing. As has been previously stated, the *ratio decidendi* of any case is an abstraction from the material facts of the case. This opens up the possibility that a court may regard the facts of the case before it as significantly different from the facts of a cited precedent and, consequentially, it will not find itself bound to follow that precedent. Judges use the device of distinguishing where, for some reason, they are unwilling to follow a particular precedent, and the law reports provide many examples of strained distinctions where a court has quite evidently not wanted to follow an authority that it would otherwise have been bound by.

2.4.6 Disadvantages of case law

It should be noted that the advantage of flexibility at least potentially contradicts the alternative advantage of certainty, but there are other disadvantages in the doctrine which have to be considered. Amongst these are the following:

- *Uncertainty*

  This refers to the fact that the degree of certainty provided by the doctrine of *stare decisis* is undermined by the absolute number of cases that have been reported and can be cited as authorities. This uncertainty is compounded by the ability of the judiciary to select which authority to follow, through use of the mechanism of distinguishing cases on their facts.

- *Fixity*

  This refers to the possibility that the law, in relation to any particular area, may become ossified on the basis of an unjust precedent, with the consequence that previous injustices are perpetuated. An example of this was the long delay in the recognition of the possibility of rape within marriage, which was only recognised a decade ago (*R v R* (1992)).

- *Unconstitutionality*

  This is a fundamental question that refers to the fact that the judiciary are in fact overstepping their theoretical constitutional role by actually making law, rather than restricting themselves to the role of simply applying it. It is now probably a commonplace of legal theory that judges do make law. Due to their position in the constitution, however, judges have to be circumspect in the way in which, and the extent to which, they use their powers to create law and impose values. To overtly assert or exercise the power would be to challenge the power of the legislature. For an unelected body to challenge a politically supreme Parliament would be unwise, to say the least.

2.4.7 Case study

Carlill v Carbolic Smoke Ball Co Ltd (1892) is one of the most famous examples of the case law in this area. A summary of the case is set out below.

Facts: Mrs Carlill made a retail purchase of one of the defendant's medicinal products: the Carbolic Smoke Ball. It was supposed to prevent people who used it in a specified way (three times a day for at least two weeks) from catching influenza. The company was very confident about its product and placed an advertisement in a newspaper, the *Pall Mall Gazette*, which praised the effectiveness of the smoke ball and promised to pay £100 (a huge sum of money at that time) to:

> ... any person who contracts the increasing epidemic influenza, colds, or any disease caused by taking cold, having used the ball three times daily for two weeks according to the printed directions supplied with each ball.

The advertisement went on to explain that the company had deposited £1,000 with the Alliance Bank (on Regent Street in London) as a sign of its sincerity in the matter. Any proper claimants could get their payment from that sum. On the faith of the advertisement, Mrs Carlill bought one of the balls at a chemist and used it as directed, but she caught influenza. She claimed £100 from the company but was refused it, so she sued for breach of contract. The company said that, for several reasons, there was no contract, the main reasons being that:

- the advert was too vague to amount to the basis of a contract;

- there was no time limit and no way of checking the way in which the customer used the ball;

- Mrs Carlill did not give any legally recognised value to the company;

- one cannot legally make an offer to the whole world, so the advert was not a proper offer;

- even if the advert could be seen as an offer, Mrs Carlill had not given a legal acceptance of that offer because she had not notified the company that she was accepting; and

- the advert was a mere puff, that is, a piece of insincere rhetoric.

Decision: The Court of Appeal found that there was a legally enforceable agreement – a contract – between Mrs Carlill and the company. The company would have to pay damages to Mrs Carlill.

Ratio decidendi: The three Lords Justice of Appeal who gave judgments in this case all decided in favour of Mrs Carlill. Each, however, used slightly different reasoning, arguments and examples. The process, therefore, of distilling the reason for the decision of the court is quite a delicate art. The *ratio* of the case can be put as follows.

Offers must be sufficiently clear in order to allow the courts to enforce agreements that follow from them. The offer here was a distinct promise, expressed in language which was perfectly unmistakable. It could not be a mere puff in view of the £1,000 deposited specially to show good faith. An offer *may* be made to the world at large, and the advert was such an offer. It was accepted by any person, like Mrs Carlill, who bought the product and used it in the prescribed manner. Mrs Carlill had accepted the offer by her conduct when she did as she was invited to do and started to use the smoke ball. She had not been asked to let the company know that she was using it.

Obiter dicta: In the course of his reasoning, Bowen LJ gave the legal answer to a set of facts which were not in issue in this case. They are thus *obiter dicta*. He did this because it assisted him in clarifying the answer to Mrs Carlill's case. He said:

> If I advertise to the world that my dog is lost, and that anybody who brings the dog to a particular place will be paid some money, are all the police or other persons whose business it is to find lost dogs to be expected to sit down and write me a note saying that they have accepted my proposal? Why, of course, they at once look [for] the dog, and as soon as they find the dog they have performed the condition.

If such facts were ever subsequently in issue in a court case, the words of Bowen LJ could be used by counsel as persuasive precedent.

Carlill was applied in *Peck v Lateu* (1973) but was distinguished in *AM Satterthwaite & Co v New Zealand Shipping Co* (1972).

2.5   Statutory Interpretation

The two previous sections have tended to present legislation and case law in terms of opposition: legislation being the product of Parliament and case law the product of the judiciary in the courts. Such stark opposition is, of course, misleading, for the two processes come together when consideration is given to the necessity for judges to interpret statute law in order to apply it.

2.5.1   Problems in interpreting legislation

In order to apply legislation, judges must ascertain its meaning and, in order to ascertain that meaning, they are faced with the difficulty of interpreting the legislation. Legislation, however, shares the general problem of uncertainty, which is inherent in any mode of verbal communication. Words can have more than one meaning and the meaning of a word can change, depending on its context.

One of the essential requirements of legislation is generality of application – the need for it to be written in such a way as to ensure that it can be effectively applied in various circumstances without the need to detail those situations individually. This requirement, however, can give rise to particular problems of interpretation; the need for generality can only really be achieved at the expense of clarity and precision of language.

Legislation, therefore, involves an inescapable measure of uncertainty, which can only be made certain through judicial interpretation. However, to the extent that the interpretation of legislative provisions is an active process, it is equally a creative process, and it inevitably involves the judiciary in creating law through determining the meaning and effect being given to any particular piece of legislation.

2.5.2 Rules of interpretation

In attempting to decide upon the precise meaning of any statute, judges use well established rules of interpretation, of which there are three primary ones, together with a variety of other secondary aids to construction.

The rules of statutory interpretation are as follows:

- *Literal rule*

  Under this rule, the judge is required to consider what the legislation actually says, rather than considering what it might mean. In order to achieve this end, the judge should give words in legislation their literal meaning; that is, their plain, ordinary, everyday meaning, even if the effect of this is to produce what might be considered an otherwise unjust or undesirable outcome.

  Inland Revenue Commissioners v Hinchy (1960) concerned s 25(3) of the Income Tax Act 1952, which stated that any taxpayer who did not complete their tax return was subject to a fixed penalty of £20 plus *treble the tax which he ought to be charged under the Act*. The question that had to be decided was whether the additional element of the penalty should be based on the total amount that should have been paid, or merely the unpaid portion of that total. The House of Lords adopted a literal interpretation of the statute and held that any taxpayer in default should have to pay triple their original tax bill.

  In *Fisher v Bell* (1961), the court, in line with general contract principles, decided that the placing of an article in a window did not amount to offering but was merely an invitation to treat, and thus the shopkeeper could not be charged with 'offering the goods for sale'. In this case, the court chose to follow the contract law literal interpretation of the meaning of 'offer' in the Act in question, and declined to consider the usual non-legal literal interpretation of the word. (The executive's attitude to the courts' legal-literal interpretation in *Fisher v Bell*, and the related case of *Partridge v Crittenden* (1968), can be surmised from the fact that later legislation, such as the Trade Descriptions Act 1968, has effectively legislated that invitations to treat are to be treated in the same way as offers for sale.)

  A problem in relation to the literal rule arises from the difficulty that judges face in determining the literal meaning of even the commonest of terms. In *R v Maginnis* (1987), the judges differed amongst themselves as to the literal meaning of the common word 'supply' in relation to a charge of supplying drugs. *Attorney General's Reference (No 1 of 1988)* (1989) concerned the meaning of 'obtained' in s 1(3) of the Company Securities (Insider Dealing) Act 1985, since replaced by the Criminal

Justice Act 1993, and led to similar disagreement as to the precise meaning of an everyday word.

- *Golden rule*

  This rule is generally considered to be an extension of the literal rule. It is applied in circumstances where the application of the literal rule is likely to result in an obviously absurd result.

  An example of the application of the golden rule is *Adler v George* (1964). In this case, the court held that the literal wording of the statute ('in the vicinity of') covered the action committed by the defendant who carried out her action within the area concerned.

  Another example of this approach is to be found in *Re Sigsworth* (1935), in which the court introduced common law rules into legislative provisions, which were silent on the matter, to prevent the estate of a murderer from benefiting from the property of the party he had murdered.

- *Mischief rule*

  This rule, sometimes known as the rule in *Heydon's Case* (1584), operates to enable judges to interpret a statute in such a way as to provide a remedy for the mischief that the statute was enacted to prevent. Contemporary practice is to go beyond the actual body of the legislation to determine what mischief a particular Act was aimed at redressing.

  The example usually cited of the use of the mischief rule is *Corkery v Carpenter* (1951), in which a man was found guilty of being drunk in charge of a 'carriage', although he was in fact only in charge of a bicycle. A much more controversial application of the rule is to be found in *Royal College of Nursing v DHSS* (1981), where the courts had to decide whether the medical induction of premature labour to effect abortion, under the supervision of nursing staff, was lawful.

2.5.3 Aids to construction

In addition to the three main rules of interpretation, there are a number of secondary aids to construction. These can be categorised as either intrinsic or extrinsic in nature:

- *Intrinsic assistance*

  This is help which is actually derived from the statute which is the object of interpretation. The judge uses the full statute to understand the meaning of a particular part of it. Assistance may be found from various parts of the statute, such as: the title, long or short; any preamble, which is a statement preceding the actual provisions of the Act; and schedules, which appear as detailed additions at the end of the Act. Section headings or marginal notes may also be considered, where they exist.

- *Extrinsic assistance*

Sources outside of the Act itself may, on occasion, be resorted to in determining the meaning of legislation. For example, judges have always been entitled to refer to dictionaries in order to find the meaning of non-legal words. The Interpretation Act 1978 is also available for consultation with regard to the meaning of particular words generally used in statutes.

Judges are also allowed to use extrinsic sources to determine the mischief at which particular legislation is aimed. For example, they are able to examine earlier statutes and they have been entitled for some time to look at Law Commission reports, Royal Commission reports and the reports of other official commissions.

Until fairly recently, *Hansard*, the verbatim report of parliamentary debate, literally remained a closed book to the courts. In *Pepper v Hart* (1993), however, the House of Lords decided to overturn the previous rule. In a majority decision, it was held that, where the precise meaning of legislation was uncertain or ambiguous, or where the literal meaning of an Act would lead to a manifest absurdity, the courts could refer to *Hansard's Reports of Parliamentary Debates and Proceedings* as an aid to construing the meaning of the legislation.

The operation of the principle in *Pepper v Hart* was extended in *Three Rivers DC v Bank of England (No 2)* (1996) to cover situations where the legislation under question was not in itself ambiguous but might be ineffective in its intention to give effect to some particular EC directive. Applying the wider powers of interpretation open to it in such circumstances, the court held that it was permissible to refer to *Hansard* in order to determine the actual purpose of the statute.

The *Pepper v Hart* principle only applies to statements made by ministers at the time of the passage of legislation, and the courts have declined to extend it to cover situations where ministers subsequently make some statement as to what they consider the effect of a particular Act to be (*Melluish (Inspector of Taxes)* v BMI (No 3) Ltd (1995)).

2.5.4   Presumptions

In addition to the rules of interpretation, the courts may also make use of certain presumptions. As with all presumptions, they are rebuttable, which means that the presumption is subject to being overturned in argument in any particular case. The presumptions operate in the following ways:

* *Against the alteration of the common law*

  Parliament can alter the common law whenever it decides to do so. In order to do this, however, it must expressly enact legislation to that end. If there is no express intention to that effect, it is assumed that statute does not make any fundamental change to the common law. With regard to particular provisions, if there are alternative interpretations, one of which will maintain the existing common law situation, then that interpretation will be preferred.

* *Against retrospective application*

As the War Crimes Act 1990 shows, Parliament can impose criminal responsibility retrospectively, where particular and extremely unusual circumstances dictate the need to do so, but such effect must be clearly expressed.

• *Against the deprivation of an individual's liberty, property or rights*

Once again, the presumption can be rebutted by express provision and it is not uncommon for legislation to deprive people of their rights to enjoy particular benefits. Nor is it unusual for individuals to be deprived of their liberty under the Mental Health Act 1983.

• *Against application to the Crown*

Unless the legislation contains a clear statement to the contrary, it is presumed not to apply to the Crown.

• *Against breaking international law*

Where possible, legislation should be interpreted in such a way as to give effect to existing international legal obligations.

• *In favour of the requirement that mens rea (a guilty mind) be a requirement in any criminal offence*

The classic example of this presumption is *Sweet v Parsley* (1969), in which a landlord was eventually found not guilty of allowing her premises to be used for the purpose of taking drugs, as she had absolutely no knowledge of what was going on in her house. Offences which do not require the presence of *mens rea* are referred to as strict liability offences.

• *In favour of words taking their meaning from the context in which they are used*

This final presumption refers back to, and operates in conjunction with, the major rules for interpreting legislation considered previously. The general presumption appears as three distinct sub-rules, each of which carries a Latin tag:

○ the *noscitur a sociis* rule is applied where statutory provisions include a list of examples of what is covered by the legislation. It is presumed that the words used have a related meaning and are to be interpreted in relation to each other (see *IRC v Frere* (1965));

○ the *eiusdem generis* rule applies in situations where general words are appended to the end of a list of specific examples. The presumption is that the general words have to be interpreted in line with the prior restrictive examples. Thus, a provision which referred to a list that included horses, cattle, sheep and other animals would be unlikely to apply to domestic animals such as cats and dogs (see *Powell v Kempton Park Racecourse* (1899)); and

○ the *expressio unius exclusio alterius* rule simply means that, where a statute seeks to establish a list of what is covered by its provisions, then anything not expressly included in that list is specifically excluded (see *R v Inhabitants of Sedgley* (1831)).

2.6 Custom

The traditional view of the development of the common law tends to adopt an overly romantic view as regards its emergence. This view suggests that the common law is no more than the crystallisation of ancient common customs, this distillation being accomplished by the judiciary in the course of their historic travels around the land in the Middle Ages. This view, however, tends to ignore the political process that gave rise to this procedure. The imposition of a common system of law represented the political victory of a State that had fought to establish and assert its central authority. Viewed in that light, the emergence of the common law can perhaps better be seen as the invention of the judges as representatives of the State and as representing what they wanted the law to be, rather than what people generally thought it was.

One source of customary practice that undoubtedly did find expression in the form of law was business and commercial practice. These customs and practices were originally constituted in the distinct form of the Law Merchant but, gradually, this became subsumed under the control of the common law courts and ceased to exist apart from the common law.

Notwithstanding the foregoing, it is still possible for specific local customs to operate as a source of law. In certain circumstances, parties may assert the existence of customary practices in order to support their case. Such local custom may run counter to the strict application of the common law and, where they are found to be legitimate, they will effectively replace the common law. Even in this respect, however, reliance on customary law as opposed to common law, although not impossible, is made unlikely by the stringent tests that have to be satisfied (see *Egerton v Harding* (1974)). The requirements that a local custom must satisfy in order to be recognised are as follows:

- it must have existed from time immemorial, that is, 1189;

- it must have been exercised continuously within that period;

- it must have been exercised peacefully and without opposition;

- it must also have been felt to be obligatory;

- it must be capable of precise definition;

- it must have been consistent with other customs; and

- it must be reasonable.

Given this list of requirements, it can be seen why local custom is not an important source of law.

2.6.1 Books of authority

In the very unusual situation of a court being unable to locate a precise or analogous precedent, it may refer to legal textbooks for guidance. Such books are subdivided, depending on when they were written. In strict terms, only certain works are actually treated as authoritative sources of law. Legal works produced after *Blackstone's Commentaries* of 1765 are considered to be of recent origin and, although they cannot be treated as authoritative sources, the courts may consider what the most eminent works by accepted experts in particular fields have said in order to help determine what the law is or should be.

2.7 Law Reform

At one level, law reform is a product of either parliamentary or judicial activity, as has been considered previously. Parliament tends, however, to be concerned with particularities of law reform and the judiciary are constitutionally and practically disbarred from reforming the law on anything other than an opportunistic and piecemeal basis. Therefore, there remains a need for the question of law reform to be considered generally and a requirement that such consideration be conducted in an informed but disinterested manner.

Reference has already been made to the use of consultative Green Papers by the Government as a mechanism for gauging the opinions of interested parties to particular reforms. More formal advice may be provided through various advisory standing committees. Amongst these is the Law Reform Committee. The function of this Committee is to consider the desirability of changes to the civil law which the Lord Chancellor may refer to it. The Criminal Law Revision Committee performs similar functions in relation to criminal law.

Royal Commissions may be constituted to consider the need for law reform in specific areas. For example, the Commission on Criminal Procedure (1980) led to the enactment of the Police and Criminal Evidence Act (PACE) 1984.

Committees may be set up in order to review the operation of particular areas of law, the most significant recent example being the Woolf review of the operation of the civil justice system. (Detailed analysis of the consequences flowing from the implementation of the recommendations of the Woolf Report will be considered subsequently.) Similarly, Sir Robin Auld conducted a review of the whole criminal justice system and Sir Andrew Leggatt carried out a similar task in relation to the tribunal system.

If a criticism is to be levelled at these committees and commissions, it is that they are all *ad hoc* bodies. Their remit is limited and they do not have the power either to widen the ambit of their investigation or initiate reform proposals.

The Law Commission fulfils the need for some institution to concern itself more generally with the question of law reform. Its general function is to keep the law as a whole under review and to make recommendations for its systematic reform.

Although the scope of the Commission is limited to those areas set out in its programme of law reform, its ambit is not unduly restricted, as may be seen from the range of matters covered in its eighth programme set out in October 2001, which includes: damages; limitation of actions; property law; housing law; the law of trusts;

partnership law; unfair terms in contracts; compulsory purchase; and the codification of criminal law. In addition, ministers may refer matters of particular importance to the Commission for its consideration. As was noted above at 1.2.5, it was just such a referral by the Home Secretary, after the Macpherson Inquiry into the Stephen Lawrence case, that gave rise to the Law Commission's recommendation that the rule against double jeopardy be removed in particular circumstances. An extended version of that recommendation was included in the Criminal Justice Act 2003.

SOURCES OF LAW

Domestic Sources of Law

- Legislation is the law produced through the parliamentary system; then it is given royal assent. The House of Lords has only limited scope to delay legislation.

- Delegated legislation is a sub-classification of legislation. It appears in the form of: Orders in Council; statutory instruments; bylaws; and professional regulations.

  Advantages of delegated legislation:

  ○ speed of implementation;

  ○ the saving of parliamentary time;

  ○ access to expertise; and

  ○ flexibility.

  The disadvantages relate to:

  ○ the lack of accountability;

  ○ the lack of scrutiny of proposals for such legislation; and

  ○ the sheer amount of delegated legislation.

  Controls over delegated legislation:

  ○ Joint Select Committee on Statutory Instruments; and

  ○ *ultra vires* provisions may be challenged in the courts.

Case Law

- Created by judges in the course of deciding cases.

- The doctrine of *stare decisis*, or binding precedent, refers to the fact that courts are bound by previous decisions of courts which are equal or above them in the court hierarchy.

- The *ratio decidendi* is binding. Everything else is *obiter dicta*.

- Precedents may be avoided through either overruling or distinguishing.

  The advantages of precedent are:

  ○ saving the time of all parties concerned;

  ○ certainty; and

  ○ flexibility.

  The disadvantages are:

ɔ uncertainty;

ɔ fixity; and

ɔ unconstitutionality.

Statutory Interpretation

This is the way in which judges give practical meaning to legislative provisions, using the following rules:

- The *literal rule* gives words everyday meaning, even if this leads to an apparent injustice.

- The *golden rule* is used in circumstances where the application of the literal rule is likely to result in an obviously absurd result.

- The *mischief rule* permits the court to go beyond the words of the statute in question to consider the mischief at which it was aimed.

There are rebuttable presumptions against:

- the alteration of the common law;

- retrospective application;

- the deprivation of an individual's liberty, property or rights; and

- application to the Crown.

And in favour of:

- the requirement of *mens rea* in relation to criminal offences; and

- deriving the meaning of words from their contexts.

Judges may seek assistance from:

- intrinsic sources as the title of the Act, any preamble or any schedules to it; and

- extrinsic sources such as: dictionaries; textbooks; reports; other parliamentary papers; and, since *Pepper v Hart* (1993), *Hansard*.

Custom

Custom is of very limited importance as a contemporary source of law, although it was important in the establishment of business and commercial law in the form of the old Law Merchant.

CHAPTER 3

THE CIVIL AND CRIMINAL
COURT STRUCTURES

This first part of the chapter looks at the civil court structure and at which type of cases are heard in which trial courts, the rules relating to transfer of cases from one level of court to another, the system of appeals and the criticisms which have been made of the various aspects of these systems. What is the difference between a criminal and civil case? There are several key distinctions:

- Criminal cases are brought by the state against individual or corporate defendants, whereas civil cases are brought by one citizen or body against another such party. The State here involves the police (or possibly Customs and Excise officers or tax inspectors), who investigate the crime and collect the evidence, and the Crown Prosecution Service, which prepares the Crown's case. In civil cases, the state is not involved, except in so far as it provides the courts and personnel so that the litigation can be judged. If a party refuses, for example, to be bound by the order a court makes in a civil case, then that party may be found in contempt of court and punished, that is, imprisoned or fined.

- The outcomes of civil and criminal cases are different. If a criminal case is successful from the point of view of the person bringing it (*the prosecutor*) because the magistrate or jury finds *the defendant* (sometimes called *the accused*) guilty as charged, then the result will be a sentence. There is a wide range of sentences available, from absolute or conditional discharges (where the convicted defendant is free to go without any conditions or with some requirement, for example, that the defendant undertakes never to visit a particular place) to life imprisonment. Criminal sentences, or 'sanctions', are imposed to mark the State's disapproval of the defendant's crime. There is often a considerable cost in imposing a punishment. In March 2006, the national prison population was 76,758 (4,428 female prisoners, and 72,330 male prisoners) (National Ofender Management Service – Prison Population date, March 2006). At an average cost of £697 per prisoner per week, (*Hansard*, 11 March 2004 Col. WA190), the average cost to the state is £36,244 per prisoner per year. By contrast, fines (the most common sentence or 'disposal') can often bring revenue to the State. In any event, however, the victim of a crime never gains from the sanction imposed on the criminal. A criminal court can order a convicted person to pay the victim compensation, but this will be in addition to and separate from the sentence for the crime.

- If a civil case is successful from the point of view of the person bringing the claim (the *claimant*), the outcome will be one of a number of civil remedies which are designed to benefit the *claimant* and in which the State, or wider community, has no direct interest. Civil remedies include damages, court orders like injunctions, orders of prohibition and specific performance. So, in civil proceedings, the *claimant* will sue the *defendant* and a successful claim will result in *judgment for* the *claimant*. In matrimonial cases, the party who brings an action is called the *petitioner* and the other party is known as the *respondent*.

- Civil and criminal cases are processed differently by the English legal system. They use different procedures and vocabulary, and they are dealt with, on the whole, by different courts. It is very important not to confuse the vocabularies of the different systems and speak, for example, about a claimant 'prosecuting' a company for breach of contract. The law of contract is civil law, so the defendant would be 'sued' or 'litigated against' or have 'a claim brought' taken against it by the claimant.

The following question then arises: 'what is the difference between a crime and a civil wrong; how am I to tell into which category a particular wrong falls?' The answer will be found simply by building up a general legal knowledge. There is nothing inherent in any particular conduct which makes it criminal. One cannot say, for example, that serious wrongs are crimes and that lesser transgressions will be civil wrongs: some crimes are comparatively trivial, like some parking offences, whilst some civil wrongs can have enormously harmful consequences, as where a company in breach of a contract causes financial harm to hundreds or thousands of people.

Sometimes a single event can be both a crime and a civil wrong. If you drive at 50 mph in a 30 mph zone and crash into another vehicle, killing a passenger, you may be prosecuted by the State for causing death by dangerous driving and, if convicted, imprisoned or fined. Additionally, you may be sued for negligence (a tortious civil wrong) by a dependant of the killed passenger and the driver.

3.1   The Civil Courts

Her Majesty's Courts Service The Courts Act 2003 provided for a new unified courts administration to be created which combined the functions of the court service and the magistrates' courts committees. The new organisation, Her Majesty's Courts Service (HMCS) was established in April 2005. The aim of the agency is to deliver improved services to the community, taxpayers, victims, witnesses and all other users of the courts. It will help to ensure the department can deliver high quality services across all the courts and develop best practice with the most effective use of resources.

The purpose of HMCS is to deliver justice efficiently and effectively. It administers the civil, family and criminal courts in England and Wales. This covers Crown, county and magistrates' courts. The organisation has 7 regions: North West, North East, Midlands, Wales & Cheshire, South East, South West and London. Below this are 42 areas all charged with providing services that meet local needs and priorities within a framework of national standards for service delivery.

The proposal to set up a new system of courts administration in England and Wales derived from Sir Robin Auld's Review of the criminal courts published in October 2001 (*A Review of the Criminal Courts of England and Wales*, The Right Honourable Lord

Justice Auld, 2001) He recommended that a 'single centrally funded executive agency, as part of the former Lord Chancellor's Department (now the Department for Constitutional Affairs) should be responsible for the administration of all courts, civil, criminal and family (save for the House of Lords), replacing the court service and magistrates' courts committees'.

The government accepted Sir Robin's proposals for a unified system of courts administration in the white paper 'Justice for All', published in July 2002. The Courts Act 2003 was passed to implement the changes and Her Majesty's Courts Service was later launched in 2005.

3.2 Magistrates' Courts

Magistrates' courts have a significant civil jurisdiction. They hear family proceedings under the Domestic Proceedings and Magistrates' Courts Act (DPMCA) 1978 and the Children Act (CA) 1989. Here, the court is termed a 'family proceedings court'. A family proceedings court must normally be composed of not more than three justices, including, as far as is practicable, both a man and a woman. Justices who sit on such benches must be members of the 'family panel' which comprises people specially appointed to deal with family matters. The magistrates' court deals with adoption proceedings, applications for residence and contact orders (the CA 1989) and maintenance relating to spouses and children. Under the DPMCA 1978, these courts also have the power to make personal protection orders and exclusion orders in cases of matrimonial violence. They have powers of recovery in relation to council tax and charges for water, gas and electricity. Magistrates grant, renew and revoke licences for selling liquor.

3.3 County Courts

The county courts were introduced in 1846 to provide local, accessible fora for the adjudication of relatively small scale litigation. There are 218 county courts. These courts are served by circuit judges and District Judges, the latter appointed by the Lord Chancellor from persons who have a seven year qualification (s 71 of the CLSA 1990).

The Civil Procedure Rules (CPR), which we examine in Chapter 7, operate the same process irrespective of whether the case forum is the High Court or the county court. Broadly speaking, county courts will hear small claims and fast track cases, while the more challenging multi-track cases will be heard in the High Court.

Over the past 10 years, the numbers of cases being resolved by the county court has increased as the financial limit of cases within its jurisdiction has increased. Also during this period, the profile of county court work has changed. The numbers both of full trials and of of small claims arbitrations have fallen sharply during the last ten years. In 1994, there were 24,219 trials and 87,885 small claims arbitrations. In 2004, there were 14,680 trials and 46,100 small claims arbitrations. The small claims limit is £5,000, except for personal injury claims which carry a £1,000 limit.

A *Practice Direction* ([1991] 3 All ER 722) states that certain types of actions set down for trial in the High Court are considered too important for transfer to a county court. These are cases involving:

- professional negligence;

- fatal accidents;

- allegations of fraud or undue influence;

- defamation;

- malicious prosecution or false imprisonment;

- claims against the police.

The county court jurisdiction also involves probate, property cases, tort, contract, bankruptcy, insolvency and relations. Regarding remedies, the county court cannot grant the prerogative remedies; that is, they cannot grant search orders (an interim mandatory injunction obtained without notice to prevent the defendant from removing, concealing or destroying evidence in the form of documents or moveable property, formerly know as the Anton Piller order) and neither, generally, can they grant freezing orders (formerly Mareva injunctions) to prevent the defendant from removing his assets out of the jurisdiction of the English courts or dissipating them. For recent authoritative guidance of both of these orders, see *Practice Direction ex p Mareva Injunctions and Anton Piller Orders* (1994).

The main advantage to litigants using the small claims process is the fact that, if sued, they can defend without fear of incurring huge legal costs, since the costs that the winning party can claim are strictly limited. The average waiting period for a trial in 2004 was 53 weeks. Although successful claimants are unable to recover costs of legal representation, the small claims procedure does not exclude litigants from seeking legal advice or engaging such legal representation. If a litigant is unrepresented, the District Judge may assist him or her by putting questions to witnesses or to the other party, and by explaining any legal terms or expressions.

A litigant simply needs to complete a claim form, available from any county court, and send it to the court with the issue fee appropriate to the amount claimed (ranging from £80 to £230, depending on the value of the claim). If the case is defended, it will be dealt with at an informal hearing, sitting around a table in the District Judge's office. This avoids the need for a trial in open court, which many litigants find daunting.

The working of the small claims system is looked at in greater detail in Chapter 8.

3.4   The High Court of Justice

The High Court was created in 1873 as a part of the Supreme Court of Judicature. The Constitutional Reform Act 2005 established a new Supreme Court of the United Kingdom (which will be operational from 2009) to replace the House of Lords as the highest court of appeal. The new official collective name for the High Court, the Court of Appeal, and the Crown Court (previously called 'The Supreme Court of Judicature') is the Senior Courts of England and Wales. The Supreme Court of Judicature of Northern Ireland was renamed the Court of Judicature of Northern Ireland.

The High Court now has three administrative divisions: the Court of Chancery, the Queen's Bench Division (QBD) and the Family Division (Divorce and Admiralty and Exchequer and Common Pleas were merged with the QBD in 1880 and 1970). High Court Judges sit mainly in the Courts of Justice in the Strand, London, although it is possible for the High Court to sit anywhere in England or Wales. Current directions from the Lord Chancellor mean that the court sits in 27 provincial cities and towns.

The High Court judiciary comprises the Lord Chancellor; the Vice Chancellor, who usually sits; the Lord Chief Justice who presides over the QBD; the President, who presides over the Family Division; the Senior Presiding Judge (s 72 of the CLSA 1990) and, in 2006, 112 High Court Judges or *puisne judges* (pronounced 'pewnee' and meaning 'lesser').

To be qualified for appointment as a *puisne* judge, a person must have 10 years' qualification within the meaning of s 71 of the CLSA 1990 – essentially, someone who has had a general right of audience on all matters in that court for at least 10 years. The Constitutional Reform Act 2005 established the Judicial Appointments Commission. This body, with 14 members drawn from the judiciary, the lay magistracy, the legal professions and the public, was launched in 2006. It is responsible for selecting candidates to recommend for judicial appointment to the Secretary of State for Constitutional Affairs. This will ensure that while merit will remain the sole criterion for appointment, the appointments system will be placed on a fully modern, open and transparent basis.

3.4.1   The Queen's Bench Division

The Queen's Bench Division, the main common law court, takes its name from the original judicial part of the general royal court which used to sit on a bench in the Palace of Westminster. It is the division with the largest workload and has some criminal jurisdiction and appellate jurisdiction. The main civil work of this court is in contract and tort cases. The court has 72 judges. In 2004, the *Judicial Statistics 2004*, (Cm 6565, 2005) show that total claims and originating proceedings increased by over 4% to 14,830. Over 65% of judgments were related to medical and personal injury cases, 59% of which were for sums in excess of £5000. In 2004, the average period between the issue of a claim and start of trial or date of disposal of actions set down for trial was 97 weeks. This was down from 164 weeks in 2003.

The Commercial Court is part of this division, being served by up to 15 judges with specialist experience in commercial law and presiding over cases concerning banking and insurance matters. The formal rules of evidence can be abandoned here, with the consent of the parties, to allow testimony and documentation which would normally be inadmissible. This informality can be of considerable benefit to the business keen to settle its dispute as quickly and easily as possible. The QBD also includes an Admiralty

Court to deal with the often esoteric issues of law-relating to shipping. Commercial Court Judges are sometimes appointed as arbitrators.

The Enterprise Act 2002 provides that the Office of Fair Trading (OFT), which investigates markets where it has reasonable grounds to suspect that competition is being prevented, restricted or distorted, may refer cases to the Competition Commission (CC). Decisions of the OFT and the CC can be reviewed by the Competition Appeal Tribunal.

The Employment Appeal Tribunal is presided over by a High Court Judge and either two or four lay persons, and hears appeals from employment tribunals. It is not part of the High Court, but is termed a superior court of record.

It is important to remember that most civil claims are settled out of court; only about 1% of cases where claim forms are issued result in civil trials.

3.4.2   The Queen's Bench Divisional Court

The nomenclature can be puzzling here. This court, as distinct from the QBD, exercises appellate jurisdiction. Here, two or sometimes three judges sit to hear appeals in the following circumstances:

- appeals on a point of law by way of case stated from magistrates' courts, tribunals and the Crown Court (there were 130 such appeals in 2004);

- by exercising judicial review of the decisions made by governmental and public authorities, inferior courts and tribunals. Leave to apply for judicial review is granted or refused by a single judge. Civil judicial reviews can be heard by a single judge (there were 4,207 applications for permission to apply for judicial review in 2004);

- applications for the writ of habeas corpus from persons who claim they are being unlawfully detained (there were 20 such cases in 2004).

3.4.3   The Chancery Division

The Chancery Division is the modern successor to the old Court of Chancery, the Lord Chancellor's court from which equity was developed. It has 17 judges. Its jurisdiction includes matters relating to:

- the sale or partition of land and the raising of charges on land;

- the redemption or foreclosure of mortgages;

- the execution or declaration of trusts;

- the administration of the estates of the dead;

- bankruptcy;

- contentious probate business, for example, the validity and interpretation of wills;

- company law;

- partnerships;

- revenue law.

Like the QBD, the Chancery Division contains specialist courts; these are the Patents Court and the Companies Court. The Chancery Division hears its cases in London or in one of eight designated provincial High Court centres. The work is very specialised and there is a Chancery Bar for barristers who practise in this area. Chancery Judges are normally appointed from this Bar. In 2004, the number of proceedings started decreased by nearly 7 per cent to 35,457.

3.4.4 The Chancery Divisional Court

Comprising one or two Chancery Judges, this appellate court hears appeals from the Commissioners of Inland Revenue on income tax cases, and from county courts on certain matters like bankruptcy.

3.4.5 The Family Division

The Family Division of the High Court was created by the Administration of Justice Act 1970. It deals with:

- all matrimonial matters, both at first instance and on appeal;

- matters relating to minors, proceedings under the CA 1989;

- legitimacy;

- adoption;

- proceedings under the Domestic Violence and Matrimonial Proceedings Act 1976 and s 30 of the Human Fertilisation and Embryology Act 1990.

3.4.6 The Family Divisional Court

The Family Divisional Court, consisting of two High Court Judges, hears appeals from decisions of magistrates' courts and county courts in family matters. Commonly these involve appeals against orders made about financial provision under the DPMCA 1978. It dealt with 50 appeals in 2004, including 41 under the Children Act, 1989.

3.5 Appeals from the High Court

Appeals from decisions made by a judge in one of the three High Court Divisions will go to the Court of Appeal (Civil Division). An exception to this rule allows an appeal to miss out or 'leapfrog' a visit to the Court of Appeal and go straight to the House of

Lords (ss 12–15 of the Administration of Justice Act 1969). In order for this to happen, the trial judge must grant a 'certificate of satisfaction' and the House of Lords must give leave to appeal. For the judge to grant a certificate, he or she must be satisfied that the case involves a point of law of general public importance, either concerned mainly with statutory interpretation or one where he or she was bound by a Court of Appeal or House of Lords' decision. Also, both parties must consent to the procedure.

3.6 The Court of Appeal (Civil Division)

The Court of Appeal was established by the Judicature Act (JdA) 1873. Together with the High Court of Justice, the Court of Appeal formed part of the Supreme Court of Judicature. Why is it called 'Supreme' if the House of Lords is a superior court? The answer is that the JdA 1873 abolished the House of Lords in its appellate capacity, and hence the Court of Appeal became part of the Supreme Court but, after a change of government, the House of Lords was reinstated as the final court of appeal by the Appellate Jurisdiction Act 1876. The Constitutional Reform Act 2005 established a new Supreme Court of the United Kingdom (which will be operational from 2009) to replace the House of Lords as the highest court of appeal. The new official collective name for the High Court, Court of Appeal and Crown Court (previously called 'The Supreme Court of Judicature') is the Senior Courts of England and Wales.

The Court of Appeal is served by senior judges, currently 37, termed Lord Justices of Appeal. Additionally, the Lord Chancellor, the President of the Family Division of the High Court, the Vice Chancellor of the Chancery Division and High Court Judges can sit. The court hears appeals from the three divisions of the High Court, the Divisional Courts, the county courts, the Employment Appeal Tribunal, the Lands Tribunal and the Transport Tribunal. The most senior judge is the Master of the Rolls. Usually, three judges will sit to hear an appeal, although for very important cases, five may sit. In the interests of business efficiency, some matters can be heard by two judges. These include:

- applications for leave to appeal;

- an appeal where all parties have consented to the matter being heard by just two judges;

- any appeal against an interim order or judgment (that is, one which is provisional).

Where such a court is evenly divided, the case must be reheard by three or five judges before it can be further appealed to the House of Lords.

There may be four or five divisions of the court sitting on any given day. The court has a heavy workload. In 1995, it disposed of a total of 2,504 cases. By 2004, the number of disposals had risen to 3,116. In cases of great urgency, this court is often *de facto* the final court of appeal, so that a party can act in reliance on its decision without waiting to see the outcome of any possible appeal to the Lords. In *C v S and Others* (1987), a case concerning a putative father's right to prevent a prospective mother from having an abortion, the woman was between 18 and 21 weeks' pregnant and her termination, if it was to be carried out, had to be performed within days of the Court of Appeal's decision. The hospital concerned was reluctant to carry out the operation in case the father appealed to the Lords and won. To have earlier terminated the pregnancy might then, the hospital believed, have been the crime of infanticide. Leave to appeal to the Lords was refused and the termination was performed but, in the Court of Appeal, Sir John Donaldson MR said [1987] 1 All ER 1230 at 1243:

> It is a fact that some thousand appeals are heard by this court every year, of which about 50 go to the House of Lords … So, in practical terms, in the every day life of this country, this court is the final court of appeal and it must always be the final court of appeal in cases of real urgency. In those circumstances, no one could be blamed in any way, *a fortiori* could they as a practical matter be prosecuted, for acting on a judgment of this court. If that be wrong, which it is not, the life of the country in many respects would grind to a halt. The purpose of any supreme court, including the House of Lords, is to review historically and on a broad front; it is not to decide matters of great urgency which have to be decided once and for all.

3.7   Reforms to the Appeal Process

3.7.1   Background

In his 1994–95 Annual Report on the Court of Appeal, the then Master of the Rolls, Lord Bingham, stated that 'the delay in hearing certain categories of appeal in the Civil Division of the Court of Appeal has reached a level which is inconsistent with the due administration of justice'.

Lord Woolf addressed this issue in his report, *Access to Justice* (July 1996), which set out his proposals for the reform of the civil justice system. At the heart of his proposals was the allocation of civil cases to 'tracks', which would determine the degree of judicial case management. Broadly speaking, cases would be allocated to the small claims track, the fast track or to the multi-track, depending upon the value and complexity of the claim. Those proposals have now been implemented in the Civil Procedure Act 1997 and the Civil Procedure Rules 1998. The principle that underlies this system of tracks is the need to ensure that resources devoted to managing and hearing a case are proportional to the weight and substance of that case. In order that the benefits arising from these reforms should not be weakened on appeal, Lord Woolf recommended that an effective system of appeals should be based on similar principles.

In 1996, Sir Jeffrey Bowman chaired a Review of the Civil Division of the Court of Appeal (*Review of the Court of Appeal (Civil Division)* – Report to the Lord Chancellor, September 1997). He identified a number of problems besetting the Court of Appeal. In particular, he noted that the court was being asked to consider numerous appeals which were not of sufficient weight or complexity for two or three of the country's most senior judges, and which had sometimes already been through one or more levels of appeal. Additionally, he concluded that existing provisions concerning the constitution of the court were too inflexible to deal appropriately with its workload. To redress this situation, Bowman's Report included recommendations to alter the jurisdiction and constitution of the Court of Appeal. The Lord Chancellor consulted on proposals to effect certain of these changes (*Reform of the Court of Appeal (Civil Division): Proposals for Change to Constitution and Jurisdiction*, LCD, July 1998).

Due to the complex nature of routes of appeal in family matters, the Bowman Report recommended that a specialist committee should examine this area, with a view to rationalising the arrangements for appeals in family cases and bringing them in line with the underlying principles for civil appeals. The Family Appeal Review Group, chaired by Lord Justice Thorpe, published recommendations in July 1998 aimed at simplifying the current appeals procedure in family cases, applying the principles outlined in Sir Jeffrey Bowman's Report.

The provisions enabling certain matters to be heard by a single High Court Judge have the same objective of ensuring that the most appropriate use is made of judicial resources.

3.7.2 The Access to Justice Act 1999 (Part IV)

In relation to civil appeals, the Access to Justice Act (AJA) 1999 made several changes:

- provide for permission to appeal to be obtained at all levels in the system (s 54);

- provide that, in normal circumstances, there will be only one level of appeal to the courts (s 55);

- introduce an order-making power to enable the Lord Chancellor to vary appeal routes in secondary legislation, with a view to ensuring that appeals generally go to the lowest appropriate level of judge (s 56);

- ensure that cases which merit the consideration of the Court of Appeal reach that court (s 57);

- give the Civil Division of the Court of Appeal flexibility to exercise its jurisdiction in courts of one, two or more judges (s 59).

Together, these measures are intended to ensure that appeals are heard at the right level, and dealt with in a way which is proportionate to their weight and complexity, that the appeals system can adapt quickly to other developments in the civil justice system and that existing resources are used efficiently, enabling the Court of Appeal (Civil Division) to tackle its workload more expeditiously. The provisions relating to the High Court (ss 61–65) allow judicial review applications.

3.7.3 Right to appeal

The AJA 1999 provides for rights of appeal to be exercised only with the permission of the court, as prescribed by rules of court. Previously, permission was required for most cases going to the Civil Division of the Court of Appeal, but not elsewhere. Under the Act, with three exceptions, permission to appeal must be obtained in all appeals to the county courts, High Court or Civil Division of the Court of Appeal. The exceptions are appeals against committal to prison, appeals against a refusal to grant habeas corpus and appeals against the making of secure accommodation orders under s 25 of the Children Act 1989 (a form of custodial 'sentence' for recalcitrant children). There is no appeal against a decision of the court to give or refuse permission, but this does not affect any right under rules of court to make a further application for permission to the same or another court.

The Act provides that, where the county court or High Court has already reached a decision in a case brought on appeal, there is no further possibility of an appeal of that decision to the Court of Appeal, unless (s 55) the Court of Appeal considers that the appeal would raise an important point of principle or practice, or there is some other compelling reason for the court to hear it.

3.7.4   Destination of appeals

Section 56 of the AJA 1999 enables the Lord Chancellor to vary, by order, the routes of appeal for appeals to and within the county courts, the High Court, and the Civil Division of the Court of Appeal. Before making an order, the Lord Chancellor will be required to consult the Heads of Division, and any order will be subject to the affirmative resolution procedure. The following appeal routes are specified by order:

- In fast track cases heard by a District Judge, appeals will be to a circuit judge.

- In fast track cases heard by a circuit judge, appeals will be to a High Court Judge.

- In multi-track cases, appeals of interim decisions made at first instance by a District Judge will be to a circuit judge, by a master or circuit judge to a High Court Judge and by a High Court Judge to the Court of Appeal.

- In multi-track cases, appeals of final orders, regardless of the court of first instance, will be to the Court of Appeal.

- The Heads of Division are the Lord Chief Justice, the Master of the Rolls, the President of the Family Division and the Vice Chancellor.

- A decision is interim where it does not determine the final outcome of the case.

The legislation provides for the Master of the Rolls or a lower court to direct that an appeal that would normally be heard by a lower court be heard instead by the Court of Appeal. This power would be used where the appeal raises an important point of principle or practice, or is a case which, for some other compelling reason, should be considered by the Court of Appeal.

3.7.5   Civil Division of Court of Appeal

The Act makes flexible provision for the number of judges of which a court must be constituted in order for the Court of Appeal to be able to hear appeals. Section 54 of the Supreme Court Act 1981 provided that the Court of Appeal was constituted to exercise any of its jurisdiction if it consisted of an uneven number of judges not less than three. In limited circumstances, it provided that a court could be properly constituted with two judges. The 1999 Act allows the Master of the Rolls, with the concurrence of the Lord Chancellor, to give directions about the minimum number of judges of which a court must consist for given types of proceedings. Subject to any directions, the Act also allows the Master of the Rolls, or a Lord Justice of Appeal designated by him for the purpose, to determine the number of judges who will sit to hear any particular appeal.

3.7.6 Jurisdiction of single judge of the High Court

The 1999 Act allows certain applications to be routinely heard by a single judge of the High Court. It does this by removing an obstacle that existed in the earlier legislation by which the route of appeal for these cases was to the House of Lords, but the Administration of Justice Act 1960 provides that the House of Lords will only hear appeals in these matters from a Divisional Court (that is, more than one judge) of the High Court. The 1999 Act amends the 1960 Act so that the House of Lords can hear appeals from a single High Court Judge.

3.7.7 The Civil Procedure Rules

Under Part 52 of the CPR, the general rule is that permission to appeal in virtually all cases is mandatory. It should be obtained immediately following the judgment from the lower court or appellate court. Permission will only be given where the court considers that the appellant shows a real prospect of success or there is some other compelling reason.

All appeals will now be limited to a review rather than a complete rehearing and the appeal will only be allowed if the decision of the lower court was wrong or unjust due to a serious procedural or other irregularity.

The rule now is that there should be only one appeal. Lord Justice Brooke emphasised in the leading case of *Tanfern v Cameron MacDonald and Another* (2000), 'The decision of the first appeal court is now to be given primacy'. An application for a second or subsequent appeal (from High Court or county court) must be made to the Court of Appeal, which will not accede unless the appeal would raise an important point of principle or practice, or there is some other compelling reason.

The route of appeal has been altered. The general rule is that the appeal lies to the next level of judge in the court hierarchy, that is, District Judge to county court judge to High Court Judge. The main exception relates to an appeal against a final decision in a multi-track claim, which will go straight to the Court of Appeal.

Great emphasis is placed on ensuring that cases are dealt with promptly and efficiently, and on weeding out and deterring unjustified appeals. The result is that the opportunity to appeal a decision at first instance in a lower court is much more restricted. It is vital, therefore, that practitioners be properly prepared at the initial hearing. For more on this, see Richard Harrison ((2000) 150 NLJ, pp 1175–76).

3.7.8   The Courts Act 2003

The Courts Act 2003 made some amendments to the jurisdiction of the civil courts.

3.7.8.1   *Civil jurisdiction and procedure*

Section 52 of the Magistrates' Courts Act 1980 limits the jurisdiction of justices to deal with civil complaints to anything done (or neglected to be done) within the commission area for which the justice acts. The Courts Act 2003 amends this provision to reflect lay magistrates being given a national jurisdiction.

3.7.8.2   *Transfer of civil proceedings (other than family proceedings)*

There were previously no provisions that allowed the transfer of civil proceedings from one magistrates' court to another. The Courts Act 2003 introduced such provisions to match the new arrangements for criminal cases. There were already detailed provisions allowing for the transfer of family proceedings between magistrates' courts and also to the county courts and the High Court. This Act made no changes to those provisions.

Section 49: family proceedings courts

This section of the 2003 Act sets out the framework whereby lay magistrates and District Judges (Magistrates' Courts) are authorised to hear family proceedings. The Lord Chancellor must authorise a Justice of the Peace before he or she can sit as a member of a family proceedings court. These personal authorisations are valid throughout England and Wales. The Lord Chancellor has power to make rules regarding (a) the allocation and removal of authorisations for justices to sit as members of family proceedings courts, (b) the appointment of chairmen of family proceedings court and (c) the composition of such family proceedings courts. It is envisaged that new rules, which provide for a more transparent selection procedure, will be published for comment. Because of the sensitive nature of family cases, and the specific knowledge and understanding that is required, these rules would help to ensure that only trained and suitable magistrates sit in family proceedings. District Judges (Magistrates' Courts) are in practice required to be 'ticketed' for this work.

Section 62: Head and Deputy Head of Civil Justice

This section requires the Lord Chancellor to appoint a Head of Civil Justice, and gives power to appoint a deputy. It has been recognised that there is an ongoing need for a Head of Civil Justice to provide consistency and an overview, although it is accepted that the level of work may decrease as the Woolf reforms (the reforms to the civil justice system contained in the *Access to Justice* Report) continue to settle down. Therefore, the need for support from a deputy may decline.

Those eligible for appointment are the Master of the Rolls, the Vice Chancellor and any ordinary judge of the Court of Appeal. The Head of Civil Justice and the Deputy Head of Civil Justice, where there is one, will be *ex officio* members of the Civil

Procedure Rule Committee (Civil PRC) as provided for in s 83. No other specific functions, duties or powers to be attached to these posts are to be provided in statute.

Section 63: ordinary judges of the Court of Appeal

This section deals with a specific problem: s 2(3) of the Supreme Court Act 1981 required an ordinary judge of the Court of Appeal to be styled a 'Lord' Justice of Appeal, whatever his or her gender. This section removes this anomaly. In 2006, three of the 37 Appeal Court judges were female: Dame Heather Hallett, Dame Janet Smith and Dame Mary Arden. Male members of the Court of Appeal are knighted (they are knighted upon elevation to the High Court), and are known, therefore, off the Bench, in that way, such as Sir David Keene. Senior female judges are invested as Dames of the British Empire (DBE). In their capacity as Appeal Court judges, both sexes are known by their judicial titles, such as Lady Justice Hallett and Lord Justice Keene.

Section 64: power to alter judicial titles

Although s 63 amends one title, Lord Justice of Appeal, s 64 provides the Lord Chancellor with a power to amend the other titles listed (which encompasses all of the judicial titles in the Supreme Court and county courts) in the future to avoid similar problems arising. Some titles may need modernisation to make them more easily understandable to court users. The acceptance commanded by titles containing a presumption of male gender might also change. Such orders may only be made after consultation with the Lord Chief Justice, Master of the Rolls, President of the Family Division and Vice Chancellor.

3.8   The House of Lords

Acting in its judicial capacity, as opposed to its legislative one, the House of Lords is the final court of appeal in civil as well as criminal law. Its judgments govern the courts in England, Wales and Northern Ireland. They can also govern civil law in Scotland. Most appeals reaching the House of Lords come from English civil cases.

In 2005, legislation created a new Supreme Court of the UK separate from the House of Lords, with its own independent appointments system, its own staff and budget. It will be situated in London. This will be the final court of appeal in the UK, except for criminal cases from Scotland. In 2009, with the approval of the Lord Chancellor, the appellate jurisdiction of the House of Lords will cease and the Supreme Court will be operational.

The Supreme Court will have 12 judges. There will be a president, a Deputy President, and ten 'Justices of the Supreme Court'. They will be appointed by the monarch on the recommendation of a Judicial Appointments Commission whose members are drawn from the judiciary, the legal professions and the lay public.

If necessary, judges in the Court of Appeal (and equivalent courts in Scotland and Northern Ireland) may be requested by the President of the Supreme Court to sit as acting judges, and so may members of a supplementary panel comprising persons who have recently held high judicial office and are under the age of 75.

The jurisdiction of the Supreme Court will not be only that which used to be exercised by the House of Lords. It also has the jurisdiction to decide devolution issues (concerning Scotland and Wales) that were previously exercised by the Judicial Committee of the Privy Council. The legislation establishing the Supreme Court, the Constitutional Reform Act 2005, declared that the creation of the Supreme Court is not 'to affect the distinctions between the separate legal systems of the parts of the United Kingdom'.

For hearing appeals, the Supreme Court must consist of an uneven number of judges (at least three), of whom more than half are permanent judges and therefore less than half are acting judges.

During 2004, there was a total of 271 appeals presented and disposed of by the House of Lords. In England and Wales, 202 were from the Civil Division of the Court of Appeal and only 34 were from the Criminal Division. There is also a 'leapfrog' procedure, introduced by ss 12–15 of the Administration of Justice Act 1969, by which an appeal may go to the Lords direct from the High Court if the High Court Judge certificates the case as being suitable for the Lords to hear and the House of Lords gives leave to appeal. All the parties must consent and the case must be one which involves a point of general public importance about a matter of statutory interpretation (sometimes called statutory 'construction' from the verb *to construe*, meaning to interpret), or where the contentious issue is one on which the trial judge is bound by a precedent of the Court of Appeal or House of Lords. In 2004, there were 7 civil and 15 such criminal appeals.

The appeals are heard by Lords of Appeal in Ordinary, of whom there are currently 12. Two of these must be from Scotland and one from Northern Ireland. Other senior judges like the Lord Chancellor sometimes sit to hear appeals. It is customary only for peers with distinguished legal and judicial careers to become Lords of Appeal in Ordinary. These judges are known as 'Law Lords'.

For most cases, five Law Lords will sit to hear the appeal, but seven are sometimes convened to hear very important cases. The House of Lords' decision which abolished the 250 year old rule against convicting a husband for rape of his wife (*R v R* (1991)) is such a case. Cases are heard in relative informality in a committee room in the Palace of Westminster. The Appellate Committee of the House of Lords, as it is technically termed, sits with its members in suits, not judicial robes. Counsel, however, do wear wigs and robes. Unlike criminal cases (s 33 of the Criminal Appeal Act (CAA) 1968), there is no requirement that the appeal is on a point of law of general public importance. An appeal from the Court of Appeal to the House of Lords must have 'leave' (that is, permission) of either court.

The judges may deliver their judgments, termed 'opinions', as speeches in the parliamentary chamber. A majority decides the case. Sometimes, however, where a case has been heard at three levels of the civil process, the final outcome is not determined, overall, by a majority of what could be described as senior judges. Consider the case of *Gillick v West Norfolk and Wisbech Area Health Authority* (1985), a case in which the plaintiff (now termed a claimant), Mrs Gillick, sought a ruling that the defendant's policy to allow contraceptive advice to be given to girls under 16 in some circumstances was illegal. Her argument was rejected by the judge hearing the case in the High Court, accepted unanimously by the three Lord Justices in the Court of Appeal and then rejected in the House of Lords by three votes to two. Thus, overall, a majority of the eight senior judges who heard her case accepted it (five out of eight), but she lost her case because she was unsuccessful in the final court.

3.9   The European Court of Justice

As we shall see in detail in Chapter 13, the Treaty of Amsterdam 1997 introduced a completely new system for numbering the Articles of the European Community treaties. In order to try to avoid confusion when readers consult other, already existing, authorities, which will refer to the old numbering, this book will refer to both the new and the previous numbering.

The function of the European Court of Justice (ECJ), which sits in Luxembourg, is to 'ensure that in the interpretation and application of this Treaty [the EEC Treaty 1957] the law is observed' (Art 220, formerly 164). The Court is the ultimate authority on European law. As the Treaty is widely composed in general terms, the Court is often called upon to provide the necessary detail for European law to operate. By virtue of the European Communities Act 1972, European law has been enacted into English law, so the decisions of the Court have direct authority in the English jurisdiction.

The Court hears disputes between nations and between nations and European institutions like the European Commission. An individual, however, can only bring an action if he is challenging a decision which affects him.

The Treaty states in Art 234 (formerly 177) that any judicial or quasi-judicial body, however low ranking, may refer a question to the ECJ if it considers that 'a decision on that question is necessary to enable it to give judgment', and that such a reference must be made where any such question is raised in a case before a national court from which there is no further appeal. So, the High Court would have a discretion as to whether to refer a point, but the House of Lords would not. The system was installed to try to ensure uniformity of interpretation of European law across all the Member States. Without such a mechanism, it would be possible for the English courts to be interpreting a point of European law one way while the Spanish courts were treating it as meaning something different.

Lord Denning MR formulated guidelines in *Bulmer v Bollinger* (1974) as to when an inferior court should refer a case to the ECJ for a preliminary ruling. He offered four guidelines to determine whether the reference was 'necessary' within the meaning of Art 234 (formerly 177):

- The decision on the point of European law must be conclusive of the case.

- The national court may choose to follow a previous ruling of the ECJ on the same point of Community law, but it may choose to refer the same point of law to the court again in the hope that it will give a different ruling.

- The national court may not make a reference on the grounds of *acte clair* where the point is reasonably clear and free from doubt.

- 'In general, it is best to decide the facts first' before determining whether it is necessary to refer the point of Community law.

If a national court decides that a reference is necessary, it still has the discretion (unlike the highest court) as to whether to refer the point. Lord Denning MR then listed some factors to help courts decide whether to refer; for example, bear in mind the expense to parties of a reference and do not send points unless they are difficult and important.

These guidelines have been influential in a number of subsequent cases. It is possible, however, for an appeal to be made against a decision of a court of first instance to refer a case to the ECJ for a preliminary ruling under Art 234 (formerly 177). The appellate court will interfere with the discretion of the trial judge who referred the case, but only if the decision was 'plainly wrong' (see *Bulmer v Bollinger*, above).

The language of Art 234 (formerly 177) is imperative, saying that courts or tribunals against whose judgments there is no appeal *must* refer a point of Community law. This does not apply where the point has already been ruled on by the ECJ. Equally, it does not apply where the national court has ruled that the issue in question is not one which requires the application of Community law. In *R v London Boroughs Transport Committee* (1992), the House of Lords decided that the case did not involve any Community law issues because it concerned the regulation of local traffic, even though the Court of Appeal had held unanimously that UK legislation was in breach of certain Community directives.

The ECJ is a court of reference: the ruling the Court makes is preliminary, in the sense that the case is then remitted to the national court for it to apply the law to the facts. The Court only addresses itself to points arising from actual cases; it will not consider hypothetical problems.

Lord Diplock (*R v Henn* (1981)) has characterised the Court's work in the following way:

> The European Court, in contrast to English courts, applies teleological rather than historical methods to the interpretation of the Treaties and other Community legislation. It seeks to give effect to what it conceives to be the spirit rather than the letter of the Treaties; sometimes, indeed, to an English judge, it may seem to the exclusion of the letter. It views the Communities as living and expanding organisms and the interpretation of the provisions of the Treaties as changing to match their growth.

The Court is made up of senior judges from each Member State (15) and a President of the Court, assisted by nine Advocates General. The latter are 'persons whose independence is beyond doubt' (Art 223, formerly 167) and their task is to give to the Court a detailed analysis of all the relevant legal and factual issues along with recommendations. The recommendations are not necessarily followed by the Court, but they can be used on later occasions as persuasive precedent. The Court attempts to ensure consistency in its decisions, but is not bound by precedent to the same extent as a court in England.

The Court of First Instance was set up to ease the mounting workload of the ECJ. It began work in 1989 and has a jurisdiction which is limited to hearing disputes between the Community and its staff, cases involving EU competition law (excluding Art 234, formerly 177, references) and some matters involving the European Coal and Steel Community.

3.10   The European Court of Human Rights

The European Court of Human Rights (ECtHR) does not arise from the European Union. The court is based in Strasbourg. It was established as a result of the European Convention on Human Rights (ECHR), created in 1950. This set out a catalogue of civil and political rights and freedoms. It allows people to lodge complaints against States which have signed up to the ECHR for alleged violations of those rights. Although founded in 1950, the court did not actually come into existence until 1959.

To start with, the number of cases coming forward was relatively few. But from 1980, they started to grow steadily. By 2001, the Court was receiving nearly 14,000 applications a year from people who felt they had a grievance against a signatory State. The Court is currently made up of 41 judges, one for every State signed up to the Convention. They are elected by the Parliamentary Assembly of the Council of Europe and serve for six years. Judges sit on the Court as individuals and do not represent their country. All the signatory nations, with the exception of Ireland and Norway, have incorporated the Convention into their own law. This means that domestic courts take full account of its provisions when considering a grievance. Only when domestic remedies are exhausted can an individual look to Strasbourg for help.

It is commonly but wrongly believed that the Convention and its institutions have been foisted upon a reluctant UK. However, the UK was one of the architects of the human rights agenda that grew out of the devastation of Second World War. Indeed, the UK was one of the first members of the Council of Europe to ratify the Convention when it did so through Parliament in 1951.

3.11   Judicial Committee of the Privy Council

The Judicial Committee of the Privy Council was created by the Judicial Committee Act 1833. Under the Act, a special committee of the Privy Council was set up to hear appeals from the Dominions. The cases are heard by the judges (without wigs or robes) in a committee room in London. The Committee's decision is not a judgment but an 'advice' to the monarch, who is counselled that the appeal be allowed or dismissed.

The Committee is the final court of appeal for certain Commonwealth countries which have retained this option, and from some independent members and associate members of the Commonwealth. The Committee comprises Privy Councillors who hold (or have held) high judicial office. In most cases, which come from places such as the Cayman Islands and Jamaica, the Committee comprises five Lords of Appeal in

Ordinary, sometimes assisted by a judge from the country concerned. The decisions of the Privy Council are very influential in English courts because they concern points of law that are applicable in this jurisdiction and they are pronounced upon by Lords of Appeal in Ordinary in a way which is thus tantamount to a House of Lords' ruling. These decisions, however, are technically of persuasive precedent only, although they are normally followed by English courts; see, for example, *The Wagon Mound* (1963), a tort case in which the Privy Council ruled, on an appeal from Australia, that in negligence claims, a defendant is liable only for the reasonably foreseeable consequences of his tortious conduct. A total of 71 appeals were entered in 2004. The Committee also hears appeals on devolution issues.

3.12 Civil Court Fees

In May 2000, the government introduced a policy to make the civil courts self-financing, and a new scale of increased court fees, some as high as 35% more, came into effect. It has continued to pursue this policy. Under the scales published in 2006, the fee for starting a claim in the county court is £30 for claims up to £300, £50 for claims up to £500, £80 for claims up to £1,000, and £120 for claims up to £5,000, which is the maximum for small claims. Fees now rise quite steeply for claims over this amount and are the same whether pursued in the county court or High Court. Now the fees are £250, £400, £700 and £900 for claims of up to £15,000, £50,000, £100,000 and £150,000 respectively. For claims over £150,000, a fee of £1,100 is charged. Additional fees are then charged as the claim proceeds through the court process, that is, £120 is charged in the High Court when the claim is allocated to a track, and a further sum of £600 is charged when the matter is set down for trial. Thus, the full court fees for pursuing a court case could be substantial. If the claimant does not pay these fees, then the claim will automatically be struck out to stop claims being issued and lying dormant in the court process only to be re-instigated at a future date.

However, the principle of running the civil courts according to business principles was, and still is, highly controversial. When the innovation was announced by the Lord Chancellor, it was denounced by Sir Richard Scott, Head of the Chancery Division of the High Court. He warned that justice should be reasonably accessible and without excessive cost. He stated that:

The policy fails to recognise that the civil justice system is, like the criminal justice system, the bulwark of a civilised State and the maintenance of order within that State. People have to use the civil courts. They can't engage in self-help in a way which would lead to chaos.

Although people who receive public funding still have their court fees paid, many unaided people can only just afford to litigate, and the raised fees may be turning a difficult hurdle into an insurmountable barrier. The policy of making litigants pay for judges and courtrooms – for that is the essence of this new court fee structure – is highly controversial. Many litigants would believe that they and others, as taxpayers, have already contributed to the funding of the legal system.

In a debate in the House of Lords (*Hansard*, 1997, Vol 581, col 863–81), the Lord Chancellor revisited the theme of at what rate, if at all, citizens should be charged fees for using the civil courts. He stated that he did not accept that all citizens had a constitutional right to go to law in the civil courts freely at the point of use. To do that, he observed, it would be necessary to find the money currently supporting the system from court fees (£257 million paid by citizens) from somewhere else, that is, he would have to cut that amount from somewhere else in his budget. He raised the possibilities of ending Criminal Legal Aid, or ending legal aid for family proceedings. The Lord Chancellor said:

Those who argue for free access to courts for all are really arguing that the government should charge taxpayers an additional £257 million and then increase my budget by that amount. The Secretary of State for Health might argue that with that money he could provide several new acute hospitals. The Secretary of State for Education might argue that with that money he could provide 30 extra secondary schools.

Many theoretical questions about 'justice' and the legal system quickly reduce to matters of political economy. The issue of court fees is a good illustration. Is the provision of free access to court services for all (including many who could easily afford to pay court fees) more important than the provision of schools and hospitals?

The principal idea here is that where people can afford to pay the costs involved in their bringing a legal action, the taxpayer should not be expected to pay for them.

There is a subsidy for costs associated with some family proceedings. This is intended to put as few barriers as possible in the way of people using the courts to protect themselves from violence or harassment, or trying to resolve disputes on the care of children.

Under the new proposals, people on low incomes will continue to be exempted from all court fees. Automatic exemptions to the fees will apply to people in receipt of Income Support, Family Credit, Disability Working Allowance, and income-based Job Seeker's Allowance.

Should fees be payable by those wishing to use the courts? Some observers point out that payments are not made by members of the public at the point of use in the education and health systems, and that justice can be seen as being just as important as those services. On the other hand, the Lord Chancellor has pointed out that were the courts to become free at the point of use, the money needed to pay for this would have to come from closing down large parts of the Civil Legal Aid or shutting schools or hospitals. Thus, legal policy is inextricably bound up with social policy in general.

3.13 Coroners' Courts

The coroners' courts are one of the most ancient parts of the English legal system, dating back to at least 1194. They are not, in modern function, part of the criminal courts, but because of historical associations, it makes more sense to classify them with the courts in this chapter rather than that dealing with civil courts. Coroners were originally appointed as *custos placitorum coronae*, keepers of the pleas of the Crown. They had responsibility for criminal cases in which the Crown had an interest, particularly a financial interest.

Today, there are 157 coroners' courts, of which 21 sit full time. These are presided over by 138 full time coroners and 240 deputy and assistant coroners. Coroners are usually lawyers (with at least a five year qualification within s 71 of the Courts and Legal Services Act (CLSA) 1990), although about 25% are medical doctors with a legal qualification. The main jurisdiction of the coroner today concerns unnatural and violent deaths, although treasure trove is also something occasionally dealt with.

The classifying of types of death is clearly of critical importance, not just to the State, politicians and policy makers, but also to the sort of campaign groups that exist in a constitutional democracy to monitor suicides, drug-related deaths, deaths in police custody and prison, accidental deaths, deaths in hospitals and deaths through industrial diseases.

In 2004, there were 514,300 registered deaths in England and Wales. Of all deaths, those that must be reported to a coroner are those of which there is evidence that they occurred in an unnatural or violent way. The coroner will order a postmortem and this may reveal a natural cause of death which can be duly registered. If not, or in certain other circumstances, such as where the death occurred in prison or police custody or if the cause is unknown, there will be an inquest. There were 229,000 deaths reported to coroners in 2004 resulting in 115,773 postmortem examinations and 28,274 inquests ('Statistics on deaths reported to coroners', *Home Office Statistical Bulletin*, September, 2005).

Most inquests (96%) are held without juries, but the State has been insistent that certain types of case must be heard by a jury in order to promote public faith in government. When, in 1926, legislation for the first time permitted inquests to be held without juries, certain types of death were deliberately marked off as still requiring jury scrutiny and these included deaths in police custody, deaths resulting from the actions of a police officer on duty and deaths in prison. This was seen as a very important way of fostering public trust in potentially oppressive aspects of the State. In 1971, the Brodrick Committee Report on the coronial system saw the coroner's jury as having a symbolic significance and thought that it was a useful way to legitimate the decision of the coroner.

The coroner's court is unique in using an inquisitorial process. There are no 'sides' in an inquest. There may be representation for people such as the relatives of the deceased, insurance companies, prison officers, car drivers, companies (whose policies are possibly implicated in the death) and train drivers, etc, but all the witnesses are the coroner's witnesses. It is the coroner who decides who shall be summoned as witnesses and in what order they shall be called.

Historically, an inquest jury could decide that a deceased had been unlawfully killed and then commit a suspect for trial at the local assizes. When this power was taken away in 1926, the main bridge over to the criminal justice system was removed. There then followed, in stages, an attempt to prevent inquest verdicts from impinging on the jurisdictions of the ordinary civil and criminal courts. Now, an inquest jury is exclusively concerned with determining who the deceased was and 'how, when and where he came by his death'. The court is forbidden to make any wider comment on the death and must not determine or appear to determine criminal liability 'on the part of a named person'.

Nevertheless, the jury may still now properly decide that a death was unlawful (that is, a crime). The verdict 'unlawful killing' is on a list of options (including 'suicide', 'accidental death' and 'open verdict') made under legislation and approved by the Home Office.

3.14   The Criminal Courts

There are over 7,500 different criminal offences in English law. These offences can be classified in different ways. You could, for example, classify them according to whether they are offences against people or property; again, you could classify them according to the type of mental element (*mens rea*) required for the offence, for example, 'intention' or 'recklessness'. One other type of classification, and the one to concern us here, is whether the offence is triable *summarily* in a magistrates' court (for relatively trivial offences like traffic offences) or is an *indictable* offence (the more serious offences like murder and rape) triable in front of a judge and jury in a Crown Court.

From the mid-19th century, magistrates were empowered to hear some indictable cases in certain circumstances. Today, there is still a class of offence which is triable 'either way', that is, summarily or in a jury trial. A typical example would be a potentially serious offence such as theft, but one which has been committed in a minor way, as in the theft of a milk bottle. These offences now account for about 80% of those tried in Crown Courts. Most defendants, however, opt for summary trial. The magistrates' court has the power to refuse jurisdiction – that means to refuse to deal with the matter – if it thinks, having considered the facts of the case, that its powers of sentencing would be insufficient if the case resulted in a conviction.

Where several defendants are charged together with either way offences, each defendant's choice can be exercised separately. So, if one elects for trial in the Crown Court, the others may still be tried summarily if the magistrates agree (*R v Brentwood Justices ex p Nicholls* (1991)).

Which types of case should be dealt with in which courts? This question was investigated by the James Committee, which reported in 1975 on *The Distribution of Business Between the Crown Court and Magistrates' Courts*. It found that for similar cases, Crown Court trials were three times more expensive than summary hearings. It concluded that the division of work between the different levels of court should reflect the public view as to what are the more serious offences justifying full trials, and those which should be dealt with by magistrates. The Committee also proposed a category of cases triable either way.

3.15   Magistrates' Courts

The office of magistrate or Justice of the Peace (JP) dates from 1195, when Richard I first appointed 'keepers of the peace' to deal with those who were accused of breaking 'the King's peace'. The JPs originally acted as local administrators for the king in addition to their judicial responsibilities. Apart from the 28,000 lay justices who sit in some 700 courts, there are also 105 District Judges (Magistrates' Courts) (formerly known as stipendiary magistrates) and 180 Deputy District Judges (Magistrates' Courts) who sit in cities and larger towns. They are qualified, experienced lawyers who are salaried justices. A Practice Direction from the Lord Chief Justice sets out details concerning the classification and allocation of Crown Court business, and some of this is relevant to the magistrates' courts. For example, upon sending someone for trial at the Crown Court, the magistrates should, if the offence is a class I offence (for example, murder, manslaughter or treason), specify the most convenient location of the Crown Court where a Hight Court judge or a circuit judge authorised to try such cases regularly sits: *Practice Direction (Criminal proceedings: Classification and allocation of business)* (2005).

3.15.1   Summary trial

Summary offences are created and defined by statute. There are thousands of different summary offences. They include traffic offences, common assault, taking a motor vehicle without consent and driving whilst disqualified: 98% of all criminal cases are dealt with by the courts summarily.

Cases are heard in the court for the district in which the offence is alleged to have been committed. In most cases, the defendant will be in court, but it is possible for the accused in road traffic offences to plead guilty by post and not to attend court.

The cases will be heard by two or three magistrates whose powers of sentencing are limited by the Acts which govern the offences in question. A District Judge (Magistrates' Courts) may sit without lay magistrates. The maximum sentence that magistrates can impose on a private individual, however, is a Level 5 fine (current maximum £5,000) and/or a 12 month prison sentence. Businesses may be fined up to £20,000 for certain offences. The maximum sentences for many summary offences are much less than these limits. Where a defendant is convicted of two or more offences at the same hearing, the maximum custodial sentence for any one offence is 12 months (s 154 of the Criminal Justice Act 2003, to be brought into law at a date to be appointed). Several sentences to be served concurrently, including more than one 12 month sentence, will be permitted. Consecutive sentences amounting to more than 12 months are not permitted, but will be to a limit of 65 weeks once s 155 of the Criminal Justice Act 2003 is brought into force. A date for its coming into force has not yet been appointed.

Many statutory offences are now given particular 'levels' according to their seriousness. This means that if a government minister wishes to raise fines (say to be in line with inflation), he does not have to go through hundreds of different offences, altering the maximum fine in relation to each one separately; the maxima for each level are simply altered. The 2006 figures are as follows: Level 5 up to £5,000; Level 4 up to £2,500; Level 3 up to £1,000; Level 2 up to £500; and Level 1 up to £200: s 37 of the Criminal Justice Act 1982.

The Criminal Justice Act (CJA) 1991 (the framework statute for many of the sentencing powers of the courts in recent times until the enactment of a consolidating statute, the Powers of the Criminal Courts (Sentencing) Act 2000) provided for a new system of fining in magistrates' courts: the 'unit fine' system. Under this system, fines were linked to the offender's income. The idea was that the rich should pay more than the poor for the same offence. Crimes were graded from one to 10 and the level of crime was then multiplied by the offender's weekly disposable income. The system's figures, however, resulted in many anomalies and it was eventually abolished. Nevertheless, in fixing the appropriate amount for a convicted defendant's fine, the magistrates will still take into account his income. Other sentences that the court may use include absolute discharge, conditional discharge, community rehabilitation orders (formerly known as probation), community punishment orders (formerly known as community service) and compensation orders.

After a conviction, the magistrates will hear whether the defendant has a criminal record and, if so, for what offences. This is to enable them to pass an appropriate sentence. If, after hearing that record, they feel that their powers of sanction are insufficient to deal with the defendant, then the defendant may be sent to the Crown Court for sentencing.

A bench of lay magistrates is legally advised by a justices' clerk who is legally qualified and guides the justices on matters of law, sentencing and procedure. The justices' clerk may give advice even when not specifically invited to do so. It is an established principle of English law that 'justice should not only be done but manifestly and undoubtedly be seen to be done' (*R v Sussex Justices ex p McCarthy* (1924), *per* Lord Hewart CJ). This is not about the proceedings being visible from a public gallery! It means there must be nothing in the appearance of what happens in a trial that might create an impression that something improper happened. In the Sussex Justices case, Mr McCarthy had been convicted of dangerous driving. He found out that the clerk to the magistrates, the person giving them legal advice, was a solicitor who happened to be representing someone who was suing him as a result of the car accident. Even though the solicitor might have been perfectly professional, there might have been an appearance that he could have framed his advice to the magistrates (even subconsciously) to help secure a conviction because a criminal conviction would have assisted his client in the civil case. The clerk had retired with the magistrates when they went to consider their verdict. The conviction was quashed because of the possibility of bias.

The magistrates are independent of the clerks and, according to the principle, the clerks should not *instruct* the magistrates what decision to make on any point, nor should they appear to be doing so. The clerk should not, therefore, normally retire with the justices when they go to consider their verdict in any case, although he may be called by them to give advice on any point. The clerk should not give any judgment on matters of fact.

The court is required in certain cases to consider a compensation order and to give reasons if it decides not to make such an order. Compensation orders are now governed by the provisions of ss 130–34 of the Powers of the Criminal Courts (Sentencing) Act (PCC(S)A) 2000. Section 130 states that a court before which a person is convicted, in addition to dealing with him in any other way, may make a compensation order. The order is to compensate personal injury, loss or damage resulting from the offence in question or any other offence 'taken into consideration' (that is, admitted by the defendant) by the court. The defendant can also be ordered to make payments for funeral expenses or bereavement in respect of a death resulting from an offence committed by the defendant (other than a death due to a motor accident). The court, s 130(3) states, 'shall give reasons, on passing sentence, if it does not make such a compensation order in a case where this section empowers it to do so'. Unlike a fine, the compensation will go to the victim rather than to the State, so these orders save victims of crime from having to claim damages against defendants in the civil courts. They are not intended as an alternative to punishment, enabling the defendant to buy his way out of the penalties for the crime. Even so, s 130(12) gives priority to the issue of a compensation order over a fine. In 1994, the Crown Court issued compensation orders in 9% of cases where the accused was sentenced – a total of 6,600 orders. The magistrates' courts issued over 88,000 orders.

3.15.2 Offences triable 'either way'

Where the defendant is charged with an offence triable 'either way', two preliminary decisions have to be made: first, should he be tried summarily (by magistrates) or on indictment (in the Crown Court by a judge and jury)? The procedure by which this matter is resolved is known as a mode of trial hearing. Secondly, if the determination is in favour of trial on indictment, is there a sufficient *prima facie* case to go before the Crown Court? This question is answered at a hearing known as *committal proceedings*. Changes to this system have been made by the Criminal Justice Act 2003.

Most defendants charged with 'either way' offences are tried by magistrates: 9% of cases go to the Crown Court because the magistrates consider their current sentencing powers to be inadequate; 4% of cases go to the Crown Court because the defendants elect for trial by jury.

Previously, the defendant could always insist on trial on indictment, but could not insist on being tried summarily if the magistrates declined jurisdiction. Similarly, the magistrates could always decide that the defendant should be tried on indictment, but could not insist that he be tried summarily. Prosecutions conducted by the Attorney General, the Solicitor General or the Director of Public Prosecutions must be tried on indictment if so requested by the prosecutor.

3.15.2.1   *The Criminal Justice Act 2003*

The Act made various changes to this area.

Section 41: allocation of offences triable either way and sending cases to the Crown Court

Section 41 introduces Sched 3, Part 1 of which sets out (through amendments to existing statutes) how it is to be decided whether cases triable either way should be tried summarily or on indictment, and provides for the sending to the Crown Court of those cases which need to go there.

Amendments to the Magistrates' Courts Act 1980

Paragraphs 3 and 4 of Sched 3 to the 2003 Act clarify that the preliminary stages of an either way case, including the plea before venue and allocation procedures, may take place at a hearing before a single justice. However, a single justice may *not* conduct a contested trial, nor – whilst he may take a guilty plea – may he impose a sentence on the offender. Paragraph 3 also limits the sentence that may be imposed where a person pleads guilty to a low-value offence.

Paragraph 5 substitutes s 19 of the Magistrates' Courts Act 1980, which makes provision for the procedure to be followed by a magistrates' court in deciding whether a case involving an offence triable either way to which the defendant has not indicated a guilty plea should be tried summarily or on indictment. The new procedure ('allocation') differs from the previous one in that the court is now to be informed about, and is to take account of, *any previous convictions* of the defendant in assessing whether the *sentencing powers available to it are adequate*. The court is to have regard not only (as previously) to any representations made by the prosecution or defence, but also to allocation guidelines which may be issued by the Sentencing Guidelines Council under s 170.

Paragraph 6 substitutes s 20 of the Magistrates' Courts Act 1980, which sets out the procedure to be followed by the magistrates' court where it decides that a case is suitable for summary trial. As previously, defendants will be told that they can either consent to be tried summarily or, if they wish, be tried on indictment. In making that decision, they may be influenced by the knowledge that, since it will generally no longer be possible to be committed for sentence to the Crown Court once the magistrates have accepted jurisdiction, they cannot receive a sentence beyond the magistrates' powers. Moreover, defendants now have the opportunity of requesting an indication from the magistrates whether, if they pleaded guilty at that point, the sentence would be custodial or not. The magistrates' court now has a discretion whether or not to give an indication to a defendant who has sought one. Where an indication is given, defendants are given the opportunity to reconsider their original indication as to plea. Where a defendant then decides to plead guilty, the magistrates' court will proceed to sentence. A custodial sentence will be available only if such a sentence was indicated, and if so – unlike after a guilty plea indication under s 17A or 17B – the option of committal to the Crown Court for sentence under s 3 of the PCC(S)A 2000 will not be available, although committal for sentence under s 3A of that Act will be available where the criteria for an extended sentence or a sentence for public protection appear to be met.

If this is not the case (that is, where the defendant declines to reconsider his plea indication, or where no sentence indication is given), the defendant will be given the choice between accepting summary trial or electing for trial on indictment, as at present. Where an indication of sentence is given and the defendant does not choose to plead guilty on the basis of it, the sentence indication is not binding on the magistrates who later try the case summarily, or on the Crown Court if the defendant elects trial on indictment.

Paragraph 7 substitutes s 21 in the Magistrates' Courts Act 1980 so that, where the court decides that trial on indictment appears more suitable, it will proceed to send the case to the Crown Court in accordance with s 51(1) of the Crime and Disorder Act 1998.

Paragraph 10 adds four new ss (24A–24D) to the Magistrates' Courts Act 1980, which apply a procedure akin to that in ss 17A–17C ('plea before venue') to cases involving defendants who are under 18. It would apply in certain cases where it falls to the court to decide whether the defendant should be sent to the Crown Court for trial, whether in his own right, or for joint trial with an adult defendant.

Paragraph 11 amends s 25 of the Magistrates' Courts Act 1980. The previous power to switch between summary trial and committal proceedings is abolished, and in its place there is a new power for the prosecution to apply for an either way case which has been allocated for summary trial to be tried on indictment instead.

Sending cases to the Crown Court

Paragraphs 15–20 amend the Crime and Disorder Act 1998. Paragraph 17 sets out the order in which a magistrates' court is to apply various procedures in respect of either way offences.

Paragraph 18 substitutes s 51 of the Crime and Disorder Act 1998 so that it applies not only (as now) to indictable only offences (and cases related to such offences), but also where an either way case involving an adult defendant is allocated for trial on indictment. The provisions for sending to the Crown Court related cases against the same defendant or another defendant (including one under 18) are preserved.

Paragraphs 21–28 amend the PCC(S)A 2000. The most important of these concerns the committal to the Crown Court for sentence of offences triable either way. This power is no longer available in cases where the magistrates' court has dealt with the case having accepted jurisdiction (whether as a contested case or a guilty plea), but is limited to cases where a guilty plea has been indicated at plea before venue.

If a defendant is charged with a number of related either way offences, pleads guilty to one of them at plea before venue and is sent to the Crown Court to be tried for the rest, the power in s 4 of the PCC(S)A 2000 – to send the offence to which he has pleaded guilty to the Crown Court for sentence – still exists.

3.15.3   Youth Courts

The procedures previously discussed apply only to those aged at least 18. Defendants who are aged less than 18 will normally be tried by a Youth Court, no matter what the classification of the offence (summary, either way, indictable only). However, a defendant under 18 must be tried on indictment where the charge is homicide, and may be tried on indictment where:

- the offence charged is punishable with at least 14 years' imprisonment, or is indecent assault, or (if the defendant is at least 14 years of age) is causing death by dangerous driving or causing death by careless driving whilst under the influence of drink or drugs;

- the defendant is jointly charged with an adult who is going to be tried on indictment and the court considers that it is in the interests of justice that both should be tried on indictment.

A defendant under 18 may be tried summarily in an adult magistrates' court where:

- he is to be tried jointly with an adult. This is subject to the power to commit both for trial on indictment, and also subject to a power to remit the defendant under 18 for trial to a Youth Court where the adult pleads guilty, or is discharged or committed for trial on indictment, but the defendant is not;

- he is charged as a principal offender and an adult is charged with aiding, abetting, etc;

- he is charged separately from, but at the same time as, an adult, and the charges against each arise out of the same or connected circumstances;

- it appears during summary trial that, contrary to the initial belief, he is under the age of 18.

There is likely to be a significant reduction in the number of defendants aged under 18 tried at the Crown Court following the introduction of s 41 of the Criminal Justice Act 2003 which, through Sched 3 to the Act, reframed the rules to produce the foregoing principles.

When defendants under 18 are tried by magistrates in the Youth Court, there will generally be three justices to hear the case, of whom at least one must be a man and one a woman. These justices will have had special training to deal with such cases. There are special provisions relating to punishments for this age group. The current maximum fine for a child (under 14 years of age) is £250, and for a young person (under 18) £1,000 (s 36 MCA 1980, as amended by s 17(2) CJA 1991 and Sched 13). Members of both groups may be made the subject of supervision orders and compensation orders. A sentence of imprisonment may be imposed only on a defendant who is at least 21 years old. A sentence of detention in a young offenders institution may be imposed only on a defendant who is at least 18 years old (the intention is to bring all those aged at least 18 within the imprisonment regime). For those under 18, the custodial sentence is a detention and training order, which may be imposed only where an adult could have been sentenced to imprisonment. Where the defendant is under 15, a detention and training order can be imposed only if he is a 'persistent' offender. In measures under Part III of the PCC(S)A 2000, the Youth Court will on some occasions be obliged, and on others will have the discretion, to refer the young offender to a youth offender panel, the members of which will agree with the young offender and his family a course of action designed to tackle the offending behaviour and its causes. This could involve actions such as making apologies, carrying out reparation, doing community work and taking part in family counselling.

Traditionally, the aim of the Youth Court system has been to take the young offender out of the normal criminal court environment, and this has involved strict rules about public access to the court. In general, members of the public have not been permitted to attend and reporting restrictions have been very tight. Parents can be required to attend, and must attend in the case of any person under the age of 16, unless such a requirement would be unreasonable in the circumstances. The name or photograph of any person under 18 appearing in a case must not be printed in any newspaper or broadcast without the authority of the court or the Home Secretary.

3.15.4 Indictable offences – committal proceedings

Where the magistrates decide that an offence triable either way should be tried in the Crown Court, they hold committal proceedings (as described at 3.15.2 above):

- *Section 51 of the Crime and Disorder Act 1998*

  These proceedings were also held where the defendant was charged with an indictable only offence (for example, murder). If, having read the papers, the magistrates took the view that there was a *prima facie* case to answer, they had to commit the defendant to the Crown Court for trial; if not, they had to discharge the defendant. Now, however, s 51 of the Crime and Disorder Act (CDA) 1998 states that, where an adult is charged with an offence triable only on indictment, the court shall send him directly to the Crown Court for trial. Where he is also charged with an either way offence or a summary offence, he may be sent directly to trial for that as well, provided the magistrates believe that it is related to the indictable offence and, in the case of a summary offence, it is punishable with imprisonment or involves obligatory or discretionary disqualification from driving. Under this procedure, the accused may apply to a Crown Court judge for the charge(s) to be dismissed, and the judge should so direct if it appears that the evidence would be insufficient to convict the accused (Sched 3 to the CDA 1998).

- *Reporting committal proceedings*

  In the old style committal proceedings, it was generally only the prosecution that would give evidence, with the defence reserving its arguments. Until 1967, this prosecution case was frequently reported on in the press so that it was virtually impossible to find an unbiased jury for the trial. A notorious instance of this was the case of Dr John Bodkin Adams in 1957. During the committal, deaths of patients other than the one for which he was to stand trial were referred to, but were not afterwards part of the evidence at the trial. The law on reporting was eventually changed in the CJA 1967 and is now in the MCA 1980. There are restrictions now on any application for dismissal put in by the defence. It is thus an offence to report on any aspect of the case if reporting restrictions have not been lifted by the bench. The bare matters which may as a matter of course be reported are:

- the identity of the court and the names of the examining magistrates;

- the names, ages, addresses and occupations of the accused and witnesses;

- the offence charged;

- the names of the lawyers engaged in the case;

- the decision of the court whether to commit or not and, if so, details of the committal, for example, to which court;

- any arrangements for bail;

- whether public funding was granted.

These restrictions, however, must be lifted by the magistrates if requested to do so by the accused. Where there are two or more accused and one objects to the reporting restrictions being lifted, then the magistrates must not lift them unless they regard it to be in the interests of justice to do so.

- *Old and new committals*

There are two sorts of committals, under the Magistrates' Courts Act 6(1) (known as 'old style', and s 6(2) 'new style'. The different possibilities give the defendant a tactical choice. Under the old style committal, the hearing is contested. The magistrates hear and examine the evidence, and the defendant's lawyer can ask the magistrates to rule that there is insufficient evidence to proceeed, that is, that there is no *prima facie* (Latin for 'at first sight') case to answer. By contrast in a new committal, the magistrates do not hear evidence or submissions. This is opted for if the defence does not wish to contest the evidence at the first stage, or if it is clear that there is a *prima facie* case to answer. Committal proceedings will be abolished when Sched 3 to the Criminal Justice Act 2003 comes into force. When that happens, 'either way' offences that are to proceed to Crown Court trial will be sent there directly.

- *Consistency of sentencing*

Concern is often expressed at the sometimes quite notable discrepancies in sentencing practices employed by different benches of magistrates. It might be that these variations are unavoidable in circumstances where the rigidity of fixed penalties is unacceptable for most offences and regional differences in types of prevalent crime prompt justices to have certain attitudes to particular offences. There are several research surveys which demonstrate the discrepancies in magistrates' sentencing. Tarling, for example (*Sentencing and Practice in Magistrates' Courts*, 1979, Home Office Study 98), showed that in the 30 courts he surveyed, the use of probation varied between 1% and 12%, suspended sentences between 4% and 16%, and fines between 46% and 76%.

3.15.4.1   Committals for sentence

Currently, cases committed to the Crown Court for sentence must be heard in the Crown Court by a bench composed of a High Court Judge, circuit judge or recorder sitting with between two and four JPs. The Powers of the Criminal Courts (Sentencing) Act 2000 ss 3–7 state that where, on a summary trial of an offence triable 'either way' a person aged 18 or over is convicted, the magistrates can commit the convicted person to the Crown Court for sentence if the magistrates are of the opinion that the offence was so serious that greater punishment should be inflicted for it than they have power to impose, or, in the case of a violent or sexual offence, that a custodial sentence for a period longer than the magistrates have power to impose is necessary to protect the public from serious harm.

3.15.4.2   *Warrant execution*

The police used to be primarily responsible for arresting fine defaulters and those in breach of community sentences. Increasingly, however, some police forces have given this work a low priority. The Courts Act 2003 extended the use of the Department for Work and Pensions' longstanding Third Party Deduction scheme which allows deductions from benefits to enforce payment of fines. The new level of deductions is contained in the Social Security Fines (Deductions from Income Support) (Amendment) Regulations 2004.

Deductions can be applied when the offender is first sentenced, subsequently applied if the offender defaults as part of a resetting of payment terms or used as a further sanction by the Fines Officer. Whilst £5 is the maximum amount which can be deducted from benefits automatically to pay a fine, the overall cap on deductions remains at £8.40. Other deductions can include council tax, rent arrears, fuel costs, housing costs and water charges.

3.16   The Crown Court

The Crown Court sits in 90 locations in England and Wales. In 2004, it held 81,750 trials. Defendants held in custody awaiting trial waited an average of 14 weeks. There were 42,185 cases where a plea of guilty was entered.

Until 1971, the main criminal courts were the Assizes and the Quarter Sessions. These courts did not sit continuously and were not held in locations which corresponded with centres of population, as had been the case when they developed. The system was very inefficient as circuit judges wasted much time simply travelling from one town on the circuit to the next, and many defendants spent long periods in gaol awaiting trial.

Change was made following the *Report of the Beeching Royal Commission on Assizes and Quarter Sessions* (1969). The Courts Act 1971 abolished the Assizes and Quarter Sessions. These were replaced by a single Crown Court, a part of the Supreme Court of Judicature. The Crown Court is not a local court like the magistrates' court but a single court which sits in over 90 centres. England and Wales are divided into six circuits, each with its own headquarters and staff. The centres are divided into three tiers. In first-tier centres, High Court Judges hear civil and criminal cases, whereas circuit judges and recorders hear only criminal cases. Second-tier centres are served by the same types of judge, but hear criminal cases only. At third-tier centres, recorders and circuit judges hear just criminal cases.

Criminal offences are divided into four classes according to their gravity. Class 1 offences are the most serious, including treason and murder, and are usually tried by a High Court Judge; exceptionally he may transfer a murder case (including attempts) to be heard by a circuit judge approved for this purpose by the Lord Chief Justice. Class 2 offences include manslaughter and rape and are subject to similar provisions. Class 3 offences include all remaining offences triable only on indictment and are usually tried by a High Court Judge, although releases of cases to circuit judges are more common here. Class 4 offences include robbery, grievous bodily harm and all offences triable 'either way', and are not normally tried by a High Court Judge.

3.16.1 The judges

The High Court Judges are usually from the Queen's Bench Division (QBD). Circuit judges are full time appointments made by the Queen on the advice of the Lord Chancellor. They are drawn from advocates with at least 10 years' experience of Crown Court practice (s 71 of the CLSA 1990) or lawyers who have been recorders. Appointment is also possible for someone who has had three years' experience in a number of other quasi-judicial offices like that of the stipendiary magistrate. Circuit judges retire at the age of 72, or 75 if the Lord Chancellor thinks it in the public interest.

A circuit judge may be removed from office by the Lord Chancellor on the grounds of incapacity or misbehaviour (s 17(4) of the Courts Act 1971). This right has not been exercised since 1983 when Judge Bruce Campbell, an Old Bailey judge, was removed from office a week after being convicted of two charges of smuggling.

To qualify for appointment as a recorder, a person must have 10 years' experience of advocacy in the Crown Court or county courts. JPs may also sit in the Crown Court, provided they are with one of the types of judge mentioned above. It is mandatory for between two and four JPs to sit when the Crown Court is hearing an appeal or dealing with persons committed for sentence by a magistrates' court.

3.16.2 Jurisdiction

The Crown Court hears all cases involving trial on indictment. It also hears appeals from those convicted summarily in the magistrates' courts. At the conclusion of the hearing, it has the power to confirm, reverse or vary any part of the decision under appeal (s 48(2) of the Supreme Court Act 1981). If the appeal is decided against the accused, the Crown Court has the power to impose any sentence which the magistrates could have imposed, including one which is harsher than the one originally imposed on the defendant.

3.16.3   Delay

Defendants committed to the Crown Court to be tried will have to wait an average of three months for their case to come to trial. This wait is sometimes in custody. Ever since the Streatfield Committee Report recommended in 1961 that the maximum time a defendant should have to wait after committal for trial should be eight weeks, there have been many schemes to help achieve this aim, but none has been particularly successful. Since 1985, for example, a person charged with an offence triable 'either way' can request the prosecution to furnish him with information (in the form of witness statements, a summary of the case, etc) of the case against him. This was aimed at increasing the number of guilty pleas by showing to the defendant at an early stage the strength of the prosecution's case.

There are 643 circuit judges, 433 district judges, and 1,350 recorders. Additionally, High Court judges sit in the Crown Court in class 1 and 2 cases. High Court judges, altogether, sat for 1,412 days (that is, if ten judges sit for 10 days each, that is 100 judge days) during 2004. When one remembers that the average time to try a case on a plea of 'not guilty' is about seven hours (one and a half court days), the burden of work on the Crown Court – dealing with about 80,000 trials a year is considerable. The consequent delay has very serious repercussions on the criminal justice system: justice delayed is justice denied. The accuracy of testimony becomes less reliable the longer the gap between the original reception of the data by a witness and his account of it in court. Also important is the stress and pain for those innocent defendants who have to wait so long before their case can be put to a jury.

The largest ever study of Crown Court cases, undertaken by Zander and Henderson for the Runciman Commission, made some worrying findings. Their research was based on responses to questionnaires by more than 22,000 people involved in 3,000 Crown Court cases. The views of lawyers, judges, clerks, jurors, police and defendants were all canvassed. There were convictions in 8% of cases that defence lawyers thought weak, 6% that prosecution barristers thought weak and 4% that judges thought weak, suggesting that innocent people were still being convicted in significant numbers. Further, 31 defendants said that they had pleaded guilty to offences they had not committed. Their reasons were varied: to avoid a trial; to gain a less severe sentence; or because they had been advised to do so by their lawyers.

Another worrying discovery, since poor defence lawyers have recently been cited as contributing to miscarriages of justice, is the large number of Crown Court cases (about one-third) that were being dealt with by clerks rather than by trained, qualified solicitors. Some defendants met with their barrister for the first time on the morning of their trial, and for about one-third of these cases, the conference lasted for just 15 minutes. In about one-third of all cases, the barristers only received their instructions the day before the trial.

3.16.4   Magistrates' courts and Crown Courts

For offences triable 'either way', there has been much debate about the merits of each venue. The introduction of the 'plea before venue' procedure previously described has significantly reduced the number of cases committed for trial to the Crown Court and significantly increased the number committed for sentence. At the same time, the proportion of cases disposed of on a not guilty plea has risen. Even so, of approximately 65,000 cases disposed of by the Crown Court in 1999, 59% were decided on a guilty plea (which actually represented a fall of almost 10% from 1998). Obviously, this means that the CPS incurs considerable costs in wasted preparation. One of the reasons defendants do this is that prosecution cases often fall apart during the delay before a Crown Court hearing, allowing the defendant to go free. Another is that juries cannot be compelled to give reasons for convicting, unlike magistrates, who can be required to justify their reasons in writing for review in the High Court which can overturn convictions or acquittals. Thus, there is a greater chance with jury convictions that an appeal court will regard a conviction (should there be one) as unsafe and unsatisfactory because the jury's reasons for having convicted will not be known. Thus, a defendant who suspects that he might be convicted can reasonably prefer to be convicted by a jury than by a magistrate because the former do not and cannot give reasons for their verdicts and are therefore perhaps easier to appeal. Jury verdicts are arguably more likely to be regarded as unsafe on appeal because it will not be known whether some improper factor (like a judge's misdirection) had entered their deliberation. The reports of the Court of Appeal (Criminal Division) contain many cases where the court states that a conviction should be quashed because the jury might have been influenced by a misleading statement from the judge. It might be said that a defendant should prefer the magistrates' court as the sentencing is generally lower, but when the defendant's antecedents are known (after a conviction), he can still be committed to the Crown Court for sentence, so the magistrates' courts are not really preferable to a defendant with a criminal record who fears another conviction is likely.

3.17   Criminal Appeals

The process of appeal depends upon how a case was originally tried, whether summarily or on indictment. The system of criminal appeals underwent some changes as a result of the Criminal Justice Act 2003.

3.17.1   Appeals from magistrates' courts

Two routes of appeal are possible. The first route allows only a defendant to appeal. The appeal is to a judge and between two and four magistrates sitting in the Crown Court and can be: (a) against conviction (only if the defendant pleaded not guilty) on points of fact or law; or (b) against sentence. Such an appeal will take the form of a new trial (a trial *de novo*).

Alternatively, the defendant can appeal 'by way of case stated' to the High Court (the Divisional Court of the QBD). This court consists of two or more judges (usually two), of whom one will be a Lord Justice of Appeal. Here, either the defence or the prosecution may appeal, but the grounds are limited to: (a) a point of law; or (b) that the magistrates acted beyond their jurisdiction. If the prosecution succeeds on appeal, the court can direct the magistrates to convict and pass the appropriate sentence. There is also an appeal by way of case stated from the Crown Court to the Divisional Court when the Crown Court has heard an appeal from the magistrates' court.

Appeal from the Divisional Court is to the House of Lords. Either side may appeal, but only on a point of law and only if the Divisional Court certifies the point to be one of general public importance. Leave to appeal must also be granted either by the Divisional Court or the House of Lords.

Section 41 of the Criminal Justice Act 2003, via paragraph 5 of Sched 3, substitutes s 19 of the Magistrates' Courts Act 1980, which makes provision for the procedure to be followed by a magistrates' court in deciding whether a case involving an offence triable either way to which the defendant has not indicated a guilty plea should be tried summarily or on indictment. The new procedure ('allocation') differs from the present one in that the court is to be informed about, and take account of, any previous convictions of the defendant in assessing whether the sentencing powers available to it are adequate. The court is to have regard, not only (as now) to any representations made by the prosecution or defence, but also to allocation guidelines which may be issued by the Sentencing Guidelines Council under s 170. This section is not yet in force.

3.17.2 Appeals from the Crown Court

Appeals from the Crown Court lie to the Court of Appeal (Criminal Division), which hears appeals against conviction and sentence. This court, replacing the Court of Criminal Appeal, was established in 1966. The Division usually sits in at least two courts: one composed of the Lord Chief Justice sitting with two judges of the QBD and the other of a Lord Justice of Appeal and two Queen's Bench judges. The court hears about 8,000 criminal appeals and applications each year. In 1999, it heard 8,274 applications, 2,104 of which were appeals against conviction and 6,170 of which concerned sentence.

Until 1996, s 2 of the Criminal Appeal Act (CAA) 1968 read:

2(1) Except as provided by this Act, the Court of Appeal shall allow an appeal against conviction if they think:

    (a) that the verdict of the jury should be set aside on the ground that, under all the circumstances of the case, it is unsatisfactory or unsafe; or

    (b) that the judgment of the court of trial should be set aside on the ground of a wrong decision of any question of law; or

    (c) that there was a material irregularity in the course of the trial, and in any other case shall dismiss the appeal:

> provided that the court may, notwithstanding that they are of opinion that the point raised in the appeal might be decided in favour of the appellant, dismiss the appeal if they consider that no miscarriage of justice has actually occurred.

January 1996 saw the introduction of the Criminal Appeal Act (CAA) 1995. The introduction of ss 1, 2 and 4 of the Act brought particularly significant changes to the criminal appeal system.

Section 1 amended the CAA 1968 so as to bring an appeal against conviction, an appeal against a verdict of not guilty by reason of insanity and an appeal against a finding of disability, *on a question of law alone*, into line with other appeals against conviction and sentence (that is, those involving questions of fact, or mixtures of law and fact). Now, all appeals against conviction and sentence must first have leave of the Court of Appeal or a certificate of fitness for appeal from the trial judge before the appeal can be taken. Before the 1995 Act came into force, it was possible to appeal without the consent of the trial judge or Court of Appeal on a point of law alone. In Parliament, the reason for this change was given as the need to 'provide a filter mechanism for appeals on a ground of law alone which are wholly without merit' (HC Official Report, SC B (Criminal Appeal Bill) Col 6, 21 March 1995).

Section 2 changed the grounds for allowing an appeal under the CAA 1968. Under the old law, the Court of Appeal was required to allow an appeal where: (1) the conviction, verdict or finding should have been set aside on the ground that, under all the circumstances, it was unsafe or unsatisfactory; or (2) that the judgment of the court of trial or the order of the court giving effect to the verdict or finding should be set aside on the ground of a wrong decision of law; or (3) that there was a material irregularity in the course of the trial. In all three situations, the Court of Appeal was allowed to dismiss the appeal if it considered that no miscarriage of justice had actually occurred. The law now requires the Court of Appeal to allow an appeal against conviction under s 1 of the CAA 1968, an appeal against verdict under s 12 (insanity) or an appeal against a finding of disability if it thinks that the conviction, verdict or finding is 'unsafe' (as opposed to the old law, which used the 'unsafe or *unsatisfactory*' formula).

During the parliamentary passage of the Act, there was much heated debate about whether the new provisions were designed to narrow the grounds of appeal. That would amount to a tilt in favour of the State in that it would make it harder for (wrongly) convicted people to appeal. Government ministers insisted that the effect of the new law was simply to re-state or consolidate the practice of the Court of Appeal. One government spokesman said that:

> In dispensing with the word 'unsatisfactory', we agree with the Royal Commission on criminal justice that there is no real difference between 'unsafe' and 'unsatisfactory'; the Court of Appeal does not distinguish between the two. Retaining the word 'unsatisfactory' would imply that we thought there was a real difference and would only lead to confusion.

There were many attempts during the legislation's passage to insert the words 'or may be unsafe' after the word 'unsafe'. The Law Society, the Bar, Liberty and JUSTICE called on the government to make such a change. Also opposed to the use of the single word 'unsafe' was the eminent criminal law expert Professor JC Smith. He has argued cogently that there are many cases where a conviction has been seen as 'unsatisfactory' rather than 'unsafe', so there is a need for both words. Sometimes, the Court of Appeal might be convinced that the defendant is guilty (so the conviction is 'safe') but still wishes to allow the appeal because fair play, according to the rules, must be seen to be done. Accepting improperly extracted confessions (violating s 76 of the Police and Criminal Evidence Act (PACE) 1984) simply because it might seem obvious that the confessor is guilty will promote undesirable interrogation practices, because police officers will think that even if they break the rules, any resulting confession will nevertheless be allowed as evidence.

Professor Smith has given the example ((1995) 145 NLJ 534) of where there has been a serious breach of the rules of evidence. In *Algar* (1954), the former wife of the defendant testified against him about matters during the marriage. The Court of Appeal allowed his appeal against conviction, but Lord Goddard said: 'Do not think that we are doing this because we think that you are an innocent man. We do not. We think that you are a scoundrel.' The idea behind such remarks is that rules are rules, and the rules of evidence must be obeyed in order to ensure justice. Once you start to accept breaches of the rules as being justified by the outcome (ends justifying means), then the whole law of evidence could begin to collapse.

The proposal to include 'or might be unsafe' was rejected for the reason probably best summarised by Lord Taylor, the then Lord Chief Justice, who argued in the Lords that there was no merit in including the words 'or may be unsafe', as the implication of such doubt is already inherent in the word 'unsafe'.

Cases decided since the new formula was introduced have tended to indicate that the Court of Appeal has not adopted a restrictive interpretation. Thus, a conviction was quashed as unsafe in *Smith (Patrick Joseph)* (1999) because of irregularities at trial, even though the accused had admitted his guilt during cross-examination. The Human Rights Act (HRA) 1998 has now introduced a further significant element into the consideration of this issue, to which the Court of Appeal is currently struggling to develop the correct approach. Article 6 of the European Convention on Human Rights (ECHR), to which English courts must give effect unless incompatible with an Act of Parliament, gives the defendant a right to a fair trial. Irregularities in a trial, including misdirections by the judge, admission of improperly obtained evidence and so on, might cast doubt on the fairness of the trial without necessarily making the conviction unsafe on a narrow view of that word. In *Davis* (2001), the Court of Appeal suggested that since a conviction might be unsafe even where there was no doubt about guilt, but there were serious irregularities at the trial, English rules on appeals were compatible with Art 6. However, it went on to argue that a violation of Art 6 did not necessarily imply that the conviction must be quashed. Subsequently, Lord Woolf CJ argued in *Togher* (2000) that obligations under the ECHR meant that it was almost inevitable that if the accused had been denied a fair trial, his conviction would have to be regarded as unsafe.

Section 4 provides a unified test for the receipt of fresh evidence in the Court of Appeal. Under the old law, the Court of Appeal had a discretion under s 23(1)(c) of the CAA 1968 to receive fresh evidence of any witness if it was thought necessary or expedient in the interests of justice. Section 23(2) added a duty to receive new evidence which was relevant, credible and admissible, and which could not reasonably have been adduced at the original trial. There was often much argument about whether new evidence should be received under the court's discretion or its duty. Gradually, the 'duty' principles came to be merged into the 'discretion' principles. The aim of the latest amendment is to reflect the current practice of the court. The general discretion under s 23(1) has been retained, but the 'duty' principle has been replaced with a set of criteria which the court must consider. They are:

- whether the evidence appears to the court to be capable of belief;

- whether it appears to the court that the evidence may afford any ground for allowing the appeal;

- whether the evidence would have been admissible at the trial on the issue under appeal; and

- whether there is a reasonable explanation for the failure to adduce the evidence at trial.

Only the accused may appeal. No leave to appeal is required if the appeal is against conviction on a point of law, but it is needed for appeals on points of fact or mixed fact and law. Leave is also required for appeals against sentence. Under s 36 of the CJA 1972, the Attorney General can refer a case which has resulted in an acquittal to the Court of Appeal where he believes the decision to have been questionably lenient on a point of law. The Court of Appeal deals just with the point of law and the defendant's acquittal is not affected even if the court decides the point against the defendant. It merely clarifies the law for future cases. Sections 35–36 of the CJA 1988 allow the Attorney General to refer indictable only cases to the Court of Appeal where the sentence at trial is regarded as unduly lenient. The court can impose a harsher sentence. Following the determination of an appeal by the Court of Appeal or by the Divisional Court, either the prosecution or the defence may appeal to the House of Lords. Leave from the court below or the House of Lords must be obtained and two other conditions fulfilled according to s 33 of the CAA 1968:

- the court below must certify that a point of law of general public importance is involved; and

- either the court below or the House of Lords must be satisfied that the point of law is one which ought to be considered by the House of Lords.

The High Court can quash tainted acquittals under s 54 of the CPIA 1996. An acquittal is 'tainted' where someone has since been convicted of conspiring to pervert the course of justice in the case by interfering with the jury.

3.17.2.1 The Criminal Justice Act 2003

Section 57: introduction

This section sets out certain basic criteria for a prosecution appeal under this Part of the Act. The right of appeal arises only in trials on indictment and lies to the Court of Appeal.

Sub-section (2) sets out two further limitations on appeals under this Part. It prohibits the prosecution from appealing rulings on discharge of the jury and those rulings that may be appealed by the prosecution under other legislation, for example, appeals from preparatory hearings against rulings on admissibility of evidence and other points of law.

Sub-section (4) provides that the prosecution must obtain leave to appeal, either from the judge or the Court of Appeal.

Section 58: general right of appeal

This section sets out the procedure that must be followed when the prosecution wishes to appeal against a terminating ruling. The section covers both rulings that are formally terminating and those that are *de facto* terminating in the sense that they are so fatal to the prosecution case that, in the absence of a right of appeal, the prosecution would offer no or no further evidence. It applies to rulings made at an applicable time during a trial (which is defined in sub-s (13) as any time before the start of the judge's summing up to the jury).

Where the prosecution fails to obtain leave to appeal or abandons the appeal, the prosecution must agree that an acquittal follow by virtue of sub-ss (8) and (9).

Section 59: expedited and non-expedited appeals

This section provides two alternative appeal routes: an expedited (fast) route and a non-expedited (slower) route. The judge must determine which route the appeal will follow (sub-s (1)). In the case of an expedited appeal, the trial may be adjourned (sub-s (2)). If the judge decides that the appeal should follow the non-expedited route, he may either adjourn the proceedings or discharge the jury, if one has been sworn (sub-s (3)). Subsection (4) gives both the judge and the Court of Appeal power to reverse a decision to expedite an appeal, thus transferring the case to the slower non-expedited route. If a decision is reversed under this sub-section, the jury may be discharged.

Section 61: determination of appeal by Court of Appeal

This section sets out the powers of the Court of Appeal when determining a prosecution appeal. This needs to be read in conjunction with s 67.

Sub-section (1) authorises the Court of Appeal to confirm, reverse or vary a ruling which has been appealed against. The section is drafted to ensure that, after the Court of Appeal has ordered one or other of these disposals, it must then always make it clear what is to happen next in the case.

When the Court of Appeal confirms a ruling, sub-ss (3) and (7) provide that it must then order the acquittal of the defendant(s) for the offence(s) which are the subject of the appeal.

When the Court of Appeal reverses or varies a ruling, sub-ss (4) and (8) provide that it must either order a resumption of the Crown Court proceedings or a fresh trial, or order the acquittal of the defendant(s) for the offence(s) under appeal. By virtue of sub-ss (5) and (8), the Court of Appeal will only order the resumption of the Crown Court proceedings or a fresh trial where it considers it necessary in the interests of justice to do so.

Section 68: appeals to the House of Lords

Sub-section (1) amends s 33(1) of the Criminal Appeal Act 1968 to give both the prosecution and defence a right of appeal to the House of Lords from a decision by the Court of Appeal on a prosecution appeal against a ruling made under this Part of the Act.

Sub-section (2) amends s 36 of the Criminal Appeal Act 1968 to prevent the Court of Appeal from granting bail to a defendant who is appealing, or is applying for leave to appeal, to the House of Lords from a Court of Appeal decision made under this Part of the Act. Bail will continue to be a matter for the trial court. This section is to come into force on a day to be appointed.

Section 69: costs

Sub-sections (2) and (3) amend ss 16(4A) and 18 of the Prosecution of Offences Act 1985 to give the Court of Appeal power, on an appeal under this Part, to award costs to and against the defendant.

The Criminal Justice Act also allows for the re-trial of serious offences.

Section 75: cases that may be re-tried – changes to the rule against 'double jeopardy'

Section 75 sets out the cases which may be re-tried under the exception to the normal rule against *double jeopardy*. These cases all involve serious offences which in the main carry a maximum sentence of life imprisonment, and which are considered to have a particularly serious impact either on the victim or on society more generally. The offences to which the provisions apply are called 'qualifying offences' and are listed in Sched 5 to the Act. They include murder, manslaughter, rape, and arson endangering life.

The cases which may be re-tried are those in which a person has been acquitted of one of the qualifying offences, either on indictment or following an appeal, or of a lesser qualifying offence of which he could have been convicted at that time. This takes into account cases of 'implied acquittals', in which, under the current law, an acquittal would have prevented a further prosecution being brought for a lower level offence on the same facts. For example, an acquittal for murder may also imply an acquittal for the lower level offence of manslaughter, but new evidence may then come to light which would support a charge of manslaughter. A person may only be re-tried in respect of a qualifying offence.

In certain circumstances, cases may also be tried where an acquittal for an offence has taken place abroad, so long as the alleged offence also amounted to a qualifying offence and could have been charged as such in the UK. This would include, for example, offences such as war crimes, and murder committed outside the UK, for which the courts in England and Wales have jurisdiction over British citizens abroad. Such cases are likely to be rare. Sub-section (5) recognises that offences may not be described in exactly the same way in the legislation of other jurisdictions.

Section 76: application to the Court of Appeal

Section 76 allows a prosecutor to apply to the Court of Appeal for an order which quashes the person's acquittal and orders him to be re-tried for the qualifying offence. A 'prosecutor' means a person or body responsible for bringing public prosecutions, such as the Crown Prosecution Service or HM Customs and Excise. Where a person has been acquitted outside the UK, the court will need to consider whether or not the acquittal would act as a bar to a further trial here and, if it does, the court can order that it must not be a bar.

Applications to the Court of Appeal require the personal written consent of the Director of Public Prosecutions (DPP). This provides a safeguard to ensure that only those cases in which there is sufficient evidence are referred to the Court of Appeal. The DPP will also consider whether it is in the public interest to proceed. This section also recognises any international obligations arising under the Treaty of the European Union, under which negotiations are taking place to support the mutual recognition of the decisions of the courts in other EU Member States.

Applications may also be brought by public prosecuting authorities if new evidence arises in cases which have previously been tried by means of a private prosecution.

Only one application for an acquittal to be quashed may be made in relation to any acquittal. In March 2006, a man accused of a 1989 murder became the first person to have his case referred to the Court of Appeal under this procedure. The body of Julie Hogg, 22, from Teesside, was found hidden behind her bath by her mother Ann Ming. William Dunlop, 42, was acquitted of Ms Hogg's murder. In April, 2005, police said they were to re-examine the case of Ms Hogg. William Dunlop previously faced two murder trials, but each time the jury failed to reach a verdict and he was formally acquitted in 1991. The Director of Public Prosecutions, Ken Macdonald, said that after looking at submissions from the Chief Crown Prosecutor for Cleveland, Martin Goldman, he was 'satisfied' the Crown Prosecution Service should apply to the Court of Appeal for a re-trial.

Section 77: determination by the Court of Appeal

Section 77 sets out the decisions which the Court of Appeal may make in response to an application for an acquittal to be quashed. The court must make an order quashing an acquittal and ordering a re-trial if it considers that the requirements set out in ss 78 and 79 of the Act are satisfied, namely that there is new and compelling evidence in the case, and that it is in the interests of justice for the order to be made. The court must dismiss an application where it is not satisfied as to these two factors.

Section 78: new and compelling evidence

Section 78 sets out the requirement for there to be new and compelling evidence against the acquitted person in relation to the qualifying offence, and defines evidence which is 'new and compelling'. Evidence is 'new' if it was not adduced at the original trial of the acquitted person. Evidence is 'compelling' if the court considers it to be reliable and substantial and, when considered in the context of the outstanding issues, the evidence appears to be highly probative of the case against the acquitted person. The court is thus required to make a decision on the strength of the new evidence. So, for example, new evidence relating to identification would only be considered 'compelling' if the identity of the offender had been at issue in the original trial. It is not intended that relatively minor evidence which might appear to strengthen an earlier case should justify a re-trial.

Section 79: interests of justice

Section 79 sets out the requirement that in all the circumstances it is in the interests of justice for the court to quash an acquittal and order a re-trial. In determining whether it is in the interests of justice, the court will consider in particular: whether there are existing factors which make a fair trial unlikely (for example, the extent of adverse publicity about the case); the length of time since the alleged offence was committed; and whether the police and prosecution acted with due diligence and expedition in relation to both the original trial and any new evidence. The court may take into account any other issues it considers relevant in determining whether a re-trial will be in the interests of justice.

3.17.3   The Access to Justice Act 1999 – jurisdiction

Section 61 of the Access to Justice Act 1999 establishes the jurisdiction of the High Court to hear cases stated by the Crown Court for an opinion of the High Court. This part of the Act (Part IV) enables these and certain other applications to the High Court to be listed before a single judge. It provides for the appointment of a Vice President of the QBD. It also prohibits the publication of material likely to identify a child involved in proceedings under the Children Act 1989, before the High Court or a county court, and allows for those under 14 years old to attend criminal trials.

3.17.4   Judicial Committee of the Privy Council

The Judicial Committee of the Privy Council was created by the Judicial Committee Act 1833. Under the Act, a special committee of the Privy Council was set up to hear appeals from the Dominions. The cases are heard by the judges (without wigs or robes) in a committee room in London. The Committee's decision is not a judgment but an 'advice' to the monarch, who is counselled that the appeal be allowed or dismissed.

The Committee is the final court of appeal for certain Commonwealth countries which have retained this option, and from some independent members and associate members of the Commonwealth. The Committee comprises Privy Councillors who hold (or have held) high judicial office. In most cases, the Committee comprises five Lords of Appeal in Ordinary, sometimes assisted by a judge from the country concerned.

Most of the appeals heard by the Committee are civil cases (see 3.11 above). In the rare criminal cases, it is only on matters involving legal questions that appeals are heard. The Committee does not hear appeals against criminal sentence.

The decisions of the Privy Council are very influential in English courts because they concern points of law that are applicable in this jurisdiction and they are pronounced upon by Lords of Appeal in Ordinary in a way which is thus tantamount to a House of Lords' ruling. These decisions, however, are technically of persuasive precedent only, although they are normally followed by English courts; see, for example, the criminal appeal case *Abbot v R* (1977). This was an appeal from Trinidad and Tobago. The Privy Council ruled that duress is no defence to the perpetrator of murder.

3.17.5 Royal Commission on Criminal Justice

Research undertaken for the Royal Commission by Kate Malleson of the London School of Economics found that judges' mistakes are by far the most common ground for successful appeals against conviction. The research discovered that in about 80% of cases where convictions were quashed, there had been an error at the trial; in most instances, it was judicial error.

Of 300 appeals in 1990, just over one-third were successful. Of those appealing, almost two-thirds of defendants appealed against conviction on the ground that the trial judge had made a crucial mistake and, of those, 43% succeeded in having their convictions quashed. Sixteen defendants were vindicated by the Court of Appeal in claims that the judge's summing up to the jury was biased or poor; a further 42 convictions were quashed because the judge was wrong about the law or evidence.

This research was critical of the way the Court of Appeal failed to consider cases where fresh evidence had emerged since the trial or where there was a 'lurking doubt' about the conviction. The Report urged that the court be given a new role allowing it to investigate the events leading up to a conviction.

The Royal Commission was set up, under the chair manship of Viscount Runciman, in March 1991, after the release of the Birmingham Six (an important case in a series of notorious miscarriages of justice in which people were found to have been wrongly convicted and sentenced for serious crimes). It reported in July 1993, with 352 recommendations largely designed to prevent wrongful conviction. Several of the recommendations are relevant to discussion of the criminal courts. The numbers here refer to those of the recommendations in the Report.

The Commission recommended (331) that the Home Secretary's power to refer cases to the Court of Appeal under s 17 of the CAA 1968 should be removed and a new body, the Criminal Cases Review Authority, should be set up to consider allegations (332) that a miscarriage of justice might have occurred. The Authority should have 'operational independence' (333), with a chairman appointed by the

Queen on the advice of the Prime Minister. The Authority should be independent of the court structure (336) and should refer meritorious cases directly to the Court of Appeal. There should be neither a right of appeal nor a right to judicial review (340) in relation to decisions reached by the authority. The Authority should consist of both lawyers and lay people, should be supported by a staff of lawyers (344) and should devise its own rules and procedures. It should be able to discuss cases directly with applicants (345) and should have powers (347) to direct its own investigations. These recommendations were largely met by the terms of the CAA 1995.

3.17.6 Criminal Cases Review Commission

The Criminal Cases Review Commission (CCRC) is an independent body set up under the CAA 1995. The CCRC came into being on 1 January 1997. There are 14 members from a wide variety of backgrounds. It is responsible for investigating suspected miscarriages of criminal justice in England, Wales and Northern Ireland. This function was previously carried out through the office of the Home Secretary. He would make occasional referrals of cases back to the Court of Appeal when a unit of civil servants in the Home Office evaluated a case (which had otherwise exhausted the formal court appeal system) as warranting further consideration. Over 250 cases were transferred from the Home Office around 31 March 1997, when the Commission took over responsibility for casework.

The CCRC cannot overturn convictions or sentences itself. Instead, it may refer to the Court of Appeal a conviction for an offence tried on indictment, or a finding of not guilty by reason of insanity, or a finding that a person was under a disability when he did the act or made the omission, and may also refer cases in respect of sentence where they were tried on indictment (s 9 of the CAA 1995). Additionally, the CCRC may refer to the Crown Court convictions and sentences imposed by magistrates' courts, though the Crown Court may not impose any punishment more severe than that of the court from which the decision is referred (s 11 of the CAA 1995). The Court of Appeal itself may direct the CCRC to carry out an investigation and it must report to the court when finished or as required to do so by the court. Once the reference has been made, it will be treated as an appeal for the purposes of the CAA 1968.

The Commission is given power by ss 17–21 of the CAA 1995 to obtain information and carry out investigations, including appointing investigating officers (who are likely to be police officers where there have been previous police investigations).

Any decision to refer a case to the relevant appellate court has to be taken by a committee of at least three members. The CCRC considers whether or not there is a real possibility that the conviction, finding, verdict or sentence would not be upheld were a reference to be made.

In order to establish that there is a real possibility of an appeal succeeding regarding a conviction, there has to be:

- an argument or evidence which has not been raised during the trial or at appeal; or

- exceptional circumstances.

In order to establish that there is a real possibility of an appeal succeeding against a sentence, there has to be a legal argument or information about the individual or the offence which was not raised in court during the trial or at appeal.

Other than in exceptional circumstances, the Commission can only consider cases in which an appeal through the ordinary judicial appeal process has failed and, once a decision is taken to refer a case to the relevant court of appeal, the Commission has no other involvement.

The CCRC referred the notorious case of Derek William Bentley to the Court of Appeal. Mr Bentley was convicted at the Central Criminal Court on 11 December 1952 of the murder of PC Sidney Miles. Mr Bentley did not actually shoot the officer. The gun was fired by his accomplice in a failed burglary attempt, but Mr Bentley was convicted under the principles of 'joint enterprise', even though he was being held under arrest by a police officer metres away from where his accomplice fired the pistol. An appeal against conviction was heard by the Court of Criminal Appeal on 13 January 1953 and dismissed. Mr Bentley was hanged on 28 January 1953.

Bentley's conviction and sentence were the subject of numerous representations to the Home Office. In July 1993, on the recommendation of the Home Secretary, Her Majesty The Queen, in the exercise of the Royal Prerogative of Mercy, granted to Mr Bentley a posthumous pardon limited to sentence.

Following submissions from the applicants' solicitors and the completion of its own inquiries, the CCRC concluded that Mr Bentley's conviction should be reconsidered by the Court of Appeal. The trial was seen as unfair in a number of respects, for example, the fact that, although 18, Bentley had a mental age of 11 was kept a secret from the jury, and the judge's summing up to the jury was astonishingly biased in favour of the police. In August 1998, on a momentous day in legal history, the Court of Appeal cleared Bentley of the murder for which he was hanged 46 years earlier. In giving judgment, the Lord Chief Justice, Lord Bingham, said: '... the summing up in this case was such as to deny the appellant that fair trial which is the birthright of every British citizen.'

The latest figures (CCRC *Case Statistics*, 31 January 2006) show that since its inception, the CCRC has had 8,401 applications. Of these, 7,693 have been completed. Of those there have been 312 referrals to the Court of appeal, of which 257 have been heard. Of those, 179 resulted in convictions being quashed, 75 convictions were upheld, and three judgments have been reserved.

Taking a global perspective on legal systems, it is unusual for any machinery of justice to provide as many opportunities for appeal and challenge as exist in the English system.

3.18 A Miscarriage of Justice

One of the English legal system's worst miscarriages of justice cases in recent history was exposed in the Court of Appeal in February 1998. In 1979, Vincent Hickey, Michael Hickey, Jimmy Robertson and Pat Molloy, who became known as the Bridgewater Four, were convicted of the murder of a 13 year old boy, Carl Bridgewater. Although the men were not angelic characters (and two had serious criminal records), they strenuously protested that they were not guilty of the horrific child murder.

Eighteen years later, and after two earlier failed visits to the Court of Appeal and seven police investigations, three of the men were released on 21 February on unconditional bail in anticipation of an appeal hearing in April. The fourth defendant, Mr Molloy, died in jail in 1981. The appeal was eventually allowed.

The Crown has conceded that the case against the men was 'flawed' by evidence falsified and fabricated by police officers. There has also come to light significant fingerprint evidence, tending to exonerate the four, which was not disclosed to the defence by the prosecution. Mr Molloy was questioned for 10 days without access to a solicitor, and a fabricated statement from Vincent Hickey was used to persuade Mr Molloy to confess to the crime. Before he died, Mr Molloy claimed he had been beaten by police officers in the course of his interrogation. The former police officers alleged to have falsified the evidence are now under investigation.

The case was given extensive coverage in the print and broadcast media in February 1997 and made a significant impact upon public consciousness. How far it will negatively affect public confidence in the criminal justice system remains to be judged. This major case raises many points germane to the operation of the criminal justice system. The following are of particular importance:

- The case was originally investigated in 1978, before PACE 1984 had been passed. The requirements under PACE 1984 for suspects to be given access to legal advice (s 58, Code C) and for interviews to be recorded (s 60, Code E) may have reduced or eliminated the opportunity for police malpractice of the sort which occurred in the Bridgewater case.

- Although the criminal justice system ultimately corrected an injustice, this result was achieved primarily through the indefatigable efforts of a few dedicated family members, campaigning journalists and Members of Parliament who would not let the issue disappear from the public forum. The case attracted attention because of the terrible nature of the crime – a child murder. It is quite possible that many other unjust convictions in cases with more mundane facts are never propelled into public discussion or overturned.

- Miscarriages of justice cases involve two types of insult to notions of legal fairness:
  (a) the wrongly imprisoned endure years of incarceration; (b) the real culprits (a child killer in the Bridgewater case) are never identified and could well go on to commit other offences.

- The men were released due to the discovery of evidence which had been fabricated and falsified, yet the CPIA 1996 restricts defence access to prosecution evidence.

- The CCRC has been established to re-evaluate alleged cases of miscarriages of justice. One criticism of it has been that it does not have its own independent investigators, but will rely on police officers to re-examine cases. How far this new body will be able to succeed in its mission statement, and carry public confidence, remains to be seen.

- The jury is only as good as the information and arguments put before it allow it to be. After the prosecution's case had been devastated by the discovery of new scientific evidence in 1993 (a forensic psychiatrist showed that Molloy's 'confession' used language the suspect would not have used), the foreman of the jury from the 1979 trial risked prosecution for contempt of court by issuing a statement to say that he thought that the men were not guilty. He, along with another juror, said they regretted that they had not been given all the evidence that was available at the time of the trial.

3.19 Reform of the Criminal Courts

At the beginning of the century, an impetus for reform came from the desire on the part of the government to subject the criminal courts to a process of review to parallel that undertaken by Lord Justice Woolf in relation to the civil courts in the 1990s. In December 1999, the Lord Chancellor appointed Lord Justice Auld to conduct on his own an independent review of the working of the criminal courts. His terms of reference required him to inquire into and report on:

> ... the practices and procedures of the criminal courts at every level, with a view to ensuring that they deliver justice fairly, by streamlining all their processes, increasing their efficiency and strengthening the effectiveness of their relationships with others across the whole of the criminal justice system, and having regard to the interests of all parties including victims and witnesses, thereby promoting confidence in the rule of law.

Lord Justice Auld's review of the criminal courts was published in September 2001. It contained a number of controversial proposals. Many of these proposals were adopted by the government and were legislated in the Courts Act 2003, which received Royal Assent on 20 November 2003 and whose 112 sections will largely be implemented from 2005. The most important features are addressed below.

The Act is divided into nine Parts. The key parts are as follows:

Part 1: maintaining the court system

- This places the Lord Chancellor under the general duty of maintaining an efficient and effective court system and gives him power to make appropriate arrangements for staff and accommodation. This Part also abolishes Magistrates' Courts Committees (MCCs) and establishes courts' boards.

The Lord Chancellor's duty will now concern all the main courts in England and Wales, namely the Court of Appeal, the High Court, the Crown Court, the county courts and the magistrates' courts. This responsibility will be discharged, in practice, by Her Majesty's Court Service.

Part 2: Justices of the Peace

- This makes provision for Justices of the Peace and other matters relating to magistrates' courts. It replaces commission areas and petty session areas with local justice areas and provides for fines officers. This Part also makes provision about the effect of the Act of Settlement 1701 on the appointment of lay magistrates.

Lay magistrates are appointed to a particular commission area on the basis of the place where they reside, and most summary offences must be tried in the commission area where the alleged offence took place. Commission areas are divided into one or more *petty sessions areas*. Petty sessions areas are the areas to which lay magistrates are assigned by the Lord Chancellor. These are the 'benches', the basic unit of local magistrates' court organisation. The 2003 Act abolished commission areas and petty sessions areas and replaced them with local justice areas. Lay magistrates are now appointed for England and Wales. This, coupled with changes in Part 3 of the Act, will have the effect of giving lay magistrates a national jurisdiction. The Lord Chancellor is however, placed under a statutory duty to assign lay magistrates to a local justice area.

The Act creates the role of a 'fines officer' to take enforcement action in certain circumstances, thus removing the need for all enforcement decisions to be taken by a court. A fines collection system (Sched 5) has been set up which introduces financial incentives to offenders to pay their fines, as well as providing a range of new disincentives for fine default, including wider powers to make attachments of earnings orders (AOE) and deductions from benefits (DFB). The system is designed to encourage payment, but will include new penalties for those who have the means and will not pay. The Act also introduces new sanctions for failing to provide information necessary to make AOE orders and DFB applications. For those who are unable to pay a fine, the Act introduces (in Sched 6) a system for discharging fines by unpaid work.

Section 21 of the Act requires the Lord Chancellor to take all reasonable and practicable steps to ensure that lay justices are kept informed on matters that affect them in the performance of their duties in a local justice area, and that their views will be taken on such matters.

Section 22 makes similar provision to s 10A(1), (3) and (4) of the Justices of the Peace Act (JPA) 1997 (as amended by the Administration of Justice Act (AJA) 1999). These provide for the appointment by the Lord Chancellor of District Judges (Magistrates' Courts), qualification requirements, payment of allowances, and removal from office. This section also replaces provisions in s 69 of the JPA 1997, which provides for the swearing-in of District Judges (Magistrates' Courts) – consequential amendments will require them to be sworn in by a circuit judge or High Court Judge.

Section 23 of the 2003 Act replaces s 10A(2) of the JPA 1997 (as amended by the AJA 1999), which deals with the appointment of a Senior District Judge and a Deputy

Senior District Judge. The section allows the Lord Chancellor to appoint one of the District Judges (Magistrates' Courts) to be the Senior District Judge and, if the Lord Chancellor decides to do this, he may appoint another District Judge (Magistrates' Courts) to be his deputy. The main function of the Senior District Judge is judicial administration. This section says that the Lord Chancellor will have a discretion, rather than a duty, to appoint a Senior District Judge (Chief Magistrate) and Deputy. This is because the government has accepted the Auld Review's recommendation that the role of the Senior District Judge should be reviewed, both as to its functions and its necessity. However, it is envisaged that in the short term at least the Senior District Judge will continue to play an important role in the management of the District Judges (Magistrates' Courts).

Part 3: magistrates' courts

- This deals with jurisdiction and procedure in criminal, civil and family proceedings in magistrates' courts.

Section 50 of the Act deals with Youth Courts. This section sets out the framework whereby lay magistrates and District Judges (Magistrates' Court) are to be authorised to hear youth cases. The Act also enables the higher judiciary including circuit judges and recorders to hear these cases, without particular authorisation, in consequence of the extension of their jurisdiction to include that of a District Judge (Magistrates' Courts) by s 66.

Part 4: judges

- This allows for alterations to the names of judicial titles and offices. This Part also allows District Judges (Magistrates' Courts) to sit as Crown Court judges and gives judges of the higher courts all the powers of justices of the peace, to give increased flexibility in judicial deployment.

Flexibility in deployment of judicial resources Section 65: District Judges (Magistrates' Courts) as Crown Court judges

Unification of the administration of the criminal courts should provide scope for rationalising the work of the magistrates' and Crown Courts, enabling both to do some of the work currently reserved to each. For example, District Judges could deal with and make orders in relation both to allocation and to other interim issues in cases reserved to the Crown Court. This will be further eased by the revised allocation of cases provided by the Criminal Justice Act 2003. Revised allocation of cases ensures that cases are dealt with by the court at the appropriate level with regard to the complexity, value and proportionality of the case.

Section 66: judges having powers of District Judges (Magistrates' Courts)

Under this section, a Crown Court judge will be able to make orders and to sentence in relation to cases normally reserved to magistrates' courts when disposing of related cases in the Crown Court. As part of implementing the policy of greater flexibility in judicial deployment, this section provides that High Court Judges, circuit judges and recorders should be able to sit as magistrates when exercising their criminal and family jurisdiction. The same is to apply to deputy High Court Judges and deputy circuit judges. It is not expected that extensive use will be made of the provision, but it would be possible for a circuit judge in the Crown Court to deal with a summary offence without the case having to go back to a magistrates' court. Historically, certain summary offences could be included in an indictment. If the person was convicted on the indictment, the Crown Court could sentence him if he pleaded guilty to the summary offence, but if he pleaded not guilty, the powers of the Crown Court ceased. It is intended in such cases that the judge of the Crown Court should be able to deal with the summary offences then and there as a magistrate. He would follow magistrates' courts' procedure.

Section 67: removal of restrictions on circuit judges sitting on certain appeals

This section provides for the repeal of s 56A of the Supreme Court Act (SCA) 1981 (as inserted by s 52(8) of the Criminal Justice and Public Order Act 1994). Repeal enables the selected circuit judges who sit in the Criminal Division of the Court of Appeal to hear or determine any appeal against either a conviction before a judge of the High Court or a sentence passed by a judge of the High Court.

Part 5: procedure rules and practice directions The Criminal Courts

The government recognised in the White Paper, *Justice for All*, that the benefits the Auld Review identified from a fully unified criminal court could be realised through closer alignment of the criminal courts. This could be achieved without a complete re-ordering of the courts system or the introduction of an 'intermediate tier'.

The White Paper announced that the government would legislate to bring the magistrates' courts and the Crown Court closer together and that these courts, when exercising their criminal jurisdiction, would be known as 'the criminal courts'. This part of the Act addresses this change.

Practice directions

The Heads of Division (the Lord Chief Justice, Master of the Rolls, President of the Family Division and Vice Chancellor) have power under the High Court's inherent jurisdiction to make directions as to practice and procedure. Section 74A of the County Courts Act (CCA) 1984 gives the Lord Chancellor overall control over practice directions to be followed in county courts. He, and any person authorised by him, may make directions as to the practice and procedure of county courts, but there is no statutory provision about practice directions for magistrates' courts. This Act will allow the Lord Chief Justice, with the concurrence of the Lord Chancellor, to make directions as to the practice and procedure of the criminal courts. It will also provide statutory authority for the President of the Family Division, with the concurrence of the Lord Chancellor, to be able to issue practice directions in his or her own name which are binding on the magistrates' courts and county courts when hearing family proceedings.

Criminal Procedure Rule Committee

The creation of the Criminal Procedure Rule Committee (Crim PRC) will establish one forum for the development of rules, to determine the practices and procedures to be used in all criminal courts in England and Wales. The Committee will be responsible for introducing consistency in procedures. Having consulted beforehand, the Committee will meet to discuss proposals and consider drafted rules.

There were previously two Committees with different purposes and differing powers: the Magistrates' Courts' Rule Committee (under s 144 of the MCA 1980) and the Crown Court Rule Committee (under ss 84 and 86 of the SCA 1981). They each dealt with rules concerning criminal and civil business. Neither Committee had over-arching responsibility for ensuring consistency across the courts. They rarely met. The Crim PRC has responsibilities that were exercised by the Magistrates' Courts' Rule Committee and the Crown Court Rule Committee, insofar as they relate to rules of criminal practice and procedure.

Part 6: miscellaneous

- This amends the procedures for appeals to the House of Lords and the Court of Appeal.

Provisions relating to criminal procedure and appeals

Appeals to Court of Appeal: procedural directions

Section 87 inserts new sections into the Criminal Appeal Act (CAA) 1968 to extend the powers of: (a) a single judge in the Court of Appeal (Criminal Division); and (b) the Registrar of the Court of Appeal (Criminal Division) prior to determination by the full court of an appeal or application for leave to appeal. The new s 31B enables either a single judge or the Registrar to give procedural directions that need not trouble the full court, thus reducing delay. Section 31C provides, in the case of a decision of a single judge, for the appellant or, under specified circumstances, the prosecution to apply to the full court to review such a direction. Section 31C also provides for the decision by the Registrar to be reviewed by a single judge in the first instance or, if the defence or prosecution so wish, further reviewed by the full court.

In the Court of Appeal (Criminal Division), single judges consider applications for leave to appeal and act as a 'filter' by carrying out certain specified functions of the full Court of Appeal. Section 31 of the CAA 1968 lists the powers of the Court of Appeal which may be exercised by a single judge. However, the inability of the single judge to make a broader range of procedural directions for the conduct and progress of an appeal can lead to delay and unnecessary complication.

The Auld Review recommended that a judge of the Court of Appeal should be empowered, when considering applications for leave to appeal, to give procedural directions for the hearing of the application or of the appeal that need not trouble the full court, subject to a right on the part of the applicant or the prosecution, as the case may be, to renew the application to the full court.

The role of the Registrar of Criminal Appeals, who is also the Registrar of the Courts-Martial Appeal Court, currently combines both judicial and administrative functions. The Registrar has ultimate responsibility for the management and running of the Criminal Appeal Office, which has a staff of 150. The Registrar also provides a key reference point for the judiciary in the criminal justice system. He undertakes the judicial responsibilities listed in s 31A of the CAA 1968. In the future, the judicial and administrative functions of the posts of Registrar of Criminal Appeals and Registrar of the Courts-Martial Appeal Court will be separated so that they become more clearly judicial offices. The Registrar's administrative duties will fall to appropriate Court Service staff. These changes will come into effect upon the appointment of the next office holder.

The aim is to enable the Registrar to give procedural directions for the preparation or hearing of the application or of the appeal, subject to a right on the part of the applicant or the prosecution, as the case may be, to submit the matter to a single judge for review. However, the intention is also to enable the Lord Chief Justice to further define by practice direction the use and operation of the Registrar's power to make procedural directions. This would allow maximum flexibility in responding to the changing needs of the Court of Appeal (Criminal Division).

Prosecution appeals from the Court of Appeal

The Act amends s 2 of the Administration of Justice Act 1960 and s 34 of the CAA 1968 by extending the time in which an application by either the defence or the prosecution for leave to appeal from a decision of the Court of Appeal (Criminal Division) can be made. It also makes clear that time begins to run against either the prosecution or the defendant from the date of the Court of Appeal's reasoned judgment, rather than from the date of its decision. The Act makes provision with the same effect in relation to Northern Ireland by amending para 1 of Sched 1 to the Judicature (Northern Ireland) Act 1978 and s 32 of the Criminal Appeal (Northern Ireland) Act 1980.

The Auld Review recommended that s 34(2) of the CAA 1968 should be amended to empower the House of Lords and Court of Appeal, as the case may be, to extend the time within which a prosecutor may apply for leave to appeal, as it does in the case of a defendant. There is a disparity between a defendant and a prosecutor as to the operation of the time limits within which each may petition the House of Lords for leave to appeal where the Court of Appeal, having certified a point of law of general public importance, has refused leave. Both have 14 days from the decision of the Court of Appeal to apply to it for leave and, if leave is refused by the court, a further 14 days from the date of refusal to petition the House of Lords. Whilst the House or the court have power at any time to extend a defendant's time for application for leave, neither has power to do so if the prosecutor wishes leave but fails to apply within time. The Act will now give both the defence and the prosecution an extra 14 days. However, it was not considered appropriate to accept the recommendation that the prosecution should be able to apply for an extension of time – this would leave a defendant with the indefinite possibility of the original conviction being restored by the House of Lords.

CIVIL AND CRIMINAL COURT STRUCTURES

The Civil Courts

The differences between civil and criminal law

There is no such thing as inherently criminal conduct. A crime is whatever the State has forbidden on pain of legal punishment. The conduct that attracts criminal sanctions changes over time and according to different social systems. The terminology and outcomes of the two systems are different. In criminal cases, the *prosecutor prosecutes the defendant* (or *accused*); in civil cases, the *claimant sues the defendant*.

Her Majesty's Court Service

The courts are now run by the HMCS, a creation of the Courts Act 2003.

Magistrates' Courts

Magistrates' courts have a significant civil jurisdiction, especially under the Children Act 1989 as 'family proceedings courts'.

County Courts

There are 218 county courts in England and Wales. They are presided over by District Judges and circuit judges. County courts hear small claims, that is, those whose value is £5,000 or under, and fast track cases. The civil justice reforms are likely to put a considerable burden of work on the county courts under the new system. The main advantage to litigants using the small claims process is the fact that, if sued, they can defend without fear of incurring huge legal costs, since the costs the winning party can claim are strictly limited.

The High Court

The High Court's judicial composition should be noted, as should the meaning of the 10 year qualification according to s 71 of the Courts and Legal Services Act (CLSA) 1990. The High Court is under considerable pressure of work, hence the CLSA 1990 provisions to ease its workload. The Queen's Bench Division deals with contract and tort, etc; its Divisional Court deals with judicial review and criminal appeals from magistrates' courts and Crown Courts. Chancery deals with cases involving land, mortgages, bankruptcy and probate, etc; its Divisional Court hears taxation appeals. The Family Division hears matrimonial and child related matters and its Divisional Court hears appeals from magistrates' courts and county courts on these issues.

The Court of Appeal (Civil Division)

The Court of Appeal (Civil Division) usually has three judges whose decision is by majority. For many purposes, it is the *de facto* final appeal court (*C v S and Others* (1987)).

Reform of the Appeal Process

Certain appeals which previously reached the Court of Appeal (Civil Division) are now heard at a lower level, and the requirement for leave to appeal has been extended to all cases coming to the Court of Appeal except for adoption cases, child abduction cases and appeals against committal orders or refusal to grant habeas corpus. The Access to Justice Act 1999 reformed the appeal process by establishing the principle that there is the need for permission to appeal at all levels in the system. The Act provides that, in normal circumstances, there will be only one level of appeal to the courts and it gives to the Civil Division of the Court of Appeal flexibility to exercise its jurisdiction in courts of one, two or more judges. Taken together, these reforms are intended to ensure that appeals are heard at the right level and in a way which is proportionate to their weight and complexity.

The Courts Act 2003

The Courts Act 2003 makes some amendments to the jurisdiction of the civil courts. Its provisions will be introduced during 2005. The changes have been designed to create a more unified civil court system. Under the Act, the Lord Chancellor will appoint a Head of Civil Justice: it has been recognised that there is an ongoing need for a Head of Civil Justice to provide consistency and an overview.

The House of Lords

In most of its cases, five Law Lords sit. They hear cases of general public importance concerning points of law, for example, *R v R* (1991), changing a 250 year old rule and allowing prosecutions for marital rape.

The European Court of Justice

The European Court of Justice (ECJ) sits in Luxembourg. Its remit is to ensure that the interpretation and application of the EEC 'Treaty of Rome' is observed consistently by all Member States. Note the importance of Art 234 (formerly 177) and the guidance provided by *Bulmer v Bollinger* (1974).

The European Court of Human Rights

The European Court of Human Rights (ECtHR) sits in Strasbourg and arose from the 1950 European Convention on Human Rights. It has no mechanism for enforcement other than of a political nature.

As a consequence of the Human Rights Act 1998, the decisions of the ECtHR are now precedents for, and binding on, domestic UK courts. In terms of human rights issues, therefore, it is superior to the House of Lords.

The Judicial Committee of the Privy Council

The Judicial Committee of the Privy Council acts as a final appeal court for some Commonwealth countries. Because it comprises senior judges from the English legal system, it gives decisions which are persuasive precedent in English law.

Civil Court Fees

A new scale of court fees for people using the civil courts came into effect in 1997, with a further increase introduced in 2003. The aim of the new fees is to make the civil court self-financing. This change raises matters of importance in legal, social and economic debates. There are those who argue, for example, that the courts should, like the National Health Service, be free to people at the point of use, and financed by general taxation. There are others who argue that some payments should be made at the point of use. The Lord Chancellor has pointed out that, were the courts to become free in this way, the money needed to pay for this would have to come from closing down large parts of the Civil Legal Aid system or closing schools or hospitals.

Criminal Courts

The main courts

The trial courts are the magistrates' courts and Crown Courts. In serious offences, known as *indictable offences*, the defendant is tried by a jury in a Crown Court; for *summary offences*, he is tried by magistrates; and for 'either way' offences, the defendant can be tried by magistrates if they agree, but he may elect for jury trial.

The main issues here concern the distribution of business between the magistrates' court and Crown Courts: what are the advantages of trial in the magistrates' court.

CHAPTER 4

THE JUDICIARY

4.1 The Constitutional Role of the Judiciary

Central to the general idea of the Rule of Law is the specific proposition that it involves the rule of *law* rather than the rule of *people*. Judges hold a position of central importance in relation to the concept of the Rule of Law. They are expected to deliver judgment in a completely impartial manner through a strict application of the law, without allowing their personal preference, or fear or favour of any of the parties to the action, to affect their decision in any way.

This desire for impartiality is reflected in the constitutional position of the judges. In line with Montesquieu's classical exposition of the separation of powers, the judiciary occupy a situation apart from the legislative and executive arms of the State, and operate independently of them. Prior to the English revolutionary struggles of the 17th century between Parliament and the monarch, judges held office at the king's pleasure. Not only did this mean that judges could be dismissed when the monarch so decided, but it highlighted the lack of independence of the law from the State in the form, and person, of the monarch. With the victory of Parliament and the establishment of a State based on popular sovereignty, and limited in its powers, the independence of the judiciary was confirmed in the Act of Settlement 1701. The centrality of the independence of the judges and the legal system from direct control or interference from the State in the newly established constitution was emphasised in the writing of the English philosopher John Locke, who saw it as one of the essential reasons for, and justifications of, the social contract on which the social structure was assumed to be based.

In order to buttress the independence of the judiciary and remove them from the danger of being subjected to political pressure, it has been made particularly difficult to remove senior judges once they have been appointed. Their independence of thought and opinion is also protected by the doctrine of judicial immunity. Both of these principles will be considered in more detail below.

After much controversy and debate, one of the final Acts passed by the last parliament in 2005 was the Constitutional Reform Act. Although it has not as yet been brought into effect, the essential features of the Act, which the government claimed were designed to inspire transparency, openness and greater public confidence in Britain's constitution, are:

- government ministers should be under a statutory duty to uphold the independence of the judiciary and specifically bars them from trying to influence judicial decisions through any special access to judges.

- the reform of the post of Lord Chancellor and the transfer of his judicial functions to President of the Courts of England and Wales who is to be the Lord Chief

Justice, currently Lord Phillips, who replaced Lord Woolf in October 2005. In this new position he will be responsible for the training, guidance and deployment of judges. He will also be responsible for representing the views of the judiciary of England and Wales to Parliament and ministers.

- the establishment of a new, independent Supreme Court, separate from the House of Lords. The newly constituted Supreme Court will have its own independent appointments system, its own staff and budget. It will eventually have its own building, although for the present it is likely that the new court will continue to occupy its present place within the House of Lords, until its new building has been refurbished.

- the 12 judges of the Supreme Court will be known as Justices of the Supreme Court and will no longer be allowed to sit as members of the House of Lords. The current Law Lords will become the first 12 Justices of the Supreme Court, with Lord Bingham as President of the Supreme Court.

- the establishment of a new system of appointing judges, independent of the patronage of politicians. Appointments will be solely on the basis of merit, and solely on the recommendation of the newly constituted Judicial Appointments Commission.

4.1.1 The Constitutional role of the Lord Chancellor

The following consideration of the constitutional position of the Lord Chancellor and the Appellate Committee of the House of Lords, as the highest court in England is correctly referred to, has to be placed within the immediate context of the proposals set out in the Constitutional Reform Act 2005., which is due to come into effect in the near future.

It should be noted that the Lord Chancellor holds an anomalous position in respect of the separation of powers in the contemporary State, in that the holder of that position plays a key role in each of the three elements of the State. The Lord Chancellor is the most senior judge in the English court structure, sitting as he does in the House of Lords. At the same time, however, the Lord Chancellorship is a party political appointment, and the occupant of the office owes his preferment to the Prime Minister of the day. Not only is the incumbent a member of the executive, having a seat in the Cabinet, but he is also responsible for the operation of his own government department. In addition to these roles, it should not be overlooked that the Chancellor is also the Speaker of the House of Lords in its general role as a legislative forum. The peculiar situation of the Lord Chancellor is also reflected in the fact that the incumbent can be dismissed or persuaded to resign by the Prime Minster and may cease to hold office on the election of a new government.

The previous Lord Chancellor, Lord Irvine of Lairg, and his immediate predecessor, Lord Mackay, did not go without criticism from within the legal profession generally and the judiciary in particular. The suggestion was made that these Lord Chancellors had represented the interests of their political masters at the expense of the interests of their legal colleagues. For some time, the legal professions have argued that economic imperatives have driven the machinery of the justice system, rather than the wish to provide the best possible service. Lord Mackay's motives and actions were continuously open to such suspicions. As Lord Steyn, one the Lords of Appeal in Ordinary in the House of Lords, was quoted as saying: 'The Lord Chancellor is always a spokesman for the government in furtherance of its party political agenda' ([1997] PL 84).

The party political role of the Lord Chancellor gave rise to a furore when, in February 2001, Lord Irvine personally wrote to lawyers who were known sympathisers of the Labour Party, asking them to donate at least £200 to the party at a fundraising dinner he was to host. His political critics made much of the fact that, as the person ultimately responsible for appointing the judiciary, his soliciting of party funds from those who might apply for such positions in the future could be represented as improper. As such, the press immediately entitled it the 'cash for wigs' affair, echoing the previous 'cash for questions' scandal in the House of Commons. The Lord Chancellor, however, refused to apologise for his action. In a statement to the House of Lords, delivered in his political persona and therefore two paces apart from the woolsack on which he sits when acting as the Speaker of the House of Lords, he stated that:

> I do not believe I have done anything wrong nor do I believe that I have broken any current rules. If I did I would be the first to apologise.

According to Lord Irvine, it was misconceived to claim that the Lord Chancellor was not a party political post, and that every minister from the Prime Minister down was involved in fundraising. The best that could be said for the Lord Chancellor was that, although he had done nothing unlawful, he had acted in an unwise, politically naïve and injudicious manner, and one which once again brought the anomalous constitutional role of his office to the political foreground and renewed calls for its reformation, if not removal.

In addition to difficulties arising directly from his responsibility for implementing political policies in relation to the legal system, the Lord Chancellor's judicial role has also come into question. As a consequence of the fact that the appointment of the Lord Chancellor is a purely political one, there is no requirement that the incumbent should have held any prior judicial office. Indeed, in the case of Lord Irvine, he had never served in any judicial capacity, making his reputation as a highly successful barrister, at one time having both the present Prime Minister and the Prime Minister's wife in his chambers. Nonetheless, as Lord Chancellor, he was the most senior judge and was entitled to sit, as he thought appropriate (see 4.3.2 below for further observations about the Lord Chancellor's residual powers).

There is, however, a much more fundamental issue relating to the manner in which the Lord Chancellor's multi-functional role may be seen as breaching the doctrine of the separation of powers. There cannot but be doubts as to the suitability, not to say propriety, of a member of the executive functioning as a member of the judiciary. Given the heightened sensitivity in relation to impartiality generated by Lord Hoffmann's participation in the *Pinochet* case (see 4.1.3 below), Lord Irvine himself withdrew from sitting in a case in March 1999 in which he recognised the possibility of a conflict of interest. That case involved an action by the family of a man who had died in police custody. The suggestion was made that the Lord Chancellor's participation in the judicial panel raised doubts as to whether the case would be decided by an independent and impartial tribunal. Given his recent guidelines warning the judiciary about the need to be sensitive to issues of conflict of interest, the Lord Chancellor clearly felt himself required to stand down from hearing the case.

In *McGonnell v UK* (2000), the European Court of Human Rights (ECtHR) confirmed the previous decision of the Commission in relation to the judicial function of the Bailiff of the island of Guernsey. It was held that the that fact that the Bailiff had acted as the judge in a case in which he had also played an administrative role was in breach of Art 6 of the European Convention on Human Rights (ECHR). In the words of the Commission decision:

> It is incompatible with the requisite appearance of independence and impartiality for a judge to have legislative and executive functions as substantial as those carried out by the Bailiff.

Although those words could apply equally to the Lord Chancellor, the actual court decision was limited to the situation of the Bailiff, and Lord Irvine made it clear that its application was limited to the particular facts of the Guernsey situation. Nonetheless, the Lord Chancellor continued not to sit on cases where there might appear to be a conflict between his judicial and other roles. In February 2003, the Lord Chancellor's dual role as judge and member of the executive came under attack in the parliamentary assembly of the Council of Europe, which oversees the operation of the ECHR (see 13.5 below). A Dutch member, Erik Jurgens, a vice president of the assembly, tabled a motion which stated that:

> The assembly ... has repeatedly stressed that judges should be a completely independent branch of government. It is undeniable that combining the function of judge with functions in other branches of government calls that independence seriously into question.

Mr Jurgens was quoted as saying that he was advising eastern European countries seeking entry to the Council of Europe that they would not be admitted unless their judges were totally independent, so it was an anomaly that one of the original members had a figure like the Lord Chancellor, and further that:

> Sooner or later a case is going to come to the European Court of Human Rights at Strasbourg, and I think they will certainly say that this is an unacceptable combination.

In April 2003, Lord Irvine defended the unique position of the Lord Chancellor in an appearance before the parliamentary select committee with oversight of the Lord Chancellor's Department. Questioned on the conflict inherent in his power to make law and still sit as a judge, he responded that he had 'difficulty seeing why this issue is so important', and argued against changing a legal system that had an enviable international reputation, simply for the sake of constitutional purity. As he put it:

> The basic point is that the higher judiciary accept this role – they believe profoundly that it is a superior system to any other.

4.1.1.1 The Constitutional Reform Act

Whilst Lord Irvine preferred to maintain his position rather than bow to constitutional purity, his views were apparently not shared by his colleagues in government and most importantly the Prime Minister, who sacked him in June 2003. As part of a cabinet reshuffle, which appeared to involve a power struggle between the Home Secretary and the Lord Chancellor, which the former won, Lord Irvine was not only removed from office, but it was announced that his office itself was to disappear. A new ministry, the Department for Constitutional Affairs, was to replace the Lord Chancellor's Department and Lord Falconer was appointed Secretary of State for Constitutional Affairs to replace Lord Irvine as Lord Chancellor. It would appear that the announcement was made without anyone having thought through the constitutional implications, or indeed practicalities, of simply abolishing the position of the Lord Chancellor. Initially Lord Falconer said he was not the Lord Chancellor and that he would not be assuming all of the functions of his predecessor. However, the realisation soon dawned that it was simply impossible to eradicate the role of the Lord Chancellor by simple dictat. Lord Falconer had to be Lord Chancellor even if by default, as someone had to perform the constitutional functions attached to the Lord Chancellor's office. So on the first day in his new role Lord Falconer was to be seen in wig and tights sitting on the woolsack in the House of Lords, for the simple reason that someone had to do it. As a consequence, Lord Falconer is, at least for the time being, both Secretary of State for Constitutional Affairs and Lord Chancellor, although in the former role he is charged with the duty of reforming the latter role. It should be noted that from the outset Lord Falconer made it clear that he would not sit as a judge.

The proposal of the original Constituional Reform Bill for the complete abolition of the officr of the Lord Chancellor was extremely controversial. Reference has already been made to the concerns of the judiciary, and those concerns were also shared by politicians and social commentators. Many of the latter argued against what they saw as the ditching of hundreds of year of history and practice for the sake of dressing up a cabinet reshuffle as a matter constitutional importance. Indeed the cross-party Commons Constitutional Affairs Committee expressed its concerns as follows:

> There is a radical difference between on the one hand, a Lord Chancellor, who as a judge is bound by a judicial oath, who has special constitutional importance enjoyed by no other member of the Cabinet and who is usually at the end of his career (and thus without temptations associated with possible advancement) and on the other hand a minister who is a full-time politician, who is not bound by any judicial oath and who may be a middle-ranking or junior member of the Cabinet with hopes of future promotion.

The government, however, insisted on pursuing its reforms justifying them on the basis of transparency and the recognition that it was no longer appropriate for one person to perform the disparate functions of the Lord Chancellor, in clear contradiction of the doctrine of the separation of powers. However, as many correctly pointed out, the constitution of the United Kingdom never actually incorporated a strict separation of powers. Nonetheless that recognition cannot be taken as justifying a situation that, as preceding analysis has shown, was clearly founded on fundamental conflicts of interest and was almost certainly contrary to the European Convention on Human Rights. In this regard the changes introduced by of the Constitutional Reform Act can be seen to be not only pertinent but also timely in their endeavour to address an issue before it became a problem. Nonetheless, as was explained above, the government did submit to the wish to retain the ancient office of Lord Chancellor, although the importance of the role will be significantly reduced under the Act.

4.1.2   The constitution and role of the House of Lords

A number of issues have come together to raise questions about the operation of the House of Lords as the final court of appeal in the English legal system and the role of the Privy Council. Amongst these are the devolution of parliamentary power to the Scottish Parliament and Welsh Assembly, the previous and proposed further reform of the House of Lords, the enactment of the Human Rights Act and the role of the House of Lords itself in the *Pinochet* case (see below). However, of far greater significance is the proposal in the Constitutional Reform Act 2005 to replace the currently constituted Appeal Committee of the House of Lords, with a new Supreme Court.

In other constitutional systems, both civil, as in France, or common law, as in the United States of America, not only is there a clear separation of powers between the judiciary, the executive and the legislature, but there is also a distinct Constitutional Court, which deals with such issues. The English Constitution provides for neither of these. It remains to consider whether, under the already changed circumstances of the contemporary constitution, not to mention the proposals for further reform under the Constitutional Reform Act, the function and powers of the highest court in the land can remain unaltered.

It is a commonplace of politics that the devolution of power from the United Kingdom Parliament in London, particularly to the Scottish Parliament in Edinburgh, will give rise to disputes as to the relationship between the two bodies. Eventually, such issues will have to be resolved in the courts and the Privy Council has been given that role.

Equally, the Human Rights Act has, for the first time, given the courts clear power to declare the United Kingdom Parliament's legislative provision contrary to essential human rights (see 1.5). Even allowing for the fact that the Human Rights Act has been introduced in such a way as to maintain the theory of parliamentary sovereignty, in practice, the courts will inevitably become involved in political/constitutional issues. Once the courts are required to act in constitutional matters, it is surely a mere matter of time before they become Constitutional Courts, as distinct from ordinary courts, with specialist judges with particular expertise in such matters.

The 1997 Labour government was elected on the promise of the fundamental reform of the House of Lords, which it saw as undemocratic and unrepresentative. After establishing a Royal Commission, the government embarked on a two-stage process of reform. The first stage of reform was achieved through the House of Lords Act 1999, which removed the right of the majority of hereditary peers to sit in the House of Lords. The second stage of reform was set out, towards the end of 2001, in a White Paper entitled *Completing the Reform*.

The most controversial aspect of the White Paper was the relatively small proportion of directly elected members it proposed, especially when compared with the large proportion of members who would be nominated rather than elected. The government faced much criticism, even from its own MPs, with regard to this suggestion and set up a joint committee of both Houses of Parliament to consider the course of future reform. Somewhat surprisingly, that committee made no recommendation and merely listed seven possible options for determining the membership of a reformed House of Lords. The options were:

- A fully appointed house.

- A fully elected house.

- 80% appointed, 20% elected.

- 80% elected, 20% appointed.

- 60% appointed, 40% elected.

- 60% elected, 40% appointed.

- 50% appointed, 50% elected.

Even more surprisingly, in February 2003, the House of Commons voted against all of the options and thus failed to approve any of them. The closest vote, for an 80% elected house, fell narrowly by 284 votes against to 281 in favour.

In September 2003, the government issued a further Consultation Paper proposing the removal of the remaining 92 hereditary peers from the House of Lords, without provision for any further reform. Following this, it was expected that a House of Lords Reform Bill would be published in February 2004, but in the face of potential disquiet in the House of Commons as to the lack of democratic input into the upper chamber, and a revolt in the House of Lords, the government delayed its issue.

It is worth noting that the case set out in the above two sections, for the reform of the Lord Chancellor's position and against the location of the most senior judges in the House of Lords, was presented in essence to the commission examining the reform of the House of Lords, by JUSTICE, the civil rights organisation. Both aspects of the challenges were strongly rejected by the then Lord Chancellor Irvine in a speech to the Third Worldwide Common Law Judiciary Conference in Edinburgh, delivered in July 1999. Nonetheless, spring 2002 saw a spate of speeches and interviews highlighting disagreement, if not actual tension, between the Lord Chancellor and some of the most senior members of the judiciary. In March of that year, Lord Steyn, the second longest serving current Law Lord, expressed the view that Lord Irvine's insistence on sitting as a judge in the House of Lords was a major obstacle to the creation of a Supreme Court to replace the House of Lords. In April, the Lord Chancellor's response was reported in the *Financial Times* newspaper. The article stated that that, 'Lord Irvine may have an impressive intellect, but his lack of diplomacy means he will seldom be short of enemies'. The point of that comment was supported by the Lord Chancellor's reaction to Lord Steyn's previous comments, dismissing them in a tone of effete arrogance, as 'rather wearisome … he's not a political scientist, he knows nothing about the internal workings of government – or very little'. As reported, he reduced Lord Steyn's argument to a demand for 'a grand new architectural venture', stating that the argument that 'the Lord Chancellor, because of his desire to continue sitting, is preventing the judges from having a new building – that's just nonsense'.

Lord Irvine's views should, however, be contrasted with those of the current senior Law Lord, Lord Bingham, expressed in the Spring Lecture given at the Constitution Unit at University College London in May 2002. In a paper entitled *A New Supreme Court for the UK*, Lord Bingham directly addressed all of the issues raised above, except for the role of the Lord Chancellor, before stating his preference for:

> … a supreme court severed from the legislature, established as a court in its own right, re-named and appropriately re-housed, properly equipped and resourced and affording facilities for litigants, judges and staff such as, in most countries of the world, are taken for granted.

As to the views and future role of the Lord Chancellor, the reduction of his direct judicial powers is implicit in the speech. As Lord Bingham concluded: '… inertia … is not an option.'

4.1.2.1   The Constitutional Reform Act

Once again Lord Irvine's political antennae appear to have lacked acuity, in that, not only was he replaced as Lord Chancellor, but his sucessor proposed the estabishment of a Supreme Court much along the lines of that suggested by Lord Bingham. Part 3 of the The Constituional Reform Act 2005 proposes the establishment of

- a new, independent Supreme Court, separate from the House of Lords with its own independent appointments system, its own staff and budget and, its own building.

- The 12 judges of the Supreme Court will be known as Justices of the Supreme Court and will no longer be allowed to sit as members of the House of Lords.

- The current Law Lords will become the first 12 Justices of the Supreme Court, with Lord Bingham as President of the Supreme Court.

This proposal can be considered in two parts, firstly to proposal to create a Supreme Court, distinct from the House of Lords and secondly the removal of the right of the members of that new Supreme Court to sit as members of the Upper House. Neither of these proposals found favour with a majority of the current members of the Law Lords, indeed in their collective response to the consultation paper on constitutional reform, six of the 12 expressed their opposition to the creation of a Supreme Court and 8 supported the retention of at least some judicial representation in the House of Lords. The minority supported the complete separation of judicial and legislative activity, as did Lord Falconer, who explained the need for reform thus:

> The present position is no longer sustainable. It is surely not right that those responsible for interpreting the law should be able to have a hand in drafting it. The time has come for the UK's highest court to move out from under the shadow of the legislature.

The relevance of Lord Falconer's argument was given added power by the decision of the Scottish Court of Sessions, the equivalent of the Court of Appeal, in *Davidson v Scottish Ministers (no 2) (2002)*. The case involved a challenge to previous court decision, on the grounds of Article 6 of the ECHR, for the reason that one of the judges in the earlier case, the former Lord Advocate Lord Hardie, had spoken on the issue before the court whilst a member of the Scottish Assembly. The Court of Sessions held that Lord Hardie should at least have declared his previous interest in the matter and that in the light of his failure to do so, it held that there was at least the real possibility of bias and ordered the case to be retried.

It has to be emphasised that the new Supreme Court will not be in the nature of most other supreme courts in that will not be a constitutional court as such and it will not have the powers to strike down legislation. Consequently, although the proposed alterations clearly increase the appearance of the separation of powers, the doctrine of parliamentary sovereignty remains unchallenged. It was presumably the a lack of such power that led Lord Woolf, the former Lord Chief Justice, to comment that the new court would effectively replace a first class appeal court House Lords with a second class Supreme Court.

4.1.3 Judicial impartiality

4.1.3.1 Re Bow Street Metropolitan Stipendiary Magistrate ex p Pinochet Ugarte (1999)

No consideration of the operation of the judiciary generally, and the House of Lords in particular, can be complete without a detailed consideration of what can only be called the *Pinochet* case (the various cases are actually cited as *R v Bartle* and *R v Evans* (House of Lords' first hearing); *Re Pinochet* (House of Lords' appeal against Lord Hoffmann); *R v Bartle* and *R v Evans* (final House of Lords' decision)).

In September 1973, the democratically elected government of Chile was overthrown in a violent army coup led by the then General Augusto Pinochet Ugarte; the President, Salvador Allende, and many others were killed in the fighting. Subsequently, in the words of Lord Browne-Wilkinson, in the final House of Lords' hearing:

> There is no doubt that, during the period of the Senator Pinochet regime, appalling acts of barbarism were committed in Chile and elsewhere in the world: torture, murder and the unexplained disappearance of individuals on a large scale.

Although it was not suggested that Pinochet had committed these acts personally, it was claimed that he was fully aware of them and conspired to have them undertaken.

In 1998, General Pinochet, by now Senator for life and recipient of a Chilean amnesty for his actions (extracted as the price for his returning his country to democracy), came to England for medical treatment. Although he was initially welcomed, he was subsequently arrested on an extradition warrant issued in Spain for the crimes of torture, murder and conspiracy to murder allegedly orchestrated by him in Chile during the 1970s. Spain issued the international warrants, but Pinochet was actually arrested on warrants issued by the metropolitan stipendiary magistrate under s 8(1)(b) of the Extradition Act 1989. The legal question for the English courts was whether General Pinochet, as Head of State at the time when the crimes were committed, enjoyed diplomatic immunity. In November 1998, the House of Lords rejected Pinochet's claim by a 3:2 majority, Lord Hoffmann voting with the majority but declining to submit a reasoned judgment.

Prior to the hearing in the House of Lords, Amnesty International, which campaigns against such things as State mass murder, torture and political imprisonment, and in favour of general civil and political liberties, had been granted leave to intervene in the proceedings, and had made representations through its counsel, Geoffrey Bindman QC. After the *Pinochet* decision, it was revealed, although it was hardly a secret, that Lord Hoffmann was an unpaid director of the Amnesty International Charitable Trust, and that his wife also worked for Amnesty. On that basis, Pinochet's lawyers initiated a very peculiar action: they petitioned the House of Lords about a House of Lords' decision; for the first time, the highest court in the land was to be subject to review, but review of itself, only itself differently constituted. So, in January 1999, another panel of Law Lords set aside the decision of the earlier hearing on the basis that Lord Hoffmann's involvement had invalidated the previous hearing. The decision as to whether Pinochet had immunity or not would have to be heard by a new, and differently constituted, committee of Law Lords.

It has to be stated in favour of this decision that the English legal system is famously rigorous in controlling conflicts of interest which might be seen to affect what should be a neutral decision making process. The rule, which applies across the board to trustees, company directors and other fiduciaries as well as to judges, is so strict that the mere possibility of a conflict of interest is sufficient to invalidate any decision so made, even if in reality the individual concerned was completely unaffected by their own interest in coming to the decision. In the words of the famous *dictum* of Lord Hewart, it is of fundamental importance that 'justice must not only be done but should manifestly and undoubtedly be seen to be done' (*R v Sussex Justices ex p McCarthy* (1924)). With regard to the judicial process, it has been a long established rule that no one may be a judge in his or her own cause, that is, they cannot judge a case in which they have an interest. This is sometimes known by the phrase *nemo judex in causa sua*. Thus, for example, judges who are shareholders in a company appearing before the court as a litigant must decline to hear the case (*Dimes v Grand Junction Canal* (1852)). It is therefore astonishing that Lord Hoffmann did not withdraw from the case, or at least declare his interest in Amnesty when it was joined to the proceedings. The only possible justification is that Lord Hoffmann assumed that all of those involved in the case, including the Pinochet team of lawyers, were aware of the connection. Alternatively, he might have thought that his support for a charitable body aimed at promoting civil and political liberties was so worthy in itself as to be unimpeachable: could not, and indeed should not, every English judge subscribe, for example, to cl 3(c) of the Amnesty International Charitable Trust memorandum, which provides that one of its objects is 'to procure the abolition of torture, extra-judicial execution and disappearance'?

In either case, Lord Hoffmann was wrong.

Once it was shown that Lord Hoffmann had a relevant interest in its subject matter, he was disqualified without any investigation into whether there was a likelihood or suspicion of bias. The mere fact of his interest was sufficient to disqualify him unless he had made sufficient disclosure. Hitherto, only pecuniary or proprietary interests had led to automatic disqualification. But, as Lord Browne-Wilkinson stated, Amnesty, and hence Lord Hoffmann, plainly had a non-pecuniary interest sufficient to give rise to an automatic disqualification for those involved with it.

The House of Lords therefore decided that Lord Hoffmann had been wrong, but it remained for the House of Lords to extricate itself, with whatever dignity it could manage, from the situation it had, through Lord Hoffmann, got itself into. This it endeavoured to do by reconstituting the original hearing with a specially extended committee of seven members. Political and legal speculation was rife before the decision of that court. It was suggested that the new committee could hardly go against the decision of the previous one without bringing the whole procedure into disrepute, yet the earlier court had actually contained the most liberal, and civil liberties minded, of the Lords. It was assumed that the new hearing would endorse the earlier decision, if with reluctance, but what was not expected was the way in which it would actually do so.

In reaching the decision that General Pinochet could be extradited, the House of Lords relied on, and established, Pinochet's potential responsibility for the alleged crimes from the date on which the UK incorporated the United Nations Convention on Torture into its domestic law through the Criminal Justice Act 1988 – 29 September 1988. Consequently, he could not be held responsible for any crimes committed before then, but was potentially liable for any offences after that date. Thus, although the later House of Lords' committee provided the same decision as the first one, it did so on significantly different, and much more limited, grounds from those on which Lords Steyn and Nicholls, with the support of Lord Hoffmann, relied. Such a conclusion is neither satisfactory in law nor political practice, and did nothing to deflect the unflattering glare of unwanted publicity that had been visited on the House of Lords.

It is important not to overstate what was decided in *Re Pinochet*. The facts of that case were exceptional and it is unlikely that it will lead to a mass withdrawal of judges from cases; however, there might well be other cases in which the judge would be well advised to disclose a possible interest. Finally, with regard to *Re Pinochet*, whatever one's views about the merits, sagacity or neutrality of the current judiciary, there is considerable evidence to support the proposition that, historically, judges have often been biased towards certain causes and social classes. For example, JAG Griffith's book, *The Politics of the Judiciary* (1997), is brimming with concrete examples of judges who have shown distinctly conservative and illiberal opinions in cases involving workers, trade unions, civil liberties, Northern Ireland, police powers, religion and other matters.

Lord Hoffmann was wrong, but it is nonetheless ironic that the first senior judge to have action taken against him for possible political bias was someone whose agenda was nothing more than being against torture and unjudicial killings.

4.1.3.2 *Locabail (UK) Ltd v Bayfield Properties Ltd (1999)*

Following a number of other cases in which lawyers sought to challenge a judgment on the grounds that through a social interest or remote financial connection the judge was potentially biased, the Court of Appeal delivered authoritative guidance on the matter in *Locabail (UK) Ltd v Bayfield Properties Ltd and Another* (1999).

The Court of Appeal ruled that all legal arbiters were bound to apply the law as they understood it to the facts of individual cases as they found them without fear or favour, affection or ill will: that is, without partiality or prejudice. Any judge, that term embracing every judicial decision maker, whether judge, lay justice or juror, who allowed any judicial decision to be influenced by partiality or prejudice deprived the litigant of his important right and violated one of the most fundamental principles underlying the administration of justice. The law was settled in England and Wales by the House of Lords in *R v Gough* (1993), and in consequence, the relevant test was whether there was in relation to any given judge a real danger or possibility of bias. When applying the real danger test, it would often be appropriate to inquire whether the judge knew of the matter relied on as appearing to undermine his impartiality. If it were shown that he did not, the danger of its having influenced his judgment was eliminated and the appearance of possible bias dispelled. It was for the reviewing court, not the judge concerned, to assess the risk that some illegitimate extraneous consideration might have influenced his decision.

There was one situation where, on proof of the requisite facts, the existence of bias was effectively presumed and in such cases, it gave rise to automatic disqualification, namely, where the judge was shown to have an interest in the outcome of the case which he was to decide or had decided: see *Dimes v Proprietors of the Grand Junction Canal* (1852), *R v Rand* (1866) and *R v Camborne Justices ex p Pearce* (1955). However, it would be dangerous and futile to attempt to define or list factors which might, or alternatively might not, give rise to a real danger of bias, since everything would depend on the particular facts. Nonetheless, the court could not conceive of circumstances in which an objection could be soundly based on the religion, ethnic or national origin, gender, age, class, means or sexual orientation of the judge. Nor, at any rate ordinarily, could an objection be soundly based on his social, educational, service or employment background or history; nor that of any member of his family; nor previous political associations, membership of social, sporting or charitable bodies; nor Masonic associations; nor previous judicial decisions; nor extra-curricular utterances, whether in textbooks, lectures, speeches, articles, interviews, reports or responses to consultation papers; nor previous receipt of instructions to act for or against any party, solicitor or advocate engaged in a case before him; nor membership of the same Inn, circuit, local Law Society or chambers.

By contrast, a real danger of bias might well be thought to arise if there existed personal friendship or animosity between the judge and any member of the public involved in the case; or if the judge were closely acquainted with any such member of the public, particularly if that individual's credibility could be significant in the decision of the case; or if in a case where the credibility of any individual were an issue to be decided by the judge, he had in a previous case rejected that person's evidence in such outspoken terms as to throw doubt on his ability to approach such a person's evidence with an open mind on any later occasion.

It might well be thought that the Court of Appeal was bound to come to this conclusion. Had it ruled that membership of certain societies, or a particular social background, or the previous political associations of a trial judge were grounds for appeal, two consequences would follow. First, there would be a rapid expansion of the use by law firms of special units that monitor and keep files on all aspects of judges' lives. Secondly, there would be a proliferation of appeals in all departments of the court structure at the very time when there is such a concerted effort to reduce the backlog of appeals. The decision in *Locabail* leaves the question of profound jurisprudential importance: how far can judges judge in an entirely neutral and socially detached manner?

4.1.3.3   R v Gough (1993)

Locabail was decided before the HRA 1998 came into force, but the Court of Appeal soon had the opportunity to assess the rules in *R v Gough* against the requirements of the European Court's approach to bias in relation to Art 6 of the ECHR. *Director General of Fair Trading v Proprietary Association of Great Britain* (2001) related to a case before the Restrictive Practices Court. Six weeks into the trial, one of the lay members of the panel hearing the case, an economist, disclosed that, since the start of the case, she had applied for a job with one of the main witnesses employed by one of the parties to the case. On learning this, the respondents argued that such behaviour must imply bias on her part and that consequently, the whole panel should stand down, or at least the member in question should stand down. The Restrictive Practices Court rejected the argument. On appeal, the Court of Appeal took the opportunity to refine the common law test as established in *R v Gough*. Previously, the court determining the issue had itself decided whether there had been a real danger of bias in the inferior tribunal. Now, in line with the jurisprudence of the ECtHR, the test was whether a fair-minded observer would conclude that there was a real possibility of bias. In other words, the test moved from being a subjective test on the part of the court to an objective test from the perspective of the fair-minded observer. In the case in question, the Court of Appeal held that there was sufficient evidence for a fair-minded observer to conclude bias on the part of one member of the panel and that consequently, at the stage the trial had reached, her discussions would have contaminated the other two members, who should also have been stood down.

4.2   Judicial Offices

Although not required to know the names of present incumbents, students should at least be aware of the various titles of judges and equally know which courts they operate in:

- *Lord Chancellor*. The peculiar and threatened nature of this office has already been commented on, but it should be pointed out that, as well as being the senior judge in the House of Lords, the Lord Chancellor is formally the most senior judge in the Court of Appeal, and holds the position of President of the Chancery Division. The present Lord Chancellor is Lord Falconer of Thoroton and he is referred to in reports as Lord Falconer LC. He is of course also Secretary of State for Constitutional Affairs.

- *Lord Chief Justice*. The holder of this position is second only to the Lord Chancellor in eminence. The Lord Chief Justice is the President of the Criminal Division of the Court of Appeal and is formally the senior judge in the Queen's Bench Division of the High Court. The present incumbent is Lord Phillips CJ.

- *Master of the Rolls*. The holder of this office is President of the Civil Division of the Court of Appeal. At present, this position is held by Lord Clarke MR.

- *President of the Family Division of the High Court of Justice*. This person is the senior judge in the Family Division and is responsible for organising the operation of the court. The current president is Sir Mark Potter.

- *Vice Chancellor*. Although the Lord Chancellor is nominally the head of the Chancery Division of the High Court, the actual function of organising the Chancery Division falls to the Vice Chancellor. The current incumbent is Sir Robert Morritt VC.

- *Senior Presiding Judge for England and Wales*. The Courts and Legal Services Act (CLSA) 1990 recognised the existing system and required that each of the six separate Crown Court circuits should operate under the administration of two Presiding Judges appointed from the High Court. In addition, a Senior Presiding Judge is appointed from the Lords Justices of Appeal (see below).

Under the proposals of the *Constitutional Reform* Act the following new offices will be created and replace current ones as follows:

- *President of the Courts of England and Wales*

  The new, additional, statutory title of President of the Courts of England and Wales will be assumed by the Lord Chief Justice. He is president of and entitled to sit in the following courts: the Court of Appeal, the High Court, the Crown Court, the county courts, the magistrates' courts. As President of the Courts of England and Wales, the Lord Chief Justice is to be responsible for representing the views of the judiciary of England and Wales to Parliament, the Minister (that is, the Secretary of State for Constitutional Affairs) and Ministers of the Crown generally. He is also to be responsible, within the resources made available by the Minister, for maintaining appropriate arrangements for the welfare, training and guidance of the judiciary of England and Wales, and for maintaining appropriate arrangements for the deployment of the judiciary of England and Wales and allocating work within courts.

- *President of the Supreme Court and Deputy President of the Supreme Court*

  These roles will be filled by the senior member of the new court and his deputy. They will sit on the appointment commission for ant new members of the Supreme Court.

- *Head and Deputy Head of Criminal Justice*

  Section 8 of the Act establishes a new statutory post of Head of Criminal Justice, which will be held *ex officio* by the Lord Chief Justice or, after consultation with the Lord Chancellor, by his nominee. It also provides that the Lord Chief Justice may appoint a Deputy Head of Criminal Justice.

- *Head and Deputy Head of Civil Justice*

  These statutory posts already exist having been established by section 62 of the *Courts Act* 2003.

- *Head and Deputy Head of Family Justice*

  Section 9 creates a new statutory post of Head of Family Justice, which will be held *ex officio* by the President of the Family Division. It also provides that the Lord Chief Justice may appoint a Deputy Head of Family Justice.

4.2.1 Judicial hierarchy

The foregoing are specific judicial offices. In addition, the various judges who function at the various levels within the judicial hierarchy are referred to in the following terms:

- *Lords of Appeal in Ordinary*. These are the people who are normally referred to as the Law Lords for the simple reason that, at least for the moment, they sit in the House of Lords and are ennobled when they are appointed to their positions. There can be between 7 and 12 Law Lords, although the maximum number is subject to alteration by Order in Council. The House of Lords is the highest domestic court in the UK. The qualifications for the position of Lord of Appeal in Ordinary will be considered later. They are referred to by their specific titles. Following the implementation of the Constitutional Reform Act, with the establishment of the new Supreme Court, the Law Lords will be known as *Justices of the Supreme Court*.

- *Lords Justices of Appeal*. This category, of which there are 37 individuals, constitutes the majority of the judges in the Court of Appeal, although the other specific office holders considered previously may also sit in that court, as may High Court Judges specifically requested so to do. They all used to be known as Lord Justice, even if they were female. The first female member of the Court of Appeal, Elizabeth Butler-Sloss, had to be referred to by the male title because the Supreme Court Act 1981 had not considered the possibility of a woman holding such high judicial office. The rules were changed subsequently to allow female judges in the Court of Appeal to be referred to as Lady Justices, and whereas their male counterparts receive knighthoods on their elevation, the women become Dames.

- *High Court Judges.* These are sometimes referred to as *'puisne'* (pronounced 'pewnee') judges, in reference to their junior status in relation to those of superior status in the Supreme Court. There are currently 107 such judges appointed. Judges are appointed to particular divisions depending on the amount of work needing to be conducted by that division, although they may be required to hear cases in different divisions and may be transferred from one division to another by the Lord Chancellor. Others, such as former High Court and Court of Appeal judges, or former circuit judges or recorders, may be requested to sit as judges in the High Court. High Court Judges are referred to by their name followed by the initial 'J'.

- The Lord Chancellor may also appoint *deputy judges* of the High Court on a purely temporary basis, in order to speed up the hearing of cases and to reduce any backlog that may have built up. The Heilbron Report on the operation of the civil justice system was critical of the use of deputy judges and recommended that more permanent High Court Judges should be appointed if necessary. The maximum numbers were subsequently increased to their present level, but the use of deputy judges has continued to provide grounds for criticism of the operation of the legal system, and has led to suggestions that the use of 'second rate' judges might eventually debase the whole judicial currency.

- *Circuit judges.* Although there is only one Crown Court, it is divided into six distinct circuits which are serviced, in the main, by circuit judges who also sit as county court judges to hear civil cases. There are currently 606 circuit judges, each being addressed as 'Your Honour'.

- *Recorders* are part time judges appointed to assist circuit judges in their functions in relation to criminal and civil law cases.

- *District Judges.* This category of judge, previously referred to as registrars, is appointed on a full time and part time basis to hear civil cases in the county court.

- The situation of *magistrates* will be considered separately and the situation of *chairmen of tribunals* will be considered in Chapter 12.

The powers of the Lord Chancellor referred to above in the management and allocation of the judiciary will be transferred to the Lord Chief Justice in the guise of *President of the Courts of England and Wales* under the Constitutional Reform Act.

4.2.2 Legal offices

In addition to these judicial positions, there are three legal offices which should be noted:

- The *Attorney General*, like the Lord Chancellor, is a political appointee whose role is to act as the legal adviser to the government. For example, in March 2003, the current Attorney General, Lord Goldsmith, advised the government that there was a legal basis for its use of military force against Iraq. The Attorney General alone has the authority to prosecute in certain circumstances and appears for the Crown in important cases. As may be recalled from 1.3.2 above, the Attorney General also has powers to appeal against points of law in relation to acquittals under the Criminal Justice Act (CJA) 1972 and can also appeal against unduly lenient sentences under the CJA 1988. The crucially important decision of the House of Lords that DNA evidence, acquired in regard to another investigation and which should have been destroyed under s 64 of the Police and Criminal Evidence Act (PACE) 1984, could nonetheless be used, was taken as the result of a reference by the Attorney General (*Attorney General's Reference (No 3 of 1999)*).

- The *Solicitor General* is the Attorney General's deputy.

- The *Director of Public Prosecutions* (DPP) is the head of the national independent Crown Prosecution Service (CPS) established under the Prosecution of Offences Act 1985 to oversee the prosecution of criminal offences. The decision of the DPP whether to prosecute or not in any particular case is subject to judicial review in the courts. In *R v DPP ex p C* (1994), it was stated that such powers should be used sparingly and only on grounds of unlawful policy, failure to act in accordance with policy and perversity. Nonetheless, successful actions have been taken against the DPP in relation to decisions not to prosecute in *R v DPP ex p Jones* (2000) and in *R v DPP ex p Manning* (2000).

4.3   Appointment of Judiciary

In the first of his Hamlyn Lectures of 1993, the then Lord Chancellor, Lord Mackay, stated that the pre-eminent qualities required by a judge are:

> ... good sound judgment based upon knowledge of the law, a willingness to study all sides of an argument with an acceptable degree of openness, and an ability to reach a firm conclusion and to articulate clearly the reasons for the conclusion.

Although the principal qualification for judicial office was experience of advocacy, Lord Mackay recognised that some people who have not practised advocacy may well have these necessary qualities to a great degree. This was reflected in the appointment of an academic and member of the Law Commission, Professor Brenda Hoggett, to the High Court in December 1993. Professor Hoggett, who sat as Mrs Justice Hale, was the first High Court Judge not to have had a career as a practising barrister, although she qualified as a barrister in 1969 and was made a QC in 1989. As Dame Brenda Hale, she sat in the Court of Appeal; now as Lady Hale of Richmond, she is the first member of the Law Lords.

The CLSA 1990 introduced major changes into the qualifications required for filling the positions of judges. Judicial appointment is still essentially dependent upon the rights of audience in the higher courts, but at the same time as the CLSA 1990 effectively demolished the monopoly of the Bar to rights of audience in such courts, it opened up the possibility of achieving judicial office to legal practitioners other than barristers.

Lawrence Collins became the first solicitor to be appointed directly to the High Court.

4.3.1 Qualifications

The main qualifications for appointment are as follows (the CLSA 1990 is dealt with in detail at 11.1 below):

- *Lord of Appeal in Ordinary*

    (a) the holding of high judicial office for two years; or

    (b) possession of a 15 year Supreme Court qualification under the CLSA 1990.

The Constitutional Reform Bill retains the same qualifications for members of the new Justices of the Supreme Court. There is, however, a new statutory appointments procedure under the proposed legislation, which is considered below at 4.3.2.

- *Lord Justice of Appeal*

    (a) the holding of a post as a High Court Judge; or

    (b) possession of a 10 year High Court qualification under the CLSA 1990.

- *High Court Judges*

    (a) the holding of a post as a circuit judge for two years;

    (b) possession of a 10 year High Court qualification under the CLSA 1990.

- *Deputy judges* must be qualified in the same way as permanent High Court Judges.

- *Circuit judges*

    (a) the holding of a post as a recorder;

    (b) possession of either a 10 year Crown Court qualification or a 10 year county court qualification under the CLSA 1990;

    (c) the holding of certain offices, such as District Judge, Social Security Commissioner, chairman of an industrial tribunal, stipendiary magistrate for three years.

- *Recorders* must possess a 10 year Crown Court or county court qualification under the CLSA 1990.

- *District Judges* require a seven year general qualification under the CLSA 1990.

4.3.2 Selection of judges

Once again, it is necessary to consider the situation as it operates at the time of writing before going on to consider the provisions of the Constitutional Reform Act 2005. However, what follows will to a large degree explain the need for the reforms proposed in the latter Act.

The foregoing has concentrated on the specific requirements for those wishing to fulfil the role of judge, but it remains to consider the more general question relating to the general process whereby people are deemed suitable and selected for such office. All judicial appointments remain, theoretically, at the hands of the Crown. The Crown, however, is guided, if not actually dictated to, in regard to its appointment by the government of the day. Thus, as has been seen, the Lord Chancellor is a direct political appointment. The Prime Minister also advises the Crown on the appointment of other senior judicial office holders and the Law Lords and Appeal Court judges. Such apparent scope for patronage in the hands of the Prime Minister has not gone without criticism.

Judges at the level of the High Court and Circuit Bench are appointed by the Crown on the advice of the Lord Chancellor, and the Lord Chancellor personally appoints District Judges, lay magistrates and the members of some tribunals. This system has not gone without challenge either, the question being raised as to how the Lord Chancellor actually reaches his decision to recommend or appoint individuals to judicial offices.

4.3.2.1   *Circuit judges and below*

All appointments up to and including circuit judges are made on the basis of open competition and the Department for Constitutional Affairs (DCA) publishes a guidance booklet entitled *Judicial Appointments*, also available on the DCA's website (www.dca.gov.uk). The guidance information sets out the criteria against which candidates are assessed as follows:

- legal knowledge;
- intellectual and analytical ability;
- sound judgment;
- decisiveness;
- communication and listening skills;
- authority and case management skills;
- integrity and independence;
- fairness and impartiality;
- understanding of people and society;
- maturity and sound temperament;
- courtesy;
- commitment, conscientiousness and diligence.

The first stage in the open competition selection procedure is an advertisement for a particular judicial vacancy which appears in the national press and/or legal journals. The candidates are required to provide the names of three members of the judiciary or the legal profession as referees.

Written assessments of candidates are then sought from those people whose names are given by the candidates themselves and 'a wide range of other judges and lawyers who are approached for assessments on the Lord Chancellor's behalf'.

The DCA, and indeed the previous Lord Chancellor himself, was adamant that there is no secrecy about those who are consulted, as lists detailing this latter group are given in the application packs and every person on this list will be invited to comment on each applicant.

All assessments are made against the criteria set out above and it is felt, not without some justification, that judges and members of the legal profession are in a good position to assess the merits of candidates, as they are familiar with the role of the judge and with the skills and qualities required to do the job well. All assessments are provided in confidence, which the DCA points out, with equal justification, is a common practice where references are sought by prospective employers.

Shortlisting of candidates is carried out by a panel of three, a judge, a lay person and one of the Lord Chancellor's senior officials, which conducts formal interviews, although the Lord Chancellor personally considers the situation of those interviewed before reaching a final decision.

The DCA provides feedback and advice to unsuccessful candidates, including, on a non-attributed basis, information about matters contained in the assessments received.

Relying on the recommendations and opinions of the existing judiciary as to the suitability of the potential candidates may appear sensible at first sight. However, it brings with it the allegation, if not the fact, that the system is over-secretive and leads to a highly conservative appointment policy. Judges are suspected, perhaps not unnaturally, of favouring those candidates who have not been troublesome in their previous cases and who have shown themselves to share the views and approaches of the existing office holders. In his 1993 Hamlyn Lecture, Lord Mackay stated that the arrangements in the UK for the collection of data about candidates for the judiciary are comparatively well developed, and provide those who have to take the decisions, essentially the Lord Chancellor himself, with fuller information than would otherwise be available to them. The reasoning behind this claim would appear to be that, because the procedure is secret and limited, people commenting on the suitability of candidates are willing to be more frank and open than would otherwise be the case were the references open to wider inspection. Such spurious justification is worrying in its complacency and its refusal to recognise that the secretive nature of the process might permit referees to make unsubstantiated derogatory comments that they would otherwise not feel free to make.

4.3.2.2   High Court Bench

In the past, appointment to the High Court Bench was by way of invitation from the Lord Chancellor. However, in 1998, the LCD issued an advertisement inviting applicants to apply for such positions. However, the Lord Chancellor retained his right to invite individuals to become High Court Judges, and since 1998, of the 46 High Court Judges who have been appointed, only 21 came through the application procedure, the other 25 being invited to accept appointment. As regards the system of invitation, the question immediately raised is as to exactly how the Lord Chancellor selects the recipients of his favour; there being no system as such, there can be no transparency and without transparency there must be doubts as to the fairness of the process. Even where a candidate applies for the post of High Court Judge, the procedure is different from applications at a lower level, for the reason that the candidate is not interviewed after the usual consultation process with the senior judiciary and the candidate's own referees. The Lord Chancellor simply decides whom to appoint on the basis of that consultation process. Thus are the doubts about the secretive nature of the consultancy procedure compounded as regards applicants for the High Court Bench.

Lord Irvine's repeated insistence on the objectivity of the judicial appointments process did little to remove the suspicion that, because it still relies on the sounding of the senior members of the judiciary and professions, it remains in the final analysis restrictive, conservative and unfair, especially to minority groups.

The current procedure of appointment to the High Court was subject to some sharp criticism in a review conducted for the Bar Council under the chairmanship of the former Appeal Court Judge, Sir Iain Glidewell. The main review concluded that the current system of appointment was not sufficiently transparent. More contentiously, however, it suggested that, given the increased role of the judiciary in matters relating to the review of administrative decisions, devolution issues and human rights, it was no longer constitutionally acceptable for judges to be appointed by the government of the day, a member of which is the Lord Chancellor. Consequently, the review recommended that:

- the Lord Chancellor should cease to be responsible for the selection and appointment of High Court Judges;

- the responsibility for such appointments should be transferred to a newly created independent body, a High Court Appointments Board; and

- the appointments to the High Court should only be made from amongst people who have made application for the position.

As a least favoured option, the review recommended that, if the Lord Chancellor continued to be responsible for appointments to the High Court, he should reach his decisions only after receiving the report and advice of a panel which should have the task of shortlisting and interviewing candidates, as is done for other judicial offices.

It is perhaps of relevance that since May 2002, the system of judicial appointments in Scotland has come under the control of a 10 member Judicial Appointments Board, consisting of five lawyers and five lay members, with the chair being one of the lay members. All judicial posts are advertised, suitable candidates are interviewed, and a short-list of appropriate candidates is drawn up and submitted to the Scottish First Minister, who, after consultation with the Lord President, makes a recommendation to the Queen. If Scotland recognised the need for transparency and to remove perceptions of political patronage, could England and the Lord Chancellor continue to hold out for much longer?

One of Lord Irvine's earliest actions as Lord Chancellor had been to declare the government's intention to inquire into the merits of establishing a Judicial Appointments Commission. However, rather than carry out that intention, he announced in 1999 that Sir Leonard Peach, the former Commissioner for Public Appointments, would be conducting an independent scrutiny of the way in which the current appointment processes for judges operated. In December of that year, Sir Leonard reported that he had been:

> ... impressed by the quality of work, the professionalism and the depth of experience of the civil servants involved [LCD Press Release, 3 December 1999].

Sir Leonard did recommend that a Commission for Judicial Appointments be established, with a Commissioner and Deputy Commissioners, whose role would be to monitor the procedures and act as an Ombudsman for disappointed applicants. It was recommended that the Commission should not have any role in the actual appointments, but should merely maintain an independent oversight of the procedure.

Not surprisingly, Lord Irvine was most happy to accept such findings and Sir Leonard's proposals, and the system of appointing the judiciary remained essentially unchanged. The appointment of Sir Colin Campbell, Vice Chancellor of Nottingham University, as the first Commissioner was announced in March 2001.

Somewhat surprisingly, Lord Irvine announced in April 2003, before the select committee with oversight of his department, that he intended to issue three separate consultation documents relating to:

- whether judges and lawyers should continue to wear wigs and gowns in court;

- whether the status of Queen's Counsel should be retained and the related appointment process; and

- the role of the Judicial Appointments Commission.

4.3.2.3   *The Constitutional Reform Act 2005 and the appointment of judges*

Once again Lord Irvine's actions were forestalled by his dismissal from office and his replacement in June 2003 by Lord Falconer who immediately issued a consultation paper on the establishment of a fully blown Judicial Appointments Commission, which subsequently formed the basis of the proposals in regard judicial appointments contained in the Constitutional Reform Act.

- **Appointment to the Supreme Court**

  Although appointment to office is by the Crown, the Act sets out the procedure for appointing a member of the Supreme Court.

  The Lord Chancellor must convene an *ad hoc* selection commission if there is, or is likely to be a vacancy. Subsequently, the Lord Chancellor will notify the Prime Minister of the identity of the person selected by that commission and under s 26 (4), the Prime Minister *must* recommend the appointment of that person to the Queen.

Schedule 8 contains the rules governing the composition and operation of the selection commission, which will consist of the President of the Supreme Court, who will chair the commission, the Deputy President of the Supreme Court and one member from each of the territorial judicial appointment commissions (see below), one of whom must be a person who is not legally qualified. The next most senior ordinary judge in the Supreme Court will take the unfilled position on the selection commission if either the President or Deputy President is unable to sit.

Section 27 sets out the process which must be followed in the selection of a justice of the Supreme Court. The commission decides the particular selection process to be applied, the criteria or competences against which candidates will be assessed, but in any event the requirement is that any selection must be made solely on merit. However, sub-s 27(8) does require that the commission must take into account the need for the Court to have among its judges, generally at least 2 Scottish judges and usually 1 from Northern Ireland. The Lord Chancellor, as provided for by sub-s 27(9), may issue non-binding guidance to the commission about the vacancy that has arisen, for example on the jurisdictional requirements of the Court, which the commission must have regard to.

Under sub-s 27(2) and (3) the commission is required to consult:

(i) senior judges who are neither on the commission nor willing to be considered for selection;

(ii) the Lord Chancellor;

(iii) the First Minister in Scotland;

(iv) the Assembly First Secretary in Wales; and

(v) the Secretary of State for Northern Ireland.

Subsection 28(1) provides that after a selection has been made the commission must submit a report nominating one candidate to the Lord Chancellor, who then must also consult the senior judges (or other judges) who were consulted by the commission, the First Minister in Scotland, the Assembly First Secretary in Wales and the Secretary of State for Northern Ireland.

Section 29 sets out the Lord Chancellor's options after he has received a name from the commission and carried out the further consultation under s 28. The procedure may be divided into three possible stages.

• Stage 1, where a person has been selected and recommended by the appointments commission. At this stage the Lord Chancellor may:

(i) accept the nomination and notify the Prime Minister;

(ii) reject the selection;

(iii) require the commission to reconsider its selection.

- Stage 2, where a person has been selected following a rejection or reconsideration at stage 1. In this event the Lord Chancellor can:

  (i) accept the nomination and notify the Prime Minister;

  (ii) reject the selection but only if it was made following a reconsideration at stage 1;

  (iii) require the commission to reconsider the selection, but only if it was made following a rejection at stage 1.

- Stage 3, where a person has been selected following a rejection or reconsideration at stage 2. At this point, the Lord Chancellor *must* accept the nomination unless he prefers to accept a candidate who had previously been reconsidered but not subsequently recommended for a second time.

In effect this means that the Lord Chancellor's options are as follows. He can:

  (i) accept the recommendation of the commission;

  (ii) ask the commission to reconsider; or

  (iii) reject the recommendation.

Where the Lord Chancellor requires the commission to *reconsider* its original selection, the commission can still put forward the same name with additional justifications for its selection. In such circumstance the Lord Chancellor will either accept the recommendation or reject it. Alternatively the commission can recommend another candidate, whom the Lord Chancellor can accept, reject or require reconsideration of.

However, if the Lord Chancellor *rejects* the original name provided by the selection commission, it must submit an alternative candidate giving reasons for their choice. At this point the Lord Chancellor can either:

  (i) accept the second candidate; or

  (ii) ask the selection commission to reconsider.

On reconsideration the commission can either resubmit the second candidate or propose an alternative candidate. At this point the Lord Chancellor must make a choice. He can either accept the alternative candidate or he can then choose the reconsidered candidate.

Under sub-s 30(1), the Lord Chancellor's right of rejection is only exercisable where in his opinion the person selected is not suitable for the office concerned. The right to require reconsideration is exercisable under three conditions:

  (i) where he feels there is not enough evidence that the person is suitable for office;

  (ii) where he feels there is not enough evidence that person is the best candidate on merit; or

  (iii) where there is not enough evidence that the judges of the Court will between them have enough knowledge of, and experience in the laws of each parts of the United Kingdom, following the new appointment.

Should the Lord Chancellor exercise either of these options he must provide the commission with his reasons in writing (s 30(3)).

- **Appointment to other juridical offices**

Part 4 of the Act creates a new independent Judicial Appointments Commission, which will assume responsibility for the process of selecting all judges for appointment in England and Wales. The Judicial Appointments Commission will make recommendations to the Lord Chancellor and no one may be appointed who has not been selected by the Commission. The Lord Chancellor may reject a candidate, once, and to ask the Commission to reconsider, once. However, if the Commission maintains its original recommendation, the Lord Chancellor must appoint or recommend for appointment whichever candidate is selected.

The appointments of Lords Justices and above will continue to be made by the Queen formally, on the advice of the Prime Minister, after the Commission has made a recommendation to the Lord Chancellor. The Act makes special provision for the appointment of the Lord Chief Justice, Heads of Division and of Lords Justices of Appeal. In these cases the Commission will establish a selection panel of four members, consisting of two senior judges, normally including the Lord Chief Justice, and two lay members of the Commission.

Members of the Judicial Appointments Commission will themselves be appointed by The Queen, on the recommendation of the Lord Chancellor.

Schedule 12 of the Act sets out the membership of the Judicial Appointments Commission, together with its powers and responsibilities. Of the total of 15 Commissioners,

- six must be lay members;
- five must be members of the judiciary (three judges of the Court of Appeal or High Court, including at least one Lord Justice of Appeal and at least one High Court Judge one Circuit Judge and one District Judge);
- two must be members of the legal profession;
- one must be a tribunal member; and
- one must be a lay magistrate.

Significantly, the Chair of the Commission will be one of the lay members.

The Act requires that all candidates must be of good character and that selection shall be made strictly on merit. In addition it gives the Lord Chancellor power to issue guidance to the Commission in regard to what considerations to take into account in assessing merit, which the Commission must have regard to. However the Act does not prescribe detailed appointments procedures and makes it clear that any such procedures are a matter for the Commission to decide.

It can be seen that although the Lord Chancellor retains the ultimate power to decide whom to appoint, or to recommend to the Queen for appointment, and thus maintains Parliamentary accountability, his discretion has been tightly circumscribed by the provisions of the Act.

The Act also provides for the establishment of a Judicial Appointments and Conduct Ombudsman to whom unsuccessful or disgruntled applicants for judicial office can apply for a consideration of their case. As the full title suggest the Ombudsman also will have a role to play in relation to matters of a disciplinary nature and section 110 allows complaints to be made to the Judicial Appointments and Conduct Ombudsman about judicial disciplinary cases.

4.3.2.4 *Gender and racial constitution of the judiciary*

Advertisements were used for the first time in 1994 to recruit likely candidates from the professions for the positions of assistant recorder, Deputy District Judge and circuit judge and, as has been seen above, advertising was extended to appointments to the High Court Bench in 1998.

The first of such advertisements stated:

The Lord Chancellor will recommend for appointment the candidates who appear to him to be best qualified regardless of ethnic origin, gender, marital status, sexual orientation, political affiliation, religion or (subject to the physical requirements of the office) disability.

By 2000, the Lord Chancellor had slightly changed the emphasis. Whilst retaining his emphasis on appointment purely on merit, he stated that:

I am particularly keen that eligible women and ethnic minority lawyers and judges should give this opportunity serious thought.

Advertising was seen as a practical step to address the matter of gender and race imbalance amongst the present judicial body. Currently, there is one woman in the House of Lords and only two in the Court of Appeal. In the High Court, the number is 10 out of 107 and, of 626 circuit judges, 67 are women. At the level of recorders, there are 197 women from a total of 1,414; and at District Judge level, the number is 85 from 433 (September 2005).

The DCA has collated statistics on ethnic origin of the judiciary, but it warns that the information they provide may be inaccurate as it is only supplied on a voluntary basis. However, using the statistics provided, it is apparent that if one restricts analysis to the black and Asian ethnic communities, for which groups statistics are available, then there are no members of those groups above the level of circuit judge and at that level, the ethnic minority representation is 1%. At the level of recorder, the percentage is 3%, at District Judge level, it is 3%, and at Deputy District Judge level, it is 2%. In the magistrates' courts, black and Asian people make up 3% of the complement of full time District Judges, as the old stipendiary magistrates are now called. The highest rate of ethnic representation is to be found at the level of Deputy District Judges in the magistrates' courts, where it stands at almost 6%.

Lord Irvine consistently encouraged women and people from ethnic backgrounds or other minorities to apply for judicial positions, as encapsulated in his sound bite, 'Don't be shy! Apply!'. As he admitted:

> Yes, it is true that many judges today are white, Oxbridge educated men. But, it is also true that they were appointed on merit, from the then available pool, at the time the vacancies arose … It does not mean that the social composition of the judiciary is immutably fixed. For too long barristers were drawn from a narrow social background. As this changes over time, I would expect the composition of the Bench to change too. That is inherent in the merit principle [Speech to the Association of Women Barristers, February 1998].

A 1997 Labour Research survey, although admittedly carried out when Lord Irvine had only been in his new job for two months, found that, in fact:

> … even greater proportions of the judiciary attended Oxbridge universities than a decade earlier … [Labour Research, July 1997].

In April 2003, the Labour MP Keith Vaz, a member of the select committee on the LCD, claimed that 78% of senior judges in England and Wales achieved the full house of being white, male, public school and Oxbridge educated. Such a situation, he claimed, represented 'a complete failure for a Labour government'.

Still, Lord Irvine remained optimistic, not to say bullish, about the way things were changing. As he pointed out:

> … things are already on the move. In December 1994, 7.6% of the main tiers of the judiciary … were women. It is now a little over 9%. Not a meteoric rise, true, but a steady one.

Accepting Lord Irvine's statistics, one certainly would have to agree that the change is not meteoric; in fact, at the rate he quotes it would take 90 years for women to hold 50% of judicial offices. According to the latest annual report on judicial appointments the current Lord Chancellor, Lord Falconer, continues to recognise he need to increase diversity amongst the judiciary. As he stated:

> One of my priorities is to increase the diversity of the judiciary by encouraging good quality candidates from ethnic minorities, women and candidates with disabilities to apply to the Bench. We need to find out why eligible people from these groups are not applying for judicial appointments in the numbers we might expect and we need to do something about removing the barriers.

4.3.2.5 *Alternative approaches to appointing judges*

A different approach, following the example of the USA, might be for the holders of the higher judicial offices to be subjected to confirmation hearings by, for example, a select committee of the House of Commons. Lord Mackay dismissed any such possibility as follows:

> The tendency of prior examination ... is to discover and analyse the previous opinions of the individual in detail. *I question whether the standing of the judiciary in our country, or the public's confidence in it, would be enhanced by such an inquiry*, or whether any wider public interest would be served by it [emphasis added].

It is perhaps unfortunate that the italicised words in the above passage can be interpreted in a way that no doubt Lord Mackay did not intend but which, nonetheless, could suggest a cover up of the dubious opinions of those appointed to judicial office.

An even more radical alternative would be to open judicial office holding to election as they also do in the USA, although in this case, one might well agree with Lord Mackay that:

> The British people would not feel that this was a very satisfactory method of appointing the professional judiciary.

Alternatively, and following Lord Mackay's emphasis on the professional nature of the judiciary, the UK could follow continental examples and provide the judiciary with a distinct professional career structure as an alternative to legal practice.

As has been seen, the proposals under the Constitutional Reform Bill have been subjected to many criticisms from the judges to the Commons Committee on Constitutional Affairs, with many social commentators and journalists joining in the attack. It is true that the reforms were an unlooked-for consequence of an ill-thought-out Cabinet reshuffle, and equally true that the proposed alterations do offer a possibility of political interference with the independence and operation of the judiciary, especially with the future possibility of a weak Secretary of State for Constitutional Affairs and an overly strong Home Secretary. Nonetheless, it is surely not appropriate, indeed it is inconsistent, for those concerned to resort to an uncritical pragmatic defence of the status quo on the basis that it has worked so far. The system may have worked, but did it do so in an open and transparent manner, and in whose interests did it operate? The opportunity for more radical reforms may not have been taken, but the measures that have been proposed surely represent an improvement in the structure and operation of the judicial system.

4.4   Training of the Judiciary

All judicial training, from the induction of new magistrates to the honing of the skills of the judges in the House of Lords, is overseen by the Judicial Studies Board (JSB). Prior to the establishment of the JSB, the training of judges in the UK was almost minimal, especially when considered in the light of the continental practice where being a judge, rather than practising as an advocate, is a specific and early career choice which leads to specialist and extensive training.

The Magisterial Committee of the JSB organises the training of newly elected chairmen of Magistrates' Benches and induction and continuation training for Deputy

District Judges (Magistrates' Courts) and District Judges (Magistrates' Courts). It is also responsible for advising on, developing and monitoring the training of lay magistrates, which is delivered locally by Magistrates' Courts Committees. With the creation of the Unified Court Administration under the Courts Act 2003, the JSB will increase its responsibility for the training of the magistracy.

The JSB provides training and instruction to all part time and full time judges in judicial skills. An essential element of the philosophy of the JSB is that the training is provided by judges for judges. The training requirements of the different jurisdictions are the responsibility of five committees (Criminal, Civil, Tribunals, Family and Magisterial). Another Committee, the Equal Treatment Advisory Committee, provides advice and support for all five committees. The JSB membership is drawn mainly from the judiciary, but also includes some leading academics and other professionals. The Board enjoys considerable autonomy from its parent department, the DCA, in deciding the need for and nature of judicial training.

Assistant recorders are required to attend seminars on procedure and sentencing before they can sit on their own in the Crown Court. Later, training takes the form of further, intermittent seminars focusing primarily on sentencing. Those sitting in the Crown Court benefit specifically from the advice contained in the *Crown Court Bench Book of Specimen Directions*. In the preface to the latest edition, produced in 1999, although it is regularly updated, Mr Justice Kay, the Chair of the JSB Criminal Committee, explained its function thus:

> This is the sixth edition of the Specimen Directions, which has become one of the most useful tools available to judges, experienced and inexperienced, in preparing a summing up. They are increasingly referred to by the Court of Appeal, Criminal Division as a starting point for a correct direction on matters of law and it is important that they are understood in that context and not simply repeated without being adapted to the facts and circumstances of a particular case. The Judicial Studies Board does not seek to lay down legal principles or to resolve difficult questions of law. It attempts to do no more than reflect the law and interpretation of the law as laid down by the courts and to that end every decision of the Court of Appeal, Criminal Division referring to these directions is studied to see if change is necessary.

The specific nature of the Specimen Directions is a delicate matter, as they do not, and indeed cannot, represent an unconditional statement of what the law and judicial practice is. They always have to be adapted by the judges to fit particular circumstances. Such a fact has to be recognised, and indeed it is enforced by an injunction not to reproduce the Directions as a part of any commercial activity. A civil law Bench Book has also been produced, and there are other Bench Books for reference in family law proceedings, Youth Court proceedings, and for the guidance of District Judges (Magistrates' Courts). There is also an *Equal Treatment Bench Book* for use by all members of the judiciary.

Judicial training has probably never been of greater public concern or been executed with such rigour since the JSB was established in 1979. For example, the judiciary were subject to thorough re-training in the new civil procedure (see Chapter 7). This training included residential seminars for all full time and part time judges dealing with civil work, local training, and conferences held at various national locations. Similarly, following the incorporation of the ECHR into English law by the HRA, the government set aside £4.5 million for human rights judicial training during 1999–2000. The JSB recently has concentrated its attention on the provision of Information Technology training for the judiciary, but it is gearing up to provide training in relation to the significant changes introduced by the Courts Act 2003, the Criminal Justice Act 2003 and the Sexual Offences Act 2003, as these important and complex pieces of legislation are gradually brought into effect.

4.4.1 Equal treatment training

Law is supposed to operate on the basis of formal equality: everyone is assumed to be equal before the law and to be treated equally, regardless of their personal attributes or situation (see 1.5 below). In the past, however, accusations have been levelled at the judiciary that allege that, at the very least, they themselves are insensitive to the sensitivities of others, particularly in matters of race, gender, sexual orientation and in relation to people with disabilities. Not only have they been accused of lacking understanding and sympathy towards others with different values or practices from their own, but it has also been claimed that many of them have been resistant to changing their attitudes.

As regards attitudes towards race, such a situation was highlighted in an article by Lincoln Crawford, a barrister, part time judge, Bar Council member and former member of the Commission for Racial Equality in *Counsel*, the journal of the Bar (February 1994).

In his article, he listed a number of reasons why judges were opposed to the race training. First, there was the belief that judges apply the law fairly and do not need to be trained in race awareness for the simple reason that they are not racist in their outlook or practice. Such an assertion sits uncomfortably, however, with the documented research that reveals that black defendants found guilty of offences are treated more harshly than equivalent white defendants. Secondly, this initial approach was supported by an attitude that considered it to be an affront to the independence of their judgments to require judges to try to take account of the different cultural backgrounds of those black and Asian people who came before them. (One white judge actually remarked that he had been called 'nigger' at his school and that it had not caused him any harm.) Thirdly, Crawford claimed that there was a bloody-mindedness amongst the judiciary, representing the view that they operated the UK legal system and that anyone within the jurisdiction should take the law as they found it, even if it was partial and discriminatory in its lack of sympathy for other cultural values. The fourth justification for resistance to race awareness training was the view that it smacked of interference with the impartiality and independence of the judiciary, the implication being that judges should not be held to account even when they were operating in a questionable, if not a patently discriminatory, manner.

All of the foregoing supposed justifications are completely spurious and represent a denial of the cultural existence of a large section of British society. As Crawford put it:

> A judiciary which fears and feels nervous about plurality and diversity runs the danger of becoming closed, narrow and brittle.

It also runs the danger of completely alienating large sections of the population over which it exercises its power and, when law is reduced to the level of mere power rather than legitimate authority, its effectiveness is correspondingly reduced. In the light of the recognition that something had to be done to forestall such potential damage, the JSB instituted seminars for training part time and circuit judges in racial awareness, for example, reminding them that, in a multi-cultural/multi-faith society, it is offensive to ask for people's 'Christian' names, as well as warning them as to the dangers of even more crassly offensive language and racial stereotyping that appears to be so much a part of the English use of metaphor.

In 1999, for the first time, JSB training included new guidance for all judges on equal treatment issues such as disability, gender and sexual orientation, and litigants-in-person. In announcing that equal treatment training was to be integral to all induction courses, Lord Justice Waller (the then chairman of the JSB) stated:

> There is absolutely no room for complacency in these areas. And I am not going to say – just because someone has been on our course, they will be perfect, but I hope that, as result, judges are better equipped to do their jobs [(1999) *The Times*, 13 July].

A key component in the JSB's strategy of overcoming the appearance of insensitivity and related perception of prejudice was the production of the *Equal Treatment Bench Book*, which it has to be said provides a truly comprehensive first class guide for the judiciary in ensuring awareness of the need to treat all those who come before them equally and with sensitivity and civility.

4.4.1.1 *Ethnic minorities in the criminal court*

An opportunity to assess the success of the JSB's policy in assuring equality of treatment was provided in March 2003 by the publication of a research report entitled *Ethnic Minorities in the Criminal Court: Perceptions of Fairness and Equality of Treatment*.

The research project investigated the extent to which ethnic minority defendants and witnesses in Crown Courts and magistrates' courts perceived their treatment to have been unfair and whether those who did perceive unfairness attributed it to racial bias. The experience of the ethnic minority group was compared with that of white defendants. The study also took into account the views of court staff, judges, magistrates and lawyers. Altogether, 1,252 people were interviewed in Manchester, Birmingham and London, and the proceedings in more than 500 cases were observed.

As regards defendants:
- The proportion who said their treatment had been unfair in court was about one-third in the Crown Court and about a quarter in the magistrates' courts.

- There was little difference between ethnic minority and white defendants (33% of black, 27% of Asian and 29% of white defendants).

- One in five black defendants in the Crown Court and one in 10 in the magistrates' courts, and one in eight Asian defendants in both types of court, thought that their unfair treatment in court related to their ethnicity.

- Very few perceived racial bias in the conduct or attitude of judges or magistrates (only 3% in the Crown Court and 1% in the magistrates' courts).

- There were no complaints about racist remarks from the bench.

- Most complaints about racial bias concerned sentences perceived to be more severe than those imposed on a similar white defendant.

- 31% of ethnic minority defendants in the Crown Court and 48% in the magistrates' courts said they would like more people from ethnic minorities sitting in judgment and amongst the staff of the courts.

As regards witnesses:

- None complained of racial bias in the Crown Court.

- 7% perceived racial bias in the magistrates' courts.

As regards the judges and magistrates:

- All the judges and two-thirds of the magistrates had received training in ethnic awareness.

- Only two judges and three magistrates said that it had 'added nothing' or been 'unhelpful'.

As regards court officials and lawyers:

- 98% of white clerks and ushers thought there was equal treatment of ethnic minorities by the courts; compared with:

  (a) 71% of Asian staff; and

  (b) 28% of black staff.

- 69% of white lawyers thought there was equal treatment of ethnic minorities by the courts; compared with:

  (a) 63% of Asian lawyers; and

  (b) 43% of black lawyers.

- 30% of black lawyers said they had personally witnessed incidents in court that they regarded as 'racist'; as opposed to:

  (a) 13% of white lawyers; and

  (b) 11% of Asian lawyers.

The conclusion of the research project was that there had been:

> ... a substantial change for the better in perceptions of ethnic minorities of racial impartiality in the criminal courts. Several judges mentioned that attitudes had altered markedly in recent years and magistrates reported a substantial decline in the frequency of racially inappropriate remarks. Many lawyers also reported that racial bias or inappropriate language was becoming 'a thing of the past'. These positive findings, taken together with the much lower than expected proportion of defendants complaining of racial bias, may be a reflection of both general social improvements in the treatment of ethnic minorities and the specific efforts begun by the Lord Chancellor's Department in the early 1990s to heighten the awareness of all involved in the system of the need to guard against racial bias.

Nonetheless, the report warned against complacency and emphasised that the fact that one in five black and one in eight Asian defendants definitely perceived racial bias in the Crown Court, and at least one in 10 in the magistrates' courts, combined with the fact that black lawyers and staff were more likely to perceive racial bias than others, was sufficient cause to continue the efforts towards eliminating the vestiges of perceived unequal treatment.

Perceptions of racial bias, more frequently held by black defendants in the Crown Court, may well arise from a belief that the disproportionately large number of black people caught up by the criminal justice and prison systems must, at least to some extent, be a reflection of racism. Every effort therefore should be made when passing sentence to demonstrate and convince defendants that no element of racial stereotyping or bias has entered into the decision.

Among black defendants and lawyers in particular, there was a belief that the authority and legitimacy of the courts, and confidence in them, would be strengthened if more personnel from ethnic minorities were seen to be playing a part in the administration of criminal justice. Indeed, in the Crown Court, many judges agreed that more could be done to avoid the impression of the courts as 'white dominated institutions'.

However, there is an undercurrent in the report which supports a more critical reading. Whilst it was concerned with '*perceptions* of racial bias', such perceptions may not wholly comprehend the underlying reality. Eliminating inappropriate language may well be a good thing in itself, but if it merely provides camouflage for a system that remains fundamentally biased in terms of its outcomes, then doubts have to be raised about its fundamental worth. The difference in perception of the black lawyers and court staff as to the true nature of the system would seem to provide grounds to support such a possibility. Given that differential sentencing remains the major ground of complaint relating to allegations of ethnic bias, that surely remains the most pressing issue in relation to equality. As the report states:

> The findings of this study may go some way to dispelling the view that most minority ethnic defendants believe that their treatment by the courts has been racially biased. But *if it could be shown that the 'cultural change' which this study has identified has had a real impact on eliminating differential sentencing of white and ethnic minority defendants*, this would further encourage the confidence of ethnic minorities in the criminal courts [emphasis added].

4.5   Retirement of Judges

All judges are now required to retire at 70, although they may continue in office at the discretion of the Lord Chancellor. The Judicial Pensions and Retirement Act 1993 reduced the retirement age from the previous 75 years for High Court Judges and 72 years for other judges.

The reduction of the retirement age may have been designed to reduce the average age of the judiciary, but of perhaps even more significance in this respect is the change that was introduced in judicial pensions at the same time. The new provision requires judges to have served for 20 years, rather than the previous 15, before they qualify for full pension rights. This effectively means that if judges are to benefit from full pension rights, they will have to take up their appointments by the time they are 50. Given that judges are predominantly appointed from the ranks of high earning QCs, this will either reduce their potential earnings at the Bar or reduce their pay package as judges by approximately 7.5%. This measure led to a great deal of resentment within both the Bar and the judiciary, Lord Chief Justice Taylor referring to its unfairness and meanness, and was one of the issues that fuelled the antagonism between Lord Mackay and the other members of the judiciary.

In any event, according to the statistics provided by the DCA, the average age for the Law Lords is 67, with Lord Nicholls being the oldest at 71, and Lady Hale the youngest at 59. In the Court of Appeal, the average age is 63, with the youngest being Sir Roger Thomas at 56 and the oldest Sir Paul Kennedy at 69.

4.6   Removal of Judges

Reference has already been made to the need, with of course the exception of the Lord Chancellorship, to protect the independence of the judiciary by making it difficult for a discomfited government to remove judges from their positions on merely political grounds. The actual provision is that judges of the House of Lords, the Court of Appeal and the High Court hold their office during good behaviour, subject to the proviso that they can be removed by the Crown on the presentation of an address by both Houses of Parliament. In actual fact, this procedure has never been used in relation to an English judge, although it was once used in 1830 to remove an Irish judge who was found guilty of misappropriating funds.

Judges below the level of the High Court do not share the same degree of security of tenure as their more senior colleagues, and can be removed, on grounds of misbehaviour or incapacity, by the action of the Lord Chancellor, who does not require the sanction of Parliament. However, even the infamous Judge Richard Gee was never actually dismissed. He was appointed as a circuit judge in February 1991 and in November 1995 was arrested and charged with conspiracy to commit offences under the Theft Act 1978 in relation to his previous solicitor's practice. He pleaded not guilty and at his trial in March 1998, the jury failed to reach a verdict. Before a retrial could be held, the Attorney General entered a *nolle prosequi* on the grounds that Gee was not fit to face another trial. This effectively meant that no further action could be taken against him. Gee had been, and remained, suspended on full pay since his original arrest in 1995. When asked in the House of Lords what was to be done about the matter, Lord Irvine answered that:

> I am considering whether the evidence disclosed in Judge Gee's criminal trial would justify me in concluding, on the standard of civil proof, that Judge Gee has been guilty of misbehaviour sufficient to allow me to remove him from office under my statutory powers to dismiss a circuit judge for misbehaviour.

The Lord Chancellor's considerations were cut short and any action pre-empted by Gee's resignation in November 1999. The Lord Chancellor had no power to prevent the payment of a judicial pension of £23,000, together with a lump sum of £46,000, both inflation proofed, when Gee reached the age of 65.

As yet, the only judge to be removed for misbehaviour remains the circuit judge who, in 1983, was found guilty of smuggling cigarettes and alcohol.

In a letter circulated in July 1994, Lord Mackay asked that judges inform him immediately if they are ever charged with any criminal offence other than parking or speeding violations. The Lord Chancellor stated that he wished to make it clear that a conviction for drink-driving would amount, *prima facie*, to misbehaviour. Causing offence on racial or religious grounds could also be seen as misbehaviour, as could sexual harassment.

The discretionary power of the Lord Chancellor not to extend the appointment of a recorder, without the need to explain or justify his action, has previously provided grounds for criticism and accusations of political interference on the part of the Lord Chancellor.

Stipendiary magistrates are subject to removal by the Crown on the recommendation of the Lord Chancellor and lay magistrates are subject to removal by the Lord Chancellor without cause or explanation.

4.6.1 Constitutional Reform Act

In relation to matters of discipline the Act proposes that both the Lord Chancellor and the Lord Chief Justice will have roles to play in relation to judicial conduct. Consistent with previous provisions, the position of all senior judicial office holders is protected, and removal from office of any judge in the High Court or above, is only possible following resolutions in both the House of Commons and the House of Lords. Under section 108 there are new powers enabling the Lord Chief Justice to:

- advise,

- warn,

- or formally reprimand judicial office holders.

He may also suspend them in certain circumstances, mainly relating to allegations relating criminal offences. Such powers are subject to the agreement of the Lord

Chancelor. The Lord Chief Justice may, also with the agreement of the Lord Chancellor, make regulations and rules about the disciplinary process.

4.7 Judicial Immunity from Suit

A fundamental measure to ensure the independence of the judiciary is the rule that they cannot be sued in relation to things said or acts done in their judicial capacity in good faith. The effect of this may be seen in *Sirros v Moore* (1975), in which a judge wrongly ordered someone's detention. It was subsequently held by the Court of Appeal that, although the detention had been unlawful, no action could be taken against the judge as he had acted in good faith in his judicial capacity. Although some judges on occasion may be accused of abusing this privilege, it is nonetheless essential if judges are to operate as independent representatives of the law, for it is unlikely that judges would be able to express their honest opinions of the law, and the situations in which it is being applied, if they were to be subject to suits from disgruntled participants.

Given the increased use of the doctrine of *ultra vires* to justify legal action by way of judicial review against members of the executive, it is satisfyingly ironic that at least one judge, Stephen Sedley, who now sits in the Court of Appeal, sees the possibility of a similar *ultra vires* action providing grounds for an action against judges in spite of their previously assumed legal immunity. As he expressed the point in the *London Review of Books* of April 1994:

> Judges have no authority to act maliciously or corruptly. It would be rational to hold that such acts take them outside their jurisdiction and so do not attract judicial immunity.

No doubt such a suggestion would be anathema to the great majority of the judiciary, but the point remains: why should judges be at liberty to abuse their position of authority in a way that no other public servant can?

Before 1991, magistrates could be liable for damages for actions done in excess of their actual authority, but the CLSA 1990 extended the existing immunity from the superior courts to cover the inferior courts, so magistrates now share the same protection as other judges.

It is worth stating at this point that this immunity during court proceedings also extends as far as advocates and witnesses, and of course jurors, although the controls of *perjury* and *contempt of court* are always available to cover what is said or done in the course of court proceedings.

Related to, although distinct from, the principle of immunity from suit is the convention that individual judges should not be subject to criticism in parliamentary debate, unless subject to an address for their removal: legal principles and the law in general can be criticised, but not judges.

In the course of 2000, it was announced that public money was to be made available to allow judges to sue for libel. Such a proposal is surprising to say the least. Surely those who benefit from immunity should not be assisted to take actions against those who do not enjoy such a benefit. And who would hear such a case? A fellow judge; hardly the stuff of transparent impartiality. It has to be reported that as yet no judge has availed himself of this opportunity.

4.8 Magistrates

The foregoing has concentrated attention on the professional and legally qualified judges. It should not be forgotten, however, that there are some 30,000 unpaid part time lay magistrates, 106 full time professional stipendiary magistrates (known as District Judges (Magistrates' Courts)) and 175 Deputy District Judges (Magistrates' Courts) operating within some 700 or so magistrates' courts in England. These magistrates are empowered to hear and decide a wide variety of legal matters and the amount and importance of the work they do should not be underestimated: 97% of all criminal cases are dealt with by the magistrates' courts. The operation of the magistrates' courts and the powers of magistrates have been considered in detail above at 4.3. It remains, however, to examine the manner in which they are appointed to their positions.

There is no requirement for lay magistrates to have any legal qualifications. On being accepted onto the bench, however, magistrates undertake a training process, under the auspices of the JSB. Magistrates are required to attend training courses, with a special emphasis being placed on Equal Treatment Training. The way in which the training programme seeks to overcome conceptions as to the politically narrow nature of the magistracy is evident in the content of the extensive training materials produced for the magistrates. These include modules on: raising awareness and challenging discrimination; discretion and decision making; prejudice and stereotype; thus, the overall emphasis may be seen to be on equality of people, and equality of treatment. There is, however, a new emphasis on the practical skills involved in performing the duties placed on magistrates, and consequently much of the training will actually be based on sitting as magistrates with the input of specially trained monitors to give guidance and advice on how the new magistrates perform their tasks and fulfil their roles.

The training course is designed to give new magistrates an understanding of the functions and powers of the bench generally, and to locate that understanding within the context of national practice, particularly with regard to sentencing. On the topic of discretion and sentencing, Lord Irvine provided the magistrates with the following strong advice, not to say warning:

> You ... must exercise your discretion in individual cases with great care within a system that needs to secure continuing public confidence. This is what makes the sentencing guidelines produced by the Magistrates' Association so important. They are guidelines – they do not curtail your independent discretion to impose sentences you think are right, case by case. But the guidelines exist to help you in that process, to give you more information in reaching your decision. And they help to assist the magistracy, to maintain an overall consistency of approach ... I urge you to follow the guidelines,

which are drawn up for your benefit and the magistracy as a whole [Speech to the Council of Magistrates' Association, March 1999].

Although particular key legal issues may be considered in the course of the training, it is not the intention to provide the magistrate with a complete grasp of substantive law and legal practice. Indeed, to expect such would be to misunderstand both the role of the magistrates and the division of responsibility within the magistrates' court. Every bench of magistrates has a legally qualified justices' clerk, whose function it is to advise the bench on questions of law, practice, and procedure, leaving matters of fact to magistrates to decide upon (see 4.3.1 above). This division of powers raises a further possible area of contention with regard to the operation of magistrates' courts, for in the case of some particularly acquiescent benches, the justices' clerks appear to run the court, and this leads to the suspicion that they actually direct the magistrates as to what decisions they should make. This perception is compounded by the fact that the bench is entitled to invite their clerk to accompany them when they retire to consider their verdicts. A *Practice Direction* (*Justices: Clerks to the Court*) (2000) set out the role and functions of the clerk to the court. Thus, the clerk, or legal adviser who stands in for the clerk, is stated to be responsible for providing the justices with any advice they require to properly perform their functions, whether or not the justices have requested that advice, on the following matters:

- questions of law (including ECHR jurisprudence and those matters set out in s 2(1) of the HRA 1998);

- questions of mixed law and fact;

- matters of practice and procedure;

- the range of penalties available;

- any relevant decisions of the superior courts or other guidelines;

- other issues relevant to the matter before the court;

- the appropriate decision making structure to be applied in any given case; and

- in addition to advising the justices, it shall be the legal adviser's responsibility to assist the court, where appropriate, as to the formulation of reasons and the recording of those reasons.

As regards when and where this advice should be given, the *Practice Direction* states that:

> At any time, justices are entitled to receive advice to assist them in discharging their responsibilities. If they are in any doubt as to the evidence which has been given, they should seek the aid of their legal adviser, referring to his/her notes as appropriate. This should ordinarily be done in open court. Where the justices request their adviser to join them in the retiring room, this request should be made in the presence of the parties in court. Any legal advice given to the justices other than in open court should be clearly stated to be provisional and the adviser should subsequently repeat the substance of the advice in open court and give the parties an opportunity to make any representations they wish on that provisional advice.

4.8.1 Appointment

Under the Justices of the Peace Act 1997, magistrates are appointed to, and indeed removed from, office by the Lord Chancellor on behalf of the Queen, after consultation with local advisory committees. There are currently 111 such advisory committees and 134 sub-committees within the UK. Section 50 of the Employment Rights Act 1996 provides that employers are obliged to release their employees, for such time as is reasonable, to permit them to serve as magistrates. In the event of an employer refusing to sanction absence from work to perform magistrate's duties, the employee can take the matter before an employment tribunal. Understandably, there is no statutory requirement for the employer to pay their employees in their absence, but magistrates are entitled to claim expenses for loss of earnings in the exercise of their office.

Proposals for office tend to be generated by local interest groups, such as political parties, trade unions, chambers of commerce and similar bodies, and this limited constituency may give rise to the view that the magistracy only represents the attitudes of a limited section of society. In a multi-cultural, multi-racial society, it is essential that the magistrates' court should reflect the composition of the wider society, and the rules relating to the appointment and training of magistrates do, at least in theory, support this conclusion.

Once candidates of a suitable quality have been identified, the local advisory committee is placed under the injunction to have regard to the need to ensure that the composition of the bench broadly reflects the community which it serves in terms of gender, ethnic origin, geographical spread, occupation and political affiliation. It may even be that individuals who are otherwise suitably qualified may not be appointed if their presence would exacerbate a perceived imbalance in the existing bench. Nonetheless, there remains a lingering doubt, at least in the minds of particular constituencies, that the magistracy still represents the values, both moral and political, of a limited section of society. A further significant step towards opening up the whole procedure of appointing magistrates was taken when local advisory committees were granted the power to advertise for people to put themselves forward for selection. As the chairman of the Mid-Staffordshire Magistrates' Bench stated in a local newspaper, although previously rank and social position were the main qualifications, nowadays:

> ... it is important a bench has a balance of sexes, professions and political allegiances.

In March 1999, the LCD launched a campaign to attract a wider section of candidates to apply to be magistrates. In announcing the campaign, Lord Irvine stated that:

> Magistrates come from a wide range of backgrounds and occupations. We have magistrates who are dinner ladies and scientists, bus drivers and teachers, plumbers and housewives. They have different faiths and come from different ethnic backgrounds, some have disabilities. All are serving their communities, ensuring that local justice is dispensed by local people. The magistracy should reflect the diversity of the community it serves ... Rest assured appointments are made on the merit, regardless of educational background, social class or ethnic background.

The campaign was supported by adverts in some 36 newspapers and magazines, from broadsheets to tabloids, from TV listings to women's magazines. The campaign was particularly aimed at ethnic minorities, its adverts being carried in such publications as the *Caribbean Times*, the *Asian Times* and *Muslim News*. The 1999 campaign was followed in 2001 by a *Judiciary for All* scheme, which aimed to encourage more people from ethnic minority groups to apply to become magistrates. The next initiative to make the Bench more reflective of the public was the 'National Strategy for the Recruitment of Lay Magistrates' announced by Lord Falconer in October 2003. As he stated:

> I consider it particularly important that the magistracy is seen to be representative of all sections of our society and that no one group of people should feel that they are under-represented on the magistrates' bench. My Department is already involved with a number of initiatives aimed at encouraging young people and minority ethnic groups to become involved in the judicial process and, although the ethnic make up of the magistracy countrywide is close to the national average for cultural representation per head of population there are still regional variations, both in age and ethnicity, that need to be addressed.

In order to achieve this aim, the Secretary of State commissioned the National Recruitment Strategy, which will examine not only how to raise the profile of the magistracy generally, but also how to develop a framework to target the recruitment and retention of magistrates from under-represented groups, whilst continuing to draw on the support of those who have traditionally provided the backbone of local recruitment. The strategy will aim to highlight the importance of the work of magistrates, particularly to employers, whom, the Lord Chancellor says, must be persuaded that, by allowing staff who are magistrates time off to carry out their duties, they are 'contributing enormously to the maintenance of local justice and the values of good citizenship'.

The statistics demonstrate that the gender balance and ethnic mix of the magistracy does not appear to pose a problem, but the same cannot be said in terms of its class mix. However, in 1998, the LCD issued a Consultation Paper relating to the political balance in the lay magistracy, which suggested that political affiliation was no longer a major issue, and therefore did not have to be controlled in relation to the make up of benches of magistrates. As support for its suggestion, the consultancy document made three points. First, that actually ensuring a political balance on the bench raises:

> ... the danger of creating a perception that politics do play a part in the administration of justice, notwithstanding that it is agreed on all sides that, in a mature democracy, politics have no place in the court room.

Secondly, that advisory committees:

> ... have increasingly found that many magistrates have declined to provide the information [relating to their political allegiance] or classed themselves as 'uncommitted'.

Thirdly, it claimed that in any case, 'geodemographic classification schemes', based on an analysis of particular personal attributes such as ethnicity, gender, marital status, occupation, home ownership and car owning status, are much more sensitive indicators for achieving social balance on benches than stated political allegiance.

Such 'geodemographics' might well represent the emergence of the truly classless society. Alternatively, they might represent a worrying denial of the importance of political attitudes within law generally, and the magistrates' bench in particular.

In any case, in March 2001, Jane Kennedy MP, Parliamentary Secretary to the LCD, announced that, at least for the moment, the Lord Chancellor had reluctantly decided that political balance would have to remain an issue. This statement was made in response to the disclosure that the Magistrates' Advisory Committee in Stoke-on-Trent had sent out a letter to several local organisations, which stated that:

> ... whilst the overriding criterion for appointment is always the suitability of the candidate, the Advisory Committee is particularly keen to receive applications from members of ethnic minorities, shop floor workers, the unemployed and Labour Party supporters.

In answering charges that such a letter was politicising the magistracy, Ms Kennedy pointed out that:

> Public confidence in lay magistrates is vital. This is achieved, first and foremost, by individual magistrates discharging their duties effectively. It is also achieved when Benches reflect the diversity of the communities which they serve. In Stoke-on-Trent the Labour vote is significantly under-reflected on the magistrates' Bench. Of those who expressed political affiliation 40% were Labour, compared to 60% who voted Labour in the area at the last General Election. This compares to 47% of the Bench being acknowledged Conservative voters, compared to 27% in the area.

The Advisory Committee was simply and correctly trying to attract more Labour voters to apply to become magistrates, in order that the composition of the Bench more broadly reflected the local voting pattern.

4.8.2   The future of the magistrates' courts

In December 2000, the results of a report, *The Judiciary in the Magistrates' Courts*, were published. The extensive report was jointly commissioned by the Home Office and the LCD and provided an extremely valuable comparison between the lay magistracy and stipendiaries. It found as follows.

As regards the lay magistracy:

- they are drawn overwhelmingly from professional and managerial ranks;

- 40% of them are retired from full time employment;

- the cost of an appearance before lay magistrates is £52.10 per hour.

As regards the stipendiaries:

- they are younger, but are mostly male and white;

- they hear cases more quickly;

- they are more likely to refuse bail and to make use of immediate custodial sentences;

- they are less likely to need legal advisers;

- the cost of an appearance before stipendiary magistrates is £61.78 per hour.

In the following January, 2001, a report entitled *Community Justice* by Professor Andrew Sanders for the Institute for Public Policy Research called for the replacement of panels of lay justices by panels composed of District Judges, the former stipendiary magistrates, assisted by two lay magistrates. According to Professor Sanders:

> These proposals would increase public confidence, and they would enhance the contribution ordinary members of the public make to our justice system.

The Magistrates' Association took a rather different view and saw the proposals as an attack on what was already an extremely representative system of justice. According to its then Chair, Harry Mawdsley, the proposed scheme would cost around £30 million annually in salaries alone, but apart from costs:

> Lay magistrates provide community justice: they are ordinary people who live and work in the local community and who have an intimate knowledge of that community.

Although praising the magistracy's gender and ethnic make up, Mr Mawdsley nevertheless recognised the need to recruit more magistrates from working class backgrounds.

When the Auld Report into the criminal court system was issued later that year, it suggested a compromise between these two positions: the retention of the magistrates' courts as one division in a unified criminal court, with the creation of a new District Division, made up of a District Judge and two magistrates, to hear mid-range either way offences (the third division, the Crown Division, retained the role of the current Crown Court). In the event, the government declined to adopt the Auld recommendations in this regard, but increased the sentencing powers of the magistrates to 12 months in detention in s 154 of the Criminal Justice Act 2003. As Lord Irvine told the Magistrates' Association in October 2002:

> What the Government's proposals cement and enhance is your position at the heart of a reformed and more joined-up Criminal Justice System; one in which we have better pre-trial preparation; a more efficient trial process; and effective and appropriate sentencing.

Nonetheless, he felt required to re-emphasise how the magistrates should use their new sentencing power:

> I cannot emphasise this to you too strongly: your greater sentencing powers are to be exercised with restraint and in accordance with these principles: 'imprisonment only when necessary and for no longer than necessary'. The proposed new Sentencing

Framework aims to encourage you to make full use of community sentences; and to reserve custodial sentences for serious, dangerous and persistent offenders.

As proposed, s 154 of the Criminal Justice Act 2003 increased the sentencing powers of the magistrates' courts to 12 months in relation to a single offence (for a detailed consideration of the impact of the Act on magistrates' courts, see 3.2 above; the changes in relation to magistrates' courts introduced by the Courts Act 2003 are considered at 3.7.8 above).

4.9   Judicial Review

The effect of the HRA on the interface between the judiciary and the executive has been considered previously at 1.7 and in this chapter, but that Act merely heightened the potential for conflict in a relationship that was already subject to some tension as a consequence of the operation of judicial review. If the interface between judiciary and executive tends now to be most sharply defined in human rights actions, the previous and continued role of judicial review in that relationship should not be underestimated.

The growth in applications for judicial review prior to the HRA was truly startling, as individuals and the judiciary recognised its potential utility as a means of challenging administrative decisions. The records show that in 1980, there were only 525 applications for judicial review; in 1996, 4,586; in 1997, 4,636 such applications; and by 1998, applications had passed the 5,000 mark and continued to rise.

At the outset, it should be noted that although this section focuses on those instances where the judiciary have decided against the exercise of executive power in a particular way, it has to be emphasised that the vast majority of judicial review cases are decided in favour of the executive.

The remedies open to anyone challenging the decisions or actions of administrative institutions or public authorities can be divided into *private* or *public* law remedies.

4.9.1   Private law remedies

There are three private law remedies:

- *Declaration*

  This is a definitive statement, by the High Court or county court, of what the law is in a particular area. The procedure may be used by an individual or body to clarify a particularly contentious situation. It is a common remedy in private law, but it also has an important part to play in regard to individuals' relations with administrative institutions. This can be seen, for example, in *Congreve v Home Office* (1976), where the Court of Appeal stated that it would be unlawful for the Home Office to revoke annual television licences after only eight months because they had been bought in anticipation of an announced price rise but before the expiry of existing licences.

Declarations, however, cannot be enforced either directly or indirectly through the contempt of court procedure. Public authorities are, as a matter of course, expected to abide by them.

- *Injunctions*

  Usually, an injunction seeks to restrain a person from breaking the law; alternatively, however, a mandatory injunction may instruct someone to undo what they have previously done, or alternatively to stop doing what they are doing. Both types of injunction may be sought against a public authority. See *Attorney General v Fulham Corp* (1921), in which a local authority was ordered to stop running a laundry service where it only had the power to establish laundries for people to wash their own clothes.

- *Damages*

  Damages cannot be awarded on their own in relation to administrative misconduct, but may be claimed in addition where one of the other remedies considered above is sought, as, for example, in *Cooper v Wandsworth Board of Works* (1863). In this case, a builder had put up a building without informing the Board of Works as he was required to do. When the Board demolished the building, he nonetheless recovered damages against them on the basis that the Board had exceeded its powers by not allowing him to defend or explain his actions.

In order to seek one of these private law remedies, an individual merely had to issue a writ against a public authority in their own name. They did not require the approval of the court.

4.9.2 The prerogative orders

The prerogative orders are so called because they were originally the means whereby sovereigns controlled the operation of their officials. As a consequence, the prerogative orders cannot be used against the Crown, but they can be used against individual ministers of State and, since *R v Secretary of State for the Home Department ex p Fire Brigades Union* (1995), it is clear that ministers cannot avoid judicial review by hiding behind the cloak of prerogative powers. The prerogative orders are as follows:

- *A quashing order*, formerly known as *certiorari*, is the mechanism by means of which decisions of inferior courts, tribunals and other authoritative bodies are brought before the High Court to have their validity examined. Where any such decision is found to be invalid, it may be set aside. An example of this can be seen in *Ridge v Baldwin* (1964). Here, the plaintiff had been dismissed from his position as Chief Constable without having had the opportunity to present any case for his defence. The House of Lords held that the committee which had taken the decision had acted in breach of the requirements of natural justice and granted a declaration that his dismissal was null and void.

- A *prohibiting order*, formerly known as *prohibition*, is similar to certiorari in that it relates to invalid acts of public authorities, but it is different to the extent that it is pre-emptive and prescriptive in regard to any such activity and operates to prevent the authority from taking invalid decisions in the first place. An example of the use of the order arose in *R v Telford Justices ex p Badham* (1991). In this case, an order was issued to stop committal proceedings in relation to an alleged rape that had not been reported until some 14 years after the alleged incident. The delay meant that the defendant would have been unable to prepare a proper defence against the charge.

- A *mandatory order*, formerly known as *mandamus*, may be seen as the obverse of a prohibiting order, in that it is an order issued by the High Court instructing an inferior court or some other public authority to carry out a duty laid on them. Such an order is frequently issued in conjunction with an order of certiorari, to the effect that a public body is held to be using its powers improperly and is instructed to use them in a proper fashion. In *R v Poplar BC (Nos 1 and 2)* (1922), the court ordered the borough council to pay over money due to the county council and to levy a rate to raise the money if necessary. Failure to comply with the order led to the imprisonment of some of the borough councillors.

In *O'Reilly v Mackman* (1982), however, the House of Lords decided that issues relating to *public* rights could *only* be enforced by means of the judicial review procedure, and that it would be an abuse of process for an applicant to seek a declaration by writ in relation to an alleged breach of a public duty or responsibility by a public authority. In deciding the case in this way, the House of Lords did much to demarcate and emphasise the role of judicial review as the method of challenging public authorities in their performance of their powers and duties in public law.

4.9.3 Grounds for application for judicial review

Judicial review allows people with a sufficient interest in a decision or action by a public body to ask a judge to review the lawfulness of:

- an enactment; or

- a decision, action or failure to act in relation to the exercise of a public function.

However, it is not an appeal on the merits of a decision.

The grounds of application can be considered under two heads: *procedural ultra vires* and *substantive ultra vires*:

- *Procedural ultra vires*, as its name suggests, relates to the failure of a person or body, provided with specific authority, to follow the procedure established for using that power. It also covers instances where a body exercising a judicial function fails to follow the requirements of natural justice by acting as prosecutor and judge in the same case or not permitting the accused person to make representations to the panel deciding the case.

- *Substantive ultra vires* occurs where someone does something that is not actually authorised by the enabling legislation. In *Associated Provincial Picture House v Wednesbury Corp* (1947), Lord Greene MR established the possibility of challenging discretionary decisions on the basis of unreasonableness.

Lord Greene's approach was endorsed and refined by Lord Diplock in *Council of Civil Service Unions v Minister for the Civil Service* (1984), in which he set out the three recognised grounds for judicial review, namely:

- illegality;

- irrationality;

- procedural impropriety.

Lord Diplock, however, introduced the possibility of a much more wide-ranging reason for challenging administrative decisions: namely, the doctrine of *proportionality*. Behind this doctrine is the requirement that there should be a reasonable relation between a decision and its objectives. It requires the achievement of particular ends by means that are not more oppressive than they need be to attain those ends. The potentially innovative aspect of this doctrine is the extent to which it looks to the substance of the decisions rather than simply focusing on the way in which they are reached.

Lord Diplock's listing of proportionality within the grounds for judicial review was controversial, if not at the very least arguably mistaken. Proportionality, however, is a key principle within the jurisdiction of the ECtHR, and is used frequently to assess the validity of State action which interferes with individual rights protected under the Convention. Consequently, as the HRA has incorporated the European Convention into UK law, proportionality will be a part of UK jurisprudence and legal practice, at least in cases which fall within the scope of the HRA. Although HRA cases and judicial review are different and distinct procedures, nonetheless, it is surely a mere matter of time before the doctrine of proportionality is applied by the judges in judicial review cases unrelated to the Convention.

Indeed, such an approach was supported by Lord Slynn in *R v Secretary of State for the Environment, Transport and the Regions ex p Holding and Barnes* (2001) in which he stated:

> The European Court of Justice does of course apply the principle of proportionality when examining such acts and national judges must apply the same principle when dealing with Community law issues. There is a difference between that principle and the approach of the English courts in *Associated Provincial Picture Houses Ltd v Wednesbury Corporation* [1948] 1 KB 223. But the difference in practice is not as great as is sometimes supposed. The cautious approach of the European Court of Justice in applying the principle is shown *inter alia* by the margin of appreciation it accords to the institutions of the Community in making economic assessments. I consider that even without reference to the Human Rights Act the time has come to recognise that this principle is part of

English administrative law, not only when judges are dealing with Community acts but also when they are dealing with acts subject to domestic law. Trying to keep the *Wednesbury* principle and proportionality in separate compartments seems to me to be unnecessary and confusing. Reference to the Human Rights Act however makes it necessary that the court should ask whether what is done is compatible with Convention rights. That will often require that the question should be asked whether the principle of proportionality has been satisfied ...

4.9.4 The exclusion of judicial review

As will be considered in Chapter 8, one of the reasons for the setting up of extensive systems of administrative tribunals was precisely the wish to curb the power of the judges. It was felt that judges, and indeed the common law itself, tended to be more supportive of *individual* rights and freedoms as opposed to *collective* notions of welfare pursued by post-war governments, and that they would not administer such policies sympathetically. The judges, however, asserted their ultimate control over such tribunals generally through the use of judicial review. There have been various attempts by parliamentary drafters to exclude the judiciary from certain areas by wording provisions in such a way as to deny the possibility of judicial review. These attempts, however, have mainly proved to be in vain and have been rendered ineffective by the refusal of the courts to recognise their declared effect. Examples are:

- *'Finality' or 'ouster' clauses*

  There is a variety of possible wordings for these clauses. For example, the legislation might provide that 'the minister's [or the tribunal's] decision shall be final', or alternatively it might attempt to emphasise the point by stating that the decision in question 'shall be final and conclusive', or it might even provide that 'it shall be final, conclusive and shall not be questioned in any legal proceedings whatsoever'. Unfortunately for the drafter of the legislation and the minister or tribunal in question, all three formulations are equally likely to be ineffective. The courts have tended to interpret such phrases in a narrow way, so as to recognise the exclusion of an appeal procedure but to introduce the possibility of judicial review, as distinct from appeal. The classic case on this point is *R v Medical Appeal Tribunal ex p Gilmore* (1957), in which Lord Denning stated that, 'The word "final" ... does not mean without recourse to certiorari'. This, however, raised the point of provisions which expressly sought to exclude certiorari.

In *South East Asia Fire Bricks Sdn Bhd v Non-Metallic Mineral Products Manufacturing Employees Union* (1980), the Privy Council decided that a Malaysian statute was sufficiently detailed in its wording to effectively exclude certiorari *for an error of law on the face of the record*. The Privy Council pointed out, however, that the exclusion could not be effective to prevent judicial review where the institution in question had acted *ultra vires* or in breach of natural justice.

The fury of the judiciary against the present government's statutory proposals found its fullest expression in respect of the Asylum and Immigration (Treatment of Claimants etc) Bill. The Bill, which was designed to speed up asylum and immigration procedures by curtailing the appeal structure, introduced the most wide-ranging of ouster clauses to the effect that no court shall have any supervisory or other jurisdiction in relation to the Asylum and Immigration Tribunal. In particular, the original cl 11 of the Bill stated that the courts could not question the decisions of the tribunal even in the event of:

- lack of jurisdiction;

- irregularity;

- error of law;

- breach of natural justice; or

- any other matter.

As was stated at the time, such a proposal was the 'mother and father' of all ouster clauses. The judiciary were extremely vocal in their opposition to cl 11, which they saw, and publicly represented, as an attack on the rule of law in its refusal to allow access to the ordinary courts. When it became apparent that the Bill was not going to pass through the House of Lords, Lord Falconer made it known that the government would change the appeal procedure to allow appellants some sort of access to the courts. Although the Lord Chancellor did not state the details of the new proposals, his promise was sufficient to win the approval of the House of Lords.

- *Partial exclusion clauses*

  Where legislation has provided for a limited time period within which parties have to apply for judicial review, then applications outside of the period will not be successful. In *Smith v East Elloe Rural DC* (1956), the House of Lords, although only by 3:2 majority, recognised the effectiveness of a six week limitation clause in the Acquisition of Land (Authorisation Procedure) Act 1946. Although that case was subject to criticism in *Anisminic Ltd v Foreign Compensation Commission* (1969), it was explained and followed in *R v Secretary of State for the Environment ex p Ostler* (1976).

In response to the Franks Committee's recommendation that judicial review should not be subject to exclusion, s 14(1) of the Tribunals and Inquiries Act 1971 was enacted to that end. Unfortunately, it only applies to pre-1958 legislation.

4.10   Politics of the Judiciary

When considering the role which the judiciary play in the process of applying the law, or indeed the process already adverted to in Chapter 2, whereby they actually make the law, criticism is usually levelled at the particular race, class and gender position of the majority of the judges. It is an objective and well documented fact that the majority of judges are 'white, middle class, middle aged to elderly men', but the question that has to be considered is whether this *necessarily* leads to the conclusion that judges reach inherently biased decisions. It is always possible, indeed the newspapers make it relatively easy, to provide anecdotal evidence which apparently confirms either the bias or the lack of social awareness of the judiciary, but the fundamental question remains as to whether these cases are exceptional or whether they represent the norm.

Why should judges' class/race/gender placement make them less objective arbiters of the law? It is worth considering the fact that *unsupported* general assertions as to the inherently partial approach of the judiciary is itself partial. Simon Lee, not totally fatuously, has highlighted the logical flaw in what he refers to as the 'Tony Benn thesis' (Benn, the former left wing Labour Party Member of Parliament who created history by being the first hereditary peer to renounce his peerage in order to remain in the House of Commons). Just because judges are old, white, rich, upper middle class, educated at public school and Oxbridge does not mean that they all necessarily think the same way; after all, Benn was a product of the same social circumstances. There is, of course, the point that people from that particular background *generally* tend to be conservative in outlook, and the apparent validity of Lee's argument is clearly the product of logic-chopping that reverses the accepted relationship and uses the exception as the rule, rather than seeing the exception as proving/testing the rule. Nevertheless, Lee's point remains true: that proof of judicial bias is needed.

As the previous chapter of this book pointed out, if law were completely beyond the scope of judges to manipulate to their own ends, then the race, class and gender placement of individual judges would be immaterial, as they would not be in any position to influence the operation of the law. That chapter also demonstrated, however, the way in which the doctrines which set the limits within which the judiciary operate are by no means as rigid and restrictive as they might at first appear. It was seen that, although judges are supposed merely to apply rather than create law, they possess a large measure of discretion in determining which laws to apply, what those laws mean, and how they should be applied. In the light of this potential capacity to create law, it is essential to ensure that the judiciary satisfactorily represent society at large in relation to which they have so much power, and to ensure further that they do not merely represent the views and attitudes of a self-perpetuating elite.

The limited class background of the judiciary was confirmed in figures issued by the Lord Chancellor's office on 17 May 1995, which revealed that 80% of Lords of Appeal, Heads of Division, Lord Justices of Appeal and High Court Justices were educated at Oxford or Cambridge. In justifying the figures, the Lord Chancellor's Permanent Secretary, Sir Thomas Legg, showing insouciance to the level of arrogance, simply stated that, 'It is not the function of the professional judiciary to be representative of the community'. Such a response, even if it is true, let alone acceptable, must surely undermine the right of such an unrepresentative body to take action in the name of the majority, as the courts do in their use of judicial review.

Unfortunately, the continuing social imbalance amongst the senior judiciary was further confirmed in a report on judicial appointments by the Commons Home Affairs Committee, presented in June 1996. It revealed that four-fifths of judges went to both public schools and Oxbridge colleges, that only seven out of 96 High Court Judges were women, and that only five out of the 517 circuit judges were black or Asian. Nevertheless, the Committee rejected proposals for positive discrimination or even for the establishment of a judicial appointments committee to replace the present informal system under the control of the Lord Chancellor.

Instead of things improving, if one actually has the temerity to consider it an improvement to have fewer Oxbridge men on the bench, a Labour Research investigation found that things were actually getting worse in terms of the wider representational make-up of the judiciary (as has been considered above at 4.3.2). Still, Lord Irvine held fast to appointment solely on merit, which appeared wholly commendable, but, as has been stated before, who decides on merit, and what qualities are they actually measuring?

A Nuffield Foundation funded report produced in November 1999 by Professor Hazel Genn in conjunction with the National Centre for Social Research, entitled *Paths to Justice*, revealed a truly remarkable lack of general confidence in the judiciary. The research surveyed a random selection of 4,125 people, from which total 1,248 people who had had experience of legal problems were selected for more detailed interview, with a smaller group of 48 being extensively interviewed. The results suggest that two out of three people think that judges are out of touch with ordinary people's lives, but more worryingly, only 53% thought that they would get a fair hearing if they ever went to court. Disappointingly, at the launch of the report, Lord Woolf claimed that this 'misconception' was due to 'irresponsible media reporting' and stated that:

> It behoves the media to learn from this and recognise the dangers posed to confidence in the judicial system.

Surely, it more behoves the judiciary and the LCD to do more to redress this negative perception than simply blame the media for focusing on silly judge stories of which, unfortunately, there are still too many.

One of the findings of the report was that judges could improve their image by getting rid of their wigs and gowns. Perish the thought: there are standards and distinctions to be maintained. Thus, in *Practice Direction (Court Dress) (No 3)* (1998), the Lord High Chancellor, Lord Irvine of Lairg, provides:

> Queens' Counsel wear a short wig and silk (or stuff) gown over a court coat; junior counsel wear a short wig and stuff gown with bands; solicitors and other advocates authorised under the Courts and Legal Services Act 1990 wear a black stuff gown, *but no wig* [emphasis added].

4.10.1   Criticisms

The treatment of some aspects of potential bias within the judiciary has already been dealt with at 4.1.3 above, but this section addresses a more amorphous form of prejudice, and therefore one that is correspondingly more difficult to recognise or deal with. Given the central position of judges in the operation of law and the legal system, particularly with regard to the growth in judicial review and their new role in relation to giving effect to the HRA, the question these reports raise is whether the social placement of the judiciary leads to any perceptible shortfall in the provision of justice.

The pre-eminent critic of the way in which the judiciary permit their shared background, attitudes and prejudices to influence their understanding and statement of the law is Professor JAG Griffith. According to Griffith, bias can occur at two levels:

- *Personal bias*

  Personal bias occurs where individual judges permit their own personal prejudices to influence their judgment and thus the effective application of the law. It is relatively easy to cite cases where judges give expression to their own attitudes and in so doing exhibit their own prejudices. As examples of this process, two cases can be cited which consider the rule of natural justice, that a person should not be both the accuser and judge in the same case. In *Hannam v Bradford Corp* (1970), the court held that it was contrary to natural justice for three school governors to sit as members of a local authority education disciplinary committee, charged with deciding whether or not to uphold a previous decision of the governors to dismiss a teacher. This was so even though the three governors had not been present at the meeting where it was decided to dismiss the teacher. On the other hand, in *Ward v Bradford Corp* (1971), the Court of Appeal refused to interfere with a decision by governors of a teacher training college to confirm the expulsion of a student, although they had instituted the disciplinary proceedings and three members of the governors sat on the original disciplinary committee. What possible explanation can there be for this discrepancy? The only tenable explanation is to be found in the latter court's disapproval of the plaintiff's behaviour in that case. The truly reprehensible judgment of Lord Denning concludes that the student lost nothing, as she was not a fit person to teach children in any case. Can such a conclusion be justified on purely legal grounds or is it based on individual morality? Lord Denning did his best to buttress his judgment with spurious legal reasoning, but it could be suggested that, in so doing, he merely brought the process of legal reasoning into disrepute and revealed its fallaciousness.

  Courts have also been notoriously unsympathetic to victims of rape and have been guilty of making the most obtuse of sexist comments in relation to such victims. Nor can it be claimed that depreciatory racist remarks have been totally lacking in court cases.

  Such cases of bias are serious and reprehensible, but the very fact that the prejudice they demonstrate appears as no more than the outcome of particular judges, who are simply out of touch with current standards of morality or acceptable behaviour, suggests that it might be eradicated by the Lord Chancellor exercising stricter control over such mavericks and appointing more appropriate judges in the first place. Professor Griffith, however, suggests that there is a further type of bias that is actually beyond such relatively easy control.

- *Corporate bias*

  Corporate bias involves the assertion that the judges *as a body* decide certain types of cases in a biased way. This accusation of corporate bias is much more serious than that of personal bias, for the reason that it asserts that the problem of bias is *systematic* rather than merely limited to particular maverick judges. As a consequence, if such a claim is justified, it has to be concluded that the problem is not susceptible to treatment at the level of the individual judge, but requires a complete alteration of the whole judicial system.

Griffith claims that, as a consequence of their shared educational experience, their shared training and practical experience at the Bar and their shared social situation as members of the Establishment, judges have developed a common outlook. He maintains that they share homogeneous values, attitudes and beliefs as to how the law should operate and be administered. He further suggests that this shared outlook is inherently conservative, if not Conservative in a party political sense.

Griffith's argument is that the highest judges in the judicial hierarchy are frequently called upon to decide cases on the basis of a determination of what constitutes the public interest and that, in making that determination, they express their own corporate values which are in turn a product of their position in society as part of the ruling Establishment. Griffith maintains that judges can be seen to operate in such a way as to maintain the status quo and resist challenges to the established authority. Underlying this argument is the implication that the celebrated independence of the judiciary is, in fact, a myth and that the courts will tend to decide cases in such a way as to buttress the position of the State, especially if it is under the control of a Conservative government.

In an attempt to substantiate his claims, Griffith examines cases relating to trade union law, personal rights, property rights and matters of national security, where he claims to find judges consistently acting to support the interests of the State over the rights of the individual. Some of the concrete examples he cites are the withdrawal of trade union rights from GCHQ at Cheltenham (*Council of Civil Service Unions v Minister for Civil Service* (1984)); the banning of publishing any extracts from the *Spycatcher* book (*AG v Guardian Newspapers Ltd* (1987)); and the treatment of suspected terrorists.

There certainly have been some overtly right wing decisions taken by the courts, and the history of trade union cases is replete with them even at the highest level. The greater strength of Griffith's argument, however, would appear to be in the way that the courts have understood and expressed what is to be meant by 'public interest' in such a way as to reflect conservative, but not necessarily illiberal, values. It is surely only from that perspective that the higher judiciary's antagonistic response to some of the electorally driven policy decisions in relation to the legal system by *both* Conservative and New Labour administrations can be reconciled.

As would be expected, Griffith, and other academics associated with the left, have expressed their reservations about the extent to which the HRA will hand power to an unelected, unaccountable, inherently conservative and unreformed body, as they claim the judiciary is.

A notable, if somewhat complacent, response to Griffith's book was provided by Lord Devlin, who pointed out that, in most cases and on most issues, there tended to be plurality rather than unanimity of opinion and decision amongst judges. He also claimed that it would be just as possible for a more conservatively minded person than Griffith to go through the casebooks to provide a list of examples where the courts had operated in an over-liberal manner. Lord Devlin also adopted a different explanation of the judiciary's perceived reluctance to abandon the status quo. For him, any conservatism on the part of judges was to be seen as a product of age rather than class. In conclusion, he asserted that even if the judiciary were biased, their bias was well known and allowances could be made for it.

The issue of the way in which the criminal appeal procedure dealt with suspected terrorist cases is of particular relevance in the light of the Runciman Commission Report. General dissatisfaction with the trials and appeals involving suspected terrorists such as the Maguire Seven, the Birmingham Six, the Guildford Four, the Tottenham Three, Stefan Kiszko and Judith Ward helped to give rise to the widespread impression that the UK criminal justice system, and in particular the British appeal system, needed to be considered for reform.

In the light of the fact that the appeal system did not seem to be willing to consider the possibility of the accused's innocence once they had been convicted, the Runciman Commission's recommendation that a Criminal Case Review Authority be established, independent of the Home Office, was widely welcomed and resulted in the establishment of the CCRC in the Criminal Appeal Act 1995 (see 3.17.2 above). The question still remains, however, whether those earlier cases reflect an inherently and inescapably conservative judiciary, or were they simply unfortunate instances of more general errors of the system which the implementation of the CCRC can overcome? And perhaps more importantly, will the Court of Appeal give a fair hearing to the cases referred to it by the CCRC?

It is apparent from the statistics produced by the DCA cited previously that senior judges are still being appointed from the same limited social and educational elite as they always have been. This gives rise to the suspicion, if not the reality, that the decisions that this elite make merely represent values and interests of a limited and privileged segment of society rather than society as a whole. Even if the accusations levelled by Professor Griffith are inaccurate, it is surely still necessary to remove even the possibility of those accusations.

4.10.2   The politics of judicial inquiries

During the summer of 2003, following the war in Iraq, the government established an inquiry to investigate the reasons why a British civil servant working for the Ministry of Defence (Dr David Kelly) apparently killed himself. The inquiry chairman was Lord Hutton, a Law Lord, and his task was set by the government as one to 'urgently conduct an investigation into the circumstances surrounding the death of Dr Kelly'. This prompts consideration of the judicial inquiry, and its place in the English legal system.

An inquiry is different from a tribunal, another quasi-judicial body with which it is sometimes compared. A tribunal is a permanent body whereas an inquiry is set up on an *ad hoc* basis to deal with one particular problematic issue. Tribunals are empowered to make decisions that affect the parties to the issue, whereas inquiries can only publish their 'findings' and make recommendations that might be implemented by the government.

A 'statutory inquiry' is one that is established because an Act permits or requires it to be set up in certain circumstances. For example, under s 78 of the Town and Country Planning 1990 Act, someone who seeks planning permission but is refused by his local planning authority has the right to appeal to the Secretary of State. In order to help decide the case, the Secretary can ask for a local public inquiry to be held.

A 'non-statutory inquiry' is one that has been set up by the government in order to examine matters of substantial public interest like disasters or scandals. These are usually, but not necessarily, chaired by senior members of the judiciary.

There are, importantly, two sorts of such judicial inquiry. First, there are those that are established under the Tribunals of Inquiry (Evidence) Act 1921. Such inquiries are similar in their formality and rules of procedure to court cases. The chair can summon witnesses under threat that they will commit an offence if they do not turn up to give evidence, and the chair can demand that documents be made available to the hearing. This type of inquiry can be established only upon a resolution of both houses of Parliament. The as yet ongoing *Bloody Sunday Inquiry* into the killing of 13 Catholic civilians by British paratroopers in Derry in 1972 and chaired by Lord Saville of Newdigate was established under the 1921 Act. Similarly, the inquiry into the Dunblane shootings, in which many children at a primary school in Scotland were shot and killed in 1996, was also established under the 1921 Act.

Secondly, there are those judicial inquiries in which a judge is simply appointed by the government to chair the process but without the full powers of running it as a court case. For example, Lord Denning investigated aspects of the Profumo affair, a scandal in 1963 involving the Secretary of State for War at the time. Lord Scarman conducted the inquiry into the Brixton riots of 1981, Lord Justice Taylor examined the safety of sports grounds following the Hillsborough stadium disaster in 1991, and Lord Justice Scott inquired into the arms-for-Iraq affair in 1994. Such investigations, however, are not necessarily conducted by a judge, as may be seen from the pertinent example of the Franks Report on the conduct of the Falklands War in 1983.

However, judges have often been selected to chair inquiries into matters of public importance because they are expert in conducting fair and methodical hearings, and are generally regarded as wise people who are well-versed in using rules of evidence justly to evaluate competing arguments. The Hutton Inquiry into the death of Dr Kelly was of this second sort.

Lord Hutton conducted his inquiry in a scrupulously forensic manner and, whilst it was ongoing, the press was particularly effusive in its praise of him. It was only with the release of the final report, which totally exonerated all members of the New Labour government and its entourage and castigated the BBC, that suggestions emerged that the Law Lord actually might not have been the best equipped person to undertake such a politically sensitive inquiry, at least from the point of view of those who were opposed to the actions of the government. For example, an article in *The Guardian* newspaper of

29 January 2004 stated that: 'Lord Hutton's report caused little surprise yesterday among lawyers who know the newly retired Law Lord. Most describe him as an establishment man and not one to rock the boat. When he set out on his task, they predicted that he would keep his remit as narrow as possible. That prediction has been proved right.'

Anthony Scrivener QC, a former chairman of the Bar, said: 'You get a conventional, conservative with a small "c" judge. You ask whether the Prime Minister and other members of the government have been lying through their teeth. As a conventional judge he applies the criminal standard of proof. You give him no right to get documents so he only sees the documents you give him. The result is entirely predictable.'

One senior QC said: 'I think the report reflects his establishment background. He is a trusting man as far as officialdom is concerned.'

Another, who knows him personally and has appeared before him, said: 'There are judges in the House of Lords who are liberal and progressive and might possibly shake the establishment branches, but not Brian Hutton.'

Whether the Hutton Report provides evidence to support Professor Griffith's thesis as to the inherently establishment nature of the judiciary as a body is a moot point, but it certainly caused Lord Woolf to question the wisdom of using members of the senior judiciary in such situations. In a *New Statesman* journal interview in February 2004, the Lord Chief Justice was quoted as disapproving of the present system. He said, 'In America they are not keen on judges doing this sort of thing', and that inquiries conducted by non-judges 'might be a better way of doing it'.

It could, once again, only be the unwonted, not to say hostile, publicity that led the Lord Chief Justice to such a conclusion: a conclusion that might suggest that judges should not be seen to be meddling in the political arena, but might also carry the implication that what is wrong is not so much the interference in itself, as the being seen to be interfering.

4.11 Politics and the Judiciary

Law is an inherently and inescapably political process. Even assertions as to the substantive autonomy of law (see Chapter 1) merely disguise the fact that, in making legal decisions, judges decide where the weight of public approval is to be placed and which forms of behaviour are to be sanctioned (see, for example, *R v Brown* (1993), where the House of Lords criminalised the sexual activities of consenting sado-masochists, arguably without fully comprehending some aspects of what was going on).

There is, however, an increasingly apparent tendency for contemporary judges to become actively, directly and openly engaged in more overtly political activity. The 1955 Kilmuir rules, named after the Lord Chancellor who introduced them, were designed to control the instances when the judiciary could express opinion in the media. The rules were abrogated in 1987 by Lord Mackay and, since then, the judiciary have been more forthcoming in expressing their views, not just on matters strictly related to their judicial functions but also on wider political matters.

4.11.1 Sentencing policy

It is surely only correct that judges should be free to express views in areas where they have particular experience and expertise. However, even there, the judges can come into direct political confrontation with the policies of elected representatives. An example of this process can be cited in the concerted action of the judiciary in response to the pronouncements of the then Home Secretary, Michael Howard, at the Conservative Party Conference in Autumn 1993, in which he asserted the success of prison as a means of dealing with crime and declared his commitment to sending more offenders to prison. First of all, Lord Woolf, architect of the government's prison reform programme and who was conducting an investigation into the operation of the whole civil law process, responded by making reference to:

> ... a fashion, not confined to the totally uninformed, to indulge in rhetoric advocating increased sentences across the board in a way which will be counter productive ...

He was quoted in *The Guardian* newspaper as stating that such talk was 'shortsighted and irresponsible'.

Perhaps the really surprising aspect of this difference of opinion was not that Lord Woolf disagreed with the Home Secretary, but that he was supported in his views by seven other judges in a series of interviews in *The Observer* (17 October 1993), including the then Law Lord, Lord Ackner, and the chairman of the JSB, Lord Justice Farquharson.

A similar scenario was replayed in February 2001, following a speech to the Social Market Foundation by the then new Labour Home Secretary, Jack Straw, in which he announced the need to target the 100,000 most persistent criminal offenders and to punish them by imprisonment. As he put it:

> Almost without exception, every persistent offender sentenced to custody has been through the mill of community sentences and has still reoffended ... If we are to get on top of this problem of persistent criminality and to process more through the system prison numbers may well have to rise.

Within hours, Lord Woolf, by now the Lord Chief Justice but still as committed to prison reform as he ever was, had responded extremely strongly. In a lecture to the Prison Reform Trust, he stated that overcrowding was the 'AIDS virus of the prison system' and went on to express his view, totally at odds with that of the Home Secretary, that:

> The judiciary must play their part in reducing the use of custody to what is the acceptable and appropriate minimum. When a custodial sentence is necessary the shortest sentence ... should be imposed. Frequently one month will achieve everything that can be achieved by three months and three months will achieve everything that can

be by six months and so on ... What has to be realised, and I include the government here, is that a short custodial sentence is a very poor alternative to a sentence to be served in the community. It is far more expensive. It will do nothing to tackle the offender's behavioural problems. It should be regarded as being no more than a necessary evil whose primary purpose is to obtain compliance with court orders.

Another instance of Lord Woolf's continued and controversial influence over sentencing policy arose towards the end of 2002. In November of that year, the government announced its Criminal Justice Bill, which it claimed would 'rebalance the system in favour of victims, witnesses and communities and deliver justice for all, by building greater trust and credibility while protecting the rights of the innocent'. Or, in the Prime Minister's sound bite, it was designed to create a 'victim justice system' rather than the present 'criminal justice system'. However in December, in *R v McInerney* (2002), Lord Woolf took the opportunity to restate sentencing policy in relation to burglary. Sitting with Mr Justice Silber and Mr Justice Grigson, he ruled that the average first time, non-professional and non-violent domestic burglar should receive a community punishment rather than be sentenced to a period of imprisonment. Consequently, the previous sentencing 'starting point' of up to 18 months in prison should no longer apply.

Lord Woolf recommended that the initial approach of the courts should be to impose a community sentence, so long as it was an effective punishment that would tackle the offender's underlying problems such as drug addiction. If, and only if, the court was satisfied that the offender had demonstrated by their behaviour that punishment in the community was not practicable should the court resort to a custodial sentence.

The new approach, and its subsequent support by the Lord Chancellor, was severely attacked in the tabloid press and by some politicians as being soft on crime and out of touch with the views of ordinary people. One Labour MP, Graham Allen, was quoted as saying that:

> We should not let burglars think that the first one is free ... I am rather surprised that the Lord Chief Justice has issued this ruling ahead of consideration of the House of Commons for sentencing in general. Is it appropriate that he can make this sort of decision, which is completely disengaged from the reality of people's lives on council estates and other parts of the country?

In the light of the attack, and some allegations that he had tried to slip it out unnoticed in the run up to Christmas, Lord Woolf took the unusual step of emailing all circuit judges and Chairmen of Magistrates' Benches in England and Wales on 23 December 2002. In his message, he stated that the new approach:

> ... is consistent with the repeated advice you have received only to resort to imprisonment when necessary and then to make the punishment as short as possible. The guidance makes clear that if the court is satisfied that the offender has demonstrated by his behaviour, that punishment in the community is not practical then there is to be a custodial sentence. As to when a community sentence is not practical the judgment recognises that the only guidance that the court can give is to say that a community

sentence may not be appropriate because of the effect of the offence on the victim, the nature of the offence or the offender's record. The guidance is intended to reduce the use of imprisonment but only if this is consistent with the protection of the public. It also makes clear that if appropriate, heavy sentences are to be imposed.

4.11.2 The politics of judicial review and the Human Rights Act

As has been stated, the HRA merely heightened the potential for conflict between the judges and the executive and Parliament, but the relationship was already subject to some tension as a consequence of the operation of judicial review, as can be seen in a number of cases.

In *M v Home Office* (1993), the House of Lords decided that the court has jurisdiction in judicial review proceedings to grant interim and final injunctions against officers of the Crown, and to make a finding of contempt of court against a government department or a minister of the Crown in either his personal *or his official capacity*.

M v Home Office is of signal importance in establishing the powers of the courts in relation to the executive. It is also interesting to note that in delivering the leading speech, Lord Woolf quoted extensively from, and clearly supported, Dicey's view of the Rule of Law as involving the subjection of all, including State officials, to the ordinary law of the land (see Chapter 1).

In November 1994, the government suffered two damaging blows from the judiciary. In *R v Secretary of State for Foreign Affairs ex p World Development Movement Ltd* (1995), the Queen's Bench Divisional Court held that the Secretary of State had acted beyond his powers in granting aid to the Malaysian government in relation to the Pergau Dam project. The financial assistance was given, not for the promotion of development *per se*, as authorised by s 1 of the Overseas Development and Co-operation Act 1980, but in order to facilitate certain arms sales. As Rose LJ stated:

> Whatever the Secretary of State's intention or purpose may have been, it is, as it seems to me, a matter for the courts and not for the Secretary of State to determine whether, on the evidence before the court, the particular conduct was, or was not, within the statutory purpose.

In *R v Secretary of State for the Home Department ex p Fire Brigades Union* (1995), the Court of Appeal held that the Home Secretary had committed an abuse of power in implementing a scheme designed to cut the level of payments made to the subjects of criminal injuries. The court held that he was under an obligation, under the CJA 1988, to put the previous non-statutory scheme on a statutory basis. It was not open for the Secretary of State to use his prerogative powers to introduce a completely new tariff scheme contrary to the intention of Parliament as expressed in the CJA 1988. The decision of the Court of Appeal was confirmed by a 3:2 majority in the House of Lords in April 1995, the majority holding that the Secretary of State had exceeded or abused powers granted to him by Parliament. It is of interest to note that in his minority judgment Lord Keith warned that to dismiss the Home Secretary's appeal would be:

… an unwarrantable intrusion into the political field and a usurpation of the function of Parliament.

In 1997, in *R v Secretary of State for the Home Department ex p Venables and Thompson*, the House of Lords decided that the Home Secretary had misused his powers in relation to two juveniles who had been sentenced to detention during Her Majesty's pleasure.

Even Lord Chancellors have not escaped the unwanted control of judicial review, and in March 1997, John Witham successfully argued that the Lord Chancellor had exceeded his statutory powers in removing exemptions from court fees for those in receipt of State income support. The exemptions had been removed as part of a wider measure to increase court income by raising fee levels, but Lord Justice Rose and Mr Justice Laws held that Lord Mackay had exceeded the statutory powers given to him by Parliament. Rose LJ stated that there was nothing to suggest that Parliament ever intended 'a power for the Lord Chancellor to prescribe fees so as to preclude the poor from access to the courts'. Laws J on the other hand stated that: 'Access to the courts is a constitutional right; it can only be denied by the government if it persuades Parliament to pass legislation which specifically permits the executive to turn people away. That has not been done in this case' (*R v Lord Chancellor ex p Witham* (1997)).

The change of government in 1997 did nothing to stem the flow of judicial review cases, with the occasional embarrassing defeat for the executive. Thus, in *R v Secretary of State for Education and Employment ex p National Union of Teachers* (2000), the Divisional Court held that the Secretary of State for Education had exceeded his statutory powers in seeking to alter teachers' contracts of employment, particularly by introducing threshold standards in relation to a new scheme of performance related pay. He had sought to introduce the changes in the Education (School Teachers' Pay and Conditions) (No 2) Order 2000 after only four days' consultation with the trade union. The court held that although the Secretary of State had the statutory powers to alter the contracts of employment under the Teachers' Pay and Conditions Act 1991, he had not adopted the correct procedure for doing so as set out in that Act. Consequently, the Education (School Teachers' Pay and Conditions) (No 2) Order was quashed. Although this decision represented a victory for the Union and an embarrassment for the Secretary of State, it was only temporary in nature and the new contracts were subsequently introduced following the proper statutory procedure.

Given his centrality in the operation of the criminal justice system and immigration, it is hardly surprising that the Home Secretary is subject to more claims for judicial review than any other minister, nor is it surprising that some of them go against him. In relation to his role in the criminal justice system, *R v Secretary of State for the Home Department ex p Tawfick* (2000) is of particular interest, in that it involved issues relating to judicial summing up and compensation for imprisonment following wrongful conviction.

The CJA 1988 introduced compensation as of right in particular and limited instances where people have been wrongly imprisoned. Prior to that, the Home

Secretary had a discretionary power to make *ex gratia* payments to such people and he retained that power in relation to cases that do not come under the CJA 1988. These discretionary payments may be made to the victim, or their family where appropriate, in 'exceptional circumstances'. The question is what amounts to 'exceptional circumstances'? An *ex gratia* payment was made to the family of Derek Bentley, who had been hanged for murder in 1953. Bentley's conviction had been referred to the Court of Appeal by the Criminal Cases Review Commission (CCRC), and his conviction was quashed as unsafe on the basis that the judge in his trial had given a summing up 'such as to deny Bentley that fair trial which is the right of every British citizen' (Lord Bingham, *R v Bentley* (1998)).

In *R v Secretary of State for the Home Department ex p Tawfick*, the Divisional Court was asked to review the Home Secretary's refusal to make a discretionary payment to the claimant. Tawfick had been found guilty of conspiracy to steal and handling stolen goods. He had already served five months in prison before the Court of Appeal quashed his conviction on the grounds that the trial judge had:

> ... allowed himself to be drawn into making observations which would in all probability have led the jury to regard the appellant as a liar.

Tawfick applied for compensation and was refused. He then successfully sought judicial review of the Home Secretary's decision but, again on reconsideration, the Home Secretary refused to make a compensation award. Subsequent to the decision to award compensation to Bentley's family, Tawfick sought a further judicial review and this time the court held that the circumstances of his case were of such an exceptional nature as to warrant payment, and that the Home Secretary had fallen into error by using the extreme circumstances of the *Bentley* case as the benchmark for making discretionary awards.

R v Secretary of State for the Home Department ex p Adan and Others (2001) considered the Home Secretary's role in relation to asylum applications. These cases concerned three applicants, two of whom had previously been refused asylum in Germany and one of whom had previously been refused asylum in France. On being refused asylum in those countries, the three had made their way to the UK and had applied for, and been refused, asylum there. The question at issue was whether the three could be returned to the countries in which they had first applied for asylum, as the Home Office had ordered. The argument for the claimants was that, whereas both Germany and France only considered those who fled 'State' persecution as coming within the definition of refugees under the Geneva Convention for the Protection of Refugees 1951, the UK recognised that persecution by 'non-State' agents could provide grounds for refugee status. All three claimed to have been subjected to 'non-State' persecution and that to return them to Germany and France would lead to their being sent back to their own States, contrary to the principles of the Geneva Convention and s 2(2) of the Asylum and Immigration Act 1996, which required that they be returned to 'safe' third countries.

The Divisional Court originally held that the applicants could be returned to Germany and France, as these were both safe countries within the meaning of the Asylum and Immigration Act. However, both the Court of Appeal and later the House of Lords held that Germany and France were not to be considered 'safe third countries' for the purposes of s 2(2) of the Asylum and Immigration Act 1996; consequently, the applicants could not be deported to either of those countries.

It can be seen from the foregoing that judicial review provided the judiciary with the means for addressing the potential for abuse that followed on from the growth of discretionary power in the hands of the modern State, particularly if it was operated on the basis of the doctrine of proportionality. Alongside the growth in the number of applications, there were also indications that at least some of the higher judiciary saw it as part of their function to exercise such control over the executive. For example, the former Master of the Rolls and former Lord Chief Justice, Lord Bingham, was quoted in *The Observer* newspaper of 9 May 1993 as saying that:

> Slowly, the constitutional balance is tilting towards the judiciary. The courts have reacted to the increase in powers claimed by the government by being more active themselves.

Judicial review is a delicate exercise and by necessity draws the judiciary into the political arena, using the word 'political' in its widest, non-party sense. That the judges were aware of this is evident from the words of Lord Woolf in the same article. As he recognised:

> Judicial review is all about balance: between the rights of the individual and his need to be treated fairly, and the rights of government at local and national level to do what it has been elected to do. There is a very sensitive and political decision to be made.

However, another former Law Lord, Lord Browne-Wilkinson, observed on a BBC radio programme, admittedly before his elevation to the House of Lords, that a great void was apparent in the political system, deriving from the fact that no government had a true popular majority and yet all governments were able to carry Parliament in support of anything they wanted. He went on to express the view that Parliament was not a place where it was easy to get accountability for abuse or misuse of powers. According to Lord Browne- Wilkinson, while judicial review could not overcome the will of Parliament, judges had a special role because *democracy was defective*. He then asked a rhetorical question as to who else but the judges could ensure that executive action is taken in accordance with law, *and not abused by increasingly polarised political stances*.

Such thinking is also evident in an article by Mr Justice Stephen Sedley (as he was then) in the May 1995 edition of the *London Review of Books*, in which he asserted that after decades of passivity, there is a new 'culture of judicial assertiveness to compensate for, and in places repair, dysfunctions in the democratic process', and that the last three decades of the 20th century may have seen the UK constitution being re-fashioned by judges 'with sufficient popular support to mute political opposition'.

The introduction of the HRA greatly increased judicial power in relation to the other two branches of the constitution, and it might have been thought that the judges would not have been reluctant to use their new powers. However, as was also seen in that section, the courts, and the Court of Appeal and the House of Lords in particular, have been reluctant to use their new powers in a radical manner. As Lord Irvine expressed it in his inaugural Human Rights Lecture at the University of Durham:

> It is all about balance. The balance between intense judicial scrutiny and reasonable deference to elected decision-makers is a delicate one to strike. But the judiciary have struck it well: and I welcome that. Whilst scrutiny is undoubtedly an important aid to better governance, there are areas in which decisions are best taken by the decision-makers entrusted by Parliament to make them. This may be for reasons of democratic accountability, expertise or complexity.

The former Lord Chancellor may well be of the view that the judges have got it right, but his views do not sound in harmony with those of his ex-colleague, the current Home Secretary, David Blunkett, who has been a consistent source of attack on the judiciary. Perhaps his most severe attack came after Collins J's decision in *R (on the Application of Q) v Secretary of State for the Home Department* (2003), which declared unlawful his power under s 55 of the Nationality, Immigration and Asylum Act 2002 to refuse to provide assistance to those who had not immediately declared their intention to claim asylum when they arrived in the UK. In the press, the Home Secretary was quoted as saying: 'Frankly, I am fed up with having to deal with a situation where Parliament debates issues and judges then overturn them. We were aware of the circumstances, we did mean what we said and, on behalf of the British people, we are going to implement it.'

Of even more concern were the reports that the Prime Minister was 'prepared for a showdown with the judiciary to stop the courts thwarting government's attempts to curb the record flow of asylum seekers into Britain', and that he was looking into the possibility of enacting legislation to limit the role of judges in the interpretation of international human rights obligations and re-assert the primacy of Parliament. There were even reports that the Prime Minister was considering withdrawing completely from the ECHR, rather than merely issuing derogations where it was thought necessary.

Given such pressure, it is perhaps not surprising that when the Court of Appeal heard the *Q* case, whilst it supported Collins J's decision, it went out of its way to provide the Home Secretary with advice on how to make the Act, and the procedures under it, compatible with ECHR rights. It is suggested that those who celebrated the decision as leaving the government's asylum policy 'in tatters' failed to fully appreciate its consequences. Certainly for once, the Home Secretary did not react with antagonism to the Court of Appeal's decision; rather he welcomed it as 'helpfully clarifying the law' and stated that he would not be taking the case to the House of Lords.

In an article in *The Guardian* newspaper in November 2001, the commentator Hugo Young expressed his puzzlement about the Home Secretary's behaviour as follows:

The judges have not been immune to the demands of the security state. Given what they are sometimes prepared to do to assist the executive, it is not easy to understand why Blunkett has marked his tenure by regularly casting aspersions on them.

It might not be too cynical to suggest that the continued favourable outcome is the justification for the continued attack. It might even not be overly cynical to suggest that the senior judiciary have been extremely circumspect in actually using their new powers, and have not been willing to use them to the extent they might have under other circumstances, when they have been generally accepted by both Parliament and the public. In April 2003, Lord Irvine entered the dispute when he offered an implicit, if no doubt stinging, criticism of the Home Secretary in his appearance before the select committee on the LCD. As he stated:

> When the judiciary gives decisions that the executive does not like, as in all governments, some ministers have spoken out against ... [them] ... I disapprove of that. I think it undermines the rule of law.

Not long after that statement, Lord Irvine was no longer Lord Chancellor, replaced by Lord Falconer, but David Blunkett remained as Home Secretary. It has been suggested that many of the fears amongst the senior judiciary in relation to the proposal in the Constitutional Reform Bill reflected a distrust of the Home Secretary and a lack of confidence in Lord Falconer's power to withstand his anti-judicial rhetoric and pressure.

Still, as Lord Woolf recognised in a speech to the Royal Academy, which linked the HRA, judicial review and the rule of law, the possibility of a major confrontation between the judges and the executive still remains:

> Just as the development of judicial review in the final quarter of last century improved administration in our increasingly complex society, so will the existence of the [HRA] protect our individual interests, which are so easily lost sight of in meeting the demands of the global economy. The real test of the [HRA] arises when individuals or minorities attract the antagonism of the majority of the public. When the tabloids are in full cry. Then, the courts must, without regard for their own interests, make the difficult decisions that ensure that those under attack have the benefit of the rule of law. At the heart of the [HRA] is the need to respect the dignity of every individual by ensuring he or she is not subject to discrimination.

The fact that the judges increasingly see it as incumbent upon them to use judicial review and the HRA as the means of questioning and controlling what they see as the abuse of executive power does, at the very least, raise very serious questions in relation to their suitability for such a role. These doubts can be set out in terms of:

- *Competence*

  This refers to the question whether the judges are sufficiently competent to participate in deciding the substantive issues that they have been invited to consider under the guise of judicial review, and may be entitled to consider under the HRA. Judges are experts in law; they are not experts in the various and highly specialised areas of policy that by definition tend to be involved in judicial review cases. They may disagree with particular decisions, but it has to be at least doubted that they are qualified to take such policy decisions. A classic example of this difficulty was the 'fares' fair' cases (*Bromley London BC v GLC* (1983) and later, *R v London Transport Executive ex p GLC* (1983)), in which the courts got involved in deciding issues relating to transport policy for London on the pretext that they were judicially defining the meaning of particular words in a statute. As was considered in Chapter 5, the apparently technocratic, and hence neutral, application of rules of interpretation simply serves to disguise a political procedure and, in these cases, the policy issue concerned was certainly beyond the scope of the judges to determine. In *Bellinger v Bellinger* (2003), the House of Lords, although obviously sympathetic to the case, admitted their incompetence as regards deciding issues relating to the rights of transsexuals. For that reason, they issued a declaration of incompatibility under the HRA 1998 and thus passed the matter to Parliament for review and appropriate reform.

- *Constitutionality*

This refers to the wider point that the separation of powers applies equally to the judiciary as it does to the executive. In interfering with substantive decisions and involving themselves in political matters, albeit on the pretence of merely deciding points of law, the judiciary may be seen to be exceeding their constitutional powers. It has to be remembered that judges are unelected and unaccountable.

- *Partiality*

This refers to the possibility of individual, and indeed corporate, bias within the judiciary.

The foregoing has indicated that the relationship between the State and the courts may, on occasion, involve a measure of tension, with the courts attempting to rein in the activities of the State. The relationship between the judiciary and the executive is well summed up in the words of Lord Justice Farquharson, again taken from an *Observer* article:

> We have to be very careful: the executive is elected. We have a role in the Constitution but, if we go too far, there will be a reaction. The Constitution only works if the different organs trust each other. If the judges start getting too frisky, there would be retaliation, renewed attempts to curb the judiciary.

Although no longer in force, the Kilmuir rules did have a valid point to make:

> ... the overriding consideration ... is the importance of keeping the judiciary in this country isolated from the controversies of the day. So long as a judge keeps silent, his reputation for wisdom and impartiality remains unassailable; but every utterance which he makes in public ... must necessarily bring him within the focus of criticism.

THE JUDICIARY

The Constitutional Role of the Judiciary

Judges play a central role in the English constitution. The doctrine of the separation of powers maintains that the judicial function be kept distinct from the legislative and executive functions of the State. Prior to the Constitutional Reform Act 2005, the Lord Chancellor filled an anomalous situation in this respect, as he was at one and the same time – the most senior member of the judiciary and could hear cases in the House of Lords as a court, a member of the legislature as speaker of the House of Lords as a legislative assembly and a member of the executive holding a position in the government.

The Constitutional Reform Act

This Act is one of the most significant pieces of legislation affecting many aspects of the constitution, but particularly addressing issues relating to the role and appointment of the judiciary.

The Act was introduced by the government to inspire transparency, openness and greater public confidence in Britain's constitution. Its major provisions are:

- government ministers should be under a statutory duty to uphold the independence of the judiciary and specifically bar them from trying to influence judicial decisions through any special access to judges.

- the reform of the post of Lord Chancellor and the transfer of his judicial functions to President of the Courts of England and Wales who is to be the Lord Chief Justice, currently Lord Phillips, who replaced Lord Woolf in October 2005. In this new position he will be responsible for the training, guidance and deployment of judges. He will also be responsible for representing the views of the judiciary of England and Wales to Parliament and ministers.

- the establishment of a new, independent Supreme Court, separate from the House of Lords. The newly constituted Supreme Court will have its own independent appointments system, its own staff and budget. It will eventually have its own building, although for the present it is likely that the new court will continue to occupy its present place within the House of Lords, until its new building has been refurbished.

- the 12 judges of the Supreme Court will be known as Justices of the Supreme Court and will no longer be allowed to sit as members of the House of Lords. The current

Law Lords will become the first 12 Justices of the Supreme Court, with Lord Bingham as President of the Supreme Court.

- the establishment of a new system of appointing judges, independent of the patronage of politicians. Appointments will be solely on the basis of merit, and solely on the recommendation of the newly constituted Judicial Appointments Commission.

Training of the Judiciary

Training of English judges is undertaken under the auspices of the Judicial Studies Board. Judges from the highest Law Lord to the lowest magistrate are subject to training. It is gratifying to note that anti-discriminatory training is a priority, although some have continued to express doubts about judicial attitudes in this regard. Special training has been instituted in relation to the Woolf reforms and the introduction of the HRA. This being said, it remains arguable that the training undergone by UK judges is not as rigorous as the training of judges on the Continent.

Removal of Judges

Senior judges hold office subject to good behaviour. They can be removed by an address by the two Houses of Parliament.

Judges below High Court status can be removed on grounds of misbehaviour or incapacity and the Lord Chancellor can remove magistrates without the need to show cause.

Judicial Immunity

To ensure judicial integrity, it is provided that judges cannot be sued for actions done or words said in the course of their judicial function.

This immunity extends to trial lawyers, witnesses and juries.

Magistrates

Magistrates have powers in relation to both criminal and civil law.

Stipendiary magistrates, now District Judges (Magistrates' Courts) are professional and are legally qualified.

Lay magistrates are not paid and they are not legally qualified.

Magistrates are appointed by the Lord Chancellor.

Important issues relate to the representative nature of the magistracy.

Politics of the Judiciary

Judges have a capacity to make law. The question is do they exercise this power in a biased way? Bias can take two forms: personal and corporate.

Accusations of corporate bias suggest that, as a group, judges represent the interest of the status quo and decide certain political cases in line with that interest.

THE CRIMINAL LAW

5.1 The General Principles of Criminal Liability

5.1.1 The nature and sources of criminal law

Criminal law obviously concerns crime, but what is a crime? There is a view that it is impossible to identify a universal definition of the nature of a crime because the essence of criminality changes with historical context. As Glanville Williams has observed:

> ... a crime (or offence) is a legal wrong that can be followed by criminal proceedings which may result in punishment [*Learning the Law*, 1983, p 27].

In other words, a crime is anything that the State has chosen to criminalise. A similar analysis was adopted by Lord Atkin:

> ... the domain of criminal jurisprudence can only be ascertained by examining what acts at any particular period are declared by the State to be crimes, and the only common nature they will be found to possess is that they are prohibited by the State and that those who commit them are punished [*Proprietary Articles Trade Association v AG for Canada* [1931] AC 324].

One way to escape the circularity of these definitions of crime is to refer to the seriousness of the wrongs. Thus, Williams eventually concedes that:

> ... a crime is an act that is condemned sufficiently strongly to have induced the authorities (legislature or judges) to declare it to be punishable before the ordinary courts [*Learning the Law*, 1983, p 29].

In an early edition of the leading theoretical text *Criminal Law* (1992), Smith and Hogan acknowledge the view of Sir Carleton Allen, who writes as follows:

> ... crime is crime because it consists in wrongdoing which directly and in serious degree threatens the security or well being of society, and because it is not safe to leave it redressable only by compensation of the party injured [p 16].

There are about 7,500 criminal offences in English law. They range from the most minor traffic offences (for example, driving a vehicle with one of the rear break lights not working) to genocide (criminalised under the Genocide Act 1969). These different criminal offences have no common denominator other than that they are things which the State has, for different reasons and at different times, decided are sufficiently serious to warrant being treated as crimes.

Much of the criminal law is now to be found in statutes, though there are a number of offences (murder and manslaughter, for example) and defences (such as automatism, intoxication and duress) which depend largely upon decisions of the courts and have not been reduced into statutory form. There is certainly no all-embracing code of criminal law, even though proposals for codification were made as long ago as the 19th century. The Law Commission has revived attempts to devise a Code and has been publishing proposals since 1989, but they have not yet been enacted.

5.1.2   Classification of crimes

There are a number of ways of classifying crimes. The more common ways of doing so include the follwing:

• by source – crimes may be treated as common law or as statutory offences, although today more and more crimes are regulated by statute;

• by method of trial – summary, indictable and triable either way;

• by reference to the powers of arrest – whether they are arrestable or non-arrestable;

• by whether they can be regarded as 'true' crimes or merely as 'regulatory' crimes – this classification may be of some value in considering whether a crime should be regarded as imposing strict liability.

5.1.3   The elements of criminal liability

It is generally argued that criminal liability consists of three components:

(1) the *actus reus* – some 'conduct' by D accompanied by the existence of legally relevant 'circumstances'. For many offences, it will also be necessary to show that the conduct 'caused' certain 'consequences'. These are the external elements of an offence and, in the traditional terminology, they comprise the *actus reus* of the offence. For example, D elbows V in the face. V is a police constable on duty. This is the *actus reus* of assaulting (meaning here a battery) a police constable in the execution of his duty. The conduct is the elbowing, the consequence is that force is inflicted on V and the circumstances are that V was not just any person (which would have made it a common assault) but a police constable acting in the execution of his duty;

(2) the *mens rea* – a blameworthy state of mind in relation to the conduct, circumstances and consequences (that is, to the *actus reus* elements identified above). Traditionally, this blameworthy state of mind is referred to as *mens rea* and encompasses intention, knowledge, recklessness (awareness of risk) and, in very limited cases, recklessness without awareness of risk. In the example above, if D was trying to elbow V in the face, he intended to inflict force. If he knew there was a risk that he would elbow V in the face (if, for instance, he had his back to V and swung his elbow back in V's direction to keep him away), he was reckless as to the infliction of force;

(3) the absence of any defence, whether general or specific, total or partial, which D could plead to avoid liability. In the example previously discussed, suppose that V was not wearing a uniform and that D thought V was an ordinary member of the public who was about to attack him. He would be entitled to use reasonable force to defend himself. So, D might avoid liability for elbowing V in the face (the issues of mistake and self-defence are discussed in 5.2).

5.1.3.1   *The* actus reus

It will be clear from the discussion above that the *actus reus* of a crime is not merely any act by D:

- criminal liability does not always require proof of an act. In some situations, an omission to act will suffice. This is why the broader term 'conduct' is used in discussing *actus reus*. For example, D will usually kill by an act such as beating, shooting or stabbing, but he may do so by withholding food from someone who is helpless. This is an omission;

- it is also usual to qualify 'conduct' by asserting that it must be 'voluntary', that is, it is at least in part the product of control by the conscious brain. So, 'voluntariness' is another element in the *actus reus* of crimes. If D is feeling a little unwell and clumsily breaks a vase on sale in a shop, he is probably still acting voluntarily because he has some conscious control of his movements. If, instead, he had received a severe blow to the head moments before he broke the vase, it may be that he was not acting voluntarily because he was concussed;

- it includes any elements appearing in the definition of the crime which are neither conduct nor consequences. These elements are generally termed 'circumstances'. As explained above, in the offence of assaulting a police constable in the execution of his duty, V must have two special characteristics: he must be a police constable; and he must be performing his duty. These are 'circumstances' to be proved, as required by the definition of the crime;

- the *actus reus* of many crimes will incorporate a required 'consequence' which must be 'caused' by D's conduct. If D kicks out at V, he will only commit the *actus reus* of inflicting grievous bodily harm if the kick lands on V and causes him serious injury. D may miss with his kick, or he may kick V and cause him only minor injury. In either case, there will be no offence of inflicting grievous bodily harm (though there may be an offence of attempt).

A general way of expressing all of this might be to say that the *actus reus* of a crime consists of all those elements which cannot be described as part of the *mens rea*.

Conduct

Criminal liability generally depends upon proof that D engaged in some act. If we think about crimes such as murder, causing grievous bodily harm with intent and theft, we envisage acts such as shooting, stabbing, kicking or punching V, or stealthily removing V's wallet from his pocket or taking items from a shop. Most of us grow up accepting the idea that we are forbidden from doing some things, however much we might want to do them. We absorb notions of prohibition and punishment from an early age and so are familiar with the general structure of criminal law and criminal justice. So, criminal liability based on the prohibition of acts creates no special problems.

By contrast, we find it difficult to envisage the factual situations in which the common crimes may be committed by failures to act (that is, omissions). How is it possible to say, for instance, that D killed V by not doing something? If D fails to help V who has been knocked down by a hit-and-run driver and is bleeding to death, how does that failure *cause* V's death? To believe that D could be responsible, we have to persuade ourselves that he ought to have intervened. But, however much we might feel morally obliged to help others, we are not accustomed to thinking that there is a general legal obligation to do so. In any case, what exactly would D be required to do, and would the same obligation be placed on every other bystander who was aware of V's injuries? Would all of them be prosecuted if they failed to help? If so, then the criminal justice system might be overwhelmed. If not, selective prosecution might bring the system into disrepute.

On the other hand, there are some situations in which we have no difficulty in regarding others as responsible for harmful consequences when they fail to act. A parent is expected to be vigilant for the health and safety of the child. A swimming pool supervisor is expected to act to ensure the safety of swimmers. The difference between the witness to the hit-and-run and the parent or supervisor is easy to see. Nothing marks out the witness to the accident from any other witness. The law would have to recognise a very broad obligation to help others, applicable to everyone, in order to impose liability on him (though some countries do recognise obligations of this kind). To impose liability on the parent or supervisor, however, is to recognise an obligation grounded in a pre-existing relationship between parent and child, or supervisor and swimmer, into which parent and supervisor have entered (more or less) freely. It does not imply that anyone else is under the obligation.

Liability for omissions to act, then, requires the following:

(a) The crime must be defined in such a way that it makes sense to say that an omission will suffice. For instance, though D will usually 'cause' grievous bodily harm by doing acts such as kicking and punching, he could also do so by failing to warn V that he is about to suffer the injury. Similarly, D could destroy or damage property by failing to put out a fire. Where a statute imposes an obligation to do something, then obviously the liability is defined in terms of an omission, for example, the obligation of a driver to stop and give certain information after being involved in an accident which resulted in personal injury or damage to property (s 170 of the Road Traffic Act 1988).

If the definition uses the word 'act', it is unlikely that an omission will suffice. So, an attempt to commit a crime requires proof of 'an act more than merely preparatory' to the commission of the full offence (s 1(1) of the Criminal Attempts Act 1981). In *Lowe* (1973), it was held that 'unlawful act manslaughter' can only be committed by an act.

In some instances, it remains unclear whether an act is required or an omission will suffice. An assault occurs when D causes V to fear the infliction of immediate personal injury. A battery is constituted by the infliction of the injury. In *Fagan v Metropolitan Police Commissioner* (1968), the court held unanimously that both assault and battery require proof of an act but, in *DPP v K* (1990), there were suggestions that an assault occasioning actual bodily harm could be committed by an omission.

(b) It must be proven that D was under a duty to do some positive act. A duty generally arises out of a relationship created, at least in part, by D's own conduct. The major examples are:

- *parental, family or equivalent.* Parents have statutory obligations to their children and there is a specific crime of neglect of a child (s 1 of the Children and Young Persons Act 1933). In *Gibbins and Proctor* (1918), D1 was convicted of the murder of his child, V, from whom food had been withheld by D2, D1's partner. In *Stone and Dobinson* (1977), even though D1 was 67 years old and V was 61, D1 was considered to be under a duty to care for V, partly because he was her brother (see below for a fuller account of this case);

- *contractual, especially employment.* Entering into a contract to perform a particular job can create a duty on the employee to both the employer and any other person who is at risk of injury or damage in the performance of that job. In *Pittwood* (1902), a level crossing keeper employed by a railway company to open and close the gates was guilty of manslaughter when he forgot to close the gates on the approach of a train and a person crossing the line was killed;

- *voluntary assumption of responsibility by D.* This is a rather controversial category, best illustrated by reference to *Stone and Dobinson*, already briefly mentioned above. V, who was anorexic, had become bedridden and had died from infected bedsores whilst living with D1 and D2. It was held that D1 and D2 had assumed responsibility for V by intervening to clean her at an earlier stage, and so were guilty of manslaughter for failing to get help for her when her condition deteriorated again;

- *the deliberate or accidental creation of a dangerous situation by D.* If D's conduct creates a danger to persons or property, he must do something to eliminate or reduce the danger. He is under this duty even if he was not initially at fault. In *Miller* (1983), D fell asleep whilst smoking a cigarette and set light to a mattress. When he woke up, he simply went off to another room and fell asleep again whilst the fire caused further damage. His initial conduct in falling asleep created the dangerous situation and thus imposed a duty on him to put the fire out or raise the alarm. His failure to do so made him guilty of criminal damage;

- *a public office.* There is a common law offence of misconduct in a public office. A police constable is the holder of a public office and he is under a duty, amongst other things, to preserve the Queen's peace, to prevent crime and to apprehend suspected offenders. The court in *Dytham* (1979) upheld the conviction of a police constable for this offence, on evidence that he had witnessed an attack outside a nightclub and had deliberately taken no action to stop V being beaten to death.

(c) The omission to act must amount to a breach of the duty.

(d) If the crime is a result crime, then it must be possible to argue that, if D had acted in fulfilment of his duty, the consequence might not have occurred. In that sense, the breach must be a legal cause of the consequence. For example, suppose that a carer did not seek help for a patient who had suddenly suffered a heart attack. If the evidence showed that the heart attack was so severe that the patient would have died no matter what treatment had been administered, then the failure to seek help did not cause the death.

Voluntariness

There can be no criminal liability in any offence requiring proof of conduct unless D's conduct was voluntary. Suppose that D slips on ice which he could not reasonably have known was there and slides into V, causing her injury. D's conduct was involuntary, and so he did not commit the *actus reus* of any personal injury offence. In this case, D was not suffering from any impaired consciousness, but issues of voluntariness more commonly arise where D asserts that his actions were not under the control of his conscious brain, such as where he is suffering from the effects of high or low blood sugar associated with diabetes. In these kinds of cases, the focus is not so much on 'voluntariness' as on 'involuntariness', and the plea is given the special name of automatism. D asserts automatism (that he was an automaton) when he asserts that he was not acting voluntarily. This plea is closely connected with the pleas of insanity and intoxication and is further explained in the analysis of the general defences in 5.2.

Causation

In any crime which requires the proof of a consequence, it will be necessary for the prosecution to prove a causal connection ('causation') between D's conduct and that consequence. In the vast majority of cases, this will present no problems and will be satisfied by proving that the consequence would not have happened 'but for' D's conduct. Suppose that D punches V and knocks him backwards towards a wall. V strikes his head on the wall and suffers a broken skull. If D had not punched V, V would not have suffered the injury, and nothing else can be said to have caused it.

But proof of causation will not be quite so straightforward in some cases, especially in those involving homicide, where there may be a significant gap between any attack by D and the occurrence of V's death (the consequence). The greater the gap, the greater the possibility that D may be able to claim that the true cause of V's death was something that occurred after the attack, such as another injury inflicted by someone else or some very poor medical treatment administered by incompetent doctors. Instead of trying to develop a comprehensive definition of causation, the courts have tended to concentrate on the commonly recurring problems. As a result, analysis has usually focused on the question of what kinds of actions and events break the chain of causation.

In broad terms, to establish that D's conduct caused a consequence, the prosecution must prove that the conduct:

- was a cause *in fact* of the consequence, that is, the consequence would not have occurred but for D's conduct; and

- was a cause *in law* of the consequence, that is, it made a significant contribution to the occurrence of the consequence (other phrases used to express this requirement include 'substantial', 'operating and substantial' and 'proximate').

Causation in fact

It is impossible to establish that D's conduct was a cause in law without first proving that it was a cause in fact. In *White* (1910), D did not cause his mother's death and so was not guilty of murder when the medical evidence showed that she had died of a heart attack rather than from the poison which D had put in her bedtime drink. It was not even established that she took any of the drink. In *Pagett* (1983), on the other hand, D's conduct in kidnapping V and using her as a human shield after he had shot at police officers was certainly a cause in fact of her death when she was killed by return fire from the police officers.

Causation in law

Evidently, there may be many 'causes in fact' of a consequence in the sense indicated above and some further test is necessary to distinguish those which are legally sufficient from those which are not. Expressions such as 'significant contribution' and 'operating and substantial' can do no more than suggest an idea of what is required. They are not formulae into which facts can be fed to unerringly produce the solution. The following points are important in understanding the approach adopted by the courts:

- whatever expression is used, the contribution of D's conduct to the occurrence of the consequence must reach a certain minimum level – it must be more than merely trivial;

- D's conduct need not be the sole cause. This may be particularly important where X's conduct later aggravates the consequences of D's original conduct. Far from breaking the chain of causation between D's conduct and the aggravated consequence, this may merely make both D and X guilty of causing the consequence. For example, there have been cases in which D has inflicted injury on V, who has then died after receiving poor or inadequate medical treatment by doctors. In such cases, it is possible that both D and the doctors can be said to have caused the death. However, it is a big step from that conclusion to the further conclusion that the doctors are actually guilty of a crime; quite rightly, the courts will not be too ready to attribute criminal liability to those who, however imperfectly, were seeking to assist V;

- in the case of death (or any other lesser consequence), if injuries inflicted by D are the immediate and sufficient cause of the consequence (the phrase 'operating and substantial' is often used in this context), then D causes that consequence no matter what has happened after D inflicted the injuries; at best, subsequent actions and events are merely additional causes. In *Smith* (1959), V was stabbed by D in a fight between several soldiers. Subsequently, his friend dragged him roughly to receive treatment from an overworked doctor, who failed to recognise the seriousness of his injuries and administered treatment which certainly did not help V and may have contributed to his death. Prompt and correct treatment, using equipment which was not available to the doctor, might have saved his life. D's act in stabbing V was held to be the 'operating and substantial' cause of his death since he died from the stab wounds, whatever the contribution made by the rough handling and poor treatment;

- if D's conduct has not caused injuries which are 'immediate and sufficient' (in the above sense) at the time that the consequence occurs, there are two possibilities. First, the immediate and sufficient cause may have been some conduct by another person, who may be either the victim or a third person. Second, injuries inflicted by D may be contributing to the consequence but may not be sufficient in themselves to bring it about. In the first case, D can only be said to have caused the consequence if some other principle can be invoked which will sufficiently connect D's conduct with the subsequent conduct of the victim or third person. In the second case, the tendency of the courts is to argue that D's conduct was a legal cause even though it would not have been sufficient in itself;

- the principle applied to connect D's conduct to that of the victim or a third person will often be reasonable foreseeability. Thus, in *Pagett*, D was held to have caused V's death, not only in fact (see above), but also in law. The acts of the police officers in returning fire were considered by the court to be reasonable acts in self-preservation and in performance of their legal duty. They were regarded as comparable with the reasonably foreseeable acts of a victim in attempting to escape from the violence of an attack by D (as in *Pitts* (1842)). However, free and voluntary action by a victim will usually prevent D from being liable for causing the consequence, even if that action was reasonably foreseeable.

It is now possible to examine the approach of the courts to some common instances where causation is in issue.

(a) *Refusal of treatment and / or aggravation of injuries by V*

If D injures V and V makes the injuries worse by neglect or maltreatment of himself, D will nonetheless be held to have caused the injuries. In *Holland* (1841), D was held to have caused V's death when V died from tetanus contracted as a result of a wound to his finger inflicted by D. V's refusal to have the finger amputated as a precaution against tetanus did not break the chain of causation. At that time, V's refusal might not have been unreasonable. Yet, in the more modern case of *Blaue* (1976), it was held that the reasonableness of a refusal of treatment is not relevant to the issue of causation. On account of her religious beliefs, V had refused a blood transfusion which might have saved her life after she had been stabbed by D. D's conviction for manslaughter was upheld. The court asserted that there would be no yardstick by which to measure reasonableness, but their reluctance to look for one might be attributable to the fact that V's refusal was neither malicious nor a mere whim but was grounded in sincerely held religious convictions. The court might have taken a different view if D had refused medical attention on other grounds, for example a moral objection to using drugs tested on animals.

(b) The especially susceptible victim (the 'thin skull' victim)

The general rule is that D must 'take his victim as he finds him'. This means that if, because of some special weakness in V, D causes greater injury to V than would normally have been expected, D will nevertheless be held to have caused the full extent of the injuries. If D hits V on the head in a way which would cause little more than bruising in most victims but V happens to have a weak skull and the blow kills him, D will be held to have caused his death. This rule was relied on in *Blaue*, where it was said that the rule extended to 'the whole man, not just the physical man'. Though V had no physical weakness, she was at special risk because of her religious beliefs.

(c) Injuries resulting from an attempted escape

If V tries to escape from an attack by D and in doing so suffers injury, D causes the injury unless V's actions were not reasonably foreseeable. In applying this rule, allowance has to be made for the fact that those in fear cannot be expected to behave entirely rationally. In *Roberts* (1971), D was held to have caused V's injuries when V jumped from D's car to avoid being sexually assaulted by him. Since the car was travelling at a moderate speed on a deserted road and V had every reason to fear a serious assault, V's actions were reasonably foreseeable. Similarly, in *Corbett* (1996), D caused V's death when V died as a result of stumbling into the path of a motor vehicle while trying to escape from an attack by D. Because of the general rule (noted above) that D 'must take his victim as he finds him', D cannot normally argue that V was excessively nervous and 'overreacted'. On the other hand, D may be able to avoid liability for V's injury if V's behaviour was completely irrational and unforeseeable; *Williams and Davies* (1992) 1 WLR 380.

(d) Negligent, poor or inappropriate medical treatment

Suppose that D injures V, who then receives poor medical treatment. If V suffers more serious injury than might have been expected, or dies, some questions are raised about the medical treatment:

- does it break the chain of causation between D's conduct and V's more serious injury or death, and so free D from liability?

- does it mean that the medical staff caused the injury or death?

- if it does, are the medical staff guilty of a crime?

Generally, negligent, poor or inappropriate treatment does not break the chain of causation. The courts do not apply the rules to such treatment that they use for other intervening acts or events. The question is not about reasonable foreseeability or even whether or not there was negligent or otherwise inappropriate treatment. As was stressed in *Mellor* (1996), the question is whether D's conduct made a significant contribution to the consequence. Negligent or inappropriate treatment will cast doubt on the extent to which D's conduct amounts to a significant contribution *only* if it is of such a kind that the original wound was 'merely the setting in which another cause operates' or where 'the second cause is so overwhelming as to make the original wound merely part of the history' *Smith* (1959).

In *Cheshire* (1991), the rule was expressed in a slightly different way. It was asserted that negligent medical treatment would only break the chain of causation if it was '… so independent of D's acts, and in itself so potent in causing death …' that the contribution made by D's acts in causing death was insignificant. So, even though V's death resulted from undetected complications some weeks after an operation, D was held to have caused his death. The operation and its complications were not causes independent of D's actions; V needed the operation because he had been shot by D. The only significant example of a successful argument that medical treatment broke the chain appears to have been in *Jordan* (1956). In that case, V had substantially recovered from injuries inflicted by D when a hospital doctor administered a drug to which he was known to be intolerant and made intravenous injections of excessive quantities of liquid, with the apparently predictable result that V died from bronchopneumonia.

Even if the chain of causation is not broken, it is possible that negligent or poor medical treatment might be regarded as an additional cause of the injury or death. Yet this would not necessarily mean that medical staff were guilty of an offence. As pointed out earlier, courts will not readily interpret the rules in such a way as to make criminals out of those who are striving to prevent injury or save life.

Circumstances

'Circumstances' is the term used to describe those elements in the definition of the *actus reus* of a crime which are neither conduct nor consequences. In the offence of murder, for instance, the required circumstances are that the victim must be a 'human being' and must be 'within the Queen's peace'.

Consequences

The meaning of 'consequences' will be apparent from earlier discussion. There is no crime of homicide unless V has died. There is no crime of assault occasioning actual bodily harm unless V has suffered some injury amounting to actual bodily harm. Of course, charges of attempt may be available in these cases if the consequence has not occurred. The requirement in many crimes for proof of a consequence inevitably means that there is an element of chance in much criminal liability. Where D beats V, intending serious injury, his liability for murder rather than the lesser offence of causing grievous bodily harm with intent depends upon the chance of V's death occurring, even though D's actions and intentions, and so arguably his blameworthiness, are the same, whatever the outcome.

5.1.3.2 *The* mens rea

In serious crimes of the kind discussed in this chapter, the prosecution will be required to prove that D had the necessary *mens rea*. Regardless of whether a crime is a statutory or a common law crime, the *mens rea* required consists of both the specific requirements of the crime itself and the general common law requirement that there must be proof of intention or recklessness in relation to the *actus reus* elements. In murder, common law prescribes that the unlawful killing must be done with malice aforethought, an intention either to kill or to cause grievous bodily harm. The intention requirement is an expression of the common law demand for proof of a sufficient mental element. So strong is this demand that there is a general common law presumption that all crimes require proof of *mens rea*. Even if no *mens rea* requirement is expressed in the statutory definition of a crime, a court will imply one unless persuaded that the presumption has been rebutted. Crimes which do not require proof of *mens rea* are known as crimes of strict liability.

When used in the sense of the common law presumption, *mens rea* means 'intention' or 'recklessness' as to the elements of the *actus reus*. The meaning of these terms is to be found only in case decisions, even though statutory definitions have been proposed on a number of occasions, most recently by the Law Commission as part of its codification project. These meanings are also applied when the terms are used in statutory crimes. So, at common law, *mens rea* requires proof that D either intended any consequence or knew of the existence of any circumstance, or that D was aware of the risk of causing the consequence or of the existence of the circumstance. Such requirements are generally said to impose a subjective test, because D can be guilty only if he intended or knew or was aware of the risk.

However, in some cases, D can be regarded as blameworthy even if he neither intended nor was reckless in the senses described above. If D does not realise that his car's brakes are not working properly though any reasonable driver would have done so, he may be liable for manslaughter if he crashes his car and kills V. In such a case, his liability will depend upon his failure to meet an objective standard, the standard of the reasonable man. This is liability for negligence. Finally, if D can be liable even though he is not subjectively or objectively blameworthy, then the crime is one of strict liability, and D is sometimes described as liable even though he is blamelessly inadvertent.

Intention

Though most offences can be committed without proof of intention to bring about a particular consequence (recklessness suffices), there are significant exceptions, murder being an obvious example.

We all have a general idea of what it means to intend to cause a particular consequence, and we all have experience of occasions on which our intentions have been fulfilled or have been thwarted. If asked to define intention, we would probably use words and phrases such as 'aim', 'purpose', 'desire', 'wanting to' or 'acting in order to'. In the vast majority of cases, magistrates or juries need no special guidance to enable them to decide whether or not D intended a particular consequence. If, for example, D is charged with causing serious injury and the evidence shows that he repeatedly kicked V about the head whilst V was on the floor, there will be little difficulty in concluding that D intended such injury. D would need to come up with a very convincing story to put reasonable doubt into the mind of any magistrate or juror. In cases where the evidence clearly suggests that it was D's purpose to cause the consequence, the prosecution would not need to show that he foresaw it as likely or probable, only that he genuinely believed that he might be able to achieve it by his conduct.

Nevertheless, there are cases where the evidence may not lead to an unambiguous, common sense answer and guidance may be required. D may aim to cause a particular consequence, which may or may not be criminal, but be prepared to risk a different, prohibited consequence in order to achieve it. Typical examples of this kind are to be found in *Hyam v DPP* (1974) and *Nedrick* (1986), cases in which D set fire to a house in pursuit of a grudge and caused the death of one or more occupants whilst claiming to have intended merely to cause fear. In other examples, violence may be used or threatened as a means of conveying some political or other message, as in *Hancock and Shankland* (1986), where D1 and D2, miners involved in the 1984 miners' strike, sought to prevent another miner from going to work by pushing concrete objects from a motorway bridge into the path of a convoy of police vehicles escorting a taxi which was taking him to work. One of the objects smashed through the windscreen of the taxi and killed the driver. They argued that their only intention was to stop the convoy and so stop the miner from getting to work.

Other cases do not fit neatly into any category. In *Woollin* (1998), D experienced a fit of rage and frustration when his three month old baby, V, choked on his food. He threw V with some violence in the direction of his pram, which was standing close to the wall. V died from a broken skull. D's only explanation was that he 'just did not want to know' V because of the feeding problem. Clearly, D did not have any obvious other aim for which he was prepared to risk death or serious injury to V, but equally, it is not immediately obvious that he intended death or serious injury.

Faced with these examples, the courts could have taken the view that there is no significant difference in moral blameworthiness between a person whose purpose is to cause a consequence and one who knows ('foresees') that his conduct will cause the consequence unless something extraordinary happens (often described as 'foresight of virtual certainty'). Intention could have been defined to include both states of mind, consistent with a recognised philosophical distinction between direct and oblique intention:

- *direct intention* – D's purpose is to cause the consequence;

- *oblique intention* – it is not D's purpose to cause the consequence but he foresees that it is virtually certain to result from his conduct.

In this scheme, any other state of mind is not sufficient to amount to intention. So, if it was not D's purpose to cause the consequence but he foresaw it as probable (or even highly probable), that would not be enough. As the explanation below will show, that state of mind is recklessness. Obviously, it might be difficult for a jury to decide whether D foresaw a consequence as virtually certain or as highly probable or merely probable, but juries are frequently faced with difficult questions of fact and they have to do their best. In cases such as *Hyam v DPP* and *Nedrick*, for instance, they would have to look at matters such as how the fire was started, what time of the day or night it occurred,

D's knowledge of how many people were in the house, what their ages were, how easy it might be to escape and so on.

Until the decision of the House of Lords in *Woollin*, however, there was considerable confusion about the meaning of intention and, in particular, about whether foresight of virtual certainty was intention or was merely evidence from which a jury was entitled to infer intention. In quashing D's conviction for murder in *Woollin*, the House of Lords acknowledged that 'a result foreseen as virtually certain is an intended result' and this ought to have cleared up the confusion. In the case itself, for example, it would not have been necessary for the prosecution to show that D's purpose was to kill the baby or to cause it serious injury. It would have been enough to show that D knew that it was virtually certain that he would kill him or (more likely) cause him serious injury by throwing him in the direction of the pram. The decision has been followed by the Court of Appeal on a number of occasions. One case involved the robbery of an 18 year old A-level student. The attackers took V's bankcard but were unable to obtain any money as the account was empty. They then threw V into the River Ouse, disregarding V's pleas that he could not swim. The defendants were convicted of murder and appealed. The Court of Appeal dismissed the appeals; *R v Matthews and Alleyne* (2003), Crim.L.R. 553.

This area of law remains unclear. In *Woolin*, the House of Lords said that in cases where there is no obvious purpose to cause the consequence, the jury is 'not entitled' to find intention unless they are satisfied that D foresaw the consequence as virtually certain to occur. This might imply that, even if they are satisfied that D foresaw the consequence as virtually certain, the jury are not obliged to find ('are entitled not to find') intention. Clearly, this would conflict with the proposition that foresight of virtual certainty is intention. Further, their Lordships said that the decision related only to the meaning of intention in the law of murder and that 'it does not follow that "intent" necessarily has precisely the same meaning in every context in criminal law'.

Before the decision in *Woollin*, the position was that foresight (of whatever degree of probability) was not intention in itself but was at best evidence of intention. In cases where it was not possible to establish that it was D's purpose to cause the consequence, the jury could be invited to infer intention if satisfied that D foresaw the consequence with virtual certainty. Yet the jury was not bound to do so and it remained within their discretion. Of course, to infer intention, the jury had to be satisfied that D did intend and that his foresight of virtual certainty was evidence of that intention. But it must be remembered that these were cases in which it did not appear to be D's purpose to cause the consequence. So, what exactly was this 'intention' which the jury were being invited to infer? The courts astutely avoided the obvious logical difficulty by adopting the simple expedient of refusing to define intention! The jury were told that they could infer it but they were not told what it was!

In both *Hancock and Shankland* and *Nedrick*, convictions for murder were quashed and convictions for manslaughter substituted because the trial judge was considered to have misdirected the jury on the intention issue. Had they been properly directed, the jury in each case could have concluded that the accused foresaw the virtual certainty of death or serious injury and yet have refused to infer intention, with the result that the offence would have been manslaughter and not murder. If *Woollin* actually decides that foresight of virtual certainty is intention, then discretion would no longer be available to the jury to say whether it did in fact amount to intention in any particular case. In *Woollin* itself, it may have been possible to persuade a jury that D foresaw the virtual certainty of serious injury to his child, but it seems more likely that he gave little thought to the consequences and that it was a very serious case of manslaughter rather than murder.

The idea that foresight of death as the virtually certain outcome of an action amounts to intention was supported by a majority of the Court of Appeal in *Re A (Children) (Conjoined twins: surgical separation)* (2000) 4 All ER 961. Some commentators lament the removal of the jury's discretion (if that is what *Woollin* has achieved – although *Matthews and Alleyne* apparently suggests otherwise), seeing in that discretion a valuable mechanism for distinguishing between degrees of moral blameworthiness. This implies that there might be some instances in which D would not be regarded as having intended a consequence despite his knowledge of virtual certainty. A controversial example might be a physician who administers a powerful painkiller such as morphine to a patient. Although the doctor's primary aim may be therapeutic (i.e. the alleviation of pain), he/she may realise that the drug used is likely/very likely to cause death, *Adams* [1957] Crim LR 365.

It is not immediately obvious why the jury should be trusted with such a discretion, or on what basis they might validly exercise it in favour of one, but against another, accused. To take *Hancock and Shankland* as an example, if the jury decided that the accused foresaw death or serious injury as a virtual certainty, what factors could legitimately influence the jury to decide against convictions for murder? Surely not the defendants' avowed aim of stopping the miner from getting to work or what lay behind the aim, that is, the circumstances of the strike and the coal industry of the time. Wherever sympathies lay in the matter of the strike, it could hardly be a significant factor in the legal issues of criminal liability for murder. Yet, what other significant factors were there? Conversely, it has also been argued that confining the 'foresight' route to intention to *foresight of virtual certainty* means that the net is not cast sufficiently wide. On this argument, D's conviction for murder in *Hyam v DPP* (where foresight of high probability was deemed to be sufficient) was correct because it satisfied perceptions of moral blameworthiness. Yet, on the facts of *Hyam*, conviction for manslaughter would now be the more likely outcome of the application of the foresight of virtual certainty rule. From a moral perspective, it may be argued that an intention to kill is not necessarily worse than recklessness as to whether lives are endangered by one's conduct. A husband who kills his cancer-stricken wife (at her request) may deserve far more respect than, for example, a drunken driver who causes a fatality.

The difficulties which persist in the interpretation of the decisions on the meaning of intention suggest that a statutory definition is desirable. The Law Commission has proposed the following definition:

> ... a person acts ... intentionally with respect to a result when:
>
> (i) it is his purpose to cause it; or
>
> (ii) although it is not his purpose to cause that result, he is aware that it would occur in the ordinary course of events if he were to succeed in his purpose of causing some other result.

[*Offences Against the Person and General Principles*, No 218, 1993.]

This definition, subsequently adopted in a 1997 Government consultation document on reform of the law on non-fatal offences against the person, is hardly very different from that which the House of Lords in *Woollin* appears to have adopted.

Recklessness

Proof of recklessness is generally sufficient to establish the *mens rea* for a criminal offence. Recklessness involves taking risks, and yet most aspects of our lives involve taking some risks. Crossing a road, driving a car and flying in an aeroplane all carry risks. Modern life would grind to a halt if it was not permissible to take such risks. Recklessness in the criminal sense consists of *unjustified* risk taking. Driving a car with defective brakes or steering creates a level of risk well beyond that associated with driving a car in general. It amounts to unjustified risk taking. To 'take' a risk, D must know of the risk, and this suggests that recklessness involves knowledge or awareness. As indicated earlier, a legal rule which requires proof that D was aware of a risk is said to impose a subjective test. D is only liable if he was aware.

It is convenient to regard the modern development of the meaning and application of recklessness as dating from the case of *Cunningham* (1957). D fractured a gas pipe in pulling a gas meter from the wall whilst committing theft. Gas escaped and permeated through to the house next door where it affected the occupant, endangering her life. D was convicted of malicious infliction of a noxious substance (s 23 of the Offences Against the Person Act 1861) after a trial in which the judge said that 'malicious' meant 'wicked'. D's conviction was quashed on appeal, when it was held that 'malicious' means 'intentionally or recklessly' and that 'recklessly' requires proof, at the very least, that D knew that injury might be caused (in other words, was aware of the risk of injury). Whether D was aware of the risk is something we do not know, precisely because the jury was not asked to consider the matter.

Therefore, recklessness is the conscious taking of an unjustified risk. D will have given thought to, and will have recognised, the risk but will have gone on to take it anyway. His reasons for doing so are irrelevant – it does not matter whether he simply could not care less or fervently hoped that no harm would result. Whether it is a risk that he was justified in taking is a question to be judged objectively. That is, would a reasonable person have taken it? The question is not whether D himself thought it was justifiable to take the risk. A reasonable person might run a low risk of causing some personal injury or damage to property in order, for instance, to save life or prevent serious injury. Yet, there are few cases in which it will be justifiable to run any risk of causing injury to the person or damage to property, and fewer still where it would be justifiable to run a high risk. Consequently, this objective component of recklessness is rarely in issue.

If, for whatever reason, D did not think about or recognise any risk of a particular consequence occurring or of a particular circumstance existing, then he is not subjectively reckless with respect to that consequence or circumstance. This remains so, no matter how obvious the risk would have been to any other person. But if D 'turns a blind eye' to the risk or deliberately refrains from making further inquiries because he has a good idea of what he will discover, that will probably be sufficient evidence of subjective recklessness. If D knows that his bank account is overdrawn and is expecting a letter from his bank to tell him that he must not use his cheque guarantee card, his deliberate refusal to open a letter to that effect from the bank will probably not save him if he tries to say that he was not aware of the risk that his authority to use the card had been withdrawn.

From 1981 to 2003 – following *Caldwell* – the courts took the view that a different form of recklessness was applicable in certain situations. Persons who were objectively reckless (i.e. behaved in a manner that created an obvious risk – even if they were unaware of it) could be convicted of offences such as criminal damage. This is no longer the case; *R v G (2003)* 3 WLR 1060.

Transferred malice

Suppose that D intends to inflict serious injury on X but unintentionally inflicts it on V. If he had succeeded in relation to X, he would have been guilty of causing grievous bodily harm with intent to cause such harm (s 18 of the Offences Against the Person Act 1861). Clearly, he had no such intention in relation to V and this might suggest that he is not guilty of the crime in relation to V. In fact, the prosecution is not required to prove that D had a separate intention against V. Provided that the *actus reus* is that of the crime intended against X, D's *mens rea* in relation to X can be transferred to the *actus reus* against V. D can be liable even if he had no idea that V was anywhere near the scene when he tried to inflict injury on X. In *Latimer* (1886), D aimed a blow with his belt at X, but the belt was deflected onto V and severely wounded him. D was taken to have the necessary *mens rea* for the wounding of V.

The doctrine applies also to recklessness and operates whether or not D succeeds in committing the *actus reus* against the intended target. In *Mitchell* (1983), D pushed or punched X, a 72 year old man who was trying to stop him pushing to the front of a post office queue. X fell back onto V, a frail 89 year old woman, who broke her femur. A few days later, a hip replacement operation had to be carried out on V, but she died two days later from pulmonary embolism caused by a blood clot resulting from the break. D's conviction for unlawful act manslaughter was upheld, partly on the grounds of transferred malice. Of course, D did succeed in causing injury to his intended target, X, but his intention to cause injury to X could also be transferred to the injury caused to V.

The only limitation on the doctrine is that D must cause the *actus reus* of the kind of crime for which he has *mens rea*. If he causes the *actus reus* of a different crime, he will be guilty of that crime only if it can be shown that he possessed the *mens rea* for that crime. Suppose that D throws a brick at V but misses. The brick breaks a window. D's intention to injure V cannot be transferred to the criminal damage in breaking the window and he will only be liable if, as well as intending injury to V, he also intended or was reckless as to the damage; *Pembliton* (1874), 22 WR 553. In a situation of this kind D might, of course, be guilty of a crime of attempt, for example, attempting to cauce grievous bodily harm to V.

5.1.3.3   Coincidence of actus reus and mens rea

Actus reus and *mens rea* must be present together at the same time (they must 'coincide') if D is to be guilty of the offence. Therefore, where the *actus reus* of a crime is instantaneous and complete, D must possess the relevant *mens rea* at that very moment. If D punches V, intending or foreseeing only minor injury, he cannot be guilty of the offence of causing grievous bodily harm with intent to cause grievous bodily harm even if V suffers such harm and, a few moments after delivering the punch, D hopes that he *does* cause grievous bodily harm. But if the offence has an *actus reus* which continues for some time, D can be guilty if he has *mens rea* at some point during the *actus reus*, even if he does not have it at the start. A famous example of this point is supplied by the case of *Fagan v MPC* (1968), in which D accidentally drove his car onto the foot of V, a policeman, when directed to stop. When he realised what he had done, D refused for a short time to move the car. His conviction for assaulting a police constable in the execution of his duty was upheld because, though he did not initially have *mens rea* (a generous interpretation of the facts!), the *actus reus* continued during the time that D 'kept' the car on V's foot, and the subsequent presence of *mens rea* during this time was sufficient.

The case of *Thabo Meli* (1954) is an example of a variation on this principle. D and others, intending to kill V, lured him to a remote spot and beat him severely. Believing they had killed him, they then rolled him down a small hill. In truth, he was not dead but he later died from the effects of exposure. D argued that, believing V already to be dead, he could not have intended death or serious injury in rolling him down the hill and leaving his 'body'. The argument was rejected on the grounds that the beating and disposal were all part of the same 'transaction', so that presence of *mens rea* in relation to the beating was sufficient coincidence of *actus reus* and *mens rea* to establish liability for murder. So, where D engages in a number of acts designed to result in a particular consequence, it may be possible to treat the presence of *mens rea* at any point in the sequence of acts (the 'transaction') as sufficient for liability, even if there was no *mens rea* in relation to the act most proximate to the consequence. More questionably, this principle was applied to manslaughter in *Church* (1965), despite the fact that D had severely injured V in a spontaneous attack arising out of a dispute and had actually killed her when disposing of what he thought to be her dead body. In the absence of a 'plan', how were these acts welded into a single 'transaction'?

5.1.3.4   *Liability without* mens rea

On the definition of *mens rea* adopted above, crimes of negligence and strict liability do not require proof of *mens rea*. Liability for negligence might be justified on the grounds that D's conduct was blameworthy in failing to meet the standard expected of a reasonable person. This requires us to accept that such failure should be enough for some criminal offences, though it would never be enough for the most serious offences such as murder, grievous bodily harm, theft and deception. Strict liability invites conviction of those who may not be blameworthy at all and certainly requires justification. As explained below, justification is usually sought in the 'regulatory' nature of the offences and consequent lack of stigma in conviction for their breach, that is, it does not matter too much if it is easy to convict D for a strict liability offence as the conviction will not be a matter of shame.

Negligence

There is no general principle which imposes liability for negligence in English criminal law. The common law view of *mens rea* is that either intention or recklessness must be proved or the offence is one of strict liability. Thus, liability for negligence is imposed:

- by statute, either in a primary manner, as in the crimes of dangerous driving and driving without due care and attention under the Road Traffic Act 1988, or in a secondary manner, as in the Misuse of Drugs Act 1971, where the statute obliges the Crown to make out a *prima facie* case of possession but then gives D the opportunity to avoid liability by proving that he was not negligent;

- (very rarely) by the common law, a notable example being gross negligence manslaughter;

- by appearing as an element in some general defences, as in duress/duress of circumstances, where D's unreasonable mistake may deprive him of the defence.

Negligence is the failure to achieve the standard of conduct to be expected of the reasonable person. D will be negligent whether or not he is aware of the risk of his failure to achieve the standard, though, of course, if he is aware of it, his culpability will be greater and his state of mind will be recklessness or intention. Since D is being judged against the standard of the reasonable person, deficiencies in D's knowledge and capacity for understanding or for reasoning are irrelevant if they would not be shared by the reasonable person (the reasonable person is not intoxicated, for instance). By contrast, if D has specialist knowledge or expertise, then he will be expected to achieve the standard of the reasonable person possessed of such knowledge or expertise.

Strict liability

Strict liability offences are predominantly regulatory in nature and tend to deal with activities which are of general concern, perhaps because of danger to the safety of the public or possible widescale fraud on the public. Examples are offences dealing with pollution and general damage to the environment, adulteration of food and drink, evasion of health and safety regulations and planning and building construction requirements and misdescriptions of the quality and price of goods and services. But they extend into many other areas, such as possession of drugs, road traffic offences and even assaults on police officers.

Justifications put forward for this remarkable form of liability include the following:

- it forces people to think actively about compliance – a butcher, for instance, is more likely to adopt measures to stop contamination of his products if he knows that even lack of negligence will not save him from liability if his products are contaminated;

- the offences are minor and conviction carries no social stigma, the penalty often being no more than a fine;

- proving fault would often be almost impossible and trying to do so would consume a lot of court time, leading to delays and inefficiency;

- the disparity between the minor nature of the offence and the considerable effort that would need to be expended in proving fault invites the obvious conclusion that proof of fault should not be required.

An offence is said to be one of strict liability where it is not necessary for the prosecution to prove intention, recklessness or negligence in relation to any one or more of the elements of the *actus reus*. For example, in *Pharmaceutical Society of Great Britain v Storkwain* (1986), D was a pharmacist who supplied prescription-only drugs when presented with a prescription which he did not realise was a forgery. Though he was 'blameless' (there was no reason for him to be suspicious of the prescription), he was convicted because the House of Lords held that it was unnecessary to prove any knowledge that the prescription was not valid.

In some offences, *mens rea* must be proved in relation to some *actus reus* elements but not in relation to others. For the offence of assaulting a police constable in the execution of his duty (s 89(1) of the Police Act 1996), it must be proved that D intended or was reckless as to the elements of the assault but, remarkably, not that he knew, suspected or even should have suspected that his victim was a police constable! The offence is a *mens rea* offence in relation to the assault but a strict liability offence in relation to the fact that the victim is a police constable and is acting in the execution of his duty.

Though most strict liability offences are statutory, they owe their status as strict liability offences not to Parliament, which has usually said nothing on the matter, but to judges who have decided to interpret them in that way. Since the House of Lords in *Sweet v Parsley* (1970) laid great stress on the importance of the general common law presumption that *mens rea* must be proved, the imposition of strict liability requires evidence to rebut that presumption. An approach frequently relied on is that suggested by Lord Scarman in *Gammon v AG for Hong Kong* (1985):

(a) there is a (rather weak) presumption that *mens rea* is required;

(b) it is particularly strong where the offence is 'truly criminal' – this is not a particularly helpful classification. It echoes the comments above about 'regulatory' and 'minor' offences. In *Blake* (1997), it was suggested that any offence for which a sentence of imprisonment may be imposed is 'truly criminal', though the court went on to hold that unlicensed broadcasting was an offence of strict liability even though it carried a sentence of imprisonment. In *Harrow London Borough v Shah* (1999), the offence of selling a national lottery ticket to a person under 16 years of age was held to be one of strict liability even though it carried a sentence of two years imprisonment. In that case, the court pointed out that the offence in *Gammon* itself carried a sentence of three years' imprisonment and yet was found to be one of strict liability. Nor can it be said that all of these offences are trivial in nature. Pollution offences or breaches of health and safety regulations may threaten the lives of scores of people. The 'truly criminal' offences are generally committed in relation only to a single victim;

(c) the presumption applies to statutory offences and can be displaced only if this is clearly or is by necessary implication the effect of the statute – evidence of this may be sought in:

- the words used – some words, such as 'knowingly', inevitably import *mens rea* notions, others, such as 'cause', are neutral;

- the relationship with other sections in the statute creating offences – if *mens rea* words appear in some sections but not others, this makes it easier for a judge to conclude that Parliament deliberately excluded *mens rea* in the latter. This was a strong factor in the *Storkwain*, where a number of other offences in the relevant statute required proof of *mens rea*;

(d) the only situation in which it can be displaced is where the statute deals with an issue of social concern – the nature of these issues has been indicated above;

(e) even then, the presumption stands unless it can be shown that the creation of strict liability will be effective to promote the objects of the statute by encouraging greater vigilance to prevent commission of the prohibited act – again, this is explained above.

The arguments in favour of the imposition of strict liability would, perhaps, be more credible if the choice were simply between liability requiring the Crown to prove fault and strict liability. In truth, there is a further possibility which Parliament has shown an increasing tendency to adopt. This is to create offences which can be interpreted as being *prima facie* of strict liability – that is, that the Crown merely has to prove that D engaged in some prohibited conduct – but which then give D the opportunity, and place on him the burden, to prove that he was not negligent (that is, there is a 'due diligence' defence).

5.2   General Defences

5.2.1   Introduction

A general defence is one which may be raised to all, or at least to most, crimes, unlike a defence such as diminished responsibility, which relates only to the offence of murder. Where a general defence is successfully pleaded, the usual effect is that D avoids liability entirely. The basis of the defences varies. For instance, automatism is a denial that the prosecution has established one of the main elements of the *actus reus* (that D's conduct must be voluntary). Intoxication, on the other hand, is usually introduced to deny that the prosecution has established the *mens rea*. Insanity may operate as a denial of either or both (though recent cases suggest that it only operates to deny *mens rea*, and so cannot be used where the offence is one of strict liability), or simply as a claim to be excused from liability because of a failure to perceive that the conduct was 'wrong'. In pleading self-defence, however, D admits the *actus reus* and the *mens rea* but claims to be justified in what he did. Some commentators see such a justificatory defence as denying that the conduct was in any way 'unlawful' (some crimes expressly incorporate the word 'unlawful' in their definition, though it might be argued that all crimes impliedly incorporate the requirement). Similarly, in duress or duress of circumstances, D admits *actus reus* and *mens rea* but claims to be justified, or at any rate excused, because of the pressure applied to him by others or by the circumstances.

The burden of proof in these defences is generally on the prosecution; that is, once the defence has been introduced, the prosecution must disprove it. Even so, D usually has to present some credible evidence in support of the defence before the prosecution is put to the task of disproving it. The defence of insanity is an exception to this rule about burden of proof. The burden is on D to prove that he was insane at the time of the commission of the alleged offence.

5.2.2 Children

Before the enactment of the Crime and Disorder Act 1998, there were three key ages for the purposes of criminal liability, namely:

(a) *under 10* – by virtue of s 50 of the Children and Young Persons Act 1933, as amended by s 16 of the Children and Young Persons Act 1963, a child under 10 years cannot incur criminal liability. There is an irrebuttable presumption against such a child having responsibility for a crime;

(b) *10 years or over but not yet 14* – under a long-standing rule, the law provided that such children could be held criminally liable, but only if they had a 'mischievous discretion', that is, they understood the distinction between right and wrong. Though the rule had been subjected to penetrating criticism in recent years, it was upheld by the House of Lords in *C v DPP* (1995) where it was asserted that in addition to proving the *mens rea* for the offence, the prosecution must also prove that the child knew that it was a 'wrong act as distinct from an act of mere naughtiness or childish mischief'. The older the child and the more obviously wrong the act, the easier it would be to rebut the presumption;

(c) *14 years and over* – full criminal responsibility.

However, the doubts expressed about the rule in (b) led to proposals for its abolition and this was achieved in s 34 of the Crime and Disorder Act. Consequently, there are now only two significant ages as far as criminal liability is concerned:

(a) *under 10 years of age* – no criminal liability; and

(b) *10 years of age or above* – full criminal liability. Of course, different procedures and sentences continue to apply to young offenders.

5.2.3 Insanity

Insanity may be relevant to criminal liability in two very distinct ways:

(a) it may prevent D from being tried at all, since he may be unfit to plead;

(b) it may provide an actual defence to the crime if D can show that he was insane at the time he allegedly committed the crime.

5.2.3.1   Unfitness to plead

D's state of mind at the time of the offence is not the issue. The issue is whether his current state of mind makes it impossible for him to be tried because he cannot understand the nature of the proceedings and cannot instruct legal advisers. If D is awaiting trial, he may be ordered to be detained in a hospital because of his mental state. Alternatively, he may be found unfit to plead at his trial. In this case, to avoid the possibility of a person found unfit to plead having the prospect of prosecution and conviction hanging over him where the evidence may not be sufficient to establish that he was guilty, the Criminal Procedure (Insanity) Act 1964, as amended by the Criminal Procedure (Insanity and Unfitness to Plead) Act 1991, enables a determination to be made of whether he did in fact 'do the act or make the omission' (though the point is currently the subject of some dispute, this probably means 'did commit the *actus reus*') which amounts to the offence charged. If not, then clearly he is innocent and is outside the criminal justice system. If it is determined that he did do the act or make the omission, the court has power to impose any one of a number of orders:

- admission to a hospital specified by the Secretary of State (with or without direction as to restriction on release);

- guardianship;

- supervision and treatment;

- absolute discharge.

In the case of a murder charge, the order must be for detention in a hospital with a restriction on release.

5.2.3.2   Insanity at the time of the crime – the M'Naghten Rules

Suppose that D is arguing that he should be excused from liability because he was insane at the time of the offence. If D succeeds in establishing this claim, then, under the Trial of Lunatics Act 1883, as amended by the Criminal Procedure (Insanity) Act 1964, the jury will return 'the special verdict' of 'not guilty by reason of insanity'. Though technically an acquittal, D will not necessarily go completely free. The judge may impose any of the orders identified above where there was a finding of unfitness to plead and, again, must make an order for detention in a hospital with a restriction on release in the case of a murder charge.

Just as in the case of unfitness to plead, the jury must be satisfied that D 'did the act or made the omission charged' before determining whether D was insane so as to be entitled to the special verdict (s 2 of the Trial of Lunatics Act 1883). In *AG's Reference (No 3 of 1998)* (1999), the Court of Appeal rejected the argument that this meant that the prosecution must prove both *actus reus* and *mens rea*. Clearly, since the whole basis of D's claim of insanity is that he lacked mental capacity and therefore did not have *mens rea*, it makes little sense to require the prosecution to prove *mens rea* before the defence of insanity can be considered. In this context, according to *AG's Reference (No 3 of 1998)*, when considering whether D 'did the act or made the omission', the jury must take into account any possible defence not founded on the insanity itself.

In the past, the insanity defence has rarely been used in anything other than murder cases and, even there, its use declined markedly following the introduction of the defence of diminished responsibility in 1957 (and, perhaps more significantly, the abolition of capital punishment in 1965). This was understandable in view of the fact that, prior to 1991, no matter what the offence charged, the judge had to direct that anyone found not guilty by reason of insanity be detained in a specified hospital. There is some evidence to suggest that the wider range of orders now available, including absolute discharge, have resulted in increased use of the defence, though the total number of successful pleas in any year is so small that it would be unwise to read too much into the statistics.

The definition of insanity is based upon the M'Naghten Rules derived from the *M'Naghten* (1843) case. These rules provide that, to succeed in a plea of insanity, D must establish (so, unusually, D bears the burden of proof) that he was suffering from:

- a defect of reason;

- arising from a disease of the mind;

- having the consequence that either he was unaware of the nature and quality of his act, or that he did not realise that he was doing what was wrong.

It must be emphasised that this is the *legal* definition of insanity. It has remained substantially unchanged since 1843. Few contemporary psychologists would be willing to adopt such an approach to severe mental illness.

Defect of reason

This is established where D was incapable of exercising powers of reason, not by a mere failure to exercise such powers. In *Clarke* (1972), D changed her plea to guilty when the trial judge ruled that her defence to a charge of theft of a small number of items from a supermarket amounted to insanity. She had claimed that she had behaved absent-mindedly in putting the items in her bag before reaching the cashier and sought to support her claim by reference to medical evidence which showed that she had been suffering from mild depression. The Court of Appeal quashed her conviction, characterising D's state of mind not as a defect of reason but merely as one of temporary absent-mindedness, confusion and failure to concentrate.

Disease of the mind

This involves disorders of brain function (described in *Kemp* (1957) as 'affecting the powers of reason, memory and understanding'). In *Sullivan* (1983), the House of Lords asserted:

> ... it matters not whether the aetiology of the impairment is organic, as in epilepsy, or functional, or whether the impairment itself is permanent or is transient and intermittent, provided that it subsisted at the time of the act ...

unless it were a temporary impairment which:

> ... results from some external physical factor such as a blow on the head causing concussion or the administration of an anaesthetic for therapeutic purposes.

So, the key distinction appears to be that between internal and external factors. Provided that the defect of reason results from an internal factor, it does not matter whether it is clearly attributable to physical (organic) disease or is only recognisable by its effects on D's behaviour (functional). Nor does it matter whether it is of long or short duration, especially where it is recurrent.

Examples of organic diseases which can cause a defect of reason and so give rise to the defence of insanity are:

- *epilepsy* – in *Sullivan*, D, whilst undergoing a *petit mal* seizure (psychomotor epilepsy), repeatedly kicked, and caused serious injury to, V, who had tried to assist him. The House of Lords held that epilepsy was a disease of the mind which had caused a defect of reason in D;

- *arteriosclerosis* (narrowing of the arteries causing constriction of blood flow to the brain) – in *Kemp*, D had struck his wife with a hammer whilst allegedly suffering from this condition, which was characterised as a disease of the mind. Logically, a tumour having the same effect ought also to be treated as a disease of the mind, so the contrary decision in *Charlson* (1955) was almost certainly wrong;

- *diabetes* – diabetes is a disease in which the body does not produce enough insulin to break down blood sugar. If not reduced, increasing levels of blood sugar lead to the condition of hyperglycaemia, resulting progressively in confusion, disorientation, possible drunken-like behaviour and aggression, lack of consciousness, coma and death. Excessively low levels of blood sugar lead to the condition of hypoglycaemia and produce almost identical effects. The former condition results from lack of insulin, the latter from too much (usually because D has injected insulin and has not eaten appropriate food to correct an excessive reduction in blood sugar). The courts have categorised the defect of reason due to hyperglycaemia as being due to a disease of the mind (an internal factor, the disease itself), and so can form the basis of the defence of insanity (*Hennessy* (1989)). On the other hand, hypoglycaemia resulting from an injection of insulin has been categorised as a defect of reason due to an external factor (the taking of the insulin) and so does not amount to insanity because it is not due to a disease of the mind (*Quick* (1973));

- *degenerative changes to the brain or other organs* resulting from (usually) persistent use of intoxicants.

Examples of functional diseases are:

- *the major psychoses* – such as schizophrenia and clinical depression;

- *brain disorder* – which results in 'sleepwalking' and its very dramatic manifestation in 'night terrors' (though whether this is functional or organic is perhaps open to question). The broad approach adopted in *Sullivan* made it almost inevitable that sleepwalking would be classified as being due to disease of the mind. How else does the brain disorder occur except as something within the brain itself, something internal? So, in *Burgess* (1991), D and V fell asleep whilst watching television. D claimed that he was still asleep when he hit V on the head with a bottle and a video recorder and put his hands round her throat. His claim of 'sleepwalking' was held to be a plea of insanity because the disorder, albeit transitory, was due to an internal factor, had manifested itself in violence, and was likely to recur, even though a further instance of serious violence was unlikely.

D does not know nature and quality of his act or does not know that what he was doing was wrong

D must prove at least one or other of these effects:

- 'does not know the nature and quality of his act' – in *Codere* (1916), the Court of Appeal held that 'nature and quality' means physical nature and quality. This would refer to very fundamental defects in awareness and understanding, such as D's lack of consciousness whilst suffering an epileptic seizure or hyperglycaemic episode, or his belief that he is strangling an animal and not, as is actually the case, his girlfriend (see the example of *Lipman* (1970) in the discussion of automatism which follows in 5.2.4, but note that D's distorted perception resulted from taking a drug). It would extend equally to his belief that strangling does not kill or his lack of understanding of what death is;

- 'does not know that he was doing what was wrong' – in *Windle* (1952), it was held that D will only escape liability under this head if his defect of reason is such that he does not appreciate that what he is doing is legally wrong. For instance, if he is convinced that he is being attacked in circumstances where he could legally use deadly force in self-defence or believes that he has been given special legal dispensation to engage in otherwise prohibited conduct, he does not believe that what he is doing is legally wrong. On the other hand, if he appreciates that it is wrong in this sense but is convinced that it is morally acceptable, the defence would fail (the Australian case of *Stapleton* (1952) took the contrary view in suggesting that D *must know* that it is morally wrong). So, in *Windle*, D's defence failed because he knew that it was legally wrong to kill his wife, who had often talked of committing suicide, even if he might have thought that it was a kindly act, given her constant unhappy state of mind.

5.2.4 Automatism

The prosecution must prove that D's conduct was voluntary. This means that he must have been sufficiently in control of his bodily movements for the conduct to be said to be truly 'his' conduct. D's claim to have been acting involuntarily is called a plea of automatism. Though such a plea will inevitably imply an absence of *mens rea*, it goes further in denying that D has committed the *actus reus*. This is especially important where the crime does not require proof of *mens rea*, as in crimes of strict liability or negligence. If automatism was merely denial of *mens rea*, D would still be guilty of an offence of strict liability even if an automaton at the time. This has proved to be important in driving offences, a number of which are strict liability offences. If D can present sufficient evidence that he may have been an automaton, the Crown must then prove that he was not. If the Crown fails to do so, then D must be acquitted.

Claims of automatism result from two distinct kinds of factual circumstances:

(1) those where D asserts a physical incapacity to control movement which is not related to any kind of brain malfunction. Examples might include:

- being propelled by superior force – for example, X pushes D into V (*Mitchell* (1983)) or D is blown off his feet by a very strong gust of wind and is thrown against V;

- slipping or skidding on ice or oil (without any prior fault);

- suffering a muscular spasm when stung by bees (a hypothetical example given by the court in *Hill v Baxter* (1958));

- experiencing mechanical, electrical or other failure in a machine which makes control of the machine temporarily impossible – as in *Burns v Bidder* (1967), where D's conviction for failing to accord precedence to a pedestrian on a pedestrian crossing (he knocked the pedestrian down!) was quashed on appeal on the grounds that his brakes had unaccountably failed, rendering him an automaton (when subsequently tested, they worked perfectly);

(2) those where D asserts that the failure to control his movement resulted from some significant malfunction of the brain. In most of these cases, there is evidence of purposeful actions by D (for example, 'striking' V or 'driving' a car). So, D's claim is that any control of movement by his brain was not at a conscious level and that only such a level of control will suffice. Examples of these claims might be:

- conduct whilst concussed or semi-concussed from some blow to the head;

- conduct whilst under the influence of a drug taken under medical advice (for example, insulin taken by a diabetic) or involuntarily taken;

- conduct whilst under the influence of a substance which was not generally known to produce intoxicating effects, as in *Hardie* (1983), where D claimed to have been unconscious when behaving aggressively and destructively after having taken tranquiliser tablets prescribed some years previously for his girlfriend.

Whatever D's explanation for the failure to control movement, his plea will not be successful unless he can present evidence of a fundamental loss of control, not merely some partial loss as might occur when movements are poorly co-ordinated through tiredness, illness or drink. Consequently, it was held in *AG's Reference (No 2 of 1992)* (1993) that D's claim to have been 'driving without awareness' (an allegedly trance-like state caused by prolonged driving on featureless motorways) when he had collided with two vehicles on the hard shoulder of a motorway and had killed two people could not amount to automatism. There was no evidence of total absence of control, merely of impaired, reduced or partial control. More questionably, in *Broome and Perkins* (1983), D, a diabetic who had suffered a hypoglycaemic attack shortly after beginning his drive home from work, was held to be 'driving' for some parts of the journey and so was unable to plead automatism. The court reasoned that, if he had somehow 'driven' the car for a distance of five miles without serious incident, there must have been periods of control, even if D could remember nothing of what had happened (this decision fails to pay sufficient attention to the different levels at which the brain can function).

Even if it appears that D was an automaton at the time of the alleged crime, the Crown may still succeed in establishing guilt if it can show that D was at fault in a way which should deprive him of the defence. There are two relevant kinds of fault (see below).

5.2.4.1   *Voluntary consumption of an intoxicant*

In this case, D's liability falls to be determined by application of the rules on intoxication (see 5.2.5). Those rules are concerned purely with issues of *mens rea*. So, when D concedes that he became an automaton as a result of, say, taking drugs, he is not allowed to argue that he did not commit the *actus reus* of the offence, only that he did not have *mens rea*. Even then, he is not allowed to argue that he did not have *mens rea* unless he is seeking to avoid liability for an offence requiring proof of nothing less than intention (a specific intent offence). If the *mens rea* of the offence includes recklessness (a basic intent offence), D will simply not be allowed to introduce the explanation that he was an automaton because of intoxication and so will inevitably be convicted. In *Lipman*, D killed his girlfriend whilst suffering from an LSD-induced hallucination that he was fighting serpents at the centre of the earth. Clearly, he was an automaton at the time since his brain functions had been fundamentally disordered by the drug. However, since he had voluntarily taken the drug, he was acquitted of the specific intent offence of murder, but convicted of the basic intent offence of manslaughter.

5.2.4.2   *Any other kind of fault in becoming an automaton*

D cannot be in a worse position than if the fault was related to intoxication, so he must at least be able to plead the automatism as a defence to a specific intent offence (you can plead intoxication as a defence to a crime requiring a 'specific intent', see 5.2.5). However, it was held in *Bailey* (1983) that there are no obvious policy reasons, such as apply to intoxication, for restricting D's defence to specific intent offences. The defence can be pleaded to any offence and the question is then whether the Crown can prove that at the time when D could have prevented himself becoming an automaton, he was aware that he might commit an offence of the kind in question. In other words, even though, as an automaton, he did not have the *mens rea* for the offence at the time of its alleged commission, does it appear that he had an equivalent *mens rea* at the earlier stage? Suppose that D, a diabetic, takes insulin and then allows himself to get into a hypoglycaemic state by subsequently not eating. In that state, he attacks and injures V. D will only be liable for the personal injury offence if, before he went into the hypoglycaemic state, he knew that he might attack someone if he did fall into such a state.

In an offence of objective recklessness (criminal damage) or negligence (for example, gross negligence manslaughter), it might be enough to prove that D ought to have been aware (a reasonable person would have been aware) before he became an automaton that he might commit an offence of the kind in question if he were to become an automaton. This is because both types of offence use an objective test of liability.

5.2.5   Intoxication

A plea of intoxication presents particular difficulties for the criminal law. On the one hand, it is generally acknowledged that a great deal of criminal behaviour, especially behaviour consisting of spontaneous acts of personal violence, aggression and damage to property, is associated with consumption of alcohol and drugs. There is also evidence to suggest that intoxication may be a factor in many instances of theft, robbery and burglary, which may be motivated by a need for funds to sustain drug-taking habits. Why allow D to plead intoxication when intoxication may be the very root of the problem? On the other hand, the Crown must prove all the elements of an offence. If D is intoxicated, so that one of those elements might not be present (intention or recklessness, say), why should D be prevented from introducing evidence of the intoxication?

A first step in confronting this dilemma is to make two crucial distinctions:

- between substances which are regarded as intoxicants and substances which are not; and

- between intoxication for which D is responsible (is at fault) (voluntary intoxication) and intoxication for which he is not (involuntary intoxication).

5.2.5.1   Substances which are intoxicants

Put in simple terms, any substance which is commonly known to produce the kind of effects generally associated with intoxication can be regarded as an intoxicant. These effects include changes of mood, perception and consciousness, reduction in inhibitions, impaired ability for self-control, reduction in motor skills and ability to react and increased difficulty in forming judgments and assessing consequences of actions. They are characteristic of the consumption of alcohol and drugs (both medical and recreational), and also of other substances such as glues and solvents. As the earlier discussion (see 5.2.4) of *Hardie* indicates, a substance may be regarded as an intoxicant when it produces the effects which would be expected of it, but not when it produces entirely unexpected effects. So, the tranquiliser was not an intoxicant in relation to the wholly unexpected violent and aggressive behaviour, but would have been had the issue been about impaired perception and responses caused by the expected tranquilising effects.

Where D suffers intoxication effects from consumption of a substance which is not an intoxicant, he may introduce the explanation in evidence as he would introduce any other explanation to cast doubt on the Crown's case.

5.2.5.2   *Voluntary and involuntary intoxication*

D will be voluntarily intoxicated where he was consuming a substance which he knew or should have known (it is commonly known) to be an intoxicant. He will be held to be voluntarily intoxicated even if he makes a mistake about the strength of the intoxicant. In *Allen* (1988), D's claim to have underestimated the alcoholic content of the wine he was drinking, and so not to have been voluntarily intoxicated, was rejected. It was enough that he knew that he was drinking wine. If D consumes a medical drug which can be characterised as an intoxicant and either does not follow medical advice or the drug has not been prescribed for him, then this will probably be voluntary intoxication.

Conversely, D will be involuntarily intoxicated when he has consumed an intoxicant without knowing that he has consumed the substance at all or, perhaps, when he neither knew nor should have known that it was an intoxicant. The obvious examples are where D's non-alcoholic drink is 'spiked' without his knowledge with alcohol or some drug, and where he innocently eats food to which a drug has been added. A further example ought to be where, without D's knowledge, a different intoxicant is added to the intoxicating substance he knows himself to be consuming, as where a mildly alcoholic drink is spiked with stronger alcohol or a drug. Theoretically, this is significantly different from the situation in *Allen*, discussed above, though the practical distinction might be hard to make.

5.2.5.3   *Liability where D is involuntarily intoxicated*

In cases of involuntary intoxication, the rule is that D is entitled to introduce evidence of the intoxication to refute the Crown's allegation of *mens rea*, whether the offence requires proof of intention or recklessness. But the effect of the intoxication must be that D did not form the required *mens rea*. D cannot claim that, though he knew what he was doing, he would not have done it but for the intoxication. Even though D could claim that it was not his fault in such a case, the broader excuse thus created would be difficult to fit within the existing legal framework and would generate considerable problems of proof. The rules on involuntary intoxication were established by the House of Lords in *Kingston* (1994) when restoring D's conviction for indecently assaulting a youth after it had been quashed by the Court of Appeal. D had claimed that he had been drugged without his knowledge as part of a deliberate plot to exploit his suppressed homosexual paedophilic tendencies and had only given way to them because of the drug. The House of Lords held that the Crown was only required to prove *mens rea* in the conventional sense and did not have to prove some extra element of moral fault.

5.2.5.4   *Liability where D is voluntarily intoxicated*

The current rules on the effect of voluntary intoxication were established by the House of Lords in *DPP v Majewski* (1976). They provide that:

- offences are divided into two categories, specific intent on the one hand, basic intent on the other. Specific intent offences are satisfied by proof of nothing less than an intention. They include murder, causing grievous bodily harm with intent to cause such harm, theft and robbery. Basic intent offences are satisfied by proof of recklessness and include manslaughter, inflicting grievous bodily harm, assault occasioning actual bodily harm, assault, battery and criminal damage. Some offences are specific intent offences as to one element but basic intent as to another. Thus, rape requires proof of intention to have sexual intercourse but merely recklessness as to V's lack of consent;

- if D is charged with a specific intent offence, he may introduce evidence of intoxication in asserting that, at the time of the offence, he did not have the required intention. This does not mean that anyone who was drunk inevitably avoids liability for such an offence. The effect of the intoxication must be evaluated by the jury and D avoids liability if it tends to show that he did not form the intention. As is well known, intoxication often simply makes people more aggressive or less inhibited and, if this was the case, it would not assist D. On the other hand, the issue is whether D did or did not form the intention; it is not whether he was capable of forming any intention at all. This distinction is important because D may argue that he did not form the *particular* intention, whilst being prepared to concede that he had formed *some* intention. In *Brown and Stratton* (1998), the trial judge erred in directing the jury that a plea of intoxication would only be relevant if D was saying, 'I was so drunk on this occasion that I was almost unconscious and I was not capable of forming any intention at all'. D's conviction for causing grievous bodily harm with intent was quashed and a conviction for the lesser offence of inflicting grievous bodily harm (requiring proof only of intention or recklessness as to some harm and, as such, a basic intent offence) was substituted;

- if D is charged with a basic intent offence, he is not allowed simply to introduce evidence of intoxication to explain why he was not aware of a risk (was not reckless). Consequently, if he has no other independent argument to advance, it is almost certain that he will be convicted. Recently, the Court of Appeal has stated that the Crown must prove that D would have foreseen the risk had he not been intoxicated (*Richardson and Irwin* (1999)). A person who raises evidence of intoxication to avoid conviction for a specific intent offence will inevitably be convicted of any associated basic intent offence. The reader should recall that, in *Lipman*, D avoided liability for murder (specific intent) but was convicted of manslaughter (basic intent);

The House of Lords in *Majewski* sought to justify this approach to the effect of voluntary intoxication on criminal liability by suggesting that voluntary consumption of intoxicants is itself a reckless course of conduct which supplies the *mens rea* element that was apparently lacking at the time of commission of the offence. Clearly, this rather general recklessness has little in common with the awareness of particular risks usually necessary in proof of *mens rea*. It might be more realistic to accept that a policy decision has been made in which the courts have tried to strike a balance between practical and theoretical concerns. The balance depends upon the arbitrary division of offences into specific and basic intent, to which distinct rules of liability are then applied when intoxication is in issue.

It is unnecessary to apply the basic intent rule to offences which can be committed with objective recklessness or negligence. In such offences, D's conduct is judged against the standard of a reasonable sober person, so his excuse of intoxication cannot succeed (*Caldwell*). Strict liability offences do not require proof of *mens rea* and so intoxication would be irrelevant.

In some cases, D may seek to raise another defence, such as self-defence, but may need to rely on proof of his intoxication to render that defence credible. Suppose, for instance, that D thinks he is being attacked by V. In reality he is not, but he thinks he is because he is intoxicated. As the discussion of mistake (see 5.2.6) and of self-defence (see 5.2.8) will reveal, D is usually entitled to defend himself by using such force as is proportionate to the danger which he genuinely, even though mistakenly, believes to exist. Yet, where this 'genuine' mistaken belief is brought about by intoxication, the rule is that D cannot rely on the intoxication to explain his mistake. Consequently, his defence of self-defence will fail. This rule was proposed in *O'Grady* (1987), where D had killed V in the drunken and mistaken belief that he needed to use deadly force to protect himself from being killed. Curiously, the courts seem to be prepared to accept that D may rely on the intoxication to explain a mistake where he is arguing that he believed that V was consenting to the risk of injury (assuming that it was a situation in which genuine consent would have been a defence). This was the effect of the decision in *Richardson and Irwin* (1999).

5.2.6 Mistake

For the most part, D's plea of mistake is merely a denial of *mens rea*. In saying that he made a mistake, D means that he could not have intended or known of the risk of a consequence, or known, or have been aware of the risk of the existence of a particular circumstance. If the offence requires proof of intention/knowledge or subjective recklessness, then an honest mistake is evidence of lack of *mens rea*. If the offence is satisfied by proof of objective recklessness or negligence, then only an honest and reasonable mistake will suffice. This approach to mistake was confirmed by the House of Lords in *DPP v Morgan* (1975), where it was held that D could not be guilty of rape if he genuinely, albeit mistakenly, believed that V was consenting. His belief did not have to be reasonable, though, of course, a reasonable mistake is more likely to be perceived as a genuine mistake. Despite the controversy generated by the ruling, D's conviction for rape was actually upheld because his belief that V was consenting was not credible. His argument had been that he genuinely believed her to be consenting, despite obvious evidence to the contrary, because V's husband had invited him to have sexual intercourse with V and had told him to expect some resistance because 'that was how [V] liked it'.

An alternative way in which mistake may be of relevance is where D pleads a defence which he cannot sustain on the actual facts but argues that it would have been available had the facts been as D mistakenly believed them to be (this is the same kind of situation as that discussed in 5.2.5). The courts have not applied a uniform rule to this kind of claim. In self-defence, for instance, D is entitled to be judged on the facts as he genuinely believed them to be. In *Beckford* (1987), D, a police officer, shot and killed a suspect, V, in the mistaken belief that V was armed and was about to shoot at D. The issue was not whether D's belief was reasonable but simply whether it was genuine. If so, was his response a use of proportionate force in the circumstances that he believed existed? By contrast, the courts have demanded that mistakes made in the context of the defence of duress must be reasonable (see 5.2.7). So, if D mistakenly believes that there is a threat of death or serious injury to himself or another, his defence will fail if the mistake is unreasonable (*Graham* (1982)).

5.2.7 Necessity, duress and duress of circumstances

5.2.7.1 The common basis of the defences

In these defences, D is claiming that he was faced with two possible courses of action: either to commit the offence alleged; or to allow some other harmful consequence to occur. In the case of necessity, it may be that D should be viewed as being in a position to choose between these courses of action. In duress and duress of circumstances, 'compulsion' may be a more appropriate expression than 'choice'. D is claiming that the nature of the harmful consequence was such that, in reality, his will was overborne. The broad concept, of which the other two are more restricted examples, is necessity, but the courts have been reluctant to accept any general defence of necessity and have been more prepared to develop the narrower forms of duress and duress of circumstances. If the defence succeeds, then D is entitled to be acquitted.

Necessity

In a general defence of necessity, D would be entitled to argue that his decision to commit any crime was excused or justified by the need to avoid an even more harmful consequence. For example, D might seek to argue that his decision to break a minor traffic regulation was justified by his desire to get V to a hospital so that V could receive medical treatment for a painful, though perhaps not serious, injury. Of course, it would be necessary to show that there was no other way of achieving this and that the other consequence would have been significantly more harmful than the commission of the offence itself. As indicated above, the judges have never quite been able to bring themselves to acknowledge this broad proposition. They rejected it in the very unusual case of *Dudley and Stephens* (1884), where D1 and D2 killed and ate the cabin boy while adrift at sea after a shipwreck. Ten days after killing the boy, D1 and D2 were rescued by a passing ship. They were charged with murder and, even after a special verdict, were found guilty (although the death sentence was commuted).

But the charge of murder is so grave that courts might be expected to balk at accepting a defence in these circumstances. There have been signs recently that the judges are beginning to accept a more general defence, as in *F v West Berkshire Health Authority* (1989), where a sterilisation operation on a patient who lacked capacity to consent was held to be lawful, as pregnancy was considered to pose risks of great psychiatric harm to the patient. Nevertheless, the development of the defence of duress of circumstances has reduced the scope for the application of the defence of necessity. Additionally, there are numerous examples of specific defences which are underpinned by the notion of necessity and which, therefore, further inhibit the development of the general defence. For example, s 5 of the Criminal Damage Act 1971 provides a defence to the charge of criminal damage where D caused the damage to protect property which he believed to be in immediate need of protection and where he believed that the measures adopted were reasonable.

Duress

In the defence of duress, D is claiming that pressure was applied to D by another to compel him to commit an offence. Examples could include the situation where terrorists kidnap members of D's family and threaten to kill them if D does not assist in the planting of a bomb, or where thieves carry out a kidnap of someone loved by D to force D to give them access to money and other valuables in a shop or bank of which D is the manager.

This defence cannot succeed if:

- *the crime is murder or attempted murder.* The House of Lords laid down this rule in *Howe* (1987) and in *Gotts* (1992), arguing that, in the case of murder, the sanctity of life must be protected and that severe anomalies would arise if duress were to be made available for a charge of attempted murder. No account was taken of the arguments that D might be saving the lives of many at the expense of the life of one, or that it may be unjust and impractical to expect D to risk the life of members of his family (rather than his own) in order to preserve the life of a stranger;

- *D has been at fault in associating himself with a person or group whom he knew might threaten him with death or serious injury to compel him to commit an offence.* This rule evolved in connection with membership of terrorist gangs but was applied to association with criminal gangs in general in the case of *Sharp* (1987), where D knew that he was joining a violent gang whose leader was willing to use firearms and would not permit him to withdraw from the armed robberies at post offices in which they were engaged. It was further extended to voluntary association with an individual in *Ali* (1995). It was held that D could not plead duress to a charge of robbery as the evidence showed that he knew that the drug dealer with whom he was involved was extremely violent and would be likely to threaten his life to compel him to commit crimes to pay money owing on a drugs deal. D may rely on this defence where he voluntarily participates in a criminal enterprise without knowing of any violent tendencies on the part of his associates *Shepherd* (1988). It seems that D may not rely on the defence if he enters into an association with a violent criminal (such as a supplier of drugs) but does not anticipate that the criminal will require him to commit offences (such as drug-trafficking); *Harmer* (2002), Crim LR 401. This principle was recently reaffirmed by the House of Lords; *R v Hasan* (2005) UKHL 22. According to Lord Bingham: 'The policy of the law must be to discourage association with known criminals, and should be slow to excuse the criminal conduct of those who do so. If a person voluntarily becomes or remains associated with others engaged in a criminal activity in a situation where he knows or ought reasonably to know that he may be made the subject of compulsion by them or their associates, he cannot rely on the defence of duress to excuse any act which he is therefore compelled to do by them'.

If the offence is not murder or attempted murder and there is no voluntary association with violent criminals, then D's plea of duress must satisfy further tests.

First, his will must have been overborne by a threat of death or serious injury to himself or any other person, made with the purpose of compelling him to commit a particular crime, which he could only avert by committing the crime.

A threat of death or serious injury

Threats of serious psychological injury (*Baker and Wilkins* (1997)) or other unpleasant consequences, such as shame at being revealed as a homosexual (*R v Valderrama-Vega* (1985)), are insufficient. Where D acts for more than one reason, the threat of death or serious injury must be the overwhelming reason (in other words, he would not have done it if there had been no such threat: *R v Valderrama-Vega*).

... to himself or any other person

Family members would be the most obvious example, but there is no reason why D should not feel compelled to prevent injury to a stranger.

... which D could only avert by committing the crime

This suggests that the threat could have been implemented immediately and before D could realistically seek any help, as in a case where, though D is himself free, his family are being held and could be injured at any time if he does not comply. However, a liberal interpretation was adopted in *Hudson and Taylor* (1971), where convictions for perjury of D1 and D2, women aged 19 and 17, were quashed. Threats to cut them up if they gave evidence against X in his criminal trial had been made by Y. Y was present at the trial and D1 and D2, even though within the protection of the court, felt too intimidated to give truthful evidence. It was held that the threat was capable of being no less real and present if it could be carried out on the streets that night, even if it could not be carried out immediately.

The approach in *Hudson and Taylor* was followed in *Abdul-Hussain and Others* (1999), where it was suggested that the threat must be 'imminent' in the sense that it hangs over D in a sufficiently powerful way as to make the threat 'immediate'. That is, that the threat is operating at the relevant time to overbear D's will. The defence does not require that D should act virtually spontaneously in response to a threat that could be carried out in the next few minutes. On the other hand, an aspect of the immediacy of the threat is that D has no opportunity to avoid it except by committing the offence. A delay between the threat and its implementation may give D the opportunity to avoid committing the offence and might deprive him of the defence if he chose not to take it. This was exactly the view taken in *Heath* (1999), where it was held that D's defence of duress failed because he had had about three days in which he could have contacted the police and thus avoided delivering a consignment of cannabis which he had been ordered to collect.

This is the subjective aspect of the defence of duress (because we are asking whether D's will was overborne), but it contains objective elements. For example, any mistake made by D as to the existence or nature of the threat or as to a possible avenue of escape, must be reasonable, otherwise the defence will be lost (*Graham*).

The second requirement is that it must appear that a sober person of reasonable firmness, sharing D's characteristics, would have responded as D did – this introduces a still stronger objective element into the requirements for duress. Even if D's will was overborne by the threats, his defence will be unsuccessful if he did not display the courage and fortitude to be expected of the average person. However, in applying this test, a concession is granted. The reasonable person will be presumed to 'share D's characteristics'. In other words, we must ask: 'Would the will of a person of average courage and fortitude, possessing the relevant characteristics of D, have been overborne by the threats?' In *Bowen* (1996), it was held that:

- mere pliability, vulnerability, timidity, and undue susceptibility to threats are not characteristics shared by the person of reasonable firmness, and nor are characteristics due to self-induced abuse such as alcohol or drug abuse or glue-sniffing;

- on the other hand, D may be in a category of persons whom the jury may think are less able to resist pressure than those not within any such category (by reason of, for example, age, possibly sex, pregnancy (because of added fear for the unborn child), serious physical disability, recognised mental illness or psychiatric condition, such as post-traumatic stress disorder leading to learned helplessness). In such cases, the correct test will be how a reasonable person with such a characteristic would have responded.

These considerations led the court to suggest that in most cases, only D's age and sex would be relevant characteristics. The court rejected D's appeal against conviction for obtaining services by deception. He claimed that he had committed the offence because two men threatened to petrol bomb him and his family if he did not obtain the goods, and that he had not told police because he was worried about repercussions. It was held that D's vulnerability was irrelevant and his low IQ of 68 fell short of mental impairment or defect and could not be classified as a characteristic which made those who possessed it less courageous and less able to withstand threats and pressure.

Duress of circumstances

In duress of circumstances, the threat which compels D to commit an offence arises out of the 'circumstances'. These circumstances may include:

- deliberate conduct by another person. Just as in duress, the threat of injury to D or others may come from another person. Unlike duress, the threat is not made with the aim of compelling D to commit the offence;

- natural events, accidental conduct and so on. The threat may result from natural catastrophes such as flooding or fire, more personal events such as the sudden onset of illness or from some accident which has befallen a person.

However, the circumstances must be in some way external to D's own thoughts and responses; they cannot be constituted entirely by those thoughts and responses. So, in *Rodger and Rose* (1998), D1 and D2, who were serving terms of life imprisonment for murder, were unable to rely on the defence. They alleged that they had tried to break out of prison because an increase in the original tariff recommended by the trial judge in each case had made them suicidal (and this constituted the threat of death). It was held that the circumstances allegedly imposing the duress were the suicidal thoughts, not the Home Secretary's decisions on raising the tariffs.

The defence of duress of circumstances was initially developed in a series of cases which all involved driving offences. A typical example is *Conway* (1989), in which D drove recklessly (as the offence then was) to escape from two men who had approached his car. He did so because, two weeks earlier, his passenger had narrowly escaped serious injury when he was the target of an attack on another vehicle, and D now feared that a further attack was about to be made. Though the two men later proved to be plain clothes police officers, it was held that there was a valid defence. Again, in *DPP v Bell* (1992), the defence was available to D when he drove with excess alcohol to escape from a gang of men intent on injuring him and stopped in a layby as soon as he believed himself to be out of danger. Until the case of *Pommell* (1995), some doubts persisted as to whether the defence was available only to driving offences. In that case, the Court of Appeal made it clear that the defence is not limited to any particular kind of offence but is of general application. Police had discovered D in possession of a firearm and the trial judge had ruled that D's claim that he was keeping it only to prevent his friend from using it to shoot someone could not found a defence. Holding that the defence of duress of circumstances should have been left to the jury, the court ordered a re-trial.

Though it is evidently a 'necessity' defence, duress of circumstances is much narrower than a true defence of necessity because its elements follow those of duress. So:

- it is not available where the charge is murder or attempted murder;

- it may not be available if D knowingly and voluntarily exposed himself to the risk of compulsion (this is merely speculation by analogy with duress, since there is no decision on the issue);

- the threat must be one of death or serious injury;

- D's will must be overborne by the threat;

- a sober person of reasonable firmness would have responded as D did.

A final important point to note is that the defence will not be available if there is a legislative provision which deals with the situation in which D finds himself. In *DPP v Harris* (1995), D was a police officer who drove across a junction against a red light and collided with another vehicle whilst following a gang believed to be intending to commit robbery. He could not use the defence of duress of circumstances because reg 34(1)(b) of the Traffic Signs Regulations and General Directions 1981 specified the circumstances in which the emergency and police services may proceed against a red light and this did not include the circumstances here.

5.2.8   Self-defence/prevention of crime

The rule that a person may use reasonable force to defend himself and his property is long established and is firmly rooted in our beliefs about our rights. Its application to particular facts, however, can often prove very difficult. In recent years, much controversy has been provoked by the criminal prosecution of ordinary people who allegedly used excessive force, usually involving a weapon, to protect themselves or their property from determined criminals. One of the most notorious examples was the case of *Revill v Newbery* (1996), in which a 76 year old man, tired of constant theft and vandalism at his allotment, had waited in his shed late at night and shot and injured V. A criminal prosecution against D failed but he was found guilty of negligence in a civil action brought by V and was required to pay V compensation (even though V had himself been convicted of criminal offences in connection with the incident). Another case involved a Norfolk famer who was convicted of murder after shooting a burglar. The conviction for murder was eventually reduced to manslaughter by the Court of Appeal; *Martin* (2000), 2 Cr App R 42.

The rule provides that D may act not only in protection of himself and his property, but also in protection of the person and property of others and, more generally, to prevent the commission of any crime. In most cases, when D acts to protect his own person and property, or those of any other person, he will be acting in the prevention of crime, but the law formerly distinguished between self-defence and prevention of crime by applying different rules. Even today, when the rules are identical, self-defence still survives because not all cases of justifiable use of force can be described as prevention of crime if 'crime' means that all the elements of an offence are present. For instance, the person allegedly committing the crime which causes D's response may be under the age of criminal responsibility, or may not have *mens rea* or may be insane.

The rule on force in the prevention of crime is expressed in s 3 of the Criminal Law Act 1967:

> A person may use such force as is reasonable in the circumstances in the prevention of crime, or in effecting or assisting in the lawful arrest of offenders or suspected offenders or of persons unlawfully at large.

The courts have gradually modified the common law defence of self-defence to bring its rules into line with the statutory requirement for prevention of crime. In doing so, they have removed special rules dealing, for instance, with the duty to 'retreat' before striking a blow in self-defence.

So, in both defences, the use of force will be reasonable if two conditions are satisfied:

(1) *the use of some force is necessary* – whether in relation to the facts as they actually were or in relation to the facts as D believed them to be, even if he was mistaken. Any mistake as to the facts (which could be about whether any attack was taking place or about the amount of force being used in the attack, or both) merely has to be genuine. It does not have to be reasonable. So, in *Beckford* (1987), a police officer was able to use the defence when he shot dead a suspect whom he had gone to arrest and whom he mistakenly believed to have a gun which he was about to use against the police officer. The only exception to this rule is that D may not rely upon a mistake which is induced by intoxication, whether the offence is one of specific or basic intent (*O'Grady* (1987));

(2) *the actual force used must be proportionate* – an objective test is applied here, that is, would a reasonable person consider that an appropriate degree of force was used in view of the danger which existed or which D genuinely believed to exist? In applying this test, it must be remembered that D may well be experiencing a great deal of fear and will probably have little time to make careful judgments about the level of force which he should use. This explains the suggestion of Lord Morris in *Palmer v R* (1971) that a sympathetic view should be taken of the level of force which D 'honestly and instinctively thought necessary' in 'a moment of unexpected anguish'. The requirement for proportion, therefore, permits the use of extreme (even deadly) force to counter a threat of death or serious injury, and the use of lesser force where less serious injury or, perhaps, damage to property, is threatened. The use of wholly disproportionate force, however, cannot be justified; *Owino* (1996) 2 Cr App R 128.

Unlike the defences of duress and duress of circumstances, there is no restriction to the offences to which self-defence/prevention of crime can be a defence. In particular, the defence can be, and often is, pleaded to a charge of murder. However, if D kills when using more force than is proportionate, even though some force was necessary, he will lose the defence entirely and will be convicted of murder, not merely of manslaughter. This proposition was starkly illustrated in the case of *Clegg* (1995), where a British soldier serving in Northern Ireland shot at a car which had broken through a checkpoint, killing a passenger. It subsequently emerged that the driver and passengers were joyriders, not terrorists. D was adjudged to have used excessive force, since the danger to other soldiers from the speeding car or anything its occupants might do had passed once the car had cleared the checkpoint. Accordingly, D's conviction for murder was upheld (later developments saw D's conviction quashed and his acquittal at a re-trial but his conviction for lesser offences arising out of the incident).

The old rules on self-defence required D to retreat if at all possible, at any rate before using deadly force. Evidence that D did retreat or did try to avoid a physical confrontation is certainly powerful evidence that he was not the aggressor and that what he did truly was done in self-defence. Even so, the modern rule is merely that it must be necessary to use force. If retreat or negotiation were possible, then force may not have been necessary. But retreat or attempts to talk may only delay the inevitable and, sometimes, striking the first blow may be the most effective form of defence. Indeed, in some cases, not to strike the first blow may be to invite inevitable disaster. These realities were recognised in *Bird* (1985), where the Court of Appeal held that there is no duty to seek to avoid a confrontation (whether by retreat or other means). The court therefore considered that even if D had struck the first blow in lashing out at V with a glass whilst being restrained by him, that was not inconsistent with the notion of self-defence.

Equally, D will not lose the defence simply because he knowingly 'walked into trouble'. A person is not required to avoid going to places where he may lawfully go but where he knows that danger may await, as occurred in *Field* (1972). In that case, D went to a café despite having been warned that V and others were waiting for him there. Nor is evidence that D was unlawfully in possession of a weapon necessarily fatal to the defence. It would be absurd to suggest that force was necessary in self-defence but that, in using proportionate force, D should not be able to use whatever was to hand. In both cases, of course, such evidence may reduce the credibility of D's claim to have been acting in self-defence or in the prevention of crime.

5.2.9 Self-defence/prevention of crime and duress of circumstances

There is clearly a very close connection between these defences and it may sometimes be difficult to decide which is the correct one to argue. If the elements were essentially the same, it would make little difference. However, duress of circumstances is a much more limited defence than that of self-defence/prevention of crime:

- duress of circumstances cannot be pleaded to a charge of murder or attempted murder;

- duress of circumstances may not be available where D has voluntarily put himself in a position where he knows there is a risk of compulsion;

- duress of circumstances requires a threat of death or serious injury;

- any mistake made by D must be reasonable if he is to rely on the defence of duress of circumstances.

None of these restrictions apply to the defence of self-defence/prevention of crime.

Symonds (1998) provides an interesting example of the close connection between the defences. D was charged with both inflicting grievous bodily harm on V and dangerous driving. He had driven off in his car whilst V's arm was trapped in the door and V had been dragged for a distance, suffering injury. D and V gave conflicting accounts of how this occurred. V was a drunken pedestrian and his story was that D was racing another car and that he (V) was forced to jump out of the way of D's car. When D's car stopped, V put his hand into the driver's window to stop D driving off so that he could remonstrate with him, but D drove off. D said that V had lurched into his path, forcing him to stop, and had then tried to pull him from the car. D was very frightened and drove off to escape. The trial judge directed the jury on self-defence as a defence to the grievous bodily harm count but did not do so in relation to the driving offence or to the lesser offence of careless driving, which the judge left to the jury without consultation with counsel. D was acquitted of the counts charged but convicted of careless driving. The Court of Appeal allowed the appeal. Though it was difficult to think in terms of self-defence in offences where D did not use force on another (careless driving, in this instance), the elements relied on for self-defence in the grievous bodily harm offence were the same as those which would make out the defence of duress of circumstances for the driving offence and the judge should have directed the jury to this effect (of course, it is not really true to say that the elements of the two defences are the same!).

5.3 Offences Against the Person

5.3.1 Introduction

The protection of individuals against physical injury is traditionally seen as one of the most important functions of the criminal law. The offence of murder itself is usually regarded as the most serious offence in criminal law (save, perhaps, for treason in times of war). This is recognised by the unusual (but increasingly common) provision of a mandatory sentence (life imprisonment) for its commission. Although all convicted murderers receive life sentences, judges have traditionally had considerable discretion when recommending how long they should serve in prison before being considered for parole. This discretion has been greatly curtailed by the Criminal Justice Act 2003. In essence, judges are required to impose minimum prison sentences according to the type of murder. The starting point for an 'ordinary' murder – if there is such a thing – is fifteen years.

Manslaughter, however, covers an enormous range of culpable killings, from those which are little short of murder to those which are barely more than accidental. Similarly, the non-fatal offences against the person encompass a range from the intentional infliction of very serious injury, in which it may be the merest chance that the victim survives and that the charge is not murder, to conduct which merely causes a person to fear violence without ever inflicting it. Murder and manslaughter are still almost entirely defined by the common law and have attracted criticism precisely because they have not been subjected to statutory reform. The non-fatal offences are largely defined in the Offences Against the Person Act 1861, a statute which has patently exceeded its useful life and the deficiencies of which have also prompted persistent calls for reform.

5.3.2 Unlawful homicide

5.3.2.1 *The* actus reus *of unlawful homicide*

The traditional definition of the *actus reus* of unlawful homicide requires proof that D:

(a) *causes death* – the difficult issues arising out of this requirement have already been considered when causation was examined in 5.1.3. The old rule that death must occur within a year and a day has been abolished by the Law Reform (Year and a Day Rule) Act 1996. However, the Attorney General must consent to any prosecution where the death occurred more than three years after the incident or where D has already been convicted of an offence committed in circumstances alleged to be connected with the death;

(b) *of a human being* – this means that aborting a foetus or damaging it in such a way that it is not born alive cannot be murder (separate offences of procuring miscarriage and child destruction exist to cover these kinds of injuries). However, as long as the baby is born alive, it may be the victim of homicide even where the conduct which eventually caused its death took place whilst the baby was unborn. In *AG's Reference (No 3 of 1994)* (1997), D caused serious injury to X whilst she was pregnant.

Consequently, V was born prematurely and survived for only a few months. It was held that D could have been guilty of the manslaughter of V on these facts. The House of Lords rejected the claim that this was murder because it was not satisfied that an appropriate *mens rea* could be found, but it did not rule out the possibility of a murder conviction where D's acts are directed at the foetus itself, rather than at the mother.

There are two other important points here:

- a comatose person who has already suffered brain-stem death is dead, even though he may appear to be alive because vital functions are being performed by a machine. When the machine is switched off, this does not break the chain of causation between D's conduct and V's death, as D had already caused V's death. The only issue here is whether a proper diagnosis of brain-stem death has been made and the courts have insisted that they will not challenge the medical diagnosis except on the strongest of evidence (*Malcherek* (1981));

- different considerations apply in the case of comatose victims in a persistent vegetative state. Such victims are neither legally nor medically dead but the House of Lords ruled in *Airedale NHS Trust v Bland* (1992) that 'treatment' may be withdrawn or withheld if in the best interests of the patient. This does not permit acts with no purpose other than to bring about V's death (such as a lethal injection), but withholding or withdrawal of treatment can be viewed as an omission (and therefore permissible) in circumstances where the doctors are under no duty to act. The distinctions between acts and omissions and treatment and general feeding are subtle in such cases. In *Airedale NHS Trust v Bland*, it was impossible to feed V except by intrusive methods which were characterised as 'treatment', and this gave the House of Lords the opportunity to permit the course of action by the doctors' withdrawal of treatment which eventually resulted in V's death;

(c) *within the Queen's peace* – in practice, this includes everyone except enemy aliens killed in the heat of battle.

Murder

The *mens rea* of murder is traditionally called 'malice aforethought', but in truth requires neither malice nor forethought but simply an intention to cause death or grievous bodily harm. Contrary to popular belief, murder does not require a 'premeditated' killing. One old case involved a butcher who killed a disrespectful customer with a meat cleaver; *Watts v Brains* (1600), Cro Eliz 778. Most of the cases on the meaning of intention were cases arising out of murder charges (see the discussion of those cases in 5.1.3).

The other aspect of the definition of malice aforethought which remains controversial is its extension to an intention to cause 'grievous bodily harm'. There is no definition of such harm, beyond the assertion that it means 'really serious' harm. There is little complaint about this in cases where D's acts are aimed at causing injury which is obviously of a life-threatening nature, such as head injuries sustained in a punching or kicking assault; Cunningham (1981) 2 All ER 863. But the liability goes further than this.

At present, D may be guilty of murder if he kills V by an act which he intends will cause serious injury but which he does not intend to be life-threatening serious injury (and which even a reasonable person would not have viewed as likely to cause life-threatening serious injury). For instance, he might deliberately break V's leg in circumstances where V will readily be able to get medical treatment but V dies because of complications which occur during surgery. A more difficult case might involve a 'glassing'. D hits V in the face with a beer glass. V dies as a result. Although D may have intended to injure V, he did not consider the possibility that the glass would shatter and sever a vital artery.

The House of Lords has criticised this rule on two occasions (*AG's Reference (No 3 of 1994)* (1997) and *Powell and Daniels* (1997)), rejecting the views of its staunch proponent, Lord Hailsham in *Cunningham* (1981), and has called for legislative intervention to change the rule.

Voluntary manslaughter

Although English law recognises manslaughter as a single offence (indictments refer to 'manslaughter'), it is customary to distinguish between voluntary and involuntary manslaughter. Voluntary manslaughter covers those killings where D has the *mens rea* for murder but the law regards the killing as partly excused due to:

- diminished responsibility; or

- provocation.

(A further excuse is provided in cases where D kills V in the course of carrying out a suicide pact to which they are both parties.)

The effect of a successful plea is that D is acquitted of murder but convicted of manslaughter, which leaves the sentence at the discretion of the judge. As was stated above, those convicted of murder can expect prison terms which range from around fifteen years to life.

The defences of diminished responsibility and provocation are only relevant if the evidence appears to show that D did have the *mens rea* of murder. If D did not have the *mens rea* then the crime can be no more than manslaughter anyway.

Diminished responsibility

This defence was created by s 2 of the Homicide Act 1957 with the aim of filling a gap left by the rules on the common law defence of insanity. As explained in 5.2.3, the defence of insanity only succeeds in cases where D either has no idea of the physical nature of what he is doing or is so disturbed that he does not realise that it is legally wrong. Yet there were obvious cases of reduced mental capacity or responsibility which would not fit within the defence and where, as a convicted murderer, D faced the death penalty. The new statutory defence enabled the law to take account of these other conditions.

Two preliminary points:

- the burden of proof lies on D unless the Crown seeks to show that D was suffering from diminished responsibility (for example, where D's state of mind is put in issue by a plea of insanity or automatism). If D does not raise the issue but it emerges through the evidence, the judge has no duty other than to point it out to D's counsel (*Campbell* (1997));

- there must be medical evidence to support the plea. Uncontradicted medical evidence entitles, but does not oblige, the judge to direct a conviction for manslaughter.

Section 2 of the Homicide Act 1957 defines diminished responsibility as:

> ... such abnormality of mind (whether arising from a condition of arrested or retarded development of mind or any inherent causes or induced by disease or injury) as substantially impaired his mental responsibility for his acts or omissions ...

It is clear from this definition that there are three requirements:

(1) *An abnormality of mind*

This was defined in the case of Byrne (1960) as requiring:

> ... a state of mind so different from that of ordinary human beings that the reasonable man would term it abnormal ...

In the case itself, D had killed and mutilated a young woman whilst suffering powerful urges which did not prevent him from knowing what he was doing but which he found impossible or very difficult to control. He was described as a sexual psychopath and his condition qualified as an abnormality of mind.

(2) *Arising from a condition of arrested or retarded development of mind or any inherent causes or induced by disease or injury*

It is not enough that there is an abnormality of mind. The abnormality has to result from a specified cause, though the causes are defined in such broad terms that this requirement is often relatively easy to satisfy. It is also clear that there is a great deal of overlap amongst the causes: 'arrested or retarded development of mind' would amply cover those whose so called 'mental age' remains far lower than their age in years; 'inherent causes' can be interpreted as including functional mental disorders and 'disease or injury' is self-explanatory. Action in the grip of powerful emotions such as jealousy would probably not qualify, unless the condition was extreme.

Pleas of diminished responsibility are often linked with intoxication. A person who is intoxicated may well be described as suffering from a temporary abnormality of mind but the intoxicant is not a specified cause within the statute. So:

- abnormality due only to intoxication is excluded. If there is evidence of intoxication as well as some other possible cause of the abnormality, the jury must ignore the intoxication and determine whether there was a sufficient abnormality due to any specified cause. This approach was established in *Fenton* (1975) and confirmed in *Gittens* (1984), where the trial judge had made the mistake of inviting the jury to examine the respective contributions of intoxication and mental illness to D's abnormality which had caused him to kill his wife and stepdaughter;

- abnormality due to disease or injury caused by the effects of drink or drugs is admissible. So, too, is abnormality due to intoxication where the drinking (or, presumably, drug taking) is involuntary in the sense that D cannot resist taking the drink. This rule emerged from *Tandy* (1987), in which D, an alcoholic, had strangled her 11 year old daughter after drinking a large amount of vodka, which was not her usual drink. However, because the evidence suggested that D could have resisted the first drink (though not subsequent drinks), her defence failed. The intoxication was not involuntary.

(3) Substantial impairment of mental responsibility

The courts have interpreted this provision as requiring an impairment which must be more than trivial but which need not be total. In the case where D is driven by an impulse, as in *Byrne*, his difficulty in controlling his impulse must merely be substantially greater than that experienced by an ordinary person.

There is some evidence that courts are willing to adopt a broad view of diminished responsibility when dealing with sympathetic cases and a more narrow interpretation when dealing with less sympathetic ones.

5.3.2.2 Provocation

Provocation was, and remains, a common law defence, though its elements have been modified significantly by s 3 of the Homicide Act 1957. Its essence is that D, though *prima facie* guilty of murder, killed whilst suffering a sudden and temporary loss of self-control in response to something said and/or done by another person. Additionally, D's response must be such as might have been expected of a reasonable person in the same situation. So, the defence will succeed if the following elements were present:

- there was provocation;

- D lost self-control and killed on account of that provocation; and

- a reasonable person would have done as D did.

If any evidence that D was provoked to lose his self-control appears at the trial, whether the issue is expressly raised by D or not (even if D asserts that he did not kill V – *Cambridge* (1994)), then the judge must put the defence to the jury, which has the task of deciding both whether D did lose his self-control on account of the provocation (the subjective test) and whether a reasonable person would have done as D did (the objective test). The onus is on the Crown to disprove the defence beyond reasonable doubt. However, there must be some evidence on which the jury can deliberate. It is not enough that there may be a strong suspicion that, if D did attack V, it was because he lost self-control. Without some evidence, there would be nothing on which the jury could determine whether a reasonable man would have done as D did (*Acott* (1997)).

Nature of provocation

Section 3 of the Homicide Act makes it absolutely clear that D can be provoked by words or conduct ('whether by things done or by things said or by both together') but does not specify who must offer the provocation nor to who it must be directed. Subsequent interpretation now seems firmly to have established that it need not come from V, nor need it be directed at D. In *Davies* (1975), D immediately sought out and killed his estranged wife, V, upon seeing her lover walking in the direction of the place where she worked. Though his conviction was upheld, the Court of Appeal ruled that the trial judge had misdirected the jury in telling them that only the conduct of V was capable of being provocation. The conduct of her lover in walking to meet her was also capable of being provocation.

Implicit in the decision in *Davies* are two further rules. First, the conduct does not have to be directed at D, since the lover was totally unaware that he was being observed by D. Second, the provocation need not consist of unlawful conduct. *Doughty* (1986), where the crying of a small baby was held to be capable of being provocation, is a dramatic illustration of both of these rules.

Incidents which have occurred well before the time of the killing are unlikely to be capable of amounting to provocation in themselves. However, evidence of such incidents may be very important in explaining why the most immediate incident, which may in itself have seemed to be very trivial, should be regarded as provocation. In *Davies*, the lover's apparently innocent conduct in walking down the street took on a totally different meaning when viewed in the light of a number of incidents arising out of D's separation from V and which had taken place over the previous nine months. Similarly, in *Humphreys* (1995), there was a considerable history of violence, exploitation and emotional abuse in D's relationship with V, as well as evidence of more immediate provocation at the time of the killing. The Court of Appeal held that it was a misdirection by the judge not to analyse for the jury's benefit the 'several distinct and cumulative strands of potentially provocative conduct'.

Since the judge must allow the jury to consider the defence if there is any evidence of provocation, he cannot withdraw it from the jury merely because the provocative conduct was itself provoked by D, as where D picks a fight in the course of which he becomes enraged at V's response. This was recognised in *Johnson* (1989), where D had stabbed V after being assaulted and threatened with a glass by V. V's actions had been in response to unpleasant behaviour and violent threats from D.

D must have lost self-control on account of the provocation

The defence does not license controlled acts (of revenge, for example) nor those where there is merely a loss of self-restraint, as occurred in *Cocker* (1989), where D eventually gave way to the persistent requests of his terminally ill wife that he should end her life. However, though it is proper to describe the loss of self-control required as being such that D was 'no longer master of his mind' (as did Devlin J in *Duffy* (1949)), this does not require that D should have suffered a complete loss of control so that he does not know what he is doing (*Richens* (1994)).

Evidence that some time elapsed between the last provocative act and D's response ('cooling off' time) will cast doubt on D's assertion that he killed whilst suffering a loss of self-control. In the highly controversial case of *Thornton* (1992) (where the main defence was diminished responsibility), the Court of Appeal considered that when directing the jury on provocation, the trial judge had been correct to emphasise the fact that the requirement for a sudden and temporary loss of self-control and D's behaviour indicated that though she had suffered threats of violence a relatively short time before, she had cooled down by the time she killed her husband. However, it is important to recognise, as the Court of Appeal strongly emphasised in the cases of *Thornton*, *Ahluwalia* (1992) and, on a further and successful appeal, *Thornton (No 2)* (1995) that the only rule is that D must have suffered a sudden and temporary loss of self-control related to words or deeds capable of being regarded as provocation. There is no rule that the response must be immediate. Two examples of possible delayed response might be:

- D immediately begins to 'seethe' on being subjected to the provocation and this builds up until there is a loss of self-control. This must be distinguished from a 'slow burn' response, where there is either no actual loss of self-control or a loss of self-control too remote from any act of provocation (as is possibly the case with battered women who kill);

- D loses self-control immediately in response to the provocation and remains out of control for some time, during which time the killing takes place. In *Baillie* (1995), on being informed by his youngest son that the drug dealer (V) who supplied all his sons was intending to punish them for switching to a different dealer, D immediately went into a rage, armed himself with a shotgun and razor, and drove to V's house. There he seriously injured V with the razor and then, as V tried to escape, shot and killed him. It was held that there was sufficient evidence that D had remained out of control during the whole of this episode.

A reasonable person would have done as D did

The Homicide Act places the responsibility for deciding whether a reasonable person would have done as D did entirely in the hands of the jury. This means that there is no longer any scope for the judge to tell the jury how the reasonable person would respond. In particular, there is no longer any rule that D's response (the act of killing) must be proportionate to the provocation.

But the courts have retained some power to direct the jury about who the reasonable person is and about the general nature of his responses. The House of Lords in *Morhall* (1995) was anxious to make it clear that the reasonable person test invites comparison with the response of an ordinary person placed in the same situation as D, not with a person using powers of reason in the way that might be expected in the application, say, of the tort of negligence. Essentially, the test serves the policy of denying the defence to those who are perceived as too quick to lose their temper and/or to react excessively.

In *DPP v Camplin* (1978), the House of Lords had held that the reasonable person must be regarded as having the power of self-control to be expected of an ordinary person (not unusually pugnacious or excitable) of the age and sex of D, and bearing such other characteristics of D as are relevant to the gravity of the provocation. In *Newell* (1980), the Court of Appeal stressed that the characteristics should have some degree of permanence and be in some way unusual and that the characteristics would affect the gravity of the provocation by being the target of that provocation (so that D's characteristic of being an alcoholic was properly regarded as irrelevant because the provocation concerned insulting remarks made by V about D's girlfriend). However, the House of Lords in *Morhall* counselled against an emphasis on 'characteristics' and preferred to stress that the jury should consider a reasonable man placed in 'the entire factual situation' in which D found himself or subject to 'all those factors' which would affect the gravity of the provocation. A solvent abuser who becomes aggressive after being insulted is therefore entitled to have his sensitivities regarding accusations of 'glue sniffing' taken into account.

It may be possible to draw a distinction between:

- factors which affect the gravity of the provocation experienced by D; and

- factors which affect D's capacity for self-control.

The argument would then be that the reasonable person should be considered to have been exposed to all the factors (including possession of any of D's personal characteristics) which would determine the degree of provocation experienced by D, but would not share any lack of capacity for self-control which D might display. Put simply, if D, an extremely bad-tempered man, had killed V after V taunted him about his big nose, the reasonable person would have a big nose (relevant to the gravity of the provocation) but would not be bad-tempered (relevant only to D's capacity for self-control).

Factors affecting the gravity of the provocation might include:

- sex, age and (im)maturity – the latter two factors may obviously affect capacity for self-control. So, in *DPP v Camplin*, D's age (15) was regarded as relevant to his capacity for self-control when taunted by V about the sexual assault which V had just performed on him. Similarly, in *Humphreys*, D's immaturity was regarded as relevant where she had suffered an unhappy childhood including drug abuse and sexual promiscuity, had been exploited as a prostitute by V and had killed him when she was 17 years old. However, age was regarded as irrelevant in *Ali* (1989) where a 20 year old man had stabbed another in a disco. At that age, D was no more immature than anyone else. The relevance of sex as such is less obvious;

- characteristics (permanent or otherwise) which are the specific target of the provocation and therefore increase its gravity, for example, addiction to glue-sniffing (*Morhall*) and attention-seeking traits (*Humphreys*);

- the general background of relevant events – for instance, the reasonable person must be assumed to have experienced any earlier instances of provocative conduct which may have produced a cumulative effect;

- other general conditions such as obsessiveness and eccentricity (*Dryden* (1995)) and battered woman syndrome (*Ahluwalia; Thornton (No 2)*, but see the comments below on *Luc Thiet Thuan v R* (1996)).

At present, there is some confusion about exactly how the courts should treat factors which merely affect D's capacity for self-control. In *Luc Thiet Thuan v R*, the Privy Council held that the reasonable person should not be invested with D's organic brain disorder which allegedly caused D to lose self-control more easily. The Privy Council stressed that characteristics which may merely have a general effect on powers of self-control may not be attributed to the reasonable person since, by definition, the reasonable person has the powers of self-control of an ordinary person and is not unusually short-tempered, aggressive or prone to lose self-control. This seems consistent with the House of Lords' decisions in *DPP v Camplin* and *Morhall* but it casts doubt on the suggestion in *Ahluwalia* and in *Thornton (No 2)* that account can be taken of the condition of 'learnt helplessness' arising from battered woman syndrome. This approach also places a question mark over the decision in *Dryden* regarding 'obsessiveness and eccentricity'.

In *Smith* (2000) 3 WLR 654, a majority of the House of Lords broadly followed the approach adopted in cases such as Morhall, Dryden and Humphreys. Evidence had been introduced at D's trial for murder (in relation to a plea of diminished responsibility) that D was suffering from a depressive illness which might have reduced his threshold for erupting with violence and might have disinhibited him. On the issue of provocation, the trial judge ruled that this characteristic was relevant only to the gravity of the provocation and not to the reasonable man's loss of self-control. On appeal against his conviction for murder, D successfully contended that the decisions in *Ahluwalia, Humphreys, Dryden* and *Thornton (No 2)* favoured a flexible approach to the reasonable man test, so that the trial judge's ruling was incorrect. The Court of Appeal considered that the defence of provocation was gradually increasing in scope and that there was nothing in *Camplin* to support the distinction between characteristics relevant only to gravity and characteristics relevant to loss of control. *Morhall* was not concerned with this distinction and there was nothing said in that case that was inconsistent with the Court of Appeal decisions in *Thornton (No 2)* and the other cases. *Luc Thiet Thuan* was not binding on the Court of Appeal; the earlier Court of Appeal decisions were. This view was upheld by the House of Lords. It seems that any characteristics of a defendant can now be taken into account by a court in deciding whether the 'objective' element of provocation is satisfied. A recent decision of the Court of Appeal suggests that these characteristics may include obsessive jealousy; *Weller* (2004), 1 Cr App R 1.

It is clear that senior judges hold different views regarding provocation. In June 2005 the Privy Council dealt with an appeal from the Court of Appeal of Jersey; *R v Holley* (2005) UKPC 23. The case arose after a chronic alcoholic killed his girlfriend with an axe. The majority judgment was that a jury should be told to judge a defendant's loss of self-control by reference to the standard of the degree of self-control to be expected of an ordinary person of the defendant's age and sex. A dissenting judgment favoured the more subjective approach adopted in *Smith*.

The concept of 'provocation' is deeply problematical. It implies that a jealous husband who intentionally kills his 'unfaithful' spouse may have a partial defence to a murder charge. In theory, he would have to show that he acted reasonably. In reality, most persons confronted with adultery do not decide to use lethal force. If this were not the case the workload of the divorce courts would be significantlt reduced. In 2004 the Law Commission published a report titled *Partial Defences* to *Murder*. It seems that a major review of the law relating to homicide is imminent.

5.3.2.3   *Involuntary manslaughter*

Involuntary manslaughter extends to all blameworthy killings in which D's *mens rea* is less than that required for murder. It may be established through two, or possibly three, different routes:

- proof that D killed in the course of committing an unlawful and dangerous act (unlawful act or constructive manslaughter);

- proof that D killed in the course of any conduct with gross negligence (gross negligence manslaughter). This was re-established in *Prentice* (1993) and affirmed in *Adomako* (1994);

- proof that D killed in the course of any conduct and was subjectively reckless as to serious (or, perhaps, some) injury (subjective reckless manslaughter). It is unclear whether the revival of gross negligence manslaughter has also revived this category.

Unlawful act manslaughter

Involuntary manslaughter by an unlawful act is also known as constructive manslaughter. Its essence is that D caused V's death whilst engaged in an act which was both a crime and created a risk of some personal injury. Typically, it occurs when D attacks V intending relatively minor injury (an act which is a crime and, self-evidently, creates a risk of some personal injury) and V sustains unexpectedly severe injuries from which death results – a very common cause is a broken skull suffered by V when falling backwards under a blow and striking his head on a wall or a kerb.

The Crown must prove the following elements.

An unlawful act ...

Though the courts insist on using this term, they actually mean a crime, despite one or two instances where they have been prepared to relax the demand. The implications are as follows:

- that other kinds of wrongdoing, such as torts, are not enough. However, many torts are also crimes;

- that all the elements of the relevant crime must be proved, both *actus reus* and *mens rea*. In *Lamb* (1967), D shot and killed his friend when he pressed the trigger of a gun during a game. He knew there were bullets in the gun but, since he did not understand the operation of a revolver, he did not believe any bullet would be ejected. He was not guilty of unlawful act manslaughter because he did not have *mens rea* for an assault or for a battery. Ill-considered comments by the House of Lords in *DPP v Newbury and Jones* (1976), that it was enough if D intentionally did an act which was unlawful but that he did not need to know that it was unlawful, have sometimes been thought to cast doubt on this proposition. Even so, it was clearly re-affirmed by the Court of Appeal in *Jennings* (1990), where D's brother, V, had been fatally but unintentionally stabbed whilst trying to take a knife from D to stop him from using it in a potential confrontation with others. It was held that the jury should have been directed to consider whether D might have had a lawful excuse for the possession of the knife. A lawful excuse would have meant that he was not guilty of the alleged crime of possession of an offensive weapon, and so not guilty of unlawful act manslaughter;

- that crimes of negligence are not enough (*Andrews v DPP* (1937)). This is because the whole liability would then be founded on negligence (the test of 'dangerousness' discussed in the following paragraph is also, essentially, one of negligence). If negligence is to be the basis of the liability, then it must satisfy the test of gross negligence which is explained below. For instance, driving without due care and attention is a crime of (minimal) negligence. D could not be guilty of unlawful act manslaughter if, whilst driving without due care and attention, he killed someone. If the driving was grossly negligent, then D might be guilty of gross negligence manslaughter;

- that it must involve an act – an omission will not suffice. This is the rule laid down in *Lowe* (1973), where D had neglected the health of his child and had been convicted of manslaughter on the basis that the crime was wilful neglect of a child under the Children and Young Persons Act 1933. The conviction was quashed because D had not engaged in any act but, rather, had made an omission. Though the decision is unsatisfactory (the court very obviously confused 'neglect' and 'negligence'), it has never been overruled.

… of a dangerous kind …

In *Church* (1965), the court defined this as being:

> … such as all sober and reasonable people would inevitably recognise must subject the other person to, at least, the risk of some harm resulting therefrom …

In *AG's Reference (No 3 of 1994)* (1997), it was held that 'the other person' need not necessarily be V. In that case, the risk of injury was to V's mother, though it was V who eventually died.

The test will be easy to satisfy where the crime alleged is actually an offence against the person, such as assault or battery. In *Larkin* (1943), for instance, D was convicted of manslaughter when he confronted his girlfriend with a 'cut throat' razor in a confined space at a party and she, 'being groggy with drink', fell against it and cut her throat. D's threatening conduct with the razor was an assault and there was an obvious risk of injury, given the high emotions, confined space and V's condition. Yet other crimes can also create a risk of personal injury and so be 'dangerous', for example, criminal damage. In *DPP v Newbury*, the probable crime (the crime was never actually specified) was criminal damage, which occurred when D threw a paving slab into the path of a train and it smashed through the window of the cab, killing the guard. In *Goodfellow* (1986), D set fire to his council house in a complicated scheme to force the council to move him, but the plan went drastically wrong and his child, wife and a friend all died in the blaze. This was clearly a case of aggravated criminal damage (criminal damage where D intends to endanger life or is reckless as to doing so), the danger to life being all too obvious.

Nevertheless, the reasonable person must be taken to possess only the knowledge that D had and should have had at the time when he committed the offence (including knowledge gained during the commission of the offence), and if the risk of injury would not have been apparent with such knowledge, then D must be acquitted. In *Dawson* (1985), V suffered a fatal heart attack during a robbery committed by D and others. Though V was apparently healthy and D had no reason to suppose otherwise, in reality he suffered from a heart condition. Since this could not have been known to D, the test applied was whether a reasonable person ignorant of V's condition would have recognised a risk of that kind of injury. D's conviction was quashed. By contrast, in *Watson* (1989), D had ample opportunity to observe the condition of his very old victim during the burglary in which he was engaged. D's conviction was quashed only because of problems about causation.

... which causes death

By now, this should be a perfectly familiar proposition and it ought to be sufficient to return to the discussion of causation in 5.1.3. In unlawful act manslaughter, unfortunately, the issue is sometimes complicated by the need to prove that the unlawful act alleged was itself dangerous. This is best illustrated by the kind of case in which V has died after voluntarily consuming a drug supplied by D (contrast these facts with those in a case such as *Cato* (1976), in which D actually injected heroin into V, with V's consent). The Crown faces formidable hurdles in proving the offence. D will object that his act of supply was neither the direct cause of V's death nor in itself dangerous. Only when V voluntarily took the drug did the danger arise.

Substantially, these were the facts of *Dalby* (1982), with the additional complication that V took the tablets by way of injection of a solution, a significantly different form from that in which D had supplied them. The court quashed D's conviction but was induced to express its decision in terms of a requirement that the unlawful act must be 'directed at' V. This was inconsistent with the position adopted in other cases, such as *Pagett*, where the court had considered that D's act in firing at the police officers, though obviously not directed at V, was a sufficient unlawful act, and *Mitchell*, where D had attacked X, who had fallen onto V. It is now generally considered that there is no requirement that the act be 'directed at V'. For instance, in *Goodfellow* (another case in which D's act was definitely not aimed at the ultimate victims), the decision in *Dalby* was explained as being concerned purely with causation and not as imposing any restriction to acts 'directed at' V or anyone else.

The use of drugs is now so prevalent in society that this issue was certain to come before the courts again, as it did in the case of *Kennedy* (1999). There, D, a dealer, had himself prepared the solution of heroin and water with which V then fatally injected himself. Upholding D's conviction for manslaughter, the court held that D's conduct was unlawful either as an offence under s 23 of the Offences Against the Person Act 1861 (which makes it an offence to 'administer to or cause to be administered to or taken by any other person any poison or other destructive or noxious thing') or because D had assisted in and wilfully encouraged V's own unlawful act in injecting himself with a mixture of heroin and water which, at the time of the injection and for the purposes of the injection, V had unlawfully taken into his possession. This unsatisfactory decision was achieved by the tortuous route of identifying V's acts of taking possession of the heroin and injecting it as unlawful, and then arguing that D's act in wilfully encouraging those acts by V was itself unlawful and dangerous because the encouragement to inject carried with it the risk of some harm. In response to the crucial objection, founded on the decision in *Dalby* that D did not cause V's death, the court returned to the significance of the preparation of the solution by D and the handing of it by him to V. Yet this appears to be nothing more than proof of causation in fact. V would not have died 'but for' the supply to him of the heroin by D, but his own decision to inject it surely broke any chain of causation. Much the same could be said in response to the argument that D committed the offence under s 23. Although the Court of Appeal is bound to follow its own decisions, it has some discretion when these are inconsistent. It recently decided to follow Dalby rather than *Kennedy*; *Dias* (2002) Crim LR 490.

Gross negligence manslaughter

Until 1983, the other major form of involuntary manslaughter was gross negligence manslaughter. Though never clearly defined by the courts, it extended to any conduct, whether unlawful in itself or not (for example, driving a car) and was said to require that:

> ... the facts must be such that, in the opinion of the jury, the negligence of the accused went beyond a mere matter of compensation between subjects and showed such disregard for the life and safety of others as to amount to a crime against the State and conduct deserving of punishment [*Bateman* (1925)].

Development of this form of manslaughter was arrested in 1983 by the House of Lords' decision in *Seymour* that, henceforth, it would be defined as *Caldwell* reckless manslaughter. It was not altogether clear whether this represented merely a change in name or extended to a change in definition of the elements of such manslaughter. This change generated a good deal of controversy and was itself abandoned when, in 1993, the House of Lords restored gross negligence manslaughter in *Adomako*.

As now defined, gross negligence manslaughter requires proof of the following:

(a) *any conduct* – it does not have to be an act, so omissions will suffice (contrast unlawful act manslaughter). It does not have to be unlawful in itself, so it may arise out of any activity which poses a risk of injury, for example, employment, medical treatment, driving, installation of domestic appliances, manufacturing, sale and distribution of food and drink;

(b) *amounting to breach of a duty* – exactly what this involves remains unclear at present. In the opinion of Lord McKay in *Adomako*, 'ordinary principles of negligence apply to ascertain whether or not the defendant has been in breach of a duty of care towards the victim who has died', but it seems unlikely that he intended an enquiry into the conditions for criminal liability to be burdened with all the technicalities which surround the notion of duty of care in the civil law of negligence. In any case, by definition, D will have engaged in conduct which created an obvious risk of death to another and this, in itself, is a powerful reason to argue that a duty of care is created. In cases of liability for omission, it will in any case be necessary to establish an appropriate duty to act (recall the duties established in cases such as *Pittwood* and *Stone and Dobinson* discussed in 5.1.3. Equally, duties will arise out of the conduct of professions and business enterprises which carry with them risks to workers, clients, consumers and, more generally, members of the public. Examples include: medical treatment (*Adomako* (1994)); domestic electrical work (*Holloway* (1993)); installation of gas fires (*Singh* (1999)); the organisation of hazardous sports and recreational pursuits (*OLL Ltd* (1994)) and sailing a ship around potentially dangerous rocks (*Litchfield* (1998));

(c) *which creates a risk of death* (or, possibly, of serious injury). This was never a formal requirement before, but it was stressed by Lord MacKay in *Adomako*;

(d) *which causes death* according to the principles of causation considered earlier;

(e) *some further element*, whether described as a state of mind or not, which supplies the requisite degree of culpability; which makes it gross negligence. In *Adomako*, Lord MacKay stressed that this is entirely a matter for the jury to determine:

> The essence of the matter, which is *supremely a jury question*, is whether, having regard to the risk of death involved, the conduct of the defendant was so bad in all the circumstances as to amount in their judgment to a criminal act or omission ... [Emphasis supplied].

There is some illogicality in requiring the conduct to be so bad as to amount to a 'criminal act or omission' if, in the first place, D's breach of duty amounted in itself to a criminal offence (that is, an offence other than manslaughter). Where this is the case, the culpability of D's conduct must lie in being something more than 'merely criminal'! Essentially, the culpability lies in its being conduct which the jury consider should amount not merely to a crime, but to the particularly grave crime of manslaughter. In *Litchfield*, D was the owner and master of a sailing ship which had foundered on rocks and smashed to pieces, with the loss of three lives. D's conduct in sailing the ship almost certainly disclosed breaches of duty which made him guilty of offences under the Merchant Shipping Act 1970. Yet the prosecution decided not to proceed with such charges, on the grounds that the penalties which could be imposed on conviction did not truly reflect D's culpability. Hence, the prosecution was prepared to show conduct which amounted not just to criminal rather than civil law negligence, but which was conduct deserving of punishment as manslaughter (and succeeded in doing so).

5.3.3 Non-fatal offences against the person

5.3.3.1 Assault

Though the word 'assault' is popularly used to describe actual physical violence, it bears a much more technical meaning in criminal law. It consists of causing V to fear violence, whilst 'battery' is the term used for the infliction of violence itself. The distinction is easily obscured by the tendency of statutes to use 'assault' when the offence can be committed by either an assault or a battery, as in assault occasioning actual bodily harm (s 47 of the Offences Against the Person Act 1861) and indecent assault (ss 14 and 15 of the Sexual Offences Act 1956).

The *actus reus* of assault is that D causes V to apprehend immediate unlawful personal violence. Typically, it occurs where D raises his fist or a weapon or makes some other menacing gesture which leads V to think that he is about to be attacked. If V does not see the gesture (if, for example, D is behind V) or does not anticipate being struck, then there is no assault. But V is not required to be literally in fear. A courageous person who does not fear the anticipated blow may still be the victim of an assault. The offence has been subject to recent important re-evaluation by the courts and the following interpretations have emerged:

- the assault may consist of words alone. This was always in doubt until the decisions in *Ireland* (1997) (assault by means of silent telephone calls) and *Constanza* (1997) (assault by means of two letters). It was never doubted that words could operate to prevent an otherwise apparently aggressive act from being an assault, as in *Tuberville v Savage* (1669) (D's gesture of putting his hand on his sword was accompanied by words indicating an intention not to use it);

- the assault must cause fear of 'immediate' personal violence but, according to *Constanza*, this is satisfied by proof that V feared that violence would be inflicted 'at some time not excluding the immediate future'. This seems to mean that it would be sufficient to show that V had thought, 'it may happen now, very soon or happen later'. Thus, V was the victim of an assault where, on receiving two letters from D (who had pursued a campaign of harassment against her for 20 months), she believed that he had 'flipped' and that he might do something at any time of the day or night. It was especially important that D lived not far from V but there was no requirement that V must be able to see the potential perpetrator of the violence. Similarly, it was held in *Ireland* that receipt of silent telephone calls from D could give rise to an assault if V feared that D might seek her out as soon as the telephone call was ended. Obviously, where the threat is clearly to inflict violence at some later time, the 'immediacy' requirement will not be satisfied. Yet, even here, it will be a question of degree as to how much later that time is;

- an act (rather than an omission) may be necessary. There are conflicting cases on this issue (*Fagan v MPC* (1969) and *DPP v K* (1990)), as explained in 5.1.3 in the discussion of liability for omissions.

The *mens rea* of an assault is intention or recklessness in relation to causing apprehension of immediate unlawful personal violence. Recklessness here is subjective.

5.3.3.2 Battery

The *actus reus* of battery requires infliction of unlawful personal violence. Though 'violence' can consist of very little, such as pushing and shoving, there is a limit below which it will not be recognised by the law (this is sometimes expressed in the maxim *de minimis non curat lex* – the law takes no account of very trifling matters). We are all taken to give our implied consent to the trivial bumps and knocks encountered in everyday life, such as when we are in crowds, in shops, at sporting events and so on. So, the following are important in understanding the *actus reus*:

- battery typically consists of a direct application of force by D on V, whether with fists or feet, by a headbutt, by the use of a weapon held or thrown or by spitting. It could also be constituted by instructing a dog to bite the victim, as occurred in *Ramsell* (1999);

- though direct and immediate contact is usually involved, it may be possible to commit battery in less direct ways. In *DPP v K*, D left acid in a hand dryer and so created the circumstances in which V would be certain to suffer injury if he used the hand dryer in the expected way. *Martin* (1881) is a more questionable example, since D's actions (putting out the lights in a theatre and barring the exit doors) only resulted in injury because of the extreme panic generated, in the course of which theatre goers trampled on each other;

- no hostility is required – if D tries to show his affections towards V by persistently kissing her against her will, this is a battery just as much as if he had punched her in anger;

- even though psychological injury is recognised as injury, it is not possible to commit a battery simply by causing V to suffer psychological injury. Violence must be inflicted (*Ireland* (1997));

- as in assault, an act *will normally* be required, although an omission *may* be enough to incur liability. A recent case arose after a police officer searched a man suspected of being a ticket tout. She asked him if he had any sharp objects in his pockets. After receiving a negative assurance she put her hand in a pocket. Her finger was pierced by a hypodermic needle. The Divisional Court took the view that D's omission could amount to an assault or battery; *DPP v Santana-Bermudez* (2004), Crim LR 471.

The *mens rea* of a battery is intention or recklessness in relation to infliction of unlawful personal violence. So, in *Venna* (1975), D was guilty of an assault (in the sense of a battery) occasioning actual bodily harm when he lashed out wildly with his feet after he realised that he had been arrested by police officers and broke a bone in the hand of one of the officers. In *Spratt* (1991), D's conviction for assault (again, in the sense of a battery) occasioning actual bodily harm was quashed when it appeared that, though he had pleaded guilty, he had not given any thought to the possibility that he might injure anyone by firing airgun pellets from a bedroom window in order to see how far they would go. Subjective recklessness had to be proved.

Since the infliction of violence must be unlawful, D will not be guilty if his intention is to inflict violence which he believes to be lawful. This may arise in two situations:

- where D believes that V expressly or impliedly consents;

- where D genuinely believes that he has a lawful excuse for inflicting violence, such as self-defence or prevention of crime. In this case, of course, D must intend to use force which is reasonably proportionate to the harm feared. In *Blackburn v Bowering* (1994), D was not guilty of battery where he defended himself against an attempt by court bailiffs to restrain him. Though the bailiffs were acting lawfully, D did not know who they were and believed that he was simply the victim of an attack.

5.3.3.3   Assault occasioning actual bodily harm

Assault occasioning actual bodily harm is a statutory offence by virtue of s 47 of the Offences Against the Person Act 1861. Its elements are entirely as for assault or battery (it is either an assault occasioning actual bodily harm or a battery occasioning actual bodily harm) but with the addition that actual bodily harm must result. Thus, as affirmed in *Ireland* (1997):

- D must cause V to apprehend immediate personal violence with the consequence that V suffers actual bodily harm (physical or psychological); or

- D must inflict violence upon V with the consequence that V suffers actual bodily harm (physical or psychological).

'Actual bodily harm' was formerly described as including 'any hurt or injury calculated to interfere with the health or comfort [of a person] ...' and so extended to mental injury (hysterical and nervous conditions) (*Miller* (1954)). However, this form of expression was disapproved of in *Chan-Fook* (1994) where, analysing all three ingredients of the offence under s 47, the Court of Appeal held that:

- 'harm' requires hurt or injury;

- 'actual' requires that it is not so trivial as to be wholly insignificant;

- 'bodily' is not limited to 'skin, flesh and bones' since the body includes organs, the nervous system and the brain. So it extends to psychiatric injury but not to mere emotions such as fear, distress or panic, nor to states of mind which are not themselves evidence of an identifiable clinical condition. To conclude that fear, distress or panic would in itself amount to actual bodily harm would be to risk equating the elements of assault with those of assault occasioning actual bodily harm, since an assault is itself constituted by fear of immediate violence.

The court warned against use of phrases such as 'injury to state of mind' or 'hysterical and nervous condition' and advised that expert evidence should be called in any case where psychiatric injury is relied upon and not admitted by the defence. This warning was ignored by the trial judge in *Morris* (1998) with the result that a new trial had to be ordered, since V's alleged injuries as a result of being 'stalked' appeared to be psychological and were unsupported by expert evidence. The inclusion of psychological/psychiatric injury within actual bodily harm (and grievous bodily harm) and the general approach adopted in *Chan-Fook* were approved by the House of Lords in *Ireland*.

The *mens rea* of the offence is purely that of the assault or battery, the actual bodily harm being entirely a matter of causation. So, an assault which causes a victim to seek to escape and in the course of which she suffers injury can satisfy the requirements of this offence (as in *Roberts* (1971), a case considered in 5.1.3 in the discussion of causation). An intentional battery accompanied by an 'accidental' act which results in actual bodily harm also suffices. In *Savage* (1991), D intentionally threw beer over V but 'accidentally' allowed the glass to slip from her hand, cutting V. Intentionally soaking V with the beer was a battery and the court was content that there was a sufficient causal connection between that act and the breaking of the glass which caused V's injuries.

5.3.3.4 Unlawful and malicious wounding or inflicting/causing grievous bodily harm

There are two different sets of offences involving wounding/grievous bodily harm. The less serious set is unlawful and malicious wounding or infliction of grievous bodily harm (s 20 of the Offences Against the Person Act 1861). The second set is unlawful and malicious wounding or causing of grievous bodily harm with intent to cause grievous bodily harm (s 18 of the 1861 Act) (a further version of this offence deals with the intent to resist arrest). In turn, each set can be committed in two distinct ways: by wounding or by bringing about grievous bodily harm. Since they have so many elements in common, it is convenient to examine them together.

5.3.3.5 *The* actus reus

- A wound requires that both layers of the skin (dermis and epidermis) be broken. In *JCC (A Minor) v Eisenhower* (1984), injury to V's eye caused by airgun pellets fired by D was not a wound. His eye was bruised just below the eyebrow and, for a time afterwards, the fluid in his eye abnormally contained red blood cells but there was no break in the layers of the skin.

- A bruise is not a wound because the outer layer of skin is not broken. A graze or scratch may not be a wound because the inner layer may not be broken.

- Wounds can be minor or serious. If serious then they may amount, in addition, to grievous bodily harm.

- Grievous bodily harm is nothing more than any really serious injury. It might be constituted by injuries such as broken bones, permanent disfigurement, serious loss of blood, significant loss of consciousness and severe psychological/psychiatric illness. In *Brown and Stratton* (1998), evidence of a broken nose, the loss of three teeth and a laceration over one eye (with other evidence available of gross facial swelling and widespread laceration and bruising) was sufficient to be left to the jury to determine whether it amounted to grievous bodily harm. It may be possible to commit grievous bodily harm by infecting a person with a disease (including sexually transmitted diseases). This area of the law is unclear (and probably requires Parliament's attention); *Dica* (2004) Crim LR 944.

- The s 20 and s 18 offences differ in requiring grievous bodily harm to have been 'inflicted' and 'caused' respectively. Until recently, this distinction was viewed as significant and had caused much judicial and academic soul searching. The House of Lords has now put an end to the anguish by declaring that there is no significant difference and that 'inflict' under s 20 is just as broad as 'cause' under s 18. In particular, an infliction can take place without the application of force, direct or indirect. This enlightened approach was prompted by the need for a judicial response to conduct generally now described as 'stalking'. In cases such as *Burstow* (1997), where D had waged a lengthy campaign against V, a former friend, it would have been impossible to achieve a conviction on the law as it stood before the decision of the House of Lords, since D did not use force. Despite this, V had been reduced to a nervous wreck by his attentions and the severe depressive illness which she suffered was easily described as grievous bodily harm. This change in the law also opens up the possibility that a s 20 charge could be brought against a person infecting a victim with, say, HIV in the course of consensual sexual activity.

5.3.3.6 *The* mens rea

- Both sets of offences use the term 'malicious'. This simply means intention or subjective recklessness, as established in *Cunningham* (1957) (see the discussion of recklessness in 5.1.3).

- In the case of s 20, no further *mens rea* is required but it is well established that D does not have to intend or be reckless as to a wound or grievous bodily harm. It is enough that he intends or is reckless as to some personal injury (*Savage; Parmenter*). So, if D pushes V over, intending at the most that V will have a painful fall, D may be guilty of the s 20 offence if V falls awkwardly and breaks bones. Similarly, an intention to inflict a minor wound might become a case of grievous bodily harm if D causes more serious injury than intended.

- In s 20, an intention to frighten alone is not enough (contrast s 47). At the very least, D must be aware that physical injury might result. In *Flack v Hunt* (1979), D, a gamekeeper, unintentionally shot V, a poacher, whom he had tried to induce to come out of hiding by firing his shotgun into an area of bushes away from where he believed that V was hiding. In fact, V was in the line of fire. D's conviction for the s 20 offence was quashed because it had not occurred to him that he might cause any injury.

- In the case of s 18, the Crown must go on to prove that, when D wounded V or caused V grievous bodily harm, he had an intention to cause grievous bodily harm. Consequently, there is little significance in the requirement for recklessness imposed by the use of the term 'malicious' in the definition of the offence (in other forms of this offence, it does have a role to play). The definition of intention follows that already discussed in 5.1.3 and this requires account to be taken of the approach now indicated by the House of Lords in *Woollin*.

5.3.3.7 Harassment

Even though the courts responded admirably to the challenge posed by a sudden surge in stalking cases, changing the law in the areas of assault and infliction of grievous bodily harm, in particular, it was evident that the problem of stalking (or, to give it a less dramatic name, harassment) could not be addressed in such piecemeal fashion. Eventually, Parliament was driven to intervene and the result was the Protection from Harassment Act 1997.

The Act creates two criminal offences:

(1) s 2 – harassing another (which includes alarming a person or causing the person distress) by a course of conduct (which includes speech and requires conduct on at least two occasions). It must be proved that D knew or ought to have known (in other words, a reasonable person in possession of the same information as D would have known) that it amounted to harassment.

(2) s 4 – causing a victim to fear violence against himself on at least two occasions by a course of conduct (which includes speech and itself requires conduct on at least two occasions). It must be proved that D knew or ought to have known (in other words, a reasonable person in possession of the same information as D would have known) that his course of conduct would cause the other to fear such violence on each occasion.

In both cases, it is a defence for D to show:

- that he pursued the course of conduct for the purpose of preventing or detecting crime; or

- that it was pursued under any enactment or rule of law or to comply with any condition or requirement imposed by any person under any enactment; or

- (in the case of s 2) that, in the particular circumstances, the pursuit of the course of conduct was reasonable; or

- (in the case of s 4) that, in the particular circumstances, the pursuit of the course of conduct was reasonable for his own or another's protection or for the protection of his own or another's property.

These provisions are supplemented and supported by civil procedures. Thus, damages may be awarded in a civil action for actual or apprehended harassment and an injunction may be granted to restrain a person from engaging in such a course of conduct. Breach of the injunction entitles the plaintiff to apply for the issue of a warrant for D's arrest and is an offence.

Following D's conviction for an offence under s 4, the court may issue, in addition to any other measure, a restraining order to protect V or any other person mentioned from further conduct amounting to harassment or likely to cause a fear of violence and may prohibit D from doing anything specified. Breach of this order is also an offence.

5.3.3.8 *Consent as a defence to offences of personal injury*

Apart from those offences (such as rape) where the definition requires that the activity be non-consensual, consent may be a defence to other non-fatal offences. It is essential that any consent is genuine and this cannot possibly be so if V lacks capacity to understand, whether because of age or other mental disability, or is under duress. On the other hand, consent obtained by some trick or fraud will not be invalid unless it concerns fundamental matters such as the identity of the other person involved or the nature of the act. In *Clarence* (1888), for instance, V's consent to sexual intercourse with D, her husband, was not invalidated by his failure to tell her that he was suffering from venereal disease, despite the fact that she would not have consented had she known. Similarly, in *Richardson* (1998), consent given to D, a dentist who, unknown to her patients, was continuing to provide treatment after being suspended from practice, was not invalidated by her fraud. The patients knew what treatment was being administered, and by whom, and the fraud was irrelevant.

The basic rule is that V can only consent to suffer injury, or the risk of injury, where that injury is less than actual bodily harm. Given the relatively minor injuries that may constitute actual bodily harm, this leaves little scope for the application of the 'defence' in the ordinary case. So, as established in *AG's Reference (No 6 of 1980)* (1981), D will not be able to avoid liability for injuries amounting to actual bodily harm (or worse) inflicted in an ordinary fight in which V has agreed to participate. In *Donovan* (1934), D's convictions for assault and indecent assault where he beat V with a cane with her consent in circumstances of indecency were quashed only because the trial judge had not directed the jury to consider whether or not the blows were likely or intended to cause bodily harm. If they were, then the consent would have been irrelevant.

However, there are exceptions to this basic rule which are generally seen as grounded in public policy, though the precise policy is not always easy to discern. So, in the following cases, consent may enable D to avoid conviction within the limits explained, even where the injury intended or risked is serious:

- in surgery, both medically indicated and for cosmetic purposes;

- in the case of 'body adornment', such as body piercing (earrings, nose studs and rings, etc) and tattooing (subject to the statutory requirement that V must be at least 18 years of age). In *Wilson* (1996), D's crude attempt to carve his initials on his wife's buttocks (at her request) by use of a hot knife was equated with body adornment;

- in the case of properly regulated sports, where the injury is inflicted, broadly speaking, within the rules of the game and, except in the case of boxing, D does not intend to inflict injury. Boxing is exceptional, in that V can consent to intentionally inflicted serious injury;

- in the case of rough 'horseplay', as in *Jones* (1986), where two younger boys were subjected to 'bumps' (being thrown in the air) by older boys who believed (so it was alleged) that their victims were consenting. This exception was also applied in the case of *Aitken* (1992) to an RAF officer who had set fire to the flying suit being worn by one of his colleagues during celebratory horseplay and inflicted serious burns and, in the case of *Richardson and Irwin* (1999), it applied to two students who had unintentionally dropped their friend when holding him over a balcony during some horseplay after they had been out drinking;

- in the case of dangerous entertainments and displays (where the skill of the performer is vital if an assistant or member of the audience is not to suffer injury);

In *Brown and Others* (1993), the House of Lords refused to extend the scope of the exceptions to cover deliberately inflicted injury for the purposes of sexual gratification. Consequently, a group of homosexual sado-masochistic men were found guilty of various offences arising out of apparently extreme practices but which caused no permanent injuries. The majority of their Lordships considered that the injuries were *prima facie* within the statute and that public policy considerations were against allowing consent as a defence (for example, the dangers of serious injury from infected blood and of events getting out of control). The minority viewed it from the opposite perspective, arguing that the activity was primarily sexual and that there were no valid public policy reasons for bringing it within the offences contained in the statute. In *Laskey and Others v UK* (1997), the European Court of Human Rights rejected a complaint by those convicted in *Brown* that their convictions for the offences constituted an unjustifiable interference with their right to respect for private life under Art 8 of the European Convention on Human Rights. Their prosecution was held to be 'necessary in a democratic society ... for the protection of health' (Art 8(2)). Though explicable on the narrow grounds already discussed, the decision in *Wilson* offered some prospect that the courts would not adopt an extreme, unliberal interpretation of *Brown*, at least where more conventional relationships were involved. However, in *Emmett* (1999), the Court of Appeal was unmoved by the fact that D and V were heterosexual partners engaged in rather extreme consensual sexual activity in private. It was held that V could not consent to the risk of the injuries which actually occurred when D put a plastic bag over her head to increase sexual excitement and when he set fire to lighter fuel which he had poured onto her breasts. It is difficult to reconcile cases such as *Brown* and *Emmett* with the recent decision of the Court of Appeal in *Dica*. If (uninformed) consent is a defence to the transmission of potentially lethal medical disorders, why can (informed) consent not be a defence to less serious injuries suffered by sexual partners?

5.3.3.9   Reform of the law on non-fatal offences against the person

The discussion of the non-fatal offences has revealed that there are many flaws in the structure and detail of the rules and that legislative reform is long overdue. The courts have struggled to adapt some of the offences to cope with modern developments, particularly the stalking phenomenon, but there is limited scope for change. A glaring anomaly, for example, is that there is no simple offence of causing injury which is not serious. The Crown must prove the elements of an assault or battery and then show that this caused the injury. So, persistent harassment which causes psychological injury is not an offence within the traditional offences against the person unless it causes V to fear immediate personal violence. By contrast, persistent harassment which causes serious psychological injury may be an offence of inflicting grievous bodily harm, which no longer requires proof of the application of force. Another example of the anomalies that keep being thrown up is revealed by *Ramsell* (1999), where D was convicted of wounding with intent to resist arrest under s 18, an offence which carries a maximum sentence of life imprisonment, when she instructed her dog to bite a police officer during a dispute with neighbours. This charge was selected because the police officer was trying to arrest her for a breach of the peace whilst the lesser, and apparently much more appropriate, offence under s 38 of assault with intent to resist arrest required that the police officer should be trying to arrest for an offence. The further alarming feature of the case was that, having been convicted under s 18, D was then at risk of incurring a mandatory sentence of life imprisonment under the Crime (Sentences) Act 1997 should she unfortunately commit another 'serious offence'.

In 1993, the Law Commission published a report in which it made proposals for such reform (No 219) and, in 1998, the government issued a consultation document on reform which closely follows those proposals. The major effect would be that the familiar Offences Against the Person Act 1861 offences (ss 18, 20 and 47) and the offences of assault and battery would disappear and be replaced by offences of:

- intentional serious injury;

- reckless serious injury;

- intentional or reckless injury;

- assault (defined as including applying force and causing V to believe force is imminent).

Law Commission definitions of intention and recklessness would be adopted. Liability for the transmission of diseases would be restricted to the offence of intentional serious injury, as would liability for an omission. 'Injury' would be defined to mean physical injury (including pain, unconsciousness and any other impairment of a person's physical condition, but excluding anything caused by disease) or mental injury (any impairment of mental health, excluding anything caused by disease). No definition of 'serious' injury would be provided.

THE CRIMINAL LAW

The rules of criminal law are derived from both common law and statute, though the latter is now much the more significant source. As well as by source, crimes may be classified in a number of ways, for instance, according to mode of trial, whether the crime is an arrestable offence, and whether it represents 'true crime' or is merely a 'regulatory' offence.

The general elements of liability

Criminal liability is generally said to require proof of an *actus reus*, accompanied by *mens rea*, in the absence of any defence (general or specific, complete or partial).

The *actus reus* of an offence is comprised of the external elements represented by the accused's conduct in the presence of any relevant circumstances and which may be required to result in prescribed consequences. In addition, the accused's conduct must be voluntary in the sense that it must be under the control of the conscious brain to a sufficient extent. Lack of voluntariness is often termed automatism, and may give rise to a defence. Conduct will usually involve an act but in many crimes liability may be based upon an omission to act. However, this will depend upon proof that the accused was under a duty to act and that the failure to do so made a significant contribution to the harmful consequence.

All crimes requiring proof of a harmful consequence require proof that the accused's conduct was the cause of that consequence. Proof of causation is established by showing that the accused's conduct was a cause in fact and a cause in law, though in most cases, proof of the former will lead inevitably to proof of the latter. The accused's conduct is a cause in fact when the consequence would not have occurred 'but for' that conduct. It is a cause in law when it makes a significant contribution to the consequence. Problems occur when the accused asserts that the consequence was attributable to the conduct of some other person (the victim or a third person) or to some natural event. It will be strongly arguable that the accused remains responsible if the conduct or natural event was reasonably foreseeable in consequence of the accused's actions. Yet such a test need not necessarily be satisfied. The accused must 'take his victim as he finds him' (the whole person, not just the physical person) and medical intervention, even if negligent, may not break the chain of causation.

Mens rea functions as a higher level fault requirement. It generally requires proof either of intention or of recklessness, though some offences are only committed if the accused intends the consequence. A clear definition of intention remains elusive despite the fact that the issue has been considered by the House of Lords on four occasions in the last **30** years. Whilst it certainly includes an aim or purpose, doubts persist about whether it extends to foresight of the virtual certainty of a consequence without aim or purpose. Subjective recklessness must be proved in almost all offences (except strict liability ones), and certainly in the non-fatal offences against the person.

In some instances, *mens rea* is not required. Negligence suffices in some common law and many statutory offences. Negligence is the failure to achieve the standard of conduct expected of a reasonable person. In yet other offences, neither *mens rea* nor negligence need be proved. These offences are termed strict liability offences and are of particular significance in the sphere of so-called regulatory crime. 'Due diligence' is sometimes a defence.

General Defences

Apart from the restriction on criminal liability to those who are at least 10 years of age, it may be possible for an accused to avoid liability by justifying or excusing his conduct.

The defence of insanity requires the accused to prove that he suffered from a defect of reason, due to disease of the mind in such a way that he did not understand what conduct he was engaged in (the 'nature and quality' of his act) or, if he did, that he did not understand that what he was doing was legally wrong. If the accused succeeds in proving these elements, he will be found not guilty by reason of insanity but may be ordered to be detained in a secure hospital. A similar condition which does not arise from a disease of the mind but which prevents awareness of the nature and quality of the act will be termed automatism. This will entitle the accused to an acquittal unless it can be shown that the accused was at fault in becoming an automaton and was aware that he might commit an offence of the kind in question if he did become an automaton. Automatism may also be pleaded in situations where the accused cannot control his movements because of the application of superior force.

Intoxication, which may result from drink or drugs, may be voluntary or involuntary. If voluntary, the accused may use it to suggest that he did not form the intention in a specific intent offence. He will be unable to rely on it in any offence requiring proof merely of recklessness (a basic intent offence). Involuntary intoxication (where the accused is unaware that he is ingesting the intoxicant) may be used in any offence to suggest that the accused neither formed any intention nor was reckless. Voluntary intoxication will usually be of no help to the accused in offences of objective recklessness, and will be irrelevant in offences of negligence and strict liability.

An accused may be able to justify or excuse his conduct by arguing that he chose to commit the 'offence' as the lesser of two evils or because he was subjected to such pressure by way of threats of death or serious injury that his will was overborne. In the first case, he will plead necessity, the existence of which as a defence still remains in doubt. In the second case, he will plead duress or duress of circumstances. A closely related defence is that of self-defence or prevention of crime. Here, the accused will be able to justify his conduct if the use of some force was necessary for either of those purposes and the force which he actually used was roughly proportionate to the harm threatened.

Offences Against the Person

Offences against the person may be divided into two categories, fatal and non-fatal. The fatal offences fall within the umbrella of unlawful homicide, which is comprised of murder and manslaughter. The *actus reus* of unlawful homicide involves proof that the accused caused the death of a human being, the differentiation between the offences being in the *mens rea* and other elements. Murder is distinguished by the requirement for proof of 'malice aforethought', which can be translated more simply as intention to kill or cause serious injury.

Manslaughter is customarily described as being voluntary or involuntary. Voluntary manslaughter consists of a *prima facie* case of murder reduced to the status of manslaughter by a successful plea of provocation or of diminished responsibility. The defence of provocation consists of a killing whilst the accused was experiencing a loss of self-control in response to something done or said by any other person and in such circumstances that a reasonable person might have responded as did the accused. Diminished responsibility is an abnormality of mind caused by one of a number of specified conditions such that the mental responsibility of the accused for his conduct was substantially impaired.

Involuntary manslaughter consists of killings where the accused is regarded as culpable but he never possessed the *mens rea* for murder. In unlawful act manslaughter, the accused kills whilst engaged in committing a crime which created an obvious risk of some injury to any person. In gross negligence manslaughter, the accused may be engaged in lawful or unlawful conduct which amounts to a breach of a duty of care, creates an obvious risk of death and is of such a nature that a jury would consider that it merits punishment as a crime. Subjective recklessness manslaughter occurs where the accused is aware of a risk of (perhaps serious) injury when engaged in any lawful or unlawful conduct.

The whole structure of the non-fatal offences of assault, battery, assault occasioning actual bodily harm, and wounding or inflicting/causing grievous bodily harm has been subjected to frequent criticism and proposals for reform. Assault is the intentional or reckless causing of fear of immediate infliction of personal violence, whilst battery is the infliction of the violence itself. Assault occasioning actual bodily harm requires proof of the elements of either assault or battery and that it caused the victim to suffer actual bodily harm, whether physical or psychological. A wound is a break in both layers of skin and may or may not be grievous bodily harm, which itself can be physical or psychological. Both versions of the offence require proof of intention or recklessness as to some injury. The more serious versions require proof that the accused wounded or caused grievous bodily harm and intended grievous bodily harm. Consent by the victim may be a defence in limited circumstances. Recently, offences involving harassment have been introduced in response to the 'stalking' phenomenon.

CHAPTER 6

THE LAW OF CONTRACT

6.1 The Nature and Function of Contract Law

6.1.1 Introduction

Ours is a market system. This means that economic activity takes place through the exchange of commodities. Individual possessors of commodities meet in the market place and freely enter into negotiations to determine the terms on which they are willing to exchange those commodities. Contract law may be seen as the mechanism for facilitating, regulating and enforcing such market activities.

It is usual for textbooks to cite how all our daily transactions, from buying a newspaper or riding on a bus to our employment, are all examples of contracts, but the point is nonetheless valid and well made. We are all players in the contract game, even if we do not realise it. In fact, we probably will not have any need to recognise that particular contractual version of reality until we enter into some transaction that goes wrong, or at least does not go as we hoped it would. Then, we seek to assert rights and to look for remedies against the person with whom we have come into dispute. It is at this time that the analytical framework of contract law principles comes to bear on the situation, to determine what, if any, rights can be enforced and what, if any, remedies can be recovered. It is perhaps paradoxical that students of contract law have to approach their study of the subject from the opposite end from that at which the layperson begins. The layperson wants a remedy and focuses on that above all else; the student, or practitioner, realises that the availability of the remedy depends upon establishing contractual responsibility and, hence, their focus is on the establishment of the contractual relationship and the breach of that relationship, before any question of remedies can be considered. Such is the nature and relationship of law and ordinary, everyday reality.

Although people have always exchanged goods, market transactions only came to be the dominant form of economic activity during the 19th century, even in the UK. The general law of contract as it now operates is essentially the product of the common law and emerged in the course of the 19th century. It has been suggested that the general principles of contract law, or the 'classical model of contract', as they are known, are themselves based on an idealised model of how the market operates.

As the following chapters will evidence, there is much tension between the fit of the theoretical classical model and the practical demands of everyday business activity. Equally of note is the extent to which statutory inroads have been made into the common law, particularly in the area of consumer protection. For example, notable pieces of legislation that will require close attention are the Unfair Contract Terms Act 1977, which restricts the use of exclusion clauses in contracts, and the Contracts (Rights of Third Parties) Act 1999, which has made inroads into the common law doctrine of privity. The extent to which employment contracts are a matter of statutory regulation.

The purpose of this short chapter is to introduce contract law as the mechanism through which market activity is conducted and regulated.

6.1.2 Definition

Given the examples of contracts cited above, it may be appreciated that the simplest possible description of a contract is a 'legally binding agreement'. It should be noted, however, that, although all contracts are the outcome of agreements, not all agreements are contracts; that is, not all agreements are legally enforceable. In order to be in a position to determine whether a particular agreement will be enforced by the courts, one must have an understanding of the rules and principles of contract law.

The emphasis placed on agreement highlights the consensual nature of contracts. It is sometimes said that contract is based on *consensus ad idem*, that is, a meeting of minds. This is slightly misleading, however, for the reason that English contract law applies an objective test in determining whether or not a contract exists. It is not so much a matter of what the parties actually had in mind as what their behaviour would lead others to conclude as to their state of mind. Consequently, contracts may be found and enforced, even though the parties themselves might not have thought that they had entered into such a relationship.

6.1.3 Formalities

There is no general requirement that contracts be made in writing. They can be created by word of mouth or by action, as well as in writing. Contracts made in any of these ways are known as *parol* or *simple* contracts, whereas those made by deed are referred to as *speciality* contracts. It is generally left to the parties to decide on the actual form that a contract is to take but, in certain circumstances, formalities are required, as follows:

- *Contracts that must be made by deed*

  Essentially, this requirement applies to conveyances of land and leases of property extending over a period of more than three years. A conveyance is the legal process of the transfer of land. It is distinct from a contract to sell land, which is merely a legal agreement to transfer the land and not the actual process of transfer, which comes later. Agreements made by deed which would not otherwise be enforceable as contracts, because the required formation element of consideration is absent, will be implemented by the courts.

- *Contracts that must be in writing (but not necessarily by deed)*

  Among this group are: bills of exchange, cheques and promissory notes (by virtue of the Bills of Exchange Act 1882); consumer credit agreements, such as hire purchase agreements (by virtue of the Consumer Credit Act 1974); and contracts of marine insurance (by virtue of the Marine Insurance Act 1906). The Law of Property (Miscellaneous Provisions) Act 1989 requires all contracts for the sale or disposition of land to be made in writing. It should also be appreciated that some such agreements, for example hire purchase, must be signed by both parties. Increasingly, agreements are conducted by electronic means and, until recently, this created a problem where the law required a contract to be signed. Now the Electronic Communications Act 2000, which resulted from an EC Directive (1999/93/EC), deals with the issue; legal recognition is given to electronic signatures in that such signatures, accompanied by certification of authenticity, are now admissible as evidence in legal proceedings.

- *Contracts that must be evidenced in writing*

This last category covers contracts of guarantee, derived from s 4 of the Statute of Frauds Act 1677.

6.1.4   The legal effect of agreement

It has already been pointed out that not all agreements are recognised as contracts in law, but it must also be borne in mind that, even where agreements do constitute contracts, they may not be given full effect by the courts. The legal effect of particular agreements may be distinguished as follows:

- *Valid contracts*

These are agreements which the law recognises as being binding in full. By entering into such contractual agreements, the parties establish rights and responsibilities and the court will enforce these by either insisting on performance of the promised action or awarding damages to the innocent party.

- *Void contracts*

This is actually a contradiction in terms, for this type of agreement does not constitute a contract: it has no legal effect. Agreements may be void for a number of reasons, including mistake, illegality, public policy or the lack of a necessary requirement, such as consideration. The ownership of property exchanged does not pass under a void contract and remains with the original owner. The legal owner may recover it from the possession of the other party or, indeed, any third party, if it has been passed on to such a person. This is so even where the third party has acquired the property in good faith and has provided consideration for it.

- *Voidable contracts*

These are agreements which may be avoided, that is, set aside, by one of the parties. If, however, no steps are taken to avoid the agreement, then a valid contract ensues. Examples of contracts which may be voidable are those which have been entered into on the basis of fraud, misrepresentation or duress.

In relation to voidable contracts, the appropriate remedy is rescission of the original agreement. The effect of rescission is that both parties are returned to their original, pre-contractual position. Consequently, anyone who has transferred property to another on the basis of misrepresentation, for example, may recover that property. However, goods which have been exchanged under a voidable contract can be sold to an innocent third party. If such a transfer occurs before the first innocent party has rescinded the original contract, then the later innocent party receives good title to the property. This means that the property is now theirs and the innocent party to the first transaction can only seek a remedy such as damages against the other, non-innocent party to that contract.

- *Unenforceable contracts*

  These are agreements which, although legal, cannot be sued upon for some reason. One example would be where the time limit for enforcing the contract has lapsed. The title to any goods exchanged under such a contract is treated as having been validly passed and cannot, therefore, be reclaimed.

The following four chapters will consider the major substantive rules relating to contracts but, first, it is necessary to issue a warning in relation to examinations. Together with company law, contract forms the main component in most syllabuses. It is not possible to select particular areas as more important and, therefore, more likely to be examined than others. Unfortunately, any aspect of contract may be asked about, and so candidates must be familiar with most, if not all, aspects of the subject. For example, it may be legitimate to expect a question on the vitiating factors in relation to contracts. It is not possible, however, to predict with any confidence which particular vitiating factor will be selected. To restrict one's study would be extremely hazardous. The candidate may have learnt mistake and misrepresentation very well, but that will be to no avail if the question asked actually relates to duress, as it might very well do. The warning, therefore, is to study contract thoroughly. Equally, students should be aware that a knowledge of remedies is of particular importance to all contractual topics; for example, an examination question on offer and acceptance or on misrepresentation may also require reference to appropriate remedies.

6.2 The Formation of a Contract

6.2.1 Introduction

As has been seen, not every agreement, let alone every promise, will be enforced by the law. But what distinguishes the enforceable promise from the unenforceable one? The essential elements of a binding agreement, and the constituent elements of the classical model of contract, are:

- offer;

- acceptance;

- consideration;

- capacity;

- intention to create legal relations; and

- there must be no vitiating factors present.

The first five of these elements must be present, and the sixth one absent, for there to be a legally enforceable contractual relationship. This chapter will consider the first five elements in turn. Vitiating factors will be considered separately, in Section 6.4.

6.2.2 Offer

An offer is a promise to be bound on particular terms, and it must be capable of acceptance. The person who makes the offer is the offeror; the person who receives the offer is the offeree. The offer sets out the terms upon which the offeror is willing to enter into contractual relations with the offeree. In order to be capable of acceptance, the offer must not be too vague; if the offeree accepts, each party should know what their rights and obligations are.

In *Scammel v Ouston* (1941), Ouston ordered a van from Scammel on the understanding that the balance of the purchase price could be paid on hire purchase terms over two years. Scammel used a number of different hire purchase terms and the specific terms of his agreement with Ouston were never actually fixed. When Scammel failed to deliver the van, Ouston sued for breach of contract. It was held that the action failed on the basis that no contract could be established, due to the uncertainty of the terms; no specific hire purchase terms had been identified.

6.2.2.1 *Identifying an offer*

An offer may, through acceptance by the offeree, result in a legally enforceable contract. It is important to be able to distinguish what the law will treat as an offer from other statements which will not form the basis of an enforceable contract. An offer must be distinguished from the following:

- *A mere statement of intention*

  Such a statement cannot form the basis of a contract, even though the party to whom it was made acts on it. See, for example, *Re Fickus* (1900), where a father informed his prospective son-in-law that his daughter would inherit under his will. It was held that the father's words were simply a statement of present intention, which he could alter as he wished in the future; they were not an offer. Therefore, the father could not be bound by them.

- *A mere supply of information*

  The case of *Harvey v Facey* (1893) demonstrates this point. The plaintiff telegraphed the defendants as follows: 'Will you sell us Bumper Hall Pen? Telegraph lowest cash price.' The defendant answered, 'Lowest price for Bumper Hall Pen £900'. The plaintiff then telegraphed, 'We agree to buy Bumper Hall Pen for £900', and sued for specific performance when the defendants declined to transfer the property. It was held that the defendants' telegram was not an offer capable of being accepted by the plaintiff; it was simply a statement of information. This clearly has similarities with asking the price of goods in a retail outlet.

- *An invitation to treat*

This is an invitation to others to make offers. The person extending the invitation is not bound to accept any offers made to him. The following are examples of common situations involving invitations to treat:

- *The display of goods in a shop window.* The classic case in this area is *Fisher v Bell* (1961), in which a shopkeeper was prosecuted for offering offensive weapons for sale, by having flick-knives on display in his window. It was held that the shopkeeper was not guilty, as the display in the shop window was not an offer for sale; it was only an invitation to treat.

- *The display of goods on the shelf of a self-service shop.* In this instance, the exemplary case is *Pharmaceutical Society of Great Britain v Boots Cash Chemists* (1953). The defendants were charged with breaking a law which provided that certain drugs could only be sold under the supervision of a qualified pharmacist. They had placed the drugs on open display in their self-service store and, although a qualified person was stationed at the cash desk, it was alleged that the contract of sale had been formed when the customer removed the goods from the shelf, the display being an offer to sell. It was held that Boots were not guilty. The display of goods on the shelf was only an invitation to treat. In law, the customer offered to buy the goods at the cash desk where the pharmacist was stationed. This decision is clearly practical, as the alternative would mean that, once customers had placed goods in their shopping baskets, they would be bound to accept them and could not change their minds and return the goods to the shelves.

- *A public advertisement.* Once again, this does not amount to an offer. This can be seen from *Partridge v Crittenden* (1968), in which a person was charged with offering a wild bird for sale, contrary to the Protection of Birds Act 1954, after he had placed an advertisement relating to the sale of such birds in a magazine. It was held that he could not be guilty of offering the bird for sale, as the advertisement amounted to no more than an invitation to treat. Also, in *Harris v Nickerson* (1873), the plaintiff failed to recover damages for his costs in attending an advertised auction which was cancelled. In deciding against him, the court stated that he was attempting 'to make a mere declaration of intention a binding contract'. As a general rule, in auctions the bids are offers to buy.

However, there are exceptional circumstances where an advertisement may be treated as an offer; where the advertisement specifies performance of a task in return for a 'reward' and, on its terms, does not admit any room for negotiation, it may be treated as an offer. In *Carlill v Carbolic Smoke Ball Co* (1893), the facts of which are given in 6.2.2.2 below, the advertisement was held to be an offer, not an invitation to treat, because it specified performance of the task of using the smoke ball as directed and catching influenza in return for the reward of £100. Furthermore, there was no room to negotiate these terms, unlike the usual advertisement (such as the one in *Partridge v Crittenden*, above) where one would commonly expect to be able to negotiate on price.

Advertisements of goods on websites (internet shopping) are of particular interest. The legal issue is whether the advertisements are offers (in which case the customer ordering the goods accepts the offer and then a binding contract is made) or invitations to treat, so that the customer's order is an offer to buy, which the advertiser can accept or reject. Many readers will be familiar with the widely reported dispute involving Argos in 1999. The Argos website advertised Sony televisions at £2.99 instead of £299 and customers placed orders at £2.99. Customers argued that they had accepted Argos' offer and that there was a binding contract to supply the goods for £2.99. A similar dispute arose where Kodak's website mistakenly advertised cameras for £100 instead of £329. Such problems are addressed by the Electronic Commerce (EC Directive) Regulations 2002 (SI 2002/2013). Regulation 9 requires Member States to ensure that certain information is given by the 'service provider' to the recipient of the service. Unless otherwise agreed by parties who are not consumers, the relevant information is:

(a)   the different technical steps to follow to conclude the contract;

(b)   whether or not the concluded contract will be filed by the service provider;

(c)   the technical means for identifying and correcting input errors before placing the order;

(d)   the languages available for conclusion of the contract; and

(e)   reference to any relevant codes of conduct and how they can be accessed.

These rules do not apply where the contract is conducted exclusively by email. The Regulations also require that:

(a)   the contract terms and general conditions provided to the recipient can be stored and reproduced by him/her; and

(b)   the service provider acknowledges receipt of the order, without delay and by electronic means.

○   *A share prospectus.* Contrary to common understanding, such a document is not an offer; it is merely an invitation to treat, inviting people to make offers to subscribe for shares in a company.

It can be seen that the decisions in both *Fisher v Bell* and *Partridge v Crittenden* run contrary to the common, non-legal understanding of the term 'offer'. It is interesting to note that later legislation, such as the Trade Descriptions Act 1968, has specifically been worded in such a way as to ensure that invitations to treat are subject to the same legal regulation as offers, where the protection of consumers from being misled is in issue.

6.2.2.2   Offers to particular people

An offer may be made to a particular person, or to a group of people, or to the world at large. If the offer is restricted, then only the people to whom it is addressed may accept it; if the offer is made to the public at large, however, it can be accepted by anyone.

In *Boulton v Jones* (1857), the defendant sent an order to a shop, not knowing that the shop had been sold to the plaintiff. The plaintiff supplied the goods, the defendant consumed them but did not pay, as he had a right to offset the debt against money the former owner owed him. The plaintiff sued for the price of the goods. The defendant argued that there was no contract obliging him to pay because his offer was an offer *only* to the former owner (because of the right of offset and lack of knowledge of the sale of the business), so only the former owner could accept, not the plaintiff. The court agreed with the defendant's argument; there was no contract, and so there was no contractual obligation to pay.

In *Carlill v Carbolic Smoke Ball Co* (1893), the company advertised that it would pay £100 to anyone who caught influenza after using their smoke ball as directed. Mrs Carlill used the smoke ball but still caught influenza and sued the company for the promised £100. Amongst the many defences argued for the company, it was suggested that the advertisement could not have been an offer, as it was not addressed to Mrs Carlill. It was held that the advertisement was an offer to the whole world, which Mrs Carlill had accepted by her conduct. There was, therefore, a valid contract between her and the company.

6.2.2.3   Knowledge of the offer

A person cannot accept an offer that he does not know about. Thus, if a person offers a reward for the return of a lost watch and someone returns it without knowing about the offer, he cannot claim the reward. Motive for accepting is not important, as long as the person accepting knows about the offer. In *Williams v Carwadine* (1883), a person was held to be entitled to receive a reward, although that was not the reason why he provided the information requested. (Acceptance is considered in detail below, at 6.2.3)

6.2.2.4   Rejection of offers

Express rejection of an offer has the effect of terminating the offer. The offeree cannot subsequently accept the original offer. A counter-offer, where the offeree tries to change the terms of the offer, has the same effect.

In *Hyde v Wrench* (1840), Wrench offered to sell his farm for £1,000. Hyde offered £950, which Wrench rejected. Hyde then informed Wrench that he accepted the original offer. It was held that there was no contract. Hyde's counter-offer had effectively ended the original offer and it was no longer open to him to accept it; Hyde was now making a new offer to buy for £1,000, which Wrench could accept or reject.

A counter-offer must not be confused with a request for information. Such a request does not end the offer, which can still be accepted after the new information has been elicited. See *Stevenson v McLean* (1880), where it was held that a request by the offeree as to the length of time that the offeror would give for payment did not terminate the original offer, which he was entitled to accept prior to revocation. The issue was considered and clarified in *Society of Lloyds v Twinn* (2000), discussed in 6.2.3.1, below.

6.2.2.5 Revocation of offers

Revocation, the technical term for cancellation, occurs when the offeror withdraws the offer. There are a number of points that have to be borne in mind in relation to revocation, as follows:

- *An offer may be revoked at any time before acceptance*

  Once revoked, it is no longer open to the offeree to accept the original offer. In *Routledge v Grant* (1828), Grant offered to buy Routledge's house and gave him six weeks to accept the offer. Within that period, however, he withdrew the offer. It was held that Grant was entitled to withdraw the offer at any time before acceptance and, upon withdrawal, Routledge could no longer create a contract by purporting to accept it.

- *Revocation is not effective until it is actually received by the offeree*

  This means that the offeror must make sure that the offeree is made aware of the withdrawal of the offer; otherwise it might still be open to the offeree to accept the offer.

  In *Byrne v Van Tienhoven* (1880), the defendant offerors carried out their business in Cardiff and the plaintiff offerees were based in New York. On 1 October, an offer was made by post. On 8 October, a letter of revocation was posted, seeking to withdraw the offer. On 11 October, the plaintiffs telegraphed their acceptance of the offer. On 20 October, the letter of revocation was received by the plaintiffs.

  It was held that the revocation did not take effect until it arrived and the defendants were bound by the contract, which had been formed by the plaintiffs' earlier acceptance (which was effective on *sending* under the postal rule: see 6.2.3.2, below).

- *Communication of revocation may be made through a reliable third party*

  Where the offeree finds out about the withdrawal of the offer from a reliable third party, the revocation is effective and the offeree can no longer seek to accept the original offer.

  In *Dickinson v Dodds* (1876), Dodds offered to sell property to Dickinson and told him that the offer would be left open until Friday. On Thursday, the plaintiff was informed by a reliable third party, who was acting as an intermediary, that Dodds intended to sell the property to someone else. Dickinson still attempted to accept the offer on Friday, by which time the property had already been sold. It was held that the sale of the property amounted to revocation, which had been effectively communicated by the third party.

- *A promise to keep an offer open is only binding where there is a separate contract to that effect*

  This is known as an *option contract*, and the offeree/promisee must provide consideration for the promise to keep the offer open. If the offeree does not provide any consideration for the offer to be kept open, then the original offeror is at liberty to withdraw the offer at any time, as was seen in *Routledge v Grant*, above.

- *In relation to unilateral contracts, revocation is not permissible once the offeree has started performing the task requested*

  A unilateral contract is one where one party promises something in return for some action on the part of another party. Rewards for finding lost property are examples of such unilateral promises, as was the advertisement in *Carlill v Carbolic Smoke Ball Co* (see 6.2.2.2, above). There is no compulsion placed on the party undertaking the action, but it would be unfair if the promisor were entitled to revoke their offer just before the offeree was about to complete their part of the contract; for example, withdrawing a 'free gift for labels' offer before the expiry date, whilst customers were still collecting labels.

  In *Errington v Errington and Woods* (1952), a father promised his son and daughter-in-law that he would convey a house to them when they had paid off the outstanding mortgage. After the father's death, his widow sought to revoke the promise. It was held that the promise could not be withdrawn as long as the mortgage payments continued to be met.

6.2.2.6   Lapse of offers

Offers lapse and are no longer capable of acceptance in the following circumstances:

- *At the end of a stated period*

  It is possible for the parties to agree, or for the offeror to set, a time limit within which acceptance has to take place. If the offeree has not accepted the offer within that period, the offer lapses and can no longer be accepted.

- *After a reasonable time*

  Where no time limit is set, then an offer will lapse after the passage of a reasonable time. What amounts to a reasonable time is, of course, dependent upon the particular circumstances of each case.

- *Where the offeree dies*

  This automatically brings the offer to a close.

- *Where the offeror dies and the contract was one of a personal nature*

  In such circumstances, the offer automatically comes to an end, but the outcome is less certain in relation to contracts that are not of a personal nature. See *Bradbury v Morgan* (1862) for an example of a case where it was held that the death of an offeror did not invalidate the offeree's acceptance.

It should be noted that the effect of death after acceptance also depends on whether or not the contract was one of a personal nature. In the case of a non-personal contract (for example, the sale of a car), the contract can be enforced by and against the representatives of the deceased. On the other hand, if performance of the contract depended upon the personal qualification or capacity of the deceased, then the contract will be frustrated (see below, 6.2.6.1).

6.2.3 Acceptance

Acceptance of the offer is necessary for the formation of a contract. Once the offeree has assented to the terms offered, a contract comes into effect. Both parties are bound: the offeror can no longer withdraw his offer and the offeree cannot withdraw his acceptance.

6.2.3.1 Form of acceptance

In order to form a binding agreement, the acceptance must correspond with the terms of the offer. Thus, the offeree must not seek to introduce new contractual terms into the acceptance.

In *Neale v Merrett* (1930), one party offered to sell some property for £280. The other party purported to accept the offer by sending £80 and promising to pay the remainder by monthly instalments. It was held that this purported acceptance was ineffective, as the offeree had not accepted the original offer as stated.

As was seen in *Hyde v Wrench* (1840), a counter-offer does not constitute acceptance. Analogously, it may also be stated that a conditional acceptance cannot create a contract relationship. Thus, any agreement subject to contract is not binding, but merely signifies the fact that the parties are in the process of finalising the terms on which they will be willing to be bound (*Winn v Bull* (1877)). However, the mere fact that a person adds a 'qualification' to their acceptance may not prevent acceptance from taking place. The dispute in *Society of Lloyds v Twinn* (2000) arose from a settlement arrangement offered to Lloyd's 'names' in July 1996. Mr and Mrs Twinn indicated that they accepted the settlement agreement but added that they were unsure of their ability to actually carry out its terms; they queried whether any 'indulgence' would be granted them in such circumstances. Subsequently, the defendants argued that their acceptance had been conditional, so there was no contract enforceable against them. It was decided that it was a question of fact in each case whether there was an unconditional acceptance plus a collateral offer (which there was in the present case) or a counter-offer (that is, a conditional acceptance – 'I only accept the offer if ...') which rejected the offer.

Acceptance may be in the form of express words, either oral or written, or it may be implied from conduct. Thus, in *Brogden v Metropolitan Railway Co* (1877), the plaintiff, having supplied the company with coal for a number of years, suggested that they should enter into a written contract. The company agreed and sent Brogden a draft contract. He altered some points and returned it, marked 'approved'. The company did nothing further about the document, but Brogden continued to deliver coal on the terms included in the draft contract. When a dispute arose, Brogden denied the existence of any contract. It was held that the draft became a full contract when both parties acted on it. More recently, acceptance by conduct was examined in *IRC v Fry* (2001). The defendant owed the Inland Revenue £100,000 and her husband sent a cheque for £10,000 to the Revenue, stating that cashing the cheque would be acceptance of his offer that it was 'full and final settlement' of the debt. As was normal practice, the Inland Revenue postroom sent the cheque for immediate banking and the accompanying letter to an inspector. The inspector informed the defendant that the cheque could not be full settlement; the defendant argued that cashing the cheque was acceptance of her husband's offer, so the debt was now fully settled. It should be noted here that part payment of a debt by a third party is an exception to the rule in *Pinnel's Case* (1602) (see below, 6.2.5.5), so the only issue was whether the husband's offer had been accepted. Jacobs J stated:

> Cashing a cheque is always strong evidence of acceptance, especially if it is not accompanied by an immediate rejection of the offer. Retention of the cheque without rejection is also strong evidence of acceptance, depending on the length of delay. But neither of these factors are conclusive and it would, I think, be artificial to draw a hard and fast line between cases where payment is accompanied by immediate rejection of the offer and cases where objection comes within a day or a few days.

It was decided that cashing the cheque raised a *rebuttable presumption* of acceptance of the offer, but the fact that the Inland Revenue did not know of the offer at the time that the cheque was cashed rebutted the presumption of acceptance (see 6.2.3, above).

6.2.3.2 Communication of acceptance

The general rule is that acceptance must be communicated to the offeror. As a consequence of this rule, silence cannot amount to acceptance. The classic case in this regard is *Felthouse v Bindley* (1863), where an uncle had been negotiating the purchase of his nephew's horse. He eventually wrote to the nephew, offering to buy it at a particular price, stating: 'If I hear no more about him I shall consider the horse mine.' The nephew made no reply. When the horse was mistakenly sold by an auctioneer, the uncle sued the auctioneer in conversion. It was held that the uncle had no cause of action, as the horse did not belong to him. Acceptance could not be imposed on the offeree on the basis of his silence.

There are, however, exceptions to the general rule that acceptance must be communicated, which arise in the following cases:

- *Where the offeror has waived the right to receive communication*

  In unilateral contracts, such as that in *Carlill v Carbolic Smoke Ball Co* (1893) or general reward cases, acceptance occurs when the offeree performs the required act. Thus, in the *Carlill* case, Mrs Carlill did not have to inform the Smoke Ball Co that she had used their treatment. Nor, in reward cases, do those seeking to benefit have to inform the person offering the reward that they have begun to perform the task that will lead to the reward.

- *Where acceptance is through the postal service*

In such circumstances, acceptance is complete as soon as the letter, properly addressed and stamped, is posted. The contract is concluded, even if the letter subsequently fails to reach the offeror.

In *Adams v Lindsell* (1818), the defendant made an offer to the plaintiff on 2 September. Due to misdirection, the letter was delayed. It arrived on 5 September and Adams immediately posted an acceptance. On 8 September, Lindsell sold the merchandise to a third party. On 9 September, the letter of acceptance from Adams arrived. It was held that a valid acceptance took place when Adams posted the letter. Lindsell was, therefore, liable for breach of contract.

As has already been seen in *Byrne v Van Tienhoven* (1880), the postal rule applies equally to telegrams. It does not apply, however, when means of instantaneous communication are used (see *Entores v Far East Corp* (1955) for a consideration of this point). It follows that when acceptance is made by means of telephone, fax or telex, the offeror must actually receive the acceptance. This also raises issues concerning acceptance by email; it has been argued that this situation should be treated as a 'face to face' situation where receipt only occurs when the recipient reads the email. This argument would be in line with the decision in *Brinkibon Ltd v Stahag Stahl und Stahlwarenhandelsgesellschaft mbH* (1983). This, of course, begs the question of the effect of culpability in not reading emails quickly. It is suggested that, as a result of the decision in *The Brimnes* (1975), a court would take account of when the sender might reasonably expect the message to be received. Where the agreement is conducted on the Internet, reg 11 of the Electronic Commerce (EC Directive) Regulations 2002 (SI 2002/2013) indicates that the contract is concluded when the service provider's acknowledgment of receipt of acceptance is received by electronic means.

It should be noted that the postal rule will apply only where it is in the contemplation of the parties that the post will be used as the means of acceptance. If the parties have negotiated either face to face, for example in a shop, or over the telephone, then it might not be reasonable for the offeree to use the post as a means of communicating their acceptance and they would not gain the benefit of the postal rule (see *Henthorn v Fraser* (1892)).

In order to expressly exclude the operation of the postal rule, the offeror can insist that acceptance is only to be effective upon receipt (see *Holwell Securities v Hughes* (1974)). The offeror can also require that acceptance be communicated in a particular manner. Where the offeror does not actually insist that acceptance can only be made in the stated manner, then acceptance is effective if it is communicated in a way that is no less advantageous to the offeror (see *Yates Building Co v J Pulleyn & Sons* (1975)).

6.2.3.3 Tenders

These arise where one party wishes particular work to be done and issues a statement requesting interested parties to submit the terms on which they are willing to carry out the work. In the case of tenders, the person who invites the tender is simply making an invitation to treat. The person who submits a tender is the offeror, and the other party is at liberty to accept or reject the offer as he pleases (see *Spencer v Harding* (1870)).

The effect of acceptance depends upon the wording of the invitation to tender. If the invitation states that the potential purchaser will require that a certain quantity of goods are supplied to him, then acceptance of a tender will form a contract and he will be in breach if he fails to order the stated quantity of goods from the tenderer.

If, on the other hand, the invitation states only that the potential purchaser may require goods, acceptance gives rise only to a standing offer. There is no compulsion on the purchaser to take any goods, but he must not deal with any other supplier. Each order given forms a separate contract and the supplier must deliver any goods required within the time stated in the tender. The supplier can revoke the standing offer, but he must supply any goods already ordered.

In *Great Northern Railway v Witham* (1873), the defendant successfully tendered to supply the company with 'such quantities as the company may order from time to time'. After fulfiling some orders, Witham refused to supply any more goods. It was held that he was in breach of contract in respect of the goods already ordered but, once these were supplied, he was at liberty to revoke his standing offer.

6.2.4 Offer, acceptance and the classical model of contract

The foregoing has presented the legal principles relating to offer and acceptance in line with the 'classical model' of contract. As has been stated, underlying that model is the operation of the market in which individuals freely negotiate the terms on which they are to be bound. The offeror sets out terms to which he is willing to be bound and, if the offeree accepts those terms, then a contract is formed. If, however, the offeree alters the terms, then the parties reverse their roles: the former offeree now becomes the offeror and the former offeror becomes the offeree, able to accept or reject the new terms as he chooses. This process of role reversal continues until an agreement is reached or the parties decide that there are no grounds on which they can form an agreement. Thus, the classical model of contract insists that there must be a correspondence of offer and acceptance, and that any failure to match acceptance to offer will not result in a binding contract.

Commercial reality, however, tends to differ from this theoretical model, and lack of genuine agreement as to terms in a commercial contract can leave the courts with a difficult task in determining whether there actually was a contract in the first place and, if there was, upon precisely which, or whose, terms it was entered into. This difficulty may be seen in relation to what is known as 'the battle of the forms', in which the parties do not actually enter into real negotiations but simply exchange standard form contracts, setting out their usual terms of trade. The point is that the contents of these standard form contracts might not agree and, indeed, might actually be contradictory. The question then arises as to whose terms are to be taken as forming the basis of the contract, if, indeed, a contract has actually been concluded.

Some judges, notably Lord Denning, have felt themselves to be too restricted by the constraints of the classical model of contract and have argued that, rather than being required to find, or construct, a correspondence of offer and acceptance, they should be able to examine the commercial reality of the situation in order to decide whether or not the parties had intended to enter into contractual relations. As Lord Denning would have had it, judges should not be restricted to looking for a precise matching of offer and acceptance, but should be at liberty to:

> ... look at the correspondence as a whole, and at the conduct of the parties, and see therefrom whether the parties have come to an agreement on everything that was material [*Gibson v Manchester CC* (1979)].

Gibson v Manchester CC (1979) concerned the sale of a council house to a tenant. The tenant had entered into negotiations with his local council about the purchase of his house. Before he had entered into a binding contract, the political make-up of the council changed and the policy of selling houses was reversed. It was clear that, under the classical model of contract, there was no correspondence of offer and acceptance, but the Court of Appeal nonetheless decided that the tenant could insist on the sale.

The status quo was restored by the House of Lords, which overturned the Court of Appeal's decision. In doing so, Lord Diplock expressed the view that:

> ... there may be certain types of contract, though they are exceptional, which do not easily fit in to the normal analysis of a contract as being constituted by offer and acceptance, but a contract alleged to have been made by an exchange of correspondence by the parties in which the successive communications other than the first are in reply to one another is not one of these.

Subsequent to this clear re-affirmation of the classical model, even Lord Denning was cowed in deciding *Butler Machine Tool Co Ltd v Ex-Cell-O Corp (England) Ltd* (1979). Although he did not hesitate to repeat his claim as to the unsuitability of the traditional offer/acceptance analysis in the particular case, which involved a clear battle of the forms, he did feel it necessary to frame his judgment in terms of the traditional analysis.

It is perhaps possible that Lord Denning's questioning of the classical model has been revitalised by the decision of the Court of Appeal in *Trentham Ltd v Archital Luxfer* (1993), another battle of the forms case, in which Steyn LJ stated that he was:

> ... satisfied that in this fully executed contract transaction a contract came into existence during performance, even if it cannot be precisely analysed in terms of offer and acceptance.

It must be pointed out, however, that the case involved a completed contract and the court was, therefore, faced with the problem of giving retrospective commercial effect to the parties' interactions and business relationship. It must also be emphasised that, in reaching its decision, the Court of Appeal relied on the authority of *Brogden v Metropolitan Railway Co* (1877). The case may not, therefore, be as significant in the attack on the classical model of contract as it appears at first sight; its full scope remains to be seen.

6.2.5 Consideration

English law does not enforce gratuitous promises unless they are made by deed. Consideration can be understood as the price paid for a promise. The element of bargain implicit in the idea of consideration is evident in the following definition by Sir Frederick Pollock, adopted by the House of Lords in *Dunlop v Selfridge* (1915):

> An act or forbearance of one party, or the promise thereof, is the price for which the promise of the other is bought, and the promise thus given for value is enforceable.

It is sometimes said that consideration consists of some benefit to the promisor or detriment to the promisee. It should be noted that both elements stated in that definition are not required to be present to support a legally enforceable agreement though, in practice, they are usually present. If the promisee acts to their detriment, it is immaterial that the action does not directly benefit the promisor. However, that detriment must be suffered at the request of the promisor; for example, in *Carlill v Carbolic Smoke Ball Co* (see above, 6.2.2.2), Mrs Carlill gave consideration by way of detriment by undertaking the inconvenience of using the smoke ball as requested by the company in their advertisement.

6.2.5.1 Forbearance

Forbearance involves non-action or the relinquishing of some right. An example is forbearance to sue. If two parties, A and B, believe that A has a cause of legal action against B, then, if B promises to pay a sum of money to A if A will give up the right to pursue the action, there is a valid contract to that effect: A has provided consideration by giving up his right to have recourse to law. Such action would not amount to consideration if A knew that the claim was either hopeless or invalid, as was illustrated in *Wade v Simeon* (1846), where it transpired that the plaintiff had no legal claim for breach of the original contract.

6.2.5.2 Types of consideration

Consideration can be divided into the following categories:

- *Executory consideration*

  This is the promise to perform an action at some future time. A contract can be made on the basis of an exchange of promises as to future action. Such a contract is known as an executory contract.

- *Executed consideration*

  In the case of unilateral contracts, where the offeror promises something in return for the offeree's doing something, the promise only becomes enforceable when the offeree has actually performed the required act. If A offers a reward for the return of a lost watch, the reward only becomes enforceable once it has been found and returned.

- *Past consideration*

This category does not actually count as valid consideration; that is, it is insufficient to make any agreement which is based on it a binding contract. Normally, consideration is provided either at the time of the creation of a contract or at a later date. In the case of past consideration, however, the action is performed before the promise for which it is supposed to be the consideration. Such action is not sufficient to support a promise, as consideration cannot consist of any action already wholly performed before the promise was made. The consideration must be given because of or in return for the other's promise.

In *Re McArdle* (1951), a number of children were entitled to a house on the death of their mother. While the mother was still alive, her son and his wife had lived with her, and the wife had made various improvements to the house. The children later promised that they would pay the wife £488 for the work she had done. It was held that, as the work was completed when the promise was given, it was past consideration and the later promise could not be enforced; she had not carried out the work because of a promise of reimbursement.

There are exceptions to the rule that past consideration will not support a valid contract, as follows:

- ○ Under s 27 of the Bills of Exchange Act 1882, past consideration can create liability on a bill of exchange.
- ○ Under s 29 of the Limitation Act 1980, a time barred debt becomes enforceable again if it is acknowledged in writing.
- ○ Where the claimant performed the action at the request of the defendant and payment was expected, then any subsequent promise to pay will be enforceable, as can be seen in *Re Casey's Patents* (1892) where the joint owners of patent rights asked Casey to find licensees to work the patents. After he had done as requested, they promised to reward him. When one of the patent holders died, his executors denied the enforceability of the promise made to Casey on the basis of past consideration. It was held that the promise made to Casey was enforceable. There had been an implied promise to reward him before he had performed his action, and the later payment simply fixed the extent of that reward. In practical terms, it is usually implied that you are promising to pay where you ask a person to undertake work which is within the course of his/her trade or profession even though you do not actually promise to pay.

6.2.5.3 *Rules relating to consideration*

It has already been seen that consideration must not be past, but that is only one of the many rules that govern the legal definition and operation of consideration. Other rules are as follows:

- *Performance must be legal*

The courts will not countenance a claim to enforce a promise to pay for any criminal act.

- *Performance must be possible*

  It is generally accepted that a promise to perform an impossible act cannot form the basis of a binding contractual agreement.

- *Consideration must move from the promisee*

  If A promises B £1,000 if B gives his car to C, then C cannot usually enforce B's promise, because C is not the party who has provided the consideration for the promise.

  In *Tweddle v Atkinson* (1861), on the occasion of the marriage of A and B, their respective fathers entered into a contract to pay money to A. When one of the parents died without having made the payment, A tried to enforce the contract against his estate. It was held that A could not enforce the contract, as he personally had provided no consideration for the promise. (This point should be considered in the context of the doctrine of privity of contract and its exceptions: see below, 6.2.6.)

- *Consideration must be sufficient but need not be adequate*

  It is up to the parties themselves to decide the terms of their contract. The court will not intervene to require equality in the value exchanged; as long as the agreement has been freely entered into, the consideration exchanged need not be *adequate*.

  In *Thomas v Thomas* (1842), the executors of a man's will promised to let his widow live in his house, in return for rent of £1 per year. It was held that £1 was sufficient consideration to validate the contract, although it did not represent an adequate rent in economic terms.

  In *Chappell & Co v Nestlé Co* (1959), it was held that a used chocolate wrapper was consideration sufficient to form a contract, even though it had no economic value whatsoever to Nestlé and was in fact thrown away after it was returned to them.

  However, the consideration must be *sufficient*; that is, something which the law recognises as amounting to consideration, as is examined below in 6.2.5.5.

6.2.5.4 Performance of existing duties

It has generally been accepted that performance of an existing duty does not provide valid consideration. The rules relating to existing duty are as follows:

- *The discharge of a public duty*

  As a matter of public policy, in order to forestall the possibility of corruption or extortion, it has long been held that those who are required to perform certain public duties cannot claim the performance of those duties as consideration for a promised reward.

In *Collins v Godefroy* (1831), the plaintiff was served with a subpoena, which meant that he was legally required to give evidence in the court case in question. Additionally, however, the defendant promised to pay him for giving his evidence. When the plaintiff tried to enforce the promised payment, it was held that there was no binding agreement, as he had provided no consideration by simply fulfilling his existing duty.

Where, however, a promisee does more than his duty, he is entitled to claim on the promise. See, for example, *Glasbrook v Glamorgan* CC (1925), where the police authority provided more protection than their public duty required; and the similar case of *Harris v Sheffield United FC* (1987), where the defendant football club was held liable to pay police costs for controlling crowds at their matches.

In cases where there is no possibility of corruption and no evidence of coercion, the courts have stretched the understanding of what is meant by 'consideration' in order to fit the facts of the case in question within the framework of the classical model of contract. See, for example, *Ward v Byham* (1956), in which a mother was held to provide consideration by looking after her child well; and *Williams v Williams* (1957), in which the consideration for a husband's promise of maintenance to his estranged wife seemed to be the fact of her staying away from him. In both of these cases, Lord Denning introduced *obiter dicta* which directly questioned the reason why the performance of an existing duty should not amount to consideration, but the cases were ultimately decided on the basis that sufficient consideration was provided.

- *The performance of a contractual duty*

Lord Denning's challenge to the formalism of the classical model of contract is particularly pertinent when considered in the context of commercial contracts, where the mere performance of a contract may provide a benefit, or at least avoid a loss, for a promisor. The long established rule, however, was that the mere performance of a contractual duty already owed to the promisor could not be consideration for a new promise.

In *Stilk v Myrick* (1809), when two members of his crew deserted, a ship's captain promised the remaining members of the crew that they would share the deserters' wages if they completed the voyage. When the ship was returned to London, the owners refused to honour the promise and it was held that it could not be legally enforced, since the sailors had only done what they were already obliged to do by their contracts of employment.

Although *Stilk v Myrick* is cited as an authority in relation to consideration, it would appear that the public policy issue in the perceived need to preclude even the possibility of sailors in distant parts exerting coercive pressure to increase their rewards was just as important. Thus, although the reason for the decision was a matter of public policy, its legal justification was in terms of consideration.

As in the case of a public duty, so performance of more than the existing contractual duty will be valid consideration for a new promise. Thus, in *Hartley v Ponsonby* (1857), the facts of which were somewhat similar to those in *Stilk v Myrick*, it was decided that the crew had done more than they previously had agreed to do, because the number of deserters had been so great as to make the return of the ship unusually hazardous. On that basis, they were entitled to enforce the agreement to increase their wages. Once again, one finds in this case a reluctance to deny the theoretical application of the classical model of contract, whilst at the same time undermining its operation in practice.

The continued relevance and application of *Stilk v Myrick* in commercial cases has been placed in no little doubt in more recent years by a potentially extremely important decision of the Court of Appeal.

In *Williams v Roffey Bros* (1990), Roffey Bros had entered into a contract to refurbish a block of flats and sub-contracted with Williams to carry out carpentry work, for a fixed price of £20,000. It became apparent that Williams was in such financial difficulties that he might not be able to complete his work on time, with the consequence that Roffey Bros would be subject to a penalty clause in the main contract. As a result, Roffey Bros offered to pay Williams an additional £575 for each flat he completed. On that basis, Williams carried on working but, when it seemed that Roffey Bros were not going to pay him, he stopped work and sued for the additional payment in relation to the eight flats he had completed after the promise of additional payment. The Court of Appeal held that Roffey Bros had enjoyed practical benefits as a consequence of their promise to increase Williams' payment: the work would be completed on time; they would not have to pay any penalty; and they would not suffer the bother and expense of getting someone else to complete the work. In the circumstances, these benefits were sufficient to provide consideration for the promise of extra money and Williams was held to be entitled to recover the extra money owed to him.

It should be emphasised that the Court of Appeal in *Williams v Roffey* made it clear that they were not to be understood as disapproving the *ratio* in *Stilk v Myrick* (1809). They distinguished the present case but, in so doing, effectively limited the application of the *ratio* in *Stilk v Myrick*. As the owners in *Stilk v Myrick* would appear to have enjoyed similar practical benefits to those enjoyed by Roffey Bros, it would seem that the reason for distinguishing the cases rests on the clear absence of any fraud, economic duress or other improper pressure. This was emphasised by the Court of Appeal in *Williams v Roffey Bros*, where it was indicated that Williams did not put pressure on Roffey Bros for extra payment; it was Roffey Bros who approached Williams with the suggestion.

The legal situation would now seem to be that the performance of an existing contractual duty can amount to consideration for a new promise in circumstances where there is no question of fraud or duress, and where practical benefits accrue to the promisor. Such a conclusion not only concurs with the approach suggested earlier by Lord Denning in *Ward v Byham* (1956) and *Williams v Williams*, but also reflects commercial practice, where contracts are frequently renegotiated in the course of their performance. However, it is important to note that in *Williams v Roffey Bros*, the court still felt constrained to find that consideration existed on the part of

Williams, though some might consider such a finding artificial. It has been suggested that the court paid 'lip service' to the concept of consideration, not being prepared to depart entirely from its constraints in the interests of commercial reality.

The foregoing has considered the situation that operates between parties to an existing contract. It has long been recognised that the performance of a contractual duty owed to one person can amount to valid consideration for the promise made by another person.

In *Shadwell v Shadwell* (1860), the plaintiff had entered into a contract to marry. His uncle promised that, if he went ahead with the marriage, he would pay him £150 per year, until his earnings reached a certain sum. When the uncle died, owing several years' payment, the nephew successfully sued his estate for the outstanding money. It was held that going through with the marriage was sufficient consideration for the uncle's promise, even though the nephew was already contractually bound to his fiancée.

6.2.5.5   Consideration in relation to the waiver of existing rights

At common law, if A owes B £10 but B agrees to accept £5 in full settlement of the debt, B's promise to give up existing rights must be supported by consideration on the part of A. In *Pinnel's Case* (1602), it was stated that a payment of a lesser sum cannot be any satisfaction for the whole. This opinion was approved in *Foakes v Beer* (1884), where Mrs Beer had obtained a judgment in debt against Dr Foakes for £2,091. She had agreed in writing to accept payment of this amount in instalments. When payment was complete, she claimed a further £360 as interest due on the judgment debt. It was held that Mrs Beer was entitled to the interest, as her promise to accept the bare debt was not supported by any consideration from Foakes.

It can be appreciated that there are some similarities between the rules in *Foakes v Beer* and *Stilk v Myrick* (1809) in respect of the way in which promisors escape subsequent liability for their promises. In the former case, however, the promisor was being asked to give up what she was legally entitled to insist on whereas, in the latter case, the promisors were being asked to provide more than they were legally required to provide.

As has been considered above in 6.2.5.4, the rule in *Stilk v Myrick* has been subsequently modified and made less strict in its application by *Williams v Roffey Bros* (1990). However, no corresponding modification has taken place in relation to *Foakes v Beer*; indeed, the Court of Appeal has rejected the argument that it should be so modified.

In *Re Selectmove Ltd* (1994), during negotiations relating to money owed to the Inland Revenue, the company had agreed with the collector of taxes that it would pay off the debt by instalments. The company began paying off the debt, only to be faced with a demand from the Revenue that the total be paid off immediately, on threat of liquidation. It was argued for the company, on the basis of *Williams v Roffey Bros*, that its payment of the debt was sufficient consideration for the promise of the Revenue to accept it in instalments. It was held that situations relating to the payment of debt were distinguishable from those relating to the supply of goods and services, and that, in the case of the former, the court was bound to follow the clear authority of the House of Lords in *Foakes v Beer*.

The practical validity of the distinction drawn by the Court of Appeal is, to say the least, arguable. It ignores the fact that payment by instalments, and indeed part payment, is substantially better than no payment at all, which is a possible, if not likely, outcome of liquidating businesses in an attempt to recover the full amount of a debt. It is surely unnecessarily harsh to deny legal enforceability to renegotiated agreements in relation to debt where the terms have been renegotiated freely and without any suggestion of fraud or coercion. Nonetheless, the Court of Appeal clearly felt itself constrained by the doctrine of binding precedent and had less scope to distinguish *Foakes v Beer* than it had with regard to *Stilk v Myrick*. It remains to be seen whether the House of Lords will be asked to reconsider the operation of *Foakes v Beer* in the light of current commercial practice.

In any case, there are a number of situations in which the rule in *Foakes v Beer* does not apply. The following will operate to fully discharge an outstanding debt:

- *Payment in kind*

  Money's worth is just as capable of satisfying a debt as money. So, A may clear a debt if B agrees to accept something instead of money.

  As considered previously, consideration does not have to be adequate; thus, A can discharge a £10 debt by giving B £5 and a bar of chocolate. Payment by cheque is no longer treated as substitute payment in this respect (see *D & C Builders Ltd v Rees* (1966)).

- *Payment of a lesser sum before the due date of payment*

  The early payment has, of course, to be acceptable to the party to whom the debt is owed.

- *Payment at a different place*

  As in the previous case, this must be at the wish of the creditor.

- *Payment of a lesser sum by a third party*

  See *Welby v Drake* (1825).

- *A composition arrangement*

  This is an agreement between creditors to the effect that they will accept part payment of their debts. The individual creditors cannot subsequently seek to recover the unpaid element of the debt (see *Good v Cheesman* (1831)).

6.2.5.6 *Promissory estoppel*

It has been seen that English law will generally not enforce gratuitous promises, that is, promises which are not supported by consideration coming from the promisee. The equitable doctrine of promissory estoppel, however, can sometimes be relied upon to prevent promisors from going back on their promises to forgo their strict contractual rights. The doctrine first appeared in *Hughes v Metropolitan Railway Co* (1877) and was revived by Lord Denning in *Central London Pty Trust Ltd v High Trees House Ltd* (1947).

In the *High Trees* case, the plaintiffs let a block of flats to the defendants in 1937 at a fixed rent. Due to the Second World War, it became difficult to let the flats and the parties renegotiated the rent to half of the original amount. No consideration was provided for this agreement. By 1945, all the flats were let and the plaintiffs sought to return to the terms of the original agreement. They claimed that they were entitled to the full rent in the future and enquired as to whether they were owed additional rent for the previous period. It was held that the plaintiffs were entitled to the full rent in the future but were estopped from claiming the full rent for the period 1941–45.

The precise scope of the doctrine of promissory estoppel is far from certain. There are a number of conflicting judgments on the point, with some judges adopting a wide understanding of its operation, whilst others prefer to keep its effect narrowly constrained. However, the following points may be made:

- *Promissory estoppel only arises where a party relies on the promise*

    The promise must have been made with the intention that it be acted upon, and it must actually have been acted on. It was once thought that the promisee must have acted to their detriment, but such detriment is no longer considered necessary (see *WJ Alan & Co v El Nasr Export and Import Co* (1972)).

- *Promissory estoppel only varies or discharges rights within an existing contract*

    Promissory estoppel does not apply to the formation of contract and, therefore, does not avoid the need for consideration to establish a contract in the first instance. This point is sometimes made by stating that promissory estoppel is a shield and not a sword (see *Combe v Combe* (1951), where it was held that the doctrine could only be used as a defence, when sued on the terms of the original agreement, and not as a cause of action).

- *Promissory estoppel normally only suspends rights*

    It is usually open to the promisor, on the provision of reasonable notice, to retract the promise and revert to the original terms of the contract for the future (see *Tool Metal Manufacturing Co v Tungsten Electric Co* (1955)). Rights may be extinguished, however, in the case of a non-continuing obligation or where the parties cannot resume their original positions. (Consider *D & C Builders v Rees* (1966), below. It is clear that, had the defendants been able to rely on promissory estoppel, the plaintiffs would have permanently lost their right to recover the full amount of the original debt.)

- *The promise relied upon must be given voluntarily*

    As an equitable remedy, the benefit of promissory estoppel will not be extended to those who have behaved in an inequitable manner. Thus, if the promise has been extorted through fraud, duress, or any other inequitable act, it will not be relied on and the common law rules will apply.

In *D & C Builders Ltd v Rees*, the defendants owed the plaintiffs £482 but would agree to pay only £300. As the plaintiffs were in financial difficulties, they accepted the £300 in full settlement of the account. The plaintiffs later successfully claimed the outstanding balance on the ground that they had been forced to accept the lesser sum. As the defendants themselves had not acted in an equitable manner, they were denied the protection of the equitable remedy and the case was decided on the basis of the rule in *Pinnel's Case* (1602).

- *Promissory estoppel might only apply to future rights*

  It is not entirely clear whether the doctrine can apply to forgoing existing rights as well as future rights, but it should be noted that, in *Re Selectmove Ltd* (1994), it was stated that promissory estoppel could not be applied where the promise related to forgoing an existing debt; it only related to debts accruing in the future, such as rent due *after* the promise was made.

6.2.5.7 *Promissory estoppel after* Williams v Roffey Bros *(1990)*

It is likely that the decision in *Williams v Roffey Bros* (1990) will reduce the need for reliance on promissory estoppel in cases involving the renegotiation of contracts for the supply of goods or services, since performance of existing duties may now provide consideration for new promises. As was stated previously with regard to *Re Selectmove Ltd* (1994), however, the same claim cannot be made in relation to partial payments of debts. Those situations are still subject to the rule in *Foakes v Beer* (1884), as modified, uncertainly, by the operation of promissory estoppel. As estoppel is generally only suspensory in effect, it is always open to the promisor, at least in the case of continuing debts, to reimpose the original terms by withdrawing their new promise.

6.2.6 Privity of contract

There is some debate as to whether privity is a principle in its own right, or whether it is simply a conclusion from the more general rules relating to consideration. In any case, it is a general rule that a contract can only impose rights or obligations on persons who are parties to it. This is the doctrine of privity and its operation may be seen in *Dunlop v Selfridge* (1915). In this case, Dunlop sold tyres to a distributor, Dew & Co, on terms that the distributor would not sell them at less than the manufacturer's list price and that they would extract a similar undertaking from anyone whom they supplied with tyres. Dew & Co resold the tyres to Selfridge, who agreed to abide by the restrictions and to pay Dunlop £5 for each tyre they sold in breach of them. When Selfridge sold tyres at below Dunlop's list price, Dunlop sought to recover the promised £5 per tyre. It was held that Dunlop could not recover damages on the basis of the contract between Dew and Selfridge, to which they were not a party.

There are, however, a number of ways in which consequences of the application of strict rule of privity may be avoided to allow a third party to enforce a contract. These occur in the following circumstances:

- *The beneficiary sues in some other capacity*

Although an individual may not originally be party to a particular contract, they may, nonetheless, acquire the power to enforce the contract where they are legally appointed to administer the affairs of one of the original parties. An example of this can be seen in *Beswick v Beswick* (1967), where a coal merchant sold his business to his nephew in return for a consultancy fee of £6 10 s during his lifetime, and thereafter an annuity of £5 per week, payable to his widow. After the uncle died, the nephew stopped paying the widow. When she became administratrix of her husband's estate, she sued the nephew for specific performance of the agreement in that capacity, as well as in her personal capacity. It was held that, although she was not a party to the contract, and therefore could not be granted specific performance in her personal capacity, such an order could be awarded to her as the administratrix of the deceased's estate. However, she *only* benefited personally because she was the beneficiary of the deceased's estate.

- *The situation involves a collateral contract*

A collateral contract arises where one party promises something to another party if that other party enters into a contract with a third party; for example, A promises to give B something if B enters into a contract with C. In such a situation, the second party can enforce the original promise, that is, B can insist that A complies with the original promise. It may be seen from this that, although treated as an exception to the privity rule, a collateral contract conforms with the requirements relating to the establishment of any other contract, consideration for the original promise being the making of the second contract. An example of the operation of a collateral contract will demonstrate, however, the way in which the courts tend to construct collateral contracts in order to achieve what they see as fair dealing.

In *Shanklin Pier v Detel Products Ltd* (1951), the plaintiffs contracted to have their pier repainted. On the basis of promises as to its quality, the defendants persuaded the pier company to insist that a particular paint produced by Detel be used. The painters used the paint but it proved unsatisfactory. The plaintiffs sued for breach of the original promise as to the paint's suitability. The defendants countered that the only contract that they had entered into was with the painters to whom they had sold the paint, and that, as the pier company was not a party to that contract, they had no right of action against Detel. The pier company was successful. It was held that, in addition to the contract for the sale of paint, there was a second collateral contract between the plaintiffs and the defendants, by which the latter guaranteed the suitability of the paint in return for the pier company specifying that the painters used it.

- *There is a valid assignment of the benefit of the contract*

A party to a contract can transfer the benefit of that contract to a third party through the formal process of assignment. The assignment must be in writing and the assignee receives no better rights under the contract than those which the assignor possessed. The burden of a contract cannot be assigned without the consent of the other party to the contract.

- *Where it is foreseeable that damage caused by any breach of contract will cause a loss to a third party*

  In *Linden Gardens Trust Ltd v Lenesta Sludge Disposals Ltd* (1994), the original parties had entered into a contract for work to be carried out on a property, with knowledge that the property was likely to be subsequently transferred to a third party. The defendants' poor work, amounting to a breach of contract, only became apparent after the property had been transferred. There had been no assignment of the original contract and, normally, under the doctrine of privity, the new owners would have no contractual rights against the defendants and the original owners of the property would have suffered only a nominal breach, as they had sold it at no loss to themselves. Nonetheless, the House of Lords held that, under such circumstances and within a commercial context, the original promisee should be able to claim full damages on behalf of the third party for the breach of contract. The issue was examined more recently, by the House of Lords, in *Alfred McAlpine Construction Ltd v Panatown Ltd* (2002).

- *One of the parties has entered the contract as a trustee for a third party*

  There exists the possibility that a party to a contract can create a contract specifically for the benefit of a third party. In such limited circumstances, the promisee is considered as a trustee of the contractual promise for the benefit of the third party. In order to enforce the contract, the third party must act through the promisee by making them a party to any action. For a consideration of this possibility, see *Les Affréteurs Réunis SA v Leopold Walford (London) Ltd* (1919).

The other main exception to the privity rule is agency, where the agent brings about contractual relations between two other parties, even where the existence of the agency has not been disclosed.

In the area of motoring insurance, statute law has intervened to permit third parties to claim directly against insurers; for example, the Road Traffic Act 1988 allows an injured third party to claim compensation from the driver's insurance company.

6.2.6.1 Contracts (Rights of Third Parties) Act 1999

Significant inroads into the operation of the doctrine of privity have been made by the Contracts (Rights of Third Parties) Act 1999, which gives statutory effect to the recommendations of the 1996 Law Commission Report into this aspect of contract law (No 242, 1996). The Act establishes the circumstances in which third parties can enforce terms of contracts. Essentially, the requirement is that, in order for the third party to gain rights of enforcement, the contract in question must either expressly confer such a right on the third party or have been clearly made for their benefit (s 1). In order to benefit from the provisions of the Act, it is required that the third party be expressly identified in the contract by name, or as a member of a class of persons, or as answering a particular description. So, for example, *Tweddle v Atkinson* (1861) (see above, 6.2.5.3) would be differently decided today because the contract expressly named the son as beneficiary *and* stated that he could enforce the contract. In *Nisshin Shipping Co Ltd v Cleaves & Co Ltd & Others* (2003), the Commercial Court examined the application of s 1 of the 1999 Act. It was decided that even though there was no express provision for third parties to enforce the contract for their own benefit, that intention could be inferred; however, the lack of an express provision did not automatically raise an inference that the third party could enforce clauses of the contract. It would be a matter of construction whether there was a mutual intention that a third party could enforce or rely on the contractual clauses. Interestingly, however, the third person need not be in existence when the contract was made, so it is possible for parties to make contracts for the benefit of unborn children or a future marriage partner. This provision should also reduce the difficulties relating to pre-incorporation contracts in relation to registered companies. The third party may exercise the right to any remedy which would have been available had they been a party to the contract. Such rights are, however, subject to the terms and conditions contained in the contract; the third party can get no better rights than the original promisee; and the actual parties to the contract can place conditions on the rights of the third party.

Section 2 of the Act provides that where a third party has rights by virtue of the Act, the original parties to the contract cannot agree to rescind it or vary its terms without the consent of the third party, unless the original contract contained an express term to that effect.

Section 3 allows the promisor to make use of any defences or rights of set-off that they might have against the promisee in any action by the third party. Additionally, the promisor can also rely on any such rights against the third party. These rights are subject to any express provision in the contract to the contrary.

Section 5 removes the possibility of the promisor suffering from double liability in relation to the promisor and the third party. It provides, therefore, that any damages awarded to a third party for a breach of the contract be reduced by the amount recovered by the promisee in any previous action relating to the contract.

Section 6 of the Act specifically states that it does not alter the existing law relating to, and confers no new rights on third parties in relation to, negotiable instruments, s 14 of the Companies Act 1985, contracts of employment or contracts for the carriage of goods. However, a third party stated as benefiting from an exclusion clause in a contract for the carriage of goods by sea may rely on such a clause if sued. So, an independent firm of stevedores damaging a cargo during loading might claim the protection of a clause in the contract of carriage between the cargo owner and the shipowner.

Although the Contracts (Rights of Third Parties) Act came into force on 11 November 1999, it does not apply in relation to contracts entered into before the end of the period of six months beginning with that date, unless the contract in question specifically provides for its application (s 10).

6.2.7 Capacity

Capacity refers to a person's ability to enter into a contract. In general, all adults of sound mind have full capacity. However, the capacity of certain individuals is limited.

6.2.7.1 Minors

A minor is a person under the age of 18 (the age of majority was reduced from 21 to 18 by the Family Reform Act 1969). The law tries to protect such persons by restricting their contractual capacity and, thus, preventing them from entering into disadvantageous agreements. The rules which apply are a mixture of common law and statute and depend on when the contract was made. Contracts entered into after 9 June 1987 are subject to the Minors' Contracts Act 1987, which replaced the Infants' Relief Act (IRA) 1874. Agreements entered into by minors may be classified within three possible categories: valid; voidable; and void.

Valid contracts

Contracts can be enforced against minors where they relate to the following:

- *Contracts for necessaries*

  A minor is bound to pay for necessaries, that is, things that are necessary to maintain the minor. Necessaries are defined in s 3 of the Sale of Goods Act 1979 as goods 'suitable to the condition in life of the minor and their actual requirements at the time of sale'. The operation of this section is demonstrated in *Nash v Inman* (1908), where a tailor sued a minor to whom he had supplied clothes, including 11 fancy waistcoats. The minor was an undergraduate at Cambridge University at the time. It was held that, although the clothes were suitable according to the minor's station in life, they were not necessary, as he already had sufficient clothing.

  The minor is, in any case, only required to pay a reasonable price for any necessaries purchased.

- *Beneficial contracts of service*

  A minor is bound by a contract of apprenticeship or employment, as long as it is, on the whole, for their benefit.

  In *Doyle v White City Stadium* (1935), Doyle, a minor, obtained a professional boxer's licence, which was treated as a contract of apprenticeship. The licence provided that he would be bound by the rules of the Boxing Board of Control, which had the power to retain any prize money if he was ever disqualified in a fight. He claimed that the licence was void, as it was not for his benefit, but it was held that the conditions of the licence were enforceable. In spite of the penal clause, it was held that, taken as whole, it was beneficial to him.

There has to be an element of education or training in the contract; thus, ordinary trading contracts will not be enforced. See, for example, *Mercantile Union Guarantee Corp v Ball* (1937), where a minor who operated a haulage business was not held liable on a hire purchase contract that he had entered into in relation to that business.

Voidable contracts

Voidable contracts are binding on the minor, unless they are repudiated by the minor during the period of minority or within a reasonable time after reaching the age of majority. These are generally transactions in which the minor acquires an interest of a permanent nature with continuing obligations. Examples are contracts for shares, leases of property and partnership agreements.

If the minor has made payments prior to repudiation of the contract, such payment cannot be recovered unless there is a total failure of consideration and the minor has received no benefit whatsoever. An example is the case of *Steinberg v Scala (Leeds)* (1923). Miss Steinberg, while still a minor, applied for, and was allotted, shares in the defendant company. After paying some money on the shares, she defaulted on payment and repudiated the contract. The company agreed that her name be removed from its register of members but refused to return the money she had already paid. It was held that Miss Steinberg was not entitled to the return of the money paid. She had benefited from membership rights in the company; thus, there had not been a complete failure of consideration.

Void contracts

Under the IRA 1874, the following contracts were stated to be absolutely void:

- contracts for the repayment of loans;
- contracts for goods other than necessaries; and
- accounts stated, that is, admissions of money owed.

In addition, no action could be brought on the basis of the ratification, made after the attainment of full age, of an otherwise void contract.

The main effect of the Minors' Contracts Act 1987 was that the contracts set out in the IRA 1874 were no longer to be considered as absolutely void. As a consequence, unenforceable, as well as voidable, contracts may be ratified upon the minor attaining the age of majority.

Although the IRA 1874 stated that such contracts were absolutely void, this simply meant that, in effect, they could not be enforced against the minor. The other party could not normally recover goods or money transferred to the minor. Where, however, the goods had been obtained by fraud on the part of the minor and where they were still in the minor's possession, the other party could rely on the doctrine of restitution to reclaim them. The minor, on the other hand, could enforce the agreement against the other party. Specific performance would not be available, however, on the ground that it would be inequitable to grant such an order to minors while it could not be awarded against them.

The Minors' Contracts Act 1987 has given the courts wider powers to order the restoration of property acquired by a minor. They are no longer restricted to cases where the minor has acquired the property through fraud; they can now order restitution where they think it just and equitable to do so.

Minors' liability in tort

As there is no minimum age limit in relation to claims in tort, minors may be liable under a tortious action. The courts, however, will not permit a party to enforce a contract indirectly by substituting a claim in tort or quasi-contract for a claim in contract.

In *Leslie v Shiell* (1914), Shiell, a minor, obtained a loan from Leslie by lying about his age. Leslie sued to recover the money as damages in an action for the tort of deceit. It was held, however, that the action must fail, as it was simply an indirect means of enforcing the otherwise void contract.

6.2.7.2   Mental incapacity and intoxication

A contract made by a party who is of unsound mind or under the influence of drink or drugs is *prima facie* valid. In order to avoid a contract, such a person must show:

* that their mind was so affected at the time that they were incapable of understanding the nature of their actions; and

* that the other party either knew or ought to have known of their disability.

The person claiming such incapacity, nonetheless, must pay a reasonable price for necessaries sold and delivered to them. The Sale of Goods Act 1979 specifically applies the same rules to such people as those that are applicable to minors.

6.2.8   Intention to create legal relations

All of the aspects considered previously may well be present in a particular agreement, and yet there still may not be a contract. In order to limit the number of cases that might otherwise be brought, the courts will only enforce those agreements which the parties intended to have legal effect. Although expressed in terms of the parties' intentions, the test for the presence of such intention is once again objective, rather than subjective. For the purposes of this topic, agreements can be divided into three categories, in which different presumptions apply.

6.2.8.1   Domestic and social agreements

In this type of agreement, there is a presumption that the parties do not intend to create legal relations.

In *Balfour v Balfour* (1919), a husband returned to Ceylon to take up employment and he promised his wife, who could not return with him due to health problems, that he would pay her £30 per month as maintenance. When the marriage later ended in divorce, the wife sued for the promised maintenance. It was held that the parties had not intended the original promise to be binding and, therefore, it was not legally enforceable.

It is essential to realise that the intention not to create legal relations in such relationships is only a presumption and that, as with all presumptions, it may be rebutted by the actual facts and circumstances of a particular case. A case in point is *Merritt v Merritt* (1970). After a husband had left the matrimonial home, he met his wife and promised to pay her £40 per month, from which she undertook to pay the outstanding mortgage on their house. The husband, at the wife's insistence, signed a note, agreeing to transfer the house into the wife's sole name when the mortgage was paid off. The wife paid off the mortgage but the husband refused to transfer the house. It was held that the agreement was enforceable, as, in the circumstances, the parties had clearly intended to enter into a legally enforceable agreement.

'Social' agreements, such as lottery syndicates, have also been the subject of legal dispute. In *Simpkins v Pays* (1955), a relatively vague agreement about contribution to postage and sharing of any winnings in competitions made between a lodger, a landlady and her granddaughter was alleged not to be a contract for lack of intention to create legal relations. However, the court decided that there was a binding contract to share winnings, despite the apparently social nature of the agreement. The agreement was commercial in nature and related to a matter unconnected with the running of a household; there was a degree of *mutuality* in the agreement which indicated an intention that it was binding. In *Albert v Motor Insurers' Bureau* (1971), an agreement between colleagues in relation to lifts to work was held to be a contract because there was intention to create legal relations. It was said to be unnecessary to show whether the parties had thought about whether there was a contract, nor did it matter that, if asked, they would have said that they would not have sued if the arrangement failed. Clearly, therefore, the presumption does not purport to find the *actual* intention of the parties. Perhaps the best advice, particularly in relation to lottery syndicates, is to reduce the agreement to writing so that there is written evidence that the parties did intend the agreement to be a binding contract.

6.2.8.2 *Commercial agreements*

In commercial situations, the strong presumption is that the parties intend to enter into a legally binding relationship in consequence of their dealings.

In *Edwards v Skyways* (1964), employers undertook to make an *ex gratia* payment to an employee whom they had made redundant. It was held that, in such a situation, the use of the term '*ex gratia*' was not sufficient to rebut the presumption that the establishment of legal relations had been intended. The former employee was, therefore, entitled to the promised payment.

As with other presumptions, this, too, is open to rebuttal. In commercial situations, however, the presumption is so strong that it will usually take express wording to the contrary to avoid its operation. An example can be found in *Rose & Frank Co v Crompton Bros* (1925), in which it was held that an express clause which stated that no legal relations were to be created by a business transaction was effective. Another example is *Jones v Vernons Pools Ltd* (1938), where the plaintiff claimed to have submitted a correct pools forecast, but the defendants denied receiving it and relied on a clause in the coupon which stated that the transaction was binding in honour only. Under such circumstances, it was held that the plaintiff had no cause for an action in contract, as no legal relations had been created.

6.2.8.3 *Collective agreements*

Agreements between employers and trade unions may be considered as a distinct category of agreement for, although they are commercial agreements, they are presumed not to give rise to legal relations and, therefore, are not normally enforceable in the courts. Such was the outcome of *Ford Motor Co v AUEFW* (1969), in which it was held that Ford could not take legal action against the defendant trade union, which had ignored previously negotiated terms of a collective agreement.

This presumption is now conclusive by virtue of s 179 of the Trade Union and Labour Relations (Consolidation) Act 1992, unless the agreement is in writing and expressly states that it is a binding agreement.

6.2.8.4 *Letters of comfort*

Letters of comfort are generally used by parent companies to encourage potential lenders to extend credit to their subsidiary companies by stating their intention to provide financial backing for those subsidiaries. It is generally the case that such letters merely amount to statements of present intention on the part of the parent company and, therefore, do not amount to offers that can be accepted by the creditors of any subsidiary companies. Given the operation of the doctrine of separate personality, this effectively leaves the creditors with no legal recourse against the parent company for any loans granted to the subsidiary.

In *Kleinwort Benson v Malaysian Mining Corp* (1989), the defendant company had issued a letter of comfort to the plaintiffs in respect of its subsidiary company, MMC Metals. However, when MMC Metals went into liquidation, the defendant failed to make good its debts to the plaintiffs.

At first instance, the judge decided in favour of the plaintiffs, holding that, in such commercial circumstances, the defendants had failed to rebut the presumption that there had been an intention to create legal relations. On appeal, it was held that, in the circumstances of the instant case, the letter of comfort did not amount to an offer; it was a statement of intention which could not bind the defendants contractually. Therefore, the Malaysian Mining Corp was not legally responsible for the debt of its subsidiary.

It is important to note that the *Kleinwort Benson* case opens up the possibility that, under different circumstances, letters of comfort might be considered to constitute offers capable of being accepted and leading to contractual relations. Under such circumstances, the presumption as to the intention to create legal relations as they normally apply in commercial situations will operate, though it is almost inconceivable that a court would decide that a letter of comfort amounted to an offer without also finding an intention to create legal relations.

6.3   Contents of a Contract

The previous section dealt with how a binding contractual agreement comes to be formed; this section will consider what the parties have actually agreed to do. What they have agreed to do form the *terms* of the contract.

6.3.1   Contract terms and mere representations

As the parties will normally be bound to perform any promise that they have contracted to undertake, it is important to decide precisely what promises are included in the contract. Some statements do not form part of a contract, even though they might have induced the other party to enter into the contract. These pre-contractual statements are called *representations*. The consequences of such representations being false will be considered below (see below, 7.3) but, for the moment, it is sufficient to distinguish them from contractual terms, which are statements which *do* form part of the contract. There are four tests for distinguishing a contractual term from a mere representation, as follows:

- Where the statement is of such major importance that the promisee would not have entered into the agreement without it, it will be construed as a term. In *Bannerman v White* (1861), the defendant wanted to buy hops for brewing purposes and he asked the plaintiff if they had been treated with sulphur. On the basis of the plaintiff's false statement that they had not been so treated, he agreed to buy the hops. When he discovered later that they had been treated with sulphur, he refused to accept them. It was held that the plaintiff's statement about the sulphur was a fundamental term (the contract would not have been made *but for* the statement) of the contract and, since it was not true, the defendant was entitled to repudiate the contract.

- Where there is a time gap between the statement and the making of the contract, the statement will most likely be treated as a representation.

In *Routledge v McKay* (1954), on 23 October, the defendant told the plaintiff that a motorcycle was a 1942 model. On 30 October, a written contract for the sale of the bike was made, without reference to its age. The bike was actually a 1930 model. It was held that the statement about the date was a pre-contractual representation and the plaintiff could not sue for damages for breach of contract. However, this rule is not a hard and fast one. In *Schawell v Reade* (1913), the court held that a statement made three months before the final agreement was part of the contract.

- Where the statement is oral and the agreement is subsequently drawn up in written form, its exclusion from the written document will suggest that the statement was not meant to be a contractual term. *Routledge v McKay* (1954) may also be cited as authority for this proposition.

- Where one of the parties to an agreement has special knowledge or skill, then statements made by them will be terms, but statements made *to* them will not.

In *Dick Bentley Productions Ltd v Harold Smith (Motors) Ltd* (1965), the plaintiff bought a Bentley car from the defendant after being assured that it had only travelled 20,000 miles since its engine and gearbox were replaced. When this statement turned out to be untrue, the plaintiff sued for breach of contract. It was held that the statement was a term of the contract and the plaintiff was entitled to damages.

In *Oscar Chess Ltd v Williams* (1957), Williams traded in one car when buying another from the plaintiffs. He told them that his trade-in was a 1948 model, whereas it was actually a 1939 model. The company unsuccessfully sued for breach of contract. The statement as to the age of the car was merely a representation, and the right to sue for misrepresentation had been lost, due to delay.

6.3.2 Conditions, warranties and innominate terms

Once it is decided that a statement is a term, rather than merely a pre-contractual representation, it is necessary to determine which type of term it is, in order to determine what remedies are available for its breach. Terms can be classified as one of three types.

6.3.2.1 Conditions

A condition is a fundamental part of the agreement and is something which goes to the root of the contract. Breach of a condition gives the innocent party the right either to terminate the contract and refuse to perform their part of it or to go through with the agreement and sue for damages.

6.3.2.2 Warranties

A warranty is a subsidiary obligation which is not vital to the overall agreement and does not totally destroy its efficacy. Breach of a warranty does not give the right to terminate the agreement. The innocent party has to complete their part of the agreement and can only sue for damages.

6.3.2.3 Distinction between conditions and warranties

The difference between the two types of term can be seen in the following cases:

- In *Poussard v Spiers and Pond* (1876), the plaintiff had contracted with the defendants to sing in an opera that they were producing. Due to illness, she was unable to appear on the first night and for some nights thereafter. When Mme Poussard recovered, the defendants refused her services, as they had hired a replacement for the whole run of the opera. It was held that her failure to appear on the opening night had been a breach of a condition and the defendants were at liberty to treat the contract as discharged.

- In *Bettini v Gye* (1876), the plaintiff had contracted with the defendants to complete a number of engagements. He had also agreed to be in London for rehearsals six days before his opening performance. Due to illness, he only arrived three days before the opening night and the defendants refused his services. On this occasion, it was held that there was only a breach of warranty. The defendants were entitled to damages but could not treat the contract as discharged.

The distinction between the effects of a breach of condition as against the effects of a breach of warranty was enshrined in s 11 of the Sale of Goods Act (SoGA) 1893 (now the SoGA 1979). For some time, it was thought that these were the only two types of term possible, the nature of the remedy available being prescribed by the particular type of term concerned. This simple classification has subsequently been rejected by the courts as being too restrictive, and a third type of term has emerged: the innominate term.

6.3.2.4 Innominate terms

In this case, the remedy is not prescribed in advance simply by whether the term breached is a condition or a warranty, but depends on the consequence of the breach.

If the breach deprives the innocent party of substantially the whole benefit of the contract, then the right to repudiate will be permitted, even if the term might otherwise appear to be a mere warranty.

If, however, the innocent party does not lose the whole benefit of the contract, then they will not be permitted to repudiate but must settle for damages, even if the term might otherwise appear to be a condition.

In *Cehave v Bremer (The Hansa Nord)* (1976), a contract for the sale of a cargo of citrus pulp pellets, to be used as animal feed, provided that they were to be delivered in good condition. On delivery, the buyers rejected the cargo as not complying with this provision and claimed back the price paid from the sellers. The buyers eventually obtained the pellets when the cargo was sold off and used them for their original purpose. It was held that, since the breach had not been serious, the buyers had not been free to reject the cargo and the sellers had acted lawfully in retaining the money paid.

Not all judges are wholly in favour of this third category of term, feeling that, in the world of commerce, certainty as to the outcome of breach is necessary at the outset and should not be dependent on a court's findings after breach has occurred (see *Bunge Corp v Tradax Export SA* (1981)).

6.3.3 Implied terms

So far, all of the cases considered in this chapter have involved express terms: statements actually made by one of the parties, either by word of mouth or in writing. Implied terms, however, are not actually stated but are introduced into the contract by implication. Implied terms can be divided into three types.

6.3.3.1 Terms implied by statute

For example, under the SoGA 1979, terms relating to description, quality and fitness for purpose are all implied into sale of goods contracts.

6.3.3.2 Terms implied by custom

An agreement may be subject to customary terms not actually specified by the parties. For example, in *Hutton v Warren* (1836), it was held that customary usage permitted a farm tenant to claim an allowance for seed and labour on quitting his tenancy. It should be noted, however, that custom cannot override the express terms of an agreement (*Les Affréteurs Réunis v Walford* (1919)).

6.3.3.3 Terms implied by the courts

Generally, it is a matter for the parties concerned to decide the terms of a contract, but on occasion the court will presume that the parties intended to include a term which is not expressly stated. It will do so where it is necessary to give business efficacy to the contract.

Whether a term may be implied can be decided on the basis of the 'officious bystander' test. Imagine two parties, A and B, negotiating a contract. A third party, C, interrupts to suggest a particular provision. A and B reply that that particular term is understood. In such a way, the court will decide that a term should be implied into a contract.

In *The Moorcock* (1889), the appellants, the owners of a wharf, contracted with the respondents to permit them to discharge their ship at the wharf. It was apparent to both parties that, when the tide was out, the ship would rest on the river bed. When the tide was out, the ship sustained damage by settling on a ridge. It was held that there was an implied warranty in the contract that the place of anchorage should be safe for the ship. As a consequence, the shipowner was entitled to damages for breach of that term.

6.3.4 The parol evidence rule

If all the terms of a contract are in writing, then there is a strong presumption that no evidence supporting a different oral agreement will be permitted to vary those terms.

In *Hutton v Watling* (1948), on the sale of a business, together with its goodwill, a written agreement was drawn up and signed by the vendor. In an action to enforce one of the clauses in the agreement, the vendor claimed that it did not represent the whole contract. It was held that the vendor was not entitled to introduce evidence on this point, as the written document represented a true record of the contract.

The presumption against introducing contrary oral evidence can be rebutted, however, where it is shown that the document was not intended to set out all of the terms agreed by the parties.

In *Re SS Ardennes* (1951), a ship's bill of lading stated that it might proceed by any route directly or indirectly. The defendants promised that the ship would proceed directly to London from Spain with its cargo of tangerines. However, the ship called at Antwerp before heading for London and, as a result, the tangerines had to be sold at a reduced price. The shippers successfully sued for damages, as it was held that the bill of lading did not constitute the contract between the parties but merely evidenced their intentions. The verbal promise was part of the final contract.

The effect of the parol evidence rule has also been avoided by the willingness of the courts to find collateral contracts which import different, not to say contradictory, terms into the written contract. An example of this may be seen in *City and Westminster Properties (1934) Ltd v Mudd* (1959), where, although the written contract expressly provided that the defendant had no right to live on particular premises, the court recognised the contrary effect of a verbal collateral contract to allow him to do so. In return for agreeing to sign the new lease, the tenant (who had previously resided on the premises) was promised that he could continue to do so, despite the term of the new lease. Thus, both parties provided consideration to support the collateral contract. (See, further, above, 6.2.6, for the use of collateral contracts to avoid the strict operation of the doctrine of privity.)

City and Westminster v Mudd at least suggests that the courts will find justification for avoiding the strict application of the parol evidence rule where they wish to do so. On that basis, it has been suggested that it should be removed from contract law entirely. Interestingly, however, a Law Commission Report (No 154) took the opposite view, stating that there was no need to provide legislation to remove the rule, as it was already a dead letter in practice.

6.3.5 Exemption or exclusion clauses

In a sense, an exemption clause is no different from any other clause, in that it seeks to define the rights and obligations of the parties to a contract. However, an exemption clause is a term in a contract which tries to exempt, or limit, the liability of a party in breach of the agreement. Exclusion clauses give rise to most concern when they are included in standard form contracts, in which one party, who is in a position of commercial dominance, imposes their terms on the other party, who has no choice (other than to take it or leave it) as far as the terms of the contract go. Such standard form contracts are contrary to the ideas of consensus and negotiation underpinning contract law; for this reason, they have received particular attention from both the judiciary and the legislature, in an endeavour to counteract their perceived unfairness.

A typical example of a standard form agreement would be a holiday booking, made on the terms printed in a travel brochure.

The actual law relating to exclusion clauses is complicated by the interplay of the common law, the Unfair Contract Terms Act (UCTA) 1977 and the various Acts which imply certain terms into particular contracts. However, the following questions should always be asked with regard to exclusion clauses:

- Has the exclusion clause been incorporated into the contract?
- Does the exclusion clause effectively cover the breach?
- What effect do UCTA 1977 and the Unfair Terms in Consumer Contracts Regulations 1999 have on the exclusion clause?

6.3.5.1   Has the exclusion clause been incorporated into the contract?

An exclusion clause cannot be effective unless it is actually a term of a contract. There are three ways in which such a term may be inserted into a contractual agreement.

By signature

If a person signs a contractual document then they are bound by its terms, even if they do not read it.

In *L'Estrange v Graucob* (1934), a café owner bought a vending machine, signing a contract without reading it, which took away all her rights under the SoGA 1893. When the machine proved faulty, she sought to take action against the vendors, but it was held that she had no cause of action, as she had signified her consent to the terms of the contract by signing it and the exclusion clause effectively exempted liability for breach.

The rule in *L'Estrange v Graucob* may be avoided where the party seeking to rely on the exclusion clause misled the other party into signing the contract, after a misleading oral explanation of the clause (*Curtis v Chemical Cleaning and Dyeing Co* (1951)).

By notice

Apart from the above, an exclusion clause will not be incorporated into a contract unless the party affected actually knew of it or was given sufficient notice of it. In order for notice to be adequate, the document bearing the exclusion clause must be an integral part of the contract and must be given at the time that the contract is made.

In *Chapelton v Barry UDC* (1940), the plaintiff hired a deck chair and received a ticket, which stated on its back that the council would not be responsible for any injuries arising from the hire of the chairs. After he was injured when the chair collapsed, Chapelton successfully sued the council. It was held that the ticket was merely a receipt, the contract already having been made, and could not be used effectively to communicate the exclusion clause.

In *Olley v Marlborough Court Hotel Ltd* (1949), a couple arrived at a hotel and paid for a room in advance. On reaching their room, they found a notice purporting to exclude the hotel's liability in regard to thefts of goods not handed in to the manager. A thief later stole the wife's purse. It was held that the hotel could not escape liability, since the disclaimer had only been made after the contract had been formed.

The notice given must be sufficient for the average person to be aware of it; if it is sufficient, it matters not that this contracting party was not aware of it. In *Thompson v LM & S Railway* (1930), a woman who could not read was bound by a printed clause referred to on a railway timetable and ticket because the average person could have been aware of it.

Whether the degree of notice given has been sufficient is a matter of fact but, in *Thornton v Shoe Lane Parking Ltd* (1971), it was stated that the greater the exemption, the greater the degree of notice required.

In *Interfoto Picture Library Ltd v Stiletto Programmes Ltd* (1988), the Court of Appeal decided that a particular clause was not to be considered as imported into a contract, even though it had been available for inspection before the contract was entered into. The clause in question sought to impose almost £4,000 liability for any delay in returning the photographic negatives which were the subject of the contract. It was held, following *Thornton v Shoe Lane Parking Ltd*, that this penalty was so severe that it could not have been fairly brought to the attention of the other party by indirect reference; explicit notification was necessary where a clause was particularly onerous and unusual. This is sometimes referred to as the *red ink* or *red hand* principle, and was recently re-examined in relation to scratch cards in *O'Brien v MGN Ltd* (2001).

By custom

Where the parties have had previous dealings on the basis of an exclusion clause, that clause may be included in later contracts (*Spurling v Bradshaw* (1956)), but it has to be shown that the party affected had actual knowledge of the exclusion clause.

In *Hollier v Rambler Motors* (1972), on each of the previous occasions that the plaintiff had had his car repaired at the defendants' garage, he had signed a form containing an exclusion clause. On the last occasion, he had not signed such a form. When the car was damaged by fire through negligence, the defendants sought to rely on the exclusion clause. It was held that there was no evidence that Hollier had been aware of the clause to which he had been agreeing and, therefore, it could not be considered to be a part of his last contract.

6.3.5.2   Does the exclusion clause effectively cover the breach?

As a consequence of the disfavour with which the judiciary have looked on exclusion clauses, a number of rules of construction have been developed which operate to restrict the effectiveness of exclusion clauses. These include the following:

- *The construction of the clause*

  The court will determine whether the clause, on its construction, covers what has occurred.

In Andrews v Singer (1934), the plaintiffs contracted to buy some new Singer cars from the defendant. A clause excluded all conditions, warranties and liabilities implied by statute, common law or otherwise. One car supplied was not new. It was held that the requirement that the cars be new was an express condition of the contract and, therefore, was not covered by the exclusion clause, which only referred to implied clauses.

- *The contra proferentem rule*

This requires that any uncertainties or ambiguities in the exclusion clause are interpreted against the person seeking to rely on it.

In *Hollier v Rambler* (1972), it was stated that as the exclusion clause in question could be interpreted as applying only to non-negligent accidental damage or, alternatively, as including damage caused by negligence, it should be restricted to the former, narrower interpretation. As a consequence, the plaintiff could recover for damages caused to his car by the defendants' negligence.

A more recent example of the operation of the *contra proferentem* rule may be seen in *Bovis Construction (Scotland) Ltd v Whatlings Construction Ltd* (1995). The details of the contract between the two parties were based on a standard form and a number of letters. One of the letters introduced a term which limited the defendants' liability in respect of time related costs to £100,000. The plaintiffs terminated the contract on the basis of the defendants' lack of diligence in carrying out the contracted work. When they subsequently sued for £2,741,000, the defendants relied on the limitation clause. The House of Lords decided that as the defendants had introduced the limitation clause, it had to be interpreted strictly, although not as strictly as a full exclusion clause. It was held that the term 'time related costs' applied to losses arising as a consequence of delay in performance, and not non-performance. The defendants had been guilty of the latter and were, therefore, fully liable for the consequences of their repudiatory breach. More recently, an ambiguous clause was considered by the Court of Appeal in *The University of Keele v Price Waterhouse* (2004). The appellant accountants claimed they were not liable to pay damages to the university, which had suffered loss of anticipated savings under a profit related pay scheme. The appellants had given negligent financial advice in relation to the scheme. A clause of the contract between the appellants and the university indicated that, subject to a cap on liability of twice the anticipated savings, the appellants accepted 'liability to pay damages in respect of loss or damage suffered by the university as a direct result of our providing the Services'. The clause went on to say, 'All other liability is expressly excluded, in particular consequential loss, failure to realise anticipated savings or benefits and a failure to obtain registration of the Scheme'. The appellants contended that the second part of the clause protected them from liability. Clearly, the clause, taken as a whole, appeared contradictory; the first part limited liability in relation to anticipated savings, whilst the second part excluded any such liability. The Court of Appeal interpreted the clause as meaning that the second part applied only to exclude liability which exceeded the cap on liability in the first part.

- *The doctrine of fundamental breach*

  In a series of complicated and conflicting cases, ending with the House of Lords' decision in *Photo Production v Securicor Transport* (1980), some courts attempted to develop a rule that it was impossible to exclude liability for breach of contract if a fundamental breach of the contract had occurred, that is, where the party in breach had failed altogether to perform the contract.

  In *Photo Production v Securicor Transport*, the defendants had entered into a contract with the plaintiffs to guard their factory. An exclusion clause exempted Securicor from liability, even if one of their employees caused damage to the factory. Later, one of the guards deliberately set fire to the factory. Securicor claimed the protection of the exclusion clause. It was ultimately decided by the House of Lords that whether an exclusion clause could operate after a fundamental breach was a matter of construction. There was no absolute rule that total failure of performance rendered such clauses inoperative. The exclusion clause in this particular case was wide enough to cover the events that took place, and so Photo Production's action failed.

6.3.5.3 What effect does the Unfair Contract Terms Act 1977 have on the exclusion clause?

This Act represents the statutory attempt to control exclusion clauses. In spite of its title, it is really aimed at unfair exemption clauses, rather than contract terms generally. It also covers non-contractual notices which purport to exclude liability under the Occupiers' Liability Act 1957. The controls under UCTA 1977 relate to two areas.

Negligence

There is an absolute prohibition on exemption clauses in relation to liability in negligence resulting in death or injury (ss 2 and 5). Exemption clauses relating to liability for other damage caused by negligence will only be enforced to the extent that they satisfy the requirement of reasonableness (s 5).

In *Smith v Bush* (1989), the plaintiff bought a house on the basis of a valuation report carried out for her building society by the defendant. The surveyor had included a disclaimer of liability for negligence in his report to the building society and sought to rely on that fact when the plaintiff sued after the chimneys of the property collapsed. The House of Lords held that the disclaimer was an exemption clause and that it failed the requirement that such terms should be reasonable.

Contract

The general rule of the Act (s 3) is that an exclusion clause imposed on a consumer (as defined in s 12(1)) or by standard terms of business is not binding unless it satisfies the Act's requirement of reasonableness. Effectively, therefore, the Act is dealing with clauses imposed by a person acting *in the course of business*. Section 12(1) states that a person deals as a consumer (so that he does *not act in the course of business*) if he neither makes the contract in the course of business nor holds himself out as so doing and the other party does make the contract in the course of business. Additionally, where goods are supplied under the contract, they must be of a type normally supplied for private consumption and they must be so used.

The precise meaning of 'acting in the course of business' for the purposes of UCTA 1977 was considered in *R & B Customs Brokers Co Ltd v UDT* (1988). In deciding that the sellers of a car to a company could not rely on an exclusion clause contained in the contract, as the transaction had not been in the course of business, the Court of Appeal stated that the purchase had been:

> ... at highest, only incidental to the carrying on of the relevant business [and] ... a degree of regularity is required before it can be said that they are an integral part of the business carried on and so entered into in the course of business.

In reaching this decision, the Court of Appeal followed the House of Lords' decision in *Davies v Sumner* (1984), which dealt with a similar provision in the Trade Descriptions Act 1968. This interpretation of s 12(1) was confirmed in *Feldaroll Foundry plc v Hermes Leasing (London) Ltd* (2004). On facts similar to *R & B Customs Brokers Co Ltd v UDT*, a company was held not to act 'in the course of business', even though the contract stated the car was acquired for use in the business. It would seem, however, that the meaning of selling 'in the course of business' for the purposes of s 14 of the SoGA 1979 is different. Section 14, which implies conditions of satisfactory quality and fitness for purpose into contracts for the sale of goods (see Chapter 9), applies where the seller 'sells in the course of business'. The meaning of selling 'in the course of business' under s 14 of the SoGA 1979 is wide enough to cover incidental sales by, for example, the professions, local and central government departments and public authorities. The meaning of selling 'in the course of business' in the context of s 14 was examined in *Stevenson v Rogers* (1999).

UCTA 1977 applies more specific rules to contracts for the sale of goods; which rules apply depends on whether the seller sells to a person 'dealing as a consumer' (as defined in s 12(1) of UCTA 1977; such sales are commonly referred to as 'consumer sales'). Under s 6(1) of UCTA 1977, the implied term of s 12(1) of the SoGA 1979 (transfer of title) cannot be excluded in consumer or non-consumer sales.

The other implied terms, namely, those as to description, fitness, satisfactory quality and sample, cannot be excluded in a consumer contract (s 6(2)); in a non-consumer transaction, any restriction is subject to the requirement of reasonableness (s 6(3)). Under s 7, similar rules apply to other contracts under which goods are supplied (for example hire contracts) by virtue of the Supply of Goods and Services Act 1982. Amendments to UCTA 1977, in so far as its provisions apply to contracts for the sale and supply of goods, are made by the Sale and Supply of Goods to Consumers Regulations 2002. These amendments are dealt with in Chapter 9.

Indemnity clauses are covered by s 4 of UCTA 1977. These are provisions in contracts by means of which one party agrees to compensate the other for any liability incurred by them in the course of carrying out the contract. Although these may be legitimate ways of allocating risk and insurance responsibilities in a commercial context, they are of more dubious effect in consumer transactions and are, therefore, required to satisfy the requirement of reasonableness.

'The requirement of reasonableness means fair and reasonable ... having regard to the circumstances ... [s 11].' Schedule 2 to UCTA 1977 provides guidelines for the application of the reasonableness test in regard to non-consumer transactions, but it is likely that similar considerations will be taken into account by the courts in consumer transactions. Amongst these considerations are:

- he relative strength of the parties' bargaining power;

- whether any inducement was offered in return for the limitation on liability;

- whether the customer knew, or ought to have known, about the existence or extent of the exclusion; and

- whether the goods were manufactured or adapted to the special order of the customer.

In *George Mitchell (Chesterhall) Ltd v Finney Lock Seeds Ltd* (1983), the respondents planted 63 acres with cabbage seed, which was supplied by the appellants. The crop failed, due partly to the fact that the wrong type of seed had been supplied and partly to the fact that the seed supplied was of inferior quality. When the respondents claimed damages, the sellers relied on a clause in their standard conditions of sale, which limited their liability to replacing the seeds supplied or refunding payment. It was held, however, that the respondents were entitled to compensation for the loss of the crop. The House of Lords decided that although the exemption clause was sufficiently clear and unambiguous to be effective at common law, it failed the test of reasonableness under UCTA 1977.

In *Watford Electronics Ltd v Sanderson CFL Ltd* (2001), a contract between two businesses for the purchase of integrated software systems stated that:

- the parties agreed no pre-contractual representations had been made;

- liability for indirect/consequential loss was excluded; and

- liability for breach of contract was limited to the contract price of £104,596.

The system was unsatisfactory and the buyer claimed damages for breach of contract, misrepresentation and negligence, totalling (including loss of expected profits) £5.5 million. The seller sought to rely on the clauses to limit/escape liability; the buyer alleged that they were unreasonable under UCTA 1977. The Court of Appeal held that the clauses were reasonable because the contract was negotiated between two experienced businesses, both of which (on the facts) were of equal bargaining strength.

It is likely that many of the situations in the cases considered under the common law prior to UCTA 1977 would now be decided under that Act. It is still important, however, to understand the common law principles, for the very good reason that UCTA 1977 does not apply in many important situations. Amongst these are transactions relating to insurance; interests in land; patents and other intellectual property; the transfer of securities; and the formation of companies or partnerships. It is evident from *Ailsa Craig Fishing Co Ltd v Malvern Fishing Co Ltd* (1983) that UCTA 1977 does not supersede common law rules.

6.3.5.4   *The Unfair Terms in Consumer Contracts Regulations*

The first Unfair Terms in Consumer Contracts Regulations were enacted in December 1994 (SI 1994/3159). They were introduced to implement the European Unfair Contract Terms Directive (93/13/EEC). Those original Regulations were repealed and replaced by the current Regulations (SI 1999/2083), which came into effect on 1 October 1999. The 1999 Regulations are intended to reflect closely the wording of the original, but they also introduced significant alterations.

It has to be stated that there was some criticism that the previous Regulations merely introduced the Directive, without engaging in a comprehensive review of this area. Concern was expressed as to the precise way in which UCTA 1977 and the 1994 Regulations impacted on one another and how their interaction would affect consumer law generally. Unfortunately, the 1999 Regulations have done nothing to improve this general problem and, in this particular respect, the criticisms of the 1994 Regulations are still relevant.

The 1999 Regulations apply to any term in a contract concluded between a seller or supplier and a consumer which has not been individually negotiated. The Regulations are, therefore, wider in scope than UCTA 1977, in that they cover all terms, not just exclusion clauses. However, reg 6(2) states that, apart from the requirement in respect of plain language, neither the core provisions of a consumer contract, which set out its main subject matter, nor the adequacy of the price paid are open to assessment in terms of fairness. The Regulations would, therefore, still appear to focus on the formal procedure through which contracts are made, rather than the substantive content of the contract in question.

By virtue of reg 5, a term is unfair if, contrary to the requirements of good faith, it causes a significant imbalance in the parties' rights and obligations arising under the contract, to the detriment of the consumer. Schedule 2 sets out a long, indicative, but non-exhaustive, list of terms which may be regarded as unfair. Examples of terms included in this list are: a term which excludes or limits liability in the event of the supplier or seller causing the death or injury of the consumer; inappropriately excluding or limiting the legal rights of the consumer in the event of total or partial non-performance or inadequate performance; a term requiring any consumer who fails to fulfil his obligations to pay a disproportionately high sum in compensation; and a term enabling the seller or supplier to alter the terms of the contract unilaterally without a valid reason which is specified in the contract.

Any such term as outlined above will be assumed to be unfair and, under reg 8, if a term is found to be unfair, it will not be binding on the consumer, although the remainder of the contract will continue to operate if it can do so after the excision of the unfair term.

Two further provisions of the Regulations which are worthy of mention have been taken from the previous Regulations. First, there is the requirement that all contractual terms be in plain, intelligible language and that, when there is any doubt as to the meaning of any term, it will be construed in favour of the consumer (reg 7). This is somewhat similar to the *contra proferentem* rule in English common law.

Secondly, although the Regulations will be most used by consumers to defeat particular unfair terms, regs 10–12 give the Director General of Fair Trading the power to take action against the use of unfair terms by obtaining an injunction to prohibit the use of such terms. However, the power of the Director General to seek injunctions to control unfair contract terms has been extended to other qualifying bodies. These qualifying bodies are listed in Sched 1 to the Regulations and include the various regulatory bodies controlling the previous public utilities sector of the economy, the Data Protection Registrar and every weights and measures authority in Great Britain.

Various aspects of the original Regulations, which have implications for the current Regulations, were examined by the House of Lords in *Director General of Fair Trading v First National Bank* (2001).

6.4 Vitiating Factors

6.4.1 Introduction

Vitiating factors are those elements which make an agreement either void or voidable, depending on which vitiating factor is present. The vitiating factors are:

• mistake;

• misrepresentation;

• duress;

• undue influence; and

• public policy, rendering contracts void/illegal.

6.4.2 Mistake

Generally speaking, the parties to a contract will not be relieved from the burden of their agreement simply because they have made a mistake. If one party makes a bad bargain, that is no reason for setting the contract aside. Very few mistakes will affect the validity of a contract at common law, but where a mistake is operative it will render the contract void. This has the effect that property which is transferred under operative mistake can be recovered, even where it has been transferred to an innocent third party.

However, in cases where the mistake is not operative, an equitable remedy such as rescission may be available. The grant of such remedies is in the court's discretion and subject to the principles of equity. In *Leaf v International Galleries* (1950), there was a contract for the sale of a painting of Salisbury Cathedral, which both parties believed to be by Constable. Five years later, the buyer discovered that the painting was not by Constable but was refused rescission because of the lapse of time since purchase.

It is also important to appreciate that a mistake cannot affect a contract unless it exists at the time of contracting. In *Amalgamated Investment & Property Co Ltd v John Walker & Sons Ltd* (1976), a company purchased property for redevelopment. Just after the contract, the property was given listed building status, which would restrict the intended development. The purchaser could not rescind the contract on the basis of a mistake that the property could be redeveloped as intended, because at the time of sale it could have been so developed.

It is usual to divide mistakes into the following three categories:

- common mistake;

- mutual mistake; and

- unilateral mistake.

6.4.2.1 Common mistake

This is where both parties to an agreement share the same mistake about the circumstances surrounding the transaction. In order for the mistake to be operative, it must be of a fundamental nature.

In *Bell v Lever Bros Ltd* (1932), Bell had been employed as chairman of the company by Lever Bros. When he became redundant, they paid off the remaining part of his service contract. Only then did they discover that Bell had been guilty of offences which would have permitted them to dismiss him without compensation. They claimed to have the payment set aside on the basis of the common mistake that neither party had considered the possibility of Bell's dismissal for breach of duty. It was held that the action must fail. The mistake was only as to quality and was not sufficiently fundamental to render the contract void. Similarly, in *Leaf v International Galleries* (1950) (above), the mistake was held to be one of quality; the court found that the contract was for the sale of a painting of Salisbury Cathedral (the value of which was mistaken) rather than a painting by Constable, and as such the mistake could not render the contract void.

These cases suggest that a mistake as to quality can never render an agreement void for mistake, and that the doctrine of common mistake is restricted to the following two specific areas:

- *Res extincta*

  In this case, the mistake is as to the existence of the subject matter of the contract.

  In *Couturier v Hastie* (1856), a contract was made in London for the sale of some corn that was being shipped from Salonica. Unknown to the parties, however, the corn had already been sold. It was held that the London contract was void, since the subject matter of the contract was no longer in existence.

It should be recognised, however, that in *Associated Japanese Bank v Credit du Nord* (1988), a contract was treated as void for common mistake on the basis of the non-existence of some gaming machines, although the agreement in point actually related to a contract of guarantee in relation to the non-existent machines. It might also be noted that there could be an argument, on the facts of *Leaf v International Galleries*, for saying that the mistake was not one of quality but as to the existence of the subject matter of the contract; that is, the contract was for the sale of a painting by Constable. Such a finding would mean that the common mistake rendered the contract void.

- *Res sua*

  In this case, the mistake is that one of the parties to the contract already own what they are contracting to receive.

  In *Cooper v Phibbs* (1867), Cooper agreed to lease a fishery from Phibbs. It later transpired that he actually owned the fishery. The court decided that the lease had to be set aside at common law. In equity, however, Phibbs was given a lien over the fishery in respect of the money he had spent on improving it, permitting him to hold the property against payment.

Though *Bell v Lever* and *Leaf v International Galleries* appear to restrict the circumstances in which a common mistake will render a contract void, it is interesting to note that not all judges are in agreement that mistakes as to quality cannot render a contract void. In *Bell v Lever*, Viscount Hailsham and Lord Warrington thought that a mistake as to quality could render the contract void; paying £50,000, when no payment need have been made to dismiss, rendered the contract fundamentally different from that intended. Similarly, in *Associated Japanese Bank v Credit du Nord*, Steyn J (*obiter*, at first instance) supported the view that a mistake as to quality might, in exceptional circumstances, render a contract void if it made the subject matter of the contract essentially and radically different from what the parties believed it to be.

Cooper v Phibbs is an example of one possible way in which equity may intervene in regard to common mistake, namely, setting an agreement aside on particular terms. Alternatively, the agreement may even be set aside completely in equity.

In *Magee v Pennine Insurance Co Ltd* (1969), a proposal form for car insurance had been improperly filled in by the plaintiff. When the car was subsequently written off, the insurance company offered Magee £375 as a compromise on his claim. After he had accepted this offer, the defendants discovered the error in the proposal form and sought to repudiate their agreement. It was held that, although it was not void at common law, the agreement could be set aside in equity.

6.4.2.2 Mutual mistake

This occurs where the parties are at cross-purposes. They have different views on the facts of the situation, but they do not realise it. However, an agreement will not necessarily be void simply because the parties to it are at cross-purposes. In order for mutual mistake to be operative, that is, to make the contract void, the terms of agreement must comply with an objective test. The court will try to decide which of the competing views of the situation a reasonable person would support, and the contract will be enforceable or unenforceable on such terms.

In *Smith v Hughes* (1871), the plaintiff offered to sell oats to the defendant, Hughes. Hughes wrongly believed that the oats were old, and on discovering that they were new oats he refused to complete the contract. It was held that the defendant's mistake as to the age of the oats did not make the contract void.

In *Scriven Bros v Hindley & Co* (1913), the defendants bid at an auction for two lots, believing both to be hemp. In fact, one of them was tow, an inferior and cheaper substance. Although the auctioneer had not induced the mistake, it was not normal practice to sell hemp and tow together. It was decided that, in such circumstances, where one party thought that he was buying hemp and the other thought that he was selling tow, the contract was not enforceable.

If the court is unable to decide the outcome on the basis of an objective 'reasonable person' test, then the contract will be void, as was illustrated in *Raffles v Wichelhaus* (1864), where the defendants agreed to buy cotton from the plaintiffs. The cotton was to arrive *ex Peerless* from Bombay. There were, however, two ships called *Peerless* sailing from Bombay, the first in October and the second in December. Wichelhaus thought that he was buying from the first, but Raffles thought that he was selling from the second. Under the exceptional circumstances, it was impossible for the court to decide which party's view was the correct one. It was decided, therefore, that the agreement was void for mutual mistake.

In respect of mutual mistake, equity follows the common law.

In *Tamplin v James* (1879), James purchased a public house at auction. He had wrongly believed that the property for sale included a field which the previous publican had used. The sale particulars stated the property for sale correctly, but James did not refer to them. When he discovered his mistake, James refused to complete the transaction. It was held that, in spite of his mistake, an order of specific performance would be granted against James. Objectively, the reasonable man would assume that the sale was made on the basis of the particulars (see also *Centrovincial Estates plc v Merchant Assurance Co Ltd* (1983) and *Great Peace Shipping Ltd v Tsavliros Salvage Ltd* (2001)).

The role of equity was considered in *Clarion Ltd v National Provident Institution* (2000), where one party's mistake as to the effect of the terms of a contract did not allow the contract to be rescinded. It was held that equity did not provide a remedy simply because of a bad bargain; mistake would only operate in equity where it related to the subject matter of the contract, the terms of the contract or the identity of the contracting party. The decision has been the subject of criticism as its effect is to narrow equitable relief to the same circumstances as common law.

6.4.2.3   Unilateral mistake

This occurs where only one of the parties to the agreement is mistaken as to the circumstances of the contract, and the other party is aware of that fact.

Most cases of unilateral mistake also involve misrepresentation (see 6.4.3, below), although this need not necessarily be so. It is important to distinguish between these two elements: whereas unilateral mistake makes a contract void and thus prevents the passing of title in any property acquired under it, misrepresentation merely makes a contract voidable and good title can be passed before the contract is avoided. This distinction will be seen in *Ingram v Little* (1960) and *Phillips v Brooks* (1919). A further important distinction relates to remedies available: damages are not available for mistake but, where there has been a misrepresentation, damages may be awarded.

The cases involving unilateral mistake relate mainly to mistakes as to identity. A contract will only be void for mistake where the seller intended to contract with a different person from the one with whom he did actually contract.

In *Cundy v Lindsay* (1878), a crook named Blenkarn ordered linen handkerchiefs from Lindsay & Co, a Belfast linen manufacturer. His order, from 37 Wood Street, was signed to look as if it were from Blenkiron & Co, a reputable firm which was known to Lindsay and which carried on business at 123 Wood Street. The goods were sent to Blenkarn, who sold them to Cundy. Lindsay successfully sued Cundy in the tort of conversion. It was held that Lindsay had intended only to deal with Blenkiron & Co, so the contract was void. Since there was no contract with Blenkarn, he received no title whatsoever to the goods and, therefore, could not pass title on to Cundy. The case is generally taken to indicate that, if you do not deal face to face, the identity of the other party is fundamental. This was confirmed in *Shogun Finance Ltd v Hudson* (2001), despite the fact that the decision defeated the objective of s 27 of the Hire Purchase Act 1964 to protect the innocent third party purchaser of a hire purchase motor vehicle. In that case, a con man obtained a car on hire purchase, using the identity of a Mr Patel, via a stolen driving licence. His contract was with the finance company, not the garage with whom he negotiated, so he did not deal face to face. The con man sold the car to Hudson and disappeared without paying the hire purchase instalments. The finance company sought damages in the tort of conversion from Hudson, on the basis that he had no title to the car. It should be noted that where goods are acquired on hire purchase, ownership does not pass until all instalments are paid, so that the con man had no title to pass to Hudson. However, s 27 gives title to the innocent third party purchaser of a motor vehicle from a 'debtor' who acquired it on hire purchase. Nevertheless, the Court of Appeal held that, as the contract was not made face to face, the contracting party's identity was crucial, so the hire purchase contract was void for mistake. As it was void, there was no 'debtor' within the meaning of s 27; Hudson was not protected and was liable in conversion. An appeal to the House of Lords in 2003 was dismissed, confirming, by a bare majority, that s 27 did not operate to give good title to Mr Hudson. Also of interest were *dicta* relating to impersonation by telephone, videophone and by e-shopping.

Although *Kings Norton Metal Co v Eldridge, Merrit & Co* (1897) appears to be similar to *Cundy*, it was decided differently, on the ground that the crook had made use of a completely fictitious company to carry out his fraud. The mistake, therefore, was with regard to the attributes of the company, rather than its identity.

Where the parties enter into a contract face to face, it is generally presumed that the seller intends to deal with the person before him; therefore, he cannot rely on unilateral mistake to avoid the contract; his concern is with the attributes (usually creditworthiness) of the other party rather than his identity. A shopkeeper will sell to you, no matter who you pretend to be, provided you pay.

In *Phillips v Brooks* (1919), a crook selected a number of items in the plaintiff's jewellery shop, and proposed to pay by cheque. On being informed that the goods would have to be retained until the cheque was cleared, he told the jeweller that he was Sir George Bullough of St James's Square. On checking in a directory that such a person did indeed live at that address, the jeweller permitted him to take away a valuable ring. The crook later pawned the ring to the defendant. Phillips then sued the defendant in conversion. It was decided that the contract between Phillips and the crook was not void for mistake. There had not been a mistake as to identity, but only as to the creditworthiness (that is, attributes) of the buyer. The contract had been voidable for misrepresentation, but the crook had passed title before Phillips took steps to avoid the contract.

A similar decision was reached by the Court of Appeal in *Lewis v Avery* (1971), in which a crook obtained possession of a car by misrepresenting his identity to the seller. The court declined to follow its earlier decision in *Ingram v Little* (1960), a very similar case. It is generally accepted that *Lewis v Avery* represents the more accurate statement of the law. It is worth noting that *Ingram v Little* was said to be wrongly decided in *Shogun Finance Ltd v Hudson*.

6.4.2.4   Mistake in respect of documents

There are two mechanisms for dealing with mistakes in written contracts:

* *Rectification*

  Where the written document fails to state the actual intentions of the parties, it may be altered under the equitable doctrine of rectification.

  In *Joscelyne v Nissen* (1970), the plaintiff agreed to transfer his car hire business to his daughter, in return for her agreeing to pay certain household expenses, although this was not stated in a later written contract. The father was entitled to have the agreement rectified to include the terms agreed.

* *Non est factum*

  Where a party signs a contract, they will usually be bound by its terms. It is assumed that the signatory has read, understood and agreed to the terms as stated, and the courts are generally reluctant to interfere in such circumstances.

  Where, however, someone signs a document under a misapprehension as to its true nature, the law may permit them to claim *non est factum*, that is, that the document is not their deed. Originally, the mistake relied on had to relate to the type of document signed, but it is now recognised that the defence is open to those who have made a fundamental mistake as to the content of the document they have signed. However, the person signing the document must not have been careless with regard to its content.

In *Saunders v Anglia Building Society* (1970), Mrs Gallie, a 78 year old widow, signed a document without reading it, as her glasses were broken. She had been told, by a person named Lee, that it was a deed of gift to her nephew, but it was in fact a deed of gift to Lee. Lee later mortgaged the property to the respondent building society. Mrs Gallie sought to repudiate the deed of gift on the basis of *non est factum*. Her action failed; she was careless in not waiting until her glasses were mended. Furthermore, the document was not fundamentally different from the one she had expected to sign. She thought that she signed a document transferring ownership and that *was* the effect of the document. The conditions laid down in *Saunders for non est factum* to apply were confirmed in *Avon Finance Co Ltd v Bridger* (1985).

This decision can be contrasted with a later successful reliance on the defence in *Lloyds Bank plc v Waterhouse* (1990), where the defendant, who was illiterate, intended to provide a guarantee in relation to his son's purchase of a farm. In actual fact, the document he signed was a guarantee in relation to all of his son's liabilities. In the Court of Appeal, it was decided that the father could rely on *non est factum*. He had not been careless – he had questioned the extent of his liability – and the document was fundamentally different from that which he had expected to sign.

6.4.3 Misrepresentation

As was seen in Section 6.4.2.3, a statement which induces a person to enter into a contract, but which does not become a term of the contract, is a representation. A false statement of this kind is a misrepresentation and renders the contract voidable. The innocent party may rescind the contract or, in some circumstances, claim damages (see below, 6.4.3.3).

Misrepresentation can be defined as 'a false statement of fact, made by one party before or at the time of the contract, which induces the other party to enter into the contract'. The following points follow from this definition.

6.4.3.1 *There must be a false statement of fact*

False

In most cases it can be proved whether a statement is false, but the following situations need consideration:

- Where the statement is a half-truth, it may be true but misleading because of facts not given; it will be treated as false.

  In *Dimmock v Hallett* (1866), when selling property, it was truthfully stated that a farm was rented to a tenant for £290 per annum. The failure to indicate that the tenant was in arrears, had left the farm and a new tenant could not be found rendered the statement false.

- Where the statement was true when made, but has subsequently become false before the contract was concluded, the change must be notified to avoid misrepresentation.

In *With v O'Flanagan* (1936), in January, the seller of a doctors' practice told the prospective buyer that it was worth an income of £2,000 per annum. By the time that the contract was concluded, its value had dropped substantially, to only £5 per week. The court held that the representation was of a continuing nature and, as it was false when it induced the contract, the buyer was entitled to rescind. The obligation to disclose changes relating to a representation of a continuing nature was affirmed by the Court of Appeal in *Spice Girls Ltd v Aprilia World Service BV* (2002).

A statement

There must be a written or oral statement. There is no general duty to disclose information, except in insurance contracts; silence does not generally amount to misrepresentation. In *Turner v Green* (1895), when negotiating a dispute settlement between T and G, T's solicitor failed to mention other legal proceedings he knew of which made the settlement to which G agreed a 'bad deal' – one he would not have made had he known. G was bound by the settlement; he was not induced by a misrepresentation, as silence is not misrepresentation. However, it should be noted that there have been cases where courts have found that there is a misrepresentation by conduct; for example, *Gordon v Selico* (1986) and, at first instance, *Spice Girls Ltd v Aprilia World Service BV*.

A fact

The following statements will not amount to representations because they are not facts:

- Mere sales puffs – the statement must have some meaningful content. Thus, in *Dimmock v Hallett*, it was held that a statement that land was fertile and improvable was not actionable as a misrepresentation.

- Statements of law – everyone is presumed to know the law and, therefore, in theory, no one can be misled as to what the law is.

- Statements of opinion – these are not actionable, because they are not statements of fact. In *Bisset v Wilkinson* (1927), the vendor of previously ungrazed land in New Zealand stated that it would be able to support 2,000 sheep. This turned out to be untrue, but it was held that the statement was only an expression of opinion and, as such, was not actionable; the purchaser knew that the vendor had no expertise. However, in *Smith v Land & House Property Corp* (1884), a statement that the tenant of a hotel was a 'desirable tenant' was a misrepresentation. Though descriptions like 'desirable' may seem to be subjective opinions, here there was expert knowledge that the tenant did not pay on time and was currently in arrears. That being so, the statement implied that there were facts on which it was based when there were not.

- A statement of intention – this does not give rise to a misrepresentation even if the intention subsequently changes, unless it can be shown that there was no such intention at the time it was stated (see *Edgington v Fitzmaurice* (1884)).

6.4.3.2   The statement must actually induce the contract

That the statement must actually induce the contract means that:

- the statement must have been made by one party to the contract to the other, and not by a third party;

- the statement must have been addressed to the person claiming to have been misled;

- the person claiming to have been misled must have been aware of the statement; and

- the person claiming to have been misled must have relied on the statement.

In *Horsfall v Thomas* (1962), Horsfall made and sold a gun to Thomas. He concealed a fault in it by means of a metal plug, and Thomas did not examine the gun. After short usage, the gun blew apart. Thomas claimed that he had been misled, by the presence of the plug, into buying the gun. It was held that the plug could not have misled him, as he had not examined the gun at the time of purchase. In *Attwood v Small* (1838), a false statement as to the profitability of a mine was not a misrepresentation as the purchaser did not rely on it; he commissioned an independent survey of the mine. On the other hand, in *Redgrave v Hurd* (1881), where the purchaser of a business declined to examine the accounts which would have revealed the falsity of a statement as to the business's profitability, there was a misrepresentation. Because he declined to examine the accounts, he clearly relied on what was said to him about profitability; he was not under a duty to check the truth of the statement.

Whether the reliance was reasonable or not is not material once the party claiming misrepresentation shows that they did, in fact, rely on the statement. See *Museprime Properties Ltd v Adhill Properties Ltd* (1990), in which an inaccurate statement contained in auction particulars, and repeated by the auctioneer, was held to constitute a misrepresentation, in spite of the claims that it should have been unreasonable for anyone to allow themselves to be influenced by the statement. This view was confirmed in *Indigo International Holdings Ltd & Another v The Owners and/or Demise Charterers of the Vessel 'Brave Challenger'; Ronastone Ltd & Another v Indigo International Holdings Ltd & Another* (2003). However, it should be noted that in *Barton v County Natwest Bank* (1999), the court indicated that an objective test would be applied to determine reliance. If, objectively, there was reliance, this was a presumption which was rebuttable.

6.4.3.3   Types of misrepresentation

Misrepresentation can be divided into three types, each of which involves distinct procedures and provides different remedies.

Fraudulent misrepresentation

In the case of fraudulent misrepresentation, the statement is made knowing it to be false, or believing it to be false, or recklessly careless as to whether it is true or false. The difficulty with this type of misrepresentation is proving the necessary mental element; it is notoriously difficult to show the required *mens rea*, or guilty mind, to demonstrate fraud.

In *Derry v Peek* (1889), the directors of a company issued a prospectus, inviting the public to subscribe for shares. The prospectus stated that the company had the power to run trams by steam power but, in fact, it only had power to operate horsedrawn trams; it required the permission of the Board of Trade to run steam trams. The directors assumed that permission would be granted, but it was refused. When the company was wound up, the directors were sued for fraud. It was held that there was no fraud, since the directors had honestly believed the statement in the prospectus. They may have been negligent, but they were not fraudulent.

Negligent misrepresentation

With negligent misrepresentation, the false statement is made in the belief that it is true, but without reasonable grounds for that belief. (It follows that the directors in *Derry v Peek* would now be liable for negligent misrepresentation.) There are two categories of negligent misrepresentation:

- *At common law*

  Prior to 1963, the law did not recognise a concept of negligent misrepresentation. The possibility of liability in negligence for misstatements arose from *Hedley Byrne & Co v Heller and Partners* (1964). In that case, however, the parties were not in a contractual or a pre-contractual relationship, so there could not have been an action for misrepresentation. But in *Esso Petroleum v Mardon* (1976), Mardon succeeded in an action for negligent misstatement, on the basis that he had been wrongly advised as to the amount of petrol he could expect to sell from a garage.

- *Under the Misrepresentation Act (MA) 1967*

  Although it might still be necessary, or beneficial, to sue at common law, it is more likely that such claims would now be taken under the statute. The reason for this is that s 2(1) of the MA 1967 reverses the normal burden of proof. In a claim in negligence, the burden of proof is on the party raising the claim to show that the other party acted in a negligent manner. However, where a misrepresentation has been made, under s 2(1) of the MA 1967 it is up to the party who made the statement to show that they had reasonable grounds for believing it to be true. In practice, a person making a statement in the course of his trade or profession might have difficulty providing such proof. In *Indigo Holdings* (1999) (see above, 6.4.3.2), the seller of a yacht could not escape liability for misrepresentation as he was unable to prove he had reasonable grounds to believe, and did believe, the facts he represented.

Innocent misrepresentation

Innocent misrepresentation occurs where the false statement is made by a person who not only believes it to be true, but also has reasonable grounds for that belief.

6.4.3.4 Remedies for misrepresentation

For fraudulent misrepresentation, the remedies are rescission and/or damages for any loss sustained. Rescission is an equitable remedy which is designed to return the parties to their original position. The action for damages is in the tort of deceit. In *Doyle v Olby (Ironmongers) Ltd* (1969), it was decided that where a contract was induced by a fraudulent misrepresentation, the measure of damages was not merely what was foreseeable, but all damage which directly resulted as a consequence of the aggrieved party having entered into the contract. An example of this principle can be seen in *Smith and New Court Securities Ltd v Scrimgeour Vickers (Asset Management) Ltd* (1996), in which the plaintiffs were induced to buy 28 million shares in Ferranti plc on the basis of a fraudulently made claim about the shares. They had been told falsely that two other companies had already bid for the package of shares, and this led them to offer and pay 82.25p per share, amounting to a total of £23,141,424. Without the false representation, they would not have offered more than 78p per share and, as the defendants would not have sold at that price, Smith New Court would not have acquired any shares in Ferranti. When it transpired that Ferranti had been subject to a completely unrelated fraud, its share price fell considerably and, although the plaintiffs managed to sell their shareholding at prices ranging from 30p–44p, they suffered an overall loss of £11,353,220. The question to be decided was as to the amount that the defendants owed in damages. Was it the difference between the market value of the shares and the price actually paid at the time, a matter of 4.25p per share, or was it the full loss, which was considerably larger? The House of Lords decided that the latter amount was due. The total loss was the direct result of the share purchase, which had been induced by the fraudulent statement; the defendants were, therefore, liable for that amount and the foreseeability test in relation to negligence, as stated in *The Wagon Mound (No 1)* (1961), did not apply (see below, Section 8.5.6, for a detailed consideration of this test).

For negligent misrepresentation, the remedies are rescission and/or damages. The action for damages may be in the tort of negligence at common law or under s 2(1) of the MA 1967. Under the statute, the measure of damages will still be determined as in a tort action (see *Royscot Trust Ltd v Rogerson* (1991), where the Court of Appeal confirmed this approach).

For innocent misrepresentation, the common law remedy is rescission. Under the MA 1967, however, the court may award damages instead of rescission, where it is considered equitable to do so (s 2(2)).

With regard to s 2(2) of the MA 1967, it was once thought that the court could only award damages, instead of rescission, where the remedy of rescission was itself available. The implication of that view was that, if the right to rescission was lost for some reason, such as the fact that the parties could not be restored to their original positions, then the right to damages under s 2(2) was also lost (*Atlantic Lines and Navigation Co Inc v Hallam* (1992)). However, in *Thomas Witter v TBP Industries* (1996) (see below), Jacob J examined and rejected that suggestion. In his opinion, the right to damages under s 2(2) depended not upon the right to rescission still being available, but upon the fact that the plaintiff had had such a right in the past. Thus, even if the right to rescission was ultimately lost, the plaintiff could still be awarded damages. This was confirmed in *Zanzibar v British Aerospace Ltd* (2000).

The right to rescind can be lost for any one of the following reasons:

- by affirmation, where the innocent party, with full knowledge of the misrepresentation, either expressly states that they intend to go on with the agreement or does some action from which it can be implied that they intend to go on with the agreement. Affirmation may be implied from lapse of time (see *Leaf v International Galleries* (1950));

- where the parties cannot be restored to their original positions; or

- where third parties have acquired rights in the subject matter of the contract (see *Phillips v Brooks* (1919)).

Section 3 of the MA 1967 provides that any exclusion of liability for misrepresentation must comply with the requirement of reasonableness, a matter that was also considered in *Thomas Witter v TBP Industries*. The facts of the *Witter* case involved the sale of a carpet manufacturing business. In the course of pre-contractual negotiation, the seller misrepresented the profitability of the business and, hence, the purchaser paid more than its real value for it. However, the eventual contract document contained the following purported exclusion clause:

> This Agreement sets forth the entire agreement and understanding between the parties or any of them in connection with the business and the sale and purchase described herein. In particular, but without prejudice to the generality of the foregoing, the purchaser acknowledges that it has not been induced to enter into this agreement by any representation warranty other than the statements contained in or referred to in Schedule 6 [of the contract document].

In analysing the legal effect of the above clause, Jacob J held that, on its own wording, it could not provide any exemption in relation to any pre-contractual misrepresentations that had been included as express warranties within the document. Moreover, he held that the clause was ineffective, even as regards those pre-contractual misrepresentations which had not been included expressly in the contract. His first ground for striking down the clause, and in spite of its apparently perfectly clear wording, was that it was not sufficiently clear to remove the purchaser's right to rely on the misrepresentation. Secondly, and as an alternative, he held that the clause did not meet with the requirement of reasonableness under s 3 of the MA 1967. The scope of the clause was held to be far too wide, in that it purported to cover 'any liability' for 'any misrepresentation'. In Jacob J's view, it could never be possible to exclude liability for fraudulent misrepresentation and, although it might be possible to exclude liability for

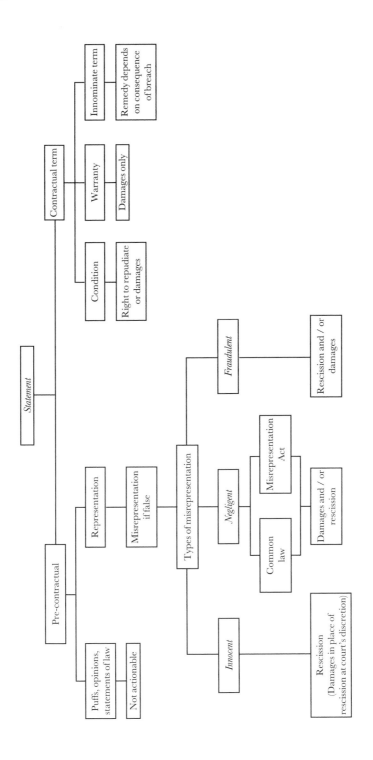

Figure 6.1   Forms of misrepresentation

negligent and innocent misrepresentation, any such exclusion had to pass the reasonableness test, which the clause in question had failed to do.

Figure 6.1, below, shows both how statements may be classified and the consequence of such classification. It should be remembered that, in some instances, a pre-contract statement may be treated as a term of the contract, rather than a misrepresentation, so that remedies for breach of contract may be claimed (see above, 6.4.3).

6.4.4 Duress

Duress is some element of force, either physical or economic, which is used to override one party's freedom to choose whether or not to enter into a particular contract. Under such circumstances, the contract is voidable at the instance of the innocent party.

Its application used to be restricted to contracts entered into as a consequence of actual physical violence or the threat of such violence to a person.

In *Barton v Armstrong* (1975), the defendant threatened Barton with death if he did not arrange for his company to buy Armstrong's shares in it. Barton sought to have the agreement set aside. It was found that the threats had been made, but that, in addition, Barton thought that the transaction was a favourable one. Barton nonetheless succeeded. The court held that the proper inference was that duress was present, and the burden of proof was on Armstrong to show that the threats had played no part in Barton's decision. He had failed to discharge this burden.

Originally, it was held that threats to a person's goods could not amount to duress, but a doctrine of economic duress has now been developed by the courts. The germ of the doctrine, that an abuse of economic power can render a contract invalid, can be found in Lord Denning's decision in *D & C Builders Ltd v Rees* (1966) and was developed in later cases such as *The Siboen and The Sibotre* (1976) and *The Atlantic Baron* (1979).

In the latter case, fully cited as *North Ocean Shipping Co v Hyundai Construction* (1979), a contract had been entered into for the building of a ship. The builders then stated that they would not complete construction unless the purchasers paid an extra 10%. Without the ship, the buyers would have lost a lucrative contract with a third party, with whom they had already agreed to charter the ship. The buyers paid the extra money and then, at a later date, sued to recover it on the basis of, *inter alia*, economic duress. It was held that the threat to terminate the contract did constitute economic duress, which rendered the contract voidable. In the event, the buyers' delay in bringing the action acted as an affirmation of the agreement and they lost their right to rescission.

There is a difficulty in distinguishing ordinary commercial pressure from economic duress (see *Pao On v Lau Yiu Long* (1979)), but the existence of economic duress as a distinct principle of contract law finally received the approval of the House of Lords in *Universe Tankships Inc v ITWF* (1982), the *Universe Sentinel* case. The facts of the case concerned the blacking of the plaintiffs' ship by the defendant trade union, which meant that it could not leave the port. As part of negotiations to lift the blacking, the plaintiffs paid money into the union's benevolent fund. They subsequently and successfully reclaimed the money from the union, on the basis that it had been induced through economic duress.

In order to benefit from the doctrine of duress, claimants must show the following two things:

- that pressure, which resulted in an absence of choice on their part, was brought to bear on them; and

- that that pressure was of a nature considered to be illegitimate by the courts.

Only under such circumstances will the court permit rescission of an agreement, as can be seen in *Atlas Express v Kafco* (1990). The defendant company had secured a highly profitable contract with Woolworths, the large retail outlet, and employed the plaintiffs as their carriers. After beginning to perform the contract, Atlas sought to increase their price. Although they protested, Kafco felt that they had no option but to agree to the demand, rather than break their contract with Woolworths, which would have proved economically disastrous for them. When Atlas sued to recover the increased charges, they failed, as it was held that the attempt to increase the charge was a clear case of economic duress. (This should be compared with the situation and outcome of *Williams v Roffey Bros* (1990); see above, 6.2.5.4.)

6.4.5 Undue influence

Transactions, either under contract or as gifts, may be avoided where they have been entered into as a consequence of the undue influence of the person benefiting from them. The effect of undue influence is to make a contract voidable, but delay may bar the right to avoid the agreement. There are two possible situations relating to undue influence.

6.4.5.1 *Special relationships*

Where there is a special relationship between the parties, there is a presumption that the transaction is the consequence of undue influence. The burden of proof is on the person receiving the benefit to rebut the presumption.

In *Re Craig* (1971), after the death of his wife, Mr Craig, then aged 84, employed a Mrs Middleton as his secretary-companion. In the course of the six years for which she was employed, he gave her money to the extent of some £30,000. An action was taken to have the gifts set aside. The action succeeded, as it was held that the circumstances raised the presumption of undue influence, which Mrs Middleton had failed to rebut.

Examples of special relationships are:

- parent and child, while the latter is still a minor;

- guardian and ward;

- religious adviser and follower;

- doctor and patient; and

- solicitor and client.

The list is not a closed one, however, and other relationships may be included within the scope of the special relationship (as in *Re Craig* (1971)).

Where a special relationship exists, then an important way in which the presumption of undue influence can be rebutted is to show that independent advice was taken by the other party, although all that is necessary is to show that the other party exercised their will freely.

Even where a special relationship exists, a transaction will not be set aside unless it is shown to be manifestly disadvantageous.

In *National Westminster Bank v Morgan* (1985), when a couple fell into financial difficulties, the plaintiff bank made financial arrangements which permitted them to remain in their house. The re-financing transaction secured against the house was arranged by a bank manager who had called at their home. Mrs Morgan had no independent legal advice. When the husband died, the bank obtained a possession order against the house in respect of outstanding debts. Mrs Morgan sought to have the refinancing arrangement set aside, on the ground of undue influence. The action failed, on the ground that the doctrine of undue influence had no place in agreements which did not involve any manifest disadvantage, and Mrs Morgan had actually benefited from the transaction by being able to remain in her home for a longer period. It might be noted, however, that recent cases are beginning to question whether this requirement of 'manifest disadvantage' is necessary before a contract can be avoided; for example, *Barclays Bank plc v Coleman* (2001).

The key element in deciding whether a relationship was a special one or not was whether one party was in a position of dominance over the other. *National Westminster Bank v Morgan* also decided that a normal relationship between a bank manager and his client is not a special relationship; but there may be circumstances where that relationship may be treated as 'special' (see *Lloyds Bank Ltd v Bundy* (1975)).

6.4.5.2 No special relationship

Where no special relationship exists between the parties, the burden of proof is on the party claiming the protection of the undue influence doctrine. It is of interest to note that relationships which are not included as special relationships include the relationships of husband and wife and bank and customer, yet these are precisely the relationships that are likely to generate the most problems.

The rule relating to manifest disadvantage, considered above in relation to special relationships, does not apply in the case where no such special relationship applies.

In *CIBC Mortgages plc v Pitt* (1993), Mrs Pitt sought to set aside a mortgage which she had signed against her home in favour of the plaintiffs, on the basis that her husband had exerted undue influence over her. Whereas the Court of Appeal had rejected her plea on the ground that the agreement was not to her manifest disadvantage, the House of Lords declared that such a principle did not apply in cases where undue influence was actual, rather than presumed. They did, however, recognise the validity of the mortgage, on the ground that the creditor had no knowledge, either actual or constructive, of the exercise of undue influence in relation to the transaction.

It is of interest to note in relation to this last case that the House of Lords in *Barclays Bank plc v O'Brien* (1993) referred to an implied duty on creditors in particular circumstances, which certainly included a marital relationship, to ensure that parties had not entered into agreements on the basis of misrepresentation or undue influence. In that particular case, the bank was held to have constructive notice of the undue influence wielded by the husband; that is, they *should* have known, whether they actually did or not. For that reason, the bank was not permitted to enforce the agreement entered into on the basis of that undue influence.

The situation relating to undue influence was most recently considered in *Dunbar Bank plc v Nadeem* (1998), in which it was clearly restated that in order to rely on the presumption of undue influence, manifest disadvantage must be shown in addition to a relationship of trust and confidence. In the case in point, the wife's claim had to fail, as there was no such disadvantage and she had failed to show actual undue influence, which could be attached to the bank on the basis of the *O'Brien* case.

6.4.6 Inequality of bargaining power

It has been suggested that undue influence and duress are simply examples of a wider principle which is based on inequality of bargaining power. The existence of such a principle was suggested in a number of decisions involving Lord Denning. It was intended to provide protection for those who suffered as a consequence of being forced into particular agreements due to their lack of bargaining power. This doctrine, however, was considered and firmly rejected by the House of Lords in *National Westminster Bank v Morgan* (1985). It could be suggested that the very idea of inequality of bargaining power is incompatible with the reality of today's economic structure, which is dominated by large scale, if not monopolistic, organisations. It should be recognised, however, that the idea of inequality of bargaining power has found a place in determining how the Unfair Contract Terms Act 1977 is to operate.

6.4.7 Contracts and public policy

It is evident that some agreements will tend to be contrary to public policy. The fact that some are considered to be more serious than others is reflected in the distinction drawn between those which are said to be illegal and those which are simply void.

6.4.7.1 *Illegal contracts*

A contract which breaks the law is illegal. The general rule is that no claim can be brought by a party to an illegal contract, though in some circumstances money or property transferred may be recovered. The contract may be either expressly prohibited by statute, or implicitly prohibited by the common law. Illegal contracts include:

- contracts prohibited by statute;

- contracts to defraud the Inland Revenue;

- contracts involving the commission of a crime or a tort;

- contracts with a sexually immoral element, although contemporary attitudes may have changed in this respect (see *Armhouse Lee Ltd v Chappell* (1996));

- contracts against the interest of the UK or a friendly State;

- contracts leading to corruption in public life; and

- contracts which interfere with the course of justice.

6.4.7.2   *Void contracts*

A void contract does not give rise to any rights or obligations. The contract is void only in so far as it is contrary to public policy; thus, the whole agreement may not be void. Severance is the procedure whereby the void part of a contract is excised, permitting the remainder to be enforced. Contracts may be void under statute or at common law.

Wagering contracts

A wagering contract is an agreement that, upon the happening of some uncertain event, one party shall give something of value to the other, the party who has to pay being dependent on the outcome of the event. Such contracts are governed by the Gaming Acts 1835–1968.

Anti-competitive practices

Certain agreements relating to matters such as price fixing and minimum resale prices may be void and unenforceable under the Competition Act 1998.

Contracts void at common law

- *Contracts to oust the jurisdiction of the court*

  Any contractual agreement which seeks to deny the parties the right to submit questions of law to the courts is void as being contrary to public policy. Agreements which provide for compulsory arbitration can be enforceable.

- *Contracts prejudicial to the status of marriage*

  It is considered a matter of public policy that the institution of marriage be maintained. Hence, any contract which seeks to restrain a person's freedom to marry, or undermines the institution of marriage in any way, will be considered void.

6.4.7.3   Contracts in restraint of trade

One area of particular importance which is subject to the control of the common law is contracts in restraint of trade. A contract in restraint of trade is an agreement whereby one party restricts their future freedom to engage in their trade, business or profession. The general rule is that such agreements are *prima facie* void, but they may be valid if it can be shown that they meet the following requirements:

- the person who imposes the restrictions has a legitimate interest to protect;

- the restriction is reasonable as between the parties; and

- the restriction is not contrary to the public interest.

The doctrine of restraint of trade is flexible in its application and may be applied to new situations when they arise. Bearing this in mind, however, it is usual to classify the branches of the doctrine as follows.

Restraints on employees

Employers cannot protect themselves against competition from an ex-employee, except where they have a legitimate interest to protect. The only legitimate interests recognised by the law are trade secrets and trade connection.

Even in protecting those interests, the restraint must be of a reasonable nature. What constitutes reasonable in this context depends on the circumstances of the case.

In *Lamson Pneumatic Tube Co v Phillips* (1904), the plaintiffs manufactured specialised equipment for use in shops. The defendant's contract of employment stated that, on ceasing to work for the plaintiffs, he would not engage in a similar business for a period of five years, anywhere in the Eastern hemisphere. It was held that such a restriction was reasonable, bearing in mind the nature of the plaintiffs' business.

This has to be compared with *Empire Meat Co Ltd v Patrick* (1939), where Patrick had been employed as manager of the company's butchers business in Mill Road, Cambridge. The company sought to enforce the defendant's promise that he would not establish a rival business within five miles of their shop. In this situation, it was held that the restraint was too wide and could not be enforced.

The longer the period of time or the wider the geographical area covered by the restraint, the more likely it is to be struck down, but in *Fitch v Dewes* (1921), it was held that a lifelong restriction placed on a solicitor was valid.

Restraints on vendors of business

The interest to be protected in this category is the goodwill of the business, that is, its profitability. Restrictions may legitimately be placed on previous owners to prevent them from competing in the future with new owners. Again, the restraint should not be greater than is necessary to protect that interest.

In *British Reinforced Concrete Engineering Co Ltd v Schleff* (1921), the plaintiffs sought to enforce a promise given by the defendant, on the sale of his business to them, that he would not compete with them in the manufacturing of road reinforcements. It was held that, given the small size and restricted nature of the business sold, the restraint was too wide to be enforceable.

However, in *Nordenfelt v Maxim Nordenfelt Guns and Ammunition Co* (1894), a worldwide restraint on competition was held to be enforceable, given the nature of the business sold.

Restraints on distributors/solus agreements

This category of restraint of trade is usually concerned with solus agreements between petrol companies and garage proprietors, by which a petrol company seeks to prevent the retailer from selling its competitors' petrol. It is recognised that petrol companies have a legitimate interest to protect, and the outcome depends on whether the restraint obtained in protection of that interest is reasonable.

In *Esso Petroleum v Harpers Garage* (1968), the parties had entered into an agreement whereby Harper undertook to buy all of the petrol to be sold from his two garages from Esso. In return, Esso lent him £7,000, secured by way of a mortgage over one of the garages. The monopoly right in respect of the garages was to last for four and a half years over one and 21 years over the other. When Harper broke his undertaking, Esso sued to enforce it. It was held that the agreements in respect of both garages were in restraint of trade. However, whereas the agreement which lasted for four and a half years was reasonable, the one which lasted for 21 years was unreasonable and void.

Until fairly recently, it was thought that *Esso v Harpers* had set down a rule that any solus agreement involving a restriction which was to last longer than five years would be void as being in restraint of trade. In *Alec Lobb (Garages) Ltd v Total Oil Ltd* (1985), however, the Court of Appeal made it clear that the outcome of each case depended on its own particular circumstances; in that case, it approved a solus agreement extending over a period of 21 years.

Exclusive service contracts

This category relates to contracts which are specifically structured to exploit one of the parties by controlling and limiting their output, rather than assisting them. The most famous cases involve musicians.

In *Schroeder Music Publishing Co v Macauley* (1974), an unknown songwriter, Macauley, entered into a five year agreement with Schroeder. Under it, he had to assign any music he wrote to them, but they were under no obligation to publish it. The agreement provided for automatic extension of the agreement if it yielded £5,000 in royalties, but the publishers could terminate it at any time with one month's notice. It was decided that the agreement was so one-sided as to amount to an unreasonable restraint of trade and, hence, was void.

Since the above case, numerous artists have made use of this ground for avoiding their contracts.

6.5 Discharge of a Contract

6.5.1 Introduction

When a contract is discharged, the parties to the agreement are freed from their contractual obligations. A contract is discharged in one of four ways:

- agreement;

- performance;

- frustration; or

- breach.

6.5.2 Discharge by agreement

Emphasis has been placed on the consensual nature of contract law, and it follows that what has been made by agreement can be ended by agreement. The contract itself may contain provision for its discharge by either the passage of a fixed period of time or the occurrence of a particular event. Alternatively, it may provide, either expressly or by implication, that one or other of the parties can bring it to an end, as in a contract of employment.

Where there is no such provision in a contract, another contract will be required to cancel it before all of the obligations have been met. There are two possible situations, as follows:

- Where the contract is executory, the mutual exchange of promises to release one another from future performance will be sufficient consideration.

- Where the contract is executed, that is, one party has performed, or partly performed, their obligations, the other party must provide consideration (that is, make a new contract) in order to be released from performing their part of the contract (unless the release is made under seal). The provision of this consideration discharges the original contract and there is said to be accord and satisfaction. This was found to have occurred in *Williams v Roffey Bros* (1990) (see above, 6.2.5.4).

6.5.3 Discharge by performance

This occurs where the parties to a contract perform their obligations under it. Performance is the normal way in which contracts are discharged. As a general rule, discharge requires complete and exact performance of the obligations in the contract.

In *Cutter v Powell* (1795), Cutter was employed as second mate on a ship that was sailing from Jamaica to Liverpool. The agreement was that he was to receive 30 guineas when the journey was completed. Before the ship reached Liverpool, Cutter died and his widow sued Powell, the ship's master, to recover a proportion of the wages due to her husband. It was held that the widow was entitled to nothing, as the contract required complete performance.

There are four exceptions to the general rule requiring complete performance:

- *Where the contract is divisible*

In an ordinary contract of employment, where it is usual for payment to be made periodically, the harshness of the outcome of *Cutter v Powell* is avoided.

In *Bolton v Mahadeva* (1972), the plaintiff had contracted to install central heating for the defendant for £560. It turned out to be defective and required a further £179 to put the defect right. It was held that Bolton could not claim any of the money, as he had failed to perform the contract. An agreement to supply a bathroom suite was divisible from the overall agreement, however, and had to be paid for.

- *Where the contract is capable of being fulfilled by substantial performance*

This occurs where the essential element of an agreement has been performed but some minor part or fault remains to be done or remedied. The party who performed the act can claim the contract price, although they remain liable for any deduction for the work outstanding.

In *Hoenig v Isaacs* (1952), Hoenig was employed by Isaacs to decorate his flat. The contract price was £750, to be paid as the work progressed. Isaacs paid a total of £400, but refused to pay the remainder, as he objected to the quality of the work carried out. Hoenig sued for the outstanding £350. It was held that Isaacs had to pay the outstanding money less the cost of putting right the defects in performance. These latter costs amounted to just under £56. A similar issue arose in *Williams v Roffey Bros* (1990).

This should be compared with *Bolton v Mahadeva*, in which no payment was allowed for work done in a totally unsatisfactory manner.

- *Where performance has been prevented by the other party*

Under such circumstances, as occurred in *Planche v Colburn* (1831), the party prevented from performance can sue either for breach of contract or on a *quantum meruit* basis (see below, 6.5.7.4).

- *Where partial performance has been accepted by the other party*

This occurs in the following circumstances: A orders a case of 12 bottles of wine from B. B only has 10, and delivers those to A. A is at liberty to reject the 10 bottles if he or she wants to; once the goods are accepted, though, he or she must pay a proportionate price for them.

6.5.3.1 Tender of performance

'Tender of performance' simply means an offer to perform the contractual obligations. For example, if a buyer refuses to accept the goods offered (where there are no legal grounds to do so, for example, where the goods are defective), but later sues for breach of contract, the seller can rely on the fact that they tendered performance as discharging their liability under the contract. The seller would also be entitled to claim for breach of contract.

In *Macdonald v Startup* (1843), Macdonald promised to deliver 10 tons of oil to the defendant within the last 14 days of March. He tried to deliver on Saturday 31 March at 8.30 pm, and Startup refused to accept the oil. It was held that the tender of performance was equivalent to actual performance, and Macdonald was entitled to claim damages for breach of contract.

Section 29(5) of the Sale of Goods Act (SoGA) 1979 now provides that tender is ineffectual unless made at a reasonable hour. It is unlikely that 8.30 pm on a Saturday evening would be considered reasonable.

6.5.4. Discharge by frustration

Where it is impossible to perform an obligation from the outset, no contract can come into existence. Early cases held that subsequent impossibility was no excuse for non-performance. In the 19th century, however, the doctrine of frustration was developed to permit a party to a contract, in some circumstances, to be excused performance on the grounds of impossibility arising after formation of the contract.

A contract will be discharged by reason of frustration in the following circumstances:

- *Where destruction of the subject matter of the contract has occurred*

  In *Taylor v Caldwell* (1863), Caldwell had agreed to let a hall to the plaintiff for a number of concerts. Before the day of the first concert, the hall was destroyed by fire. Taylor sued for breach of contract. It was held that the destruction of the hall had made performance impossible and, therefore, the defendant was not liable under the contract.

- *Where government interference, or supervening illegality, prevents performance*

  The performance of the contract may be made illegal by a change in the law. The outbreak of war, making the other party an enemy alien, will have a similar effect.

  In *Re Shipton, Anderson & Co* (1915), a contract was made for the sale of some wheat, which was stored in a warehouse in Liverpool. Before the seller could deliver, it was requisitioned by the Government under wartime emergency powers. It was held that the seller was excused from performance. Due to the requisition, it was no longer possible to lawfully deliver the wheat.

- *Where a particular event, which is the sole reason for the contract, fails to take place*

  In *Krell v Henry* (1903), Krell let a room to the defendant for the purpose of viewing the Coronation procession of Edward VII. When the procession was cancelled, due to the King's ill health, Krell sued Henry for the due rent. It was held that the contract was discharged by frustration, since its purpose could no longer be achieved. This only applies where the cancelled event was the sole purpose of the contract.

In *Herne Bay Steamboat Co v Hutton* (1903), a naval review, which had been arranged as part of Edward VII's coronation celebrations, also had to be cancelled due to illness. Hutton had contracted to hire a boat from the plaintiffs for the purpose of seeing the review. It was held that Hutton was liable for breach of contract. The sole foundation of the contract was not lost, as the ship could still have been used to view the assembled fleet.

- *Where the commercial purpose of the contract is defeated*

This applies where the circumstances have so changed that to hold a party to their promise would require them to do something which, although not impossible, would be radically different from the original agreement.

In *Jackson v Union Marine Insurance Co* (1874), the plaintiff's ship was chartered to proceed to Newport to load a cargo bound for San Francisco. On the way, it ran aground. It could not be refloated for over a month, and needed repairs. The charterers hired another ship and the plaintiff claimed under an insurance policy which he had taken out to cover the eventuality of his failure to carry out the contract. The insurance company denied responsibility, on the basis that the plaintiff could claim against the charterer for breach of contract. The court decided, however, that the delay had put an end to the commercial sense of the contract. As a consequence, the charterers had been released from their obligations under the contract and were entitled to hire another ship.

- *Where, in the case of a contract of personal service, the party dies or becomes otherwise incapacitated*

In *Condor v Barron Knights* (1966), Condor contracted to be the drummer in a pop group. After he became ill, he was medically advised that he could only play on four nights per week, not every night as required. It was decided that the contract was discharged by reason of the failure in the plaintiff's health preventing him from performing his duties under it; thus, any contractual obligations were unenforceable. In *Hare v Murphy Bros* (1974), a foreman's employment contract was frustrated when he was jailed for unlawful wounding. This was not self-induced frustration (see below, 6.5.4.1), though there was fault on the part of the foreman; he did not have a choice as to his availability for work.

6.5.4.1 Situations in which the doctrine of frustration does not apply

In *Tsakiroglou & Co v Noblee and Thorl* (1962), it was stated that frustration is a doctrine which is only too often invoked by a party to a contract who finds performance difficult or unprofitable, but it is very rarely relied on with success. It is, in fact, a kind of last resort, and is a conclusion which should be reached rarely and with reluctance. A contract will not be discharged by reason of frustration in the following circumstances:

- *Where the parties have made express provision in the contract for the event which has occurred*

In this case, the provision in the contract will be applied.

- *Where the frustrating event is self-induced*

An example of such a situation is the case of *Maritime National Fish Ltd v Ocean Trawlers Ltd* (1935). Maritime were charterers of a ship, equipped for otter trawling, which was owned by Ocean Trawlers. Permits were required for otter trawling, and Maritime, which owned four ships of its own, applied for five permits. They were only granted three permits, however, and they assigned those permits to their own ships. They claimed that their contract with Ocean Trawlers was frustrated, on the basis that they could not lawfully use the ship. It was held, however, that the frustrating event was a result of their action in assigning the permits to their own ships and, therefore, they could not rely on it as discharging their contractual obligations. Effectively, self-induced frustration amounts to breach of contract (see below, 6.5.5).

- *Where an alternative method of performance is still possible*

In such a situation, the person performing the contract will be expected to use the available alternative method.

In *Tsakiroglou & Co v Noblee and Thorl*, a 'cif' contract was entered into to supply 300 tons of Sudanese groundnuts to Hamburg. It had been intended that the cargo should go via the Suez Canal, and the appellants refused to deliver the nuts when the canal was closed. It was argued that the contract was frustrated, as to use the Cape of Good Hope route would make the contract commercially and fundamentally different from that which was agreed. The court decided that the contract was not fundamentally altered by the closure of the canal and, therefore, was not discharged by frustration. Thus, the appellants were liable for breach of contract. Obviously, if the cargo had been perishable, performance may not have been possible.

- *Where the contract simply becomes more expensive to perform*

In such circumstances, the court will not allow frustration to be used as a means of escaping from a bad bargain.

In *Davis Contractors v Fareham UDC* (1956), the plaintiffs contracted to build 78 houses in eight months, at a total cost of £94,000. Due to a shortage of labour, it actually took 22 months to build the houses, at a cost of £115,000. The plaintiffs sought to have the contract set aside as having been frustrated, and to claim on a *quantum meruit* basis. The court determined that the contract had not been frustrated by the shortage of labour and the plaintiffs were, thus, bound by their contractual undertaking with regard to the price.

6.5.4.2   The effect of frustration

At common law, the effect of frustration was to make the contract void as from the time of the frustrating event. It did not make the contract void *ab initio*, that is, from the beginning. The effect of this was that each party had to perform any obligation which had become due before the frustrating event, and was only excused from obligations which would arise after that event. On occasion, this could lead to injustice. For example, in *Krell v Henry* (1903), the plaintiff could not claim the rent, as it was not due to be paid until after the coronation event had been cancelled. However, in *Chandler v Webster* (1904), the plaintiff had already paid £100 of the total rent of £141 15 s for a room from which to watch the coronation procession, before it was cancelled. He sued to recover his money. It was decided that not only could he not recover the £100, but he also had to pay the outstanding £41 15 s, as the rent had fallen due for payment before the frustrating event had taken place.

6.5.4.3   Law Reform (Frustrated Contracts) Act 1943

Statute intervened to remedy the potential injustice of the common law with the introduction of Law Reform (Frustrated Contracts) Act 1943. The position is now as follows:

• any money paid is recoverable;

• any money due to be paid ceases to be payable;

• the parties may be permitted, at the discretion of the court, to retain expenses incurred from any money received; or to recover those expenses from money due to be paid before the frustrating event. If no money was paid, or was due to be paid, before the event, then nothing can be retained or recovered; and

• a party who has received valuable benefit from the other's performance before the frustrating event may have to pay for that benefit.

The Act does not apply to contracts of insurance, contracts for the carriage of goods by sea and contracts covered by s 7 of the SoGA 1979 (see below, 7.2.1).

6.5.5   Discharge by breach

Breach of a contract occurs where one of the parties to the agreement fails to comply, either completely or satisfactorily, with their obligations under it. A breach of contract may occur in three ways:

• where a party, prior to the time of performance, states that they will not fulfil their contractual obligation;

• where a party fails to perform their contractual obligation; or

• where a party performs their obligation in a defective manner.

6.5.5.1   Effect of breach

Any breach will result in the innocent party being able to sue for damages. In addition, however, some breaches will permit the innocent party to treat the contract as having been discharged. In this situation, they can refuse either to perform their part of the contract or to accept further performance from the party in breach. The right to treat a contract as discharged arises in the following instances:

- where the other party has repudiated the contract before performance is due, or before they have completed performance; and

- where the other party has committed a fundamental breach of contract. There are two methods of determining whether a breach is fundamental or not: the first is by relying on the distinction between conditions and warranties; the other is by relying on the seriousness of the consequences that flow from the breach.

6.5.5.2 Anticipatory breach

Anticipatory breach arises where one party, prior to the actual due date of performance, demonstrates an intention not to perform their contractual obligations. The intention not to fulfil the contract can be either express or implied, as follows:

- *Express*

  This occurs where a party actually states that they will not perform their contractual obligations.

  In *Hochster v De La Tour* (1853), in April, De La Tour engaged Hochster to act as courier on his European tour, starting on 1 June. On 11 May, De La Tour wrote to Hochster, stating that he would no longer be needing his services. The plaintiff started proceedings for breach of contract on 22 May and the defendant claimed that there could be no cause of action until 1 June. It was held, however, that the plaintiff was entitled to start his action as soon as the anticipatory breach occurred (that is, when De La Tour stated that he would not need Hochster's services).

- *Implied*

  This occurs where a party carries out some act which makes performance impossible.

  In *Omnium D'Enterprises v Sutherland* (1919), the defendant had agreed to let a ship to the plaintiff. Prior to the actual time for performance, he sold the ship to another party. It was held that the sale of the ship amounted to repudiation of the contract and the plaintiff could sue from that date.

With regard to anticipatory breach, the innocent party can sue for damages immediately, as in *Hochster v De La Tour*. Alternatively, they can wait until the actual time for performance before taking action, thus giving the other party a chance to perform. In the latter instance, they are entitled to make preparations for performance and claim for actual breach if the other party fails to perform on the due date, even though this apparently conflicts with the duty to mitigate losses (see below, 6.5.7.2).

In *White and Carter (Councils) v McGregor* (1961), McGregor contracted with the plaintiffs to have advertisements placed on litter bins which were supplied to local authorities. The defendant wrote to the plaintiffs, asking them to cancel the contract. The plaintiffs refused to cancel, and produced and displayed the adverts as required under the contract. They then claimed payment. It was held that the plaintiffs were not obliged to accept the defendant's repudiation. They were entitled to perform the contract and claim the agreed price. Thus, the duty to mitigate loss did not place the plaintiffs under an obligation to accept anticipatory breach and stop their own performance; as they were allowing the defendants a 'second chance', the plaintiffs had to commence their performance in case the defendants did perform on the due date.

Where the innocent party elects to wait for the time of performance, they take the risk of the contract being discharged for some other reason, such as frustration, and, thus, of losing their right to sue.

In *Avery v Bowden* (1856), Bowden chartered the plaintiff's ship in order to load grain at Odessa within a period of 45 days. Although Bowden later told the ship's captain that he no longer intended to load the grain, the ship stayed in Odessa in the hope that he would change his mind. Before the end of the 45 days, the Crimean War started and, thus, the contract was discharged by frustration. Avery then sued for breach of contract. It was held that the action failed. Bowden had committed anticipatory breach, but the captain had waived the right to discharge the contract on that basis. The contract continued and was brought to an end by frustration, not by breach.

A more recent case sheds some light on the operation and effect of anticipatory breach. In *Vitol SA v Norelf Ltd* (1996), the parties entered into a contract for the purchase of a cargo of propane gas by the plaintiff. The contract was made on 11 February, but on 8 March, Vitol sent a telex to Norelf which purported to repudiate the agreement on the basis of an alleged breach by the latter party. As the allegation of breach on the part of Norelf subsequently turned out to be unfounded, the telex of 8 March was itself an anticipatory breach of the contract on the part of Vitol. Norelf did not communicate with Vitol and sold the cargo to another party on 15 March. In arbitration, it was decided that this subsequent sale effectively represented Norelf's acceptance of the anticipatory breach and left Vitol with no action in relation to the cargo. In the Court of Appeal, however, it was held that Norelf should have indicated their acceptance of the anticipatory breach in a clear and unequivocal manner, and that silence could not amount to such acceptance. In restoring the decision of the arbitrator, the House of Lords decided that the fact that Norelf had not taken the next step in the contract by delivering a bill of lading was sufficient notification that they had accepted Vitol's repudiatory breach. In so doing, they set out three principles that govern the acceptance of repudiatory breach, as follows:

• In the event of repudiatory breach, the other party has the right either to accept the repudiation or to affirm the contract.

• The aggrieved party does not specifically have to inform the other party of their acceptance of the anticipatory breach, and conduct which clearly indicates that the injured party is treating the contract as at an end is sufficient (though, of course, each case must be considered on its specific facts).

- The aggrieved party need not personally notify the other of the decision to accept the repudiation; it is sufficient that they learn from some other party.

6.5.6 Remedies for breach of contract

The principal remedies for breach of contract are:

- damages;

- *quantum meruit*;

- specific performance;

- injunction;

- action for the agreed contract price; and

- repudiation.

Which of these remedies is available for a particular breach depends on issues such as whether the breach is of a condition or a warranty.

6.5.7 Damages

According to Lord Diplock in *Photo Productions Ltd v Securicor Transport Ltd* (1980):

> Every failure to perform a primary obligation is a breach of contract. The secondary obligation on the part of the contract breaker to which it gives rise by implication of the common law is to pay monetary compensation to the other party for the loss sustained by him in consequence of the breach.

Such monetary compensation for breach of contract is referred to as 'damages'. The estimation of what damages are to be paid by a party in breach of contract can be divided into two parts: remoteness and measure.

6.5.7.1 Remoteness of damage

What kind of damage can the innocent party claim? This involves a consideration of causation and the remoteness of cause from effect, in order to determine how far down a chain of events a defendant is liable. The rule in *Hadley v Baxendale* (1854) states that damages will only be awarded in respect of losses which arise naturally, that is, in the natural course of things; or which both parties may reasonably be supposed to have contemplated, when the contract was made, as a probable result of its breach.

In *Hadley v Baxendale*, Hadley, a miller in Gloucester, had engaged the defendant to take a broken mill-shaft to Greenwich so that it could be used as a pattern for a new one. The defendant delayed in delivering the shaft, thus causing the mill to be out of action for longer than it would otherwise have been. Hadley sued for loss of profit during that period of additional delay. It was held that it was not a natural consequence of the delay in delivering the shaft that the mill should be out of action. The mill might, for example, have had a spare shaft. So, the first part of the rule stated above did not apply. In addition, Baxendale was unaware that the mill would be out of action during the period of delay, so the second part of the rule did not apply, either. Baxendale, therefore, although liable for breach of contract, was not liable for the loss of profit caused by the delay.

The effect of the first part of the rule in *Hadley v Baxendale* is that the party in breach is deemed to expect the normal consequences of the breach, whether they actually expected them or not.

Under the second part of the rule, however, the party in breach can only be held liable for abnormal consequences where they have actual knowledge that the abnormal consequences might follow.

In *Victoria Laundry Ltd v Newham Industries Ltd* (1949), the defendants contracted to deliver a new boiler to the plaintiffs, but delayed in delivery. The plaintiffs claimed for normal loss of profit during the period of delay, and also for the loss of abnormal profits from a highly lucrative contract which they could have undertaken had the boiler been delivered on time. In this case, it was decided that damages could be recovered in regard to the normal profits, as that loss was a natural consequence of the delay. The second claim failed, however, on the ground that the loss was not a normal one; it was a consequence of an especially lucrative contract, about which the defendant knew nothing.

The decision in the *Victoria Laundry* case was confirmed by the House of Lords in *Czarnikow v Koufos* (*The Heron II*) (1967), although the actual test for remoteness was reformulated in terms of whether the consequence should have been within the reasonable contemplation of the parties at the time of the contract.

In *The Heron II*, the defendants contracted to carry sugar from Constanza to Basra. They knew that the plaintiffs were sugar merchants, but did not know that they intended to sell the sugar as soon as it reached Basra. During a period in which the ship was delayed, the market price of sugar fell. The plaintiffs claimed damages for the loss from the defendants. It was held that the plaintiffs could recover. It was common knowledge that the market value of such commodities could fluctuate; therefore, the loss was within the reasonable contemplation of the parties (see also *Bailey v HSS Alarms* (2000)).

As a consequence of the test for remoteness, a party may be liable for consequences which, although within the reasonable contemplation of the parties, are much more serious in effect than would be expected of them.

In *H Parsons (Livestock) Ltd v Uttley Ingham & Co* (1978), the plaintiffs, who were pig farmers, bought a large food hopper from the defendants. While erecting it, the plaintiffs failed to unseal a ventilator on the top of the hopper. Because of a lack of ventilation, the pig food stored in the hopper became mouldy. The pigs that ate the mouldy food contracted a rare intestinal disease and died. It was held that the defendants were liable for the loss of the pigs. The food that was affected by bad storage caused the illness as a natural consequence of the breach, and the death from such illness was not too remote.

6.5.7.2 *Measure of damages*

Damages in contract are intended to compensate an injured party for any financial loss sustained as a consequence of another party's breach. The object is not to punish the party in breach, so the amount of damages awarded can never be greater than the actual loss suffered. The aim is to put the injured party in the same position they would have been in had the contract been properly performed. There are a number of procedures which seek to achieve this end, as follows:

- *The market rule*

  Where the breach relates to a contract for the sale of goods, damages are usually assessed in line with the market rule. This means that if goods are not delivered under a contract, the buyer is entitled to go into the market and buy similar goods, paying the market price prevailing at the time. They can then claim the difference in price between what they paid and the original contract price as damages. Conversely, if a buyer refuses to accept goods under a contract, the seller can sell the goods in the market and accept the prevailing market price. Any difference between the price they receive and the contract price can be claimed in damages (see ss 50 and 51 of the SoGA 1979, and below, 7.2.1).

- *The duty to mitigate losses*

  The injured party is under a duty to take all reasonable steps to minimise their loss. So, in the above examples, the buyer of goods which are not delivered has to buy the replacements as cheaply as possible, and the seller of goods which are not accepted has to try to get as good a price as they can when they sell them.

  In *Payzu v Saunders* (1919), the parties entered into a contract for the sale of fabric, which was to be delivered and paid for in instalments. When the purchaser, Payzu, failed to pay the first instalment on time, Saunders refused to make any further deliveries unless Payzu agreed to pay cash on delivery. The plaintiff refused to accept this and sued for breach of contract. The court decided that the delay in payment had not given the defendant the right to repudiate the contract. As a consequence, he had breached the contract by refusing further delivery. The buyer, however, should have mitigated his loss by accepting the offer of cash on delivery terms. His damages were restricted, therefore, to what he would have lost under those terms, namely, interest over the repayment period.

  A more recent case highlights the problems that can arise in relation to both the market rule and the duty to mitigate losses. In *Western Web Offset Printers Ltd v Independent Media Ltd* (1995), the parties had entered into a contract under which the plaintiff was to publish 48 issues of a weekly newspaper for the defendant. In the action which followed the defendant's repudiation of the contract, the only issue in question was the extent of damages to be awarded. The plaintiff argued that damages should be decided on the basis of gross profits, merely subtracting direct expenses such as paper and ink, but not labour costs and other overheads; this would result in a total claim of some £177,000. The defendant argued that damages should be on the basis of net profits, with labour and other overheads being taken into account; this would result in a claim of some £38,000. Although the trial judge awarded the lesser sum, the Court of Appeal decided that he had drawn an incorrect analogy from cases involving sale of goods. In this situation, it was not simply a matter of working out the difference in cost price from selling price in order to reach a nominal profit. The plaintiff had been unable to replace the work, due to the recession in the economy, and, therefore, had not been able to mitigate the loss. In the circumstances, the plaintiff was entitled to receive the full amount that would have been due in order to allow it to defray the expenses that it would have had to pay during the period that the contract should have lasted.

- *Non-pecuniary loss*

At one time, damages could not be recovered where the loss sustained through breach of contract was of a non-financial nature. The modern position is that such non-pecuniary damages can be recovered.

In Jarvis v Swan Tours Ltd (1973), the defendant's brochure stated that various facilities were available at a particular ski resort. The facilities available were, in fact, much inferior to those advertised. The plaintiff sued for breach of contract. The court decided that Jarvis was entitled to recover not just the financial loss he suffered, which was not substantial, but also damages for loss of entertainment and enjoyment. The Court of Appeal stated that damages could be recovered for mental distress in appropriate cases, and this was one of them. The scope of recovery of damages for 'distress and disappointment' was recently examined by the House of Lords in *Farley v Skinner* (2001).

Particular problems arise in relation to estimating the damages liable in relation to construction contracts. Where a builder has either not carried out work required or has carried it out inadequately, they will be in breach of contract and the aggrieved party will be entitled to claim damages. The usual measure of such damages is the cost of carrying out the work or repairing the faulty work. However, this may not be the case where the costs of remedying the defects are disproportionate to the difference in value between what was supplied and what was ordered.

In *Ruxley Electronics and Construction Ltd v Forsyth* (1995), the parties had entered into a contract for the construction of a swimming pool and surrounding building. Although the contract stated that the pool was to be 7 ft 6 in deep at one end, the actual depth of the pool was only 6 ft 9 in. The total contract price was £70,000. Fixing the error would have required a full reconstruction at a cost of £20,000. The trial judge decided that the measure of damages for the plaintiff's breach was the difference between the value of the pool actually provided and the value of the pool contracted for. He decided that the difference was nil, but awarded the defendant £2,500 for loss of amenity. On appeal, the Court of Appeal overturned that award, holding that Forsyth was entitled to the full cost of reconstruction. On further appeal, the House of Lords reinstated the decision of the trial judge. They considered that, in building contracts, there were two possible ways of determining damages: either the difference in value, as used by the trial judge; or the cost of reinstatement, as preferred by the Court of Appeal. As the costs of reinstatement would have been out of all proportion to the benefit gained, the House of Lords awarded the difference in value. According to Lord Jauncey, 'damages are designed to compensate for an established loss and not to provide a gratuity to the aggrieved party'. Lord Lloyd said that the plaintiff could not, in all cases, 'obtain the monetary equivalent of specific performance'.

It should be noted that such construction contracts are evidently to be treated differently from contracts for the sale of goods, for purchasers of goods can reject them under s 13 of the SoGA 1979 where they do not match their description, even if they are otherwise fit for the purpose for which they were bought (see below, 7.2).

Recently, in *Kingston-upon-Hull City Council v Dunnachie* (2003), the Court of Appeal decided that employment tribunals could award damages, under statute, for non-pecuniary losses (such as injury to self-respect) resulting from unfair dismissal. Referral to the House of Lords seems likely to clarify the situation.

6.5.7.3   Liquidated damages and penalties

It is possible, and common in business contracts, for the parties to an agreement to make provisions for possible breach by stating in advance the amount of damages that will have to be paid in the event of any breach occurring. Damages under such a provision are known as liquidated damages. They will only be recognised by the court if they represent a genuine pre-estimate of loss and are not intended to operate as a penalty against the party in breach. If the court considers the provision to be a penalty, it will not give it effect but will award damages in the normal way, that is, unliquidated damages assessed by the court.

In *Dunlop v New Garage & Motor Co* (1915), the plaintiffs supplied the defendants with tyres under a contract designed to achieve resale price maintenance. The contract provided that the defendants had to pay Dunlop £5 for every tyre they sold in breach of the resale price agreement. When the garage sold tyres at less than the agreed minimum price, they resisted Dunlop's claim for £5 per tyre, on the grounds that it represented a penalty clause. On the facts of the situation, the court decided that the provision was a genuine attempt to fix damages and was not a penalty. It was, therefore, enforceable.

In deciding the legality of such clauses, the courts will consider the effect, rather than the form, of the clause, as can be seen in *Cellulose Acetate Silk Co Ltd v Widnes Foundry (1925) Ltd* (1933). In that case, the contract expressly stated that damages for late payment would be paid by way of penalty at the rate of £20 per week. In fact, the sum of £20 was in no way excessive and represented a reasonable estimate of the likely loss. On that basis, the House of Lords enforced the clause, in spite of its actual wording.

In *Duffen v FRA Bo SpA* (1998), it was held that a term in an agency contract which established so-called 'liquidated damages' for the dismissal of the agent at £100,000 was, in fact, a penalty clause and could not be enforced. This was in spite of the fact that the agreement specifically stated that the £100,000 was 'a reasonable pre-estimate of the loss and damage which the agent will suffer on the termination of the agreement'. In reaching its conclusion, the court held that although the wording of the agreement was persuasive, it was outweighed by the fact that the level of damages did not alter in proportion to the time remaining to be served in the agreement. The claimant was consequently only allowed to claim for normal damages, although these could be augmented under the Commercial Agents (Council Directive) Regulations 1993 (SI 1993/3053) (see below, 9.1.1).

The whole question of penalty clauses is fraught. It is obviously advantageous, in a business context, for the parties to a contract to know with certainty what the financial consequences of any breach of the contract will be, so as to allow them to manage their risk properly. However, the possibility of the courts subsequently holding a damages clause to be punitive introduces the very uncertainty that the clause was designed to avoid.

In any case, why should businesses not be bound by clauses, as long as they have been freely negotiated? This point leads to a comparison of liquidated damages clauses and limitation and exclusion clauses. Usually, penalty clauses are thought of as overestimating the damages, but it should be considered that such a pre-estimation may be much lower than the damages suffered, in which case the clause will effectively operate as a limitation clause. It would surely be better all round if the liquidated damages/penalties clause question was subject to a similar regime as regulates exclusion/limitation clauses under the Unfair Contract Terms Act 1977. The courts would then be required to examine whether the clause was the product of truly free negotiation and not the outcome of an abuse of power, in which case it would be effective, or, alternatively, whether it was imposed on one of the parties against their wishes, in which case it would be inoperative.

6.5.7.4　Quantum meruit

The term *quantum meruit* means that a party should be awarded as much as he had earned, and such an award can be either contractual or quasi-contractual (see below, 8.12) in nature. If the parties enter into a contractual agreement without determining the reward that is to be provided for performance, then, in the event of any dispute, the court will award a reasonable sum.

Payment may also be claimed on the basis of *quantum meruit* where a party has carried out work in respect of a void contract and the other party has accepted that work.

In *Craven-Ellis v Canons Ltd* (1936), the plaintiff had acted as the managing director of a company under a deed of contract. However, since he had not acquired any shares in the company, as required by its articles, his appointment was void. He sued to recover remuneration for the service he had provided prior to his removal. The court decided that, although he could not claim under contract, he was entitled to recover a reasonable sum on the basis of *quantum meruit*.

Furthermore, where the defendant has prevented the claimant from completing performance, the claimant may be entitled to payment for work done so far. In *Planche v Colburn* (1831), the plaintiff was under contract to write a book for the defendants, with payment to be made on completion of the manuscript. The defendants abandoned publication plans before the manuscript was completed; the plaintiff, having done some of the research for and writing of the manuscript, could claim for that work done.

6.5.8 Specific performance

It will sometimes suit a party to break their contractual obligations and pay damages; through an order for specific performance, however, the party in breach may be instructed to complete their part of the contract. The following rules govern the award of such a remedy:

- An order of specific performance will only be granted in cases where the common law remedy of damages is inadequate. It is not usually applied to contracts concerning the sale of goods where replacements are readily available. It is most commonly granted in cases involving the sale of land and where the subject matter of the contract is unique (for example, a painting by Picasso).

- Specific performance will not be granted where the court cannot supervise its enforcement. For this reason, it will not be available in respect of contracts of employment or personal service.

In *Ryan v Mutual Tontine Westminster Chambers Association* (1893), the landlords of a flat undertook to provide a porter, who was to be constantly in attendance to provide services such as cleaning the common passages and stairs and delivering letters. The person appointed spent much of his time working as a chef at a nearby club. During his absence, his duties were performed by a cleaner or by various boys. The plaintiff sought to enforce the contractual undertaking. It was held that, although the landlords were in breach of their contract, the court would not award an order of specific performance. The only remedy available was an action for damages.

Similarly, in *Co-operative Insurance Society Ltd v Argyll Stores (Holdings) Ltd* (1997), the House of Lords held that it would be inappropriate to enforce a covenant to trade entered into by the defendant company. The case concerned a shopping centre owned by the claimants, in which the defendant's Safeway supermarket was the largest attraction. Although it had contracted in its lease to keep its supermarket open during usual trading hours, the defendant company decided to close the shop, causing significant threat to the continued operation of the shopping centre. The plaintiff's action for specific performance to force Argyll to keep the store open was unsuccessful at first instance, although it was supported in the Court of Appeal. The House of Lords, however, restored the traditional approach by refusing to issue an order for specific performance in such circumstances where it would require constant supervision by the court. Damages were held to be the appropriate remedy.

- Specific performance is an equitable remedy which the court grants at its discretion. It will not be granted where the claimant has not acted properly; neither will it be granted where mutuality is lacking. Thus, a minor will not be granted specific performance, because no such order could be awarded against a minor.

6.5.9   Injunction

This is also an equitable order of the court, which directs a person not to break their contract. It can have the effect of indirectly enforcing contracts for personal service.

In *Warner Bros v Nelson* (1937), the defendant, the actress Bette Davis, had entered a contract which stipulated that she was to work exclusively for the plaintiffs for a period of one year. When she came to England, the plaintiffs applied for an injunction to prevent her from working for someone else. The court granted the order to Warner Bros. In doing so, it rejected Davis's argument that granting it would force her either to work for the plaintiffs or not to work at all.

An injunction will only be granted to enforce negative covenants within the agreement and cannot be used to enforce positive obligations.

In *Whitwood Chemical Co v Hardman* (1891), the defendant had contracted to give the whole of his time to the plaintiffs, his employers, but he occasionally worked for others. The plaintiffs applied for an injunction to prevent him working for anyone else. No injunction was granted. Hardman had said what he would do, not what he would not do; therefore, there was no negative promise to enforce.

6.5.10   Action for the agreed contract price

In some circumstances, a party may sue for non-payment of the price rather than seeking damages for breach. For example, s 49 of the SoGA 1979 gives this right to the seller where either the buyer fails to pay on the agreed date, or ownership in the goods has been transferred to the buyer.

6.5.11   Repudiation

As already discussed in this chapter, where there is a breach of condition, the party not in breach has the option of treating the contract as repudiated, so that he need not perform his contractual obligations (see above, 6.5.1).

6.5.12   Quasi-contractual remedies

Quasi-contractual remedies are based on the assumption that a person should not receive any undue advantage from the fact that there is no contractual remedy to force them to account for it. An important quasi-contractual remedy is an action for money paid and received.

If no contract comes into existence by reason of a total failure of consideration, then, under this action, any goods or money received will have to be returned to the party who supplied them.

A case of particular interest is *HM Attorney General v Blake* (2000). Blake, jailed for treason for spying for the Soviet Union, escaped and subsequently wrote his autobiography. This was alleged to be a breach of his contract of employment with the British Intelligence Service and the Attorney General sought an injunction to prevent the publishers from paying Blake £90,000 royalties on the book. The Court of Appeal granted the injunction on the ground that it was against public policy for a criminal to profit from his crime.

The House of Lords did not uphold grant of the injunction as they could find no statutory or common law authority for such grant; accordingly, the money could be paid to Blake. However, Blake's treachery made the case exceptional, allowing application of the principle of restitution to Blake's breach of contract. Accordingly, the Attorney General was allowed an account of all profits resulting from the breach. Effectively, therefore, the Attorney General recovered the royalties from Blake.

THE LAW OF CONTRACT

The Nature and Function of Contract Law

Definition

- A 'legally binding agreement' – enforceable in law.

- Enforceability is determined by legal rules.

Formalities

- Not normally required for *simple/parol* contracts.

- Some *simple* contracts need to be in writing/evidenced in writing.

The legal effect of agreements

- Valid contracts are enforceable.

- Void contracts have no legal effect.

- Voidable contracts can be set aside at one party's option; the contract is valid unless/until it is avoided.

- Unenforceable contracts are valid but no court action may be taken to enforce them.

The Formation of a Contract

n order to create a contract, the following factors have to be present.

Offer

- An offer is a promise, which is capable of acceptance, to be bound on particular terms.

- An offer may be restricted to a particular person(s) or made to the public at large.

- A person can only accept an offer they are aware of.

- An offer may be revoked *before* acceptance or may come to an end in other ways.

- An offer must be distinguished from an invitation to treat, a statement of intention and a supply of information.

Acceptance

- Acceptance must correspond with the terms of the offer.

- Acceptance must be communicated to the offeror (subject to certain exceptions such as the *postal rule*).

Consideration

- Consists of some benefit to the promisor or detriment to the promisee.

- Consideration can be *executed* or *executory*, but not *past*.

- Consideration must be *sufficient*, but need not be *adequate*.

Promissory estoppel

- The doctrine may prevent a person from going back on a promise to forgo strict contractual rights.

- The doctrine operates as a defence, not a cause of action.

Privity

- Only a party to a contract can sue or be sued on it.

- There are common law and statutory exceptions to the doctrine of privity, notably the Contracts (Rights of Third Parties) Act 1999.

Capacity

- Minors, those of unsound mind or under the influence of drugs or alcohol have limited capacity to make binding contracts; nevertheless, contracts for necessaries bind them.

- Minors are also bound by beneficial contracts of service.

- Some contracts made by minors are voidable and only bind them if not repudiated by them before or within a reasonable time after reaching the age of majority.

Intention to create legal relations

- In social/domestic agreements, there is a rebuttal presumption that legal relations were not intended.

- In commercial/business agreements, there is a rebuttal presumption that legal relations were intended.

- Collective agreements are usually presumed not to create legal relations.

Contents of a Contract

Contract terms and mere representations

A pre-contract statement is likely to be a term if:

- the contract would not have been made but for the statement;

- the time gap between the statement and the contract is short; or

- the statement is made by a person with special skill/knowledge.

A pre-contract statement is likely to be a representation only if:

- there is a long time gap between the statement and the contract;

- the statement is oral and the written contract does not refer to it; or

- the person making the statement had no special skill/knowledge.

Terms

- A *condition* is a fundamental term, going to the root of the contract, breach of which gives a right to repudiate the contract.

- A *warranty* is a subsidiary term, breach of which gives a right to claim damages.

- If a term is *innominate*, the seriousness of the breach determines the remedies available.

Express and implied terms

- Express terms are those specifically agreed by the parties.

- Implied terms are not specifically agreed by the parties, but are implied into the contract by statute or custom or the courts.

The parol evidence rule

- Where there is a written contract, it is *presumed* that evidence cannot be adduced to show a differing oral agreement.

Exemption or exclusion clauses

The validity of such a clause depends on:

- whether it was incorporated into the contract;

- whether, on its wording, it covers the breach;

- whether a common law rule of construction, such as the *contra proferentem* rule, restricts its effect; and

- the effect of statutory provisions.

Statutory regulation of exemption clauses

Under the Unfair Contract Terms Act 1977

- Liability for negligence causing death or injury cannot be excluded.

- Liability for breach of the implied terms of the Sale of Goods Act 1979 cannot be excluded in consumer sales.

- Liability for breach of s 12(1) of the Sale of Goods Act 1979 cannot be excluded in non-consumer sales, but liability for breach of the other implied terms may be excluded, subject to the requirement of *reasonableness*.

Under the Unfair Terms in Consumer Contracts Regulations 1999

- Contract clauses not made *in good faith* are void.

- Authorised bodies may obtain injunctions to prevent the use of unfair terms.

Vitiating Factors

Mistake

- Operative (fundamental) mistake renders a contract void.

- Equitable remedies may be available where mistakes are not fundamental.

- Operative common mistake usually involves *res sua* or *res extincta*.

- An objective test is applied to determine whether a mutual mistake is operative.

- Generally, unilateral mistake is not operative where the parties deal face to face.

- Where the mistake relates to a written contract, rectification or *non est factum* may be claimed.

Misrepresentation

- Misrepresentation can be defined as 'a false statement of fact, made by one party before or at the time of the contract, which induces the other party to contract'.

- Some statements will not amount to representations, for example, statements of opinion and law.

- Some pre-contract statements may be treated as terms of the contract. This gives rise to an alternative cause of action for breach of contract, which should be noted for examination purposes.

- Rescission and damages in the tort of deceit are available for *fraudulent misrepresentation.*

- Rescission and/or damages under s 2(1) of the Misrepresentation Act 1967 are available for *negligent misrepresentation.*

- Rescission or damages under s 2(2) of the Misrepresentation Act 1967 are available for *innocent misrepresentation.*

Duress

- A contract entered into in consequence of duress is voidable.

- Economic duress may render a contract voidable if there was illegitimate pressure, negating consent to the contract.

Undue influence

- Subject to delay, undue influence renders a contract voidable.

- Where there is a special relationship between the contracting parties, a rebuttal presumption of undue influence arises.

- Where there is no special relationship between the contracting parties, the party claiming undue influence has the burden of proof.

Contracts and public policy

- A contract rendered illegal by statute or common law cannot be the subject of legal action.

- Contracts rendered void as contrary to public policy (for example, contracts in restraint of trade) do not give rise to legal rights or obligations.

Discharge of a Contract

Discharge by agreement

- Executory contracts may be discharged by mutual exchange of promises to discharge.

- Where one party has executed the contract, the other is only released from the obligation to perform by providing new consideration.

Discharge by performance

- As a general rule, discharge by performance requires complete and exact performance of the obligations in the contract, except where the contract is divisible, is capable of being fulfilled by substantial performance, performance has been prevented by the other party or partial performance has been accepted by the other party.

Tender of performance

- Tender of performance (an offer to perform the contractual obligations) discharges liability under a contract.

Discharge by frustration

- Frustrating events, such as destruction of the subject matter of the contract, discharge the contract.

- A contract will not be frustrated where the contract expressly provides for the frustrating event, nor where the frustration is self-induced nor where an alternative method of performance is available.

- Contracts frustrated at common law are void from the time of frustration.

- Under the Law Reform (Frustrated Contracts) Act 1943, money paid before frustration is recoverable and money due is recoverable/not payable. In the court's discretion, claims may be made for expenses incurred prior to frustration.

Discharge by breach

- Breach may be anticipatory or by failure to perform/defective performance of the contract.

- Breach of a contract entitles the innocent party to damages. Additionally, a breach of condition entitles the innocent party to treat the contract as being discharged.

Damages

- Damages may be *liquidated* or *unliquidated*.

- Assessment of unliquidated damages is determined by the rules of *remoteness* (reasonable forseeability) and *mitigation of loss*.

CHAPTER 7

CONSUMER PROTECTION

7.1 Introduction to Consumer Protection

The previous chapter has focused on what has been described as the 'Classical Model of Contract Law'. The assumptions underlying such a model are based on the appearances of a competitive, free market, system, in which the parties to contracts are truly free to determine their own economic/market relationships. It has to be recognised, however, that this competitive market model of contractual relationships is no longer an accurate representation of what actually takes place in the contemporary market place. We now live in economies that are dominated by huge economic organisations which wield extensive economic power. In such situations of oligopolistic, if not monopolistic, power it is simply nonsensical to think in terms of consumer sovereignty, or its legal equivalent, equality of bargaining power. It would be a misrepresentation of reality, for example, to suggest that individual consumers negotiate the terms of their individual purchases in supermarkets in the way that is assumed in the invitation to treat-offer-acceptance description portrayed in cases such as *Pharmaceutical Society of Great Britain v Boots* (1953). In reality, consumers are faced with the simple, single, choice; take it or leave it, and go elsewhere to be met by the same conditions.

With the collapse of the notion of equality of bargaining power, the modern state has intervened to protect individual consumers who would otherwise be left at the mercy of those who might abuse the market relationship. The introduction of consumer protection legislation, of course, has also been aimed at safeguarding the individual from the depredations of the mere crooked and criminal trader. Given the nature of this book, it is impossible to do justice to all the aspects of consumer protection, and it is recognised that extremely important areas, such as the product liability and the consumer protection legislation, cannot be covered in the limited space available. It is hoped, however, that what is dealt with in this chapter will follow on from, and build upon, the previous chapter of contract law, whilst providing an indication of the role of consumer protection. The areas to be dealt with are:

- Sale of Goods Act 1979;

- Consumer Protection Act 1987;

- Trade Descriptions Act 1968;

- Consumer Credit Act 1974.

Furthermore, the SSGA 1982 provides protection for the victims of poor.

7.2   Sale and Supply of Goods

One of the most common transactions entered into by businesses is the contract for the sale of goods to other businesses or consumers. However, goods may be supplied under contracts other than sale, as follows, for example:

- *Contracts of hire*

  Here, the owner of goods transfers possession for a fixed period but retains ownership; common examples are television rental and car hire.

- *Contracts of hire purchase*

  The owner of goods transfers possession of the goods, but does not transfer ownership of them unless and until the hirer has paid all of the agreed instalments and has exercised his or her option to purchase.

Furthermore, a person may be supplied with goods other than under a contract; for example:

- *By gift*

  Gifts are voluntary transfers of ownership to a person who does not give any consideration in return for the ownership.

It should also be appreciated that the sale and supply of goods can give rise to both civil and criminal liability, the latter being of particular importance in relation to the protection of consumers.

  A detailed examination of the laws relating to all transactions for the sale or supply of goods is outside the remit of this book; civil and criminal laws relating to the commonest of such transactions will be considered, namely:

- *Civil liability*:
  - Sale of Goods Act (SoGA) 1979;
  - Supply of Goods and Services Act (SGSA) 1982;
  - Consumer Protection (Distance Selling) Regulations 2000;
  - Part I of the Consumer Protection Act 1987.

- *Criminal liability*:
  - Part II of the Consumer Protection Act 1987;
  - General Product Safety Regulations 1994;
  - Trade Descriptions Act 1968.

7.2.1   The Sale of Goods Act 1979

This Act has been amended by the Sale and Supply of Goods Act (SSGA) 1994, the Sale of Goods (Amendment) Act 1994 and the Sale of Goods (Amendment) Act 1995. All references to the SoGA 1979 are to the provisions as amended.

Note should also be taken of the Sale and Supply of Goods to Consumers Regulations 2002 (2002 Regulations); these result from an EC Directive (1999/44/EC). The 2002 Regulations make amendments to the SoGA 1979, mainly where the buyer of goods is a consumer; the Regulations define a 'consumer' as a natural person who is acting for purposes which are outside his business.

7.2.1.1 Definition

Under s 2(1), a contract for the sale of goods is 'a contract by which the seller transfers or agrees to transfer the property in the goods to the buyer for a money consideration, called the price'.

In this context, 'property' means 'ownership', so the object of such a contract is to transfer ownership in the goods to the buyer; however, the contract is only covered by the SoGA 1979 if the buyer's consideration is money. Accordingly, an exchange of goods is not within the Act; following the decision in *Connell Estate Agents v Begej* (1993), however, it can be argued that part exchange contracts are within the Act, particularly where the value of the goods given in part exchange is apparent. Section 2(1) also requires that 'goods', as defined in s 61(1) of the SoGA 1979, are the subject matter of the contract. In general, the word 'goods' includes personal property of a moveable type (that is, anything which can be physically possessed in some way and is not attached to the land). For example, crops become goods on harvesting and money becomes goods when antique or collectable. However, there are specific exclusions from the definition of 'goods', for example:

- real property (for example, land and buildings); and

- choses in action (for example, debts, cheques and currency in circulation).

7.2.1.2 Form of the agreement

The basic essentials for forming any contract (see Section 6.2), such as capacity to contract, must be met, but there are no formal requirements: the contract can be oral, written or even inferred from conduct, as might be the case in a supermarket sale, where the parties are unlikely to actually state that they wish to buy and sell the goods!

7.2.1.3 The Price of the goods

Being an essential part of the contract by virtue of s 2(1), the price of the goods is usually expressly agreed; for example, when buying goods in a shop, the buyer agrees to pay the marked price. Section 8(1) of the SoGA 1979 confirms that the price may be fixed by the contract and also indicates that the price can be determined by a course of dealing between the parties or in a manner agreed by the contract. Thus, when re-ordering goods without reference to the price, the parties could be taken to agree that the price paid in a previous transaction was applicable to this contract. Equally, the parties might validly agree that an independent third party should determine the price payable. Of course, the question arises of what happens if that third party does not make, or is prevented from making, that determination of the price payable. Section 9 of the SoGA 1979 solves these issues:

(1) Where there is an agreement to sell goods on the terms that the price is to be fixed by the valuation of a third party, and he cannot or does not make the valuation, the agreement is avoided; but if the goods or any part of them have been delivered to and appropriated by the buyer, he must pay a reasonable price for them.

(2) Where the third party is prevented from making the valuation by the fault of the seller or buyer, the party not at fault may maintain an action for damages against the party at fault.

Some problems arising from determination of the price, however, are not specifically addressed by the SoGA 1979. Though the Act indicates in s 8(2) that 'a reasonable price' is payable where the price has not been determined under s 8(1), it has been suggested that failure to agree a price or a manner of fixing it means that there is no contract concluded and s 8(2) cannot operate to make such an arrangement a contract.

In *May and Butcher v The King* (1934), an agreement for the purchase of government tentage provided that the price was to be agreed from time to time; effectively, they agreed to make later agreements as to the price. Had there been no mention of the price at all, then failure to actually agree a price would not mean that there was no contract: a 'reasonable price' would have been payable, under the SoGA 1893. However, as the parties had expressly stated that the price was to be agreed later, it was held that they were simply agreeing to agree and had not intended to make a binding contract.

In *Foley v Classique Coaches Ltd* (1934), the defendants agreed to purchase supplies of petrol from the plaintiffs, at a price 'to be agreed by the parties from time to time'. Failing agreement, the price was to be settled by arbitration. The agreement was held to be a binding contract by the Court of Appeal.

The distinction between the two cases would appear to be based on the fact that, by providing a method (arbitration) by which the price could be fixed, the parties had shown an intention to make a legally binding agreement. Accordingly, it would seem that intention to be bound can be regarded as the key issue, and agreement as to price is merely a factor in determination of such intention.

7.2.1.4 Seller's implied obligations

As well as performing any express undertakings in the contract, the seller must also comply with certain terms implied into the contract by the SoGA 1979, regardless of whether he or she sells to a consumer or a business. These implied terms are of particular interest to the consumer, who rarely negotiates and agrees express terms. In supermarket sales, for example, it is unlikely that there will be any discussion, let alone specific undertakings given, as to the quality and functions of the goods sold. Nevertheless, the implied terms will place a seller under an obligation as to matters such as quality and functions of the goods that he or she sells. It is also important to note that the seller's obligations under the implied terms apply even though the seller is not actually at fault; he or she undertakes liability by the act of selling the goods. Thus, if a new stereo system does not function properly because of a manufacturing defect, the buyer may still sue the seller for breach of contract. Furthermore, in some cases, the Contracts (Rights of Third Parties) Act 1999 (considered above, Chapter 6) might give a non-buyer the same rights against the seller.

Finally, it should be realised that the implied terms of the SoGA 1979 are classified as conditions or warranties (see above, Chapter 6), which give rise to different remedies for breach (see below, 7.2.1.7).

Title (s 12 of the SoGA 1979)

We have already seen that the objective of a contract for the sale of goods is to buy ownership in the goods; accordingly, s 12(1) implies a condition into the contract that the seller has the 'right to sell' the goods. If the seller cannot transfer ownership, he or she does not have the 'right to sell'. In *Rowland v Divall* (1923), the buyer of a car did not receive ownership, as the garage which sold him the car did not own it. There was a breach of s 12(1) and he was able to recover the full purchase price paid, even though he had used the car for four months. Where ownership is not transferred, there is a total failure of consideration, as the buyer does not receive what he contracted to buy. Clearly, legal ownership is of paramount importance and transferring use and possession of goods is not sufficient for performance of a sale of goods contract.

Section 12(2) also implies into the contract warranties of quiet possession and freedom from encumbrances (s 12(2) of the SoGA 1979). Effectively, the seller undertakes that the buyer's title will not be interfered with or be subject to anyone else's rights, except in so far as such are known by or disclosed to the buyer before the contract is made.

In *Microbeads AC v Vinhurst Road Markings* (1975), the seller sold some road marking machines to the buyers. Unbeknown to the seller at the time of the sale, another firm was in the process of patenting this type of equipment, although rights to enforce the patent did not commence until after the contract between the seller and buyer was made. A patent action was subsequently brought against the buyer, who then claimed that the seller was in breach of the implied condition, as he had no right to sell and was in breach of the warranty of quiet possession. It was held that, at the time of sale, the seller had every right to sell the goods, but was in breach of the warranty for quiet possession, because that amounted to an undertaking as to the future.

Description (s 13 of the SoGA 1979)

Where the sale of goods is by description, the goods must correspond with that description. Goods are sold 'by description' either where the buyer does not see the goods but relies on a description of them or where the buyer sees the goods but relies on terms describing features of the goods or a description on the goods themselves. So, descriptive words printed on packaging could form part of the description; one would buy a packet labelled 'Cornflakes' because one would rely on that word as indicating that the contents were cornflakes.

Not all words used by the seller will be part of the contract description (it might be a 'moot' point whether the ingredients list on the 'Cornflakes' packet also forms part of the contract description under s 13). *Reliance* on the words as *identifying* the goods being bought is the important issue (see *Harlingdon and Leinster Enterprises Ltd v Christopher Hull Fine Art Ltd* (1990)), as was illustrated in *Beale v Taylor* (1967), where the buyer answered an advertisement for the sale of a 'Herald Convertible 1961'. On the back of the car was a disc which stated '1200'. He bought the car. Later, he found that the car consisted of the back half of a 1961 model welded to the front half of an earlier model. It was held that the description in the advertisement was clearly relied on in buying the car and was, therefore, part of the contract description under s 13, which had not been complied with.

The description may be very simple; in *Grant v Australian Knitting Mills* (1936), the buyer asked for 'underpants', which was held to be the contract description, as that was the way in which the buyer identified what he was purchasing. It is interesting to note that the court also indicated that retail sales, where goods were asked for over the counter or chosen from a display, were still sales by description. In other contracts, the description may be a very detailed one, such as a formula (see, for example, *Ashington Piggeries v Christopher Hill Ltd* (1972)) or design specifications. It is not always easy to determine which words used are part of the contract description. In *Re Moore & Co and Landauer & Co* (1921), the contract required tins of fruit to be packed in cases of 30. The correct quantity of tins was delivered, but some were in cases of 24 tins; there was held to be a breach of the contract description. The court decided that a stipulated method of packaging was part of the contract description. However, as we have seen that later authority leans towards looking only to those words which the buyer relies on as identifying the goods being bought, the case might be decided differently today.

Where goods are 'sold as seen', this is an indication that the goods are not sold under any description within the meaning of s 13.

Once the contractual description of the goods has been established, the question arises of whether or not it has been complied with. This may be easy to determine in some cases, but is often less obvious. In *Arcos Ltd v Ronaasen & Son* (1933), a delivery of staves which were nine-sixteenths of an inch thick instead of half an inch thick, as required by the contract, was a breach of description. In *Ashington Piggeries v Christopher Hill*, in a written contract, the seller agreed to make up a formula specified by the buyer to produce a 'vitamin fortified' mink food to be called 'King Size'. One of the ingredients in the formula was herring meal, and the herring meal used by the seller was contaminated and harmful to mink. If 'mink food' was part of the contract description under s 13, there would have been a breach of condition, as a product which harmed mink could hardly be correctly described as 'mink food'. However, the House of Lords decided that the statement that the end product was to be a 'mink food' was not part of the contract description; the contract description was the specified formula which indicated what the end product was. Therefore, it was the words 'herring meal' which were in issue as regards compliance with the contract description. Despite the fact the contaminated herring meal was harmful to mink, and even potentially harmful to other animals, it was decided that the contract description was complied with, as the meal was still identifiable as 'herring meal'. This finding has been criticised on the basis that 'herring meal' should be regarded as meaning 'a food which can be safely fed to animals'; if it cannot fulfil that function, it is not 'herring meal'.

Though strict compliance with the description was required in cases such as *Arcos Ltd v Ronaasen & Son*, where there was a breach of s 13 even though the staves could still have been used as the buyer intended, namely, to make barrels, the *de minimis* rule may allow minor deviations in certain situations. Where a description has acquired a meaning in the trade, goods which comply with that trade meaning will comply with s 13 even if they do not comply with the strict wording of the contract description. In *Peter Darlington Partners Ltd v Gosho Co Ltd* (1964), there was a contract for the purchase of canary seed on a 'pure basis'. The buyers refused to accept 98% pure seed but, because 98% pure was the highest standard in the trade, there was no breach of description and the buyers were in breach themselves for wrongfully refusing the seed.

Section 13 also indicates that, where goods are sold by sample and description, there must be compliance with both sample and description. It is not sufficient that the goods comply with either description or sample. Sale by sample is the subject of s 15 of the SoGA 1979 (see below).

Finally, it should be noted that s 13 does not require that the seller is undertaking a business transaction, so the private seller, such as a person selling goods through a classified advertisement column, has the obligation to supply goods complying with the contract description.

Satisfactory quality (s 14(2) of the SoGA 1979)

The SSGA 1994 repealed the implied condition of 'merchantable quality' and replaced it with the current s 14(2).

There is an implied term that the goods shall be of satisfactory quality, according to s 14(2) of the SoGA 1979. While s 14(2) uses the word 'term', it is clear from s 14(6) that the term is a condition. Unlike s 13, s 14 does not apply to private sales; that is, the goods must be sold in the course of a business. The term 'sale in the course of a business' is not defined in the SoGA 1979, but in *Stevenson v Rogers* (1999), it was held that a fisherman 'acted in the course of business' when he sold his trawler. Even though he did not deal in vessels, it was a sale connected with his business. (Note, however, *R & B Customs Brokers Ltd v UDT* (1988), which discusses the meaning of 'in the course of business' in the context of s 12(1) of the Unfair Contract Terms Act (UCTA) 1977 (see above, 6.3.5.3). Thus, goods which come within s 14(2) include not only goods sold in the normal course of business, but also goods used in or connected with the business, for example, the sale of a van which has been used in a grocery business.

The meaning of the requirement of 'satisfactory quality' must also be considered. Section 14(2A) states that 'goods are of satisfactory quality if they meet the standard that a reasonable person would regard as satisfactory, taking account of any description of the goods, the price (if relevant) and all other relevant circumstances'. In *Jewson v Kelly* (2003), the buyer purchased heating boilers for the flats he was refurbishing for sale as low cost/energy efficient. The boilers did not comply with low cost/energy efficient ratings but did provide adequate heating. At first instance, the boilers were found not to be of satisfactory quality under s 14(2A), because a reasonable person buying such a flat would expect it to be possible to show evidence of the low cost/energy efficient claim, that is, what a 'reasonable person' would expect had to be looked at in the context of the particular requirements of the contract. However, the Court of Appeal found there was no breach of s 14(2A); the particular requirements of a buyer in the context of a particular contract were a matter for s 14(3) of the SoGA 1979 (see below), not s 14(2). Under s 14(2A), the factor to consider was the intrinsic quality of the goods; the court should determine what quality a reasonable person would expect from a heating boiler. The court decided a reasonable person would expect a boiler to heat adequately, which these boilers did; the expectations of a reasonable person in relation to these particular boilers (that they were low cost/energy efficient) should be decided under s 14(3). Section 14(2A) must be read subject to s 14(2B), which states:

> ... the quality of the goods includes their state and condition and the following factors (among others) are in appropriate cases aspects of the quality of goods:
> (i)   fitness for all the purposes for which goods of the kind in question are commonly supplied;
> (ii) appearance and finish;
> (iii) freedom from minor defects;
> (iv) safety; and
> (v)   durability.

The SSGA 1994, in replacing s 14(6) of the SoGA 1979, attempted to clarify the meaning of 'satisfactory quality'. An objective test based on the reasonable man was introduced, as well as statutory recognition that second hand goods may have some acceptable minor defects. The factors are to be regarded as a non-exhaustive list, and failure to comply with one of the factors will not necessarily result in goods being classified as being of unsatisfactory quality. Earlier case law may still be relevant in interpreting both ss 14(2A) and 14(2B). For example, the price of the goods may be extremely relevant in the case of second hand goods, but may not be of significance in relation to new goods sold at a reduced price in a sale (see *Business Appliances Specialists Ltd v Nationwide Credit Corp Ltd* (1988)).

In *Rogers v Parish (Scarborough) Ltd* (1987), the buyer bought a Range Rover for £16,000. It transpired that it had a defective engine, gear box and bodywork, all of which were below the standard normally expected of a vehicle costing that much. It was held that the vehicle was not of merchantable quality. The fact that it was driveable and repairable did not satisfy s 14 of the SoGA 1979, as this could only be judged by considering whether it was of a reasonable standard for a vehicle of its type. As a result, the buyer's rejection was valid and he was entitled to recover the purchase price and damages.

With regard to new cars, in *Bernstein v Pamsons Motors (Golders Green) Ltd* (1987), the buyer purchased a new Nissan car for £8,000. He drove it for three weeks, covering some 140 miles. The engine then seized and had to undergo extensive repairs. The buyer rejected the car and refused to take it back after it had been repaired. The court felt that the buyer of a new car was entitled to expect more than the buyer of a second hand car, although how much more was dependent upon the nature of the defect, the length of time that it took to repair it and the price of the vehicle. The court distinguished between 'the merest cosmetic blemish on a new Rolls Royce which might render it unmerchantable, whereas on a humbler car it might not'. However, whilst the car was unmerchantable at the time of delivery, it was further held that a period of three weeks and 140 miles was a reasonable time to examine and try out the goods. The buyer was, therefore, deemed to have accepted the goods within the meaning of s 35 (see below, 7.2.1.8) and could, therefore, only claim for breach of warranty.

It is unlikely that the decisions in *Rogers v Parish* and *Bernstein v Pamsons* in relation to breach of s 14(2) would have been different in the light of the new definition. However, the goods have to be suitable for all their common purposes under s 14(2B), which is an extension of the s 14(6) definition. As a result, *Aswan Engineering Establishment v Lupdine* (1987) (where containers which could fulfil some, though not all, of their normal uses, as now required by s 14(2B), were of merchantable quality) may need to be reconsidered. However, the decision would probably stand in *Kendall (Henry) & Sons v William Lillico & Sons Ltd* (1968) (where groundnut extraction which harmed pheasants was still of merchantable quality, as it could be safely fed to other poultry, which was one of its normal uses) and *Brown & Sons Ltd v Craiks Ltd* (1970) (where cloth which was suitable for its normal industrial use was of merchantable quality, though it was not fit for the buyer's intended purpose of dressmaking).

The factors now specifically include appearance and finish, as well as freedom from minor defects. The former clearly refer to cosmetic defects which may or may not affect the quality of the goods by reference to the type of goods, price, etc. The same is true of minor defects. For example, a scratch on a Rolls Royce may affect quality, whereas a scratch on a second hand Ford Fiesta may not.

Safety is now a specific factor in assessing satisfactory quality, and it would appear that any matter which results in the goods being unsafe will fall within s 14(2).

Finally, durability of the goods also falls to be considered. This raises the contentious issue of the length of time for which a buyer can expect goods to remain of satisfactory quality. However, the test to be applied is that of the reasonable man, that is, an objective test. Again, an assessment of durability can only be made by reference to description, purpose, price, etc. Indeed, it would appear that it will only be in rare situations that these factors are considered in isolation from each other. Where the 2002 Regulations apply, the 'six month' rule will clarify the durability issue in some circumstances (see below, 7.2.1.8).

From the foregoing analysis of s 14(2), it seems clear that the new legislation was designed to address the shortcomings of the old law which the courts had striven to overcome. A clear illustration of this can be found in the fact that the condition of satisfactory quality applies not simply to the goods sold, but to the 'goods supplied under the contract', which could clearly include 'free gifts' supplied with goods and is a confirmation of the Court of Appeal's decision in *Wilson v Rickett Cockerell* (1954). There, an argument that explosives supplied in a bag of Coalite did not amount to a breach of s 14(2), as the section only applied to the goods purchased – the Coalite – was rejected.

Lastly, note should be taken of s 14(2C), which provides for exceptions to the 'satisfactory quality' requirement. Section 14(2C) states that the term does not extend to any 'matter' making the quality of goods unsatisfactory:

- which is specifically drawn to the buyer's attention before the contract is made;

- which examination ought to reveal, where the buyer examines the goods before the contract is made; or

- which, in the case of a contract for sale by sample, would have been apparent on reasonable examination of the sample.

These exceptions are essentially the same as those found previously in the SoGA 1979; so, for example, if somebody buys a sweater labelled 'shop soiled', he or she cannot later argue that marks on the goods rendered them of unsatisfactory quality. Of course, if the sweater also had a hole in the sleeve which had not been drawn to the buyer's attention, this defect could mean that the sweater was not of satisfactory quality.

Nevertheless, it could be argued that the seller may now be able to invoke this exception not by actually specifying the defect (as was previously necessary), but by simply mentioning a 'matter' which could affect quality. Case law on this point is awaited with interest. The relationship of s 14(2C) to goods 'sold as seen' was considered in *Bramhill and Bramhill v Edwards and Edwards* (2004).

It should be remembered that the buyer is under no obligation to actually examine the goods before sale. If, however, the buyer chooses to undertake such an examination, then defects which that examination actually reveal, or ought to have revealed, will be excluded from s 14(2).

The 2002 Regulations add four new sub-sections to s 14(2), which apply where the buyer is a consumer, as defined in the 2002 Regulations. The effect of these additions is that, in determining whether goods are of 'satisfactory quality', the s 14(2B) factors that the court should consider will also include any 'public statements on the specific characteristics of the goods made about them by the seller, the producer or his representative, particularly in advertising or on labelling'. A 'producer' is not only the manufacturer but also a person who imports the goods into the EC or puts his name, sign or trademark on the goods. The English courts have already taken account of this factor but, as far as the retailer is concerned, having the obligation specifically stated in the 2002 Regulations will mean that more care must be taken to check advertisements and labelling of goods. Of course, many such statements will be taken to be 'sales puff', which will not affect the legal position; this was one of the arguments put forward by the company in *Carlill v Carbolic Smoke Ball Co* (1893) as to why their advertisement was not an offer.

It should be noted that this additional factor will not apply if the seller shows that he was not/could not have been aware of the statement, or it had been corrected at the time of contracting, or the buyer could not have been influenced to buy by the statement or the statement had been publicly withdrawn before sale.

Though the additional factor, relating to advertising and labelling statements, only has to be considered by the courts where the buyer is a consumer, nevertheless, where the buyer is a business, the factor may be considered as a 'relevant circumstance' determining 'satisfactory quality' for the purposes of s 14(2A). Thus, those who sell to businesses (for example, manufacturers) may consider their advertising and labelling more carefully.

Reasonable fitness for purpose (s 14(3) of the SoGA 1979)

There is an implied condition in a contract for the sale of goods that the goods supplied are reasonably fit for any purpose expressly or impliedly made known to the seller or credit-broker under s 14(3) of the SoGA 1979. A breach of this section is to be treated as a breach of a condition. A credit-broker is an intermediary; for instance, a furniture shop might allow a buyer to have goods under a credit sale. To achieve this, the goods are sold, 'on paper', to a finance company with whom the buyer then contracts to buy the goods and pay by instalments. Where goods have a normal purpose, the law implies that one buys those goods for that purpose, unless stated otherwise. For example, in the case of *Grant v Australian Knitting Mills* (1936), the purpose of 'underpants' was that they could be worn; in *Godley v Perry* (1960), in purchasing a toy catapult, the buyer did not have to state specifically the purpose for which the object was being bought. Note, also, *Kendall & Sons v Lillico & Sons Ltd* (1969), where resale was held to be a normal purpose of goods. If the purpose is unusual or the goods have several normal but distinct uses, for example, timber for paper or for furniture, then the purpose must be made known expressly – that is, it must be spelt out clearly, either orally or in writing – to the seller before the buyer can rely on this section. An example of this is the case of *Ashington Piggeries v Christopher Hill Ltd* (1972), where the buyers made it clear to the seller that the end product would be fed to mink, even though they supplied the formula.

Whether goods are reasonably fit for the purpose is a question of fact. In *Crowther v Shannon Motor Co* (1975), in determining whether a second hand car which needed a new engine after 2,300 miles was 'reasonably fit', the court said that the age, condition and make of the car should be considered in order to determine what could reasonably be expected of it.

It should also be noted that poor instructions for use, or a failure to give warning of dangers related to the use of the goods which are not generally known, can render the goods unfit for the buyer's purpose (see *Vacwell Engineering Co Ltd v BDH Chemicals Ltd* (1969) and *Wormell v RHM Agriculture (East) Ltd* (1986)). This may explain rather bizarre warnings in instruction booklets, such as advice not to dry underwear or newspapers in microwave ovens!

Section 14(3) indicates that this condition does not apply where the buyer does not rely on the skill and judgment of the seller or credit-broker, for example, where a brand other than that recommended by the seller is chosen or where it is unreasonable for the buyer to have relied on that skill and judgment if he or she had greater expertise (see *Teheran-Europe Corp v ST Belton Ltd* (1968) and *Jewson v Kelly* (2003)). However, even if the buyer selects the product him or herself (for example, from a supermarket shelf), he or she still relies on the seller that the product will fulfil its normal functions.

In *Slater v Finning Ltd* (1996), the seller installed a camshaft in the buyer's vessel. Following a number of repairs and replacements, a new engine had to be installed. The old engine was installed in another vessel with no problems. On the facts, it was concluded that excessive torsional resonance in the vessel caused damage to the camshaft. The buyer argued that, as the seller knew that the camshaft was to be installed in a particular ship, there was reliance on the seller to supply a suitable camshaft for that ship. It was held that there was no breach of condition where the failure of the goods to meet a particular purpose arose from an abnormal feature or idiosyncrasy in the buyer or, as in this case, in the circumstances in which the buyer used the goods, and such was not made known to the seller. In the present case, the camshaft was suitable for use on this type of vessel, which was the extent of the buyer's reliance on the seller. It was only a particular idiosyncrasy of this vessel which made the usual type of camshaft unsuitable. (Compare this case with *Manchester Liners Ltd v Rea* (1922) and see also *Griffiths v Peter Conway Ltd* (1939).)

A final point to note is that reliance on the seller's skill and judgment may be partial, as was shown in *Ashington Piggeries v Christopher Hill Ltd*, where it was held that the buyer, in supplying the formula, did not rely on the seller's skill and judgment that the end product would be suitable for mink (in the sense that he did not rely on the seller that the specified combination of ingredients was suitable for mink), but he did rely on the seller to use ingredients which were not defective. Accordingly, there was a breach of s 14(3).

Sale by sample (s 15 of the SoGA 1979)

Section 15 of the SoGA 1979 imposes an implied condition that, where goods are sold by sample, they will comply with that sample. Furthermore, such goods will be free from any defect making their quality unsatisfactory which would not be apparent on reasonable examination of the sample.

This section applies only if there is a term of the contract which states that it is a contract of sale by sample. This could be an oral term, but if it is in writing then the term about sale by sample must be written into the contract. The mere act of showing a sample of the goods during negotiations does not make the sale one of sale by sample unless the parties agree to this. In *Drummond v Van Ingen* (1887), Lord MacNaughten examined the function of a sample, stating that:

> ... the office of a sample is to present to the real meaning and intention of the parties with regard to the subject matter of the contract, which, owing to the imperfection of language, it may be difficult or impossible to express in words. The sample speaks for itself.

Everyday examples could be the purchase of carpets or wallpaper by reference to a sample book.

It is no defence under s 15(2) to say that the bulk can easily be made to correspond with the sample. In *E & S Ruben Ltd v Faire Bros & Co Ltd* (1949), a material known as Linatex was sold which was crinkled, whereas the sample had been soft and smooth. The seller argued that, by a simple process of warming, the bulk could have been made as soft as the sample. It was held that there had been a breach of s 15(2) and the sellers were, therefore, liable to pay damages to the buyer.

A buyer may not be able to claim damages under s 15(2) of the SoGA 1979 for defects which he or she could reasonably have discovered upon examination of the goods. He or she may still have a claim under s 14(2) and (3). It is important to remember that the implied conditions under s 15 are that:

- the bulk shall correspond with the sample;

- the buyer shall have a reasonable opportunity to compare the goods with the sample; and

- the goods will be free from any defect rendering them unsatisfactory which would not be apparent on reasonable examination of the sample.

7.2.1.5 *Delivery and payment obligations*

By virtue of s 27 of the SoGA 1979, the seller has an obligation to deliver the goods to the buyer, and the buyer has a duty to accept the goods and pay for them, as follows:

- *Seller's delivery obligation*

    The seller's obligation is to deliver the goods at the right time and place and by the correct method.

    A stipulated time for delivery will be considered to be 'of the essence' (that is, a condition of the contract), as will a specified date of shipment of goods. Where the time of delivery is not complied with or, in the absence of an agreed time, a reasonable time has elapsed, the buyer may treat the contract as repudiated for breach of condition. Alternatively, he or she can accept late delivery and sue for damages only.

    In *Rickards v Oppenheim* (1950), the seller contracted to build a car for the buyer by 20 March. It was not ready by that date. The buyer did not repudiate the contract, but pressed for early delivery. When it was still not finished by the end of June, the buyer informed the seller that, if it was not ready in another four weeks, he would regard the contract as repudiated. At the end of four weeks, the car was still not ready. It was held that the buyer had acted within his rights. He lost the right to regard the contract as repudiated on 20 March by his waiver, but it was a condition of that waiver, under those circumstances, that delivery should take place as soon as possible. The buyer could, therefore, revive his right to repudiate the contract by giving reasonable notice. The buyer was under no obligation, after four weeks, to buy the car.

- *Buyer's obligation to accept and pay for the goods*

    Unless the buyer has a right to repudiate the contract for the seller's breach (for example, due to delivery of defective goods), he or she must take and pay for the goods. Failure to do so means that the buyer is in breach of contract and the seller will be able to maintain a claim against him or her for the contract price or for damages for non-acceptance (see below, 7.2.1.6). It should be noted, however, that the *time* of payment is not normally perceived as a condition of the contract unless the parties have expressly agreed otherwise.

7.2.1.6   Seller's personal remedies

Where the buyer is in breach of contract, the seller may seek a remedy against the buyer personally, as follows:

- *Action for the price of the goods*

  The seller can sue for the contract price, under s 49 of the SoGA 1979, where the buyer has failed to pay on the date fixed in the contract, or he or she wrongfully fails to pay, the property in the goods having passed to the buyer (see below, 7.2.1.12).

  If neither of these conditions applies and the buyer wrongfully refuses to take and pay for the goods, he or she cannot be sued for the contract price. If this were allowed, the seller would have both the money and the goods. Instead, the seller may sue for damages for non-acceptance.

  The Late Payment of Commercial Debts (Interest) Act 1998 provides for statutory interest to accrue on debts paid late in certain circumstances.

- *Damages for non-acceptance of the goods*

  This right is given by s 50(1) and, according to sub-s (2), the measure of damages, as in *Hadley v Baxendale* (1854), is the loss arising naturally from the breach. However, in this context, note should be taken of sub-s (3), which imposes an obligation on the seller to mitigate his or her loss by reselling the goods that the buyer has refused to accept. Where there is an available market for the goods in question, the measure of damages is *prima facie* to be ascertained by the difference between the contract price and the market or current price at the time or times when the goods ought to have been accepted, or, if no time was fixed for acceptance, at the time of refusal to accept (see *WL Thompson Ltd v Robinson Gunmakers Ltd* (1955) and *Charter v Sullivan* (1957)). Currently, problems might arise in applying sub-s (3) because of constant 'price wars', which may make it difficult to determine the 'market' or 'current' price.

7.2.1.7   Seller's real remedies

A seller may not be able to pursue personal remedies against the buyer because, for example, the buyer has gone into liquidation. However, in such circumstances, he or she may be able to use his or her 'real' remedies by taking action against the goods, as follows:

- *Lien (ss 41–43 of the SoGA 1979)*

  The seller has the right to retain possession of the goods, even though the property has passed to the buyer. The SoGA 1979 assumes that delivery and payment are normally concurrent events, except where sales are on credit. The lien, or right to keep the goods, is based on possession of the goods and is only available for the price of the goods, and not for other debts such as storage charges. It may be a useful remedy in times of economic stress where there are rumours of bankruptcies and liquidations. The unpaid seller may well be better off financially with the goods in his or her possession than if he or she had simply become a creditor in the bankruptcy.

Delivery of part of the goods will not destroy the unpaid seller's lien unless the circumstances show an intention to waive the lien. The unpaid seller will lose his or her lien if the goods are delivered for carriage to the buyer and he or she does not reserve the right of disposal over them or if the buyer lawfully obtains possession of the goods.

- *Stoppage in transit (ss 44–46 of the SoGA 1979)*

If the buyer becomes insolvent and the goods are still in transit between the seller and the buyer, the unpaid seller is given the right of stoppage in transit and can recover the goods from the carrier. The cost of re-delivery must be borne by the seller in this case.

- *Right of resale*

An unpaid seller can pass a good title to the goods to a second buyer after exercising a right of lien or stoppage in transit. In these cases, the contract with the first buyer is automatically rescinded, so that the property in the goods reverts to the seller, who can keep any further profit made from the resale and any deposit put down by the buyer. If a loss is made on the resale, then he or she can claim damages from the original buyer. There is no requirement that the second purchaser takes delivery or buys in good faith (that is, without knowledge of the first sale).

In *Ward (RV) Ltd v Bignall* (1967), two cars were being sold for £850. After paying a deposit of £25, the buyer refused to pay the remainder. The seller informed the buyer in writing that, if he did not pay the balance by a given date, he would resell the cars. The buyer did not pay. The seller sold one car at £350 but failed to find a purchaser for the other. He brought a claim against the purchaser for the balance of the price and advertising expenses. It was held that the seller could not recover any of the price, since the ownership had reverted back to him, but he could recover damages. The remaining car was worth £450, so that his total loss on resale would be £50, minus the £25 deposit originally paid. He was entitled to this £25 plus advertising expenses.

- *Reservation of title (s 19 of the SoGA 1979)*

Section 19(1) of the SoGA 1979 indicates that in contracts for the sale of specific goods, or where goods have been appropriated to the contract (see below, 7.2.1.12), the seller can reserve the right to dispose of the goods. Effectively, he or she can insert a clause in the contract under which the property in the goods does not pass to the buyer (even if he or she is in possession of the goods) until payment is made. This could protect an unpaid seller where the buyer is in liquidation. If the buyer owns the goods, the liquidator can sell them and the money raised goes towards paying all creditors. The seller would merely be a creditor for the purchase price and might only receive a small part of the price if there is insufficient to pay all creditors in full. Clearly, it is better for the seller to retain ownership, so that he or she can resell the goods.

• *The Romalpa clause*

This arose from the case of *Aluminium Industrie Vassen BV v Romalpa Aluminium Ltd* (1976), which established that the manufacturer or supplier of goods had rights to retain some proprietary interest over the goods until paid for, even when the goods supplied had been processed or sold. Furthermore, proprietary rights could be maintained even after a sub-sale of the goods (sale by the buyer to another party), so that debts owed to the buyer could be transferred to the manufacturer or supplier if an appropriate *Romalpa* clause had been inserted.

7.2.1.8 Buyer's remedies

Action for specific performance (s 52(1) of the SoGA 1979)

The court can make an order of specific performance against the seller in the case of a contract to deliver specific or ascertained goods; the order cannot be made for unascertained or future goods (see below, 7.2.1.12). The seller is required to deliver the goods and is not given the option of paying damages instead. The courts will not make the order for such a remedy unless damages for non-delivery would not be adequate. Damages will generally be adequate, except where the goods are in some way unique or rare.

Remedies for breach of condition

Where the seller is in *breach of condition*, the buyer can treat the contract as repudiated. Accordingly, he or she can *reject* the goods, claim a *refund* of the price paid or refuse payment and claim *damages* for further loss suffered; however, where the seller is in *breach of warranty*, the buyer may only sue for damages for breach of contract.

It is useful to note that, from a practical point of view, the buyer who sues for breach of implied terms of the SoGA 1979 would be well advised to sue for breach of more than one implied term, in order to increase his or her chances of success. In *Godley v Perry* (1960) (see above, 7.2.1.4), the child successfully pleaded breaches of s 14(2) and (3). There may appear to be an overlap of the provisions of the implied terms on the facts of some cases, but all the implied terms are needed to protect a buyer. For example, if one purchased a brand new washing machine and it was delivered badly dented but in full working order, one could claim that it was not of satisfactory quality under s 14(2). However, as it worked properly, there would be no breach of s 13 or 14(3).

Rejection of goods means refusing to take delivery or informing the seller that they are rejected and returning the goods. A buyer in possession of rejected goods will often take them back to the seller, but is under no obligation to do so; the seller has the obligation to collect rejected goods from the buyer (s 36 of the SoGA 1979). The buyer does not have a lien over rejected goods and must hand them back, even if the purchase price paid has not been refunded.

Section 15A of the SoGA 1979 may now limit the right to reject goods for 'technical' breaches of condition, as occurred in cases such as *Re Moore & Co v Landauer & Co* (1921). The courts are now given the right to refuse to allow rejection of goods by a business buyer for breach of s 13, 14 or 15 where 'the breach is so slight that it would be unreasonable for him to reject them'. In such circumstances, the buyer may instead sue for damages for breach of warranty, though it should be noted that the effect of s 15A can be circumvented by a 'contrary intention' in or be 'implied from' the contract. Whether the breach is 'slight' is a question of fact in each case. Section 15A does not apply where the buyer is a consumer. Guidance on whether or not a person 'deals as consumer' can be found in UCTA 1977, which provides that a person deals as consumer if the contract is not made in the course of a business, if the other party does not make the contract in the course of a business and if the goods are of a type ordinarily supplied for private use or consumption. This has a wide remit and, since the burden is on the seller to prove that the buyer does not deal as consumer, the average sale of goods contract is unlikely to be affected. However, it should be noted that the 2002 Regulations omit the requirement that the goods are of a type 'ordinarily supplied for private use or consumption'.

Section 35A of the SoGA 1979 deserves consideration, as it gives the buyer a wider right of *partial* rejection than did s 30(4), which has been repealed. In line with what many businesspersons would do in practice, the buyer has now been given the right to choose to accept those goods which do conform with the contract and to reject those which do not.

Where the buyer claims a *refund* of the price paid, he or she can recover all payments made if the consideration has failed. This may apply to cases of non-delivery, but may also apply where there has been a breach of condition of the sale. If the contract is severable (for example, where there are separate delivery times and instalments for different parts of the goods), the buyer can accept part and reject part of the goods and recover the price paid on the rejected goods.

The buyer's *claim for damages* may be for non-delivery or for breach of condition or warranty. Where the claim is for damages for non-delivery, damages may be recovered for losses arising naturally from the breach (s 51(2) of the SoGA 1979), but this may not allow a buyer to claim the whole of the profit he or she expected to gain by resale of the goods which the seller has failed to deliver. He or she is required to mitigate his or her loss by purchasing replacement goods for resale, and the measure of damages to which he or she is entitled is the difference between the contract price and the current or market price which he or she would have to pay for replacements, assuming that it is higher (s 51(3) of the SoGA 1979).

Damages for breach of condition are assessed according to the usual contractual rules, but it should be noted that if the buyer has 'accepted' a breach of condition, he or she can only treat it as a breach of warranty (s 11(4) of the SoGA; but note also that s 11(4) must be read subject to s 35, which is discussed below, 7.2.1.9). Claims for damages for breach may include a claim for loss of a sub-sale or for damages payable to a sub-buyer, if the seller knew or ought to have known of the possibility of a sub-sale. The whole issue of sub-sales was examined in *Louis Dreyfus Trading Ltd v Reliance Trading Ltd* (2004).

Damages for breach of warranty

These are assessed according to the provisions of s 53 of the SoGA 1979, which, in particular, indicate the measure as *prima facie* the difference between the value of the goods at the time of delivery to the buyer and the value they would have had if they had fulfilled the warranty.

The buyer's right to claim any of the remedies described above may be affected by:

- acceptance of a breach of condition; or

- an exclusion or limitation clause.

Additional remedies under the 2002 Regulations

The 2002 Regulations give additional remedies to the buyer of goods which do not conform with the contract of sale, who deals as a 'consumer', by adding s 48(A)–(D) to the SoGA 1979. The additional remedies are replacement, repair, reduction in price and rescission. Whilst such remedies were previously given voluntarily by sellers, there was no legal obligation to do so. The 2002 Regulations also indicate that if the buyer chooses replacement or repair, he cannot reject for breach of condition until he has given the seller a reasonable time to carry out the chosen remedial action. The right to such remedies is further limited by reference to whether they are disproportionate in relation to other remedies available or are impossible. So, for example, if repair costs more than replacement, a claim for repair could not be enforced.

Section 48(A)(3) of the SoGA 1979 indicates that if the goods do not conform with the contract of sale at any time within six months of the transfer of ownership to the buyer, it will be presumed that they did not conform at the time property was transferred. The effect of this provision is that the buyer would not bear the burden of proving that non-conformity existed at the time the goods were supplied to him. However, it should be appreciated that:

- as a presumption, it is rebuttable by evidence to the contrary; and

- the 'six month' rule only applies in relation to a claim for the additional remedies given by the Regulations.

7.2.1.9 *Acceptance*

As already stated above, acceptance of a breach of condition deprives the buyer of the right to reject the goods and claim a refund or refuse payment. It does not deprive him or her of all remedies; he or she is still entitled to claim damages for breach of warranty.

The rules relating to what amounts to 'acceptance' are contained in s 35 of the SoGA 1979 (these rules were amended by the SSGA 1994), which indicates that acceptance occurs when either:

- the buyer states to the seller that the goods are acceptable, for example, where an acceptance note is signed; or

- the goods have been delivered to the buyer and he or she does an act in relation to them which is inconsistent with the ownership of the seller, for example, selling the goods or processing them.

The rules on when acceptance takes place are subject to s 35(2), which provides the buyer with an opportunity to examine the goods in the following circumstances:

> Where goods are delivered to the buyer, and he has not previously examined them, he is not deemed to have accepted them until he has had a reasonable opportunity of examining them for the purpose –
> (a) of ascertaining whether they are in conformity with the contract; and
> (b) in the case of a contract for sale by sample, of comparing the bulk with the sample.
> This right cannot be removed or excluded in consumer sales.

Although s 34(1) of the SoGA 1979 has been repealed, s 34 continues to provide that, subject to agreement, the seller is bound on request to afford the buyer a reasonable opportunity of examining the goods for the purpose of ascertaining whether they conform with the contract. Following s 35(2), acceptance cannot take place until this examination has been carried out.

Section 35(4) continues to provide that acceptance is also deemed to have taken place when the buyer retains the goods after a reasonable length of time without intimating to the seller that they will be rejected. What amounts to a reasonable length of time has to be considered in conjunction with the reasonable opportunity to examine the goods. It will be a question of fact in each case, as illustrated in *Bernstein v Pamsons Motors* (1987) (see above, 7.2.1.4), where the car was held to be neither of merchantable quality nor fit for the purpose, but the plaintiff was deemed to have accepted the car under s 35 and, therefore, could only treat the breach of condition as a warranty and claim damages. The court felt that 'reasonable time' meant a reasonable time to try out the goods, not a reasonable time to discover the defect.

As a result of the new provisions, the decision in *Bernstein* would be different today. In *Clegg v Andersson* (2003), a yacht did not comply with the manufacturer's specifications, as required by the contract of sale. The buyer asked the seller for information to enable him to decide whether to have repairs carried out; whilst awaiting the information, the buyer registered and insured the yacht. After five months, the information was supplied, and three weeks later the buyer rejected the yacht. The Court of Appeal decided that registration and insurance of the vessel were not acts inconsistent with the seller's ownership and that the request for information was not an intimation of acceptance. Furthermore, the buyer had not retained the yacht for more than a reasonable time, given the circumstances, and *Bernstein* was no longer good law. Accordingly, the buyer had not accepted the yacht.

A further clarification of the rules on acceptance has been provided by s 35(6). A buyer is not deemed to have accepted the goods merely because he or she has requested or agreed to their repair. As it had been thought that agreeing to repair might amount to acceptance, this section provides a useful addition to consumer protection.

Whilst the 'traditional' remedies of rejection and refund are lost by acceptance, the 2002 Regulations make no correlation between acceptance and the new remedies (see above, 7.2.1.8). Therefore, it is arguable that the new remedies could be available for the six year limitation period for breach of contract claims.

7.2.1.10   Exclusion and limitation of liability

The rules of UCTA 1977 relating to the ability to exclude or limit liability for breach of contract are discussed above (see Chapter 6) but, in so far as they apply to contracts for the sale of goods, they can be summarised as follows:

- Section 12 of the SoGA 1979 cannot be excluded in consumer or non-consumer sales (the distinction between consumer and non-consumer sales is covered by s 12(1) of UCTA 1977).

- In consumer sales (for example, where an individual buys goods from a shop), liability for breach of ss 13–15 of the SoGA 1979 cannot be excluded. Businesses should be aware that it is a criminal offence to include a term in a contract, or to display a notice, which purports to exclude the statutory implied terms or restrict liability for their breach as against a person who deals as a consumer (by virtue of the Consumer Transactions (Restrictions on Statements) Order 1976 (SI 1976/1813), as amended by SI 1998/127; the power to make such orders is now given to the Secretary of State by the Enterprise Act 2002). Accordingly, a notice in a shop which states 'No refunds' is a criminal offence, but one which states 'No refunds, except on faulty goods' does not contravene the Order, as there is no obligation to give refunds, except where they are legally faulty under ss 13–15 of the SoGA 1979.

The 2002 Regulations indicate that, for the purposes of ss 13–15 of the SoGA 1979, the definition of a consumer sale in s 12(1) of UCTA 1977 will not apply. Instead, there is a new definition:

> ... a party deals as a consumer where –
> (a) he is a natural person who makes the contract otherwise than in the course of a business; and
> (b) the other party does make the contract in the course of a business.

Thus, the s 12(1) of UCTA 1977 requirement that the goods be of a type ordinarily supplied for private use and consumption is omitted. However, there will not be a consumer sale for the purposes of exclusion of liability for breaches of ss 13–15 of the SoGA 1979 if the buyer is an individual buying second hand goods at a public auction which consumers may attend in person. Nor will there be a consumer sale where an individual buys at auction or by competitive tender.

- In non-consumer sales, it is possible to exclude liability for breach of ss 13–15 of the SoGA 1979, provided that the exclusion clause satisfies the test of 'reasonableness'. The requirement of reasonableness means that the exclusion clause 'shall be a fair and reasonable one to be included, having regard to the circumstances which were or ought to have been known to or in the contemplation of the parties when the contract was made'.

  UCTA 1977 provides that, in determining 'reasonableness', regard shall be had in particular to guidelines stated in Sched 2 (as listed above, Chapter 6), such as 'whether the customer received an inducement to agree to the term'. A clause in a contract which states that 'The seller undertakes no liability for defects in the goods sold in return for granting the purchaser a 20% price discount' could be considered under this guideline.

- Any other liability for breach of contract can be excluded or restricted only to the extent that it is reasonable.

- Exclusion of liability for death and personal injury caused by negligence is prohibited.

- It is possible to exclude liability for other loss or damage arising from negligence or misrepresentation only to the extent that the clause is deemed to be reasonable.

  In addition, the Unfair Terms in Consumer Contracts Regulations 1999 (SI 1999/2083) provide further protection with respect to exclusion or other unfair terms in consumer contracts where the term has not been individually negotiated, such as may be found in a standard form contract. 'Consumer' in this context is confined to natural persons not acting in the course of business and is, therefore, currently narrower than UCTA 1977 (see 6.3.5.3).

  A basic requirement of the Regulations is that written contractual terms are 'expressed in plain, intelligible language'.

  An unfair term is defined in regs 5 and 6 as 'any term which, contrary to the requirement of good faith, causes a significant imbalance in the parties' rights and obligations under the contract to the detriment of the consumer'. Such terms are not unlawful *per se*, but can be challenged on the basis that they are contrary to good faith. Schedule 2 contains an indicative, though not exhaustive, list of terms which may be unfair.

  A consumer wishing to challenge a term under the Regulations can ask the court to find that the unfair term should not be binding. This allows the remaining terms of the contract to stand. In addition, the Office of Fair Trading, on receipt of a complaint, has the power to obtain an injunction against unfair terms which would allow a challenge to be made against particular terms in standard form contracts. This power is also given to other bodies, such as Weights & Measures Authorities and the Data Protection Registrar.

7.2.1.11   Guarantees

Many consumer goods, such as electrical appliances, are sold with a voluntary guarantee given by the seller or manufacturer. These often give the right to replacement or repair. It should be noted that these rights are not given *instead* of statutory rights under ss 13–15 of the SoGA 1979; they are simply rights which the consumer may choose to exercise against the person giving the guarantee. The person giving the guarantee is obliged by law to insert a statement to the effect that 'Statutory rights are not affected' (Consumer Transactions (Restrictions on Statements) Order 1976 (SI 1976/1813), as amended). Furthermore, it should be noted that exercising the right to repair under a guarantee does not necessarily amount to 'acceptance' of the goods depriving the buyer of the right to reject them for breach of condition (see above, 7.2.1.9).

Under the 2002 Regulations, these voluntary (or 'commercial') guarantees are further controlled. The new controls operate where a natural person who acts outside the course of a business is supplied with goods under a contract and is also given a guarantee. The main provisions of the 2002 Regulations are as follows:

- The guarantee creates a contract between the consumer and the guarantor, subject to any conditions stated in the guarantee or associated advertising.

- The guarantee must be in plain, intelligible language, written in English where the goods are supplied within the UK, and must indicate how to claim under the guarantee, its duration and the name and address of the guarantor. Furthermore, the consumer may require that a copy of the guarantee, in writing or other durable medium, be made available to him or her within a reasonable time.

Failure to comply with these provisions allows enforcement of an injunction against the guarantor.

From 6 April 2005, the rules of the Supply of Extended Warranties on Domestic Electrical Goods Order 2005 (SI 2005/37) apply to retailers and to manufacturers who supply directly to consumers. The Order is aimed at businesses who charge for the extended warranties they supply with domestic electrical goods, and results from findings of the Competition Commission that consumers were often pressurised to buy such warranties and that prices charged were often higher than was necessary. The Order seeks to regulate such practices by, for instance, requiring retailers to show the price of extended warranties alongside the goods, in stores, catalogues, printed advertisements and on websites. Consumers must also be given detailed information about their statutory rights in relation to the warranty and have the right to cancel the extended warranty agreement.

7.2.1.12   Transfer of property and risk

The main essential of the s 2 of the SoGA 1979 definition is the transfer of property (ownership) to the buyer. It is important to know when property is transferred because:

- if the property has passed, the unpaid seller can sue the buyer for the agreed contract price (s 49(1) of the SoGA 1979; see above, 7.2.1.6); and

- as a general rule, risk passes with property (s 20(1) of the SoGA 1979), although this rule may be varied by agreement or custom. In such circumstances, it will become necessary to ascertain who bears the financial risk of loss of the goods – the seller or the buyer. ('Risk' determines who bears the cost of accidental loss or damage; that is, loss or damage caused by reasons beyond the control of the seller, buyer or their employees.) Various possibilities can complicate the situation. It is possible that the title to the goods has passed to the buyer and yet he or she still does not have possession. Similarly, it is possible that the buyer has the goods in his or her possession but the title to the goods, and therefore the risk, has not yet passed. The 2002 Regulations add s 20(4) to the SoGA 1979, which indicates that s 20(1) does not apply where the buyer deals as a consumer; the goods remain at the seller's risk until they are delivered to the buyer. Section 20(4) also applies to s 20(2) (below).

The Act gives detailed rules for determining when property is transferred and divides goods into four categories:

- *Specific goods*

  These are goods which are identified and agreed upon at the time of contracting (for example, a contract to buy a particular second hand car). The term also includes a share in a specific bulk which has not been divided up at the time of contracting, expressed as a percentage or fraction (s 61 of the SoGA 1979). For example, a contract for the sale of '50% of the seller's 100 tons of grain in the warehouse' would be a sale of specific goods, but the sale of '50 tons of the 100 tons of grain in the seller's warehouse' would not be a sale of specific goods, as the goods are not expressed as a percentage or fraction of the 100 tons.

- *Unascertained goods*

  This means that the seller possesses goods of the type that the buyer (B) agrees to buy but, at the time of contracting, B does not know exactly which goods he or she will get. For example, B agrees to buy a sofa like the one on show but, at the time of contracting, B does not know which of six such sofas in stock he or she will actually get. In this context, note s 16, which states: '... where there is a contract for the sale of unascertained goods, no property in the goods is transferred to the buyer unless and until the goods are ascertained.' However, s 16 must now be read subject to s 20A (see below).

- *Ascertained goods*

  These are goods identified after the making of the contract. Thus, when B agrees to buy one of the six sofas that the shop has in stock, the goods will not be ascertained until one of the sofas is labelled/set aside for B.

- *Future goods*

  These are goods to be manufactured or acquired by the seller after the making of the contract of sale. As a general rule, future goods will be unascertained.

Subject, of course, to the provisions of s 16, s 17 of the SoGA 1979 provides that the property passes when the parties intend it to pass and, in determining this, regard should be had to the terms of the contract, the conduct of the parties and all other circumstances. A reservation of title clause (see above, 7.2.1.7) is a common example of an expression of the parties' intention. Where the parties have not agreed on a time at which property is to pass (as would be common in consumer transactions), s 18 determines the time of transfer, as described below.

The passing of property in specific goods

The general rule for the passing of property in specific goods is that, if a contract of sale is unconditional, property passes to the buyer when the contract is made (s 18 r 1). This is subject to the intention of the parties. In *Re Anchor Line (Henderson Bros Ltd)* (1937), a crane was sold to buyers, who agreed to pay annual sums for depreciation. It was held that the buyers would not have paid depreciation on their own goods, so the intention must be inferred that the property in the goods remained with the sellers until the price was fully paid.

In *Dennant v Skinner and Collam* (1948), a gentleman bought a car at an auction and, later, signed a form to the effect that the ownership of the vehicle would not pass to him until his cheque had been cleared. He sold the car to a third party and there followed a dispute about the ownership of the car. It was held that the contract was complete and ownership passed as the auctioneer's hammer fell. The third party therefore acquired a good title to the car. If s 18 r 1 is satisfied, property passes immediately.

If the contract is for the sale of specific goods, but the seller is bound to do something to them to put them in a deliverable state, then ownership does not pass until that thing is done and the buyer has notice that it is done (s 18 r 2).

In *Underwood v Burgh Castle Brick and Cement Syndicate* (1922), the parties entered a contract for the sale of an engine weighing 30 tons. At the time that the contract was made, the engine was embedded in a concrete floor. Whilst it was being removed and loaded onto a truck, it was damaged. The seller still sued for the price. It was held that the engine was not in a deliverable state when the contract was made and, applying r 2, property would not pass until the engine was safely loaded on the truck; the seller must, therefore, bear the risk.

If the goods are to be weighed, tested or measured by the seller, or are to be subjected to some other act or thing for the purpose of ascertaining the price, the property will not pass until the process is complete and the buyer is informed, unless there is a specific agreement to the contrary (s 18 r 3).

Where goods are supplied on sale or return or on approval, property passes to the buyer when:

- the buyer signifies approval or acceptance to the seller (see *Kirkham v Attenborough* (1897));

- the buyer does any other act adopting the transaction; or

- the buyer, whilst not giving approval or acceptance, retains the goods beyond the agreed time or, if no time is agreed, beyond a reasonable time (s 18 r 4). In *Poole v Smith's Car Sales (Balham) Ltd* (1962), following several requests by the seller for the return of his car, which had been left at a garage on a sale or return basis, the car was returned damaged. It was held that, as the car had not been returned within a reasonable time, property had passed to the defendant, who would then be liable for the price.

Section 18 rr 1–4 clearly apply where the specific goods are those identified and agreed upon at the time of sale, but the s 61 of the SoGA 1979 definition of specific goods also includes a share in a specific bulk which has not been divided up at the time of contracting and which is expressed as a percentage or fraction. Though such goods would be unascertained at the time of contracting, they are defined as 'specific goods'. Unfortunately, there is no statutory provision stating when the property is to pass.

The passing of property in unascertained goods

No property passes in unascertained or future goods, unless and until the goods become ascertained (s 16). Section 18 r 5 provides that:

> ... where there is a contract for the sale of unascertained or future goods by description, and goods of that description and in a deliverable state are unconditionally appropriated to the contract, either by the seller with the assent of the buyer or by the buyer with the assent of the seller, the property in the goods then passes to the buyer and the assent may be express or implied, and may be given either before or after the appropriation is made.

In *Carlos Federspiel & Co v Charles Twigg & Co Ltd* (1957), it was held that goods are unconditionally appropriated to the contract if they have been 'irrevocably earmarked' for use in that contract.

Where the seller places the goods in the hands of a carrier for transmission to the buyer, this is deemed to be 'unconditional appropriation', unless he or she reserves the right to dispose of the goods (s 18 r 5(2)).

This is further illustrated by the case of *McDougall v Aeromarine of Emsworth Ltd* (1958), in which the seller agreed to build a yacht for the buyer. As part of the agreement, after the first instalment was paid, the yacht and all the materials were intended to become the 'absolute property' of the buyer. It was held that no property could pass to the buyer, since the goods were not physically in existence at that time.

In *Healy v Howlett* (1917), 190 boxes of fish were carried by rail. The buyer was to purchase 20 boxes and the seller directed the railway company to set aside 20 boxes. However, before this could be done, the fish went rotten. The seller had sent the buyer an invoice, stating that the fish were carried at the buyer's sole risk. It was held that since the fish had gone rotten before the goods were ascertained, property could not pass to the buyer, who was, therefore, entitled to reject the goods. Obviously, the critical factor in this case was the failure on the part of the railway company to identify the

20 boxes by setting them aside for the buyer. It would have been untenable for future buyers if the courts had made the buyer 'bear the loss' in these circumstances.

Section 18 r 5(3) provides for ascertainment by exhaustion. This occurs where the goods are part of a designated bulk and the bulk is reduced to a quantity which is equal or less than the contract quantity. In these circumstances, the goods will be deemed to be appropriated. For example, a buyer agrees to buy 200 cases of wine from 500 cases stored in the seller's warehouse. The seller then sells and delivers 300 cases to another buyer. The remaining 200 cases are then deemed to be appropriated to the contract and property passes to the buyer when the 300 cases are removed from the warehouse.

Section 16 must be considered in the light of the new s 20A, which provides that where the buyer purchases a specified quantity (for example, 100 tons, but not a quantity expressed as a percentage or fraction of the whole) from an identified bulk source, and has paid for some or all of the goods forming part of the bulk, the buyer becomes co-owner of the bulk. No specific provision is made for the passing of risk in such situations, but it has been suggested that if the bulk is partially destroyed before the shares of several buyers are divided, they bear the risk, and so suffer loss proportionate to the size of their undivided shares. (See Dobson, P, 'Sale of goods forming part of a bulk' (1995) 16 SLR 11.)

Exceptions to s 20(1) of the SoGA 1979

Though the general rule is that property and risk pass together, there are exceptions to this rule, as follows:

- Under s 20(2), 'where delivery has been delayed through the fault of either buyer or seller, the goods are at the risk of the party at fault as regards any loss which might not have occurred but for such fault'. The rule is subject to s 20(4) (above).

- The contract or trade custom may indicate that the passing of property and risk is separated. For example, in a 'cif' (cost, insurance and freight) contract, goods are sold abroad and carriage by sea is part of the contract. In such contracts, property passes to the buyer on loading for sea transit; risk does not pass until later, when the seller sends the shipping documents to the buyer against payment.

Consequences of bearing the 'risk'

- If the buyer bears the risk at the time of loss or damage, he or she must pay for the goods and cannot claim for breach of condition when he or she receives no goods or damaged goods.

- If the seller bears the risk at the time of loss or damage and the contract was for future or unascertained goods, he or she must, at his or her own expense, get a replacement to deliver; otherwise, he or she will be in breach of condition by failure to deliver or by delivering damaged goods.

- Under s 7 of the SoGA 1979, where there is a contract for the sale of specific goods and they perish whilst at the seller's risk, the contract is frustrated (see above, 6.5.3).

Note that the rules of the Law Reform (Frustrated Contracts) Act 1943 do not apply to s 7 situations.

7.2.1.13   *Sale by a person who is not the owner*

There is an implied condition in s 12 of the SoGA 1979 that the seller has a right to sell the goods, that is, pass on a good title to them. The rule *nemo dat quod non habet* means that a person cannot give what he or she has not got, so that, in general, ownership is protected. The general rule is that where goods are sold by a person who is not the owner, the buyer acquires no better title than the seller (s 21 of the SoGA 1979). However, there are exceptions, and the law may often have to choose between the rights of two innocent parties – the innocent purchaser and the real owner of the goods. Generally, the buyer will have to return the goods to the true owner, usually without any recompense, although where the goods have been 'improved', the buyer may be entitled to some reimbursement.

If the innocent purchaser does not get good title, he or she may sue the seller for breach of s 12(1) f the SoGA 1979. See *Rowland v Divall* (1923) (above, 7.2.1.4). The exceptions to the *nemo dat* rule are as follows:

* *Estoppel*

   If the seller or buyer, by his or her conduct, makes the other party believe that a certain fact is true, and the other party alters his or her position, then that same party will later be estopped (or prevented) from saying that the fact is untrue. This has arisen where a party has, for complicated reasons, signed a statement that their own property belongs to someone else and then ends up 'buying back' their own property. They may be estopped from denying the statement that they made falsely about the ownership of the property (*Eastern Distributors Ltd v Goldring* (1957)).

   In order to make a successful claim, estoppel can only be raised against a person who had actual knowledge of the facts and actually agreed to them, knowing that a third party might rely on the 'apparent' authority.

* *Agency*

   If a principal appoints an agent to sell his or her goods to a third party, then any sale by the agent, in accordance with the instructions given, will pass on a good title to the third party. If, however, the agent has exceeded the instructions in some way, then no title will pass to the third party unless the agent had apparent authority (*Central Newbury Car Auctions v Unity Finance* (1957)).

* *Mercantile agency*

   A third party has an even stronger claim to the title of the goods where the agent is a mercantile agent. A mercantile agent is one 'having in the customary course of business as such agent, authority either to sell goods or to consign goods for the purposes of sale or to buy goods, or to raise money on the security of goods' (s 1(1) of the Factors Act 1889). So, for example, where the third party, as a consumer, buys a car from an agent who is in the car trade, this provision may apply.

The Factors Act 1889 states that the owner is bound by the actions of a mercantile agent in the following circumstances:

- ○ If the agent has possession of the goods or the documents of title, with the owner's consent, and makes any sale, pledge or other disposition of them in the ordinary course of business, whether or not the owner authorised it (s 2(1); *Folkes v King* (1923)). Any third party claiming against the owner in this situation must prove, *inter alia*, that, at the time of the sale, he or she had no notice of the lack of authority on the part of the agent.

- ○ In *Pearson v Rose and Young* (1951), the owner of a car took it to a dealer and asked him to obtain offers. The owner did not intend to hand over the registration book, but left it with the dealer by mistake. The dealer sold the car with the book to an innocent buyer. The question of true ownership of the car was raised. It was held that the dealer had obtained the car 'with the consent of the owner' but this consent did not extend to the registration book; hence, the sale must be treated as a sale without registration book which was not in the ordinary course of business, and the buyer could not get a good title to the car.

- ○ If the mercantile agent pledges goods as security for a prior debt, the pledgee acquires no better right to the goods than the factor has against his or her principal at the time of the pledge (s 4).

- ○ If the mercantile agent pledges goods in consideration of either the delivery of the goods or a document of title to goods or a negotiable security, the pledgee acquires no right in the goods pledged beyond the value of the goods, documents or security when so delivered in exchange (s 5).

- ○ If the mercantile agent has received possession of goods from their owner for the purpose of consignment or sale and the consignee has no notice that the agent is not the owner, the consignee has a lien on the goods for any advances he or she has made to the agent (s 7).

- *Sales authorised by law*

There are cases in which the title does not pass directly from the owner, because the sale is authorised by the court, for example, the sale of goods which are the subject matter of legal proceedings. Similarly, in common law or by statute, it is sometimes declared that a non-owner is entitled to sell goods, for example, an unpaid seller (see above, 7.2.1.7).

- *Sale in market overt (s 22 of the SoGA 1979)*

This was a rule relating to well established open public markets in England and shops within the City of London. These rules did not apply in Scotland and Wales. When goods were sold in such 'markets', at business premises, in the normal hours of business between sunrise and sunset, the buyer would obtain a good title as long as he bought the goods in good faith and without notice of the defect in title on the part of the seller (*Reid v Metropolitan Police Commissioner* (1974)). The Sale of Goods (Amendment) Act 1994, which came into force in January 1995, has abolished this exception to the *nemo dat* rule, although it should be noted that its effect is not retrospective.

- *Sale under a voidable title (s 23 of the SoGA 1979)*

Where a buyer obtains goods by fraud, he or she acquires a voidable title in them and has title unless and until the seller avoids the contract, so that the title in the goods reverts to him or her. The seller may avoid the contract by telling the buyer that he or she avoids or by, for example, informing the police. If the person who obtained the goods by fraud resells them before the original seller avoids the contract, the buyer in good faith who did not know that the person who sold the goods to him or her had a defective title acquires good title and keeps the goods. In *Car & Universal Finance Co v Caldwell* (1965), the buyer obtained a car by fraud, paying by a cheque, which was dishonoured. The seller told the police and then the buyer resold the car to a purchaser, who was later found by the court not to have acted in good faith. The original owner had good title and could recover the car, because he had avoided the buyer's title *before* he resold the car *and* the person who subsequently purchased the car was not an innocent purchaser.

- *Disposition by a seller in possession (s 24 of the SoGA 1979)*

A contract of sale can be complete and valid even where the goods are still in the possession of the seller, for example, when they are awaiting delivery. If, in this scenario, the seller sells the goods to a second buyer, the second buyer will obtain a good title to those goods if delivery of them is taken. However, the goods must be taken in good faith and without notice of the original sale. This leaves the first buyer in the position of having to sue the seller for breach of contract.

In *Pacific Motor Auctions Ltd v Motor Credits (Hire Finance)* Ltd (1965), a car dealer sold a number of vehicles to the plaintiffs under a 'display agreement'. This allowed the seller to retain possession of the cars for display in their showroom. He was paid 90% of the purchase price and was authorised to sell the cars as agent for the plaintiff. The seller got into financial difficulties and the plaintiffs revoked their authority to sell the cars. However, the dealer sold a number of them to the defendants, who took them in good faith and without notice of the previous sale. Whilst the defendants knew about the 'display agreement', it was presumed that the dealer had the authority to sell the cars; as a result, it was held that s 24 applied and that, as the defendant had obtained a good title to the car, the plaintiff would fail in their claim for the return of the vehicles.

- *Disposition by a buyer in possession (s 25 of the SoGA 1979)*

Disposition by a buyer in possession is a corresponding situation, where the buyer possesses the goods but the seller has retained property in them. Then, if the buyer has the goods and any necessary documents of title with the consent of the seller and transfers these to an innocent transferee (second buyer), that transferee will obtain a good title to the goods; again, this is subject to the proviso that the second buyer takes the goods in good faith and without notice of any lien or other claim on the goods by the original seller. In *Cahn v Pockett's Bristol Channel Co* (1899), it was held that possession of a bill of lading (a document of title) with the owner's consent was sufficient to pass a good title to a third party under s 25(1); in *Re Highway Foods International Ltd* (1995), it was held that where there is a reservation of title clause, the sub-purchaser may not be able to rely on s 25.

In *Newtons of Wembley Ltd v Williams* (1965), a car was sold with an agreement that the property would not pass until the price was paid. The cheque for payment was dishonoured, which meant that no title had passed because of the provisions of the contract; the buyer was, therefore, a buyer in possession without any title when he sold the car in a London street market. The car was then sold to the defendant. It was held that, as the buyer took the car in good faith when it was resold in the market, he obtained a good title under s 25, which he then transferred by sale to the defendant. It should be stressed, however, that s 25 only applies where the buyer in possession resells as if he were 'a mercantile agent'; in the *Newtons of Wembley case*, this aspect was satisfied by sale in the street market.

It is worth comparing *Newtons of Wembley* with *Car & Universal Finance Co v Caldwell*; once the buyer's title was avoided in *Caldwell*, he became a buyer in possession within the meaning of s 25. However, s 25 could not have operated because the subsequent purchaser did *not* act in good faith.

- *Sale of motor vehicles which are subject to hire purchase agreements*

The law changed in 1964 (by Pt III of Hire Purchase Act 1964 (re-enacted in the Consumer Credit Act 1974)) to protect 'private purchasers' of motor vehicles which were subject to a hire purchase agreement. The original hirer will still have the same obligation to the finance company. The purchaser who takes the car in good faith, without notice of the hire purchase agreement, gets a good title thereto. However, it appears that the original hire purchase contract must be valid for the third party to be protected (see *Shogun Finance Ltd v Hudson* (2001), above, 6.4.2.3).

In conclusion, it should be noted that if none of the exceptions to the *nemo dat* rule applies, the original owner retains title and may sue in the tort of conversion anyone who does possess or has possessed the goods since they were obtained from the original owner.

7.3 The Supply of Goods and Services Act 1982

7.3.1 Implied terms

The SGSA 1982 provides protection in respect of agreements which do not fulfil the definition of the SoGA 1979 but under which goods are supplied, usually along with a service. For example, an exchange contract and a car service which included purchase of new parts would come within the Act. The SGSA 1982 itself mirrors the

SoGA 1979, in that it implies conditions with respect to goods supplied. These implied conditions are contained in ss 2–5 and are very similar to ss 12–15 of the SoGA 1979; that is, there are implied conditions regarding title, description, quality and fitness for purpose, as well as sample. The SGSA 1982 also applies to contracts of hire, in that ss 6–10 imply in hire contracts terms similar to those implied by ss 12–15 of the SoGA 1979 in sale of goods contracts. The SGSA 1982 is also subject to similar amendments, introduced by the SSGA 1994. These amendments can be found in Sched 2. The 2002 Regulations amend the rules relating to implied terms and remedies in the same way as for contracts for the sale of goods (see above, 7.2.1.8).

Furthermore, the SGSA 1982 provides protection for the victims of poor quality workmanship, including the time it takes to provide services and the price for such services. It applies to all contracts where a 'person agrees to carry out a service in the course of a business'. Dry cleaning and window cleaning contracts would come within this definition. The implied terms as to services can be found in ss 13–15.

Section 13 of the SGSA 1982 states that there is an implied term that where the supplier is acting in the course of a business, the supplier will carry out the service with reasonable skill and care.

Section 14 states that where the supplier is acting within the course of a business and the time for the service to be carried out is not fixed by the contract or determined by a course of dealings between the parties, the supplier will carry out the service within a reasonable time.

Section 15 states that where the consideration is not determined by the contract or in a manner agreed in the contract or by the course of dealing between the parties, the party contracting with the supplier will pay a reasonable price.

Obviously, some contracts coming within the SGSA 1982 are 'hybrids'; for example, a decorating contract would involve supply of goods (paint, wallpaper, etc) and supply of a service (the labour involved in carrying out the decorating). In such a case, the provisions of ss 2–5, relating to the supply of goods, apply to the paint and wallpaper and the provisions of ss 13–15, relating to the supply of a service, apply to the carrying out of the work.

7.3.2   Exclusion clauses

UCTA 1977 governs exclusion and limitation of liability under the SGSA 1982. Title cannot be excluded and any attempt to exclude renders the clause void. In consumer sales, any attempt to exclude the terms contained in ss 2–5 will render the clause void. If the buyer does not deal as a consumer, any attempt to exclude these terms will be subject to the test of reasonableness. The 2002 Regulations make similar amendments to such rules as for sale of goods (see above, 7.2.1.10).

However, where there is a contract of hire, the terms as to title and quiet possession can be excluded or restricted by an exemption clause, subject to the test of reasonableness.

Where an exclusion clause relates to s 13, it must satisfy the test of reasonableness. Liability for death or personal injury cannot be excluded.

7.4 The Consumer Protection (Distance Selling) Regulations 2000

7.4.1 Application

The Regulations apply to contracts for the supply of goods or services which are concluded solely by distance communication (no face to face meeting) where the supplier normally contracts in this way (not a one-off transaction). For example, they apply to press advertisements with order forms, catalogues, telephone sales, internet shopping, email, fax and letter. However, some contracts are specifically excluded; for example, financial services, vending machine sales, contracts concluded via pay phone operator and internet auctions.

7.4.2 Main provisions

- The consumer must receive clear information about the goods/services *before* he or she decides whether to contract. For example, he or she must be told the name of the supplier, the price, delivery arrangements and costs, the cost of using distance communication (for example, premium telephone rate) and (where it applies) of his or her right to cancel the contract.

  So, for example, internet shopping channels should allow access to this information at the time people might order; catalogues should contain such information.

- The consumer must also receive confirmation of this information in a 'durable medium' (for example, email, fax, letter) and the confirmation must also contain certain other information, such as details of any guarantee and how to exercise the right to cancel. The confirmation must be received by the consumer, at the latest, on delivery of the goods or commencement of the supply of services.

- The consumer can withdraw from the contract without liability on it (that is, exercise the right of cancellation) up to seven working days (excluding weekends and bank holidays) from receipt of the confirmation of information (see above). However, the right of cancellation is not available in some circumstances, for example, perishable goods (such as supermarket 'home shopping' via the internet); sale of videos and software which the customer has 'unsealed'; supply of newspapers and magazines; goods made to order. If the consumer is not given prior notice of the right to cancel, the cancellation period is extended by three months. The consumer has to give written notice of cancellation (by, for example, email, letter, fax), but cannot cancel where he or she has used or damaged the goods. If the consumer who cancels already has possession of the goods, then (unless the details sent of the right to cancel state otherwise) the supplier must collect them within 21 days of cancellation, after giving the consumer notice of when they will be collected.

Whilst awaiting collection, the consumer must take reasonable care of the goods. On cancellation, the consumer is entitled to a refund of money paid.

In 2004, the Department of Trade and Industry consulted interested parties on proposed amendments to the Regulations:

- requiring suppliers to inform consumers specifically whether or not they have the right to cancel; and

- requiring suppliers of services to provide cancellation information in 'good time' during performance of the service (the current requirement, to provide information before the contract, may cause delays).

7.5 The Consumer Protection Act 1987

7.5.1 Introduction

The Consumer Protection Act (CPA) 1987 was passed to implement the EC Directive on Product Liability (85/374/EEC). The CPA 1987 provides a means of redress for a consumer against the 'producer' of a product for injury or property damage caused by that product. This means of redress is of particular importance to the non-buyer (for example, the recipient of a gift), but a buyer might pursue a claim under the CPA 1987 where, for example, it is not worth suing an insolvent seller. Although a consumer would have had a claim against the manufacturer in negligence (*Donoghue v Stevenson* (1932); see below, Chapter 8), this would involve establishing fault; the CPA 1987 does not require such evidence in order to establish liability.

A consumer might also encounter problems in suing a manufacturer abroad; apart from the expense involved, English law may not be applied by a foreign court to determine the issue. The CPA 1987 solves this problem by providing for the possibility of proceeding against a person or body in this country. Accordingly, a business which does not manufacture the defective goods or sell them to the consumer may nevertheless find itself liable to compensate a consumer who suffers loss because of the defects in the goods, because it is a 'producer'.

In order to succeed in a claim, the claimant must show that:

- the product contained a defect; and

- the claimant suffered damage; and

- the damage was caused by the defect; and

- the defendant was a producer, own brander or importer of the product into the EU.

7.5.2 Meaning of 'producer'

A 'producer' of a product is defined as including the manufacturer of a finished product or of a component; any person who won or abstracted the product; or, where goods are not manufactured or abstracted, any person responsible for an industrial or other process to which any essential characteristic of the product is attributable, for example, a person who processes agricultural produce (s 2(2) of the CPA 1987).

Although a supplier of a defective product (for example a retail outlet) does not have primary liability, the supplier will be liable if he or she fails to identify the producer or importer when requested to do so (s 2(2)).

A person may be deemed to be a 'producer' of a defective product if that person claims to be a producer by putting his or her name or trademark on the product.

7.5.3 'Defective' product

A product will be 'defective' within the meaning of s 3 of the CPA 1987 if the safety of the product is not such as persons generally are entitled to expect, taking all circumstances into account, including: the marketing of the product; the presentation of the product, including instructions and warnings; the use to which it might reasonably be expected to be put; and the time when it was supplied, that is, the state of the product at the time of supply. In *A & Others v National Blood Authority* (2001), claims were made under the CPA 1987 by people infected by hepatitis C through blood transfusions. At the time, it was known by doctors that there could be such infection, but no warnings were given as there was then no test to detect the virus in blood. As no warnings of the risk were given, the public were found to have a legitimate expectation that no risk existed. Thus, the transfused blood was 'defective'. In *Worsley v Tambrands* (2000), a woman suffering toxic shock syndrome from tampon use alleged the tampons were not as safe as people were entitled to expect; though the risks of use were stated in the leaflet in the tampon box, the information was not printed on the box and regular users would not always read the leaflet. The court held that the warnings in the leaflet were sufficient to meet the expectations of users under s 3 of the CPA 1987.

A 'product' is 'any goods or electricity and ... includes a product which is comprised in another product, whether by virtue of being a component part or raw materials or otherwise' (s 1 of the CPA 1987). 'Goods' includes substances (which can be natural or artificial, solid, liquid, gaseous or in the form of a vapour), things comprised in land by virtue of being attached to it (but not land itself), ships, aircraft and vehicles (s 45).

Thus, for example, all processed and manufactured goods supplied by a business are covered by the CPA 1987, as are raw materials and components incorporated into them. However, services such as advice are not included and agricultural produce and game which have not undergone an industrial process were specifically exempted from the provisions of the CPA 1987. So, for example, a farmer who supplied eggs infected with salmonella would not be liable under the CPA 1987, though, of course, the seller of such could be liable to a buyer under the SoGA 1979. However, probably because of the BSE crisis, EC Directive 99/34 required a change in the law by 4 December 2000 to include primary agricultural products within the scope of the CPA 1987, which has now been implemented.

7.5.4   Extent of liability

A person suffering loss because of a defective product can claim but, under s 5, damages can only be awarded for property damage over £275 and for death or injury. No claim can be made for 'pure' economic loss, or for damage to the defective product itself.

7.5.5   Exclusion of liability

Under s 7, liability cannot be excluded, though a claim for damages is subject to the defences of the CPA 1987 and the time limitations of the Limitation Act 1980.

7.5.6   Defences

Although the CPA 1987 imposes strict liability, there are a number of defences provided by s 4.

Any person has a defence if it can be shown that:

- the defect is attributable to compliance with a domestic or EC enactment;
- the person was not at any time the supplier of the product;
- the supply was not in the course of business;
- the defect did not exist in the product at the time it was supplied;
- the state of scientific and technical knowledge at the relevant time was not such that the producer might be expected to have discovered the defect;
- the defect was in a product in which the product in question had been comprised and was wholly attributable to the design of the subsequent product; or
- more than 10 years has elapsed since the product was first supplied.

The 'development risks' defence allows the producer to show that the defect was not discoverable at the time of supplying the product. What is required of a producer for this defence to operate is an area of contention, awaiting clarification by the courts. Should the producer make sure that he or she is aware of all available knowledge related to the product and then ensure that it is applied, or will it suffice to do limited research, bearing in mind the cost of development and the potentially small risk to the consumer? The issue was examined in *Abouzaid v Mothercare (UK) Ltd* (2000).

Section 6(4) indicates that the defence of contributory negligence is available.

7.5.7 Limitations on claims

There is a three year limitation period for claims, the start date being the date of the injury or damage. Where the injury or damage is not apparent, the date runs from the time that the claimant knew or could reasonably have known of the claim.

It should also be made clear that products supplied before 1 March 1988 cannot be the subject of claims under the CPA 1987, as the Act is not retrospective.

7.6 Criminal Liability

7.6.1 Introduction

The businessman must be aware that, as well as seeking to protect buyers and consumers generally by providing remedies, the law also strives to prevent consumers being misled and defective products being supplied by imposing criminal liability. The conviction of a business could cause harm to its commercial reputation, apart from any other consequences, such as payment of a fine and seizure of dangerous goods.

7.6.2 Part II of the Consumer Protection Act 1987

This part of the Act provides protection for the public from unsafe consumer goods by imposing criminal liability. It enables the Secretary of State to make safety regulations in respect of specific products. Safety regulations already exist in respect of a wide range of products, including children's nightdresses and the coverings and fillings of upholstered furniture.

The CPA 1987 creates a criminal offence of 'supplying consumer goods which are not reasonably safe' (s 10). It allows the Secretary of State to serve either a 'prohibition notice' on a supplier, prohibiting him or her from supplying goods which are unsafe, or a 'notice to warn', which requires the supplier to publish warnings about the unsafe goods (s 13).

A consumer may have a civil claim for breach of statutory duty against the supplier of unsafe goods under this part of the CPA 1987.

Note should also be taken of 'Stop Now' Orders, introduced by the Stop Now Orders (EC Directive) Regulations 2001 (SI 2001/1422) and now covered by the Enterprise Act 2002. The Office of Fair Trading and Trading Standards officers can inspect and seize goods for testing and inspect documents before consumers receive goods; by way of speeded up process, an injunction can be obtained to prevent the goods being supplied onto the market.

7.6.3   The General Product Safety Regulations 1994

Even if there are no specific safety regulations relating to a particular product, the General Product Safety Regulations (GPSR) 1994 (SI 1994/2328) can impose criminal liability for supplying *unsafe products* onto the market.

The GPSR 1994 arose out of EC Directive 92/59, which requires Member States to introduce general product safety requirements and develop and implement procedures for the notification and exchange of information relating to dangerous products. The Regulations apply to all manufacturers and producers within the EC. If the manufacturer/producer does not have a base within the EC, the onus will fall on the distributor/importer (reg 2). The main requirement states that no producer shall place a product on the market unless the product is safe (reg 7).

The GPSR 1994 apply to any product intended for or likely to be used by consumers. They also cover second hand and reconditioned goods, subject to reg 3 (reg 2). 'Product' has a wider meaning than that found in the CPA 1987; for example, tobacco was specifically excluded from the CPA 1987 but is covered by the GPSR 1994.

A 'safe product' is further defined by reg 2 of the GPSR 1994 as:

> ... any product which, under normal or reasonably foreseeable conditions of use, including duration, does not present any risk or only the minimum risks compatible with the product's use, considered as acceptable and consistent with a high level of protection for the safety and health of persons, taking into account in particular:
>
> (a) the characteristics of the product, including its composition, packaging, instructions for assembly and maintenance;
>
> (b) the effect on other products, where it is reasonably foreseeable that it will be used with other products;
>
> (c) the presentation of the product, the labelling, any instructions for its use and disposal and any other indication or information provided by the producer; and
>
> (d) the categories of consumers at risk when using the product, in particular children.

Clearly, the packaging itself, or misleading or inadequate instructions on it, can render a product unsafe and result in a breach of the Regulations.

Where the producer or distributor is accused of an offence under the GPSR 1994, the due diligence defence may be raised (reg 14), that is, it can be shown that all reasonable steps were taken and all due diligence was exercised to avoid committing the offence.

On conviction of an offence under the GPSR 1994, the penalty may either be imprisonment for up to three months and/or a fine (reg 17).

The GPSR 1994 specifically preserve application of s 13 of the CPA 1987 in relation to products coming under the GPSR 1994 (provisions regarding prohibition notices and notices to warn – see above, 7.6.2).

7.6.4 Misleading price indications

It has been common practice for businesses to mislead or give inadequate information to consumers in relation to prices. For example, a notice stating '10% off' with no reference to the original price means that the consumer is unable to determine whether the price now charged is a 'bargain'.

Section 20 of the CPA 1987 provides that a person is guilty of an offence if, in the course of a business, consumers are given a misleading indication as to the price at which any goods, services, accommodation or facilities are available (see *Toyota (GB) Ltd v North Yorkshire CC* (1998)). Evidence of an offence is provided by compliance or non-compliance with the Consumer Protection (Code of Practice for Traders on Price Indications) Approval Order 1988 (SI 1988/2078). Under the guidelines of the Code, where goods are 'reduced' in price, the last previous price during the preceding six months must also be shown and the product must have been available at that price for at least 28 consecutive days in those six months at the same outlet where the reduced price is now offered. Also, a retailer should not compare his prices with an amount described only as 'worth' or 'value', for example, 'worth £20, our price £15'. Under s 20(2) of the CPA 1987, a criminal offence is also committed where the price indication, though not misleading when given, has become misleading before the consumer enters a contract (see *Link Stores Ltd v Harrow LBC* (2001)).

A number of defences are provided in s 24 of the CPA 1987. The defendant may prove that all reasonable precautions were taken and that he or she exercised all due diligence to avoid the commission of an offence, or that he or she was an innocent publisher/advertiser who was unaware of the fact that, and had no grounds to suspect that, the advertisement contained a misleading price indication.

The provisions of the CPA 1987 and the Code of Practice can be supplemented by regulations made by the Secretary of State under s 26 of that Act. Under the Price Indications (Method of Payment) Regulations 1991 (SI 1991/199), where a trader charges different prices according to the method of payment, the differences must be made clear to consumers. It is common practice for garages to charge more for payment by credit card than for cash. Further regulations have been made; for example, the Price Indications (Bureaux de Change) Regulations 1992 (SI 1992/316), deal with matters such as commission rates on currency and travellers' cheques.

7.6.5 The Trade Descriptions Act 1968

The Trade Descriptions Act (TDA) 1968 provides criminal sanctions for offences relating to the sale of goods involving the use of false or misleading descriptions, as well as misleading statements about services. It also provides facilities for the court to make a compensation order for the consumer who has suffered loss.

Under the TDA 1968, it is a criminal offence to apply, in the course of a trade or business, a false description to goods or to sell goods where such a description is applied (ss 1 and 3 of the TDA 1968; see *Formula One Autocentres Ltd v Birmingham CC* (1998)). Private sales are outside the remit of the TDA 1968.

The professions fall within the scope of the TDA 1968. For example, in *Roberts v Leonard* (1995), a veterinary surgeon was held to be carrying on a trade or business. 'False' means 'false to a material degree'; therefore, in effect, any deviation from the description must be significant. The meaning of 'trade description' is indicated in s 2(1) as including statements about quantity, size and method of manufacture; fitness for purpose; other physical characteristics; testing and the results of such tests; approvals by any person; place, date and name of manufacturer, producer or processor; and any history, including ownership and use.

In *Sherratt v Geralds The American Jewellers Ltd* (1970), a watch, described by the maker as a 'diver's watch' and inscribed 'waterproof', filled with water and stopped on its first immersion. The defendant was found guilty of a breach of s 1 of the TDA 1968 in supplying goods to which a false description had been applied by another person.

The TDA 1968 not only makes it unlawful for the trader to apply a false trade description to goods, but extends to supplying goods, exposing goods for supply or having goods in his or her possession for the purposes of supply and to services, accommodation or facilities (ss 6 and 14 of the TDA 1968). In *Yugo Tours Ltd v Wadsley* (1988), a tour operator advertised a holiday on board a three-masted schooner under full sail and included a photograph. It was held that the tour operator was in breach of the TDA 1968, as customers, having relied on the brochure to book their holiday, then found themselves on a two-masted schooner without sails.

A person may be guilty of an offence, even where the description is technically correct, where it is likely to mislead a customer without specialist knowledge, although this is subject to the general provision that the description must be false or misleading to a material degree. For example, to describe a car as 'beautiful' when it is in a poor mechanical state could be a false description to a material degree (*Robertson v Dicocco* (1972)).

The TDA 1968 provides two defences (s 24), which are:

- that the misdescription was due to a mistake; or to reliance on information supplied by a third party; or to the act or default of a third party or some other cause beyond the control of the defendant; and

- that all reasonable precautions were taken and due diligence was exercised to avoid the commission of an offence. The defence of due diligence was recently examined in *DSG Retail Ltd v Oxfordshire CC* (2001).

In *Lewin v Rothersthorpe Road Garage* (1984), a defendant raised the second s 24 defence by establishing that he was a member of the Motor Agents Association and had adopted the code of practice drawn up by the Association, as approved by the Office of Fair Trading. This was sufficient for the court to accept that the defendant had taken reasonable precautions to avoid commission of an offence by his employee.

It is also open to a 'trader' who is supplying goods to issue a disclaimer. This will provide a defence as long as it is sufficiently bold to equal that of the description supplied.

In *Norman v Bennett* (1974), though the mileage recorded on a car's odometer was incorrect, there was no contravention of s 1(1)(b) of the TDA 1968 because the buyer signed a sales agreement which he knew contained the words 'odometer reading not guaranteed'. (Compare this with *Holloway v Cross* (1981).) Such a disclaimer is not available where the trader is actually applying the trade description him or herself, as occurred in *Newham LBC v Singh* (1988). It seems fair that a dealer should be able to say that he is not liable for odometer readings which he cannot check but, clearly, he should not be allowed to exclude liability where he knows, or ought to know, that a description is false.

7.7   Consumer Credit

In our 'live now, pay later' society, credit is a fact of everyday life for most people. Credit is obtained by a wide range of methods, for example, loans, credit cards and mail order catalogues; for many years, the media has related stories of 'loan sharks' and unscrupulous money lenders taking advantage of consumers. The Consumer Credit Act (CCA) 1974 was passed following the Crowther Committee Report (*Report of the Committee on Consumer Credit* (Cmnd 4569, 1971)) and its purpose was to provide greater protection to those buying on credit – for example, the CCA 1974 repealed and replaced most of the Hire Purchase Act 1964 – and to rectify the imbalance in the bargaining positions of the respective parties.

European Community directives have been issued (for example, 87/02/EEC, to harmonise the laws relating to consumer credit in Member States), but the directives largely follow the pattern of the CCA 1974 and so major legislative changes have not been necessary in the UK.

It is extremely important that any business providing credit is aware of and complies with the regulatory framework of control of the CCA 1974, as it creates criminal offences for non-compliance, controls on advertising and a licensing system for credit providers, outside which businesses cannot operate.

It should be noted, however, that new regulations, resulting from the Department of Trade and Industry's White Paper, *Fair, Clear and Competitive; The Consumer Credit Market in the 21st Century*, and its consultation paper of December 2003, *Establishing a Transparent Market*, reform consumer credit legislation. The Consumer Credit (Advertisement) Regulations 2004 (SI 2004/1484) largely came into effect on 31 October 2004; the Consumer Credit (Disclosure of Information) Regulations 2004 (SI 2004/1481), the Consumer Credit (Agreements) (Amendment) Regulations 2004 (SI 2004/1482) and the Consumer Credit (Early Settlement) Regulations 2004 (SI 2004/1483) have effect from 31 May 2005. Furthermore, new legislation is proposed to amend the current financial limits for application of various provisions of the CCA 1974 and associated regulations and a Consumer Credit Bill was published in December 2004. The Bill aims to reform the CCA 1974 in several key areas, for example, regulation of consumer credit and hire agreements, and licensing of credit providers. The Bill also seeks to allow debtors to challenge unfair relationships with creditors and to provide an Ombudsman Scheme to hear complaints made about licensed credit providers.

7.7.1   Examples of credit agreements

- *Hire purchase*

  Under such an agreement, the customer is given use and possession of goods in return for payment by instalments. The ownership in the goods is not transferred unless and until all payments are made and the option to purchase is exercised (usually by payment of an additional nominal sum). Accordingly, the customer may never acquire ownership in the goods, even though that could have been his or her objective from the outset, and the goods may be repossessed for non-payment.

- *Credit sale*

  In this type of agreement, the customer agrees to buy the goods but pays the purchase price by instalments. Ownership passes immediately and the goods cannot be repossessed for non-payment. If a buyer fails to pay, he or she can only be sued for the arrears.

- *Conditional sale*

  At first sight, this agreement appears to be similar to both credit sale and hire purchase, but in legal terms it is a distinct type of agreement. Here, the buyer agrees to purchase ownership and pay by instalments but ownership does not actually pass to him or her until he or she has made a specified number of payments. The distinction between conditional sale and credit sale lies in the time at which ownership is transferred.

- *Personal loans*

  Fixed term loans are available from banks and other financial institutions and are repaid by instalments, which include interest payments. Such loans are commonly obtained to purchase goods and holidays; it should be realised that, if the loan was used, for example, to pay for a car, there would be two separate contracts – a contract for the sale of goods and a loan agreement.

- *Overdraft*

  Under an overdraft agreement, the holder of a current account at a bank is able to draw against his or her account up to an agreed amount when the account is in debit. Therefore, the customer is borrowing money and usually has to pay interest on the borrowing.

7.7.2   The terminology of the Consumer Credit Act 1974

The specific terminology of the CCA 1974 must be explained before the provisions of the Act can be understood:

Creditor   The person/body who supplies the credit/finance.

Credit broker   A person/body who carries on a business, which includes introducing individuals requiring credit to persons/bodies carrying on a consumer credit business or to other credit brokers. So, a garage which arranges for a customer to obtain hire purchase finance for a car from a finance company is a credit broker.

Debtor   The customer/borrower/person who is obliged to repay the finance.

Credit   Not only cash loans, but also any other form of financial accommodation (s 9(1) of the CCA 1974), such as hire purchase.

7.7.3   Agreements within the scope of the Consumer Credit Act 1974

The CCA 1974 applies to regulated agreements. There are three main types:

• consumer credit agreements;

• consumer hire agreements; and

• linked transactions.

7.7.3.1   Consumer credit agreements

Section 8(2) of the CCA 1974 states that:

> A consumer credit agreement is a personal credit agreement by which the creditor provides the debtor with credit not exceeding [£25,000].

A 'personal credit agreement' is defined in s 8(1) as an agreement between an individual (a debtor) and any other person (a creditor) whereby the creditor provides the debtor with credit of any amount.

Section 8(3) indicates such agreements are 'regulated'. It should be noted that the credit limit for application of the Act was increased from £15,000 to £25,000 by the Consumer Credit (Increase of Monetary Limits) Order 1998 (SI 1998/996).

In such agreements, the amount of the credit extended determines the application of the CCA 1974. The Act does not apply where the credit extended exceeds £25,000 and 'credit extended' refers to the principal sum advanced. Accordingly, charges such as interest payments should not be included in the calculation of whether the credit extended is within the current statutory limit. This is aimed at preventing the creditor from including all sums payable under the credit agreement (such as administration fees and insurance premiums) so that the agreement appears to fall outside the ambit of the CCA 1974. Thus, the 'credit' extended has to be distinguished from the 'total payable';

it must also be distinguished from the 'total charge for credit', which means the cash price deducted from the 'total payable' (see *Huntpast Ltd v Leadbetter* (1993)). For details of matters to be or not be included in the 'total charge for credit', the Consumer Credit (Total Charge for Credit Agreements and Advertisements) (Amendment) Regulations 1999 (SI 1999/3177), which came into force on 14 April 2000, should be referred to.

It should further be appreciated that the Act only applies where the credit is extended to an 'individual', but s 189 indicates that this 'includes a partnership or other unincorporated body of persons not consisting entirely of bodies corporate'. Arguably, Parliament felt that businesses such as sole traders needed the same protection from the unscrupulous as did private individuals.

7.7.3.2 Consumer hire agreements

Under s 15 of the CCA 1974, this is an agreement:

> ... made by an individual (the 'hirer') for the bailment of goods to the hirer, being an agreement which:
>
> (a) is not a hire purchase agreement; and
>
> (b) is capable of subsisting for more than three months; and
>
> (c) does not require the hirer to make payments exceeding £25,000.

The nature of regulated consumer credit and consumer hire agreements was examined by the House of Lords in *Dimond v Lovell* (2000). L damaged D's car and, whilst it was being repaired, D hired a car from A. Under the hire agreement, payment was not required until the claim against L's insurers was settled, so credit was extended. L's insurers refused to pay the hire charge on the basis that the hire agreement was a regulated consumer credit agreement which was unenforceable because it did not contain all the terms required by regulations made under the CCA 1974 (see below, 7.7.5); as the agreement was not enforceable, D did not have to pay the hire charge and therefore L's insurers were not liable for it. L's insurers also argued that D had not 'mitigated' her loss (see above, 6.5.7.2) because she could have hired a car much more cheaply at 'spot rate' (the prevailing price in the market generally). On this latter argument, the House of Lords indicated that, if the hire agreement was enforceable, she could only have obtained, as damages, the 'spot rate' hire charge (see also *Burdis v Livsey* (2002)). In relation to the nature of the hire agreement, the House of Lords decided that it was a regulated consumer credit agreement rather than a regulated consumer hire agreement because, technically, it did not indicate that it was capable of lasting more than three months. It was agreed that this regulated consumer credit agreement was unenforceable for non-compliance with regulations; as D did not have to pay, the hire charge was not a loss suffered within her claim against L and L's insurers were not liable.

7.7.3.3   Linked transactions (s 19 of the CCA 1974)

These are agreements which are entered into by the debtor with the creditor or a third party in relation to the regulated agreement but which are not part of the regulated agreement. Linked transactions take one of three forms:

- *Compulsory*

  One which has to be entered into by the terms of the principal agreement, for example, a maintenance agreement on a washing machine.

- *Financial*

  Where the transaction is a debtor-creditor-supplier agreement (see below, 7.7.4) and is financed by the principal agreement, for example, if A pays for goods by credit card, the contract under which he obtains the credit card is the principal agreement which finances A's purchase of the goods, because the credit card company pays the supplier of the goods and A repays the card company later with interest. A credit card agreement is a regulated agreement under s 14 of the CCA 1974, but it should be noted that cheque guarantee cards are outside the definition of s 14 (see *Metropolitan Police Commissioner v Charles* (1977)). However, some cards have multi-functions, one or more of which may bring them within s 14, for example, a cheque guarantee card which is also a credit card.

- *Suggested*

  This may occur where a person is induced to enter another transaction by the suggestion of the creditor, owner or credit broker, in order to persuade the creditor to enter the principal agreement. For example, a credit broker might suggest that he can arrange a loan with a creditor if A is willing to insure repayment of the loan under an insurance policy which he will also arrange. Here, the loan agreement would be the principal agreement, and the insurance policy would be the linked transaction.

The significance of a linked transaction is that it will be affected by any action taken in respect of the principal agreement. So, if the principal agreement is cancelled under s 69, the related insurance policy would be discharged. The right of cancellation is discussed below, 7.7.9.3.

7.7.4   Types of regulated consumer credit agreements

Depending on the nature of the particular situation, a regulated agreement may be one of various types. The distinction can be important in determining which provisions of the CCA 1974 will apply. (Some agreements will fall into more than one category and are known as *multiple agreements* (s 18(1)) and each divisible part is regulated by the CCA 1974 accordingly.)

7.7.4.1 Debtor-creditor agreement

This is an agreement where finance only is supplied by the creditor to the debtor, as in the case of a bank loan. Such an agreement could be a *restricted* or *unrestricted use* credit agreement (see s 11 of the CCA 1974).

7.7.4.2 Unrestricted use credit agreements

This is an agreement where the creditor has no control over how the credit extended to the debtor is used. Thus, if the debtor gets a bank loan for home improvements by a credit to his current account, the bank cannot physically prevent him from using that loan to pay for a holiday. Of course, he may be in breach of his loan agreement in such circumstances.

7.7.4.3 Restricted use credit agreements

In such agreements, the creditor can control the use to which the credit extended to the debtor is put. If a debtor obtained a loan from a bank to buy a car, it could be part of the agreement that the bank pays the money borrowed directly to the seller of the car. This clearly prevents the debtor from misleading the bank as to the purpose of any loan applied for. Possibly, such agreements protect consumers from themselves! In *Dimond v Lovell* (2000) (see above, 7.7.3), the Court of Appeal said that the hire agreement was (*inter alia*) a restricted use credit agreement.

7.7.4.4 Debtor-creditor-supplier agreements

These are agreements where there is a link between the creditor and the supplier of the goods/services given to the debtor. Common examples would be as follows:

- *Purchase by credit card*

  The debtor is the purchaser, who must repay the credit card company; the supplier is the retailer; and the creditor is the credit card company, because, under a pre-existing arrangement with retailers (which is the *link* between creditor and supplier), the card company pays the retailer for the debtor 's purchase. Incidentally, this type of transaction would be an unrestricted use agreement, as the card company does not dictate what the card is used for.

- *Purchase of goods on credit from a retailer who himself finances the credit*

  This can be done by allowing the debtor to pay by instalments; this would be usual for purchases by store card.

- *Hire purchase agreements*

  A retailer of expensive goods such as cars will not be able to sell them unless customers can buy on credit, but he or she may not be in a financial position to wait two or three years for his or her money. Therefore, the retailer will have to enter into a contract with a finance company, under which any car a customer wants is sold ('on paper') to the finance company by the retailer and the finance company lets the customer have the car on hire purchase terms. In this situation, the customer's contract is with the finance company, *not* the retailer, though the agreement forms are usually filled out at the retailer's premises. Hire purchase is a restricted use consumer credit agreement and fulfils the CCA 1974 definition of a debtor-creditor-supplier agreement. (The finance company is the creditor, the person acquiring the car on hire purchase is the debtor and the retailer (though merely a credit broker in this case) is treated as the supplier.)

In relation to debtor-creditor-supplier agreements, the consumer gets special protection under s 75 of the CCA 1974, which allows the debtor to bring an action *against the creditor* for any misrepresentation or breach of contract *by the supplier*. (But whether misrepresentation or breach by the supplier would give the debtor the right to rescind or treat the credit contract as repudiated is not clear, despite the decision in *United Dominions Trust v Taylor* (1980).) To put s 75 into context, the following situations can be considered:

- The consumer pays a travel company for his holiday by credit card. Before the date that he is due to go on holiday, the travel company goes into liquidation, so that the consumer gets no holiday and the travel company will not have the funds to repay him.

  Here, the consumer could claim his refund from the credit card company.

- A furniture retailer induces a consumer to purchase a three-piece suite by a negligent misrepresentation that the covers are machine washable.

  Here, the consumer may bring an action for misrepresentation against the credit card company which issued the card.

Whilst, in theory, s 75 of the CCA 1974 appears to place a heavy burden on the creditor, if the debtor pursues a claim against the creditor, the creditor can claim an indemnity from the supplier – presuming that he or she is still in existence. There are limitations on the use of s 75, in that it does not apply to a non-commercial agreement (defined in s 189 of the CCA 1974 as a consumer credit agreement where the creditor/owner does not act in the course of business), nor does it apply to a claim in respect of any item where the cash price does not exceed £100 or is more than £30,000. However, in these circumstances, the debtor could still take action against the supplier.

The application of s 75 has not proved to be straightforward, particularly where credit card holders have used the section to pursue claims against banks. First, it does not apply to credit card agreements made before 1 July 1977; secondly, where there is a main card holder and a second authorised user, only the main card holder has the right to use s 75, which means that, if defective goods are purchased by the second user, s 75 may not operate; and, thirdly, where the card has been used abroad, banks are keen to avoid liability on the basis that the law of the country in which the purchase is made should apply (see *Jarrett v Barclays Bank plc* (1996)). In *Office of Fair Trading v Lloyds TSB Bank plc & Others* (2004), it was decided that s 75 does not apply to foreign transactions where the contract is made wholly outside the UK, is governed by a foreign law, and the goods or services contracted for are delivered or supplied outside the UK.

7.7.4.5   Fixed sum credit

Fixed sum credit is where the actual amount of the loan is fixed from the start of the agreement, subject to the statutory limit for regulated agreements. The relevant figure is the actual amount of the sum being loaned, excluding the amount payable as interest or deposit. It is irrelevant that it may be repaid or received by instalments. A hire purchase agreement is one of fixed sum credit. The actual amount of fixed sum credit determines whether the agreement is covered by or is outside the financial limits of the CCA 1974. In *Dimond v Lovell* (2000) (see above, 7.7.3), the hire agreement was said to be a fixed sum credit in the Court of Appeal.

7.7.4.6   Running account credit

Running account credit is where credit is fixed up to an agreed limit, for example, credit card agreements and bank overdrafts. Again, such agreements will be regulated agreements within the CCA 1974, as long as the credit limit does not exceed the current specified figure (£25,000).

7.7.5   Exempt and partially exempt agreements

Though apparently falling within the definition of the CCA 1974, some agreements are exempt from the provisions of that Act. 'Extortionate credit bargains' (see below, 7.7.9.1) are not exempt; others are only partially regulated by the CCA 1974.

7.7.5.1   Small agreements (s 17 of the CCA 1974)

A small agreement is either a regulated consumer credit agreement or a regulated consumer hire agreement where the amount of credit or hire/rental charges do not exceed £50. (Note that the Department of Trade and Industry consultative document, Deregulation of UK Consumer Credit Legislation (1995), proposes raising the sum to £150.) The rules for determining whether the credit exceeds the limit are by reference to fixed sum and running account credit (explained above).

Small agreements are *exempt* from some, but not all, of the provisions of the CCA 1974; for example, the rules relating to formation of credit agreements (see below, 7.7.5.1) do not apply. However, the main provisions contained in Pt IV, relating to seeking business, the requirement on the creditor to supply information on request and the provisions restricting remedies on default, will apply (see below, 7.7.9.2 and 7.7.9.6).

7.7.5.2   Exempt agreements

Certain agreements are exempt from the provisions of the CCA 1974 by virtue of s 16 of that Act and the Consumer Credit (Exempt Agreements) Order 1989 (SI 1989/869) (as amended by SI 1999/1956).

The exemptions cover situations where it is probably unnecessary to provide protection for debtors and, accordingly, though the 1989 Order exempts debtor-creditor-supplier agreements where there are no more than four payments in a 12 month period, this exemption does not apply to any hire purchase or conditional sale agreement. (One of the purposes of the CCA 1974 was to protect consumers in relation to hire purchase agreements.) Everyday examples of exempt agreements are milk and newspaper bills, which are usually paid in arrears, so credit is given. In *Dimond v Lovell* (2000) (see above, 7.7.3.2) in the House of Lords, Lord Hoffmann indicated that the hire car company could have made the agreement 'exempt', and therefore enforceable, by stating in the agreement that the hire charge had to be paid within 12 months.

Other examples of exempt agreements are:

- mortgages;

- debtor-creditor-supplier agreements for running account credit where the whole of the credit given has to be paid off in a lump sum. Certain charge cards will require the whole of the outstanding balance to be repaid at the end of each month; and

- credit sale agreements where no interest is charged when the purchase price is repaid over an agreed period. This type of arrangement is what is commonly offered by furniture retailers in their television advertising.

7.7.5.3   Non-commercial agreements

Such agreements are made by a creditor who is not acting in the course of any business carried on by him (s 189 of the CCA 1974), for example, a private individual giving a loan to a friend. In *Hare v Schurek* (1993), a business only giving credit very occasionally was not required to be licensed under the CCA 1974 (see below, 7.7.6, for CCA 1974 licensing provisions). Thus, in relation to the definition of a non-commercial agreement, such a business should not be regarded as acting in the course of a business it carries on when giving credit.

Non-commercial agreements are exempt from the CCA 1974 provisions relating to, for example, form and contents (see below, 7.7.8.3); the right to cancel (see below, 7.7.9.3); cooling off periods (see below, 7.7.9.3); and licensing (see below, 7.7.6).

7.7.6   Licensing

The licensing system was introduced to regulate creditors and thereby protect consumers, but it is clear that there are still unlicensed money lenders who charge exorbitant rates of interest and enforce payment by threats. The people who are most likely to be caught in this trap are the poor, because banks and other financial institutions which are licensed under the CCA 1974 are loath to extend credit to them because of their low income; perhaps those who need the protection of the law most are not receiving it.

Businesses which provide facilities for regulated agreements must be licensed by the Office of Fair Trading (OFT); a licence is required whether the business's main activity is the provision of credit or whether such provision is ancillary to its main activities (for example, debt collection, debt counselling and credit references).

The licences which can be granted are *standard* licences (given on an individual basis) and *group* licences (for example, covering a group of professionals such as solicitors or accountants). Standard licences are granted for five years; group licences for 15 years. Licences under the CCA 1974 are not required by local authorities or businesses granting credit over £25,000 or granting credit only to companies. A licence may be granted to cover only stated aspects of the credit business; if a licence was granted to cover debt collection and debt counselling only, the holder could not legally extend credit within the provisions of the CCA 1974.

Applicants for licences have to satisfy the Director General of Fair Trading as to their fitness to be granted the licence. In considering such fitness, the Director General will take account of such matters as convictions for fraud, theft and breaches of the Trade Descriptions Act 1968 (s 25 of the CCA 1974). In *North Wales Motor Auctions Ltd v Secretary of State* (1981), the refusal of a licence because the applicant was not a fit person, on account of convictions for fraud on the Inland Revenue, was upheld. The Director General will also ensure that the applicant is not applying to trade under a name which is misleading. In *Hunter-Jaap v Hampshire Credit Consultants Ltd* (1986), it was held that a trader may be prevented from using a name (even his own name) which, with intent to deceive, might mislead the public into thinking that it is someone else's business.

The Director General also has the power to vary, withdraw or suspend current licences (ss 30–32 of the CCA 1974). In the second quarter of 2004, the OFT refused nine licence applications and revoked three licences; a further 201 applications were withdrawn after applicants were asked to provide further information. Licensees or applicants for licences may appeal against the Director General's decision to the Secretary of State (as occurred in *North Wales Motor Auctions Ltd v Secretary of State*). Where an unlicensed trader makes an agreement which comes within the provisions of the CCA 1974, that agreement is not enforceable unless the Director General makes an order allowing enforcement (s 40 of the CCA 1974). Failure to get such an order would mean that the unlicensed trader would not be able to sue the debtor for non-payment under the agreement; however, this provision would not protect the consumer against an unlicensed money lender who used unlawful means, such as coercion, to obtain payment.

Unlicensed trading is a criminal offence, as is trading under a name other than that on the licence (s 39 of the CCA 1974). Conviction may result in a fine of up to £5,000 and/or up to two years' imprisonment (s 167 of the CCA 1974).

In September 2004, a consultation document, *The Consumer Credit Act 1974: Review of the Group Licensing Regime*, was published. In the document, the OFT makes proposals to update the group licensing regime, such as tightening policy on the issue of group licences and ensuring that group licence holders take primary responsibility for action on issues of fitness. The CCA 1974 permits courts to notify the OFT of judgments or convictions relevant to a licence holder's fitness to hold the licence. It is proposed to require the licence holder to report to the OFT any changes (such as convictions) to the information given when the licence was applied for.

7.7.7 Promotion of credit agreements

7.7.7.1 Introduction

People are often caught in the 'credit trap' because they do not appreciate the practical consequences of using credit; equally, many consumers do not realise how much credit costs them and find it difficult to assess what is the best credit deal for them. So, a person wishing to buy a freezer might not be sure whether to buy by credit card, by bank loan or on hire purchase.

The law seeks to protect the consumer in these situations by measures such as controls on advertising and specifying the information that a prospective debtor must be given.

7.7.7.2 Canvassing offences

The CCA 1974 creates the following criminal offences:

- sending documents to a minor, inviting him or her to enter a credit agreement or to apply for information about credit (s 50 of the CCA 1974); a defence is available if there was no reasonable cause to believe that the addressee was a minor;

- giving a person an unsolicited credit token (s 51 of the CCA 1974), for example, a credit card, though the provisions of s 51 do not render renewals unlawful; and

- canvassing off trade premises for debtor-creditor agreements (ss 48 and 49 of the CCA 1974).

It is a criminal offence to make an unsolicited call at a person's home and to make oral statements to him or her about credit terms available in relation to debtor-creditor agreements. Commission of the offence can be avoided where the 'canvasser' has a written request to call at premises. Most people are familiar with salesmen calling round and saying that they are 'not trying to sell anything, but if you would like to know more about our product or service you can fill out our card for one of our salesman to call'. By responding positively, the consumer makes a written request, soliciting the salesman to call, and no offence is committed. Of course, the subsequent sales talk will then include reference to credit terms available.

In May 2004, the OFT reported on its study of doorstep selling (OFT 716), highlighting psychological techniques used by doorstep salespersons, such as making the consumer feel like a friend rather than a party to a business transaction by giving samples, services and discounts; this may make it difficult for the consumer to refuse to contract. As a result, the OFT has recommended that the Government should extend the right to cancel to solicited doorstep selling visits (see below, 7.7.9.3). It should also be noted that the OFT has drawn up proposals for legislation in relation to sales techniques such as pressurised cold-calling.

7.7.7.3 Advertising of credit

In the context of control of the advertising of credit, the word 'advertisement' is a wide concept, encompassing television and radio advertising, labels, distribution of samples, films, circulars and catalogues, to mention just a few (see the full definition in s 189 of the CCA 1974).

The CCA 1974 creates two main criminal offences relating to advertising credit, which apply even to the advertising of 'exempt' agreements:

- Conveying information which, in a material respect, is false or misleading (s 46(1) of the CCA 1974). In *Metsoja v Pitt & Co Ltd* (1989), a car dealer was able to advertise a '0% finance' deal by giving smaller part-exchange allowances. This was held to be misleading and the dealer was convicted of an offence under s 46(1) of the CCA 1974.

- Advertising the supply of goods under a restricted use credit agreement where the advertiser is not also prepared to sell those goods for cash. If there is no comparable cash price, the consumer is unable to assess the advisability of acquiring the goods on credit.

There are further criminal offences relating to non-compliance with regulations made under s 44 of the CCA 1974 as to the form and content of advertisements of credit (s 47(1) of the CCA 1974). For example, most advertisements of credit are required to include a statement of the Annual Percentage Rate (APR) of interest payable. The APR has also been called the 'true rate of interest' and is the rate which should be used to compare one method of obtaining credit against another, rather than a simple comparison of flat rates of interest. The method of calculating the APR is provided for in the Consumer Credit (Total Charge for Credit, Agreements and Advertisements) (Amendment) Regulations 1999, in line with EC Directive 98/7.

The Consumer Credit (Content of Quotations) and the Consumer Credit (Advertisements) (Amendment) Regulations 1999 (SI 1999/2725), as amended by the Consumer Credit (Advertisement) Regulations 2004, regulate the information to be included in the quotation.

However, the Consumer Credit (Advertisement) Regulations 2004 took effect on 31 October 2004. The main changes to existing law were:

- the imposition of a duty on the advertiser to ensure compliance with the regulations;

- that advertisements must use plain and intelligible language, be easily legible/audible and specify the name of the advertiser; and

- in addition to the existing definition of the APR, the concept of the 'typical APR' is created, which may also be quoted in advertisements; this is an APR, at or below which, at the date of publication, the advertiser reasonably expects that credit will be given in at least 66% of transactions resulting from the advertisement. This provision clearly impacts on advertisers who have previously used phrases such as 'typical/guideline APR' in advertisements.

7.7.7.4 *Adequacy of protection*

Whilst the laws relating to promotion of credit go a long way to protecting the consumer, the problem still remains that many consumers either do not read or do not understand the information made available. Despite the attempts to protect young people from being persuaded into obtaining credit, application forms for 'plastic' cards are common magazine inserts and television advertising of credit is on the increase. Finally, it is worth noting that an offence against the advertising provisions does not in itself affect the validity and enforceability of a credit agreement (s 170 of the CCA 1974).

7.7.8   Pre-contract protection of the consumer

7.7.8.1   Introduction

The desire to protect the consumer from entering into a credit agreement without a full realisation of what he is undertaking extends to the making of the contract and, accordingly, the CCA 1974 makes the following provisions:

- Section 55(1) enables regulations to be made requiring disclosure of specific information to the debtor before the contract is made. Section 55(2) indicates that failure to comply with regulations renders the agreement unenforceable, unless a court orders that it can be enforced (s 65(1) of the CCA 1974), for example, *Eastern Distributors Ltd v Goldring* (1957) (decided under previous legislation). In such circumstances, the creditor could not recover possession of goods from a debtor who defaulted on payment, nor could he recover any arrears. The Consumer Credit (Disclosure of Information) Regulations 2004 will require a pre-disclosure document to be provided to the hirer/debtor before a regulated agreement is made. The document must be separate from the agreement document and it must be possible for the consumer to take the document away. The contents of the document must be legible and all information must have equal prominence; the required information largely mirrors that to be included in any resulting agreement (see below, 7.7.8.2).

- Section 60(1) requires the Secretary of State to make regulations concerning the form and content of the consumer credit agreement, so that the debtor can be aware of his or her rights and obligations under the agreement. (Section 61 of the CCA 1974 requires that such regulations are complied with for the agreement to be properly executed and s 65 renders an improperly executed agreement unenforceable in the absence of a court order that action may be taken to enforce it.)

- To reflect the growth in the number of *credit reference agencies* and to provide protection and redress for those persons who are incorrectly rated as to their creditworthiness, ss 157–59 allow someone who has been refused credit to request the name and address of the credit reference agency from the creditor/owner. The customer is then entitled to make a written request to the agency for a copy of his or her file (subject to a fee of £2). The customer can then take steps to have the file amended, if necessary.

7.7.8.2   The Consumer Credit (Agreements) Regulations 1983

The Consumer Credit (Agreements) Regulations 1983 (SI 1983/155, as amended by SI 1999/3177) relate to the provisions of s 60. Accordingly, the contractual document must:

- be printed or typed (though 'blanks' can be filled in handwriting) and signed by *both* parties. The debtor must sign *personally*, but the creditor (often a company) can sign through an agent;

- indicate APR, amount of any deposit, amount and timing of instalments, number of instalments, amount of credit given, difference between cash and credit price, total charge for credit and total amount payable;

- give details of the debtor's right to terminate and (where applicable) the restriction on the creditor's right to repossess 'protected goods' (see below, 7.7.9.6);

- give details of any security provided by the debtor;

- include details of the right of cancellation (if applicable) (see below, 7.7.9.3) and the details must be stated in a box; this draws the debtor's attention to his or her right; and

- include the names and postal addresses of the parties and, if goods are involved (as in, for example, hire purchase and credit sale), details of the goods.

All copies of the agreement must contain the same information, subject to some exceptions in relation to signatures (see below, 7.7.8.3).

These provisions should mean that the debtor has all the information that he or she needs before signing the agreement, but the question must arise as to how many consumers actually avail themselves of the opportunity to read all of the information before signing. The Consumer Credit (Agreements) (Amendment) Regulations 2004 amend the 1983 Regulations from 31 May 2005; the main amendment is to require prescribed information to be given in a strict order in the agreement. Furthermore, there cannot be any 'small print' and the print size must be legible.

7.7.8.3 Copies of regulated agreements (ss 62 and 63 of the Consumer Credit Act 1974)

When the debtor signs the agreement, he or she must receive a copy of what he or she signs (the *first* statutory copy); if the creditor does not sign at the same time, the debtor must also receive the *second* statutory copy, which is a copy of the concluded contract with both signatures, within seven days of the creditor signing. Where only the first statutory copy is required, the creditor must send, by post to the debtor, within seven days of conclusion of the contract, a *notice of his or her right to cancel* (if applicable).

In order to determine how many copies of the agreement are required, consider the following examples of debtor-creditor-supplier agreements on hire purchase terms:

Situation 1

1 Sales assistant completes details of hire purchase agreement on the proposal form;

2 debtor signs the form = his or her *offer* to contract;

3 debtor is given first statutory copy (of what he or she has just signed);

4   shop sends form to finance company for signature;

5   creditor signs = *acceptance* = *contract made* (up to this point, the debtor could withdraw his or her offer, in which case no contract would be made). Under s 57 of the CCA 1974, notice of withdrawal of offer can be given to people other than the prospective creditor, for example, the credit broker or supplier who conducted the antecedent negotiations; and

6   within seven days of signing, creditor sends second statutory copy (with both signatures) to debtor = copy of contract.

Situation 2

1   Sales assistant completes details on hire purchase proposal form;

2   debtor signs = *offer* to contract;

3   creditor's representative (for example, shop manager) signs immediately after debtor = *acceptance* = contract; and

4   shop gives debtor a copy of the contract (with both signatures).

Failure to comply with these regulations renders the contract unenforceable without a court order under s 65(1) of the CCA 1974.

It is clear from this section that failure to comply with the legal rules relating to formalities renders the contract unenforceable unless the court grants an enforcement order. Section 127 of the CCA 1974 restricts or denies the power of a court to grant such orders; in *Wilson v First County Trust* (2001), the Court of Appeal held that preventing the court from making such an order (s 127(3)) was incompatible with the rights of the lender under Art 6 of the European Convention on Human Rights. On appeal by the Secretary of State to the House of Lords (*Wilson & Others v The Secretary of State for Trade & Industry* (2003)), it was decided that Art 6 did not apply to this agreement because it was made before the HRA 1998 came into force. However, their Lordships determined that s 127(3) was not incompatible with Art 6 of the Convention; Art 6 did not create civil rights but guaranteed the right to take a civil claim to court. Section 127(3) did not prevent a person making a civil claim; rather, it indicated that the court might find the claim was unenforceable where the agreement was improperly executed.

7.7.9   Protecting the debtor after the contract is made

A wide range of provisions continue to protect debtors even after the contract is made. A specific instance that is known to many consumers is that there are legal restrictions on the right of a finance company to repossess hire purchase goods for non-payment.

7.7.9.1   *Extortionate credit bargains (ss 137–40 of the Consumer Credit Act 1974)*

The CCA 1974 gives the court power to reopen a credit agreement and take action if it finds that a credit agreement is extortionate. A 'bargain' is defined as extortionate when payments imposed on the debtor are grossly exorbitant or grossly contravene the ordinary principles of fair dealing. The court will take into account the prevailing interest, age, capacity and experience of the hirer/debtor. In considering whether the agreement is extortionate, the court must also consider the degree of risk accepted by the creditor and the nature and value of the security. The court can rewrite the agreement or set aside the contract. They do, however, seem to be reluctant to intervene on some occasions.

In *Ketley v Scott* (1981), Mr Scott had negotiated a loan for which he was paying interest at the rate of 48% per annum. He had an overdraft at the bank and the loan was negotiated in a hurry, without full enquiries being made. He defaulted on the loan and the plaintiffs sued him. Mr Scott claimed that the interest rate was extortionate. It was held that there was a high degree of risk involved in the loaning of money and, therefore, the interest charged was not disproportionately high. (See also *Davies v Direct Loans Ltd* (1986).)

Application may be made to the court under these provisions in respect of *any* consumer credit agreement – the £25,000 limit does not apply here.

It should be noted, however, that the creditors who impose extortionate demands are likely to be unlicensed ones who deal with the most vulnerable members of society, who either do not know their rights or may be 'persuaded' not to exercise them. Furthermore, lawyers have speculated that courts will be reluctant to intervene under the provisions of the CCA 1974 – perhaps the *caveat emptor* principle has left its mark on the judiciary.

7.7.9.2 *Disclosure of information*

It is important that consumers are regularly made aware of the current state of their obligations under a credit agreement; most consumers will receive monthly statements of their current bank accounts so as to enable them to check their financial position. The CCA 1974 places obligations on the creditor to ensure that consumers are aware of their financial situation, as follows:

- If the debtor under a fixed term credit agreement makes a written request for a statement of his or her current position under the agreement, the creditor must respond in writing within 12 days (s 77(1) of the CCA 1974) and the creditor's statement is binding (s 172(1) of the CCA 1974). Thus, if a creditor stated that the sum owed was less than it actually was, he or she would be unable to enforce payment of the true sum owed unless, by virtue of s 172(3)(b), the court thinks that the enforcement is just. In relation to running account credit agreements, the information provided by the creditor must include a statement of what is currently owed, amounts which will become payable and the dates on which such amounts will be payable (s 78(1) of the CCA 1974).

- Regardless of any request by the debtor, statements of running account credit agreements must be sent to the debtor at least once every 12 months (s 78(4) of the CCA 1974).

7.7.9.3   The debtor's right to cancel the agreement

The right is given by s 67 of the CCA 1974 and the Consumer Protection (Cancellation of Contracts Concluded away from Business Premises) Regulations 1987 (SI 1987/2117).

It has already been seen (see above, 7.7.8.3) that the prospective debtor can withdraw his or her offer to contract before the creditor accepts; the right to cancel allows a debtor to cancel a validly concluded contract without being in breach. The right may apply to regulated agreements, subject to certain exceptions such as small agreements and overdrafts (see s 74 of the CCA 1974).

In order for the right to cancel to be available, the following conditions must be fulfilled:

- Oral representations (such as 'sales talk') were made in the hirer's (under a consumer hire agreement) or debtor's presence about the agreement before it was made. In *Moorgate Services Ltd v Kabir* (1995), it was indicated that the representation must be material/capable of inducing the agreement, though proof that it was so intended or in fact induced the agreement, was not necessary.

- Such representations were made by the creditor, a party to a 'linked' transaction or the person conducting antecedent negotiations.

- The hirer or debtor signed the agreement off trade premises. The general idea here was to protect people who signed agreements in their own homes, perhaps to 'get rid of' a door-to-door salesman. However, an agreement signed in the pub could also be cancellable because the definition of 'trade premises' means the premises of the creditor, owner, a party to a 'linked transaction' or the person who conducted the antecedent negotiations (s 67(b)). It should also be noted that, under SI 1987/2117 (see above), where an agreement is made during an unsolicited visit by a trader, for example, at the consumer 's home or place of work, it is unenforceable against the consumer unless he or she is sent a notice of his or her right to cancel within seven days, and he or she has a seven day 'cooling off' period. In the past, some businesses tried to avoid the cancellation provisions by driving the consumer to their premises to sign the agreement!

In order to cancel the agreement, the hirer/debtor must give written notice to the creditor (or to any other person specified in s 69 of the CCA 1974) that he or she is cancelling. The usual 'cooling off' period or time allowed for cancellation is five days from receipt of the second statutory copy of the agreement, or the notice of cancellation where the hirer/debtor receives only one copy of the agreement (see above, 7.7.8.3).

The effect of cancellation (ss 70–73 of the CCA 1974) is as follows:

- the agreement is erased and there is no liability under it;

- all sums cease to be payable and all sums paid out are recoverable (for example, a deposit);

- the hirer or debtor is not obliged to return the goods but must hand them over if the owner calls at a reasonable time;

- the hirer or debtor has a duty to take care of the goods for 21 days after notice of cancellation. During that period, he or she is liable if he or she accidentally damages the goods; on expiry of the 21 days, he or she is only liable if he or she deliberately damages the goods;

- the hirer has a lien on the goods for the repayment of sums paid under the agreement;

- any part-exchange goods can be recovered within 10 days or a part-exchange allowance must be given to the hirer;

- any linked transaction is also terminated; and

- if a debtor has received credit under a loan agreement, no interest is payable if he or she repays it within one month of cancellation or before the first repayment is due. If he or she fails to repay within that period, he or she must pay the interest agreed on the loan.

7.7.9.4   The debtor's right to terminate the agreement

The CCA 1974 gives debtors the right to terminate certain credit agreements during the currency of the agreement; the right can be exercised in relation to regulated hire purchase and conditional sale agreements. Termination must be distinguished from cancellation, which wipes out the contract and means that no liability accrues under it. Termination brings the contract to an end at the date of termination, but any obligations already accrued are enforceable. At first sight, the fact that a debtor can bring the contract to an end and does not have to pay future instalments appears to be a protection for the debtor in financial difficulties. In practice, however, termination may not prove to be a financially sound decision.

The right to termination is exercised by notice to the creditor (s 99(1) of the CCA 1974) or any other person entitled to receive the payment under the agreement (for example, the dealer or supplier of the goods). Although termination might appear to be a problem in conditional sales where the ownership has already passed, the CCA 1974 provides that, on termination, ownership reverts to the previous owner (s 99(5) – but subject to s 99(4)).

Termination has the following consequences (s 100 of the CCA 1974):

- arrears due at the date of termination are payable;

- the debtor is liable to pay damages if he or she has failed to take reasonable care of the goods (fair wear and tear excepted);

- the debtor must return the goods when the creditor calls to collect them; and

- the debtor must pay to the creditor such sum (if any) as brings the total paid by the debtor up to half the total price agreed. However, this provision does not apply where the agreement makes no such provision or provides that a smaller sum is payable or a court orders that a smaller sum is payable. It is this provision which the debtor should consider carefully before terminating, as termination could prove very costly. As an alternative to termination, he or she might be able to re-negotiate the contract and pay smaller amounts over a longer period. The debtor might also consider the possibility of re-financing the debt, so that the creditor can be paid off in full.

It should also be noted that s 101 of the CCA 1974 provides for termination of consumer hire agreements. The hirer must give written notice, which is subject to a minimum period. The agreement must have run for at least 18 months before the right to terminate can operate.

7.7.9.5 *The creditor's right of termination*

Most hire purchase and conditional sale agreements give the creditor the right to terminate the agreement and repossess the goods for breach of contract. The commonest form of breach is default in payment.

Of course, the creditor could merely sue for arrears owing, but this is rather an onerous undertaking where the debtor continually defaults. The creditor would clearly prefer to terminate the agreement and recover the goods, which he or she could then sell. Some consumer credit agreements may contain accelerated payment clauses, allowing the creditor to claim the whole of the outstanding balance where the debtor is in default; this, again, is preferable to suing for arrears for each default in payment. Accelerated payment clauses are valid, provided that they are not interpreted as penalty clauses (see above, Chapter 8); this can be avoided by providing for an appropriate rebate on interest for early repayment.

Despite the fact that the law may allow the creditor to terminate the contract and make claims for the balance outstanding or repossession of the goods, the debtor still receives protection because the provisions of the CCA 1974 control the exercise of such rights. Where the debtor is in breach and the creditor wishes to terminate the contract, he or she must serve a default notice on the debtor (s 87 of the CCA 1974). The default notice must state the nature of the breach and what is to be done to remedy it; at least seven days must be given to remedy the breach (s 88 of the CCA 1974). The form of the notice is prescribed by the Consumer Credit (Enforcement, Default and Termination) Regulations 1983 (SI 1983/1561). If the debtor complies, the contract continues as if there had been no breach (s 89 of the CCA 1974). In the case of a default in payment, the default notice should specify the amount owed (see *Woodchester Lease Management Services Ltd v Swain & Co* (1998)), the date by which it must be paid and the consequences of non-compliance; if the debtor fails to comply with the notice, the contract can be treated as terminated. The debtor's liability on such termination would be to:

- pay arrears owing up to date of termination;

- return goods to the creditor when he or she calls for them, after having given the debtor a written request for re-delivery;

- pay damages if he or she has failed to take reasonable care of goods; or

- possibly pay such sum as brings the total paid up to half the total price (see above, 7.7.9.4).

However, these consequences will not automatically follow. The debtor or hirer, having been served with a default notice or in the event of any other action being taken to enforce a regulated agreement, may apply to the court for a time order, allowing him or her extra time to make payments or rectify the breach. Such orders can be varied, extended or revoked by the court (s 129 of the CCA 1974). The terms of a time order will depend on the debtor's circumstances. The court will also consider what is 'just', bearing in mind the creditor's position and the debtor's future prospects. During the period of the time order, the creditor cannot take any action to terminate the agreement, recover possession of any land or goods or remove or vary any rights of the debtor (s 130 of the CCA 1974). Following the decision in *Southern District Finance v Barnes* (1995), where a default notice has been served, the court will have the power under s 129 to rewrite the agreement, resulting in the rescheduling of the whole of the outstanding balance under the loan and, if necessary, where it is 'just', vary the rate of interest.

The CCA 1974 does not actually state the consequences of failing to send a default notice or of sending one which does not comply with the prescribed form, but it has been suggested that a repossession of the goods in such circumstances would give the debtor the right to sue for damages for conversion or trespass to goods or for breach of an implied warranty of quiet possession.

However, there is one limitation on the liability of the debtor who fails to comply with a default notice provided by the rules relating to 'protected goods' (see below, 7.7.9.6).

7.7.9.6   Protected goods

Where the debtor under a hire purchase or conditional sale agreement has paid one-third or more of the total price but the ownership is still with the creditor who terminates the agreement for the debtor's default, the goods cannot be repossessed, unless the debtor consents, without a court order (s 90 of the CCA 1974). A creditor who repossesses goods in contravention of this provision does so at his or her peril. Although the creditor may keep the repossessed goods which he or she owns, the agreement is at an end and the debtor is released from all liability and is entitled to recover all sums already paid (s 91 of the CCA 1974). In such a case, the debtor will have had free use and possession of goods for a period. Furthermore, any guarantor of the credit agreement would be released from liability and could recover any security given. A guarantor is someone who guarantees that the creditor will receive payment due to him or her from the hirer/debtor. It is a secondary responsibility based solely on the responsibility of the hirer to pay.

In *Capital Finance Co Ltd v Bray* (1964), Bray acquired a car under a hire purchase agreement. He fell behind with the repayments and an agent of the finance company repossessed the car without obtaining Bray's consent or a court order. The finance company realised that it had made a mistake and the car was duly returned to Bray. Unfortunately, Bray continued to default on the repayments and the company sued for repossession. It was held, on granting a repossession order, that Bray was entitled to recover all the money he had previously paid to the finance company.

In *Bentinck Ltd v Cromwell Engineering* (1971), a car was the subject of a hire purchase agreement. The car was involved in an accident. The hirer took the car to a garage for repair; he then failed to pay any more hire purchase instalments and did not collect the car. The finance company traced the car and repossessed it. They sold the car and sought to recover depreciation costs from the hirer. He claimed that they had repossessed the car without consent. It was held that, when a hirer has abandoned goods and shows that he or she no longer has any interest in them, the owner can repossess even 'protected goods' without a court order.

7.7.9.7 *Action to recover possession of protected goods*

The CCA 1974 gives the county court jurisdiction over actions relating to protected goods. All those concerned, including any guarantor or indemnifier, must be made parties to the court action. The court can make the following orders in relation to the goods (s 133 of the CCA 1974).

Return order

The hirer is asked to return the goods to the owner/creditor. If the hirer fails to return the goods, the only fallback position is to send in the bailiffs.

Suspended return order

This is awarded when the hirer has a reasonable excuse for default, for example, redundancy or ill health. The court can vary the terms of the original agreement in order to enable the hirer to meet his or her obligations. It can reduce the amount of each instalment and extend the period of time to pay, if this is deemed to be necessary. These are known as time orders. The effect of a suspended order can therefore be summarised as follows:

- the agreement continues but with a variation in terms;

- the owner cannot claim extra interest for the longer period of time;

- if the hirer breaks any terms specified in the varied agreement, it is possible for the court to make an order that the creditor can repossess without going back to court, that is, implement the suspended order;

- the court can vary the time order upon application from the hirer or the owner, if the hirer's financial circumstances get better or worse; and

- the hirer may avoid the suspended order by paying off the unpaid balance and becoming the owner of the goods.

Transfer order

This order gives part of the goods back to the owner and allows the hirer to retain part of the goods and become owner of them. The hire purchase agreement is then at an end.

7.7.9.8 *Early settlement of debts*

The CCA 1974 allows a debtor to pay off his or her debt earlier than agreed (s 94 of the CCA 1974). In order to do so, he or she must give written notice to the creditor of his or her intention and settle the outstanding debt in full. As the creditor gets paid earlier than he or she expected, it would be unfair for him or her to claim interest payments in full; a rebate on the interest must be allowed, which is calculated in accordance with the Consumer Credit (Rebate on Early Settlement) Regulations 1983 (SI 1983/1562). From 31 May 2005, these Regulations are revoked and replaced by the Consumer Credit (Early Settlement) Regulations 2004, which contain transitional arrangements for agreements made before that date. The new Regulations contain an actuarially-based formula for calculating rebates on early settlement.

7.7.10 Defective goods acquired on credit terms

Under credit sale, conditional sale, consumer hire and hire purchase agreements, the debtor/hirer will receive goods. If such goods prove to be defective, the law provides protection by way of statutory implied terms as follows:

- *Credit sale and conditional sale agreements*

  The implied terms of ss 12–15 of the Sale of Goods Act 1979, as amended, apply to such agreements (see above, 7.2.1).

- *Consumer hire*

  The implied terms of ss 6–10 of the Supply of Goods and Services Act 1982, as amended, apply to consumer hire agreements (see above, 7.3).

- *Hire purchase agreements*

  The implied terms of ss 8–11 of the Supply of Goods (Implied Terms) Act 1973 apply to hire purchase agreements. The implied terms are similar to those relating to sale of goods contracts, namely: title; description; satisfactory quality; fitness for purpose; and correspondence with sample. The Sale and Supply of Goods to Consumers Regulations 2002 make amendments to these implied terms in the same way as for the implied terms of a sale of goods or a hire contract.

7.7.11 The dealer/supplier as agent of the creditor – a summary

We have seen that the dealer or supplier is often regarded as the agent of the creditor under the CCA 1974; for example, the garage supplying a vehicle to a debtor is usually the agent of the finance company which lets the debtor have the car on hire purchase terms.

To summarise, he or she is agent in the following circumstances:

- to receive notice of cancellation;
- to receive the goods;

- to receive notice of withdrawal of offers;

- to receive notice of the rescission of the contract; and

- to receive notice of termination.

Also, by virtue of s 56(2) of the CCA 1974, the dealer is to be treated as the agent of the creditor in antecedent negotiations.

CONSUMER PROTECTION

Sale and Supply of Goods

Goods may be supplied onto the market by several means, such as sale and hire. As a result of supply, there may be civil liability to a person suffering loss and a criminal offence may be committed in respect of supplying defective goods.

Sale of Goods Act 1979

- The price may be expressly agreed by the parties, but otherwise a reasonable price is payable.

- The Act implies conditions into contracts for the sale of goods: the goods must correspond with the contract description, must be of satisfactory quality, must be reasonably fit for the purpose made known by the buyer and must correspond with any sample by reference to which the goods are sold. The Sale and Supply of Goods to Consumers Regulations 2002 make amendments to s 14(2).

- It is the duty of the seller to deliver the goods and of the buyer to accept and pay for them.

- Acceptance of a breach of condition deprives the buyer of the right to reject the goods and claim a refund; however, damages may be claimed.

- The seller's remedies for breach of contract are an action for the price, damages for non-acceptance, lien, stoppage in transit and the right of resale.

- The buyer's remedies for breach of contract are specific performance, rejection of the goods, damages and recovery of the price paid. Additional remedies are given by the Sale and Supply of Goods to Consumers Regulations 2002.

- Liability for loss caused by breach of the contract cannot be excluded in consumer sales. In non-consumer sales, liability for failure to transfer title cannot be excluded, but exclusion of liability for other implied conditions of the Act may be valid, subject to the requirement of reasonableness.

- Guarantees must state that 'Statutory rights are not affected'. New controls on voluntary guarantees are made by the Sale and Supply of Goods to Consumers Regulations 2002.

- The purpose of sale of goods contracts is the transfer of property (ownership). The time of such transfer is important because, once property has passed to the buyer, the risk of accidental loss is usually transferred and an unpaid seller can sue for the contract price. The time of transfer of property depends on whether the contract is for the sale of specific, ascertained or unascertained goods. Section 20 of the Sale of Goods Act 1979 is amended in relation to consumer buyers by the 2002 Regulations.

Sale of goods by non-owners

- Generally, a person who does not own goods cannot transfer title in them by sale. There are several statutory exceptions to this rule, contained mainly in the Sale of Goods Act 1979.

The Supply of Goods and Services Act 1982

- Where goods are supplied, terms similar to those of ss 13–15 of the Sale of Goods Act 1979 are implied.
  The ability to exclude these terms is governed by the Unfair Contract Terms Act 1977. Amendments are made by the Sale and Supply of Goods to Consumers Regulations 2002.

- In relation to any service aspect of the contract, there are implied terms that the work will be carried out with reasonable skill and care, that the work will be carried out within a reasonable time (if no time is agreed) and that a reasonable price is payable where none was agreed.

The Consumer Protection (Distance Selling) Regulations 2000

- The Regulations control contracts for the supply of goods and services which are not made face to face, such as online shopping. Some such contracts are not covered, such as internet auctions.

- The Regulations cover information to be given to the consumer before contracting, require confirmation of orders by the supplier and give consumers the right to cancel the contract.

Part I of the Consumer Protection Act 1987

- The Act imposes strict liability on the 'producer' of 'defective' products in relation to a person suffering property loss over £275, death or injury.

- Liability cannot be excluded (s 7) but defences are available under the Act (ss 4 and 6(4)).
- To succeed in proceedings under the Act, the claimant must show that he or she suffered loss, that the product was defective and that it was the defective product which caused the loss.

Part II of the Consumer Protection Act 1987

- Breach of safety regulations made under the Act is a criminal offence.
- The Secretary of State may make safety regulations and issue prohibition notices and notices to warn.

General Product Safety Regulations 1994

- It is a criminal offence to supply unsafe goods on to the market.
- The regulations can apply to new, second hand and reconditioned goods.

Misleading price indications

- It is a criminal offence to give a misleading indication to consumers as to the price of goods, services, accommodation or facilities available.
- Evidence of an offence is provided by non-compliance with the Office of Fair Trading's Code of Practice.

Trade Descriptions Act 1968

- It is a criminal offence for a trader to apply a false description to goods or to sell goods to which such a description applied.
- The trader may plead as a defence that he or she exercised all due diligence and took all reasonable precautions to avoid committing the offence.

Consumer Credit

- Consumer credit is regulated for the most part by the Consumer Credit Act 1974. This applies to 'regulated agreements' (for example, consumer credit and consumer hire agreements) and primarily controls the provision of credit to individuals as opposed to companies.
- In order for the provisions of the Consumer Credit Act 1974 to apply, the credit extended must not exceed £25,000. *Small* agreements are exempted from some of the provisions of the Consumer Credit Act 1974. *Exempt* agreements are not

regulated by the provisions of the Consumer Credit Act 1974 (subject to a few exceptions).

Licensing

- Businesses providing finance for regulated agreements must be licensed by the Office of Fair Trading.

- Issue of a licence is subject to the applicant being a fit person to hold a licence. Licences can be refused, revoked or varied and may limit the credit facilities that the licence holder can offer. Unlicensed trading is a criminal offence.

Promotion of credit agreements

- The Consumer Credit Act 1974 creates criminal offences, such as soliciting a minor to take credit. There are specific criminal offences in relation to non-compliance with provisions in relation to the form and content of advertisements of credit.

Pre-contract protection of the consumer

- The Act enables a person who is refused credit to see any information held by a credit reference agency and to amend it if necessary.

- The Consumer Credit (Disclosure of Information) Regulations 2004 require disclosure of prescribed information to the debtor/hirer before the contract is made.

- The Consumer Credit (Agreements) Regulations 1983 (as amended by the Consumer Credit (Agreements) (Amendment) Regulations 2004) specify the form and content of credit agreements and copies thereof; non-compliance renders the agreement unenforceable without a court order.

Protection of the debtor after the contract is made

- Extortionate credit bargains can be re-opened by the courts.

- The debtor is entitled to statements of the current state of the credit agreement.

- Credit agreements signed off trade premises after oral representations are made can be cancelled within five days of receipt of the second statutory copy of the agreement, by written notice to the creditor/credit broker.

- The debtor can terminate hire purchase, conditional sale and consumer hire agreements by written notice to the creditor/credit broker.

CHAPTER 8

THE TORT OF NEGLIGENCE

8.1 Introduction

Negligence is a tort. It is, however, necessary to define what is meant by 'a tort' before considering the essentials of negligence. A tort is a wrongful act against an individual or body corporate and his, her or its property, which gives rise to a civil claim (usually for damages, although other remedies are available). Principally, liability is based on fault, although there are exceptions to this, for example, breach of statutory duty, vicarious liability and the tort established in *Rylands v Fletcher* (1865). The motive of the defendant in committing the tort is generally irrelevant.

Negligence is the most important of all the torts, not only because an understanding of it is vital to the comprehension of other torts, such as employers' and occupiers' liability, but also because it is the one tort which is constantly developing in the light of social and economic change. This can be seen by reference to product liability, professional negligence and economic loss, all of which were originally only compensated if there was in existence a valid contract; in other words, 'no contract, no claim'. After a period of continual development in the scope and application of this tort, there are signs that the courts are beginning to be more cautious. They are aware of the economic implications on the public and private sector if they continue to extend the scope of actions in negligence. Whether this should be an issue for the courts is always open to debate, but if the courts are to be pragmatic, then they may have no choice but to be restrained in the current economic climate.

A professional person, such as an auditor, accountant, lawyer or doctor, may find themselves in a non-contractual relationship with another who will have little choice but to pursue a claim in negligence if they are injured as a result of professional malpractice. Indeed, in order to cover potential claims in negligence and contract, many professional bodies require, as part of membership approval and the issue of practising certificates, that their members take out insurance cover to meet the cost of potential claims (usually, a minimum amount of cover is stipulated for an individual claim). This is known as professional indemnity insurance.

The prime object of the tort of negligence is to provide compensation for the injured person. It has also been suggested that liability in tort provides a deterrent and that negligence is no exception; that is, it helps to define what is or is not acceptable conduct and, therefore, sets the boundaries of such behaviour. Unfortunately, people rarely act by reference to the civil law and the only real deterrent is through market forces – the economic impact being passed on to those who have a higher risk of causing injury. Alternative compensation systems have been considered, as these would largely eradicate the need of the injured party to pursue legal action. The alternatives on offer are no fault compensation schemes – see the Pearson Commission's *Report on*

Civil Liability and Compensation for Personal Injury (Cmnd 7054, 1978) – and extending public and private insurance schemes.

The impact of the Human Rights Act (HRA) 1998 in opening up the boundaries of the duty of care also needs to be considered. This may be particularly relevant where, for example, the duty of care is restricted on policy grounds. As a result of the decision in *Osman v United Kingdom* (2000), an individual may be able to pursue a claim using the HRA 1998 as the basis of the claim. In the *Osman* case, a claim against the police failed in the Court of Appeal on the basis of public service immunity. However, the claimant succeeded before the European Court of Human Rights on the basis of a breach of Art 6 of the European Convention on Human Rights (ECHR), which guarantees access to justice.

Now that the HRA 1998 is in force, the courts have to implement the ECHR and interpret existing law so as to avoid conflict with the ECHR's underlying principles. Article 13 in particular may provide a remedy where UK law fails to do so. Article 13 provides that 'everyone whose rights and freedoms as set out in this convention are violated, shall have an effective remedy before a national authority notwithstanding the violation has been committed by persons acting in an official capacity'. As a result, there is an increased likelihood that public authorities may be subject to negligence claims (see *Z & Others v United Kingdom* (2001)).

8.2 Elements of the Tort

There are specific elements of the tort of negligence which have to be established in the correct order if a claim by an injured party is to succeed. The burden of proof is on the claimant to show, on a balance of probabilities, that certain elements exist.

8.2.1 Duty of care

A person is not automatically liable for every negligent act that he or she commits. The need to establish the essentials, particularly a duty of care, sets a legal limit on who can bring a claim, as a duty is not owed to the world at large. The onus is on the claimant to establish that the defendant owes him or her a duty of care. Unless this first hurdle is crossed, no liability can arise. The test for establishing whether a duty of care exists arises out of the case of *Donoghue v Stevenson* (1932). Prior to this case, the duty of care was only owed in limited circumstances. Now, it is said that the categories of negligence are never closed, in that the law can change to take into account new circumstances and social or technical change. Where, therefore, there is unintentional damage, there is, potentially, a claim in negligence.

In *Donoghue v Stevenson*, a lady went into a café with her friend, who bought her a bottle of ginger beer. After she had drunk half the bottle, she poured the remainder of the ginger beer into a glass. She then saw the remains of a decomposed snail at the bottom. She suffered nervous shock and sued the manufacturer, as the snail must have got into the bottle at the manufacturer's premises, since the bottle top was securely sealed when her friend bought it. It was held that a manufacturer owes a duty of care to the ultimate consumer of his or her goods. He or she must therefore exercise reasonable care to prevent injury to the consumer. The fact that there is no contractual relationship between the manufacturer and the consumer is irrelevant to this action.

The most important aspect of this case is the test laid down by Lord Atkin. He stated that:

> You must take reasonable care to avoid acts and omissions which you could reasonably foresee would be likely to injure your neighbour. Who, then, in law is my neighbour? … any person so closely and directly affected by my act that I ought reasonably to have them in contemplation as being so affected when I am directing my mind to the acts and omissions which are called in question.

This test forms the basis for deciding the existence of a duty. It follows that, if a duty of care is to exist, the question for the court is somewhat hypothetical, in that the court does not look at the reality (that is, 'did you contemplate the effect of your actions on the injured party?') but asks, 'should you have done so?'; that is, the question is objective, rather than subjective. This does not require specific identity of the injured person; it merely requires ascertainment of the identity of the class of person, for example, pedestrians, children, etc.

The test in *Donoghue v Stevenson* was qualified in *Anns v Merton LBC* (1978). Lord Wilberforce in this case introduced the two stage test for establishing the existence of a duty, as follows:

- Is there a sufficient relationship of proximity or neighbourhood between the alleged wrongdoer and the person who has suffered damage such that, in the reasonable contemplation of the former, carelessness on his part may be likely to cause damage to the latter?

- If the first question is answered in the affirmative, are there then any considerations which ought to negate, reduce or limit the scope of the duty or the class of persons to whom it is owed or the damages to which a breach of duty may give rise?

The first question clearly corresponds with the 'neighbour test' in *Donoghue v Stevenson* (1932), although it is referred to as the 'proximity test'. The second question introduces the consideration of public policy issues, which may be grounds for limiting the situations where a duty of care is found to exist. As far as new situations are concerned, the following are some of the policy reasons which, if justified, may prevent a duty of care from being actionable:

- The 'floodgates' argument, that is, will an extension of duty to cover this situation lead to a flood of litigation?

- Will it lead to an increase in the number of fraudulent claims either against insurance companies or in the courts?

- What are the financial or commercial consequences of extending the duty?

The impact of *Anns* led to the expansion of negligence, as the policy reasons acted only to limit liability once a duty had been found to exist, as opposed to limiting the existence of the duty itself. This was illustrated in the case of *Junior Books Ltd v Veitchi Co Ltd* (1983), in which the House of Lords extended the duty of care because of the close proximity between the parties, in that their relationship was quasi-contractual. As a result, the defendants were found to be liable for pure economic loss resulting from their negligent actions. It should be noted that the decision in *Junior Books* has come to be regarded as a special case, providing a narrow exception to the rule that, in general, there can be no liability in negligence for pure economic loss. However, there was gradual criticism of and retraction from the approach taken by Lord Wilberforce, as can be seen in two cases: *Peabody Donation Fund v Sir Lindsay Parkinson & Co Ltd* (1984), in which the court stressed that the proximity test had to be satisfied before a duty of care could be found to exist; and *Leigh and Sullivan Ltd v Aliakmon Shipping Co Ltd* (1986) (known as *The Aliakmon*), in which Lord Brandon stated that when Lord Wilberforce laid down the two stage test in *Anns*, he was:

> ... dealing with the approach to the questions of existence and scope of duty of care in a novel type of factual situation, which was not analogous to any factual situation in which the existence of such a duty had already been held to exist. He was not suggesting that the same approach should be adopted to the existence of a duty of care in a factual situation in which the existence of such a duty had repeatedly been held not to exist.

This further limitation was developed in *Yuen Kun Yeu v AG of Hong Kong* (1987), in which Lord Keith stated that Lord Wilberforce's approach 'had been elevated to a degree of importance greater than it merits and greater, perhaps, than its author intended'. Finally, the decision in *Anns* was overruled by *Murphy v Brentwood DC* (1990), where it was held that local authorities owed a duty of care to a building owner to avoid damage to the building which would create a danger to the health and safety of the occupants. The duty arose out of the local authority's powers to require compliance with building regulations. However, as the damage was held to be pure economic loss, it was irrecoverable.

The present position, following this rapid retraction from *Anns*, appears to be that in establishing the existence of a duty of care in negligence, an incremental approach must be taken.

The claimant must show that the defendant foresaw that damage would occur to the claimant, that is, that there was sufficient proximity in time, space and relationship between the claimant and the defendant (see *Bourhill v Young* (1943)). In practical terms, foreseeability of damage will determine proximity in the majority of personal injury cases. The courts will then, where appropriate, consider whether it is just and reasonable to impose a duty and whether there are any policy reasons for denying or limiting the existence of a duty, for example, under the floodgates argument. The courts will not necessarily consider these in all cases.

The final retraction from *Anns* and support for the incremental approach was seen in *Caparo Industries plc v Dickman* (1990), where the application of a three stage test for establishing a duty of care was recommended. This requires consideration of the following questions:

* Was the harm caused reasonably foreseeable?

* Was there a relationship of proximity between the defendant and the claimant?

* In all the circumstances, is it just, fair and reasonable to impose a duty of care?

This decision has since been followed in *Marc Rich Co AG v Bishop Rock Marine Co Ltd (The Nicholas H)* (1994). The Court of Appeal held in this case that a duty of care would only be imposed if the three aims of the test expounded in *Caparo* could be satisfied. These would have to be applied irrespective of the type of loss suffered. If anything, this takes the retraction from *Anns* one step further, as, in the past, it could always be argued that *Anns* applied to new duty situations, as opposed to all situations.

A clear application of policy reasons limiting the existence of a duty of care can be seen in *Hill v CC of West Yorkshire* (1989). Mrs Hill's daughter was the last victim of the Yorkshire Ripper. She alleged that the police had failed to take reasonable care in apprehending the murderer, as they had interviewed him but had not arrested him prior to her daughter's unlawful killing. The House of Lords had to determine whether the police owed her a duty of care. After confirming the need to establish foresight and proximity, the court went on to state that there were policy reasons for not allowing the existence of a duty in this case, namely, that any other result might lead to police discretion being limited and exercised in a defensive frame of mind. This might, in turn, distract the police from their most important function – 'the suppression of crime'.

A further illustration of public policy influences on whether there is a duty of care owed by the police can be seen in *Alexandrou v Oxford* (1993), in which it was held that there was no duty owed by the police to the owners of premises that had a burglar alarm system connected to a police station.

It is apparent that the courts' current position is to continue to retreat from *Anns* to a more 'category-based' approach, as referred to in the *ratio* of *Donoghue v Stevenson*. This was clearly summed up by Lord Hoffmann in *Stovin v Wise* (1996), as follows:

> The trend of authorities has been to discourage the assumption that anyone who suffers loss is *prima facie* entitled to compensation from a person ... whose act or omission can be said to have caused it. The default position is that he is not.

Public policy or not, it is still the case that, unless harm to the claimant can be foreseen, a duty of care cannot be established. In *Goodwin v British Pregnancy Advisory Service* (1996), the defendants performed a vasectomy on a man who was subsequently to become Goodwin's lover. It transpired that the vasectomy had not been a success, and the plaintiff became pregnant. The plaintiff claimed that the defendants owed her a duty of care and were negligent in not warning her lover that a small number of vasectomies spontaneously reverse, leading to the possibility of fertility being restored. Her claim was struck out. The only possible duty of care would have been to the wife of the patient, had he been married at the time of the vasectomy. The plaintiff, however, could not be foreseen by the defendants, as she fell within an indeterminate class of women with whom the patient could have a sexual relationship.

Even where harm to the claimant is foreseen, an omission to act will not result in liability unless there is an existing relationship between the parties, for example, between a member of the public and the fire service or a doctor and patient. Liability may also arise through custom and practice resulting in wilful neglect (see *X v Bedfordshire CC* (1995)). This can be seen in *Vellino v Chief Constable of Greater Manchester* (2001), in which the claimant sustained serious injuries whilst trying to escape from police custody. The claimant had a history of being arrested at his flat, and of trying to evade arrest by jumping out of his flat windows. He argued that two police officers had sought to arrest him, but made no attempt to prevent him from jumping out of the window. The Court of Appeal held that a police officer carrying out an arrest did not owe the person being arrested a duty of care to prevent him from injuring himself in a foreseeable attempt to escape. The act of escaping from custody constituted a common law crime and therefore could not attract tortious liability (*ex turpi causa*).

8.2.2 Nervous shock

Nervous shock (or post-traumatic stress disorder, to give it its medical name) is a form of personal injury and, thus, may give rise to a claim for damages. The Law Commission Report, *Liability for Psychiatric Illness* (No 249, 1998) highlights the continuing problem for the courts in determining the extent of liability for post-traumatic stress disorder. If damages are to be recoverable, nervous shock must take the form of a recognised mental illness; mental suffering, such as grief, is generally not recoverable (see *Vernon v Bosley (No 1)* (1997)). No physical injury need be suffered. The basis of liability for nervous shock depends on whether this type of injury was reasonably foreseeable and whether there was sufficient proximity between the claimant and the defendant.

In *Bourhill v Young* (1943), the plaintiff, a pregnant woman, heard a motor accident as she alighted from a tram. A little while later, she saw some blood on the road. She alleged that, as a result of seeing the aftermath of the accident, she suffered nervous shock, which led to a miscarriage. It was held that the plaintiff did not fall within the class of persons to whom it could be reasonably foreseen that harm might occur.

Indeed, it was made clear in this case that one could expect passers-by to have the necessary 'phlegm and fortitude' not to suffer nervous shock as a result of seeing the aftermath of an accident. As a result, the abnormally sensitive claimant will not recover for nervous shock unless the person with normal phlegm and fortitude would have sustained shock in those circumstances (see *Jaensch v Coffey* (1984)).

At present, the courts appear to be treating the professional rescuer as a bystander for the purposes of nervous shock claims and expect them to have the requisite phlegm and fortitude, as described in *Bourhill v Young*.

As far as the courts are concerned, persons claiming for nervous shock fall into distinct categories, as follows:

- *The claimant experiences shock and illness after fearing for his or her own safety*

  In this situation, the claimant is a primary victim. In claiming nervous shock, there is a clear distinction between how the courts view primary and secondary victims (the latter being those who are not in danger themselves but who witness the aftermath). In *Dulieu v White* (1901), a pregnant woman was serving in a public house when the defendant's employee negligently drove a van into the front of the building. The plaintiff was not physically injured, but suffered severe shock, which led to illness. It was held that she was allowed to recover damages, as the shock and illness arose out of a fear of immediate personal injury to herself.

Further application of the decision in *Dulieu* can be seen in *Page v Smith* (1995), where the House of Lords held that foreseeability of physical injury was sufficient to enable the plaintiff, who was directly involved in an accident, to recover damages for nervous shock, even though he had not actually been physically hurt. Interestingly, Lord Keith, in a dissenting judgment, felt that the plaintiff's claim for nervous shock should be defeated on the basis of remoteness of damage; that is, the class of injury was unforeseen.

- *Where the claimant fears for the personal safety of a close relative*

In *Hambrook v Stokes Bros* (1925), an unattended lorry began to roll down a hill. A mother had just left her children when she saw the lorry go out of control. She could not see her children, but heard the crash. She was told that a child wearing glasses had been hurt. One of her children wore glasses. She suffered shock, which was so severe that it eventually led to her death. It was held that her estate could recover damages, even though her illness was caused by fear for her children, not for herself. The defendant, the lorry driver, should have foreseen that his negligence might put someone in such fear of bodily injury, that is, that they would suffer nervous shock, and that this could be extended to cover fear for one's children.

Nervous shock can arise from a series of events which can be viewed holistically rather than as a single traumatising event. In *North Glamorgan NHS Trust v Walters* (2002), a mother, having been informed that her 10 month old baby, who was suffering from hepatitis, would survive, then witnessed the baby have a major fit. As a result, both mother and baby were immediately transferred to another hospital for the baby to undergo a liver transplant. However, in the interim, the baby had suffered severe brain damage. Within 36 hours the life support machine had to be switched off and the baby died in its mother's arms. As a result, the mother suffered a recognised psychiatric illness and successfully sued the hospital. It was held by the Court of Appeal that the chain of events should be viewed as having an immediate impact on the mother and could therefore be distinguished from cases involving psychiatric illness over a period of time.

In *McLoughlin v O'Brian* (1982), a mother was informed at home that her family had been injured in a road accident two miles away. As a result, she suffered psychiatric illness, caused by the shock of hearing this news and seeing her family in hospital, who were still in a particular bloody state because they had not yet received any treatment; also, one child had been killed. It was held that she should recover damages, as the shock was a foreseeable consequence of the defendant's negligence. The courts felt that the proximity of the plaintiff to the accident was relevant. However, 'proximity' here meant closeness in time and space. Furthermore, the shock must be caused by the sight or hearing of the event or its immediate aftermath.

The essential elements for establishing a duty in similar cases arose out of Lord Wilberforce's *dictum in McLoughlin*, which was that, in addition to foresight, the claimant must show that there was a close relationship between him or her and the person suffering injury; secondly, that there was sufficient proximity between the claimant and the accident in terms of time and space; and, finally, it was concluded that being told about the accident by a third party was outside the scope of the duty. The application of Lord Wilberforce's *dictum* was seen in *Alcock & Others v Chief Constable of South Yorkshire* (1991). This case arose out of the accident at Hillsborough stadium in Sheffield, involving Liverpool supporters who were crushed as a result of a surge of supporters being allowed into the ground by the police. The nervous shock claim was made by those friends and relatives who witnessed the scenes either first hand at the ground or saw or heard them on television or radio. The House of Lords repeated the requirements for establishing duty of care in cases of nervous shock. There should be:

○ a close and loving relationship with the victim if reasonable foresight is to be established;

○ proximity in time and space to the accident or its aftermath; and

○ nervous shock resulting from seeing or hearing the accident or its immediate aftermath.

It is still open to debate whether viewing live television is equivalent to seeing the accident. It is generally considered not to be, because broadcasting guidelines prevent the showing of suffering by recognisable individuals. Furthermore, any such transmission may be regarded as a *novus actus interveniens*.

• *Where the claimant suffers nervous shock through seeing injury to others, even though he or she is in no danger himself or herself*

In *Dooley v Cammell Laird & Co* (1951), a faulty rope was being used on a crane to secure a load as it was hoisted into the hold of a ship. The rope broke, causing the load to fall into the hold, where people were working. The crane driver suffered shock arising out of a fear for the safety of his fellow employees. It was held that the crane driver could recover damages, as it was foreseeable that he was likely to be affected if the rope broke.

It would appear that the decision in Dooley is confined to situations where the employee making the claim was directly involved in the incident, rather than a mere 'bystander'. In *Robertson and Rough v Forth Road Bridge Joint Board* (1995), two employees claimed damages for nervous shock after witnessing another colleague, who was working alongside them on the Forth Road Bridge, fall to his death. It was held that their claim would fail, as they were in effect mere bystanders and their illness was not, therefore, reasonably foreseeable.

This was confirmed in *Hegarty v EE Caledonia Ltd* (1996), in which the plaintiff, who was on one of the support vessels, witnessed at close range the Piper Alpha oil rig disaster, in which over 150 men died. He claimed nervous shock but was found to be a person of normal fortitude who, as a 'mere bystander', was close to the danger but not actually in danger himself. However, it could now be argued that damages for psychiatric harm suffered by an employee who witnesses the event and is in danger himself may be recoverable, following the decision in *Young v Charles Church (Southern) Ltd* (1996), in which an employee working alongside a man who was electrocuted and killed was also held to be a 'primary victim'.

In *Chadwick v British Railways Board* (1967), Chadwick took part in the rescue operation after a train crash. He suffered a severe mental condition as a result of the horrific scenes. He had a previous history of mental illness. It was held that the British Railways Board was liable. It was reasonably foreseeable that, in the event of an accident, someone other than the defendant's employees would intervene and suffer injury. Injury to a rescuer in the form of shock was reasonably foreseeable, even if he suffered no physical injury.

One of the more controversial decisions arose in *White (formerly Frost) v CC of South Yorkshire* (1999), in which a number of policemen involved in the Hillsborough stadium disaster (in which 95 football supporters were crushed to death) brought claims for psychiatric damage attributable to witnessing the events. It was held by the Court of Appeal that the police who attended the scene in the immediate aftermath of the incident were rescuers and were entitled to recover on that basis. It was further held that a rescuer, whether a policeman or layperson, may recover against a tortfeasor for physical or psychiatric injury sustained during a rescue. Among the factors to be considered in determining whether a particular person is a rescuer are: the character and extent of the initial incident caused by the tortfeasor; whether that incident has finished or is continuing; whether there is any danger, continuing or otherwise, to the victim or to the claimant; the character of the claimant's conduct, both in itself and in relation to the victim; and how proximate, in time and place, the claimant's conduct is to the incident.

However, the findings of the Court of Appeal were reversed by the House of Lords (*White v Chief Constable of South Yorkshire Police* (1999)). The House of Lords concluded that the police officers who were present should not be treated as primary victims. They were secondary victims, like any person who witnesses injury to others but is not in danger himself or herself. As such a victim, the conditions laid down in *Alcock* (1991) must, therefore, be met. Furthermore, they were not to be treated as a special category of rescuer. To claim as 'rescuers', the police officers would still have to show that they met the criteria under which rescuers could recover as secondary victims. (For further discussion of the law in this area, see Mullany and Handford, 'Hillsborough replayed' (1997) 113 LQR 410; and Teff, 'Liability for negligently inflicted psychiatric harm: justifications and boundaries' [1998] CLJ 91.)

It is certainly possible for the law to be extended in this area. For example, in *Attia v British Gas* (1987), the plaintiff was able to recover damages for nervous shock resulting from the sight of her house being burned down as a result of the defendant's negligence.

Finally, returning to the principle that grief alone will not normally sustain a claim for nervous shock, the case of *Vernon v Bosley (No 1)* (1997) shows that it may be possible to recover for a condition which falls short of post-traumatic stress disorder, but which amounts to pathological grief disorder. In *Vernon*, the plaintiff's children were killed when their car, which was being driven by their nanny, left the road and crashed into a river. The plaintiff was called to the scene of the accident and witnessed the attempts of the emergency services to rescue the children. He subsequently became mentally ill and his business and marriage failed. The plaintiff accepted that his illness was due to the deaths of his children, but argued that it was not caused by shock, but by pathological grief. The Court of Appeal held that, as a secondary victim who met the general preconditions for such a claim, he could recover, even though his illness was linked to pathological grief rather than post-traumatic stress disorder. It could, however, be argued that, given the facts of this case, there is a very fine dividing line between the two notional heads of claim.

8.2.3 Economic loss

There are two categories of economic loss which may form the basis of a claim in negligence. First, there is economic loss arising out of physical injury or damage to property; and, secondly, there is what is known as 'pure' economic loss, which is the sole loss sustained, unconnected with physical damage. Following more recent developments, only the former is now recoverable, unless the claimant can show that there was a 'special relationship' between him or her and the defendant, in which the defendant assumed responsibility for the claimant's economic welfare (see *Williams v Natural Life Health Foods Ltd* (1998)). In effect, the law has reverted to the decision in the following case for defining the extent of liability for economic loss.

In *Spartan Steel and Alloys Ltd v Martin & Co* (1973), the plaintiffs manufactured steel alloys 24 hours a day. This required continuous power. The defendant's employees damaged a power cable, which resulted in a lack of power for 14 hours. There was a danger of damage to the furnace, so this had to be shut down and the products in the process of manufacture removed, thereby reducing their value. The plaintiffs also suffered loss of profits. It was held that the defendants were liable for physical damage to the products and the loss of profit arising out of this. There was, however, no liability for economic loss which was unconnected with the physical damage.

The rule that economic loss was only recoverable where it was directly the consequence of physical damage was challenged in *Junior Books Ltd v Veitchi Ltd* (1983), in which a claim for pure economic loss was allowed on the basis of there being sufficiently close proximity between the plaintiffs and the sub-contractor who had carried out the work for the main contractor. However, following this case, there was a gradual retraction from recovery for pure economic loss: see *Muirhead v Industrial Tank Specialties Ltd* (1986), where it was held that there was insufficient proximity between the purchaser of goods and the manufacturer of the goods with respect to a claim for economic loss. This was reinforced in the cases of *Simaan General Contracting Co v Pilkington Glass Ltd (No 2)* (1988) and *Greater Nottingham Co-operative Society Ltd v Cementation Piling and Foundations Ltd* (1988), where the courts refused to find sufficient proximity in tripartite business relationships, although the decision in *Junior Books* appears to stand, at least for the moment.

The expansion of the law in this area was seen to result from Lord Wilberforce's two stage test in *Anns v Merton LBC* (1978). As the gradual withdrawal from that decision grew apace, it was inevitable that a final blow would be dealt to this test. First, in *D and F Estates Ltd v Church Commissioners for England* (1988), it was held that a builder was not liable in negligence to the owner for defects in quality, only for personal injury or damage to other property, thereby bringing back the distinction between actions in tort and contract. Additionally, it was held that pure economic loss could only be recovered in an action for negligent misstatement or where the circumstances fell within *Junior Books*. Secondly, in *Murphy v Brentwood DC* (1990), the decision in *Anns* was overruled; it was made clear that liability for pure economic loss could only be sustained in an action for negligent misstatement based on *Hedley Byrne & Co v Heller and Partners* (1964).

For further discussion of this area, see Cane, *Tort Law and Economic Interests*, 2nd edn, 1996.

8.2.4 Negligent misstatements

The importance of the neighbour, or proximity, test can be seen in the extension of the duty of care to cover negligent misstatements which result in economic loss. Indeed, as we have seen, this is the only heading under which pure economic loss can be claimed. This expansion of the duty arose out of the case of *Hedley Byrne & Co v Heller and Partners* (1964). Prior to this case, there was only liability for negligent misstatements causing physical damage, intentionally dishonest or fraudulent statements, or where there was a fiduciary or contractual relationship between the parties (*Derry v Peek* (1889)).

In *Hedley Byrne*, Hedley Byrne asked their bank to make inquiries into the financial position of Heller, one of their clients. The bank made enquiries of Heller's bank, which gave a favourable reply about the client's financial position, adding the words 'without responsibility'. Hedley Byrne relied on this advice and lost a lot of money when their clients went into liquidation. However, they lost their action against the bank because of the exclusion clause, which at that time was held to be valid. The importance of the case is the *dictum* on negligent misstatements. It was held that a duty of care exists where:

> ... one party seeking information and advice was trusting the other to exercise such a degree of care as the circumstances required, where it was reasonable for him to do that, and where the other party gave the information or advice when he knew or ought to have known the enquirer was relying on him.

Liability for negligent misstatements is based on the existence of a special relationship; that is, the defendant must hold himself out in some way as having specialised knowledge, knowing that any information that he or she gives will be relied upon by the claimant. Interestingly, it has recently been decided that there may be concurrent liability in tort and contract, so that the claimant may choose which cause of action provides him or her with the best remedy. This is illustrated in *Henderson v Merrett Syndicates Ltd* (1994), in which it was held that an assumption of responsibility by a person providing professional or quasi-professional services, coupled with reliance by the person for whom the services were provided, could give rise to tortious liability, irrespective of whether there was a contractual relationship between the parties. (This decision finally lays to rest the decision in *Tai Hing Cotton Mill Ltd v Liu Chong Hing Bank Ltd* (1986), which excluded concurrent liability in contract and tort.) Obviously, lawyers, accountants, bankers, surveyors, etc, come within this 'special relationship'. (See Hepple, R, 'The search for coherence' (1997) 50 CLP 69.)

However, as the law has developed, some attempts to limit liability can be found in the case law. For example, in *Mutual Life and Citizens Assurance Co v Evatt* (1971), it was held that the defendant should be in the business of giving such advice, although the minority in this case required the plaintiff to make it clear to the defendant that he was seeking advice which he may then have relied on. There is, in general, no liability for information given on a purely social occasion, but advice from friends on other occasions may result in liability, as can be seen in *Chaudry v Prabhakar* (1988). Silence or inaction can rarely amount to misstatement, unless there was a duty on the defendant to disclose or take action. In *Legal and General Assurance Ltd v Kirk* (2002), the Court of Appeal held that for a claim based on negligent misstatement in respect of an employment reference, a statement must actually have been made to a third party. The fact that Mr Kirk had not applied for a reference in the knowledge that the contents of the reference would inevitably have led to his being rejected by a prospective employer was insufficient to establish liability on the part of the employer. The courts have recognised that it is possible for there to be a voluntary assumption of responsibility by the defendant and reliance by the claimant on that assumption (*La Banque Financière de la Cité v Westgate Insurance Co Ltd* (1990)). Any attempt at excluding liability may be subject to the Unfair Contract Terms Act (UCTA) 1977 and would then have to satisfy the test of reasonableness laid down in s 2(2). It should also be noted that any attempt to exclude liability for death or personal injury is not permitted by virtue of s 2 of UCTA 1977.

8.3   Professional Negligence

In considering whether a duty of care is owed by the defendant to the claimant, it is necessary to consider the particular position of the professional person who, through the nature of his or her job, will be giving advice or carrying out acts which may leave him or her open to a claim in negligence.

8.3.1   Accountants and auditors

While there may be a contractual relationship between an accountant and his client, on which the client can sue, the contentious legal area arises in respect of other people who may rely on reports made or advice given in a non-contractual capacity. Indeed, in many situations, the potential claimant may be unknown to the accountant. Whether there is liability appears to depend upon the purpose for which reports are made or accounts prepared.

In *JEB Fasteners v Marks Bloom & Co* (1983), the defendant accountants negligently overstated the value of stock in preparing accounts for their client. At the time of preparation, the accountants were aware that their client was in financial difficulties and was actively seeking financial assistance. After seeing the accounts, the plaintiff decided to take over the company. They then discovered the true financial position and sued the accountants for negligent misstatement. It was held that a duty of care was owed by the accountants, as it was foreseeable that someone contemplating a takeover might rely on the accuracy of the accounts; they were not liable, however, as their negligence had not caused the loss to the plaintiff. The evidence revealed that when they took over the company, they were interested not in the value of the stock but in acquiring the expertise of the directors. Thus, although they relied on the accounts, the accounts were not the cause of the loss, as they would have taken over the company in any event.

In *Law Society v KPMG Peat Marwick* (2000), a firm of accountants hired by solicitors to prepare their annual accounts was found also to owe a duty to the Law Society. This was on the grounds that there was a statutory and professional duty on solicitors to produce annual accounts for the Law Society, and because the Law Society was also liable to solicitors' clients for mis-management of solicitors' accounts, resulting in the possible payment of compensation by the Law Society. It was therefore reasonable that a duty should be owed.

The case of *Caparo Industries plc v Dickman* (1990) served to limit the potential liability of auditors in auditing company accounts. Accounts were audited in accordance with the Companies Act 1985. The respondents, who already owned shares in the company, decided to purchase more shares and take over the company after seeing the accounts. The accounts were inaccurate. The respondents then incurred a loss, which they blamed on the negligently audited accounts. It was held that, when the accounts were prepared, a duty of care was owed to members of the company (that is, the shareholders), but only so far as to allow them to exercise proper control over the company. This duty did not extend to members as individuals and potential purchasers of shares. The onus was clearly on the appellants in these circumstances to make their own independent inquiries, as it was unreasonable to rely on the auditors.

However, where express representations are made about the accounts and the financial state of a company by its directors or financial advisers, with the intention that the person interested in the takeover will rely on them, a duty of care is owed (*Morgan Crucible Co plc v Hill Samuel Bank Ltd* (1991)).

The case of *James McNaughten Paper Group Ltd v Hicks Anderson & Co* (1991) reaffirmed the key elements in determining liability for negligent misstatements. In this case, the accountants were asked, at short notice, to draw up draft accounts for a company chairman. The plaintiffs, who were planning a takeover bid, inspected the accounts, and on that basis took over the company. They subsequently claimed that the draft accounts were inaccurate and that they had suffered a loss. The Court of Appeal held that in determining liability, the following needed to be considered:

- the purpose for which the statement is made;

- the purpose for which the statement is communicated;

- the relationship between the adviser, the one advised and any relevant third party;

- the size of any class to which the person advised belonged; and

- the state of knowledge of the adviser.

8.3.2 Lawyers

Solicitors are usually in a contractual relationship with their client; however, there may be circumstances outside this relationship where they are liable in tort for negligent misstatements. The definitive position was stated in *Ross v Caunters* (1980), where the defendant solicitors prepared a will, under which the plaintiff was a beneficiary. The solicitors sent the will to the person instructing them, but failed to warn him that it should not be witnessed by the spouse of a beneficiary. When the will was returned to them, they failed to notice that one of the witnesses was the plaintiff's spouse. As a result, the plaintiff lost her benefit under the will. It was held that a solicitor may be liable in negligence to persons who are not his clients, either on the basis of the principle in *Hedley Byrne & Co v Heller and Partners* (1964) or under *Donoghue v Stevenson* (1932). The latter was specifically applied in this case, the plaintiff being someone so closely and directly affected by the solicitors' acts that it was reasonably foreseeable that they were likely to be injured by any act or omission.

The decision in *Ross v Caunters* was further supported by the decision of the House of Lords in *White v Jones* (1995), in which the plaintiff was cut out of his father's will. The father then instructed his solicitors to reinstate him. Unfortunately, the solicitors delayed some six weeks in carrying out the change and, in the meantime, the father died. It was held that the solicitors owed a duty of care to the son as a potential beneficiary. The loss to the plaintiff was reasonably foreseeable and the duty of care was broken by their omission to act promptly.

Barristers are in the position of not being in a contractual relationship with their 'client', that is, the person they are representing; neither are they liable in tort for the way in which they conduct a case in court. There are policy reasons for this, as the duty to the court is higher than the duty to the client and must be put first, as can be seen in *Rondel v Worsley* (1969). In *Saif Ali v Sidney Mitchell* (1980), it was confirmed that a barrister was neither liable for conduct of the case in court, nor was he liable for pre-trial work connected with the conduct of the case in court. However, he would be liable in tort for negligent opinions, that is, written advice where there was no error on the part of the solicitor briefing him.

Further limits on immunity for solicitors can be seen in *Arthur JS Hall & Co v Simons* (2000), in which solicitors who were being sued for negligence in civil proceedings attempted to rely on *Rondel v Worsley*. The House of Lords held that public policy arguments in favour of exemption were no longer appropriate and that *Rondel v Worsley* was disapproved. It was felt that the courts would be able to judge between errors of judgment which were an inevitable part of advocacy and true negligence and, as a result, the floodgates would not be opened. This has resulted in immunity being removed in both criminal and civil proceedings.

Lawyers may also be liable for psychiatric injury resulting from negligence. In *McLoughlin v Jones* (2001), a person who was wrongly convicted and imprisoned as a result of his solicitor's negligence was able to claim psychiatric injury as a result of the trauma involved.

8.3.3 Surveyors

A duty of care is owed by surveyors, builders and architects, etc, to the client, with whom they are usually in a contractual relationship. However, there may also be liability in tort as a result of *Hedley Byrne & Co v Heller and Partners* (1964), although this hinges on the questions of reasonable reliance by the third party and whether the defendant ought to have foreseen such reliance.

In *Yianni v Edwin Evans & Sons* (1982), surveyors who were acting for the defendant building society valued a house at £15,000 and, as a result, the plaintiffs were able to secure a mortgage of £12,000. The house was, in fact, suffering from severe structural damage and repairs were estimated at £18,000. The basis of the plaintiffs' claim was not only the surveyor's negligence, but also the fact that he ought reasonably to have contemplated that the statement would be passed on by the building society to the plaintiffs and that they would rely on it, which they did. It was held that a duty of care was owed by the defendants. An important factor was that the price of the house indicated that the plaintiff was of modest means, would not be expected to obtain an independent valuation and would, in all probability, rely on the defendant's survey, which was communicated to them by the building society. The court was also confident that the defendants knew that the building society would pass the survey to the purchasers and that they would rely on it.

The decision in *Yianni* was approved in *Smith v Eric Bush* (1989) and *Harris v Wyre Forest DC* (1989). The facts of the former case are very similar to *Yianni*, in that the plaintiff was sent a copy of the surveyor's report by the defendant building society. This report stated that no essential repairs were necessary and, although it contained a recommendation on obtaining independent advice, the plaintiff chose to rely on the report. In fact, the property had defective chimneys. In *Harris*, the plaintiffs did not see the surveyor's report, as it was stated on the mortgage application that the valuation was confidential and that no responsibility would be accepted for the valuation. However, the plaintiff paid the valuation fee and accepted the 95% mortgage on offer. When they attempted to sell the house three years later, structural defects were revealed and the property was deemed to be uninhabitable and unsaleable. It was held, in both cases, that there was sufficient proximity between the surveyor and the purchaser and that it was foreseeable that the plaintiff was likely to suffer damage as a result of the negligent advice. It was felt that, in general, surveyors knew that 90% of purchasers relied on their valuation for the building society; it was, therefore, just and reasonable for a duty to be imposed. The limitation on this decision is that it does not extend protection to subsequent purchasers or where the property is of a high value (although this will need to be determined on the facts of each case). The attempt to exclude liability in this case was seen as an attempt to exclude the existence of a duty of care, which, it was felt, was not within the spirit of UCTA 1977 and could not be permitted. In *Merrett v Babb* (2001), the defendant was held to have assumed personal responsibility to the buyers of a house he surveyed. This was despite the fact that he had not met the client, nor was the fee paid to him individually. However, he signed the valuation report personally and this report proved to be defective.

The decision in *Murphy v Brentwood DC* (1990) has seriously limited the potential liability of builders, architects and quantity surveyors in respect of claims arising out of defective buildings. Where the defect is discovered prior to any injury to person or health, or damage to property other than the defective premises itself, this is to be regarded as pure economic loss, not physical damage to property, and is not, therefore, recoverable in negligence.

8.4   Breach of the Duty of Care

Once the claimant has established that the defendant owes him or her a duty of care, he or she must then establish that the defendant is in breach of this duty. The test for establishing breach of duty was laid down in *Blyth v Birmingham Waterworks Co* (1856). A breach of duty occurs if the defendant:

> ... fails to do something which a reasonable man, guided upon those considerations which ordinarily regulate the conduct of human affairs, would do; or does something which a prudent and reasonable man would not do [*per* Alderson B].

The test is an objective test, judged through the eyes of the reasonable man. The fact that the defendant has acted less skilfully than the reasonable man would expect will usually result in breach being established. This is the case even where the defendant is inexperienced in his particular trade or activity. One cannot condone the incompetence of such defendants. For example, a learner driver must drive in the manner of a driver of skill, experience and care (*Nettleship v Weston* (1971)). It is, however, clear from the case law that, depending on the age of the child, the standard of care expected from a child may be lower than that of an adult. Children should be judged on whether they have the 'foresight and prudence of a normal child of that age' (see *Mullin v Richards* (1998)). The degree or standard of care to be exercised by such a person will vary, as there are factors, such as the age of the claimant, which can increase the standard of care to be exercised by the defendant. The test is, therefore, flexible. The following factors are relevant:

8.4.1   The likelihood of injury

In deciding whether the defendant has failed to act as the reasonable man would act, the degree of care must be balanced against the degree of risk involved if the defendant fails in his duty. It follows, therefore, that the greater the risk of injury or the more likely it is to occur, the more the defendant will have to do to fulfil his duty.

In *Bolton v Stone* (1951), a cricket ground was surrounded by a 17 ft high wall and the pitch was situated some way from the road. A batsman hit a ball exceptionally hard, driving it over the wall, where it struck the plaintiff, who was standing on the highway. It was held that the plaintiff could not succeed in his action, as the likelihood of such injury occurring was small, as was the risk involved. The slight risk was outweighed by the height of the wall and the fact that a ball had been hit out of the ground only six times in 30 years.

8.4.2   The seriousness of the risk

The degree of care to be exercised by the defendant may be increased if the claimant is very young, old or less able bodied in some way. The rule is that 'you must take your victim as you find him' ('the egg-shell skull rule'). This is illustrated in *Haley v London Electricity Board* (1965), in which the defendants, in order to carry out repairs, had made a hole in the pavement. Haley, who was blind, often walked along this stretch of pavement. He was usually able to avoid obstacles by using his white stick. The precautions taken by the Electricity Board would have prevented a sighted person from injuring himself, but not a blind person. Haley fell into the hole, striking his head on the pavement, and became deaf as a consequence. It was held that the Electricity Board was in breach of its duty of care to pedestrians. It had failed to ensure that the excavation was safe for all pedestrians, not just sighted persons. It was clearly not reasonably safe for blind persons, yet it was foreseeable that they may use this pavement.

There are other cases in this field which should be referred to, for example: *Gough v Thorne* (1966), concerning young children; *Daly v Liverpool Corp* (1939), concerning old people; and *Paris v Stepney BC* (1951), concerning disability.

8.4.3   Cost and practicability

Another factor in deciding whether the defendant is in breach of his duty to the claimant is the cost and practicability of overcoming the risk. The foreseeable risk has to be balanced against the measures necessary to eliminate it. If the cost of these measures far outweighs the risk, the defendant will probably not be in breach of duty for failing to carry out these measures. This is illustrated by the case of *Latimer v AEC Ltd* (1952). A factory belonging to AEC became flooded after an abnormally heavy rainstorm. The rain mixed with oily deposits on the floor, making the floor very slippery. Sawdust was spread on the floor, but it was insufficient to cover the whole area. Latimer, an employee, slipped on a part of the floor to which sawdust had not been applied. It was held that AEC Ltd was not in breach of its duty to the plaintiff. It had taken all reasonable precautions and had eliminated the risk as far as it practicably could without going so far as to close the factory. There was no evidence to suggest that the reasonably prudent employer would have closed down the factory and, as far as the court was concerned, the cost of doing that far outweighed the risk to the employees.

Compare this case with *Haley*, where the provision of 2 ft barriers around excavations in the pavement would have been practicable and would have eliminated the risk to blind people.

8.4.4   Social utility

The degree of risk has to be balanced against the social utility and importance of the defendant's activity. If the activity is of particular importance to the community, then the taking of greater risks may be justified in the circumstances.

In *Watt v Hertfordshire CC* (1954), the plaintiff, a fireman, was called out to rescue a woman trapped beneath a lorry. The lifting jack had to be carried on an ordinary lorry, as a suitable vehicle was unavailable. The jack slipped, injuring the plaintiff. It was held that the employer was not in breach of duty. The importance of the activity and the fact that it was an emergency were found to justify the risk involved.

8.4.5   Common practice

If the defendant can show that what he or she has done is common practice, then this is evidence that a proper standard of care has been exercised. However, if the common practice is in itself negligent, then his or her actions in conforming to such a practice will be actionable, as can be seen in *Paris v Stepney BC* (1951). There, the common practice of not wearing safety glasses could not be condoned, as it was in itself inherently negligent.

8.4.6   Skilled persons

The standard of care to be exercised by people professing to have a particular skill is not to be judged on the basis of the reasonable man. The actions of a skilled person must be judged by what the ordinary skilled man in that job or profession would have done, for example, the reasonable doctor, plumber, engineer, etc. Such a person is judged on the standard of knowledge possessed by the profession at the time that the accident occurred. Obviously, there is an onus on the skilled person to keep himself abreast of changes and improvements in technology.

In *Roe v Minister of Health* (1954), a patient was paralysed after being given a spinal injection. This occurred because the fluid being injected had become contaminated with the storage liquid, which had seeped through minute cracks in the phials. It was held that there was no breach of duty, since the doctor who administered the injection had no way of detecting the contamination at that time.

Furthermore, the common practice of the profession may, if this is followed, prevent liability. This can be seen in *Bolam v Friern Hospital Management Committee* (1957). Bolam broke his pelvis whilst undergoing electro-convulsive therapy treatment at the defendant's hospital. He alleged that the doctor had not warned him of the risks; he had not been given relaxant drugs prior to treatment; and no one had held him down during treatment. It was held that the doctor was not in breach of duty (and there was, therefore, no vicarious liability), because this form of treatment was accepted at that time by a certain body of the medical profession. This has been qualified by the decision in *Bolitho v City and Hackney HA* (1998): in order to be accepted, expert opinion must be shown to be reasonable and responsible and to have a logical basis (*per* Lord Browne-Wilkinson). There is continued criticism of the decision in *Bolam*, particularly in so far as, in determining the standard of care, professionals are allowed to set their own standard which is not measured against that of the reasonable man. It can therefore be argued that professionals operate from a subjective standard determined by other professionals. As a result, they have a great degree of protection from allegations of negligence. However, if professionals are to push back the boundaries in their area of expertise, then it can also be argued that they should be given this leeway.

8.4.7 *Res ipsa loquitur*

The burden of proof in establishing breach of duty normally rests on the claimant. In certain circumstances, the inference of negligence may be drawn from the facts. If this can be done, the claimant is relieved of the burden, which moves to the defendant to rebut the presumption of negligence. This is known as *res ipsa loquitur*, that is, the thing speaks for itself. It can only be used where the sole explanation for what happened is the negligence of the defendant, yet the claimant has insufficient evidence to establish the defendant's negligence in the normal way. There are three criteria for the maxim to apply:

- *Sole management or control*

  It must be shown that the damage was caused by something under the sole management or control of the defendant, or by someone for whom he or she is responsible or whom he or she has a right to control (*Gee v Metropolitan Railway* (1873)).

- *The occurrence cannot have happened without negligence*

  This depends on the facts of each case. If there are other possible explanations as to how the incident occurred, *res ipsa loquitur* will fail. In *Mahon v Osborne* (1939), a patient died after a swab was left in her body after an operation. No one could explain how this had happened; therefore, *res ipsa loquitur* applied.

- *The cause of the occurrence is unknown*

  If the defendant can put forward a satisfactory explanation as to how the accident occurred which shows no negligence on his part, then the maxim is inapplicable. In *Pearson v NW Gas Board* (1968), the plaintiff's husband was killed and her house destroyed when a gas main fractured. She pleaded *res ipsa loquitur*. However, the Gas Board put forward the explanation that the gas main could have fractured due to earth movement after a heavy frost. This explanation was plausible and, as it showed no negligence on the board's part, it was not liable.

If the defendant can rebut the presumption of negligence by giving a satisfactory explanation, it is open to the claimant to establish negligence in the normal way. In practice, he or she is unlikely to succeed because, if sufficient evidence were available in the first place, *res ipsa loquitur* would not have been pleaded.

8.5   Resultant Damage

The claimant must show that he or she has suffered some injury, but it does not necessarily have to be physical injury. Furthermore, he or she must show that this injury was caused by the defendant's negligence. This is known as causation in fact. The 'but for' test is used to establish whether the defendant's negligence was the cause of the injury to the claimant.

8.5.1   The 'but for' test

In order to satisfy the test, the claimant must show that, 'but for' the defendant's actions, the damage would not have occurred. If the damage would have occurred irrespective of a breach of duty on the part of the defendant, then the breach is not the cause.

In *Cutler v Vauxhall Motors Ltd* (1971), the plaintiff suffered a grazed ankle whilst at work, due to the defendant's negligence. The graze became ulcerated because of existing varicose veins and the plaintiff had to undergo an immediate operation to remove the veins. It was held that the plaintiff could not recover damages for the operation, because the evidence was that he would have to undergo the operation within five years anyway, irrespective of the accident at work.

In medical cases, failure to warn of the risks of surgery, for example, may satisfy the 'but for' test even though the actual surgery carried out was not negligent. In *Chester v Afshar* (2002), a surgeon failed to give the full information on the risks of nerve damage from an operation even though the risk was very small. He was found by the Court of Appeal to have failed in his duty to warn the patient of the risks, and that failure had caused the injury even though the operation had not been carried out negligently.

If the same result would have occurred regardless of the breach, then the courts are unlikely to find that the breach caused the injury. This is illustrated in *Barnett v Chelsea and Kensington HMC* (1969), in which a doctor in a casualty department sent home a patient without treating him, telling him to go and see his own doctor. The patient died from arsenic poisoning. While it was held that the doctor was negligent, the evidence indicated that the patient would have died anyway. The doctor's conduct did not, therefore, cause his death. This is further supported by the case of *Robinson v Post Office* (1974), where a doctor failed to test for an allergic reaction before giving an anti-tetanus injection. However, it was held that the doctor would not be liable for the reaction of the patient, because the test would not have revealed the allergy in time.

Recent case law has not been sympathetic to the claimant where there has been a number of potential causes of the injury. The onus is on the claimant to show that the defendant's breach was a material contributory cause of his or her injury.

Where there are a number of possible causes, establishing causation may prove difficult, particularly in medical negligence cases. In *Wilsher v Essex AHA* (1988), the plaintiff was born three months premature. He suffered almost total blindness as a result of a condition known as retrolental fibroplasia. It was claimed on behalf of the plaintiff that this was caused by the negligence of the doctor, who had failed to notice that the device for adding oxygen to the blood had been wrongly attached, resulting in an excessive dose of oxygen. However, medical evidence showed at least six potential causes of the plaintiff's blindness, the majority of which were inherent in premature babies. The House of Lords held that there was insufficient evidence to show which of the six caused the injury to the plaintiff.

The court in *Hotson v East Berkshire AHA* (1987) considered whether the defendant could be liable for loss of a chance. Here, a boy fell from a tree and injured his hip. At the hospital, his injury was misdiagnosed and, by the time the mistake was discovered, he was left with a permanent disability. It was held that, as 75% of such cases were inoperable, there was no lost chance and, therefore, the plaintiff could not recover. Where there are two or more independent tortfeasors, there can also be problems in establishing how far each one is responsible for the damage caused.

In *Baker v Willoughby* (1970), the plaintiff injured his leg through the defendant's negligence, and he was left partially disabled. Subsequently, the plaintiff was shot in the same leg by another person and, as a result of the shooting, the leg had to be amputated. It was held that the first defendant was liable only for the first injury (and not the amputation). Irrespective of the amputation, it would have been a continuing disability, and this was reflected in the responsibility imposed on the defendant. The liability for the existing disability did not cease when the second incident took place.

Determining liability where there have been multiple consecutive causes can be difficult. The courts have at times taken a pragmatic approach. This can be seen in *Fairchild v Glenhaven Funeral Services Ltd & Others* (2002). In this case, the employees concerned had contracted mesothelioma due to a prolonged exposure to asbestos fibres gained during their employment with a number of different employers. It was therefore almost impossible to identify which period of employment was responsible for the employees contracting the disease. As the disease could be generated through exposure to just one fibre of asbestos – although the greater the exposure, the greater the chances of contracting the disease – the House of Lords was prepared to impose liability on all of the employers. It felt that all of the defendants, by failing to take reasonable care, had contributed to the risk.

This is an exceptional case, subject to an exceptional principle in establishing causation, which is that where the defendant's negligence materially increased the risk, the defendant would be liable. There is also the policy argument that in cases involving asbestos related disease, because of the nature of the disease, it can be extremely difficult to establish a sole cause, and therefore some flexibility in applying the legal principles is justifiable.

The 'but for' test cannot solve all questions of factual causation. Indeed, where there has been an omission to act, or an act which does not in itself have physical consequences, it may not be an appropriate test. In *Joyce v Merton, Sutton and Wandsworth HA*

(1996), the plaintiff underwent an operation which resulted in a partially blocked artery. This, in turn, resulted in total paralysis. The procedure itself was not necessarily negligent; however, it was concluded that the immediate aftercare *was* negligent, in that the plaintiff was discharged from hospital without proper instruction and advice. A vascular surgeon should have seen the plaintiff within the first 48 hours and he should have operated to deal with the blockage. In order to succeed on the point of causation, it was held that the plaintiff would have to prove either that, had the vascular surgeon been summoned, he would have operated, or that it would have been negligent for him not to do so. The correct test in these circumstances was to satisfy one of two questions. First, what steps would have been taken if proper care had been taken? Or, secondly, what would have been the outcome of any further steps that ought to have been taken? In this case, the plaintiff was able to satisfy the first question by establishing that his injuries would have been avoided if proper care had been taken.

Recovery for a lost opportunity or chance may at times be problematic. In *Spring v Guardian Assurance plc* (1995), an employee who was provided with a poor reference by his employer recovered for his lost chance of employment, even though he could not prove that he would have got the job.

The 'but for' test can be used to establish causation on the facts. However, once this has been established, it does not mean that the defendant will be liable for all of the damage to the claimant. There must be causation in law. This can be seen through the maxim, *novus actus interveniens*, or 'a new intervening act'.

8.5.2 *Novus actus interveniens*

Where there is a break in the chain of causation, the defendant will not be liable for damage caused after the break. The issues are whether the whole sequence of events is the probable consequence of the defendant's actions and whether it is reasonably foreseeable that these events may happen. This break in the chain is caused by an intervening act and the law recognises that such acts fall into three categories, as follows:

8.5.3 A natural event

A natural event does not automatically break the chain of causation. If the defendant's breach has placed the claimant in a position where the natural event can add to that damage, the chain will not be broken unless the natural event was totally unforeseen.

In *Carslogie Steamship Co Ltd v Royal Norwegian Government* (1952), a ship which was owned by Carslogie had been damaged in a collision caused by the defendant's negligence. The ship was sent for repair and, on this voyage, suffered extra damage, caused by the severe weather conditions. This resulted in the repairs taking 40 days longer than anticipated. It was held that the bad weather acted as a new intervening act, for which the defendant was not liable. The effect of the new act in this case prevented the plaintiff from recovering compensation for the time that it would have taken to repair the vessel in respect of the collision damage, as the ship would have been out of use in any case, due to the damage caused by the weather.

8.5.4   Act of a third party

Where the act of a third party following the breach of the defendant causes further damage to the claimant, such an act may be deemed to be a *novus actus*; the defendant will not then be liable for damage occurring after the third party's act.

In *Lamb v Camden LBC* (1981), due to the defendant's negligence, a water main was damaged, causing the plaintiff's house to be damaged and the house to be vacated until it had been repaired. While the house was empty, squatters moved in and caused further damage to the property. It was held that the defendant was not liable for the squatters' damage. Although it was a reasonably foreseeable risk, it was not a likely event. Furthermore, it was not the duty of the council to keep the squatters out.

The third party's act need not be negligent in itself in order to break the chain of causation, although the courts take the view that a negligent act is more likely to break the chain than one that is not negligent, as can be seen in *Knightley v Johns* (1982).

8.5.5   Act of the claimant himself or herself

In *McKew v Holland, Hannen and Cubbitts (Scotland) Ltd* (1969), the plaintiff was injured at work. As a result, his leg sometimes gave way without warning. He was coming downstairs when his leg gave way, so he jumped in order to avoid falling head first and badly injured his ankle. It was held that the defendants were not liable for this additional injury. The plaintiff had not acted reasonably in attempting to negotiate the stairs without assistance and his actions amounted to a *novus actus interveniens*.

The case of *Reeves v Commissioner of Police* (2000) questions whether an act of suicide amounts to a *novus actus*. In this case, D, apparently of sound mind, committed suicide in police custody. At first instance, the police were held to be in breach of their duty of care, but the court treated the deceased's behaviour as a totally voluntary act, which broke the chain of causation. The Court of Appeal initially allowed the Commissioner's appeal. However, the House of Lords found the police liable on the basis that they were under a specific duty to protect D from the risk of suicide and had failed to do so. The defence of voluntary assumption of risk was not compatible with this duty.

The House of Lords allowed the appeal, reducing the amount of damages. A deliberate act of suicide was not a *novus actus interveniens* negating the casual connection between breach of duty and death. To hold as such would lead to the absurd result that the very act which the duty sought to prevent would be fatal to establishing a causative link. On the issue of causation, both the police, who had been negligent in leaving the door hatch open, and the deceased, who had responsibility for his own life, were the causes of his death. The deceased was held to be contributorily negligent and damages were reduced by 50%.

Where it is the act of the claimant which breaks the chain, it is not a question of foresight but of unreasonable conduct.

8.5.6 Remoteness of damage

It must be understood that, even where causation is established, the defendant will not necessarily be liable for all of the damage resulting from the breach. This was not always the case and the way in which the law has developed must be considered.

In *Re Polemis and Furness, Withy & Co* (1921), the plaintiff's ship was destroyed by fire when one of the employees of the company to whom the ship had been chartered negligently knocked a plank into the hold. The hold was full of petrol vapour. The plank caused a spark as it struck the side and this ignited the vapour. It was held that the defendants were liable for the loss of the ship, even though the presence of petrol vapour and the causing of the spark were unforeseen. The fire was the direct result of the breach of duty and the defendant was liable for the full extent of the damage, even where the manner in which it took place was unforeseen.

The case of *Re Polemis* is no longer regarded as the current test for remoteness of damage. The test currently used arose out of *The Wagon Mound (No 1)* (1961). The defendants negligently allowed furnace oil to spill from a ship into Sydney harbour. The oil spread and came to lie beneath a wharf, which was owned by the plaintiffs. The plaintiffs had been carrying out welding operations and, on seeing the oil, they stopped welding in order to ascertain whether it was safe. They were assured that the oil would not catch fire, and so resumed welding. Cotton waste, which had fallen into the oil, caught fire. This in turn ignited the oil and a fire spread to the plaintiff's wharf. It was held that the defendants were in breach of duty. However, they were only liable for the damage caused to the wharf and slipway through the fouling of the oil. They were not liable for the damage caused by fire because damage by fire was at that time unforeseeable. This particular oil had a high ignition point and it could not be foreseen that it would ignite on water. The court refused to apply the rule in *Re Polemis*.

The test of reasonable foresight arising out of *The Wagon Mound* clearly takes into account such things as scientific knowledge at the time of the negligent act. The question to be asked in determining the extent of liability is whether the damage is of such a kind as the reasonable man should have foreseen. This does not mean that the defendant should have foreseen precisely the sequence or nature of the events. Lord Denning in *Stewart v West African Air Terminals* (1964) said:

> It is not necessary that the precise concatenation of circumstances should be envisaged. If the consequence was one which was within the general range which any reasonable person might foresee (and was not of an entirely different kind which no one would anticipate), then it is within the rule that a person who has been guilty of negligence is liable for the consequences.

This is illustrated in the case of *Hughes v Lord Advocate* (1963), where employees of the Post Office, who were working down a manhole, left it without a cover but with a tent over it and lamps around it. A child picked up a lamp and went into the tent. He tripped over the lamp, knocking it into the hole. An explosion occurred and the child was burned. The risk of the child being burned by the lamp was foreseeable. However, the vapourisation of the paraffin in the lamp and its ignition were not foreseeable. It was held that the defendants were liable for the injury to the plaintiff. It was foreseeable that the child might be burned and it was immaterial that neither the extent of his injury nor the precise chain of events leading to it was foreseeable.

The test of remoteness is not easy to apply. The cases themselves highlight the uncertainty of the courts. For example, in *Doughty v Turner Manufacturing Co Ltd* (1964), an asbestos cover was knocked into a bath of molten metal. This led to a chemical reaction, which was at that time unforeseeable. The molten metal erupted and burned the plaintiff, who was standing nearby. It was held that only burning by splashing was foreseeable and that burning by an unforeseen chemical reaction was not a variant on this. It could be argued that the proper question in this case should have been 'was burning foreseeable?', as this was the question asked in *Hughes*.

A similar issue surrounding the questions asked to establish whether the harm is foreseeable can be seen in *Tremain v Pike* (1969), in which a farmhand contracted a rare disease transmitted by rat's urine. It was foreseeable that the plaintiff might sustain injury from rat bites or from contaminated food, but not from the contraction of this disease. Once again, this case raises the issue of whether the correct question was asked (see *Robinson v Post Office* (1974), 8.5.1, above).

In *Jolley v London Borough of Sutton* (2000), the House of Lords, overruling the Court of Appeal, decided that it was sufficient to satisfy the test of remoteness if some harm was foreseeable, even though the precise way in which the injuries occurred could not be foreseen. In this particular case, the Council failed to move an abandoned boat for two years. It was known to the Council that children were attracted to and played in the boat even though it was dangerous. A 14 year old boy was seriously injured when he and a friend tried to jack-up the boat to repair it.

8.6　Defences

The extent of the liability of the defendant may be reduced or limited by one of the defences commonly pleaded in negligence proceedings.

8.6.1　Contributory negligence

Where the claimant is found in some way to have contributed through his or her own fault to his or her injury, the amount awarded as damages will be reduced accordingly (under the Law Reform (Contributory Negligence) Act 1945). The onus is on the defendant to show that the claimant was at fault and that this contributed to his or her injury.

The court, if satisfied that the claimant is at fault, will reduce the amount of damages by an amount which is just and reasonable, depending on the claimant's share of the blame. For example, damages may be reduced by anything from 10% to 75%.

However, a 100% reduction has been made, as can be seen in *Jayes v IMI (Kynoch) Ltd* (1985).

8.6.2 *Volenti non fit injuria*

Volenti, or consent, as it applies to negligent acts, is a defence to future conduct of the defendant which involves the risk of a tort being committed. *Volenti* may arise from the express agreement of the claimant and defendant, or it may be implied from the claimant's conduct.

In *ICI v Shatwell* (1965), the plaintiff and his brother ignored the safety precautions issued by their employer and breached the regulations in testing detonators. As a result, the plaintiff was injured in an explosion. The action against the employer was based on vicarious liability and breach of statutory duty on the part of the plaintiff's brother. It was held that the defence of *volenti* would succeed. The plaintiff not only consented to each act of negligence and breach of statute on the part of his brother, but also participated in them quite willingly.

It must be stressed that this particular case highlights extreme circumstances where *volenti* is likely to succeed. However, if the defence is to succeed, it must be shown that the claimant was fully informed of the risks when he or she gave his or her consent.

In *Dann v Hamilton* (1939), a girl accepted a lift in the car of a driver whom she knew to be drunk. She could have used alternative transport. She was injured as a result of his negligent driving. It was held that, although she knew of the risk, this was insufficient to support the defence of *volenti*. It was necessary to show that she had consented to the risk, which could not be established. She therefore succeeded in her action against the driver.

Following this case, it is unlikely that this defence will succeed where the implied consent is given before the negligent act occurs. In practice, the courts do not look favourably on this defence in respect of negligent actions and, therefore, it is not usually pleaded.

8.7 Limitation of Claims

Finally, there is a limitation period for commencing a claim in tort. The Limitation Act 1980 states that, generally, proceedings must be brought within six years from the date on which the negligent act occurred. If the claim is for personal injury, the period is three years from the date on which it occurred or the date of knowledge, that is, the date that the injury becomes attributable to another person's negligent actions, whichever is the later.

THE TORT OF NEGLIGENCE

The tort of negligence imposes a duty to take reasonable care to prevent harm or loss occurring from one's actions.

The elements of the tort which must be established by the claimant are:

- duty of care;

- breach of duty; and

- resultant damage.

Duty of Care

- Established by the 'neighbour' test:

  ○ *Donoghue v Stevenson* (1932);

  ○ *Peabody Donation Fund v Sir Lindsay Parkinson & Co Ltd* (1984); *Leigh and Sullivan Ltd v Aliakmon Shipping Co Ltd* (1986); *Anns v Merton LBC* (1978);

  ○ *Caparo Industries plc v Dickman* (1990), which introduced a three stage test for establishing the existence of a duty of care. This test appears to apply to all situations.

- The test is incremental, requiring consideration of:

  ○ foresight;

  ○ proximity; and

  ○ 'just and reasonable'.

It was approved in *Marc Rich & Co AG v Bishop Rock Marine Co Ltd (The Nicholas H)* (1994).

Nervous Shock

The tort of negligence also recognises liability for nervous shock, sometimes known as post-traumatic stress disorder. The claimant must establish:

- a recognised medical condition which goes beyond grief and distress;

- foresight; and

- proximity.

The courts clearly distinguish between:

- fearing for one's own safety (*Dulieu v White* (1901)); and

- merely being a passing witness to an accident (*Bourhill v Young* (1943); *Hegarty v EE Caledonia Ltd* (1996)).

A further contentious issue arises where the claimant who witnesses the accident or its immediate aftermath has a close relationship with the victim. In these circumstances, the claimant must establish:

- a close loving relationship;

- proximity to the accident in terms of time and space;

- *Hambrook v Stokes Bros* (1925);

- *McLoughlin v O'Brian* (1982);

- *Alcock & Others v Chief Constable of South Yorkshire* (1991); and

- *North Glamorgan NHS Trust v Walters* (2002).

Rescuers are usually treated as a special case, particularly where they are not professional rescuers:

- *Chadwick v BRB* (1967); and

- *White v Chief Constable of South Yorkshire* (1998).

Economic Loss

Liability for economic loss arising out of physical injury or damage to property may be compensated in negligence. Liability for pure economic loss cannot, in general, be compensated:

- *Spartan Steel & Alloys Ltd v Martin & Co* (1973).

- *Junior Books Ltd v Veitchi Ltd* (1983).

- Liability for pure economic loss will generally only be upheld where negligent misstatement is proven (*Murphy v Brentwood DC* (1990)).

- Where a special relationship is found to exist between the parties which falls short of contract, the defendant may be liable for giving negligent advice (*Hedley Byrne & Co v Heller & Partners* (1964); see also *Mutual Life and Citizens Assurance Co v Evatt* (1971); *Chaudry v Prabhakar* (1988)); *Law Society v KPMG Peat Marwick* (2000).

- *McLoughlin v Jones* (2001).

However, the claimant will have to show that he or she actually relied on the advice:

- *JEB Fasteners v Marks Bloom & Co* (1983).

- *Caparo Industries plc v Dickman* (1990).

- *White v Jones* (1995).

- *Merrett v Babb* (2001).

Breach of Duty

Once the claimant has established a duty of care, breach of duty must be proven. The test for establishing breach of duty is whether the defendant has acted as a reasonable person in all the circumstances of the case. The courts will take the following into account:

- likelihood of harm occurring (*Bolton v Stone* (1951));

- egg-shell skull rule (*Haley v London Electricity Board* (1965); *Paris v Stepney BC* (1951));

- cost and practicability of taking precautions (*Latimer v AEC* (1952));

- social utility of the act (*Watt v Hertfordshire CC* (1954)); and

- common practice (*Roe v Minister of Health* (1954); *Chester v Afshar* (2002)).

In certain circumstances, the claimant may rely on the maxim *res ipsa loquitur* in order to establish breach. However, it must be shown that:

- there was sole management or control on the part of the defendant;

- the occurrence could not have happened without negligence; and

- the cause of the occurrence is unknown.

Resultant Damage

Finally, the claimant must show that the breach of duty on the part of the defendant was the cause of his or her loss. The test for establishing causation in fact is the 'but for' test:

- If there is another acceptable explanation for the injury, causation may not be proven (see *Cutler v Vauxhall Motors Ltd* (1971)).

- The onus rests on the claimant to show that the defendant's breach was a material contributory cause, as in *Wilsher v Essex AHA* (1988); *Hotson v East Berkshire AHA* (1987).

- The extent of the defendant's liability may be further limited by the rules for determining remoteness of damage (for example, *novus actus interveniens*).

- Where the cause and extent of the harm is unforeseen, the loss will not be recoverable. The test for establishing remoteness is that of reasonable foresight, as expounded in *The Wagon Mound (No 1)* (1961).

- As a general rule, it is not necessary to foresee the exact cause of the harm, as long as it is within the general range which any reasonable person might foresee:

  ○ *Stewart v West African Air Terminals* (1964).

  ○ *Hughes v Lord Advocate* (1963).

- *Doughty v Turner Manufacturing Co Ltd* (1964).

- *Tremain v Pike* (1969).

- *Jolley v London Borough of Sutton* (2003).

There may be exceptional circumstances where for policy reasons, the normal legal rules may not be applied strictly:

- *Fairchild v Glenhaven Funeral Services Ltd* (2002).

Defences

Damages may be reduced by the claimant's contributory negligence (Law Reform (Contributory Negligence) Act 1945).

The defence of *volenti* or consent may operate as a complete defence (*ICI v Shatwell* (1965); *Dann v Hamilton* (1939)).

CHAPTER 9

BUSINESS AND CORPORATE LAW

9.1 Agency

The principles of agency law provide the basis for an understanding of many issues relating to partnerships and some of those relating to registered companies. The general assumption is that individuals engaging in business activity carry on that business by themselves, and on their own behalf, either individually or collectively. It is not uncommon, however, for such individuals to engage others to represent them and negotiate business deals on their behalf. Indeed, the role of the 'middleman' is a commonplace one in business and commerce. The legal relationship between such a representative, or middleman, and the business person making use of them is governed by the law of agency. Agency principles also apply in relation to companies registered under the companies legislation and the directors and other officers of such companies.

9.1.1 Definition of agency

An agent is a person who is empowered to represent another legal party, called the principal, and brings the principal into a legal relationship with a third party. It should be emphasised that the contract entered into is between the principal and the third party. In the normal course of events, the agent has no personal rights or liabilities in relation to the contract. This outcome represents an accepted exception to the usual operation of the doctrine of privity in contract law (see above, (6.2.6)).

Since the agent is not actually entering into contractual relations with the third party, there is no requirement that the agent has contractual capacity, although, based on the same reasoning, it is essential that the principal has full contractual capacity. Thus, it is possible for a principal to use a minor as an agent, even though the minor might not have contractual capacity to enter into the contract on their own behalf.

There are numerous examples of agency relationships. For example, as their names imply, estate agents and travel agents are expressly appointed to facilitate particular transactions. Additionally, employees may act as agents of their employers in certain circumstances; or friends may act as agents for one another.

Some forms of agency merit particular consideration, as follows:

- A general agent, as the title indicates, has the power to act for a principal generally in relation to a particular area of business, whereas a special agent only has the authority to act in one particular transaction.

- A *del credere* agent is one who, in return for an additional commission by way of payment, guarantees to the principal that, in the event of a third party's failure to pay for goods received, the agent will make good the loss.

- A commission agent is a hybrid form which lies midway between a full principal/agent relationship and the relationship of an independent trader and client. In essence, the agent stands between the principal and the third party and establishes no contract between those two parties. The effect is that, although the commission agent owes the duties of an agent to his or her principal, he or she contracts with the third party as a principal in his or her own right. The effectiveness of this procedure is undermined by the normal operation of the agency law relating to an undisclosed principal (see below, 9.1.7.2).

- The position of a mercantile agent/factor is defined in the Factors Act 1889 as an agent:

    ... having in the customary course of his business as such agent authority either to sell goods, or to consign goods for the purpose of sale, or to buy goods, or to raise money on the security of goods.

    However, of perhaps more contemporary importance are marketing agents, distribution agents and the question of franchising.

- Marketing agents have only limited authority. They can only introduce potential customers to their principals and do not have the authority either to negotiate or to enter into contracts on behalf of their principals.

- Distribution agents are appointed by suppliers to arrange the distribution of their products within a particular area. The distributors ordinarily cannot bind the supplier, except where they have expressly been given the authority to do so.

- Franchising arrangements arise where the original developer of a business decides, for whatever reason, to allow others to use their goodwill to conduct an independent business, using the original name of the business. Two prominent examples of franchises are McDonalds and The Body Shop, although there are many others. It is essential to emphasise that any such relationship does not arise from, or give rise to, a relationship of principal and agent. Indeed, it is commonplace, if not universal, that franchise agreements include an express clause to the effect that no such relationship is to be established.

- Commercial agents are specifically covered by the Commercial Agents (Council Directive) Regulations 1993, which were enacted in order to comply with EC Directive 86/653. The Regulations define a commercial agent as a self-employed intermediary who has continuing authority to negotiate the sale or purchase of goods on behalf of another person, or to negotiate and conclude such transactions on behalf of that person. Although intended to harmonise the operation and effect of agency law within the European Union, the regulations do not introduce any major substantive change into UK agency law. The effect of the Regulations will be considered in more detail below at 9.1.6.1.

- A power of attorney arises where an agency is specifically created by way of a deed.

9.1.2 Creation of agency

No one can act as an agent without the consent of the principal, although consent need not be expressly stated.

In *White v Lucas* (1887), a firm of estate agents claimed to act on behalf of the owner of a particular property, though that person had denied them permission to act on his behalf. When the owner sold the property to a third party, who was introduced through the estate agents, they claimed their commission. It was held that the estate agents had no entitlement to commission, as the property owner had not agreed to their acting as his agent.

The principal/agent relationship can be created in a number of ways. It may arise as the outcome of a distinct contract, which may be made either orally or in writing, or it may be established purely gratuitously, where some person simply agrees to act for another. The relationship may also arise from the actions of the parties.

It is usual to consider the creation of the principal/agency relationship under five distinct categories.

9.1.2.1 Express appointment

This is the most common manner in which a principal/agent relationship comes into existence. In this situation, the agent is specifically appointed by the principal to carry out a particular task or to undertake some general function. In most situations, the appointment of the agent will itself involve the establishment of a contractual relationship between the principal and the agent, but need not necessarily depend upon a contract between those parties.

For the most part, there are no formal requirements for the appointment of an agent, although, where the agent is to be given the power to execute deeds in the principal's name, they must themselves be appointed by way of a deed (that is, they are given power of attorney).

9.1.2.2 Ratification

An agency is created by ratification when a person who has no authority purports to contract with a third party on behalf of a principal. Ratification is the express acceptance of the contract by the principal. Where the principal elects to ratify the contract, it gives retrospective validity to the action of the purported agent. There are, however, certain conditions which have to be fully complied with before the principal can effectively adopt the contract, as follows:

- *The principal must have been in existence at the time that the agent entered into the contract*

  Thus, for example, in *Kelner v Baxter* (1866), where promoters attempted to enter into a contract on behalf of the as yet unformed company, it was held that the company could not ratify the contract after it was created and that the promoters, as agents, were personally liable on the contract. (This is now given statutory effect under s 36C of the Companies Act 1985.)

- *The principal must have had legal capacity to enter into the contract when it was made*

  When the capacity of companies to enter into a business transaction was limited by the operation of the doctrine of *ultra vires*, it was clearly established that they could not ratify any such *ultra vires* contracts. Similarly, it is not possible for minors to ratify a contract, even though it was made in their name.

- *An undisclosed principal cannot ratify a contract*

  The agent must have declared that he or she was acting for the principal. If the agent appeared to be acting on his or her own account, then the principal cannot later adopt the contact (see *Keighley, Maxted & Co v Durant* (1901)).

- *The principal must adopt the whole of the contract*

  It is not open to the principal to pick and choose which parts of the contract to adopt; they must accept all of its terms.

- *Ratification must take place within a reasonable time*

  It is not possible to state with certainty what will be considered as a reasonable time in any particular case. Where, however, the third party with whom the agent contracted becomes aware that the agent has acted without authority, a time limit can be set, within which the principal must indicate their adoption of the contract for it to be effective.

9.1.2.3   Implication

This form of agency arises from the relationship that exists between the principal and the agent and from which it is assumed that the principal has given authority to the other person to act as his or her agent. Thus, it is implied from the particular position held by individuals that they have the authority to enter into contractual relations on behalf of their principal. So, whether an employee has the actual authority to contract on behalf of his or her employer depends on the position held by the employee; and, for example, it was decided in *Panorama Developments v Fidelis Furnishing Fabrics Ltd* (1971) that a company secretary had the implied authority to make contracts in the company's name relating to the day to day running of the company.

Problems most often occur in relation to the implied extent of a person's authority, rather than their actual appointment (but see *Hely-Hutchinson v Brayhead Ltd* (1967) as an example of the latter).

9.1.2.4   Necessity

Agency by necessity occurs under circumstances where, although there is no agreement between the parties, an emergency requires that an agent take particular action in order to protect the interests of the principal. The usual situation which gives rise to agency by necessity occurs where the agent is in possession of the principal's property and, due to some unforeseen emergency, the agent has to take action to safeguard that property:

- *In order for agency by necessity to arise, there needs to be a genuine emergency*

  In *Great Northern Railway Co v Swaffield* (1874), the railway company transported the defendant's horse and, when no one arrived to collect it at its destination, it was placed in a livery stable. It was held that the company was entitled to recover the cost of stabling, as necessity had forced them to act as they had done as the defendant's agents.

- *There must also be no practical way of obtaining further instructions from the principal*

  In *Springer v Great Western Railway Co* (1921), a consignment of tomatoes arrived at port after a delayed journey due to storms. A railway strike would have caused further delay in getting the tomatoes to their destination, so the railway company decided to sell the tomatoes locally. It was held that the railway company was responsible to the plaintiff for the difference between the price achieved and the market price in London. The defence of agency of necessity was not available, as the railway company could have contacted the plaintiff to seek his further instructions.

- *The person seeking to establish the agency by necessity must have acted bona fide in the interests of the principal (see Sachs v Miklos (1948))*

9.1.2.5 *Estoppel*

This form of agency is also known as 'agency by holding out' and arises where the principal has led other parties to believe that a person has the authority to represent him or her. (The authority possessed by the agent is referred to as 'apparent authority' – see below, 9.1.3.2.) In such circumstances, even though no principal/agency relationship actually exists in fact, the principal is prevented (estopped) from denying the existence of the agency relationship and is bound by the action of his or her purported agent as regards any third party who acted in the belief of its existence:

- *To rely on agency by estoppel, the principal must have made a representation as to the authority of the agent*

  In *Freeman and Lockyer v Buckhurst Park Properties Ltd* (1964), a property company had four directors, but one director effectively controlled the company and made contracts as if he were the managing director, even though he had never actually been appointed to that position and, therefore, as an individual, had no authority to bind the company. The other directors, however, were aware of this activity and acquiesced in it. When the company was sued in relation to one of the contracts entered into by the unauthorised director, it was held that it was liable, as the board which had the actual authority to bind the company had held out the individual director as having the necessary authority to enter such contracts. It was, therefore, a case of agency by estoppel.

- *As with estoppel generally, the party seeking to use it must have relied on the representation*

    In *Overbrooke Estates Ltd v Glencombe Properties Ltd* (1974), a notice which expressly denied the authority of an auctioneer to make such statements as actually turned out to be false was successfully relied on as a defence by the auctioneer 's employers.

9.1.3 The authority of an agent

In order to bind a principal, any contract entered into must be within the limits of the authority extended to the agent. The authority of an agent can be either actual or apparent.

9.1.3.1 Actual authority

Actual authority can arise in two ways:

- *Express actual authority*

    This is explicitly granted by the principal to the agent. The agent is instructed as to what particular tasks are required to perform and is informed of the precise powers given in order to fulfil those tasks.

- *Implied actual authority*

    This refers to the way in which the scope of express authority may be increased. Third parties are entitled to assume that agents holding a particular position have all the powers that are usually provided to such an agent. Without actual knowledge to the contrary, they may safely assume that the agent has the usual authority that goes with their position. (This has been referred to above in relation to implied agency.)

    In *Watteau v Fenwick* (1893), the new owners of a hotel continued to employ the previous owner as its manager. They expressly forbade him to buy certain articles, including cigars. The manager, however, bought cigars from a third party, who later sued the owners for payment as the manager's principal. It was held that the purchase of cigars was within the usual authority of a manager of such an establishment and that for a limitation on such usual authority to be effective, it must be communicated to any third party.

9.1.3.2 Apparent authority

Apparent authority is an aspect of agency by estoppel considered above at 9.1.2.5. It can arise in two distinct ways:

- *Where a person makes a representation to third parties that a particular person has the authority to act as their agent without actually appointing the agent*

In such a case, the person making the representation is bound by the actions of the apparent agent (see *Freeman and Lockyer v Buckhurst Park Properties Ltd* (1964)). The principal is also liable for the actions of the agent where it is known that the agent claims to be his or her agent and yet does nothing to correct that impression.

- *Where a principal has previously represented to a third party that an agent has the authority to act on their behalf*

  Even if the principal has subsequently revoked the agent's authority, he or she may still be liable for the actions of the former agent, unless he or she has informed third parties who had previously dealt with the agent about the new situation (see *Willis Faber & Co Ltd v Joyce* (1911)).

9.1.3.3 *Warrant of authority*

If a person claims to act as agent, but without the authority to do so, the supposed principal will not be bound by any agreement entered into. Neither is there a contract between the supposed agent and the third party, for the reason that the third party intended to deal not with the purported agent but with the supposed principal. However, the supposed agent may lay themselves open to an action for breach of warrant of authority.

If an agent contracts with a third party on behalf of a principal, the agent impliedly guarantees that the principal exists and has contractual capacity. The agent also implies that he or she has the authority to make contracts on behalf of that principal. If any of these implied warranties prove to be untrue, then the third party may sue the agent in quasi-contract for breach of warrant of authority. Such an action may arise even though the agent was genuinely unaware of any lack of authority.

In *Yonge v Toynbee* (1910), a firm of solicitors was instructed to institute proceedings against a third party. Without their knowledge, their client was certified insane, and although this automatically ended the agency relationship, they continued with the proceedings. The third party successfully recovered damages for breach of warrant of authority, since the solicitors were no longer acting for their former client.

9.1.4 The relationship of principal and agent

The following considers the reciprocal rights and duties that principal and agent owe to each other.

9.1.5 The duties of agent to principal

The agent owes a number of duties, both express and implied, to the principal. These duties are as follows:

- *To perform the agreed undertaking according to the instructions of the principal*

A failure to carry out instructions will leave the agent open to an action for breach of contract. This, of course, does not apply in the case of gratuitous agencies, where there is no obligation whatsoever on the agent to perform the agreed task. See *Turpin v Bilton* (1843), where an agent was held liable for the loss sustained by his failure to insure his principal's ship prior to its sinking.

• *To exercise due care and skill*

An agent will owe a duty to act with reasonable care and skill, regardless of whether the agency relationship is contractual or gratuitous. The level of skill to be exercised, however, should be that appropriate to the agent's professional capacity and this may introduce a distinction in the levels expected of different agents. For example, a solicitor would be expected to show the level of care and skill that would be expected of a competent member of that profession, whereas a layperson acting in a gratuitous capacity would only be expected to perform with such degree of care and skill as a reasonable person would exercise in the conduct of their own affairs. See *Keppel v Wheeler* (1927), where the defendant estate agents were held liable for failing to secure the maximum possible price for a property.

• *To carry out instructions personally*

Unless expressly or impliedly authorised to delegate the work, an agent owes a duty to the principal to act personally in the completion of the task. The right to delegate may be agreed expressly by the principal, or it may be implied from customary practice or arise as a matter of necessity. In any such case, the agent remains liable to the principal for the proper performance of the agreed contract.

• *To account*

There is an implied duty that the agent keep proper accounts of all transactions entered into on behalf of the principal. The agent is required to account for all money and other property received on the principal's behalf and should keep his or her own property separate from that of the principal.

In addition to these contractual duties, there are general equitable duties which flow from the fact that the agency relationship is a fiduciary one, that is, one based on trust. These general fiduciary duties are as follows:

• *Not to permit a conflict of interest to arise*

An agent must not allow the possibility of personal interest to conflict with the interests of his or her principal without disclosing that possibility to the principal. Upon full disclosure, it is up to the principal to decide whether or not to proceed with the particular transaction. If there is a breach of this duty, the principal may set aside the contract so affected and claim any profit which might have been made by the agent.

In *McPherson v Watt* (1877), a solicitor used his brother as a nominee to purchase property which he was engaged to sell. It was held that since the solicitor had allowed a conflict of interest to arise, the sale could be set aside. It was immaterial that a fair price was offered for the property.

The corollary to the above case is that the agent must not sell his or her own property to the principal without fully disclosing the fact (see *Harrods v Lemon* (1931)). This leads into the next duty.

- *Not to make a secret profit or misuse confidential information*

An agent who uses his or her position as an agent to secure financial advantage for him or herself, without full disclosure to his principal, is in breach of fiduciary duty. Upon disclosure, the principal may authorise the agent's profit, but full disclosure is a necessary precondition (see *Hippisley v Knee Bros* (1905) for a clear-cut case). An example of the strictness with which this principle is enforced may be seen in the case of *Boardman v Phipps* (1967), in which agents were held to account for profits made from information which they had gained from their position as agents, even though their action also benefited the company for which they were acting.

- *Not to take a bribe*

This duty may be seen as merely a particular aspect of the general duty not to make a secret profit, but it goes so much to the root of the agency relationship that it is usually treated as a distinct heading in its own right. Again, for clear-cut cases, see *Boston Deep Sea Fishing & Ice Co Ltd v Ansell* (1957), in which the managing director of the company was held to have breached his fiduciary duties as an agent by accepting a bribe in return for orders. See also *Mahesan v Malaysian Government Officers Co-operative Housing Society* (1978), where the plaintiff received a bribe to permit a third party to profit at his principal's expense.

Where it is found that an agent has taken a bribe, the following civil remedies are open to the principal:

- to repudiate the contract with the third party;
- to dismiss the agent without notice;
- to refuse to pay any money owed to the agent or to recover such money already paid;
- to claim the amount of the bribe; and
- to claim damages in the tort of deceit for any loss sustained as a result of the payment of the bribe.

The payment of the bribe may also have constituted a breach of criminal law.

9.1.6 The rights of an agent

It is a simple matter of fact that the common law does not generally provide agents with as many rights in relation to the number of duties that it imposes on them. The agent, however, does benefit from the clear establishment of three general rights. These rights are as follows:

- *To claim remuneration for services performed*

  It is usual in agency agreements for the amount of payment to be stated, either in the form of wages or commission or, indeed, both. Where a commercial agreement is silent on the matter of payment, the court will imply a term into the agreement, requiring the payment of a reasonable remuneration. Such a term will not be implied in contradiction of the express terms of the agreement. See *Re Richmond Gate Property Co Ltd* (1965), where it was held that no remuneration could be claimed where an agreement stated that payment would be determined by the directors of the company, but they had not actually decided on any payment.

- *To claim indemnity against the principal for all expenses legitimately incurred in the performance of services*

  Both contractual and non-contractual agents are entitled to recover money spent in the course of performing their agreed task. In the case of the former, the remedy is based on an implied contractual term; in the case of a gratuitous agent, it is based on the remedy of restitution. Money can, of course, only be claimed where the agent has been acting within his or her actual authority.

- *To exercise a lien over property owned by the principal*

  This is a right to retain the principal's goods, where they have lawfully come into the agent's possession, and hold them against any debts outstanding to him or her as a result of the agency agreement. The nature of the lien is usually a particular one relating to specific goods which are subject to the agreement, not a general one which entitles the agent to retain any of the principal's goods, even where no money is owed in relation to those specific goods. The general lien is only recognised on the basis of an express term in the contract, or as a result of judicially recognised custom, as in the area of banking.

9.1.6.1 Commercial Agents (Council Directive) Regulations 1993

These Regulations implement Council Directive 86/653/EEC on the Co-ordination of the Laws of Member States relating to Self-Employed Commercial Agents, and came into force at the beginning of 1994. Regulations 3–5 set out the rights and obligations as between commercial agents and their principals; regs 6–12 deal with remuneration; and regs 13–16 deal with the conclusion and termination of the agency contract. Regulations 17–19 contain provisions relating to the indemnity or compensation payable to a commercial agent on termination of his agency contract, and reg 20 relates to the validity of restraint of trade clauses.

Considering the provisions in more detail:

- reg 3 provides that agents must act dutifully and in good faith in the interests of their principal. The agents must negotiate in a proper manner, execute the contracts they are contracted to undertake, communicate all necessary information to, and comply with all reasonable instructions from, their principal;

- reg 4 relates to principals' duties and requires that they provide their agents with the necessary documentation relating to the goods concerned, obtain information necessary for the performance of the agency contract and, in particular, notify the commercial agent within a reasonable period once they anticipate that the volume of commercial transactions will be significantly lower than that which the commercial agent could normally have expected. Additionally, a principal shall inform the commercial agent, within a reasonable period, of their acceptance or refusal of a commercial transaction which the commercial agent has procured for them;

- reg 14 provides that agents are entitled to notice of termination of their situation;

- reg 17 states that commercial agents are entitled to indemnity or compensation on termination of the agency agreement; and

- reg 20 states that any agreements in restraint of trade in agency contracts are only effective if they are in writing. Such restraints must relate solely to the type of goods dealt with under the agency agreement and must be limited to the geographical area, or the particular customer group, allocated to the agent. In any case, such restraints may only be valid for a maximum period of two years (cf general contracts in restraint of trade above at 6.4.7.3).

The relationship of the Commercial Agents (Council Directive) Regulations 1993 (SI 1993/3053) and the common law was considered in *Duffen v FRA Bo SpA* (1998), in which it was held that although a dismissed agent could not enforce a 'liquidated damages' clause in his contract because it was really a penalty clause, he might not be restricted to merely claiming common law damages, as the Regulations allowed him to claim 'compensation' which might well involve a premium over the level of ordinary damages (see further, above, 6.5.7).

Recently, however, controversy, not to say confusion, has arisen over the way in which the level of compensation provided for in reg 17 should be calculated. As has been stated, the regulation itself simply provides that, in the event of a principal terminating a relationship with a commercial agent, the latter is entitled to compensation. The Regulations do not, however, state precisely how such compensation should be calculated, and it this lack of detail that has led to the confusion, as follows:

- In *Douglas King v T Tunnock Ltd* (2000), the Inner House of the Scottish Court of Session determined that, as the EC Directive was based on French law, it would be appropriate to operate the system for the calculation of compensation on the same basis as was adopted by the French courts. On that basis, the Inner House held that the agent should receive compensation equal to the gross commission paid during the previous two years of the agency. Alternatively, the court held that a multiple of twice the average commission earned during the last three years could be used.

- In *Barrett McKenzie & Co Ltd v Escada (UK) Ltd* (2001), the High Court reached a different conclusion as to the way in which compensation should be calculated. It did so on the basis that the aim of the original Directive was simply to establish a general right to an entitlement and that the particular method of assessing the value of that entitlement was to be left to the individual Member States to decide upon. The Court, therefore, thought it inappropriate simply to follow the method of calculation operated by the French courts. Following *Duffen v FRA Bo SpA*, the High Court, contrary to general common law principles, held that, under the Regulations, an independent agency had a value, which was akin to the value of the goodwill in a business. Any assessment of that value, at or just before termination, required consideration of various factors, including the agent's expenditure incurred in earning the commission, the duration and history of the agreement, provision for notice, etc, and was not susceptible to the application of a simple formula.

- In *Ingmar GB Ltd v Eaton Leonard Inc (formerly Eaton Leonard Technologies Inc)* (2001), whilst Morland J felt himself bound to recognise the hierarchical superiority of the Scottish Court of Session decision as stated in *Douglas King v T Tunnock Ltd* in relation to a piece of British legislation, he nonetheless felt more in sympathy with the approach adopted by the High Court in *Barrett McKenzie & Co Ltd v Escada (UK) Ltd*. His mechanism for achieving both ends was to decide that the Scottish court had laid down 'not a principle of law but a guideline that in many cases … may be appropriate'. However, in the present case, he found it not appropriate and thus he could effectively avoid following the Court of Session's decision.

The situation as to the precise way in which reg 17 compensation payments are to be calculated remains uncertain. Although much academic work supports the approach of the English High Court, it remains for the final resolution to be determined by the House of Lords, either in that form or as the Privy Council in relation to Scottish cases.

9.1.7 Relations with third parties

In the words of Wright J in *Montgomerie v UK Mutual Steamship Association* (1891), once an agent creates a contract between the principal and a third party, *prima facie* at common law, 'the only person who can sue is the principal and the only person who can be sued is the principal'. In other words, the agent has no further responsibility. This general rule is, however, subject to the following particular exceptions, which in turn tend to depend upon whether or not the agent has actually disclosed the existence of the principal.

9.1.7.1 *Where the principal's existence is disclosed*

Although the actual identity of the principal need not be mentioned, where the agent indicates that he is acting as an agent, the general rule is as stated above; only the principal and the third party have rights and obligations under the contract.

Exceptionally, however, the agent may be held liable as a party to the contract. This can occur in the following ways:

- *At third party insistence*

  Where the agent has expressly accepted liability with the principal in order to induce the third party to enter the contract, he or she will attract liability.

- *By implication*

  Where the agent has signed the contractual agreement in his or her own name, without clearly stating that he or she is merely acting as a representative of the principal, he or she will most likely be liable on it.

- *In relation to bills of exchange*

  As in the previous situation, where an agent signs a bill of exchange without sufficiently indicating that he or she is merely acting as the agent of a named principal, he or she will become personally liable on it.

- *In relation to the execution of a deed*

  Where the agent signs the deed other than under a power of attorney, he or she will be personally liable on it.

- *Where the agent acts for a non-existent principal*

  In such circumstances, the other party to the agreement can take action against the purported agent.

9.1.7.2   *Where the principal's existence is not disclosed*

Even in the case of an undisclosed principal, where the agent has authority but has failed to disclose that he or she is acting for a principal, the general rule is still that a contract exists between the principal and the third party, which can be enforced by either of them. The following, however, are some modifications to this general rule:

- The third party is entitled to enforce the contract against the agent and, in turn, the agent can enforce the contract against the third party. In both cases, the principal can intervene to enforce or defend the action on his or her own behalf.

- As stated previously, an undisclosed principal cannot ratify any contract made outside of the agent's actual authority.

- Where the third party had a special reason to contract with the agent, the principal may be excluded from the contract. This will certainly apply in relation to personal contracts, such as contracts of employment and, possibly, on the authority of *Greer v Downs Supply Co* (1927), where the third party has a right to set off debts against the agent.

- Authority exists in *Said v Butt* (1920), where a theatre critic employed someone to get him a ticket for a performance he would not have been allowed into, for claiming that an undisclosed principal will not be permitted to enforce a contract where particular reasons exist as to why the third party would not wish to deal with him or her. This decision appears to run contrary to normal commercial practice and is of doubtful merit.

It is certain, however, that where the agent actually misrepresents the identity of the principal, knowing that the third party would not otherwise enter into the contract, the principal will not be permitted to enforce the contract (see *Archer v Stone* (1898)).

9.1.7.3 Payment by means of an agent

Payment by means of an agent can take two forms:

- *Payment by the third party to the agent to pass on to the principal*

  In this situation, if the principal is undisclosed, then the third party has discharged liability on the contract and is not responsible if the agent absconds with the money. However, if the principal is disclosed, then any payment to the agent only discharges the third party's responsibility if it can be shown that the agent had authority, either express or implied, to receive money.

- *Payment by the principal to the agent to pass on to the third party*

  In this situation, the general rule is that if the agent does not pay the third party, the principal remains liable. This remains the case with an undisclosed principal (see *Irvine & Co v Watson & Sons* (1880)).

9.1.7.4 Breach of warrant of authority

As has been stated above (9.1.3.3), where an agent purports to act for a principal without actually having the necessary authority, the agent is said to have breached his or her warrant of authority. In such circumstances, the third party may take action against the purported agent.

9.1.7.5 Liability in tort

An agent is liable to be sued in tort for any damages thus caused. However, the agent's right to indemnity extends to tortious acts done in the performance of his or her actual authority. In addition, the principal may have action taken against him or her directly, on the basis of vicarious liability.

9.1.8 Termination of agency

The principal/agent relationship can come to end in two distinct ways: either by the acts of the parties themselves, either jointly or unilaterally; or as an effect of the operation of law.

9.1.8.1 Termination by the parties

There are a number of ways in which the parties can bring an agency agreement to an end, as follows:

- *By mutual agreement*

  Where the agency agreement is a continuing one, the parties may simply agree to bring the agency relationship to an end on such terms as they wish. Where the agency was established for a particular purpose, then it will automatically come to an end when that purpose has been achieved. Equally, where the agency was only intended to last for a definite period of time, then the end of that period will bring the agency to an end.

- *By the unilateral action of one of the parties*

  Because of the essentially consensual nature of the principal/agency relationship, it is possible for either of the parties to bring it to an end simply by giving notice of termination of the agreement. Although the agency relationship will be ended by such unilateral action, in situations where the principal has formed a contractual relationship with the agent, such unilateral termination may leave the principal open to an action for damages in breach of contract.

- *Irrevocable agreements*

  In some circumstances, it is not possible to revoke an agency agreement. This situation arises where the agent has authority coupled with an interest. Such an irrevocable agency might arise where a principal owes money to the agent and the payment of the debt was the reason for the formation of the agency relationship. For example, where, in order to raise the money to pay off his debt, the principal appoints his creditor as his agent to sell some particular piece of property, the principal may not be at liberty to bring the agency to an end until the sale has taken place and the debt has been paid off.

9.1.8.2 Termination by operation of law

This refers to the fact that an agency relationship will be brought to an end by any of the following:

- *Frustration*

  Contracts of agency are subject to discharge by frustration in the same way that ordinary contracts are (see above, 6.5.4, for the general operation of the doctrine of frustration).

- *The death of either party*

  Death of the agent clearly brings the agreement to an end, as does the death of the principal. The latter situation may, however, give rise to problems where the agent is unaware of the death and continues to act in the capacity of agent. In such circumstances, the agent will be in breach of his or her warrant of authority and will be personally liable to third parties.

- *Insanity of either party*

  As in the previous situation, the insanity of either party will bring the agency to an end; similarly, agents will have to be careful not to breach their warrant of authority by continuing to act after the principal has become insane (see *Yonge v Toynbee* (1910), above, 9.1.3.3).

- *Bankruptcy*

  Generally, the bankruptcy of the principal will end the agency agreement, but the bankruptcy of the agent will only bring it to an end where it renders him or her unfit to continue to act as an agent.

9.2   Partnership

The partnership is a fundamental form of business/commercial organisation. Historically, the partnership predated the registered limited company as a means for uniting the capital of separate individuals, and it was of the utmost importance in financing the Industrial Revolution in the UK in the 18th and 19th centuries.

As an economic form, the partnership is still important. However, since the last quarter of the 19th century, as unlimited partnerships have transformed themselves into private limited companies, partnership law has given way to the control of company law as a form of legal regulation. It could be argued that, nowadays, the important partnership cases take place in the Companies Court. The continued relevance of partnership law should not be underestimated, however, since it remains the essential form of organisation within the sphere of such professional activities as the law, accountancy and medicine, where there is no wish, or need, for limited liability.

The situation has been further complicated by the availability of the new legal form of the incorporated and limited partnership under the Limited Liability Partnership Act 2000.

9.2.1   The Partnership Acts

9.2.1.1   *Standard partnerships*

The legal regulation of standard partnerships is mainly to be found in the Partnership Act (PA) 1890. The PA 1890 recognised the existing business and commercial practice and at least some of the previous decisions of common law and equity as they affected partnerships.

In line with the consensual nature of partnership undertakings, the PA 1890 did not seek to achieve a complete codification of the law; it merely sought to establish a basic framework, whilst leaving open the possibility of partners establishing their own terms. The limited nature of the PA 1890 means that reference has to be made to cases decided by the courts both before and after the PA 1890 in order to understand the full scope of partnership law (s 46 expressly maintains all the rules of the common law and equity, except where they are inconsistent with the provisions of the PA 1890).

9.2.1.2 Limited partnerships

A key attribute of the standard partnership is the fact that its members are liable to the full extent of their personal wealth for the debts of the business. The Limited Partnership Act 1907, however, allows for the formation of limited partnerships. In order for members of a partnership to gain the benefit of limited liability under this legislation, the following rules apply:

- Limited partners are not liable for partnership debts beyond the extent of their capital contribution but, in the ordinary course of events, they are not permitted to remove their capital.

- One or more of the partners must retain full, that is, unlimited, liability for the debts of the partnership.

- A partner with limited liability is not permitted to take part in the management of the business enterprise and cannot usually bind the partnership in any transaction (contravention of this rule will result in the loss of limited liability).

- The partnership must be registered with the Companies Registry.

In practice, the Limited Partnership Act 1907 has had little effect and has been seldom used. The simple reason for such a situation is the emergence, legal recognition and development of the private limited company as an alternative form of organisation. At least to the extent that it affords the protection of limited liability, limited small businesses have seen the private company as the better and preferred form. The famous company law case of *Salomon v Salomon & Co* (1897) recognised the legal validity of the private limited company and predestined the failure of the Limited Partnership Act 1907 (see, further below, 9.3.1.2).

9.2.1.3 Limited liability partnerships

The Limited Liability Partnership Act (LLPA) 2000 provides for a new form of business entity, the limited liability partnership (LLP). Although stated to be a partnership, the new form is a corporation, with a distinct legal existence apart from its members. It will have perpetual succession and, consequently, alterations in its membership will not have any effect on its existence. Most importantly, however, the new legal entity will allow all of its members to benefit from limited liability, in that they will not be liable for more than the amount they have agreed to contribute to its capital.

This last advantage is significantly different from the previous limitation on liability available under the Limited Partnership Act 1907, which, as has been seen, required at least one general partner to remain fully liable for partnership debts. The provisions of the LLPA 2000 will be considered in detail below at 9.2.10, and what follows before then will relate to the ordinary standard partnership.

9.2.2 Definition of 'partnership'

Section 1 of the PA 1890 states that partnership is the relation which subsists between persons carrying on a business in common with a view to profit.

In relation to this definition, the following points should be noted:

- *Membership numbers*

  There must be a minimum of two and a maximum of 20 members in a partnership, except for some professional partnerships (see 9.2.4.2).

- *Registered companies*

  Section 1 of the PA 1890 expressly excludes companies registered under the companies legislation from being treated as partnerships. However, as legal persons (see 9.3.2.2) such companies can be members of partnerships.

- *The nature of the relationship is a contractual one*

  Partners enter into the agreement on the terms that they themselves have negotiated and acceded to. As a consequence, they are contractually bound by those terms, as long as they do not conflict with the express provisions of the PA 1890, and they may be enforced by the law in the same way as other contractual terms.

- *It is a requirement that a business be carried on*

  The term 'business' includes any trade, occupation or profession. The mere fact that individuals jointly own property does not necessarily mean that they are partners if the property is not being used by them to pursue some collective business activity. See also *Britton v Commissioners of Customs & Excise* (1986), where it was held that the fact that a wife received a share of the profits of her husband's business did not make her a partner in the business, since this was a purely domestic arrangement.

- *Any business must be carried out in common*

  Partnerships are by definition collective organisations. Under English law, however, they are no more than a collection of individuals and do not enjoy the benefits of separate personality (see below, 9.2.4.1).

- *Partnerships may be created for the purposes of a single venture*

  It is usually the case that partnerships continue over an extended period of time, but this is not necessarily the case.

- *The business must be carried on with a view to profit*

An immediate result of this provision is that neither charitable nor mutual benefit schemes are to be considered as partnerships.

It used to be the case that the mere receipt of a share of profit was enough to make a person a partner and responsible for partnership debts (see *Waugh v Carver* (1793)). Nowadays, although the receipt of a share of profits may be *prima facie* evidence of a partnership relationship, it is not conclusive.

Section 2(2) of the PA 1890 expressly states that the sharing of gross returns does not in itself indicate the existence of a partnership agreement, since such an arrangement may simply represent a form of payment for the individual concerned. Thus, by way of example, the authors of this book will receive a percentage of the total sales value of the book. That, however, does not make them partners of the publishers so, if publication of the book results in massive losses for the publishers, third parties cannot look to the authors for any money owed. In *Cox v Coulson* (1916), the defendant, who owned a theatre, agreed with another party, Mill, that he (Mill) could use the premises to put on a play. Coulson was to receive 60% of gross profits by way of payment. During a performance, the plaintiff was shot and she sued Coulson as Mill's partner for compensation for her injuries. Her action failed as the mere sharing of gross profits did not in itself create partnership relations.

Even receiving a share of net profits does not necessarily indicate a partnership. For example, a person would not be treated as a partner where they received payment of a debt by instalments made from business profits; or where they received wages in the form of a share of profit; or where they received interest on a loan to a business, the rate of which varied in relation to the level of the business profits. Thus, in *Strathearn Gordon Associates Ltd v Commissioners of Customs & Excise* (1985), the company acted as management consultant to seven separate enterprises, receiving a share of their individual profits as part of its payment. The company argued that the consultancy was part of seven separate partnership agreements and, therefore, did not accrue value added tax (VAT), as would be the case if it were merely supplying its services to the various enterprises. The VAT tribunal found against the company, on the basis that merely receiving a share of profit was not sufficient to establish a partnership relationship. (See also *Britton v Commissioners of Customs & Excise*.)

9.2.3 Types of partners

It is sometimes thought to be necessary to distinguish between different types of partners but, in reality, such a division is of most use in pointing out particular dangers inherent in a failure to adopt an active, if only supervisory, role in a partnership enterprise. Thus, a general partner is the typical member of a partnership. The term is actually used in the Limited Partnership Act 1907 to distinguish that usual type from the unusual limited partner. The general partner is one who is actively engaged in the day to day running of the business enterprise, whereas the limited partner is actually precluded from participating in the management of the enterprise.

Section 24(5) of the PA 1890 provides that every partner is entitled to take part in the management of the partnership business. The partnership agreement may place limitations on the actual authority of any such person but, unless an outsider is aware of the limitation, the partnership is responsible for any business transaction entered into by a partner within his or her usual authority. (For further consideration of these types of authority, see below, 9.2.7.1.)

A dormant or 'sleeping' partner is a person who merely invests money in a partnership enterprise but, apart from receiving a return on capital invested, takes no active part in the day to day running of the business. The limited partner in a limited partnership may be seen as a dormant partner. The term is used more generally, however, to refer to people who simply put money into partnership enterprises without taking an active part in the business and yet do not comply with the formalities required for establishing a limited partnership. The essential point that has to be emphasised in this regard is that, in so doing, such people place themselves at great risk. The law will consider them as general partners in the enterprise and will hold them personally and fully liable for the debts of the partnership to the extent of their ability to pay. By remaining outside the day to day operation of the business, such people merely surrender their personal unlimited liability into the control of the active parties in the partnership.

The term 'salaried partner' applies in professional partnerships to someone who, although appropriately qualified, is not a partner in the full sense of the word. They will be recognised as partners and will have the satisfaction of having their name on the partnership's letterhead, but they will not fully participate in the business profits as the other, ordinary partners do – they will merely receive a salary. They might also be restricted in their participation in partnership meetings. Nonetheless, such partners are liable for partnership debts in the same way, and to the same extent, as the ordinary partners.

9.2.4 The legal status of a partnership

The standard partnership is an organisation established by individuals to pursue some business activity. Although the law is permissive in relation to the establishment of such enterprises, there are particular ways in which the law impinges on and controls not just the operation of partnerships, but their very formation and existence.

9.2.4.1 Legal personality

The definition of a partnership expressly states that it is a relationship between persons. The corollary of this is that the partnership has no existence outside of, or apart from, that relationship. In other words, the partnership has no separate legal personality apart from its members, unlike a joint stock company.

Although Scots law does grant corporate personality to the partnership without the benefit of limited liability, in English law a partnership is no more than a group of individuals collectively involved in a business activity. Section 4 of the PA 1890, however, does recognise an element of unity within the partnership organisation, to the extent that it permits the partnership to be known collectively as a firm and permits the business to be carried out under the firm's name. In addition, the procedural Rules of the Supreme Court, Ord 81, as stated in the Civil Procedure Rules 1998, provides that legal action may be taken by, and against, the partners in the firm's name, although any award against the partnership may be executed against any of the individual partners.

LLPs formed under the LLPA 2000 are incorporated and, as such, have a distinct legal personality apart from their members. (See below, 9.2.10 for LLPs and below, 9.3.1 for an analysis of corporations.)

In November 2003, the Law Commission and the Scottish Law Commission produced a joint proposal for the major alteration of partnership law under which partnerships would be extended the privilege of full legal personality. In relation to liability, the proposal is for the partnership, as a legal person, to assume primary liability for debts but for the members to retain secondary liability for any debts beyond the assets of the partnership.

It follows from the current lack of separate personality in the standard partnership that the partners are self-employed. The partnership can, of course, employ others. However, an interesting juxtaposition of the requirement to carry out a business collectively in the pursuit of profit and the requirements of employment law may be found in *Rennison & Sons v Minister of Social Security* (1970). It is essential for the purposes of employment law to distinguish between those who are self-employed (or in contracts for services) and those who are employees (in contracts of service), as different rights appertain to the different categories. In deciding any question, the courts will look at the reality of the situation, rather than the mere title that someone bares.

In the *Rennison* case, a firm of solicitors had purported to enter into contracts of service with their clerical staff and, subsequently, all of the staff had entered into a partnership agreement, under which the profits and losses were to be divided on terms to be agreed. In fact, the clerical staff continued to work as they had done before and continued to be paid at exactly the same hourly rate that they had previously been paid. The only difference was that the wages were paid in a lump sum to one of them who was responsible for dividing it out amongst the rest. When the issue of responsibility for payment of national insurance was raised, as was required in relation to employees but not the self-employed, the court held that neither of the devices successfully removed the reality that the staff concerned were employees. Simply calling them 'self-employed' did not alter their status as employees, nor did calling them 'partners'. In reality, the agreement simply affected the way in which they were paid, rather than their employment status. (See below, for more detailed treatment of the employment law issues.)

9.2.4.2 Illegal partnerships

A partnership is illegal if it is formed to carry out an illegal purpose, or to carry out a legal purpose in an illegal manner. In such circumstances, the courts will not recognise any partnership rights between the persons involved, but will permit innocent third parties who have no knowledge of any illegality to recover against them.

Partnerships are generally not lawful if they consist of more than 20 persons, as provided by s 716 of the Companies Act (CA) 1985. However, certain professional partnerships, such as solicitors, accountants and surveyors, etc, are exempt from this maximum limit.

9.2.4.3　Capacity

There are two distinct aspects relating to capacity, as follows:

- *Capacity of individuals to join a partnership*

  The general common law rules relating to capacity to enter into contracts apply in the particular case of the membership of a partnership. Thus, any partnership agreement entered into by a minor is voidable during that person's minority and for a reasonable time after they have reached the age of majority. If the former minor does not repudiate the partnership agreement within a reasonable time of reaching the age of majority, then they will be liable for any debts as a *de facto* partner. Third parties cannot recover against partners who are minors, but they can recover against any other adult partners.

  Mental incapacity does not necessarily prevent someone from entering into a partnership, but subsequent mental incapacity of a partner may be grounds for the dissolution of a partnership.

- *Capacity of the partnership*

  A particular consequence of the fact that the partnership is, at least in the perception of the law, no more than a relationship between individuals is that there are no specific rules controlling the contractual capacity of partnerships, other than those general rules which constrain individuals' capacity to enter into contracts. This point was of more significance when companies were more strictly constrained by the operation of the *ultra vires* doctrine but, as will be seen below at 9.3.4.1, company law doctrine has been much relaxed.

  Section 5 of the PA 1890 provides that each partner is the agent of the firm and the other partners for the purpose of the business of the partnership but, as that purpose is determined by the members, and as it is not fixed by law, it can be changed by the unanimous agreement of those members. (See below, 9.2.5.2, on the alteration of the partnership agreement.)

9.2.5　Formation of a partnership

There are no specific legal requirements governing the formation of a partnership. Partnerships arise from the agreement of the parties involved and are governed by the general principles of contract law. An agreement to enter into a partnership, therefore, may be made by deed, in writing or by word of mouth. Such agreement may even be implied from the conduct of the parties.

9.2.5.1 The partnership agreement

It is usual for the terms of the partnership to be set out in written form. The document produced is known as the 'articles of partnership'. The parties involved, no doubt after some negotiation, decide what they wish to be specifically included in the articles. Any gaps in the articles will be filled in by reference to the PA 1890 or the existing common law and equitable rules relating to partnerships, but it is necessary for the future partners to provide for any unusual or specialised terms to be included in the articles.

The detailed provisions in articles of partnership usually refer to such matters as the nature of the business to be transacted, the name of the firm, the capital contributions to be made by the individual partners, the drawing up of the business accounts, the method of determining and sharing profits and the dissolution of the partnership. It is also usual for there to be a provision for disputes between partners to be referred to arbitration for solution.

The partnership agreement is an internal document and, although it has effect between the partners, it does not necessarily affect the rights of third parties. Thus, where the agreement seeks to place limitations on the usual authority of a partner, it is effective with regard to the internal relations of the partners but does not have any effect as regards an outsider who deals with the partner without knowledge of the limitation.

In *Mercantile Credit v Garrod* (1962), Parkin and Garrod were partners in a garage business, which was mainly concerned with letting garages and repairing cars. The partnership agreement expressly excluded the sale of cars. After Parkin had sold a car, to which he had no title, to the plaintiffs, they claimed back the money they had paid from Garrod.

It was held that since selling cars was within the usual scope of a garage business, it was within the usual authority of a partner in such a business. Parkin, therefore, had acted within his implied authority and the partnership was responsible for his actions. The plaintiffs had no knowledge of the limitation contained within the articles and could not be subject to it.

9.2.5.2 Alteration of the partnership agreement

Just as the consensual nature of the partnership relationship allows the parties to make the agreement in such terms as they wish, so are they equally free to alter those terms at a later date. Section 19 of the PA 1890, however, enacts the common law rule that any decision to alter the terms of partnership articles must be made unanimously. Consent does not have to be expressed but may be inferred from the conduct of the partners.

In *Pilling v Pilling* (1887), the articles of partnership entered into between a father and his two sons stated that the business was to be financed by the father's capital and that such capital was to remain his personal property and was not to be treated as the partnership property. The articles also stated that the father should receive interest on his capital. In practice, however, the sons, as well as the father, received interest on partnership capital. It was held that the capital originally provided by the father was partnership property and that the conduct of the parties in treating it as such had amounted to a valid alteration of the written agreement.

9.2.5.3 *The firm's name*

Partnerships may use the words 'and Company', or its alternative form 'and Co', in their name; for example, a firm of solicitors may call itself 'Brown, Smith and Co'. This merely indicates that the names of all the partners are not included in the firm's name. As has been seen above, it in no way indicates that the partnership has any existence apart from its constituent members, or that those members have the benefit of limited liability. Even in the case of limited partnerships, someone must accept full liability for partnership debts. Section 34 of the CA 1985 consequently makes it a criminal offence for a partnership to use the word 'Limited' (or the abbreviation 'Ltd') in its name.

A partnership may trade under the names of the individual partners or it may trade under a collective name. Any name must comply with both the Business Names Act (BNA) 1985 and the common law provisions relating to the tort of passing off.

9.2.5.4 *The Business Names Act 1985*

Section 4 of the BNA 1985 requires that where a partnership does not trade under the names of all of its members, the names of individuals must be displayed on the business premises and on the firm's business documents. Where the partnership is a large one with more than 20 members, the individual names do not have to be listed on business documents, but a list of all partners must be available for inspection at the firm's principal place of business. Any failure to comply with this requirement may result in the person in breach not being able to enforce a claim against another party who was disadvantaged by the breach.

There is no longer any requirement that business names be registered as such, but the BNA 1985 requires the approval of the Secretary of State for Trade and Industry before certain names can be used. Such names may imply that the business is related in some way to the Crown, the Government, local authorities or other official bodies.

9.2.5.5 *Passing off*

The BNA 1985 does not prevent one business from using the same, or a very similar, name as another business. However, the tort of passing off prevents one person from using any name which is likely to divert business their way by suggesting that the business is actually that of some other person or is connected in any way with that other business. It thus enables people to protect the goodwill they have built up in relation to their business activity. See *Ewing v Buttercup Margarine Co Ltd* (1917), where the plaintiff successfully prevented the defendants from using a name that suggested a link with his existing dairy company. For a more up to date and less serious case, see *Stringfellow v McCain Foods GB Ltd* (1984), in which the owner of the famous Stringfellow's night club failed to prevent a manufacturer of long, thin oven chips from calling their product by the same name.

9.2.6 Arbitration clauses

The consensual nature of the relationship on which any partnership is based has been repeatedly emphasised. It should always be remembered, however, that even the best of friends can fall out; when they are engaged in a joint business venture, any such conflict may be disastrous for the business. In an attempt to forestall such an eventuality, and to avoid the cost, delay and publicity involved in court procedure, it is standard practice for partnership articles to contain a clause referring disputes to arbitration for solution.

The actual procedure of arbitration has been considered in Chapter 3, above, but it should be recognised that arbitration, although relatively cheaper than the court system, is not cheap in absolute terms. Nor can it deal with situations where the partners have reached the stage where their continued conflict prevents the effective operation of the business. In such circumstances, it is probably wiser if the partnership is wound up on just and equitable grounds under s 35 of the PA 1890. (See below, 9.2.8.1 and see also *Re Yenidje Tobacco Co Ltd* (1916) as an example of the partnership principle being extended to a quasi-partnership company.)

9.2.7 The relation of partners to one another

The partnership agreement is contractual in nature. The partnership also involves a principal/agency relationship, but is complicated by the fact that partners are, at one and the same time, both agents of the firm and their fellow partners, and principals as regards those other partners. Partners are equally subject to the equitable rights and duties that derive from their being in a fiduciary position in relation to another. Thus, the legal nature of the partnership involves a complicated mixture of elements of contract, agency and equity.

Section 24(8) of the PA 1890 provides that, subject of course to any agreement to the contrary, any differences arising as to the ordinary matters connected with the partnership business are to be decided by a majority of the partners, although they must not impose their views without actually consulting the minority (see *Const v Harris* (1824)). Thus, the day to day business is conducted in line with the wishes of the majority. However, s 24(8) also states that the nature of that business cannot be changed without the unanimous agreement of the partners.

9.2.7.1 Duties of partners

The fiduciary nature of the partnership relationship imports the usual duties that derive from such a relationship, which can be summed up under the general heading of a duty to act in good faith. In addition to these general fiduciary duties, ss 28–30 of the PA 1890 lay down specific duties as follows:

- *The duty of disclosure*

  Section 28 provides that partners must render true accounts and full information in relation to all things affecting the partnership to the other partners or their legal representatives.

  In *Law v Law* (1905), one partner accepted an offer from the other to buy his share of the firm. He later discovered that certain partnership assets had not been disclosed to him and sought to have the contract set aside. The court decided that, as the purchasing partner had breached the duty of disclosure, the agreement could have been set aside. In actual fact, the parties had come to an arrangement, so it was not necessary for such an order to be granted.

- *The duty to account*

  Section 29 of the PA 1980 provides that partners must account to the firm for any benefit obtained, without consent, from any transaction concerning the partnership; its property, including information derived from membership of the partnership; its name; or its business connection. As with fiduciary duties generally, such profit is only open to challenge where it is undisclosed. Full disclosure is necessary and sufficient to justify the making of an individual profit from a partnership position.

  In *Bentley v Craven* (1853), Craven was in partnership with the plaintiff in a sugar refinery business. He bought sugar on his own account and later sold it to the partnership at a profit, without declaring his interest to the other partners. It was held that the partnership was entitled to recover the profit from the defendant.

- *The duty not to compete*

  Section 30 provides that where a partner competes with the partnership business, without the consent of the other partners, then that person shall be liable to account to the partnership for any profits made in the course of that business. In *Glassington v Thwaites* (1823), a member of a partnership, which produced a morning paper, was held to account for the profit he made from publishing an evening paper. Once again, it is essential to note that full disclosure is necessary to validate any such profits made in competition with the partnership. (See *Trimble v Goldberg* (1906), where the court declined to recognise competition in relation to a partnership; but the likely severity of the courts' approach can be surmised from the company law case of *Industrial Development Consultants v Cooley* (1972).)

9.2.7.2 *Rights of partners*

Subject to express provision to the contrary in the partnership agreement, and it should be remembered that the consensual nature of the partnership allows the parties to avoid the provisions of the Act, s 24 of the PA 1890 sets out the rights of partners. Amongst the most important of these are the following rights:

- *To share equally in the capital and profits of the business*

  Even where the partnership agreement is silent on the matter, s 24 does not mean that someone who has contributed all, or the greater part, of the capital of a firm must share it equally with the other partners. In such circumstances, it would most likely be decided that the facts of the case provided evidence of such contrary intention as to rebut the statement in the PA 1890. What the section does mean is that, even in the same circumstances, the partners will share profits equally, although it is not unusual to find clauses in agreements which recognise differences in capital input by providing for profits to be shared on an unequal basis. The same effect can be achieved by permitting interest to be paid on capital before profits are determined. Where partners advance additional capital to the firm by way of a loan, they are entitled to interest at 5% unless there is an agreement to the contrary.

  The corollary of this right is the duty to contribute equally to any losses of capital, even where no capital was originally brought into the business. For example, if A and B enter into a partnership, with A providing all of the capital of £10,000 but A and B sharing the profits equally, and, upon winding up, the business has accrued a loss of £2,000, then both parties are required to contribute to the loss. In effect, B will have to contribute £1,000 and A will only receive a return of £9,000.

- *To be indemnified by the firm for any liabilities incurred or payments made in the course of the firm's business*

  This may be seen as merely an express declaration of the usual right of an agent to indemnity. The right of an agent to act outside their authority in the case of necessity is also expressly set out in s 24.

- *To take part in the management of the business*

  The unlimited nature of the ordinary partnership means that involvement in such a business brings with it the risk to one's personal wealth. It is essential under such circumstances, therefore, that partners are able to protect their interests by taking an active part in the operation of the business in order to assess and control the level of their risk. It is for this reason that the right to take part in the management of the business is stated expressly. In the case of quasi-partnership companies, the courts will imply such a right.

  A partner is generally not entitled to receive any salary for acting in the partnership business, but it is not unusual for the agreement effectively to provide for the payment of a salary to particular partners before the determination of net profit.

- *To have access to the firm's books*

  This right follows from, and is based on, the same reasoning as the previous provision. The books are normally kept at the firm's principal place of business.

- *To prevent the admission of a new partner or prevent any change in the nature of the partnership business*

As has been seen, any differences relating to the partnership business can be decided by the majority, but unanimity is required to change the nature of the business. Again, this reflects the need for individual partners to accept risk voluntarily. They have only accepted existing business risks and cannot be forced to alter or increase that risk.

Similarly, as principals, they have agreed to give their authority to bind them and make them liable for partnership debts to particular individuals. They cannot be forced to extend that authority against their wishes.

In addition to the above rights, s 25 of the PA 1980 provides that no majority can expel another partner, unless such power is contained in the partnership agreement. Even where such a power is included, it must be exercised in good faith. See *Blisset v Daniel* (1853), where the majority attempted to expel a partner in order to acquire his share of the business cheaply; and *Green v Howell* (1910), where a partner was properly expelled for a flagrant breach of his duties. For somewhat more recent cases, see *Kerr v Morris* (1987) and *Walters v Bingham* (1988).

9.2.7.3 *Partnership property*

Property may be owned collectively by all of the partners and may thus amount to partnership property. Alternatively, it is possible for property to be used by the partnership as a whole and yet remain the personal property of only one of the partners.

Section 20 of the PA 1890 states that partnership property consists of all property brought into the partnership stock or acquired on account for the purposes of the firm. Section 21 further states that any property bought with money belonging to the firm is deemed to have been bought on account of the firm.

Whether or not any particular item of property belongs to the firm is always a matter of fact, to be determined in relation to the particular circumstances of any case. If there is no express agreement that property is to be brought into the firm as partnership property, the court will only imply such a term to the extent required to make the partnership agreement effective.

In *Miles v Clarke* (1953), Clarke had carried on a photography business for some time before taking Miles into partnership. The partnership agreement merely provided that the profits should be divided equally. When the partners fell out, a dispute arose as to who owned the assets used by the partnership. It was held that only the consumable stock-in-trade could be considered as partnership property. The leases of the business premises and other plant and equipment remained the personal property of the partner who introduced them into the business.

It is important to distinguish between partnership property and personal property for the following reasons:

- *Partnership property must be used exclusively for partnership purposes (s 20 of the PA 1980)*

  This may been seen as a statement of the general duty not to make a personal profit from a fiduciary position without full disclosure. Thus, partners are not supposed to use partnership property for their own personal benefit or gain, and if they were to do so they would be liable to account to the partnership for any profit made.

It is also made clear that partners do not own the firm's assets directly. All they have, under s 30, is the partnership lien over those assets, which entitles them, on dissolution, to participate in any surplus after their realised value has been used to pay off partnership debts.

- *Any increase in the value of partnership property belongs to the partnership*

  As a consequence, the increased value when realised will be divided amongst all the partners.

- *Any increase in the value of personal property belongs to the person who owns the property*

  Consequently, the increased value will not have to be shared with the other partners.

- *On the dissolution of the firm, partnership property is used to pay debts before personal property*

  This is clearly stated in s 39, which has been considered above in relation to the nature of the partnership lien.

- *Partnership and personal property are treated differently in the satisfaction of claims made by partnership creditors, as opposed to personal creditors*

  Under s 23, a writ of execution can only be issued against partnership property in respect of a judgment against the partnership. A personal creditor of a partner may not, therefore, take action against partnership property. They can, however, apply for a charging order against that partner's share in the partnership, which would entitle them to receive the partner's share of profits, or assets on dissolution, to the extent of the debt and interest. The other partners may redeem the charge at any time by paying off the debt, in which case the charge becomes vested in them.

- *On the death of a partner, any interest in partnership land will pass as personalty, whereas land owned personally will pass as realty*

  In effect, this means that the interest may pass to different people, depending on whether or not the party has made an appropriate will.

  Specifically in relation to land, s 22 enacts the equitable doctrine of conversion by providing that any such partnership property is to be treated as personal property.

9.2.7.4 Assignment of a share in a partnership

Unless the partnership agreement states otherwise, partners are at liberty to mortgage or assign absolutely their shares in partnerships to outsiders. The assignee is, however, only entitled to the share of profits due to the partner assigning the shares or, on dissolution, to the appropriate share of partnership assets. Section 31 makes it clear that any such assignee does not become a partner and has no right whatsoever to become involved in the management of the business. In *Garwood v Paynter* (1903), Garwood charged his shares to a trust, of which his wife was one of the beneficiaries. When the other partners began to pay themselves salaries, Mrs Garwood objected on the ground that such payment reduced the net profit of the firm and, hence, indirectly, the income to the trust. It was held that the payment of salaries was an internal management matter and, therefore, the trustees, who were assignees, by virtue of s 31 could not interfere in the absence of fraud.

The assignee does not take over responsibility for partnership debts. These remain the liability of the assignor. Where, however, the assignment is absolute, the assignee must indemnify the assignor in respect of future liabilities arising from the business.

9.2.8   The relation of partners to outsiders

Of equal importance to the internal relationships of the partnership is the relationship of the members of the partnership to outsiders who deal with the partnership and, in particular, the extent to which the partnership and, hence, the partners are liable for the actions of the individual partners.

9.2.8.1   *The authority of partners to bind the firm*

As stated in s 5 of the PA 1890, every partner is an agent of the firm and of the other partners. Each partner, therefore, has the power to bind co-partners and make them liable on business transactions. The partnership agreement may, however, expressly seek to limit the powers of particular members. The effect of such limitations depends on the circumstances of each case. They do not apply where the other partners have effectively countermanded the restriction. This can occur in two ways:

- If the other partners give their prior approval for a partner to exceed his actual authority, then the partner in question has express actual authority and the firm is bound by his action.

- If the other partners give their approval after the event, then they have ratified the transaction and the partnership is again liable.

The firm may be liable even where the other partners have not expressly approved the action in excess of authority, as long as the partner has acted within his or her implied powers, that is, within the usual scope of a partner's powers in the particular business concerned (see *Mercantile Credit v Garrod* (1962) above, 9.2.5.1). If, however, the outsider had actual knowledge of the partner's lack of authority, then the partnership is not bound by the transaction.

Every partner other than a limited partner is presumed to have the implied authority to enter into transactions:

- to sell the firm's goods;

- to buy goods of a kind normally required by the firm;

- to engage employees;

- to receive payment of debts due to the partnership;

- to pay debts owed by the partnership and to draw cheques for that purpose; and

- to employ a solicitor to act for the firm in defence of an action or in pursuit of a debt.

The above implied powers apply equally to trading and non-trading partnerships. Partners in trading firms, that is, those which essentially buy and sell goods, have additional implied powers:

- to accept, draw, issue or endorse bills of exchange or other negotiable instruments on behalf of the firm;

- to borrow money on the credit of the firm; and

- to pledge the firm's goods as security for borrowed money.

9.2.8.2   The nature of partners' liability

Every partner is responsible for the full amount of the firm's liability. Outsiders have the choice of taking action either against the firm collectively or against the individual partners. Where damages are recovered from one partner only, the other partners are under a duty to contribute equally to the amount paid, as follows:

- *Liability on debts and contracts*

    Under s 9 of the PA 1890, the liability of partners as regards debts or contracts is joint. The effect of joint liability used to be that, although the partners were collectively responsible, a person who took action against one of the partners could take no further action against the other partners, even if they had not recovered all that was owing to them.

    That situation was remedied by the Civil Liability (Contributions) Act 1978, which effectively provided that a judgment against one partner *does not* bar a subsequent action against the other partners.

- *Liability for torts*

    Under s 10 of the PA 1890, the liability of partners with regard to torts or other wrongs committed in the ordinary course of the partnership business is joint and several. In such a situation, there is no bar on taking successive actions against partners in order to recover all that is due.

    It should be emphasised that, in order for the partnership to be responsible, the wrong sued on must have been committed in the ordinary course of partnership business or with the express approval of all the partners. If a tort is committed outside this scope, then the partner responsible is personally liable.

    In *Hamlyn v Houston & Co* (1905), one of the partners in the defendant company bribed a clerk employed by the plaintiff, in order to get information about their rival's business. Hamlyn sued the defendant partnership to recover the loss he claimed to have suffered as a consequence. It was held that the defendant firm was liable for the wrongful act of the individual partner, as he had acted within the usual scope of his authority, although he had used illegal methods in doing so.

However, see *Arbuckle v Taylor* (1815), where the partnership was not liable because the individual partner had gone beyond the general scope of the partnership business.

As was stated in 9.2.4.1, partners may be sued in the firm's name, although they remain individually liable for any awards made as a consequence of any such claim.

9.2.8.3 *The liability of incoming and outgoing partners*

A person who is admitted into an existing firm is not liable to creditors of the firm for anything done before they became a partner (see s 17 of the PA 1890). The new partner can, however, assume such responsibility by way of a device known as novation. This is the process whereby a retiring partner is discharged from existing liability and the newly constituted partnership takes the liability on themselves. Novation is essentially a tripartite contract involving the retiring partner, the new firm and the existing creditors. As creditors effectively give up rights against the retiring partner, their approval is required. Such approval may be express, or it may be implied from the course of dealing between the creditor and the firm.

In *Thompson v Percival* (1834), Charles Thompson and James Percival had been in partnership until Thompson retired. The plaintiff creditors, on applying for payment, were informed that Percival alone would be responsible for payment, as Thompson had retired. As a consequence, they drew a bill for payment against Percival alone. Subsequently, it was held that they no longer had a right of action against Thompson, since their action showed that they had accepted his discharge from liability.

Creditors do not have to accept a novation. A creditor may still hold the retired partner responsible for any debts due at the time of retirement. The newly constituted firm may, however, agree to indemnify the retiring partner against any such claims.

Apart from novation, a retired partner remains liable for any debts or obligations incurred by the partnership prior to retirement. The date of any contract determines responsibility: if the person was a partner when the contract was entered into, then they are responsible, even if the goods under the contract are delivered after they have left the firm. The estate of a deceased person is only liable for those debts or obligations arising before death.

Where someone deals with a partnership after a change in membership, they are entitled to treat all of the apparent members of the old firm as still being members, until they receive notice of any change in membership. In order to avoid liability for future contracts, a retiring partner must:

- ensure that individual notice is given to existing customers of the partnership; and

- advertise the retirement in the *London Gazette*. This serves as general notice to people who were not customers of the firm prior to the partner's retirement but who knew that that person had been a partner in the business. Such an advert is effective whether or not it comes to the attention of third parties.

A retired partner owes no responsibility to someone who had neither dealings with the partnership nor previous knowledge of his or her membership.

In *Tower Cabinet Co Ltd v Ingram* (1949), Ingram and Christmas had been partners in a firm known as Merry's. After it was dissolved by mutual agreement, Christmas carried on trading under the firm's name. Notice was given to those dealing with the firm that Ingram was no longer connected with the business, but no notice was placed in the *London Gazette*. New note paper was printed without Ingram's name. However, the plaintiffs, who had had no previous dealings with the partnership, received an order on old note paper, on which Ingram's name was included. When Tower Cabinet sought to enforce a judgment against Ingram, it was held that he was not liable, since he had not represented himself as being a partner, nor had the plaintiffs been aware of his membership prior to dissolution.

9.2.8.4 *Partnership by estoppel*

Failure to give notice of retirement is one way in which liability arises on the basis of estoppel or holding out. Alternatively, anyone who represents themselves, or knowingly permits themselves to be represented, as a partner is liable to any person who gives the partnership credit on the basis of that representation. Although they may become liable for partnership debts, they are not, however, partners in any other sense. (In *Tower Cabinet Co Ltd v Ingram* (1949) (see above, 9.2.7.3), the defendant was not affected by partnership by estoppel, since he was never actually aware that he had been represented as being a partner.)

9.2.9   Dissolution and winding up of the partnership

There are a number of possible reasons for bringing a partnership to an end. It may have been established for a particular purpose and that purpose has been achieved, or one of the partners might wish to retire from the business, or the good relationship between the members, which is essential to the operation of a partnership, may have broken down. In all such cases, the existing partnership is dissolved, although, in the second case, a new partnership may be established to take over the old business.

9.2.9.1 *Grounds for dissolution*

As has been repeatedly emphasised, the partnership is based on agreement. It is created by agreement and it may be brought to an end in the same way. However, subject to any provision to the contrary in the partnership agreement, the PA 1890 provides for the automatic dissolution of a partnership on the following grounds:

- *The expiry of a fixed term or the completion of a specified enterprise (s 32(a) and (b))*

    If the partnership continues after the pre-set limit, it is known as a 'partnership at will' and it can be ended at any time thereafter at the wish of any of the partners.

- *The giving of notice (s 32(c))*

  If the partnership is of indefinite duration, it can be brought to an end by any one of the partners giving notice of an intention to dissolve the partnership.

- *The death or bankruptcy of any partner (s 33(1))*

  Although the occurrence of either of these events will bring the partnership to an end, it is usual for partnership agreements to provide for the continuation of the business under the control of the remaining/solvent partners. The dead partner's interest will be valued and paid to his or her personal representative, and the bankrupt's interest will be paid to his or her trustee in bankruptcy.

- *Where a partner's share becomes subject to a charge under s 23 (s 33(2))*

  Under such circumstances, dissolution is not automatic; it is open to the other partners to dissolve the partnership.

- *Illegality (s 34)*

  The occurrence of events making the continuation of the partnership illegal will bring it to an end. An obvious case would be where the continuation of the partnership would result in trading with the enemy (see *R v Kupfer* (1915)). The principle applied equally, however, in the more recent and perhaps more relevant case of *Hudgell, Yeates & Co v Watson* (1978). Practising solicitors are legally required to have a practice certificate. However, one of the members of a three-person partnership forgot to renew his practice certificate and, thus, was not legally entitled to act as a solicitor. It was held that the failure to renew the practice certificate brought the partnership to an end, although a new partnership continued between the other two members of the old partnership.

In addition to the provisions listed above, the court may, mainly by virtue of s 35 of the PA 1890, order the dissolution of the partnership in the following circumstances:

- *Where a partner becomes a patient under the Mental Health Act 1983*

  The procedure is no longer taken under s 35 of the PA 1890 but, where the person is no longer able to manage their affairs because of mental incapacity, the Court of Protection may dissolve a partnership at the request of the person's receiver or the other partners.

- *Where a partner suffers some other permanent incapacity*

  This provision is analogous to the previous one. It should be noted that it is for the other partners to apply for dissolution and that the incapacity alleged as the basis of dissolution must be permanent. It is not unusual for partnerships to include specific clauses in their agreement in order to permit dissolution on the basis of extended absence from the business (see *Peyton v Mindham* (1971), where a clause in a partnership covering medical practice provided for termination after nine months' continuous absence or a total of 300 days in any period of 24 months).

- *Where a partner engages in an activity prejudicial to the business*

Such activity may be directly related to the business, such as the misappropriation of funds. Alternatively, it may take place outside the business but operate to its detriment; an example of this might be a criminal conviction for fraud.

- *Where a partner persistently breaches the partnership agreement*

This provision also relates to conduct which makes it unreasonable for the other partners to carry on in business with the party at fault.

- *Where the business can only be carried on at a loss*

This provision is a corollary of the very first section of the PA 1890, in which the pursuit of profit is part of the definition of the partnership form. If such profit cannot be achieved, then the partners are entitled to avoid loss by bringing the partnership to an end.

- *Where it is just and equitable to do so*

The courts have wide discretion in relation to the implementation of this power. A similar provision operates within company legislation and the two provisions come together in the cases involving quasi-partnerships. On occasion, courts have wound up companies on the ground that they would have been wound up had the business assumed the legal form of a partnership. For examples of this approach, see *Re Yenidje Tobacco Co Ltd* (1916) and *Ebrahimi v Westbourne Galleries Ltd* (1973).

After dissolution, the authority of each partner to bind the firm continues so far as is necessary to wind up the firm's affairs and complete transactions that have begun but are unfinished at the time of dissolution (s 38 of the PA 1980). Partners cannot, however, enter into new contracts.

9.2.9.2 Dissolution and winding up

Since the introduction of the Insolvency Act (IA) 1986, partnerships as such are not subject to bankruptcy, although the individual partners may be open to such procedure. Partnerships may be wound up as unregistered companies under Pt V of the IA 1986 where they are unable to pay their debts.

9.2.9.3 Treatment of assets on dissolution

Upon dissolution, the value of the partnership property is realised and the proceeds are applied in the following order:

- in paying debts to outsiders;

- in paying to the partners any advance made to the firm beyond their capital contribution; and

- in paying the capital contribution of the individual partners.

Any residue is divided between the partners in the same proportion as they shared in profits (s 44 of the PA 1890).

If the assets are insufficient to meet debts, partners' advances and capital repayments, then the deficiency has to be made good out of any profits held back from previous years, or out of partners' capital, or by the partners individually in the proportion to which they were entitled to share in profits.

An example will clarify this procedure. Partners A, B and C contribute £5,000, £3,000 and £1,000 respectively. In addition, A makes an advance to the firm of £1,000. Upon dissolution, the assets realise £8,000, and the firm has outstanding debts amounting to £2,500. The procedure is as follows:

First, the creditors are paid what is due to them from the realised value of the assets. Thus, £8,000 – £2,500 = £5,500.

Secondly, an advance of £1,000 is paid back, leaving £4,500.

Assuming that there was no agreement to the contrary, profits and losses will be shared equally. The actual loss is determined as follows:

Original capital:	£9,000
Minus money left:	£4,500
	£4,500

This loss of £4,500 has to be shared equally in this case. Each partner has to provide £1,500 in order to make good the shortfall in capital. In the case of A and B, this is a paper transaction, as the payment due is simply subtracted from their original capital contribution. C, however, actually has to make a contribution of £500 from his personal wealth, as his due payment exceeds his original capital. The outcome is as follows:

- A's share of net assets: £5,000 – £1,500 = £3,500
- B's share of net assets: £3,000 – £1,500 = £1,500
- C's share of net assets: £1,000 – £1,500 = –£500

A provision in the partnership agreement for profits to be shared in proportion to capital contribution, that is, in the ratio 5:3:1, would have the following effect:

- A would contribute five-ninths of the £4,500 loss, that is, £2,500
- B would contribute three-ninths of the £4,500 loss, that is, £1,500
- C would contribute one-ninth of the £4,500 loss, that is, £500

Their shares in net assets would, therefore, be as follows:

- A: (£5,000 – £2,500) = £2,500
- B: (£3,000 – £1,500) = £1,500
- C: (£1,000 – £500) = £500

9.2.9.4 Bankruptcy of partners

Where a partner is bankrupt on the dissolution of a firm, the partnership assets are still used to pay partnership debts. It is only after the payment of partnership debts that any surplus due to that partner is made available for the payment of the partner's personal debts.

Where one partner is insolvent and there is a deficiency of partnership assets to repay the firm's creditors and any advances, the burden of making good the shortfall has to be borne by the solvent partners in proportion to their share in profits. If, however, the shortfall only relates to capital, then the situation is governed by the rule in *Garner v Murray* (1904). This rule means that, in any such situation, the solvent partners are not required to make good the capital deficiency due to the insolvency of t   h   e   i   r co-partner. However, as a consequence, there will be a shortfall in the capital fund, which has to be borne by the solvent partners in proportion to their capitals.

To return to the original example, the net assets were £4,500 and the capital deficiency was £4,500. All three partners were to contribute £1,500. In effect, C was the only one who actually had to pay out any money, since A and B merely suffered an abatement in the capital returned to them. However, if it is now assumed that C is insolvent and can make no contribution, the situation is as follows:

C loses his right of repayment, so this reduces the capital fund required to pay back partners' contributions to £8,000.

As previously, A and B contribute their portion of the total loss, taking the available capital fund up to £7,500 (that is, £4,500 + (2 × £1,500)).

There still remains a shortfall of £500. This is borne by A and B in proportion to their capital contribution. Thus, A suffers a loss of five-eighths of £500; and B suffers a loss of three-eighths of £500.

So, from the capital fund of £7,500 they receive the following:

- A: £5,000 − (5/8 × £500) = £4,687.50   (in reality, he or she simply receives £3,187.50)

- B: £3,000 − (3/8 × £500) = £2,812.50   (in reality, he or she simply receives £1,312.50)

9.2.10 Limited liability partnerships

As has already been seen, the main shortcoming with regard to the standard partnership is the lack of limited liability for its members: members have joint and several liability for the debts of their partnership to the full extent of their personal wealth. The risk of such unlimited liability is increased by the fact that, due to the nature of the partnership, all members can enter into contracts on behalf of the partnership, and is further compounded when the membership of the partnership is extensive, as it is in the case of many professional partnerships. The dangers inherent in such partnerships were revealed in the US in the early 1990s, with the collapse of the savings and loans system. Many firms of accountants and lawyers who had advised on such schemes found themselves being sued for negligence and the partners in those firms found themselves personally liable for extremely large amounts of debt, even though they had had absolutely nothing to do with the transaction in question. Whilst such firms of professionals were reluctant to incorporate and turn themselves into limited liability companies, they clearly saw the benefit of limiting the liability of the individual partners in relation to the misbehaviour of one of their fellow members. The LLP was the device for achieving the desired end of limiting claims for such vicarious liability. It should be noted, however, that although the LLP was introduced to offer protection to the large scale professional firms, it is not in any way limited to them, and it is open to any type of partnership, no matter how small, no matter what their business, to register as an LLP.

The possibility of registering as an LLP was introduced into the UK in 2000 with the passage of the LLPA 2000, although the Act did not come into effect until April 2001. The Act itself was a remarkable example of enabling legislation, merely providing a general framework and leaving the details to be supplied by the Limited Liability Partnership Regulations (LLPR) 2001 (SI 2001/1090). Section 1 of the LLPA 2000 states quite clearly that the LLP is a new form of legal entity, but before going on to consider the LLP in detail, it has to be stated at the outset that the LLP is something of a hybrid legal form, seeking, as will be seen, to amalgamate the advantages of the company's corporate form with the flexibility of the partnership form. However, s 1(5) states categorically that:

> ... except as far as otherwise provided by this Act ... the law relating to partnerships does not apply to a limited liability partnership.

9.2.10.1 Legal personality and limited liability

Although called a partnership, the LLP is a corporation with a distinct legal existence apart from its members. As such, it has the ability to:

- hold property in its own right;
- create floating charges over its property;
- enter into contracts in its own name; and
- sue and be sued in its own name.

It also has perpetual succession and, consequently, alterations in its membership will not have any effect on its existence. Similarly, the death or personal insolvency of a member will not affect the existence of the LLP. Most importantly, however, the new legal entity allows its members to benefit from limited liability, in that they are not liable for more than the amount they have agreed to contribute to its capital. There is no minimum amount for such agreed capital contribution. (For a further consideration of these attributes of incorporation, see below, 9.3.1.)

9.2.10.2   Creation

In order to form an LLP, the appropriate form must be registered with the Registrar of Companies. The form must contain:

- the signatures of at least two persons who are associated for the purposes of carrying on a lawful business with a view to profit;
- the name of the LLP, which must end with the words 'Limited Liability Partnership' or the abbreviation 'LLP';
- the location of the LLP's registered office in England and Wales, in Wales or in Scotland;
- the address of the registered office of the LLP;
- the names and addresses of those persons who will be members on the incorporation of the LLP and a statement whether some or all of them are to be designated members (see below); and
- a statement of compliance.

On registration of the company, the Registrar will issue a certificate of incorporation.

9.2.10.3   Membership

There must be a minimum of two members of the LLP. If the membership should fall below two for a period of six months, then the remaining member will lose their limited liability and will assume personal liability for any liabilities incurred during that period that the LLP cannot meet.

There is no maximum limit on membership. This is clearly indicative of the fact that LLPs were initially designed to offer limited liability to large scale professional firms, which were not limited to 20 members as were ordinary trading partnerships. However, as has been seen, the LLP form is in fact open to any partnership. Membership is not limited to individuals, and other incorporated bodies can be members of an LLP, as can other LLPs.

Within the LLP, there is a special type of membership, known as *designated membership*. As will be seen, such members are responsible for ensuring that the LLP conforms with its duty to file its accounts with the Registrar of Companies.

Becoming a member

Section 4(1) states that the original subscribers to the incorporation document are automatically members of the LLP. Other members may join with the agreement of the existing members (s 4(2)).

Ceasing to be a member

Under s 4(3), membership ceases on the occurrence of any of the following eventualities:

- death;

- dissolution (if the member is a corporation);

- on gaining the agreement of the other members; or

- after the giving of reasonable notice.

9.2.10.4   Disclosure requirements

Just as with limited companies, members of LLPs get the benefit of limited liability; equally, however, as with limited companies, such a benefit has to be paid for in the form of publicity and disclosure. People dealing with limited business are put on notice of that fact by the need to indicate their limited status in the names of the LLPs; this applies to both companies and LLPs. In addition, both are required to submit their accounts and some of their affairs to public scrutiny by filing them with the Registrar of Companies. In respect of LLPs, the essential filing requirements relate to:

- accounts;

- annual returns;

- changes in membership generally;

- changes in designated membership; and

- change to the registered office.

Accounts

The provisions that apply to limited companies with regard to auditing apply equally to LLPs, and therefore they will be required to submit properly audited accounts which give a true and fair view of the affairs of the LLP. However, the exemptions open to small and medium sized companies also apply to LLPs.

9.2.10.5   Relationship between members and the limited liability partnership

Section 6(1) provides that every member of the LLP is an agent of the LLP and, consequently, they will bind the LLP to any agreement entered into within the scope of their actual or apparent authority. However, the LLP will not be liable where the third party is aware of the lack of authority or does not know, or believe, that the other party is a member of the LLP. The LLP is also liable to the same extent as the member for any wrongful acts or omissions of individual members.

9.2.10.6   Relationship between members

Section 5 makes clear the intention to retain the flexible and consensual nature of the internal regulation of standard partnerships by providing that the mutual rights and duties of the members shall be governed 'by agreement between the members'. It is expected that LLPs will draw up specific agreements but, in the absence of any agreement, the default provisions of the LLPR 2001 will apply, which in turn are generally based on the previous rules set out in the PA 1890.

9.2.10.7 *Relationship between members and third parties*

As the LLP is a distinct legal person in its own right with full contractual capacity, it follows that there is usually no relationship between a member as agent and third parties who contract with the LLP as principal. However, it is possible that, as stated previously, the member may be personally liable for any wrongful act or omission, in which case he or she will consequently make the LLP equally liable.

9.2.10.8 *Creditor protection*

Members' liability is limited to the amount of capital introduced into the partnership. However, unlike limited companies, there are no controls on the withdrawal of capital by members, so creditors are not protected by the doctrine of capital maintenance. Creditors, however, are protected by the following general mechanisms:

- the requirement for LLPs to file audited accounts;
- the rules relating to fraud or misconduct under the IA 1986;
- actions to recover money from members in relation to misfeasance, fraudulent and wrongful trading and other potential compensatory provisions under the IA 1986 (see further below, 9.2.10.10); and
- the power to disqualify members.

9.2.10.9 *Taxation*

Although the LLP enjoys corporate status, it is not taxed as a separate entity from its members. Section 10 of the LLPA 2000 expressly provides that where a LLP carries on business with a view to profit, the members will be treated for the purposes of income tax, corporation tax and capital gains tax as if they were partners in a standard partnership. Thus, members of LLPs gain the benefits of limited liability whilst retaining the tax advantages of a partnership.

9.2.10.10 *Insolvency and winding up*

The LLPR 2001 extend the provisions relating to the insolvency and winding up of registered companies to LLPs. Thus, the relevant sections of the CA 1985, the IA 1986, the Company Directors Disqualification Act 1986 and the Financial Services and Markets Act 2000 have been appropriately modified to apply to LLPs.

Of particular interest are two alterations to the IA 1986. Section 1(4) of the LLPA 2000 merely stated that members of LLPs should have liability to contribute to its assets in the event of its winding up as 'is provided for by virtue of this Act'. The actual extent of that liability is established by a new s 74, introduced into the IA 1986 under the LLPR 2001.

The new section provides that:

> ... when a limited liability partnership is wound up every present and past member of the limited liability partnership who has agreed with the other members or with the limited liability partnership that he will, in circumstances which have arisen, be liable to contribute to the assets of the limited liability partnership in the event that the limited liability partnership goes into liquidation is liable, to the extent that he has so agreed, to contribute to its assets to any amount sufficient for payment of its debts and liabilities, and the expenses of the winding up, and for the adjustment of the rights of the contributories among themselves.

Thus, it is a matter for the members to agree the level of their potential liability, which may be set at a nominal level, as there is no minimum level established in the section. Indeed, there is no compulsion for the members to agree to pay any debts of the LLP.

As has been stated previously, members of LLPs are subject to the usual controls exerted over company members in relation to their conduct in relation to their insolvent companies, such as actions for misfeasance, fraudulent trading and wrongful trading (see further below, 9.3.1.1). In addition to these, however, the LLPR 2001 introduce a new s 214A into the IA 1986, which allows a liquidator to recover assets from members who have previously withdrawn property from their LLP. This measure strengthens the degree of creditor protection and is necessary in the light of the lack of the capital maintenance provisions which apply to companies. Section 214A applies in the following circumstances:

- A member withdrew property from the LLP in the two years prior to the start of its winding up. The property may be in the form of a share of profits, salary, repayment or payment of interest on a loan to the limited liability partnership, or any other withdrawal of property.

- It can be shown that, at the time of the withdrawal, the member knew or had reasonable grounds to believe that the LLP:
  - was unable to pay its debts; or
  - became unable to pay its debts as a result of the withdrawal.

In deciding whether a person had reasonable grounds to believe in the continued solvency of the LLP, the court will apply a minimum objective test, based on what they ought to have known in their position, as well as a potentially more onerous subjective test – what they ought to have known, given their personal attributes.

Under s 214A, the court may declare that the person who made the withdrawal is liable to make such contribution (if any) to the LLP's assets as it thinks proper. However, the court cannot make a declaration which exceeds the aggregate of the amounts of all the withdrawals made by that person within the period of two years previously referred to.

9.2.10.11   The future of the limited liability partnership

As yet, the availability of the LLP form of business organisation is too new to accurately assess its impact on traditional partnerships. It is generally thought that the relatively slow take-up of the new form is due to a reluctance on the parts of professional partnerships to comply with the publicity requirements under the LLP regime. It would appear that they would rather not have limited liability than have to reveal their finances to the public. Whether this remains the case is a matter for speculation for the moment, but there are indications that interest in the new form is increasing as awareness of it spreads. It is certainly an area of business law to be watched in the future.

9.3 Company Law

This chapter deals with the formation and regulation of a common alternative form of business association to the partnership, namely, the registered company. The flexibility of the company form of organisation is shown by the fact that it is used by businesses of widely different sizes and needs, from the one-man business to the transnational corporation. In fact, the register of all companies shows that the overwhelming number (almost 99%) are, in fact, private companies which may be seen as sole traders, or partnerships which have assumed the legal form of the registered company (see below, 9.3.2).

As yet, it is too early to estimate the likely impact of the availability of the limited liability partnership (LLP) form (see 9.2.10, above), but it may be reasonably expected that it will provide a useful alternative to the private company form.

The major general legislation governing company law is the Companies Act (CA) 1985, as amended by the CA 1989. There are, however, other Acts that govern specific aspects of company law, such as the Insolvency Act (IA) 1986, the Company Directors Disqualification Act (CDDA) 1986 and the Criminal Justice Act (CJA) 1993, which covers insider dealing. In this chapter, if no reference is made to any specific Act, then it can be assumed that reference is to the CA 1985. All other Acts will be specifically named.

9.3.1 Corporations and their legal characteristics

Partnerships may trade as, for example, 'J Smith and Co', but the use of the term 'company' in this instance does not mean that such a business is to be understood, or treated in the same way, as a company registered under the companies legislation. In terms of legal form, companies differ from partnerships, in that they are bodies corporate or corporations. In other words, they have a legal existence in their own right, apart from and independent of their members. Such is not the case with respect to partnerships.

9.3.1.1 Types of corporation

Corporations can be created in one of four ways, which are as follows:

- *By grant of royal charter*

Such corporations are governed mainly by the common law. The very earliest trading companies were created by royal charter, but this was essentially in order to secure monopoly privileges from the Crown, which could not be given to individuals. Nowadays, this method of incorporation tends to be restricted to professional, educational and charitable institutions and is not used in relation to business enterprises.

- *By special Act of Parliament*

Such bodies are known as statutory corporations, although this method of incorporation was the only alternative to charters before the introduction of registration and was common during the 19th century. This was particularly true in relation to railway and public utility companies, which usually required powers of compulsory purchase of land. It is not greatly used nowadays, and certainly not by ordinary trading companies.

- *By registration under the Companies Acts*

Since 1844, companies have been permitted to acquire the status of a corporation simply by complying with the requirements for registration set out in general Acts of Parliament. This is the method by which the great majority of trading enterprises are incorporated. The current legislation is the CA 1985, as subsequently amended by various other Acts of Parliament.

- *By registration under the Limited Liability Partnership Act (LLPA) 2000*

As has already been seen above, at 9.2.10, LLPs are granted the privilege of incorporation on registration with the Companies' Registry.

9.3.1.2   *The doctrine of separate personality*

English law, unlike continental or Scots law, treats a partnership simply as a group of individuals trading collectively. The effect of incorporation, however, is that a company, once formed, has its own distinct legal personality, separate from its members.

The doctrine of separate, or corporate, personality is an ancient one and may be found in Roman law. An early example of its application in relation to English business law can be seen in *Salmon v The Hamborough Co* (1671). That being said, the usual case cited in relation to separate personality is *Salomon v Salomon & Co* (1897). Salomon had been in the boot and leather trade for some time. Together with other members of his family, he formed a limited company and sold his previous business to it. Payment was in the form of cash, shares and debentures (the latter is loan stock which gives the holder priority over unsecured creditors if the company is wound up; see below, 9.3.11.2). When the company was eventually wound up, it was argued that Salomon and the company were the same and, as he could not be his own creditor, Salomon's debentures should have no effect. Although previous courts had decided against Salomon, the House of Lords held that, under the circumstances, in the absence of fraud, his debentures were valid. The company had been properly constituted and, consequently, it was, in law, a distinct legal person, completely separate from Salomon.

It is important to note that, contrary to what some, if not most, textbooks state, the *Salomon* case did not establish the doctrine of separate personality. It merely permitted its application to one-man and private companies (see below, 9.3.2.2).

Following the European Community's 12th Directive on Company Law (89/667), which was enacted in the UK in the form of the Companies (Single Member Private Limited Companies) Regulations 1992 (SI 1992/1699), provision has been made for the establishment of true one-man companies. These Regulations permit the incorporation of private limited companies by one person and with only one member. Thus, there is no longer any need for any pretence in the registration of sole traders as companies. As a matter of interest, it should be noted that the LLPA 2000 does not permit individuals to register as an LLP as, by definition, a partnership involves more than one person.

9.3.1.3 The effects of incorporation

A number of consequences flow from the fact that corporations are treated as having legal personality in their own right, as follows:

- *Limited liability*

  No one is responsible for anyone else's debts unless they agree to accept such responsibility. Similarly, at common law, members of a corporation are not responsible for its debts without agreement. However, registered companies, that is, those formed under the CA 1985 and CA 1989, are not permitted unless the shareholders agree to accept liability for their company's debts. In return for this agreement, the extent of their liability is set at a fixed amount. In the case of a company limited by shares, the level of liability is the amount remaining unpaid on the nominal value of the shares held. In the case of a company limited by guarantee, it is the amount that shareholders have agreed to pay in the event of the company being wound up.

- *Perpetual succession*

  As the corporation exists in its own right, changes in its membership have no effect on its status or existence. In contrast to the partnership, members of companies may die or be declared bankrupt or insane without any effect on the company. More importantly, however, members may transfer their shares to a third party without having any effect on the continuation of the business. In public limited companies, and certainly those listed on the stock exchange, freedom to transfer shares is unrestricted, although it is common for some restrictions to be placed on the transferability of shares in private companies (this is merely one of the many legal differences between the two forms of company, which reflects their essential difference as economic forms; see below, 9.3.2).

As an abstract legal person, the company cannot die, although its existence can be brought to an end through the winding up procedure (see below, 9.3.11).

- *Business property is owned by the company*

Any business assets are owned by the company itself, not the shareholders. This is normally a major advantage, in that the company's assets are not subject to claims based on the ownership rights of its members. It can, however, cause unforeseen problems.

In *Macaura v Northern Assurance* (1925), the plaintiff owned a timber estate. He later formed a one-man company and transferred the estate to it. He continued to insure the estate in his own name. When the timber was lost in a fire, it was held that Macaura could not claim on the insurance, since he had no personal interest in the timber, which belonged to the company.

What the member owns is a number of shares in the company. The precise nature of the share will be considered below (see below, 9.3.5.1).

- *The company has contractual capacity in its own right and can sue and be sued in its own name*

The nature and extent of a company's contractual capacity will be considered in detail later (see below, 9.3.4.3). For the moment, it should be noted that contracts are entered into in the company's name and it is liable on any such contracts. The extent of the company's liability, as opposed to the members' liability, is unlimited, and all of its assets may be used to pay off debts.

As a corollary of this, the members of the board of directors are the agents of the company. Members as such are not agents of the company; they have no right to be involved in the day to day operation of the business and they cannot bind the company in any way. This lack of power on the part of the members is one of the key differences between the registered company and the partnership, as partners have the express power to bind the partnership (s 5 of the Partnership Act 1890). However, members of private, quasi-partnership companies may have a legitimate expectation to be involved in the management of their company and may take action under s 459 of the CA 1985 to remedy any exclusion from the management.

- *Liability in crime and tort*

Certain offences can be committed without regard to the mental element (*mens rea*) normally required for the commission of a crime, that is, guilty intention. Companies may be liable in relation to such strict liability offences. The situation, however, is less clear in relation to the potential liability of companies in relation to offences which normally do require the presence of the necessary degree of *mens rea*. It is immediately obvious that, as an artificial rather than a real legal person, a company cannot have any *mens rea*. However, in certain circumstances, the *mens rea* of the company's servants or agents may be ascribed to the company in order to make it liable for a particular criminal offence. In *Tesco Supermarkets v Nattrass* (1971), it was held that the *mens rea* of minor employees or agents could not normally be imputed to the company, and that to make the company liable the *mens rea* had to be presented by someone, such as a director, who could be said to be the embodiment of the company. This requirement has made it particularly difficult for successful cases of manslaughter to be brought against large companies, although such a charge was successfully used in relation to a small private company, where the director was directly involved in the day to day operation of the business (*R v Kite and OLL Ltd* (1994)).

Companies, like other employers, are vicariously liable for the torts of their employees.

- *The rule in Foss v Harbottle (1843)*

    This states that where a company suffers an injury, it is for the company, acting through the majority of the members, to take the appropriate remedial action. Perhaps of more importance is the corollary of the rule, which is that an individual cannot raise an action in response to a wrong suffered by the company (exceptions to the rule in *Foss v Harbottle*, both at common law and under statute, will be considered in detail below, at 9.3.10).

Contemporary company lawyers explain the foregoing attributes as being the consequence of, and see them as following from, the doctrine of separate personality. It is possible, however, to reverse the causality contained in such conventional approaches. Consequently, it may be suggested that the doctrine of separate personality, as we now know it, is itself the product, rather than the cause, of these various attributes, which were recognised and developed independently by the courts.

9.3.1.4 Lifting the veil of incorporation

There are a number of occasions, both statutory and at common law, when the doctrine of separate personality will not be followed. On these occasions, it is said that the veil of incorporation, which separates the company from its members, is pierced, lifted or drawn aside, and the members are revealed and made responsible for the actions of the company. Such situations arise in the following circumstances:

- *Under the companies legislation*

    Section 24 of the CA 1985 provides for personal liability of the member where a company carries on trading with fewer than two members; s 229 requires consolidated accounts to be prepared by a group of related companies. In relation to the name of companies, officers are personally liable if they issue bills of exchange or enter into contracts without using their company's full name (s 349 of the CA 1985).

    Section 213 of the IA 1986 provides for personal liability in relation to fraudulent trading; s 214 does the same in relation to wrongful trading (see below, 9.3.6.6). And, as has already been seen, the new s 214A, introduced into the IA 1986 by the LLPR 2001, operates in a similar way with regard to LLPs.

- *At common law*

As in most areas of law that are based on the application of policy decisions, it is difficult to predict with any certainty when the courts will ignore separate personality. What is certain is that the courts will not permit the corporate form to be used for a clearly fraudulent purpose or to evade a legal duty. In such instances, the courts tend to refer to the company using terms such as sham, cloak and mask, and ignore it in order to fix ultimate responsibility on the person who tries to hide behind it. For example, in *Gilford Motor Co Ltd v Horne* (1933), an employee had entered into a contractual agreement not to solicit his former employers' customers. After he left their employment, he formed a company to solicit those customers. It was held that the company was a sham and the court would not permit it to be used to avoid the prior contract.

As would be expected, the courts are prepared to ignore separate personality in times of war to defeat the activity of shareholders who might be enemy aliens. See *Daimler Co Ltd v Continental Tyre and Rubber Co (GB) Ltd* (1917).

Where groups of companies have been set up for particular business ends, the courts will not usually ignore the separate existence of the various companies, unless they are being used for fraud. *Adams v Cape Industries plc* (1990) is a particularly strong example of this approach. In that case, it was held that an award made in relation to asbestos-related injuries against a company in the US could not be enforced against the UK parent company. The basis for the decision was the doctrine of separate personality, even though it might have appeared that the company structure had been deliberately set up to avoid such a claim. Such ingenuity was not fraud.

There is authority for treating separate companies as a single group, as in *DHN Food Distributors Ltd v Borough of Tower Hamlets* (1976), but later authorities have cast extreme doubt on this decision and, although it has never been overruled, it is probably true to say that it is no longer an accurate statement of the law (see *Woolfson v Strathclyde Regional Council* (1978); *National Dock Labour Board v Pinn and Wheeler Ltd* (1989); and *Adams v Cape Industries plc*).

At one time, it appeared that the courts were increasingly willing to use and extend their essential discretionary power in such a way as to achieve results they considered right. However, in *Ord v Bellhaven Pubs Ltd* (1998), Hobhouse LJ expressed what appears to be the contemporary reluctance of the courts to ignore separate personality simply to achieve what might be considered a subjectively fair decision. In overturning the decision at first instance, and at the same time overruling *Creasey v Breachwood Motors* (1993), he stated that:

> The approach of the judge in the present case was simply to look at the economic unit, to disregard the distinction between the legal entities that were involved and then to say: since the company cannot pay, the shareholders who are the people financially interested should be made to pay instead. That, of course, is radically at odds with the whole concept of corporate personality and limited liability and [from] the decision of the House of Lords in *Salomon v Salomon and Co Ltd* it is clear that ... there must be some impropriety before the corporate veil can be pierced.

9.3.2   Types of companies

Although the distinction between public and private companies is probably the most important, there are a number of ways in which companies can be classified.

9.3.2.1   *Limited and unlimited companies*

One of the major advantages of forming a company is limited liability, but companies can be formed without limited liability. Such companies receive all the benefits that flow from incorporation, except limited liability, but, in return, they do not have to submit their accounts or make them available for public inspection.

The great majority of companies, however, are limited liability companies. This means, as explained above, that the maximum liability of shareholders is fixed and cannot be increased without their agreement. There are two ways of establishing limited liability:

- *By shares*

  This is the most common procedure. It limits liability to the amount remaining unpaid on shares held. If the shareholder has paid the full nominal value of the shares, plus any premium that might be due to the company, then that is the end of their responsibility with regard to company debts. So, even if the company goes into insolvent liquidation with insufficient assets to pay its creditors, the individual shareholder cannot be required to make any further contribution to its funds.

- *By guarantee*

  This type of limited liability is usually restricted to non-trading enterprises such as charities and professional and educational bodies. It limits liability to an agreed amount, which is only called on if the company cannot pay its debts on being wound up. In reality, the sum guaranteed is usually a nominal sum, so no real risk is involved on the part of the guarantor.

9.3.2.2   *Public and private companies*

Rather oddly, previous legislation defined the public company in relation to the private company. The current legislation, however, makes the public company the essential form, with the private company as the exceptional form. Thus, the CA 1985 defines a public company as essentially a company:

(a) the memorandum of which states that it is a public company;

(b) in relation to which the appropriate registration requirements have been complied with.

The Act then defines a private company as any company which is not a public company.

The essential difference between these two forms is an economic one, although different legal rules have been developed to apply to each of them, as follows:

- *Private companies*

  Private companies tend to be small scale enterprises, owned and operated by a small number of individuals who are actively involved in the day to day running of the enterprise. Outsiders do not invest in such companies and, indeed, private companies are precluded from offering their shares to the public at large. Their shares are not quoted on any share market, and in practice tend not to be freely transferable, with restrictions being placed on them in the company's articles of association. Many such companies – and they make up the vast majority of registered companies – are sole traders or partnerships which have registered as companies in order to take advantage of limited liability. When limited liability was made available to registered companies in 1855 and under the later CA 1862, it was clearly not intended that it should be open to partnerships or individuals. Nonetheless, it became apparent that such businesses could acquire the benefit of limited liability by simply complying with the formal procedures of the CA 1862, and a great many businesses converted to limited companies. The legal validity of such private companies was clearly established only in the House of Lords' decision in *Salomon v Salomon & Co* (1897), but since then the courts and the legislature have developed specific rules governing their operation.

- *Public limited companies*

  Public companies, on the other hand, tend to be large and are controlled by directors and managers rather than the shareholders. This division is sometimes referred to as the separation of ownership and control. These public companies are essentially a source of investment for their shareholders and have freely transferable shares which may be quoted on the stock exchange.

As a consequence of the difference with regard to ownership and control, many of the provisions of the companies legislation, which is designed to protect the interests of shareholders in public companies, are not applicable to private companies. In his leading text on company law, Professor John Farrar lists some 18 differences in the way in which the legislation operates as between public and private companies (Farrar, JH, *Company Law*, 4th edn, 1998). The most important of these are as follows:

- Public companies must have at least two directors, whereas private companies need only have one. This recognises the reality of the true one-man business. It is important to note that the Companies (Single Member Private Companies) Regulations 1992 (SI 1992/1699) provide for the formation of a limited company with only one member. These Regulations are in line with the 12th European Company Law Directive.

- Public companies must have a minimum issued capital of £50,000, which must be paid up to the extent of 25%. There is no such requirement in relation to private companies (see further at 9.3.5, below).

- The requirement to keep accounting records is shorter for private companies – three years, as opposed to six years for public companies.

- The controls over distribution of dividend payments are relaxed in relation to private companies.

- Private companies may purchase their own shares out of capital, whereas public companies are strictly forbidden from doing so.

- Private companies can provide financial assistance for the purchase of their own shares where public companies cannot.

- There are fewer and looser controls over directors in private companies with regard to their financial dealings with their companies than there are in public companies.

- In a private company, anything that might be done by way of a resolution of a general meeting or a meeting of a class of members may instead be achieved by a resolution in writing, signed by all the members of the company, without the need to convene any such meeting.

- Private companies may pass an elective resolution dispensing with the need to appoint auditors annually, to lay accounts before an annual general meeting (AGM) or, indeed, to hold AGMs at all. An elective resolution also permits private companies to reduce the majority needed to call meetings at short notice from 95% to 90%.

It may also be suggested that, in cases involving private limited companies, which the courts view as quasi-partnerships, other general company law principles are applied less rigorously, or not at all. See, for example, *Ebrahimi v Westbourne Galleries Ltd* (1973) (otherwise known as *Re Westbourne Galleries*), where the court seemed to play down the effect of separate personality in such instances. Consider also *Clemens v Clemens Bros Ltd* (1976), over which much ink has been spilled in trying to establish a general rule concerning the duties owed by majority to minority shareholders. The reality is that there was no general principle that could be applied: the case merely reflects the courts' willingness to treat what they see as quasi-partnerships in an equitable manner. What is certain about the *Clemens* case is that it would find no application in public limited companies.

Many of the above issues will be dealt with in more detail below but, for the moment, it might be pointed out that there is much to be said for the suggestion that private limited companies should be removed from the ambit of the general companies legislation and be given their own particular legislation. It is apparent that they are not the same as public companies and cannot be expected to submit to the same regulatory regime as applies to the latter. In practice, the law recognises this, but only in a roundabout way, by treating them as exceptions to the general law relating to public companies. The argument, however, is that they are not exceptions; they are completely different, and this difference should be clearly recognised by treating them as a legal form *sui generis*. The introduction of the possibility of LLPs may be seen as a measure to address and rationalise this particular matter, although, as yet, it is too early to assess its impact.

9.3.2.3 *Parent and subsidiary companies*

This description of companies relates to the way in which large business enterprises tend to operate through a linked structure of distinct companies. Each of these companies exists as a separate corporate entity in its own right but, nonetheless, the group is required to be treated as a single entity in relation to the group accounting provisions under s 229 of the CA 1985.

Section 736 of the CA 1985 states that one company, S, is a subsidiary of another company, H, its holding company, in any of the following circumstances:

- where H holds a majority of voting rights in S;

- where H is a member of S and has a right to appoint or remove a majority of its board of directors;

- where H is a member of S and controls a majority of the voting rights in it; or

- where S is a subsidiary of a company which is in turn a subsidiary of H.

Section 258, which relates to accounting requirements, defines the relationship of parent and subsidiary companies in a similar way but introduces the additional idea of the parent exercising a dominant influence over the subsidiary company.

9.3.2.4 *Small, medium and large companies*

Companies can be categorised in relation to their size. Small and medium sized companies are subjected to relaxation in relation to the submission of accounts under s 246 of the CA 1985. Which category a company fits into depends on its turnover, balance sheet valuation and number of employees.

A small company must satisfy two of the following requirements:

Turnover	not more than £5.6 million
Balance sheet	not more than £2.8 million
Employees	not more than 50

A medium sized company must satisfy two of the following requirements:

Turnover	not more than £22.8 million
Balance sheet	not more than £11.4 million
Employees	not more than 250

It should be remembered that, as discussed above at 9.3.1, it is now open to individuals to form companies, and the companies legislation will apply, subject to appropriate alterations.

9.3.2.5   Overseas companies

Part XXIII of the CA 1985 relates to what are known as overseas companies, and these are defined in s 744 as companies incorporated elsewhere than in Great Britain but which have a place of business in that country. Such companies are required to maintain an address within the jurisdiction, at which all official communications can be served. Overseas companies are also required to register copies of their constitutional documents and to submit their accounts in the same way as domestic companies.

9.3.3   Formation of companies

The CA 1985 establishes a strict procedure with which companies have to comply before they can operate legally. The procedure, which in the case of public companies involves two stages, is described below.

9.3.3.1   Registration

There are two Companies Registries in the UK, one in Cardiff, which deals with companies registered within England and Wales, and one in Edinburgh, which deals with Scottish companies. A registered company is incorporated when particular documents are delivered to the Registrar of Companies (s 10 of the CA 1985). On registration of these documents, the Registrar issues a certificate of incorporation (s 13 of the CA 1985). The documents required under s 10 are:

- a memorandum of association;

- articles of association (unless Table A articles are to apply – see 9.3.4.1, below);

- form 10: a statement detailing the first directors and secretary of the company with their written consent and the address of the company's registered office; and

- form 12: a statutory declaration that the necessary requirements of the CA 1985 have been complied with must be submitted under s 12. This declaration can be made by a solicitor engaged in the formation of the company, or a director, or the company secretary.

The duty of the Registrar of Companies is to ensure that:

- the requirements of the Companies Act have been complied with;

- the memorandum and articles of association do not infringe the CA 1985;

- the objects of the company are lawful;

- the name of the company is lawful; and

- in the case of a public company, its share capital is not less than the authorised minimum.

If the Registrar is satisfied that the above requirements have been complied with, a certificate of incorporation will be issued. Such a certificate is conclusive evidence that the company has been properly incorporated (see *Jubilee Cotton Mills v Lewis* (1924)).

The Registrar can refuse to register a company if he or she considers it to have been formed for some unlawful purpose. Such a refusal can be challenged under judicial review (*R v Registrar of Joint Stock Companies ex p Moore* (1931)), as can the improper registration of a company formed for unlawful purposes (*R v Registrar of Companies ex p AG* (1991), where the company had been formed for the purposes of conducting prostitution).

9.3.3.2   Commencement of business

A company exists from the date of its registration, and a private company may start its business and use its borrowing powers as soon as the certificate of registration is issued. A public company, however, cannot start a business or borrow money until it has obtained an additional certificate from the registrar under s 117 of the CA 1985. In relation to public companies, there is a requirement that they have a minimum allotted share capital, at present £50,000 (ss 11 and 118 of the CA 1985), and, under s 101, they must not allot shares unless they have been as paid up at least as to one-quarter of their nominal value (it follows that the statutory minimum issued and paid up capital for a public company is £12,500). The s 117 certificate confirms that the company has met these requirements.

9.3.3.3   Re-registration

A company may initially register as one type of company, only to decide at a later date that a different form is more appropriate. The CA 1985 makes the following provisions for such alterations:

- *Re-registration of a private company as public*

  This procedure, set out in ss 43–47 of the CA 1985, requires the passing of a special resolution (75% and 21 days' notice), not only expressing the intention to re-register but altering the company's constitutional documents to bring them in line with the requirements applicable to public companies. The company must also comply with the requirements as to minimum issued and paid up capital.

- *Re-registration of a public company as private*

  This procedure, set out in ss 53–55 of the CA 1985, also requires a special resolution and the appropriate alteration of the company's constitutional documents. Under s 54, a minimum of 50 members, or holders of 5% or more of the voting share capital of the company, may seek to have the resolution to re-register as a private company overturned by the courts. Where a public company's issued share capital is reduced to below the authorised minimum, the company is required to re-register as a private company (s 139 of the CA 1985).

- *Re-registration of a limited company as unlimited*

This form of re-registration, as provided for under ss 49–50 of the CA 1985, requires the agreement of all members as well as the alteration of the constitutional documents. As public companies cannot be unlimited, a public limited company seeking to re-register as unlimited would first of all have to re-register as a private company before changing its status in terms of liability.

- *Re-registration of an unlimited company as limited*

  This procedure, under ss 51–52, requires a special resolution of the company together with the appropriate alteration of the constitutional documents.

  Since there is the danger that members of an insolvent unlimited company might seek to avoid liability for the company's debts by converting it into a limited company, s 77 of the IA 1986 provides that if the company goes into liquidation within three years of its conversion to limited liability status, any person who was a member at the time of the conversion continues to have unlimited liability in regard to any outstanding debts incurred while the company was unlimited.

9.3.4 The constitution of the company

The constitution of a company is established by two documents: the memorandum of association and the articles of association. If there is any conflict between the two documents, the contents of the memorandum prevail over anything to the contrary contained in the articles, although provisions in the articles may be used to clarify particular uncertainties in the memorandum.

As will be seen, there is a large measure of freedom as to what is actually included in such documents, but this latitude is extended within a clearly established framework of statutory and common law rules. Model memoranda and articles of association are set out in the Companies (Tables A to F) Regulations 1985 (SI 1985/805), although companies may alter the models to suit their particular circumstances and requirements.

9.3.4.1 The memorandum of association

The memorandum of association is a compulsory document which mainly governs the company's external affairs. It represents the company to the outside world, stating its capital structure, its powers and its objects. The document submitted to the registrar of companies must be signed by at least two subscribers from amongst the company's first shareholders. Every memorandum must contain the following clauses:

- *The name clause*

  Except in relation to specifically exempted companies such as those involved in charitable work, companies are required to indicate that they are operating on the basis of limited liability. Thus, private companies are required to end their names either with the word 'Limited' or the abbreviation 'Ltd', and public companies must end their names with the words 'public limited company' or the abbreviation 'plc'. Welsh companies may use the Welsh language equivalents (ss 25 and 27).

Equally, it amounts to a criminal offence to use the words 'public limited company' or 'Limited' in an improper manner (ss 33 and 34).

A further aspect of this requirement for publicity is that companies display their names outside their business premises, on business documents and on their seal. In addition to committing a criminal offence, any person who fails to use a company's full name on any document will be personally liable for any default. See *Penrose v Martyr* (1858), where a company secretary was held personally liable when he failed to indicate that the company against which he had drawn a bill of exchange was in fact a limited company.

A company's name must not be the same as any already registered, nor should it constitute a criminal offence or be offensive (s 26(1)). Any suggestion of connection with the Government or any local authority in a company's name requires the approval of the Secretary of State (s 26(2)), as does the use of any of the many words listed in the Company and Business Names Regulations 1981 (SI 1981/1699) (s 29). Among the words in the Regulations are such as imply connection with royalty, such as 'king', 'queen', 'prince', 'princess', 'royal', etc. Other controlled words in titles include abortion, benevolent and co-operative, through to stock exchange, trade union and university.

A passing off action may be taken against a company, as previously considered in relation to partnership law (see above, 9.2.5.5).

The name of a company can be changed by a special resolution of the company (s 28).

- *The registered office clause*

This is the company's legal address. It is the place where legal documents such as writs or summonses can be served on the company. It is also the place where particular documents and statutory registers such as the register of members (s 353), the register of directors' interests in shares (s 325), the register of debenture holders (s 190) and the register of charges held against the company's property (s 407) are required to be kept available for inspection. The memorandum does not state the actual address of the registered office, but only the country within which the company is registered, be it Scotland or England and Wales. The precise location of the registered office, however, has to be stated on all business correspondence (s 351). It is not necessary that the registered office be the company's main place of business and, indeed, it is not unusual for a company's registered office to be the address of its accountant or lawyer.

- *The objects clause*

Companies registered under the various Companies Acts are not corporations in the same way as common law corporations are. It was established in *Ashbury Railway Carriage and Iron Co Ltd v Riche* (1875) that such companies were established only to pursue particular purposes. Those purposes were stated in the objects clause of the company's memorandum of association and any attempt to contract outside of that limited authority was said to be *ultra vires* and, as a consequence, was void.

It was felt for a long time that the operation of the *ultra vires* doctrine operated unfairly on outsiders and various attempts were made to reduce the scope of its application. Since the introduction of the CA 1989, it is fortunately no longer necessary to enter into a detailed consideration of the history and operation of the doctrine of *ultra vires*. After the CA 1989, *ultra vires* has been effectively reduced to an internal matter and does not affect outsiders; even as a means of limiting the actions of directors it has been considerably weakened (see ss 35, 35A and 35B of the CA 1989).

Whereas in the past companies used to register extended objects clauses to provide for unforeseen eventualities, they can now simply register as a general commercial company, which will empower them to carry on any trade or business whatsoever and to do all such things as are incidental or conducive to the carrying on of any trade or business (s 3A).

Companies can alter their objects clause by passing a special resolution, by virtue of s 4, although such procedure is subject to a right of appeal to the courts within 21 days, by the holders of 15% of the issued capital of the company. However, given the effect of the CA 1989, this element of control will only have indirect effect on the external relations of the company to the extent that members may bring proceedings to prevent directors from acting beyond the stated objects of the company (s 35(2) of the CA 1989).

- *The limited liability clause*

  This clause simply states that the liability of the members is limited. It must be included even where the company has permission not to use the word 'Limited' in its name.

- *The authorised share capital clause*

  This states the maximum amount of share capital that a company is authorised to issue. The capital has to be divided into shares of a fixed monetary amount, as no-fixed-value shares are not permissible in UK law.

- *The association clause*

  This states that the subscribers to the memorandum wish to form a company and agree to take the number of shares placed opposite their names.

It should also be recalled that the memorandum of public companies must contain a clause stating that they are public companies.

9.3.4.2   *The articles of association*

The articles primarily regulate the internal working of the company. They govern the rights and relations of the members to the company and vice versa, and the relations of the members between themselves. As provided in s 14 of the CA 1989, the articles are to be treated as an enforceable contract, although it has to be stated that it is a peculiar contract, in that its terms can be altered by the majority of the members without the consent of each member.

The articles deal with such matters as the allotment and transfer of shares, the rights attaching to particular shares, the rules relating to the holding of meetings and the powers of directors.

A company is at liberty to draw up its own articles, but regulations made under the CA 1989 provide a set of model articles known as Table A. Companies do not have to submit their own articles and, if they do not, then Table A applies automatically. The provisions contained in Table A also apply to the extent that they have not been expressly excluded by the company's particular articles. Usually, companies adopt Table A and modify it to suit their own situation.

Alteration of articles

Articles can be altered by the passing of a special resolution (s 9 of the CA 1985). Any such alteration has to be made *bona fide in the interest of the company as a whole*, but the exact meaning of this phrase is not altogether clear. It is evident that it involves a subjective element in that those deciding the alteration must actually believe they are acting in the interest of the company. There is additionally, however, an objective element. In *Greenhalgh v Arderne Cinemas Ltd* (1951), it was stated that any alteration had to be in the interests of the individual hypothetical member; thus, the alteration that took a pre-emptive right from a particular member was held to be to the advantage of such a hypothetical member, although it severely reduced the rights of a real member. Such differentiation between concrete and hypothetical benefits is a matter of fine distinction, although it can be justified. In any case, persons suffering from substantive injustice are now at liberty to make an application under s 459 for an order to remedy any unfairly prejudicial conduct (see below, 9.3.10.2).

The following two cases may demonstrate the difference between the legitimate use and the abuse of the provision for altering articles; each of them relates to circumstances where existing shareholders' rights were removed.

In *Brown v British Abrasive Wheel Co* (1919), an alteration to the articles of the company was proposed, to give the majority shareholders the right to buy shares of the minority. It was held, under the circumstances of the case, that the alteration was invalid, since it would benefit the majority shareholders rather than the company as a whole.

In *Sidebottom v Kershaw Leese & Co* (1920), the alteration to the articles gave the directors the power to require any shareholder who entered into competition with the company to transfer their shares to nominees of the directors at a fair price. It was held that, under these circumstances, the alteration permitting the expropriation of members interests was valid, since it would benefit the company as a whole.

As the power to alter their articles is a statutory provision, companies cannot be prevented from using that power, even if the consequence of so doing results in a breach of contract. Thus, in *Southern Foundries Ltd v Shirlaw* (1940), it was held that the company could not be prevented from altering its articles in such a way that eventually would lead to the breach of the managing director's contract of employment. Shirlaw was, of course, entitled to damages for the breach.

9.3.4.3 Effect of memorandum and articles

Section 14 of the CA 1985 provides that:

> ... the memorandum and articles, when registered, bind the company and its members to the same extent as if they had respectively had been signed and sealed by each member and contained covenants on the part of each member to observe all the provision of the memorandum and articles.

Thus, the memorandum and articles constitute a statutory contract. The effect of this is that:

- the constitutional documents establish a contract between each member and the company and bind each member to the terms of that contract. Thus, in *Hickman v Kent or Romney Marsh Sheep Breeders Association* (1915), the company was able to insist that a member complied with an article which provided that disputes between the company and any member should go to arbitration;

- the company is contractually bound to each member to abide by the terms of the documents. Thus, in *Pender v Lushington* (1877), a member was able to enforce his constitutional right in the face of the company's refusal to permit him to vote at a company meeting; and

- the members are bound *inter se*, that is, to each other. Authority for this was provided by *Rayfield v Hands* (1960), in which the directors of a company were required to abide by the articles of association, which required them to buy the shares of any members who wished to transfer their shares.

It is essential to note, however, that the memorandum and articles only create a contractual relationship in respect of membership rights. Consequently, although members can enforce such rights, non-members, or any member suing in some other capacity than that of a member, cannot enforce the provisions contained in those documents. In *Eley v Positive Government Life Assurance* (1876), the company's articles stated that the plaintiff was to be appointed as its solicitor. It was held, however, that Eley could not use the article to establish a contract between himself and the company. The articles only created a contract between the company and its members, and although Eley was a member of the company, he was not suing in that capacity but in a different capacity, namely, as the company's solicitor.

9.3.4.4 Class rights

A company might only issue one class of shares giving the holders the same rights. However, it is possible, and quite common, for companies to issue shares with different rights. Thus, preference shares may have priority rights over ordinary shares with respect to dividends or the repayment of capital. Nor is it uncommon for shares to carry different voting rights. Each of these instances is an example of class rights and the holders of shares which provide such rights constitute distinct classes within the generality of shareholders. It is usual for class rights to attach to particular shares and to be provided in the memorandum of association, although it is more usual for such rights to be provided for in the articles of association. It is now recognised, however, that such class rights may be created by external agreements and may be conferred upon a person in the capacity of shareholder of a company, although not attached to any particular shares. Thus, in *Cumbrian Newspapers Group Ltd v Cumberland and Westmorland Herald Newspaper and Printing Co Ltd* (1986), following a merger between the plaintiff and defendant companies, the defendant's articles were altered so as to give the plaintiff certain rights of pre-emption and also the right to appoint a director, so long as it held at least 10% of the defendant's ordinary shares. Scott J held that these rights were in the nature of class rights and could not be altered without going through the procedure for altering such rights.

As the *Cumbrian Newspapers* case demonstrates, class rights become an issue when the company looks to alter them. When it is realised that class rights usually provide their holders with some distinct advantage or benefit not enjoyed by the holders of ordinary shares, and that the class members are usually in a minority within the company, it can be appreciated that the procedure for varying such rights requires some sensitivity towards the class members.

Alteration of class rights

The procedure for altering class rights is set out in ss 125–27 of the CA 1985. The precise procedure depends upon two matters: first, where the rights are set out; and, secondly, whether there is a pre-established procedure for altering the rights, as follows:

- Where the original articles set out a procedure for varying class rights, then that procedure should be followed, even if the rights are provided by the memorandum (s 125(4)).

- Where the rights are attached to a class of shares otherwise than by the memorandum, that is, by the articles or an external contract, and there is no pre-established procedure for altering them, then the consent of a three-quarters majority of nominal value of the shares in that class is necessary. The majority may be acquired in writing or by passing a special resolution at a separate meeting of the holders of the shares in question. This is the most common way of attaching and varying class rights (s 125(2)).

- Where the articles are attached by the memorandum and there is no pre-established procedure for alteration, then the consent of all members of the company is required to alter the rights (s 125(5)).

Any alteration of class rights under s 125 is subject to challenge in the courts. To raise such a challenge, any objectors must:

- hold no less than 15% of the issued shares in the class in question (s 127(2));

- not have voted in favour of the alteration (s 127(2)); and

- apply to the court within 21 days of the consent being given to the alteration (s 127(3)).

The court has the power to either confirm the alteration or cancel it as unfairly prejudicial.

In *Greenhalgh v Arderne Cinemas* (1946), it was held that the sub-division of 50p shares, which had previously carried one vote each, into five 10p shares, which each carried one vote, did not vary the rights of another class of shares. Note that although, strictly speaking, such an alteration did not affect the rights held by the other shares, it did alter their real voting power. Also, in *House of Fraser plc v ACGE Investments Ltd* (1987), it was held that the return of all the capital held in the form of preference shares amounted to a total extinction of right. It could not, therefore, be seen as a variation of those rights and the s 125 procedure did not have to be followed. However, in *Re Northern Engineering Industries plc* (1994), it was held that a specific provision in the articles, designed to prevent the reduction of preference share capital with the approval of its holders, was equally effective to prevent to the complete extinction of the preference share capital.

9.3.5 Capital

There are many different definitions of 'capital'. For the purposes of this chapter, attention will be focused on the way in which companies raise such money as they need to finance their operation. The essential distinction in company law is between share capital and loan capital.

9.3.5.1 Share capital

Company law and company lawyers have been extremely hesitant in offering any precise definition of the share, being content to deal with shares in a pragmatic rather than a theoretical manner. The most generally accepted definition of the share states that it is:

> ... the interest of the shareholder in the company measured by a sum of money, for the purposes of liability in the first place and of interest in the second, but also consisting of a series of mutual covenants entered into by all the shareholders [*Borlands Trustees v Steel* (1901)].

This definition can be divided into three elements, as follows:

- *Liability*

  The nominal value of the share normally fixes the amount which the shareholder is required to contribute to the assets of the company. Shareholders must pay at least the full nominal value of any shares issued to them (that is, shares must not be issued at a discount (s 100)), but where, as is quite common, the company issues shares at a premium, that is, at more than the nominal value of the shares, then the holders of those shares will be liable to pay the amount owed over and above the nominal value. The excess will form part of the company's capital and be included in the share premium account (s 130).

- *Interest*

Legal definitions usually state that the share is a form of property, representing a proportionate interest in the business of the company, but tend to be much less certain as to the precise nature of such an interest. What is clear is that, as a consequence of separate personality, the share does not represent, in any other than a very contingent way, a claim against the assets owned by the company. What shareholders possess is not a right to own and control the capital assets operated by their company but, rather, a right to receive a part of the profit generated by the use of those assets. As McPherson put it:

> The market value of a modern corporation consists not of its plant and stocks of material but its presumed ability to produce a revenue for itself and its shareholders by its organisation of skills and its manipulation of the markets. Its value as a property is its ability to produce a revenue. The property of its shareholders have is the right to a revenue from that ability ['Capitalism and the changing concept of property', in Kamenka, E and Neale, RS (eds), *Feudalism, Capitalism and Beyond*, 1975].

It also has to be recognised that even this right is contingent upon the company making a profit and the directors of the company recommending the declaration of a dividend.

- *Mutual covenants*

The effect of s 14 of the CA 1985 has already been considered above, at 9.3.4.3.

Section 182 of the CA 1985 provides that shares are personal property and are transferable in the manner provided for in the company's articles of association. Although the articles of private limited companies tend to restrict the transfer of shares within a close group of people, it is an essential aspect of shares in public limited companies that the investment they represent is open to immediate realisation; to that end, they are made freely transferable, subject to the appropriate procedure being followed.

9.3.5.2 *Types of share capital*

The word 'capital' is used in a number of different ways in relation to shares:

- *Nominal or authorised capital*

This is the figure stated in the company's memorandum of association. It sets the maximum number of shares that the company can issue, together with the value of each share. There is no requirement that companies issue shares to the full extent of their authorised capital.

- *Issued or allotted capital*

This represents the nominal value of the shares actually issued by the company. It is more important than authorised capital as a true measure of the substance of the company. If a company is willing to pay the registration fee, it can register with an authorised capital of £1 million yet only actually issue two £1 shares. Public companies must have a minimum issued capital of £50,000 (s 11 of the CA 1985).

- *Paid up capital*

  This is the proportion of the nominal value of the issued capital actually paid by the shareholder. It may be the full nominal value, in which case it fulfils the shareholders' responsibility to outsiders; or it can be a mere part payment, in which case the company has an outstanding claim against the shareholder. Shares in public companies must be paid up to the extent of at least one-quarter of their nominal value (s 101 of the CA 1985).

- *Called and uncalled capital*

  Where a company has issued shares as not fully paid up, it can at a later time make a call on those shares. This means that the shareholders are required to provide more capital, up to the amount remaining unpaid on the nominal value of their shares. Called capital should equal paid up capital; uncalled capital is the amount remaining unpaid on issued capital.

- *Reserve capital*

  This arises where a company passes a resolution that it will not make a call on any unpaid capital. The unpaid capital then becomes a reserve, only to be called upon if the company cannot pay its debts from existing assets in the event of its liquidation.

The following could be a theoretical capital structure for a public limited company:

Authorised capital	£100,000
Issued capital	£50,000
Paid up capital	£12,500

9.3.5.3 Types of shares

Companies can issue shares of different value, and with different rights attached to them. Such classes of shares can be distinguished and categorised as follows:

- *Ordinary shares*

  These shares are sometimes referred to as 'equity in the company'. Of all the various types of shares, they carry the greatest risk, but in recompense receive the greatest return. The nominal value of shares is fixed but the exchange value of the shares in the stock market fluctuates in relation to the performance of the company and the perception of those dealing in the stock exchange. It is perhaps a matter of regret that the typical shareholder – and that includes the institutional investor – relates more to the performance of their shares in the market than to the actual performance of their company in productive terms. Ownership of ordinary shares entitles the holder to attend and vote at general meetings, although, once again, it is a matter of regret that very few shareholders actually exercise these rights.

- *Preference shares*

These shares involve less of a risk than ordinary shares. They may have priority over ordinary shares in two respects: dividends and repayment. They carry a fixed rate of dividend which has to be paid before any payment can be made to ordinary shareholders. Such rights are cumulative unless otherwise provided. This means that a failure to pay a dividend in any one year has to be made good in subsequent years.

As regards repayment of capital, preference shares do not have priority unless, as is usually the case, this is specifically provided for. Also, without specific provision, preference shares have the same rights as ordinary shares, but it is usual for their voting rights to be restricted. Preference shareholders are entitled to vote at class meetings convened to consider any alteration to their particular rights but, apart from that, they are usually restricted to voting in general meetings when their dividends are in arrears.

- *Deferred shares*

This type of share postpones the rights of its holder to dividends until after the ordinary shareholders have received a fixed return. In effect, the ordinary shares are treated as preference shares and the deferred shares as ordinary shares. It is no longer a common form of organisation.

- *Redeemable shares*

These are shares issued on the understanding that they may be bought back by the company (s 159). Redemption may be at the option of either the company or the shareholder, depending on the terms of issue. Companies, in any case, now have the right, subject to conditions, to purchase their own shares and, therefore, are no longer restricted to buying redeemable shares (s 162).

9.3.5.4 Issue of shares

Directors generally are not allowed to issue shares without the authority of the members. In practice, however, it is usual for them to be granted general authority to issue the company's shares as they see fit, as long as that authority does not extend beyond a period of five years (s 80). The directors must not use their power to issue shares for an improper purpose. Thus, it was held in *Hogg v Cramphorn* (1967) that the issue of shares as a way of defeating a takeover bid was an improper use of the directors' power. Conversely, in *Howard Smith v Ampol Petroleum* (1974), issuing shares in order to facilitate a takeover bid was also unlawful.

It should be noted that any such breach of directors' powers can be ratified by a subsequent vote of the members in a general meeting (*Bamford v Bamford* (1970)).

9.3.5.5 *Payment for shares*

Under s 99 of the CA 1985, shares are only treated as paid up to the extent that the company has received money or money's worth. Any shortfall in payment will have to be made up in the future, and this is especially true if the company goes into insolvent liquidation.

Issuing shares at a discount

This responsibility to make good any difference between consideration provided and the nominal value of the shares received is re-emphasised in s 100, which expressly prohibits the issuing of shares at a discount. The strictness of the rule may be seen in *Ooregeum Gold Mining Co of India Ltd v Roper* (1892). The £1 shares of the company were trading at only 12.5p and, in an attempt to refinance it, new £1 preference shares were issued and credited with 75p already paid. When the company subsequently went into liquidation, the holders of the preference shares were required to pay their full value and, therefore, had to subscribe a further 75p. The court does have the power to grant relief from such payment in appropriate circumstances (s 113). Section 314 extends criminal liability to both the company and any officer of the company who has breached the rules relating to issuing shares at a discount.

Issuing shares at a premium

It is possible, and indeed quite common, for companies to issue their shares at a premium, that is, to charge those who take the shares more than their nominal value. In such circumstances, any additional payment received must be transferred into a share premium account, which may only be used for specific limited purposes, such as paying any premium due on the redemption of preference shares or paying for previously unissued shares to be issued to the existing members. As a capital reserve, the share premium account certainly cannot be used to finance dividend payments.

It was held in *Henry Head v Ropner Holdings* (1952), and subsequently confirmed in *Shearer v Bercain* (1980), that the requirement to create a share premium account applied to situations where non-cash assets were transferred to pay for shares. The perceived inequity of this decision led to the provision of specific relief relating to mergers where assets are transferred in consideration of shares between formerly distinct companies (ss 131 and 132 of the CA 1985).

Where public companies accept non-cash consideration for the issue of shares, they are required to have the value of the consideration provided independently reported on by some person who is qualified to act as a company auditor (ss 103 and 108). Such reports must be filed with the Companies Registry (s 111). Private companies, as usual, are less restricted in what they can do and they may accept non-cash consideration without the need to have it independently valued, as long as a copy of the contract is delivered to the registry (s 88).

Bonus issues and rights issues

It should be recognised that although both of these procedures operate to the benefit of the existing shareholders, they are not contrary to the above rules relating to payment for shares. In relation to bonus issues, the company rather than the individual shareholders pays fully for the shares issued. Such payment can come from retained profits, or from the company's share premium account or capital redemption reserve fund, but it must never be funded from the company's ordinary capital.

Rights issues offer existing shareholders additional shares in the company in proportion to their existing shareholding. The inducement in such a procedure is that the offer price is usually less than the prevailing market price of the shares and so includes an element of potential profit for the shareholders.

9.3.5.6   Capital maintenance

The immediately preceding section focused on the way in which the law insists on companies receiving the full capital value for the shares they issue. Once the capital has been received by the company, there are equally as important rules controlling what can be done with it, or, more accurately, controlling what cannot be done with it.

Thus, in *Flitcroft's Case* (1882), Jessel MR stated:

> The creditor has no debtor but the impalpable thing the corporation, which has no property except the assets of the business. The creditor, therefore, I may say, gives credit to that capital, gives credit to the company on the faith of the implied representation that the capital shall be applied only for the purposes of the business, and he has therefore a right to say that the corporation shall keep its capital and not return it to the shareholders ...

This quotation highlights two aspects of the doctrine of capital maintenance: first, that creditors have a right to see that the capital is not dissipated unlawfully; and, secondly, that members must not have the capital returned to them surreptitiously. These two aspects of the single doctrine of capital maintenance are governed by the rules relating to capital reduction and company distributions.

Capital reduction

The procedures under which companies can reduce the amount of their issued share capital are set out in ss 135–41 of the CA 1985. Section 135 states that a company may reduce its capital in any way, if so authorised in its articles, by passing a special resolution to that end. The section sets out three particular ways in which such capital can be reduced, which are as follows:

- removing or reducing liability for any capital remaining as yet unpaid, that is, deciding that the company will not need to make any call on that unpaid capital in the future;

- cancelling any paid up share capital which has been lost through trading and is unrepresented in the current assets of the company, that is, bringing the balance sheet into balance at a lower level by reducing the capital liabilities in acknowledgment of the loss of assets; or

- paying off any already paid up share capital that is in excess of the company's requirement, either now or in the future, that is, giving the shareholders back some of the capital that they have invested in the company.

Any proposal to reduce a company's capital is subject to confirmation by the court (s 136), on such terms as it thinks fit (s 137). For example, it is possible that the court will require the company to add the words 'and reduced' after its name, in order to warn the general public that the company has undergone such an alteration to its capital structure. In considering any capital reduction scheme, the court will take into account the interests not just of the members and creditors of the company, but of the general public as well. It should be noted that the process of capital reduction is distinct from, and treated more restrictively than, the process of capital alteration, which is governed by s 121 and is an essentially internal affair which does not affect the interests of creditors. Amongst the alterations governed by s 121 is the procedure for increasing a company's capital. As long as its articles allow for such a process, this may be achieved by the passing of an ordinary resolution to that effect. Clearly, outside creditors have no say in relation to any such decision to increase the company's capital, as it would actually increase their security. Of equal importance is the fact that existing members cannot be required to subscribe for any of the increased capital.

Distribution/dividend law

As has been seen, it is a fundamental rule of company law that capital must be maintained and that any reduction in capital is strictly controlled by the courts. This doctrine of capital maintenance led to two statements of a general rule with respect to the payment of dividends, which are that:

- dividends may only be paid out of profits; and

- dividends may not be paid out of capital.

However, just as with capital, there are a number of different, not to say contradictory, ways to determine profit. The lack of certainty in this regard led to an extremely lax regulation of the manner in which dividends could be paid out to shareholders, which was only remedied by the introduction of clear and stricter rules under the CA 1980. The current rules about what may be distributed to shareholders are to be found in Pt VIII of the CA 1985 and, once again, the rules relating to public limited companies are more restrictive than those governing private companies.

Section 263 of the CA 1985 imposes restrictions on companies generally and sets out the basic requirement that any distribution of a company's assets to its members must come from 'profits available for that purpose'. This latter phrase is then defined as 'accumulated realised profits (which have not been distributed or capitalised) less accumulated realised losses (which have not been written off in a reduction of capital)'. Any such profits may be either revenue or capital in origin, the key requirement being that they are realised, that is, that they are not merely paper profits.

Public companies are subject to the additional controls of s 264, which imposes a balance sheet approach to the determination of profits by requiring that:

- net assets at the time of distribution must exceed the total of called up capital plus undistributable reserves; and

- the distribution must not reduce the value of the net assets below the aggregate of the total called up capital plus undistributable reserves.

The undistributable reserves include the share premium account, capital redemption reserve fund, and the excess of accumulated unrealised profits. There are special and distinct rules relating to investment companies.

At common law, directors who knowingly paid dividends out of capital were liable to the company to replace any money so paid out, although they could seek to be indemnified by shareholders who knowingly received the payments. Section 277 of the CA 1985 additionally provides that shareholders who receive payments, with reasonable grounds to know that they are made in breach of the rules, shall be liable to repay the amount received to the company.

Purchase of own shares

It was once an extremely strict rule of company law that companies were not allowed to buy their own shares. Any such purchase was treated as a major contravention of the capital maintenance rules (*Trevor v Whitworth* (1887)). Subsequently, companies were granted the power to issue specifically redeemable shares and such a power still finds expression in s 159 of the CA 1985, although there are strict controls over how any such redemption has to be financed (s 160). However, in a Green Paper in 1980, the leading academic company lawyer, Professor Gower, recommended that the right to buy back should be extended to cover all, rather than just redeemable, shares. Professor Gower's recommendations were accepted and are currently enacted in ss 162–81 of the CA 1985.

The Act provides for three distinct ways in which companies can buy their own shares:

- through a market purchase, conducted under the rules of recognised investment exchange (s 166);

- through an off-market purchase, which effectively relates to any other method of purchase (s 164); or

- through a contingent purchase contract, which essentially relates to options to buy shares (s 165).

The rules for financing the purchase by a company of its own shares are the same as those that apply to the redemption of redeemable shares, and are to be found in s 160 of the CA 1985. The most essential rule is that no purchase or redemption is to be financed from the company's capital, and can only be paid from profits properly available for distribution to the company's members (see immediately above).

However, as in most areas of company law, there are relaxations of the strict rules in relation to private limited companies. Thus, in ss 171–75, private companies are permitted to use the company's capital to finance the purchase of their own shares, although even here the controls established are extremely rigorous. Thus, any payment out of capital will not be lawful unless:

- the company has passed a special resolution approving the procedure;

- the directors of the company have made a statutory declaration to the effect that the company is solvent and will remain so for the following year;

- the directors' declaration is supported by auditors; or

- the company, within a week of the resolution to that end, advertises its proposed conduct.

Further:

- the procedure cannot be implemented less than five weeks or more than seven weeks after the resolution;

- any member who did not vote in favour, or any creditor of the company, can apply to the courts for the cancellation of the resolution;

- s 173 of the CA 1985 provides that any director who made the statutory declaration without reasonable grounds for so doing is guilty of a criminal offence;

- s 76 of the IA 1986 provides that directors who signed the statutory declaration, together with those former shareholders from whom shares were purchased, are liable to make any shortfall in assets up to the level of the payment from capital if the company goes into insolvent liquidation within 12 months of the capital repayment.

Financial assistance for the purchase of the company's own shares

Section 151 of the CA 1985 makes it illegal for a company to provide financial assistance to any person to enable them to buy shares in the company. The company, and any officer, in breach of the section is liable to criminal sanctions. The section applies to both direct and indirect assistance, no matter whether it is given before or after the share purchase. Thus, it covers gifts, loans and any other transactions that allow the purchaser of the shares to use the company's assets to pay for those shares.

Section 153, however, provides for general exceptions to the application of s 151. Thus, lending in the ordinary course of business is not covered, nor is assistance provided for employees' share schemes. The most significant exception, however, is that provided under s 153(1), which allows the company to finance share purchases as long as it is done in good faith and in the pursuit of some larger purpose. The precise extent of this relaxation is uncertain and was not helped by the refusal to consider it in the *Guinness* trials or the House of Lords' confused, and confusing, decision in *Brady v Brady* (1989).

As usual, exceptions to the general rule are to be found in relation to private companies (ss 155–58), which are allowed to provide financial assistance, as long as it does not come out of the company's capital, but only from profits available for distribution. The procedure involved is similar to that governing the purchase of a private company's own shares. Thus, a special resolution must be passed and the directors must issue a declaration of solvency supported by auditors. However, in this situation, members holding 10% of the nominal share capital may object to the proceedings within four weeks of the resolution to put it into effect.

9.3.5.7   Loan capital

Companies usually acquire the capital they need to engage in their particular business through the issue of shares. It is, however, also common practice for companies to borrow additional money to finance their operation. It is usual for the memorandum of association of companies to contain an express power allowing the company to borrow money but, in any event, such power is implied as incidental to the conduct of the business of any trading company. Nonetheless, it should be remembered that public limited companies are prohibited from using their borrowing powers until they have been issued with a trading certificate under s 117 of the CA 1985. It is also possible for the articles of association to attempt to limit the borrowing powers of the directors, to whom the general power to borrow is delegated. Again, it should be remembered that, as a consequence of s 35, any such purported limitation remains an internal issue and is not effective as against an outsider.

Loans may be provided simply by a company's bank extending to it an overdraft facility. Alternatively, however, the company may use special facilities to borrow from individuals, either individually or as a group. In either case, the lender is likely to require that security is given for the loan, in order to allow them to recover the value of the loan from the company if it defaults on its interest payments or its final repayment. Even where the lender is given such security, it is essential to realise that borrowing, even when it is secured, does not give the lender any interest in the company but represents a claim against the company. The relationship between the company and the provider of loan capital is the ordinary relationship of debtor/creditor, even where specific mechanisms exist to facilitate the borrowing of companies and to secure the interests of their creditors.

Debentures

In strict legal terms, a debenture is a document which acknowledges the fact that a company has borrowed money and does not refer to any security that may have been given in relation to the loan. In business practice, however, the use of the term 'debenture' is extended to cover the loan itself and usually designates a secured loan, as opposed to an unsecured one. Debentures may be issued in a variety of ways:

- *Single debentures*

  A debenture may be issued to a single creditor, for example, a bank or other financial institution or, indeed, an individual. The debenture document will set out the terms of the loan: interest, repayment and security.

- *Debentures issued in series*

  Alternatively, the company may raise the specific capital that it requires from a number of different lenders. In this case, the global sum of the loan is made up from all of the individual loans. In such a situation, the intention is that each of the participant lenders should rank equally (*pari passu*) in terms of rights and security. Thus, although each lender receives a debenture, they are all identified as being part of a series and consequently have equality of rights.

- *Debenture stock*

  This third method is the way in which companies raise loans from the public at large. The global sum of the loan is once again raised from a large number of people, each of whom holds a proportional part of the total loan stock. The individual lender receives a debenture stock certificate, which in some ways is similar to a share certificate, at least to the extent that such debenture stock is freely transferable and may be dealt with on the stock exchange.

  The loan and the rights appertaining to it are set out in a deed of trust, and a trustee for the debenture stockholders is appointed to represent and pursue the interests of the individual stockholders. In law, it is the trustee, rather than the individual lender, who is the creditor of the company, and the individual debenture stockholders have no direct relationship with the company. In this way, the individuals are relieved of the need to pursue their own causes and the company is relieved of the need to deal with a multiplicity of lenders. Of course, if the trustee fails to pursue the interests of the beneficiaries, they can have recourse to the courts to instruct him to pursue his duties. The content of the trust deed sets out the terms relating to the loan, and in particular it will detail any security and the powers of the trustee to act on behalf of the lenders to enforce that security.

Debentures may be issued as redeemable or irredeemable under s 193 of the CA 1985. In addition, they may carry the right to convert into ordinary shares at some later time. Just as with shares, debentures may be transferred from the current holder to another party, subject to the proper procedure under s 183 of the CA 1985.

However, debentures differ from shares in the following respects:

- Debenture holders are creditors of the company; they are not members, as shareholders are.

- As creditors, they receive interest on their loans; they do not receive dividends, as shareholders do.

- They are entitled to receive interest, whether the company is profitable or not, even if the payment is made out of the company's capital; shareholders' dividends must not be paid out of capital.

- Debentures may be issued at a discount, that is, at less than their nominal value; shares must not be issued at a discount and the company must receive the equivalent to the shares' nominal value.

Company charges

As has been stated previously, it is usual for debentures to provide security for the amount loaned. 'Security' means that, in the event of the company being wound up, the creditor with a secured debt will have priority as regards repayment over any unsecured creditor. There are two types of security for company loans, which are as follows:

- *Fixed charge*

  In this case, a specific asset of the company is made subject to a charge in order to secure a debt. The company cannot thereafter dispose of the property without the consent of the debenture holders. If the company fails to honour its commitments, then the debenture holders can sell the asset to recover the money owed. The asset most commonly subject to fixed charges is land, although any other long term capital asset may also be charged, as may such intangible assets as book debts. It would not be appropriate, however, to place a fixed charge against stock in trade, as the company would be prevented from freely dealing with it without the prior approval of the debenture holders. This would obviously frustrate the business purpose of the enterprise.

- *Floating charge*

  This category of charge does not attach to any specific property of the company until it crystallises through the company committing some act or default in relation to the loan. On the occurrence of such a crystallising event, the floating charge becomes a fixed equitable charge over the assets detailed, the value of which may be realised in order to pay the debt owed to the floating charge holder. It is usual for the document creating the floating charge to include a list of events which will effect crystallisation of the floating charge. Examples of such occurrences are typically that the company is in a position where it is unable to pay its debts; or some other holder of a charge appoints a receiver; or it ceases business or goes into liquidation.

  The floating charge is most commonly made in relation to the undertaking and assets of a company. In such a situation, the security is provided by all the property owned by the company, some of which may be continuously changing, such as stock in trade. The use of the floating charge permits the company to deal with its property without the need to seek the approval of the debenture holders.

Registration of charges

All charges, including both fixed and floating charges, have to be registered with the Companies Registry within 21 days of their creation (ss 395 and 396 of the CA 1985). If they are not registered, then the charge is void, that is, ineffective, against any other creditor or the liquidator of the company, but it is still valid against the company. This means that the charge holder loses priority as against other creditors.

Under s 404 of the CA 1985, the court has the power to permit late registration, that is, at some time after the initial 21 day period. In allowing any late registration, the court can impose such terms and conditions 'as seem to the court to be just and expedient'. Where the court accedes to a request for late registration, as a matter of custom, it does so with the proviso that any rights acquired as a consequence of the late registration are deemed to be without prejudice to the rights of any parties acquired before the time of actual registration. Thus, parties who lent money to the company and received security for their loans will be protected and will not lose out to the rights given under the late registration.

In addition to registration at the Companies Registry, companies are required to maintain a register of all charges on their property (s 407 of the CA 1985). Such a register has to be available for inspection by members and creditors of the company. Failure to comply with this requirement constitutes an offence but it does not invalidate the charge.

Priority of charges

In relation to properly registered charges of the same type, charges take priority according to their date of creation. Thus, although it is perfectly open for a company to create a second fixed or floating charge over assets that are already subject to such preexisting charges, it is not possible for the company to give the later charge equality with, let alone priority over, the charge already in existence.

However, with regard to charges of different types, a fixed charge takes priority over a floating charge even though it was created after it. Generally, there is nothing to prevent the creation of a fixed charge after the issuing of a floating charge and, as a legal charge against specific property, that fixed charge will still take priority over the earlier floating charge. The reason for this apparent anomoly lies in the whole purpose of the floating charge.

As has been seen, the floating charge was designed specifically to allow companies to continue to deal with their assets in the ordinary course of their business, without being subject to the interference of the holder of the floating charge. Consequently, the courts have held that this freedom extended to the ability to create fixed charges over the assets in order to secure later borrowings in the course of the business (*Wheatley v Silkstone and Haigh Moor Coal Co* (1885)). It is possible, however, for the debenture creating the original floating charge to include a provision preventing the creation of a later fixed charge taking priority over that floating charge. The question then is whether the registration of that restriction has any effect on subsequent debenture holders. The current position is that, for such a restrictive provision to be effective, it is necessary that the holder of the subsequent charge should have knowledge of the specific restriction in the original debenture. As registration has been held only to give constructive notice of the existence of a debenture, and not its contents, it is likely that the courts will maintain the position that subsequent charge holders are not subject to limitations contained in previous debentures, unless they actually have knowledge of the existence of such restrictions. Sections 92–107 of the CA 1989 set out procedures to deal with this particular problem, amongst others, in relation to the operation of the registration process for debentures, but unfortunately, due to several inadequacies of the proposed alterations, it was decided that the new procedures would not be introduced.

9.3.6   Directors

Shareholders in public limited companies typically remain external to the actual operation of the enterprise in which they have invested. They also tend to assess the performance of their investment in relation to the level of dividend payment and the related short term movement of share prices on the stock exchange rather than in relation to any long term business strategy. These factors have led to the emergence of what is known as the separation of ownership and control. As it suggests, this idea refers to the fact that those who provide a company's capital are not actually concerned in determining how that capital is used within the specific business enterprise. In effect, the day to day operation of the business enterprise is left in the hands of a small number of company directors, whilst the large majority of shareholders remain powerless to participate in the actual business from which they derive their dividend payments.

In theory, the shareholders exercise ultimate control over the directors through the mechanism of the general meeting. The separation of ownership and control, however, has resulted in the concentration of power in the hands of the directors and has given rise to the possibility that directors might operate as a self-perpetuating oligarchy which seeks to run the company in its own interests, rather than in the interests of the majority of shareholders. In light of the lack of fit between theory and practice, statute law has intervened to place a number of specific controls on the way in which directors act.

9.3.6.1   *The position of directors*

It is a feature of the companies legislation that it tends to define terms in a tautological way, using the term to be defined as part of the definition. Thus, s 741 of the CA 1989 defines the term 'director' to include any person occupying the position of director, by whatever name that person is called. The point of this definition is that it emphasises the fact that it is the function that the person performs, rather than the title given to them, that determines whether they are directors or not. Section 741 also introduces the concept of the shadow director. This is a person who, although not actually appointed to the board, instructs the directors of a company as to how to act. A person is not to be treated as a shadow director if the advice is given in a purely professional capacity. Thus, a business consultant or a company doctor would not be liable as a shadow director for the advice they might give to their client company.

A distinction is sometimes drawn between *de facto* directors who hold themselves out to be directors without actually being formally appointed, and shadow directors who deny being directors (see *Re Hydrodan (Corby) Ltd* (1994)). However, as was pointed out by the Court of Appeal in *Secretary of State for Trade and Industry v Deverell* (2001), in most cases the distinction is irrelevant, and in any event both categories are covered by s 741. The point is that such a person is subject to all the controls and liabilities to which the ordinary directors are subject.

The actual position of a director may be described in a number of ways:

• They are officers of the company (s 744 of the CA 1985).

- The board of directors is the agent of the company and, under Art 84 of Table A, the board may appoint one or more managing directors. They are, therefore, able to bind the company without incurring personal liability. It should be noted that directors are not the agents of the shareholders (see below in relation to the powers of directors).

- Directors are in a fiduciary relationship with their company. This means that they are in a similar position to trustees. The importance of this lies in the nature of the duties that it imposes on directors (see below).

- Directors are not employees of their companies *per se*. They may, however, be employed by the company, in which case they will usually have a distinct service contract detailing their duties and remuneration. Apart from service contracts, the articles usually provide for the remuneration of directors in the exercise of their general duties.

9.3.6.2 *Appointment of directors*

A public company must have at least two directors, whilst a private company can operate with only one director as long as that person does not also act as the company secretary.

The first directors are usually named in the articles or memorandum. Form 10, which is submitted to the Companies Registry prior to the incorporation of a company, requires the inclusion of the names and signatures of those individuals who agree to be the first directors of the company. Subsequent directors are appointed under the procedure stated in the articles. The usual procedure is for the company in a general meeting to elect the directors by an ordinary resolution.

Casual vacancies are usually filled by the board of directors co-opting someone to act as director. That person then serves until the next AGM, when they must stand for election in the usual manner.

Anyone can become a director of a company as long as they are not disqualified from so acting (see below, 9.3.6.3). As a distinct legal person, one company can be a director of a second company. There is no minimum qualification to act as a director; neither is there a requirement for a director to be a member of the company. However, the articles of some companies do require the directors to hold shares in them. If the director does not acquire such qualifying shares within a two month period of being appointed, or subsequently disposes of those shares, then they will be required to resign their position (s 291 of the CA 1985). Even where the director does not comply with this provision, their acts are nonetheless binding on the company.

9.3.6.3 *Removal of directors*

There are a number of ways in which a person may be obliged to give up their position as a director:

- *Rotation*

Table A provides that one-third of the directors shall retire at each AGM, being those with longest service. They are, however, open to re-election and in practice are usually re-elected.

- *Retirement*

Directors of public companies are required to retire at the first AGM after they have reached the age of 70. They may retire at any time before then.

- *Removal*

A director can be removed at any time by the passing of an ordinary resolution of the company (s 303). The company must be given special notice (28 days) of the intention to propose such a resolution.

The power to remove a director under s 303 cannot be taken away or restricted by any provision in the company's documents or any external contract (see *Southern Foundries v Shirlaw* (1940), above at 9.3.4.2). It is possible, however, for the effect of the section to be avoided in private companies by the use of weighted voting rights.

In *Bushell v Faith* (1969), the articles of association of a company which had three equal shareholders, each of whom was a director, provided that, on a vote to remove a director, that person's shares would carry three votes as against its usual one. The effect of this was that a s 303 resolution could never be passed. The House of Lords held that such a procedure was legitimate, although it has to be recognised that it is unlikely that such a decision would be extended to public limited companies.

As regards private/quasi-partnership companies, it has been held, in *Re Bird Precision Bellows Ltd* (1984), that exclusion from the right to participate in management provides a ground for an action for a court order to remedy unfairly prejudicial conduct under s 459 of the CA 1985 (see below, 9.3.10.2).

- *Disqualification*

The articles of association usually provide for the disqualification of directors on the occurrence of certain circumstances: bankruptcy; mental illness; or prolonged absence from board meetings. In addition, there are statutory controls over directors, other officers and promoters of companies.

9.3.6.4   Company Directors Disqualification Act 1986

Individuals can be disqualified from acting as directors up to a maximum period of 15 years under the CDDA 1986. The Act was introduced in an attempt to prevent the misuse of the company form. One of its specific aims was the control of what are described as 'phoenix companies'. These are companies which trade until they get into financial trouble and accrue extensive debts. Upon this eventuality, the company ceases trading, only for the person behind the company to set up another company to carry on essentially the same business, but with no liability to the creditors of the former company. Such behaviour is reprehensible and is clearly an abuse of limited liability. The CDDA 1986 seeks to remedy this practice by preventing certain individuals from acting as company directors, but the ambit of the Act's control is much wider than this one instance.

The CDDA 1986 identifies three distinct categories of conduct which may, and in some circumstances must, lead the court to disqualify certain persons from being involved in the management of companies:

- *General misconduct in connection with companies*

  This first category involves the following:

  ○ A conviction for an indictable offence in connection with the promotion, formation, management or liquidation of a company or with the receivership or management of a company's property (s 2 of the CDDA 1986). The maximum period for disqualification under s 2 is five years where the order is made by a court of summary jurisdiction, and 15 years in any other case.

  ○ Persistent breaches of companies legislation in relation to provisions which require any return, account or other document to be filed with, or notice of any matter to be given to, the Registrar (s 3 of the CDDA 1986). Section 3 provides that a person is conclusively proved to be persistently in default where it is shown that, in the five years ending with the date of the application, he has been adjudged guilty of three or more defaults (s 3(2) of the CDDA 1986). This is without prejudice to proof of persistent default in any other manner. The maximum period of disqualification under this section is five years.

  ○ Fraud in connection with winding up (s 4 of the CDDA 1986). A court may make a disqualification order if, in the course of the winding up of a company, it appears that a person:

    (a) has been guilty of an offence for which he is liable under s 458 of the CA 1985, that is, that he has knowingly been a party to the carrying on of the business of the company either with the intention of defrauding the company's creditors or any other person or for any other fraudulent purpose; or

    (b) has otherwise been guilty, while an officer or liquidator of the company or receiver or manager of the property of the company, of any fraud in relation to the company or of any breach of his duty as such officer, liquidator, receiver or manager (s 4(1)(b) of the CDDA 1986).

The maximum period of disqualification under this category is 15 years.

- *Disqualification for unfitness*

  The second category covers:

  ○ disqualification of directors of companies which have become insolvent, who are found by the court to be unfit to be directors (s 6 of the CDDA 1986). Under s 6, the minimum period of disqualification is two years, up to a maximum of 15 years; and

○ disqualification after investigation of a company under Pt XIV of the CA 1985 (s 8 of the CDDA 1986).

A disqualification order may be made as the result of an investigation of a company under the companies legislation. Under s 8 of the CDDA 1986, the Secretary of State may apply to the court for a disqualification order to be made against a person who has been a director or shadow director of any company, if it appears from a report made by an inspector under s 437 of the CA or s 94 or 177 of the Financial Services Act 1986 that 'it is expedient in the public interest' that such a disqualification order should be made. Once again, the maximum period of disqualification is 15 years.

The CDDA 1986 sets out certain particulars to which the court is to have regard where it has to determine whether a person's conduct as a director makes them unfit to be concerned in the management of a company (s 9). The detailed list of matters to be considered is set out in Sched 1 to the Act.

In addition, the courts have given indications as to what sort of behaviour will render a person liable to be considered unfit to act as a company director. Thus, in *Re Lo-Line Electric Motors Ltd* (1988), it was stated that:

> Ordinary commercial misjudgment is in itself not sufficient to justify disqualification. In the normal case, the conduct complained of must display a lack of commercial probity, although ... in an extreme case of gross negligence or total incompetence, disqualification could be appropriate.

A 'lack of commercial probity', therefore, will certainly render a director unfit, but, as Vinelott J stated in *Re Stanford Services Ltd* (1987):

> ... the public is entitled to be protected, not only against the activities of those guilty of the more obvious breaches of commercial morality, but also against someone who has shown in his conduct of a company a failure to appreciate or observe the duties attendant on the privilege of conducting business with the protection of limited liability.

Consequently, even where there is no dishonesty, incompetence may render a director unfit. Thus, in *Re Sevenoaks Stationers (Retail) Ltd* (1990), the Court of Appeal held that a director was unfit to be concerned in the management of a company on the basis that:

> His trouble is not dishonesty, but incompetence or negligence in a very marked degree, and that is enough to render him unfit; I do not think it is necessary for incompetence to be 'total' to render a director unfit to take part in the management of a company.

• *Other cases for disqualification*

This third category relates to:

○ participation in fraudulent or wrongful trading under s 213 of the IA 1986 (s 10 of the CDDA 1986);

○ undischarged bankrupts acting as directors (s 11 of the CDDA 1986); and

○ failure to pay under a county court administration order (s 12 of the CDDA 1986).

Disqualification orders

For the purposes of most of the CDDA 1986, the court has a discretion to make a disqualification order. Where, however, a person has been found to be an unfit director of an insolvent company, the court has a duty to make a disqualification order (s 6 of the CDDA 1986).

The precise nature of any such order is set out in s 1, under which the court may make an order preventing any person (without leave of the court) from being:

- a director of a company;
- a liquidator or administrator of a company;
- a receiver or manager of a company's property; or
- in any way, whether directly or indirectly, concerned with or taking part in the promotion, formation or management of a company.

However, a disqualification order may be made:

- with leave to continue to act as a director for a short period of time, in order to enable the disqualified director to arrange his business affairs (*Re Ipcon Fashions Ltd* (1989));
- with leave to continue as a director of a named company, subject to conditions (*Re Lo-Line Electric Motors Ltd* (1988)); or
- with leave to act in some other managerial capacity but not as director (*Re Cargo Agency Ltd* (1992)).

Period of disqualification

With regard to the period of disqualification, in *Re Sevenoaks Stationers (Retail) Ltd* (1990), Dillon LJ in the Court of Appeal divided the potential maximum 15 year period of disqualification into three distinct brackets:

- over 10 years for particularly serious cases (for example, where a director has been disqualified previously);
- two to five years for 'relatively not very serious' cases; and
- a middle bracket of between 6 and 10 years for serious cases not meriting the top bracket.

Penalty for breach of a disqualification order

Anyone who acts in contravention of a disqualification order is liable to:

- imprisonment for up to two years and/or a fine, on conviction on indictment; or
- imprisonment for up to six months and/or a fine not exceeding the statutory maximum, on conviction summarily (s 13 of the CDDA 1986).

Under s 14, where a company is guilty of an offence under s 13, then any person who consented or contributed to its so doing will also be guilty of an offence. In addition, s 15 imposes personal liability for company debts arising during a period when a person acts as a director whilst disqualified, either under an order or whilst personally bankrupt. The Secretary of State is required to maintain a register of disqualification orders which is open to public inspection (s 18).

Case study: Re Uno (2004)

The operation of the CDDA 1986 was considered extensively in *Re Uno, Secretary of State for Trade and Industry v Gill* (2004). This case related to a group of two furniture companies which, although in severe financial difficulties, continued to trade whilst the directors investigated possible ways of saving the businesses. During this period, one of the companies, Uno, continued to raise its working capital from deposits taken from customers to secure orders that were never to be met, when the company eventually went into liquidation. Although the directors were advised that they could have safeguarded the deposits by placing the money in a trust account for the customers, they decided not to do so, as they needed the money to keep the business going in the short term. An application from the Department of Trade and Industry for the disqualification of the directors on the basis of this behaviour was unsuccessful. In refusing the application, the court emphasised the fact that in order to justify disqualification there had to be behaviour that was either dishonest or lacking in commercial probity. Moreover, that behaviour had to be such as to make the person concerned unfit to be involved in the management of a company. In the circumstances of the case, the court found that the directors had pursued realistic opportunities to save the businesses and consequently were blameless for the eventual failure of the businesses and the loss to the customers.

9.3.6.5   Directors' powers

In considering the topic of directors' powers, it is necessary to distinguish between the power of the directors as a board and the powers of individual directors.

The power of directors as a board

Article 70 of Table A provides that the directors of a company may exercise all the powers of the company. It is important to note that this power is given to the board as a whole and not to individual directors, although Art 72 does allow for the delegation of the board's powers to one or more directors.

Article 70 gives the board of directors general power, but the Articles may seek to restrict the authority of the board within limits expressly stated in the company's constitutional documents. The effectiveness of such restrictions has been greatly reduced by the operation of s 35 of the CA 1985, as amended by the CA 1989. As a consequence of s 35, as it now is, not only can the power of a company not be challenged on the grounds of lack of capacity: neither can the actions of its directors be challenged on the basis of any limitation contained in the company's documents. This provision is subject to the requirement that any third party must act in good faith, although such good faith is presumed, subject to proof to the contrary.

The power of individual directors

There are three ways in which the power of the board of directors may be extended to individual directors. These ways are, however, simply particular applications of the general law of agency, considered above (see above, 9.1):

- *Express actual authority*

   This category is unproblematic, in that it arises from the express conferral by the board of a particular authority onto an individual director. For example, it is possible for the board to specifically authorise an individual director to negotiate and bind the company to a particular transaction.

- *Implied actual authority*

   In this situation, the person's authority flows from their position. Article 84 of Table A's model articles (see above, 9.3.4.2) provides for the board of directors to appoint a managing director. The board of directors may confer any of their powers on the managing director as they see fit. The mere fact of appointment, however, will mean that the person so appointed will have the implied authority to bind the company in the same way as the board, whose delegate they are. Outsiders, therefore, can safely assume that a person appointed as managing director has all the powers usually exercised by a person acting as a managing director.

   Implied actual authority to bind a company may also arise as a consequence of the appointment of an individual to a position other than that of managing director.

   In *Hely-Hutchinson v Brayhead Ltd* (1968), although the chairman and chief executive of a company acted as its *de facto* managing director, he had never been formally appointed to that position. Nevertheless, he purported to bind the company to a particular transaction. When the other party to the agreement sought to enforce it, the company claimed that the chairman had no authority to bind it. It was held that although the director derived no authority from his position as chairman of the board, he did acquire such authority from his position as chief executive; thus, the company was bound by the contract he had entered into on its behalf.

- *Apparent or ostensible authority / agency by estoppel*

   This arises where an individual director has neither express nor implied authority. Nonetheless, the director is held out by the other members of the board of directors as having the authority to bind the company. If a third party acts on such a representation, then the company will be estopped from denying its truth.

   Problems tend to arise where someone acts as a managing director without having been properly appointed to that position. In such a situation, although the individual concerned may not have the actual authority to bind the company, they may still have apparent authority and the company may be estopped from denying their power to bind it to particular transactions.

   In *Freeman and Lockyer v Buckhurst Park Properties (Mangal) Ltd* (1964), although a particular director had never been appointed as managing director, he acted as such with the clear knowledge of the other directors and entered into a contract with the plaintiffs on behalf of the company. When the plaintiffs sought to recover fees due to them under that contract, it was held that the company was liable: a properly appointed managing director would have been able to enter into such a contract and the third party was entitled to rely on the representation of the other directors that the person in question had been properly appointed to that position.

9.3.6.6   Directors' duties

At common law, the duties owed by directors to their company and the shareholders, employees and creditors of that company were at worst non-existent or at best notoriously lax. Statute has, by necessity, been forced to intervene to increase such duties in order to provide a measure of protection for those concerned.

Fiduciary duties

As fiduciaries, directors owe the following duties to their company (it is imperative to note that the duty is owed to the company as a distinct legal person and not to the shareholders of the company, so the rule in *Foss v Harbottle* applies – see above, 9.3.1.3):

- *The duty to act bona fide in the interests of the company*

  In effect, this means that directors are under an obligation to act in what they genuinely believe to be the interests of the company.

- *The duty not to act for any collateral purpose*

  This may be seen as a corollary of the preceding duty, in that directors cannot be said to be acting *bona fide* if they use their powers for some ulterior or collateral purpose. For example, directors should not issue shares to particular individuals in order merely to facilitate, or indeed prevent, a prospective takeover bid (see *Howard Smith v Ampol Petroleum* (1974) and *Hogg v Cramphorn* (1967)). The breach of such a fiduciary duty is, however, subject to *post hoc* ratification (see *Bamford v Bamford* (1970)).

- *The duty not to permit a conflict of interest and duty to arise*

  This equitable rule is strictly applied by the courts and the effect of its operations may be seen in *Regal (Hastings) v Gulliver* (1942), where the directors of a company which owned one cinema provided money for the creation of a subsidiary company to purchase two other cinemas. After the parent and subsidiary companies had been sold at a later date, the directors were required to repay the profit they had made on the sale of their shares in the subsidiary company on the ground that they had only been in the situation to make that profit because of their positions as directors of the parent company. (The profits made went back to the parent company, which was by then in the hands of the person who had paid the money to the directors in the first place.)

  One obvious area where directors place themselves in a position involving a conflict of interest is where they have an interest in a contract with the company. The common law position was that in the event of any such situation arising, any contract involved was voidable at the instance of the company (*Aberdeen Railway Co v Blaikie* (1854)). However, Art 85 of Table A specifically excludes the no-conflict rule where the director in question has declared the nature and extent of his interest. Section 317 of the CA 1985 also places a duty on directors to declare any interest, direct or indirect, in any contracts with their companies, and provides for a fine if they fail in this regard. A director's disclosure can take the form of a general declaration of interest in a particular company, which is considered sufficient to put the other directors on notice for the future. Any declaration of interest must be made at the board meeting that first considers the contract, or, if the director becomes interested in the contract after that, at the first meeting thereafter. Article 94 of Table A generally prohibits directors from voting in regard to contracts in which they have an interest. Failure to disclose any interest renders the contract voidable at the instance of the company and the director may be liable to account to the company for any profit made in relation to it.

Duty of care and skill

Common law did not place any great burden on directors in this regard. Damages could be recovered against directors for losses caused by their negligence but the level of such negligence was high. As was stated in *Lagunas Nitrate Co v Lagunas Syndicate* (1989), it must, in a business sense, be culpable or gross. The classic statement is to be found in *Re City Equitable Fire Assurance Co* (1925), which established three points:

- First, in determining the degree of skill to be expected, the common law applied a subjective test and established no minimum standard. A director was expected to show the degree of skill which might reasonably be expected of a person of their knowledge and experience. As a result, if they were particularly experienced and skilled in the affairs of their business, then they would be expected to exercise such skill in the performance of their functions. On the other hand, however, if the director was a complete incompetent, he would only be expected to perform to the level of a complete incompetent. The reasoning behind this seemed to be that the courts left it to the shareholders to elect and control the directors as their representatives. If the shareholders elected incompetents, then that was a matter for them and the courts would not interfere.

- Secondly, the duties of directors were held to be of an intermittent nature and, consequently, directors were not required to give continuous attention to the affairs of their company. In *Re Cardiff Savings Bank* (the *Marquis of Bute's case*) (1892), it emerged that the Marquis had inherited his position as president of the bank at the age of six months and, in the course of 38 years, he had only ever attended one board meeting.

- Thirdly, in the absence of any grounds for suspicion, directors were entitled to leave the day to day operation of the company's business in the hands of managers and to trust them to perform their tasks honestly.

Fraudulent and wrongful trading

The laxity of the situation at common law has been much tightened by statute, particularly by the development of the possibility of wrongful trading, which was introduced by s 214 of the IA 1986.

It should be noted that there has long been civil liability for any activity amounting to fraudulent trading. Thus, s 213 of the IA 1986 governs situations where, in the course of a winding up, it appears that the business of a company has been carried on with intent to defraud creditors, or for any fraudulent purpose. In such cases, the court, on the application of the liquidator, may declare that any persons who were knowingly parties to such carrying on of the business are liable to make such contributions (if any) to the company's assets as the court thinks proper. There is a major problem in making use of s 213, however, and that lies in meeting the very high burden of proof involved in proving dishonesty on the part of the person against whom it is alleged. It should be noted that there is also a criminal offence of fraudulent trading under s 458 of the CA 1985, which applies to anyone who has been party to the carrying on of the business of a company with intent to defraud creditors or any other person, or for any other fraudulent purpose. Wrongful trading does not involve dishonesty but, nonetheless, it still makes particular individuals potentially liable for the debts of their companies. Section 214 applies where a company is being wound up and it appears that, at some time before the start of the winding up, a director knew, or ought to have known, that there was no reasonable chance of the company avoiding insolvent liquidation. In such circumstances, then, unless the directors took every reasonable step to minimise the potential loss to the company's creditors, they may be liable to contribute such money to the assets of the company as the court thinks proper. In deciding what directors ought to have known, the court will apply an objective test, as well as a subjective one. As in common law, if the director is particularly well qualified, they will be expected to perform in line with those standards. Additionally, however, s 214 of the IA 1986 establishes a minimum standard by applying an objective test which requires directors to have the general knowledge, skill and experience which may reasonably be expected of a person carrying out the same functions as are carried out by that director in relation to the company.

The manner in which incompetent directors will become liable to contribute the assets of their companies was shown in *Re Produce Marketing Consortium Ltd* (1989), in which two directors were held liable to pay compensation from the time that they ought to have known that their company could not avoid insolvent liquidation, rather than the later time when they actually realised that fact. In that case, the two directors were ordered to contribute £75,000 to the company's assets. In reaching that decision, Knox J stated that:

> In my judgement, the jurisdiction under s 214 is primarily compensatory rather than penal. *Prima facie*, the appropriate amount that a director is declared to be liable to contribute is the amount by which the company's assets can be discerned to have been depleted by the director's conduct which caused the discretion under s 214(1) to arise ... The fact that there was no fraudulent intent is not of itself a reason for fixing the amount

at a nominal or low figure, for that would amount to frustrating what I discern as Parliament's intention in adding s 214 to s 213 in the Insolvency Act 1986 ...

It should also be recalled, as considered previously, that directors may be disqualified from holding office for a period of up to 15 years under the provisions of the CDDA 1986 if they are found liable for either fraudulent or wrongful trading (see above, 9.3.6.4)

Interestingly, the common law approach to directors' duty of care has been extended to accommodate the requirements of s 214. Thus, in *Re D'Jan of London Ltd* (1993), Hoffmann LJ, as he then was, held that the common law duty of care owed by a director to his company was stated in s 214 of the IA 1986, and contained both objective and subjective tests. In that particular case, the managing director of a small company had signed a proposal for fire insurance which had been filled in by his insurance broker and which contained inaccurate answers to some questions. When the insurers subsequently declined liability for a fire which destroyed the company's premises and stock, Hoffmann LJ held that the director was liable to the company for breaching his duty of care.

9.3.7 Company secretary

Section 744 of the CA 1989 includes the company secretary among the officers of a company. Every company must have a company secretary and, although there are no specific qualifications required to perform such a role in a private company, s 286 of the CA 1985 requires that the directors of a public company must ensure that the company secretary has the requisite knowledge and experience to discharge their functions. Section 286(2) sets out a list of professional bodies, including the ICA, ACCA, ICMA and ICSA, membership of which enables a person to act as a company secretary.

9.3.7.1 *Duties of company secretaries*

The duties of company secretaries are set by the board of directors, and therefore vary from company to company but, as an officer of the company, the secretary will be responsible for ensuring that the company complies with its statutory obligations.

Some of the most important duties undertaken by company secretaries are to:

- ensure that the necessary registers required to be kept by the Companies Acts are established and properly maintained;

- ensure that all returns required to be lodged with the Companies Registry are prepared and filed within the appropriate time limits;

- organise and attend meetings of the shareholders and directors;

- ensure that the company's books of accounts are kept in accordance with the Companies Acts and that the annual accounts and reports are prepared in the form and at the time required by the Acts;

- be aware of all the statutory requirements placed on the company's activities and to ensure that the company complies with them; and

- sign such documents as require their signature under the Companies Acts.

9.3.7.2 *Powers of company secretaries*

Although old authorities, such as *Houghton & Co v Northard Lowe and Wills* (1928), suggest that company secretaries have extremely limited authority to bind their company, later cases have recognised the reality of the contemporary situation and have extended to company secretaries potentially significant powers to bind their companies. As an example, consider *Panorama Developments Ltd v Fidelis Furnishing Fabrics Ltd* (1971), in which a company secretary hired cars for his own use, although he signed the documents as 'company secretary'. His company was held liable to pay for the hire of the cars. In the Court of Appeal, Lord Denning stated that a company secretary was entitled:

> ... to sign contracts connected with the administrative side of a company's affairs, such as employing staff and ordering cars and so forth. All such matters now come within the ostensible authority of a company's secretary.

Although Lord Denning dealt with the secretary's authority on the basis of ostensible authority, it would be more accurate to define it as an example of implied actual authority (see above, 9.1.3.1).

9.3.8 Company auditor

Section 384 of the CA 1985 requires all companies to appoint an auditor, whose duty it is under s 235 of the CA 1985 to report to the company's members as to whether or not the company's accounts have been properly prepared and to consider whether the directors' report is consistent with those accounts.

In the case of a newly registered company, the first auditors are appointed by the directors until the first general meeting, at which they may be reappointed by the members of the company. Thereafter, auditors are appointed annually at general meetings at which accounts are laid (s 385 of the CA 1985). It should be recalled that private companies may, by means of an elective resolution, dispense with the requirement to appoint auditors annually. In such circumstances, the existing auditor is deemed to be reappointed for each succeeding year (s 386 of the CA 1985). The Secretary of State has the power to appoint an auditor where the company has not appointed one (s 387 of the CA 1985).

Section 389 provides that a person can only be appointed as an auditor where he is a member of a recognised supervisory body such as the Institute of Certified Accountants or the Chartered Association of Certified Accountants. A person cannot be appointed where he is an officer or employee of the company in question.

Auditors are appointed to ensure that the company is being run on a proper basis. They represent the interests of the shareholders and report to them. They are, however, employed by the company and owe their contractual duty to the company rather than the shareholders. As partnerships may now be appointed as auditors (s 26 of the CA 1989), some concern has been expressed that the large accountancy firms might offer auditor services as a loss leader, in order to acquire more lucrative accountancy deals with the company. The concern is that this might lead to a conflict of interest between the accountancy firm's role as auditor and its other roles in relation to the company.

Auditors are required to make a report on all annual accounts laid before the company in a general meeting during their tenure of office (s 235(1)). The report must state the names of the auditors and must be signed by them (s 236(1) and (3)).

The auditors are required to report (s 235(2)) whether the accounts have been properly prepared in accordance with the CA 1989, and whether the individual and group accounts show a true and fair view of the profit or loss and state of affairs of the company and of the group, so far as concerns the members of the company.

Auditors are required to make the necessary investigations and consider the following, which need only be reported on if there are deficiencies: whether the company has kept proper accounting records and obtained proper accounting returns from branches (s 237(1) and (2)); whether the accounts are in agreement with the records (s 237(1) and (2)); whether they have obtained all the information and explanations that they considered necessary (s 237(3)); whether the requirements of Sched 6, concerning disclosure of information about directors and officers remuneration, loans and other transactions, have been met; and whether the information in the directors' report is consistent with the accounts (s 235(3)).

Where the company circulates a summary financial statement, the auditors are required to give a report on whether the summary statement is consistent with the company's annual accounts and directors' report, and whether it complies with the requirements of the CA 1985 and regulations in relation to this statement (s 251(4)(b)).

If the auditors' report does not state that, in their unqualified opinion, the accounts have been properly prepared in accordance with the relevant legislation governing the relevant undertakings' accounts (s 262(1)), then the accounts are said to be qualified.

Auditors have the right of access at all times to the company's books and accounts, and officers of the company are required to provide such information and explanations as the auditors consider necessary (s 389A of the CA 1985). It is a criminal offence to make false or reckless statements to auditors (s 389A). Auditors are entitled to receive notices and other documents in connection with all general meetings, to attend such meetings and to speak when the business affects their role as auditors (s 390). Where a company operates on the basis of written resolutions rather than meetings, then the auditor is entitled to receive copies of all such proposed resolutions as are to be sent to members (s 381B).

An auditor may be removed at any time by ordinary resolution of the company (s 391(1) of the CA 1985). This does, however, require special notice. Any auditor who is to be removed or not reappointed is entitled to make written representations and require these to be circulated or have them read out at the meeting (s 391A).

An auditor may resign at any time (s 392 of the CA 1985). Notice of resignation must be accompanied by a statement of any circumstances that the auditor believes ought to be brought to the attention of members and creditors, or, alternatively, a statement that there are no such circumstances (s 394). The company is required to file a copy of the notice with the registrar of companies within 14 days (s 392). Where the auditor's resignation statement states that there are circumstances that should be brought to the attention of members, then he may require the company to call a meeting to allow an explanation of those circumstances to the members of the company (s 392A(1)).

The power of auditors will be significantly increased when the Companies (Audit, Investigations and Community Enterprise) Act C(AICE)A 2004 comes into force (see below, 9.3.14).

The tortious liability of auditors is considered above, at 8.2.1.

9.3.9   Company meetings

In theory, the ultimate control over a company's business lies with the members in general meeting. In practice, however, the residual powers of the membership are restricted to their ultimate control over the company's memorandum and articles of association, although this control has been reduced by the introduction of the new s 35 of the CA 1985, as effected by the CA 1989, together with their control over the composition of the board of directors. The reality of such limited theoretical powers are further constrained by the practicalities involved with the operation of company meetings.

In line with this approach, some powers are specifically reserved to the members by statute, such as the right to petition for voluntary winding up; Art 70 of Table A provides that the shareholders, by passing a special resolution, can instruct the directors to act in a particular way. In reality, the ideal typical shareholder tends either not to be bothered to take an active part in the conduct of company meetings or to use their votes in a way directed by the board of directors.

One would obviously conclude that a meeting involved more than one person and, indeed, there is authority to that effect in *Sharp v Dawes* (1876). In that case, a meeting between a lone member and the company secretary was held not to be validly constituted. It is possible, however, for a meeting of only one person to take place in the following circumstances:

- in the case of a meeting of a particular class of shareholders and all the shares of that class are owned by the one member; or

- by virtue of s 371 of the CA 1985, the court may order the holding of a general meeting, at which the quorum is to be one member. This eventuality might arise in a quasi-partnership where a recalcitrant member of a two-person company refused to attend any meetings, thus preventing the continuation of the enterprise.

9.3.9.1   *Types of meetings*

There are three types of meeting:

- *Annual general meeting*

    By virtue of s 366 of the CA 1985, every company is required to hold an AGM every calendar year, subject to a maximum period of 15 months between meetings. This means that, if a company holds its AGM on 1 January 2005, then it must hold its next AGM by 31 March 2006 at the latest.

    In line with the recognised distinction between public and private companies, the CA 1989 introduced a provision in the form of a new s 366A, which permitted private companies, subject to approval by a unanimous vote, to dispense with the holding of an AGM.

    If a company fails to hold an AGM, then any member may apply to the Secretary of State, under s 367 of the CA 1989, to call a meeting in default.

- *Extraordinary general meeting*

    An extraordinary general meeting (EGM) is any meeting other than an AGM. EGMs are usually called by the directors, although members holding 10% of the voting shares may requisition such a meeting.

- *Class meeting*

    This refers to the meeting of a particular class of shareholder, that is, those who hold a type of share providing particular rights, such as preference shares (considered above, 9.3.5.3).

Under s 381A of the CA 1985, it is no longer necessary for a private company to convene a general meeting where the members have unanimously signed a written resolution setting out a particular course of action.

9.3.9.2   *Calling meetings*

Meetings may be convened in a number of ways by various people, for example:

- by the *directors* of the company under Art 37 of Table A. Apart from this usual power, directors of public limited companies are required, under s 142 of the CA 1985, to call meetings where there has been a serious loss of capital, defined as the assets falling to half or less than the nominal value of the called up share capital;

- by the *members* using the power to requisition a meeting under s 368 of the CA 1985. To require the convening of a company meeting, any shareholders must hold at least one-tenth of the share capital carrying voting rights. If the directors fail to convene a meeting as required within 21 days of the deposit of the requisition, although the actual date of the meeting may be within eight weeks of the date of requisition, then the requisitionists may themselves convene a meeting and recover any expenses from the company;

- by the *auditor* of a company under s 392A of the CA 1985, which provides for a resigning auditor to require the directors to convene a meeting in order to explain the reason for the auditor's resignation;

- the *Secretary of State* may, under s 367 of the CA 1985, on the application of any member, call a meeting of a company where it has failed to hold an AGM as required under s 366; or

- the *court* may order a meeting under s 371 of the CA 1985 where it is otherwise impracticable to call a meeting.

9.3.9.3 *Notice of meetings*

Proper and adequate notice must be sent to all those who are entitled to attend any meeting, although the precise nature of the notice is governed by the articles of association.

Details of the following must be given:

- *Time*

    This is set out in s 369 of the CA 1985. The minimum period of notice is 21 clear days for an AGM and 14 clear days for all other meetings, except those called to consider a special resolution, which also require 21 clear days' notice. Shorter notice is permissible in the case of an AGM where all the members entitled to attend agree, and in the case of any other meeting where holders of 95% of the nominal value of the voting shares agree. Private companies, by means of an elective resolution, may reduce this latter requirement to 90%.

- *Content*

    Adequate notice of the content of any resolution must be sent to members, so that they can decide whether to attend the meeting or to appoint a proxy to vote in line with their instructions. In respect of anything other than standard business, it is desirable that the full text of any resolution to be put to the meeting be circulated to all of the members entitled to vote on it.

9.3.9.4 *Agenda*

It is usually the prerogative of the directors to decide which motions will be put to the company in the general meeting. Members, however, may set the agenda where they have requisitioned an EGM under the procedure established in s 368 (see above, 9.3.9.1). In relation to an AGM, s 376 provides a procedure whereby a minority of members, amounting to one-20th of the total voting rights or 100 members holding an average of £100 worth of shares, may have a motion considered. This mechanism is complicated and expensive, and the difficulties involved in putting it into practice, especially in large public companies, mean that it is not often used.

The difficulties involved in ordinary members getting issues onto the agenda also extend to resolutions to remove directors. Although s 303 provides for the removal of directors on the passing of an ordinary resolution, it was held in *Pedley v Inland Waterways Association Ltd* (1977) that a disgruntled member could only get such a resolution onto the agenda if he satisfied the requirements of s 376.

9.3.9.5 *Types of resolutions*

There are essentially three types of resolution:

- *Ordinary resolution*

  This requires a simple majority of those voting. Members who do not attend or appoint a proxy, or who attend but do not vote, are disregarded.

  Notice in relation to an ordinary resolution depends on the type of meeting at which it is proposed: the required period is 21 days for an AGM and 14 days for an EGM, although, in relation to an ordinary resolution to remove a director under s 303, the company must be given special notice of 28 days. It should be noted that, in this latter case, the notice is given to the company, whereas it is usually the company that is required to give notice to the members.

- *Extraordinary resolution*

  Section 378(1) of the CA 1985 provides that an extraordinary resolution is one passed by a three-quarters majority of votes cast at a meeting convened by a notice specifying the intention to propose such a resolution. As no period of notice is stated in s 378, it would appear that, unless the articles provide for a longer period, the minimum period of notice will be the 14 days ordinarily laid down for EGMs, or 21 days for AGMs, under s 369 of the CA 1985. The effect of linking the notice of the resolution to the notice for the meeting is that the minimum 14 day period of notice can be reduced with the approval of the appropriate majority, that is, those representing at least 95% of the authorised capital of the company (s 369(4) of the CA 1985). This latter majority may be reduced by the passing of an elective resolution to that effect in a private company (see below).

  The requirement for meetings to pass extraordinary resolutions is not a common one. However, s 125 of the CA 1985 provides for the variation of class rights, other than those contained in the memorandum, by an extraordinary resolution of the class concerned, where the articles of association do not provide for variation. Also, although it is normally necessary for the company to pass a special resolution in order to be wound up voluntarily, an extraordinary resolution can be used on the grounds of insolvency (s 84 of the IA 1986).

- *Special resolution*

  A special resolution is one that has been passed by a majority of not less than three-quarters at a general meeting, of which not less than 21 days' notice has been given, such notice having specified the intention to propose the resolution as a special resolution (s 378(2) of the CA 1985). The 21 day notice period may be shortened, as with extraordinary resolutions, under s 368 of the CA 1985. The companies legislation requires special resolutions to be passed in so many situations that they cannot all be listed here. Amongst those in the CA 1985 are the following examples:

ɔ   alteration to objects clause (s 4);

ɔ   alteration of articles (s 9);

ɔ   change of company name (s 28);

ɔ   re-registration of a private company as a public company (s 430) and vice versa (s 53); and

ɔ   reduction of capital (s 135).

Written resolutions

By virtue of s 381A of the CA 1985, anything which in the case of a private company might be done by resolution in a general or class meeting may be done by resolution in writing, signed by, or on behalf of, all members who would be entitled to attend and vote at such a meeting. However, resolutions for the removal of directors or auditors before expiry of their term of office cannot be the subject of written resolutions. The effect of s 381A is that private companies no longer have to call meetings or give notice for resolutions.

The written resolution requires unanimity. The members can, however, sign different pieces of paper, so long as each accurately states the terms of the resolution (s 381A(2) of the CA 1985).

Directors or the secretary must ensure that the company's auditor receives a copy of the resolution before the members receive it but, although failure to comply with this provision may render the person liable to a fine, it does not affect the validity of the resolution. The date of a written resolution is the date when the last member signs it (s 381B(3) of the CA 1985) and the company is required to keep a record of any written resolutions.

Elective resolutions

Under s 379A of the CA 1985, a private company may dispense with certain procedural requirements of the Act by passing an elective resolution to that effect. Five possibilities are set out in s 379A, but the Secretary of State can alter the list by statutory instrument (s 117 of the CA 1989).

Elective resolutions may be passed to:

•   provide directors with permanent authority to allot shares (s 80A);

•   dispense with laying accounts and reports before the general meeting (s 252);

•   dispense with the holding of AGMs (s 366A);

•   reduce the majority required to consent to short notice of a meeting (s 369); and

•   dispense with the appointment of auditors annually (s 386).

An elective resolution requires 21 days' notice to be given of the meeting at which it is to be proposed. It also requires unanimity of all members entitled to attend and vote. The members may agree unanimously to dispense with the notice requirement. An elective resolution may be revoked by an ordinary resolution. Finally, it should be noted that an elective resolution may be passed by written resolution.

It *was* the case that elective resolutions required 21 days' notice; however, under the Deregulation (Resolutions of Private Companies) Order 1996 (SI 1996/1471), itself made under the Deregulation and Contracting Out Act 1994, that requirement has been removed and such a resolution is effective notwithstanding that less than 21 days' notice was given. It is still the case that unanimity is required both to pass the resolution and to accept the shorter notice. So, all those entitled to attend and vote at a meeting must approve of the resolution, but it should also be noted that elective resolutions can themselves be passed, using the procedure for passing written resolutions.

9.3.9.6   Quorum

This is the minimum number of persons whose presence is required for the transaction of business at any meeting. The precise details are set out in the articles of association, although s 370 and Art 41 of Table A set the minimum at two, who must be continuously present at the meeting.

9.3.9.7   Votes

A resolution is decided upon initially by a show of hands, unless a poll is demanded. On a show of hands, every member has one vote. In a poll, it is usual for each share to carry a vote and, thus, for the outcome of the poll to reflect concentration of interest in the company (for exceptions to this, see *Bushell v Faith* (1969), above, 9.3.6.3).

Article 41 of Table A enables any two members or the chairman to call for a poll.

9.3.9.8   Proxies

Section 372 of the CA 1985 provides that any member of a company who is entitled to attend and vote at a meeting may appoint another person as their proxy, that is, to act as their agent in exercising the member's voting right. Every notice of a meeting must state the member's right to appoint a proxy and, although the articles may require notice of the appointment of a proxy to be given to the company, they may not require more than 48 hours' notice. Proxies need not be members of the company. They have no right to speak at meetings of public companies but may speak in private companies. They are not allowed to vote on a show of hands, but only in regard to a poll vote.

9.3.9.9   Chairman

Although s 370 provides that any member may act as chair, Art 43 of Table A (see above, 9.3.6.1) states that the chairman of the board of directors shall preside. The chairman conducts the meeting and must preserve order and ensure that it complies with the provisions of the companies legislation and the company's articles. He or she may adjourn it with the consent of, or where instructed to do so by, the meeting. The chairman has a casting vote in the case of equality. He or she is under a general duty at all times to act *bona fide* in the interests of the company as a whole, and thus must use his or her vote appropriately.

9.3.9.10   Minutes

Section 382 requires that minutes of all general meetings and directors' meetings must be kept and are regarded as evidence of the proceedings when signed by the chairman.

9.3.10   Majority rule and minority protection

It has been seen how the day to day operation of a company's business is left in the hands of its directors and managers, with shareholders having no direct input into business decisions. Even when the members convene in general meetings, the individual shareholder is subject to the wishes of the majority, as expressed in the passing of appropriate resolutions. In normal circumstances, the minority has no grounds to complain, even though the effect of majority rule may place them in a situation with which they do not agree. Even where the minority shareholders suspect that some wrong has been done to the company, it is not normally open to them to take action. This situation is encapsulated in what is known as the rule in *Foss v Harbottle* (1843) (see above, 9.3.1.3), where individual members were not permitted to institute proceedings against the directors of their company. It was held that if any wrong had been committed, it had been committed against the company, and it was for the company acting through the majority to decide to institute proceedings. A more recent example of the operation of this rule may be seen in *Stein v Blake* (1998), in which the court refused to allow an individual shareholder to pursue an action against a sole director for his alleged misappropriation of the company's property. Although the shareholder did suffer a loss as a consequence of the fall of value in his shares, that loss was a reflection of the loss sustained by the company; consequently, it was for the company, and not the shareholder, to take any action against the director.

It is important to distinguish the various ways in which one or more minority shareholders may take action against the company, the directors or the majority shareholders.

In a personal action, shareholders sue in their own name to enforce personal rights. An example might be where the individuals' voting rights are denied, as in *Pender v Lushington* (1877).

A representative action is a collective action taken where the rights of other shareholders have been affected by the alleged wrongdoing. Once again, if the rights in question are membership rights, the rule in *Foss v Harbottle* does not apply.

A derivative action is the usual form of action, where minority shareholders sue under the fraud on the minority exception to the rule in *Foss v Harbottle* (see below, 9.3.10.1). The claimants sue in their own name, usually in representative form on behalf of themselves and all the other shareholders, except those who are named as defendants. The defendants in the action are, first, the alleged wrongdoers and, secondly, the company itself. As the claimant shareholders are seeking to redress a corporate wrong, they are actually seeking a remedy on the company's behalf. As a result, if the action is successful, the judgment takes the form of an order against the first defendants and in favour of the company as second defendant. With regard to the costs of such an action, it was held in *Wallersteiner v Moir (No 2)* (1975) that where the minority shareholder has reasonable grounds for bringing the action, the company itself should be liable, on the basis that the individual was acting not for himself but for the company.

Particular problems may arise where those in effective control of a company use their power in such a way as either to benefit themselves or cause a detriment to the minority shareholders. In the light of such a possibility, the law has intervened to offer protection to minority shareholders. The source of the protection may be considered in three areas.

9.3.10.1 *Common law – fraud on the minority*

At common law, it has long been established that those controlling the majority of shares are not to be allowed to use their position of control to perpetrate what is known as a fraud on the minority. In such circumstances, the individual shareholder will be able to take legal action in order to remedy their situation. Thus, in *Menier v Hooper's Telegraph Works* (1874), the plaintiff, who was the majority shareholder in the company, had entered into a contract with it to lay a submarine telegraph cable. However, he was approached by another party with a more lucrative offer to lay a cable for them. As a result, he used his majority power to cause his company to abandon its contract, allowing him to pursue the other one. It was held that, in the face of such an abuse of power amounting to fraud, a minority shareholder could pursue a derivative action, the result of which required the majority shareholder to account to the company for any profits made on the second contract. Similarly, in *Cook v Deeks* (1916), directors who were also the majority shareholders of a company negotiated a contract on its behalf. They then took the contract for themselves and used their majority voting power to pass a resolution declaring that the company had no interest in the contract. On an action by the minority shareholder in the company, it was held that the majority could not use their votes to ratify what was a fraud on the minority. The contract belonged to the company in equity and the directors had to account to the company for the profits they made on it. Thus, the minority shareholder was not excluded from benefiting from the contract.

Fraud

The forgoing cases provide clear cut examples of fraudulent activity, but there are less clear cut situations relating to the issue of fraud. What is certain is that mere negligence, in the absence of any more serious allegation of fraud, will not permit a derivative action. Thus, in *Pavlides v Jensen* (1956), a company sold an asbestos mine for £182,000, although a minority shareholder claimed that it was worth £1 million. An action by the minority shareholder failed, on the basis that the directors had done nothing unlawful and, in the absence of any assertion of fraud on their part, any negligence they had shown could have been ratified by the majority of shareholders. The case, therefore, clearly fell within the scope of the rule in *Foss v Harbottle* (1843). However, the meaning of fraud, with specific reference to fraud on the minority, was extended in *Daniels v Daniels* (1977). In this case, a married couple were the directors and majority shareholders in the company. The company bought land for £4,250 and later sold it, at the same price, to the female director. She subsequently sold it for £120,000. A minority shareholder's action was successful, in spite of *Pavlides v Jensen* and the fact that no allegation of fraud was raised against the majority shareholders. In the view of Templeman J:

> If a minority shareholder can sue if there is fraud, I see no reason why they cannot sue where the action of the majority, and the directors, though without fraud, confers some benefit on those directors or majority shareholders.

Thus, it can be seen that the meaning of 'fraud' in this regard has been extended to cover negligence on the part of the majority where the majority themselves benefit from that negligence.

Minority

In normal circumstances, control is the correlation of holding the majority of the voting shares in a company. However, the meaning of 'control' has also been extended by the courts in relation to fraud on the minority. In *Prudential Assurance Co Ltd v Newman Industries Ltd (No 2)* (1980), the chair and vice chair of a public company controlled a substantial, but nonetheless minority, shareholding in that company through another company. They proposed that the public company should buy the share capital of the second company, on the basis of the latter's supposed asset value. It was subsequently alleged that the information provided by the chair and vice chair to the general meeting which approved the purchase was incomplete and misleading. Prudential, which was a minority shareholder in the company, sought to pursue a derivative action on the basis of the common law exceptions to the rule in *Foss v Harbottle*. At first instance, it was held that the action could proceed as, although the chair and vice chair did not constitute majority shareholders, they did control the flow of information to the company's board, its advisers and the general meeting. On that basis, they could be said to control the company. Although the directors' appeal on the substance of the allegation was upheld in the Court of Appeal, the above point was not overruled, and so remains effective.

In relation to voting rights, it was stated in *Greenhalgh v Arderne Cinemas Ltd* (1950) that shareholders were entitled to pursue their own interests when voting. However, there is judicial authority for the suggestion that special restrictions apply to the way in which majority shareholders are permitted to use their voting powers. Thus, in *Clemens v Clemens Bros Ltd* (1976), a majority shareholder was prevented from using her voting power in such a way as would affect the rights of a minority shareholder. Much time has been spent trying to explain, and justify, the decision in *Clemens*, but it should be recognised that the case involved a private, family-run company and its application should be restricted to such a case. It certainly will not be applied in regard to public companies (*Re Astec (BSR) plc* (1998)).

The Law Commission Report, *Shareholder Remedies* (No 246, Cm 3769), which was issued in October 1997, recommended the partial abolition of the rule in *Foss v Harbottle* and its exceptions and the replacement of the existing procedure by a new statutory action.

9.3.10.2   Statutory protection

In circumstances where the minority shareholders disagree with the actions of the majority, but without that action amounting to fraud on the minority, one remedy is simply to leave the company. In a listed public limited company, this procedure is easily achieved by selling the shares held, but things are more difficult in the case of small, private companies. In these quasi-partnership cases, an alternative to bringing a derivative action in the name of the company is to petition to have the company wound up, or to apply to the court for an order to remedy any unfairly prejudicial conduct.

Just and equitable winding up

Section 122(g) of the IA 1986 gives the court the power to wind up a company if it considers it just and equitable to do so. Such an order may be applied for where there is evidence of a lack of probity on the part of some of the members. It may also be used in small private companies to provide a remedy where either there is deadlock on the board or a member is removed from the board altogether or refused a part in the management of the business.

In *Re Yenidje Tobacco Co Ltd* (1916), the company only had two shareholders, who also acted as its directors. After quarrelling, the two directors refused to communicate with one another, except through the company secretary. It was held that the company was essentially a partnership and that, as a partnership would have been wound up in this eventuality, the company should be wound up as well.

In *Re Westbourne Galleries* (1973), a business which two parties had previously carried on as a partnership was transformed into a private limited company. After a time, one of the two original partners was removed from the board of directors of the company. It was held that the removal from the board and the consequential loss of the right to participate in the management of the business were grounds for winding up the company. In reaching his decision in the House of Lords, Lord Wilberforce made the following observations, which go a long way to explain *Clemens v Clemens Bros Ltd* (1976) and have important implications for the operation of actions for unfairly prejudicial conduct under s 459 of the CA 1985 (see below):

> The words ['just and equitable'] are a recognition of the fact that a limited company is more than a mere judicial entity, with a personality in law of its own; that there is room in company law for recognition of the fact that behind it, or amongst it; there are individuals, with rights, expectations and obligations *inter se* which are not necessarily submerged in the company structure ... The 'just and equitable' provision does not, as the respondents suggest, entitle one party to disregard the obligation he assumed by entering a company, nor the court to dispense him from it. It does, as equity always does, enable the court to subject the exercise of legal rights to equitable considerations; considerations, that is, of a personal character arising between one individual and

another, which may make it unjust, or inequitable, to insist on legal rights or to exercise them in a particular way.

It would be impossible, and wholly undesirable, to define the circumstances in which these considerations may arise. Certainly, the fact that a company is a small one, or a private company, is not enough. There are very many of these where the association is a purely commercial one, of which it can safely be said that the basis of association is adequately and exhaustively laid down in the articles. The superimposition of equitable considerations requires something more, which typically may include one, or probably more, of the following elements: (a) an association formed or continued on the basis of a personal relationship, involving mutual confidence – this element will often be found where a pre-existing partnership has been converted into a limited company; (b) an agreement, or understanding, that all, or some (for there may be 'sleeping' members), of the shareholders shall participate in the conduct of the business; (c) restriction on the transfer of the members' interest in the company so that, if confidence is lost, or one member is removed from management, he cannot take out his stake and go elsewhere.

Unfairly prejudicial conduct

Use of the procedure under s 122 of the IA 1986 is likely to have extremely serious consequences for a business. Indeed, the fact that the company has to be wound up will probably result in losses for all the parties concerned. It is much better if some less mutually destructive process can be used to resolve disputes between members of private companies.

Under s 459 of the CA 1985, any member may petition the court for an order on the ground that the affairs of the company are being conducted in a way that is unfairly prejudicial to the interests of some of the members or the members generally. Section 461 gives the court general discretion as to the precise nature and content of any order it makes to remedy the situation. The following case demonstrates the operation and scope of the procedure.

In *Re London School of Electronics* (1986), the petitioner held 25% of the shares in the company LSE. The remaining 75% were held by another company, CTC. Two directors of LSE, who were also directors and the principal shareholders in CTC, diverted students from LSE to CTC. The petitioner claimed that such action deprived him of his share in the potential profit to be derived from those students. It was held that the action was unfairly prejudicial and the court instructed CTC to purchase the petitioner's shares in LSE at a value which was to be calculated as if the students had never been transferred.

In *Re Ringtower Holdings plc* (1989), Gibson J made the following four points in relation to the operation of s 459:

(1) the relevant conduct (of commission or omission) must relate to the affairs of the company of which the petitioners are members;

(2) the conduct must be both prejudicial (in the sense of causing prejudice or harm) to the relevant interests and also unfairly so: conduct may be unfair without being prejudicial or prejudicial without being unfair and in neither case would the section be satisfied;

(3) the test is of unfair prejudice, not of unlawfulness, and conduct may be lawful but unfairly prejudicial;

(4) the relevant interests are the interests of members (including the petitioners) as members, but such interests are not necessarily limited to strict legal rights under the company's constitution, and the court may take into account wider equitable considerations such as any legitimate expectation which a member has which go beyond his legal rights.

The s 459 procedure has also been used in cases where a member has been excluded from exercising a 'legitimate expectation' of participating in the management of a company business (see *Re Bird Precision Bellows Ltd* (1984)). And, in *Re Sam Weller & Sons Ltd* (1990), the court decided that a failure to pay dividends may amount to unfairly prejudicial conduct.

In *Re Elgindata Ltd* (1991), it was held that, depending on the circumstances of the case, serious mismanagement could constitute unfairly prejudicial conduct, although the court would normally be reluctant to make such a finding. On the facts of that case, evidence of mismanagement was found, together with a lack of managerial purposefulness, but it was not sufficient to amount to unfairly prejudicial conduct. However, in *Re Macro (Ipswich) Ltd* (1994), the court found that mismanagement in relation to two companies had been so bad as to warrant the requirement that the majority shareholder and sole director in both companies should buy out the minority. The order was made to the effect that the price to be paid should ignore the current value of the shares and value them as if the mismanagement had not taken place.

Although s 459 is referred to, and tends to be thought of, as a minority shareholders' remedy, it has been held that it is equally open to the majority shareholders to use it under appropriate circumstances (*Re Legal Costs Negotiators Ltd* (1998)).

As stated previously, the powers of the court under s 461 are extremely wide and extend to making 'such orders as it thinks fit for giving relief in respect of the matters complained of'. Section 461(2) provides examples of such orders but expressly states that any such are 'without prejudice to the generality of sub-s (1)'. The examples cited in the section are powers to:

• regulate the conduct of the company's affairs in the future;

• require the company to refrain from doing or continuing an act complained of by the petitioner or to do an act which the petitioner has complained that it omitted to do;

• authorise civil proceedings to be brought in the name and on behalf of the company, by such person or persons and on such terms as the court may direct; and

• provide for the purchase of the shares of any members of the company by other members or by the company itself, and, in the case of a purchase by the company itself, the reduction of the company's capital accordingly.

The ambit of judicial discretion extends to not providing a remedy, even where there has been unfairly prejudicial conduct (*Re Full Cup International Trading Ltd* (1998)).

It should be noted, however, that when the House of Lords came to consider the ambit of s 459 in *O'Neill v Phillips* (1999), it adopted a restraining role in the extent to which the term 'legitimate expectation' should be interpreted in order to permit access to the remedies available under s 459. As Lord Hoffmann put it, the term should not be allowed to 'lead a life of its own' as a way of justifying judicial intervention in business relationships. On the facts of the case, the House of Lords declined to award a remedy under s 459 simply on the basis of a breakdown of a previous relationship of trust and confidence. Rather, it required that prejudicial conduct should be clearly demonstrated, which was not the situation in the immediate case.

Section 459 is an extremely active area of company law and has replaced s 122 of the IA 1986 as the most appropriate mechanism for alleviating the distress suffered by minority shareholders. It is essential, however, to note that the cases considered above all involved economic partnerships which had merely assumed the company legal form as a matter of internal and external convenience. The same outcomes would not be forthcoming in relation to public limited companies. The statutory protections still apply in the case of public companies but it is extremely unlikely that they would be used as freely or as widely as they are in quasi-partnership cases. As evidence of this claim, see *Re A Company 003843* (1986), in which the exclusion of a party from management was held not to be unfairly prejudicial, as the business had not been established on a quasi-partnership basis (see also *Re Astec (BSR) plc* (1998)).

The Law Commission Report, *Shareholder Remedies* (see above, 9.3.10.1), made a number of proposals designed to reduce the number of, and speed up the trials of, such actions. Amongst the recommendations were:

- that there should be greater use of case management powers by the courts;

- that there should be a statutory presumption that, in quasi-partnerships instances, the exclusion of a member from management is unfairly prejudicial conduct justifying the award of a buyout order on a *pro rata* basis;

- that actions under s 459 of the CA 1985 should be subject to a limitation period; and

- that a petitioner should, with the leave of the court, be able to seek the winding up of the company as a form of s 459 of the CA 1985.

In addition, the Report recommended that there should be a new but non-compulsory provision in Table A, providing 'exit rights' for shareholders. This would give shareholders the right to require their fellow shareholders to buy out their shareholding.

9.3.10.3 Investigations

In order for minority shareholders to complain, they must know what is going on in their company. It is part of their situation as minority shareholders, however, that they do not have access to all the information that is available to the directors of the company. As a possible means of remedying this lack of information and, thus, as a means of supporting minority protection, the Department of Trade and Industry has been given extremely wide powers to conduct investigations into the general affairs of companies, their membership and their dealings in their securities. Such powers are framed extremely widely and the courts have accepted the need for such wide powers. As Lord Denning stated in *Norwest Holst Ltd v Secretary of State for Trade* (1978):

> It is because companies are beyond the reach of ordinary individuals that this legislation has been passed so as to enable the Department of Trade to appoint inspectors to investigate the affairs of a company.

Such theoretical power as is possessed by the Secretary of State for Trade and Industry is much diluted in practice by a reluctance on the part of government to finance their use.

Bearing in mind the forgoing caveat, the Secretary of State has the power under s 431 of the CA 1985 to appoint inspectors to investigate the affairs of a company on application by:

- the company itself, after passing an ordinary resolution;
- members holding 10% of the company's issued share capital; or
- 200 or more members.

However, s 431(3) requires that any such application must be supported by such evidence as the Secretary of State may require for the purpose of showing that the applicant has good reason for requiring the investigation. This at least somewhat undermines the whole purpose of the exercise. Shareholders may want an investigation because, although they might suspect that something untoward is going on, they do not know exactly what is happening in their company. Yet, before they can get such an investigation, they have to supply evidence that something is going on, which is exactly the reason why they want the investigation in the first place.

The Secretary of State may also require the applicant to give security of up to £5,000 before appointing inspectors (s 431(4)).

Under s 432 of the CA 1985, the Secretary of State may order such an investigation where:

- the company's affairs have been conducted with intent to defraud creditors, or for an unlawful or fraudulent purpose;
- the company's affairs have been conducted in a manner which is unfairly prejudicial to some of the members;
- the promoters or managers have been found guilty of fraud; or
- the shareholders have not been supplied with proper information.

Once appointed, the investigators have very wide powers. Thus, inspectors appointed under s 431 or 432 of the CA 1985 may also investigate the affairs of any other body corporate which is or has been in the same group, if they consider it necessary (s 433).

The inspectors also have extensive powers to require production of company documents, that is, any information recorded in any form. Information which is not in legible form can be required to be produced in legible form. All officers and agents of the company being investigated and of any related company that is being investigated are required:

- to produce for the inspectors all documents concerning the company or related company which are in their custody or power;

- to attend before the inspectors when required to do so; and

- otherwise to give the inspectors all assistance in connection with the investigation which they are reasonably able to give (s 434(1) of the CA 1985).

The inspectors' powers extend to any person who is or may be in possession of information relating to a matter which the inspectors believe may be relevant to the investigation (s 434(2) of the CA 1985); so, for example, banks may be required to provide information about any clients who are under investigation.

Failure to comply with these requirements renders an individual liable for contempt of the court (s 436 of the CA 1985).

Both during and at the end of an investigation, inspectors are required to report to the Secretary of State (s 437 of the CA 1985). Inspectors may or, if the Secretary of State so directs, must inform the Secretary of State of any matters coming to their knowledge as a result of their investigations (s 437).

The Secretary of State may, if he thinks fit, cause the report to be printed and published (s 437(3)(c)). The Secretary of State has a discretion as to whether to publish the report (*R v Secretary of State for Trade and Industry ex p Lonrho plc* (1989)).

Where the investigation has been carried out on the order of the court under s 432 of the CA 1985, the Secretary of State must provide a copy of any report to the court.

Under s 439 of the CA 1985, the expenses of an investigation are met in the first instance by the Secretary of State. The following persons, however, may be liable to reimburse the Secretary:

- any person who is convicted on a prosecution as a result of the investigation or who is ordered to pay damages or restore property may, in the same proceedings, be ordered to pay the expenses or part of them;

- any company in whose name proceedings are brought is liable to the amount or value or any sums or property recovered as a result of the proceedings;

- any company dealt with by the report where the inspector was not appointed at the Secretary of State's initiative, unless the company was the applicant for the investigation and the Secretary of State directs otherwise; and

- the applicants for the investigation, where the inspector was appointed under s 431 or 442, to the extent that the Secretary of State directs.

In an investigation, individuals cannot only be required to attend; they must answer any questions that are put to them. There is no privilege against self-incrimination and all the evidence given may be used in subsequent proceedings. Section 441 renders the report admissible evidence of the inspectors' opinion in any legal proceedings. In contrast, where a disqualification order is sought under s 8 of the CDDA 1986, it may be treated as 'evidence of any fact stated therein'.

In *R v Seelig* (1991), the Court of Appeal rejected an argument that answers given under s 434 should be inadmissible in criminal proceedings as being oppressive under s 76(2) of the Police and Criminal Evidence Act 1984 (see also *Re London United Investments plc* (1992)).

However, the European Court of Human Rights (ECtHR) has decided that the use in criminal proceedings of evidence obtained by inspectors under their compulsory powers is an infringement of Art 6(1) of the European Convention on Human Rights (*Saunders v United Kingdom* (1996)). Even before the Human Rights Act 1998 was introduced, the Secretary of State had made it clear that, in light of the *Saunders* decision in the ECtHR, the prosecution would no longer rely on evidence compelled from the accused under the mandatory powers conferred on company inspectors. However, it has been decided subsequently that evidence acquired through the use of such powers of compulsion can still be used in actions taken in relation to the CDDA 1986. The reason for such a conclusion, and the means of distinguishing *Saunders*, was that such actions are not criminal in nature (*R v Secretary of State for Trade and Industry ex p McCormick* (1998)). It remains to be seen whether such a fine distinction can survive the increased emphasis on human rights ushered in by the Human Rights Act 1998.

On receipt of the final report of the investigation, the Secretary of State may:

- institute criminal proceedings against any person believed to be guilty of offences;

- petition to have the company wound up under s 124 of the IA 1986;

- petition for an order under s 459;

- bring a civil action in the name of the company against any party; or

- apply to the courts to have any director disqualified from acting as a director in future, under s 8 of the CDDA 1986.

In addition to the above investigation into the affairs of a company, the Secretary of State has the power, under s 442, to appoint inspectors to investigate the ownership and control of companies. In this regard, the general powers of the inspector are the same as those relating to an investigation into the affairs of the company (s 443). Additionally, however, an inspector may require documents and evidence from all persons who are or have been, or whom the inspector has reasonable cause to believe to be or to have been financially interested in, the success or failure of the company or related company. This provision also applies to those able to control or materially to influence the policy of the company or related company (s 444).

Where there is difficulty in finding out the relevant facts about the ownership of particular shares, the court may impose restrictions on those shares (s 454). These restrictions, commonly known as 'freezing orders', provide that:

- any transfer of the securities or, in the case of unissued securities, any transfer of the right to be issued with securities, and any issue of them, will be void;

- voting rights may not be exercised in respect of those securities;

- no further securities shall be issued in right of those securities or in pursuance of any offer made to the holder of them;

- except in a liquidation, no payment shall be made of any sums due from the company on the securities.

Investigations may also be instigated into directors' share dealings under s 446 of the CA 1985, and into insider dealing under s 177 of the Financial Services Act 1986.

The forgoing has focused on full scale investigation, but it has to be recognised that such investigations can be not only extremely time consuming, but also extremely expensive, not to mention potentially very damaging to the company that is the object of the investigation. In the light of these patent disadvantages of a full investigation, a possible alternative, and perhaps a precursor to a full investigation, exists in the investigation of a company's documents, supported by the power to require an explanation of such documents, where necessary. These investigations are carried out by officials of the Department of Trade and Industry.

Thus, under s 447 of the CA 1985, the Secretary of State may require a company, or any person who is in possession of them, to produce specified documents. Section 447 also empowers the Secretary of State to take copies of the documents and to require the person who produces them, or any other person who is a present or past officer or employee of the company, to provide an explanation of them.

The Secretary of State may obtain a search warrant, enabling the police to enter and search premises and take possession of documents (s 448 of the CA 1985). Any information obtained under s 447 of the CA 1985 may not be published or disclosed, except for specified purposes set out in s 449 of that Act, including criminal proceedings and proceedings for a disqualification order under the CDDA 1986. Any company officer who destroys, mutilates or falsifies a document relating to the company's property or affairs is guilty of an offence (s 450 of the CA 1985), and any person who makes a materially false statement in relation to a requirement under s 447, whether recklessly or deliberately, is also liable to a criminal charge.

Powers under s 447 will be significantly increased when the C(AICE)A 2004 comes into force (see 9.3.14, below).

Given the extent of the powers possessed by the Secretary of State and the investigators appointed by him, it is a little ironic, if not symptomatic of the failures in the system of company investigations, that some of the most famous cases of the early 1970s, that is, *Re Pergamon Press Ltd* (1971) and *Maxwell v Department of Trade and Industry* (1974), involved the late, and generally unlamented, publishing mogul,

Robert Maxwell. Maxwell's death in 1991 revealed the corruption and criminal illegality on which his business empire was based and had been sustained. The blameworthy part of the Maxwell saga was, however, that his corrupt behaviour was an open secret that should have been investigated before it reached its inevitably disastrous conclusion. The manner in which Maxwell used the threat of libel actions to ensure his immunity from criticism is also to be regretted, but is a matter beyond the scope of this book.

9.3.11   Winding up and administration orders

Winding up and administrative orders are alternative mechanisms for dealing with companies whose business activity is in a state of potentially terminal decline.

9.3.11.1   *Winding up*

Winding up, or liquidation, is the process whereby the life of the company is terminated. It is the formal and strictly regulated procedure whereby the business is brought to an end and the company's assets are realised and distributed to its creditors and members. The procedure is governed by the IA 1986 and may be divided into three distinct categories, which are as follows:

* *Members' voluntary winding up*

   This takes place when the directors of a company are of the opinion that the company is solvent, that is, capable of paying off its creditors. The directors are required to make a statutory declaration to that effect and the actual liquidation process is initiated by a special resolution of the company.

   Section 89 of the IA 1986 requires that the directors of the company which wishes to go into voluntary winding up must make a declaration that the company will be able to pay its debts within 12 months from the date of the commencement of the winding up. If the directors make a false declaration, they may be criminally liable under s 89(4).

   A company may be wound up voluntarily in the following ways:

   ○ where an event takes place, which the articles provide should bring about the liquidation of the company, then the members need only pass an ordinary resolution;

   ○ where the company is to be wound up for any other reason, a special resolution is required; except

   ○ where the company's liabilities make it advisable to wind up, in which case an extraordinary resolution has to be passed.

   On the appointment of a liquidator, all directors' powers cease, although the liquidator may continue to employ them. On appointment, the liquidator proceeds to wind up the affairs of the company. When this is achieved, the liquidator calls a final meeting of the members and presents a report to members of how the procedure has been carried out. The liquidator must also send a copy of the report and a notice that the final meeting has been held to the registrar of companies. Three months after registration, the company is deemed to be dissolved and no longer exists.

If at any time during the winding up process the liquidator forms the opinion that the company will not be able to pay its debts in full, then a meeting of the company's creditors must be called and the winding up will proceed as a creditors' winding up.

- *Creditors' voluntary winding up*

This occurs when the directors of the company do not believe that it will be able to pay off its debts and thus do not make the necessary declaration required for a members' voluntary winding up. The liquidation is initiated by an extraordinary resolution of the company. Within 14 days of the passing of the resolution to wind up the company, a meeting of its creditors has to be called, at which the directors are required to present a full statement of the company's affairs together with a list of its creditors and an estimation of how much is owed to them. The creditors' meeting may require the formation of a committee of inspection, consisting of representatives of the creditors and the members. The purpose of the committee is to assist the liquidator and it does away with the need to call full creditors' meetings to get approval for particular actions. In the event of any disagreement as to who should act as liquidator, the nomination of the creditors prevails over that of the members.

As in a members' voluntary winding up, once appointed, the liquidator proceeds to wind the company up and on completion of that task calls meetings of both the members and creditors to account for his actions in so doing. Once again, a copy of the account has to be sent to the registrar of companies and, three months after registration, the company is deemed to be dissolved.

- *Compulsory winding up*

This is a winding up ordered by the court under s 122 of the IA 1986. Although there are seven distinct grounds for such a winding up, one of which, depending upon just and equitable grounds, has already been considered (see above, 9.3.10.2), the most common reason for the winding up of a company is its inability to pay its debts. Section 123 provides that if a company with a debt exceeding £750 fails to pay it within three weeks of receiving a written demand, then it is deemed unable to pay its debts.

On the presentation of a petition to wind up a company compulsorily, the court will normally appoint the Official Receiver to be the company's provisional liquidator. The Official Receiver will require the present or past officers, or indeed employees of the company, to prepare a statement of the company's affairs. This statement must reveal:

o particulars of the company's assets and liabilities;

○ names and addresses of its creditors;

○ any securities held by the creditors (fixed or floating charges) and the dates on which they were granted; and

○ any other information which the Official Receiver may require.

After his appointment, the Official Receiver calls meetings of the company's members and creditors in order to select a liquidator to replace him and to select a liquidation committee if required. Once again, in the event of disagreement, the choice of the creditors prevails.

Section 142 of the IA 1986 states that the functions of the liquidator are 'to secure that the assets of the company are got in, realised and distributed to the company's creditors and, if there is a surplus, to the persons entitled to it'. Once the liquidator has performed these functions, he must call a final meeting of the creditors, at which he gives an account of the liquidation and secures his release from the creditors. Notice of the final meeting has to be submitted to the registrar of companies and, three months after that date, the company is deemed to be dissolved.

9.3.11.2 Order of payment of company debts

The assets of a company being wound up are to be applied in the following order:

- *Secured creditors holding fixed charges*

  This category of creditor is entitled to have their debt met from the assets before any other payment is made. If, however, the security is insufficient to meet the full amount owed, then the creditor ranks merely as an unsecured creditor for the balance.

- *Expenses incurred in the winding up*

  Thus, liquidators are entitled to recover their remuneration plus the costs of the winding up.

- *Preferential creditors who all rank equally*

  Section 175 of and Sched 6 to the IA 1986 set out what are to be treated as preferred payments and these are essentially wages of employees together with all accrued holiday pay (£800 maximum).

  The Enterprise Act 2002 removed the previous Crown preference in relation to moneys owed in relation to national insurance, income tax and VAT. These now lose their priority and stand as unsecured debts.

  In removing Crown preference, it would appear that the Enterprise Act 2002 ensured that more potential assets would be made available to holders of floating charges who stand next in terms of priority. However, in order to improve the position of unsecured creditors, the Act also introduced the concept of ring-fencing some of a company's assets for the exclusive use of unsecured creditors. Under the new regime, s 176A of the IA 1986, which applies to floating charges created after

15 September 2003, a liquidator, administrator or receiver is required to make a prescribed part of the company's net assets available for the satisfaction of unsecured debts before any money can be paid in satisfaction of a floating charge. Currently, the procedure does not apply if the company's assets are less than £10,000; thereafter, the prescribed amount is set at 50% of the first £50,000 and 20% of any assets above that value up to a maximum of £600,000.

- *Creditors secured by a floating charge*

  See above, 9.3.5.7.

- *Ordinary unsecured creditors*

  This category is the one that stands to lose most. It comprises the customers and trade creditors of the company. As creditors, they rank equally but, as is likely, if the company cannot fully pay its debts, they will receive an equal proportion of what is available.

- *The deferred debts of the company*

  These are debts owed to the members as members, for example, dividends declared but not paid.

- *Members' capital*

  After the debts of the company are paid, the members are entitled to the return of their capital, depending on, and in proportion to, the provisions of the articles of association.

Any remaining surplus is distributed amongst the members, subject to the rights given in the articles of association or other documents.

9.3.11.3   Administration orders

Administration, as a means of safeguarding the continued existence of business enterprises in financial difficulties, was first introduced in the IA 1986. The aim of the administration order is to save the company, or at least the business, as a going concern by taking control of the company out of the hands of its directors and placing it in the hands of an administrator. Alternatively, the procedure is aimed at maximising the realised value of the business assets.

Once an administration order had been issued, it was no longer possible to commence winding up proceedings against the company, or enforce charges, retention of title clauses or even hire-purchase agreements against the company. This major advantage was in no small way undermined by the fact that, under the previous regime, an administration order could not be made after a company had begun the liquidation process. Since companies are required to inform any person who is entitled to appoint a receiver of the fact that the company is applying for an administration order, it was open to any secured creditor to enforce their rights and to forestall the administration procedure. This would cause the secured creditor no harm, since their debt would more than likely be covered by the security, but it could well lead to the end of the company as a going concern.

The Enterprise Act 2002 introduced a new scheme, which limited the powers of floating charge holders to appoint administrative receivers, whose function had been essentially to secure the interest of the floating charge holders who had appointed them rather than the interests of the general creditors. By virtue of the Enterprise Act 2002, which amends the previous provisions of the IA 1986, floating charge holders no longer have the right to appoint administrative receivers, but must now make use of the administration procedure as provided in that Act. As compensation for this loss of power, the holders of floating charges are given the right to appoint the administrator of their choice.

The function of the administrator is to:

- rescue the company as a going concern;

- achieve a better result for the company's creditors *as a whole* than would be likely if the company were to be wound up; or

- realise the value of the property in order to make a distribution to the secured or preferential creditors.

The administrator is only permitted to pursue the third option where:

- he or she thinks it is not reasonably practicable to rescue the company as a going concern;

- he or she thinks that he or she cannot achieve a better result for the creditors as a whole than would be likely if the company were to be wound up; and

- he or she does not unnecessarily harm the interests of the creditors of the company as a whole.

An application to the court for an administration order may be made by a company, the directors of a company, or any of its creditors but, in addition, the Enterprise Act 2002 allows the appointment of an administrator without the need to apply to the court for approval. Such 'out of court' applications can be made by the company or its directors, but may also be made by any floating charge holder.

The company, or its directors, will be permitted to appoint an administrator only where:

- the company has not been in administration in the previous 12 months;

- the company either cannot, or is likely to become unable to, pay its debts;

- there is no existing application for either winding up or the administration of the company and the company is not in the process of liquidation; or

- no administrative receiver has already been appointed.

Floating charge holders may appoint the administrator of their choice subject to the following conditions:

- they have a qualifying floating charge over the whole or substantially the whole of the company's property;

- the floating charge is enforceable, that is, the circumstances are such that the creditor is in a position to seek to enforce their security;

- the floating charge holder has notified other such charge holders who may have priority over their own claim. This allows the prior chargee to appoint their own preferred administrator;

- the company is not in the process of liquidation; or

- neither a receiver nor an administrator is already in position.

The consequences of administration are that:

- winding up orders are either suspended (if the administrator is appointed by a floating charge holder) or dismissed (if the appointment is by order of the court);

- no further procedures to have the company wound up may be pursued whilst the administration is in effect;

- creditors are prevented from taking action to recover debts without the approval of the administrator; and

- all company documents must state that the company is in the process of administration.

The process of administration requires the administrator to:

- notify the registrar of companies and all creditors of his or her appointment;

- require a statement of the company's affairs to be produced by the company's officers and employees, giving details of the company's assets, liabilities, details of creditors and any security they might hold;

- produce, within eight weeks, a statement of proposed actions to be delivered to the registrar and all creditors of the company; and

- arrange a meeting of creditors to consider the proposals of the administrator. The meeting may modify the proposals only with the consent of the administrator.

During the administration process, the administrator has the powers to:

- do anything necessary for the management of the company;

- remove or appoint directors;

- pay out moneys to secured or preferential creditors *without the need to seek the approval of the court*;

- pay out moneys to unsecured creditors *with the approval of the court*;

- take custody of all property belonging to the company; and

- dispose of company property. This power includes property which is subject to both fixed and floating charges, which may be disposed of without the consent of the charge holders, although they retain first call against any money realised by such a sale.

The administration period is usually 12 months, although this may be extended by six months with the approval of the creditors, or longer with the approval of the court. When the administrator concludes that the purpose of his or her appointment has been achieved, a notice to this effect is sent to the creditors, the court and the Companies Registry. Such a notice terminates the administrator's appointment. If the administrator forms the opinion that none of the purposes of the administration can be achieved, the court should be informed, and it will consider ending the appointment. Creditors can always challenge the actions of the administrator through the courts.

9.3.12   Insider dealing

It is essential to distinguish between the nominal value of a share and its market value, that is, what it is actually worth. Whilst the former is fixed, the latter is free to fluctuate with demand. The fluctuation in the exchange value of shares in listed public limited companies is readily apparent in the constantly changing value of shares on the stock exchange. It is, of course, the fact that share prices do fluctuate in this way that provides the possibility of individuals making large profits, or losses, in speculating in shares. Speculation, which is not unlike gambling, refers to the purchase of shares in the hope of a quick capital gain and should be distinguished from investment, which refers to the purchase of shares as a longer term basis for income as well as capital gain. The stock exchange is insistent on its role as a mechanism for facilitating investment rather than speculation but, nonetheless, that does not prevent it from being a mechanism for a huge amount of such short term speculation. The question remains to be asked, however, as to what actually causes the fluctuation in share prices. The obvious answer, that it is the result of the working out of the law of supply and demand, merely begs the question and prompts the further question as to why particular shares should be in more demand than others. A more fundamental answer to the original question may be located in the nature of the share itself.

It will be recalled that one of the essential attributes of the share is the right it provides to participate in the profits generated by the company. At least at a very basic level, the value of shares may be seen as a reflection of the underlying profitability of the company: the more profitable the company, the greater its potential to pay dividends and the higher the value of its shares. In such a simplified model, the function of the market is to act in a rational way to ascribe a fitting capital value to the business undertaking of the company. However, it will be appreciated that the accuracy of any such valuation relies on the information provided intermittently in the company's published accounts. Once the actual performance of a company is revealed in its accounts and statements, the market value of its share capital will be adjusted in the market to reflect its true worth: either upwards, if it has done better than expected; or downwards, if it has done worse than was expected. It will be seen, therefore, that the accuracy of any current valuation is always uncertain in the face of a shortage of accurate information relating to the company's current performance, which itself may fluctuate considerably over time.

The market's valuation of the company's performance and, consequently, the market value of the individual share in that company can never be completely accurate. Speculators, in particular, look to make large capital gains by capitalising on large disparities between performance and share value through buying shares that are currently undervalued and selling them at a profit when the market adjusts the share value in line with performance. It has actually been claimed that the distorting effect of speculation is so strong that it undermines the rational operation of the market. Consequently, share prices are described as assuming a 'random walk' pattern; that is, there is no way of accurately predicting which direction they will go in, rather like a drunk man staggering back from the pub. It might be thought that the short term success of many internet '.com' companies before their ultimate collapse undermined the forgoing analysis, in that very few of them had generated any profit to sustain the value of the many millions of pounds they had been valued at. The answer to this apparent anomaly is that, in those cases, individuals were investing in the prospects of future large scale profits, not to mention the immediate short term capital gains to be made as interest in such shares intensified.

Substantial capital gains can also be made as a result of a takeover bid, for it is usual for the predator company to pay a premium, over and above the market value of the shares in the company it has targeted for takeover. Once again, speculators may buy shares in companies which they think will be likely targets of a takeover bid, in the hope of receiving such premium payoffs.

To reiterate, it can be seen that share valuation depends upon accurate information as to a company's performance or its prospects. To that extent, knowledge is money, but such price sensitive/affected information is usually only available to the individual share purchaser on a *post hoc* basis, that is, after the company has issued its information to the public. If, however, the share buyer could gain prior access to such information, then they would be in the position to predict the way in which share prices would be likely to move and, consequently, to make substantial profits. Such dealing in shares, on the basis of access to unpublished price sensitive information, provides the basis for what is referred to as 'insider dealing' and is governed by Pt V of the CJA 1993.

9.3.12.1 The Criminal Justice Act 1993

Section 52 of the CJA 1993 sets out the three distinct offences of insider dealing:

- An individual is guilty of insider dealing if they have information as an insider and deal in price-affected securities on the basis of that information.

- An individual who has information as an insider will also be guilty of insider dealing if they encourage another person to deal in price-affected securities in relation to that information.

- An individual who has information as an insider will also be guilty of insider dealing if they disclose it to anyone other than in the proper performance of their employment, office or profession.

It should be noted that s 52(3) of the CJA 1993 makes it clear that any dealing must be carried out on a regulated market or through a professional intermediary.

The CJA 1993 goes on to explain the meaning of some of the above terms. Thus, s 54 defines which securities are covered by the legislation. These are set out in the second Schedule to the Act and specifically include: shares; debt securities, for example, debentures; warrants; options; futures; and contracts for differences (the last do not involve the exchange of the security but merely require one party to pay or receive any change in value of the security in question).

'Dealing' is defined in s 55 as, amongst other things, acquiring or disposing of securities, whether as an principal or agent, or agreeing to acquire securities.

Who are insiders and what amounts to insider information are clearly crucial questions, and s 56 defines 'inside information' as:

- relating to particular securities;

- being specific or precise;

- not having been made public; and

- being likely to have a significant effect on the price of the securities (this latter definition applies the meaning of 'price sensitive' and 'price affected').

Section 57 of the CJA 1993 goes on to provide that a person has information as an insider only if they know that it is inside information and they have it from an inside source. The section then considers what might be described as primary and secondary insiders. The first category of primary insiders covers those who get the inside information directly, through either:

- being a director, employee or shareholder of an issuer of securities; or

- having access to the information by virtue of their employment, office or profession.

Significantly, the term 'insider' is extended to the secondary category of anyone who receives, either directly or indirectly, any inside information from anyone who is a primary insider. Thus, anyone receiving information from an insider, even second or third hand, is to be treated as an insider. It is important to note that if the primary insider merely recommends that the second party should buy shares, without passing on information, then, although the tipper has committed an offence under s 52(2) in recommending the shares, the tippee does not commit any offence under the CJA 1993 because they have not received any specific information, as required by s 56.

The requirement that information must not have been made public is dealt with in s 58 of the CJA 1993, although not exhaustively. Of interest is the fact that information is treated as public even if it can only be acquired through the exercise of skill or expertise.

Schedule 1 to the CJA 1993 sets out special defences for those who act in good faith in the course of their jobs as market makers, but perhaps of more importance are the general defences set out in s 53 of the Act. These require the individual concerned to show one of three things:

- that they did not expect the dealing to result in a profit attributable to the price sensitive information; or

- that they reasonably believed that the information had been previously disclosed widely enough to ensure that those taking part in the dealing would be prejudiced by not having the information; or

- that they would have done what they did even if they did not have the information.

Remembering that the legislation applies to individuals who are seeking to avoid losses, as well as to those seeking to make gains, an example of the last defence listed above would be where an individual who had access to inside information nonetheless had to sell shares in order to realise money to pay a pressing debt because they had no other funds to pay it.

The seriousness of the offence is highlighted by penalties available to the courts in the event of a conviction for insider dealing. Thus, on summary conviction, an individual who is found guilty of insider dealing is liable to a fine not exceeding the current statutory maximum and/or maximum of six months' imprisonment. On indictment, the penalty is an unlimited fine and/or a maximum of seven years' imprisonment.

9.3.12.2   *The reality of insider dealing*

From the forgoing exposition of the CJA 1993, it can be seen that insider dealing is viewed as a very serious offence, with severe penalties for those found guilty of engaging in it. However, doubts have to be expressed about how the law actually operates in practice in order to control the activities of insiders. The fact that insider dealing continues to be carried out is reflected in the 'spike' that quite often appears in the graph of share prices just before a takeover bid is announced. This spike reflects a sudden, and otherwise inexplicable, rise in market value of the shares in question and suggests, if it cannot categorically prove, that some people have been trading on the basis of inside information about the takeover. The stock exchange employs a small body of people to monitor and investigate such abnormal share price rises, and they pass any doubtful cases to the Department of Trade and Industry for further investigation (see below).

When legislation against insider dealing was first introduced in the CA 1980, there was no provision for any independent investigation of suspected dealing. This shortcoming was remedied, at least to a degree, by the provision of s 177 of the Financial Services Act 1986, which gives the Secretary of State for Trade and Industry power to appoint inspectors to carry out investigations into suspected insider dealing. The powers of any such inspectors appointed are considerable (see above, 9.3.10.3).

It has been claimed that insider dealing is a 'victimless crime', to the extent that no one is forced to sell or buy shares that they would not have bought or sold in any case. Take, for example, a company that is the target of a takeover bid. The insider knows about the bid and, equally, knows that if they buy shares before the bid becomes public knowledge, they will stand to make a considerable profit on any shares bought. It is quite clear that the possessor of inside information will benefit from that knowledge, but the question is as to who actually loses in the share dealing. One argument is that the sellers of the shares are in no way coerced into selling at the prevailing price, so they get what they want and, therefore, have no grounds for complaint. From this perspective, the only shareholder who could complain about losing would be the one who was mistakenly persuaded to sell by the market activity generated by the insider dealing. Some have even gone as far as to suggest that the profits derived from insider dealing are a legitimate perk of those in the know, and that they cut down the need to pay such people even higher salaries than those that they already enjoy.

There is, however, an overpowering argument against the practice of insider dealing, and not just in the fact that it unjustly rewards particular individuals. Perhaps more importantly, in so doing, it undermines the faith in, and the integrity of, the whole investment mechanism. In a system designed to encourage the concept of shareholder democracy, how can ordinary individuals be persuaded to invest in shares if they are faced with the reality of insider dealing?

9.3.13 Electronic communications

No treatment of company law can be considered complete without reference to the Companies Act 1985 (Electronic Communications) Order 2000 (SI 2000/3373), but, as its consequences are so disparate, it is better to postpone any mention of it until a general understanding of at least some of the areas on which it impacts have been considered. As its title suggests, the Electronic Communications Order recognises the impact of the computer revolution and the Internet on communication by allowing electronic communication to replace what were formerly requirements for paper-based systems. The Order applies to communication between the company and the Registrar of Companies, the company and its member, and the members and the company. Although there are many consequential amendments to the Companies Act, the most significant alterations recognise electronic statements of compliance as equivalent to statutory declarations. Thus, for example, it applies in relation to statements regarding:

- company registration;

- company re-registration;

- public companies' share capital requirements; and

- the provision of financial assistance for the purchase of shares in private companies.

The Order also allows companies to issue their annual reports electronically. This can be done by either emailing individual members or, if the members agree, placing them on a web page for members to access on notification by email. Similar arrangements can be made with regard to the notification of company meetings and the appointment of proxies.

Not only does the Order alter Table A as regards future companies, but it also provides that existing companies can take advantage of its provisions, even if there is anything contrary in their existing articles.

9.3.14   The Companies (Audit, Investigations and Community Enterprise) Act 2004

The C(AICE)A 2004 received royal assent in October 2003. Although its provisions will only be brought into effect over an extended period of time through regulations, its effect will be significant in the extent to which it will strengthen the auditing and company investigation regimes, in the hope of ensuring confidence in the UK corporate framework. Its major provisions relate to the following matters.

9.3.14.1   Independence of auditors

One aim of the Act is to improve the reliability of financial reporting and the *independence of auditors and auditor regulation*. This is to be achieved by:

- requiring the professional accountancy bodies that supervise auditors to sign up to independent auditing standards, monitoring and disciplinary procedures;

- strengthening the role of the Financial Reporting Review Panel (FRRP) in enforcing good accounting and reporting, by giving it new powers to require documents and broadening its scope;

- allowing the Inland Revenue to pass information about suspect accounts to the FRRP; and

- giving the Government the power to require large and quoted companies to publish details of non-audit services provided by their auditors.

9.3.14.2   Powers of auditors

The Act also significantly strengthens the power of auditors. Under s 389A of the CA 1985, a company's auditors are currently entitled to require from the *company's officers* such information and explanations as they think necessary for the performance of their duties as auditors. It is a criminal offence for an officer of the company to provide misleading, false or deceptive information or explanations. However, it is not an offence for them to fail to provide any information or explanation that the auditors require of them. Under the C(AICE)A 2004:

- s 8 will make it a criminal offence to fail to provide information or explanations required by the auditor;

- s 8 also entitles the auditor to require information and explanations from a wider group of people than merely the officers of the company. Consequently, employees may now be subject to the auditor's authority;

- s 8(4) makes it an offence for a parent company to fail to take all steps reasonably open to it to obtain the information or explanations which the auditor has required it to obtain from its non-GB subsidiary and those associated with it. The offence applies also to any officer of the company who knowingly and wilfully authorises or permits the failure; and

- s 9 will require that directors' reports contain a statement that the directors are not aware of relevant information which has not been disclosed to the company's auditors. The directors will be placed under the duty to ensure that they have taken all the steps they should have taken as directors to make themselves aware of such information and to establish that the auditors are aware of it. It will be a criminal offence to issue a false statement. The stated purpose of s 9 is to ensure that each director will have to think hard about whether there is any information that they know about or could ascertain, which is needed by the auditors in connection with preparing their report.

9.4.13.3 *Powers of investigation*

The Secretary of State has a range of powers under companies legislation to investigate the affairs of a company and related matters (see above, 13.11.3). The vast majority of company investigations exercise powers under s 447 of the CA 1985. The C(AICE)A 2004 strengthens those powers, without changing the basis for inspections or making any change of substance to the grounds for an investigation. Changes have been made to:

- give s 447 investigators a general power to require relevant information and strengthen their powers to require relevant documents (s 21);

- provide statutory immunity from liability for breach of confidence where people voluntarily provide information to members of the Department of Trade and Industry's Companies Investigations Branch (CIB) in certain circumstances (s 22);

- give inspectors and investigators a power to require entry to premises used for company business, and a right to remain there for the purposes of the investigation (s 23); and

- provide a more effective sanction for non-compliance with s 447 requirements, and provide a sanction for non-compliance with the power to require entry to premises (s 24).

9.3.14.4   Directors' indemnity

The C(AICE)A 2004 also relaxes the current prohibition on companies indemnifying directors against liability, and permits companies to pay directors' defence costs as they are incurred.The Act requires disclosure in the directors' report by companies that indemnify directors. Shareholders will also have the right to inspect any indemnification agreement.

9.3.14.5   Community interest companies

Part 2 of the C(AICE)A 2004 makes provision for the establishment of a new corporate vehicle, the 'community interest company' (CIC), intended to make it simpler and more convenient to establish a business whose profits and assets are to be used for the benefit of the community. There will be a statutory 'lock' on the profits and financial assets of CICs and, where a CIC is limited by shares, power to impose a 'cap' on any dividend. Companies wishing to become a CIC are required to pass a community interest test and to produce an annual report showing that they have contributed to community interest aims. A new, independent regulator will be responsible for approving the registration of CICs and ensuring they comply with their legal requirements. He or she will have powers to obtain information from CICs, to appoint, suspend or remove CIC directors, to make orders in respect of the property of CICs, to apply to the court for a CIC to be wound up and to set the dividend cap.

9.4   Employment Law

Most businesses employ a workforce of some size, no matter how limited. This section examines the nature of the employment relationship.

9.4.1   Contract of Employment

The relationship between employee and employer is governed by the contract of employment, which forms the basis of the employee's employment rights. The distinction between contracts of employment and those of self-employment is of fundamental importance, because only 'employees' qualify for employment rights such as unfair dismissal, redundancy payments, minimum notice on termination, etc. Wider protection is provided under the discrimination and equal pay legislation, which applies to both a contract of service and a contract 'personally to execute any work or labour', which in effect includes some self-employed relationships. The Health and Safety at Work etc Act 1974 is also broader in scope, as it protects employees, the self-employed and, indeed, the general public. It is, therefore, important to understand the meaning of the term 'employee'. Employees are employed under a contract of employment or contract of service, whereas self-employed persons, that is, independent contractors, are employed under a contract for services. The following example assists in distinguishing between employees and independent contractors.

If A employs a plumber to install his washing machine, A does not become an employer, as the plumber is an independent contractor, although a firm of plumbers may employ him or her. If A was to employ a nanny, then, as a general rule, he or she would become A's employee and would, therefore, be responsible for such things as deductions from his or her salary (for example, tax, national insurance, etc); as well as this, the nanny would benefit from employment protection rights.

There is very limited guidance in the legislation as to what is meant by the term 'employee'. However, s 230 of the Employment Rights Act (ERA) 1996 offers the following definition:

(1) In this Act, 'employee' means an individual who has entered into or works under (or, where the employment has ceased, worked under) a contract of employment.

(2) In this Act, 'contract of employment' means a contract of service or apprenticeship, whether express or implied, and (if it is express) whether oral or in writing.

Tests have been developed through the case law for determining whether a person is an employee and, therefore, employed under a contract of service or employment, or whether he or she is self-employed and engaged under a contract for services. (See *Chung and Shun Sing Lee v Construction and Engineering Co Ltd* (1990), in which Lord Griffith argued that the question of employee status was largely one of fact.) These enable the courts to distinguish between the two types of contract and, clearly, s 230 should be read in the light of those tests. Although, for the majority of people at work, there is no problem in deciding whether they are employees or independent contractors, there may be occasions on which the distinction is not clear-cut. These tests will be considered in chronological order since, although the early tests are still of relevance, the multiple test and the mutuality of obligations test are now at the forefront, should the question of employment status arise.

9.4.1.1 Control test

In applying the control test, the question to be asked is does the person who is to be regarded as the employer control the employee or servant? Control extends to not just what the employee does, but how it is done. If the answer is in the affirmative, there is an employer/employee relationship. The reasoning behind this question was that an independent contractor might be told what to do, but probably had discretion as to how to do the work. However, in the modern workplace, this question has become a little unreal and, therefore, has fallen into decline as the sole test applied by the courts, although it is still a vital element in the multiple test.

In *Walker v Crystal Palace Football Club* (1910), Walker was employed as a professional footballer with the defendant club. It became necessary to decide whether he was employed under a contract of service or a contract for services. It was held that he was employed under a contract of service (or employment) because he was subject to the control of his master in the form of training, discipline and method of play.

One problem in applying the control test was that, if interpreted strictly, it resulted in skilled and professional people being categorised as independent contractors, which, at a time when there were limited employment rights, was not a problem for them, but proved to be a problem for persons injured as a result of their negligence at work, as such a person would be unable to rely on the principle of vicarious liability to claim against the employer. As a result, the courts saw fit to develop another test which would reflect this development in the workplace by recognising that skilled and professional people could also be employees.

9.4.1.2   Integration test

This test was developed to counter the deficiencies of the control test. In applying the integration test, the question to be asked is how far is the servant/employee integrated into the employer's business? If it can be shown that the employee is fully integrated into the employer's business, then there is in existence a contract of employment. It is clear that an independent contractor does not become part of the employer's business. The use of this test was confirmed in *Stevenson Jordan and Harrison Ltd v MacDonald and Evans* (1952), in which Lord Denning expressed the following view:

> One feature which seems to run through the instances is that, under a contract of service, a man is employed as part of the business and his work is done as an integral part of the business; whereas, under a contract for services, his work, although done for the business, is not integrated into it but is only accessory to it.

In *Whittaker v Minister of Pensions and National Insurance* (1967), Whittaker was employed as a trapeze artist in a circus. She claimed industrial injury benefit as a result of an accident sustained at work. Initially, this was refused, on the basis that she was not an employee of the circus. She was, however, able to show that, for at least half of her working day, she was expected to undertake general duties other than trapeze work, such as acting as usherette and working in the ticket office. It was held that her general duties showed that she was an integral part of the business of running a circus and was, therefore, employed under a contract of employment.

Although this test developed due to the impracticalities of the control test, it never gained popularity with the courts. It was successfully used in cases such as *Cassidy v Ministry of Health* (1951) to establish that highly skilled workers, such as doctors and engineers, can be employed under a contract of employment, and may even have a type of duel employment, where in some circumstances they are to be regarded as employees and in others they are seen as self-employed. The control test was clearly inapplicable to these situations. The need to develop a test which would suit all circumstances became of paramount importance. Employers were able to avoid various aspects of the statutory provisions by categorising employees as self-employed when, in reality, this was not necessarily the case, but at that time there was no test to cover these situations. For example, an employer could avoid tax and national insurance provisions, as well as liability for accidents caused by these persons whilst going about their jobs. As a result, the following test was developed.

9.4.1.3   Multiple test

The multiple test is, by definition, much wider than either the control test or the integration test. It requires numerous factors to be taken into account in deciding whether a person is employed under a contract of service or a contract for services. It arose out of the case of *Ready Mixed Concrete (South East) Ltd v Minister of Pensions and National Insurance* (1968). RMC previously employed a number of lorry drivers under a contract of employment. The company then decided to dismiss the drivers as employees. However, it allowed them to purchase their vehicles, which had to be painted in RMC's colours. The contract between the drivers and the company stated that the drivers were independent contractors. The Minister of Pensions, who believed that the drivers were employees and, therefore, that RMC was liable for national insurance contributions, disputed this. There were a number of stipulations under the contract. The drivers had to wear the company's uniform and the company could require repairs to be carried out to the vehicles at the drivers' expense. The vehicle could only be used for carrying RMC's products for a fixed period and the drivers were told where and when to deliver their loads, although, if a driver was ill, a substitute driver could be used. It was held by MacKenna J that a contract of service exists if the following three conditions are fulfilled:

- The servant agrees that, in consideration of a wage or other remuneration, he or she will provide his or her own work and skill in the performance of some service for his or her master.

- He or she agrees, expressly or impliedly, that, in the performance of that service, he or she will be subject to the other's control in a sufficient degree to make that other master.

- The other provisions of the contract are consistent with its being a contract of service.

In this case, it was decided that the drivers were independent contractors, as there were factors which were inconsistent with the existence of a contract of employment, for example, the ability to provide a replacement driver if the need arose.

This test has proved to be most adaptable, in that it only requires evaluation of the factors which are inconsistent with the existence of a contract of employment. It is important to appreciate that there is no exhaustive list of inconsistent factors. The courts will ask questions such as: who pays the wages? Who pays income tax and national insurance? Is the person employed entitled to holiday pay?

They will treat as irrelevant the fact that there is a contract in which someone is termed 'independent contractor' when the other factors point to him or her being an employee. This is illustrated in *Market Investigations Ltd v Minister of Social Security* (1969), in which Market Investigations employed Mrs Irving as an interviewer on an occasional basis. If she was selected from the pool of interviewers maintained by the firm, she was not obliged to accept the work. However, if she accepted, she would be given precise instructions of the methods to be used in carrying out the market research and the time in which the work had to be completed. However, she could choose the hours she wanted to work and do other work at the same time, as long as she met Market Investigations' deadlines. It was held that she was an employee of the company every time she decided to undertake work for them. It was felt that the question to be asked is, 'is the person who has engaged himself to perform these services performing them as a person in business on his own account?'. If the answer is yes, then there is a contract for services; if the answer is no, there is a contract of service. Cooke J in that case stated that no exhaustive list could be compiled of the considerations which are relevant to this question, nor could strict rules be laid down as to the relevant weight which the various considerations should carry in particular cases. The most that could be said is that control will always have to be considered, although it will not be the sole determining factor. Whilst this multifactorial test found approval in *Lee v Chung and Shun Sing Construction and Engineering Co Ltd* (1990), the Court of Appeal in *Hall (HM Inspector of Taxes) v Lorimer* (1994) warned against adopting a mechanistic application of Cooke J's checklist.

A further illustration of the problem of defining status and the implications for the individual can be seen in *Lane v Shire Roofing Co (Oxford) Ltd* (1995). The plaintiff was a roofer who traded as a one-man firm and was categorised as self-employed for tax purposes. In 1986, he was hired by the defendants, a newly established roofing business, which had not wanted to take on direct labour and so had taken on the plaintiff on a 'payment by job' basis. While re-roofing a porch of a house, he fell off a ladder, sustaining serious injuries. It was held initially that the defendants did not owe the plaintiff a duty of care, as he was not an employee. However, on appeal, the Court of Appeal found for the plaintiff. They concluded, in recognition of greater flexibility in employment patterns, that many factors had to be taken into account in determining status. First, control and provision of materials were relevant but were not decisive factors; secondly, the question may have to be broadened to 'whose business was it?'; finally, these questions must be asked in the context of who is responsible for the overall safety of the men doing the work in question. There were clear policy grounds for adopting this interpretation, the safety of the individual being of paramount importance. Whether such an interpretation would have been adopted in an unfair dismissal case is open to debate.

Obviously, as was seen in the *Ready Mixed Concrete* case, there are other factors which may have to be taken into account, even though there may be some reluctance on the part of the courts to articulate what these other factors might be, with the exception of control. It is important that the multiple test continues to be flexible, so that it can adapt with changes in the labour environment. Unfortunately, these tests have tended to result in the atypical worker, that is, those with irregular working patterns, being categorised as self-employed. This is particularly true of casual or seasonal workers, even though, in practical terms, they may see themselves tied to a particular firm and, therefore, have an obligation to that business. There have, however, been some developments in this area which provide possible redress for such workers.

The test which has developed is known as the 'mutuality of obligation' test. This arose out of the case of *O'Kelly v Trusthouse Forte plc* (1983). O'Kelly and his fellow appellants worked on a casual basis as wine waiters at the Grosvenor House Hotel. They were regarded as regular casuals, in that they were given preference in the work rota over other casual staff. They had no other employment. They sought to be classified as employees, so that they could pursue an action for unfair dismissal. They argued that if they were to be classified as employees, then each independent period of work for the defendant could be added together and the qualifying period of employment under the Employment Protection (Consolidation) Act 1978 would be met. It was held that the regular casuals in this case were self-employed, as there was no mutuality of obligation on the part of either party, in that Trusthouse Forte was not obliged to offer work, nor were O'Kelly and his colleagues obliged to accept it when it was offered. The preferential rota system was not a contractual promise.

The court made it clear that an important factor in determining whether there is a contract of service in this type of situation is the custom and practice of the particular industry. The case of *Wickens v Champion Employment* (1984) supports the decision in *O'Kelly*. In *Wickens*, 'temps' engaged by a private employment agency were not accorded employment status because of the lack of binding obligation on the part of the agency to make bookings for work and the absence of any obligation on the worker to accept them. Such an approach by the courts is obviously disadvantageous to atypical workers. However, a more liberal approach was taken in *Nethermore (St Neots) v Gardiner and Taverna* (1984), in which home workers who were making clothes on a piecework basis were accorded employee status, on the basis that a mutuality of obligation arose out of an irreducible minimum obligation to work for that company 'by the regular giving and taking of work over periods of a year or more'.

However, it was held by the Court of Appeal in *McMeecham v Secretary of State for Employment* (1997) that a temporary worker can have the status of employee of an employment agency in respect of each assignment actually worked, notwithstanding that the same worker may not be entitled to employee status under his or her general terms of engagement.

While the decision in *McMeecham* goes some way to supporting the position of the temporary worker, the same cannot be said of the decision in *Express and Echo Publications Ltd v Tanton* (1999). There, Mr Tanton worked for the claimants as an employee until he was made redundant. He was then re-engaged as a driver, ostensibly on a self-employed basis. One clause in his contract stated that if he was unable or unwilling to perform the services personally, he should, at his own expense, find another suitable person. Mr Tanton found the agreement unacceptable and refused to sign it. He did, however, continue to work in accordance with its terms and, on occasions, utilised a substitute driver. He then brought a claim to an employment tribunal that he had not been provided with written particulars – thereby confirming his employee status. The employment tribunal found in Mr Tanton's favour on the basis of what had actually occurred, particularly the element of control exercised by the company. It was also concluded by the employment tribunal, and then on appeal by the Employment Appeal Tribunal (EAT), that the substitution clause was not fatal to the existence of a contract of employment. However, the Court of Appeal ruled that the right to provide a substitute driver was 'inherently inconsistent' with employment status, as a contract of employment must necessarily contain an obligation on the part of the employee to provide services personally.

There has been some criticism of this judgment (see Rubenstein, M, 'Highlights' [1999] IRLR 337), as it may allow unscrupulous employers to:

> ... draft contracts which will negate employment status for certain workers by including a substitution clause in their contracts. Clearly, the whole issue of employment status needs clarification. The position of atypical workers or those on zero hours contracts is particularly vulnerable until this issue is resolved.

A return to the *Wickens* approach is again in evidence in *Montgomery v Johnson Underwood Ltd* (2001). Mrs Montgomery was registered with an agency and was sent to work as a receptionist for the same client company for more than two years. Following her dismissal, she named both the agency and the client as respondents. The employment tribunal and the EAT both held that she was an employee of the agency, but this view was rejected by the Court of Appeal. Buckley J stated that 'mutuality of obligation' and 'control' are the 'irreducible minimum legal requirement for a contract of employment to exist'. According to Buckley J, 'a contractual relationship concerning work to be carried out in which one party has no control over the other could not possibly be called a contract of employment'. In Mrs Montgomery's case, there may have been sufficient mutuality, but a finding of fact that there was no control by the agency was fatal to the argument that she was an employee of the agency.

Yet more confusion relating to the status of agency work was introduced by the decision of the Scottish EAT in *Motorola v Davidson and Melville Craig* (2001). Davidson worked for Motorola as a mobile telephone repairer. His contract was with Melville Craig, who assigned him to work for Motorola. Motorola paid Melville Craig for his services, and Melville Craig paid Davidson. Davidson was largely subject to Motorola's control. They gave him instructions, provided tools, and he arranged holidays with them. He wore their uniform and badges, and obeyed their rules. If Davidson chose not to work for Motorola, that might have breached his contract with Melville Craig, but not a contract with Motorola. The agreement between Motorola and Melville Craig gave Motorola the right to return Davidson to them if they found him 'unacceptable'. His assignment was terminated by Motorola following a disciplinary hearing held by one of their managers. Mr Davidson claimed unfair dismissal against Motorola, who maintained that he was an employee of Melville Craig. However, the employment tribunal concluded that there was sufficient control to make Motorola the employer and the EAT agreed. In the view of the EAT, in determining whether there is a sufficient degree of control to establish a relationship of employer and employee, there is no good reason to ignore practical aspects of control that fall short of legal rights. Nor is it a necessary component of the type of control exercised by an employer over an employee that it should be exercised only directly between them and not by way of a third party acting upon the directions, or at the request of the third party.

In the case of *Carmichael v National Power plc* (1998), where a tourist guide employed on a casual basis was found to be an employee, the Court of Appeal held that there was the requisite mutuality of obligations between the parties, because there was an implied term in the contract that the applicants would take on a reasonable amount of work and that the employers would take on a reasonable share of such guiding work as it became available. *Carmichael* went on appeal to the House of Lords (*Carmichael v National Power plc* (2000)). It was held that the relationship, on its facts, did not have the mutuality of obligations necessary to create an employment relationship. However, in determining the terms of the contract of employment, the House of Lords concluded that where the parties intended all of the terms of the contract to be contained in documents, the terms should be determined solely by reference to these documents. In other situations, the court can look beyond the written documentation to the evidence of the parties in relation to what they understand their respective obligations to be, and to their subsequent conduct as evidence of the terms of the contract. It is argued that this approach, while it did not assist Carmichael, would assist many other marginal workers.

A number of wider implications flow from *Carmichael*. The decision has erected significant obstacles in the way of any attempts to extend employment status to casual workers. Furthermore, it could be used by employers to try to question the employment status of other workers on the margins of employment protection, for example, agency workers and homeworkers. Finally, 'highly evolved' human resource practitioners have always faced an uphill struggle in trying to convince line managers that it was not sufficient to label a worker as 'casual' and then assume that they possessed no employment rights. The *Carmichael* decision does not aid the HR manager's cause (see Leighton, P and Painter, RW, 'Casual workers: still marginal after all these years' (2001) 23(1/2) Employee Relations 75).

Finally, in *Stevedoring & Haulage Services Ltd v Fuller & Others* (2001), workers who voluntarily accepted redundancy were then re-employed as casual workers. A letter from the company offering employment made it clear that they were not employees and that there was no obligation on either the part of the company to provide work or on the applicants to accept it. However, they worked for the company on more days than not and did not work for any other employer. After three years, they applied to an employment tribunal for written particulars of their employment under s 1 of the ERA 1996. The employment tribunal and EAT concluded that the applicants were employed because there was an 'overarching contract of employment', evidenced by the implied mutuality of obligation which reflected the reality of the agreement. However, the company successfully appealed to the Court of Appeal on the basis that the implied term and express terms contained in the documents could not be reconciled.

This case therefore opens up the possibility that employers will be able to avoid legal responsibilities by including express terms denying 'employee' status to their workers. In effect, an express term will be able to override statutory employment rights.

It is still open to the Government to ensure that legislation is extended to provide cover to such workers. Section 23 of the Employment Relations Act 1999 provides the Secretary of State with such a power, and the broadening of the scope of legislative provisions can be seen in the Working Time Regulations 1998 and the National Minimum Wage Act 1998, both of which extend protection to 'workers' (see Painter,

RW, Puttick, K and Holmes, AEM, *The Gateway to Employment Rights, Employment Rights*, 2nd edn, 1998, Chapter 1).

9.4.1.4 Part time workers

Part time workers as well as casuals have also found themselves to be in a vulnerable position in the labour market (see Dickens, L, *Whose Flexibility? Discrimination and Equality Issues in Atypical Work*, 1992). The Part-Time Workers Directive (EC 97/81), which the UK Government had originally opposed on the ground that it would have a negative employment effect, has finally been adopted in the Part-Time Workers (Prevention of Less Favourable Treatment) Regulations 2000. The main thrust of the Regulations is to ensure that part time employees will be treated no less favourably than comparable full time employees in relation to a variety of matters, including pay, leave, training and pensions. A part time employee is defined under the Regulations as 'one who is not identifiable as a full time employee'. Comparison will be made with a full time employee 'who is engaged in the same or broadly similar work as a part time employee ... [and] works at the same establishment or, where no full time employee working at the establishment meets the preceding criteria, works at a different establishment and satisfies those requirements'. This means that part time employees are entitled to:

- the same hourly rate of pay;

- the same access to company pension schemes;

- the same entitlement to annual leave and maternity/parental leave on a pro rata basis;

- the same entitlement to contractual sick pay; and

- no less favourable treatment in access to training.

It has been recognised by the Department of Trade and Industry (DTI) in its regular impact assessment that the Regulations are likely to have a limited effect. Although there are over 6 million part time employees in Great Britain, less than 17% of all part time workers work alongside a potential full time comparator, and less than 7% stand directly to benefit through an increase in pay and long term wage benefits. The right of part timers not to be treated less favourably than a comparable full timer applies only if the treatment is not justified on objective grounds within reg 5(4). Regulation 5(4) allows the employer to justify his action if it is to achieve a legitimate objective, for example, a genuine business objective, and it is necessary to achieve that objective, and it is an appropriate way to achieve the objective. (See Jeffery, M, 'Not really going to work? Of the Directive on part time work, atypical work and attempts to regulate it' (1998) 27 ILJ 193.)

Despite the broadening of the coverage of the 2000 Regulations to 'workers' as opposed to 'employees', the Regulations retain the potential to disenfranchise many economically dependent workers from the scope of their protection. This is because comparisons under the Regulations can only be employed under the Regulations between an actual comparator (cf the Sex Discrimination Act 1975 and the Race

Relations Act 1976) employed under the same contract. Thus, for example, a part time worker employed as a fixed term contract worker cannot compare his or her treatment with that of a full time worker employed on a permanent contract. Similarly, workers employed under contracts for services ('workers') cannot compare their treatment with full time workers employed under contracts of employment ('employees') – see reg 2(3). In other words, the *Carmichael v National Power plc* (2000) problem is not resolved. The only cases in which a claim may be made without reference to an actual full time comparator are set out in the Regulations. Broadly, these exceptions cover (a) a full time worker who becomes part time (reg 3), and (b) full time workers returning to work part time for the same employer within a period of 12 months (reg 4). In the past, the threshold qualifying hours also imposed a barrier for part time and casual workers in qualifying for employment protection rights, for example, the requirement that a worker had worked 16 hours per week for a minimum of two years in order to qualify for unfair dismissal or redundancy payments. However, this was changed by the decision in *R v Secretary for Employment ex p Equal Opportunities Commission* (1995). As a result of this, the Employment Protection (Part-Time Employees) Regulations 1995 (SI 1995/31) were introduced, which removed the 16 hours per week qualification. The decision of the European Court of Justice in *R v Secretary of State for Employment ex p Seymour-Smith* (1999) went one step further, in concluding that the two year qualifying period discriminated against part time employees, who are predominantly female. Such a qualifying period may, therefore, contravene Art 141 of the EC Treaty. However, in *R v Secretary of State for Employment ex p Seymour-Smith and Perez* (2000), the House of Lords concluded that although the qualifying period was discriminatory, it was justified on the basis that, when it was introduced, there was evidence that a shorter qualifying period might inhibit employers recruiting employees. The Employment Relations Act 1999, in which the qualifying period for unfair dismissal was reduced to one year, has overtaken the decision in the *Seymour-Smith* case.

The Part-Time Workers (Prevention of Less Favourable Treatment) Regulations (Amendment) Regulations 2002 (SI 2002/2035) attempt to address the issue of the comparator by recognising that fixed term and permanent workers may be regarded as 'employed under the same contract'. The two year time limit on remedies has also been removed.

9.4.2 Unfair dismissal

Employees who qualify for protection under the ERA 1996 have the right not to be unfairly dismissed; that is, the employer must show that the reason for the dismissal was reasonable. The ERA 1996 provides greater protection and a wider range of remedies for the unfairly dismissed employee and, in this respect, is a much needed provision in the light of the inadequacies of the common law. Further procedural protection is provided by the Employment Act 2002 (Dispute Resolution) Regulations 2004 (SI 2004/752), which introduce significant changes for dealing with employment disputes. All employers must have written dismissal, disciplinary and grievance procedures in line with the statutory model; if such procedures are not followed, the employee is to be regarded as automatically unfairly dismissed; failure to follow the procedures will result in an additional penalty in any subsequent tribunal proceedings; where the statutory grievance procedures apply, the normal time for bringing a complaint will be extended to six months.

The Employment Rights (Dispute Resolution) Act 1998 contains provisions to implement those aspects of the Green Paper, *Resolving Employment Rights Disputes: Options for Reform* (Cm 2707, 1994), which attracted wide support and required primary legislation. The most significant change under the Act is to grant the Advisory, Conciliation and Arbitration Service (ACAS) powers to fund and provide an arbitration scheme for unfair dismissal claims. This is available as an alternative to an employment tribunal hearing and is voluntary on both sides. After some delay, the ACAS Arbitration Scheme came into force in England and Wales on 21 May 2001 and in Scotland by April 2004. The Scheme has got off to a sluggish start, with 23 cases heard in its first full year of operation and only 8 in 2003/04 (ACAS Annual Report 2003/04).

In the White Paper *Fairness at Work* (Cm No 3968, 1998), the Government put forward a number of proposals aimed at strengthening the unfair dismissal remedy. These included:

- abolishing the maximum limit on the compensatory award;

- index-linking limits on the basic award, subject to a maximum rate;

- prohibiting the use of waivers for unfair dismissal claims but continuing to allow them for redundancy payments;

- creating a legal right for individuals to be accompanied by a fellow employee or trade union representative of their choice during grievance and disciplinary hearings; and

- reducing the qualifying period for claimants to one year.

The Employment Relations Act 1999 and a ministerial order have implemented these proposals with one exception. The ceiling on the compensation award has not been completely removed but the maximum limit has been raised to £56,800.

The Employment Relations Act 1999 provides a right for workers who are subject to a disciplinary or grievance hearing to be accompanied (s 10), as amended by the Employment Relations Act 2004. In respect of disciplinary hearings, the right to be accompanied is triggered by a hearing which could result in (a) the administration of a formal warning to a worker by his employer, or (b) the taking of some other action in respect of the worker by his employer. If the outcome of a hearing could result in an entry on an employee's disciplinary record, then he or she is entitled to be accompanied at that hearing – *London Underground Ltd v Ferenc-Batchelor* (2003). Section 10(2B) of the 1999 Act clarifies the role of the worker's companion.

Finally, the Employment Act 2002 amends the statutory unfair dismissal regime. A new statutory dispute resolution procedure has been introduced and every contract of employment will require employers and employees to comply with it. The statutory procedures set out in Sched 2 to the Act deal with disciplinary and dismissal issues, and employee grievances.

9.4.2.1   Who qualifies under the Employment Rights Act 1996?

Protection from unfair dismissal is only available to employees, that is, those employed under a contract of service. The basic rule is that an employee must have at least one year's continuous employment in order to qualify. This significant change to the qualifying period arose out of the Government's White Paper, *Fairness at Work* (Cm 3968, 1998), which resulted in the Unfair Dismissal and Statement of Reasons for Dismissal (Variation of Qualifying Period) Order 1999 (SI 1999/1436). This change from two years to one took effect on 1 June 1999. The two year qualifying period was held indirectly to discriminate against women in *R v Secretary of State for Employment ex p Seymour-Smith and Perez (No 2)* (2000). However, the House of Lords ruled that the Secretary of State was objectively justified under EC law in increasing the qualifying period from one to two years in 1985. This decision has largely been overtaken by the subsequent statutory amendment, although this does not have retrospective effect. There is a presumption that continuity exists. The onus is therefore on the employer to show that it does not.

The following people are specifically excluded from the unfair dismissal provisions of the ERA 1996:

- share fishermen;

- any employee who has reached the normal retirement age (this is recognised as 65 for both men and women under the Sex Discrimination Act 1986); or, if relevant, the contractual retirement age;

- persons ordinarily employed outside Great Britain;

- workers on fixed term contracts who have waived in writing their right to claim if the contract is not renewed;

- the police and armed forces;

- employees who are affected by a dismissal procedure agreement between the employer and an independent trade union which has been approved by the Secretary of State;

- employees who, at the time of their dismissal, are taking industrial action or are locked out, where there has been no selective dismissal or re-engagement of those taking part. Unofficial strikers may be selectively dismissed or re-engaged (ss 237 and 238 of the Trade Union Labour Relations (Consolidation) Act (TULR(C)A) 1992); and

- where the settlement of a claim for dismissal has been agreed with the involvement of ACAS and the employee has agreed to withdraw his or her complaint.

In *Secretary of State for Trade and Industry v Rutherford (No 2)* (2003), the EAT allowed the Government's appeal. It held that the exclusion of employees aged 65 and over from the statutory rights not to be unfairly dismissed and the right to receive redundancy payments did not discriminate against men and was not contrary to EU law. The EAT ruled that the correct pool of comparison was a pool consisting of the entire workforce, which would then have shown no disparate impact on men and therefore no discrimination. The EAT was also satisfied that even if a disparate impact had been established, this was justified on the basis that the Secretary of State could demonstrate responsible policy objectives for the age limits, reflecting legitimate aims of social policy.

9.4.2.2   Claims

An applicant must bring a claim within three months of the effective date of termination (s 111 of the ERA 1996). The employment tribunal may extend this limit if it considers that it was not reasonably practicable for the applicant to present it in time (*Palmer v Southend-on-Sea BC* (1984)). However, the time limit tends to be rigorously applied. Such is the stringency of the approach that it has been held that an applicant may not use the excuse that his or her failure to claim was due to a mistake of 'a skilled adviser' such as a lawyer, trade union official or Citizen's Advice Bureau worker (see *Riley v Tesco Stores Ltd* (1980)). Thus, the date of termination, as well as the length of service, etc, is of importance in deciding whether a claim is made in time.

9.4.2.3   Effective date of termination

The same rules apply for unfair dismissal and redundancy, although with respect to redundancy it is known as 'the relevant date':

- Where the contract of employment is terminated by notice, whether by the employer or employee, the date of termination is the date on which the notice expires (s 97(1) of the ERA 1996). If an employee is dismissed with notice but is given a payment in lieu of notice, the effective date of termination is the date when the notice expires, as illustrated in *Adams v GKN Sankey* (1980).

- Where the contract of employment is terminated without notice, the date of termination is the date on which the termination takes effect, that is, the actual date of dismissal, not the date on which the notice would expire. In *Robert Cort & Sons Ltd v Charman* (1981), where an employee was summarily dismissed with wages in lieu of notice, the effective date of termination was the actual date on which he was told of his dismissal, not the date on which the notice would expire. The exception to this rule is provided by s 97(2) of the ERA 1996, by which the effective date is extended either where summary dismissal has occurred, despite the employee being entitled to the statutory minimum notice, or where the actual notice given was less than that required by statute. In both cases, the effective date is the expiration of the statutory notice period.

- Where the employer is employed under a contract for a limited term, the date of termination is the date on which the term expires.

One important issue has been what the effective date of termination is where the employee invokes an internal appeals procedure. It appears that, if the appeal is subsequently rejected, the effective date is the date of the original dismissal (*J Sainsbury Ltd v Savage* (1981)), unless the contract provides for the contrary (*West Midlands Co-operative Society v Tipton* (1986)).

9.4.2.4 What is meant by dismissal?

The onus is on the employee to show that he or she has been dismissed within the meaning of the Act (s 95 of the ERA 1996). There are three ways in which dismissal can take place, which are as follows:

- *Express termination of the contract of employment by the employer*

  The employer may terminate the contract with or without notice. Such a dismissal may be made orally or in writing; however, if it is made orally, the words used should be unambiguous. For example, in *Futty v Brekkes Ltd* (1974), in a row with his foreman, the employee was told, 'If you do not like the job, fuck off'. This was interpreted by the employee as a dismissal and he left and found a job elsewhere. The employer argued that there had been no dismissal, as the words were to be interpreted in the context of the workman's trade. Furthermore, if a dismissal had been intended, the words used would have been formal. This argument was accepted by the industrial tribunal, which concluded that the employee had terminated his own employment.

  Where the words are ambiguous, the effect of the statement is determined by an objective test; that is, would the reasonable employer or employee have understood the words to be tantamount to a dismissal? One of the problems for the courts has been deciding whether there has been a dismissal within the meaning of the ERA 1996.

  A termination which is mutually agreed between the employer and employee is not a dismissal. However, the courts have, with some reluctance, upheld this practice, as it may work to the advantage of the employer in avoiding employment rights and thereby lead to an abuse of a dominant position. The courts will look closely to see whether there is genuine mutual agreement; this will be a question of fact in each case.

  In *Igbo v Johnson Matthey Chemicals Ltd* (1986), the applicant requested extended leave to visit her husband and children in Nigeria. This was granted by her employers on the condition that she signed a document which stated that she agreed to return to work on 28 September 1986 and, if she failed to do so, her contract of employment would automatically terminate on that date. She signed the document. She failed to return on the due date because she was ill and, as a result, her contract was terminated. The Court of Appeal held that the contract had been terminated, not by mutual agreement, but by dismissal. The document amounted to a means of avoiding employment rights and was, therefore, void by virtue of s 140(1) of the Employment Protection (Consolidation) Act 1978 (now s 203 of the ERA 1996).

It should be noted that, where the employee is under notice of termination and gives the employer a counter notice indicating an intention to leave before the expiry of the employer's notice, the employee is still deemed to have been dismissed for the purposes of the ERA 1996. Any counter notice must be in writing with respect to a claim for redundancy, but this is not a requirement in respect of unfair dismissal.

- *Where the employee invites a termination of his contract either by his inaction or conduct*

In *Martin v Yeoman Aggregates Ltd* (1983), Martin refused to get a spare part for the director's car. The director angrily told the employee to get out. Five minutes later, the director took back what he had said and instead suspended Martin without pay until he could act more rationally. Martin insisted that he had been dismissed. It was held that it was vital to industrial relations that both the employer and employee should have the opportunity to withdraw their words. It was up to a tribunal to decide whether the withdrawal had come too late to be effective.

Certainly, immediate retraction is effective. However, a subsequent retraction will only be effective with the consent of the other party.

Where the employer invites the employee to resign, this may amount to a dismissal. In *Robertson v Securicor Transport Ltd* (1972), Robertson had broken one of the works rules by signing for a load which had not actually been received. When his employers discovered what he had done, they gave him the option of resignation or dismissal. He chose resignation. It was held that resignation in these circumstances amounted to a dismissal by the employer because, in effect, there was no alternative action open to the employee. He would have been dismissed if he had not opted to resign on the invitation of his employer.

- *Expiration of a fixed or limited term contract*

As we have seen, in certain situations, a fixed term contract may be excluded from the protection afforded by the ERA 1996; that is, where the employee agrees before the term expires to forgo any claim for unfair dismissal. However, if a fixed term contract is not renewed and it is not within the excluded category, the failure to renew amounts to a dismissal (whether it is a fair dismissal is another issue).

Section 95 of the ERA 1996 states that an employee is dismissed by his employer if he is employed under a limited term contact and that contract terminates by virtue of the limiting event, without being renewed under the same contract.

Section 235 states that a contract is for a limited term if the employment under the contract is not intended to be permanent and provision is accordingly made in the contract for it to terminate by virtue of the limiting event. A limiting event includes the expiry of a fixed term contract, the performance of a specific task, or the occurrence of a particular event as specified in the contract. Previously, the courts drew a distinction between a fixed term contract deemed to be a dismissal under the legislation and a contract for the completion of a particular task, at the end of which there was no dismissal. A task contract was therefore discharged by performance of the particular task and could not give rise to a dismissal (see *Brown v*

Knowsley BC (1986)). However, s 95, as amended by s 235, removes this distinction and provides protection to both fixed term and task contracts.

Section 2 of the ERA 1996 further requires that, if the agreement amounts to a fixed term contract, the duration of the contract must be certain, that is, there must be a date on which the contract expires. It follows, therefore, that a contract to do a specific job, which does not refer to a completion date, cannot be a fixed term contract, since the duration of the contract is uncertain.

Furthermore, at one time, it was thought that a fixed term contract must run for the whole of the term and must not be capable of termination before the term expired, for example, by a clause giving either party the right to terminate (see *BBC v Ioannou* (1975)). However, in *Dixon v BBC* (1979), it was held that a fixed term contract could exist even though either party could terminate it before it had run its full term.

Constructive dismissal

Constructive dismissal is an important concept, since the law recognises that an employee may be entitled to protection where he or she is put in a position in which he or she is forced to resign. Constructive dismissal arises where the employee is forced to terminate the contract with or without notice due to the conduct of the employer (s 95(1)(c) of the ERA 1996). One issue for the courts is whether the words or actions of the employee in resigning are unambiguous. In *Sovereign House Security Services Ltd v Savage* (1989), Savage, a security officer, was told that he was to be suspended pending police investigations into the theft of money from the employer's offices. Savage told his immediate superior to pass on the fact that he was 'jacking it in'. The Court of Appeal held that the employer was entitled to treat these words as amounting to a resignation.

The courts will, however, make some allowance for 'heat of the moment' utterances (see *Tanner v Kean* (1978)). The main focus for the courts is to decide whether the employer's conduct warrants the action taken by the employee. It is now firmly decided that, in order to permit the employer to constructively dismiss him or her, the employee's actions must amount to a breach of contract and must, therefore, be more than merely unreasonable conduct.

In *Western Excavating Ltd v Sharp* (1978), Sharp took time off from work without permission. When his employer discovered this, he was dismissed. He appealed to an internal disciplinary board, which substituted a penalty of five days' suspension without pay. He agreed to accept this decision but asked his employer for an advance on his holiday pay, as he was short of money; this was refused. He then asked for a loan of £40, which was also refused. As a result, he decided to resign, since this would at least mean that he would receive his holiday pay. At the same time, he claimed unfair dismissal on the basis that he was forced to resign because of his employer's unreasonable conduct. Initially, the tribunal found in Sharp's favour; that is, the employer's conduct was so unreasonable that Sharp could not be expected to continue working there. However, the case eventually went to the Court of Appeal, where it was decided that, before a valid constructive dismissal can take place, the employer's conduct must amount to a breach of contract such that it entitles the employee to resign. In this particular case, there was no breach by the employer and, therefore, there was no constructive dismissal.

It would appear that if the breach by the employer is to allow the employee to resign, it must be a breach of some significance and must go to the root of the contract, for example, a unilateral change in the employee's terms (express or implied) and conditions of employment. For example, in *British Aircraft Corp v Austin* (1978), a failure to investigate a health and safety complaint was held to be conduct amounting to a breach of contract on the part of the employer which was sufficient to entitle the employee to treat the contract as terminated. If the employee does not resign in the event of a breach by the employer, the employee will be deemed to have accepted the breach and to have waived any rights. However, the law recognises that he or she need not resign immediately but may, for example, wait until he or she has found another job (see *Cox Toner (International) Ltd v Crook* (1981)).

It is also recognised that a series of minor incidents can have a cumulative effect, which results in a fundamental breach amounting to repudiation of the contract by the employer. In *Woods v WM Car Services (Peterborough)* (1982), it was held that the general implied contractual duty that employers will not, without reasonable or proper cause, conduct themselves in a manner calculated as being likely to destroy the relationship of trust and confidence between employer and employee, is an overriding obligation independent of and in addition to the literal terms of the contract. See also *London Borough of Waltham Forest v Omilaju* (2004).

In *Simmonds v Dowty Seals Ltd* (1978), Simmonds was employed to work on the night shift. His employer attempted to force him to work on the day shift by threatening to take industrial action if he refused to be transferred from the night shift. He resigned. It was held that he was entitled to resign and could regard himself as having been constructively dismissed because the employer's conduct amounted to an attempt to unilaterally change an express term of his contract, namely, that he was employed to work nights.

The employee may also be able to claim where he or she is forced to resign when the employer is in breach of an implied term in the contract of employment. However, it must be stressed that the employee must be able to show not only the existence of the implied term, but also what is required by the implied term, that is, its scope (see *Gardner Ltd v Beresford* (1978)). An implied term in a contract which provided for demotion in the event of incompetence defeated a claim of constructive unfair dismissal when applied to a helicopter pilot who was demoted following a dangerous incident (*Vaid v Brintel Helicopters Ltd* (1994)).

It is also possible for the conduct of an immediate superior to amount to a fundamental breach on the part of the employer, as long as the test for establishing vicarious liability is satisfied (*Hilton International Hotels (UK) Ltd v Protopapa* (1990)).

The case law illustrates that a wide range of conduct on the part of the employer may entitle the employee to resign. For example, in *Bracebridge Engineering Ltd v Darby* (1990), failing to properly investigate allegations of sexual harassment or failing to treat such a complaint with sufficient seriousness was held to be constructive dismissal. The employee is not expected to tolerate abusive language from his or her employer, particularly when he or she is being accused of something which he or she did not do (*Palmanor Ltd v Cedron* (1978)). Even where the employer orders his or her employee to relocate as a result of a mobility clause in the employee's contract, if the employee is given very short notice and no financial assistance, he or she may resign and claim constructive dismissal (*United Bank Ltd v Akhtar* (1989)). Finally, where an employee lodges a grievance which is not investigated because of a failure to implement a proper procedure, the employee's resignation may be justified (*WA Goold (Pearmak) Ltd v McConnell & Another* (1995)).

As a result of the decision in *Western Excavating Ltd v Sharp*, it is clear that unreasonable conduct alone which makes life difficult for the employee, so that he or she is put in a position where he or she forced to resign, will not automatically be deemed to be a constructive dismissal, unless it can be found to be a breach of the express or implied terms on the part of the employer. The employee may have to depend on the generosity of the courts in establishing a breach of an implied term.

In the case of *Pepper and Hope v Daish* (1980), in December 1978, Pepper, who was employed by the defendants, negotiated for himself an hourly wage rate. In January 1979, his employers increased the hourly rate of all workers by 5%, with the exception of Pepper. As a result, Pepper resigned and claimed constructive dismissal. It was held that Pepper would succeed in his claim. The tribunal was prepared to imply a term into his contract that he would be given any wage increases received by the hourly rate workers. Such a term had therefore been broken by his employer, forcing him to resign. Whether the courts will always be as generous in their interpretation is open to debate.

9.4.2.5 Reasons for the dismissal

An employee who is dismissed within the meaning of the ERA 1996 is entitled to a written statement of the reasons for his dismissal (s 92 of the ERA 1996). He or she must, however, have been continuously employed for one year (s 92(3) of the ERA 1996). However, this qualifying period is not applicable where a female employee is dismissed while she is pregnant or in connection with childbirth (s 92(4) of the ERA 1996). The employee must request the statement and it must be supplied within 14 days of this request. Failure to do so or providing particulars which are inadequate or untrue will allow the employee to make a complaint to an employment tribunal. If the tribunal finds in favour of the employee, it may declare the real reason for the dismissal and award the employee two weeks' pay. It has been held that a 'conscientiously formed belief that there was no dismissal was a reasonable ground for refusing to provide a written statement' (*Brown v Stuart Scott & Co* (1981)). The written statement is admissible in proceedings and any inconsistency between the contents of the statement and the reason actually put forward could seriously undermine the employer's case.

9.4.2.6 Fair dismissals

Once the employee has established dismissal, be it by the employer or constructively, the onus moves to the employer to show that he or she acted reasonably in dismissing the employee and, therefore, that the dismissal was fair (s 98 of the ERA 1996). Prior to 1980, the burden of proof in unfair dismissal claims at this stage was on the employer. The Employment Act 1980 amended the test, primarily by removing the requirement that the employer shall satisfy the employment tribunal as to the reasonableness of his or her action, and so rendered the burden of proof 'neutral'. A further amendment required tribunals to have regard to the size and administrative resources of the employer's undertaking in assessing the reasonableness of the dismissal. The specific reference to size and administrative resources is an encouragement to tribunals to be less exacting in their examination of the disciplinary standards and procedures of small employers.

The test of reasonableness requires consideration of what a reasonable employer would have done in the circumstances; that is, does it fall within 'the band of reasonable responses to the employee's conduct within which one employer might take one view, another quite reasonably another?' (*Iceland Frozen Foods v Jones* (1982), *per* Browne-Wilkinson J). Whether the test is satisfied is a question of fact in each case. More recently, in *Haddon v Van Den Bergh Foods Ltd* (1999), the EAT held that the 'range of reasonable responses' test was an unhelpful gloss on the statute and should no longer be applied by employment tribunals. The EAT qualified its decision in *Haddon* in the case of *HSBC v Madden* (2000). In this case, the EAT stated that, whilst only the Court of Appeal or a higher court can discard the range of reasonable responses test, a tribunal is free to substitute its own views for those of the employer as to the reasonableness of dismissal as a response to the reason shown for it. Instead, the test of fairness should be applied 'without embellishment and without using mantras so favoured by lawyers in this field'. The EAT recommended the approach adopted in *Gilham v Kent CC (No 2)* (1985), in which the Court of Appeal emphasised that whether a dismissal was fair or unfair is a pure question of fact for the tribunal. However, the Court of Appeal in *Post Office v Foley; HSBC Bank v Madden* (2000) has now restored the 'band of reasonable responses' test. The proper function of the employment tribunal is to determine objectively whether the decision to dismiss the employee fell within the band of reasonable responses which a reasonable employer might have adopted. In practice, this may not be required in every case; nor is there a requirement to show that the employer's decision was so unreasonable as to be perverse.

In *Sainsbury's Supermarkets Ltd v Hitt* (2003), the Court of Appeal held that the range of reasonable responses test applied to the question of whether the employer's investigation into suspected misconduct was reasonable in the circumstances. As a result, a dismissal which occurs without an opportunity for the employee to explain his conduct is fair unless no reasonable employer could take the view that no explanation was necessary.

However, employment tribunals continue to have regard to the substantive merits of a case, for example, length of service, previous disciplinary record and any other mitigating circumstances, with a view to maintaining consistency of treatment and procedural fairness. In other words, they will ask whether the employer has adhered to the ACAS Code of Practice on Disciplinary and Grievance Procedures, which involves the provision of formal warnings, internal hearings, appeals procedures, etc. The Code may be used as evidence to show that the employer has not acted reasonably (s 207 of the TULR(C)A 1992). ACAS has updated the Code of Practice to take account of the new statutory procedures set out in the Employment Act 2002. The revised Code came into effect in October 2004, at the same time as the regulations giving effect to the new dispute resolution procedures. Further rights in respect of disciplinary and grievance hearings can be found in ss 10–12 of the Employment Relations Act 1999, in particular, the right to be accompanied at a hearing; the right to complain to an employment tribunal if the employer fails to allow a worker to be accompanied; and the right not to be subjected to any detriment by his or her employer for pursuing his or her rights under ss 10 and 11.

Schedule 2 to the Employment Act 2002 introduces new statutory dispute resolution procedures and every contract of employment will require employers and employees to comply with them. A standard procedure for dismissal and disciplinary procedures is found in Chapter 1 of the provisions. It extends to the conduct of the meetings, as well as procedural fairness, and may have implications for the decision in *Polkey v AE Dayton Services Ltd* (1987) (below).

The leading case on procedural fairness is *Polkey v AE Dayton Services Ltd*. Polkey was employed as a van driver. In order to avoid more financial losses, his employer decided to make three van drivers redundant. There was no prior consultation; Polkey was merely handed a letter informing him that he was being made redundant. Polkey claimed that this amounted to unfair dismissal, as the failure to consult showed that the employer had not acted reasonably in treating redundancy as a sufficient reason for dismissing him. It was held that, in deciding whether the employer had acted reasonably, the tribunal should have regard to the facts at the time of the dismissal and should not base their judgment on facts brought to light after the dismissal, such as whether the failure to consult would have made any difference to the dismissal or whether the employee had in practice suffered an injustice.

The implementation of the disciplinary procedure is also of paramount importance. In *Westminster CC v Cabaj* (1996), the council's disciplinary code required three members of the council to be in attendance to hear appeals. The complainant's appeal was heard by the Chief Executive and two other members. The EAT held that this amounted to a significant error, as the appeals panel should have been constituted in a particular way. As a result, the dismissal was unfair.

The grounds on which a dismissal is capable of being fair are laid down in s 98 of the ERA 1996. In *Wilsorky v Post Office* (2000), the Court of Appeal held that it was a question of legal analysis to determine in which part of s 98 of the ERA 1996 a reason for dismissal falls. If it was incorrectly 'characterised', this was an error of law which would therefore be corrected on appeal.

Capability or qualifications

Section 98(3) states that capability is 'assessed by reference to skill, aptitude, health or any other physical or mental quality', whereas qualifications means 'any degree, diploma, or other academic, technical or professional qualification relevant to the position which the employee held'. In *Blackman v Post Office* (1974), Blackman was a telegraph officer. He was required to pass an aptitude test. He was allowed the maximum number of attempts (three), and he still failed. He was then dismissed. It was held that, as the taking of an aptitude test was a qualification requirement of that job, his dismissal was fair.

Before dismissing an employee for incompetence, the employer should have regard to the ACAS Code of Practice on Disciplinary Practices and Procedures in Employment, which offers some guidance on improving poor performance; certainly, no dismissal should take place without formal warnings providing the employee with an opportunity to redress his or her position, unless the potential consequences of the incompetence are so serious that warnings are inappropriate. In *Taylor v Alidair* (1978), a pilot was dismissed for a serious error of judgment when he landed a plane so badly that it caused extensive damage. The Court of Appeal held that the company had reasonable grounds for honestly believing that he was incompetent.

The employer must not only be able to show that, for example, the employee was incompetent or inadequately qualified, but also that, in the circumstances, it was reasonable to dismiss him or her – that is, what would the reasonable employer have done? The court will have regard to all the surrounding circumstances, such as training, supervision and what alternatives were available, for example, could the employee have been redeployed in another job, etc? The employer may also have to show that the employee was given a chance to improve his or her standing. If the employer is to be deemed to have acted reasonably, he or she must be able to show that dismissal was the last resort.

In *Davison v Kent Meters Ltd* (1975), Davison worked on an assembly line. She was dismissed as a result of assembling 500 components incorrectly. She alleged that she had merely followed the instructions of the chargehand. The chargehand maintained that he had not given her any instructions. It was held that the dismissal was unfair. Davison should have received supervision and training in the assembly of the components. It was clear from the evidence that she had not received any; therefore, her employer had not acted reasonably in dismissing her.

Persistent absenteeism may be treated as misconduct and should be dealt with under the disciplinary procedure. However, a long term absence, such as long term sickness, should be treated as incapability. Whether the employer's action to dismiss for long term sickness absence is reasonable will depend on the particular circumstances of each case, for example, the nature of the illness, the length of the absence, the need to replace the absent employee and the carrying out of an investigation of the illness (*London Fire and Civil Defence Authority v Betty* (1994)). The employer will be expected to make a reasonable effort to inform him or herself of the true medical position of the employee, although the consent of the employee is needed before access to medical records can be gained.

Conduct

In deciding whether a dismissal for misconduct is to be regarded as fair, attention must be paid to the nature of the offence and the disciplinary procedure. For example, gross or serious misconduct may justify instant dismissal, whereas a trivial act may only warrant a warning in line with the disciplinary procedure. In *Hamilton v Argyll and Clyde Health Board* (1993), it was found that the fact that the employer was prepared to offer the employee an alternative post did not mean that the misconduct could not be classified as 'gross'. The word 'misconduct' is not defined in the ERA 1996, but it is established that it covers assault, refusal to obey instructions, persistent lateness, moonlighting, drunkenness, dishonesty, failing to implement safety procedures, etc. Whether the commission of a criminal offence outside employment justifies a dismissal will depend upon its relevance to the actual job carried out by the employee.

Before any dismissal for misconduct takes place, the employer must have established a genuine and reasonable belief in the guilt of the employee. This may involve carrying out a reasonable investigation. A false accusation without reasonable foundation may result in the employee resigning and claiming constructive dismissal (*Robinson v Crompton Parkinson Ltd* (1978)). It should be remembered that reference must also be made to what the reasonable employer would have done; that is, the test is an objective one.

In *Taylor v Parsons Peebles Ltd* (1981), a works rule prohibited fighting. It was also the policy of the company to dismiss anyone caught fighting. The company had employed the applicant for 20 years without complaint. He was caught fighting and was dismissed. It was held that the dismissal was unfair. Regard must be had to the previous 20 years of employment without incident. The tribunal decided that the reasonable employer would not have applied the sanction of instant dismissal as rigidly because of the mitigating circumstances.

In *Whitbread & Co v Thomas* (1988), it was held that an employer who could not identify which member of a group was responsible for an act could fairly dismiss the whole group, even where it was probable that not all were guilty of the act, provided that the following three conditions were satisfied:

- the act of misconduct warranted dismissal;

- the industrial (now employment) tribunal is satisfied that the act was committed by at least one of the group being dismissed and all were capable of committing the act; and

- the tribunal is satisfied that the employer had carried out a proper investigation to attempt to identify the persons responsible.

In *Parr v Whitbread plc* (1990), Parr was employed as a branch manager at an off-licence owned by the respondents. He and three other employees were dismissed after it was discovered that £4,000 had been stolen from the shop in circumstances which suggested that it was an inside job. Each of the four had an equal opportunity to commit the theft and the employers found it impossible to ascertain which of them was actually guilty. It was held, applying the test in the *Thomas* case, that the dismissals were fair.

Redundancy

Redundancy is *prima facie* a fair reason for dismissal. However, the employer must show that the reason for the dismissal was due to redundancy (s 98(2) of the ERA 1996). He or she must, therefore, be able to establish redundancy within the meaning of the ERA 1996. A dismissal for reason of redundancy will be unfair if the employer had not acted as the reasonable employer would have acted in the circumstances. The following matters, as laid down in *Williams v Compair Maxam Ltd* (1982), should be considered before the redundancies are put into effect:

- to give as much warning as possible;

- to consult with the trade union (see ss 188–92 of the TULR(C)A 1992, as amended by the Collective Redundancies and Transfer of Undertakings (Protection of Employment) (Amendment) Regulations 1995 (SI 1995/2587));

- to adopt an objective rather than a subjective criteria for selection;

- to select in accordance with the criteria; and

- to consider the possibility of redeployment rather than dismissal.

In *Allwood v William Hill Ltd* (1974), William Hill Ltd decided to close down 12 betting shops. Without any warning, they made all the managers redundant. They offered no alternative employment. The managers, as employees, complained that this amounted to unfair dismissal. It was held that, in the circumstances, this amounted to unfair dismissal. The employer should have considered possible alternatives, such as transfers to other betting shops. Furthermore, the way in which the redundancies had taken place was not the way in which a reasonable employer would have acted.

It is important to realise that just because there is a redundancy situation within the meaning of the ERA 1996, it does not automatically follow that any dismissal due to redundancy will be fair. An important issue is whether the criteria used for selection of those employees who are to be made redundant are fair, for example, first in, first out (FIFO); last in, first out (LIFO); or part time staff first, which may also amount to discrimination. Contravention of customary practices may be evidence that the dismissal is unfair.

In *Hammond-Scott v Elizabeth Arden Ltd* (1976), the applicant was selected for redundancy because she was close to retirement age. The defendants had employed her for many years, but this was not taken into account when she was selected for redundancy. It was held that her selection for redundancy amounted to unfair dismissal because the employer had not acted reasonably in the circumstances. In view of her age, the length of service and the fact that she was close to retirement age, it would have had little financial effect on the company if they had continued to employ her until she retired.

Transferring the responsibility for deciding who will be made redundant from the employer to the employees involved in the redundancy may also amount to unfair dismissal. In *Boulton and Paul Ltd v Arnold* (1994), when an employee complained about her selection for redundancy, the employer offered to retain her, but on the terms that another employee would be made redundant in her place. She rejected this offer and claimed unfair dismissal. Her claim was upheld, as the EAT did not accept the employer's defence that she could have remained in employment. It also declared that it was unfair to move the onus to the employee in order to decide whether she or another employee would be selected for dismissal.

Where employees in similar positions are not made redundant and the reason why a particular employee was selected for redundancy was because he or she was a member or non-member of a trade union or participated in trade union activities, dismissal will be deemed to be automatically unfair (s 153 of the TULR(C)A 1992). This is no longer subject to any qualifying period of service.

Statutory restrictions (s 98(2)(d) of the Employment Rights Act 1996)

If the dismissal is because the continued employment of the employee would result in a contravention of a statute or subordinate legislation on the part of either the employer or the employee, the dismissal will be *prima facie* fair, for example, if the employee has been banned from driving, yet the job requires him or her to hold a current driving licence – if the employee continues to fulfil the job specification, he or she would be in breach of the Road Traffic Acts (*Fearn v Tayford Motor Co Ltd* (1975)); or if the employer, in continuing to employ someone, was found to be contravening the Food and Drugs Act 1955.

As with all cases of dismissal, the employer must act as the reasonable employer and must, therefore, consider any possible alternatives if the dismissal is to be regarded as fair (*Sandhu v Department of Education and Science and London Borough of Hillingdon* (1978)).

Some other substantial reason

Where the employer is unable to show that the reason for the dismissal was one of those referred to above, he or she may show 'some other substantial reason' (s 98(1)(b) of the ERA 1996). There is no exhaustive list of what is recognised in law as some other substantial reason. The employer must show not only that his or her actions were reasonable, but also that the reason was 'substantial'. The following have been held to be valid reasons for dismissal, although it should be appreciated that it is a question of fact in each case:

- a conflict of personalities which is primarily the fault of the employee. In *Tregonowan v Robert Knee and Co* (1975), the atmosphere in the employer's office was so bad, due to the complainant constantly talking about her private life, that her fellow employees could not work with her. Accordingly, she was dismissed and the tribunal upheld the dismissal. Dismissal should be a last resort after attempts to improve relations have taken place;

- failure to disclose material facts in obtaining employment, for example, mental illness (see *O'Brien v Prudential Assurance Co Ltd* (1979));

- commercial reasons, for example, pressure from important customers to dismiss the employee (*Grootcon (UK) Ltd v Keld* (1984));

- failure to accept changes in the terms of employment (see *Storey v Allied Brewery* (1977)). Any change must be justified by the employer as being necessary;

- non-renewal of a fixed term contract – the employer must show a genuine need for temporary contracts and that the employee knew of the temporary nature of the contract from the outset (*North Yorkshire CC v Fay* (1985)); and

- a dismissal which satisfies reg 8(2) of the Transfer of Undertakings (Protection of Employment) Regulations 1981 (SI 1981/1794) in so far as the dismissal is for an 'economic, technical or organisational reason entailing changes in the workforce and the employer is able to show that his actions were reasonable'. Where the employer can satisfy reg 8, the employee may be able to claim redundancy, as in *Gorictree Ltd v Jenkinson* (1984). Any other dismissal in connection with the transfer of the business is automatically unfair: see *Litster & Others v Forth Dry Dock and Engineering Co Ltd* (1989), considered below.

9.4.2.7 Special situations

The following are situations where dismissal is automatically unfair:

- *Trade union membership or activity (s 152(1) of the TULR(C)A 1992)*

  Where the employee is dismissed because of an actual or proposed membership of an independent trade union, or because he or she is not a member of a trade union or refuses to become a member, the dismissal is automatically unfair. This is also the case where the employee has taken part or proposes to take part in any trade union activities. The employee need not have the required qualifying period of employment in order to bring an action for unfair dismissal under this section.

- *Pregnancy or childbirth*

  Section 99 of the ERA 1996 provides that an employee is automatically unfairly dismissed where the principal reason for the dismissal is pregnancy or a reason connected with pregnancy; or, following maternity leave, dismissal for childbirth or a reason connected with childbirth, adoption leave, parental leave, paternity leave, etc.

  In *O'Neil v Governors of St Thomas Moore RCVA Upper School* (1996), a religious instruction teacher was dismissed whilst on maternity leave when it was discovered that the father of her child was the local Roman Catholic priest. The employer argued that the reason for the dismissal was the paternity of the child and her particular post at the school. The EAT declined to accept this and held that the main reason related to pregnancy and was, therefore, unlawful.

- *Industrial action*

  Dismissals during strike or lock-out are governed by s 238 of the TULR(C)A 1992. Generally, dismissal of the participants during a strike, lock-out or other industrial action is not unfair, as long as all those participating are dismissed and none are re-engaged within three months of the dismissal. However, if only some of the participants are dismissed or have not been offered re-engagement within the three month period, an unfair dismissal claim may be brought. This exception is subject to the action being regarded as official by trade unions (s 20 of the TULR(C)A 1992).

- *Industrial pressure*

  Where an employer dismisses an employee because of industrial pressure brought to bear by other employees, the dismissal may be unfair. Section 107 of the ERA 1996 provides that industrial pressure such as the threat of a strike if the applicant continues to be employed by the employer should be ignored by the tribunal, which must consider the dismissal on the basis of whether the employer had acted reasonably.

  Where pressure is put on an employer to dismiss the applicant by a trade union, because the applicant was not a member of a trade union, the trade union may be joined by the employer or applicant as party to the proceedings. The tribunal may then make an award against the trade union if it finds that the dismissal was unfair.

Sections 99 and 105 of the ERA 1996 made it automatically unfair to select an employee for redundancy on grounds of pregnancy or childbirth, or because he or she has made a health and safety complaint or has asserted a statutory right.

Section 100 of the ERA 1996 provides that an employee has the right not to be dismissed:

- for carrying out, or proposing to carry out, any health and safety activities which he or she is designated to do by the employer;

- for bringing to his or her employer's attention, by reasonable means and in the absence of a safety representative or committee who could do so on his or her behalf, a reasonable health and safety concern (see *Harris v Select Timber Frame Ltd* (1994));

Entitlement:	Age	Weeks' pay for each year of employment
	18–21	$\frac{1}{2}$
	22–40	1
	41–65	$1\frac{1}{2}$

- in the event of danger which he or she reasonably believes to be serious and imminent and which he or she could not reasonably be expected to avert, for leaving or proposing to leave the workplace or any dangerous part of it, or (while the danger persisted) refusing to return; or

- in circumstances of danger which he or she reasonably believes to be serious and imminent, for taking or proposing to take appropriate steps to protect him or herself or other persons from danger. In *Lopez v Maison Bouquillon Ltd* (1996), an assistant in a cake shop complained to the police that a chef, who was married to the shop manageress, had assaulted her. She was then dismissed from her job. She claimed unfair dismissal, stating that it was reasonable for her to leave the workplace because of the assault. The tribunal found that the incident came within s 100 and, therefore, the dismissal was unfair.

- *Dismissal for exercising rights under the Part-Time Workers (Prevention of Less Favourable Treatment) Regulations 2000*

  Part time employees will be held to be unfairly dismissed (or selected for redundancy), regardless of length of service or age, if the reason, or the main reason, for the dismissal is: that they exercised or sought to enforce their rights under the Regulations, refused to forgo them or allege that the employer had infringed them; they requested a written statement; they gave evidence or information in connection with proceedings brought by an employee under the Regulations; or that the employer believed that the employee intended to do these things. The same rights are provided for a dismissal for exercising rights under the Fixed-Term Employees (Prevention of Less Favourable Treatment) Regulations 2002.

- *To dismiss someone because they are entitled to working tax credits, or they took any action with a view to enforcing or securing their rights to working tax credits, also amounts to an unfair dismissal*

- *A dismissal for making an application for flexible working arrangements, if this is the main reason for the dismissal, also amounts to unfair dismissal*

The ERA 1996 also extends protection to the following: workers who refuse to comply with working hours which would contravene the Working Time Regulations 1998 (s 101A of the ERA 1996); workers who are dismissed on the grounds of asserting a statutory right, for example, bringing proceedings against an employer to enforce a statutory right (s 104 of the ERA 1996) – see *Mennell v Newell and Wright (Transport Contractors) Ltd* (1997); employees who are dismissed for making protected disclosures (s 103A of the ERA 1996) – protective disclosures are defined in ss 43A–J of the ERA 1996 and cover such matters as crime, protection of the environment, disclosure to a legal adviser, to the Crown or to a prescribed person. This protection arises from the Public Interest Disclosure Act 1998. Finally, s 25 of the National Minimum Wage Act 1998 amends the ERA 1996 by inserting new ss 104A and 105(7A), which provide that employees who are dismissed or selected for redundancy will be regarded as unfairly dismissed if the sole or main reason for the dismissal or selection was that, *inter alia*, they had asserted their right to the national minimum wage; or the employer was prosecuted for an offence under the National Minimum Wage Act 1998; or they qualify for the national minimum wage.

9.4.2.8 Remedies

Where the dismissal is found to be unfair, the tribunal has the power to make an order for reinstatement, re-engagement or compensation (ss 112–24 of the ERA 1996).

Reinstatement

In the case of reinstatement, the tribunal must ask the applicant whether he or she wishes such an order to be made. The effect of an order for reinstatement is that the employer must treat the employee as if he or she had not been dismissed, that is, as if his or her employment is on the same or improved terms and conditions.

Re-engagement

If the applicant so wishes, the tribunal may make an order for re-engagement (s 115 of the ERA 1996). The effect of this is that the applicant should be re-engaged by the employer, or by an associated employer in employment which is comparable to the previous employment or amounts to other suitable employment. The tribunal will specify the terms on which the applicant should be re-engaged and this may make provision for arrears of pay. The making of orders for reinstatement and re-engagement is at the discretion of the tribunal, which will consider whether it is just and equitable to make such an order considering the conduct of the employee and whether it is practicable to do so.

Failure to comply fully with the terms of an order for reinstatement or re-engagement will result in an award of compensation being made by the employment tribunal, having regard to the loss sustained by the complainant, which is usually the basic award plus an additional award. The employer may raise 'impracticability' as a defence to such a claim.

Compensation

Certain employment protection awards are now automatically index-linked – see the Employment Relations Act 1999 (Commencement No 3 and Transitional Provision) Order 1999 (SI 1999/3374). It should be noted that compensation for unfair dismissal cannot include any award for non-economic loss – see *Dunnachie v Kingston-upon-Hull CC* (2004). However, where the injury, including psychiatric harm, resulted prior to and separately from the act of dismissal, a cause of action will exist at common law – see *Eastwood & Another v Magnox Electric plc; McCabe v Cornwall CC & Others* (2004).

An award of compensation will be made where an order for reinstatement or re-engagement is not complied with or it is not practicable to make such an order. The various types of compensation are described below.

Basic award (s 118 of the ERA 1996)

The calculation of the basic award is dependent upon the number of years of continuous service which the applicant has attained:

The maximum number of years which can be counted is 20 and the maximum amount of weekly pay is currently £280. The maximum basic award is at present £8,400. The tribunal may reduce the basic award on the grounds of contributory conduct on the part of the applicant. Where there is also an award of a redundancy payment, the basic award will be reduced by the amount of that payment, as long as it is established that the dismissal was for reason of redundancy.

A 'week's pay' relates to gross pay; if the applicant is over 64, the award is reduced by one-twelfth for each month after the complainant's 64th birthday. The basic award will be two weeks' pay where the reason for the dismissal was redundancy and the employee unreasonably refuses to accept a renewal of the contract or suitable alternative employment.

Any statutory limits placed on awards are now to be index-linked and reviewed in September of each year (s 34 of the Employment Relations Act 1999).

Compensatory award (s 123 of the ERA 1996)

A compensatory award is in addition to the basic award and is awarded at the discretion of the tribunal. The amount of the award is decided upon by the tribunal by reference to what is 'just and equitable in all the circumstances, having regard to the loss sustained by the applicant in consequence of the dismissal'. At present, the maximum amount of this award is £56,800. The amount of the award may be reduced by failure on the part of the employee to mitigate his or her loss, contributory conduct and any *ex gratia* payment made by the employer.

In making the award, the tribunal will take into account loss of wages; expenses incurred in taking legal action against the employer; loss of future earnings; loss of pension rights and other benefits, for example, a company car; and the manner of the dismissal.

Additional award

An additional award can be made where the employer fails to comply with an order for reinstatement or re-engagement and fails to show that it was not practicable to comply with such an order. The amount of this additional award will be between 13 and 26 weeks' pay; if the dismissal is unfair because it is based on sex or race discrimination, the additional award will be between 26 and 52 weeks' pay.

Interim relief

There are now minimum awards of compensation for dismissal in 'special situations'. For example, the minimum amount for contravening s 100 is £3,600.

Where an employee alleges dismissal for union/non-union membership or trade union activities, he or she can apply to the employment tribunal for an order for interim relief (s 161 of the TULR(C)A 1992).

Such an order will preserve the status quo until a full hearing of the case and has the effect, therefore, of reinstating or re-engaging the employee. In order to obtain an order for interim relief, an application must be made to the employment tribunal within seven days immediately following the effective date of termination. This must be supported by a certificate signed by an authorised trade union official where the allegation relates to dismissal for trade union membership or taking part in trade union activities. Finally, it must appear to the employment tribunal that the complaint is likely to succeed at a full hearing.

Even where these conditions are satisfied, the employment tribunal must then determine whether the employer is willing to reinstate or re-engage the employee. If the employer is not so willing, then the employment tribunal must make an order for the continuation of the employee's contract of employment until the full hearing, thus preserving continuity, pay and other employment rights.

Where the employer fails to comply with an interim relief order, the employment tribunal must:

- make an order for the continuation of the contract; and

- order the employer to pay such compensation as the tribunal believes is just and equitable, having regard to the loss suffered by the employee.

Where an employer fails to observe the terms of a continuation order, the employment tribunal shall:

- determine the amount of any money owed to the employee; and

- order the employer to pay the employee such compensation as is considered to be just and equitable.

There has been much academic debate about the success or otherwise of the unfair dismissal provisions. It has been said that the law has been unsuccessful in providing effective control over what is seen as managerial prerogative in relation to dismissals (see, for example, Collins, H, 'Capitalist discipline and corporatist law' (1982) 11 ILJ 78). One general weakness expounded by academics is the attitude of the appeal court judges to the legislation. They perceive that judges feel that they are being asked to intervene in areas which they believe individuals should resolve; as a result, judges end up endorsing the ordinary practices of employers, even though these may be flawed (see *Saunders v Scottish National Camps Association Ltd* (1980)). The right to protection from unfair dismissal can be seen as a fundamental human right, which therefore demands a complete overhaul of the current legislative provisions (see Hepple, R, 'The fall and rise of unfair dismissal', in McCarthy, W (ed), *Legal Intervention in Industrial Relations: Gains and Losses*, 1992, p 95).

9.4.3 Redundancy

When an employee's services are no longer required by the business, either through the closing down of that business or perhaps because of the introduction of new technology, he or she will in general have been made redundant. Whether or not the employee is entitled to redundancy pay will depend upon whether the qualification rules and the key essentials are satisfied. The law in this area is weighted in favour of the employer, who, in order to avoid the higher compensation limits for unfair dismissal, may well try to disguise an unfair dismissal situation as redundancy. The law relating to redundancy can be found in the ERA 1996. The purpose of the ERA 1996 is to provide for the payment of compensation based on an employee's service and wages, in order to tide the employee over during the period in which he or she is without a job. However, any entitlement to redundancy payments only exists where it is established that the employee's dismissal was by reason of redundancy within the meaning of the ERA 1996.

9.4.3.1 Qualifications

In assessing whether an employee qualifies for redundancy payment, the rules are similar to the unfair dismissal provisions. The qualifying period for redundancy is two years. The final outcome of the decision in *R v Secretary of State for Employment ex p Seymour-Smith and Perez (No 2)* (2000) does not change this, even though a two year qualifying period was found by the House of Lords to discriminate indirectly against women and was contrary to EC law. The onus is on the employer to show that continuity has been broken or that there are weeks which do not count towards continuity; once again, the same rules apply regarding continuity. Certain categories of employee are excluded from the provisions of the ERA 1996 (as referred to earlier), in some cases because existing arrangements between their employer and their trade union are better than the protection afforded by the ERA 1996.

9.4.3.2 Dismissal

The burden of proof in the initial stages of any claim for redundancy is on the employee to show dismissal. There is then a presumption that the dismissal was for reason of redundancy and the burden moves to the employer to show that redundancy was not the reason for the dismissal.

Where an employee meets the basic qualification requirements, it must be shown that he or she has been 'dismissed' within the meaning of s 136 of the ERA 1996. Again, the provisions which determine dismissal are the same as for unfair dismissal. According to s 139 of the ERA 1996, an employee shall be treated as dismissed by the employer if, but only if:

- the contract of employment is terminated by the employer with or without notice; or

- it is a fixed term contract which has expired without being renewed; or

- the employee terminates the contract with or without notice in circumstances such that he or she is entitled to terminate it without notice by reason of the employer's conduct; or

- the contract is terminated by the death of the employer or on the dissolution or liquidation of the firm.

It is clear, however, that the initiative to dismiss the employee must come from the employer. An employee who resigns is not entitled to redundancy payment unless the constructive dismissal provision is satisfied (*Walley v Morgan* (1969)).

Whether a dismissal is within s 136 or 139 is a question of fact in each case. For example, a variation in the terms of the employee's contract will amount to a dismissal if he or she does not agree to the new terms. If, however, the employee accepts the new terms, there can be no dismissal and continuity is preserved.

In *Marriot v Oxford and District Co-operative Society Ltd* (1970), the defendants employed Marriot as a foreman. He was informed that, from a certain date, he would be employed on a lower grade and his rate of pay would be reduced accordingly. It was held that the variation in the terms of the existing contract amounted to termination by the employer, which Marriot could treat as a dismissal.

Clearly, there may be a term in the contract which allows the employer to vary the terms. If the employee in this situation does not like the new terms and chooses to leave his or her employment, this will not amount to a dismissal for the purposes of the ERA 1996. One type of contentious term has proved to be the 'mobility clause' which many executive contracts contain. Where an employee refuses to comply with an express mobility clause requiring him or her to move, the refusal amounts to misconduct and, therefore, any dismissal cannot be treated as redundancy, but it could leave the employer open to a claim of unfair dismissal. Furthermore, if the employee attempts to anticipate the employer's actions and resigns, the resignation will not amount to a dismissal.

In *Morton Sundour Fabrics v Shaw* (1967), Morton employed Shaw as a foreman. He was informed that there might be some redundancies in the near future, but nothing specific was decided. In the light of what he had been told, he decided to leave the firm in order to take another job. It was held that he had not been dismissed and, therefore, was not entitled to redundancy payments. His precipitous action could not be shown to relate to the subsequent redundancies made by his employer.

Obviously, he would have succeeded had he waited until he received his notice of redundancy. However, when he resigned, there was no way of knowing exactly who would be made redundant (see *Doble v Firestone Tyre and Rubber Co Ltd* (1981), which followed the decision in *Morton*).

9.4.3.3 *Dismissals for reasons of redundancy*

In order for the employee to be entitled to redundancy payments, he or she must have been dismissed 'for reason of redundancy'. There is a presumption that, once the employee has shown dismissal, the reason for the dismissal was redundancy (s 163(2) of the ERA 1996). The onus is on the employer to show that the dismissal was for some reason other than redundancy.

Section 139(1) of the ERA 1996 provides a definition of 'redundancy':

[This is where] dismissal is attributable wholly or mainly to:

(a) the fact that his employer has ceased, or intends to cease, to carry on the business for the purposes of which the employee was employed by him, or has ceased, or intends to cease, to carry on that business in the place where the employee was so employed; or

(b) the fact that the requirements of that business for employees to carry out work of a particular kind, or for employees to carry out work of a particular kind in the place where they were so employed have ceased or diminished or are expected to cease or diminish.

In effect, there are three situations in which the dismissal can be said to be for redundancy. These are as follows.

9.4.3.4 Cessation of the employer's business

This covers both temporary and permanent closures of the employer's business in respect of the type of work carried on at the premises and is, on the whole, straightforward. In *Gemmell v Darngavil Brickworks Ltd* (1967), a brickworks closed for a period of 13 weeks in order for substantial repairs to be carried out. Some of the employees were dismissed. It was held that the dismissal was for reason of redundancy, even though part of the premises was still in use.

9.4.3.5 Closure or change in the place of work

Where the employer ceases to trade at a particular place, as opposed to the cessation of the type of work, the dismissal of any employees will usually be for reason of redundancy. This is subject to any term in the contract of employment which contains a 'clear and unambiguous mobility clause'. Such clauses will rarely be implied.

In *O'Brien v Associated Fire Alarms Ltd* (1969), O'Brien was employed by the defendants at their Liverpool branch. There was a shortage of work and he was asked to work in Barrow-in-Furness. He refused and was dismissed by his employer. He contended that the dismissal amounted to redundancy. It was held that, as there was no clause in O'Brien's contract of employment which would have allowed his employer to move him to a different location, the dismissal was for reason of redundancy.

Where the employer only moves his place of work a short distance and/or remains within the same town or conurbation, any offer of work to his existing employees at the new place of employment may prevent any dismissal from being for reason of redundancy. Obviously, this will depend on accessibility to the new premises, as well as the terms on which the offer is made – it should be remembered that the terms must not be worse than existing terms. It can, therefore, be within the employer's expectations that his or her employees will move to different premises without there being a redundancy situation if such an expectation is reasonable in all the circumstances of the case.

In *Managers (Holborn) Ltd v Hohne* (1977), the defendants occupied premises in Holborn, of which Hohne was a manageress. They decided to move their business to Regent Street, which was only a short distance away. Hohne refused to move there and claimed redundancy, on the basis that there was no term in her contract which required her to move. It was held that the new premises were just as accessible as the old ones and, therefore, it was reasonable for her employer to expect her to move without there being any issue of redundancy. There was no evidence of any additional inconvenience to Hohne if she agreed to move to the new premises. She did not, therefore, succeed in her action.

Finally, this provision has been interpreted in such a way that it will only be satisfied if the place where the employee actually works, rather than is expected to work, closes or changes. In *High Table Ltd v Horst* (1997), Mrs Horst was employed as a silver service waitress. Her letter of appointment specified that she was appointed as waitress to one particular client and she worked at their premises from July 1988 until she was dismissed. The staff handbook stated:

> Your place of work is as stated in your letter of appointment, which acts as part of your terms and conditions. However, given the nature of our business, it is sometimes necessary to transfer staff on a temporary or permanent basis to another location. Whenever possible, this will be within reasonable travelling distance of your existing place of work.

The client for whom Horst worked reduced its catering needs and, as a result, Horst was dismissed as redundant. She claimed unfair dismissal. The main issue for the Court of Appeal was, what is the test for determining redundancy? It held that the test was primarily a factual one and, on the facts, the place where she was employed no longer needed her. There was, therefore, a redundancy situation, which caused her to be dismissed. This decision casts doubt on the decision in *UK Automatic Energy Authority v Claydon* (1974). In that case, Claydon's contract of employment included a mobility clause. When he was asked to move from his employer's Suffolk plant to their Aldermaston premises, he refused and was dismissed. It was held that the mobility clause was valid and, although the work had ceased in Suffolk, it was reasonable for the employer to request a transfer to Aldermaston. The dismissal was therefore fair.

Whilst the decision in *Horst* appears to recognise the importance of an employee's redundancy rights and the desire to ensure that those rights are not negated by the unscrupulous use of mobility clauses, in real terms the employer in this case wanted it to be a redundancy situation without any obligation to redeploy staff or increase the amount of compensation payable.

9.4.3.6   Diminishing requirements for employees

As a general rule, where the employer is forced to dismiss employees because of a reduction in the work available, such employees are surplus to the requirements of the business and any dismissal is for reason of redundancy. Furthermore, where there is a change in systems of work so that fewer employees are actually needed to do the job, this, too, can amount to redundancy. The courts are, from time to time, faced with the difficult task of deciding whether dismissal for failing to keep up with modern working practices is for reason of redundancy.

In *North Riding Garages v Butterwick* (1967), Butterwick had been employed at the same garage for 30 years and had risen to the position of workshop manager. The garage was taken over by the appellants and Butterwick was dismissed for inefficiency, on the ground that he was unable or unwilling to accept new methods of work, which would involve him in some administrative work. It was held that the dismissal was not for reason of redundancy because the employee was still expected to do the same type of work, subject to new working practices. As far as the court was concerned, employees who remain in the same employment for many years are expected to adapt to new techniques and methods of work and even higher standards of efficiency. It is only when the new practices affect the nature of the work so that, in effect, there is no requirement to do that particular kind of work that a redundancy situation may arise.

In *Hindle v Percival Boats Ltd* (1969), Hindle had been employed to repair wooden boats for many years. This type of work was in decline because of the increasing use of fibreglass. He was dismissed because he was 'too good and too slow' and it was uneconomical to keep him. He was not replaced; his work was merely absorbed by existing staff. It was held that Hindle's dismissal was not for reason of redundancy. The court felt that the employer was merely shedding surplus labour and that this was not within the ERA 1996.

Clearly, there are situations where shedding surplus labour will amount to redundancy; each case must be considered on its merits.

In *Haden Ltd v Cowen* (1982), Cowen was employed as a regional supervisor. He was based in Southampton and had to cover a large part of southern England as part of his job. He suffered a mild heart attack. His employer then promoted him to divisional contracts surveyor, as it was thought that this would make his life less stressful. One of the terms of his contract required him to undertake, at the discretion of the company, any duties which reasonably fell within the scope of his capabilities. The company was later forced to reduce the number of employees at staff level. Cowen was not prepared to accept demotion and was dismissed. He claimed both redundancy and unfair dismissal. It was held that Cowen was dismissed for reason of redundancy because there was no other work available within the terms of his contract, that is, as divisional contracts manager.

It is suggested that the true test of redundancy is to be found in this case and the issue to be considered is 'whether the business needs as much work of the kind which the employee could, by his contract, lawfully be required to do'. This is a question not of the day to day function of the employee, but of what he or she could be expected to do under his or her contract of employment (see *Pink v White & Co Ltd* (1985)). Recent case law suggests that, even where a contract contains a 'flexibility clause', for example, 'and any work which may be required by the employer', there may still be a redundancy situation. In *Johnson v Peabody Trust* (1996), Johnson was employed as a roofer. A flexibility clause was introduced into his contract, which stated that he was expected to undertake general building work. By 1993, Johnson was doing more general work than roofing. He was then laid off. The EAT concluded that he was redundant. In looking at the basic task which he was expected to perform, it was determined that he was first and foremost a roofer and the need for such employees had diminished. However, a move from day shift to night shift work or vice versa may be 'work of a particular kind', as was held in *Macfisheries Ltd v Findlay* (1985).

In *Shawkat v Nottingham City Hospital NHS Trust (No 2)* (2001), the Court of Appeal held that the mere fact of a reorganisation of the business, as a result of which the employer requires one or more employees to do a different job from which he or she was previously doing, is not conclusive of redundancy. The tribunal must go on to decide whether that change had any, and if so what, effect on the employer's requirements for employees to carry out work of a particular kind. It does not necessarily follow from the fact that a new post is different in kind from the previous post or posts that the requirements of the employer's business for employees to carry out work of a particular kind must have diminished. Nor does the fact that an employee of one skill was replaced by an employee of a different skill compel the conclusion that the requirements for work of a particular kind have ceased or diminished. That is always a question of fact for the tribunal to decide.

In *Shawkat's* case, a tribunal was entitled to find that dismissal of a thoracic surgeon, following a reorganisation as a result of which he was asked to carry out cardiac surgery in additional to thoracic surgery, was not by reason of redundancy. The requirements for employees to carry out thoracic surgery had not diminished even though the reorganisation changed the work which the employees in the thoracic department, including the applicant, were required to carry out.

Finally, the definitive test, which upholds an earlier decision in *Safeway Stores plc v Burrell* (1997), can be found in *Murray & Another v Foyle Meats* (1999). The House of Lords in this case determined that a dismissal must now be regarded as being by reason of redundancy wherever it is attributable to redundancy; that is, did the diminishing requirement for employees cause the dismissal? This is a straightforward causative test.

9.4.3.7 Lay-off and short time (ss 147–49 of the Employment Rights Act 1996)

Redundancy payment may be claimed where an employee has been laid off or kept on short time for either four or more consecutive weeks or for a series of six or more weeks (of which not more than three are consecutive) within a period of 13 weeks. The employee must give written notice to his or her employer, no later than four weeks from the end of the periods referred to, of his or her intention to claim redundancy payment, and should terminate the employment by giving either at least one week's notice or notice during the period stipulated in the contract of employment. Following this action by the employee, the employer may serve a counter-notice within seven days of the employee's notice, contesting the claim and stating that there is a reasonable chance that, within four weeks of the counter-notice, the employee will commence a period of 13 weeks' consecutive employment. This then becomes a matter for the tribunal.

If the employer withdraws the counter-notice or fails to employ the employee for 13 consecutive weeks, the employee is entitled to the redundancy payment.

9.4.3.8 Change in ownership and transfer of undertakings

Under the ERA 1996, continuity is preserved in the following situations, so that past service will count in the new employment:

- change of partners;

- where trustees or personal representatives take over the running of the company when the employer dies;

- transfer of employment to an associated employer; and

- transfer of an undertaking, trade or business from one person to another.

Where there is a change in the ownership of a business and existing employees either have their contract renewed or are re-engaged by the new employer, this does not amount to redundancy and continuity is preserved (s 218(2) of the ERA 1996); an example of this is where the business is sold as a going concern, rather than a transfer of the assets. However, if the employee has reasonable grounds for refusing the offer of renewal, he or she may be treated as redundant (s 141(4)).

The Transfer of Undertakings (Protection of Employment) Regulations 1981 (SI 1981/1794) apply to the sale or other disposition of commercial and noncommercial undertakings (see s 33 of the Trade Union Reform and Employment Rights Act (TURERA) 1993, which brought the UK in line with EC Directive 77/187 – the Acquired Rights Directive). The transfer must be of the whole or part of a business, not merely a transfer of assets (*Melon v Hector Powe Ltd* (1980)); nor do the Regulations apply to a change in ownership resulting from a transfer of shares. Where there is the transfer of a business which falls within the Regulations, the contracts of employment of the employees are also transferred, as if they had been made by the transferee. This not only protects continuity, but also puts the new employer in the same position as the original employer. As a result, all existing rights, etc, attained by employees are preserved and become enforceable against the new business. Such transfers are subject to the consent of the employee. If the employee objects, the transfer will in effect terminate the contract of employment, but this termination will not amount to a dismissal (s 33(4) of the TURERA 1993). If, following a transfer, there is a subsequent dismissal, the employee may claim unfair dismissal, or, if it is for 'an economic, technical or organisational reason', redundancy payment may be claimed.

In *Astley v Celtic Ltd* (2002), the Court of Appeal held that the wording of the EC Acquired Rights Directive is sufficiently wide in its terms to embrace a transfer of an undertaking which takes place over a period of time and does not imply that the transfer must take place at a particular moment in time.

The Court of Appeal in *RCO Support Services v Unison* (2002) held that there can be a TUPE transfer even where there is no transfer of significant assets and none of the relevant employees were taken on by the new employer. In the present case, there was a change in hospitals providing inpatient care within the same NHS trust area and new contractors took over the provision of cleaning and catering. In determining whether there had been a transfer of an undertaking, the tribunal had correctly applied the retention of identify test as well as considering the reasons why the employees were not taken on by the new employer.

The contentious issue concerning the position of employees who are dismissed prior to a transfer (thus potentially enabling the employers to evade the Regulations) has been resolved by *Litster & Others v Forth Dry Dock and Engineering Co Ltd* (1989), in which it was decided that where employees are dismissed in these circumstances, they must be treated as if they were still employed at the time of transfer. As a result, the Regulations are to be applied to such employees. The transferee employer will be responsible for any unfair dismissals, unless they can be shown to be for an 'economic, technical or organisational' reason entailing a change in the workforce.

By virtue of reg 8(2), such dismissals are deemed to be for a substantial reason for the purposes of s 98(1) of the ERA 1996 and are fair, provided that they pass the statutory test of reasonableness. If the employer successfully establishes the 'economic, technical or organisational' (ETO) defence, an employee can claim a redundancy payment if the transfer was the reason for the redundancy dismissal. The Court of Appeal considered the scope of the ETO defence in *Berriman v Delabole Slate Ltd* (1985). The court held that in order to come within reg 8(2), the employer must show that a change in the workforce is part of the economic, technical or organisational reason for dismissal. It must be an *objective* of the employer's plan to achieve changes in the workforce, not just a possible consequence of the plan. So, where an employee resigned following a transfer, because the transferee employer proposed to remove his guaranteed weekly wage so as to bring his pay into line with the transferee's existing workforce, the reason behind the plan was to produce uniform terms and conditions and was not in any way intended to reduce the numbers in the workforce.

A further contentious issue relating to the position of contracted out services has been resolved by the decision in *Dines & Others v Initial Health Care Services & Another* (1994). The Court of Appeal held that where employees are employed by the new contracting company, the new company is obliged to take over the contract of employment on exactly the same terms (following the decision in *Kenny v South Manchester College* (1993)).

Following *Dines*, cases have extended the meaning of 'relevant transfer'. In *Betts v Brintel Helicopters and KLM* (1996), Brintel had, until 1995, exclusive rights to provide and service Shell's helicopter requirements for all of their North Sea oil rigs. In 1995, Shell decided to split the contract between Brintel and KLM, and 66 Brintel employees were left without jobs. Betts and six others claimed successfully that they were now employed by KLM. The High Court held that there had been a transfer of the 'activity' from Brintel to KLM, even though there was no transfer of employees or assets. (See also *ECM (Vehicle Delivery Service) Ltd v Cox & Others* (1999).)

An attempt to avoid the application of the Transfer of Undertakings (Protection of Employment) Regulations 1981 (SI 1981/1794) by 'hiving down' the transfer first to a subsidiary company and then to the ultimate transferee has been thwarted. In *Re Maxwell Fleet and Facilities Management Ltd (No 2)* (2000), the High Court held that liability for employees dismissed before the purported 'hive down' passed to the ultimate transferee by virtue of the application of the *Litster* principle. The employees in this situation were dismissed for a reason connected with the transfer and were, therefore, deemed to have been employed immediately before the transfer.

Following the decision in *Abler & Others v Sodexho MM Catering Gesellschaft mbH* (2004), the courts make a clear distinction between 'asset reliant' businesses and 'labour intensive' businesses. For there to be a transfer in respect of the former, all of the key assets must be transferred; in respect of the latter, the labour force must be transferred. In this particular case, catering was held to be asset intensive.

Finally, the Government is proposing to reform the Transfer of Undertakings (Protection of Employment) Regulations 1981 and issued a Consultation Paper: *Government Proposals for Reform (Employment Relations Directorate)* (DTI, September 2001).

Draft regulations and a further Consultation Paper have been produced (see www.dti.gov.uk).

The Collective Redundancies and Transfer of Undertakings (Protection of Employment) (Amendment) Regulations 1995 have amended the 1981 Regulations. In particular, reg 8(5) was introduced to reverse the decision in *Milligan v Securicor Cleaning Ltd* (1995) to the effect that an employee did not need to have two years' continuous employment in order to claim unfair dismissal on a transfer pursuant to reg 8. The effect of the decision was that someone who was dismissed after one week's employment because of a transfer could claim unfair dismissal, whereas an employee of 23 months' duration who was dismissed in a non-transfer situation could not! The decision has been overruled by the High Court in *R v Secretary of State for Trade and Industry ex p Unison* (1996).

9.4.3.9 *Offer of alternative employment*

The offer of alternative employment is covered by s 141 of the ERA 1996. The general rule is that where the employer makes an offer of suitable alternative employment, which is unreasonably refused by the employee, the employee will be unable to claim redundancy. This contract, which is either a renewal or a re-engagement, must take effect on the expiry of the old contract or within four weeks. Clearly, the main issue is what amounts to 'suitable'. Consideration must be had of the old terms and conditions as compared with the new ones, that is, the nature of the work; remuneration; hours; place; skills; and experience, including qualifications, etc. Where the conditions of the new contract do not differ materially from the old contract regarding place, nature of the work, pay, etc, then the question of suitability does not arise. It is a question of fact in each case as to whether an offer can be deemed 'suitable', with the onus resting on the employer to establish suitability. However, the facts must be considered objectively.

In *Taylor v Kent CC* (1969), Taylor was made redundant from his post as headmaster of a school. He was offered a place in the pool of supply teachers from which temporary absences were filled in schools. There was no loss of salary or other rights, other than status. Taylor refused the offer. It was held that his refusal was reasonable. The offer was not suitable because of the loss of status, since he was being removed from a position as head of a school to an ordinary teacher.

A loss of fringe benefits has been held to be a reasonable refusal (*Sheppard v NCB* (1966)). However, the refusal of an offer of a job which may only last a short period could be deemed to be unreasonable (*Morganite Crucible v Street* (1972)). It was decided in *Spencer and Griffin v Gloucestershire CC* (1985) that the issue for the industrial (now employment) tribunal is twofold: first, whether the job offered is suitable; and, secondly, whether the employee has acted reasonably in refusing the offer.

In considering whether a refusal by the employee is reasonable, regard must be had for the personal circumstances of the employee, such as housing and domestic problems. It may be reasonable for an employee to refuse a job offer which involves a move to London when he or she lives in the Midlands, because of the housing problems associated with a move to the Home Counties. However, a refusal based upon a personal whim will be unreasonable. In *Fuller v Stephanie Bowman (Sales) Ltd* (1977), the applicant refused to move with her employers from a West End address to one in Soho, where the new business premises were above a sex shop. After a site visit to the premises, it was decided that the dislike of the sex shop was not enough to make the refusal of the offer reasonable, as it was not one of the worst streets in Soho and it was unlikely that the applicant would be mistaken for a prostitute. In *Rawe v Power Gas Corp* (1966), it was held to be reasonable to refuse a move from the south-east of England to Teeside because of marital difficulties.

Finally, even where the employment tribunal finds that the offer was suitable, it does not automatically follow that a refusal by the employee is unreasonable. For example, in *Cambridge and District Co-operative Society Ltd v Ruse* (1993), although the job was deemed to be suitable by the industrial tribunal, the employee had personal objections to the job offered, as he perceived a lack of status which supported his refusal of the offer.

It must be remembered that the onus is on the employer to show that the employee's rejection of the offer is unreasonable. Where the offer of alternative employment is accepted by the employee, there is deemed to be continuity of employment between the former contract and the new contract.

The offer of alternative employment following the transfer of an undertaking must not be on less favourable terms than the original contract. If the alteration of the employment relationship is connected to the transfer, it is invalid – see *Martin v South Bank University* (2004).

By virtue of s 132 of the ERA 1996, the employee is entitled to a trial period of four weeks (or longer, if agreed with the employer) if the contract is renewed on different terms and conditions. If the employee terminates his or her employment during the trial period for a reason connected with the new contract, he or she will be treated as having been dismissed on the date that the previous contract was terminated. Whether he or she will be entitled to redundancy will depend on whether it was a suitable offer of alternative employment and whether the refusal to accept it was reasonable (see *Meek v Allen Rubber Co Ltd and Secretary of State for Employment* (1980)). If the employer dismisses the employee during the trial period for any reason, the dismissal is to be treated as redundancy.

An employee is entitled to a reasonable amount of time off to seek work or retrain once notice of redundancy has been received (s 52 of the ERA 1996). This right is confined to those employees who meet the qualifying periods. Failure to provide time off may result in the employee making a complaint to an employment tribunal, which may award two-fifths of a week's pay.

9.4.3.10 *Calculation of redundancy payment*

The employee must inform the employer, in writing, of any intention to claim a redundancy payment. If the employer does not make the payment or there is a dispute over entitlement, the matter is referred to an employment tribunal. As a general rule, the claim must be made within six months of the date of termination of the contract of employment. This period can be extended at the discretion of the employment tribunal but cannot exceed 12 months.

9.4.3.11   Method of calculation

Although those under 20 years of age or who have reached retirement age do not qualify, the method of calculation is the same for unfair dismissal (considered above). The maximum award at present is, therefore, £8,400. An employee may lose entitlement to all or part of his or her redundancy payments in the following circumstances:

- if the claim is made out of time, that is, after a period of six months from the relevant date. However, as with unfair dismissal, an employment tribunal may allow an extension within the time limit if it is just and equitable to do so (s 164 of the ERA 1996);

- if employment is left prematurely, the employee having been warned of the possibility of redundancy in the future. An employee under notice of dismissal who leaves before the notice expires may also lose the right to payment. This will depend on whether the employer objects to the premature departure (s 142 of the ERA 1996);

- where the employee is guilty of misconduct, allowing the employer to terminate the contract for this reason (s 140(1) of the ERA 1996); and

- strike action – if the employee is involved in a strike during his or her period of notice, he or she will still be entitled to redundancy payment. However, if his or her notice of dismissal is received whilst on strike, he or she will not be entitled to claim redundancy payment.

9.4.3.12   Procedure for handling redundancies

This is governed by s 188 of the TULR(C)A 1992 (as amended by the Trade Union Reform and Employment Rights Act (TURERA) 1993) and the Collective Redundancies and Transfer of Undertakings (Protection of Employment) (Amendment) Regulations 1995 (SI 1995/2587). There is an obligation on the employer to consult a recognised trade union or elected employee representative 'in good time', as opposed to 'at the earliest opportunity'. Such consultation must take place even if only one employee is being made redundant. Where consultation cannot take place at the earliest opportunity, the fall back rules are as follows:

- at least 90 days before the first dismissal takes effect, where he or she proposes to make 100 or more employees redundant at one establishment within a period of 90 days or less; or

- at least 30 days before the first redundancy takes effect, where he or she proposes to make 20 or more employees redundant at one establishment within a 30 day period.

Consultation must include consideration of the ways in which the redundancies can be avoided; a possible reduction in the numbers of employees being dismissed; anything which might mitigate the effects of the redundancy *ex gratia* payment, etc (ss 188–98 of the TURERA 1993). Durng the consultations, the employer must also disclose (s 188(4) of the TULR(C)A 1992):

- the reasons for the proposed redundancies;

- the number and description of the employees whom it is proposed to make redundant;

- the total number of employees of that description employed at that establishment;

- the method of selection, for example, FIFO, LIFO, part timers first, etc; and

- the method of carrying out the redundancies, having regard to any procedure agreed with the trade union.

During these consultations, the trade union may make any representations which it sees fit. The employer may not ignore these representations and must give the reasons if he or she chooses to reject them. However, in considering the fairness of the employer's conduct, in *British Aerospace plc v Green* (1995) the Court of Appeal adopted a broad brush approach in judging the overall fairness of the employer's conduct of the selection procedure and did not feel that it was necessary to examine individual applications of it too closely. Where there are special circumstances, such as insolvency, the employer need only do what is reasonably practicable to comply with the consultation requirements.

9.4.3.13 *Effect of non-compliance with the procedure*

Where the employer fails to comply with the consultation procedure in circumstances where it was reasonably practicable to expect him or her to do so, the trade union can complain to the employment tribunal. If the tribunal finds in favour of the trade union, it must make a declaration to this effect and may make a protective award to those employees who were affected. This award, which is discretionary, takes the form of remuneration for a protected period. The length of the protected period usually reflects the severity of the breach by the employer. However, the protected period:

- must not exceed 90 days, where it was proposed to make 100 or more employees redundant within 90 days; or

- is 30 days, where it was proposed to make 20 or more redundant.

All employees covered by the protective award are entitled to up to 13 weeks' pay (Collective Redundancies and Transfer of Undertakings (Protection of Employment) (Amendment) Regulations 1995 (SI 1995/2587)).

9.4.3.14 *Notification of redundancies to the Secretary of State*

By virtue of s 193 of the TULR(C)A 1992, an employer must notify the Secretary of State of his or her intentions where he or she proposes:

- to make 100 or more employees redundant at one establishment within a 90 day period – here, the notification must take place within 90 days; or

- to make 20 or more employees redundant within a 30 day period – in which case the notification must take place within 30 days.

Failure to meet these requirements may result in prosecution. However, there is a 'special circumstances' defence where it is not reasonably practicable for the employer to comply with the law on notification.

BUSINESS AND CORPORATE LAW

Agency

Definition

An agent is a person who is empowered to represent another legal party, called the principal, and brings the principal into a legal relationship with a third party.

Agency agreements may be either contractual or gratuitous.

Commercial agents are specifically covered by the Commercial Agents (Council Directive) Regulations 1993.

Creation of agency

Agency may arise:

- expressly;

- by ratification;

- by implication;

- by necessity; or

- by estoppel.

Nature of agent's authority

Actual authority may be divided into:

- express actual authority; and

- implied actual authority.

Apparent authority is based on estoppel and operates in such a way as to make the principal responsible for their action or inaction as regards someone who claims to be their agent.

Warrant of authority

If an agent contracts with a third party on behalf of a principal, the agent impliedly guarantees that the principal exists and has contractual capacity and that he or she has that person's authority to act as his or her agent. If this is not the case, the agent is personally liable to third parties for breach of warrant of authority.

The duties of agent to principal

The duties of the agent to the principal are:

- to perform the undertaking according to instructions;
- to exercise due care and skill;
- to carry out instructions personally;
- to account;
- not to permit a conflict of interest to arise;
- not to make a secret profit or misuse confidential information; and
- not to take a bribe.

The rights of an agent

The rights of an agent are:

- to claim remuneration for services performed;
- to claim indemnity for all expenses legitimately incurred in the performance of services; and
- to exercise a lien over property owned by the principal.

Commercial Agents (Council Directive) Regulations 1993

- Regulations 3–5 set out the rights and obligations as between commercial agents and their principals.
- Regulations 6–12 deal with remuneration.
- Regulations 13–16 deal with the conclusion and termination of the agency contract.
- Regulations 17–19 contain provisions relating to the indemnity or compensation payable to a commercial agent on termination of his agency contract.
- Regulation 20 relates to the validity of restraint of trade clauses.

Relations with third parties

Where the agent indicates that he or she is acting as an agent, the general rule is that only the principal and the third party have rights and obligations under the contract.

There are exceptions to this:

- at the insistence of the third party;
- by implication;

- in relation to bills of exchange; and
- in relation to deeds.

  Where the principal's existence is not disclosed:
- the agent can enforce the contract against the third party;
- the principal can enforce the contract against the third party;
- the third party can choose to enforce the contract against the agent or the principal; or
- an undisclosed principal cannot ratify any contract made outside of the agent's actual authority.

Where the third party had a special reason to contract with the agent, the principal may be excluded from the contract.

Where the agent misrepresents the identity of the principal, the third party may not be bound by the contract.

Payment by means of an agent

- If the agent does not pay the third party, the principal remains liable.
- If the agent absconds with money paid by the third party, then, if the principal is undisclosed, he or she sustains the loss. If, however, the principal is disclosed, the agent must have had authority to accept money, or else the third party is liable.

Termination of agency

Agreements may end:

- by mutual agreement;
- by the unilateral action of one of the parties;
- through frustration; or
- due to the death, insanity or bankruptcy of either party.

Partnership

Definition of 'partnership'

- Section 1 of the Partnership Act 1890 states that partnership is the relation which subsists between persons carrying on a business in common with a view to profit.

The legal status of a partnership

- A partnership, unlike a joint stock company, has no separate legal personality apart from its members, although the limited liability partnership formed under the

Limited Liability Partnership Regulations 2000 does have separate legal personality.

- Partnerships are generally limited to 20 members; however, certain professional partnerships are exempt from this maximum limit.

Formation of a partnership

- There are no specific legal requirements governing the formation of a partnership. Partnerships arise from the agreement of the parties involved and are governed by the general principles of contract law.

Duties of partners

- General fiduciary duties.

- Sections 28–30 of the PA 1890 lay down the specific duties:
  - of disclosure;
  - to account; and
  - not to compete.

Rights of partners

Subject to express provision to the contrary in the partnership agreement, s 24 of the PA 1890 sets out the rights of partners. Among the most important of these are the rights:

- to share equally in the capital and profits of the business;
- to be indemnified by the firm for any liabilities incurred or payments made in the course of the firm's business;
- to take part in the management of the business;
- to have access to the firm's books;
- to prevent the admission of a new partner; and
- to prevent any change in the nature of the partnership business.

Partnership property

It is important to distinguish between partnership property and personal property for the following reasons:

- partnership property must be used exclusively for partnership purposes;

- any increase in the value of partnership property belongs to the partnership;

- any increase in the value of personal property belongs to the person who owns the property;

- on the dissolution of the firm, partnership property is used to pay debts before personal property;

- partnership and personal property are treated differently in the satisfaction of claims made by partnership creditors, as opposed to personal creditors; and

- on the death of a partner, any interest in partnership land will pass as personalty, whereas land owned personally will pass as realty.

The authority of partners to bind the firm

Authority can be actual or implied on the basis of the usual authority possessed by a partner in the particular line of business carried out by the firm.

Partners' liability on debts

Every partner is responsible for the full amount of the firm's liability.

Outsiders have the choice of taking action against:

- the firm collectively; or

- against the individual partners.

Where damages are recovered from one partner only, the other partners are under a duty to contribute equally to the amount paid.

Partnership by estoppel

Failure to give notice of retirement is one way in which liability arises on the basis of estoppel or holding out. Alternatively, anyone who represents themselves, or knowingly permits themselves to be represented, as a partner is liable to any person who gives the partnership credit on the basis of that representation.

Dissolution

Grounds for dissolution are:

- the expiry of a fixed term or the completion of a specified enterprise;

- the giving of notice;

- the death or bankruptcy of any partner;

- where a partner's share becomes subject to a charge;

- illegality;
- where a partner becomes a patient under the Mental Health Act 1893;
- where a partner suffers some other permanent incapacity;
- where a partner engages in activity prejudicial to the business;
- where a partner persistently breaches the partnership agreement;
- where the business can only be carried on at a loss; and
- where it is just and equitable to do so.

Winding up

Since the introduction of the Insolvency Act 1986, partnerships as such are not subject to bankruptcy. Partnerships may be wound up as unregistered companies under Pt V of the Insolvency Act 1986.

Treatment of assets on dissolution

On dissolution, the value of the partnership property is applied in the following order:

- in paying debts to outsiders;
- in paying to the partners any advance made to the firm beyond their capital contribution;
- in paying the capital contribution of the individual partners; and
- any residue is divided between the partners in the same proportion as they shared in profits.

Limited liability partnerships

The Limited Liability Partnership Act 2000, together with the Limited Liability Partnership Regulations 2001, provides for a new form of business entity, the limited liability partnership. Although stated to be a partnership, the new form is a corporation, with a distinct legal existence apart from its members. As such, it will have the ability:

- to hold property in its own right; and
- to sue and be sued in its own name.

It will have perpetual succession and, consequently, alterations in its membership will not have any effect on its existence.

Most importantly, however, the new legal entity will allow its members to benefit from limited liability, in that they will not be liable for more than the amount they have agreed to contribute to its capital.

Formation

To form a limited liability partnership:

- two or more persons must subscribe to an incorporation document;

- the incorporation document must be delivered to the Companies' Registry; and

- a statement of compliance must be completed by a solicitor or subscriber to the incorporation document.

The incorporation document must include:

- the name of the limited liability partnership (subject to restrictions);

- the address of the registered office;

- the names and addresses of those who will be members on incorporation of the limited liability partnership; and

- the names of at least two designated members whose duty it is to ensure that the administrative and filing duties of the LLP are complied with. If no such members are designated, then all members will be assumed to be designated members.

Regulation between members

The rights and duties of members will be governed by any agreement entered into. In the absence of any agreement, the default provisions of the Limited Liability Partnership Regulations 2001 will apply. These default rules are based on the previous rules set out in the Partnership Act 1890.

Section 6 of the Limited Liability Partnership Act 2000 provides that every member of the limited liability partnership is an agent of the limited liability partnership rather than a principal, and agent of the other members, as in an ordinary partnership. The extent of such authority is subject to the usual agency rules.

Liability and creditor protection

Members' liability is limited to the amount of capital introduced into the partnership. However, unlike limited companies, there are no controls on the withdrawal of capital by members, so creditors are not protected by the doctrine of capital maintenance. Creditors are protected by the following general mechanisms:

- the requirement for limited liability partnerships to file audited accounts; and

- the rules relating to fraud or misconduct under the Insolvency Act 1986.

Insolvency and winding up

The Limited Liability Partnership Regulations 2001 extend the provisions relating to the insolvency and winding up of registered companies to limited liability partnerships. Thus, the relevant sections of the Companies Act 1985, the Insolvency Act 1986, the Company Directors Disqualification Act 1986 and the Financial Services and Markets Act 2000 have been appropriately modified to apply to limited liability partnerships.

Company Law

The effects of incorporation

- *Separate personality* is where the company exists as a legal person in its own right, completely distinct from the members who own shares in it.

- *Limited liability* refers to the fact that the potential liability of shareholders is fixed at a maximum level, equal to the nominal value of the shares held.

- *Perpetual succession* refers to the fact that the company continues to exist, irrespective of any change in its membership. The company only ceases to exist when it is formally wound up.

- The company owns the business property in its own right. Shareholders own shares; they do not own the assets of the business in which they have invested.

- The company has contractual capacity in its own right and can sue and be sued in its own name. Members, as such, are not able to bind the company.

Lifting the veil of incorporation

The courts will, on occasion, ignore separate personality. Examples include:

- statutory provisions; and

- the use of the company form as a mechanism for perpetrating fraud.

It is difficult, however, to provide a general rule to predict when the courts will lift the veil of incorporation.

Public and private companies

This is an essential distinction which causes/explains the need for different legal provisions to be applied to the two forms. The essential difference is to be found in the fact that the private company is really an economic partnership seeking the protection of limited liability.

The company's documents

- The memorandum of association governs the company's external affairs. It represents the company to the outside world, stating its capital structure, its powers and its objects.

- The articles of association regulate the internal working of the company.

- If there is any conflict between the two documents, the contents of the memorandum prevail.

Share capital

A 'share' has been defined as 'the interest of the shareholder in the company measured by a sum of money, for the purposes of liability in the first place and of interest in the second, but also consisting of a series of mutual covenants entered into by all the shareholders' (*Borlands Trustees v Steel* (1901)).

The main ways of categorising shares are in terms of:

- nominal or authorised capital;

- issued or allotted capital;

- paid up and unpaid capital; and

- called and uncalled capital.

Types of shares

Shares can be divided into:

- ordinary;

- preference;

- deferred; and

- redeemable shares.

Loan capital

The term 'debenture' refers to the document which acknowledges the fact that a company has borrowed money, and also refers to the actual debt:

- A fixed charge is a claim against a specific asset of the company.

- A floating charge does not attach to any specific property of the company until it crystallises through the company committing some act or default.

- All charges, both fixed and floating, have to be registered with the Companies Registry within 21 days of their creation.

- A fixed charge takes priority over a floating charge, even though it was created after the floating charge.

- Similar charges take priority according to their date of creation.

Directors

- The board of directors is the agent of the company and may exercise all the powers of the company.

- Individual directors may be described as being in a fiduciary relationship with their companies.

A director can be removed at any time by the passing of an ordinary resolution of the company (s 303 of the Companies Act 1985).

Individuals can be disqualified from acting as directors up to a maximum period of 15 years under the Company Directors Disqualification Act 1986.

As fiduciaries, directors owe the following duties to their company:

- to act *bona fide* in the interests of the company;

- not to act for a collateral purpose; and

- not to permit a conflict of interest to arise.

They also owe the company a duty of care and skill. This has been enhanced by s 214 of the IA 1986.

Meetings

In theory, the ultimate control over a company's business lies with the members in a general meeting. In practice, however, the residual powers of the membership are extremely limited.

There are three types of meeting:

- annual general meeting;

- extraordinary general meeting; and

- class meeting.

Proper and adequate notice must be sent to all those who are entitled to attend any meeting, although the precise nature of the notice is governed by the articles of association.

There are three types of resolutions:

- ordinary resolutions;

- extraordinary resolutions; and

- special resolutions.

Voting is by a show of hands or according to the shareholding on a poll. Proxies may exercise voting rights if properly appointed.

Majority rule and minority protection

The majority usually dictate the action of a company and the minority is usually bound by the decisions of the majority. Problems may arise where those in effective control of a company use their power in such a way as to benefit themselves or to cause a detriment to the minority shareholders.

Three remedies are available to minority shareholders, which are as follows:

- The minority may seek court action to prevent the majority from committing a fraud on the minority.

- An order to have the company wound up on just and equitable grounds may be applied for where there is evidence of a lack of probity on the part of some of the members. It may also be used in small private companies to provide a remedy where there is either deadlock on the board or a member is removed from the board altogether or refused a part in the management of the business.

- Under s 459 of the Companies Act 1985, any member may petition the court for an order, on the ground that the affairs of the company are being conducted in a way that is unfairly prejudicial to the interests of some of the members.

In addition to the above remedies, the Secretary of State has the power under s 431 of the Companies Act 1985 to appoint inspectors to investigate the affairs of a company.

Winding up

Liquidation is the process whereby the life of the company is brought to an end.

There are three possible procedures:

- compulsory winding up;
- a members' voluntary winding up; and
- a creditors' voluntary winding up.

Administration

This is a relatively new procedure, aimed at saving the business as a going concern by taking control of the company out of the hands of its directors and placing it in the hands of an administrator. Alternatively, the procedure is aimed at maximising the realised value of the business assets. The Enterprise Act 2002 introduced a new scheme which reduced the powers of floating charge holders to appoint administrative receivers to the potential detriment of the company.

Insider dealing

Insider dealing is governed by Pt V of the Criminal Justice Act 1993:

- Section 52 of the Criminal Justice Act 1993 states that an individual who has information as an insider is guilty of insider dealing if they deal in securities that are price affected securities in relation to the information.

- They are also guilty of an offence if they encourage others to deal in securities that are linked with this information, or if they disclose the information otherwise than in the proper performance of their employment, office or profession.

- Section 56 makes it clear that securities are price affected in relation to inside information if the information, made public, would be likely to have a significant effect on the price of those securities.

- Section 57 defines an insider as a person who knows that they have inside information and knows that they have the information from an inside source. 'Inside source' refers to information acquired through:

  ○ being a director, employee or shareholder of an issuer of securities; or

  ○ having access to information by virtue of their employment.

  It also applies to those who acquire their information from primary insiders previously mentioned.

- Section 53 makes it clear that no person can be so charged if they did not expect the dealing to result in any profit or the avoidance of any loss.

- On summary conviction, an individual found guilty of insider dealing is liable to a fine not exceeding the statutory maximum and/or a maximum of six months' imprisonment.

- On indictment, the penalty is an unlimited fine and/or a maximum of seven years' imprisonment.

Companies Act 1985 (Electronic Communications) Order 2000

This allows electronic communication to replace what were formerly requirements for paper-based systems. It also alters Table A articles of association.

Companies (Audit, Investigations and Community Enterprise) Act 2004

This Act will strengthen the auditing and company investigation regimes. It also introduces the possibility of community interest companies.

CHAPTER 10

THE LAW OF EQUITY AND TRUSTS

10.1 Introduction

In this chapter, we will look at the trust, a curious feature of English law. A trust is the relationship that exists between a person who holds property for another (trustee) and that other person (beneficiary). It is a relationship between the parties that was originally recognised only by a court of equity. The key scenario is where A transfers property to B telling him to hold it on trust for C. In this situation, A is the donor or 'settlor' if he makes a formal settlement or transfers property by will, B is the trustee (armed with the legal title) and C is the beneficiary (who acquires the equitable title). In order to properly understand this area of law, it is necessary to have an understanding of the basic principles of Equity and how this peculiar feature of English law developed historically.

The branch of law known as Equity developed in England and Wales in the Middle Ages in circumstances where the ordinary common law had failed to give proper redress. Many legal actions, for example, were commenced by the issue of a writ (basically a claim form in modern civil law) which was drafted in complex legal language. The slightest error on the writ had the effect of invalidating the whole action. Another deficiency in the ordinary common law concerned the fact that the only remedy was damages (that is monetary compensation) – thus, court orders did not exist to require individuals to do something such as to sell a plot of land according to an agreement, or to desist from some conduct, for example, to prohibit the use of a particular title.

Dissatisfied litigants often chose to petition the King to intervene in cases of injustice – the courts were, after all, the King's courts. These petitions for justice were dealt with by the King's Chancellor (Lord Chancellor) who decided each case according to his own discretion. Over the years, the decisions made by the Lord Chancellor became known as the rules of equity (derived from the Latin expression, *aequitas* meaning levelling). These new rules came to be applied in a special court, the Chancellor's Court, which became known as the Court of Chancery. Thus equity is a body of rules which have legal significance although sometimes, rather confusingly, lawyers distinguish 'equity' from 'law'. The significance of this distinction lies in the fact that it is sometimes important to know whether the origin of a rule existed in the ordinary common law as it was evolved by judges in the ordinary courts of law or from the Court of Chancery. Different principles concerning how a rule should be enforced and applied come into play depending on whether the rule derives from 'equity' or 'law'. For example, the equitable remedy of specific performance is discretionary so the court may refuse to give this remedy to a claimant even if the defendant is technically in breach of a rule of trusts law, whereas the remedy of damages is a legal remedy and must be granted to a claimant by the court where a legal rule has been violated by the defendant.

Probably the most important branch of equity is the law of trusts, although equitable remedies, like specific performance and injunctions are also widely used today. The order of specific performance allows the court to order a recalcitrant party to carry out his side of a contract, and the injunction is a court order which can be used to require someone to refrain from acting in a particular way or to require some sort of positive conduct. Where there is a case of conflict or variance between the rules of common law and the rules of equity, equity will prevail. Historically, there were often conflicts in specific cases where a litigant who had received satisfaction through the ordinary common law courts could then find himself taken to the Court of Chancery, whereupon a different judge may come to a different conclusion on the basis of different principles. This rather odd state of affairs continued until 1875, when the Judicature Acts 1873/75 came into effect and allowed all courts to administer the principles of both equity and law.

Consider the following case (which we take from Glanville Williams, *Learning the Law*, 11th edn, p 28, Stevens). One of the principles of equity is that 'he who comes to equity must come with clean hands'. This rule applies whenever a claimant is relying on an equitable right but not when he is relying on a common law right. In the case, a landlord brought an action against his tenant, Mr Isaacson, for ejectment. Mr Isaacson had what is known as an equitable lease of the premises, that is not a formal lease under seal but an informal lease valid only in equity. For nearly all practical purposes, these equitable leases were just as good as legal leases even though they were technically void at law. This particular tenant, however, had broken a term of his equitable lease by assigning it to a company by the name of Saxon Ltd, contrary to a covenant in the lease not to assign. Mr Isaacson awkwardly explained to the court that he did not act improperly because the company was his own creation and 'Saxon' was none other than the latter part of his name. Mr Isaacson's real defence however was that although he might be liable to pay damages for having broken his covenant not to assign, that was not a reason for his being ejected altogether from the premises. If the document had been a legal lease, the defence would have been a good one, for the lease did not contain a proviso for re-entry on breach of covenant. But, unfortunately for the tenant, it was an equitable lease, and by being in breach of an important term, he had soiled his hands and had accordingly lost his lease.

The trust developed historically from the 'use'. The 'use' arose in the Middle Ages where a person conveyed property of any sort to another on the understanding that the other was to become seised of it on behalf of the donor or on behalf of some third party (*cestui que use* or beneficiary). The person thus trusted with the property (*a feoffee to* use or trustee) was in a position of confidence, which could easily be abused. Consequently, the rights of the *cestui que* use required protection. The ordinary common law courts did not recognise such uses and therefore did nothing to provide protection but at an early date the Court of Chancery acting as a court of conscience intervened to force the *feoffee to* use to administer the property for the benefit of the *cestui que* use according to the terms of the grant. Thus over time, and accumulation of a great many decisions by the Court of Chancery, the *cestui que* use came to have a special interest in the property which could be enforced by the Court of Chancery. This interest was known as an equitable interest. Eventually, the *cestui que* use became a *cestui que* trust (that is, a beneficiary) and the *feoffee to* use became a trustee.

A modern definition of the trust was formulated and included in Art 12 of the Hague Convention on the Recognition of Trusts enacted in the Recognition of Trusts Act 1987. This provides that:

> ... the term 'trust' refers to the legal relationship created – '*inter vivos*' or on death – by a person, the settlor, when assets have been placed under the control of a trustee for the benefit of a beneficiary or for a specified purpose.

A trust has the following characteristics:

(a) the assets constitute a separate fund and not a part of the trustee's own estate;

(b) title to the trust assets stands in the name of the trustee or in the name of another person on behalf of the trustee;

(c) the trustee has the power and the duty, in respect of which he is accountable, to manage, employ or dispose of the assets in accordance with the terms of the trust and the special duties imposed on him by law.

> The reservation by the settlor of certain rights and powers, and the fact that the trustee may himself have rights as a beneficiary are not necessarily inconsistent with the existence of a trust.

In general, trusts enable people to take the benefit of property where they are for one reason or another unable or unwilling to hold the legal ownership themselves. Groups or aggregations of people such as unincorporated associations can enjoy the benefit of property held in trust even though the law would not recognise the legal personality (that is, individual status) of their group. One of the key issues in understanding trusts law is to appreciate that the two titles (legal and equitable) may be separated. When this is the case a trust is created. The legal title is acquired by the trustee but the beneficial interest or equitable title is acquired by the equitable owner.

In this chapter, we will examine the current law governing the creation of trusts including secret trusts, resulting and constructive trusts, the nature of charitable trusts, the appointment and retirement and removal of trustees, the duties and powers of trustees and the variation of trusts.

10.2   Express Trusts

Here, we examine the resulting trust (where the court will imply a trust), the constructive trust (created by the court to satisfy the demands of justice) and the charitable trust (a public trust designed to benefit the public). We start, though, by looking at the express trust.

10.2.1   Creation of an express trust

A settlor is a person who makes a settlement of his land or personal property. A settlement is a deed (a legal document, signed, sealed and delivered) whereby property may be subjected to a string of limitations. A settlor who wishes to create an express trust is required to adopt either of the following methods:

- a self-declaration of trust; or

- a transfer of property to the trustees subject to a direction to hold upon trust for the beneficiaries.

This is known as the rule in *Milroy v Lord* (1862):

(a) *self-declaration*. A settlor may declare that he holds property on trust for a beneficiary by declaring his intention and specifying the terms of the trust. Generally, no special form is required, so long as the intention of the settlor is sufficiently clear so as to constitute himself a trustee, for 'equity looks at the intent rather than the form'. Thus, the declaration may be in writing or be evidenced by conduct, or may take the form of an oral statement. It can also be a combination of these (see *Paul v Constance* (1977); contrast *Jones v Lock* (1865). For an interesting case, see *Re Kayford* (1975) where a company created a trust for its customers). What is required from the settlor is a firm commitment on his part to undertake the duties of trusteeship in respect of the relevant property, on behalf of the specified beneficiaries (see 10.3). In this respect, there is no obligation to inform the beneficiaries that a trust has been created in their favour. The effect of this mode of creation is to alter the status of the settlor from beneficial owner to that of trustee. For example, S, the absolute owner of 50,000 shares in BP plc, declares that henceforth he holds the entire portfolio of shares upon trust for B, his son, absolutely. In these circumstances, an express trust is created. S retains the legal title to the shares, but B acquires the entire equitable interest in the shares;

(b) *transfer to the trustees*. A settlor may create a trust by transferring the property to another person (or persons), subject to a valid declaration of trust. In this context, the settlor must comply with two requirements, namely, a transfer of the relevant property or interest to the trustees, complemented by a declaration of the terms of the trust (see 10.3). If the settlor intends to create a trust by this method, and declares the terms of the trust but fails to transfer the property to the intended trustees, it is clear that no express trust is created. The ineffective transaction will amount to a conditional declaration of trust but without the condition (the transfer) being satisfied. For example, S, a settlor, nominates T1 and T2 to hold 50,000 BT plc shares upon trust for A for life with remainder to B absolutely (the declaration of trust). In addition, S is required to transfer the title to the shares to T1 and T2. The declaration of trust on its own, without the transfer, is of no effect.

The formal requirements (if any) for the transfer of the legal title to property vary with the nature of the property involved. Thus, in order to transfer legal title to registered land, the settlor is required to execute the prescribed transfer form and register the transfer in the names of the trustees at the appropriate Land Registry. The transfer of tangible moveable property requires that the settlor deliver the property to the trustees accompanied by the appropriate intention to donate. The transfer of the legal title to shares in a private company involves the execution of the appropriate transfer form and registration of the transfer in the company's share register.

If, as stated above, a settlor manifests an intention to create a trust by naming another as trustee and setting out the terms of the trust, but fails to deliver the property to the named trustees, the purported trust will not be effective or constituted. In this event, the court will not imply a self-declaration of trust (which would make the settlor the trustee) because this would mean that all imperfect trusts would become perfect. (See *Milroy v Lord* (1862) – ineffective transfer of the legal title to the trustees.) But if the settlor appoints multiple trustees, including himself, the trust declared will be perfect even if there is no transfer to the third party trustees. The retention of the property by the settlor will be as trustee and, as the office of trusteeship is joint, the acquisition of the property by one trustee will be treated as if all the trustees had acquired the same, see *Choithram v Pagarani* [2001] 1 WLR 1.

However, it appears that, if the settlor intends to transfer the legal title to property and has done everything which is necessary for him to do to effect the transfer, but the last act remaining to be done is required to be done by a third party (this being outside the control of the settlor), the transfer or conveyance *will* be effective in equity. In other words, the transfer of the equitable title may be effective even though the transfer of the legal title has not yet taken place (see *Re Rose* (1952) and *Mascall v Mascall* (1985); contrast *Re Fry* (1946)). This principle was recently endorsed by the Court of Appeal in *Pennington v Waine* [2002] All ER (D) 24.

10.2.1.1   *No trust of future property*

A trust may only be created in respect of existing property. Accordingly, no trust is created in respect of an 'expectancy' or 'future property', such as an anticipated interest under a will during the lifetime of the testator, the reason being that there is no property actually capable of being subject to the protection of equity. The anticipated property may or may not be acquired by the settlor in the future; in the meantime, there is only a hope of acquiring the same. (See *Re Ellenborough* (1903); *Re Cook's Settlement Trust* (1965).)

10.2.1.2   *Trust of a chose in action*

A '*chose in action*' is a right that exists in intangible personal property, such as the right to be paid royalties (copyright), the right to receive dividends (shares), the creditor's right to have a loan repaid, etc. The *chose* may be assigned to the trustees, in accordance with the intention of the settlor. Accordingly, the *chose* is capable of being the subject matter of a trust. In *Don King Productions Inc v Warren* (1998), the court decided that the benefit of promotion and management agreements created by boxing promoters was capable of being the subject matter of a trust. Likewise, a trust may be created in respect of the 'benefit of a covenant', which is a *chose in action*. In *Fletcher v Fletcher* (1844), the court decided that, on the execution of the covenant between the settlor and the trustees, the benefit of the covenant was transferred to the trustees and the trust was perfect. However, in *Re Cook's Settlement Trust*, the court distinguished *Fletcher v Fletcher* on the ground that, in the former case, the underlying property intended as the subject matter of the trust (the proceeds of a possible sale of paintings) did not exist and was thus incapable of being trust property.

10.2.1.3   Effect of a perfect trust

On the creation of an express trust, the beneficiaries are given a recognisable interest in the property. They are entitled to protect their interest against anyone, except the *bona fide* purchaser of the legal estate for value without notice. The beneficiaries are entitled to sue directly for either the common law remedy of damages or, in appropriate cases, an equitable remedy, irrespective of whether they have provided consideration or not (see *Fletcher v Fletcher*, above). In any event, the trustees (as representatives of the trust) are entitled to bring or defend a claim on behalf of the trust. Of course, this can only be the case if the trust is perfect.

If the trust is imperfect, the intended beneficiaries may only commence an action if they have provided consideration, that is, if they are non-volunteers (see below). In other words, a non-volunteer of an imperfect trust is placed in almost the same position as that of a beneficiary under a trust. The non-volunteer of an imperfect trust may force the intended trustee to bring or defend an action concerning the relevant property. Similarly, the non-volunteer may bring a claim to enforce rights in respect of the property (see *Pullan v Koe* (1913)).

A 'volunteer' is a person who has not provided valuable consideration. 'Valuable consideration' refers to either common law consideration in money or money's worth or marriage consideration. Common law consideration is the price contemplated by each party to an agreement. Marriage consideration takes the form of an ante-nuptial settlement made in consideration of marriage or a post-nuptial settlement made in pursuance of an ante-nuptial agreement. A post-nuptial settlement *simpliciter* is not within the marriage consideration. An ante-nuptial agreement is one made before or at the time of a marriage, on condition that the marriage takes place, or on the occasion of the marriage and for the purpose of facilitating the marriage (see *Re Park (Deceased) (No 2)* (1972)). The persons who are treated as providing marriage consideration are the parties to the marriage and the issue of the marriage, including remoter issue. Any other children affiliated to the parties to the marriage are volunteers. Thus, illegitimate, legitimate and adopted children, as well as children of a subsequent marriage, are volunteers.

10.2.1.4   Effect of an imperfect trust

The imperfect trust operates as an agreement to create a trust and, subject to the Contracts (Rights of Third Parties) Act 1999, only a party is entitled to sue for breach of contract. This principle is subject to the limitation that the claimant must have provided valuable consideration for the promise, for 'equity will not assist a volunteer' and 'equity will not perfect an imperfect gift'. For example, A voluntarily promises to transfer 10,000 BP plc shares to B to hold on trust for C, a volunteer and non-party, absolutely. A fails to transfer the shares to B. The trust is, therefore, imperfect. Since B and C are volunteers, neither may bring a claim against A to enforce the promise.

The general rule, that only persons who have provided consideration may claim rights under a promise to create a trust, is subject to one limitation, namely that a party to a voluntary covenant (deed) may claim a remedy of damages for breach of covenant. The rule at common law is that in a 'specialty' contract (deed), the absence of consideration does not prevent a party from enforcing the contract at law by claiming damages. In this respect, 'equity follows the law' and does not prevent the party from enforcing his legal rights. At the same time, the volunteer is not entitled to claim equitable assistance. In the above example, if the voluntary promise between A and B is incorporated in a deed for the benefit of C, B, in theory, is entitled to claim damages at common law for breach of contract, even though B and C are volunteers. (See *Re Cavendish Browne's Settlement Trust* (1916) (substantial damages were awarded); contrast *Re Kay's Settlement* (1939) (B was prevented from bringing an action for damages on behalf of C).) The quantum of damages may sometimes pose a problem. But, if C is also a party to the covenant, he will be entitled to claim damages in his own right. In the above example, neither B nor C is entitled to claim equitable assistance (see *Cannon v Hartley* (1949)). Under the Contracts (Rights of Third Parties) Act 1999, the decision in *Re Kay* was reversed. Under s 1 of the Act, a third party to a contract is entitled in his own right to enforce a term of the contract if, *inter alia*, a 'term of the contract purports to confer a benefit on him'. This is clearly covered by a contract, albeit voluntary, to create a trust for the benefit of C. Today, C would be entitled to claim substantial damages from A, even though he is not a party to the contract. Notwithstanding the reforms enacted in the 1999 Act, C, a volunteer, will not be entitled to an equitable remedy of specific performance. Such a remedy would not have been available to him even if he had been a party to the contract, for 'equity will not assist a volunteer'.

10.2.2 Exceptions to the rule that 'equity will not assist a volunteer'

There are a number of occasions when, although a gift or trust is imperfect, equity would give assistance to volunteers and force the defendant to complete the intended gift or trust.

10.2.2.1 *The rule in* Strong v Bird

The rule in *Strong v Bird* (1874) is that, if an *inter vivos* gift is imperfect by reason only of the fact that the transfer to the intended donee is incomplete, the gift will become perfect when the donee acquires the property in the capacity of executor of the donor's estate. In probate law, a deceased's estate devolves upon his executor as appointed in his will. The executor is treated in law as the *alter ego* of the deceased. The intended donee/executor will take the property beneficially, in accordance with the intention of the donor, even though he acquires the asset in a different capacity. In short, the defective gift will be cured by operation of law. In *Strong v Bird*, a loan without consideration was effectively eliminated in favour of the debtor/executor. This rule has been extended to imperfect transfers to trustees (see *Re Ralli* (1964)).

The donor's intention is of paramount importance. The donor is required to manifest a present, continuous intention to make an *inter vivos* gift. Accordingly, the test will not be satisfied if the donor declares an intention to transfer the property to the donee in the future (see *Re Freeland* (1952)). If the donor changes his mind at any time before his death, the test will not be satisfied (*Re Wale* (1956)). In *Re James* (1935), the principle was extended to the acquisition of property by the next of kin on an intestate succession.

10.2.2.2   *Donatio mortis causa* (DMC)

A DMC is an *inter vivos* delivery of property by a person contemplating death, subject to the condition that the gift will take effect only on the donor's death. The effect is that on the donor's death, the conditional transfer becomes complete and the donee (volunteer) is entitled to retain the property or compel the personal representatives of the deceased to transfer the property to him. For example, T, by his will, appoints A, his executor, and declares an intention to dispose of all his property to B. However, on his death bed, T gives C his watch and his building society passbook showing a credit balance of £1,000. These transfers were made conditional on death. On T's death, the gift of the watch becomes complete. The transfer of the building society funds is incomplete, but C will be entitled to compel A to perfect the intended gift.

10.2.2.3   *Proprietary estoppel*

Proprietary estoppel is a right given to a volunteer whenever a landowner stands by and permits a volunteer to incur expenditure in order to improve his (the landowner's) property, on the promise or assumption that there will be a transfer of an interest to him. The principle may be used as a cause of action entitling the volunteer to acquire an interest in land. The landowner and his successors in title will be estopped from denying the interest in land acquired by the volunteer. The court will decide the nature of the interest that may be acquired by the volunteer. The test today is: having regard to all the circumstances of the case, would it be unconscionable to deny the promisee an interest or right in the land? For example, L, a landowner, encourages his son, S, to build a house on his farm. No conveyance is made to S. On L's death, S may be entitled to claim the freehold interest in the house (*Dillwyn v Llewellyn* (1862)).

10.3   The Three Certainties

An established test to determine whether a valid declaration of trust has been effected is the 'three certainties test'. These certainties are certainty of intention, subject matter and objects. The declaration of trust may take effect as a self-declaration by the settlor, or may complement a transfer of property to the trustees.

10.3.1 Certainty of intention

The issue here is to identify whether the settlor manifested a 'present irrevocable intention' to create a trust. This is a subjective question, and the focus of attention is on the spoken or written words of the settlor and his conduct. In the event of a dispute, the question is decided by the court. An intention to benefit another *simpliciter* is distinct from the narrow question of whether the settlor intended to create a trust obligation (see *Jones v Lock*).

Use of the expressions 'trust' and 'trustees', although desirable, is not obligatory. Substitute expressions vary in the degree of precision insisted on by the court in order to create a trust. A testator who intends to create a trust should avoid the use of 'precatory' words. Such words express a 'hope', 'recommendation', 'desire', 'confidence', etc, that the transferee of property will deal with the property in a particular way. Precatory words impose a moral obligation on the transferee to accomplish the stated result, but whether they create a trust obligation will depend on the facts of each case. Unless the document and the surrounding circumstances establish the existence of an obligation to hold the property upon trust, the transferee will be entitled to take the property beneficially. (See *Re Adams and the Kensington Vestry* (1884); contrast *Comiskey v Bowring-Hanbury* (1905).)

10.3.2 Certainty of subject matter

It is obvious that an express trust cannot be created if the subject matter is uncertain. The property (including the appropriate interest) which is intended to be subject to the trust is required to be ascertainable to such an extent that the court may impose an order in respect of the property. Assuming that the property can be identified, its type and nature is irrelevant. All kinds of property, whether legal, equitable, real or personal, are capable of being the subject matter of a trust. If the property cannot be identified with certainty, then there can be no trust and the transferee may take the property beneficially. In this respect, uncertainty in identifying the property creates a 'reflex action on the words of the settlor and creates doubt as to his intention' (*Missoorie Bank v Raynor* (1882), *per* Hobhouse J). Examples of failure of a trust for uncertainty of subject matter include directions regarding 'the bulk of my estate' (*Palmer v Simmonds* (1854)); 'the remaining part of what is left that he does not want for his own use to be equally divided between A, B and C' (*Sprange v Barnard* (1789)); where a claimant argued that he was entitled to a number of bottles of wine from a wine company, but where the claim failed because it could not be shown which bottles of wine the claimant was entitled to (*Re London Wine Co* (1986)); and shares and debentures in the 'blue chip' category (*Re Kolb's Will Trust* (1961)). On the other hand, trusts were created in respect of declarations of '5% of the issued share capital' of a company (*Hunter v Moss* (1994)) and 'reasonable income from my properties' *(Re Golay* (1965)).

If the beneficial interest (as opposed to the property) is uncertain, the trust will not be void *ab initio* but the transferee (trustee) will hold the property on resulting trust for the settlor. Failure to exercise a personal obligation to select one property from two trust properties resulted in failure of the express trust in *Boyce v Boyce* (1849).

10.3.3   Certainty of objects

No express trust can be created if it is unclear in whose favour the trust was intended to be created. The settlor has a duty to identify the beneficiaries with sufficient clarity. The effect of uncertainty of objects (assuming that there is certainty of intention and subject matter) is that the intended express trust fails and a resulting trust is set up in favour of the settlor or his estate.

The test for certainty of objects varies with the nature of the trust. There is a narrow test for fixed trusts and a broad test for discretionary trusts. If the trust is 'fixed', the test is whether the trustees are capable of identifying all the members of the class. In other words, the test is whether the trustees are capable of drawing up a comprehensive list of all the beneficiaries (see *IRC v Broadway Cottages Ltd* (1955)). A 'fixed' trust is one where the trustees are required to distribute the property amongst all the beneficiaries in the proportion of the shares specified (fixed) by the settlor, for example, £20,000 to be divided *equally* by the trustees among four named beneficiaries. In the recent case *OT Computers Ltd v First National Tricity Finance Ltd* [2003] EWHC 1010, the court decided that an intended express trust for 'urgent suppliers' failed on the ground of uncertainty of objects. On the other hand, a trust is 'discretionary' if the trustees are obliged to exercise their discretion to distribute the property (subject to the terms of the trust) among such of the objects, and in such proportions, as the trustees may decide in their discretion. An example of this is a direction to distribute 'the income from £50,000, held by the trustees, for 10 years, in favour of such of my relatives and on such terms as the trustees may decide in their absolute discretion. Subject thereto, the property is to be held upon trust in favour of a named charity'.

The test for certainty of objects in the context of discretionary trusts was laid down in *McPhail v Doulton* (1971). The test is whether the trustees may say with certainty that any given individual is or is not a member of a class of objects. Thus, there is no need to identify all the objects, but the class (or classes) of objects is required to be clearly defined so that the trustees are able to say who comes within or falls outside the class. In the example above, the trustees are required to be aware of and apply the legal definition of 'relatives'. In so doing, the trustees are capable of deciding whether X or Y is a relative. It is unnecessary to identify all the relatives of the settlor. The expression, 'relatives' was defined by the Court of Appeal in *Re Baden (No 2)* (1972) as anyone who can prove a common ancestry with the relevant person (the settlor).

10.4   Formalities

In addition to the tests stated above, in order to create an express trust, a settlor is required to comply with any formal statutory requirements. These formalities vary with the subject matter of the trust (for example, land or personalty), the nature of the interest involved (for example, a legal or equitable interest and the mode of creation (*inter vivos* or by will).

10.4.1 *Inter vivos* declarations of trusts of land

Section 53(1)(b) of the Law of Property Act 1925 provides that 'a declaration of trust concerning land or any interest therein must be manifested and proved by some writing, signed by some person who is able to declare the same or by his will'.

This sub-section concerns the creation of an express trust of realty. It is not applicable to personalty. The declaration of trust is not required to be created in writing, but must be proved in writing. Failure to comply with the sub-section leads to the trust being unenforceable, but not void. The writing may be supplied subsequently, and the trust will then be enforceable.

Resulting and constructive trusts are exempt from the above formal requirement, because s 53(2) of the Law of Property Act 1925 provides that: 'This section shall not affect the creation or operation of implied, resulting and constructive trusts.' Accordingly, a resulting trust of land may arise without the terms being reduced into writing. (See *Hodgson v Marks* (1971).)

10.4.1.1 Inter vivos *dispositions of equitable interests*

Section 53(1)(c) of the Law of Property Act 1925 provides that:

> ... a disposition of an equitable interest or trust subsisting at the time of disposition must be in writing, signed by the person disposing of the same or by his agent thereunto lawfully authorised in writing or by his will.

The policy of the sub-section is to prevent oral hidden transfers of equitable interests which exist under trusts. The wording of the sub-section, as opposed to that of s 53(1)(b), is mandatory in effect. Accordingly, non-compliance with the provision results in the purported disposition being void, subject to limited exceptions. The sub-section is applicable to transactions concerning interests in both realty and personalty subsisting under a trust. The provision is not applicable in relation to the original creation of a trust. For example, on day one, S creates a trust by transferring shares to T, a trustee, on trust for B, a beneficiary. This transaction does not come within s 53(1)(c). On day two, B verbally declares himself a trustee of his interest for C. This arrangement falls within s 53(1)(c) and, as the transaction is not in writing, it is void.

The key feature of s 53(1)(c) is the meaning of the term 'disposition'. This has not been defined in the statute. But the term 'conveyance' has been defined in s 205(1)(ii) of the Law of Property Act 1925 as including a disposition. However, Romer LJ, in *Timpson's Executors v Yerbury* (1936), went some way to defining the expression when he classified four types of dispositions that can be made by a beneficiary under a trust:

- an assignment to a third party;

- a direction to the trustees to hold on trust for a third party;

- a contract for valuable consideration to assign the equitable interest; and

- a self-declaration by the beneficiary under a trust in favour of another.

In *Grey v IRC* (1960), the House of Lords decided that an oral direction by an equitable owner to the trustees to hold upon trust for another was void for non-compliance with s 53(1)(c).

In *Vandervell v IRC* (1967), the House of Lords held that s 53(1)(c) has no application where the equitable owner under a trust directs the legal owner to transfer his title to a third party and where, in the same transaction, the equitable owner, in the absence of writing, transfers his interest to the same third party. In other words, the sub-section is not applicable where the equitable owner terminates the trust by a transfer of both equitable and legal title in favour of a third party.

In *Neville v Wilson* (1996), the Court of Appeal held that s 53(2) restricts the operation of s 53(1)(c) by exempting constructive trusts from the operation of the sub-section. In *Re Vandervell Trusts (No 2)* (1974), the Court of Appeal decided that equitable estoppel was also excepted from the provision. The same court decided in *Re Paradise Motor Co* (1968) that a disclaimer of an equitable interest under a trust was not a disposition; and in *Re Danish Bacon Staff Pension Fund* (1971), the High Court held that nominations by staff pension fund holders are outside the provision.

It appears that a self-declaration of trust of part of an equitable interest in favour of another is outside the operation of s 53(1)(c). The reason for this is that such an arrangement operates as the creation of a new trust. For example, T, a trustee, holds the legal title to 50,000 BT plc shares upon trust for B, a beneficiary. B subsequently orally declares himself trustee of his interest for himself for life with remainder to C. Since B has active duties to perform, he does not drop out of the picture and his self-declaration of trust is outside s 53(1)(c).

10.4.2 Contracts for the sale of land

Section 2 of the Law of Property (Miscellaneous Provisions) Act 1989 declares that a contract for the sale or other disposition of land or an interest in land must be in writing. The need for writing is mandatory; informal transactions concerning land, such as mortgages and options, which fail to comply with the section are treated as void. Excluded from the provision are constructive and resulting trusts.

10.4.3 Testamentary dispositions

Any donation of property (including a gift by way of a trust) must be made by will if the property is intended to take effect on the death of the donor. The testamentary document is revocable by the testator during his lifetime. The will must comply with the provisions of s 9 of the Wills Act 1837, as amended by s 17 of the Administration of Justice Act 1982. Broadly, the formalities are threefold: the will must be in writing, signed by the testator (that is, the person who makes the will), and his signature must be witnessed by two or more witnesses, who are also required to sign. Failure to fulfil any of these requirements renders the purported will void and the deceased's property will be distributed on an intestacy. Excepted from these provisions are secret trusts. These are considered below.

10.5   Secret Trusts

A secret trust is an equitable obligation, communicated to an intended trustee during the testator's lifetime, but which is intended to attach to a gift arising under the testator's will.

On a testator's death, his will becomes a public document. But the testator may wish to make provision for what he considers to be an embarrassing object, such as his mistress or an illegitimate child. To avoid adverse publicity, he may make an apparent gift by will to an intended trustee, subject to an understanding created outside the will that the trustee will hold the property for the benefit of the secret beneficiary.

In enforcing such trusts, equity does not contradict s 9 of the Wills Act 1837, as amended, because the trust operates outside (*dehors*) this Act. Indeed, the secret trust complements the will, in that a valid will is assumed, but it is recognised that the will on its own does not reflect the true intention of the testator. The bare minimum requirements to create a secret trust are a validly executed will which transfers property to the trustees, whether or not named as such under the will, and the *inter vivos* acceptance by the trustees of an equitable obligation. It is immaterial that one of the intended beneficiaries under the trust, as distinct from the will, witnesses the will. Section 15 of the Wills Act 1837 is not applicable in this context (see *Re Young* (1951)).

There are two types of secret trusts – fully and half secret trusts.

10.5.1   Fully secret trusts

These trusts are fully concealed on the face of the will. The testator transfers property by will apparently beneficially to the intended trustees, but subject to an understanding created outside the will that they will hold on trust for beneficiaries when they acquire the property. For example, T, a testator, transfers '50,000 BT plc shares by will to my legatee, L'. Prior to his death, T orally informs L that he wishes him to hold the shares on trust for B, the secret beneficiary, absolutely. L becomes a trustee for B on T's death and is not allowed to claim the property beneficially.

The following conditions need to be fulfilled in order to create a fully secret trust:

*   it is essential that, during his lifetime, the testator communicates the terms of the intended trust to the trustee (legatee or devisee). This requirement reflects the distinction between a gift on trust and an absolute gift to the legatee. It follows that, if the legatee or devisee only hears of the trust after the testator's death, no secret trust is created and the legatee or devisee may take the property beneficially. In this event, s 9 of the Wills Act 1837 may be used as a defence by the legatee or devisee (see *Wallgrave v Tebbs* (1865));

- if the testator communicates to the legatee the fact that he is to hold the legacy on trust, but fails to disclose the terms of the trust before his death, the intended secret trust fails. The legatee will not take the property beneficially, but will instead hold the property on resulting trust for the testator's estate or next of kin (see *Re Boyes* (1884));

- the communication of the terms of the trust may be made before or after the execution of the will, provided that it is made during the lifetime of the testator. Communication may either be made directly with the legatee or be effected constructively, that is, the testator may deliver a sealed envelope to the legatee, marked with a direction such as 'Not to be opened before my death'. Once the legatee is aware that the contents of the envelope are connected with a transfer of property by will, the communication is effective. The communication is deemed to be made on the date of the delivery of the envelope (see *Re Keen* (1937));

- the legatee may 'expressly' or 'impliedly' accept the obligation imposed by the testator. An 'implied' acceptance is signified by silence or acquiescence on the part of the legatee. Thus, if the legatee does not wish to become a trustee, it is incumbent on him to inform the testator during his lifetime. Failure to do so amounts to an acceptance of the obligation by the legatee;

- the fully secret trust obligation may take the form of the trustee holding the property on trust for the secret beneficiary absolutely. Alternatively, the obligation may require the legatee to execute a will in favour of the secret beneficiary. In this event, the legatee may enjoy the property beneficially during his lifetime (see *Ottoway v Norman* (1972));

- where a testator leaves property to two or more legatees but informs one or some of them (but not all of them) of the terms of the trust, the issue arises as to whether the uninformed legatees are bound by the communication to the informed legatees. The solution here depends on the timing of the communication and the status of the legatees. If: (a) the communication is made to the legatees before or at the time of the execution of the will; and (b) they take as joint tenants, the uninformed legatees are bound to hold for the purposes communicated to the informed legatees. The justification commonly ascribed to this principle is that no one is allowed to take property beneficially under a fraud committed by another. If any of the above conditions is not satisfied, the uninformed legatees are entitled to take the property beneficially (see *Re Stead* (1900)).

10.5.2 Half secret trusts

This classification arises where the legatee or devisee takes as trustee on the face of the will, but the terms of the trust are not specified in the will. For example, T, a testator, transfers property to L, a legatee, to 'hold upon trust for purposes that have been communicated to him'. The will acknowledges the existence of the trust, but the terms are concealed.

The following points are relevant in order to establish a half secret trust:

- the will is irrevocable on the death of the testator. Thus, evidence is not admissible to contradict the terms of the will. To adduce such evidence would have the potential to perpetrate a fraud. For example, if the will points to a past communication (that is, a communication of the terms of the trust before the will was made), evidence is not admissible to prove a future communication. Similarly, since the will names the legatee as trustee, evidence is not admissible to prove that he is a beneficiary (see *Re Rees* (1950));

- where the communication of the terms of the trust is made before or at the time of the execution of the will, evidence may be adduced to prove the terms of the trust (see *Blackwell v Blackwell* (1929));

- if the communication of the terms of the trust is made after the execution of the will, but during the lifetime of the testator, the courts have ruled that such communication is inadmissible. The justification commonly given for this principle is that a testator is prohibited from making a future unattested disposition by naming a trustee in the will and supplying the purposes subsequently (see *Blackwell v Blackwell*; *Re Keen* (1937)). This principle is not without its critics;

- the persons named as trustees on the face of the will are not entitled to take any part of the property beneficially. For these purposes, it is immaterial that the testator intended the trustees to take part of the property beneficially (see *Re Rees*). Likewise, on a failure, whole or in part, of the secret trust, the trustee holds the property on resulting trust for the testator's estate or next of kin.

10.6   Resulting Trusts

A resulting trust, unlike an express trust, is implied by the court in favour of the settlor/transferor (or his estate if he is dead). Such trusts arise by virtue of the unexpressed or implied intention of the settlor or testator. The settlor (or his estate) becomes the beneficial owner under the resulting trust. The trust is created as a result of defective drafting. The expression 'resulting trust' derives from the Latin verb '*resultare*', meaning to spring back (in effect, the trust 'springs back' to the original owner). Examples are the transfer of property subject to a condition precedent which cannot be achieved, and the creation of an express trust which becomes void.

In *Re Vandervell's Trusts (No 2)* (1974), Megarry J classified resulting trusts into two categories, namely, 'automatic' and 'presumed'.

10.6.1   Automatic resulting trusts

Sometimes the legal title to property has been transferred but the destination of the beneficial interest remains unclear. Automatic resulting trusts arise in order to fill a gap in ownership. This type of resulting trust arises in a variety of situations, as follows:

- on the failure of an intended express trust (see *Re Ames* (1946), where a purported marriage settlement was void);

- on the transfer of property to trustees where the terms of the trust have not been specified (see *Vandervell v IRC* (1967), where there was vagueness as to the destination of the equitable interest in a share option scheme);

- on the transfer of property subject to a condition precedent which has not been achieved (see *Barclays Bank v Quistclose* (1970), where a loan that was created for a specific purpose was not fulfilled);

- where the trust exhausts only part of the trust property. The surplus may be held on resulting trust (see *Re Abbott* (1900)). By way of contrast, the court may decide, on construction of the instrument, that the ulterior purpose of the settlor/transferor may be achieved by permitting the transferee to retain the property beneficially. In these circumstances, there is no room for a resulting trust (see *Re Osoba* (1979)).

10.6.2 Presumed resulting trusts

A presumed resulting trust is, *prima facie*, a rule of evidence that creates a rebuttable presumption of law. Where (a) there is a purchase of property in the name of another or the voluntary transfer of property to another; and (b) there is no definitive evidence in the first place concerning the transferor's real intention, equity *prima facie* declares that the transferee is a trustee for the transferor. In short, the transferor is presumed to have retained the equitable title and the transferee is presumed to obtain a nominal interest in the property. The rule is arbitrary, but the presumption has the advantage of determining the ownership of the beneficial interest, subject to evidence of the contrary.

There are two occasions when the presumption arises, namely:

- a purchase of property in the name of another; and

- a voluntary conveyance of property in the name of another.

10.6.2.1 Purchase in the name of another

The rule is that, where a purchaser contracts with a vendor to acquire real or personal property, but directs the vendor to transfer the legal title in the name of another, the transferee is presumed to hold the property on trust for the purchaser. Parol evidence is admissible in order to identify the purchaser.

Thus, if A purchases shares in the name of B (that is, B becomes the legal owner), the latter is presumed to hold the shares on trust for A. B is a mere nominee for A until he rebuts the presumption.

Similarly, where A and B jointly purchase a house and have it conveyed in the name of B, so that B becomes the legal owner of the house, B is presumed to hold the house on trust for both A and B in proportion to the contribution made by each of them. If A provides four-fifths and B provides one-fifth of the purchase moneys, B is presumed to hold the house for himself beneficially as to one-fifth and to hold the remainder on trust for A (see *Bull v Bull* (1955)).

10.6.2.2   *Voluntary transfer in the name of another*

Another state of affairs which gives rise to a presumed resulting trust is the occasion of a voluntary transfer of personal property in the name of another. No consideration is provided by the person in whose favour the transfer is made.

For example, if A transfers the legal title to shares in the name of B, a resulting trust is presumed in favour of A (see *Re Vinogradoff* (1935)).

By virtue of s 60(3) of the Law of Property Act 1925, this principle does not extend to realty. Nevertheless, the circumstances may give rise to a presumption of resulting trust (see *Hodgson v Marks* (1971)).

10.6.3   Presumption of advancement

A presumption of advancement, unlike a presumption of a resulting trust, is a presumption of a gift in favour of the transferee. Where there is a 'special relationship' between the transferor and transferee, a purchase or voluntary transfer of property in the name of the transferee gives rise to a presumption of a gift. In short, the transferee is presumed to own both the legal and equitable interests. This presumption, like the presumption of a resulting trust, may be rebutted by evidence of the intention of the transferor.

The courts have, in the past, recognised the 'special relationship' as giving rise to a moral obligation on the part of the transferor to benefit the transferee.

These are occasions where:

- the transferee is the wife of the transferor. This presumption has been considerably weakened with regard to the family home (see later);

- there is a transfer by a father to his legitimate child (see *Shephard v Cartwright* (1955));

- the transferor stands in the shoes of the male parent (*loco parentis patris*) towards the child (see *Re Paradise Motor Co* (1968)).

10.6.4   Rebuttal of the presumptions

The presumptions of resulting trust and advancement are, in a sense, artificial rules adopted for deciding the intention of the transferor or purchaser and may give way to the real intention of the parties. Although the weight of the presumptions depends on the circumstances of each case, the courts will consider all the surrounding facts and decide whether the presumptions have been rebutted or not. The quality of the rebutting evidence varies from case to case. Much depends on the relationship between the parties, their conduct and any statements made by them. For example, strong evidence will be needed to rebut the presumption of a resulting trust where a transfer of the legal title to property is made by a client to his solicitor. On the other hand, less evidence will be needed to rebut the presumption where a transfer is made by an uncle to his favourite nephew.

Recently, the courts have considered the position of a transferor who disposes of property to another in pursuance of an intended fraudulent or illegal purpose, but subsequently repents and withdraws from the illegal purpose, and wishes to recover the property from the transferee. The law was reviewed by the House of Lords in *Tinsley v Milligan* (1994). It was decided that, if a party does not rely on the illegality in order to establish a claim to an equitable interest, the illegality is no bar to a successful action. In other words, if the claimant enjoys an equitable interest by way of a resulting trust, his subsequent illegality is not decisive. On the other hand, in the different context of the presumption of advancement, the transferor is generally prevented from establishing his equitable interest by virtue of his intended fraudulent conduct. The principle here is, 'he who comes to equity must come with clean hands' (see *Tinker v Tinker* (1970)). However, in *Tribe v Tribe* (1995), the Court of Appeal decided that the claimant was entitled to rebut the presumption on the ground that he had withdrawn from the unlawful venture.

10.7 Constructive Trusts

A constructive trust is fundamentally different from an express or resulting trust. The constructive trust is not created in accordance with the express or implied intention of the settlor. It is a device adopted by the courts in the interests of justice and good conscience. The constructive trust is a residual category of trusts which is called into play whenever the court desires to impose a trust and no other category of trust is suitable. The courts reserve the power to interpret a transaction as giving rise to a constructive trust.

For example, T1 and T2 hold property on trust but, in breach of trust, purport to sell the property to X, a third party, who has knowledge of the breach of trust. Although T1 and T2 are already express trustees and are liable to the beneficiaries for the breach of trust, they will become constructive trustees of any unauthorised profit made from their office as trustees, such as the proceeds of sale received from X. By virtue of X's participation in the breach with knowledge of the facts, he will be treated as a constructive trustee.

Thus, constructive trusts may be imposed on express trustees and other 'fiduciaries' in respect of any unauthorised benefits received by them. In addition, strangers or third parties who have misconducted themselves with knowledge that their actions constitute an unwarranted interference with the interest of the beneficiary will become constructive trustees.

The effect of a constructive trust is similar in many ways to any other type of trust, in that the beneficiary retains a proprietary interest in the subject matter of the trust. In the event of the constructive trustee becoming bankrupt, the trust property is held in trust for the beneficiaries who take precedence over the trustee's creditors. If the trustee disposes of the assets, the beneficiary is entitled to 'trace' his property in the hands of a third party, not being a *bona fide* transferee of the legal estate for value without notice.

The courts have adopted a pragmatic, broad based approach towards constructive trusts which, although classified into various categories, remain subject to extension and development.

Per Edmund-Davies LJ in *Carl Zeiss Stiftung v Herbert Smith and Co* (1969):

> English law provides no clear and all-embracing definition of a constructive trust. Its boundaries have been left perhaps deliberately vague, so as not to restrict the court by technicalities in deciding what the justice of a particular case may demand.

10.7.1 Categories of constructive trusts

10.7.1.1 *Trustee or fiduciary making an unauthorised profit*

The rule is that a person occupying a position of confidence (such as a trustee or fiduciary) is prohibited from deriving any personal benefit from the property in the absence of authority from the beneficiaries, the trust instrument or the court. In other words, the trustee or fiduciary should not place himself in a position where his duties may conflict with his personal interest. If such a conflict occurs and the trustee obtains a benefit or profit, the advantage is held on constructive trust for the beneficiary. In particular, a trustee, without specific authority to the contrary, is not entitled to purchase trust property for his own benefit. The position remains the same even if the purchase appears to be fair. If such a purchase takes place, the transaction is treated as voidable, that is, valid until avoided. In *Keech v Sandford* (1726), an unauthorised renewal of a lease (trust property) by a trustee for his own benefit was treated as voidable.

The rule in *Keech v Sandford* (as it is sometimes called) has been extended to other fiduciary relationships, including: agents acting on behalf of principals, directors in favour of companies, partners vis à vis co-partners and solicitors in respect of clients. A 'fiduciary' is an individual who is aware that his judgment and confidence is, and has been, relied on by the claimant. Apart from the traditional categories of fiduciaries, the existence of such a relationship is a question for the court to decide.

In claims concerning breach of fiduciary duties, the claimant is required to establish each of the following three complementary propositions:

- the defendant holds a fiduciary position towards the claimant;

- the defendant obtained a benefit; and

- there is a causal connection between the relationship and the benefit.

In *Holder v Holder* (1968), the claimant failed to establish that the defendant held a fiduciary position. Normally, trustees cannot purchase trust property because they cannot be both vendors and purchasers. The circumstances of this case, however, were special. The trustee in question (executor) took no part in instructing the valuer or in the preparations for the auction. He had never assumed the duties of an executor.

In *English v Dedham Vale Properties* (1978), the prospective purchasers of land were held to be fiduciaries when they obtained planning permission without the vendor's authority. In *Boardman v Phipps* (1967), the House of Lords held that a solicitor was a fiduciary when, acting on behalf of the trust, he obtained confidential information and made an unauthorised profit therefrom.

In *AG v Blake* [2000] 3 WLR 625, the House of Lords decided that a former member of the Secret Service who unlawfully disclosed information for reward, in breach of his duty of confidentiality, was liable to disgorge the profits.

In accordance with the rule in *Keech v Sandford*, a trustee is not entitled to receive any remuneration or benefit for his services as trustee without appropriate authority (see *Williams v Barton* (1927)). But the trustee may be reimbursed in respect of expenditure properly incurred in connection with his trusteeship (s 31 of the Trustee Act 2000 replacing 30(2) of the Trustee Act 1925). Similarly, where a fiduciary accepts a bribe in breach of his fiduciary duty, the bribe, including property representing the unauthorised profit, is held upon trust for the persons to whom the duty is owed (see *AG for Hong Kong v Reid* (1993)). A similar result was reached by the High Court in *Daraydan Holdings Ltd v Solland Interiors Ltd* [2004] EWHC 622: a fiduciary who received a bribe was liable to account as a constructive trustee.

Likewise, trustees who are appointed directors of a company by virtue of their trust shareholding are accountable to the trust for their remuneration (see *Re Macadam* (1946)).

10.7.1.2 Occasions when a trustee may be paid

The general rule, as illustrated in *Williams v Barton*, is subject to the following four exceptions.

Authority in the trust instrument

The settlor may authorise the trustees to be paid from the trust funds, but such a power is required to be expressed in the trust instrument. Professional trustees normally insist on an adequate charging clause before they undertake the duties of trusteeship.

However, in the event of any ambiguity, charging clauses are strictly construed against the trustees. Furthermore, trustees may only charge a reasonable amount which would vary with the circumstances of each case. Section 29 of the Trustee Act 2000 authorises reasonable remuneration for a trust corporation or professional trustee where the trust instrument is silent as to the remuneration of trustees.

Authority of the court

The court will only authorise reasonable remuneration for services performed by trustees which are of exceptional benefit to the trust (see *Boardman v Phipps* (1967)).

Agreement with all the beneficiaries

Where the beneficiaries are all *sui juris* and absolutely entitled to the trust property, they may make an agreement with the trustees for the latter to be remunerated. This is an application of the *Saunders v Vautier* rule.

The rule in Cradock v Piper (1850)

A solicitor/trustee may charge his usual fees for acting on behalf of his co-trustees in litigation concerning the trust, but is not permitted fees for representing himself.

Company directors stand in a fiduciary relationship to the company and are subject to the rigours of the trust principle. If a director places himself in a position where his duties to the company conflicts with his personal interest, any benefits obtained in consequence are accountable to the company. In *Regal (Hastings) Ltd v Gulliver* (1942), the unauthorised purchase by directors of shares in a subsidiary company gave rise to a constructive trust.

Contracts for the sale of land

Once a specifically enforceable contract for the sale of land is made, the purchaser becomes the equitable owner of the property. Thus, on the date of the exchange of contracts, the vendor becomes a constructive trustee for the purchaser until the date of the completion of the sale (see *Lysaght v Edwards* (1876)).

10.7.1.3   Equity will not allow a statute to be used as an engine for fraud

Acts of Parliament are binding on all courts, even a court of equity. However, if a strict compliance with a statutory provision (for example, in the case of formalities) has the incidental effect of perpetrating a fraud, the court is entitled to suspend such a provision in order to prevent a fraud, (see *Rochefoucauld v Boustead* (1897)).

10.7.1.4   Strangers to the trust

The general rule is that third parties or persons who have not been appointed trustees (such as agents of trustees, for example, accountants and solicitors) are not constructive trustees if they merely act in breach of their duties. Instead, in appropriate cases they may be personally liable in damages for breach of contract or tort. Provided that the agent acts within the limits of his authority, does not receive the trust property for his own benefit and is unaware that he is acting in a manner inconsistent with the terms of the trust, he does not become a constructive trustee (see *Barnes v Addy* (1874), where a solicitor to a trust was not a constructive trustee when he gave the sole trustee sound advice which was disregarded and resulted in loss to the trust).

However, there are three occasions when a stranger to a trust may become a constructive trustee:

- *The stranger becomes a trustee de son tort (that is, a trustee of his own wrong)*

    To fall within this category, the stranger is required to undertake acts that are characteristic of trusteeship, and act on behalf of the trust and not for his own benefit. In short, this type of constructive trustee is one who, by mistake, believes that he was properly appointed to act on behalf of the trust (see *Boardman v Phipps* (1967) and *James v Williams* (1999)).

- *The stranger knowingly receives trust property for his benefit*

  The rationale for liability under this head is that a stranger who knows that trust property has been transferred to him in breach of trust cannot take possession of the property for his own benefit, but is subject to the claims of the trust. He is not a *bona fide* transferee of the legal estate for value without notice.

  The contest in this context is based on the assertion of proprietary rights. The trust sues the stranger claiming that he/it has better title to the property. Equity is entitled to make the most strenuous efforts in order to protect the beneficiary's interest under the trust. In the majority of cases, the view is that any form of knowledge on the part of the trustee, subjective or objective, will be sufficient to make him liable under this head (see *Belmont Finance Corp Williams Furniture (No 2)* (1980)). On the other hand, in *Re Montagu* (1987), the court advocated the rationale that only subjective knowledge is relevant to make the stranger liable under this head. In *BCCI v Akindele* [2004] 4 All ER 221, the Court of Appeal endorsed the approach in *Re Montagu* and decided that the basis of liability is unconscionability. The test is whether the defendant may in the opinion of the court conscientiously retain the property.

- *The stranger who dishonestly assists in a fraudulent transaction*

  Under this head of liability, a stranger to a trust becomes a constructive trustee (a form of personal liability) if he dishonestly assists in a fraudulent scheme devised by another (perhaps the settlement trustee), see *Brunei Airlines v Tan* [1995] 3 WLR 64. This is the position even though the stranger does not receive the trust property. In effect, the stranger acts as an accomplice to the principal fraudulent trustee or other party.

The following three elements must be established in order to attach liability to the stranger: (a) the existence of the trust (or a fiduciary relationship); (b) the existence of a dishonest or fraudulent design (c) the assistance by the stranger in that design. In *Twinsectra v Yardley* [2002] UKHL 12, the House of Lords adopted the test for dishonesty that exists in criminal law in order to determine whether the accessory is liable to account. This test is the combined objective/subjective standard. If the defendant's conduct is dishonest by reference to the ordinary standards of reasonable and honest people (objective) and the defendant subjectively realised that that is the case, then he will be treated as acting dishonestly. For these purposes the standard of proof exceeds a balance of probabilities, see *Heinl v Jyske Bank* (1999) The Times, 28 September.

10.7.1.5 The family home

The family home is regarded by the majority of families as their most valuable asset. The legal title may be vested in the joint names of the partners or, as is sometimes the case, one partner acquires the legal title. The question for determination by the courts is in respect of the ownership of the home in equity. The principles of property law are applicable here in order to determine this question. The following principles emerge from case and statute law:

(a) The presumptions of resulting trusts and advancement are regarded as outmoded principles, better suited to a different society (see *Pettit v Pettit* (1970)).

(b) The same common law principles are applicable to married and unmarried partners and other relationships.

(c) If the parties have expressly declared their beneficial interests in writing, then, in the absence of fraud or mistake, this will be conclusive as to their interests (see *Goodman v Gallant* (1986) and *Goodman v Carlton* [2002] All ER (D) 284.

(d) If the express intention of the parties is not declared in writing, the intention becomes unenforceable for non-compliance with s 53(1)(b) of the Law of Property Act 1925.

(e) The court may infer the intention of the parties based on all the circumstances of the case under s 53(2) of the Law of Property Act 1925 (that is, resulting and constructive trusts). The overriding consideration in creating such trusts is not primarily to achieve justice between the parties, but to give effect to their intentions.

(f) The two governing principles are that, at any time prior to the acquisition of the property (or exceptionally afterwards), there is:

- evidence of an agreement, arrangement or understanding reached between the parties, based on express discussion between them, concerning the beneficial interest in the property. In addition, the claimant has acted to his or her detriment in reliance on such agreement; or
- evidence of the conduct of the parties which gives rise to a constructive trust, such as direct contributions (including mortgage payments) to the purchase price of the home (see *Lloyds Bank v Rosset* (1990)).

(g) Ordinary domestic services, such as looking after the children and other household chores, without more, are insufficient to create an interest in the home (see *Burns v Burns* (1984)).

(h) With regard to married couples, in addition to the principles as outlined above, ss 23–25 of the Matrimonial Causes Act 1973 give the court wide discretionary powers to declare or vary the interests of spouses in family assets on a divorce, decree of nullity or judicial separation.

(i) Under s 37 of the Matrimonial Proceedings and Property Act 1970, spouses (but not unmarried couples) who contribute in a substantial way in money or money's worth to the improvement of real (or personal) property may enjoy a share or enlarged share in the asset. The court decides whether a contribution is substantial or not by having regard to all the circumstances of the case.

(j) Once the claimant has established an interest in the property, the value of that interest is quantified at the time the property is sold. Accordingly, any increases or decreases in the value of the property are taken into consideration. In *Oxley v Hiscock* [2004] EWCA 546, the Court of Appeal identified three judicial approaches to quantification:

- The approach adopted by Lord Diplock in *Gissing v Gissing* [1971] AC 886 and Nourse LJ in *Stokes v Anderson* [1991] 1 FLR 391. The respective shares of the parties are not to be determined at the time of the acquisition of the property but are left to be determined when their relationship comes to an end or the property sold. Thus, a complete picture of the whole course of dealing is available to the court in order to determine what is fair.

- The approach suggested by Waite LJ in *Midland Bank v Cooke* [1995] 2 FLR 915. The court undertakes a survey of the whole course of dealing between the parties in order to determine what proportions the parties must be assumed to have intended from the outset for their beneficial ownership. Thus evidence of what the parties intended at the time of the acquisition may be inferred from the conduct of the parties while they were living together.

- The suggestion put forward by Browne-Wilkinson V.C. in *Grant v Edwards* [1986] 1 Ch 638 and approved by Walker LJ in *Yaxley v Gotts* [2000] Ch 162. The court in its discretion makes such an order as the circumstances require in order to give effect to the beneficial interest in the property of the one party, the existence of which the party with the legal title is estopped from denying.

In *Oxley v Hiscock* the court expressed a preference for the third approach. The second approach was capable of leading to an artificial or fictional intention of the parties. Likewise, the same point could be made of the first approach, that is, at the time of the acquisition the parties' intention was that their shares should be left for late determination.

(k) The claimant is entitled to apply to the court, under s 14 of the Trusts of Land and Appointment of Trustees Act 1996, for an order of sale.

10.8   Purpose Trusts

A purpose trust is designed to promote a purpose as an end in itself, such as the discovery of an alphabet of 40 letters, to provide a cup for a yacht race or the boarding up of certain rooms in a house. Such intended trusts are void, for the court cannot give effect to a trust which it cannot supervise. There is no beneficiary with a *locus standi* capable of enforcing such trust. In *Re Astor's Settlement Trust* (1952), a gift on trust for 'the maintenance of good understanding between nations and the preservation of the independence and integrity of newspapers' was void.

This general rule is subject to a number of exceptions:

- charitable trusts (see 10.9);

- gifts for the care of animals are generally charitable, but trusts for the care of specific animals, such as pets, are treated as private purpose trusts (see *Pettingall v Pettingall* (1842));

- a trust for the building of a memorial or monument for an individual is not charitable, but may exist as a valid private purpose trust if the trustees express a desire to perform the trust. In *Re Hooper* (1932), a gift for the maintenance of particular graves 'for as long as the law allows' was valid as a private purpose trust;

- the '*Denley* approach': it is a question of construction for the court to ascertain whether a gift or trust is for the promotion of a purpose *simpliciter* (within the *Astor* principle), which is void, or, alternatively, whether the trust is for the benefit of persons who are capable of enforcing the trust. The settlor may, in form, create what appears to be a purpose trust but, in substance, the trust may be construed as being for the benefit of human beneficiaries (see *Re Denley's Trust Deed* (1969), where land was conveyed on trust for use as a sports ground by a specific group of employees of a company);

- a trust for the promotion of fox hunting was held to be valid in *Re Thompson* (1934);

- a trust for the saying of masses in private is not charitable, but may create a valid private trust (*Bourne v Keane* (1919)). In *Khoo Cheng Teow* (1932), a trust for the performance of non-Christian ceremonies was upheld.

10.8.1   The rule against perpetuities

The grant of future interests is void unless the property vests within the perpetuity period. At common law, the perpetuity period is a life or lives in being and/or 21 years from the date that the instrument creating the gift takes effect. Only human lives are taken into consideration (including an embryonic child (*en ventre sa mère*)). A life or lives in being, whether connected with the gift or not, may be chosen expressly by the donor or settlor, or may be implied. A life is implied if it is so related to the gift that it is capable of being used to measure the date of the vesting of the interest. A group of lives may be selected by the settlor, provided that it is possible to say when the last member of the group dies. Indeed, the settlor may select persons who have no connection with the settlement, such as royal lives, for example, 'the lineal descendants of Queen Elizabeth II living at my death'. If no lives are selected or implied, the perpetuity period at common law is 21 years.

In substance, the perpetuity rule not only requires a future interest to vest within the perpetuity period, but also stipulates the maximum period of duration in which such an interest may be enjoyed following the vesting of the interest. On analysis, the rule may be classified into two categories, namely:

- the rule against remote vesting; and

- the rule against excessive duration.

10.8.1.1   The rule against remote vesting

This rule stipulates the maximum period of time in which the vesting of a future interest may be postponed. Before 1964, if there was a possibility, however slight, that a future interest may vest outside the perpetuity period, the gift was void. The Perpetuities and Accumulations Act 1964 introduced three major reforms to the law. Under the Act, a future interest is no longer void on the ground that it 'might' vest outside the perpetuity period. It is void if, in the circumstances, the interest does not vest within the perpetuity period. In the meantime, the court will 'wait and see' whether or not the gift vests. Second, the Act introduced a certain and fixed period not exceeding 80 years which the grantor may nominate as the perpetuity period. Third, s 3(5) of the Act introduced a variety of persons who may be treated as a 'statutory life'. These are: the grantor, the beneficiary or potential beneficiary, the donee of a power, option or other right, parents and grandparents of the grantor and any person entitled in default. Where there are no lives within any of these categories, the wait and see period is 21 years from the date the instrument takes effect.

10.8.1.2   The rule against excessive duration

Closely related to the rule against remote vesting is the rule against the inalienability of property. This rule renders void any trust or interest which is required to be enjoyed for longer than the perpetuity period. Charitable trusts are exempt from this principle (see 10.9). The issue here is not whether the property or interest is, in reality, tied up forever, but whether the owner is capable of disposing of the same within the perpetuity period. Thus, property may be owned perpetually by persons, companies or unincorporated associations if these bodies are entitled to dispose of the same at any time but have refrained from exercising the right of disposal.

Unincorporated associations

In *Conservative and Unionist Central Office v Burrell* (1982), Lawton LJ defined an unincorporated association as follows:

> ... two or more persons bound together for one or more common purposes, not being business purposes, by mutual undertakings, each having mutual duties and obligations, in an organisation which has rules which identify in whom control of it and its funds rests and on what terms and which can be joined or left at will.

The difficulty concerning unincorporated associations is that they are not separate legal persons. They are bodies with labels which identify their members. Such bodies may only act through their members or officers. Accordingly, such associations cannot hold property, except through their officers, and likewise, gifts cannot be made to such organisations *per se*. The following solutions have been adopted from time to time by the courts in respect of gifts to unincorporated associations:

(a) a donor may make a gift to an association which, on a true construction, is a gift to the members of that body who take as joint tenants free from any contractual fetter.

Any member is entitled to sever his share. In these circumstances, the association is used as a label or definition of the class which is intended to take. In *Cocks v Manners* (1871), a gift by will to the Dominican Convent at Carisbrooke 'payable to the supervisor for the time being' was treated as a gift to the members of the community;

(b) more frequently, a gift to an association may be construed as a gift to the members of the association, not beneficially, but as an accretion to the funds of the society regulated by the contract (evidenced by the rules of the association) that was made by the members *inter se*. A member who leaves the association by death or resignation will have no claim to the property in the absence of any rules to the contrary. In *Re Recher* (1972), a gift to the London and Provincial Anti-Vivisection Society was held to be a gift to the members as an addition to the funds of the society, but subject to the contract created by the members, as set out in the rules;

(c) a gift to an association may be construed by the court as a gift to both present and future members of the association. In coming to this conclusion, the courts are required to consider the rules of the association and its function, in addition to the intention of the donor. But, if the members of the society (in accordance with its constitution) are incapable of disposing of the assets of the society or are incapable of altering the rules of the association, the gift may fail for infringing the perpetuity rule. In *Re Grant's Will Trust* (1980), a gift to the Chertsey Labour Party was void for infringing the perpetuity rule. The members did not have the power to change the rules of the association. Such control was vested in the National Executive Committee of the Labour Party;

(d) a transfer of property to an association may be construed as a transfer on trust for the function or operation of the society and not for its members. If this construction is adopted, the court may decide that the trust fails under the *Astor* principle, owing to the intention to promote a purpose. Such a construction would be exceptional. Moreover, if the intention of the settlor is to set up an endowment in favour of the beneficiary (that is, the association), the gift may fail on the separate ground of the infringement of the perpetuity rule. In *Leahy v AG for New South Wales* (1959), a gift of a sheep station for 'such order of nuns of the Catholic Church or the Christian brothers as my trustees shall select' was construed as an intended gift on trust to promote a purpose, and thus failed. The gift also failed on the separate ground of infringing the perpetuity rule, as the capital could not be spent;

(e) a gift of property to an association may be construed as a transfer on trust for the current members of the association and not on trust for its purposes. In this event, provided that the rules of the association empower the members to liquidate and distribute the assets, the perpetuity rule will not be infringed and the trust will be valid. The position remains the same even though the settlor specifies a purpose for which the fund may be used. Such a stipulation may be construed as insufficient to prevent the members (beneficiaries) from disposing of the property in any way they consider appropriate within the rules of the society. In *Re Lipinski* (1977), a testator bequeathed half of his residuary estate on trust for an association to be used 'solely' in constructing or maintaining the association's buildings. This transfer was valid as a gift to the members, subject to the contract between them as members.

Dissolution of unincorporated associations

The issue here concerns the occasions when the rules are silent as to the destination of assets following a dissolution of an unincorporated association. In effect, there are a number of issues involved, namely, whether the members of the association are entitled to the assets on a distribution (and if so, whether only members on the date of dissolution or all members, past and present may participate in the distribution), or whether the Crown should be entitled as *bona vacantia*. If the members are entitled, how much ought they to claim? In short, the question is: on what basis should a distribution of assets of a society be made?

So far, the courts have adopted the following three approaches to this question:

(1) The resulting trust

This was the original remedy adopted and it represents, in theory, a solution to the problem, although the more recent cases have considered this basis of distribution with disfavour. The approach was adopted in *Re Printers and Transferrers Society* (1899). On a dissolution of a trade union society, the court decided that the surplus was acquired by the subsisting members at the time of the dissolution. This approach was followed (with some adaptation) *in Re Printers and Transferrers Society* (1899). In this case, the surplus funds were held on resulting trust for everyone who contributed, past and present, in proportion to their contribution, but with a reduction for any benefits received from the fund.

(2) Bona vacantia

A second solution adopted by the courts is to assume that the members of a society who make their contributions for the benefit of others do not expect the return of their subscriptions or assets of the society on the date of liquidation. The members parted 'out and out' with their subscriptions. Accordingly, the assets of the society may be taken by the Crown as *bona vacantia*. This solution is adopted only as a last resort when the settlor and beneficiary, and no one else, is entitled to claim the property. The property being ownerless, the Crown steps in to fill the gap. In *Cunnack v Edwards* (1896), a society was formed to raise funds to provide annuities for the widows of deceased members. The personal representatives of the last widow unsuccessfully claimed the surplus funds.

A similar result was reached by the court in *Re West Sussex Constabulary's Widows, Children and Benevolent Fund Trusts* (1971). A fund was established for providing payments to widows of deceased members of the West Sussex Constabulary. Receipts were derived from four classes of contributors, namely: (a) identifiable donations and legacies, (b) members' subscriptions, (c) collecting boxes and (d) proceeds of entertainment, sweepstakes and raffles. In 1968, the Constabulary was amalgamated with other police forces and the purpose came to an end, leaving a surplus of funds. It was held that, with the exception of contributors in category (a) (a resulting trust was set up for these contributors), the balance of the fund passed to the Crown as *bona vacantia*. The contributors within category (b) got what they bargained for, following *Cunnack v Edwards*. In any event, members' contributions were received by way of contract for the benefit of others (dependants of deceased members) and not by reference to the trust institution. The contributors in category (c) were treated as parting with their money 'out and out'. Contributors in category (d) received what they were contractually entitled to.

(3) Contractual basis

In *Cunnack v Edwards* (1896) and *Re West Sussex* (1971), the courts adopted the notion that members contributed to the society on a contractual basis, but decided on the facts that such contributions were taken by the Crown as *bona vacantia*. In more recent cases, the courts have decided that subsisting members of the association are entitled to participate in the distribution of the society's funds. Their contributions are made as an accretion to the funds of the association, by reference to the contract made *inter se*, in accordance with the rules of the society. The members control the association, subject to the constitution of the society. Equally, the subsisting members alone are entitled to the surplus funds on a dissolution, in the absence of any agreement to the contrary between the members. In *Re Bucks Constabulary Widows' and Orphans' Fund Friendly Society (No 2)* (1979), the fund was established for purposes similar to those in *Re West Sussex*, but the court decided that the fund belonged to the subsisting members of the association. At all times, the members could have altered the rules and obtained the funds.

Date of dissolution

In the ordinary course of events, the date of the dissolution of an association will not be in dispute. This will be the date when a formal resolution is passed to wind up the association. But, exceptionally, an association may become inactive for an exceptionally long period of time, and the formal resolution to wind up the body may not, in itself, reflect the true state of affairs concerning the date of termination of operations. In these circumstances, the extraordinarily prolonged period of inactivity may offer strong evidence of spontaneous dissolution. The court will decide, on the facts, the precise date of dissolution. The subsisting members of the association will then be entitled to participate in the distribution of the assets. But mere inactivity, by itself, is insufficient to constitute spontaneous dissolution. The association may be treated as going through a dormant period (see *GKN Bolts and Nuts Ltd Sports and Social Club* (1982)).

10.9 Charitable Trusts

A charitable trust is a trust set up to benefit society as a whole or a sufficiently large section of society.

10.9.1 Characteristics of charitable trusts

Donations for charitable purposes have always been recognised as sentiments to be encouraged, as a matter of public policy. Generally, charitable trusts are subject to the same rules as private trusts but, as a result of the public nature of such bodies, they enjoy a number of advantages over private trusts in respect of certainty of objects, the perpetuity rule, the *cy-près* rule and fiscal privileges.

10.9.1.1 Certainty of objects

A charitable trust is subject to a unique test for certainty of objects, namely, whether the objects are exclusively charitable. In other words, if the trust funds may be used solely for charitable purposes, the test will be satisfied. Indeed, it is unnecessary for the settlor or testator to specify the charitable objects. A gift 'on trust for charitable purposes' will satisfy this test. The Charity Commissioners and the courts have the jurisdiction to establish a scheme for application of the funds. In *Moggridge v Thackwell* (1807), a bequest 'to such charities as the trustee sees fit' was valid as a gift for charitable purposes.

On the other hand, if the trust funds are capable of being devoted for both charitable and non-charitable purposes, the gift may be construed as being non-charitable for these purposes. In *IRC v City of Glasgow Police Athletic Association* (1953), the association promoted both a charitable purpose (efficiency of the police force) and a non-charitable purpose (promotion of sport). The court decided that the association was not charitable.

In two circumstances, an objects clause which seeks to benefit both charitable and non-charitable purposes will not fail as a charity if:

- the non charitable purpose is construed as being incidental to the main charitable purpose. This involves a question of construction for the courts to evaluate the importance of each class of objects (see *Re Coxen* (1948)); and

- the court is able to sever the fund and devote the charitable portion of the fund for charitable purposes. This is the case where only part of the fund is payable for charitable purposes and the rest is for non-charitable purposes. In the absence of circumstances requiring a different division, the court will apply the maxim 'equality is equity' and order an equal division of the fund. In *Salusbury v Denton* (1857), severance was permitted where an unspecified part of a fund was made for charitable purposes (the relief of poverty) and the remainder for a private purpose (testator's relatives).

10.9.1.2 *Perpetuity*

Charities are not subject to the rule against excessive duration. But charitable gifts, like private gifts, are subject to the rule against remote vesting, that is, the subject matter of the gift is required to vest in the charity within the perpetuity period.

10.9.1.3 Cy-près *doctrine*

When a charitable trust fails to vest in the relevant association, the funds may be applied *cy-près* (to the nearest alternative).

10.9.1.4 *Fiscal advantages*

A variety of tax relief are enjoyed by both charitable bodies and members of the public (including companies) who donate funds for charitable purposes. A detailed analysis of such concessions is outside the scope of this book.

10.9.2 Charitable purposes

There is no statutory or judicial definition of a charity. It has been recognised that a definition of charities would have the undesirable effect of restricting the flexibility which currently exists in permitting the law to keep abreast of the changing needs of society. Most charitable bodies are required to be registered with the Charity Commissioners under s 3(2) of the Charities Act 1993. The effect of registration creates a conclusive presumption of charitable status. (See s 4(1) of the Charities Act 1993.)

Ever since the passing of the Charitable Uses Act 1601 (sometimes referred to as the Statute of Elizabeth I), the courts developed the practice of referring to its Preamble for guidance as to charitable purposes. The preamble contained a catalogue of purposes which, at that time, was regarded as charitable. It was not intended to constitute a definition of charities. The Preamble has been expressly preserved by the s 38(4) of the Charities Act 1960.

Lord MacNaghten, in *IRC v Pemsel* (1891), classified charitable purposes into four categories: trusts for relief of poverty, trusts for the advancement of education, trusts for the advancement of religion and trusts for other purposes beneficial to the community. An additional requirement for charitable status is that the trust exists for the public benefit, that is, the institution is required to confer some tangible benefit on the public at large or a sufficiently large section of the public. Trusts for the relief of poverty are exempt from this requirement.

The extent to which the purpose will be required to benefit the public varies according to the type of charitable purpose in question. Judges must rely on their own subjective views. The test will not be satisfied if there is a personal nexus, in blood or contract, between the donor and the beneficiaries or between the beneficiaries themselves. In *Re Compton* (1945), the test was not satisfied where the gift was on trust for the education of the children of three named relatives. In *Oppenheim v Tobacco Securities Trust Co Ltd* (1951), a gift for the education of employees and ex-employees of a company did not satisfy the public element test. The majority of their Lordships decided that, to constitute a section of the public, the beneficiaries must neither be numerically negligible nor be subject to a personal nexus. In *Gilmour v Coats* (1949), a community of 20 cloistered nuns did not satisfy this test. On the other hand, in *Neville Estates v Madden* (1962), the members of the Catford Synagogue satisfied the public element test.

10.9.2.1 Classification of charitable purposes

Relief of poverty

'Poverty' connotes that the beneficiaries are in straitened circumstances and unable to maintain a modest standard of living (determined objectively). The beneficiaries need not be destitute but must suffer from a standard of living lower than that generally enjoyed in the community. Relief may take many forms, as, for example, direct payments to the poor (*Pemsel's* case (1891)) the funding of soup kitchens (*Biscoe v Jackson* (1887)) and the provision of rest homes or flats let out at below commercial rents (*Re Cottam* (1955)). The practice of the courts has always been to exclude such trusts from the public element test. At the same time, the courts have drawn a subtle distinction between private trusts for the relief of poverty and public trusts for the same purpose. For example, a gift for the settlor's 'poor relations, A, B and C', may not be charitable but may exist as a private trust, whereas a gift for the benefit of the settlor's 'poor relations', without identifying them, may be charitable. It appears that the distinction between the two types of trust lies in the degree of precision with which the objects have been identified. The more precise the language used by the settlor in identifying the poor relations, the stronger the risk of failure as a charitable trust. This is a question of degree. In *Re Scarisbrick* (1951), a bequest was made on trust 'for such relations of my said son and daughters as in the opinion of the survivor shall be in needy circumstances'. The court held that the gift was charitable.

The advancement of education

'Education' has been interpreted generously and is not restricted to the classroom mode of disseminating knowledge, but it does require some element of instruction or supervision. Research is capable of being construed as providing education if: (a) the subject matter is a useful object of study, (b) the knowledge acquired from the research will be disseminated to others and (c) the public element test is satisfied (see Slade J in *McGovern v AG* (1981)). Examples of the provision of education are: gifts for the provision of scholarships and academic prizes, donations to specific educational institutions, such as universities or museums, the publication of law reports which record the development of judge made law, the promotion of artistic and cultural activities of value to the community and the promotion of concerts and choral works of renowned composers. Expert evidence is admissible as to the value of the activity (see *Re Pinion* (1965)).

The advancement of religion

The advancement of religion was described by Donovan J in *United Grand Lodge of Freemasons in England and Wales v Holborn Borough Council* (1957):

> To advance religion means to promote it, to spread its message ever wider among mankind ... It should include religious instruction, a programme for the persuasion of unbelievers, and religious supervision to see that its members remain active and constant in the various religions they may profess.

Religion may be advanced in a variety of ways, such as: the maintenance of places of worship, including the upkeep of churchyards, gifts for the clergy, the provision of an organ or maintenance of a choir and the active spread of religion at home and abroad. A gift for 'parish work' will be void for including many objects which are not charitable (see *Farley v Westminster Bank* (1939)). On the other hand, in *Re South Place Ethical Society* (1980), it was decided that the study and dissemination of ethical principles which did not involve faith in a deity could not constitute religion. The society was charitable on the ground of advancement of education.

Unlike trusts for the advancement of education, the courts do not evaluate the merit of one religion as opposed to another or, indeed, the benefit of religious instruction to the public. Provided that the religious gift is not subversive of all morality, the gift will be charitable.

A gift for the saying of masses in public is charitable, for the gift promotes an integral part of religion, namely, the saying of prayers. The *prima facie* assumption is that prayers are assumed to be said in public, until the contrary is established (see *Re Hetherington* (1989)).

Other purposes beneficial to the community

The approach of the courts under this head is to treat the examples stated in the Preamble as guidance for deciding on the validity of the relevant purpose. Two approaches have been adopted by the courts:

- *Reasoning by analogy*

  The approach here is to ascertain whether a purpose has some resemblance to an example stated in the Preamble or to an earlier decided case which was considered charitable. For example, the provision of a crematorium was considered charitable by analogy with 'the repair of churches' as stated in the Preamble in *Scottish Burial Reform and Cremation Society v City of Glasgow Corporation* (1968). In that case, a crematorium was found to be a charitable body.

- *The spirit and intendment of the Preamble*

  This approach is much wider than the previous approach. The courts decide if the purpose of the organisation is 'within the spirit and intendment' or 'within the equity' of the statute, unhindered by the specific purposes as stated in the Preamble (see *Incorporated Council of Law Reporting v AG* (1972): law reporting was a charitable activity).

10.9.2.2   Illustrations of charitable purposes under this head

Animals

A trust which promotes the welfare of animals generally, as opposed to benefiting specific animals, is charitable because it promotes public morality (see *Re Wedgewood* (1915)).

It is essential to establish that the welfare of the animals provide some benefit to mankind, albeit indirect. Failure to establish such a benefit was fatal in *National Anti-Vivisection Society v IRC* (1948).

The relief of the aged and impotent

The Preamble specifically refers to 'the relief of the aged, impotent and poor people'. The words have been construed disjunctively and objects need not qualify on all three grounds. (See *Joseph Rowntree Memorial Trust Housing Association v AG* (1983)). In this case, a scheme of dwelling houses for the elderly (males aged at least 65 and females aged 60 and over) was charitable.

Recreational facilities

The promotion of sport *simpliciter* is not charitable, as such an activity is not within the Preamble or the spirit and intendment of the Preamble (see *IRC v City of Glasgow Police Athletic Association* (1953) (sport within the police force)). However, with appropriate drafting, sport within a school may be treated as charitable for the advancement of education (see *IRC v McMullen* (1981), which concerned the encouragement of the playing of football in schools).

In *IRC v Baddeley* (1955), the House of Lords was in doubt as to whether the provision of recreational facilities was charitable. The Recreational Charities Act 1958 was passed in order to clarify the law. The Act stipulates that the provision of recreational facilities shall be charitable if two criteria are fulfilled: the public benefit test and the test of 'social welfare'.

Under the Act, the 'social welfare' test will be satisfied if two conditions are complied with. The first requirement is that the facilities are provided with the object of improving the conditions of life of the beneficiaries (s 1(2)(a)). The second requirement may be satisfied in alternative ways, by proving either that the facilities are available to a limited class of objects who have a need for such facilities by virtue of one or more of the factors enumerated within s 1(2)(b)(i) (such as a youth club or an organised outing for orphaned children) or that the facilities are available to 'the entire public' (such as a public swimming pool or a public park) or 'female members of the public' (women's institutes, etc).

In *Guild v IRC* (1992), the House of Lords decided that the material issue concerns the nature of the facilities rather than the status of the participants. *Per* Lord Keith: 'Hyde Park improves the conditions of life for residents in Mayfair and Belgravia as much as those in Pimlico or the Portobello Road.' In this case, a devise of land by will for use as a sports centre in North Berwick gained charitable status.

Miscellaneous examples

Other charitable purposes decided under Lord MacNaghten's fourth heading include: the encouragement and advancement of choral singing (*Royal Choral Society v IRC* (1943)), gifts for the promotion of the defence of the UK (*Re Good* (1905)), gifts for the production of better organists and better organ music (*Re Levien* (1955)), a gift to provide a local fire brigade (*Re Wokingham Fire Brigade Trusts* (1951)), a trust to relieve hardship and suffering by the local people as a result of a disaster (*Re North Devon and West Somerset Relief Fund Trusts* (1953)) (but it is imperative that the size of the class of beneficiaries be sufficiently large to satisfy the public element test), the promotion of industry, commerce and art (*Crystal Palace Trustees v Minister of Town and Country Planning* (1950)), the general improvement of agriculture (*IRC v Yorkshire Agricultural Society* (1928)), a gift to the inhabitants of a town or village (*Goodman v Saltash Corporation* (1882)), a gift 'to my country, England' (*Re Smith* (1932) and a gift 'to the Queen's Chancellor of the Exchequer' (*Nightingale v Goulburn* (1849)).

10.9.2.3 Political purposes

Political purposes include attempts to change the law and gifts to further the objects of political parties. A trust for political purposes is incapable of subsisting as a charity because the court may not stultify itself by deciding that it is in the public good for the law to be changed (see *National Anti-Vivisection Society v IRC* and *McGovern v IRC* (1948)).

Cy-près *doctrine*

Where property is donated for charitable purposes but the purposes cannot be carried out (initially or subsequently), the trust objectives will not necessarily fail. The *cy-près* doctrine enables the court and the Charity Commissioners to make a scheme for the application of the funds for other charitable purposes as closely as possible (*cy-près*) to those intended by the donor.

There are only two conditions to be satisfied for a *cy-près* application:

- the impossibility or impracticality of carrying out the original charitable purpose or the existence of a surplus of funds after the charitable purpose has been fulfilled; and

- the manifestation of a general charitable intention by the donor, as opposed to a specific charitable intention.

Impossibility

Section 13 of the Charities Act 1993 (which re-enacts s 13 of the Charities Act 1960) consolidates to some extent and substantially extends the powers of the Charity Commissioners and the courts to apply property *cy-près*. The circumstances when the purposes of the charity will become impractical or impossible are enacted in s 13(1)(a)–(e) of the Charities Act 1993:

> 13(1)(a) ... where the original purposes wholly or partly have been as far as may be fulfilled, or cannot be carried out according to the directions given and to the spirit of the gift.

This sub-section gives the court the jurisdiction to decide that the original purposes of the gift have been fulfilled or have become impractical. The only restriction on the discretion of the court is in regard to the construction of the expression 'spirit of the gift'. This phrase has been interpreted by Pennycuick VC, in *Re Lepton's Charity* (1972), as meaning 'the basic intention underlying the gift, as ascertained from its terms in the light of admissible evidence'. In this case, a testator who died in 1716 devised specific property to trustees on trust to pay an annual sum of £3 to the Protestant Minister in Pudsey, and the surplus income to the poor and aged people of Pudsey. In 1716, the total income was £5. On the date of the application to the court, that income was £790 per annum. The court held that, on a construction of the will, the minister was not entitled to three-fifths of the annual income but only a fixed sum of £3 per annum. However, having regard to the spirit of the gift, a *cy-près* scheme would be approved, entitling the minister to £100 per annum:

> 13(1)(b) ... where the original purposes provide a use for part only of the property available by virtue of the gift.

The approval of the court may be granted under this paragraph where a surplus of funds are left over after the original charitable purposes have been carried out. This paragraph merely declares the law that existed before 1960 (see *Re North Devon and West Somerset Relief Fund* (1953)):

> 13(1)(c) ... where the property available by virtue of the gift and other property applicable for similar purposes can be more effectively used in conjunction with property held for common purposes, regard being had to the spirit of the gift.

This provision enables a number of small charities with common purposes to be amalgamated in order to create larger funds (see *Re Faraker* (1912)):

> 13(1)(d) ... where the original purposes were laid down by reference to an area which has ceased to be a unit, or by reference to a class of persons or to an area which has ceased to be suitable or practicable, regard being had to the spirit of the gift.

Under this sub-section, the court is entitled to consider that the original class of beneficiaries has become difficult to identify or that the class of beneficiaries has dwindled over the years. See *AG v City of London* (1790), where a fund for the advancement of the Christian religion among infidels in Virginia was applied *cy-près*:

> 13(1)(e) ... where the original purposes, in whole or in part, have, since they were laid down:
>
> (i) been adequately provided for by other reasons; or
>
> (ii) ceased, as being useless or harmful to the community, or, for other reasons, to be in law charitable; or
>
> (iii) ceased in any other way to provide a suitable and effective method of using the property given, regard being had to the spirit of the gift.

Sub-section (e)(i) empowers the court to modify the original purposes as stated by the donor, in view of the charitable purposes being provided for by other bodies.

Sub-section (e)(ii) will rarely be used. It assumes that a purpose was once charitable but, owing to changed circumstances, the purpose ceases to be charitable. An example of this is the Anti-Vivisection Society.

Sub-section (e)(iii) enacts a wide ranging provision giving the courts the power to consider whether the original purposes selected by the donor represent an effective method of using the property. In *Re Lepton's Charity* (1972), the court assumed jurisdiction under, *inter alia*, s 13(1)(e)(iii) to sanction the scheme.

10.9.2.4 General charitable intention

This is the second condition which is required to be fulfilled before the charitable funds may be applied *cy-près*.

Subsequent failure

The courts have dispensed with the need to prove a general charitable intention when the charitable body exists at the appropriate date of vesting but which ceases to exist subsequently. In *Re Wright* (1954), a remainder interest by will to found and maintain a convalescent home for needy women was viable on the date of the testatrix's death but impracticable on the subsequent death of the life tenant. The court decided that the fund was applied *cy-près*.

Initial failure

In the event of an initial failure of the charitable institution, it is essential to prove a general charitable intention before the funds are applied *cy-près*. The intention of the donor is essentially a question of fact. The courts are required to consider all the circumstances in order to determine whether the donor intended to benefit a charitable 'purpose' *simpliciter*, identified by reference to a charitable institution (paramount charitable intention), or whether the settlor's intention was to benefit a specifically identified charitable body.

The court adopted a broad approach to this question in *Re Lysaght* (1966), where a bequest by will was made to the Royal College of Surgeons (the trustees) to apply the income in establishing studentships, subject to a religious bar. The college declined to accept the gift with the religious bar. The court decided that, in accordance with the paramount charitable intention of the testatrix (to make the college a trustee), the religious bar would be deleted.

Form and substance

A gift may appear, in form, to provide for a particular purpose but, on construction, the court may decide that the paramount intention of the donor in substance is to promote a general charitable intention. *Re Lysaght* (above) is an example of this principle. Alternatively, the donor may make a gift which, in both form and substance, promotes a specific charitable intention. In the latter type of case, there is no room for the application of the *cy-près* principle. In *Re Good* (1950), the provision of a detailed scheme for the provision of rest home in Hull proved impracticable. This was evidence of a specific charitable intention.

Non-existent charitable bodies

The identification by the donor of a named charitable institution which had never existed may be construed as a reference to a purpose for which the donor intended to devote his funds. This is evidence of a general charitable intention. In *Re Harwood* (1936), a donation to a non-existent body referred to as the 'Peace Society of Belfast' was construed a general charitable intention to promote peace in Belfast.

Incorporated and unincorporated associations

An incorporated association, as distinct from an unincorporated association, has an independent legal existence distinct from its members. In *Re Vernon's Will Trust* (1972), Buckley J expressed the view that a gift to a corporate charity is *prima facie* intended to take effect as a beneficial gift to the named body and will lapse if the charity ceases to exist before the testator's death. On the other hand, a gift to an unincorporated association *prima facie* takes effect for the purposes of the association. The named unincorporated association is treated as the trustee in order to carry out the charitable purpose. Accordingly, if the association ceases to exist, the court is entitled to use its inherent jurisdiction to ensure that the trust will not fail for want of a trustee, and may appoint new trustees to continue the charitable purposes. (This *prima facie* rule may be rebutted by evidence which shows that the gift was dependent upon the continued existence of the particular trustees.) In *Re Finger's Will Trust* (1972), a testatrix left shares of her residuary estate to various charities, two of which had ceased to exist by the date of her death. One of these was an unincorporated association. It was held that the gift was for charitable purposes and, as such purposes were still sought, a *cy-près* scheme was ordered. The other charity was a corporation and, *prima facie*, the gift was to the corporation itself and not for its purposes. However, on the facts, it was possible to find a general charitable intention.

Section 14 of the Charities Act 1993 (re-enacting s 14 of the Charities Act 1960)

The general rule, as detailed above, is that property given for a specific charitable purpose which fails from the outset cannot be applied *cy-près* if no general charitable intention can be imputed to the donor. Such property will be held on resulting trust for the donor.

By way of exception to that general rule, s 14 of the Charities Act 1993 enacts that property given for specific charitable purposes which fail shall be applicable *cy-près* as if given for charitable purposes generally. This is generally the case where the property belongs to a donor who cannot be identified or found after reasonable inquiries and advertisements have been made or who disclaims his right to the property in writing.

10.10 Appointment, Retirement and Removal of Trustees

There are only two occasions when it may be necessary to appoint trustees:

- on the creation of a new trust – whether *inter vivos* or by will; and

- during the continuance of an existing trust, either in replacement of a trustee or as an additional trustee.

10.10.1 Creation of a new trust

Where, in the purported creation of a trust *inter vivos*, the settlor fails to nominate trustees, the intended trust will be imperfect.

Where a trust is created by will but the testator does not name trustees in his will, or the trustees named are unwilling or unable to act, a replacement trustee will be appointed as on a continuance of the trust (see 10.10.2). The principle applied here is that 'equity will not allow a trust to fail for want of a trustee'.

10.10.2 Continuance of the trust

When a trust is created (whether *inter vivos* or by will), the trust property (real or personal) vests in all the trustees as joint tenants. The effect is that, on the death of a trustee, the property devolves on the survivors (see s 18(1) of the Trustee Act 1925).

On the death of the sole or surviving trustee, the property vests in his personal representatives, subject to the trust, until replacement trustees are appointed (see s 18(2) of the Trustee Act 1925).

The authority to appoint replacement trustees is derived from three sources:

- express power;

- statutory power;

- the courts.

In *Re Higginbottom* (1892), the majority of the beneficiaries under a trust were not able to prevent the sole executrix of the sole surviving trustee from appointing new trustees.

10.10.2.1 *Express power*

The trust instrument may confer the authority to appoint a trustee. This is exceptional, for the statutory power to appoint is generally regarded as adequate. The express authority may be 'general' or 'special'. A general authority is one which confers an authority to appoint trustees in any circumstances. If the authority is special (that is, exercisable in limited circumstances), it would be strictly construed by the courts. In *Re Wheeler and De Rochow* (1896), a nominee was entitled to appoint trustees in specified circumstances, including the occasion when a trustee became 'incapable' of acting. One of the trustees became bankrupt. The court decided that this made him 'unfit' but not incapable of acting as a trustee. Thus, the nominee did not have the authority to appoint.

10.10.2.2 Statutory power (s 36 of the Trustee Act 1925)

The statutory power to appoint trustees is contained in s 36 of the Trustee Act 1925 (replacing the Trustee Act 1893). The occasions giving rise to the need to appoint trustees are enacted in s 36(1) (replacement trustees) and s 36(6) (additional trustees).

10.10.3 Replacement trustees (s 36(1))

There are seven circumstances listed in s 36(1) when a replacement trustee may be appointed. These are:

(1) Where a trustee is dead. Under s 36(8), this includes the person nominated as trustee under a will but predeceasing the testator.

(2) Where a trustee remains outside the UK for a continuous period of 12 months or more. The motive for remaining outside the UK is irrelevant, so this condition will be satisfied even if the trustee remains outside the UK against his will.

(3) Where a trustee desires to be discharged from all or any of the trusts or powers reposed in or conferred on him. Thus, a trustee may retire from part only of the trust.

(4) Where a trustee refuses to act. This includes the occasion when the trustee disclaims his office. It is advisable that the disclaimer be executed by deed.

(5) Where a trustee is unfit to act. Unfitness refers to some defect in the character of the trustee which creates an element of risk in leaving the property in the hands of the individual. For example, a conviction for an offence involving dishonesty or bankruptcy (see *Re Wheeler and De Rochow* (1896)).

(6) Where a trustee is incapable of acting. Incapacity refers to some physical or mental inability to adequately administer the trust, but does not include bankruptcy (see *Re Wheeler and De Rochow* (1896)).

(7) Where the trustee is an infant, that is, under the age of 18. Such a person may become a trustee under an implied trust (resulting or constructive).

10.10.3.1 Persons who may exercise the statutory power

Section 36(1) of the Trustee Act 1925 lists, in chronological order, the persons who are entitled to exercise the statutory power of appointing replacement trustees. These are:

(a) the person or persons nominated in the trust instrument for the purpose of appointing new trustees (see 10.10.2);

(b) the surviving or continuing trustee, if willing to act. Section 36(1) was enacted to empower a sole retiring trustee to appoint his successor. It enables a 'retiring' or 'refusing' trustee to participate with the surviving trustees in appointing a successor (sub-ss (6), (8) of the Trustee Act 1925);

(c) the personal representatives of the last surviving or continuing trustee.

10.10.4 Additional trustees (s 36(6))

Section 36(6) authorises the appointment of additional trustees, although no trustee needs to be replaced when:

...

(a) the person or persons nominated for the purpose of appointing new trustees by the instrument, if any, creating the trust; or

(b) if there is no such person, or no such person able and willing to act, then the trustee or trustees for the time being,

may, by writing, appoint another person or other persons to be an additional trustee or additional trustees ...

This sub-section is self-explanatory, but it may be observed that a trust corporation (corporate professional trustee, such as a bank or an insurance company) has the power of two or more individual trustees. No power exists under s 36(6) to increase the number of trustees beyond four.

10.10.5 Direction of the beneficiaries

Sections 19–21 of the Trusts of Land and Appointment of Trustees Act (TLATA) 1996 have invested new powers in the beneficiaries to direct a retirement and/or appoint trustees. These provisions relate to trusts of all types of property (whether land or personalty). But the provisions may be excluded in whole or in part by the trust.

Section 19 applies where there is no person nominated under the trust instrument to appoint new trustees, and all the beneficiaries are of full age and capacity and collectively are absolutely entitled to the trust property. The beneficiaries have either one or both of the following rights: a right to direct in writing that one or more of the trustees shall retire from the trust; and/or a right that a named person or persons be appointed, in writing, as new trustee or trustees. The direction may be by way of substitution for a trustee or trustees directed to retire or as an additional trustee or trustees.

Section 20 of TLATA 1996 enacts a similar provision where the trustee becomes mentally incapable of exercising his functions.

Section 36(7) of the Trustee Act 1925 (as amended by TLATA 1996) enacts that the effect of an appointment under s 36 or ss 19 or 20 of TLATA shall have the same consequences 'as if he had been originally appointed a trustee by the instrument, if any, creating the trust'.

10.10.6   The number of trustees

10.10.6.1   Realty

Section 34 of the Trustee Act 1925 (as amended by TLATA 1996) provides that where land is held on trust, there may not be more than four trustees. If the instrument purports to appoint more than four trustees, only the first four named as trustees will take the property.

On the other hand, while a sole trusteeship is not forbidden, s 14(2) of the Trustee Act 1925 enacts that a sole trustee (other than a trust corporation) may not give a valid receipt for the proceeds of sale.

10.10.6.2   Personalty

In theory, there is no restriction on the number of persons who may be appointed trustees of personalty. The office of trusteeship requires unanimous approval of all the trustees (charities are treated as an exception).

In practice, it may be inconvenient and cumbersome to have too many trustees. But the law does not recognise a 'sleeping' or inactive trustee. A breach may be committed by a 'sleeping' trustee in failing to oppose a decision taken by his colleagues (see *Bahin v Hughes* (1886)).

There are rarely more than four trustees and, if the appointment is made under s 36 of the Trustee Act 1925, there will be not more than four trustees.

On the other hand, a sole trustee is most unsatisfactory because of the danger or risks of fraud or misconduct in administering the trust.

10.10.7   Vesting of trust property in trustees

On an appointment of replacement or additional trustees, the trust property is required to be vested in the new trustee or trustees to enable him or them to carry out his or their duties. Trustees hold the property as joint tenants so that the right of survivorship applies.

The vesting of the property in new trustees may be effected in one of two ways:

* by a conveyance or transfer effective to vest the property in the transferee; or

* by recourse to ss 40(1) and (2) of the Trustee Act 1925. These provisions create short forms and inexpensive methods of vesting the trust property in the new trustee or trustees. Under s 40(1)(a), if the deed merely declares that the property vests in the new trustee, this would be sufficient without a conveyance, etc. Section 40(1)(b) enacts that, if the deed of appointment omits to include a vesting declaration, it will be treated as if it had contained one.

However, s 40(4) of the Trustee Act 1925 excludes certain types of properties from the general provisions in ss 40(1) and (2). These include land held by trustees on a mortgage, certain leases, and stocks and shares.

These properties are required to be transferred in accordance with the appropriate formalities for that type of property.

10.10.8 Appointment by the court

Section 41 of the Trustee Act 1925 gives the court sweeping powers to appoint new trustees, either as replacement or additional trustees:

> The court may, whenever it is expedient to appoint a new trustee or new trustees, and it is found inexpedient, difficult or impracticable so to do without the assistance of the court, make an order appointing a new trustee or new trustees either in substitution for or in addition to any existing trustee or trustees, or although there is no existing trustee ...

The court will only exercise its power to appoint trustees when all other avenues have been exhausted. The most popular occasions when this power may be exercised are: where a sole surviving trustee dies intestate, where an appointor is incapable of making an appointment because he is an infant, where all the trustees of a testamentary trust predecease the testator or where there is friction between the trustees.

In exercising its discretion under s 41, the court will have regard to the wishes of the settlor, the interests of the beneficiaries and the efficient administration of the trust. In *Re Tempest* (1866), the court decided that a nominated person was unsuitable to be appointed as trustee, in order to avoid family dissension.

10.10.9 Retirement

A trustee may retire from the trust in one of five ways:

(1) by taking advantage of a power in the trust instrument;

(2) by taking advantage of a statutory power under:

- s 36(1) of the Trustee Act 1925 when a new trustee is appointed; or
- s 39 of the Trustee Act 1925 where no new trustee is appointed;

(3) by obtaining the consent of all the beneficiaries who are *sui juris* and absolutely entitled to the trust property under the *Saunders v Vautier* principle;

(4) by direction from the relevant beneficiaries under s 19 of TLATA 1996; or

(5) by obtaining the authority of the court.

Unlike a retirement under s 36(1) of the Trustee Act 1925, a trustee is not allowed to retire from part of a trust under s 39 of the Trustee Act 1925. The procedure for retirement under s 39 of the Trustee Act 1925 is as follows:

- at least two individuals will continue to act as trustees or a trust corporation;
- the remaining trustees (or trustee) and other persons empowered to appoint trustees consent to the retirement by deed; and

- the retiring trustee makes such a declaration by deed.

It should be noted that a retiring trustee remains liable for breaches of trust committed whilst he was a trustee. He is absolved from liability in respect of subsequent breaches, unless he retired in order to facilitate a breach of trust (see *Head v Gould* (1898)).

10.10.9.1 Retirement under a court order

Generally speaking, the court will not discharge a trustee under its statutory jurisdiction under s 41 of the Trustee Act 1925 unless it appoints a replacement trustee. However, the court has an inherent jurisdiction to discharge a trustee without replacement, in accordance with its responsibility to administer the trust. This will be the position when s 39 of the Trustee Act 1925 is not applicable because the appropriate consent cannot be obtained.

10.10.10 Removal of trustees

A trustee may be removed from office in one of the following four ways:

- by virtue of a power contained in the trust instrument. This is highly unusual and requires construction of the trust instrument;

- under s 36 of the Trustee Act 1925. This involves the removal of and appointment of a replacement trustee in circumstances laid down in s 36(1) (see 10.10.3);

- in the circumstances specified in ss 19 and 20 of TLATA 1996;

- under a court order under s 41 of the Trustee Act 1925 or under the inherent jurisdiction of the court.

10.10.10.1 Court order

Under s 41 of the Trustee Act 1925, the court has the jurisdiction to remove an existing trustee and appoint a replacement trustee (see above).

Under its inherent jurisdiction to secure the proper administration of the trust, the court has the power to remove a trustee without appointing a replacement trustee. In *Letterstedt v Broers* (1884), the Privy Council declared that the court has a general duty to ensure that the trusts were properly executed and their main guide was the welfare of the beneficiaries. Accordingly, friction and hostility between the trustees and beneficiaries which is likely to prejudice the proper administration of the trust may be a ground for the removal of trustees.

10.11 Duties and Powers of Trustees

The duties of a trustee are varied and extremely onerous. They are required to be executed with the utmost diligence and good faith. Otherwise, he will be liable for breach of trust. The primary duty of the trustee is to comply with the terms of the trust and, subject thereto, to act in the best interests of the beneficiaries. In order to carry out these duties, the trustee is invested with a variety of powers and discretions which are required to be exercised for the benefit of the beneficiaries.

10.11.1   The duty and standard of care

Throughout the administration of the trust, the trustees are required to exhibit an objective standard of skill as would be expected from an ordinary prudent man of business (see *Learoyd v Whiteley* (1887)). This is the common law standard of care. However, s 1 of the Trustee Act 2000 reformulates the duty of care applicable to powers exercisable by trustees under the Act. This provision replaces the common law standard of care as indicated above. The section enacts that the trustees are required to exercise such care and skill as is reasonable in the circumstances:

(a) having regard to any special knowledge or experience he has or holds himself out as having, and

(b) if he acts as a trustee in the course of a business or profession, to any special knowledge or experience that it is reasonable to expect of a person acting in the course of that kind of business or profession.

Thus, the section has created an objective/subjective test of the standard of care required from the trustees. The minimum degree of care and skill expected from a trustee is to be determined objectively by the court. But this standard of care may be increased by reference to the trustees' special knowledge or experience acquired personally or held out by him.

In the case of a power of investment, the duty must be exercised so as to yield the best return for all the beneficiaries, judged in relation to the risks inherent in the investments, the prospects of the yield of income and capital appreciation.

The courts will have regard to all the circumstances of each case in order to ascertain whether the trustees' conduct fell below the standard expected of such persons.

In considering the investment policy of the trust, the trustees are required to put their own personal interests and views on one side. They may have strong social or political views. They may be firmly opposed to any investments in companies connected with alcohol, tobacco, armaments or many other things. In the conduct of their own affairs, trustees are free to abstain from making any such investments. However, in performance of their fiduciary duties, if investments of the morally reprehensible type would be more beneficial to the beneficiaries than other investments, the trustees must not refrain from making the investments by reason of the views that they hold. Trustees may even act dishonourably (though not illegally) if the interests of their beneficiaries require it, as in *Buttle v Saunders* (1950). Here, trustees struck a bargain for the sale of trust property, but the bargain was not legally binding. The court held that the trustees were under a duty to consider and explore a better offer received by them. Similarly, in *Cowan v Scargill and Others* (1984), the defendants were trustees of the Mineworkers Pension Scheme who raised an objection to a new investment plan of trust funds in competing forms of energy. The court decided that the plan would yield the best return for the beneficiaries and refused the application.

In an action for breach of trust, the claimant is required to establish that the trust has suffered a loss which is attributable to the conduct or omission of the trustees. If the trustees' conduct or omission fell below the required standard imposed on trustees, they become personally liable, whether they acted in good faith or not. In *Re Lucking's Will Trust* (1968), a trustee-director of a company was liable to the trust when he allowed the managing director to appropriate £15,000 of the company funds through the delivery of blank cheques to the managing director which were signed by the trustee.

With regard to professional trustees, such as banks and insurance companies, the standard of care imposed on such bodies is higher than the degree of diligence expected from a non-professional trustee. The professional trustee is required to administer the trust with such a degree of expertise as would be expected from a specialist in trust administration. This objective standard is applied by the courts after due consideration of the facts of each case.

In *Bartlett v Barclays Bank* (1980), a trust corporation, in managing a property development company, did not actively participate in the company's deliberations, nor was it provided with regular information concerning the company's activities, but was content to rely on the annual balance sheet and profit and loss account. One of the schemes pursued by the company proved to be disastrous. In an action brought against the trustee, the court held that the trustee was liable, because it (the trust corporation) had not acted reasonably in the administration of the trust.

On the other hand, the claimant failed in her action in *Nestle v National Westminster Bank* (1993) on the ground that she failed to prove positively that the defendant's action or inaction resulted in a loss to the trust.

10.11.2   Duty to act unanimously

Trustees are required to act unanimously. The settlor has given all of his trustees the responsibility to act on behalf of the trust. Subject to provisions to the contrary in the trust instrument, the acts and decisions of some of the trustees (even a majority of trustees) are not binding on the others. Thus, once a trust decision is made, the trustees become jointly and severally liable to the beneficiaries in the event of a breach of trust. In *Bahin v Hughes* (1886), 'passive' trustees were liable to the beneficiaries for breach of trust along with an 'active' trustee.

A claim by one trustee against his co-trustee is now subject to the Civil Liability (Contribution) Act 1978. A trustee who is sued for breach of trust may claim a contribution from his co-trustee. The court has a discretion to make a contribution order if it 'is just and equitable, having regard to the extent of the (co-trustee's) responsibility for the damage in question'.

10.11.3 Duty to act personally

Generally speaking, a trustee is appointed by a settlor because of his personal qualities. It is expected that the trustee will act personally in the execution of his duties. The general rule is *delegatus non potest delegare* (one to whom something is delegated cannot [further] delagate).

However, in the current commercial climate, it is unrealistic to expect trustees to act personally in all matters relating to the trust. Accordingly, trustees are entitled to appoint agents to perform acts in respect of the trust.

Under s 23(1) of the Trustee Act 1925 (consolidating previous provisions), trustees may appoint agents to transact trust business, even if the trustees themselves could have properly conducted the transaction. Of course, the trustees are required to exercise care in making the appointment and are entitled to pay the agent for his services.

In *Fry v Tapson* (1884), trustees were liable for loss in failing to exercise care in appointing an agent.

But s 23(1) of the Trustee Act 1925 declares that the trustee 'shall not be responsible for the default of such agent if employed in good faith'. Furthermore, s 30(1) of the Trustee Act 1925 enacts that the trustee is answerable for his own acts, receipts, neglects or defaults and not for those of other persons 'unless the same happens through his own wilful default'. The question in issue is, to what extent may a trustee be liable for the acts of an agent if the latter was appointed in good faith? In other words, what is meant by the phrase 'wilful default'?

In the leading case of *Re Vickery* (1931), the expression was described as involving 'a consciousness of negligence or breach of duty or recklessness'.

Part IV of the Trustee Act 2000 reformed the law as to the trustees' powers of delegation. It repeals ss 23 and 30 of the Trustee Act 1925 and introduces provisions with a clearer framework for delegation. Generally, the new provisions deal with the appointment of agents, nominees and custodians and the liability of the trustees for such persons.

Sections 11 to 20 of the Trustee Act 2000 deal with the appointment of agents, nominees and custodians. Sections 21 to 23 of the 2000 Act deal with the review of acts of the agents, nominees and custodians and the question of liability for their acts.

Section 11(1) of the Trustee Act 2000 enacts that the trustees of a trust 'may authorise any person to exercise any or all of their *delegable functions* as their agent'. Section 11(2) of the 2000 Act defines 'delegable functions' as *any function* of the trustee subject to four exceptions. These are:

(a) functions relating to the distribution of assets in favour of beneficiaries, that is, dispositive functions,

(b) any power to allocate fees and other payments to capital or income,

(c) any power to appoint trustees, and

(d) any power conferred by the trust instrument or any enactment which allows trustees to delegate their administrative functions to another person.

Thus, the trustees cannot delegate their discretion under a discretionary trust to distribute the funds or to select beneficiaries from a group of objects. But they may delegate their investment decision making power and thereby obtain skilled professional advice from an investment manager.

In the case of charitable trusts, the trustees' *delegable functions* are set out in s 11(3) of the Trustee Act 2000. These are:

(a) any function consisting of carrying out a decision that the trustees have taken;

(b) any function concerning investment of assets subject to the trust;

(c) any function relating to the raising of funds for the trust otherwise than by means of profits of a trade which is an integral part of carrying out the trust's charitable purpose;

(d) any other function prescribed by order of the Secretary of State.

Section 12 of the Trustee Act 2000 provides who may or may not be appointed an agent of the trustees. The trustees may appoint one of their number to act as an agent but cannot appoint a beneficiary to carry out that function. If more than one person is appointed to exercise the same function, they are required to act jointly. Section 14 authorises the trustees to appoint agents on such terms as to remuneration and other matters as they may determine. But certain terms of the agency contract are subject to a test of reasonableness. These are terms permitting the agent to sub-delegate to another agent or to restrict his liability to the trustees or the beneficiaries or to allow the agent to carry out functions that are capable of giving rise to a conflict of interest. Thus, sub-delegation to another trustee or the insertion of an exclusion clause in the contract appointing the agent is subject to a test of reasonableness.

Section 15 of the Trustee Act 2000 imposes special restrictions within certain types of agency contracts. With regard to asset management functions the agreement is required to be evidenced in writing. In addition, the trustees are required to include a 'policy statement' in the agreement giving the agent guidance as to how the functions ought to be exercised, and should seek an undertaking from the agent that he will secure compliance with the policy statement. In the ordinary course of events, the policy statement will refer to the 'standard investment criteria' and, in the case of beneficiaries entitled in succession, require the agent to provide investments with a balance between income and capital. Section 24 provides that a failure to observe these limits does not invalidate the authorisation or appointment.

10.11.3.1 Power to appoint nominees

Section 16 of the Act of 2000 authorises trustees to appoint nominees in relation to such of the trust assets as they may determine (other than settled land). In addition, the trustees may take steps to ensure the vesting of those assets in the nominee. Such appointments are required to be evidenced in writing.

10.11.3.2 *Power to appoint custodians*

Section 17 of the Trustee Act 2000 authorises the trustees to appoint a person to act as custodian in relation to specified assets. A custodian is a person who undertakes the safe custody of the assets or any documents or records concerning the assets. The appointment is required to be evidenced in writing.

10.11.3.3 *Persons who may be appointed as nominees or custodians*

Section 19 of the Trustee Act 2000 provides that a person may not be appointed as a nominee or custodian unless he carries on a business which consists of or includes acting as a nominee or custodian, or is a body corporate controlled by the trustees. The trustees may appoint as a nominee or custodian, one of their number if that is a trust corporation, or two (or more) of their number if they act jointly.

10.11.3.4 *Review of acts of agents, nominees and custodians*

Provided that the agent, nominee or custodian continues to act for the trust, the trustees are:

- required to keep under review the arrangements under which they act, and how those arrangements are put into effect;

- required to *consider* whether to exercise any powers of intervention, if the circumstances are appropriate;

- required to intervene if they consider a need has arisen for such action.

10.11.3.5 *Liability for the acts of agents, nominees and custodians*

Section 23 of the Trustee Act 2000 provides that a trustee will not be liable for the acts of agents, nominees and custodians provided that he complies with the general duty of care laid down in s 1 and Schedule 1 (see 10.11.1), both in respect of the initial appointment of the agent, etc and when carrying out his duties under s 22 (review of acts of agents, etc). The effect of this provision is that it lays to rest the eccentric principles that were applied under the 1925 Act, and introduces one standard objective test concerning the trustees' duty of care.

10.11.4 Delegation under the Trusts of Land and Appointment of Trustees Act 1996

Section 9 of TLATA 1996 enacts that trustees of land may delegate any of their powers in relation to the land by a power of attorney to adult beneficiaries who are currently entitled to interests in possession. The powers of trustees are 'all the powers of an absolute owner' (s 6). In exercising their powers, trustees may not favour or prejudice the interest of any beneficiary. It should be noted that the powers included in s 6 relate only to a trust of land and not to any personal property. In addition, the s 6 powers may be amended or excluded by the settlement, or made subject to obtaining the consent of any person (s 8). Thus, the settlor may prevent any dealing with the land (although this could be challenged under s 14 (see 10.7.1). In the case of charitable trusts, the trustees' powers may not be amended or excluded, but they may be made subject to obtaining consent.

10.11.5 Protection of purchasers from delegate

In respect of land, it is presumed that the trustees were entitled to delegate to a certain person, unless the purchaser had knowledge at the time of the transaction that the trustees were not entitled to delegate to that person (s 9(2) of the 1996 Act). 'Knowledge' for these purposes has not been defined in the legislation, but it is submitted that, since we are concerned here with a proprietary interest, any type of cognisance will suffice for these purposes, even constructive knowledge.

10.11.6 Exclusion clauses

Exclusion clauses which are validly inserted into trust instruments may have the effect of limiting the liability of trustees. Such clauses are not, without more, void on public policy grounds. Moreover, provided the clause does not purport to exclude the basic minimum duties ordinarily imposed on trustees, it may be valid. Some of the minimum duties which cannot be excluded are the duties of honesty, good faith and acting for the benefit of the beneficiaries (see *Armitage v Nurse* (1997)). Much depends on the wording of such clauses. *Prima facie*, any ambiguities are construed against the trustees. See *Wight v Olswang* (1999). In this case, a trust settlement incorporated two conflicting exemption clauses, one protecting all trustees from liability for breach of trust (a general exemption clause) and the other applied only to unpaid trustees. The court decided that the paid trustees could not rely on the general exemption clause.

10.11.7 Duty to provide accounts and information

Owing to the nature of the fiduciary character of trustees, a duty is imposed on them to keep proper accounts for the trust. In pursuance of this objective, the trustees may employ an agent (an accountant) to draw up the trust accounts. The beneficiaries are entitled to inspect the accounts, but if they need copies they are required to pay for these from their own resources.

In addition, the beneficiaries are entitled to inspect documents created in the course of the administration of the trust. These are trust documents and are *prima facie* the property of the beneficiaries. Indeed, 'trust documents' were described by Salmon LJ in *Re Marquess of Londonderry's Settlement* (1965) as possessing the following characteristics:

- they are documents in the possession of the trustees as trustees;

- they contain information about the trust which the beneficiaries are entitled to know; and

- the beneficiaries have a proprietary interest in the documents and, accordingly, are entitled to see them.

In the recent case, *Schmidt v Rosewood Trust Ltd* [2003] 3 All ER 76, the Privy Council reviewed the right to seek disclosure of trust documents and concluded that it is one aspect of the court's inherent jurisdiction to supervise, and if necessary to intervene in, the administration of trusts. Thus, the beneficiary's right to inspect trust documents (including objects under a discretionary trust) is founded not on an equitable proprietary right in respect of those documents, but upon the trustee's fiduciary duty to inform the beneficiary and to render accounts.

10.11.8   Powers of investment

Trustees have an obligation to maintain the real value of trust funds and may need to consider investing the trust property. An 'investment' for these purposes refers to property which will produce an income yield (see *Re Wragg* (1918–19)). The trustees are required to consider the investment policy of the trust with the standard of care and skill as is reasonable in the circumstances. This standard was enacted in s 1 of the Trustee Act 2000 (see 10.11.1). The powers of investment may exist in the trust instrument or may be implied by statute, or the court may enlarge the power of the trustees.

10.11.8.1   *Express power*

A prudent settlor will include a wide investment clause in the trust instrument, in order to give the trustees the maximum flexibility in the selection of investments. The modern approach of the courts is to construe investment clauses liberally (see *Re Harari's Settlement* (1949)).

10.11.9   Statutory power under the Trustee Act 2000

The Trustee Act 2000 (which came into force on 1 February 2001) repeals and replaces the Trustee Investment Act 1961. The new statutory power of investment is found in s 3(1) of the Trustee Act 2000. Under s 3, 'a trustee may make any kind of investment that he could make if he were absolutely entitled to the assets of the trust'. The trustee must, of course, comply with the general duty of care as stated in s 1 of the Act of 2000 (see 10.11.1). This new power is required to be considered in the light of the new powers of delegation (see 10.11.1). As will be seen trustees will be able to delegate their discretion as well as their duty to invest.

The new power is treated as a *default provision* and will only operate in so far as there is no contrary provision in the trust instrument. It should be noted that restrictions imposed by the trust instrument prior to 3 August 1961 are treated as void (see s 7(2) of the Trustee Act 2000). This new power operates retrospectively in the sense that trusts existing before or after the commencement of the 2000 Act are subject to this default provision. However, the new regime does not apply to occupational pensions schemes, authorised unit trusts and schemes under the Charities Act 1993.

Section 4 of the 2000 Act requires trustees to have regard to the 'standard investment criteria' when investing. This is defined in s 4(3) to mean the suitability of the investment to the trust and the need for diversification as is appropriate in the circumstances. Thus, trustees are no longer restricted as to the type of investments they make but are restricted by reference to the standard investment criteria. The standard investment criteria are important because the suitability of investments vary from trusts to trusts. Having exercised the power of investment the trustees are required to review the trust investments periodically by reference to the standard investment criteria (s 4(2)). The purpose of this provision is to require the trustees to determine whether the trust fund ought to be re-invested or not.

By virtue of s 5 of the Trustee Act 2000, trustees are required to obtain and consider proper advice before investing, unless in the circumstances they reasonably conclude that it is unnecessary to do so, for example, if funds are paid in to an interest-bearing account pending investment by the trustees, it may be unnecessary to take advice regarding the interim account, or one or more of the trustees may be suitably qualified to give proper advice. Section 5(4) of the 2000 Act defines 'proper advice' as 'advice of a person who is *reasonably believed* by the trustee to be qualified to give it by his ability in and practical experience of financial and other matters relating to the proposed investment'. This is an objective issue and the test is not restricted to individuals with paper qualifications but includes those with practical experience. Although the provision does not require the advice to be in writing, a prudent trustee will require advice to be in such form.

10.11.9.1   *Mortgages*

Prior to the Trustee Act 2000, the trustees' powers to invest in mortgages was laid down in the Trustee Investment Act 1961 and s 8 of the Trustee Act 1925. The effect of these provisions was that trustees were authorised to invest in mortgages of freehold or leasehold property provided that in the latter case the lease had at least 60 years to run. Section 8 of the Trustee Act 1925 provided that a trustee was not impeachable for breach of trust if the amount of the loan did not exceed two-thirds of the value of the property, and he acted on the written advice of a suitable and independent valuer.

The Trustee Act 2000 repeals and replaces these provisions. Section 3 of the Act of 2000 authorises the trustees to invest by way of a loan secured on land. Although the point is far from clear, it is generally advisable for the trustees to invest in a legal estate by way of a legal mortgage as under the previous law. In addition the security is restricted to land in the UK.

10.11.9.2 Acquisition of land

Before the passing of the Trustee Act 2000, trustees had no general power to purchase land as an investment. There were two exceptions to this rule. First, the trust instrument may authorise trustees to purchase land as an investment. For these purposes and subject to any contrary provision, the land was required to be bought in order to generate an income. Second, s 6(4) of the Trusts of Land and Appointment of Trustees Act 1996 empowered trustees of land to purchase land as an investment, or for the occupation by a beneficiary or for other purposes. The trustees may sell all of the land subject to the trust and purchase further land with the proceeds of sale (s 17 of the 1996 Act). The trustees of land have wide powers to mortgage or lease the land, though not to make a gift of the property, or sale at an undervalue (for such action will involve a loss to the trust, but may be lawful if all the beneficiaries, being of full age and capacity consent to such action). The trustees under s 6 are subject to the statutory duty of care under s 1 of the Trustee Act 2000 and will be in breach of trust if they enter into a dealing for less than the full market value of the land. In exercising their powers under s 6 the trustees are required to have regard to the rights of the beneficiaries and any rule of law or equity or statute. The trustees are required to consult the beneficiaries entitled to possession and give effect to the wishes of the majority, measured by reference to the value of their interest (if consistent with the general interests of the trust). Moreover, the trust deed may impose an obligation on the trustees to obtain the consent of any person prior to a dealing. Failure to consult such a person may not necessarily invalidate the transaction, but will give rise to liability for breach of trust, unless the court dispenses with the need to obtain consent by an order under s 14 of the 1996 Act.

Under s 8 of the Trustee Act 2000, trustees are now entitled to purchase freehold or leasehold land in the UK:

- as an investment; or

- for the occupation by a beneficiary; or

- for any other purpose.

Thus, the new power mirrors the power of trustees under s 6(4) of the Trusts of Land and Appointment of Trustees Act 1996, which has been repealed and replaced by s 8 of the 2000 Act. Once trustees have acquired the relevant land they will be vested with the same powers as an absolute owner of land. Accordingly, the trustees will be able to sell, lease and mortgage the land. This new power is a *default* provision which may be excluded by a contrary intention in the trust instrument.

10.11.9.3 Duty of care

Section 1 of the Trustee Act 2000 reformulates the duty of care applicable to powers exercisable by trustees under the Act. This provision replaces the common law standard of care as indicated above.

10.11.10   The right of beneficiaries to occupy land

Section 12 of TLATA 1996 confers on a beneficiary entitled to an interest in possession under a trust of land the right to occupy the land. But this right does not apply where the land is not available or is unsuitable for occupation by the beneficiary.

10.11.11   Enlargement of investment powers

Trustees are entitled to apply to the court under either s 57 of the Trustee Act 1925 or the Variation of Trusts Act 1958 in order to widen these investment powers. The approach of the courts has been encouraging in granting approval in order to update the investment policy of trusts beyond the scope of the old Trustee Investments Act 1961. In *Mason v Farbrother* (1983), the court approved a scheme to widen the investment powers of trustees of the employees of the Co-operative Society's pension fund owing to the effects of inflation and the size of the funds (some £127 million). Prior to the introduction of the Trustee Act 2000 such applications were regularly made by trusts of long standing. With the changes introduced by the 2000 Act the popularity of such applications is likely to be reduced.

10.11.12   Powers of maintenance and advancement

10.11.12.1   Power of maintenance

A power of maintenance is a discretion granted to the trustees to pay or apply income for the benefit of an infant beneficiary at a time prior to the beneficiary acquiring a right to the income or capital of the trust. Maintenance payments are expenditure incurred out of the income of a fund for routine recurring purposes, such as food, clothing, rent and education.

The issues that are required to be considered by the trustees are:

* whether they have a power to maintain an infant beneficiary;

* whether there is any income available for maintenance;

* whether the trustees are prepared to exercise their discretion to maintain the beneficiary.

Express power

A settlor may expressly include a power of maintenance in the trust instrument. Most professionally drafted settlements will include this power. If this is the case, the trustees' duties will be encapsulated in the clause.

Inherent power

The court has an inherent power to authorise the trustees to maintain beneficiaries. The underlying unexpressed intention of the settlor must have been consistent with the maintenance payments in favour of infant beneficiaries.

Statutory power

Section 31 of the Trustee Act 1925 authorises the trustees, in their discretion, to pay the whole or part of the income from the trust to the parent or guardian of an infant beneficiary, or otherwise apply the relevant amount towards the maintenance, education or benefit of the infant beneficiary during his infancy or until his interest fails.

This statutory power may be modified or excluded by the settlor in the trust instrument (see s 69(2) of the Trustee Act 1925). An exclusion of the power may be express or implied in the settlement. Section 31 of the Trustee Act 1925 is intended to be implied into every settlement, subject to any contrary intention expressed by the terms of the instrument. A contrary intention will be established if the settlor has specifically disposed of the income, for example, a payment of the income to another or a direction to accumulate income.

10.11.12.2   *Availability of income*

The issue here is whether the income of the trust is available to maintain the infant beneficiary. The effect of complex rules of case law, s 175 of the Law of Property Act 1925 and s 31(3) of the Trustee Act 1925 is that a vested interest carries the intermediate income, unless someone else is entitled to it or the income is required to be accumulated. Contingent interests created *inter vivos* or by will carry the intermediate income (save insofar as the settlor or testator has otherwise disposed of the income). A contingent pecuniary legacy does not carry the income, except where the gift was made by the infant's father or a person standing *in loco parentis*, and the contingencies are attaining the age of majority and that no other fund is set aside for the maintenance of the legatee.

10.11.12.3   *Exercise of power during infancy*

The trustees have a discretion to maintain infant beneficiaries. This discretion is required to be exercised responsibly and objectively, as ordinary prudent men of business. Thus, trustees who applied the income automatically to the infant's father, without consciously exercising their discretion, were liable to the beneficiaries for breach of trust when the father used the sums for his own benefit (see *Wilson v Turner* (1883)).

Under the proviso to s 31(1) of the Trustee Act 1925, the trustees are required to take a number of factors into account, such as the age and requirements of the infant, whether other income is applicable for the same purpose and, generally, all the surrounding circumstances. The exercise of the power will vary with the facts of each case.

10.11.12.4   *Accumulations*

The trustees may accumulate the income instead of maintaining the infant with the fund. Such accumulations (or capitalised income) will produce further income when invested. The additional income, as well as accumulations of income, become available for the maintenance of the infant beneficiary in the future, should the need arise (proviso to s 31(2) of the Trustee Act 1925).

10.11.12.5 *Attaining the age of majority*

If the beneficiary attains the age of majority without attaining a vested interest under the terms of the trust, the trustees are required to pay the income to the beneficiary until he acquires a vested interest, dies or his interest fails (s 31(1)(ii)). The payment includes accumulated income. Accordingly, a beneficiary acquires a vested interest in the income of the trust by statute on attaining the age of majority even though, under the trust, he does not enjoy a vested interest. Take, for example, a gift 'on trust for A, provided he attains the age of 25'. On attaining the age of 18, A becomes entitled to an interest in possession.

However, this provision is subject to any contrary intention stipulated by the settlor. Such contrary intention may be manifested by the settlor directing the income to be accumulated beyond the age of majority (see *Re Turner's Will Trust* (1937)).

Power of advancement

An advancement is a payment from the capital funds of a trust to, or on behalf of, a beneficiary in respect of some long-term commitment, such as the purchase of a house or establishment of a business. A potential beneficiary may be in need of capital from the trust fund prior to his becoming entitled, as of right, to the capital from the fund. In such a case, the trustees may be entitled to accelerate the enjoyment of his interest by an advance payment of capital.

For example, S transfers £50,000 to T1 and T2 on trust for B, contingent on B's attaining the age of 25. While B is only 14 years old, a legitimate need for capital arises. But for special provisions to the contrary, the trustees would be prevented from making an advancement to B on the grounds that the contingency entitling B to the capital has not taken place, and in any event B, as a minor, is incapable of giving a valid receipt for the payment of capital. If, on the other hand, the trustees validly exercise their power of advancement, capital may be released in favour of B before the satisfaction of the contingency and B will be prevented from claiming the capital a second time.

10.11.12.6 *Authority to advance*

The authority to exercise a power of advancement may originate from a variety of sources such as the trust instrument, the inherent jurisdiction of the courts or statutory power. Only the statutory power is considered below.

Statutory power

Section 32 of the Trustee Act 1925 creates a statutory power of advancement, which is not limited to minors, but empowers the trustees with a discretion to distribute an amount not exceeding one-half of the beneficiary's presumptive share capital in favour of any beneficiary, who may become entitled to the whole or part of the capital in the future.

However, this statutory power may be excluded expressly or impliedly by the settlor. An implied exclusion involves any power of advancement which is inconsistent with the statutory power, such as an express power which exceeds the statutory maximum amount (see *IRC v Bernstein* (1961)).

10.11.12.7   Advancement or benefit

Under s 32 of the Trustee Act 1925, the trustees are entitled to pay or apply capital in their discretion for the 'advancement or benefit' of a beneficiary. This expression has been interpreted widely by the courts, and 'benefit' was interpreted by Viscount Radcliffe in *Pilkington v IRC* (1964) as extending the wide ambit of 'advancement':

> The word 'advancement' itself means ... the establishment in life of the beneficiary ... The expression ['benefit'] means any use of the money which will improve the material situation of the beneficiary.

Thus, the phrase includes the use of money not only for the immediate personal benefit of the beneficiary but also for an indirect benefit, such as a moral obligation to give to a charity (see *Re Clore's Settlement* (1966)). Similarly, in *Re Kershaw* (1868), the power was exercised, with the intention of benefiting the object under a trust, by making a loan to the beneficiary's husband to help him set up a business in England in order to keep the family together.

Scope of s 32 of the Trustee Act 1925

The policy of s 32 of the 1925 Act is to invest trustees with a discretion to appoint up to one-half of the presumptive share of the capital of the beneficiary for his advancement or benefit. The value of the presumptive share of the beneficiary is measured on the date of the advancement. If the ceiling concerning the statutory power of advancement has been reached (that is, 50% of the presumptive share of capital), the statutory power of advancement would be exhausted even if the value of the capital increases subsequently (see *Marquess of Abergavenny v Ram* (1981)).

The settlor may expressly increase the ceiling of sums which may be advanced. The sum advanced is credited to the prospective share of the beneficiary so that if he becomes absolutely entitled to a share as of right, the sum advanced is taken into account (s 32(1)(b) of the Trustee Act 1925).

Prior interests

If a beneficiary is entitled to a prior interest (life interest), whether vested or contingent, his consent in writing must be obtained prior to the exercise of the power of advancement. The reason for this is that an advancement reduces the income available to other beneficiaries (s 32(1)(c) of the Trustee Act 1925).

Trustees' duties

The trustees are required to exercise their power of advancement in a fiduciary manner. The exercise will not be *bona fide* and will be void if the trustees advance funds to a beneficiary on condition that the sum is used to repay a loan made by one of the trustees (*Molyneux v Fletcher* (1898)). Moreover, the trustees may transfer the capital to the beneficiary directly if they reasonably believe that he can be trusted with the money. If the trustees specify a particular purpose which they reasonably believe the beneficiary is capable of fulfilling, they (the trustees) may pay the fund over to him. But the trustees are under an obligation to ensure that the beneficiary, the recipient of the fund, expends the sum for the specific purpose (see *Re Pauling Settlement Trust* (1964)).

10.12 Variation of Trusts

Trustees are required to administer the trust in accordance with its terms. They have a primary duty to obey the instructions as detailed by the settlor or as implied by law. Any deviation from the terms of the trust is a breach, making the trustees personally liable, irrespective of how well intentioned they may have been. But circumstances may have arisen since the setting up of the trust which indicate that the trust may be more advantageously administered if the terms were altered.

In these circumstances, the trustees are in need of some mechanism whereby authority may be conferred on them to depart from or vary the terms of the trust. Such authority may be conferred in a variety of ways. Under the rule in *Saunders v Vautier* (1841), where the beneficiaries are of full age and of sound mind and are absolutely entitled to the trust property, they may deal with the equitable interest in any way they wish. They may sell, exchange or gift away their interest. As a corollary to this rule, such beneficiaries acting in unison are entitled to terminate the trust.

10.12.1 Management and administration

10.12.1.1 *Inherent jurisdiction of the court*

The court has an inherent jurisdiction to depart from the terms of a trust in the case of an 'emergency', that is, on an occasion when no provision was made in the trust instrument and the event could not have been foreseen by the settlor. This power is very narrow and arises in order to 'salvage' the trust property, for example, to order essential repairs to buildings (see *Re New* (1901)).

10.12.1.2 *Section 57 of the Trustee Act 1925*

This section is drafted in fairly wide terms and empowers the court to confer authority on the trustees to perform functions whenever it is 'expedient' to do so. The policy of s 57 of the 1925 Act is to ensure that the trust property is managed as advantageously as possible in the interests of the beneficiaries and to authorise specific dealings with the trust property that are outside the scope of the inherent jurisdiction of the court. It may not be possible to establish that the situation is an emergency or that the settlor could not reasonably have foreseen the circumstances which have arisen. In these circumstances, the court may sanction the scheme presented.

Under this provision, the courts have sanctioned schemes for the following: partitioning of land (*Re Thomas* (1939)), a sale of land where the necessary consent could not be obtained (*Re Beale's Settlement Trust* (1932)), the sale of a reversionary interest which the trustees had no power to sell until it fell into possession (*Re Heyworth's Contingent Reversionary Interest* (1956)), two charitable trusts blended into one (*Re Shipwrecked Fishermen's and Mariners' Benevolent Fund* (1959)), extended investment powers of pension fund trustees (*Mason v Farbrother* (1983)), a power created to invest abroad (*Trustees of the British Museum v AG* (1984)) and a power created to invest as if the trustees were beneficial owners, subject to certain guidelines (*Steel v Wellcome Custodian Trustee* (1988)).

10.12.1.3 Variation of beneficial interest

The courts have the jurisdiction both to approve schemes which go beyond an alteration of the management powers of trustees and to effect arrangements which vary the beneficial interests under a trust.

10.12.1.4 Section 53 of the Trustee Act 1925

Where an infant is beneficially entitled to real or personal property and the property does not produce income which may be used for the infant's maintenance, education or benefit, the court may adopt a proposal authorising a 'conveyance' of the infant's interest, with a view to the application of the capital or income for the maintenance, education or benefit of the infant.

10.12.1.5 Section 64 of the Settled Land Act 1925

The jurisdiction of the courts under s 64 of the 1925 Act is much wider than their jurisdiction under s 57 of the Trustee Act 1925. Section 64 of the Settled Land Act 1925 not only entitles the courts to sanction schemes connected with the management and administration of the trust; they are also entitled to alter beneficial interests under the settlement.

10.12.1.6 Compromise

The court has the jurisdiction to approve compromise arrangements governing the rights of beneficiaries, including infants and unborn persons under trusts. The House of Lords in *Chapman v Chapman* (1954) clarified the meaning of the expression 'compromise' by deciding that its jurisdiction concerned cases of genuine disputes about the existence of rights.

10.12.1.7   Variation of Trusts Act 1958

The Variation of Trusts Act 1958 was passed in order to reverse the decision of the House of Lords in *Chapman v Chapman* and to introduce sweeping changes in the law.

The court is entitled, at its discretion, to sanction 'any arrangement varying or revoking all or any trusts or enlarging the powers of the trustees of managing or administering any of the property subject to the trusts', provided that the beneficiary (actual or potential) falls within at least one of the following categories as enumerated in s 1(1) of the 1958 Act:

(a)   any person having, directly or indirectly, an interest, whether vested or contingent, under the trusts who by reason of infancy or other incapacity is incapable of assenting; or

(b)   any person (whether ascertained or not) who may become entitled, directly or indirectly, to an interest at a future date or on the happening of a future event, a person of any specified description or a member of any specified class of persons, but not including any person who would be of that description or a member of that class if the said date had fallen or the said event had happened at the date of the application to the court; or

(c)   any person unborn; or

(d)   any person in respect of any discretionary interest of his under protective trusts where the interest of the principal beneficiary has not failed or determined,

provided that, with the exception of para (d) above, the arrangement was carried out for the benefit of that person.

The purpose of the 1958 Act is to permit the court to approve arrangements on behalf of beneficiaries who cannot give their consent by reason of infancy or other incapacity or because their identity is unascertained, for example, a future spouse. It follows, therefore, that the court has no jurisdiction to approve arrangements on behalf of beneficiaries who are *sui juris*, adult and ascertained. Thus, the consent of all adult, ascertained beneficiaries must be obtained before a court grants its approval to a scheme.

The only exception to the above rule is to be found in s 1(1)(d) of the 1958 Act. The court may consent on behalf of an adult 'beneficiary' who may become entitled to an interest on the failure of the principal beneficiary's interest under a protective trust.

10.12.1.8   Settlor's intention

In deciding whether to approve an arrangement or not, the intention of the settlor (if relevant) or testator is only a factor to be taken into consideration by the court. But the settlor's or testator's intention is certainly not an overriding factor, nor is it even a weighty consideration in determining how the discretion of the court is to be exercised. The role of the court is not to act as a representative of the settlor or testator in varying the trusts. Thus, the court approved a scheme, despite the contradiction of the clear intention of the testatrix, in *Goulding v James* (1997).

10.12.1.9 *Benefit*

The notion of benefit is not restricted to financial benefits, though variations have been made to avoid tax. In *Re Weston's Settlement* (1969), the Court of Appeal refused to approve a scheme because, despite being financially advantageous, it would have been morally and socially detrimental to the beneficiaries. In appropriate cases, the court may have regard to the financial instability of an infant beneficiary and approve a scheme by postponing the vesting of such beneficiary's interest in capital (see *Re T's Settlement* (1964)). Likewise, the court may approve an arrangement if its effect would be to prevent real or potential conflict within a family (*Re Remnant's Settlement Trust* (1970)).

10.13 Breach of Trust

A trustee is liable for a breach of trust if he fails to perform his duties, either by omitting to do any act which he ought to have done, or by doing an act which he ought not to have done. The beneficiary is required to establish a causal connection between the breach of trust and the loss suffered either directly or indirectly by the trust. Indeed, even if the trust suffers no loss, the beneficiary is entitled to claim any profit accruing to the trustees as a result of a breach.

10.13.1 Measure of liability

Trustees' liability for breach of trust is based on principles of restitution to the trust estate. The trustee in default is required to restore the trust property, or its equivalent, to the trust estate. In respect of a breach of trust claim, the basic right of the beneficiary is to have the trust duly administered in accordance with the trust instrument and general law. In this regard, the common law rules on remoteness of damage and causation are not applied strictly, but there still has to be some causal link between the breach of trust and loss to the estate. Once the trust fund is 'reconstituted', the defaulting trustee becomes a bare trustee for the claimant and will have no answer to a claim by him for the payment of the moneys in the 'reconstituted' fund.

The fact that there is an accrued cause of action as soon as the breach is committed does not mean that the quantum of the compensation payable is ultimately fixed as at the date when the breach occurred. The quantum is fixed at the date of judgment, according to circumstances which would put the beneficiary back into the position he would have been in, but for the breach. The claimant's actual loss is assessed with the full benefit of hindsight. In *Target Holdings v Redfern* (1995), the court rejected a claim that the loss is to be measured at the time of the breach. This would have entitled the claimants to obtain compensation of an amount which exceeded its loss and would not have reflected the basic principles of equitable compensation.

10.13.1.1 Interest

As a general rule, the court is entitled to award simple interest under s 35A of the Supreme Court Act 1981. There is no consistent view as to the rate of interest. In recent years, some courts have taken the view that the rate is 1% above the minimum lending rate (see *Belmont Finance Corp v Williams Furniture Ltd (No 2)* (1980)). Other courts have suggested that the appropriate rate is that allowed from time to time on the court's short-term investment account (see *Bartlett v Barclays Bank (No 2)* (1980)).

The court has a discretion to award compound interest against trustees. The principle here stems from the policy of preventing the trustees from profiting from their breach. Their Lordships in *Westdeutsche Landesbank Girozentrale v Islington BC* (1996) decided that, in the absence of fraud, this jurisdiction is exercised against a defendant who is a trustee or otherwise stands in a fiduciary position and makes an unauthorised profit, or is assumed to have made such profit. The majority of their Lordships decided that, since the defendant local authority did not owe fiduciary duties to the bank, compound interest would not be awarded against it.

10.13.1.2 Contribution and indemnity between trustees

Trustees are under a duty to act jointly and unanimously. In principle, the liability of the trustees is joint and several. The innocent beneficiary may sue one or more or all of the trustees.

If a successful action is brought against one trustee, he has a right of contribution from his co-trustees, with the effect that each trustee will contribute equally to the damages awarded in favour of the claimant, unless the court decides otherwise. The position today is that the right of contribution is governed by the Civil Liability (Contribution) Act 1978. The court has a discretion concerning the amount of the contribution which may be recoverable from any other person liable in respect of the same damage.

The Act does not apply to an indemnity which is governed entirely by case law. There are three circumstances when a trustee is required to indemnify his co-trustees in respect of their liability to the beneficiaries:

- where one trustee has fraudulently obtained a benefit from a breach of trust (see *Bahin v Hughes* (1886));

- where the breach of trust was committed on the advice of a solicitor–trustee (see *Re Partington* (1887)). In *Head v Gould* (1898), the claim for an indemnity against a solicitor–trustee failed because the co-trustee actively encouraged the solicitor–trustee to commit the breach of trust. The mere fact that the co-trustee is a solicitor is insufficient to establish the claim;

- the rule in *Chillingworth v Chambers* (1896): where a trustee is also a beneficiary (whether he receives a benefit or not is immaterial) and the trustees are liable for breach of trust, the beneficiary/trustee is required to indemnify his co-trustee to the extent of his beneficial interest. If the loss exceeds the beneficial interest, the trustees will share the surplus loss equally, insofar as it exceeds the beneficial interest.

10.13.1.3   Defences to an action for breach of trust

In pursuance of an action against trustees for breach of trust, there are a number of defences which the trustees are entitled to raise. These are as follows.

Knowledge and consent of the beneficiaries

A beneficiary who has freely consented to or concurred in a breach of trust is not entitled to renege on his promise and sue the trustees.

In order to be prevented from bringing an action against the trustees, the beneficiary is required to be of full age and sound mind, with full knowledge of all the relevant facts, and must exercise an independent judgment. The burden of proof will be on the trustees to establish these elements (see *Nail v Punter* (1832)).

Impounding the interest of a beneficiary

Under the inherent jurisdiction of the court, a beneficiary who instigated a breach of trust may be required to indemnify the trustees. The rule of equity was extended in s 62 of the Trustee Act 1925. Under that section, the court has a discretion which it will not exercise if the beneficiary was not aware of the full facts. Section 62 is applicable irrespective of whether the beneficiary has an intention to receive a personal benefit or not. The beneficiary's consent is required to be in writing.

Relief under s 61 of the Trustee Act 1925

Section 61 of the Trustee Act 1925 provides three main ingredients for granting relief. The trustee: (a) must have acted honestly, (b) must have acted reasonably and (c) ought fairly to be excused in respect of the breach. The trustee bears the burden of proof.

The expression 'honestly' means that the trustee acted in good faith. This is a question of fact. The word 'reasonably' indicates that the trustee acted prudently. If these two criteria are satisfied, the court has a discretion to excuse the trustee. The test in exercising the discretion is to have regard to both the interests of the trustees and the beneficiaries and to decide whether the breach of trust ought to be forgiven in whole or in part. In the absence of special circumstances, a trustee who has acted honestly and reasonably ought to be relieved.

In *Perrins v Bellamy* (1899), the trustees of a settlement, acting on the erroneous advice of their solicitor, executed a sale of leaseholds, thereby diminishing the income of the claimant (who was a tenant for life). In an action for breach of trust, the trustees successfully claimed relief under the predecessor to s 61 of the Trustee Act 1925.

But each case is decided on its own facts. A factor which is capable of influencing the court is whether or not the trustee is a professional. In *Bartlett v Barclays Bank* (1980), the professional trustee company was refused relief under s 61 of the Trustee Act 1925 because it acted unreasonably in failing to keep abreast or informed of the changes in the activities of the investment company.

Limitation and laches

The limitation periods concern the time limits during which a beneficiary is required to pursue a cause of action in respect of trust property:

- *Six year limitation period*: under s 21(3) of the Limitation Act 1980, the general rule concerning the limitation period for actions for breach of trust is six years from the date on which the cause of action accrued. A cause of action does not accrue in respect of future interests (remainders and reversions) until the interest falls into possession. In addition, time does not begin to run against a beneficiary suffering from a disability (infancy or mental incapacity) at the time of the breach until the disability ends. For these purposes, a 'trustee' includes a personal representative, and no distinction is drawn between express, implied or constructive trustees.

- *Exceptions*: under s 21(1) of the Limitation Act 1980, where a beneficiary brings an action in respect of any fraud by the trustee or to recover trust property or the proceeds of sale from trust property (that is, actions *in rem* (see below)), the limitation period fixed shall not apply. A transferee is in the same position as the trustee unless he is a *bona fide* transferee of the legal estate for value without notice.

  Where the right of action has been concealed by fraud or where the action is for relief from the consequences of a mistake, time does not begin to run until the plaintiff discovers the fraud or mistake or ought, with reasonable diligence, to have discovered it (s 32 of the 1980 Act).

- *Laches:* where no period of limitation has been specified under the Act (see s 21(1)), the doctrine of laches will apply to equitable claims. Section 36(2) of the Limitation Act 1980 states that 'nothing in the Act shall affect any equitable jurisdiction to refuse relief on the grounds of acquiescence or otherwise'.

The doctrine of laches consists of a substantial lapse of time coupled with the existence of circumstances which make it inequitable to enforce the claimant's action. The doctrine is summarised in the maxim 'equity aids the vigilant and not the indolent'. It may be treated as inequitable to enforce the claimant's claim where the delay has led the defendant to change his position to his detriment, in the reasonable belief that the claim has been abandoned, where the delay has led to the loss of evidence which might assist the defence, or where the claim is related to a business (because the claimant should not be allowed to wait and see if it prospers).

In order to raise a successful defence, the defendant is required to establish the following three elements, as laid down in *Nelson v Rye* (1996):

- there has been unreasonable delay in bringing the action by the claimant;

- there has been consequential substantial prejudice or detriment to the defendant; and

- the balance of justice requires the claimant's action to be withheld.

10.13.1.4   Proprietary remedies

A beneficiary is entitled to 'trace' the trust assets in the hands of the trustees or third parties (not being *bona fide* transferees of the legal estate for value without notice) and recover such property, or obtain a charging order in priority over the trustees' creditors. This is known as a proprietary remedy, or a claim *in rem* or tracing order.

A tracing order is a process whereby the claimant establishes and protects his title to assets that are in the hands of another. The remedy is 'proprietary' in the sense that the order is attached to specific property under the control of another or may take the form of a charging order, thereby treating the claimant as a secured creditor. The remedies at common law and equity are mainly 'personal', in the sense that they are remedies which force the defendant to do or refrain from doing something in order to compensate the claimant for the wrong suffered. But the proprietary remedy exists as a right to proceed against a particular asset in the hands of the defendant.

Advantages of the proprietary remedy over personal remedies

The proprietary remedy has a number of advantages over the personal remedy, namely:

- the claimant's action is not dependant on the solvency of the defendant. Indeed, the claim is based on an assertion of ownership of the asset in question;

- the claimant may be able to take advantage of increases in the value of the property in appropriate cases; and

- on a proprietary claim, interest accrues from the date the property was acquired by the defendant, while claims *in personam* carry interest only from the date of the judgment.

10.13.1.5   Tracing at common law

The approach at common law is that, provided the claimant's property is 'identifiable' and recognised at law, the process of tracing may continue through any number of transformations. The main restrictions to the common law right to trace are when the property ceases to be 'identifiable' perhaps because it becomes comprised in a mixed fund or when the asset ceases to be wholly owned by the claimant (see *Taylor v Plumer* (1815)). In *Lipkin Gorman v Karpnale* (1991), a partner in a firm of solicitors fraudulently misappropriated some of the firm's funds, part of which were lost at a casino. Although the claimant had not sought a tracing order, Lord Goff considered that such a claim may have had a reasonable chance of success. The relationship of banker and customer created a *chose in action* in favour of the claimant. The customer (claimant) was entitled to trace his property in its unconverted form.

10.13.1.6 Tracing in equity

Equity had conceived the notion that, once property was identifiable, recognition of the claimant's right could be given by:

- attaching an order to specific property; or

- by charging the asset for the amount of the claim.

Unmixed fund

Equity followed the common law and declared that, where the trust property has been transformed into property of a different form by the trustees and has been kept separate and distinct from the trustees' resources, the beneficiary may take the proceeds. If the proceeds of sale have been used to acquire further property, the beneficiary may elect:

- to take the property which has been acquired wholly with the trust property; or

- to charge the property for the amount belonging to the trust.

See *Banque Belge pour l'Estrange v Hambrouck* (1921).

Mixed fund

Where the trustee or fiduciary mixes his funds with that of the beneficiary or purchases further property with the mixed fund, the beneficiary loses his right to elect to take the property acquired. The reason for this is that the property would not have been bought with the beneficiary's money, pure and simple, but with the mixed fund. However, in the exercise of the exclusive jurisdiction of equity, the beneficiary would be entitled to have the property charged for the amount of the trust money (see *Re Hallett's Estate* (1880)).

The rule in *Re Hallett's Estate* seems to be that, if a trustee or fiduciary mixes trust moneys with his own:

- the beneficiary is entitled in the first place to a charge on the amalgam of the fund in order to satisfy his claim; and

- if the trustee or fiduciary withdraws moneys for his own purposes, he is deemed to draw out his own moneys, so that the beneficiary may claim the balance of the fund as against the trustee's general creditors.

Assets purchased

Since the beneficiaries are entitled to trace their property (including a charge) into a mixed fund, it follows that that right (to trace) may extend to property (assets) acquired with the mixed fund. Accordingly, if a part of the fund is used to purchase an asset which is identifiable and the remainder of the fund has been exhausted (the right to trace against the fund becoming otiose), the beneficiary may claim to trace against the asset acquired by the trustees.

In short, from the point of view of the beneficiary, the trustee and his successors in title are prevented from denying the interest deemed to be acquired with the mixed fund. In *Re Oatway* (1903), the trustees mixed their funds with trust moneys and bought shares with part of the fund. The remaining funds in the account were exhausted. The court held that the beneficiaries were entitled to claim the proceeds of sale of the shares.

Lowest intermediate balance

If the funds in the account fall below the amount of the trust funds originally paid in, that part of the trust fund (the depreciation) is presumed to have been spent. The right to trace into the balance held in the bank account will be depreciated to the extent of the lowest balance in the account. The lowest intermediate balance is presumed to be the trust property (see *Re Goldcorp Exchange Ltd* (1994)). Subsequent payments are not *prima facie* treated as repayments to the trust fund in order to repair the breach, unless the trustee earmarks such repayments as having that effect.

10.13.1.7 Rule in Clayton's Case

The rule in *Clayton's Case* (1816) is a rule of banking law and one of convenience which had been adopted in the early part of the 19th century to ascertain the respective interests in a bank account of two innocent parties *inter se*. Where a trustee mixes trust funds subsisting in an active current bank account belonging to two beneficiaries, the amount of the balance in the account is determined by attributing withdrawals in the order of sums paid into the account. This is referred to as 'first in first out' (FIFO).

The rule is applied as between beneficiaries (or innocent parties) *inter se* in order to:

- ascertain ownership of the balance of the fund; and

- ascertain ownership of specific items bought from funds withdrawn from the account.

The basis of the rule lies in the fact that, as between the beneficiaries (or innocent parties), the 'equities are equal'. That is, there is no need to give one beneficiary any special treatment over the other (see *Clayton's Case; Devaynes v Noble* (1816)). But it is worth noting that, as between the trustee and beneficiary, the rule in *Re Hallett*, not *Clayton's Case*, applies. The wrongdoer may never take advantage of the FIFO rule.

However, *Clayton's Case* was distinguished in *Barlow Clowes International Ltd v Vaughan* (1992). The rule in *Clayton's Case* was considered to be impractical, unjust, and contrary to the intention of the investors. Accordingly, the court was entitled to refuse to apply it, provided that an alternative method of distribution was available. Recently, in *Commerzbank Aktiengesellschaft v IMB Morgan* [2004] EWHC 2771, the High Court resisted the rule in *Clayton's case* in the interests of fairness and justice.

Limitations

The Court of Appeal, in *Re Diplock* (1948), enunciated the limits surrounding the right to trace. The principles discerned are as follows:

- The equitable remedy does not affect rights obtained by a *bona fide* transferee of the legal estate for value without notice. All equitable claims are extinguished against such persons.
- Tracing will not be permitted if the result will produce inequity, for 'he who comes to equity must do equity'. Accordingly, if an innocent volunteer spends money

improving his land, there can be no declaration of charge because the method of enforcing the charge would be by way of sale, thus forcing the volunteer to convert his property. In *Lipkin Gorman (A Firm) v Karpnale* (1991), Lord Goff advocated a defence of change of position which ought to be adopted in English law in respect of restitution claims. This defence is to be developed on a case by case basis.

- The right to trace is extinguished if the claimant's property is no longer identifiable, for example, if the trust moneys have been spent on a dinner or a cruise or in paying off a loan (see *Re Diplock*).

- It is essential that the claimant proves that the property was held by another on his behalf in a fiduciary or quasi-fiduciary capacity in order to attract the jurisdiction of equity. This fiduciary need not be the person who mixes the funds or the assets. The mixture may be effected by an innocent volunteer, as was the case in *Re Diplock*. In *Chase Manhattan Bank v Israel–British Bank* (1979), the court decided that a payment by mistake of funds from the claimant bank to the defendant bank affected the conscience of the latter to such an extent that the defendant bank became subject to a fiduciary duty to repay the fund to the claimant.

THE LAW OF EQUITY AND TRUSTS

Express Trusts

An express trust is created when the settlor either:

- vests the legal title to the trust property in the trustee(s), subject to the terms of the trust; or

- declares himself a trustee and sets out the terms of the trust.

A principle for deciding whether the terms of the trust have been validly declared is 'the three certainties' test, that is, certainties of intention, subject matter and objects.

The creation of an express trust has the following consequences:

- the settlor, in his capacity as settlor, cannot change his mind and recover the property;

- the trustees are required to deal with the property in accordance with the terms of the trust and the general law;

- the beneficiaries acquire equitable interests and are entitled to protect these against anyone except a *bona fide* transferee of the legal estate for value without notice.

An express trust may be classified as 'fixed' or 'discretionary'. Fixed trusts aim to benefit a specified list of individuals as laid down by the settlor whereas discretionary trusts impose a duty on the trustees to distribute the trust property in favour of any or all of the members of a class of objects. The test for certainty of objects under a discretionary trust is much broader than the test for fixed trusts.

If the intended trust is not perfectly created, the arrangement involving the intended settlor operates as an agreement to create a trust. The claimant is required to establish that he has furnished consideration, for 'equity will not assist a volunteer' or 'equity will not perfect an imperfect gift'. However, the Contracts (Rights of Third Parties) Act 1999 made huge inroads to the privity rule and permits a non-party (volunteer) to bring a claim for damages, in his own right, for breach of contract. Exceptionally, equity will assist a volunteer under any of the following principles, the *Strong v Bird* rule, *donatio mortis causa* or proprietary estoppel.

Resulting Trusts

A resulting trust is a device, which is implied by the court, whereby the equitable interest in property is returned to the settlor or transferor. The trust is created in order to fill a gap in ownership. These trusts may be classified into two categories namely, automatic and presumed. The automatic resulting trust arises in a variety of situations. Examples are a failure of an express trust, or a transfer of property subject to a condition precedent which has not been achieved or when a surplus of funds is left over after the purpose has been fulfilled. The presumed resulting trust is created when property is bought or transferred in the name of another. This presumption may be rebutted by evidence which establishes that the settlor or transferor did not intend to retain a beneficial interest.

Constructive Trusts

A constructive trust is created by the court in order to satisfy the demands of justice and good conscience without reference to the express or presumed intention of the parties. The categories of constructive trusts are never closed because the occasions when there is a need to maintain a balance between the trustees and the beneficiaries are limitless. Instances are a conflict of fiduciary duty and interest, specifically enforceable contracts of sale, proprietary rights in the family home, the frustration of fraudulent or unfair conduct. In addition, a constructive trust arises whenever a stranger to a trust intermeddles with trust property.

Charitable Trusts

A charitable trust is distinctive in that it is a public trust designed to benefit society as a whole or a sufficiently large section of society. This type of trust enjoys a number of privileges not accorded to other trusts. Charitable purposes are schemes which relieve poverty, advance education or religion and promote other purposes which are beneficial to the community.

Breach of Trusts

Generally, the duties of trustees, in respect of all types of trusts, are primarily to comply with the terms of the trust and the general law. Subject thereto, the trustees are required to act in the best interests of the beneficiaries. Failure to perform his or her duties exposes the trustee to liability for breach of trust. A disappointed beneficiary is entitled to bring a personal action against the trustee or an action *in rem* to recover the trust property.

CHAPTER 11

THE CIVIL PROCESS

Jarndyce [v] Jarndyce drones on. This scarecrow of a suit has, in the course of time, become so complicated that no man alive knows what it means. The parties to it understand it least; but it has been observed that no two Chancery lawyers can talk about it for five minutes without coming to a total disagreement as to all the premises. Innumerable children have been born into the cause; innumerable young people have married into it; innumerable old people have died out of it. Scores of persons have deliriously found themselves made parties in Jarndyce [v] Jarndyce, without knowing how or why; whole families have inherited legendary hatreds with the suit. The little plaintiff or defendant, who was promised a new rocking horse when Jarndyce [v] Jarndyce should be settled, has grown up, possessed himself of a real horse, and trotted away into the other world. Fair wards of court have faded into grandmothers; a long procession of Chancellors has come in and gone out ... there are not three Jarndyces left upon the earth perhaps, since old Tom Jarndyce in despair blew his brains out at a coffee-house in Chancery Lane; but Jarndyce [v] Jarndyce still drags its dreary length before the Court, perennially hopeless [*Bleak House*, Charles Dickens].

> Many critics believe that the adversarial system has run into the sand, in that, today, delay and costs are too often disproportionate to the difficulty of the issue and the amount at stake. The solution now being followed to that problem requires a more interventionist judiciary: the trial judge as the trial manager [Henry LJ, *Thermawear v Linton* (1995) CA].

The extent of delay, complication and therefore expense of civil litigation may have changed since the time of Dickens' observations about the old Court of Chancery, but how far the civil process is as efficient as it might be is a matter of some debate.

11.1 The Need for Reform

A survey by the National Consumer Council in 1995 found that three out of four people in serious legal disputes were dissatisfied with the civil justice system (*Seeking Civil Justice: A Survey of People's Needs and Experiences*, 1995, NCC). Of the 1,019 respondents, 77% claimed the system was too slow, 74% said it was too complicated and 73% said that it was unwelcoming and outdated.

According to the Civil Justice Review (CJR) 1988, delay in litigation 'causes continuing personal stress, anxiety and financial hardship to ordinary people and their families. It may induce economically weaker parties to accept unfair settlements. It also frustrates the efficient conduct of commerce and industry'. Despite some of the innovations in the five years following that CJR, the problems continued.

The Heilbron Hodge Report, *Civil Justice on Trial: The Case for Change* (1993), recommended many changes in civil procedure. The Report resulted from an independent working party set up in 1992 by the Bar Council and the Law Society. The 39-member working party was chaired by Hilary Heilbron QC; its vice chair was solicitor Henry Hodge OBE. The Report called for a 'radical reappraisal of the approach to litigation from all its participants'.

The Report painted a depressing picture of the civil justice system, where delays are endemic and often contrived and procedures are inflexible, rule ridden and often incomprehensible to the client. It noted that, incongruously for a multi-million pound operation, technology scarcely featured. All High Court and county court records, for example, were kept manually. The main plank of the Report was concerned with making the operation of the courts more 'litigant-friendly'. It said that judges, lawyers and administrators should develop a culture of service to the litigant. The report made 72 recommendations for change.

Historically, change has come very slowly and gradually to the legal system. The report of the CJR was largely ignored and, with the exception of a shift in the balance of work from the High Court to the county court (under the Courts and Legal Services Act (CLSA) 1990), no major changes came from its recommendations. The whole process began again with the Woolf Review of the civil justice system. In March 1994, the Lord Chancellor set up the Woolf Inquiry to look at ways of improving the speed and accessibility of civil proceedings, and of reducing their cost. Lord Woolf was invited by the government to review the work of the civil courts in England and Wales. He began from the proposition that the system was 'in a state of crisis ... a crisis for the government, the judiciary and the profession'. The recommendations he formulated – after extensive consultation in the UK and in many other jurisdictions – form the basis of major changes to the system that came into effect in April 1999. David Gladwell, head of the Civil Justice Division of the Lord Chancellor's Department (LCD), stated (*Civil Litigation Reform*, 1999, LCD, p 1) that these changes represent 'the greatest change the civil courts have seen in over a century'.

In the system that Lord Woolf examined, the main responsibility for the initiation and conduct of proceedings rested with the parties to each individual case, and it was normally the plaintiff (now claimant) who set the pace. Thus, Lord Woolf also noted the following:

> Without effective judicial control ... the adversarial process is likely to encourage an adversarial cultural and to degenerate into an environment in which the litigation process is too often seen as a battlefield where no rules apply. In this environment, questions of expense, delay, compromise and fairness have only a low priority. The consequence is that the expense is often excessive, disproportionate and unpredictable; and delay is frequently unreasonable [*Access to Justice*, Interim Report, 1995, p 7].

The system had degenerated in a number of other respects. Witness statements, a sensible innovation aimed at 'cards on the table', began after a very short time to follow the same route as pleadings, with the drafter's skill often used to obscure the original words of the witness. In addition, the use of expert evidence under the old system left a lot to be desired:

> The approach to expert evidence also shows the characteristic range of difficulties: instead of the expert assisting the court to resolve technical problems, delay is caused by the unreasonable insistence on going to unduly eminent members of the profession and evidence is undermined by the partisan pressure to which party experts are subjected.

When Lord Woolf began his examination of the civil law process, the problems facing those who used the system were many and varied. His Interim Report published in June 1995 identified these problems. He noted, for example, that:

> ... the key problems facing civil justice today are cost, delay and complexity. These three are interrelated and stem from the uncontrolled nature of the litigation process. In particular, there is no clear judicial responsibility for managing individual cases or for the overall administration of the civil courts. Just as the problems are interrelated, so too the solutions, which I propose, are interdependent. In many instances, the failure of previous attempts to address the problem stems not from the solutions proposed but from their partial rather than their complete implementation [*Access to Justice*, Interim Report of Lord Woolf, 1995].

Many potential litigants are deterred from taking action by the high costs. It is also relevant to remember that whichever party loses the claim must pay for his own expenses and those of the other side – a combined sum which will, in many cases, be more than the sum in issue. An appeal to the Court of Appeal will increase the costs even further (in effect, fees and expenses for another claim) and the same may be true again if the case is taken to the House of Lords. There is in such a system a great pressure for parties to settle their claims. The CJR found that 90–95% of cases were settled by the parties before the trial.

The cost of taking legal action in the civil courts has been gigantic. Two cases cited by Adrian Zuckerman in an address to Lord Woolf's Inquiry illustrate the point. In one, a successful claim by a supplier of fitted kitchens to stop a £10,000-a-year employee from taking up a job with a competitor cost the employer £100,000, even though judgment was obtained in under five weeks from the start of the proceedings. The expense of this case was in fact double the stated amount when the cost of the Legal Aid Fund's bill for the employee's defence was added to the total. In another case, a divorced wife had to pay £34,000 in costs for a judgment which awarded her £52,000 of the value of the family home.

It was the spiralling costs of civil litigation, to a large extent borne by the taxpayer through legal aid, which prompted the Lord Chancellor to move to cap the Legal Aid Fund. The legal aid budget rose from £426 million in 1987–88 to £1,526 million in 1997–98.

The system of civil procedure entails a variety of devices. Very complex cases may require the full use of many of these devices, but most cases could be tried without parties utilising all the procedures. Exorbitant costs and long delays often resulted from unduly complicated procedures being used by lawyers acting for parties to litigation.

Zuckerman has argued that this problem arose from the fact that the legal system was evolved principally by lawyers with no concern for cost efficiency. In both the High Court and the county court, the system allowed parties to quarrel as much over procedural matters as the actual merits of the substantive dispute. In one case, for example, the issue of whether a writ had been properly served on the other side had to be considered by a Master (the High Court judicial officer empowered to deal with procedural matters) and then on appeal, by a judge, and then on another appeal, by the Court of Appeal. Thus, cost and delay could build up before the parties even arrived at the stage of having their real argument heard. If a claim or defence was amended, the fate of the amendment could take two appeal hearings to finally resolve. The pre-trial proceedings often degenerated into an intricate legal contest separate from the substantive issue.

The CJR 1988 recommended unification of the county courts and the High Court. It accepted the need for different levels of judiciary, but argued that having different levels of courts was inefficient. This recommendation carried what Roger Smith, then director of the Legal Action Group, called an 'unspoken sting', namely, that a divided legal profession could hardly survive a unified court. The Bar rebelled and the judiciary were solidly opposed to such change. The recommendation was not legislated.

The Courts and Legal Services Act (CLSA) 1990, following other recommendations in the CJR, legislated for large numbers of cases in the High Court being sent down to the county courts to expedite their progress. No extra resources were given to the county courts to cope with the influx of cases and so, not surprisingly, there has been a growing backlog of cases and a poorer quality of service in the county courts. This problem may well have worsened rather than been helped by the introduction of the Civil Procedure Rules (CPR), as more cases are now heard in the county courts.

There were tactical reasons why parties were tempted to use the full panoply of procedural rules. The rule that 'costs follow success' (that is, the losing side usually has to pay the legal costs of the other side) can operate to encourage the building up of expense. Wealthy litigants could employ protracted procedures in an effort to worry poorer opponents to settle on terms determined by the former. Conditional fee arrangements (see 11.13 below) have made very little impact on the system, so lawyers who are paid by the hour regardless of success are unlikely to be especially anxious about the speed and efficiency of their work.

Zuckerman has argued for the introduction of a more efficient system like the one used in Germany. There, legal fees are determined by law. A lawyer is paid for litigation in units that represent a small proportion of the value of the claim. Payment is in three stages. The first is made at the commencement of the claim; the second when representation begins at a hearing where the judge will attempt to procure a settlement. If this fails, he will give directions for the preparation of evidence. The third payment will be made if the case goes to a full hearing. Since lawyers earn only a fixed fee, there is no systemic incentive for them to prolong any stage of the litigation; on the contrary, they have an incentive to work as expeditiously as possible so as to maximise their rate of pay at any given stage (that is, to get a reasonable return per hour). There was evidence, however, that this system encourages some lawyers to go to the final stage even where there might have been a reasonable chance of settlement at the second stage. To overcome that difficulty, it has now been regulated that a lawyer can get a full three-part fee even if the case is settled at the second stage.

In January 1995, instructions to judges from Lord Taylor, the then Lord Chief Justice, and Sir Nicholas Scott, the Vice Chancellor, have had an effect on the length and therefore cost of High Court cases. Judges were instructed to use their discretion to set strict time limits to lawyers' speeches and cross-examination, to limit the issues in cases and the documents to be disclosed ahead of trial and to curb reading aloud from documents and case reports (*Practice Direction, Civil Litigation: Case Management* (1995)). Lawyers who violated these instructions would stand to lose some of their fees as the Direction states that failure by practitioners to conduct cases economically would be visited by appropriate orders for costs, including wasted costs orders (that is, some of the costs incurred would not be recoverable). Now, lawyers are no longer allowed to examine their own witnesses in court (examination-in-chief) without the express permission of the judge. These rules apply to actions in the Queen's Bench Division (QBD) and Chancery Division of the High Court and the county courts, and are modelled on those which have been used for some time in the Commercial Court where cases are dealt with most expeditiously.

In a statement to launch the rules (24 January 1995), the Lord Chief Justice said that:

> The aim is to try and change the whole culture, the ethos, applying in the field of civil litigation. We have over the years been too ready to allow those who are litigating to dictate the pace at which cases proceed. Time is money, and wasted time in court means higher charges for litigants and for the taxpayer. It also means that everyone else in the queue has to wait longer for justice.

For this system to operate well, however, there is a need for judges to be better assisted by researchers and assistant lawyers, so that they can be properly briefed on the contents and significance of witness statements, and so forth. So far, there has been little improvement in the provision of such services for judges.

The CJR recommended that more cases should be devolved from the county court to arbitration in the small claims procedure. Such a policy was facilitated by changes to the rule in 1992 and 1996, which raised the limit of the value of claims on which the county court small claims procedure can adjudicate to £1,000 and £3,000, respectively (now the limit is £5,000; see 11.4 below). Cases in the small claims procedure are heard without the ordinary formal rules of evidence and procedure, the consequential informality being seen as conducive to quicker settlement of issues. The full width of jurisdiction of the court has been confirmed by the Court of Appeal's decision in *Afzal and Others v Ford Motor Company Ltd* (1994). The court gave guidance on the approach to be adopted by county court judges when deciding whether small claims involving amounts below £1,000 should be tried in court instead of being automatically referred to arbitration under Ord 19, r 3 of the County Court (Amendment No 2) Rules 1992 (SI 1992/1965). The court allowed an appeal by Ford against the decision of a judge who had declined to refer to arbitration 16 employees' claims for damages for personal injuries sustained in the workplace. The employees were supported by their trade union and the employer's case was handled by its insurer.

The employees had argued that compulsory arbitration was unsuitable for their claims and that the issues of liability involved were too complex for summary resolution. Moreover, it was argued that the denial of the right to recover the cost of legal advice and representation at arbitration would deter trade unions from assisting claimants, who would be at a disadvantage in negotiating compensation settlements out of court. In a submission to the Woolf Inquiry in 1995, Marlene Winfield of the National Consumer Council argued that companies and insurance firms are the real beneficiaries of this law. As neither public funding nor costs are generally available for arbitrated disputes, many people who suffer relatively minor injuries now no longer go to law because they cannot afford the assistance of a lawyer. How far the new system for small claims (see 11.4.1 below) is able to ensure greater fairness remains to be judged, but the limited costs regime in the new system and absence of public funding do not provide for much optimism.

When Lord Woolf came to examine the system, small claims hearings played a very important part in the resolution of disputes. He noted that:

> ... in 1994, 24,219 cases where disposed of by full trial [in the county courts] while the number of small claims hearings was 87,885 [*Access to Justice*, Interim Report, 1995, p 102].

What had begun life in 1973 as a new system, designed to facilitate ordinary individuals using the law, had degenerated by 1995 into a system in which business and organisations played the major part. Lord Woolf noted:

> ... in a sample [by RDA Bowles] of 134 county court cases, in one court including a hundred small claims, only 12% of the cases were brought by private individuals, although individuals formed a large proportion of defendants. More recently, Professor John Baldwin of the University of Birmingham found that some 40% of the 109 plaintiffs in his 1994 research for the Office of Fair Trading were individuals [*Access to Justice*, Interim Report, 1995, p 106].

Professor Baldwin's research also identified some fundamental differences among District Judges in the way in which they dealt with evidence and applied the substantive law to small claims. Additionally, Lord Woolf found a real problem in the way that ordinary citizens were expected to present their cases in court (see *Access to Justice*, Interim Report, 1995, pp 102–10).

11.2 The New Civil Process

Following the Civil Procedure Act 1997, the changes have been effected through the new Civil Procedure Rules (CPR) 1998. These have been supplemented by new practice directions and pre-action protocols. The principal parts of all of these new rules and guidelines are examined below. The rules are divided into 76 parts, each dealing with a particular aspect of procedure. Within each part is a set of rules laying down the procedure relating to that aspect. Also, under most parts can be found new practice directions which give guidance on how the rules are to be interpreted. In addition, the rules are kept under constant review and there are regular updates; between 1999 and April 2005, there have been some 39 amendments. Of major importance has been the accessibility of the CPR, which can be found on the LCD website, including practice directions and updates. A further method of improving the civil process has been the introduction of pre-action protocols for certain types of cases, which are designed to increase the opportunity for settling cases as early in the proceedings as possible by improving communication between the parties and their advisers. The rules are quoted as, for example, 'rule 4.1', which refers to Part 4, r 1 of the CPR.

The reforms work towards conflict resolution as the main purpose for civil legal proceedings, rather than a case being a prolonged opportunity for lawyers to demonstrate a range of legalistic skills.

The main features of the new civil process are as follows.

The case control

The progress of cases is monitored by using a computerised diary monitoring system. Parties are encouraged to co-operate with each other in the conduct of the proceedings; which issues need full investigation and trial are decided promptly and others disposed of summarily.

Court allocation and tracking

The county courts retain an almost unlimited jurisdiction for handling contract and tort claims. Where a matter involves a claim for damages or other remedy for libel or slander, or a claim where the title to any toll, fair, market or franchise is in question then the proceedings cannot start in the county court unless the parties agree otherwise. Some matters are expressly reserved to the county court such as Consumer Credit Act claims and money claims under £15,000.

Issuing proceedings in the High Court is now limited to personal injury claims with a value of £50,000 or more; other claims with a value of more than £15,000; claims where an Act of Parliament requires a claim to start in the High Court; or specialist High Court claims.

Cases are allocated to one of three tracks for a hearing, that is, small claims, fast track or multi-track, depending on the value and complexity of the claim.

The documentation and procedures

Most claims will be begun by a multi-purpose form and the provision of a response pack, and the requirement that an allocation questionnaire is completed is intended to simplify and expedite matters.

11.2.1 The Civil Procedure Rules

The CPR are the same for the county court and the High Court. The vocabulary is more user-friendly, so, for example, what used to be called a 'writ' will be a 'claim form' and a *guardian ad litem* will be a 'litigation friend'.

Although in some ways all the fuss about the new CPR being so far reaching creates the impression that the future will see a sharp rise in litigation, the truth may be different. It seems likely that a fall off in litigation in the 1990s will continue. Judge John Frenkel ('On the road to reform' (1998) Law Soc Gazette, 16 December) has pointed to the data. QBD writs were down from 50,295 in 1993–94 to 22,483 in 1997–98 and county court summonses from 2,577,704 to 1,959,958. During the same period, the number of District Judges increased from 289 to 337. In 2001, claims continued to decrease, with 21,613 in the QBD and 1,739,090 being issued in the county court, which was a 7% decrease on 2000.

11.2.2 The overriding objective (CPR Part 1)

The overriding objective of the CPR is to enable the court to deal justly with cases. The first rule reads:

> 1.1(1) These rules are a new procedural code with the overriding objective of enabling the court to deal with cases justly.

This objective includes ensuring that the parties are on an equal footing and are saving expense. When exercising any discretion given by the CPR, the court must, according to r 1.2, have regard to the overriding objective and a checklist of factors, including the amount of money involved, the complexity of the issue, the parties' financial positions and how the case can be dealt with expeditiously and fairly and by allotting an appropriate share of the court's resources while taking into account the needs of others. In future, as Judge John Frenkel observes ('On the road to reform' (1998)), 'the decisions of the Court of Appeal are more likely to illustrate the application of the new rules to the facts of a particular case as opposed to being interpretative authorities that define the meaning of the rules'.

11.2.3 Practice directions

Practice directions (official statements of interpretative guidance) play an important role in the new civil process. In general, they supplement the CPR, giving the latter fine detail. They tell parties and their representatives what the court will expect of them in respect of documents to be filed in court for a particular purpose, and how they must co-operate with the other parties to their action. They also tell the parties what they can expect of the court, for example, they explain what sort of sanction a court is likely to impose if a particular court order or request is not complied with. Almost every part of the new rules has a corresponding practice direction. They supersede all previous practice directions in relation to civil process.

11.2.4 Pre-action protocols

The pre-action protocols (PAPs) are an important feature of the reforms. They exist for cases of *clinical disputes* (formerly called medical/clinical negligence, but now extended to cover claims against dentists, radiologists *et al*), *personal injury, disease and illness, construction and engineering disputes, defamation, professional negligence, housing disrepair and judicial review*. Further protocols are likely to follow.

In the *Final Report on Access to Justice* (1996), Lord Woolf stated (Chapter 3) that PAPs are intended to 'build on and increase the benefits of early but well informed settlements'. The purposes of the PAPs, he said, are as follows:

(a) to focus the attention of litigants on the desirability of resolving disputes without litigation;

(b) to enable them to obtain the information they reasonably need in order to enter into an appropriate settlement;

...

(d) if a pre-action settlement is not achievable, to lay the ground for expeditious conduct of proceedings.

The protocols were drafted with the assistance of The Law Society, the Clinical Disputes Forum, the Association of Personal Injury Lawyers and the Forum of Insurance Lawyers. Most clients in personal injury and clinical dispute claims want their cases settled as quickly and as economically as possible. The new spirit of co-operation fostered by the Woolf reforms should mean that fewer cases are pushed through the courts. The PAPs are intended to improve pre-action contact between the parties and to facilitate better exchange of information and fuller investigation of a claim at an earlier stage. Both clinical disputes and personal injury PAPs recommend the following:

- the claimant sending a reasonably detailed letter of claim to the proposed defendant, including details of the accident/medical treatment/negligence, a brief explanation of why the defendant is being held responsible, a description of the injury and an outline of the defendant's losses. Where the matter involves a road traffic accident, the name and address of the hospital where treatment was received along with the claimant's hospital reference number should be provided. Unlike a 'pleading' in the old system (which could not be moved away from by the claimant), there will be no sanctions applied if the proceedings differ from the letter of claim. However, as Gordon Exall has observed ('Civil litigation brief' (1999) SJ 32, 15 January), letters of claim should be drafted with care because any variance between them and the claim made in court will give the defendant's lawyers a fruitful opportunity for cross-examination;

- the defendant in personal injury cases should reply to the letter within 21 days of the date of posting, identifying insurers if applicable and if necessary identify specifically anything omitted from the letter. The healthcare provider in clinical dispute cases should acknowledge the letter within 14 days of receipt and should identify who will be dealing with the matter. The defendant/healthcare provider then has a maximum of three months to investigate/provide a reasoned answer and tell the claimant whether liability is admitted. If it is denied, reasons must be given;

- within that three-month period or on denial of liability, the parties should organise disclosure of key documents. For personal injury cases, the protocol lists the main types of defendant's documents for different types of cases. If the defendant denies liability, then he should disclose all the relevant documents in his possession which are likely to be ordered to be disclosed by the court. In clinical dispute claims, the key documents will usually be the claimant's medical records, and the protocol includes a *pro-forma* application to obtain these;

- the personal injury PAP also includes a framework for the parties to agree on the use of expert evidence, particularly in respect of a condition and prognosis report from a medical expert. Before any prospective party instructs an expert, he should give the other party a list of names of one or more experts in the relevant specialty which he considers are suitable to instruct. Within 14 days, the other party may indicate an objection to one or more of the experts; the first party should then instruct a mutually acceptable expert. Only if all suggested experts are objected to can the sides instruct experts of their own. The aim here is to allow the claimant to get the defendant to agree to one report being prepared by a mutually agreeable non-partisan expert. The clinical dispute PAP encourages the parties to consider sharing expert evidence, especially with regard to quantum (that is, the amount of damages payable);

- both PAPs encourage the parties to use alternative dispute resolution (ADR) or negotiation to settle the dispute during the pre-action period.

At the early stage of proceedings, when a case is being allocated to a track (that is, small claims, fast track or multi-track), after the defence has been filed, parties will be asked whether they have complied with a relevant protocol, and if not, why not. The court will then be able to take the answers into account when deciding whether, for example, an extension of time should be granted. The court will also be able to penalise poor conduct by one side through costs sanctions – an order that the party at fault pay the costs of the proceedings or part of them.

11.3   Case Control (CPR Part 3)

Case control by the judiciary, rather than leaving the conduct of the case to the parties, is a key element in the reforms resulting from the Woolf Review. The court's case management powers are found in Part 3 of the CPR, although there is a variety of ways in which a judge may control the progress of the case. A judge may make a number of orders to give opportunities to the parties to take stock of their case-by-case management conferences, check they have all the information they need to proceed or settle by pre-trial reviews or halt the proceedings to give the parties an opportunity to consider a settlement. When any application is made to the court, there is an obligation on the judge to deal with as many outstanding matters as possible. The court is also under an obligation to ensure that witness statements are limited to the evidence that is to be given if there is a hearing, and expert evidence is restricted to what is required to resolve the proceedings. Judges receive support from court staff in carrying out their case management role. The court monitors case progress by using a computerised diary monitoring system which:

- records certain requests, or orders made by the court;

- identifies the particular case or cases to which these orders/requests refer, and the dates by which a response should be made; and

- checks on the due date whether the request or order has been complied with.

Whether there has been compliance or not, the court staff will pass the relevant files to a procedural judge (a Master in the Royal Courts of Justice, a District Judge in the county court) who will decide if either side should have a sanction imposed on them.

In the new system, the litigants have much less control over the pace of the case than in the past. They will not be able to draw out proceedings, or delay in the way that they once could have done, because the case is subject to a timetable. Once a defence is filed, the parties get a timetable order that includes the prospective trial date. The need for pre-issue preparation is increased, and this benefits litigants because, as Professor Hazel Genn's research has shown (*Hard Bargaining: Out of Court Settlement in Personal Injury Claims* (1987)), in settled personal injury actions, 60% of costs were incurred before proceedings. The court now has a positive duty to manage cases. Rule 1.4(1) states that 'The court must further the overriding objective by actively managing cases'. The rule goes on to explain what this management involves:

> 1.4(2) Active case management includes–
>
> (a) encouraging the parties to co-operate with each other in the conduct of the proceedings;
>
> (b) identifying the issues at an early stage;
>
> (c) deciding promptly which issues need full investigation and trial and accordingly disposing summarily of the others;
>
> (d) deciding the order in which issues are to be resolved;
>
> (e) encouraging the parties to use an alternative dispute resolution procedure if the court considers that appropriate;
>
> (f) helping the parties to settle the whole or part of the case;
>
> (g) fixing timetables or otherwise controlling the progress of the case;
>
> (h) considering whether the likely benefits of taking a particular step justify the cost of taking it;
>
> (i) dealing with as many aspects of the case as it can on the same occasion;
>
> (j) dealing with the case without the parties needing to attend court;
>
> (k) making use of technology; and
>
> (l) giving directions to ensure that the trial of a case proceeds quickly and efficiently.

It is worth noting here that District Judges and Deputy District Judges have had extensive training to promote a common approach (see 3.15 above). Training is being taken very seriously by the judiciary. District Judges now occupy a pivotal position in the civil process.

Part 3 of the CPR gives the court a wide range of substantial powers. The court can, for instance, extend or shorten the time for compliance with any rule, practice direction or court order, even if an application for an extension is made after the time for compliance has expired. It can also hold a hearing and receive evidence by telephone or 'by using any other method of direct oral communication'.

The Association of District Judges, the Association of Personal Injury Lawyers and the Forum of Insurance Lawyers, who meet at six-monthly intervals to discuss how the operation of the CPR might be improved ((2000) 13 Law Soc Gazette 11), agreed that telephone hearings are now working very well (on the whole), but contested interim applications are often not suitable for telephone hearings and should not be disguised as case management conferences. Furthermore, not all courts have yet received the right equipment to be able to conduct a telephone hearing. The District Judge cannot be put in the role of a go-between, which happens in some judges' rooms where there is no conference facility but one party has attended in person and the opponent is on the other end of a standard telephone.

Part 3 of the CPR also gives the court powers to:

- strike out a statement of case;

- impose sanctions for non-payment of certain fees;

- impose sanctions for non-compliance with rules and practice directions;

- give relief from sanctions.

There is, though, a certain flexibility built into the rules. A failure to comply with a rule or practice direction will not necessarily be fatal to a case. Rule 3.10 of the CPR states:

> Where there has been an error of procedure such as a failure to comply with a rule or practice direction:
>
> (a) the error does not invalidate any step taken in the proceedings unless the court so orders; and
>
> (b) the court may make an order to remedy the error.

The intention of imposing a sanction will always be to put the parties back into the position they would have been in if one of them had not failed to meet a deadline. For example, the court could order that a party carries out a task (like producing some sort of documentary evidence) within a very short time (for example, two days) in order that the existing trial dates can be met.

11.3.1 Case management conferences

Case management conferences may be regarded as an opportunity to 'take stock'. Many of these are now conducted by telephone. There is no limit to the number of case management conferences which may be held during the life of a case, although the cost of attendance at such hearings against the benefits obtained will always be a consideration in making the decision. They will be used, among other things, to consider:

- giving directions, including a specific date for the return of a listing questionnaire;

- whether the claim or defence is sufficiently clear for the other party to understand the claim they have to meet;

- whether any amendments should be made to statements of case;

- what documents, if any, each party needs to show the other;

- what factual evidence should be given;

- what expert evidence should be sought and how it should be sought and disclosed; and

- whether it would save costs to order a separate trial of one or more issues.

11.3.2   Pre-trial reviews

Pre-trial reviews will normally take place after the filing of listing questionnaires and before the start of the trial. Their main purpose is to decide a timetable for the trial itself, including the evidence to be allowed and whether this should be given orally, instructions about the content of any trial bundles (bundles of documents including evidence, such as written statements, for the judge to read) and confirming a realistic time estimate for the trial itself.

Rules require that, where a party is represented, a representative 'familiar with the case and with sufficient authority to deal with any issues likely to arise must attend every case management conference or pre-trial review'.

Both the Chancery Guide and the Queens Bench Guide provide that where it is estimated that a case will last more than 10 days or where a case warrants it the court may consider directing a pre-trial review.

11.3.3   Stays for settlement (CPR Part 26) and settlements (CPR Part 36)

Under the new CPR, there is a greater incentive for parties to settle their differences.

The court will take into account any pre-action offers to settle when making an order for costs. Thus, a side which has refused a reasonable offer to settle will be treated less generously in the issue of how far the court will order their costs to be paid by the other side. For this to happen, the offer must be one which is made to be open to the other side for at least 21 days after the date it was made (to stop any undue pressure being put on someone with the phrase 'take it or leave it, it is only open for one day then I shall withdraw the offer'). Also, if the offer is made by the potential defendant if proceedings were commenced, it must be an offer to pay the claimant's costs up to 21 days after the offer was made.

Several aspects of the new rules encourage litigants to settle rather than take risks in order (as a claimant) to hold out for unreasonably large sums of compensation, or try to get away (as a defendant) with paying nothing rather than some compensation. The system of Part 36 payments or offers does not apply to small claims but, for other cases, it seems bound to have a significant effect. Thus, if at the trial, a claimant does not get more damages than a sum offered by the defendant in what is called a 'Part 36' payment (that is, an offer to settle or a payment into the court), or obtain a judgment more favourable than a Part 36 offer, the court will, unless it considers it unjust to do so, order the claimant to pay any costs incurred by the defendant after the latest date for accepting the payment or offer without requiring the courts permission. The court now has the discretion to make a different order for costs than the normal order. District Judge Frenkel has given the following example:

> Claim, £150,000 – judgment, £51,000 – £50,000 paid into court. The without prejudice correspondence shows that the claimant would consider nothing short of £150,000. The claimant may be in trouble. The defendant will ask the judge to consider overriding principles of Part 1 'Was it proportional to incur the further costs of trial to secure an additional £1,000?'. Part 44.3 confirms the general rule that the loser pays but allows the court to make a different order to take into account offers to settle, payment into court, the parties' conduct including pre-action conduct and exaggeration of the claim [(1999) 149 NLJ 458].

Similarly, where at trial, a defendant is held liable to the claimant for more money than the proposals contained in a claimant's Part 36 offer (that is, where the claimant has made an offer to settle), the court may order the defendant to pay interest on the award at a rate not exceeding 10% above the base rate for some or all of the period, starting with the date on which the defendant could have accepted the offer without requiring the courts permission. In addition, the court may order that the claimant be entitled to his costs on an indemnity basis together with interest on those costs at a rate not exceeding 10% above base rate for the period from the latest date when the defendant could have accepted the offer without requiring the courts permission.

Active case management imposes a duty on the courts to help parties settle their disputes. A 'stay' is a temporary halt in proceedings, and an opportunity for the court to order such a pause. Either party to a case can also make a written request for a stay when filing their completed allocation questionnaire. Where all the parties indicate that they have agreed on a stay to attempt to settle the case and provided the court agrees, they can have an initial period of one month to try to settle the case. If the court grants a stay, the claimant must inform the court if a settlement is reached, because otherwise at the expiry of the stay it will effectively be deemed that a settlement has not been reached and the file will be referred to the judge for directions as considered appropriate.

The court will always give the final decision about whether to grant the parties more time to use a mediator or arbitrator or expert to settle, even if the parties are agreed they wish to have more time. A stay will never be granted for an indefinite period.

11.3.4 Applications to be made when claims come before a judge (CPR Part 1)

The overriding objective in Part 1 requires the court to deal with as many aspects of the case as possible on the same occasion. The filing of an allocation questionnaire, which is to enable the court to judge in which track the case should be heard, is one such occasion. Parties should, wherever possible, issue any application they may wish to make, such as an application for summary judgment (CPR Part 24), or to add a third party (CPR Part 20), at the same time as they file their questionnaire. Any hearing set to deal with the application will also serve as an allocation hearing if allocation remains appropriate.

11.3.5 Witness statements (CPR Part 32)

In the *Final Report on Access to Justice*, Lord Woolf recognised the importance of witness statements in cases, but observed that they had become problematic because lawyers had made them excessively long and detailed in order to protect against leaving out something which later proved to be relevant. He said 'witness statements have ceased to be the authentic account of the lay witness; instead they have become an elaborate, costly branch of legal drafting' (para 55).

Under the new rules, witness statements must contain the evidence that the witness will give at trial, but they should be briefer than those drafted under the previous rules: they should be drafted in lay language and should not discuss legal propositions. Witnesses will be allowed to amplify on the statement or deal with matters that have arisen since the report was served, although this is not an automatic right and a 'good reason' for the admission of new evidence will have to be established.

11.3.6 Experts (CPR Part 35)

The rules place a clear duty on the court to ensure that 'expert evidence is restricted to that which is reasonably required to resolve the proceedings'. That is to say that expert evidence will only be allowed either by way of written report, or orally, where the court gives permission. Equally important is the rules' statement about experts' duties. Rule 35.3 states that it is the clear duty of experts to help the *court* on matters within their expertise, bearing in mind that this duty overrides any obligation to the person from whom they have received instructions or by whom they are paid.

There is greater emphasis on using the opinion of a single expert. Experts are only to be called to give oral evidence at a trial or hearing if the court gives permission. Experts' written reports must contain a statement that they understand and have complied with, and will continue to comply with, their duty to the court. Instructions to experts are no longer privileged and their substance, whether written or oral, must be set out in the expert's report. Thus, either side can insist, through the court, on seeing how the other side phrased its request to an expert.

11.4   Court and Track Allocation (CPR Part 26)

Part 7 of the CPR sets out the rules for starting proceedings. A new restriction is placed on which cases may be begun in the High Court. The county courts retain an almost unlimited jurisdiction for handling contract and tort claims (that is, negligence cases, nuisance cases but excluding a claim for damages or other remedy for libel or slander unless the parties agree otherwise). Issuing proceedings in the High Court is now limited to:

- personal injury claims with a value of £50,000 or more;

- other claims with a value of more than £15,000;

- claims where an Act of Parliament requires proceedings to start in the High Court; or

- specialist High Court claims which need to go to one of the specialist 'lists', like the Commercial List, the Technology and Construction List.

The new civil system works on the basis that the court, upon receipt of the defence, requires the parties to complete 'allocation questionnaires' (giving all the relevant details of the claim, including how much it is for and an indication of its factual and legal complexity). Under Part 26 of the CPR, the case will then be allocated to one of three tracks for a hearing. These are: (a) small claims track; (b) fast track and (c) multi-track. Each of the tracks offers a different degree of case management.

The new small claims limit is £5,000, although personal injury and housing disrepair claims for over £1,000, illegal eviction and harassment claims will be excluded from the small claims procedure. The limit for cases going into the fast track system is £15,000, and only claims for over £15,000 can be issued in the High Court. Applications to move cases 'up' a track on grounds of complexity will have to be made on the allocation questionnaire (see 11.5.10).

Directions (instructions about what to do to prepare the case for trial or hearing) will be proportionate to the value of the claim, its importance, complexity and so on. Each track requires a different degree of case monitoring, that is, the more complex the claim, the more milestone events there are likely to be (that is, important points in the process, like the date by which the allocation questionnaire should be returned). Time for carrying out directions, no matter which track, may be extended or shortened by agreement between parties, but must not, as a result, affect any of the milestones relevant to that track. The time for carrying out directions will be expressed as calendar dates rather than periods of days or weeks. Directions will include the court's directions concerning the use of expert evidence.

11.4.1   The small claims track (CPR Part 27)

There is no longer any 'automatic reference' to the small claims track. Claims are allocated to this track in exactly the same way as to the fast track or multi-track. The concept of an '*arbitration*' therefore disappears and is replaced by a *small claims hearing*. Aspects of the old small claims procedure which are retained include their informality, the interventionist approach adopted by the judiciary, the limited costs regime and the limited grounds for appeal (misconduct of the District Judge or an error of law made by the court).

Changes to the handling of small claims are:

- *an increase in the jurisdiction from £3,000 to no more than £5,000* (with the exception of claims for personal injury where the damages claimed for pain and suffering and loss of amenity do not exceed £1,000 and the financial value of the whole claim does not exceed £5,000; and for housing disrepair where the claim for repairs and other work does not exceed £1,000 and the financial value of any other claim for damages is not more than £1,000);

- *hearings to be generally public hearings* – but subject to some exceptions (CPR Part 39);

- *paper adjudication, if parties consent* – where a judge thinks that paper adjudication may be appropriate, parties will be asked to say whether or not they have any objections within a given time period. If a party does object, the matter will be given a hearing in the normal way;

- *parties need not attend the final hearing* – a party not wishing to attend the final hearing will be able to give the court written notice before the hearing that they will not be attending. The notice must be filed with the court seven days before the start of the hearing. This will guarantee that the court will take into account any written evidence that the party has sent to the court. A consequence of this is that the judge must give reasons for the decision reached which will be included in the judgment;

- *use of experts* – expert witnesses will only be allowed to give evidence with the permission of the court;

- *costs* – these are not generally awarded, but a small award may be made to cover costs in issuing the claim, court fees for legal advice and assistance relating to proceedings which included a claim for an injunction or an order for specific performance, the costs assessed by summary procedure in relation to an appeal and expenses incurred by the successful party, witnesses and experts. Under r 27.14 of the CPR, additional costs may be awarded against any party who has behaved unreasonably;

- *preliminary hearings* – these may be called:

  (a) where the judge considers that special directions are needed to ensure a fair hearing and where it appears necessary that a party should attend court so that it can be ensured that the party understands what he is required to do to comply with the special directions;

(b) to enable the judge to dispose of the claim where he is of the view that either of the parties has no real prospect of success at a full hearing;

(c) to enable the judge to strike out either the whole or part of a statement of case on the basis that it provides no reasonable grounds for bringing such a claim.

- *the introduction of tailored directions* – to be given for some of the most common small claims, for example, spoiled holidays or wedding videos, road traffic accidents or building disputes.

Parties can consent to use the small claims track even if the value of their claim exceeds the normal value for that track, but subject to the court's approval. The limited cost regime will not apply to these claims, but trial costs are at the discretion of the court and will be limited to the costs that might have been awarded if the claim had been dealt with in the fast track. Generally, the parties will be restricted to a maximum one day hearing.

The milestone events for the small claims track are the date for the return of the allocation questionnaire and the date of the hearing.

11.4.2 The fast track (CPR Part 28)

In accordance with one of the main principles of the Woolf reforms, the purpose of the fast track is to provide a streamlined procedure for the handling of moderately valued cases – *those with a value of more than £5,000 but less than £15,000* – in a way which will ensure that the costs remain proportionate to the amount in dispute. The features of the procedure which aim to achieve this are:

- standard directions for trial preparation which avoid complex procedures and multiple experts, with minimum case management intervention by the court;

- a standard limited period between directions and the start of the trial, it will not be more than 30 weeks;

- a maximum of one day (five hours) for trial;

- trial period must not exceed 3 weeks and parties must be given 21 days' notice of the date fixed for trial unless in exceptional circumstances the court directs shorter notice;

- normally, no oral expert evidence is to be given at trial, but where allowed, it will be limited to one expert party in any expert field and expert evidence in two expert fields; and

- costs allowed for the trial are fixed depending on the level of advocacy.

Directions given to the parties by the judge will normally include a date by which parties must file a listing questionnaire. As with allocation questionnaires, the procedural judge may impose a sanction where a listing questionnaire is not returned by the due date. Listing questionnaires will include information about witnesses, confirm the time needed for trial, parties' availability and the level of advocate for the trial.

The milestone events for the fast track are *the date for the return of allocation* and *listing questionnaires* and *the date for the start of the trial or trial period*.

11.4.3 The multi-track (CPR Part 29)

The multi-track is intended to provide a flexible regime for the handling of the higher value, more complex claims, that is, those with a *value of over £15,000*.

This track does not provide any standard procedure, such as those for small claims or claims in the fast track. Instead, it offers a range of case management tools – *standard directions, case management conferences* and *pre-trial reviews* – which can be used in a 'mix and match' way to suit the needs of individual cases. Whichever of these is used to manage the case, the principle of setting a date for trial, or a trial period at the earliest possible time, no matter that it is some way away, will remain paramount.

Where a trial period is given for a multi-track case, this will be one week. Parties will be told initially that their trial will begin on a day within the given week. The rules and practice direction do not set any time period for giving notice to the parties of the date fixed for trial.

11.5 Documentation and Procedures

One of the main aims of the Woolf reforms is to simplify court forms. Under the old system, there were various forms that needed to be completed at the outset of a claim – different types including summonses, originating applications, writs and petitions. Under the new system, most claims will be begun by using a 'Part 7' claim form.

11.5.1 How to start proceedings – the claim form (CPR Part 7)

A Part 7 claim form has been designed for multi-purpose use. It can be used if the claim is for a *specified* amount of money (the old term was *liquidated* damages) or an *unspecified* amount (replacing the term *unliquidated* damages). The form can also be used for non-monetary claims, for example, where the claimant just wants a court order, not money. The person issuing the claim form is called a claimant (plaintiff in old vocabulary) and the person at whom it is directed will continue to be known as a defendant.

Under the new rules, the court can grant any remedy to which the claimant is entitled, even if the claimant does not specify which one he wants. It is, though, as Gordon Exall has observed ((1999) SJ 162, 19 February), dangerous to start a claim without having a clear idea of the remedy you want. The defendant might be able to persuade the court not to allow the claimant a certain part of his costs if he (the defendant) finds himself having to consider a remedy which had not been mentioned prior to the trial.

In the longer term, it seems clear that a plain set of language forms designed all at one time as a part of one coherent system will provide a more efficient system than that afforded by a collection of outdated forms which have been generated reactively over a long period. The most important change to come out of the 21st CPR update was the new allocation questionnaire. All the questions were revised in the light of experience since April 1999.

11.5.2 Alternative procedure for claims (CPR Part 8)

Part 8 of the rules introduced the *alternative procedure for claims*. This procedure is commenced by the issue of a Part 8 claim form. It is intended to provide a speedy resolution of claims which are not likely to involve a substantial dispute of fact, for example, applications for approval of infant settlements, or for orders enforcing a statutory right such as a right to have access to medical records (under the Access to Health Records Act 1990). The Part 8 procedure is also used where a rule or practice direction requires or permits its use.

The main differences between this and the Part 7 procedure are as follows:

- a hearing may be given on issue or at some later stage if required;

- only an acknowledgement of service is served with the claim form by way of a response document;

- a defendant must file an acknowledgement of service to be able to take part in any hearing;

- a defendant must serve a copy of the acknowledgement on the other parties, as well as filing it with the court;

- no defence is required;

- default judgment is not available to the claimant; the court must hear the case;

- there are automatic directions for the exchange of evidence (in this case, in the form of witness statements);

- Part 8 claims are not formally allocated to a track; they are automatically multi-track cases.

11.5.3 Statement of case – value (CPR Part 16)

The 'value' of a claim is the amount a claimant reasonably expects to recover. Unless the amount being claimed is a specified amount, a claimant will be expected (Part 16) to state the value band into which the claim is likely to fall. The value bands reflect the values for the different tracks (for example, £1 to £5,000 for small claims). Value is calculated as the amount a claimant expects to recover, ignoring any interest, costs, contributory negligence, or the fact that a defendant may make a counterclaim or include a set-off in the defence. If a claimant is not able to put a value on the claim, the reasons for this must be given.

11.5.4 Statement of case – particulars of claim (CPR Part 16)

Particulars of claim may be included in the claim form, attached to it or may be served (that is, given or sent to a party by a method allowed by the rules) separately from it. Where they are served separately, they must be served within 14 days of the claim form being served. The time for a defendant to respond begins to run from the time the particulars of claim are served.

Part 16 is entitled *Statements of case* (replacing the term *pleadings*). Statements of case include documents from both sides: claim forms, particulars of claims, defences, counterclaims, replies to defences and counterclaims, Part 20 (third party) claims and any *further information* provided under CPR Part 18 (replacing the term *further and better particulars*). Part 16 also sets out what both particulars of claim and defences should contain.

The particulars of claim must contain:

- a concise statement of facts on which the claimant relies;

- details of any interest claimed;

- specific details if exemplary, provisional or aggravated damages are claimed

- any other matters that may be set out in a practice direction

The Woolf Report was against obliging the claimant to state the legal nature of the claim as this would prejudice unrepresented defendants. If the nature of the claim is uncertain, then the court can take its own steps to clarify the matter.

Where a claimant is going to rely on the fact that the defendant has been convicted for a crime arising out of the same circumstances for which the claimant is now suing, then the particulars of claim must contain details of the conviction, the court which made it and exactly how it is relevant to the claimant's arguments.

It is optional for the claimant also to mention any point of law on which the claim is based and the names of any witnesses which he proposes to call.

All statements of case must also contain a statement of truth.

11.5.5 Statements of truth (CPR Part 22)

A statement of truth is a statement that a party believes that the facts or allegations set out in a document, which they put forward, are true. It is required in statements of case, witness statements and expert reports. Any document which contains a statement of truth may be used in evidence. This will avoid the previous need to swear affidavits in support of various statements made as part of the claim.

Any document with a signed statement of truth which contains false information given deliberately, that is, without an honest belief in its truth, will constitute a contempt of court (a punishable criminal offence) by the person who provided the information. Solicitors may sign statements of truth on behalf of clients, but on the understanding that it is done with the clients' authority, and with clients knowing that the consequences of any false statement will be personal to them.

11.5.6 Response to particulars of claim (CPR Part 9)

When a claim form is served, it will be served with a response pack. The response pack will contain an acknowledgment of service, a form of admission and a form of defence and counterclaim. The response pack will be served with a claim form containing the particulars of claim, which are attached to it or, where particulars of claim are served after the claim form, with the particulars. A defendant must respond within 14 days of service of the particulars of claim. If a defendant ignores the claim, the claimant may obtain judgment for the defendant to pay the amount claimed. A defendant may:

- pay the claim;

- admit the claim, or partly admit it;

- file an acknowledgement of service; or

- file a defence.

Requirements have also been introduced regarding the content of a defence. A defence which is a simple denial is no longer acceptable and runs the risk of being struck out by the court (that is, deleted so that it may no longer be relied upon). A defendant must state in any defence:

- which of the allegations in the particulars of claim are denied, giving reasons for doing so and must state his own version of the events if he intends to put forward a different version to that of the claimant;

- which allegations the defendant is not able to admit or deny but which the claimant is required to prove;

- which allegations are admitted; and

- if the defendant disputes the claimant's statement of value, the reasons for doing so and, if possible, stating an alternate value.

These rules mark a significant change of culture from the old civil procedure rules. Under the old rules, a defendant could, in his defence, raise a 'non-admission' or a 'denial'. The first meant that the defendant was putting the plaintiff (now claimant) to proof, that is, challenging him to prove his case on the balance of probabilities. The second meant that the defendant was raising a specific defence, for example, a 'development risks defence' under the Product Liability Act 1987. Defendants were allowed under the old rules to keep as many avenues of defence available for as long as possible. Under the new rules, the defendant must respond according to the choices in the four options above. According to r 16.5(5), if the defendant does not deal specifically with an allegation, then it will be deemed to be admitted. However, where a defendant does not specifically deal with an allegation, but in any event sets out in his defence the nature of his case on that issue, it will be deemed that the matter be proved.

11.5.7 Service (CPR Part 6)

Where the court is to serve any document (not just claim forms), it is for the court to decide the method of service. This will generally be by first class post. The deemed date of service is two days after the day of posting for all defendants, including limited companies. Where a claim form originally served by post is returned by the Post Office, the court will send a notice of non-service to the claimant stating the method of service attempted. The notice will tell the claimant that the court will not make any further attempts at service. Service therefore becomes a matter for claimants. The court will return the copies of the claim form, response pack, etc, for claimants to amend as necessary and re-serve.

Claimants may serve claim forms, having told the court in writing that they wish to do so, either personally, by post, by fax, by document exchange (a private courier service operated between law firms) or by email or other electronic means. A claimant who serves the claim form must file a certificate of service within seven days of service with a copy of the document served attached.

11.5.8 Admissions and part admissions (CPR Part 14)

The possibility of admitting liability for a claim for a specific amount and making an offer to pay by instalments, or at a later date, applies to both county court and High Court cases. Where the claim is for a specific amount, the admission will be sent direct to the claimant. However, if a claimant objects to the rate of payment offered, there are changes which affect the determination process, that is, the process by which a member of a court's staff or a judge decides the rate of payment.

Cases involving a specific amount where the balance outstanding, including any costs, is less than £50,000, will be determined by a court officer. Those where the balance is £50,000 or more, or for an unspecified amount of any value, must be determined by a Master or District Judge. The Master or Judge has the option of dealing with the determination on the papers without a hearing or at a hearing.

A defendant in a claim for an unspecified amount of money (damages) will be able to make an offer of a specific sum of money in satisfaction of a claim, which does not have to be supported by a payment into court. A claimant can accept the admission and rate of payment offered as if the claim had originally been for a specific amount. The determination procedure described above will apply where a claimant accepts the amount offered, but not the rate of payment proposed.

If a claimant does not accept the amount offered, a request that judgment be entered for liability on the strength of the defendant's admission may be made to the court. This is referred to as *judgment for an amount and costs to be decided by the court* (replacing *interlocutory judgment for damages to be assessed*). Where judgment is entered in this way, the court will at the same time give case management directions for dealing with the case.

Where a request for such a judgment is received, the court file will be passed to a procedural judge. The judge may allocate the case to the small claims track and give directions if it is of appropriate value, ask that the case be set down for a *disposal* hearing or where the amount is likely to be heavily disputed, order a trial. Directions will be given as appropriate. A disposal hearing in these circumstances may be a hearing either at which the court gives directions, or at which the amount and costs are decided.

11.5.9 Defence and automatic transfer (CPR Part 26)

Claims for specified amounts will be transferred automatically to the defendant's 'home court' where the defendant is an individual who has filed a defence. The defendant's home court will be the court or district registry, including the Royal Courts of Justice, for the district in which the defendant's address for service as shown on the defence is situated. This means that, where the defendant is represented by a solicitor, this will be the defendant's solicitor's business address.

Where there is more than one defendant, it is the first defendant to file a defence who dictates whether or not automatic transfer will take place. For example, if there were two defendants to a claim, one an individual and one a limited company, there would be no automatic transfer if the limited company was the first defendant to file a defence.

11.5.10 Allocation questionnaire (Form N150)

The purpose of this document is to enable the judge to allocate in which track the case should be heard. When a defence is filed, the issuing court will send out a copy of the defence to all other parties to the claim, together with an allocation questionnaire, a notice setting out the date for returning it and the name and address of the court (or district registry or the Royal Courts of Justice (that is, High Court), as appropriate) to which the completed allocation questionnaire must be returned. A notice of transfer will also be sent if the case is being automatically transferred. The allocation questionnaire will not be served on the parties when a defendant files a defence if r 14.5 or r 15.10 applies or if the court decides to dispense with its service.

When all the parties have filed their allocation questionnaire, or at the end of the period for returning it, whichever is the sooner (providing the questionnaires have not been dispensed with or the case stayed under r 26.4) the court will allocate the claim to a track. If there is sufficient information, the judge will allocate the case to a track and a notice of allocation and directions will be sent out to each party. Where the judge has insufficient information, an order may be made for a party to provide further information. In particularly complex cases, for those allocated to the multi-track, the judge may first list the matter for a case management conference to formulate directions.

Where only one party has filed a questionnaire the judge may allocate the claim to a track providing he has enough information or will order that an allocation hearing be listed and that all parties must attend. Where none of the parties has filed a questionnaire, the file will be returned to the judge who will usually decide to impose a sanction by ordering that the claim and any counterclaim be struck out unless a completed questionnaire is filed within three days from service of the order.

The questionnaire asks a number of questions, for example:

- Do you wish there to be a one month stay to attempt to settle this case?

- Which track do you consider most suitable for your case (small claims, fast track or multi-track)? A party wishing a case to be dealt with on a track which is not the obviously suitable track must give reasons.

- At this stage, you are asked whether you have complied with any relevant protocols, and if not, why not and the extent of the non-compliance.

- You are asked for an estimate of costs to date and the overall costs up to trial.

- You are asked if you wish to use expert evidence at the trial, whether expert reports have been copied to the other side, who the expert is and, if the parties have not agreed upon a common expert, why not.

The purpose of this questionnaire is to make both sides have a clear overview of the case at an early stage, so it becomes very difficult for lawyers to bumble along buffeted by developments in a case. To reduce delays and therefore costs, it is desirable that a lawyer should be able to purposefully stride through a case along a planned route.

11.5.11 Default judgment (CPR Part 12)

If a defendant (to a Part 7 claim) files an acknowledgment stating an intention to defend the claim, this extends the period for filing a defence from 14 to 28 days from the date of service of the particulars. Failure to file an acknowledgement with the court or, later, failure to file a defence can result in 'default judgment'. That means the court will, without a trial, find in favour of the claimant, so the defendant will lose the case.

If the defendant does not to reply to the claim, a claimant may apply for default judgment for the amount claimed if the amount claimed is a specified amount, or on liability if the amount claimed is unspecified, after the 14-day period from service has elapsed.

There are a number of cases in which it is not possible to obtain judgment in default, notably in claims for delivery of goods subject to an agreement controlled by the Consumer Credit Act 1974.

11.5.12 Summary judgment (CPR Part 24)

Summary judgment is available to both claimants and defendants. Where either party feels that the other does not have a valid claim or defence, they can apply to the court for the claim or defence to be struck out and for judgment to be entered in their favour. The applicant, either claimant or defendant, must prove to the court's satisfaction that the other party has no real prospect of success and that there is no other compelling reason why the case or issue should be dealt with at trial.

Application for summary judgment cannot be made without the court's permission (replacing the term 'leave') or where a practice direction provides otherwise, before an acknowledgement of service or defence has been filed. Where an application is made by the claimant before a defendant files a defence, the defendant against whom it is made need not file a defence. If a claimant's application is unsuccessful, the court will give directions for the filing of a defence.

11.6 Public and Private Hearings (CPR Part 39)

In the new rules, the distinction between 'public' and 'private' hearings is not whether a claim or application is heard in a court room or the *judge's room* (formerly called *chambers*), but whether members of the public are allowed to sit in on the hearing wherever it takes place.

Courts are not required to make any special arrangements to accommodate members of the public, for example, if the judge's room is too small to accommodate more than those directly concerned with the claim. However, where a hearing is 'public', anyone may obtain a copy of the order made upon payment of the appropriate fee.

11.7 Appeals (CPR Part 52)

The appeal system is covered in Chapter 3 above.

There is generally no automatic right to appeal under the CPR, except as provided for in r 52.3 or statute and parties will need permission to appeal and will be granted only where:

(a) the court considers that the appeal would have a real prospect of success; or

(b) where there is some other compelling reason why the appeal should be heard.

Permission to appeal will usually be made to the lower court at the hearing against which it is to be appealed. Alternatively, an appeal can be made to the appeal court in an appeal notice usually within 14 days after the date of the decision to be appealed unless directed otherwise by the lower court.

The important procedural points and the routes to appeal will vary depending on whether the matter involves a final decision.

Generally, an appeal will lie to the next court above. From a district judge of the county court, appeal lies to a circuit judge. From a master or district judge of the High Court, or a circuit judge, appeal lies to a High Court judge and from a High Court judge, appeal lies to the Court of Appeal. In almost all cases, permission is needed in order to appeal.

Paragraph 2A.2 of the Practice Direction to Part 52 provides:

Where the decision to be appealed is a final decision -

(1) in a Part 7 claim allocated to the multi track; or

(2) made in specialist proceedings (under the Companies Act 1985 or 1989 or to which sections I,II,or III of part 57 or any of Parts 58 to 63 apply)

the appeal is to be made to the Court of Appeal (subject to obtaining any necessary permission)

A final decision 'is a decision of a court that would finally determine (subject to any possible appeal or detailed assessment of costs) the entire proceedings whichever way the court decides the issues before it'. A decision will not be deemed a final decision where an order is made on a summary or detailed assessment of costs or on an application to enforce a final decision. In these circumstances the appeal will follow the general appeal route.

If a decision of a circuit judge in relation to fast track claims, claims on the multi track except for final decisions, and Part 8 claims including final decisions but excluding final decisions in specialist proceedings, appeal lies to the High Court. However, a Part 8 claim that is a final decision and is treated as allocated to the multi track may be sent direct to the Court of Appeal if the court considers it appropriate.

Under CPR 52.14 a lower court may order the appeal to be sent directly to the Court of Appeal, where it considers that the appeal would raise an important point of principle or practice or that there is some other compelling reason for the Court of Appeal to hear it.

Generally an appeal will be limited to a review of the decision of the lower court unless a practice direction provides otherwise or the court considers that in the circumstances of the particular appeal it would be in the interests of justice to order a re-hearing. The appeal court will not hear any oral evidence or new evidence unless it orders otherwise. An appeal will be allowed where the decision in the lower court was wrong, or unjust due to a serious procedural or other irregularity in the lower courts proceedings.

When the court deals with appeals it must have regard to the overriding objective in CPR 1.1. Consequently, the appeal court is only likely to deal with appeals where they are founded on an error of law, against a finding of fact, in respect of the exercise of a discretion, involving new evidence or a change of circumstances or where a serious procedural or other irregularity arise causing injustice.

Appeals from the Court of Appeal lie to the House of Lords, but the appellant must be granted leave either by the Court of Appeal or by the House of Lords. The application for leave must first be made to the Court of Appeal, and then if refused, by petition for leave to appeal which will be heard by the House of Lords sitting in public. Only cases involving points of public importance reach the House of Lords and there are usually fewer than 50 civil appeals heard by the Lords each year. It is possible, under the Administration of Justice Act 1969, for the House of Lords to hear an appeal direct from the High Court, 'leapfrogging' the Court of Appeal. The agreement of both parties and the High Court judge is required. Such cases must concern a point of statutory interpretation (including the construction of a statutory instrument) which has been fully explored by the High Court judge, or concern a point which he was bound by precedent to follow.

11.8 Remedies

The preceding sections of this chapter have examined the institutional and procedural framework within which individuals pursue civil claims. What it has not addressed is the question why people pursue such claims. Taking a claim to court can be expensive, time consuming and very stressful, but people accept these costs, both financial and personal, because they have a grievance that they require to be settled. In other words, they are seeking a remedy for some wrong they have suffered, or at least that they believe they have suffered. In practice, it is the actual remedy available that the litigant focuses on, rather than the finer points of law or procedure involved in attaining that remedy; those are matters for the legal professionals. It is appropriate, therefore, to offer a brief explanation of remedies, although students of the law will engage with the details of remedies in the substantive legal subjects, such as contract and tort. As will be seen, it is essential to distinguish between the common law remedy of damages, available as of right, and equitable remedies, which are awarded at the discretion of the court (see 1.3.2 above).

11.9 Damages

As has been said, the whole point of damages is compensatory: to recompense someone for the wrong they have suffered. There are, however, different ways in which someone can be compensated. For example, in contract law, the object of awarding damages is to put the wronged person in the situation they would have been in had the contract been completed as agreed; that is, it places them in the position they would have been after the event. In tort, however, the object is to compensate the wronged person, to the extent that a monetary award can do so for injury sustained; that is, to return them to the situation they were in before the event.

11.9.1   Types of damages

(a) *Compensatory damages*: these are the standard awards considered above, intended to achieve no more than to recompense the injured party to the extent of the injury suffered. Damages in contract can only be compensatory.

(b) *Aggravated damages*: these are compensatory in nature, but are additional to ordinary compensatory awards and are awarded in relation to damage suffered to the injured party's dignity and pride. They are, therefore, akin to damages being paid in relation to mental distress. In *Khodaparast v Shad* (2000), the claimant was awarded aggravated damages after the defendant had been found liable for the malicious falsehood of distributing fake pictures of her in a state of undress, which resulted in her losing her job.

(c) *Exemplary damages*: these are awarded in tort in addition to compensatory damages. They may be awarded where the person who committed the tort intended to make a profit from their tortious action. The most obvious area in which such awards might be made is in libel cases, where the publisher issues the libel to increase sales. An example of exemplary awards can be seen in the award of £50,000 (originally £275,000) to Elton John as a result of his action against *The Mirror* newspaper (*John v MGN Ltd* (1996)).

(d) *Nominal damages*: these are awarded in the few cases which really do involve 'a matter of principle', but where no loss or injury to reputation is involved. There is no set figure in relation to nominal damages; it is merely a very small amount.

(e) *Contemptuous damages*: these are extremely small awards made where the claimant wins their case, but has suffered no loss and has failed to impress the court with the standard of their own behaviour or character. In *Reynolds v Times Newspaper Ltd* (1999), the former Prime Minister of Ireland was awarded one penny in his libel action against *The Times* newspaper; this award was actually made by the judge after the jury had awarded Reynolds no damages at all. Such an award can be considered nothing if not contemptuous.

11.9.2   Damages in contract

The estimation of what damages are to be paid by a party in breach of contract can be divided into two parts: remoteness and measure.

11.9.2.1   *Remoteness of damage*

What kind of damage can the innocent party claim? This involves a consideration of causation, and the remoteness of cause from effect, in order to determine how far down a chain of events a defendant is liable. The rule in *Hadley v Baxendale* (1845) states that damages will only be awarded in respect of losses that arise naturally, that is, in the natural course of things, or in which both parties may reasonably be supposed to have contemplated, when the contract was made, as a probable result of its breach.

The effect of the first part of the rule in *Hadley v Baxendale* is that the party in breach is deemed to expect the normal consequences of the breach, whether they actually expected them or not.

Under the second part of the rule, however, the party in breach can only be held liable for abnormal consequences where they have actual knowledge that the abnormal consequences might follow. In *Victoria Laundry Ltd v Newham Industries Ltd* (1949), the defendants contracted to deliver a new boiler to the plaintiffs, but delayed in delivery. The plaintiffs claimed for normal loss of profit during the period of delay, and also for the loss of abnormal profits from a highly lucrative contract which they could have undertaken had the boiler been delivered on time. In this case, it was decided that damages could be recovered in regard to the normal profits, as that loss was a natural consequence of the delay. The second claim failed, however, on the grounds that the loss was not a normal one, but was a consequence of an especially lucrative contract, about which the defendant knew nothing.

As a result of the test for remoteness, a party may be liable for consequences which, although within the reasonable contemplation of the parties, are much more serious in effect than would be expected.

In *H Parsons (Livestock) Ltd v Uttley Ingham and Co* (1978), the plaintiffs, who were pig farmers, bought a large food hopper from the defendants. While erecting it, the plaintiffs failed to unseal a ventilator on the top of the hopper. Because of lack of ventilation, the pig food stored in the hopper became mouldy. The pigs that ate the mouldy food contracted a rare intestinal disease and died. It was held that the defendants were liable for the loss of the pigs. The food affected by bad storage caused the illness as a natural consequence of the breach, and the death from such illness was not too remote.

11.9.2.2   Measure of damages

Damages in contract are intended to compensate an injured party for any financial loss sustained as a consequence of another party's breach. The object is not to punish the party in breach, so the amount of damages awarded can never be greater than the actual loss suffered. The aim is to put the injured party in the same position they would have been in had the contract been properly performed. Where the breach relates to a contract for the sale of goods, damages are usually assessed in line with the market rule. This means that, if goods are not delivered under a contract, the buyer is entitled to go into the market and buy similar goods, and pay the market price prevailing at the time. They can then claim the difference in price between what they paid and the original contract price as damages. Conversely, if a buyer refuses to accept goods under a contract, the seller can sell the goods in the market and accept the prevailing market price. Any difference between the price they receive and the contract price can be claimed in damages.

11.9.2.3 *Non-pecuniary loss*

At one time, damages could not be recovered where the loss sustained through breach of contract was of a non-financial nature. The modern position is that such non-pecuniary damages can be recovered. In *Jarvis v Swan Tours Ltd* (1973), the defendant's brochure stated that various facilities were available at a particular ski resort. The facilities available were in fact much inferior to those advertised. The plaintiff sued for breach of contract. The court decided that Jarvis was entitled to recover not just the financial loss he suffered, which was not substantial, but also for loss of entertainment and enjoyment. The Court of Appeal stated that damages could be recovered for mental distress in appropriate cases, and this was one of them.

11.9.3   **Damages in tort**

11.9.3.1 *Remoteness of damage*

Even where causation is established, the defendant will not necessarily be liable for all of the damage resulting from the breach. The question to be asked in determining the extent of liability is whether the damage is of such a kind as the reasonable person should have foreseen, but this does not mean that the defendant should have foreseen precisely the sequence or nature of the events. The test for remoteness of damage in tort was set out in *The Wagon Mound (No 1)* (1961). The defendants negligently allowed furnace oil to spill from a ship into Sydney harbour. The oil spread and came to lie beneath a wharf owned by the plaintiffs. The plaintiffs had been carrying out welding operations and, on seeing the oil, they stopped welding in order to find out whether it was safe to continue. They were assured that the oil would not catch fire and resumed welding. However, cotton waste that had fallen into the oil caught fire, which in turn ignited the oil, and the resultant fire spread to the plaintiff's wharf. It was held that the defendants were liable in tort, as they had breached their duty of care. However, they were only held liable for the damage caused to the wharf and slipway through the fouling of the oil. They were not liable for the damage caused by fire because that damage was unforeseeable due to the high ignition point of the oil.

11.9.3.2 *Economic loss*

There are two categories of economic loss that may form the basis of a claim in negligence. First, there is economic loss arising out of physical injury or damage to property and, second, there is what is known as 'pure economic loss', which is unconnected with physical damage. Following recent developments, only the former is recoverable unless the claimant can show that there was 'a special relationship' between them and the defendant (*Williams v Natural Life Health Foods Ltd* (1998)).

11.10　Equitable Remedies

Equitable remedies are not available as of right and are only awarded at the discretion of the court. They will not be granted where the claimant has not acted properly. There are a number of maxims that relate to the awarding of equitable remedies. Thus, for example, it is frequently stated that '*He who comes to equity must come with clean hands*', which simply means that persons looking for the remedy must have behaved properly themselves (*D & C Builders v Rees* (1966)). The actual remedies are as follows.

11.10.1　Specific performance

It will sometimes suit a party to break their contractual obligations and pay damages; however, through an order for specific performance, the party in breach may be instructed to complete their part of the contract. An order of specific performance will only be granted in cases where the common law remedy of damages is inadequate, and providing the matter does not fall into a category where the courts will not order specific performance. It is not usually applied to contracts concerning the sale of goods where replacements are readily available. It is most commonly granted in cases involving the sale of land, where the subject matter of the contract is unique.

Generally, specific performance will not be available in respect of contracts of employment or personal service. However, in light of *C H Giles & Co Ltd v Morris and others* [1972], it would appear that the courts may be prepared to depart from this principle in certain circumstances.

Specific performance will not be granted if the court has to constantly supervise its enforcement. In *Ryan v Mutual Tontine Westminster Chambers Association* (1893), the landlords of a flat undertook to provide a porter, who was to be constantly in attendance to provide services such as cleaning the common passages and stairs, and delivering letters. The person appointed spent much of his time working as a chef at a nearby club. During his absence, his duties were performed by a cleaner or by various boys. The plaintiff sought to enforce the contractual undertaking. It was held that, although the landlords were in breach of their contract, the court would not award an order of specific performance. The reason given was that to enforce the contract would require constant supervision by the court. In addition, it was held that damages were an adequate remedy and hence the only available course of action. By comparison, in *Posner and others v Scott-Lewis and others* [1986] an order for specific performance was granted. In this case, the landlord had covenanted (so far as it was in his power) with the tenants, to employ a resident porter to carry out certain specified tasks. The court held that the covenant was specifically enforceable as they could order the landlord to employ a resident porter within a specified time as this would not require constant supervision by the court. If the landlord failed to adhere to the order the tenants could go back to the court and take appropriate action.

11.10.2 Injunction

This is the term used in relation to the courts' powers to order someone to either do something or, alternatively, to refrain from doing something. Injunctions are governed by s 37 of the Supreme Court Act 1981 and they may be granted on an interim or a permanent basis. Breach of an injunction is a contempt of court. Examples of specific injunctions are 'freezing orders', formerly known as Mareva injunctions, which are interim orders which prevent defendants from moving their assets out of the jurisdiction of the English courts before their case can be heard. Another well-known order is the search order, formerly known as an Anton Piller order, which prevents the concealment or disposal of documents which might be required in evidence at a later time. It can also authorise the searching of premises for such evidence.

In contract, an injunction directs a person not to break their contract. It can have the effect of indirectly enforcing contracts for personal service. In *Warner Bros v Nelson* (1937), the defendant, the actress Bette Davis, had entered a contract that stipulated that she was to work exclusively for the plaintiffs for a period of one year. When she came to England, the plaintiffs applied for an injunction to prevent her from working for someone else. The court granted the order to Warner Bros. In doing so, the court rejected Nelson's argument that granting it would force her either to work for the plaintiffs or not to work at all. An injunction will only be granted to enforce negative covenants within the agreement, and cannot be used to enforce positive obligations (*Whitwood Chemical Co v Hardman* (1891)).

11.10.3 Rectification

This award allows for the alteration of contractual documents. It is generally assumed that written contractual documents accurately express the parties' terms, especially where the document has been signed. There are occasions, however, when the court will allow the written statement to be altered where it does not represent the true agreement (*Joscelyne v Nissen* (1970)).

11.10.4 Rescission

This action sets aside the terms of a contractual agreement and returns the parties to the situation they were in before the contract was entered into. The right to rescind a contact may be available as a result of fraud, misrepresentation of any type or the exercise of undue influence. The right can be lost, however, for a number of reasons, such as it being impossible to return the parties to their original position, affirmation, delay or the intervention of third party rights.

11.11 Court Fees

The fee structure is designed so that fees become payable as various stages of a claim are reached (a 'pay as you go' regime).

Courts are proactive in collecting fees, in particular those which are payable at allocation and listing stages, but *without interrupting* a case's progress. There are sanctions for non-payment of allocation and listing questionnaire fees, which could lead to a party's statement of case being struck out.

11.12   Costs (CPR Parts 44–48)

11.12.1   Fixed costs (CPR Part 45)

There are rates for the fixed costs allowed on issue of a claim and on entry of judgment where a party is represented by a solicitor.

11.12.2   Assessment (CPR Part 47)

The terms *taxed* costs and *taxation* are now redundant and have been replaced by assessment. Costs will either be assessed summarily, that is, there and then, or there will be a *detailed assessment* at some later stage where one party has been ordered to pay another's costs.

11.12.3   Summary assessment

Judges will normally summarily assess costs at the end of hearings, both interim and final, and particularly at the end of fast track trials. Parties will be expected to bring any necessary documentation to the hearing for this purpose. In this way, the need for detailed assessment of costs is avoided so far as possible.

11.13   What Has the New System Achieved?

The new CPR, the most fundamental changes in civil process for over 100 years, have radically altered the operation of civil justice. Since the new rules came into force (26 April 1999), they have been regularly reformed. The 39th update came into force on 4 April 2005.

Part of the rationale of the new rules was to expedite the way cases were dealt with and to allow more cases to be settled early through negotiation between the parties or ADR. In this respect, there is some evidence of success. During the May–August period in 1999, there was a 25% reduction in the number of cases issued in the county courts compared with the same period the previous year. By the end of January 2000, there was a further fall to 23%. There is also evidence (speech by David Lock MP, Parliamentary Secretary to the LCD, 15 October 1999) that changes to pre-action behaviour as a result of the pre-action protocols have been partly responsible for the reduction in the number of cases going all the way through to trial.

An interesting assessment of the new rules was presented by Mr Justice Burton of the QBD. Speaking at the City law firm, Kennedys, he outlined five benefits of the reforms, five problems, and what he referred to as 'one big question mark' ((2000) Law Soc Gazette, 10 February).

The five problems with the reforms were: the courts' inflexibility in not allowing parties to agree upon extensions of time between themselves; the danger of the judiciary pushing time guillotines onto parties; the risk that lawyers and clients could exploit 'standard' disclosure to conceal important documents; single joint experts possibly usurping the role of judges and summary assessments of costs leading to judges making assumptions replacing detailed costs analysis. The benefits were listed as: pre-action protocols; emphasis on encouraging settlement; judicial intervention; Part 24 strike-out provisions and Part 36 offers to settle.

Mr Justice Burton said there had been three options for reforming appeals: (1) to extend the present system in order to discourage more than one appeal; (2) to refuse appeals without leave or (3) to abolish the present system, giving no right to rehearings, only appeals. He said he regretted that all three had been adopted (in the Access to Justice Act 1999). The consequence will be pressure on judges 'to get it right first time' and higher costs for parties.

Richard Burns, a barrister and recorder sitting in the county court, and thus someone who has experienced the new rules from both sides of the bench, has made some interesting observations about the new system ('A view from the ranks' (2000) 150 NLJ, pp 1829–30). On the positive side, Burns says that 'the transition has been far smoother than many had anticipated and there have been a number of very worthwhile gains'. He notes, however, that set against the ambitious aims Lord Woolf had for the reforms, they were a 'relative failure'. Among the gains, the judge lists: the unified system of procedure in all civil courts; awareness that the costs of litigation should bear a 'passing resemblance to the value of the claim'; vastly improved pre-action co-operation; more sensible and open pleadings which force the parties to define the issues at an early stage; the wider use of jointly instructed (and therefore impartial) experts and, in CPR Part 36, rules cunningly devised to encourage the parties to settle.

One way in which the system is not working properly, according to Richard Burns, is in relation to costs. He argues that the system is in fact proving more expensive than the old system for many litigants, as the timetable imposed usually compels the parties 'to spend time and money progressing claims to trial whether or not they expect to settle. Paradoxically the procedures, encouraging as they do the front end loading of expenditure on cases, may lead to more trials – certainly this appears to have been happening in some of the court centres where I appear'.

Another difficulty concerns the system of case management, which Lord Woolf envisaged would be the engine to drive forward the litigation cheaply and expeditiously. Burns regards this as a system which is 'excessively bureaucratic and makes too many demands on the parties'. It is also, he argues, very poorly resourced, as the Court Service received very little extra money to finance the sort of increases in judicial staffing and information technology Woolf had seen as essential.

Concealed delays are also blighting the system, according to Judge Burns. While recognising that, on the whole, cases come to trial more quickly than they did, he notes that:

> ... the overall delay experienced by litigants is much the same as it ever was. This is because solicitors, feeling daunted by the demands made on them by the CPR and lacking the time and resources to manage more than a certain quota of cases through the system, are delaying the issue of proceedings. The delay frequently runs into years.

Eversheds, the corporate law claims firm, has conducted an 'access to justice' survey for five years. It canvasses the opinions and experiences of lawyers and those using the legal system. Results published in 2000, after one year of the Woolf reforms, showed that of its respondents, 54% said that the civil litigation process had improved in the past year, a big increase on 1998s 15%. Some 52% of respondents believed that litigation was quicker, but only 22% thought costs were lower.

John Heaps, head of litigation at Eversheds, has stated ((2000) *The Times*, 2 May) that: 'The UK legal system historically has been plagued by unsatisfactory delays and expense. The style of dispute resolution is changing as a result of the Woolf reforms; people no longer seek aggressive uncompromising lawyers, but those who look for commercial solutions.'

The survey sought the views of heads of legal departments of UK companies and public sector bodies: 70% of respondents were in the private sector, with 30% in London. The replies suggested that a change in culture is emerging. Nearly two-thirds of respondents did not think the reforms would make them less likely to start proceedings, but 43% said they were settling cases earlier and almost half said their lawyers were handling disputes differently. Mediation, or ADR, is also becoming more popular: 41% had used it, compared with 30% in 1998.

There is, however, concern that while judges are managing cases more effectively, the courts do not have adequate resources (this was expressed by 50% of respondents). Only 24% believed that litigants were now getting better justice; 44% said they were not.

On the matter of costs, opinions were sharply divided. Nearly half did not believe costs to have been affected by the introduction of the new rules. Disturbingly, however, 19% said costs had risen, particularly in the regions. But a conference on the Woolf reforms held by the Centre for Effective Dispute Resolution (CEDR) found that although costs had increased at the start of litigation (front loading), overall they were down, as settlements came sooner.

Conditional, or 'no win, no fee', work is attractive in principle but little used: 48% of respondents said they would pay lawyers a higher fee for winning if they could pay a lower fee, or none, if the case was lost. However, only 24% had discussed such a deal.

Litigation may be quicker and less likely to go to court, but 52% of respondents expected to have the same number of business disputes in the following year, with as many being resolved through litigation. One in five was more optimistic and thought fewer disputes would be resolved in court.

John Heaps argues that, overall, the findings are positive. He has said: 'Over half the respondents feel the speed of resolving disputes has improved. But there are concerns that the aims and aspirations are not matched by court resources.'

A survey carried out by the City Research Group of the firm Wragge & Co obtained similar findings ((2000) *The Times*, 2 May). It suggests that among in-house lawyers from FTSE 100 companies, a lack of resources has become 'a major stumbling block'. Some 81% of respondents thought courts did not have the resources to process claims quickly enough, and some complained of 'inconsistent interpretation' between courts. But 89% of respondents backed the changes and said litigation was quicker with fewer 'frivolous claims'. Some 41% thought costs had been cut, and there was strong backing for ADR, with 80% saying it had proved popular. Nine out of 10 lawyers thought clients were more involved in the management of the dispute, but 38% believed that the reforms had compromised justice at the expense of cost cutting. As with the CEDR survey, the change singled out for the biggest impact is that which allows either party to make a formal settlement offer at any stage – or potentially face cost penalties.

A senior litigation partner at Wragge & Co, Andrew Manning Cox, observed that the survey mirrored the firm's experiences. Among surprise findings was the low awareness of the Woolf reforms among businesses. Their lawyers were apparently not using the new rules to the best tactical advantage of their companies.

Another City law firm, Lovells, found 71% of respondents now treating litigation as a last resort, with 72% willing voluntarily to exchange documents with the other side. Where litigation was unavoidable it was quicker, with 66% saying that judges now set tighter timetables. Two-thirds found the court 'rubber stamped' joint requests by the parties to move back dates in the timetable, but this flexibility did not extend to trial dates.

One of the findings that will be very disappointing for many involved with the project of the Woolf reforms is the apparently low use of a jointly appointed expert. According to the survey, only 7% of respondents were involved in cases with such an expert.

The survey also highlights a low level of case management. Only 9% found that the court monitored case progress and chased lawyers to meet deadlines; 42% found that the court had sought to narrow the issues as early as it could. The Commercial Court, Lovells found, was managing cases better than other High Court divisions. Courts did not penalise parties who failed to comply with the new rules. This certainly ties in with the experience of the barrister and county court judge, Richard Burns. He has noted that the burden of work on many civil judges is so heavy that they cannot properly manage each case:

> Their burden in the busier courts is so huge that all they can do is skim the surface of files that cross their desks. It is rare, in my experience, for the same judge to be able to deal with all the interlocutory stages of even the bigger cases and so there is little or no continuity [(2000) 150 NLJ, 8 December, p 1830].

Asked for the worst aspect of the reforms, respondents chose the rule on summary assessment of costs in preliminary hearings, criticised as a lottery. In fact, the main deficiency in the new system seems to be one of variable application according to the style or interpretation of them favoured in any given court or region. This, though, may well become more uniform over time and if that occurs, then the new rules really can claim to have radically and successfully altered the civil process in England and Wales.

11.14 The Division of Work between the High Court and County Courts after the Woolf Reforms

In *A Programme for the Future*, the LCD's strategic plan for 1993/94–1995/96, a number of aims were set out in relation to the civil process. One of the plan's objectives was stated to be the need 'To match fora [that is, each type of court being a different forum] and resources to different types and levels of cases'. The problem of allocating the right sort and volume of cases to the appropriate courts is a long-running challenge. It is a matter of debate how far the problems highlighted by the CJR and tackled by the CLSA 1990 have been significantly reduced.

The differences in procedure between the High Court and the county court were considerable and applied from the inception of litigation until the enforcement of court judgments. The arguments for a single court were rehearsed over many years, beginning not long after the establishment of the county courts (1846) when the Judicature Commission considered the proposal in 1869. The Law Society supported the idea in 1980, arguing that: 'A one court system would lead to the expedition, standardisation and simplification of proceedings and to a saving in judicial time.'

A merger of the High Court and county court was considered by the Beeching Royal Commission in 1969, but was rejected. Instead, it recommended a more flexible use of the judiciary. Some judges are more experienced and expert than others. Clearly, it makes sense for the judges with greater expertise to preside in the more important cases, but how is 'importance' to be judged? The sum involved may not be very large, but the legal point in issue may be of enormous significance. Conversely, a case where the sum claimed is very great may not raise any particularly difficult or consequential point of law. Beeching recommended that the allocation of cases to the different tiers of judges should be determined to some extent by judges, rather than by simply looking at the sum claimed. Now, because there is just one set of rules (the CPR) governing both the High Court and the county courts, the courts in one sense have been unified. We now have a single procedural system.

11.15 Do We Need Two Sorts of Court after Woolf?

The introduction of the Woolf reforms in 1999 added new impetus to the case for having only one type of civil court. With a unified set of forms and procedures applicable to both the High Court and the county courts, the question is raised as to why we need to have two sorts of venue. In an article entitled 'Why have two types of civil court?' ((1999) 149 NLJ 65), Richard Harrison has argued for unification.

Lord Woolf came close to recommending that the two sorts of court be merged, but stopped short of that because such a suggested merger would have involved him in dealing with matters beyond his remit. There are three main issues:

- the need to preserve the special status of High Court judges;

- the existence of inherently specialist jurisdictions in each court;

- the problem with rights of audience.

Harrison presents cogent arguments against all three points being raised as obstacles to change. He argues:

- under the new system, cases could be allocated simply to judges 'at the right level', without levels being characterised by special conditions of service and the trappings of prestige. Now, a High Court judge is given a knighthood or a Damehood and his/her tenure is under letters patent, with removal from office being only theoretically possible under address by both Houses of Parliament. Her Majesty's judges are the fount of the common law, as opposed to being creatures of statute like circuit judges and District Judges. Harrison states that: 'I do not think it is possible to argue sensibly that there should be a distinction between levels of the judiciary with increased prestige, respect and remuneration being afforded to an elite band';

- resistance to change relies on the view that High Court Judges should not have to deal with small claims and that county court judges should not be able to judge in cases like those involving judicial review. Harrison says that specialist judges (from the High Court) could carry on, as at present, dealing with highly complex or sensitive cases without having a separate rank;

- in future, rights of audience will depend upon fitness and qualification, not on whether one is a solicitor or barrister or practising in the High Court or county court. In these circumstances, it does not appear, argues Harrison, that this will present any problem for a unified court.

Harrison recognises that unification of the civil court structure may be some time away. He therefore proposes an interim practical solution – ignoring the distinction in procedural terms. Cases could be headed 'Before the Civil Courts ...' without worrying the claimant about through which type of court his case is going. Case management decisions on allocation could then be made in accordance with the spirit of the Woolf reforms.

11.16   Enforcement of Civil Remedies

It is one thing to be awarded a remedy by the court against another party, but it is another thing to actually enforce that remedy. Consequently, an effective enforcement system is essential to providing access to justice. Statistics in the 2001 Green Paper,

Towards Effective Enforcement, reveal that as regards warrants of execution, which account for about 85% of all enforcement effort, only 35% of all warrants issued are paid It was also estimated that the value of unpaid post-judgment debt is more than £600 million per year. With specific regard to small claims, once again 35% of successful claimants had received no part of the sum awarded to them, several months after judgment.

In March 2003, the LCD issued the White Paper, *Effective Enforcement*, in which it claimed to set out a strategy for reforming the current system by:

- improving methods of recovering civil debt; and

- establishing a more rigorous system of controls for enforcement agents, previously known as bailiffs.

In announcing the White Paper, Baroness Scotland, Civil Justice Minister, said:

> Society wants those who owe money judgments to pay their dues but also wants to protect the vulnerable. It's about getting the balance right in a system that is firm but fair in enforcing decisions of the court. So the system we propose will utilise the full weight of the law on those who won't pay while at the same time safeguarding vulnerable individuals who simply can't pay.

The response of a significant number of individuals and organisations which specialise in the provision of debt advice has, however, been less than enthusiastic about the approach set out in the White Paper, seeing it as being far from balanced and as favouring the interest of debt recovery at the expense of those who genuinely cannot pay.

To enforce court decisions, the White Paper proposes:

- giving the courts the power to issue data disclosure orders which will require parties to disclose information about their financial circumstances;

- making attachment of earnings faster, more effective and, it is suggested, fairer;

- streamlining the system for charging orders which allow creditors to gain security against the debtor's house.

To safeguard those who are genuinely unable to repay their debt, the White Paper proposes:

- an adequate regulatory system, unified law and fairer fee structure for all enforcement agents. The Security Industry Authority (SIA) will license all enforcement agents and would aim to ensure that their work is carried out appropriately, effectively and fairly in relation to both debtors and creditors;

- a complete overhaul of distress for rent (taking legal control of goods as security for payment of, or in satisfaction of, rent arrears) laws. In the future, it is proposed that these rules will not be used for residential properties, but solely as a commercial rent arrears recovery system.

When the White Paper was issued, some commentators appeared to be more interested in the fact that the ancient title of 'bailiff' was to be replaced by the modern usage 'enforcement agent'. It would have been better had the commentators actually focused more carefully on the details of the proposals it contained. Currently, 'bailiffs' are not entitled to use force to enter debtors' homes in order to effect warrants. They can seize goods outside the home, but they can only gain access to goods inside after being invited to enter. Under the White Paper proposals, 'enforcement agents', subject to the requirement to obtain a warrant from a judge, will be able to use force to gain entry into domestic premises. It is unlikely that those who suffer the forced invasion of their homes will be particularly concerned as to the lineage of the title borne by the invaders. The proposals, which extend the rights of forced entry in all cases, are set out in paras 165–67 as follows:

> 165   We seek to establish the principle that refusing to open a door or unlock a gate will not stop legitimate enforcement action, nor should superior technology to protect the entrance to a property prevent enforcement from taking place. For example, currently there is little scope for entering private homes that are protected by video cameras and electronic gates. *Forcible entry in domestic premises will be permitted – but only with prior judicial authority.*

> 166   Forcible entry in commercial premises is currently allowed for those enforcement agents who undertake civil enforcement on behalf of the High Court and County Court. It will continue to be permitted for those who presently have this power. *Forcible entry to commercial premises will also be permitted for other enforcement agents with prior judicial authority.* Having failed to gain normal entry, enforcement agents, save for those who are currently officers of the court, may apply to the court for permission to undertake forcible entry in commercial premises with or without notice.

> 167   Normal entry to third party premises will be appropriate. However, the agent should be certain that the goods are on the premises before attempting to gain entry. *Forcible entry to third party premises will require prior judicial authority in all cases* [emphasis added in all cases].

Of equal concern is the White Paper's approval of the continuation of the pernicious charging order mechanism as a means of securing debts. This permits creditors to apply to the courts, where debtors are in default, to have existing unsecured debts charged against the interest debtors might have in their houses. Consequently, the debtors risk losing their houses if they subsequently fail to pay off their debts. Thus, the debt is effectively transformed into a second mortgage, but of course the interest rate on the debt remains at the level of the original unsecured debt and at a much higher level than would be charged by a genuine mortgage lender.

When the review of civil enforcement procedures was first announced, it was felt by many that it would lead to the reduction in the powers of bailiffs, if only to bring them into compliance with the debtors' rights under the European Convention on Human Rights (ECHR). It would appear, however, that the government has decided that not only are existing bailiffs' powers ECHR compliant, but that they can safely be extended, subject to the safeguard of improved regulation of the area. Many debt advisers and civil liberties lawyers would disagree and if the White Paper ever becomes an Act of Parliament, it will undoubtedly face challenge in the courts on that issue.

THE CIVIL PROCESS

The Need for Reform

The Woolf Inquiry into the civil justice system was set up by the government in 1994 to examine why civil litigation was generally very costly, protracted, complicated and subject to long delays.

The Inquiry published its final report in 1996 and its proposals resulted in the Civil Procedure Act 1997 and the Civil Procedure Rules 1998. The new Civil Procedure Rules (CPR) are the same for the county court and the High Court. They apply to all cases except those listed in CPR 2.1 which include insolvency proceedings, family proceedings, adoption proceedings and non-contentious probate proceedings.

The New Civil Process

The changes are effected through the Civil Procedure Act 1997 and the CPR 1998. These have been supplemented by new practice directions and pre-action protocols.

The overriding objective (CPR Part 1)

The overriding objective of the new CPR is to enable the court to deal justly with cases. The first rule reads:

> 1.1(1) These rules are a new procedural code with the overriding objective of enabling the court to deal with cases justly.

Practice directions

Practice directions (official statements of interpretative guidance) play an important role in the new civil process. In general, they supplement the CPR, giving the latter fine detail. They tell parties and their representatives what the court will expect of them in respect of documents to be filed in court for a particular purpose, and how they must co-operate with the other parties to their action. They also tell the parties what they can expect of the court.

The pre-action protocols

The pre-action protocols (PAPs) are an important feature of the reforms. They exist for cases of clinical disputes, personal injury, disease and illness, construction and engineering disputes, defamation, professional negligence, housing disrepair and judicial review. They are likely to be followed, over time, with similar protocols for cases involving other specialisms like debt.

Case Control (CPR Part 3)

Judges will receive support from court staff in carrying out their case management role. The court will monitor case progress by using a computerised diary monitoring system.

Active case management includes:

(a) encouraging the parties to co-operate with each other in the conduct of the proceedings;

(b) identifying the issues at an early stage;

(c) deciding promptly which issues need full investigation and trial and, accordingly, disposing summarily of the others;

(d) deciding the order in which issues are to be resolved.

Case Management Conferences

Case management conferences may be regarded as an opportunity to 'take stock'. There is no limit to the number of case management conferences which may be held during the life of a case, although the cost of attendance at such hearings measured against the benefits obtained will always be a consideration in making the decision.

Pre-trial reviews

Pre-trial reviews will normally take place after the filing of listing questionnaires and before the start of the trial. Their main purpose is to decide a timetable for the trial itself (including the evidence to be allowed and whether this should be given orally), instructions about the content of any trial bundles (bundles of documents including evidence such as written statements, for the judge to read) and confirming a realistic time estimate for the trial itself.

Rules require that where a party is represented, a representative 'familiar with the case and with sufficient authority to deal with any issues likely to arise must attend every case management conference or pre-trial review'.

Stays for settlement (CPR Part 26) and settlements (Part 36)

Under the new CPR, there is a greater incentive for parties to settle their differences.

The court will take into account any pre-action offers to settle when making an order for costs. Thus, a side which has refused a reasonable offer to settle will be treated less generously in the issue of how far the court will order their costs to be paid by the other side. For this to happen, the offer, though, must be one which is made open to the other side for at least 21 days after the date it was made (to stop any undue pressure being put on someone with the phrase: 'take it or leave it; it is only open for one day, then I shall withdraw the offer'). Also, if the offer is made by the potential defendant if proceedings were commenced, it must be an offer to pay the claimant's costs.

Witness statements (CPR Part 32)

Under the new rules, witness statements must contain the evidence that the witness will give at trial, but they should be briefer than those drafted under the previous rules; they should be drafted in lay language and should not discuss legal propositions. Witnesses will be allowed to amplify on the statement or deal with matters that have arisen since the report was served, although this is not an automatic right and a 'good reason' for the admission of new evidence will have to be established.

Experts (CPR Part 35)

New rules place a clear duty on the court to ensure that 'expert evidence is restricted to that which is reasonably required to resolve the proceedings'. That is to say, expert evidence will only be allowed either by way of written report or orally, where the court gives permission. Equally important is the rules' statement about experts' duties. They state that it is the clear duty of experts to help the court on matters within their expertise, bearing in mind that this duty overrides any obligation to the person from whom they have received instructions or by whom they are paid.

Court and Track Allocation (CPR Part 26)

Part 7 of the CPR sets out the rules for starting proceedings. A new restriction is placed on which cases may be begun in the High Court. The county courts retain an almost unlimited jurisdiction for handling contract and tort claims (that is, negligence cases, nuisance cases but excluding a claim for damages or other remedy for libel or slander unless the parties agree otherwise). Issuing proceedings in the High Court is now limited to:

- personal injury claims with a value of £50,000 or more;

- other claims with a value of more than £15,000;

- claims where an Act of Parliament requires an action to start in the High Court; or

- specialist High Court claims which need to go to one of the specialist 'lists', like the Commercial List, the Technology and Construction List.

The new civil system works on the basis of the court, upon receipt of the claim (accompanied by duly filled in forms giving all the relevant details of the claim, including how much it is for and an indication of its factual and legal complexity), allocating the case to one of three tracks for a hearing. These are:

- small claims;

- fast track;

- multi-track.

The new small claims limit is £5,000, although personal injury and housing disrepair claims for over £1,000, illegal eviction and harassment claims will be excluded from the small claims court. The limit for cases going into the fast track system is £15,000, and only claims for over £15,000 can be issued in the High Court. Applications to move cases 'up' a track on grounds of complexity will have to be made on the new allocation questionnaire.

Documentation and Procedures

How to start proceedings – the claim form (CPR Part 7)

Under the new system, most claims will be begun by using a 'Part 7' claim form – a form which has been designed for multi-purpose use. It can be used if the claim is for a *specified* amount of money (the old term was *liquidated* damages) or an *unspecified* amount (replacing the term *unliquidated* damages) and for non-monetary claims.

Under the new rules, the court can grant any remedy to which the claimant is entitled, even if the claimant does not specify which one he wants.

Alternative procedure for claims (CPR Part 8)

Part 8 of the new rules introduces the alternative procedure for claims. This procedure is commenced by the issue of a Part 8 claim form. It is intended to provide a speedy resolution of claims which are not likely to involve a substantial dispute of fact, for example, applications for approval of infant settlements, or for orders enforcing a statutory right such as a right to have access to medical records (under the Access to Health Records Act 1990). The Part 8 procedure is also used where a rule or practice direction requires or permits its use.

Statement of case – particulars of claim (CPR Part 16)

Particulars of claim may be included in the claim form, attached to it, or may be served (that is, given or sent to a party by a method allowed by the rules) separately from it. Where they are served separately, they must be served within 14 days of the claim form being served. The time for a defendant to respond begins to run from the time the particulars of claim are served.

Part 16 of the CPR is entitled 'statements of case' (replacing the word 'pleadings'). Statements of case include documents from both sides: claim forms, particulars of claims, defences, counterclaims, replies to defences and counterclaims, Part 20 (third party) claims and any further information provided under Part 18 of the CPR (replacing the term 'further and better particulars'). Part 16 of the rules also sets out what both particulars of claim and defences should contain.

Statements of truth (CPR Part 22)

A statement of truth is a statement that a party believes that the facts or allegations set out in a document, which they put forward, are true. It is required in statements of case, witness statements and expert reports. Any document which contains a statement of truth may be used in evidence. This will avoid the previous need to swear affidavits in support of various statements made as part of the claim.

Defence and Automatic Transfer (CPR Part 26)

Claims for specified amounts will be transferred automatically to the defendant's 'home court' where the defendant is an individual who has filed a defence. The defendant's home court will be the court or district registry, including the Royal Courts of Justice, for the district in which the defendant's address for service as shown on the defence is situated. This means that where the defendant is represented by a solicitor, this will be the defendant's solicitor's business address.

Where there is more than one defendant, it is the first defendant to file a defence who dictates whether or not automatic transfer will take place. For example, if there were two defendants to a claim, one an individual and one a limited company, there would be no automatic transfer if the limited company was the first defendant to file a defence.

Allocation Questionnaire (Form N150)

The purpose of this document is to enable the judge to allocate in which track the case should be heard. When a defence is filed, the issuing court will send out a copy of the defence to all other parties to the claim together with an allocation questionnaire, a notice setting out the date for returning it and the name and address of the court (or district registry or the Royal Courts of Justice – that is, High Court – as appropriate) to which the completed allocation questionnaire must be returned. A notice of transfer will also be sent if the case is being automatically transferred. The allocation questionnaire will not be served on the parties when a defendant files a defence if r 14.5 or r 15.10 applies or if the court decides to dispense with its service.

When all the parties have filed their allocation questionnaire, or at the end of the period for returning it, whichever is the sooner (providing the questionnaires have not been dispensed with or the case stayed under r 26.4) the court will allocate the claim to a track. If there is sufficient information, the judge will allocate the case to a track and a notice of allocation and directions will be sent out to each party. Where the judge has insufficient information, an order may be made for a party to provide further information.

Where only one party has filed a questionnaire the judge may allocate the claim to a track providing he has enough information or will order that an allocation hearing be listed and that all parties must attend. Where none of the parties has filed a questionnaire, the file will be returned to the judge who will usually decide to impose a sanction by ordering that the claim and any counterclaim be struck out unless a completed questionnaire is filed within three days from service of the order.

Default judgment (CPR Part 12)

If a defendant (to a Part 7 claim) files an acknowledgment stating an intention to defend the claim, this extends the period for filing a defence from 14 to 28 days from the date of service of the particulars. Failure to file an acknowledgment or, later, failure to file a defence can result in default judgment, that is, the court will find for the claimant, so the defendant will lose the case.

Remedies

It is essential to distinguish between the common law remedy of damages, available as of right, and equitable remedies, which are awarded at the discretion of the court.

Damages

Damages are compensatory, to recompense someone for the wrong they have suffered. There are, however, different ways in which someone can be compensated.

In contract law, the object of awarding damages is to put the wronged person in the situation they would have been in had the contract been completed as agreed: that is, it places them in the position they would have been in after the event. In tort, however, the object is to compensate the wronged person, to the extent that a monetary award can do so, for injury sustained: that is, to return them to the situation they were in before the event.

Types of damages

(i) Compensatory damages.

(ii) Aggravated damages.

(iii) Exemplary damages.

(iv) Nominal damages.

(v) Contemptuous damages.

Equitable Remedies

Specific performance

This remedy will only be granted in cases where the common law remedy of damages is inadequate. It is not usually applied to contracts concerning the sale of goods where replacements are readily available. It is most commonly granted in cases involving the sale of land, where the subject matter of the contract is unique.

Injunction

This is the term used in relation to the courts' powers to order someone either to do something or alternatively to refrain from doing something.

Rectification

This award allows for the alteration of contractual documents.

Rescission

This action sets aside the terms of a contractual agreement and returns the parties to the situation they were in before the contract was entered into.

Court Fees

A new fee structure takes account of the different procedures, a movement towards a 'pay as you go' fees regime and the need for full cost recovery. 'Pay as you go' means that parties will be expected to contribute more in fees, the more court and judicial time they use, for example, if they do not settle but carry on to trial.

CHAPTER 12

ARBITRATION, TRIBUNAL ADJUDICATION AND ALTERNATIVE DISPUTE RESOLUTION

12.1 Introduction

Although attention tends to be focused on the courts as the forum for resolving conflicts when they arise, the court system is not necessarily the most effective way of deciding disputes, especially those which arise between people, or indeed businesses, which have enjoyed a close relationship. The problem with the court system is that it is essentially an antagonistic process, designed ultimately to determine a winner and a loser in any particular dispute. As a consequence, court procedure tends to emphasise and heighten the degree of conflict between the parties, rather than seek to produce a compromise solution. For various reasons, considered below, it is not always in the best long term interests of the parties to enter into such hostile relations as are involved in court procedure. In recognition of this fact, a number of alternative procedures to court action have been developed for dealing with such disputes.

The increased importance of alternative dispute resolution (ADR) mechanisms has been signalled in both legislation and court procedures. For example, the Commercial Court issued a *Practice Statement* in 1993, stating that it wished to encourage ADR, and followed this in 1996 with a further *Direction* that allows judges to consider whether a case is suitable for ADR at its outset, and to invite the parties to attempt a neutral, non-court settlement of their dispute. In cases in the Court of Appeal, the Master of the Rolls now writes to the parties, urging them to consider ADR and asking them for their reasons for declining to use it. Also, as part of the civil justice reforms, r 26.4 of the Civil Procedure Rules (CPR) 1998 enables judges, either on their own account or with the agreement of both parties, to stop court proceedings where they consider the dispute to be better suited to solution by some alternative procedure, such as arbitration or mediation.

If, subsequently, a court is of the opinion that an action it has been required to decide could have been settled more effectively through ADR then, under r 45.5 of the CPR 1998, it may penalise the party who insisted on the court hearing by awarding them reduced (or no) damages should they win the case.

In *Cowl v Plymouth CC* (2001), the Court of Appeal, with Lord Woolf as a member of the panel, made it perfectly clear that lawyers for both parties are under a heavy duty only to resort to litigation if it is unavoidable and the dispute cannot be settled by some other non-court based mechanism. In *Kinstreet Ltd v Bamargo Corp Ltd* (1999), the court actually ordered ADR against the wishes of one of the parties to the action, requiring that:

> [T]he parties shall take such serious steps as they may be advised to resolve their disputes by ADR procedures before the independent mediator ... [and] if the actions are not

finally settled by 30 October 1999 the parties are to inform the court by letter within three working days what steps towards ADR have been taken and why such steps have failed.

The potential consequences of not abiding by a recommendation to use ADR may be seen in *Dunnett v Railtrack plc* (2002). When Dunnett won a right to appeal against a previous court decision, the court granting the appeal recommended that the dispute should be put to arbitration. Railtrack, however, refused Dunnett's offer of arbitration and insisted on the dispute going back to a full court hearing. In the subsequent hearing, in the Court of Appeal, Railtrack proved successful. The Court of Appeal, however, held that if a party rejected ADR out of hand when it had been suggested by the court, they would suffer the consequences when costs came to be decided. In the instant case, Railtrack had refused even to contemplate ADR at a stage prior to the costs of the appeal beginning to flow. In his judgment, Brooke LJ set out the modern approach to ADR:

> Skilled mediators are now able to achieve results satisfactory to both parties in many cases which are quite beyond the power of lawyers and courts to achieve. This court has knowledge of cases where intense feelings have arisen, for instance in relation to clinical negligence claims. But when the parties are brought together on neutral soil with a skilled mediator to help them resolve their differences, it may very well be that the mediator is able to achieve a result by which the parties shake hands at the end and feel that they have gone away having settled the dispute on terms with which they are happy to live. A mediator may be able to provide solutions which are beyond the powers of the court to provide ... It is to be hoped that any publicity given to this part of the judgment of the court will draw the attention of lawyers to their duties to further the overriding objective in the way that is set out in Part 1 of the Rules and to the possibility that, if they turn down out of hand the chance of alternative dispute resolution when suggested by the court, as happened on this occasion, they may have to face uncomfortable costs consequence.

The Court of Appeal subsequently applied *Dunnett* in *Leicester Circuits Ltd v Coates Bros plc* (2003), where, although it found for Coates, it did not award it full costs on the grounds that it had withdrawn from a mediation process. The Court of Appeal also dismissed Coates' claim that there was no realistic prospect of success in the mediation. As Judge LJ stated:

> We do not for one moment assume that the mediation process would have succeeded, but certainly there is a prospect that it would have done if it had been allowed to proceed. That therefore bears on the issue of costs.

It is possible to refuse to engage in mediation without subsequently suffering in the awards of costs. The test, however, is an objective rather than a subjective one and a difficult one to sustain, as was shown in *Hurst v Leeming* (2002). Hurst, a solicitor, started legal proceedings against his former partners. He instructed Leeming, a barrister, to represent him. When the action proved unsuccessful, Hurst sued Leeming in professional negligence. When that action failed, Hurst argued that Leeming should not be awarded costs, as he, Hurst, had offered to mediate the dispute but Leeming had rejected the offer. Leeming cited five separate justifications for his refusal to mediate. These were:

- the heavy costs he had already incurred in meeting the allegations;

- the seriousness of the allegation made against him;

- the lack of substance in the claim;

- the fact that he had already provided Hurst with a full refutation of his allegation; and

- the fact that, given Hurst's obsessive character, there was no real prospect of a successful outcome to the litigation.

Only the fifth justification was accepted by the court, although even in that case it was emphasised that the conclusion had to be supported by an objective evaluation of the situation. However, in the circumstances, given Hurst's behaviour and character, the conclusion that mediation would not have resolved the complaint could be sustained objectively. In *Halsey v Milton Keynes General NHS Trust* (2004), the Court of Appeal emphasised that the criterion was the reasonableness of the belief that there was no real prospect of success through ADR.

The former Lord Chancellor, Lord Irvine, was very favourably disposed to ADR, as is evident in his inaugural lecture to the Faculty of Mediation and ADR, in which he said:

> ADR has many supporters. But they, too, have a responsibility to proceed with care. ADR is not a panacea, nor is it cost free. But, I do believe that it can play a vital part in the opening of access to justice.

And in its 1999 Consultation Paper, *Alternative Dispute Resolution*, the Lord Chancellor's Department (LCD) redefined 'access to justice' as meaning:

> [W]here people need help there are effective solutions that are proportionate to the issues at stake. In some circumstances, this will involve going to court, but in others, that will not be necessary. *For most people most of the time, litigation in the civil courts, and often in tribunals too, should be the method of dispute resolution of last resort* [emphasis added].

12.2 Arbitration

The first and oldest of these alternative procedures is arbitration. This is the procedure whereby parties in dispute refer the issue to a third party for resolution, rather than taking the case to the ordinary law courts. Studies have shown a reluctance on the part of commercial undertakings to have recourse to the law to resolve their disputes. At first sight, this appears to be paradoxical. The development of contract law can, to a great extent, be explained as the law's response to the need for regulation in relation to business activity, and yet businesses decline to make use of its procedures. To some degree, questions of speed and cost explain this peculiar phenomenon, but it can be explained more fully by reference to the introduction to this chapter. It was stated there that informal procedures tend to be most effective where there is a high degree of mutuality and interdependency, and that is precisely the case in most business relationships. Businesses seek to establish and maintain long term relationships with other concerns. The problem with the law is that the court case tends to terminally rupture such relationships. It is not suggested that, in the final analysis, where the stakes are sufficiently high, recourse to the law will not be had; such action, however, does not represent the first, or indeed the preferred, option. In contemporary business practice it is common, if not standard, practice for commercial contracts to contain express clauses referring any future disputes to arbitration. This practice is well established and its legal effectiveness has long been recognised by the law.

12.2.1 Arbitration procedure

The Arbitration Act 1996 repeals Pt 1 of the Arbitration Act 1950 and the whole of the Arbitration Acts of 1975 and 1979. As the Act is a relatively new piece of legislation, it is necessary to consider it in some detail.

Section 1 of the 1996 Act states that it is founded on the following principles:

(a) the object of arbitration is to obtain the fair resolution of disputes by an impartial tribunal without necessary delay or expense;

(b) the parties should be free to agree how their disputes are resolved, subject only to such safeguards as are necessary in the public interest;

(c) in matters governed by this part of the Act, the court should not intervene except as provided by this part.

This provision of general principles, which should inform the reading of the later detailed provisions of the Act, is unusual for UK legislation, but may be seen as reflecting the purposes behind the Act, a major one of which was the wish to ensure that London did not lose its place as a leading centre for international arbitration. As a consequence of the demand-driven nature of the new legislation, it would seem that court interference in the arbitration process has had to be reduced to a minimum and replaced by party autonomy. Under the 1996 Act, the role of the arbitrator has been increased and that of the court has been reduced to the residual level of intervention where the arbitration process either requires legal assistance or is seen to be failing to provide a just settlement.

The Act follows the Model Arbitration Law, which was adopted in 1985 by the United Nations Commission on International Trade Law.

Whilst it is possible for there to be an oral arbitration agreement at common law, s 5 provides that Pt 1 of the Arbitration Act 1996 only applies to agreements in writing. What this means in practice, however, has been extended by s 5(3), which provides that, where the parties agree to an arbitration procedure which is in writing, that procedure will be operative, even though the agreement between the parties is not itself in writing. An example of such a situation would be where a salvage operation was negotiated between two vessels on the basis of Lloyds' standard salvage terms. It would be unlikely that the actual agreement would be reduced to written form but, nonetheless, the arbitration element in those terms would be effective.

In analysing the Arbitration Act 1996, it is useful to consider it in four distinct parts: autonomy of the parties; arbitrators and their powers; powers of the court; and appellate rights.

12.2.1.1 Autonomy of the parties

It is significant that most of the provisions set out in the Arbitration Act 1996 are not compulsory. As is clearly stated in s 1, it is up to the parties to an arbitration agreement to agree on what procedures to adopt. The main purpose of the Act is to empower the parties to the dispute and to allow them to decide how it is to be decided. In pursuit of this aim, the mandatory parts of the Act only take effect where the parties involved do not agree otherwise. It is actually possible for the parties to agree that the dispute should not be decided in line with the strict legal rules; rather, it should be decided in line with commercial fairness, which might be a different thing altogether.

12.2.1.2 Arbitrators and their powers

The arbitration tribunal may consist of either a single arbitrator or a panel, as the parties decide (s 15). If one party fails to appoint an arbitrator, then the other party's nominee may act as sole arbitrator (s 17). Under s 20(4) of the Arbitration Act 1996, where there is a panel and it fails to reach a majority decision, the decision of the chair shall prevail.

The tribunal is required to fairly and impartially adopt procedures which are suitable to the circumstances of each case. It is also for the tribunal to decide all procedural and evidential matters. Parties may be represented by a lawyer or any other person, and the tribunal may appoint experts or legal advisers to report to it.

Arbitrators will be immune from action being taken against them, except in situations where they have acted in bad faith.

Section 30 provides that, unless the parties agree otherwise, the arbitrator can rule on questions relating to jurisdiction, that is, in relation to:

- whether there actually is a valid arbitration agreement;

- whether the arbitration tribunal is properly constituted; and

- what matters have been submitted to arbitration in accordance with the agreement.

Section 32 allows any of the parties to raise preliminary objections to the substantive jurisdiction of the arbitration tribunal in court, but provides that they may only do so on limited grounds, which require either: the agreement of the parties concerned; the permission of the arbitration tribunal; or the agreement of the court. Permission to appeal will only be granted where the court is satisfied that the question involves a point of law of general importance.

Section 28 expressly provides that the parties to the proceedings are jointly and severally liable to pay the arbitrators such reasonable fees and expenses as are appropriate. Previously, this was only an implied term.

Section 29 of the Arbitration Act 1996 provides that arbitrators are not liable for anything done or omitted in the discharge of their functions unless the act or omission was done in bad faith.

Section 33 provides that the tribunal has a general duty:

- to act fairly and impartially between the parties, giving each a reasonable opportunity to state their case; and

- to adopt procedures suitable for the circumstance of the case, avoiding unnecessary delay or expense.

Section 35 provides that, subject to the parties agreeing to the contrary, the tribunal shall have the power:

- to order parties to provide security for costs (previously a power reserved to the courts);

- to give directions in relation to property subject to the arbitration; and

- to direct that a party or witness be examined on oath, and to administer the oath.

The parties may also empower the arbitrator to make provisional orders (s 39 of the Arbitration Act 1996).

12.2.1.3   Powers of the court

Where one party seeks to start a court action in the face of a valid arbitration agreement to the contrary, then the other party may request the court to stay the litigation in favour of the arbitration agreement under ss 9–11 of the Arbitration Act 1996. Where, however, both parties agree to ignore the arbitration agreement and seek recourse to litigation, then, following the party consensual nature of the Act, the agreement may be ignored.

The courts may order a party to comply with an order of the tribunal and may also order parties and witnesses to attend and to give oral evidence before tribunals (s 43).

The court has power to revoke the appointment of an arbitrator, on application of any of the parties, where there has been a failure in the appointment procedure under s 18, but it also has powers to revoke authority under s 24. This power comes into play on the application of one of the parties in circumstances where the arbitrator:

- has not acted impartially;

- does not possess the required qualifications;

- does not have either the physical or mental capacity to deal with the proceedings;

- has refused or failed to properly conduct the proceedings; or

- has been dilatory in dealing with the proceedings or in making an award, to the extent that it will cause substantial injustice to the party applying for their removal.

Under s 45, the court may, on application by one of the parties, decide any preliminary question of law arising in the course of the proceedings.

12.2.1.4   Appellate rights

Once the decision has been made, there are limited grounds for appeal. The first ground arises under s 67 of the Arbitration Act 1996, in relation to the substantive jurisdiction of the arbitral panel, although the right to appeal on this ground may be lost if the party attempting to make use of it took part in the arbitration proceedings without objecting to the alleged lack of jurisdiction. The second ground for appeal to the courts is on procedural grounds, under s 68, on the basis that some serious irregularity affected the operation of the tribunal. Serious irregularity means either:

- failure to comply with the general duty set out in s 33;

- failure to conduct the tribunal as agreed by the parties;

- uncertainty or ambiguity as to the effect of the award; or

- failure to comply with the requirement as to the form of the award.

Parties may also appeal on a point of law arising from the award under s 69 of the Arbitration Act 1996. However, the parties can agree beforehand to preclude such a possibility and, where they agree to the arbitral panel making a decision without providing a reasoned justification for it, they will also lose the right to appeal.

The issue of rights to appeal under s 69 has been recently considered in a number of cases by the Court of Appeal. In March 2002, in *North Range Shipping Ltd v Seatrams Shipping Corp* (2002), the court confirmed that there was no further right of appeal against a judge's refusal to grant permission for an appeal against an arbitrator's decision, except on the grounds of unfairness. In *CMA CGM SA v Beteiligungs KG* (2002), it insisted that judges in the High Court should not be too hasty in allowing appeals. In the case in point, the Court of Appeal decided that the present appeal should not have been allowed. In reaching this decision, the court set out the new standard that had to be met to justify an appeal, that 'the question should be one of general importance and the decision of the arbitrators should be at least open to serious doubt'. This standard was higher than that applied under the previous test as stated in *Antaios Compania Naviera SA v Salen Redereierna AB* (1985).

In *BLCT Ltd v J Sainsbury plc* (2003), the Court of Appeal held that not only had the appellant no real prospect of succeeding in its appeal but also rejected the argument that, by curtailing the right of appeal, s 69 was incompatible with Art 6 of the European Convention on Human Rights.

12.2.2   Relationship to ordinary courts

In general terms, the courts have no objection to individuals settling their disputes on a voluntary basis but, at the same time, they are careful to maintain their supervisory role in such procedures. Arbitration agreements are no different from other terms of a contract and, in line with the normal rules of contract law, courts will strike out any attempt to oust their ultimate jurisdiction as being contrary to public policy. Thus, as has been stated above, arbitration proceedings are open to challenge, through judicial review, on the ground that they were not conducted in a judicial manner.

The Arbitration Act 1950 allowed for either party to the proceedings to have questions of law authoritatively determined by the High Court through the procedure of case stated. The High Court could also set aside the decision of the arbitrator on grounds of fact, law or procedure. Whereas the arbitration process was supposed to provide a quick and relatively cheap method of deciding disputes, the availability of the appeals procedures meant that parties could delay the final decision and, in so doing, increase the costs. In such circumstances, arbitration became the precursor to a court case, rather than a replacement of it. The Arbitration Act 1979 abolished the case stated procedure and curtailed the right to appeal and, as has been seen, the Arbitration Act 1996 has reduced the grounds for appeal to the court system even further.

12.2.3 Advantages

There are numerous advantages to be gained from using arbitration rather than the court system:

- *Privacy*

  Arbitration tends to be a private procedure. This has the twofold advantage that outsiders do not get access to any potentially sensitive information and the parties to the arbitration do not run the risk of any damaging publicity arising out of reports of the proceedings.

  The issue of privacy was considered by the Court of Appeal in *Department of Economic Policy and Development of the City of Moscow v Bankers Trust* 2004), in which the decision of an arbitration panel was challenged in the High Court under s 68 of the Arbitration Act 1996. The details of the original arbitration had remained confidential between the parties and in the High Court Cooke J decided that the details of his judgment against the appellants should also remain confidential. On appeal, Cooke J's decision not to publish his judgment in full was confirmed, although the Court of Appeal did allow the publication of a Lawtel summary of the case.

- *Informality*

  The proceedings are less formal than a court case and they can be scheduled more flexibly than court proceedings.

- *Speed*

  Arbitration is generally much quicker than taking a case through the courts. Where, however, one of the parties makes use of the available grounds to challenge an arbitration award, the prior costs of the arbitration will have been largely wasted.

- *Cost*

  Arbitration is generally a much cheaper procedure than taking a case to the normal courts. Nonetheless, the costs of arbitration and the use of specialist arbitrators should not be underestimated.

- *Expertise*

  The use of a specialist arbitrator ensures that the person deciding the case has expert knowledge of the actual practice within the area under consideration and can form their conclusion in line with accepted practice.

It can be argued that arbitration represents a privatisation of the judicial process. It may be assumed, therefore, that, of all its virtues, perhaps the greatest (at least as far as the Government is concerned) is the potential reduction in costs for the State in providing the legal framework within which disputes are resolved.

12.2.4 The small claims track (Pt 27 of the CPR 1998)

After 1973, an arbitration service was available within the county court specifically for the settlement of relatively small claims. This small claims procedure, known as arbitration, was operated by county court district judges. However, under the civil justice reforms, there is no longer any automatic reference to arbitration, which is replaced by reference to the small claims track. Claims are allocated to this track in exactly the same way as they are allocated to the fast track or multi- track. The concept of an arbitration therefore disappears and is replaced by a small claims hearing. Aspects of the old small claims procedure that are retained include their informality, the interventionist approach adopted by the judiciary, the limited costs regime and the limited grounds for appeal (misconduct of the district judge or an error of law made by the court).

Changes to the handling of small claims are:

- *an increase in the jurisdiction from £3,000 to no more than £5,000* (with the exception of claims for personal injury where the damages claimed for pain and suffering and loss of amenity do not exceed £1,000 and the financial value of the whole claim does not exceed £5,000; and for housing disrepair where the claim for repairs and other work does not exceed £1,000 and the financial value of any other claim for damages is not more than £1,000);

- *hearings to be generally public hearings* – but subject to some exceptions (Pt 39 of the CPR 1998);

- *paper adjudication, if parties consent* – where a judge thinks that paper adjudication may be appropriate, parties will be asked to say whether or not they have any objections within a given time period. If a party does object, the matter will be given a hearing in the normal way;

- *parties need not attend the hearing* – a party not wishing to attend a hearing will be able to give the court and the other party or parties written notice that they will not be attending. The notice must be filed with the court seven days before the start of the hearing. This will guarantee that the court will take into account any written evidence which that party has sent to the court. A consequence of this is that the judge must give reasons for the decision reached, which will be included in the judgment;

- *use of experts* – expert witnesses will only be allowed to give evidence with the permission of the court;

- *costs* – these are not generally awarded, but a small award may be made to cover costs in issuing the claim, court fees, and expenses incurred by the successful party, witnesses and experts. Under r 27.14 of the CPR 1998, additional costs may be awarded against any party who has behaved unreasonably;

- *preliminary hearings* – these may be called:
  - where the judge considers that special instructions are needed to ensure a fair hearing;
  - to enable the judge to dispose of the claim where he is of the view that either of the parties has no real prospect of success at a full hearing; or
  - to enable the judge to strike out either the whole or part of a statement of action on the basis that it provides no reasonable grounds for bringing such an action.

- *the introduction of tailored directions* – to be given for some of the most common small claims, for example, spoiled holidays or wedding videos, road traffic accidents, building disputes.

Parties can consent to use the small claims track even if the value of their claim exceeds the normal value for that track, although subject to the court's approval. The limited cost regime will not apply to these claims. But costs will be limited to the costs that might have been awarded if the claim had been dealt with in the fast track. Parties will also be restricted to a maximum one day hearing.

The milestone events for the small claims track are the date for the return of the allocation questionnaire and the date of the hearing.

The right to appeal under the CPR 1998 is governed by new principles. An appeal can be made on the grounds that:

- there was a serious irregularity affecting the proceedings; or

- the court made a mistake of law.

An example would be where an arbitrator failed to allow submissions on any crucial point upon which he rested his judgment.

12.2.5   Small claims procedure

Arbitration proceedings begin with an individual filing a statement of case at the county court. This document details the grounds of their dispute and requests the other party to be summonsed to appear. There may be preliminary hearings, at which the issues involved are clarified, but it is possible for the dispute to be settled at such hearings. If no compromise can be reached at this stage, a date is set for the small claims hearing.

Arbitration hearings are usually heard by the district judge, although the parties to the dispute may request that it be referred to the circuit judge or even an outside arbitrator. The judge hearing the case may, at any time before or after the hearing, with the agreement of the parties, consult an expert on the matter under consideration and, again with the approval of the parties, invite an expert to sit on the arbitration in the role of assessor.

If one of the parties fails to appear at the hearing, the dispute can be decided in their absence. Alternatively, the parties may agree to the case being decided by the arbitrator, solely on the basis of documents and written statements.

The arbitration procedure is intended to be a less formal forum than that provided by the ordinary courts and, to that end, the CPR 1998 provide that the strict rules of evidence shall not be applied. Parties are encouraged to represent themselves rather than make use of the services of professional lawyers, although they may be legally represented if they wish.

The CPR 1998 give judges wide discretion to adopt any procedure they consider helpful to ensure that the parties have an equal opportunity to put their case. This discretion is not limitless, however, and it does not remove the normal principles of legal procedure, such as the right of direct cross-examination of one of the parties by the legal representative of the other party (see *Chilton v Saga Holidays plc* (1986), where the Court of Appeal held that a registrar was wrong to have refused to allow solicitors for the defendant in the case to cross-examine the plaintiff on the ground that that person was not also legally represented).

On the basis of the information provided, the judge decides the case and, if the claimant is successful, makes an award for appropriate compensation. A no-costs rule operates to ensure that the costs of legal representation cannot be recovered, although the losing party may be instructed to pay court fees and the expenses of witnesses. Judgments are legally enforceable.

12.2.6 Evaluation

Problems have become evident in the operation of the arbitration procedure, particularly in cases where one party has been represented whilst the other has not. In spite of the clear intention to facilitate the resolution of disputes cheaply and without the need for legal practitioners, some individuals, particularly large business enterprises, insisted on their right to legal representation. As legal assistance, formerly known as legal aid, is not available in respect of such actions, most individuals cannot afford to be legally represented and, therefore, find themselves at a distinct disadvantage when opposed by professional lawyers.

One solution to this difficulty would have been to make legal assistance available in the case of arbitration. Such a proposal is very unlikely ever to come to fruition, mainly on economic grounds, but also on the ground that the use of professional lawyers in such cases would contradict the spirit and the whole purpose of the procedure.

Alternatively, it might have been provided that no party could be legally represented in arbitration procedures, but to introduce such a measure would have been a denial of an important civil right.

The actual method chosen to deal with the problem was to lift the restrictions on the rights of audience in small debt proceedings. Parties to the proceedings were entitled to be accompanied by a McKenzie friend to give them advice, but such people had no right of audience and, thus, had no right actually to represent their friend in any arbitration (see *McKenzie v McKenzie* (1970)). In October 1992, under the Courts and Legal Services Act 1990, the Lord Chancellor extended the right of audience to lay representatives in small claims courts. This decision has the effect of allowing individuals access to non-professional, but expert, advice and advocacy. Members of such organisations as citizens advice bureaux and legal advice centres will now be permitted to represent their clients, although they will still not be permitted to issue proceedings. In cases involving claims of more than £1,000, they may even charge a fee.

The increase in the maximum amount to be claimed to £5,000 introduces two particular difficulties with regard to representation. The first, and by far the more serious, is the fact that the raising of the ceiling to what is a not inconsiderable sum of money means that individuals will lose legal aid to fund their claims in such cases and, therefore, may not have access to the best possible legal advice with respect to their case. The second, and apparently contradictory, point is that the number of lawyers appearing in small claims proceedings may actually increase as a result of the rise in the limit. Whereas it might not be worth paying for legal representation in a £3,000 claim, it might make more economic sense to pay for professional help if the sum being claimed is much higher. Which alternative actually occurs remains to be seen.

In evaluating the small claims procedure, regard has to be had to the Civil Justice Review of 1996, which specifically considered the arbitration procedure and concluded that it generally works in a satisfactory way to produce a relatively quick, cheap and informal mechanism for resolving many smaller cases without the need to overburden the county courts.

In March 2003, the LCD issued the recommendations that followed from its Civil Enforcement Review. Unsurprisingly, its conclusion was that creditors who have established a legitimate claim should be able to pursue it through a straightforward and accessible system and, if necessary, enforce a judgment by the most appropriate means. As it stated:

> ... without effective means of enforcement people ordered to pay a court judgment or criminal penalty would have little or no incentive to do so and the authority of the courts, the effectiveness of penalties, and confidence in the justice system would all be undermined.

This has been considered in some detail at 1.2.2 above.

12.2.7 Arbitration under codes of conduct

When it was first established in 1973, the small claims procedure was seen as a mechanism through which consumers could enforce their rights against recalcitrant traders. In reality, the arbitration procedure has proved to be just as useful for, and used just as much by, traders and businesses as consumers. There remains one area of arbitration, however, that is specifically focused on the consumer: arbitration schemes that are run under the auspices of particular trade associations. As part of the regulation of trade practices and in the pursuit of effective measures of consumer protection, the Office of Fair Trading has encouraged the establishment of voluntary codes of practice within particular areas. It is usual to find that such codes of practice provide arbitration schemes to resolve particularly intractable problems between individual consumers and members of the association. Such schemes are never compulsory and do not seek to replace the consumers' legal rights, but they do provide a relatively inexpensive mechanism for dealing with problems without the need even to bother the county court. Such schemes are numerous; the most famous one is probably the travel industry scheme operated under the auspices of the Association of British Travel Agents, but other associations run similar schemes in such areas as car sales, shoe retailing, dry cleaning, etc. Again, the point of such schemes is to provide a quick, cheap means of dealing with problems without running the risk of completely alienating the consumer from the trade in question.

Although many of the trade arbitration schemes offered consumers distinct advantages, some did not and, in order to remedy any abuses, the Consumer Arbitration Act 1988 was introduced. This statute provides that, in the case of consumer contracts, no prior agreement between the parties that subsequent disputes will be referred to arbitration can be enforced. However, consumers will be bound by arbitration procedures where they have already entered into them as a consequence of a prior agreement, or have agreed to them subsequently.

12.3 Administrative Tribunals

Although attention tends to be focused on the operation of the courts as the forum within which legal decisions are taken, it is no longer the case that the bulk of legal and quasi-legal questions are determined within that court structure. There are, as alternatives to the court system, a large number of tribunals which have been set up under various Acts of Parliament to rule on the operation of the particular schemes established under those Acts. There are at least 70 different types of administrative tribunal and, within each type, there may well be hundreds of individual tribunals operating locally all over the country to hear particular cases. Almost one million cases are dealt with by tribunals each year and, as the Royal Commission on Legal Services (Cmnd 7648) pointed out in 1979, the number of cases then being heard by tribunals was six times greater than the number of contested civil cases dealt with by the High Court and county court combined. It is evident, therefore, that tribunals are of major significance as alternatives to traditional courts in dealing with disputes.

The generally accepted explanation for the establishment and growth of tribunals in Britain since 1945 was the need to provide a specialist forum to deal with cases involving conflicts between an increasingly interventionist welfare State, its functionaries and the rights of private citizens. It is certainly true that, since 1945, the Welfare State has intervened more and more in every aspect of people's lives. The intention may have been to extend various social benefits to a wider constituency but, in so doing, the machinery of the Welfare State, and in reality those who operate that machinery, has been granted powers to control access to its benefits. As a consequence, they have been given the power to interfere in, and control the lives of, individual subjects of the State. By their nature, welfare provision tends to be discretionary and dependent upon the particular circumstance of a given case. As a consequence, State functionaries were given extended discretionary power over the supply/withdrawal of welfare benefits. As the interventionist State replaced the completely free market as the source of welfare for many people, so access to the provisions made by the State became a matter of fundamental importance and a focus for potential contention, especially given the discretionary nature of its provision. At the same time as Welfare State provisions were being extended, the view was articulated that such provisions and projects should not be under the purview and control of the ordinary courts. It was felt that the judiciary reflected a culture which tended to favour a more market centred, individualistic approach to the provision of rights and welfare and that their essentially formalistic approach to the resolution of disputes would not fit with the operation of the new projects.

12.3.1 Tribunals and courts

There is some debate as to whether tribunals are merely part of the machinery of administration of particular projects, or whether their function is the distinct one of adjudication. The Franks Committee (Cmnd 218, 1957) favoured the latter view, but others have disagreed and have emphasised the administrative role of such bodies. Parliament initiated various projects and schemes, and included within those projects specialist tribunals to deal with the problems that they inevitably generated. On that basis, it is suggested that tribunals are merely adjuncts to the parent project and that this, therefore, defines their role as more administrative than adjudicatory.

If the foregoing has suggested the theoretical possibility of distinguishing courts and tribunals in relation to their administrative or adjudicatory role, in practice it is difficult to implement such a distinction, for the reason that the members of tribunals may be, and usually are, acting in a judicial capacity. See *Pickering v Liverpool Daily Post and Echo Newspapers* (1991), in which it was held that a mental health review tribunal was a court whose proceedings were subject to the law of contempt. Although a newspaper was entitled to publish the fact that a named person had made an application to the tribunal, together with the date of the hearing and its decision, it was not allowed to publish the reasons for the decision or any conditions applied.

If the precise distinction between tribunals and courts is a matter of uncertainty, what is certain is that tribunals are inferior to the normal courts. One of the main purposes of the tribunal system is to prevent the ordinary courts of law from being overburdened by cases, but tribunals are still subject to judicial review on the basis of breach of natural justice, or where it acts in an *ultra vires* manner, or, indeed, where it goes wrong in relation to the application of the law when deciding cases.

In addition to the control of the courts, tribunals are also subject to the supervision of the Council on Tribunals, which was originally established under the Tribunals and Inquiries Act 1958, as subsequently amended by the Tribunals and Inquiries Acts 1971 and 1992, the latter of which is the current legislation. Members of the Council are appointed by the Lord Chancellor and their role is to keep the general operation of the system under review.

In May 2000, Lord Irvine LC appointed High Court judge Sir Andrew Leggatt to review the current operation of the tribunal system as a whole. However, consideration of Sir Andrew's findings and recommendations will be postponed until later in this chapter.

12.3.2   Composition of tribunals

Tribunals are usually made up of three members, only one of whom, the chair, is expected to be legally qualified. The other two members are lay representatives. The lack of legal training is not considered to be a drawback, given the technical and administrative, as opposed to specifically legal, nature of the provisions they have to consider. Indeed, the fact of there being two lay representatives on tribunals provides them with one of their perceived advantages over courts. The non-legal members may provide specialist knowledge and, thus, may enable the tribunal to base its decision on actual practice, as opposed to abstract legal theory or mere legal formalism. An example of this can be seen with regard to the tribunals having responsibility or determining issues relating to employment, which usually have a trade union representative and an employers' representative sitting on the panel, and are, therefore, able to consider the immediate problem from both sides of the employment relationship.

The procedure for nominating tribunal members is set out in the parent statute but, generally, it is the Minister of State with responsibility for the operation of the statute in question who ultimately decides the membership of the tribunal. As tribunals are established to deal largely with conflicts between the general public and government departments, this raises at least the possibility of suspicion that the members of tribunals are not truly neutral. In response to such doubts, the 1957 Franks Committee recommended that the appointment of the chairmen of tribunals should become the prerogative of the Lord Chancellor and that the appointment of the other members should become the responsibility of a Council on Tribunals. This recommendation was not implemented, and ministers, by and large, still retain the power to appoint tribunal members. As a compromise, however, the minister selects the chairperson from a panel appointed by the Lord Chancellor.

12.3.3 Statutory tribunals

There are a number of tribunals which have considerable power in their areas of operation, and it is necessary to have some detailed knowledge of a selection of the most important of these. Examples of such tribunals are as follows:

- *Employment tribunals*

    These are governed by the Employment Tribunals Act 1996, which sets out their composition and major areas of competence and procedure. In practice, such tribunals are normally made up of a legally qualified chairperson, a representative chosen from a panel representing employers and another representative chosen from a panel representing the interests of employees.

    Employment tribunals have jurisdiction over a number of statutory provisions relating to employment issues. The majority of issues arise in relation to such matters as disputes over the meaning and operation of particular terms of employment, disputes in respect of redundancy payments, disputes involving issues of unfair dismissal and disputes as to the provision of maternity pay.

    They also have authority in other areas, under different legislation. Thus, they deal with complaints about racial discrimination in the employment field under the Race Relations Act 1976; complaints about sexual discrimination in employment under the Sex Discrimination Act 1975; complaints about equal pay under the Equal Pay Act 1970, as amended by the Sex Discrimination Act 1975; complaints under the Disability Discrimination Act 1995; complaints about unlawful deductions from wages under the Wages Act 1986; and appeals against the imposition of improvement notices under the Health and Safety at Work etc Act 1974. In addition, employment tribunals have to deal with various ancillary matters relating to trade union membership and activities.

    The tribunal hearing is relatively informal. As in arbitration hearings, the normal rules of evidence are not applied and parties can represent themselves, or be represented by solicitors or barristers. And, as appropriate, in an employment context they may also be represented by trade union officials or representatives, or indeed by any other person they wish to represent them. Appeal, on a point of law only, is to the Employment Appeal Tribunal, which also sits with lay representatives.

- *Social security appeals tribunals*

    Various Social Security Acts have provided for safety net provisions for the disadvantaged in society to ensure that they enjoy at least a basic standard of living. In the pursuit of this general goal, various State functionaries have been delegated the task of implementing the very complex provisions contained in the legislation and have been granted considerable discretionary power in the implementation of those provisions. The function of the social security tribunals is to ensure that such discretion is not abused and that the aims of the legislation are generally being met.

The tribunals, of which there are some 200 in England and Wales, are charged with the duty of hearing and deciding upon the correctness of decisions made by adjudication officers, who are the people who actually determine the level of benefit that individuals are entitled to receive.

- *Immigration Appeal Tribunal*

This body hears appeals from individuals who have been refused entry into the UK or who have been refused permission to extend their stay. Given the contemporary world situation, it can be appreciated that the work of this particular tribunal is not only politically sensitive but on the increase.

- *Mental health review tribunals*

These operate under the Mental Health Act 1983. The tribunals have wide powers to decide whether individuals should be detained for the purposes of compulsory treatment. They can also dispose of the property of such individuals. Given the particular area within which the mental health review tribunals operate, it is essential that there are medical experts present to decide on medical issues. This latter requirement also applies in respect of social security issues relating to the state of the individual claimant's health.

- *Lands Tribunal*

Established under the Lands Tribunal Act 1949, the Lands Tribunal's essential function is to determine the legality of, and the levels of compensation in relation to, compulsory purchase orders over land. It also considers matters relating to planning applications.

- *Rent Assessment Committee*

This committee deals with matters specifically relating to the rent charged for property. It resolves disputes between landlords and tenants of private accommodation, hears appeals from decisions of rent officers and has the power to fix rent in relation to furnished and unfurnished residential tenancies.

12.3.4 Domestic tribunals

The foregoing has focused on public administrative tribunals set up under particular legislative provisions to deal with matters of public relevance. The term 'tribunal', however, is also used in relation to the internal disciplinary procedures of particular institutions. Whether these institutions are created under legislation or not is immaterial; the point is that domestic tribunals relate mainly to matters of private, rather than public, concern, although, at times, the two can overlap. Examples of domestic tribunals are the disciplinary committees of professional institutions such as the Bar, The Law Society or the British Medical Association; trade unions; and universities. The power that each of these tribunals has is very great and is controlled by means of the ordinary courts, ensuring that the rules of natural justice are complied with and that the tribunal does not act *ultra vires*, that is, beyond its powers. Matters relating to trade union membership and discipline are additionally regulated by the Employment Rights Act 1996.

12.3.5 Advantages of tribunals

Advantages of tribunals over courts relate to such matters as follows:

- *Speed*

  The ordinary court system is notoriously dilatory in hearing and deciding cases. Tribunals are much quicker to hear cases. A related advantage of the tribunal system is the certainty that it will be heard on a specific date and will not be subject to the vagaries of the court system. That being said, there have been reports that the tribunal system is coming under increased pressure and is falling behind in relation to its caseload.

- *Cost*

  Tribunals are a much cheaper way of deciding cases than using the ordinary court system. One factor that leads to a reduction in cost is the fact that no specialised court building is required to hear the cases. Additionally, because those deciding the cases are less expensive to employ than judges and complainants do not have to rely on legal representation, the tribunal procedure is considerably less expensive than using the traditional court system. These reductions are further enhanced by the fact that there are no court fees involved in relation to tribunal proceedings and costs are not normally awarded against the loser.

- *Informality*

  Tribunals are supposed to be informal, in order to make them less intimidating than full court cases. The strict rules relating to evidence, pleading and procedure which apply in courts are not binding in tribunal proceedings. The lack of formality is strengthened by the fact that proceedings tend not to be inquisitorial or accusatorial, but are intended to encourage and help participants to express their views of the situation before the tribunal. Informality should not, however, be mistaken for a lack of order, and the Franks Committee Report itself emphasised the need for clear rules of procedure. The provision of this informal situation and procedure tends to suggest that complainants do not need to be represented by a lawyer in order to present their grievance. They may represent themselves or be represented by a more knowledgeable associate, such as a trade union representative or some other friend. This contentious point will be considered further below.

- *Flexibility*

  Tribunals are not bound by the strict rules of precedent, although some pay more regard to previous decisions than others. It should be remembered that, as tribunals are inferior and subject to the courts, they are governed by precedents made in the courts.

- *Expertise*

  Reference has already been made to the advantages to be gained from the particular expertise that is provided by the laymembers of tribunals, as against the more general legal expertise of the chairperson.

- *Accessibility*

  The aim of tribunals is to provide individuals with a readily accessible forum in which to air their grievances, and gaining access to tribunals is certainly not as difficult as getting a case into the ordinary courts.

- *Privacy*

  The final advantage is the fact that proceedings can be taken before a tribunal without triggering the publicity that might follow from a court case.

12.3.6 Disadvantages of tribunals

It is important that the supposed advantages of tribunals are not simply taken at face value. They represent significant improvements over the operation of the ordinary court system, but it is at least arguable that some of them are not as advantageous as they appear at first sight to be, and that others represent potential, if not actual, weaknesses in the tribunal system.

Tribunals are cheap, quick, flexible and informal, but their operation should not be viewed with complacency. These so-called advantages could be seen as representing an attack on general legal standards, and the tribunal system could be portrayed as providing a second rate system of justice for those who cannot afford to pay to gain access to real law in the court system. Vigilance is required on the part of the general community to ensure that this does not become an accurate representation of the tribunal system.

In addition to this general point, there are particular weaknesses in the system of tribunal adjudication. Some of these relate to the following:

- *Appeals procedures*

  There is ground for confusion due to the lack of uniformity in relation to appeals from tribunals. Rights of appeal from decisions of tribunals and the route of such appeals depend on the provision of the statute under which a particular tribunal operates. Where such rights exist, they may be exercised variously – to a further tribunal, to a minister or to a court of law. A measure of coherence would not come amiss in this procedure.

  Prior to the Report of the Franks Committee, tribunals were not required to provide reasons for their decisions and this prevented appeals in most cases. Subsequent to the Report, however, most tribunals, though still not all of them, are required to provide reasons for their decisions under s 10 of the Tribunals and Inquiries Act 1992. The importance of this provision is that, in cases where a tribunal has erred in its application of the law, the claimant can appeal to the High Court for an application for judicial review to have the decision of the tribunal set aside for error of law on the face of the record. All tribunals should be required to provide reasons for their decisions.

- *Publicity*

It was stated above that lack of publicity in relation to tribunal proceedings was a potential advantage of the system. A lack of publicity, however, may be a distinct disadvantage, because it has the effect that cases involving issues of general public importance are not given the publicity and consideration that they might merit.

- *The provision of public funding*

It was claimed previously that one of the major advantages of the tribunal system is its lack of formality and non-legal atmosphere. Research has shown, however, that individual complainants fare better where they are represented by lawyers. Additionally, as a consequence of the Franks recommendations, the fact that chairpersons have to be legally qualified has led to an increase in the formality of tribunal proceedings. As a consequence, non-law experts find it increasingly difficult, in practice, to represent themselves effectively. This difficulty is compounded when the body which is the object of the complaint is itself legally represented; although the parties to hearings do not have to be legally represented, there is nothing to prevent them from being so represented.

This leads to a consideration of the major weakness in the operation of tribunals. Except for the Lands Tribunal, employment appeals tribunals, mental health tribunals and the Commons Commissioners, legal assistance is not available to people pursuing cases at tribunals. They may be entitled to legal advice, but such limited help as is available is unlikely to provide potential complainants with sufficient help to permit them to pursue their case with any confidence of achieving a satisfactory conclusion.

The effect of the replacement of legal aid by the Community Legal Service Fund, under the Access to Justice Act 1999, remains to be seen and fully assessed. It is probably accurate to say, however, that in this particular area, it certainly cannot make matters worse and that the establishment of Community Legal Service Partnerships may well improve the availability of quality advice for those with problems to be decided by tribunals.

If, by and large, tribunals are quicker, cheaper and less formal than courts, then arbitration has similar advantages over tribunals. In the field of employment law, employers have accused employment tribunals of being over-formal, over-complicated, time consuming and expensive. Such complaints led to the setting up of an alternative arbitration procedure to replace the employment tribunal in relation to straightforward unfair dismissal cases. The new arbitration system operates under the auspices of the Advisory, Conciliation and Arbitration Service (ACAS) and came into force in May 2001.

The intention is that the resolution of disputes under the scheme will be confidential, relatively fast and cost-efficient. Procedures under the scheme are non-legalistic and far more informal and flexible than the employment tribunal. The process is inquisitorial rather than adversarial, with no formal pleadings or cross-examination by parties or representatives. Instead of applying strict law, the arbitrator will have regard to general principles of fairness and good conduct in employment relations. The latter will include, for example, principles referred to in the ACAS Code of Practice *Disciplinary and Grievance Procedures* and the ACAS Handbook *Discipline at Work*, which were current at the time of the dismissal. In addition, as it is only possible to appeal or otherwise challenge an arbitrator's award (decision) in very limited circumstances, the scheme should also provide quicker finality of outcome for the parties to an unfair dismissal dispute. Alternatively, this requirement to give up rights that could be insisted upon in the tribunal system might render the ACAS alternative inoperative from the outset.

12.3.7 The Leggatt Review of Tribunals

The obviously apparent proliferation of tribunals operating under a variety of powers gave rise to the perceived need to investigate the whole tribunal system. In May 2000, the Lord Chancellor announced a wide-ranging, independent review of tribunals in England and Wales, to be conducted by Sir Andrew Leggatt. In his report, Sir Andrew found that there were 70 different administrative tribunals in England and Wales, not counting regulatory bodies. Between them they dealt with nearly one million cases a year, but only 20 each heard more than 500 cases a year and many were defunct. He concluded that it was necessary to rationalise and modernise the structure and operation of the tribunal system, and to that end his Review suggested the pursuit of the following main objects:

- *To make the 70 tribunals into one tribunals system*

  This would be achieved by combining the administration of different tribunals, which are concerned with disputes between citizen and State (in the guise of either central or local government) and those which are concerned with disputes between parties within one organisation. It was suggested that only on that basis would tribunals acquire a collective standing to match that of the court system and a collective power to fulfil the needs of users in the way that was originally intended. Within the overall system, the tribunals should be grouped by subject matter into divisions dealing with, for example, education, financial matters, health and social services, immigration, land and valuation, social security and pensions, transport and employment.

- *To render the tribunals independent of their sponsoring departments by having them administered by one Tribunals Service*

  At present, departments of State may provide the administrative support for a tribunal, may pay the fees and expenses of tribunal members, may appoint some of them, may provide IT support (often in the form of access to departmental systems), and may promote legislation prescribing the procedure which it is to follow. On such a basis, the tribunal simply does not appear to be independent of the department it is regulating, nor is it independent in fact. The establishment of a distinct Tribunals Service with the duty to provide all of those services would stimulate both the appearance and reality of independence.

- *To improve the training of chairmen and members*

The review felt that there was a necessity to improve training in the interpersonal skills peculiar to tribunals, the aim being to encourage an atmosphere which would permit the people who use tribunals to represent themselves effectively. It also felt that every effort should be made to reduce the number of cases in which legal representation is needed. That could only be attained, however, by seeking to ensure that:

- ○ decision-makers give comprehensible decisions;
- ○ the Tribunals Service provides users with all requisite information;
- ○ voluntary and other advice groups are funded so that they can offer legal advice; and
- ○ the tribunal chairmen are trained to afford such assistance as they legitimately can by ensuring that the proceedings are intelligible and by enabling users to present their cases.

Sir Andrew recognised that there will always be complex cases in which legal representation is a necessity. However, he suggested that voluntary and community bodies should be funded to provide it and that *only as a last resort should it be provided by legal aid.*

- *There should be clear and effective rights of appeal, replacing the confused and confusing variety of appeal procedures that operate at present*

He recommended that there should be a right of appeal on a point of law, by permission, on the generic ground that the decision of the tribunal was unlawful:

- ○ from the first-tier tribunals in each division to its corresponding appellate tribunal;
- ○ from appellate tribunals to the Court of Appeal; and
- ○ where there was no corresponding appellate tribunal, to any such court as may be prescribed by statute, or in default to such appellate tribunal as may be appointed by the Senior President.

- *Lay members should not sit automatically in any particular case or category of cases*

It was suggested that there was no justification for any members to sit, whether expert or lay, unless they have a particular function to fulfil, as they clearly do in the employment tribunal. In all other divisions, the President (or regional or district chairmen) should have a discretion to decide whether or not lay members should sit in particular classes of cases.

- *There should be active case management of actions*

It was found that, at present, too many cases took too long and were often ill prepared. It was suggested that their length should be measured from the date of the decision giving rise to the action, and that rigorous time constraints should be applied to them, supported by sanctions. In each division, one or more registrars should be responsible for determining what attention each case or type of case should receive.

In March 2003, the LCD revealed the Government's intention to follow Sir Andrew Leggatt's recommendations and to institute a new unified Tribunals Service. The detail of the proposals would appear in a White Paper but, according to Lord Irvine:

> A unified tribunal service will have at its core the top 10 non-devolved tribunals which currently exist throughout departments in Whitehall. By combining the administration we will deliver a more efficient and effective service to the users of tribunals. The new Service will be established as a distinct part of the justice system, *accountable to the Lord Chancellor*. The Service will bring together the 10 largest tribunals from across central Government, with smaller tribunals joining as appropriate.

The 10 tribunals concerned are:

- the Appeals Service;

- the Immigration Appellate Authority;

- the Employment Tribunals Service;

- the Criminal Injuries Compensation Appeals Panel;

- the Mental Health Review Tribunal;

- the Office for Social Security and Child Support Commissioners;

- Tax tribunals;

- the Special Education Needs and Disability Tribunal;

- the Pensions Appeal Tribunal; and

- the Lands Tribunal.

12.4 Ombudsman

As with tribunals, so the institution of the ombudsman reflects the increased activity of the contemporary State. As the State became more engaged in everyday social activity, it increasingly impinged on, and on occasion conflicted with, the individual citizen. Courts and tribunals were available to deal with substantive breaches of particular rules and procedures, but there remained some disquiet as to the possibility of the adverse effects of the implementation of general State policy on individuals. If tribunals may be categorised as an ADR procedure to the ordinary court system in relation to substantive decisions taken in breach of rules, the institution of ombudsman represents a procedure for the redress of complaints about the way in which such decisions have been taken. It has to be admitted, however, that the two categories overlap to a considerable degree. The ombudsman procedure, however, is not just an alternative to the court and tribunal system; it is based upon a distinctly different approach to dealing with disputes. Indeed, the Parliamentary Commissioner Act 1967, which established the position of the first ombudsman, provides that complainants who have rights to pursue their complaints in either of those fora will be precluded from making use of the ombudsman procedure. (Such a prohibition is subject to the discretion of the ombudsman, who tends to interpret it in a generous manner in favour of the complainant.)

The concept of the ombudsman is Scandinavian in origin, and the function of the office holder is to investigate complaints of maladministration; that is, situations where the performance of a government department has fallen below acceptable standards of administration. The first ombudsman, appointed under the 1967 legislation, operated, as the present ombudsman still operates, under the title of the Parliamentary Commissioner for Administration (PCA) and was empowered to consider central government processes only. Since that date, a number of other ombudsmen have been appointed to oversee the administration of local government in England and Wales, under the Local Government Act 1974. Scotland and Northern Ireland have their own local government ombudsmen, who fulfil the same task. There are also Health Service Commissioners for England, Wales and Scotland, whose duty it is to investigate the administration and provision of services in the health service and, in October 1994, Sir Peter Woodhead was appointed as the first Prisons Ombudsman. The ombudsman system has also spread beyond the realm of government administration and there are ombudsmen overseeing the operation of, amongst other things, legal services, banking and insurance. Some schemes, such as the legal services scheme, have been established by statute, but many others have been established by industry as a means of self-regulation; as regards this latter type, the Newspaper Ombudsman does not appear to have been a great success and it has been rumoured that the position might be disbanded.

The European Parliament appointed an ombudsman under the powers extended to it by Art 195 (formerly Art 138(e)) of the Treaty Establishing the European Community (now the EC Treaty). The European Ombudsman has the function of investigating maladministration in all Community institutions, including the non-judicial operation of the European Court of Justice.

Before going on to consider the work of the Parliamentary Commissioner in some detail, mention should also be made of the various regulatory authorities which were established to control the operation of the privatised former State monopolies such as the water, gas, telephone and railway industries. Thus, OFWAT, OFGAS and OFTEL were set up, with part of their remit being to deal with particular consumer complaints as well as the general regulation of the various sectors.

12.4.1 Procedure

Although maladministration is not defined in the Parliamentary Commissioner Act 1967, it has been taken to refer to an error in the way that a decision was reached, rather than an error in the actual decision itself. Indeed, s 12(3) of the Parliamentary

Commissioner Act 1967 expressly precludes the PCA from questioning the merits of particular decisions taken without maladministration. Maladministration, therefore, can be seen to refer to the procedure used to reach a result, rather than the result itself. In an illuminating and much quoted speech introducing the Act, Richard Crossman, then leader of the House of Commons, gave an indicative, if non-definitive, list of what might be included within the term 'maladministration'. The list included the following: bias; neglect; inattention; delay; incompetence; ineptitude; perversity; turpitude; and arbitrariness.

Members of the public do not have the right to complain directly to the PCA; they must channel any such complaint through a Member of Parliament (MP). Complainants do not have to provide precise details of any maladministration; they simply have to indicate the difficulties they have experienced as a result of dealing with an agency of central government. It is the function of the PCA to discover whether the problem arose as a result of maladministration. There is a 12 month time limit for raising complaints, but the PCA has discretion to ignore this.

The powers of the PCA to investigate complaints are similar to those of a High Court judge; thus, they may require the attendance of witnesses and the production of documents, and wilful obstruction of the investigation is treated as contempt of court.

On conclusion of an investigation, the PCA submits reports to the MP who raised the complaint and to the principal of the government office which was subject to the investigation. The ombudsman has no enforcement powers but, if his recommendations are ignored and existing practices involving maladministration are not altered, he may submit a further report to both Houses of Parliament in order to highlight the continued bad practice. The assumption is that, on the submission of such a report, MPs will exert pressure on the appropriate minister of State to ensure that any necessary changes in procedure are made.

Annual reports are laid before Parliament and a Parliamentary Select Committee exists to oversee the operation of the PCA. The operation of the PCA is subject to judicial review (*R v PCA ex p Balchin* (1997)); however, the Parliamentary Commissioner for Public Standards, established after the Nolan Inquiry into 'cash for questions' in Parliament, is not subject to judicial review (*R v Parliamentary Commissioner for Standards ex p Al Fayed* (1997)).

The relationship between the PCA and government is highlighted by three case studies.

12.4.1.1 Barlow Clowes

The first of these concerned the Barlow Clowes group of companies. In 1988, Peter Clowes and three others were arrested and charged with offences in connection with the Prevention of Fraud (Investments) Act 1958 and theft. The prosecution alleged that there had been an investment fraud of over £115 million. The main allegation was that members of the public were induced to deposit their moneys in the belief that they would be invested in gilt-edged securities, but that only £1.9 million was in fact so invested. The rest was misappropriated by the defendants. Clowes alone faced charges of theft totalling some £62 million. The PCA received hundreds of complaints from investors who had lost their money in relation to the Barlow Clowes affair, all alleging maladministration on the part of the Department of Trade and Industry (DTI), which had responsibility for licensing such investment companies. The PCA made five findings of maladministration against the DTI and recommended that compensation should be paid to those who had suffered as a result of it. Surprisingly, the Government initially denied any responsibility for providing compensation. Subsequently, after the PCA had expressed his regret at the Government's initial stance, the latter agreed to pay the recommended compensation payments, amounting to £150 million, but with the rider that it still accepted no legal liability.

12.4.1.2   Child Support Agency

The much criticised Child Support Agency (CSA) had been established in an endeavour to ensure that absent parents, essentially fathers, would have to accept financial responsibility for the maintenance of their children as determined by the Agency. The PCA's report followed complaints referred to him by 95 MPs, covering the time that the Agency started its operations in April 1994 until the end of 1995. Although the PCA investigated 70 complaints, the report focused on seven of those as being representative of the whole. These complaints highlighted a number of failures on the part of the CSA: mistakes as to the identity of individuals subject to the determinations of the CSA; failure to answer correspondence; delay in assessing and reviewing maintenance assessments; delay in actually securing payments due; and the provision of incorrect or misleading advice. The conclusion of the PCA was that the CSA was liable for maladministration, inexcusable delays and slipshod service. In response to the report, the chief executive of the CSA wrote to the PCA, informing him that steps were being taken to deal with the problems highlighted in the report. Such changes in the way that the CSA operated has not staved off its proposed replacement by a more sympathetic and efficient organisation.

12.4.1.3   Channel Tunnel Rail Link

As a consequence of the four year delay on the part of the Department of Transport in deciding on a route for the Channel Tunnel Rail Link, the owners of properties along the various possible routes found the value of their properties blighted, if not unsaleable. The situation was not finalised until the Department announced its final selection in 1994.

According to the PCA:

> The effect of the Department of Transport's policy was to put the project in limbo, keeping it alive when it could not be funded.

As a consequence, he held that the Department:

... had a responsibility to consider the position of such persons suffering exceptional or extreme hardship and to provide redress where appropriate. They undertook no such considerations. That merits my criticism.

The unusual thing about this case, however, was the reaction of the Department of Transport, which rejected the findings of the PCA and refused to provide any compensation. The refusal of the Department of Transport led the PCA to lay a special report before Parliament, consequent upon a situation where an injustice has been found which has not, or will not be, remedied (s 10(3) of the Parliamentary Commissioner Act 1967). Even in the face of the implementation of this extremely rare form of censure, the Government maintained its original policy that it was not liable for the consequences of either general or particular blight. The matter was then taken up by the Select Committee on the Parliamentary Commissioner for Administration, which supported the conclusions of the PCA and recommended that:

... the Department of Transport reconsider its response to the Ombudsman's findings, accept his conclusions that maladministration had occurred ... It would be most regrettable if the department were to remain obdurate. In such an event, we recommend that as a matter of urgency a debate on this matter be held on the floor of the House on a substantive motion in government time [Sixth Report of the PCA].

Such a demonstration of solidarity between the PCA and the Committee had the desired effect, leading to the Government's climb down and payments of £5,000 to those property owners who had suffered as a consequence of the housing blight.

12.4.1.4   Equitable Life Assurance Society

This more recent investigation took place into the role of the Financial Services Authority (FSA) in regulating the conduct of the Equitable Life Assurance Society. In the 1950s the society started selling pension policies with a guaranteed annuity rate (GAR) that allowed policyholders to opt for minimum pension payouts and a bonus when their policy matured. Such policies were sustainable during the high inflation rates of the 1970s, but with current low inflation and interest rates Equitable found it hard to fund its commitments.

Consequently, in an attempt to maintain payments to the majority of its customers who did not hold guarantees, it tried to withdraw the guaranteed payouts. However, in July 2000 the House of Lords ruled that Equitable was required to make good its promises to the 90,000 holders of guaranteed annuity pension policies. As a consequence of this decision, it was apparent that Equitable was not in a position to maintain its payment to its policyholders, and in December 2000 it closed its doors to new business and in July 2001 it announced that it was reducing the value of pension policies for with-profits policyholders by about 16%. Later, in September 2001, Equitable published a compromise proposal for policyholders aimed at salvaging the company's finances and meeting its liabilities. This ensured that the existing GAR policyholders would get a 17.5% increase in the value of their policies, but they would have to sign away their guaranteed pension rights. The other policyholders who were not GAR holders were offered a 2.5% increase on the value of their policies, but they were required to sign away their rights to any legal claims. It has been estimated that some 800,000 policyholders have lost money as a result of the actions of Equitable.

In August 2001, the Government announced the independent Penrose Inquiry into events at Equitable Life; in October 2001, the then parliamentary ombudsman, Michael Buckley, announced that he would be carrying out a statutory investigation into the FSA's handling of events at Equitable Life beginning in 1999, when it had assumed responsibility for the prudential regulation of the life insurance industry.

The investigation by the ombudsman took 20 months, and when the report was issued by the current ombudsman, Ann Abraham, in July 2003, it was not met with uniform approval. The ombudsman 'found no evidence to suggest that the FSA … had failed their regulatory responsibilities during the period under investigation'. As she pointed out:

> … the responsibility for what individual potential investors were actually told when purchasing new policies or annuities was not a matter for the regulator. Given all the publicity surrounding Equitable's high-profile court case and their subsequent decision to put up the company for sale, I would have expected potential investors to have sought independent advice before investing in Equitable.

However, the investigation had highlighted a specific issue that she wished to draw to Parliament's attention. That was the apparent mismatch between public expectations of the role of the prudential regulator and what the regulator could reasonably be expected to deliver. It was never envisaged by those who framed the legislation establishing the regulatory regime that it would provide complete protection for all policyholders. The emphasis was on a 'light touch' approach to regulation and the avoidance of over-interference in a company's affairs.

Referring to calls for her to extend her investigation to an earlier period, the ombudsman stated that:

> I have the very deepest sympathy for those who have suffered financial loss as a result of events at Equitable. However, given my very limited remit and the conclusions I have drawn from the investigation, I do not believe that anything would be gained from my further intervention, nor do I believe I could meet the expectations of policyholders in terms of the remedies they are seeking. It would be offering policyholders false hope were I to suggest otherwise. I have therefore decided not to investigate further complaints about the prudential regulation of Equitable.

The placing of blame on the management of Equitable rather than on the regulator was confirmed when Lord Penrose issued his report in March 2004. The report laid the blame for the affair at the door of Equitable's management in its finding that 'a culture of manipulation and concealment on the part of some of the company's previous senior management allowed a bonus policy to develop that led to the society's financial weakening – a policy left unchecked by its own board'.

In July 2004, the ombudsman reported to Parliament that she would, after all, be conducting a further investigation into the prudential regulation of Equitable Life. As she stated:

> The concerns surrounding the prudential regulation of Equitable Life remain despite the publication of the Penrose Report and the Government's response to it. I took the view that I should consider whether a new investigation by my Office was justified as Lord Penrose did not deal with questions of maladministration – or redress.

In her report, the ombudsman asked the Government to bring the Government Actuary's Department (GAD) into her jurisdiction so that she could assess the GAD's role in the prudential regulation of Equitable. As she stated:

> I consider that there is sufficient initial evidence to suggest that the actions of GAD are key to an assessment of whether maladministration by the prudential regulators caused an injustice to complainants that has not been put right. I believe therefore that GAD's actions must be brought within my jurisdiction.

It was stated that the investigation would cover the actions of the government departments responsible for the prudential regulation of Equitable Life but not concerns around the management of Equitable Life itself, or complaints about the alleged mis-selling of its policies, neither of which is within the ombudsman's remit.

12.4.2 Evaluation

All in all, the ombudsman system appears to function fairly well within its restricted sphere of operation, but there are major areas where it could be improved. The more important of the criticisms levelled at the PCA relate to the following:

- *The retention of MPs as filters of complaints*

  It is generally accepted that there is no need for such a filter mechanism. At one level, it represents a sop to the idea of parliamentary representation and control. However, at the practical level, PCAs have referred complaints made to them directly to the constituent's MP, in order to have them referred back to them in the appropriate form. It is suggested that there is no longer any need or justification for this farce.

- *The restrictive nature of the definition of maladministration*

  It is possible to argue that any procedure that leads to an unreasonable decision must involve an element of maladministration and that, therefore, the definition as currently stated is not overly restrictive. However, even if such reverse reasoning is valid, it would still be preferable for the definition of the scope of the PCA's investigations to be clearly stated, and be stated in wider terms than they are at present.

- *The jurisdiction of the PCA*

This criticism tends to resolve itself into the view that many areas that should be covered by the PCA are not in fact covered by it. For example, as presently constituted, the ombudsman can only investigate the operation of general law. It could be claimed, not without some justification, that the process of making law in the form of delegated legislation could equally do with investigation.

- *The lack of publicity given to complaints*

It is sometimes suggested that sufficient publicity is not given to either the existence of the various ombudsmen or the results of their investigations. The argument is that, if more people were aware of the procedure and what it could achieve, then more people would make use of it, which would lead to an overall improvement in the administration of governmental policies.

- *The reactive role of the ombudsman*

This criticism refers to the fact that the ombudsmen are dependent upon receiving complaints before they can initiate investigations. It is suggested that a more proactive role, in which the ombudsmen would be empowered to initiate investigation on their own authority, would lead to an improvement in general administration, as well as an increase in the effectiveness of the activity of the ombudsman. This criticism is related to the way in which the role of ombudsmen is viewed. If they are simply a problem solving dispute resolution institution, then a reactive role is sufficient; if, however, they are seen as the means of improving general administrative performance, then a more proactive role is called for.

In his Hamlyn Lectures of 1994, the former Lord Chancellor, Lord Mackay, approvingly categorised the ombudsman as:

> Popularly representing justice for the small against the great justice that is quick, inexpensive and unfettered by legalistic procedures, acceptance of the institution of ombudsman now extends well beyond central and local government administration. The concept is widely viewed as a desirable, and even necessary, avenue to fairness wherever the individual is perceived to be at the mercy of an impenetrable administrative system.

12.5 Mediation and Conciliation

The final alternative dispute mechanisms to be considered – mediation and conciliation – are the most informal of all.

12.5.1 Mediation

Mediation is the process whereby a third party acts as the conduit through which two disputing parties communicate and negotiate, in an attempt to reach a common resolution of a problem. The mediator may move between the parties, communicating their opinions without their having to meet or, alternatively, the mediator may operate in the presence of both parties. However, in either situation, the emphasis is upon the parties themselves working out a shared agreement as to how the dispute in question is to be settled.

In his Hamlyn Lecture, Lord Mackay considered three alternative systems of mediation and examined the possibility of annexing such schemes to the existing court system. One, involving lawyers advising parties as to the legal strengths of their relative positions, he rejected on the ground that it merely duplicated, without replacing or extending, what was already available in the courts. A second, based on judges adopting the role of mediators, he rejected on the ground that it might be seen as undermining the traditional impartiality of the judiciary. The third type, and the one that found most favour with him, broadened the issues beyond the legal, to explore solutions that were not available to the court. His approval, however, did not extend to financing such a system; the implication being that public money should, and does, finance the civil justice system and that any benefits that flow from a different system should be financed privately.

In March 1998, the LCD reported that take up of the voluntary mediation procedure offered in the pilot schemes had been fairly low. As regards the pilot scheme established in the Central London County Court, a monitoring report found that only 5% of cases referred to the ADR scheme actually took it up. However, in a more positive mode, the report did find that, in cases that did go to mediation, 62% settled during the process, without going on to court. The conclusion of the report was that mediation was capable of dealing with a wider range of cases than might have been expected, including personal injury cases. It also found that those who participated found the process satisfying and that it led to outcomes that the parties generally found acceptable.

12.5.2   Mediation in divorce

Mediation has an important part to play in family matters, where it is felt that the adversarial approach of the traditional legal system has tended to emphasise, if not increase, existing differences of view between individuals and has not been conducive to amicable settlements. Thus, in divorce cases, mediation has traditionally been used to enable the parties themselves to work out an agreed settlement, rather than having one imposed on them from outside by the courts.

This emphasis on mediation was strengthened in the Family Law Act 1996, but it is important to realise there are potential problems with mediation. The assumption that the parties freely negotiate the terms of their final agreement in a less than hostile manner may be deeply flawed, to the extent that it assumes equality of bargaining power and knowledge between the parties to the negotiation. Mediation may well ease pain but, unless the mediation procedure is carefully and critically monitored, it may gloss over and perpetuate a previously exploitative relationship, allowing the more powerful participant to manipulate and dominate the more vulnerable and force an inequitable agreement. Establishing entitlements on the basis of clear legal advice may be preferable to apparently negotiating those entitlements away in the non-confrontational, therapeutic atmosphere of mediation.

Under the Divorce Reform Act 1969, the concept of no fault divorce was introduced for those couples who had been separated for two years, and it was assumed that this would provide the main grounds for divorce applications. This has not proved to be the case and it is commonly accepted that, because of the two year delay involved, 75% of those seeking divorces still apply on the basis of adultery or unreasonable behaviour, permitting them to complete the procedure in between three and six months.

The Family Law Act 1996 proposed to introduce real no fault divorce by abolishing the grounds of adultery and unreasonable behaviour, but couples would have to wait a minimum of 12 months before their divorce was confirmed. Instead of filing a divorce petition, the person seeking to be divorced would merely be required to submit a statement certifying that their marriage has broken down. The process of divorce would require that the parties attend an informal meeting three months before they made their statement of marital breakdown. They would then have to wait a further nine months for their divorce, during which time they should reflect on whether the marriage could be saved, have an opportunity for reconciliation and consider arrangements relating to finance, property and children. The Act encourages the use of mediation in appropriate cases and allows the court, after it has received a statement of marital breakdown, to direct the parties to attend a meeting with a mediator for an explanation of the mediation process. The role of the mediator is restricted to sorting out the aspects of the divorce relating to finance and children, and should refer the case to an appropriate counsellor if it appears that the parties to the marriage might be open to reconciliation. During the cooling off period, State funding would be available for meetings with marriage guidance counsellors for those eligible for legal aid, and others would be encouraged to take advantage of such marriage support services.

Although the Family Law Act was passed in 1996, the proposed reforms were not implemented immediately and trials were conducted as to the appropriateness of the new procedures. Additionally, the fact that the Act was passed under the previous Conservative administration as a consequence of the strenuous endeavours of the then Lord Chancellor, Lord Mackay, did not prevent the incoming Labour administration's continued support for the proposed reforms. As Lord Irvine LC stated:

> ... in government, we have continued to encourage the use of mediation, most notably in the area of family law, where it is a central tenet of divorce law reform. The importance of mediation and ADR in family law cases can scarcely be understated, given the high incidence of family breakdown and the appaling social consequences which result [Lord Irvine LC, Speech to Faculty of Mediators, 1999].

However, in June 1999, Lord Irvine, the then Lord Chancellor, announced that the Government would not be implementing the new proposals in the Family Law Act in 2000, as had been previously intended. It has to be said that much academic and legal practitioner opinion was dubious about, if not hostile to, the way in which the mediation procedure would operate. It was accepted generally that mediation might work in relation to children, but it was thought that it would be less likely to work where money was concerned and, in those circumstances, it was suggested that people would still be likely to look for their own personal legal representative rather than submit to mediation. It would appear that the results of the trials support such scepticism. Lord Irvine stated that the results of the mediation pilot schemes were disappointing, in that fewer than 10% of divorcing couples in the pilot areas were willing to make use of the preliminary information meetings, which would become compulsory under the Family Law Act's proposals. Of those attending the meetings, only 7% were successfully encouraged to opt for mediation and only 13% took up the offer to see a marriage counsellor. Almost 40% of those attending the meetings stated that they were more convinced of the need to see an independent lawyer to protect their legal rights.

In a speech at the UK Family Law Conference in London on 25 June 1999, Lord Irvine recognised that his decision to postpone the implementation of Pt II of the Family Law Act 1996 raised a question mark over its future, but he went on to say that the final decision depended on the outcome of current and future research into the area.

Unfortunately, at least for proponents of no fault divorce, the outcome of the research proved disagreeable to the LCD and, on 16 January 2001, Lord Irvine announced the Government's intention to repeal Pt II of the Family Law Act 1996. Six versions of the compulsory information meetings, intended to help couples either to save their marriages or to end them with minimum distress and acrimony, had been tested in pilot schemes over a period of two years. The research showed that, although those attending such meetings valued the information gained, it actually tended to incline those who were uncertain about their marriage towards divorce. The Lord Chancellor, however, stated that his concerns did not only relate to information meetings as the complex procedures in Pt II would be likely also to lead to significant delay and uncertainty in resolving arrangements for the future. The Government concluded that such delay would not be in the best interests of either couples or their children.

It is important to note that the repeal of Pt II of the Family Law Act 1996 does not mean the end of mediation. Both the Lord Chancellor and the Government remain strongly committed to advancing the role of mediation in family breakdown.

In March 2004, the Department for Constitutional Affairs (the new name for the LCD) announced that it had given up its intention to pilot 'early intervention' schemes under which separating parents would be presented with parenting plans from which to choose. The schemes were to have been based on a practice that, it was claimed, had reduced the number of court battles over children in the United States. Under the scheme, divorced parents would have been given sample templates for parenting plans, with both being provided generous contact time with their children.

It was also announced in the Green Paper *Parental Separation: Children's Needs and Parents' Responsibilities* that the original planned schemes would be replaced by a more *ad hoc* 'family resolution' scheme, under which parents would be helped by mediation to work out their own plans. The new initiative, under the auspices of the Department for Education and Skills, established pilot mediation schemes in London, Brighton and Sunderland to run from September 2004. Parents who apply to court for contact orders are encouraged to go to mediation to try to agree their own arrangements within two weeks, instead of waiting 16 weeks for a court hearing. Each applicant to the scheme receives an information pack and attends group sessions in which they watch a video showing the experiences of children who have experienced parental separation. Participants are encouraged to produce their own parenting plan with the assistance of a CAFCASS (the Children and Family Court Advisory and Support Service) officer.

12.5.3 Conciliation

Conciliation takes mediation a step further and gives the mediator the power to suggest grounds for compromise and the possible basis for a conclusive agreement. Both mediation and conciliation have been available in relation to industrial disputes, under the auspices of the government funded ACAS. One of the statutory functions of ACAS is to try to resolve industrial disputes by means of discussion and negotiation, or, if the parties agree, it might take a more active role as arbitrator in relation to a particular dispute.

The essential weakness in the procedures of mediation and conciliation lies in the fact that, although they may lead to the resolution of a dispute, they do not necessarily achieve that end. Where they operate successfully, they are excellent methods of dealing with problems as, essentially, the parties to the dispute determine their own solutions and, therefore, feel committed to the outcome. The problem is that they have no binding power and do not always lead to an outcome.

ARBITRATION, TRIBUNAL ADJUDICATION AND ALTERNATIVE DISPUTE RESOLUTION

Alternative dispute resolution has several features that make it preferable to the ordinary court system.

Its main advantages are that it is less antagonistic than the ordinary legal system and it is designed to achieve agreement between the parties involved:

- *Arbitration* is the procedure whereby parties in dispute refer the issue to a third party for resolution, rather than take the case to the ordinary law courts. Arbitration procedures can be contained in the original contract or agreed after a dispute arises. The procedure is governed by the Arbitration Act 1996.

- Advantages over the ordinary court system are:
  - privacy;
  - informality;
  - speed;
  - lower cost;
  - expertise; and
  - less antagonistic.

- *Administrative tribunals* deal with cases involving conflicts between the State, its functionaries and private citizens. Tribunals are subject to the supervision of the Council on Tribunals but are subservient to, and under the control of, the ordinary courts.

Examples of tribunals are:

- employment tribunals;

- social security appeals tribunals; and

- mental health review tribunals.

Advantages of tribunals over ordinary courts relate to:

- speed;

- cost;

- informality;

- flexibility;

- expertise;

- accessibility; and

- privacy.

Disadvantages relate to:

- appeals procedure;

- lack of publicity; and

- the lack of legal aid in most cases.

The Leggatt Review of Tribunals recommended:

- the creation of a single tribunals system with different divisions;

- the creation of a single tribunals service;

- an improvement in training of tribunal chairs;

- active case management of claims; and

- discretion to appoint lay members.

Ombudsmen investigate complaints of maladministration in various areas of State activity. Members of the public must channel complaints through an MP. On conclusion of an investigation, the Parliamentary Commissioner for Administration (PCA) submits reports to the MP who raised the complaint, and to the principal of the government office which was subject to the investigation. He can also report to Parliament.

Shortcomings in the procedure include:

- the MP filter;

- uncertain, if not narrow, jurisdiction;

- lack of publicity; and

- the reactive rather than proactive nature of the role.

Mediation is where a third party only acts as a go-between and cannot decide the matter at issue.

Conciliation is where the third party is more active in facilitating a reconciliation or agreement between the parties than is the case with mediation.

CHAPTER 13

THE CRIMINAL PROCESS: (1) THE INVESTIGATION OF CRIME

13.1   General Introduction to the Criminal Process

13.1.1   The criminal justice system in the 21st century

The criminal justice system has recently been the subject of widespread heated debate in Parliament, the broadcast media and the print media, and in academic and professional journals. The Criminal Justice Act 2003, for example, has 339 sections and makes hundreds of quite significant changes to the operation of the criminal justice system. The changes are in many areas, including those of criminal evidence, bail, juries, and appeals. We examine some of these, where relevant, in this chapter.

Crime levels are notoriously difficult to calculate. Much depends on how crime is defined, perceived and measured. The most recent British Crime Survey (BCS) (*Crime in England and Wales 2003/2004*, Home Office, 2004) indicates that crime levels are declining. Criminal activity seems to have peaked in 1995. The 2003/2004 Survey suggests that crime has fallen by 39% since then. More specifically, crimes of violence have apparently declined by 36% over this period. Acquisitive property crime (for example theft as opposed to criminal damage) has fallen by 46%. Offences involving firearms receive considerable media attention. In 1997/98, there were 4,903 crimes involving firearms (excluding air weapons). In 2003/04, there were 10,340. Although this is a disturbing trend, it should be noted that most firearms offences do not result in fatalities. In 2003/04, 68 homicides involved the use of firearms (compared with 80 in 2002/03).

The 2003/04 Survey also suggests that public anxieties about crime and anti-social behaviour are also declining. It is difficult to reconcile this evidence with the amount of criminal justice legislation recently enacted by Parliament (or with the fact that the prison population has doubled since 1993). The Queen's Speech to Parliament in November proposed 37 pieces of legislation. Eleven of these were relevant to the criminal justice system (Jason Schone, 'The Politics of Fear' (2004), 154, NLJ, 1797).

This chapter and the following one refer to the 'criminal justice system'. This has been for many years an accepted descriptive term used by social scientists, journalists and occasionally lawyers. Officially, however, there is no such thing as the 'criminal justice system'. Governmental responsibilities, for example, overlap in this area. The Home Secretary is responsible for the Metropolitan Police, criminal statistics, the probation service and the Crown Prosecution Service (CPS) (and, more broadly, for 'law and order'), while the Lord Chancellor is responsible for all the criminal law courts, the appointment of magistrates and the judges. Nonetheless, in recent times, there has been increasing governmental recognition of something called the 'criminal justice system'. On 30 December 1998, for example, a single official statement entitled

'Joint Press Release on the Criminal Justice System Public Service Agreement' was issued on behalf of the Home Office, the Lord Chancellor's Department (LCD) and the Attorney General's Office. It stated:

> The overarching aims, objectives and performance measures for the criminal justice system have been published for the first time in a cross departmental Public Service Agreement. The three Departments, and their respective services, will be working more closely than ever before to ensure that the criminal justice system protects the public and delivers justice. Inter-agency co-operation will be promoted at regional, local, as well as at the national level. Ministers believe that these arrangements are a good example of 'joined-up government' in practice.

The significance of such a pronouncement is that it reveals an attempt to make co-ordinated policy in respect of each of these branches of operation. In fact, the statement goes on to become quite explicit:

> The three ministers have set two overarching aims to provide a strategic direction for the system as a whole. They have made clear that every part of the criminal justice system (including the police, courts, Crown Prosecution Service, prison and probation services) should work together so as to best serve and protect the public.
>
> The two overarching aims are:
>
> • to reduce crime and the fear of crime and their social and economic costs; and
>
> • to dispense justice fairly and efficiently and to promote confidence in the rule of law.
>
> Supporting the aims are the following eight objectives:
>
> In support of the first aim:
>
> (1) to reduce the level of actual crime and disorder;
>
> (2) to reduce the adverse impact of crime and disorder on people's lives;
>
> (3) to reduce the economic costs of crime.
>
> In support of the second aim:
>
> (4) to ensure just processes and just and effective outcomes;
>
> (5) to deal with cases throughout the criminal justice process with appropriate speed;
>
> (6) to meet the needs of victims, witnesses and jurors within the system;
>
> (7) to respect the rights of defendants and to treat them fairly;
>
> (8) to promote confidence in the criminal justice system.

In pursuit of these general aims, and in a more recent manifestation of the desire on the part of the government to treat the system as an integrated whole, in February 2001, the Home Office, the LCD and the Attorney General's Office jointly published *Criminal Justice: The Way Ahead* (Cmnd 5074, 2001). There, the government set out its vision for a modern, efficient criminal justice system to help police, prosecutors, courts, prisons and probation officers deal more effectively with offenders, provide a professional service to the general public and step up support for victims and witnesses. The paper proposes that, in order to deliver a new criminal justice 'service', every part of the existing system, from detection, prosecution and punishment to resettlement of prisoners, will be subject to reform and modernisation. Proposals include:

- improved policing – enhanced detective capability, a police service-wide strategic approach to information technology, scientific and technical developments, more officers, greater police visibility and accessibility;

- more effective prosecution – increased investment in the CPS, a specialist body of prosecutors to deal with organised and serious crime, a new consolidated criminal code;

- punishments to fit the criminal as well as the crime – continued oversight and intervention by the criminal justice system of drug addicted offenders, more regard to crime reduction and reparation with new, more flexible community sentences, increase in severity of punishments for persistent offenders, improved supervision and support of short sentence prisoners after release from prison;

- improvements in the experience of victims and witnesses in the criminal justice system – court familiarisation visits and improved court waiting facilities, introduction of victim personal statements enabling victims to indicate the effect of the crime on their lives, better information on progress of the case from the CPS, a possible 'Victim's Fund' to ensure victims are more swiftly compensated, possible introduction of a Victims' Ombudsman to champion victims' interests and the opportunity for victims to report minor crime online.

13.2   Mistrust of the System

There exists mistrust of the criminal justice system from both those who believe innocent people have been convicted and those who think guilty people escape justice. The number of exposed miscarriages of justice involving malpractice and disastrous errors by agencies of the criminal justice system has grown rapidly. On 19 March 1991, the day the Birmingham Six were released from prison having wrongly served 16 years in jail, the Home Secretary announced a Royal Commission on Criminal Justice to examine the system with a view to reducing the chances of wrongful conviction. The Commission published its report with 352 recommendations in July 1993. Some of these recommendations have been implemented in subsequent legislation (like the establishment of the Criminal Cases Review Commission (CCRC) by the Criminal Appeal Act (CAA) 1995). For a useful discussion of these issues, see Annabelle James, 'Miscarriages of justice in the 21st century' (2002) 66(4) Journal of Criminal Law, pp 326–37. Great concern has been expressed by pressure groups about the government's rejection of the Royal Commission's findings in relation to the so called 'right to silence'. This right was effectively undermined by ss 34–37 of the Criminal Justice and Public Order Act (CJPOA) 1994, and this change will arguably increase the chances of miscarriages occurring rather than reduce them. Confidence in the criminal justice system appears to be in decline. In a national survey for the 1962 Royal Commission on the Police (Cmnd 1728, 1962, HMSO), 83% of respondents indicated that they had 'a great deal of respect' for the way the police operated. In a national poll in 1993, conducted by MORI for *The Sunday Times* and the Police Federation, under 50% of respondents indicated that they had 'a great deal of respect' for the way the police operated. The poll also showed that one in six adults (7 million people) actually distrust the police ((1993) *The Sunday Times*, 25 July). In another nationwide poll ((1993) *The Independent*, 21 June), 28% of respondents indicated that they would be 'concerned at what might be going to happen' if stopped by the police, with only 36% of respondents indicating they would be confident that they would be treated fairly.

Public confidence in the police continued to fall in the late 1990s (see, for example, 'Lack of trust at heart of attitude problem' (1999) *The Guardian*, 25 February; 'One in four say police racist' (1999) *The Guardian*, 9 February). This drop in confidence plummeted with particular sharpness after the publication of the Macpherson Report into the racist killing of the black London teenager, Stephen Lawrence. The Report identified various fundamental operational failings of the police and, more significantly, 'institutional racism'. According to a recent survey, 75% of respondents believed that the police did 'a very good' or 'fairly good' job. Of these, 14% thought the police did a 'very good job'. Twenty years earlier, 43% of respondents to a similar survey had answered in this way. Although 76% of respondents were 'confident' or 'fairly confident' that the rights of defendants were respected, 56% believed that the criminal justice system was 'fairly ineffective' or 'totally ineffective'. The survey also revealed widespread dissatisfaction with the sentencing of offenders: 76% believed that sentences were too lenient while only 3% thought they were too severe (Tendler, 'Justice system is failing victims of crime say public' (2003) *The Times*, 10 January).

The amount of bureaucracy associated with modern policing is a related area of public concern. A recent Home Office report revealed that officers in Nottinghamshire spend just 8% of their time 'on the beat'. This figure includes time spent in patrol cars; J. Grimston, 'Police spend up to 90% of their time on red tape', *Sunday Times*, 25 January 2004.

13.2.1 The Macpherson Report

Following the stabbing of Stephen Lawrence, a black teenager from south London, by a group of racist thugs in 1993, defects in several aspects of the English legal system failed to bring his killers to justice. There was a catalogue of profoundly incompetent errors in the way the police handled events. These included: the failure to administer proper first aid at the scene of the attack; a failure to properly search for evidence and suspects; a failure to properly log and investigate tip-offs about the identity of the killers and a failure to treat the family of Stephen Lawrence with proper respect and sensitivity. A judicial inquiry headed by a former High Court Judge, Sir William Macpherson, was set up by the government in 1997 and its report was published in February 1999 (Cm 4262-I, The Stationery Office).

The Report accused the Metropolitan Police (in London) of 'institutional racism'. Its recommendation that the police and several other public services should now be brought fully within the Race Relations Act 1976 has been acted upon by amendments to the 1976 Act contained in the Race Relations (Amendment) Act 2000. The Act now makes it unlawful for a public authority (including the police) to discriminate against a person on racial grounds in carrying out any of its public functions. It also imposes a general duty on specified public authorities (including the police), in carrying out their functions, to have due regard for the need to eliminate unlawful discrimination and to promote equality of opportunity and good relations between persons of different racial groups.

Another recommendation in the Report, to end the ancient principle against 'double jeopardy' – whereby a person cannot be tried more than once for the same, or substantially the same, crime – has now been enacted. The rule arose in an ancient era when there existed none of today's multifarious checks and balances against the abuse of official power (committal proceedings, independent magistrates and judges, random juries, stringent laws of evidence; see Chapter 10). The law was changed by s 75 of the Criminal Justice Act 2003 and retrials are now permitted for certain serious crimes like murder, manslaughter and rape. At the time of the origin of the rule against double jeopardy, powerful aristocrats could, effectively, terrorise individual enemies with the threat of repeated prosecutions. By contrast, in today's setting, provided some form of high level and independent authorisation were to be required before a second prosecution could be brought, there would be no real risk that the threat of re-prosecution would constantly hang over an acquitted defendant's head. Only those fearful of new, viable incriminating evidence for serious crimes would have reason to worry.

The recommendation arose from one twist in the developments in the Lawrence case, in which three suspects were sent for trial at Crown Court after a private prosecution brought by Stephen's father. The trial was stopped by the judge, who ruled that there was insufficient evidence to proceed and ordered the jury to acquit the defendants. The rule of double jeopardy (*autrefois acquit* – the person has been otherwise acquitted) will now prevent any further prosecution being brought against the main suspects, even if strong evidence against them is subsequently found. The feeling that the guilty have got away with such a serious and repulsive crime is widespread. One national newspaper, beneath the banner headline 'Murderers', printed the names and photographs of the five chief suspects of the killing.

The Report recommended (Recommendation 38) that the Court of Appeal should have the power to permit prosecution after acquittal 'where fresh and viable evidence is presented'.

The Home Secretary referred this issue to the Law Commission, which recommended (Law Com 267, 2001) that the rule against double jeopardy should be subject to an exception where new evidence, which appears reliable and compelling as to the accused's guilt, is discovered after acquittal. The exception should apply retrospectively. However, the exception should apply only to murder cases and to genocide cases involving the killing of any person (and also to reckless manslaughter cases should proposals for reform of the law on involuntary manslaughter be enacted). These proposals have now been largely legislated by s 75 of the Criminal Justice Act 2003. The Law Commission also recommended extending the grounds for quashing a tainted acquittal (currently, acquittals resulting from conduct which is an offence involving interference with or intimidation of jurors, witnesses or potential witnesses) to include an offence involving interference with or intimidation of a judge, magistrate or magistrates' clerk. In both instances, the power to quash the acquittal should lie with the Court of Appeal (Criminal Division).

The Report's other recommendations include:

(1) that a ministerial priority be established for all police services 'to increase trust and confidence in policing among minority ethnic communities'.

Comment: Unfortunately, only days after this Report was published, it came to light that a special report commissioned 15 months *previously* showed that 17 out of the 43 police forces of England and Wales did not have any community and race relations policy, despite having been urged to establish one ((1999) *The Times*, 2 March).

(9) that a Freedom of Information Act should apply to all areas of policing, subject only to a 'substantial harm' test for withholding information.

Comment: Both during the investigation and at various stages after the failed public prosecution, the friends and relatives of Stephen Lawrence found it impossible to get clear and accurate information from the police about how the case had been handled and was being taken forward. The more open and transparent a system, the more likely it is to carry public confidence. It seems more likely that this hope will be realised by establishing a role for the CPS in keeping victims informed of the progress of the case (in accordance with the proposals in *Criminal Justice: The Way Ahead*) than by resort to the rather limited rights of access to information given by the Freedom of Information Act 2000.

(11) that the Race Relations Acts should apply to police officers and that Chief Constables should be vicariously liable for the acts and omissions of their officers in this area.

Comment: This proposal would help focus police attention on what might otherwise be unconscious or unintended racist behaviour and has been implemented by amendments to the 1976 Act made by the Race Relations (Amendment) Act 2000.

(33) that the CPS should, in deciding whether to prosecute a racist crime, consider that once the 'evidential test' is satisfied (that is, that there is a 'realistic prospect of conviction'), there is a rebuttable presumption that the public interest test is in favour of prosecution.

Comment: Racism in a crime is currently a factor which should strengthen the chances of a prosecution according to the Code for Crown Prosecutors; the change would make a prosecution more certain in such circumstances. The Code was issued in a revised form in October 2000. It has not been amended to state this proposition specifically but, commenting on the relationship between the evidential and public benefit tests, the Director of Public Prosecutions (DPP), Sir David Calvert-Smith, remarked that the Code creates 'a general presumption in favour of prosecution for all cases in which there is sufficient evidence, unless there are public interest factors that clearly outweigh those in favour of prosecution' ((2000) 150 NLJ 1495). The public interest factor in favour of prosecution relating to (*inter alia*) racist crime has been amended so that it extends beyond an actual racial motivation to encompass a demonstration of hostility towards the victim based on such a factor.

(34) that the police and CPS should take particular care to recognise and to include any evidence of a racial motivation in a crime. The CPS should take care to ensure that any such motivation is referred to at trial and in the sentencing process. No plea bargaining should ever exclude such evidence.

Comment: This highlights that racism is a serious aggravating factor in any crime, as it shows that the innocent victim has been specially and vindictively selected for a reason that is irrational, and therefore, especially terrifying. The Crime and Disorder Act (CDA) 1998 contains provisions which make the committing of various non-fatal offences, harassment, criminal damage and some public order offences separate and more serious offences where they are *racially aggravated* (ss 28–32). It also provides that in all offences, racial aggravation is to be taken into account when determining sentence (s 82). A report of the Crown Prosecution Service Inspectorate has suggested that many racists escape with lenient sentences because prosecutors downgrade charges before cases go to court. In the Inspectorate's survey, one-fifth of race-related charges were found not to properly reflect the gravity of the crime ((2004) *The Independent*, 19 March). The Anti-Terrorism, Crime and Security Act (ACSA) 2001 broadened the scope of s 28 of the CDA 1998. It now refers to 'racially and religiously aggravated offences'.

(41) that consideration be given to the proposition that victims or victims' families should be allowed to become 'civil parties' to criminal proceedings, to facilitate and to ensure the provision of all relevant information to victims and their families.

Comment: Unlike civil litigation, it is the State that prosecutes where there has been a crime; the victim neither determines whether to prosecute nor, if someone is convicted, can they influence the sentence for the crime. Recommendation 41 is therefore a controversial proposal, as there has traditionally been great resistance to permitting citizens to participate in the prosecution of crimes. The essentially communicative role suggested here, however, is arguably different from an influential role.

(42) that there should be advance disclosure of evidence and documents as of right to parties who have leave from a coroner to appear at an inquest.

Comment: Presently, relatives often only discover the terrible details of the death of their loved ones at the inquest in open court, as some coroners will not release any information even to bereaved next of kin before the hearing.

(43) that consideration be given to the provision of legal aid to victims or the families of victims to cover representation at an inquest in appropriate cases.

Comment: This is a recommendation that has been made for many years by various bodies and committees. There is a very strong case for bereaved people *in extremis*, who cannot afford to have representation at the inquest of their loved one, to receive public funding.

Britain is a multi-cultural and ethnically diverse community. Its policing is based on consent rather than sheer strength: there are 60 million citizens and only 127,000 police officers, so it can only work on consent. At the heart of the debate about policing, the law and the criminal justice system in the wake of the Macpherson Report is the question of whether ethnic minorities, especially visible minorities, can quickly be made to feel confident about the way they are treated by the English legal system.

A report produced by the Metropolitan Police Service (MPS) entitled *Stop and Search: Reviewing the Tactic* and two Home Office research papers, *Entry into the Criminal Justice System: A Survey of Police Arrests and their Outcomes* (1998) and *Statistics on Race and the Criminal Justice System* (1998), recognise the disproportionate use of stop and search powers against black people (see Cragg, 'Stop and search powers: research and extension' (1999) Legal Action 3, February). Cragg argues that, 'with the figures already showing that almost 90% of those stopped are not arrested (and therefore, the implication must be that there were, in fact, no grounds to stop and search these people), the training and management strategy proposed by the MPS "to manage the tactic more fairly and effectively" must be rigorously imposed and monitored if it is to have any chance of success'. A study by Miller, Quinton and Bland (Police Research Series Papers 127–32, September 2000) examined the disproportionate use of stops and searches by measuring populations 'available' to be stopped and searched by the police (those in public places where and when stops or searches are carried out). It found that in areas with high stop and search activity, young men and people from minority ethnic backgrounds tended to be over-represented in the available population. On the other hand, the findings suggested that, within the available population, no general pattern of bias against people from minority ethnic groups was evident, either as a whole or for particular groups. Comparing statistics on stops and searches with available populations showed that white people tended to be over-represented, Asian people tended to be under-represented (with some exceptions), and black people's representation varied (with examples of both over and under-representation). However, the report concluded that despite these findings, the possibility of discrimination by officers in their use of stops and searches could not be dismissed. The exercise of stop and search powers by the police is governed by the revised Code of Practice A (see 13.3.14 below), which states that it is important that these powers are used fairly and responsibly. It warns, 'any misuse of the powers is likely to be harmful to policing and can lead to mistrust of police'.

13.2.2   Lack of confidence in the system

The British Crime Survey 2003–2004 (Home Office, 2004) suggests that most people (77%) believe that the criminal justice system respects the rights of individuals accused of offences and generally treats them fairly. This may reflect widespead confidence in the system. Alternatively, it may imply that many people feel that the system attaches too much importance to the rights of possible offenders.

People seem to have much less confidence regarding the *effectiveness* of the criminal justice system. Only 35% of those surveyed expressed confidence that the system is effective at reducing crime. A mere 24% believed that it is effective in dealing with young people accused of offences.

Although the BCS survey suggests that crime against individuals living in private households may be declining (11.7 million incidents in 2003/04 compared with 11.2 million a year earlier), most people seem to think that crime is increasing. Curiously, individuals seem to believe that the situation is less bad in their own areas than in 'the country as a whole'. When asked about the national situation, 65% of the BCS respondents claimed that crime had increased in the previous two years; 31% said that crime had increased 'a lot'.

When asked about their own areas, the figures were 48% and 20% respectively.

In 2003–04, the police in England and Wales recorded a total of 5.9 million offences (*Crime in England and Wales 2003/2004*, Home Office, 2002). This figure is 1% higher than the one for 2002–03. Certain types of offence, like domestic burglary, theft of and from vehicles and vandalism against vehicles and other household and personal property, have greatly vexed large sections of the population. Just over 11.7 million BCS crimes are comparable with those recorded by police statistics. However, a large proportion of crime is unrecorded, as many offences are not reported to the police.

13.2.3 A contradiction

There is a friction between the sort of policies that these two concerns generate, that is, people seem to want the police to have greater powers to combat crime, and yet contradictorily want greater controls on the police and evidence so as to avoid more miscarriages of justice. It is argued that if we wish to avoid unjust convictions like those of the Winchester Three, the Guildford Four, the Birmingham Six, the Maguire Seven, the Tottenham Three, Stefan Kiszko, Judith Ward and the Bridgewater Three ((1997) *The Guardian*, 21, 22 February), we should tighten the rules of evidence and procedure that govern the investigation and prosecution of crime. Against this, it has been argued (for example, by Charles Pollard, Chief Constable of the Thames Valley Police: letter (1995) *The Times*, 12 April; article (1995) *The Sunday Times*, 9 July) that the police should have greater powers and that the trial process should be tilted less in favour of the defendant. The rules on disclosure of evidence in criminal trials, for example, have been radically changed by the Criminal Procedure and Investigations Act (CPIA) 1996. In particular, the material the prosecution has to disclose to the defence is now staged and brought within a more restrictive framework and now, for the first time, the defence has a duty to disclose its case in advance of trial.

One problem, therefore, in this area of the English legal system is that as the growing problems of crime, and the fear of crime, become more important concerns of government, there are two lobbies for change that are emerging, lobbies which are diametrically opposed.

The criminal process is examined here in two chapters. This chapter considers the law relating to important pre-trial matters up to and including the admissibility of confession evidence in court. Chapter 10 looks at institutional and procedural aspects of prosecution and matters relating to bail, the classification of offences, trials, plea bargaining and the jury. In examining all these topics, it is important to keep in mind the various aims of the criminal justice system and the extent to which the existing law serves these aims. Amongst the aims to be borne in mind are the following:

- to detect crime and convict those who have committed it;

- to have rules relating to arrest, search, questioning, interrogation and admissibility of evidence which do not expose suspects to unfair treatment likely to lead to unjust convictions;

- to have rules as above which do not unnecessarily impede the proper investigation of crime;

- to ensure that innocent persons are not convicted;

- to maintain public order;

- to maintain public confidence in the criminal justice system;

- to properly balance considerations of justice and fair procedure with those of efficiency and funding.

13.2.4 Contemporary issues

The criminal justice system is bearing signs of strain as it tries to cope with a society in the throes of major transitions: changes in the pattern of family life, changes in the nature of employment expectations and a revolution in information and communications technology.

In 1993, the prison population of England and Wales was 42,000 (this includes those incarcerated in young offender institutions). By 31 May 2005 this had risen to 76,607. The prison population is currently near capacity and rising at a rate of approximately 200 per month.

The Police and Magistrates' Courts Act 1994 amended the Police Act 1964, permitting Home Secretaries now to 'determine objectives for the policing of all of the areas of all police authorities'. Under this power, a new police mission statement was announced in 1999. The purpose of the police according to this is 'to help secure a safe and just society in which the rights and responsibilities of individuals, families and communities are properly balanced'. This raises many contentious issues, as the determination of, for example, what is a 'just society' becomes something which is more overtly a matter for policing policy than in previous times when the police role was more simply (in the words of Robert Peel, the 19th century founder of modern policing) to 'prevent and detect crime'.

Yet, can 135,000 police officers do well enough to retain credibility in a society of 60 million people undergoing all sorts of social upheavals? In 1998, the police had to respond to 17.8 million incidents and 7.5 million 999 calls. The racist canteen culture revealed in the wake of the Stephen Lawrence Inquiry (see 13.2.1 above) and the recognition in 1998 by the Commissioner for the Metropolitan Police that he probably had 250 corrupt officers on his force did not help raise public confidence. In October 2003 BBC1 broadcast an extremely disturbing undercover documentary titled 'Secret Policeman'. It revealed strong evidence of racism amongst new recruits at a police training centre in Cheshire.

It is not clear yet what the main thrust of governmental policy is in relation to the criminal justice system. Thus far, we have seen an unusual cocktail consisting of several privatisation measures and a good dose of centralisation.

Criminal justice has historically been regarded by government as a matter for the State. Recently, however, first under the Conservative government in the early 1990s and now under Labour, various parts of the system have been privatised. Such moves have not generally been seen as runaway successes. In November 1998, there was public scandal at the extent of injury to prison officers and trainers and damage to the premises of the country's leading private institution for young offenders. It was revealed that over £100,000 of damage had been wrought by wild 12–14 year olds at the Medway Secure Training Centre in Kent. After more than one fiasco, privatised prison escort services have come in for severe criticism, and a provision of the CJPOA 1994 allowing for private sponsorship of police equipment has been a boon for satirical cartoonists.

By contrast, there are several ways in which aspects of the criminal justice system, historically all independent from each other and detached from governmental control, have been drawn within the influence of central government. It has, for example, been a hallowed precept of the British constitution that police forces are local and not governmental agencies. Yet, under Conservative legislation, the Home Secretary became allowed to 'determine objectives for the policing of the areas of all police authorities'.

More worryingly, there has been a notable governmental move to integrate different organisational functions. The CPS has been restructured so that its erstwhile 13 regions are turned into 42 to match the 43 police forces of England and Wales. This is a remarkable swerve from previous policy. Close and often cosy relations between police officers and the lawyers who used to prosecute their cases (sometimes with atrocious malpractice) were the very reason for the establishment of the CPS.

However, moves towards criminal justice system unification go further than this. The Lord Chancellor announced in 1997 (*Ministerial Statement to the House of Lords*, 29 October) that the 96 Magistrates' Courts Committees (which administer the courts dealing with 95% of all criminal cases) should enjoy much greater alignment with the police and the CPS.

Most disturbing of all for some are the foundations for the Criminal Defence Service (CDS) (laid in the Access to Justice Act 1999 and finally established in April 2001) which will give the government greater control over legal representation. The

Law Society has pointed out that campaigning lawyers like Gareth Pierce, who represented the Guildford Four, and Jim Nicol, who represented the appellants in the Carl Bridgewater case, could be avoided by the new body.

There is also reason for disquiet about the law contained in the Terrorism Act 2000, which makes the opinion of a police officer admissible evidence in court – proof of membership of a proscribed organisation may be based in part upon the opinion of a senior police officer. In the wake of considerable evidence (from miscarriage of justice cases, especially those involving suspects of terrorism from Northern Ireland) that some police officers were apparently prepared to lie and falsify evidence to secure convictions, the new law has caused some people to become alarmed at the prospect that a person could be convicted of a serious offence on evidence taken mainly from the opinion of a police officer.

Proactive 'intelligence-led' policing has become increasingly commonplace in recent years, especially in relation to drugs and organised crime. Such techniques inevitably involve deception by police officers and their informers (see C Dunnighan and C Norris, 'A risky business: the recruitment and running of informers by English police officers' (1996) 19 Police Studies 1). This may involve testing whether a person is willing to commit an offence. Although English law has never recognised a defence of entrapment, entrapment may be a mitigating factor and a ground for excluding evidence; *R v Looseley; Attorney General's Reference (No 3 of 2000)* (2002). See Andrew Ashworth, 'Re-drawing the boundaries of entrapment' [2002] Crim LR 161–79.

Until recently, foreign persons (that is, non-British nationals) suspected of involvement in terrorist activities could be detained without trial under the provisions of Part 4 of the Anti-terrorism, Crime and Security Act 2001. Detention without trial obviously breached Art 5(1) of the European Convention on Human Rights. The policy was justified under Art 15 which permits derogation from Art 5(1) in time of war 'or other public emergency threatening the life of the nation'. The House of Lords addressed the issue in 2004; *A and X and Others* [2004].

UKHL 56. Their Lordships decided the case against the Government. Lord Hoffmann rejected the view that modern terrorists a threat to the life of the nation (and therefore that a 'state of emergency' was appropriate): 'The real threat to the life of the nation ... comes not from terrorism but from laws such as these'. See P. Mendelle, 'No detention please, we're British?' (2005), 155, NLJ, 77. Although the Government could (theoretically) have ignored this decisive rebuff, it accepted the constitutional reality that the law had to change. Recent legislation makes provision for 'control orders'. Although controversial, these are less restrictive than formal detention without trial. See M. Zander, 'The Prevention of Terrorism Act 2005' (2005), 155, NLJ, 438–39. According to Doug Jewell, Liberty's campaign director: 'The Prevention of Terrorism Act 2005 is a fundamentally flawed piece of legislation. No one knows how [the orders] are going to be enacted ... It's going to be a policing nightmare'. See ' "Profound unese" over control orders' (2005), 155, NLJ, 394.

13.3 Arrest

According to AV Dicey, 'individual rights are the basis not the result of the law of the constitution' (*Law of the Constitution*, 6th edn, p 203; cited by Judge LJ in *R v Central Criminal Court ex p The Guardian, The Observer and Bright* (2002)). Before considering the rights of the citizen and the law governing arrest and detention, what happens in the police station and what evidence is admissible in court, it is appropriate to look first at what the citizen can do if those rights are violated.

13.3.1 Remedies for unlawful arrest

Like other areas of law where the liberty of the subject is at stake, the law relating to arrest is founded upon the principle of *justification*. If challenged, the person who has attempted to make an arrest must justify his actions and show that the arrest was lawful. Failing this, the arrest will be regarded as unlawful.

There are three possible remedies:

- The person, or someone on his behalf, can bring proceedings of habeas corpus. This ancient prerogative writ used to begin with the words 'habeas corpus', meaning 'you must have the body'. It is addressed to the detainer and asks him to bring the detainee in question before the court at a specified date and time. The remedy protects the freedom of those who have been unlawfully detained in prison, hospital, police station or private custody. The writ is applied for from a judge in chambers and can, in emergencies, be made over the telephone. It must be issued if there is *prima facie* evidence that the detention is unlawful. As every detention is unlawful, the burden of proof is on the detainer to justify his conduct. If issued, the writ frees the detainee and thus allows him to seek other remedies (below) against the detainer.

- To use the illegality of the detention to argue that any subsequent prosecution should fail. This type of argument is very rarely successful as illegally obtained evidence is not, *ipso facto*, *automatically rendered* inadmissible. The House of Lords ruled in *R v Sang* (1979) that no discretion existed to exclude evidence simply because it had been illegally or improperly obtained. A court could only exclude relevant evidence where its effect would be 'unduly prejudicial'. This is reflected in s 78(1) of the Police and Criminal Evidence Act (PACE) 1984. This perhaps surprising rule was supported by the Royal Commission on Criminal Justice (although the argument there was chiefly focused on the admissibility of confession evidence). Professor Zander, however, in a note of dissent, contested the idea that a conviction could be upheld despite serious misconduct by the prosecution if there is other evidence against the convicted person. He states: 'I cannot agree. The moral foundation of the criminal justice system requires that, if the prosecution has employed foul means, the defendant must go free if he is plainly guilty ... the conviction should be quashed as an expression of the system's repugnance.' An extreme case might involve the admissibility of confession evidence obtained by torture by the authorities in another country. Since the Human Rights Act (HRA)

1998 became fully operative in October 2000, it has no longer been possible to treat such issues merely as involving interpretation of s 78(1) of PACE 1984 itself. Additionally, any court must take Art 6 of the European Convention on Human Rights (ECHR) into account in appropriate circumstances. For further discussion of this aspect, see 13.5.26 below.

- An action for damages for false imprisonment. In some cases, the damages for such an action would be likely to be nominal if the violation by the detainer does not have much impact on the detainee. Consider cases under this heading like *Christie v Leachinsky* (1947). Damages can, however, be considerable. In *Reynolds v Commissioner of Police for the Metropolis* (1982), a jury awarded £12,000 damages to the plaintiff. She had been arrested in the early hours in connection with charges of arson for gain, that is, that insured houses, which had been set alight deliberately, would be the subject of 'accidental fire' insurance claims. She was taken by car to a police station, a journey which took two and a half hours. She was detained until about 8 pm when she was told there was no evidence against her. She arrived home about 11 pm. The judge, Caulfield J, ruled that the police had no reasonable grounds for suspecting the plaintiff of having committed an arrestable offence and he directed the jury in relation to damages. The jury awarded £12,000 and the defendant's appeal against this sum as excessive was dismissed.

  In a review of trends in actions against the police, Sadiq Khan and Matthew Ryder ((1998) Legal Action 16, September) comment on two cases in relation to damages. In *Goswell v Commissioner of Police for the Metropolis* (1998), a jury awarded damages totalling £302,000 to Mr Goswell, comprising £120,000 for assault, £12,000 for false imprisonment and £170,000 exemplary damages. On appeal, Simon Brown LJ held that £100 was an appropriate award for basic damages for false imprisonment for 20 minutes. He allowed for the fact that the unlawfulness of the detention was a consequence of a breach of s 28 of PACE 1984 and expressed the opinion that the case 'does not in the fullest sense involve a wrongful deprivation of liberty'. Basic damages were assessed at £22,500, aggravated damages at £10,000 and £15,000 for exemplary damages. Overall, the figure was reduced from £302,000 to £47,500. In a second case against the police, *Commissioner of Police for the Metropolis v Gerald* (1998), an initial award by a jury of £125,000 for assault, false imprisonment and malicious prosecution was reduced to £50,000 on appeal by the Commissioner.

Apart from the question of civil remedies, it is important to remember the following:

- If the arrest is not lawful, there is the right to use reasonable force to resist it: *R v Waterfield* (1964); *Kenlin v Gardner* (1967). This is a remedy, however, of doubtful advisability, as the legality of the arrest will only be properly tested after the event in a law court. If a police officer was engaged in what the courts decide was a lawful arrest or conduct, then anyone who uses force against the officer might have been guilty of an offence of assaulting an officer in the execution of his duty, contrary to s 89(1) of the Police Act 1996.

- That, for our purposes in considering the consequences for an unlawfully arrested person faced with prosecution, s 78 of PACE 1984 states:

78(1) In any proceedings, the court may refuse to allow evidence on which the prosecution proposes to rely to be given if it appears to the court that, having regard to all the circumstances, including the circumstances in which the evidence was obtained, the admission of the evidence would have such an adverse effect on the fairness of the proceedings that the court ought not to admit it.

13.3.2   General powers of arrest

In *Spicer v Holt* (1977), Lord Dilhorne stated:

> Whether or not a person has been arrested depends not upon the legality of the arrest, but on whether he has been deprived of his liberty to go where he pleases.

So, a person detained by the police against his will is arrested. Whether this arrest is lawful will depend on whether the conditions for a lawful arrest have been satisfied.

Lawful arrests are those: (1) under warrant (2) without warrant at common law or (3) without warrant under legislation.

13.3.3   Arrest under warrant

The police lay a written information on oath before a magistrate that a person 'has, or is suspected of having, committed an offence' (s 1 of the Magistrates' Courts Act 1980). The Criminal Justice Act (CJA) 1967 provides that warrants should not be issued unless the offence in question is indictable or is punishable with imprisonment.

Until recently, complex extradition arrangements existed between the Member States of the European Union (EU). In December 2001, the EU agreed in principle to introduce European arrest warrants. The decision was formally adopted in June 2002. The traditional approach (found in extradition agreements) embodied the principle of 'dual criminality'; that is, a person would not be extradited from one State to another unless his alleged offence was an extraditable crime in both countries. This requirement has now been removed from a list of 32 offences. The inclusion of 'racism and xenophobia' has aroused some controversy. See Susie Allegre, 'The myth and the reality of a modern European judicial space' (2002) 152 NLJ 986–87.

13.3.4   Common law arrests

The only power to arrest at common law is where a breach of the peace has been committed and there are reasonable grounds for believing that it will be continued or renewed, or where a breach of the peace is reasonably apprehended. Essentially, it requires *conduct* related to violence, real or threatened. A simple disturbance does not, in itself, amount to a breach of the peace unless it results from violence, real or threatened.

In 1981, two cases decided within months of each other offered definitions of a breach of the peace, in an attempt to bring some clarification to an area of law that previously was in doubt. In *R v Howell* (1981), the defendant was arrested after being involved in a disturbance at a street party in the early hours of the morning. Watkins LJ, who delivered the judgment of the court, observed that there was a power of arrest for anticipated breach of the peace provided the arrestor had been witness to the earlier shouting and swearing of H, and therefore had reasonable grounds for belief, and did believe at the time that the defendant's conduct, either alone or as part of a general disturbance, was likely to lead to the use of violence by the defendant or someone else in the officer's presence.

The court adopted the following definition of 'breach of the peace' – it occurs:

> Wherever harm is actually done or is likely to be done to a person or in his presence his property or a person is in fear of being so harmed through an assault, an affray, a riot, unlawful assembly or other disturbance.

In the second of the two cases, *R v Chief Constable of the Devon and Cornwall Constabulary ex p Central Electricity Generating Board (CEGB)* (1981), Lord Denning MR suggested that breach of the peace might be considerably wider than this. This case involved a group of protesters who had occupied private land in order to prevent CEGB employees from carrying out a survey to assess its suitability for a nuclear power station. The protest was intended to be peaceful and non-violent. Lord Denning MR suggested that:

> There is a breach of the peace whenever a person who is lawfully carrying out his work is unlawfully and physically prevented by another from doing it … If anyone unlawfully and physically obstructs the worker, by lying down or chaining himself to a rig or the like, he is guilty of a breach of the peace.

He appears to have been saying (Feldman, *Civil Liberties and Human Rights in England and Wales* (1993), pp 788–89) not that a breach of the peace is automatic in such circumstances, but that in the context of the *CEGB* case, any obstruction or unlawful *resistance* by the trespasser could give the police a reasonable apprehension of a breach of the peace, in the sense of violence.

However, in cases that have followed (such as *Parkin v Norman* (1982), *Percy v DPP* (1995) and *Foulkes v Chief Constable of Merseyside Police* (1998)), it is the definition in *R v Howell* that has been preferred. Despite earlier doubts, argues Parpworth ('Breach of the peace: breach of human rights?' (1998) 152 JP 6, 7 November), the recent decision of the European Court of Human Rights (ECtHR) in *Steel and Others v UK* (1998) brings clear and authoritative clarification to this area of law. This case represents 'a clear endorsement by a court largely unfamiliar with the common law concept of a breach of the peace that such a concept is in accordance with the terms of the European Convention on Human Rights'.

At common law, a constable may arrest a person for conduct which he genuinely suspects might be likely to cause a breach of the peace even on private premises where no member of the public is present: *McConnell v Chief Constable of Manchester* (1990). Although mere shouting and swearing alone will not constitute a breach of the peace, it is an offence under s 28 of the Town Police Causes Act 1847 and could lead to an arrest under s 25 of PACE 1984 (general arrest conditions). If it causes harassment, alarm or distress to a member of the public, it may constitute an offence under s 5 of the Public Order Act 1986.

13.3.5 Arrest under legislation

The right to arrest is generally governed by s 24 of PACE 1984. Originally, this provided that the police may arrest without a warrant for 'arrestable offences' and certain other offences. An arrestable offence is one for which the sentence is fixed by law (there are very few of these, life imprisonment for murder being the most common); any offence for which a person could be liable to a sentence of five years' imprisonment or more on first conviction; any one of the offences which were listed in s 24(2); and any attempt to commit any of the above. The offences listed in s 24(2) involved Customs and Excise, the Official Secrets Acts, indecent assaults on women, taking a motor vehicle without authority, going equipped for stealing and certain offences relating to obscenity and indecent photographs and pseudo-photographs of children.

There are differences between the powers of arrest given by s 24 of PACE 1984 to police constables and ordinary citizens.

Prof J. R. Spencer QC noted that 'In essence, the only real limit on the powers of the police to arrest without warrant for offences taking place before their eyes is that they cannot automatically use it for minor offences (for example dropping litter), as a means of enforcing social discipline.' ('Extending the Police State' (2005), 155, NLJ, 477).

The law has recently been changed.

13.3.5.1 Serious Organised Crime and Police Act 2005

Part 3 of this Act, which came into force in 2006, makes a number of changes to police powers set out in the Police and Criminal Evidence Act 1984 (PACE) and extends the powers of Community Support Officers (CSOs) and other persons designated or accredited under the provisions of the Police Reform Act 2002.

Sections 110, 111, 113 and 114 and Schedule 7 revise the framework of arrest and search powers in PACE. In particular they provide, in the case of a constable's power of arrest, for all offences to be 'arrestable' subject to a necessity test. This means that someone who has committed a relatively low order criminal offence, like littering, could, in theory, be arrested if an officer deemed it necessary and was able to satisfy his or her desk sergeant at the police station that this was so. That might occur, for example, if the person being requested to pick up the litter refused to do so, and then refused to give his or her name to the officer.

Section 110 states:

(1) For section 24 of PACE (arrest without warrant for arrestable offences) substitute-24 Arrest without warrant: constables

    (1) A constable may arrest without a warrant-

        (a) anyone who is about to commit an offence;

        (b) anyone who is in the act of committing an offence;

        (c) anyone whom he has reasonable grounds for suspecting to be about to commit an offence;

(d) anyone whom he has reasonable grounds for suspecting to be committing an offence.

(2) If a constable has reasonable grounds for suspecting that an offence has been committed, he may arrest without a warrant anyone whom he has reasonable grounds to suspect of being guilty of it.

(3) If an offence has been committed, a constable may arrest without a warrant-

(a) anyone who is guilty of the offence;

(b) anyone whom he has reasonable grounds for suspecting to be guilty of it.

(4) But the power of summary arrest conferred by subsection (1), (2) or (3) is exercisable only if the constable has reasonable grounds for believing that for any of the reasons mentioned in subsection (5) it is necessary to arrest the person in question.

(5) The reasons are-

(a) to enable the name of the person in question to be ascertained (in the case where the constable does not know, and cannot readily ascertain, the person's name, or has reasonable grounds for doubting whether a name given by the person as his name is his real name);

(b) correspondingly as regards he person's address;

(c) to prevent the person in question-

(i) causing physical injury to himself or any other person;

(ii) suffering physical injury;

(iii) causing loss of or damage to property;

(iv) committing an offence against public decency (subject to subsection (6)); or

(v) causing an unlawful obstruction of the highway;

(d) to protect a child or other vulnerable persons from the person in question;

(e) to allow the prompt and effective investigation of the offence or of the conduct of the person in question;

(f) to prevent any prosecution for the offence from being hindered by the disappearance of the person in question.

(6) Subsection (5)(c)(iv) applies only where members of the public going about their normal business cannot reasonably be expected to avoid the person in question.

24A Arrest without warrant: other persons

(1) A person other than a constable may arrest without a warrant-

(a) anyone who is in the act of committing an indictable offence;

(b) anyone whom he has reasonable grounds for suspecting to be committing an indictable offence.

(2) Where an indictable offence has been committed, a person other than a constable may arrest without a warrant-

(a) anyone who is guilty of the offence;

    (b) anyone whom he has reasonable grounds for suspecting to be guilty of it.

  (3) But the power of summary arrest conferred by subsection (1) or (2) is exercisable only if-

    (a) the person making the arrest has reasonable grounds for believing that for any of the reasons mentioned in subsection (4) it is necessary to arrest the person in question; and

    (b) it appears to the person making the arrest that it is not reasonably practicable for a constable to make it instead.

  (4) The reasons are to prevent the person in question-

    (a) causing physical injury to himself or any other person;

    (b) suffering physical injury;

    (c) causing loss of or damage to property; or

    (d) making off before a constable can assume responsibility for him."

(2) Section 25 of PACE (general arrest conditions) shall cease to have effect.

(3) In section 66 of PACE (codes of practice), in subsection (1)(a)-

  (a) omit 'or' at the end of sub-paragraph (i),

  (b) at the end of sub-paragraph (ii) insert 'or (iii) to arrest a person;'

(4) The sections 24 and 24A of PACE substituted by subsection (1) are to have effect in relation to any offence whenever committed.

Section 112 introduces a new offence of failing to obey a police direction to leave an exclusion area. Section 115 extends the powers of the police, in s 1 of PACE, to stop and search persons suspected of carrying prohibited fireworks.

Sections 116 to 118 enable the police to take photographs and fingerprints of persons away from a police station and to take impressions of a person's footwear at a police station. The power to take photographs is extended to CSOs and accredited persons in limited circumstances. Section 116(3) amends s 64A of PACE to allow the police to pass a photograph to the court for the purposes of enforcing the orders of the court. This new power is in addition to that which already allows the police to pass a photograph to the court for the purposes of prosecution. Section 119 amends the definition of an intimate and non-intimate sample.

Sections 120 and 121 create a new category of designated person under the Police Reform Act 2002, namely a 'staff custody officer', thereby enabling police staff to undertake custody functions previously restricted to police officers.

Sections 122 and 123 and Schedules 8 and 9 extend the powers of CSOs, other designated police staff and accredited persons and enable police staff to access certain information relating to drivers, vehicle registration plate suppliers and motor insurance.

These are highly controversial new powers. The case to extend powers for the police is built on the idea that those who have done nothing wrong will have nothing to fear from the exercise of the powers. The extension of police powers is also defended on the grounds that any arrest, to be lawful, must be 'necessary' (see s 24(5) of PACE as amended, above, by s110 of the Serious Organised Crime and Police Act.

There are, however, clear reasons for concern at this development. A society in which the police have unlimited powers can be described as a 'police state', and such tyranny is almost universally disfavoured. That of course, is very far from the position now in the UK, a country which has what are among the best protected liberties in the world. However, the closer that law in the UK moves towards giving the police very wide powers to arrest, the greater the need for concern. A society in which people can be arrested for any offence, in which CCTV is ubiquitous (Surveillance UK, *The Independent*, 22 December 2005) and in which police 'success' is progressively measured by how many arrests and crimes solved, might reduce certain sorts of offending (although many sorts of criminality are not reduced by such policies) but how comfortable a place would it be to live? The inhabitants of many countries in which there are dictatorial governments and no respect for civil liberties do not seem to rejoice in the crime-free streets. At all events, the most desirable balance between *freedom not to be interfered with by police officers* and *policing which improves society by effectively reducing crime* is ultimately a political question for the public rather than the small section of the public comprised by judges, lawyers and police officers.

13.3.6 *G v DPP* (1989)

In *G v DPP* (1989), the appellant (G) with other juveniles, including a co-accused, Gill, went to a police station to complain about being ejected from a public service vehicle. On being asked for their names and addresses by the officer, G, the appellant, refused to do so; some of the others gave false particulars, but Gill gave his real name and address. The officer did not accept that Gill's particulars were correct because in his experience people who committed offences did not give correct details (even though the juveniles had only gone to the police station to complain about the way they had been treated on the bus). The juveniles would not accept the officer's advice about their complaint and became threatening and abusive. Gill was arrested for 'disorderly behaviour in a police station' and he struggled and resisted; the appellant joined in, punching the officer and causing him to lose hold of Gill. Both Gill and G were convicted of assaulting a police officer in the execution of his duty. The Divisional Court quashed their convictions. The offence of 'violent behaviour' or 'disorderly behaviour' under the Town Police Causes Act 1847 was not an arrestable offence. The only power the officer therefore had to arrest Gill was under s 25(3) of PACE 1984 if there were genuine doubts about Gill's name and address. But the ground given by the officer – about people who commit offences not giving their proper name, etc – was not a proper ground because there was no evidence that the youths had committed any offences; they had gone to the police simply to complain. Therefore, in purporting to arrest Gill, the officer had not been acting in the execution of his duty and the appellant could not, therefore, have been guilty of obstructing him in the performance of such duty.

It should be noted in particular that, under s 24(6), no offence need actually have been committed. All that is required is that the police officer reasonably believes that an arrestable offence has been committed.

The differences in the powers of arrest in s 24 are based on whether an offence:

- *is being* committed: anyone may make the arrest; see s 24(4);

- *has been* committed: anyone may make the arrest; see s 24(5) or the wider powers of the police (s 24(6)) who can arrest where they have 'reasonable grounds for suspecting that an arrestable offence has been committed' whether one has in fact been committed or not;

- *is about to be* committed: only a police officer may act here; see s 24(7).

PACE 1984 preserves an old common law distinction in respect of the powers of constables and private individuals when making such arrests. Where an arrest is being made *after* an offence is thought to have been committed, then PACE 1984 confers narrower rights upon the private individual than on the police officer.

13.3.7 *Walters v WH Smith & Son Ltd* (1914)

In *Walters v WH Smith & Son Ltd* (1914), the defendants had reasonably suspected that Walters had stolen books from a station bookstall. At his trial, Walters was acquitted, as the jury believed his statement that he had intended to pay for the books. No crime had therefore been committed in respect of any of the books. Walters sued the defendants, *inter alia*, for false imprisonment, a tort which involves the wrongful deprivation of personal liberty in any form, as he had been arrested for a crime which had not in fact been committed. The Court of Appeal held that, to justify the arrest, a private individual had to show not only reasonable suspicion but also that the offence for which the arrested person was given over into custody had in fact been committed, even if by someone else. A police officer making an arrest in the same circumstances could legally justify the arrest by showing 'reasonable suspicion' alone without having to show that an offence was, in fact, committed.

This principle is now incorporated in s 24 of PACE 1984. It is worthy of note that the less prudent arrestor who acts against a suspect when the latter is suspected of being in the act of committing an arrestable offence (s 24(4)) can justify his conduct simply by showing that there were 'reasonable grounds' on which to base the suspicion. They need not show that an offence was in fact being committed. If the arrestor waits until he thinks the crime has been committed, then, whereas a police officer will only have to show 'reasonable grounds for suspecting that an arrestable offence has been committed' (s 24(6)), a citizen can only justify his behaviour if an offence 'has been committed' (s 24(5)).

13.3.8   *R v Self* (1992)

This analysis is supported by the decision in *R v Self* (1992). The defendant was seen by a store detective in Woolworths to pick up a bar of chocolate and leave the store without paying. The detective followed him out into the street and, with the assistance of a member of the public, she arrested the suspect under the powers in s 24(5) of PACE 1984. The suspect resisted the arrest and assaulted both his arrestors. He was subsequently charged with theft of the chocolate and with offences of assault with intent to resist lawful apprehension or detainer, contrary to s 38 of the Offences Against the Person Act 1861. At his trial, he was acquitted of theft (apparently for lack of *mens rea*) but convicted of the assaults. These convictions were quashed by the Court of Appeal on the grounds that, as the arrest had not been lawful, he was entitled to resist it. The power of arrest conferred upon a citizen (s 24(5)) in circumstances where an offence is thought to *have been committed* only applies when an offence *has* been committed, and as the jury decided that Mr Self had not committed any offence, there was no power to arrest him. It is not easy to justify the considerable legal protection available to police officers when compared with the near total lack of protection available to ordinary British subjects/citizens. In the article mentioned above, Professor Spencer states: '[I]f a citizen, reacting to the words "Stop thief!" tackles someone who looks for all the world like a fleeing robber, he has no defence if it later turns out that no robbery has actually occurred. The person he tackles can hit him with impunity, and sue him for damages at leisure later' ('Extending the Police State', *ibid.*). This seems far from satisfactory.

13.3.9   *John Lewis & Co v Tims* (1952)

In *John Lewis & Co v Tims* (1952), Mrs Tims and her daughter were arrested by store detectives for shoplifting four calendars from the appellant's Oxford Street store. It was a regulation of the store that only a managing director or a general manager was authorised to institute any prosecution. After being arrested, Mrs Tims and her daughter were taken to the office of the chief store detective. They were detained there until a chief detective and a manager arrived to give instructions whether to prosecute. They were eventually handed over to police custody within an hour of arrest. In a claim by Mrs Tims for false imprisonment, she alleged that the detectives were obliged to give her into the custody of the police immediately upon arrest. The House of Lords held that the delay was reasonable in the circumstances as there were advantages in refusing to give private detectives a 'free hand' and leaving the determination of such an important question as whether to prosecute to a superior official.

13.3.10   What is the meaning of 'reasonable grounds for suspecting'?

Many of the powers of the police in relation to arrest, search and seizure are founded upon the presence of reasonable 'suspicion', 'cause' or 'belief' in a state of affairs, usually that a suspect is involved actually or potentially in a crime.

In *Castorina v Chief Constable of Surrey* (1988), detectives reasonably concluded that the burglary of a company's premises was an 'inside job'. The managing director told them that she had recently dismissed someone (the plaintiff), although she did not think it would have been her, and that the documents taken would be useful to someone with a grudge. The detectives interviewed the plaintiff, having found out that she had no criminal record, and arrested her under s 2(4) of the Criminal Law Act (CLA) 1967 (which has now been replaced by s 24(6) of PACE 1984). She was detained at the police station for almost four hours, interrogated and then released without charge. On a claim for damages for wrongful arrest and detention, a jury awarded her £4,500. The trial judge held that the officers had had a *prima facie* case for suspicion, but that the arrest was premature. He had defined 'reasonable cause' (which the officers would have needed to show they had when they arrested the plaintiff) as 'honest belief founded upon reasonable suspicion leading an ordinary cautious man to the conclusion that the person arrested was guilty of the offence'. He said an ordinary man would have sought more information from the suspect, including an explanation for any grudge on her part. In this he relied on the *dicta* of Scott LJ in *Dumbell v Roberts* (1944) that the principle that every man was presumed innocent until proved guilty also applied to arrests. The Court of Appeal allowed an appeal by the Chief Constable. The court held that the trial judge had used too severe a test in judging the officers' conduct.

Purchas LJ said that the test of 'reasonable cause' was objective and therefore the trial judge was wrong to have focused attention on whether the officers had 'an honest belief'. The question was whether the officers had had reasonable grounds to suspect the woman of the offence. There was sufficient evidence that the officers had had sufficient reason to suspect her.

Woolf LJ thought there were three things to consider in cases where an arrest is alleged to be unlawful:

- Did the arresting officer suspect that the person who was arrested had committed the offence? This was a matter of fact about the officer's state of mind.

- If the answer to the first question is yes, then was there reasonable proof of that suspicion? This is a simple objective matter to be determined by the judge.

- If the answers to the first two questions are both yes, then the officer did have a discretion to arrest, and the question then was whether he had exercised his discretion according to *Wednesbury* principles of reasonableness.

This case hinged on the second point and, on the facts, the Chief Constable should succeed on the appeal.

Note: The *Wednesbury* principles come from *Associated Provincial Picture Houses Ltd v Wednesbury Corp* (1948). Lord Greene MR laid down principles to determine when the decision made by a public authority could be regarded as so perverse or unreasonable that the courts would be justified in overturning that decision. The case actually concerned whether a condition imposed by a local authority on cinemas operating on Sundays was reasonable. Lord Greene MR said:

... a person entrusted with a discretion must, so to speak, direct himself properly in law. He must call his own attention to matters which he is bound to consider. He must exclude from his consideration matters which are irrelevant to what he has to consider. If he does not obey those rules, he may be truly said, and often is said, to be acting 'unreasonably'.

Sir Frederick Lawton, the third judge in the Court of Appeal in *Castorina*, agreed. The facts on which 'reasonable cause' was said to have been founded did not have to be such as to lead an ordinary cautious man to conclude that the person arrested *was* guilty of the offence. It was enough if they could lead an ordinary person to *suspect* that he was guilty.

This allows quite a latitude to the police. Additionally, the House of Lords has decided in *Holgate-Mohammed v Duke* (1984) that, where a police officer reasonably suspects an individual of having committed an arrestable offence, he may arrest that person with a view to questioning him at the police station. His decision can only be challenged on *Wednesbury* principles if he acted improperly by taking something irrelevant into account. The police arrested a former lodger for theft of jewellery from the house where she had lived in order to question her at the police station. The trial judge awarded her £1,000 damages for false imprisonment. The Court of Appeal set aside the award and the decision was upheld by the House of Lords. The following passage from a judgment in the Court of Appeal in *Holgate-Mohammed* was approved in the House of Lords:

> As to the proposition that there were other things which [the police officer] might have done. No doubt there were other things which he might have done first. He might have obtained a statement from her otherwise than under arrest to see how far he could get. He might have obtained a specimen of her handwriting and sent that off for forensic examination against a specimen of the writing of the person who had obtained the money by selling the stolen jewellery, which happened to exist in the case. All those things he might have done. He might have carried out finger print investigations if he had first obtained a print from the plaintiff. But, the fact that there were other things which he might have done does not, in my judgment, make that which he did do into an unreasonable exercise of the power of arrest if what he did do, namely, to arrest, was within the range of reasonable choices open to him.

It has been forcefully contended, however, that, in some circumstances, a failure to make inquiries before making an arrest could show that there were insufficient grounds for the arrest. See Clayton and Tomlinson, 'Arrest and reasonable grounds for suspicion' (1988) Law Soc Gazette, 7 September.

Note, however, that the powers are *discretionary. See Simpson v Chief Constable of South Yorkshire Police* (1991).

13.3.11 Detention short of arrest

For there to be an arrest, the arrestor must regard his action as an arrest. If he simply detains someone to question him without any thought of arrest, the action will be unlawful. It is often reported in criminal investigations that a person is 'helping police with their inquiries'. In *R v Lemsatef* (1977), Lawton LJ said:

> It must be clearly understood that neither customs officers nor police officers have any right to detain somebody for the purposes of getting them to help with their inquiries.

There is no police power to detain someone against his will in order to make inquiries about that person. See also *Franchiosy* (1979). This is confirmed by s 29 of PACE 1984, which states that where someone attends a police station 'for the purpose of assisting with an investigation', he is entitled to leave at any time unless placed under arrest. He must be informed at once that he is under arrest 'if a decision is taken by a constable to prevent him from leaving at will'. There is, however, no legal duty on the police to inform anyone whom they invite to the station to help with their inquiries that he may go.

13.3.12   Suspects stopped in the street

In *Kenlin v Gardiner* (1967), a police officer took hold of the arm of a boy he wanted to question about the latter's suspicious conduct. The boy did not believe the man was a policeman, despite having been shown a warrant card, and punched the officer in order to escape. The other boy behaved similarly but their convictions for assaulting an officer in the execution of his duty were quashed by the Divisional Court. The court held that the boys were entitled to act as they did in self-defence as the officer's conduct in trying to physically apprehend them had not been legal. There is no legal power of detention short of arrest. As Lawton LJ observed in *R v Lemsatef* (see above), the police do not have any powers to detain somebody 'for the purposes of getting them to help with their inquiries'.

It is important, however, to examine the precise circumstances of the detaining officer's conduct, because there are cases to suggest that if what the officer does amounts to only a *de minimis* interference with the citizen's liberty, then forceful 'self-defence' by the citizen will not be justified. In *Donnelly v Jackman* (1970), an officer approached a suspect to ask some questions. The suspect ignored the request and walked away from the officer. The officer followed and made further requests for the suspect to stop and talk. He tapped the suspect on the shoulder and the suspect reciprocated by tapping the officer on the shoulder and saying 'Now we are even, copper'. The officer tapped the suspect on the shoulder again which was replied to with a forceful punch. Mr Donnelly's conviction was upheld and the decision in *Kenlin v Gardiner* was distinguished as, in the earlier case, the officer had actually taken hold of the boys and detained them. The court stated that, 'it is not every trivial interference with a citizen's liberty that amounts to a course of conduct sufficient to take the officer out of the course of his duties'.

In *Bentley v Brudzinski* (1982), the facts were very close to those in question. A constable stopped two men who had been running barefoot down a street in the early hours. He questioned them about a stolen vehicle as they fitted the description of suspects in an earlier incident. They waited for about 10 minutes while the officer checked their details over a radio and then they began to leave. Another constable, who had just arrived on the scene, then said, 'Just a minute', and put his hand on the defendant's shoulder. The defendant then punched that officer in the face. Unlike the decision in *Donnelly v Jackman*, the Divisional Court held that the officer's conduct was more than a trivial interference with the citizen's liberty and amounted to an unlawful attempt to stop and detain him. The respondent was thus not guilty of assaulting an officer in the execution of his duty.

Note, also, that a person may be arrested for being silent or misleading under s 25 of PACE 1984 if the officer has reasonable doubts about the suspect's name and address or whether the summons procedure can be used at the address given.

13.3.13 Stop and search

PACE 1984 gives the police power to search 'any person or vehicle' and to detain either for the purpose of such a search (s 1(2)). A constable may not conduct such a search 'unless he has reasonable grounds for suspecting that he will find stolen or prohibited articles' (s 1(3)). Any such item found during the search can be seized (s 1(6)). An article is 'prohibited' if it is either an offensive weapon or it is 'made or adapted for use in the course of or in connection with burglary, theft, taking a motor vehicle without authority or obtaining property by deception or is intended by the person having it with him for such use by him or by some other person' (s 1(7)). An offensive weapon is defined as meaning 'any article made or adapted for use for causing injury to persons or intended by the person having it with him for such use by him or by some other person' (s 1(9)). This definition is taken from the Prevention of Crime Act 1953. It has two categories: things that are offensive weapons *per se* (that is, in themselves), like a baton with a nail through the end or knuckle-dusters, and things that are not offensive weapons, like a spanner, but which are intended to be used as such. If the item is in the first category, then the prosecution need prove only that the accused had it with him to put the onus onto the accused to show that he had a lawful excuse. Stop and search powers can now also be exercised under s 8A regarding items covered by s 139 of the CJA 1988. These items are any article which has a blade or is sharply pointed, except folding pocket knives with a blade of less than three inches. It is an offence to possess such items without good reason or lawful authority, the onus of proof being on the defendant. The courts will not accept the carrying of offensive weapons for generalised self-defence unless there is some immediate, identifiable threat.

Under s 2 of PACE 1984, a police officer who proposes to carry out a stop and search must state his name and police station, and the purpose of the search. A plain clothes officer must also produce documentary evidence that he is a police officer. The officer must also give the grounds for the search. Such street searches must be limited to outer clothing; the searched person cannot be required to remove any article of clothing other than a jacket, outer clothes or gloves. The officer is required to make a record of the search immediately, or as soon as is reasonably practicable afterwards (s 3). The record of the search should include the object of the search, the grounds of the search and its result (s 3). A failure to give grounds as required by s 2(3)(c) will render the search unlawful (*R v Fennelley* (1989)).

A recent case involved a protester who wore a skeleton-type mask at a demonstration. A police officer asked her to remove it. When she failed to do so, he tried to remove it himself. The protester responded by hitting him in the face. She was charged with assaulting a police officer in the course of his duty. The charge was dismissed by magistrates (partly because the policeman had failed to give his name, the location of his police station or the reason why he wanted the mask to be removed). The Divisional Court took the view that an assault had been committed: *DPP v Avery* (2002).

13.3.14 The Code of Practice for the exercise of statutory powers of stop and search

In view of the wide powers vested in the police in the exercise of stop and search, Code A has been revised to reflect the new legislation and to clarify how searches under stop and search powers are to be conducted. A revised Code A came into effect on 1 April 2003. Codes A, B, C, D and F have subsequently been revised. The latest versions took effect on 1 August 2004 (for details see http://www.homeoffice.gov.uk/crimpol/police/ system/pacecodes.html).

The primary purpose of stop and search powers is to enable officers to allay or confirm suspicions about individuals without exercising their powers of arrest. The Code applies to powers of stop and search and states at para 2.1(a) that these are 'powers which require reasonable grounds for suspicion before they may be exercised; that articles unlawfully obtained or possessed are being carried'.

Reasonable suspicion can never be supported on the basis of personal factors alone. For example, 'a person's race, age, appearance, or the fact that the person is known to have a previous conviction' cannot be used alone or in combination with each other as the reason for searching that person (para 2.2). Paragraph 2.6 states that:

> Where there is reliable information or intelligence that members of a group or gang habitually carry knives unlawfully or weapons or controlled drugs, and wear a distinctive item of clothing or other means of identification to indicate their membership of the group or gang, that distinctive item of clothing or other means of identification may provide reasonable grounds to stop and search.

Other means of identification might include jewellery, insignias, tattoos or other features which are known to identify members of the particular gang or group (Note 9).

Any search involving the removal of more than an outer coat, jacket, gloves, headgear or footwear, or any other item concealing identity, may only be made by an officer of the same sex as the person searched and may not be made in the presence of anyone of the opposite sex unless the person being searched specifically requests it (para 3.6). All searches involving exposure of intimate parts of the body shall be conducted in accordance with para 11 of Annex A to Code C. All stops and searches must be carried out with courtesy, consideration and respect for the person concerned. Every reasonable effort must be made to reduce to the minimum the embarrassment that a person being searched may experience (para 3.1).

The revised Code A at para 2.15 introduces new powers to require removal of face coverings. These powers were added by s 60A of the Criminal Justice and Public Order Act 1994. Paragraph 2.15 states:

> The officer exercising the power must reasonably believe that someone is wearing an item wholly or mainly for the purpose of concealing identity. There is also a power to seize such items where the officer believes that a person intends to wear them for this purpose. There is no power for stop and search for disguises. An officer may seize any such item which is discovered when exercising a power of search for something else, or which is being carried, and which the officer reasonably believes is intended to be used for concealing anyone's identity.

Where there may be religious sensitivities about asking someone to remove headgear using a power under s 45(3) of the Terrorism Act 2000, the police officer should offer to carry out the search out of public view (for example, in a police van or police station if there is one nearby) (Note 8).

13.3.15   Search of arrested persons

The power to search after arrest somewhere other than at the police station is governed by s 32 of PACE 1984 (searches of detained persons are dealt with by s 54 and Code C, para 4.1). Section 32(1) allows the police to search someone arrested where there are grounds for believing that he may present a danger to himself or to others; s 32(2) allows a search for anything that might be used to effect an escape or which might be evidence relating to any offence. Additionally, s 32(2)(b) gives the police power to enter and search the premises in which he was when arrested, or immediately before he was arrested, for evidence relating to the offence for which he was arrested. Unlike the power to search under s 18, this is not limited to arrestable offences, nor do the searched premises need to be occupied or controlled by him. Such searches, however, are only lawful where there are reasonable grounds for believing that the search might find something for which a search is permitted under s 18(5) and (6). Random or automatic searching is not lawful. Section 32(4) states that a person searched in public cannot be required to take off more than outer garments like coats, jackets and gloves. In 2004 new paragraphs were added to Code A (4.11–4.20). In essence, police officers are now required to record stops that do not lead to searches. This will normally involve giving the person stoped a brief account of the incident and the outcome of the encounter.

13.3.16   Search on detention

Section 54 of PACE 1984 and Code C, para 4.1 require the custody officer (a particular officer with special responsibilities in police stations) to take charge of the process of searching detainees. He must make sure a record is made of all the suspect's property unless he is to be detained for only a short time and not put in a cell. The person detained can be searched to enable this to happen, but the custody officer needs to believe it to be necessary; it is not an automatic right (s 54(6)). Anything the detainee has can be seized and retained, although clothes and personal effects can only be kept if the custody officer *believes* that the detained person *may* use them to escape, interfere with evidence or cause damage or injury to himself, to others or to property. The police are not permitted, however, to retain anything protected by legal professional privilege, that is, private legal communications between the detainee and his legal adviser. The police can also seize things they *reasonably believe* to be evidence of an offence. A search must be carried out by a constable and only one who is the same sex as the person to be searched. Strip searches can only be made where the custody officer thinks it necessary to get some item that the detainee would not be allowed to keep; the officer must make a record of the reason for the search and its result.

13.3.17 Procedure on arrest

At common law (that is, before PACE 1984), it was necessary for the arrestor to make it clear to the arrestee that he was under compulsion either: (a) by physical means, such as taking him by the arm or (b) by telling him, orally, that he was under compulsion. There was a danger, where words alone were used, that they might not be clear enough. Consider *Alderson v Booth* (1969). Following a positive breathalyser test, the officer said to the defendant: 'I shall have to ask you to come back to the station for further tests.' D did accompany the officer to the station. Lawful arrest was a condition precedent to anyone being convicted of driving with excess alcohol in their blood. At his trial, the defendant said he had not been arrested. He was acquitted and the prosecution appeal failed. Compulsion is a necessary element of arrest and the magistrates were not convinced that it was present in this case. The Divisional Court was not prepared to contradict the factual finding of the magistrates.

Additionally, where words alone were used, it was necessary for the arrestee to accede to the detention. There was no arrest where the arrestor said 'I arrest you' and the arrestee ran off before he could be touched (see *Sandon v Jervis* (1859)).

These principles remain good law after PACE 1984; see, for example, *Nichols v Bulman* (1985).

According to s 28(3) of PACE 1984, no arrest is lawful unless the arrestee is informed of the ground for the arrest at the time of or as soon as reasonably practicable after the arrest. Where a person is arrested by a constable, this applies (s 28(4)) regardless of whether the ground for the arrest is obvious.

The reasons for this rule were well put by Viscount Simon in *Christie v Leachinsky* (1947):

> ... a person is *prima facie* entitled to personal freedom [and] should know why for the time being his personal freedom is being interfered with ... No one, I think, would approve of a situation in which when the person arrested asked for the reason, the policeman replied 'that has nothing to do with you: come along with me' ... And there are practical considerations ... If the charge ... is then and there made known to him, he has the opportunity of giving an explanation of any misunderstanding or of calling

attention to other persons for whom he may have been mistaken, with the result that further inquiries may save him from the consequences of false accusation ...

An arrest, however, becomes lawful once the ground is given. In *Lewis v Chief Constable of the South Wales Constabulary* (1991), the officers had told the plaintiffs of the fact of arrest but delayed telling them the grounds for 10 minutes in one case and 23 minutes in the other. The Court of Appeal said that arrest was not a legal concept but arose factually from the deprivation of a person's liberty. It was also a continuing act and therefore what had begun as an unlawful arrest could become a lawful arrest. The remedy for the plaintiffs was the damages they had been awarded for the 10 minutes and 23 minutes of illegality: £200 each.

In *DPP v Hawkins* (1988), the Divisional Court held that an exception to the rule requiring information to be given to the arrestee exists where the defendant makes it impossible (for example, by his violent conduct) for the officer to communicate the reasons for the arrest to him. In that situation, the arrest is lawful and remains lawful until such a time as the reasons should have been given. The fact that the reasons were not given then does not invalidate the original arrest. The arrest would only become unlawful from the moment when the reasons for it should have been given to the arrested person.

In *R v Telfer* (1976), a police officer knew that the defendant was wanted for questioning about certain burglaries. The officer checked that the suspect was wanted, but not for which particular burglaries. He then stopped the defendant and asked him to come back to the station; when the defendant refused, he was arrested 'on suspicion of burglary'. The arrest was held to be unlawful. The person arrested was entitled to know the particular burglary of which he was suspected.

In *Nicholas v Parsonage* (1987), N was seen riding a bicycle without holding the handlebars by two police officers. They told him twice to hold the bars and then he did so. When they drove off, N raised two fingers. They then stopped N and PC Parsonage asked him for his name, telling him it was required as he had been riding his bicycle in a dangerous manner. N refused. P then informed him of his powers under PACE 1984 and requested N's name and address. N again refused. P then arrested him for failing to give his name and address. N attempted to ride off and a struggle ensued. N was subsequently convicted of, *inter alia*, assaulting a police officer in the execution of his duty contrary to s 51(1) of the Police Act 1964. His appeal was dismissed by the Divisional Court, which held that the arrest under s 25 of PACE 1984 had been lawful as a constable exercising power under s 25(3) was not required to say why he wanted the suspect's name and address. N had been adequately informed of the ground of arrest under s 28(3) of PACE 1984. N was not arrested for failing to give his name and address, he was arrested because, having committed the minor offence of 'riding in a dangerous manner', it then became necessary to arrest him because the conditions in s 25(3)(a) and (c) were satisfied. These conditions were that an arrest for a minor offence is possible where the officer believes that the service of a summons is impracticable because he has not been given a proper name and address.

As to the extent of the explanation that has to be given on arrest under s 28 of PACE 1984, *Christie v Leachinsky* (above) was considered in *R v Chalkley and Jeffries*

(1998). In this case, an arrest for an alleged credit card fraud was made for an ulterior motive, namely, to place recording equipment in the arrested defendant's house in order to record his discussions about planned robberies. The Court of Appeal held that, as there were reasonable grounds for suspecting the arrested defendant's involvement in the credit card frauds, and given that the police had informed him of this, the trial judge had been correct to rule that the arrest was lawful notwithstanding the ulterior motive.

Is it necessary for an arrestor to indicate to the arrestee the grounds on which his 'reasonable suspicion' was based? In *Geldberg v Miller* (1961), the appellant parked his car outside a restaurant in London while he had a meal. He was asked by police officers to move the car. He refused, preferring to finish his meal first. On being told that the police would remove the car, he removed the rotor arm from the distributor mechanism. He also refused to give his name and address or show his driving licence and certificate of insurance. He was arrested by one of the officers for 'obstructing him in the execution of his duty by refusing to move his car and refusing his name and address'. There was no power to arrest for obstruction of the police as no actual or apprehended breach of the peace was involved. The court held, however, that the arrest was valid for 'obstructing the thoroughfare', an offence under s 56(6) of the Metropolitan Police Act 1839, an offence the officer had not mentioned. Lord Parker CJ said:

> In my judgment, what the appellant knew and what he was told was ample to fulfil the obligation as to what should be done at the time of an arrest without warrant.

An arrest will be unlawful, however, where the reasons given point to an offence for which there is no power of arrest (or for which there is only qualified power of arrest) and it is clear that no other reasons were present in the mind of the officer: *Edwards v DPP* (1993). This principle was confirmed in *Mullady v DPP* (1997). A police officer arrested M for 'obstruction', an offence with the power of arrest only if the defendant's conduct amounted to a breach of the peace (for which there is a common law power of arrest) or if one of the general arrest conditions as set out in s 25 is satisfied. The police argued that the officer could have arrested M for a breach of the peace and merely gave the wrong reason. The Divisional Court held that the officer had acted unlawfully and that it would be wrong for the justices to go behind the reason given and infer that the reason for the arrest was another lawful reason.

In some circumstances, the court may infer a lawful reason for an arrest if the circumstantial evidence points clearly to a lawful reason (*Brookman v DPP* (1997)). However, if there is insufficient evidence to determine whether a lawful or unlawful reason was given for the arrest, then the police will fail to show that the arrest was lawful (*Clarke v DPP* (1998)). The issue seems to be what degree of evidence is necessary to allow the court to infer a lawful reason for arrest (see further, Khan and Ryder (1998) Legal Action 16, September).

13.3.18 Police powers under s 60 of the Criminal Justice and Public Order Act 1994

Section 60 of the CJPOA 1994 provides for a stop and search power in anticipation of violence, and was introduced to deal with violent conduct, especially by groups of young men. The section provides that where authorisation for its use has been granted:

(4) A constable in uniform may:

(a) -stop any pedestrian and search him or anything carried by him for offensive weapons or dangerous instruments;

(b) stop any vehicle and search the vehicle, its driver and any passenger for offensive weapons or dangerous instruments.

(5) A constable may, in the exercise of those powers, stop any person or vehicle and make any search he thinks fit whether or not he has any grounds for suspecting that the person or vehicle is carrying any weapons or articles of that kind.

(6) If, in the course of such a search under this section, a constable discovers a dangerous instrument or an article which he has reasonable grounds for suspecting to be an offensive weapon, he may seize it.

The authorisation required by s 60 must be given by a police officer of, or above, the rank of superintendent (or a chief inspector or inspector where such an officer reasonably believes that incidents involving serious violence are imminent and no superintendent is available). The authorising officer must reasonably believe that:

(a) incidents involving serious violence may take place in any locality in his area; and

(b) it is expedient to grant an authorisation to prevent their occurrence.

Such an authorisation, which must be in writing, will permit the exercise of stop and search powers within that locality for a period up to 24 hours. The authorisation could conceivably be given in fear of a single incident, even though the CJPOA 1994 requires fear of 'incidents'. This is because s 6 of the Interpretation Act 1978 states that the plural includes the singular unless a contrary intention is shown.

There are several aspects of this section which have been drafted in what appears to be a deliberately vague way. 'Serious violence' is not defined and this will be very much within the judgment of the senior officer concerned, provided of course that his view is based upon reasonable belief. Richard Card and Richard Ward, in a commentary on the Act (*The Criminal Justice and Public Order Act 1994* (1994)), have noted that the dictionary includes 'force against property' as within the definition of violence, and this may well become an important matter for decision by the courts.

The word 'locality' is left undefined in the CJPOA 1994. It could be an area outside a particular club or pub, or it might extend to a large estate. The courts have the power to declare an authorisation invalid because of an over-expansive geographical area; they are unlikely to substitute their own view for that of the operational officer.

13.3.19 Other aspects of s 60 of the Criminal Justice and Public Order Act 1994

'Offensive weapon' (s 60(4), (11)) means the same as for s 1(9) of PACE 1984. It is: (a) any article made or adapted for use for causing injury to persons; or (b) intended by the person having it with him for such use by him or some other person. There is no provision for reasonable excuse for the possession of such weapons.

'Dangerous instruments' (s 60(4)) will often be caught within the definition of offensive weapons, but the definition extends to cover instruments which have a blade or are sharply pointed (s 60(11)).

The authorising officer must reasonably believe that it is 'expedient' to give an authorisation in order to prevent the occurrence of incidents of serious violence. Thus, the authorisation need not be the only way in which such incidents may be prevented. Various policing factors may have to be balanced, including the ability of the police force to remain effective and efficient if it were to use other methods.

There is no power to detain especially conferred on officers by s 60 in order to carry out the search, but it does make failure to stop a summary offence. As it stands, there is nothing in s 60 which would permit an officer to use any force to conduct a non-consensual search. It is possible that the courts will imply such a power. When conducting the search, the officer must give the suspect his name, the police station to which he is attached, the authorisation for the search and the reason for the search. It seems that failure to comply with these conditions will make the search unlawful (see *Fennelley* (1989), a case where the defendant was not told why he was stopped, searched and arrested in the street. Evidence from the search, some jewellery, was excluded at the trial. Evidence of drugs found on him at the police station was also excluded).

The scope of s 60 and police powers to stop and search are being incrementally extended through various Acts of Parliament. They include the following: s 8 of the Knives Act 1997 amended s 60 to allow *initial* authorisations by an inspector or above thus obviating the need for an officer of at least the rank of superintendent, s 60(1)(b) extends the criteria under which an authorising officer may invoke this power to include reasonable belief that incidents involving serious violence may take place or that such instruments of weapons are being carried in a particular area and s 60(3) provides that authorisations may be extended up to 24 hours instead of six, although only an officer of the rank of superintendent or above may do this. A new sub-s (11A) was inserted under s 60 by s 8 of the Knives Act 1997 and states that, 'for the purposes of this section, a person carries a dangerous instrument or an offensive weapon if he has it in his possession'.

'Offensive weapon' means the same as for s 1(9) of PACE 1984 (see 13.3.13 above). 'Dangerous instruments' means instruments which have a blade or are sharply pointed.

These amendments are intended to deal with anticipated violence in situations where gangs or persons may be 'tooled-up' and travelling through various police areas en route to an intended scene of confrontation. Thus, the power may be invoked even where it is believed that the actual anticipated violence may occur in another police jurisdiction, for example, by football hooligans travelling to and from matches.

Further amendments to s 60 have been made under the CDA 1998. This is mainly to deal with the problem of troublemakers deliberately wearing facial coverings to conceal their identities, especially when the police are using CCTV cameras. Section 25 of the CDA 1998 inserted a new sub-s (4A) under s 60, which conferred a power on any constable in uniform to demand the removal of, or seize, face coverings where an authority had been given under s 60, if the officer reasonably believed that the face covering was being worn or was intended to be used to conceal a person's identity. The Anti-Terrorism, Crime and Security Act 2001 replaced s 60(4A) with s 60AA. This is broader than the earlier sub-section and provides for the removal of 'disguises'. Section 25 also extends s 60(8) and makes it a summary offence if a person fails to stop, or to stop a vehicle or to remove an item worn by him when required by the police in the exercise of their powers under s 60. This is punishable by a term of imprisonment not exceeding one month and/or a maximum fine of £1,000. Section 60A inserted by s 26 of the CDA 1998 provides that things seized under s 60 may be retained in accordance with regulations made by the Secretary of State. (See L Jason-Lloyd (1998) 162 JP 836, 24 October.)

13.3.20 Accountability and s 60 of the Criminal Justice and Public Order Act 1994

There are dangers that the powers under s 60 could be misused, as no reasonable suspicion is required and the requirements for authorisation are rather nebulous.

The safeguards against misuse include the fact that the admissibility of evidence gained through the use of a dubious stop and search event may be in doubt if there are serious breaches of the revised Code A. Someone charged with obstructing a police officer in the exercise of duty may raise breaches of the Code in defence. Unlawful search or seizure may also provide a basis for an application for exclusion of evidence thus obtained under s 78 of PACE 1984.

As the police have a common law power to take whatever action is necessary in order to prevent an imminent breach of the peace (*Moss v Mclachlan* (1985)), then, even if a challenge to the use of a s 60 power is technically successful, the police conduct in question may often be thus justified.

13.3.21 The Terrorism Act 2000

The Terrorism Act 2000 gives exceptional powers of stop and search to uniformed police constables. A person of at least the rank of commander or assistant chief constable, who considers it expedient to do so for the prevention of acts of terrorism, may issue an authorisation specifying a particular area or place (to last for not more than 28 days). This gives a constable powers to stop vehicles and pedestrians within that area or place and search the vehicle, driver, passengers, pedestrian (and anything with them) for articles of a kind which could be used in connection with terrorism. These powers may be exercised whether or not the constable has grounds for suspecting the presence of articles of that kind. The constable may seize and retain an article which he discovers in the course of such a search and which he reasonably suspects is intended to be used in connection with terrorism (ss 44 and 45). By s 47, it is an offence to fail to stop a vehicle when required to do so, fail to stop when required to do so and wilfully to obstruct a constable in the exercise of these powers. The offences are punishable with six months' imprisonment and/or a fine of up to £5,000.

These provisions are not confined to terrorism in connection with Northern Ireland or international terrorism. 'Terrorism' means the use or threat of action involving serious violence against a person, serious damage to property, endangering the life of a person other than the 'terrorist', creating a serious risk to the health or safety of the public or a section of the public, or designing seriously to interfere with or seriously to disrupt an electronic system. The above action(s) must be designed to influence the government or to intimidate the public or a section of the public, and made for the purpose of advancing a political, religious or ideological cause. However, where the use or threat of action involves the use of firearms or explosives, it need not be designed to influence the government or to intimidate the public or a section of the public.

Clearly, these are extensive powers which are available for activities which go well beyond political terrorism and may be used in the struggle to control various kinds of disaffected groups. Perhaps the most obvious example might be the animal rights groups, some of which have resorted to significant violence against those carrying on commercial activities involving animal experiments.

13.3.22 The use of force to effect an arrest

The use of force by a member of the public when arresting someone is governed by s 3 of the CLA 1967. This states:

> (1) A person may use such force as is reasonable in the circumstances in the prevention of crime, or in effecting or assisting in the lawful arrest of offenders or suspected offenders or of persons unlawfully at large.

Reasonable force will generally mean the minimum necessary to effect an arrest.

The use of force by police officers is governed by s 117 of PACE 1984. This states:

Where any provision of this Act:

(a) confers a power on a constable; and

(b) does not provide that the power may only be exercised with the consent of some person, other than a police officer,

the officer may use reasonable force, if necessary, in the exercise of the power.

13.3.23 Duties after arrest

A person arrested by a constable, or handed over to one, must be taken to a police station as soon as is 'practicable', unless his presence elsewhere is 'necessary in order to carry out such investigations as it is reasonable to carry out immediately' (s 30(1), (10) of PACE 1984). Where a citizen makes an arrest, he 'must, as soon as he reasonably can, hand the man over to a constable or take him to the police station or take him before a magistrate', *per* Lord Denning in *Dallison v Caffery* (1965). There is no requirement, however, that this be carried out immediately: *John Lewis & Co v Tims* (see 13.3.9 above).

13.4   Entry, Search and Seizure

Powers of search and seizure consequent upon the exercise of general stop and search powers under PACE 1984, the CJPOA 1994 and the Terrorism Act 2000 have already been considered, though it must be remembered that other powers are available, conferred by statutes such as the Misuse of Drugs Act 1971. Apart from stop and search powers, there are various other powers involving entry into property and subsequent search and seizure. Once again, general powers of this nature are contained in PACE. Powers of search and seizure must be used proportionately. They are generally inappropriate when less intrusive routes to the same goals are available. 'Seize and sift' operations (where officers remove numerous items for examination away from the premises) are controversial: *R v Chesterfield Justices ex p Bramley* (2001). Although permitted by Part II of the Criminal Justice and Police Act (CJPA) 2001, these powers should only be exercised when there is no practicable alternative.

Note: PACE 1984 came into force on 1 January 1986. The Act was accompanied by four Codes of Practice: Code A on Stop and Search, Code B on Search of Premises, Code C on Detention, Questioning and Treatment of Persons in Custody and Code D on Identification. Codes E and F, on the tape-recording and visual recording of interviews respectively, were added later. The Codes were produced after consultation with a wide range of interested groups and people, and were debated and approved by both Houses of Parliament before being promulgated. The first revised versions of Codes A–D came into force in April 1991. The Codes have been subjected to review and amendment. As stated above, the most recent revised versions of Codes A–E came into force on 1 August 2004. The Codes are not technically law and s 67(10) of PACE 1984 states that a breach of them can lead to neither a claim for damages nor a criminal prosecution against police officers. A breach of the Codes can, however, result in a police officer being subject to a disciplinary hearing. Referring to 'stop and search' powers, for example, Code A of PACE states in 1.4: 'Any misuse of powers is likely to be harmful to policing and lead to mistrust of the police … the misuse of these powers can lead to disciplinary action.'

The chief significance of a breach of the Codes is that a judge may exclude otherwise relevant evidence if it has been obtained in such a way and an appeal court may quash a conviction where a trial judge has not excluded such evidence (s 67(7)).

13.4.1 Entry of premises under the common law

Premises can be searched by consent. Here, the constable must get written consent from the occupier of the premises on a special 'Notice of Powers and Rights' form before the search takes place. The officer must make inquiries to ensure that the person concerned is in a position to give that consent. Before seeking the consent, the officer in charge must state the purpose of the proposed search and inform the person concerned that he is not obliged to consent, that anything seized may be produced in evidence and if such is the case, that he is not suspected of any offence. These propositions come from the governing *Code of Practice (B) for the Searching of Premises by Police Officers and the Seizure of Property found by Police Officers on Persons or Premises*. An officer cannot enter and search, or continue to search premises by consent, if the consent is given under duress or is withdrawn before the search is completed (Code B, para 5.3). Consent need not be sought if this would cause disproportionate inconvenience to the occupiers of premises, for example, where the police wish to briefly check a number of gardens on a suspected escape route.

Police officers may enter premises with permission or under implied permission, but then must leave when required unless remaining under some particular power. In *Davis v Lisle* (1936), Sidney Davis was a member of a firm that occupied a railway arch as a garage. Two police officers entered the garage to ask about a lorry that had been obstructing the highway. The lorry had since been moved into the garage. D, using obscene language and abuse, told the officers to leave. L was in the act of producing his warrant card when D struck him in the chest and stomach, damaging his tunic. The convictions of D for assaulting and obstructing a police officer in the execution of his duty were quashed by the Divisional Court. Lord Hewart CJ held that the officers were not acting in the course of their duty once they had remained on premises, having been told in forthright terms by the occupiers to leave: 'From that moment on, while the officers remained where they were, it seems to me that they were trespassers.'

13.4.2 Entry of premises to prevent an offence being committed

There is a common law right for police officers to enter a building to deal with or prevent a breach of the peace. In *Thomas v Sawkins* (1935), the Divisional Court held that police officers were entitled to enter and remain on premises, despite being asked by the occupiers to leave, in circumstances where the officers believed that certain offences (seditious speeches, incitements to violence) would be committed if they were not present. Lord Hewart CJ said:

> I am not at all prepared to accept the doctrine that it is only where an offence has been, or is being, committed, that the police are entitled to enter and remain on premises. On the contrary, it seems to me that a police officer has, *ex virtute officii*, full right so to act when he has reasonable grounds for believing that an offence is imminent or is likely to be committed.

Sections 17(5) and (6) of PACE 1984 abolishes all common law powers of entry except to deal with or prevent a breach of the peace.

Note, however, that a licensee must be given a reasonable time to leave premises before his continued presence on the land constitutes a trespass, unless he makes it clear that he will not leave voluntarily (*Robson v Hallet* (1967)).

The power has even extended to private homes. In *McGowan v Chief Constable of Kingston upon Hull* (1967), the Divisional Court held that the police were entitled to enter and remain in a private dwelling where they feared there would be a breach of the peace arising out of a private quarrel.

13.4.3   Entry and search of premises to make an arrest

This is governed by s 17 of PACE 1984, which says that a constable may enter and search premises for the purposes of arresting someone for an arrestable offence or under warrant, recapturing a person unlawfully at large whom he is pursuing, saving life or limb or preventing serious damage to property. This power can only be exercised if the constable has 'reasonable grounds' for believing that the person whom he is seeking is on the premises.

A police officer exercising his power to enter premises by the use of reasonable force to arrest a person for an arrestable offence (pursuant to ss 17 and 117 of PACE 1984) should, unless circumstances make it impossible, impracticable or undesirable, announce to the occupier the reason why he is exercising that power. In *O'Loughlin v Chief Constable of Essex* (1998), a police officer who had a lawful right to enter premises but failed to announce why he was entering when it was practicable and possible to do so was held to be acting unlawfully. In such circumstances, the occupier is entitled to use reasonable force to prevent the entry.

The relevant powers here are those discussed below under ss 18 and 32 of PACE 1984. In practice, the police act routinely under s 18 and rarely under s 32.

Section 18 of PACE 1984 gives a constable power to enter and search:

> ... any premises occupied or controlled by a person who is under arrest for an arrestable offence, if he has reasonable grounds for suspecting that there is on the premises evidence other than items subject to legal privilege that relates (a) to the offence; or (b) to some other arrestable offence which is connected with or similar to that offence.

If, therefore, the police suspect that evidence of other unconnected offences is to be found at the address, then they must get a search warrant or seek the householder's consent to the search. Until recently, the search of someone's address after they have been arrested normally required written permission from an officer of the rank of inspector or above. This is not now the case: revised Code B; para 6.14. A search must not go beyond what is normally required to find the particular item(s) being sought; no general search is permitted (s 18(3)). The time constraint when the police use s 32 (the search has to be made at the time of the arrest) (see below) does not appear to apply to a s 18 search (see *R v Badham* (1987), below). It is perhaps because of this and the comparative narrowness of s 32 in respect of searches of premises (see below) that s 18 is much more frequently used by police. Research by Ken Lidstone, for example, found that in a survey of two city forces, s 18 accounted for 75% of searches compared with 2% for s 32: 'Entry, search and seizure' (1989) 40 NILQ 333, p 355, n 67.

Section 32(2)(b) gives the police power to enter and search premises in which the suspect was when arrested, or immediately before he was arrested, for *evidence relating to the offence for which he was arrested*. Unlike the power to search under s 18, this is not limited to arrestable offences, nor do the searched premises need to be occupied or controlled by him. Such searches, however, are only lawful where there are reasonable grounds for believing that the search might find something for which a search is permitted under s 32(5) and (6). Random or automatic searching is not lawful.

Section 32(7) states that where a person is arrested in premises consisting of two or more separate dwellings, only the premises in which he was arrested or was in immediately beforehand and any common parts (like stairways and common corridors) can be searched.

The powers here are narrower than those given under s 18 to enter and search the premises of an arrested person. Under s 18, the police may enter and search for evidence of the offence for which the person was arrested or *any* offence which is 'connected with or similar to that offence'. Section 32 only covers searches for evidence relating to the actual offence for which the suspect was arrested. The police can, however, under s 32, search the person himself for evidence of any offence. It was held in *R v Badham* that s 32 only applies to a search made at the time of the arrest. It does not permit the police to return to the premises several hours after the arrest.

In *R v Churchill* (1989), the defendant was arrested on suspicion of burglary and placed in a police car. The police asked him to hand over the keys to the car he had been in so that they could lock it, thus keeping it safe for a later scientific examination. C was convicted of assault when, after refusing to hand over the keys, a struggle ensued and he hit an officer. On appeal, he contended that the police had no power to take the keys since they had no evidence of any crime. The court quashed the conviction, saying that the case could have been argued on the basis of the officer's duty to preserve the property, but the prosecution had not used that argument. The police could, alternatively, have searched the car under s 32 as that section confers a power to search any 'premises' the defendant was in immediately before arrest and this includes a vehicle (s 23(a)). See also 13.7 below for the changes to be made to this area by the Criminal Justice Act 2003 during 2004–06.

13.4.4 Seizure of articles from searches

Seizure of articles from searches is controlled by s 19 and Code B, para 7. These state that an officer who is lawfully on any premises has power to seize anything which is on the premises if he has reasonable grounds to believe that an item has been obtained in consequence of the commission of an offence, or that it is evidence in relation to an offence, and that it is necessary to seize the item in order to prevent that item being concealed, lost, disposed of, altered, damaged, destroyed or tampered with (s 19(2) and (3) and para 7.1(b)). Items exempted from seizure are those reasonably believed to be subject to legal professional privilege (s 19(6)). The scope of the seizure rights is therefore quite wide and Zander has argued that the insistence since *Entick v Carrington* (1765) that general warrants are unlawful must now be qualified by the knowledge that once the police have entered premises lawfully, it is difficult to hold them to a search restricted to the specific purpose of the search. The only serious restraint is the requirement in s 16(8) that a search under warrant must be carried out in a manner consistent with the items being looked for and in Code B, para 6.9, which states that 'premises may be searched only to the extent necessary to achieve the object of the search having regard to the size and nature of whatever is sought'.

13.4.5   Search warrants and safeguards

Section 8 of PACE 1984 provides for the issue of warrants by magistrates to enter and search premises for evidence of serious arrestable offences. This gives justices of the peace the power, on written application from a constable, to issue a search warrant where he is satisfied that there are reasonable grounds for believing that a 'serious arrestable offence' has been committed. A 'serious arrestable offence' (as distinct from an 'arrestable offence' defined by s 24) is defined by s 116 of and Sched 5 to PACE 1984. The definition divides offences into two categories. One category comprises offences so serious that they are always 'serious arrestable offences'; they are listed in Sched 5 and include treason, murder, manslaughter, rape, kidnapping, incest and possession of firearms with intent to injure, and attempts or conspiracies are treated as if they were completed. Any other arrestable offence is serious only if its commission has led, or is likely to lead, to any of the consequences specified in s 116(6), namely:

(a) serious harm to the security of the State or public order;

(b) serious interference with the administration of justice or with the investigation of offences;

(c) the death of anyone;

(d) serious injury to anyone;

(e) substantial financial gain to anyone;

(f) serious financial loss to anyone in the sense that, having regard to all the circumstances, it is serious for the person suffering loss (the seriousness of the loss is therefore to be measured by the financial position of the potential loser).

The magistrate must also be satisfied that:

- there is material on the premises likely to be of substantial value to the investigation (s 8(1)(b));

- it is likely to be relevant evidence (s 8(1)(c));

- it does not include 'excluded material' (for example, human tissue taken for medical diagnosis and held in confidence); journalistic material held in confidence (see s 11), or 'special procedure material' (for example, confidential business/professional material, see s 14); or material subject to legal privilege (s 10); and

- any of the conditions in s 8(3) applies. These are, essentially, that it is not practicable to gain entry to the premises in question without a search warrant or that the reasons for the search would be frustrated if the constable did not gain immediate entry upon arrival.

Section 15 incorporates proposals made by the Philips Royal Commission on Criminal Procedure (Cmnd 8092, 1981, HMSO) to protect against warrants being too easily obtained. Clearly, it is highly contentious at what point there is the correct, desirable balance between the State's concern to prevent and detect crime and the interests of the public at large in having the civil liberty of freedom from speculative entry into their homes by the police. If police officers could legally enter any home at any time without permission from anyone, then the detection of crime would arguably be easier than now, but there would be a significant price to pay in the consequential public resentment against the police and the probably profound loss of faith in the legal and political system.

An application for a search warrant must now state the grounds for making the application, the statutory authority under which the claim is made and the object of the proposed search in as much detail as possible. Research by Lidstone (see 13.4.3 above) has shown a tendency for informations (the applications) and warrants to use very generalised terms like 'electrical goods', which he argues is not desirable. The applications are normally made *ex parte* (that is, from one side – the police, without the presence of the person whose premises are to be searched) and the information must be made in writing by an officer who must answer any questions (from the magistrate) under oath. Lidstone's research also suggests that, both before and after PACE 1984, there is evidence of reliance on formulaic informations, for example, 'As a result of information received from a previously reliable source ...', and a lack of any probative questioning by magistrates on such informations. The warrant may only be used to gain entry on one occasion; if the police find nothing relevant and wish to return, they must apply for another warrant. On each search, the occupier must be given a copy of the warrant authorising entry.

One part of s 15 has caused some difficulty for the courts. It relates to the word 'it' in s 15(1), which states that 'an entry on or search of premises under a warrant is unlawful unless it complies with this section and s 16 below'.

What must comply – the warrant or the whole entry and search? In *R v Longman* (1988), Lord Lane CJ said, *obiter*:

> With some hesitation, we are inclined to think it probably refers to the warrant, but the real probability is that the intention of the framers of the Act was to provide that the warrant should comply with the terms of s 25 and the entry and search should comply with s 16. But, unhappily, that is not what it says. So, we leave that problem unresolved.

Section 16 and Code B govern the actual search of premises and seek to ensure that warrants are executed in a proper and reasonable manner. Section 16 states that any constable, not just the one named in the warrant, may execute that warrant (s 16(1)) and it must be carried out within one month of its date of issue (s 16(3)). The search must be at a 'reasonable hour' unless 'it appears to the constable executing it that the purpose of a search may be frustrated on an entry at a reasonable hour' (s 16(4)). Notice that here the test is subjective; it is what 'appears to the constable' that is critical, not whether such a belief is reasonable or not. If the occupier is present, he must be given a copy of the warrant (s 16(5)); if he is not there, then a copy must be left in a prominent place (s 16(7)). A constable executing a warrant must identify himself and, if he is not in uniform, he must produce documentary evidence that he is a constable, even if he is not asked (s 16(5)).

In *R v Longman* (above), a plain clothes police officer posed as a delivery girl from Interflora to gain entry to premises without alerting the occupants. She had come to the premises with other officers with a warrant to search for drugs. It was not the first time that the premises had been searched and the officers knew that entry would be very difficult. When the door was opened, the officers burst in. They did not, therefore, properly identify themselves as officers according to s 16(5), nor had they shown the householder their search warrant as required by para 5.5 of the 1991 revision of Code B. The Court of Appeal held that force or subterfuge could lawfully be used for the purposes of gaining entry with a search warrant. The warrant was 'produced' for the purposes of s 16(5) when the occupier was given the opportunity of inspecting it. In this case, the occupier had not attempted to look at the warrant, he had shouted a warning to others on the premises and then tried to stab the officers with a knife. The court held that it would be prepared to overlook failures to comply with the precise provisions of ss 15 and 16 regarding production of the warrant whenever circumstances made it wholly inappropriate, such as a search for drugs or in a terrorism case. In any event, it was not necessary that the formalities set out in s 16(a)–(c), on identification of the searcher as a police officer and production of the warrant, be carried out before *entry* but only before the search begins. The revised Code B states that the officer shall first attempt to get access by asking the occupier unless (Code B, para 6.4(iii)):

> ... there are reasonable grounds for believing that alerting the occupier or any other person entitled to grant access would frustrate the object of the search or endanger officers or other people.

A search under a warrant 'may only be a search to the extent required for the purpose of which the warrant was issued' (s 16(8)). In *Chief Constable of the Warwickshire Constabulary ex p Fitzpatrick* (1998), the Divisional Court disapproved of the police practice of using a warrant phrased in broad terms to seize every possible item that could broadly fall within those terms. They should ensure both that the material seized falls within the terms of the warrant and, because such a warrant is granted to search for material of evidential value, that there are reasonable grounds for believing so and that such material is likely to be of substantial value in the investigation. In this case, in relation to one of the warrants, the police officers went on a 'fishing expedition' and seized a large selection of documents not on their face related to the offence under investigation. In doing so, they exceeded the ambit of the warrant. Thus, the entire search was a trespass and unlawful under ss 16(8) and 15(1) of PACE (see further, Khan and Ryder, 'Police and the law' (1998) Legal Action 16, September).

A search warrant does not entitle the executing officers to search persons on the premises. Such persons may only be searched if arrested or if there is a specific power in the warrant, for example, as in warrants issued under s 23 of the Misuse of Drugs Act 1971 (Home Office Circular on PACE 1984, 1985, No 88/1855).

13.5 Interrogation, Confession and Admissibility of Evidence

Before moving into the specific provisions of PACE 1984 and the Codes of Practice, it is important to be aware of the general issues at stake in this area of law. Are the rights of suspects being interrogated by the police sufficiently protected by law? Is there scope for abuse of power by the police? Are the police burdened by too many legal requirements when trying to induce a suspect to confess to a crime? What effects are likely to flow from the undermining of the right to silence (see ss 34–37 of the CJPOA 1994, 13.5.17 below)? See also 13.7 below for the changes to be made to this area by the Criminal Justice Act 2003 during 2004–06.

Once again, it is also necessary to bear in mind the significance of the ECHR in this context. Unless impossible because of conflicting primary legislation, English courts must interpret rules of law so as to be compatible with obligations under the ECHR. Article 5 guarantees a right to liberty. To justify depriving a person of his liberty before conviction for an offence, for example, Art 5 requires that there be a lawful arrest or detention for the purpose of bringing the person before a competent authority on a reasonable suspicion of having committed an offence, or that arrest or detention is considered reasonably necessary to prevent him from committing an offence. Moreover, every person arrested shall be informed promptly in a language which he understands of the reasons for his arrest and of any charge against him, shall be brought promptly before a judge and shall be entitled to trial within a reasonable time or to release pending trial. Clearly, PACE requirements in relation to arrest and detention must be measured against Art 5. Equally, Art 6 requires a fair trial and declares a presumption of innocence, matters which bear on the conduct of the trial, the evidence presented, and the obligation to offer explanations or risk the consequences of adverse inferences being drawn from silence.

13.5.1 Time limits on detention without charge

Under s 42 of PACE 1984, a suspect can be held without being charged for 24 hours before any further authorisation needs to be given. At this point, the situation must be reviewed and further detention must be authorised by an officer of at least the rank of superintendent. The period is measured from arrival at the police station. If he is arrested by another force, the time runs from his arrival at the station of the area where he is wanted. If further detention is authorised, this can continue for up to the 36-hour point. After 36-hours from the beginning of the detention, there must be a full hearing in a magistrates' court with the suspect and, if he wishes, legal representation (s 43). The magistrates can grant a warrant of further detention for up to a further 60 hours – making a total of 96 hours (ss 43 and 44). However, the police could not be granted the 60-hour period as a whole because the maximum extension that a magistrates' court can grant at one time is 36 hours (ss 43(12) and 44). The magistrates can only grant such extensions if the offence being investigated is a serious arrestable offence (s 116), is being investigated diligently and expeditiously and provided that the further detention is necessary to secure or preserve evidence relating to an offence for which the suspect is under arrest or to obtain such evidence by questioning him (s 43(4)).

Section 38 states that, *after being charged*, the arrested person must be released with or without bail, unless:

- it is necessary to hold him so that his name and address can be obtained; or

- the custody officer reasonably thinks that it is necessary to hold him for his own protection or to prevent him from causing physical injury to anyone or from causing loss of or damage to property; or

- the custody officer reasonably thinks that he needs to be held because he would otherwise fail to answer bail or to prevent him from interfering with witnesses or otherwise obstructing the course of justice; or

- if he is a juvenile and ought to be held 'in his own interests'.

If the suspect is charged and not released, he will have to be brought before a magistrates' court 'as soon as practicable' and not later than the first sitting after being charged (s 46(2)). See also 13.7 below for the changes to be made to this area by the Criminal Justice Act 2003 during 2004–06.

13.5.2   Searches of detained persons

Searches of people detained at police stations are governed by s 54 and Code C. The Act also allows 'speculative searches' in which fingerprints, samples or information in respect thereof can be checked against other similar data held by the police. Section 82 of the CJPA 2001 retrospectively amended s 64 of PACE 1984, giving the police the right to retain DNA samples and fingerprints. The Court of Appeal has decided that this does not contravene Arts 8 or 14 of the ECHR: *R v Chief Constable of South Yorkshire* (2002). For an analysis of this decision, see Charles Bourne, 'Retaining fingerprints and DNA samples' (2002) 152 NLJ 1693.

A person may only be searched if the custody officer considers this necessary in order to make a complete list of his property (s 54(6)). There is no automatic right to search all suspects as a matter of routine. The police can, however, search anyone to ascertain whether he has with him anything which he could use to cause physical injury, damage property, interfere with evidence or assist him to escape (s 55, as amended). Section 65 deals with intimate searches:

> ... a search which consists of the physical examination of a person's body orifices other than the mouth.

A physical examination of the mouth is therefore allowed in the circumstances where a non-intimate search of the person may occur, subject to the ordinary safeguards (Code of Practice A, para 3; Code C, para 4). A search of the mouth for drugs is not the taking of a sample as defined by s 65 of PACE 1984, so the restrictions which apply to the taking of samples do not apply here. A search of an arrested person's mouth may thus be carried out by a police officer at the station, subject to the safeguards in Code C. The officer carrying out the search must be of the same sex as the arrested person (s 54(9)). Nonetheless, an officer of either sex may search the arrested person's mouth at the time of the arrest if he or she has reasonable grounds to believe that the arrested person is concealing therein evidence related to the offence (s 32(2)(b)). The powers to take fingerprints and non-intimate samples have recently been extended: revised Code D; para 4.3).

Intimate searches must be authorised by an officer of the rank of superintendent or above, on the basis of reasonable belief that the arrested person in police detention has concealed on him anything which could be used to cause physical injury to himself or to others and that he might so use it. Intimate searches for weapons can, if a doctor or registered nurse is not available, be carried out by a police officer of the same sex as the suspect. If the search is for drugs, it can only be carried out by a doctor or registered nurse and it cannot be carried out at a police station (s 55(4)). Intimate searches for drugs are limited to those for hard drugs, defined as Class A drugs in Sched 2 to the Misuse of Drugs Act 1971. Regarding the property of detained persons, see 13.7 below for the changes to be made by the Criminal Justice Act 2003 during 2004–06.

13.5.3   The right to have someone informed when arrested

The effect of s 56 and Code C is that when a detainee is under arrest and is being held in custody in a police station, he is entitled, if he so requests, to have 'one friend or relative or other person who is known to him or who is likely to take an interest in his welfare' to be told as soon as practicable that he is under arrest and his whereabouts (s 56(1), Code C, para 5.1). If such a person cannot be contacted, the Code allows for two alternates to be nominated, following which any further alternates can be called at the discretion of the custody officer. Delay is only permissible in the case of a 'serious arrestable offence' (see s 116) and only if authorised by an officer of at least the rank of superintendent. The grounds for delaying appear in Annex B. They are essentially that there are reasonable grounds for believing that telling the named person of the arrest will lead to interference with, or harm to, evidence of witnesses or the alerting of others involved in such an offence; or will hinder the recovery of property obtained as a result of the offence. No one, however, may be prevented from notifying someone outside the police station for longer than 36 hours after 'the relevant time' (s 41(2)), usually the time that he arrived at the station. Unless the reasons for a lawful delay (see Annex B) exist, Code C states that the detainee should be allowed to speak on the telephone 'for a reasonable time to one person' (para 5.6) and that this privilege is in addition to the right to phone someone under para 5.1 to inform him or her of the arrest or under para 6.1 to obtain legal advice. Children and young persons are afforded additional rights by s 57; the section says that the police should contact a person 'responsible for his welfare' to inform the person about the arrest.

13.5.4 The right to consult a solicitor

Section 58(1) of PACE 1984 states that, 'A person who is in police detention shall be entitled, if he so requests, to consult a solicitor privately at any time'. The rules relating to persons held under suspicion of terrorist offences are different and will not be covered here. Where the detained person is a juvenile, mentally disordered or otherwise vulnerable, then 'the appropriate adult' may exercise the right to ask for legal advice. There is effectively a human right to custodial legal advice. This is guaranteed by Art 6(3)(c) of the ECHR: *Murray v UK* (1996); *Averill v UK* (2000); *Condron and Condron v UK* (2000). See Ed Cape, 'Incompetent police station advice and the exclusion of evidence' [2002] Crim LR 471–83.

Where the detainee has been allowed to consult a solicitor, and the solicitor is available, the solicitor must be allowed to sit in on any interview the police hold with the detainee (Code C, para 6.8). Normally, the request must be allowed as soon as practicable (s 58(4)).

13.5.5 Notifying the suspect of the right to free legal advice

There is clearly the danger that a person's right to legal advice can be effectively curtailed if he is not aware of it. Code C therefore goes to some lengths to ensure the detainee is aware of the right. The custody officer is required (para 3.5), when he authorises a person's detention in the police station, to make sure that the detainee signs the custody record signifying whether he wishes to have legal advice at that point.

The Code stipulates that police stations must advertise the right to free legal advice in posters 'prominently displayed in the charging area of every police station' (para 6.3). The Code also gives precise rules concerning at what point and in what form a person should be notified of the right to get free legal advice. For example, a person who comes to the station *under arrest* must be told immediately both orally and in writing (paras 3.1 and 3.2). A person who comes to the police station voluntarily (that is, someone who is helping the police with their inquiries) is to be given a leaflet if he requests information, but strangely there is no police duty to notify if that person does not ask.

A person who asks for legal advice should be given the opportunity to consult a specific solicitor (for example, his own) or the duty solicitor (see 13.5.6 below). Alternatively, he should be given an opportunity to choose one from a list of those available to give advice. Ultimately, the custody officer has discretion to allow further requests if the others are unsuccessful. The advice may be given by a solicitor or some other accredited representative. The revised Code C carries the provision that 'No police officer should, at any time, do or say anything with the intention of dissuading a detainee' (para 6.4) and that reminders of the right to consult legal advice should be given at specified times, for example, on commencement and re-commencement of interviews.

The revised Code also states (para 6.15) that if a solicitor arrives at the station to see a particular person, that person must (unless Annex B applies) be informed of the solicitor's arrival and asked whether they would like to see the solicitor. This applies even if the person concerned has already declined legal advice. This would be important, for example, where the lawyer had been sent by a friend or family member.

Under Code C, para 3.1(ii), the detainee must be told that they have the right to consult privately with a solicitor and that free independent legal advice is available. The solicitor or some other accredited representative is paid from public funds. At his discretion, a solicitor may give the advice over the telephone. The Law Society advises the solicitor when he is considering whether the telephone is a suitable medium to have regard to certain issues, for example, whether the detainee would be likely to be inhibited from speaking freely by fear of being overheard and whether the detainee has already been charged and no further police interview is proposed.

There has been notable judicial concern that the suspect's rights to be informed about the availability of legal advice is enforced. In *R v Absolam* (1989), the Court of Appeal quashed a conviction for the supply of cannabis and substituted one for simple possession because the defendant had not been informed of his right to see a solicitor before he had been questioned. The trial judge had held that the series of preliminary questions and answers did not amount to an 'interview', but the Court of Appeal disagreed; the questions were an 'interview' within the meaning of the Code because they were directed at a suspect with the aim of obtaining admissions on which a prosecution could be based. The reference in s 58(4) to seeing a solicitor 'as soon as practicable' was not relevant to the suspect's right to be informed of his right to legal advice from the outset of his detention.

In *R v Beycan* (1990), the defendant was arrested in connection with a charge of supplying heroin. He was taken to a police station where he was asked, 'Are you happy to be interviewed in the normal way we conduct these interviews without a solicitor, friend or representative?'. The Court of Appeal held that this did not amount to informing him of his right to legal advice and it quashed his conviction which was based on his subsequent confession.

13.5.6 Duty solicitors

The Duty Solicitor Schemes at police stations and magistrates' courts are run locally but organised under the auspices of the Legal Services Commission (LSC) acting through the CDS. At police stations, the duty solicitor is contacted through a special national telephone network provided by a company, Air Call plc. When a detainee asks for a duty solicitor (at any time of the day or night), a call is made to Air Call who then contact either the rota duty solicitor or telephone duty solicitors on the panel until, in the latter case, one is found who is able and willing to attend. In rota schemes, there is always (in theory) someone on duty; in panel schemes, the panellists are called one after the other on a list beginning with the name after the last solicitor to have come out.

It will be apparent that when a detainee at a police station requests legal advice, that advice may be provided by a number of different categories of advisers. Broadly speaking, the advice may be supplied as a result of a choice of adviser made by the suspect himself, or as a result of using the duty solicitor. Where the suspect makes his own choice of adviser, that person may be a solicitor or an accredited, probationary or non-accredited representative who may not be a solicitor. Under the new arrangements, public funding for such advice will only be available where the advice supplied by a firm which has a contract with the CDS to do criminal work and the advice is given by a solicitor, an accredited representative or a probationary representative. An accredited representative will be registered on the police station register and will have successfully undergone testing, including producing a portfolio and completing written tests. A probationary representative will be registered, but will not yet have completed the relevant tests. A probationary representative cannot give advice in connection with an indictable only offence. Any adviser who is a duty solicitor will have fulfilled the requirements for publicly funded advice. Eventually, such advice should also be available from salaried defenders engaged by the CDS.

Since PACE 1984 was enacted, the precise arrangements for who may give advice at police stations have altered significantly. In the early days of the operation of the Duty Solicitor Scheme, considerable disquiet was expressed about advice given to suspects at the police station. This disquiet tended to focus on delay in receiving advice, the lack of availability of a solicitor, the provision of advice over the telephone rather than in person and the quality of advice and advisers, including advice from unqualified advisers (for a review of the evidence, see Sanders and Bridges, 'The right to legal advice', in *Miscarriages of Justice*, 1999). For example, the Runciman Royal Commission on Criminal Justice noted the problem of inadequate professional advice in some cases. Its Report states (para 69):

> The Legal Aid Board should commission occasional empirical research as a means of checking on the quality of performance of legal advisers at police stations.

The inadequacy of much legal advice given to suspects was highlighted when Stephen Millar, one of the Cardiff Three, had his conviction quashed on appeal ((1992) *The Times*, 11 December). In his judgment, the Lord Chief Justice criticised the defence solicitor for not intervening to halt the questioning. In his research for the Royal Commission on Criminal Justice, Professor John Baldwin analysed 600 police interviews (see 13.5.25 below) and found that in 66.5% of them, the adviser said nothing at all ((1993) 33 British J of Criminology 3). In one recent unreported case, a defence solicitor repeatedly claimed during interviews that his client was being untruthful. He apparently said: 'I'd better shut up or I'll be accused of prosecuting the case!' The Court of Appeal concluded that the solicitor had 'evinced a quite open hostility' towards his client: *R v M* (2000), cited by Ed Cape and Jane Hickman, 'Bad lawyer, good defence' (2002) 152 NLJ 1194–95. Confession evidence may be excluded under s 76(2)(b) of PACE if rendered unreliable by a person other than the suspect.

Following significant criticism, including that in the Runciman Report, The Law Society and Legal Aid Board introduced a scheme for the accreditation of non-solicitor representatives, which was implemented progressively from 1995 and which paved the way for the current arrangements described above.

13.5.7 Delaying access to legal advice

The police have no right to delay a detainee's access to legal advice except in the case of a serious arrestable offence (Annex B to Code C). If the detainee is being held in connection with a serious arrestable offence (s 116), he can be delayed access to legal advice, but the delay must be authorised by an officer of the rank of superintendent and only where he has reasonable grounds for believing that the exercise of the right:

- will lead to interference with, or harm to, evidence connected with a serious arrestable offence or interference with or physical harm to other persons; or

- will lead to the alerting of other persons suspected of having committed such an offence but not yet arrested for it; or

- will hinder the recovery of any property obtained as a result of such an offence.

If a delay is authorised, the suspect must be told the reason for it and the reason must be recorded in the custody record. The maximum period of delay is 36 hours (Annex B, para 6).

13.5.8 *R v Samuel* (1988)

In *R v Samuel* (1988), the defendant was arrested on suspicion of robbery and taken to a police station. During that day and the following day, he was interviewed several times about the robbery and other offences. He asked for a solicitor during the second interview. His request was refused by a superintendent on the grounds that two of the offences under investigation were serious arrestable offences and there would be a danger of accomplices being inadvertently alerted. At the fourth interview, Samuel confessed to two burglaries. A little later, a solicitor instructed by the family was notified of the charges, but he was refused access to the suspect. Shortly after that, Samuel confessed to the robbery charge. The trial judge admitted evidence of the last interview. Samuel was convicted of robbery and sentenced to 10 years' imprisonment. The Court of Appeal quashed the conviction. Two important issues were clarified:

- The police were not entitled to deny a suspect access to a solicitor after he has been charged, even if other charges are still being investigated. This follows from the plain and natural meaning of Annex B (para 1), which states that the right to legal advice can be delayed where:

  ... the person is in police detention ... in connection with a serious arrestable offence, has not yet been charged with an offence and an officer of superintendent rank or above, or inspector rank or above ... has reasonable grounds for believing ...

- The right of access to a solicitor was a 'fundamental right of a citizen' and if the police sought to justify refusing that right, they must do so by reference to specific aspects of the case; it was insufficient to suppose that giving the suspect access to a solicitor *might* lead to the alerting of accomplices. The officer had to believe that it probably would and that the solicitor would either commit the criminal offence of alerting other suspects, or would be hoodwinked into doing so inadvertently or unwillingly. Either belief could only be genuinely held by an officer on rare occasions. The belief that a solicitor would commit the criminal offence had to be based on knowledge of that particular solicitor. It could not be advanced successfully in relation to solicitors generally. As to the other point, Hodgson J observed (p 626):

> But, what is said is that the detained person will be able to bring about one or more of the happenings (a) to (c) [in Annex B] by causing the solicitor to pass on unwittingly some form of coded message. Whether there is any evidence that this has or may have happened in the past we have no way of knowing. Solicitors are intelligent, professional people; persons detained by the police are frequently not very clever and the expectation that one of (a) to (c) will be brought about in this way seems to contemplate a degree of intelligence and sophistication in persons detained, and perhaps a naïveté and lack of common sense in solicitors which we doubt often occurs.

This is not perhaps a view of offenders and solicitors which would be immediately agreed with by all those whose work brings them into contact with either group. Hodgson J said there were two tests. First, did the officer have the belief? This was a subjective question. Second, was that belief reasonable? This is an objective matter. In this case, the solicitor was well known and highly respected. He was unlikely to be hoodwinked by a 24-year old. The suspect's mother had been informed of her son's arrest hours before the solicitor was refused access to the son. If anyone was to have been alerted, it could easily have been done already. The solicitor would have advised his client to have said nothing at that stage. Samuel would not have made his admission having been denied his 'fundamental freedom' to consult with a solicitor. The evidence of the admission should, therefore, have been excluded under s 78.

13.5.9 *R v Alladice* (1988)

In *R v Alladice* (1988), the Court of Appeal allowed the evidence of an admission made during an interview where the suspect had had access to a solicitor delayed. The decision has been regarded as based on the narrow facts of the case. Alladice had made admissions of involvement in an armed robbery and was convicted, but argued on appeal that the evidence should have been excluded because there had been no valid reason for delaying his access to a solicitor. He argued that the real reason for the delay was that the police believed that a solicitor would have advised him to remain silent and that, as the Code and *Samuel* showed, this was not a valid reason. The court found that, on the facts, there had been a breach of s 58, but that this did not mean that the evidence obtained in breach of the section should automatically be excluded. There was no suggestion of oppression nor was there evidence of bad faith on the part of the police. The court took the view that it would be wrong to regard the admission as having resulted from the refusal to grant access to a solicitor. Alladice had stated that he understood the caution, that he was aware of his rights and that he was able to cope with the interview. He argued that the alleged admissions had not been made, although that argument was rejected by the judge. In any event, it seemed to the Court of Appeal that the presence of a solicitor would not have made any difference to the suspect's knowledge of his rights. There was no causal link between the absence of Alladice's solicitor and the admission.

13.5.10   *R v Davidson* (1988)

In *R v Davidson* (1988), the trial judge stated that *Samuel* meant that, in order for the police to validly delay access to advice, they had to be 'nearly certain' that the solicitor granted access to a suspect would warn an accomplice or get rid of the proceeds of the crime. Davidson had been arrested for handling a stolen ring, the fruit of an armed robbery. The power to delay access to a solicitor could not be exercised until D had nominated a particular lawyer. As this had not been done when the superintendent came to consider the matter, he could not have had a reasonable fear that the lawyer would pass a message to another person involved in the crime. The suspect had already spoken to his wife twice, so the reality of the police fears that he would use the lawyer as a messenger had to be doubted. The court excluded the crucial confessions and the prosecution's case collapsed.

13.5.11   *R v Parris* (1989)

In *R v Parris* (1989), the court quashed a conviction for armed robbery because of breaches of s 58. The police arrested Parris for armed robbery and took him to the station where he was kept incommunicado (under s 56). He asked to see a solicitor at his first interview and was refused. He refused to answer any questions. During his second interview, he agreed to answer some questions, provided nothing was written down. He then allegedly made oral admissions although, at trial, he denied these took place. The Crown did not deny that there had been a breach of s 58(8) as there had been no valid reason for refusing access to a solicitor; the incommunicado order under s 56 was wrongly assumed to also exclude access to a solicitor under s 58. Had there been a solicitor present at the second interview, he would probably have advised Parris not to speak; at the least he would have discouraged the alleged fabrication of admissions. The appeal succeeded.

13.5.12   Interviewing before solicitor arrives

The police have a right to start questioning detainees before a solicitor has arrived at the police station if the situation is an emergency or the solicitor is not likely to arrive for a considerable period. The power is governed by Code C, para 6.6, which states:

> A detainee who wants legal advice may not be interviewed or continue to be interviewed until they have reached such advice unless:

(a) Annex B applies, when the restriction on drawing adverse inferences from silence in Annex C will apply because the detainee is not allowed an opportunity to consult a solicitor; or

(b) an officer of superintendent rank or above has reasonable grounds for believing that:

(i) the consequent delay might:

- lead to interference with, or harm to, evidence connected with an offence;

- lead to interference with, or physical harm to, other people;

- lead to serious loss of, or damage to, property;

- lead to alerting other people suspected of having committed an offence but not yet arrested for it;

- hinder the recovery of property obtained in consequence of the commission of an offence;

(ii) when a solicitor, including a duty solicitor, has been contacted and has agreed to attend, awaiting their arrival would cause unreasonable delay to the process of investigation.

It will not normally be appropriate to begin an interview if the solicitor has said he is on his way (Note 6A). Another exception is where the solicitor cannot be contacted or declines to attend and the detainee, having been told about the Duty Solicitor Scheme, declines to ask for the duty solicitor or the duty solicitor is unavailable.

13.5.13 Answering police questions and the right to silence

The police are free to ask anyone any questions. The only restriction is that all questioning is supposed to cease once a detainee has been charged. Code C, para 11.6 states that:

> The interview or further interview of a person about an offence with which that person has not been charged or for which they have not been informed they may be prosecuted must cease when the officer in charge of the investigation:
>
> (a) is satisfied all the questions they consider relevant to obtaining accurate and reliable information about the offence have been put to the suspect, this includes allowing the suspect an opportunity to give an innocent explanation and asking questions to test if the explanation is accurate and reliable, eg, to clear up ambiguities or clarify what the suspect said;
>
> (b) has taken account of any other available evidence; and
>
> (c) the officer in charge of the investigation, or in the case of a detained suspect, the custody officer, see *paragraph 16.1*, reasonably believes there is sufficient evidence to provide a realistic prospect of conviction for that offence if the person was prosecuted for it. See Note 11B.
>
> This paragraph does not prevent officers in revenue cases or acting under the confiscation provisions of the Criminal Justice Act 1988 or the Drug Trafficking Act 1994 from inviting suspects to complete a formal question and answer record after the interview is concluded.

There is no obligation on a citizen to answer police questions. A person cannot be charged, for example, with obstructing the police in the execution of their duty simply by failing to answer questions. Although a judge or prosecutor cannot suggest to the jury that such silence is evidence of guilt, adverse inferences might be drawn in court from a defendant's earlier refusal to answer police questions (s 34 of the CJPOA 1994). Judges seem to have interpreted this section rather narrowly. Lord Bingham CJ, for example, said in *R v Bowden* (1999):

> Proper effect must of course be given to these provisions ... But since they restrict rights recognised at common law as appropriate to protect defendants against the risk of injustice, they should not be construed more widely than the statutory language allows.

It could be argued that s 34 is difficult to reconcile with the fair trial guarantees found in Art 6 of the ECHR. The Strasbourg Court has said, for example, that 'the very fact that an accused is advised by his lawyer to maintain his silence must be given appropriate weight by the domestic court. There may be good reason why such advice is given'; *Condron and Condron v UK* (2001). See generally, Ian Dennis, 'Silence in the police station: the marginalisation of s 34' [2002] Crim LR 25–38 and 13.5.15 below.

In *Rice v Connolly* (1966), the appellant was seen by officers in the early hours of the morning behaving suspiciously in an area where house-breaking had taken place on the same evening. On being questioned, he refused to say where he was going or where he had come from. He refused to give his full name and address, though he did give a name and the name of a road which were not untrue. He refused to accompany the officer to a police box for identification purposes, saying: 'If you want me, you'll have to arrest me.' He was arrested and charged with wilfully obstructing a police officer contrary to s 51(3) of the Police Act 1964.

His appeal against conviction succeeded. Lord Parker CJ noted that the police officer was acting within his duty in inquiring about the appellant and that what the appellant did was obstructive. The critical question, though, was whether the appellant's conduct was 'wilful' within the meaning of s 51. Lord Parker CJ, in the Divisional Court, took that word to mean 'intentional [and] without lawful excuse'. He continued:

> It seems to me quite clear that, though every citizen has a moral duty or, if you like, a social duty to assist the police, there is no legal duty to that effect, and, indeed, the whole basis of the common law is the right of the individual to refuse to answer questions put to him by persons in authority, and to refuse to accompany those in authority to any particular place; short, of course, of arrest.

The court was unanimous, although one judge, James J, cautioned that he would not go as far as to say that silence coupled with conduct could not amount to obstruction. It would depend on the particular facts of any given case.

In *Ricketts v Cox* (1982), two police officers who were looking for youths responsible for a serious assault approached the defendant and another man in the early hours of the morning. The justices found that the officers acted in a proper manner in putting questions to the men. The defendant was abusive, unco-operative and possibly hostile to the officers, using obscene language calculated to provoke and antagonise the officers, and tried to walk away. The justices were satisfied that this conduct amounted to an obstruction for the purposes of a charge under s 51(3) of the Police Act 1964. The defendant's appeal was dismissed by the Divisional Court which found that the case raised the point reserved by James J in *Rice v Connolly* – the combination of silence and hostility without lawful excuse. As Zander has observed, the state of the law here is now unclear.

13.5.14   Duties to answer

There are certain circumstances where the citizen is under a duty to answer police questions. Where a constable has reasonable grounds for believing that a vehicle has been involved in an accident and he seeks the particulars of the driver, he may arrest that person if the information is not given. With the Home Secretary's consent, and on the authority of a chief constable, coercive questioning (that is, where a suspect's silence can be used in evidence against him) can be used in matters under s 11 (as amended) of the Official Secrets Act 1911. There are also wide powers under the Companies Act 1985 to require officers and agents of companies to assist inspectors appointed to investigate the company. Refusal to answer questions can be sanctioned as a contempt of court (s 431) and as a criminal offence (s 447). A person can also be required to answer questions put to him by a liquidator of a company (*Bishopsgate Management Ltd v Maxwell Mirror Group Newspapers* (1993)).

Under s 2 of the CJA 1987, the Director of the Serious Fraud Office (SFO) (dealing with frauds worth over £5 million) can require anyone whom he has reason to think has relevant information to attend to answer questions and to provide information including documents and books. Such statements, however, cannot be used in evidence against the persons who make them unless they go into the witness box and give inconsistent testimony. Even this power, though, does not require the breach of legal professional privilege. Failure to comply with s 2 requests is a criminal offence and can result in an application for a magistrates' search warrant. These powers have been widely used. The SFO Annual Report for 1991–92 revealed that a total of 793 notices had been given during that year. In *R v Director of the Serious Fraud Office ex p Smith* (1993), the House of Lords held that the SFO could compel a person to answer questions relating to an offence with which he had already been charged. It followed that in relation to such questions, the suspect did not have to be further cautioned.

Other powers to compel answers on pain of penalties for refusal exist under the Terrorism Act 2000, and refusal to answer certain allegations from the prosecutor can be treated as acceptances of them under the Drug Trafficking Act 1994.

The closest English law comes to creating a duty to give one's name and address is the power given to the police under s 25(3) of PACE 1984. This is the power to arrest for a non-arrestable offence where the officer cannot find out the suspect's particulars for the purpose of serving a summons on him.

There is no duty to offer information about crime to the police. However, s 19 of the Terrorism Act 2000 makes it an offence for a person who believes or suspects that another person has committed an offence under any of ss 15–18 (offences involving funding of terrorism), and bases his belief or suspicion on information which comes to his attention in the course of a trade, profession, business or employment to not disclose to an officer as soon as is reasonably practicable his belief or suspicion and the information on which it is based. Additionally, s 5 of the CLA 1967 creates the offence of accepting money or other consideration for not disclosing information that would lead to the prosecution of an arrestable offence. The House of Lords has also held that it is the duty of every citizen in whose presence a breach of the peace is being committed to attempt to stop it, if necessary by detaining the person responsible. It is, however, except in the case of a citizen who is a police officer, 'a duty of imperfect obligation' (*Albert v Lavin* (1982), *per* Lord Diplock).

13.5.15 What can be said in court about silence in the face of police questioning

There is an established common law rule that neither the prosecution nor the judge should make adverse comment on the defendant's silence in the face of questions. The dividing line, however, between proper and improper judicial comment was a matter of great debate. There are many reasons why a suspect might remain silent when questioned (for example, fear, confusion, reluctance to incriminate another person) and the 'right to silence' enjoyed the status of a long-established general principle in English law. Thus, in *R v Davis* (1959), a judge was ruled on appeal to have misdirected the jury when he told them that 'a man is not obliged to say anything but you are entitled to use your common sense ... can you imagine an innocent man who had behaved like that not saying anything to the police ... He said nothing'.

An exception, though, was that some degree of adverse suggestion was permitted where two people were speaking on equal terms and one refused to comment on the accusation made against him by the other. In *R v Parkes* (1974), the Privy Council ruled that a judge could invite the jury to consider the possibility of drawing adverse inferences from silence from a tenant who had been accused by a landlady of murdering her daughter. The landlady and tenant, for the purposes of this encounter, were regarded as having a parity of status unlike a person faced with questions from the police. It was held in *R v Chandler* (1976) that the suspect was on equal terms with the police officer where the former was in the company of his solicitor. Chandler had refused to answer some of the questions he had been asked by the police officer before the caution, and the judge told the jury that they should decide whether the defendant's silence was attributable to his wish to exercise his common law right or because he might incriminate himself. The Court of Appeal quashed Chandler's conviction since the judge had gone too far in suggesting that silence before a caution could be evidence of guilt.

It was proper for the judge to make some comment on a defendant's reticence before being cautioned provided that the jury were directed that the issue had to be dealt with in two stages: (i) was the defendant's silence an acceptance of the officer's allegations?; and, if so, (ii) could guilt of the offence charged be reasonably inferred from what the defendant had implicitly accepted? The court said that it did not accept that a police officer always had an advantage over a suspect. Everything depended on the circumstances. In an inquiry into local government corruption, for example, a young officer might be at a distinct disadvantage when questioning a local dignitary.

That type of interview was very different from a 'tearful housewife' being accused of shoplifting.

The Court of Appeal's decision in *Chandler* asserted that silence might only be taken as acquiescence to police allegations before a caution. The court excluded silence after the caution as being something from which anything adverse can be inferred, because a suspect could not be criticised for remaining silent having been specifically told of that right. This, however, seemed like an irrational dichotomy. If the suspect did, in fact, have a legal right to silence whether or not he had been cautioned, it is very odd that full enjoyment of the right could only be effective from the moment of it being announced by the police. Additionally, any questioning of a suspect at a police station prior to a caution being given is probably in contravention of Code C, para 10, which requires a caution to be given at the beginning of each session of questioning. Violation of the Code affords grounds for an appeal under s 78 of PACE 1984. Cautions need not be given according to para 10.1:

> ... if questions are for other necessary purposes, eg:
>
> (a) solely to establish their own identity or ownership of any vehicle;
>
> (b) to obtain information in accordance with any relevant statutory requirement, see *paragraph 10.9*;
>
> (c) in furtherance of the proper and effective control of a search, eg, to determine the need to search in the exercise of powers of stop and search or to seek co-operation while carrying out a search ...

13.5.16 Right to silence in courts

Before the changes to the right to silence that were eventually made by the CJPOA 1994, the value of maintaining the traditional approach was subjected to considerable scrutiny. Since 1988, the right to silence was effectively abolished in Northern Ireland. It became possible for a court to draw adverse inferences from a defendant's silence when he was arrested. Adverse inferences could also be drawn from the defendant's failure to provide an explanation for any 'object, substance or mark' on his clothing, footwear or in his possession which the arresting officer found suspicious and questioned the suspect about (Criminal Justice (Evidence etc) (Northern Ireland) Order 1988).

Similar recommendations were made by the Home Office Working Group on the Right to Silence in 1989. The question was also considered by the Runciman Royal Commission on Criminal Justice. It had to decide whether to adopt a practice like the Northern Ireland system and the one recommended by the Home Office, or whether to retain the right to silence, as the Philips Royal Commission on Criminal Procedure had recommended in 1981. In evidence to the Runciman Royal Commission, the proposal to retain the right to silence was supported by The Law Society, the Bar Council and the Magistrates' Association. It was opposed by the police, the CPS, HM Council of circuit judges and senior judges.

Professor Michael Zander's research on this issue suggested that the role of the right to silence in the real workings of the criminal justice system was in fact not as significant as often argued. In one of his studies, 'Investigation of crime' [1979] Crim LR 211, he looked at 150 cases randomly drawn from those heard at the Old Bailey. According to police statements, of the 286 defendants (in many cases, there was more than one defendant), only 12 were said to have relied on their right to silence when confronted by police accusations. Of these, 9 were convicted. Zander has also made the following points:

- Most defendants plead guilty, so the right to silence is unimportant in such a context.

- Common law rules permit the judge to *mention* the defendant's silence and, in some limited circumstances, to comment on it.

- In any event, the jury may draw adverse conclusions about the defendant's silence to police questions, that is, whether the judge is permitted to comment on this or not.

In a study commissioned by the LCD, only 2% of 527 suspects exercised their right to silence; see Sanders *et al, Advice and Assistance at Police Stations and the 24 Hour Duty Solicitor Scheme*, 1989, LCD.

In a study by Stephen Motson, Geoffrey Stephenson and Tom Williamson ((1992) 32 British J of Criminology 23–40), the researchers looked at 1,067 CID interviews carried out in nine London police stations in 1989. By carefully matching cases where the right to silence had been exercised with like cases where it had not and then comparing the outcomes, the researchers found that decisions as to whether to prosecute were based on factors like the strength of the evidence against the suspect and the seriousness of the offence; they were not correlated with whether the suspect responded to questions or not. There was no evidence that silence at the police station gave the suspect any advantage at court. They commented:

> The high proportion of silence cases who ultimately plead guilty might be taken to suggest that the use of silence is a ploy – adopted for the most part by previously convicted offenders, [it] is abandoned in favour of a guilty plea when prosecution, probable conviction and (especially) sentencing are nigh.

The Runciman Royal Commission eventually decided to recommend retaining the right to silence. Its Report (1993) states (para 82):

> The majority of us believe that adverse inferences should not be drawn from silence at the police station and recommend retaining the present caution and trial direction.

The Commission did, however, recommend (para 84) the retention of the current law regarding silence in investigations of serious and complex fraud under which adverse consequences can follow from silence. The Report notes that a large proportion of those who use the right to silence later plead guilty. The majority of the Commission felt that the possibility of an increase in convicting the guilty by abolishing the right would be outweighed by the considerable extra pressure on innocent suspects in police stations. The Commission did, however, meet the police and CPS concern about 'ambush defences', where a defence is entered late in a trial, thus leaving the prosecution no time to check and rebut the defence. The Commission recommends that if the defence introduces a late change or departs from the strategy it has disclosed in advance to the prosecution, then it should face adverse comment (para 136). Professor Zander, however, issued a note of dissent that the principle must remain that the burden of proof always lies with the prosecution. He states:

> The fundamental issue at stake is that the burden of proof throughout lies with the prosecution. Defence disclosure is designed to be helpful to the prosecution and, more generally, to the system. But, it is not the job of the defendant to be helpful either to the prosecution or the system.

Since the abolition of the court of Star Chamber in 1641, no English court has had the power to use torture or force to exact confessions from suspects. The so called 'right to silence' really meant that a suspect could remain silent when questioned by police or in court without prosecution counsel or the judge being allowed to make adverse comment to the jury about such a silence. Traditionally, silence could not be used in court as evidence of guilt.

In support of the old rule, it could be said that:

- people are innocent until proven guilty of a crime by the State; and that

- people should never be under force to condemn themselves; and that

- there are several reasons other than genuine guilt why someone may wish to remain silent in the face of serious accusations – they might be terrified, confused, retarded, wish to protect someone else or fear that the truth would get them in some other type of trouble. The 11th Report of the Criminal Law Revision Committee (1972) gives several examples. The accused might be so shocked at an accusation that he forgets a vital fact which would acquit him of blame; his excuse might be embarrassing, like being in the company of a prostitute; or he may fear reprisals from another party;

- the 'right' is widely protected in other aspects of society: the police, for example, when facing internal disciplinary charges, are not bound to answer questions or allegations put to them.

13.5.17 Effective abolition of the right to silence

The government ignored the recommendations of the Runciman Commission and, in ss 34–37 of the CJPOA 1994, effectively abolished the right to silence. 'Abolished' may be too strong a word because everyone still has the right to remain silent in the same circumstances as they did before the CJPOA 1994; what has changed is the entitlement of a judge or prosecuting counsel to make adverse comment on such a silence.

Notwithstanding the 1994 Act, therefore, any person may refuse to answer questions put to him out of court. There are only a few exceptions to this (as with s 2 of the CJA 1987, which concerns the investigation of serious fraud, and requires certain questions to be answered under pain of punishment for refusal) and they existed before the Act. The CJPOA 1994 does not alter the position of the accused person as a witness – he remains a competent but not compellable witness in his own defence (s 35), although now the prosecution as well as the judge may comment upon such a failure to give evidence (s 168).

Except in so far as the new law makes changes, the old law still applies.

In enacting ss 34–37 of the CJPOA 1994, the government was adopting a particular policy. The general purpose of the Act was to assist in the fight against crime. The government took the view that the balance in the criminal justice system had become tilted too far in favour of the criminal and against the public in general, and victims in particular. The alleged advantage of the change in law is that it helps convict criminals who, under the old law, used to be acquitted because they took advantage of the right to keep quiet when questioned without the court or prosecution being able to comment adversely upon that silence. Introducing the legislation, the Home Secretary said that change in law was desirable because 'it is professional criminals, hardened criminals and terrorists who disproportionately take advantage of and abuse the present system'.

Section 34 states that where anyone is questioned under caution by a police officer, or charged with an offence, then a failure to mention a fact at that time which he later relies on in his defence will allow a court to draw such inferences as appear proper about that failure. Inferences may only be drawn if, in the circumstances, a suspect could reasonably have been expected to mention the fact when he was questioned. The inferences which can be drawn can be used in determining whether the accused is guilty as charged. The section, however, permits adverse inferences to be drawn from silence in situations that do not amount to 'interviews' as defined by Code C of PACE 1984, and thus which are not subject to the safeguards of access to legal advice and of contemporaneous recording which exist where a suspect is interviewed at the police station. The caution to be administered by police officers is as follows (with appropriate variants for ss 36 and 37):

> You do not have to say anything. But, it may harm your defence if you do not mention when questioned something which you later rely on in court. Anything you do say may be given in evidence.

Section 58 of the Youth Justice and Criminal Evidence Act (YJCEA) 1999 amends s 34 by adding a new s 34(2A). This restricts the drawing of inferences from silence in an interview at a police station (or similar venue) where the suspect was not allowed an opportunity to consult a solicitor prior to being questioned or charged (see Code D, Annex C). This amendment is intended to meet the ruling of the ECtHR in *Murray v UK* (1996) that delay in access to legal advice, even if lawful, could amount to a breach of Art 6, given the risk of adverse inferences being drawn.

Section 35 allows a court or jury to infer what appears proper from the refusal of an accused person to testify in his own defence, or from a refusal without good cause to answer any question at trial. In para 44 of the *Practice Direction (Criminal: Consolidated)* (2002), the Lord Chief Justice indicated that where the accused is legally represented, the following should be said by the judge to the accused's lawyer at the end of the prosecution case if the accused is not to give evidence:

> Have you advised your client that the stage has now been reached at which he may give evidence and, if he chooses not to do so or, having been sworn, without good cause refuses to answer any question, the jury may draw such inferences as appear proper from his failure to do so?

If the lawyer replies to the judge that the accused has been so advised, then the case will proceed. If the accused is not represented, and still chooses not to give evidence or answer a question, the judge must give him a similar warning, ending: '... the jury may draw such inferences as appear proper. That means they may hold it against you.'

Section 36 permits inferences to be drawn from the failure or refusal of a person under arrest to account for any object, substances or mark in his possession, on his person, in or on his clothing or footwear or in any place at which he is at the time of arrest. Section 37 permits inferences to be drawn from the failure of an arrested person to account for his presence at a particular place where he is found.

Thus, as the late Lord Taylor, the then Lord Chief Justice, observed, the legal changes do not, strictly speaking, abolish the right to silence:

> If a defendant maintains his silence from first till last, and does not rely on any particular fact by way of defence, but simply puts the prosecution to proof, then [ss 34–37] would not bite at all.

The change has been widely and strongly opposed by lawyers, judges and legal campaign groups. Liberty, for example, has said that drawing adverse inferences from silence would undermine the presumption of innocence. Silence is an important safeguard against oppressive questioning by the police, particularly for the weak and vulnerable.

John Alderson, former chief constable of Devon and Cornwall (1973–82) and a respected writer on constitutional aspects of policing, has written of the impending danger when police are able to 'exert legal and psychological pressure on individuals held in the loneliness of their cells'. He stated ((1995) *The Independent*, 1 February) that:

> History tells us that, when an individual has to stand up against the entire apparatus of the modern State, he or she is very vulnerable. That is why, in criminal cases, the burden of proof has always rested on the State rather than on the accused. The Founding Fathers of America amended their constitution to that effect in 1791.

A topical recent example might be persons detained indefinitely at the Home Secretary's discretion at HMP Belmarsh and HMP Woodhill (see J. Cooper, 'Guantanamo Bay, London' (2004), 154, NLJ, 41.

Undermining the right to silence may constitute a significant constitutional change in the relationship between the individual and the State. It may be doubted whether the majority of suspects should be put under greater intimidation by the system because of the conduct of a few 'hardened criminals' – the justification for the legislation given by the Home Secretary when he introduced it.

Two points should be noted, however, to put the debate in its proper historical context. First, it should not be forgotten that there were, prior to the Act, several instances in English law where there was already a legal obligation for a suspect to answer questions. These included the obligation to speak under s 2 of the CJA 1987 (see above); the obligations under ss 431–41 of the Companies Act 1985 (concerning investigations in respect of company officers and agents whose companies are being investigated by the Department of Trade and Industry); and the obligations under ss 22 and 131 of the Insolvency Act 1986 (concerning inquiries upon the winding up of companies). Note, however, that in *Saunders v UK* (1997), the ECtHR held that where evidence obtained under compulsion is subsequently used in a trial, this amounts to a breach of the right to a fair trial in Art 6. Consequently, s 59 of and Sched 3 to the YJCEA 1999 amend the various existing statutes to provide that, in any criminal proceedings, the prosecution will not be able to introduce evidence of, or put questions about, answers given under compulsion unless the evidence is first introduced or a question is asked by or on behalf of the accused in the proceedings.

Second, in the few cases where the right to silence was used under the pre-Act law, we need to ask how far juries were genuinely sympathetic to the judge's directions that they could not assume guilt from silence. Juries convicted in half of such cases, so there is evidence that jurors were suspicious and sceptical about people who exercised the right, just as they may be today where someone exercises the right (that is, remains silent from arrest until the jury retires without relying on any fact he could have mentioned earlier).

In research undertaken in 1995 and 1996, Bucke, Street and Brown (Home Office Research Study 199, 2000) found that the provisions had had a marked impact on various aspects of the investigation and trial of criminal offences, including suspects' use of silence at the police station, police practices in relation to interviewing and disclosure, the advice given at police stations by legal advisers and the proportion of defendants testifying at trial. However, they concluded that there was no discernible increase in charges or convictions and reported that there was considerable scepticism about the effect on professional criminals. For an interesting account of these controversial reforms, see Ian Dennis, 'The Criminal Justice and Public Order Act 1994: the evidence provisions' [1995] Crim LR 4. For a more detailed discussion, see S. Easton, *The Case for the Right to Silence*, 2nd edn (1998).

13.5.18 Directions to the jury on silent defendants

Following the enactment of the CJPOA 1994, there has been a steady stream of case law as to correct judicial practice when directing the jury about the drawing of adverse inferences under s 34 and s 35.

In *R v Cowan* (1995), the Court of Appeal considered what should be said in the summing up if the defendant decides not to testify. The jury must be directed that (as provided by s 38(3) of the CJPOA 1994) an inference from failure to give evidence could not on its own prove guilt. The jury had to be satisfied (on the basis of the evidence called by the prosecution) that the prosecution had established a case to answer before inferences could be drawn from the accused's silence. The jury could only draw an adverse inference from the accused's silence; they concluded that the silence could only be sensibly attributed to the accused having no answer to the charge or none that could stand up to cross-examination.

The difficult issue as to correct judicial practice when the accused remains silent during interview on the advice of his solicitor was considered in *R v Condron* (1997) and *R v Argent* (1997). These cases make it clear that such advice was only one factor to be taken into consideration, along with all the other circumstances, in any jury determination as to whether adverse inferences could be drawn from a 'no comment' interview. In *Condron*, the Court of Appeal considered the guidelines set out in *Cowan* (above) and concluded that they were equally applicable to failure to answer questions (s 34) and failure to testify (s 35).

Stuart-Smith LJ, giving the judgment of the court, went on to say that it was desirable to direct the jury that if, despite any evidence relied upon to explain the failure (to answer questions), or in the absence of such evidence, it concluded that the failure could only sensibly be attributed to the accused having fabricated the evidence subsequently, the jury might draw an adverse inference.

More detailed guidance was given in *Argent*, where Lord Bingham set out the conditions that had to be met before s 34 could operate. They include:

(a) the failure to answer had to occur before the defendant was charged;

(b) the alleged failure must occur during questioning under caution;

(c) the questioning must be directed at trying to discover whether and by whom the offence has been committed;

(d) the failure must be a failure to mention any fact relied on in the person's defence;

(e) the fact the defendant failed to mention had to be one which this particular defendant could reasonably be expected to have mentioned when being questioned, taking account of all the circumstances existing at that time (for example, the time of day, the defendant's age, experience, mental capacity, state of health, sobriety, personality and access to legal advice).

The Court of Appeal in *Argent* took a similar view to that of the Judicial Studies Board (JSB) as regards the relevance of legal advice to remain silent. This, of course, puts the solicitor who attends the interview under some difficulty, especially as The Law Society guidelines suggest that to remain silent is inappropriate when the police have made less than full disclosure of the evidence available. However, Lord Bingham in *Argent* added that the jury is neither concerned with the correctness of the solicitor's advice, nor with whether it complies with the Law Society guidelines, but with the reasonableness of the defendant's conduct in all circumstances.

The court approved the trial judge's direction to the jury:

> You should consider whether or not he is able to decide for himself what he should do or having asked for a solicitor to advise him he would not challenge that advice [at p 34].

Finally, in *R v Daniel (Anthony Junior)* (1998), it was held that the *dicta* of Stuart-Smith LJ in *Condron* (1997) need not be confined to a subsequent fabrication. In addition to the JSB specimen direction, it is desirable for the judge in an appropriate case to include a passage to the effect that, if the jury conclude that the accused's reticence could only sensibly be attributed to his unwillingness to be subjected to further questioning, or that he had not thought about all the facts, or that he did not have an innocent explanation to give, they might draw an adverse inference. This was upheld soon after by the Court of Appeal in *R v Beckles and Montague* (1999), when the defendant gave a 'no comment' interview on legal advice. It was held that the proper inference under s 34 was not limited to recent fabrication.

Where, however, a judge concludes that the requirements of s 34 have not been satisfied and therefore that it is not open to him to leave to the jury the possibility of drawing adverse inferences, he must direct the jury that it should not in any way hold against the accused the fact that he did not answer questions in interview (*R v McGarry* (1998)).

The provisions as to silence must now also meet the requirements of Art 6 of the ECHR. The ECtHR had already held in *Murray v UK* that this right is not absolute and that a system under which inferences could be drawn from silence did not in itself constitute a breach of Art 6, though particular caution when drawing inferences was necessary. This was re-affirmed in *Condron v UK* (2000), where the Court asserted that though silence could not be the only or even the main basis for any conviction, it was right that it should be taken into account in circumstances which clearly called for an explanation from the accused (examples might be having to account for presence at the scene of the crime, or having to account for the presence of fibres on clothing). It should be noted that although the specimen direction issued by the JSB and used by judges emphasises that silence cannot be the only basis for a conviction, it does not make any reference to whether it can be the main basis for conviction. Thus, there is a possible conflict between the approach under the ECHR and that currently adopted in English courts.

The ECtHR considers that legal advice is of great significance in this system. Thus, both *Murray v UK* and *Condron v UK* stressed the importance of access to legal advice at the time of any interview. As explained earlier, the finding in *Murray v UK* that denial of access to legal advice, in conjunction with the drawing of inferences, amounted to a breach of Art 6 led to the amendment to the CJPOA 1994 contained in s 34(2A). However, access in itself is not the end of the matter. The question which then arises is whether the drawing of inferences may be improper under the ECHR where silence results from legal advice. The approach of the English courts to this aspect has been discussed above. The ECtHR has held in both *Condron v UK* and *Averill v UK* (2000) that legal advice may be a proper reason for declining to answer questions and that it may not be fair to draw adverse inferences in such cases. A solicitor representing a young or otherwise vulnerable person may recognise that the evidence against the client is very weak. Advising such a client to 'say nothing' will often make good sense. See A. Keogh, 'The right to silence – revisited again' (2003), 153, NLJ, 1352–3.

The jury should be informed that no adverse inference should be drawn where a defendant 'genuinely and reasonably' relies on a solicitor's advice to remain silent in interview; *R v Beckles* [2004] All ER (D) 226.

In *R v Robert Webber* (2004), the House of Lords decided that, for the purposes of working out whether a silent defendant in court was 'relying on a fact' used in his defence (and therefore something which could prompt the judge to allow the jury to draw adverse inferences about the defendant's silence), answers given by a witness for the prosecution who was being cross-questioned by the defendant's counsel were facts.

A positive suggestion put to a witness by or on behalf of a defendant could amount to a fact relied on in his defence for the purpose of s 34 of the CJPOA 1994 even if that suggestion was not accepted by a witness.

The defendant (W) appealed from a decision (summarised below) that the trial judge was correct to give a direction under s 34 of the CJPOA 1994. W and two co-defendants had been charged with conspiracy to murder. The prosecution case against W was based on three incidents. When interviewed by police about each incident, W had either denied involvement in any conspiracy or said that he was not present. At trial, W's counsel put it to several prosecution witnesses that their evidence relating to the incidents was wrong. The witnesses rejected counsel's suggestions. The certified question for the House was whether a suggestion put to a witness by or on behalf of a defendant could amount to a 'fact relied on in his defence' for the purpose of s 34 of the Act, if that suggestion was not adopted by the witness. W submitted that s 34 was directed to evidence and that suggestions of counsel were not evidence unless or until accepted by a witness. The prosecution submitted that such suggestions were matters on which a defendant relied, whether or not he supported them by his own or other evidence, and whether or not prosecution witnesses accepted them.

The court held that a positive suggestion put to a witness by or on behalf of a defendant could amount to a fact relied on in his defence for the purpose of s 34 even if that suggestion was not accepted by a witness. The word 'fact' in s 34 covered any alleged fact that was in issue and was put forward as part of the defence case. If the defendant advanced at trial any pure fact or exculpatory explanation or account that, if true, he could reasonably have been expected to advance at earlier, s 34 was potentially applicable. A defendant relied on a fact or matter in his defence not only when he gave or adduced evidence of it, but also when counsel, acting on his instructions, put a specific and positive case to prosecution witnesses, as opposed to asking questions intended to probe or test the prosecution case. That was so, whether or not the prosecution witness accepted the suggestion put. The appeal was dismissed.

13.5.19 Tape-recording of interrogations

The police were initially very hostile to the recommendation of the Philips Royal Commission on Criminal Procedure that there should be tape-recording of interviews with suspects. After a while, however, the police became more enthusiastic when it became apparent that the tape-recording of the interrogations increased the proportion of guilty pleas and reduced the challenges to prosecution evidence. Tape-recording of interviews is conducted in accordance with Code of Practice E. The tapes are time-coded so that they cannot be interfered with. It is now compulsory for all police stations to record all interviews with suspects interrogated in connection with indictable offences.

13.5.20 Confessions and the admissibility of evidence

It was long established by the common law that a confession would not be admitted in evidence if it was 'involuntary' in the sense that it was obtained by threat or promise held out by a person in authority. This would include 'even the most gentle, if I may put it that way, threats or slight inducements', *per* Lord Parker CJ in *R v Smith* (1959). In that case, a sergeant major had put the whole company on parade and told them no one would be allowed to move until one of them gave details about which of them had been involved in a fight resulting in a stabbing. A confession resulting from this incident was ruled to have been something that should not have been admitted (although the conviction was not quashed as there was other evidence against the defendant).

In *R v Zavekas* (1970), a conviction was quashed where it had resulted from an improper promise. Z was told that the police were arranging an identification parade and that he would be free to go if he was not picked out. He asked whether he could be allowed to go at once if he made a statement. The officer agreed and then Z made a statement admitting guilt. The admission was given in evidence and Z was convicted. His conviction was quashed even though the inducement had not been proffered by the police. Similarly, the Court of Appeal regarded it a 'fatal inducement' for a police officer to have agreed to a request by the defendant, in *R v Northam* (1968), for a second offence to be taken into account at a forthcoming trial rather than tried as a separate matter.

Apart from threats and promises, 'oppression' leading to a confession would render such a statement inadmissible. The Judges Rules were a set of guidelines made by Divisional Court judges for excluding unreliable evidence, but they left it as discretionary whether violation of the rules should result in the exclusion of any resultant evidence.

There had been a significant change in the approach of the courts by the 1980s. The new approach was to ask, even where there had been promises or threats, as a matter of fact and causation, had there been an involuntary confession? In *R v Rennie* (1985), Lord Lane CJ stated that even where a confession was made 'with a hope that an admission may lead to an earlier release or a lighter sentence' and the hope was prompted by something said or done by a person in authority, the confession would not automatically be regarded as involuntary. The same applied where, as in the present case, a confession was prompted by a fear that otherwise the police would interview and perhaps charge the defendant's sister and mother. The judge should apply his 'common sense' and assume that voluntary meant 'of one's own free will'.

This approach was much criticised as it was often impossible for even trained psychologists to realise which pressures on a suspect being questioned were the ones that prompted him to confess.

The law is now contained in s 76 of PACE 1984, which renders inadmissible any confession (i) obtained as a result of oppression (s 76(2)(a)) or (ii) which was obtained in consequence of something 'likely in the circumstances to render unreliable any confession which might be made by the accused in consequence thereof' (s 76(2)(b)). 'Oppression' is defined by s 76(8) to include 'torture, inhuman or degrading treatment, and the use or threat of violence'.

13.5.21 Oppression

The judge rules on whether evidence is admissible on these lines: if it is admitted, then the jury decides whether to believe it. There should be a 'trial within a trial' – without the jury – to determine whether the evidence is admissible (*R v Liverpool Juvenile Court ex p R* (1988)).

The courts have not found much evidence of 'oppression' in police questioning. In *Miller* (1986), a paranoid schizophrenic had confessed to killing his girlfriend. He had admitted the killing in an interview which contained both reliable and unreliable matter. He later retracted his confession. It was argued for him at trial that the confession should be excluded under s 76(2)(a) – that it had been obtained by 'oppression of the person who made it', as it had come as the result of protracted and oppressive interviews which had caused him to suffer an episode of 'schizophrenic terror'. Medical evidence was given that the style and length of questioning had produced a state of voluntary insanity in which his language reflected hallucinations and delusion. The judge would not exclude the evidence and the defendant was convicted of manslaughter. The Court of Appeal held that the mere fact that questions triggered off hallucinations in the defendant was not evidence of oppression.

In *R v Fulling* (1987), the Court of Appeal held that it was not oppression for the police to tell the defendant that her lover had been having an affair with another woman, which so affected her that she made a confession. The word 'oppression', the court held, should be given its ordinary dictionary meaning as stated in the *Oxford English Dictionary*:

> The exercise of authority or power in a burdensome, harsh or wrongful manner; unjust or cruel treatment of subjects, inferiors, etc; the imposition of unreasonable or unjust burdens.

13.5.22 Unreliability

Evidence of a confession can be excluded if it was given:

> ... in consequence of anything said or done which was likely in the circumstances existing at the time, to render unreliable any confession which might be made by him in consequence thereof ... [s 76(2)(b)].

The phrase 'anything said or done' means by someone other than the suspect. In *R v Goldenberg* (1988), G, a heroin addict, was arrested on a charge of conspiracy to supply diamorphine. He requested an interview five days after his arrest and during this he gave information about a man whom he said had supplied him with heroin. It was argued for G at trial that he had given the statement to get bail and thus to be able to feed his addiction; that the words 'in consequence of anything said or done ...' included things said or done by the suspect and that the critical thing here was the things G had said and done, namely, requested the interview and given any statement that would be likely to get him out of the station. G was convicted and his appeal was dismissed. Neill LJ stated:

> In our judgment, the words 'said or done' in s 76(2)(b) of the 1984 Act do not extend so as to include anything said or done by the person making the confession. It is clear from the wording of the section and the use of the words 'in consequence' that a causal link must be shown between what was said or done and the subsequent confession. In our view, it necessarily follows that 'anything said or done' is limited to something external to the person making the confession and to something which is likely to have some influence on him.

The reasoning in cases like *R v Zavekas* (see 13.5.20, above) has now clearly been rejected. This view is confirmed by Code C – that if a suspect asks an officer what action will be taken in the event of his answering questions, making a statement or refusing to do either, the officer may inform him what action he proposes to take in that event 'provided that the action is itself proper and warranted' (para 11.3).

13.5.23   *R v Heaton* (1993)

In *R v Heaton* (1993), the appellant was convicted of manslaughter of his 26 day old son. The evidence of the mother, who was of limited intelligence, was that the appellant had shaken the child hard to quieten him and that the child subsequently went limp and breathless. She had also said that she had given the child Calpol (a children's medicine containing paracetamol).

Due to difficulties in contacting the appellant's solicitor, he had been in custody overnight for some 15 and a half hours by the time he was able to see a solicitor. As he said he had been ill, he was examined by a doctor who said he was fit to be interviewed. He was interviewed for about 75 minutes in the presence of the solicitor and the interview was tape-recorded. The first part of the interview dealt with his background details. When asked about the events leading up to the child's death, he at first denied that he had held the child. Later, he admitted holding the child but denied holding him up in the air. Under further questioning, he admitted holding the child up in the air and finally conceded that he had shaken the child about four times to and fro to keep him quiet and that the child's head was flopping.

The defence case was that the death could have been caused solely by the administration of the wrong drug by the mother; although she claimed to have given the child Calpol, which contained paracetamol, no evidence of any paracetamol was found in the child's body on postmortem. However, promethazine was found in the blood and was the active ingredient of Phenergen, a drug which the mother also had in the house for the older children. In his evidence, the appellant said that he came downstairs to find the baby purplish in the face and breathless and had seen the mother giving him some medicine, following which she became hysterical and shook the baby. In the interview, he had been upset and as the police would not believe what he was saying, in the end he had told them that he had shaken the child. He denied that he had done so violently or in order to quieten the child.

On the *voir dire* (the trial within a trial where the judge, having asked the jury to go out, decides a dispute between counsel as to whether certain evidence is admissible), the defence sought to exclude the evidence of the appellant's interview under ss 76 and 78 of PACE 1984. An application was made to call a psychiatrist, Dr Z, on the *voir dire*. The trial judge ruled against admitting Dr Z's evidence and ruled that the interview should be admitted.

On appeal, it was argued on the appellant's behalf that the trial judge was wrong to exclude the evidence of Dr Z, and that the trial judge should have excluded the interview because the officers concerned had applied pressure to the appellant, raising their voices and repeating their questions.

13.5.24   The Court of Appeal's decision

The Court of Appeal dismissed the appeal, holding:

- The trial judge had considered Dr Z's report, which was based upon a single interview with the appellant, sight of the case papers, hearing of the interview tapes and a conversation with the probation officer. Dr Z had noted in particular: 'My impression is that he is not exceptionally bright and is possibly of dull normal intelligence and is very suggestible.' In *R v Turner* (1975), Lawton LJ said at p 83:

  > ... an expert's opinion is admissible to furnish the court with scientific information which is likely to be outside the experience and knowledge of a judge or jury. If, on the proven facts, a judge or jury can form their own conclusions without help, then the opinion of an expert is unnecessary. In such a case, if it is given dressed up in scientific jargon, it may make judgment more difficult. The fact that an expert witness has impressive scientific qualifications does not, by that fact alone, make his opinion on matters of human nature or behaviour within the limits of normality any more helpful than that of the jurors themselves; but there is a danger that they may think it does.

In the more recent case of *R v Raghip, Silcott and Braithwaite* (1991), the Court of Appeal had drawn a distinction between psychiatric or psychological evidence going to *mens rea* and such evidence going to the reliability of a confession, but had not criticised the general principle laid down in *Turner*. The court had rejected a 'judge for yourself' approach by the judge in respect of the jury and, it would seem, in respect of his own task on a *voir dire*, where there was expert evidence which would have been of assistance in assessing the defendant's mental condition. In that case, Alliott J said:

... the state of the psychological evidence before us ... is such that the jury would have been assisted in assessing the mental condition of Raghip and the consequent reliability of the alleged confessions. Notwithstanding that Raghip's IQ was at 74 just in the borderline range, a man chronologically aged 19 years seven months at the date of the interview with a level of functioning equivalent to that of a child of nine years, and the reading capacity of a child of six years, cannot be said to be normal. It would be impossible for the layman to divide that data from Raghip's performance in the witness box, still less the abnormal suggestibility of which [the expert witness] spoke.

- There was in *Heaton* no suggestion of mental handicap or retardation; the appellant was within the normal range of intelligence, albeit towards the duller end of it. There was nothing more than Dr Z's bare impression that the appellant was very suggestible; there was no data on which to found that assertion nor was it clear that 'very suggestible' was outside the normal range. The judge expressly indicated that he should be told if there was anything more to Dr Z's evidence than was contained in his report and he was not informed of anything else. In those circumstances, he concluded that there was nothing in the doctor's impression which complied with the tests laid down in *Turner* and illustrated by *Raghip*; in the court's judgment, he was justified in ruling as he did. Unless the medical evidence sought to be introduced on an issue of this kind was truly based on some scientific data or expert analysis outside the experience of judge and jury, a mere impression, even of a highly qualified doctor, that the defendant 'is not exceptionally bright' or was 'very suggestible' was not admissible for the reasons set out by Lawton LJ.

- The court had read the transcript of the interview and heard the tape-recordings. The appellant had a full opportunity to consult with a solicitor before the interview and the solicitor was present throughout. A doctor had examined the appellant and pronounced him fit to be interviewed. The questioning lasted in all only some 75 minutes and much of the first two tapes was concerned merely with taking the appellant's history. Voices were slightly raised but there was no shouting and no oppressive hostility; the pace of the interview was slow and the appellant was given time to consider his replies. Some questions were repeated several times but not inappropriately. In *R v Paris, Abdullahi and Miller* (1994), where similar arguments were raised, the court said:

Of course, it is perfectly legitimate for officers to pursue their interrogation of their suspect with a view to eliciting his account or gaining admissions. They are not required to give up after the first denial or even after a number of denials.

In that case, the questioning had continued for some 13 hours and the tapes had shown hostility and bullying on the part of the interviewing officers. In the present case, the situation was wholly different, with the appellant changing his story gradually over a comparatively short period and providing further details without the police putting them in. The judge had been right to conclude that the prosecution had discharged the burden upon them to exclude oppression and the possibility that the circumstances might have rendered the admission unreliable.

In a commentary on *Heaton* in the Criminal Law Review, it is pointed out that the law on confessions is developing in a number of ways to prevent, as far as is possible, the conviction of weak minded and suggestible persons on the basis of their own unreliable statements. In addition to the exclusionary rule in s 76(2)(b) of PACE 1984 and the discretion in s 78, defendants labouring under a 'significant degree of mental handicap' are protected by the rule in *McKenzie* (1994), which requires an unconvincing case based solely on confessions to be withdrawn from the jury.

'Confessions' made to fellow prisoners are particularly controversial. In 1996, Lin, Megan and Josie Russell were attacked while taking their dog for a walk. Lin and Megan were killed; Josie suffered serious injuries. Michael Stone was arrested and charged with the murders. He was then remanded into custody. At his trial in 1998, two fellow inmates, Damien Daley and Harry Thompson, were called as witnesses. Both alleged that Stone had 'confessed' to them. Stone was convicted. The next day Thompson contacted national newspapers. He said that he had lied in court because of police pressures. In 2001, Stone's convictions were quashed by the Court of Appeal. At his re-trial, the prosecution used Daley's evidence and Stone was re-convicted. A strong argument could be made for excluding such dubious evidence under s 78 of PACE. The central problem has been described by Gwyn Morgan in 'Cell confessions' (2002) 152 NLJ 453:

> There may be a strong incentive for 'grasses' to come up with their incriminating stories. Deals may be done with the police as to the withdrawal of charges. Even where this is not the case, those on remand may well feel – even if they are wrong – that giving evidence for the prosecution will ease the way when their own cases come up. And where the grasses are already convicted, they may be anxious (again rightly or wrongly) to give a favourable impression to the prison authorities or the parole board. What's more, in contrast to most witnesses, coming to court does not adversely interfere with their lives; it's a day out.

See also 'Cell confessions – no stone left unturned' (2005), 155, NLJ, 550–551.

13.5.25 Research findings

In an interesting study of police interview techniques ('Police interview techniques: establishing truth or proof?' (1993) 33 British J of Criminology 3), John Baldwin analysed 400 videoed police interviews with suspects – 100 from each of four police stations – and 200 audio-taped interviews taken from two busy stations. As he observes, an interrogation leading to a confession can be of great importance to the police, as it can provide an alternative to a time-consuming investigation of the crime. Baldwin did not find much evidence of oppression, but rather of deficiency in questioning technique:

> ... coercion or belligerence in police interviews strike the observer much less frequently than feebleness and ineptitude. Instances of heavy handedness were much less common than unduly timorous questioning. It must, nonetheless, be acknowledged that the boundaries between officers acting, say, upon an assumption of guilt, or failing

adequately to listen to suspects' responses, and exerting undue pressures to induce a confession, are thoroughly blurred.

Baldwin concluded that, evaluated as a search for 'the truth', most police interviews were 'thoroughly deficient'. But such a judgment would be to miss the point of interrogation, a central feature of which is concerned with the future rather than past events. Interrogations are, he argued, conducted with an eye to any subsequent trial:

> A main purpose of the interrogation is thus to seek to limit, close down, or pre-empt the future options available to the subject. It will be very difficult for suspects to claim in court that, say, goods were taken by accident or that they were not at the scene when precisely the opposite was established in an earlier taped interview.

13.5.26 Evidence illegally or improperly obtained

There is an overlap between the subject of this discussion and that above because sometimes the illegally or improperly obtained evidence will be a confession, in which case the rules above will also apply.

There was for a long time a judicial discretion to exclude otherwise admissible evidence on the basis that it would be unfair to the defendant. The *dictum* of Lord Goddard CJ on this was often cited. He said: 'If, for instance, some admission or piece of evidence, for example, a document, had been obtained from a defendant by a trick, no doubt the judge might properly rule it out.' (See *Kuruma Son of Kaniu v R* (1955), a Privy Council case dealing with an appeal from Kenya. It held that, if evidence was relevant, it did not matter how it was obtained.)

In *R v Sang* (1979), the House of Lords took a very restrictive view of the discretion, holding that it could not be used to exclude evidence merely on the basis that it was given by an *agent provocateur*. The defendant claimed he had been induced to commit an offence by an informer acting on the instructions of the police. All the judges ruled that there was no defence of entrapment in English law. They were also unanimous in ruling that (except for confessions or issues of self-incrimination) no discretion existed to exclude evidence simply on the basis that it had been improperly or illegally obtained. Such illegality might lead to civil proceedings or disciplinary action within the police, but not to the exclusion of evidence. The only basis for excluding relevant evidence was if its prejudicial effect outweighed its probative value. This reasoning has been reconfirmed by the Court of Appeal in *R v Spurthwaite and Gill* (1993).

The approach of s 78 of PACE 1984 is to widen the discretion. It does not go so far as the system in the USA where improperly obtained evidence is inadmissible – the doctrine that the fruit of the poisoned tree should not be eaten. It states that the court *may* refuse to allow evidence on which the prosecution proposes to rely:

> ... if it appears to the court that, having regard to all the circumstances, including the circumstances in which the evidence was obtained, the admission of the evidence would have such an adverse effect on the fairness of the proceedings that the court ought not to admit it.

The courts have been persuaded on many occasions to exclude evidence using this section. In fact, Zander has suggested that 'the judges have forged the somewhat ambiguous words of s 78 into a powerful weapon to hold the police accountable for breaches of the law and the Codes of Practice'. Most cases have involved access to solicitors or the law relating to interrogations. In *R v Absolam* (1989), the Court of Appeal quashed a conviction for supplying cannabis where A, in contravention of the Code, had not been told of his right to a solicitor and rules about the tape-recording of interviews were broken.

Unlike the rule applying to s 76 (see 13.5.22 above), there does not need to be a trial within a trial under s 78 to determine whether the evidence is admissible. The admissibility of a confession can be opposed under both s 76 and s 78. The court will be less willing to exclude evidence where there were technical breaches but the defendant had experience of police stations. In *R v Dunford* (1991), the Court of Appeal refused to quash a conviction in spite of a serious breach of s 58 (see 13.5.4 above) because D, who had several previous convictions, answered 'No comment' to awkward questions by the police and refused to sign a record of the interview. The court thought it was extremely doubtful 'whether the solicitor's advice would have added anything to [his] knowledge of his rights'.

Since the HRA became fully operative in October 2000, it has no longer been possible to treat such issues merely as involving interpretation of s 78(1) of PACE 1984 itself. Additionally, Art 6 of the ECHR must be taken into account by any court in appropriate circumstances. Article 6 guarantees the right to a fair trial, and a trial may not be fair if there are irregularities in the investigative process which result in evidence being unlawfully obtained. It has already been seen that the Court of Appeal has wavered over whether a lack of fairness in a trial contrary to Art 6 should essentially require a conviction to be quashed as being unsafe (see 13.5.2 above). In the context currently under consideration, the interesting issue may well be whether the illegal or improper manner of obtaining the evidence means that its use in the trial renders the trial itself unfair. If it does not, then Art 6 clearly has no effect. In *Khan* (1996), it was held by the House of Lords that evidence obtained from a secret listening device planted by the police, and which was the only evidence on which the accused was convicted of drug-dealing, was rightly admitted. Since the authority to engage in such conduct was not properly established by legal rules, this form of covert surveillance was a breach of the right to respect for private life, home and correspondence as guaranteed by Art 8. When, in *Khan v UK* (2000), the accused subsequently argued before the ECtHR that his Convention rights had been violated, the Court agreed in respect of Art 8, but denied that that meant that his right to a fair trial had been violated under Art 6, even though the conviction was based only on that evidence. Criticising this approach, Ashworth has argued strongly that when exercising the discretion to exclude evidence under s 78, English courts should give extra weight to the fact that the evidence was obtained in breach of a Convention right, rather than in breach of domestic law ([2000] Crim LR 684).

13.5.27   Runciman Royal Commission proposals

The Commission's recommendations in this area are of particular interest, as it was set up in the wake of a number of grave miscarriages of justice in which people had been wrongly convicted on the basis of subsequently discredited confession evidence. The Commission was announced on the day the Birmingham Six were released from jail having served 16 years for crimes which later scientific evidence showed they could not have confessed to in the way the police alleged.

13.5.28   Confession evidence

The Commission said:

- (para 85) when PACE 1984 is next revisited, attention should be given to the fact that s 77 (judge's duty to caution the jury of the need for care in cases where mentally handicapped people have made confessions without independent witnesses) is limited to the 'mentally handicapped' and does not include the 'mentally ill' or other categories of the 'mentally disordered';

- (para 86) the law should be changed so that a judge may stop any case if the prosecution evidence is demonstrably unsafe or unsatisfactory or too weak to be allowed to go to the jury;

- (para 87) wherever a confession has allegedly been made to the police outside the police station, whether tape-recorded or not, it should be put to the suspect at the beginning of the first tape-recorded interview at the station. Failure to do this may render the alleged confession inadmissible, but, if the suspect does not confirm the confession on the tape, it should not automatically be inadmissible;

- (para 88) an alleged confession to an investigating official should be allowed to go before the jury even if not tape-recorded, provided it meets the tests contained in PACE 1984 and the judge believes the jury could safely consider it.

13.5.29   Corroboration of confessions

The Commission recommended that:

- (para 89) there should be a judicial warning in cases where confession evidence is involved. The precise terms of the warning should depend on the circumstances of the case. If it remains possible for a confession to be admitted without other supporting evidence, the jury should be warned that great care is needed before convicting on the basis of the confession alone;

- (para 90) the majority of the Commission believed that where a confession is credible and has passed the tests laid down in PACE 1984, the jury should be able to consider it even in the absence of other evidence. The judge should in all such cases give a strong warning to the jury. The other evidence which the jury should be advised to look for should be supporting evidence (that is, of a different kind) in the *R v Turnbull* (1977) sense.

There was considerable disquiet among defence lawyers and civil liberty groups that the Commission had not recommended the automatic inadmissibility of uncorroborated confessions (see, for example, (1993) *The Guardian*, 7 July). Consider, for example, the case of the Guildford Four. Three men and a woman were jailed for life in 1975 after being convicted of bombing pubs in 1974, which killed five people. The evidence against them amounted to confessions they were alleged to have made. Fourteen years after conviction, a rough set of typed notes was discovered with handwritten addenda which matched one of the men's supposedly contemporaneously recorded interview. The Lord Chief Justice, Lord Lane, concluded that the police officers involved must have lied. The three former officers, however, were acquitted later on charges of attempting to pervert the course of justice. Alistair Logan, solicitor for two of the men, has pointed out that the men would not necessarily have been saved by Runciman's recommendations, because these accept the possibility of uncorroborated confessions going to the jury.

The Commission's Report notes that it is now generally accepted that people do on occasions confess to crimes they have not committed, perhaps due to a desire for notoriety, to protect somebody else or for immediate advantage like wanting to get out of the police station. The long-held belief that people will not make false statements against themselves can no longer be sustained. The Report advocates the introduction of continuous video-recording of all police custody suites at a cost of about £9 million. The Report states (para 50):

> Continuous video-recording (including sound track) of all the activities in the custody office, the passages and stairways leading from the custody office to the cells and, if feasible, the cell passage and the doors of individual cells of all police stations designated under PACE 1984 as suitable for detaining suspects should be introduced as soon as practicable.

John Baldwin has argued ('Power and police interviews' (1993) 143 NLJ 1194, 14 August) that the Royal Commission's Report was sadly lacking in not providing recommendations for a better legal regulation of police questioning of suspects. He says in the Report:

> There is little new thinking or analysis; rather, the emphasis is upon re-working old ideas and offering encouragement to those professional groups which are striving to improve their own procedures.

The problem needing to be addressed, argues Baldwin, is basically one of power:

> Legal advisers and their clients are bound to be relatively powerless in a situation in which it is police officers who decide when an interview takes place, how it is to be conducted and for how long. Interviews take place on police territory and on police terms. Police officers can even determine who sits where in the interview room and they may deliberately prevent eye contact between legal representatives and their clients by physically bolting the chairs to the floor. Their power to eject troublesome advisers from the interview room [Code of Practice C, para 6.9], though very infrequently exercised, underlines still further who is in charge.

13.6   Revised PACE Codes

In April 2003, revised PACE Codes of Practice A–E came into force. Although the essential structure remains substantially intact, there are numerous amendments.

Code A – stop and search. It is anticipated that the revised Code A will make it clear beyond doubt that searches must not take place unless the necessary legal power exists. Police officers will also be expected to record encounters which do not involve searches. If an officer asks a member of the public to account for his 'actions, behaviour, presence in the area or possession of anything', a record must be made. The person stopped will be entitled to a copy.

Code B – entry and search of premises. Paragraph 1.3 states:

> The right to privacy and respect for personal property are key principles of the Human Rights Act 1998. Powers of entry, search and seizure should be fully and clearly justified before use because they may significantly interfere with the occupiers' privacy. Officers should consider if the necessary objectives can be met by less intrusive means.

Paragraph 7.7 states:

> The Criminal Justice and Police Act 2001, Part 2, gives officers limited powers to seize property from premises or persons so that they can sift or examine it elsewhere. Officers must be careful they only exercise these powers when it is essential and they do not remove any more material than necessary. The removal of large quantities of material, much of which may not ultimately be retainable, may have serious implications for the owners … Officers must carefully consider if removing copies or images of relevant material or data would be a satisfactory alternative to removing originals.

Code C – treatment and questioning in the police station. The revised version of Code C restricts the drawing of adverse inferences by a detainee's decision to remain silent until he has received legal advice. This has implications for the cautioning of suspects. The revisions are largely a response to *Murray v UK* (1996).

Code D – identification procedures. These have been amended partly to take account of the increasing use of video evidence.

Code E – tape recordings. Revisions to Code E largely reflect changes to cautioning procedures.

13.7   The Criminal Justice Act 2003 Amendments of the Police and Criminal Evidence Act 1984

The following changes were made by the 2003 Act and these are to be implemented, in the main, during 2005.

Section 1: extension of powers to stop and search

This section extends the definition of prohibited articles under s 1 of PACE 1984 so that it includes articles made, adapted or intended for use in causing criminal damage. It does this by amending the list of offences in s 1(8) of PACE 1984 to include offences under s 1 of the Criminal Damage Act 1971. The effect is to give police officers power to stop and search where they have reasonable suspicion that a person is carrying, for example, a paint spray can which they intend to use in producing graffiti.

Section 1(1) of the Criminal Damage Act 1971 made it a criminal offence for a person to destroy or damage any property belonging to another without lawful excuse if he intends to destroy or damage that property or is reckless as to whether that property would be destroyed or damaged. Section 1(2) of that Act created a related offence of destroying or damaging property with intent to endanger life.

Section 2: warrants to enter and search

This section enhances the powers of persons authorised to accompany constables executing search warrants. Section 16(2) of PACE 1984 allows a search warrant to authorise persons to accompany any constable who is executing the warrant.

A new sub-s (2A) provides that any such person has the same powers as the constable whom he is accompanying in relation to executing the warrant and seizing anything to which the warrant relates. Sub-section (2B) ensures that the person can only exercise these powers when he is accompanied by a constable and under that constable's supervision.

This addition to PACE 1984 will ensure that persons who accompany police officers in the execution of warrants can play an effective role in searching and seizure. For example, it will often be necessary for someone who is an expert in computing or financial matters to assist a constable in searching premises where particular types of records are likely to be found. This provision enables such experts to take an active role in carrying out searches and in seizing material, rather than being present in a merely advisory or clerical capacity.

Section 3: arrestable offences

Section 3 adds the following offences to the list of specified offences which are arrestable offences:

- the offence of making a false application for a passport;

- the offence of possession of cannabis or cannabis resin (which are controlled drugs);

- the offence of making a false application for a driving licence, etc.

In relation to drugs, this provision allows the police to continue to arrest without a warrant persons in possession of cannabis or cannabis resin following the drug's re-classification from Class B to Class C under the Misuse of Drugs Act 1971, which took place on 29 January 2004.

Section 6: use of telephones for review of police detention

This provision enables reviews of the continuing need for detention without charge carried out under s 40 of PACE 1984 to be conducted over the telephone rather than in person at the police station. Such reviews have to be carried out by an officer of at least inspector rank. PACE 1984 currently only allows telephone reviews where it is not reasonably practicable for the reviewing officer to be present at the police station.

The new s 40A(1) allows a review to be carried out by means of a discussion over the telephone with one or more persons at the police station where the arrested person is held. In practice, the reviewing officer would normally speak to the custody officer at the police station, as well as to the detained person or their legal representative if they wanted to exercise their right to make representations about the continuing need for detention.

The new s 40A(2) specifies that telephone reviews are not applicable where it is reasonably practicable to carry out the review using video conferencing facilities in accordance with regulations under s 45A of PACE 1984. Where such video conferencing facilities are readily available, it is appropriate that they should be used.

Section 7: limits on periods of detention without charge

This provision extends the scope for an officer of at least superintendent rank to authorise detention without charge up to a maximum of 36 hours. As the law currently stands, an officer of superintendent rank or above can extend detention without charge up to an overall period of 36 hours if satisfied that detention is necessary to secure, preserve or obtain evidence, that the investigation is being conducted diligently and expeditiously and that the relevant offence is a serious arrestable offence. Serious arrestable offences are defined in s 116 of PACE 1984 and are either offences which are specified to be 'always serious' (for example, murder) or offences which give rise to serious consequences.

The amendment will allow detention to be extended for up to an overall period of 36 hours where the relevant offence is an arrestable offence, provided the other conditions are satisfied. Section 24 of PACE 1984 defines an arrestable offence as: (a) any offence for which the sentence is fixed by law; (b) any offence for which a sentence of imprisonment of five years or more may be imposed; or (c) any offence specifically listed in Sched 1A to PACE 1984.

This broadened capacity for extended detention without charge will assist the police in dealing effectively with a range of offences, for example, robbery, where it will sometimes be extremely difficult or impossible to complete the necessary investigatory processes within 24 hours.

Section 8: property of detained persons

This provision removes the requirement of the custody officer, currently in s 54(1) of PACE 1984, to record or cause to be recorded everything a detained person has with him on entering custody. The custody officer will still be under a duty to ascertain what the person has with him, but the nature and detail of any recording will be at the custody officer's discretion. He will also have discretion as to whether the record is kept as part of the custody record or as a separate record. This seeks to reduce the serious burden on officers which can arise from recording large volumes of property. Clearly, it will still be necessary to make records, not least to ensure against claims that property has been mishandled or removed. However, it will now be open to the police to make judgments about how to balance the need for recording against the amount of administrative work involved.

Section 9: taking fingerprints without consent

This section extends the circumstances in which the police may take a person's fingerprints without consent to include taking fingerprints from a person arrested for a recordable offence and detained in a police station.

Section 61 of PACE 1984 currently provides powers for taking fingerprints from those in police detention without consent in the following circumstances:

- following charge with a recordable offence or notification that a suspect will be reported for such an offence;

- on the authority of an inspector, which can only be given where the officer has reasonable grounds for believing the suspect is involved in a criminal offence and the fingerprints will tend to confirm or disprove his involvement or facilitate the ascertainment of his identity.

An authorisation may only be given for the purpose of facilitating the ascertainment of the person's identity where the person has either refused to identify themselves or the authorising officer has reasonable grounds to suspect they are not who they claim to be.

Fingerprints may also be taken from a person convicted of a recordable offence or cautioned, warned or reprimanded in respect of such an offence.

Sub-section (2) replaces the existing provisions about the taking of fingerprints on the authority of an inspector with a *wider power* to take fingerprints *from any person detained in consequence of his arrest for a recordable offence.*

The existing requirement to give a person whose fingerprints are taken without consent reasons for doing so and for recording the reason as soon as practical applies to the new power (see s 9(5)).

This amendment to s 61 of PACE 1984 will prevent persons who come into police custody and who may be wanted on a warrant or for questioning on other matters from avoiding detection by giving the police a false name and address. Using Livescan technology, which enables the police to take fingerprints electronically and which is linked to the national fingerprint database (NAFIS), the police will be able to confirm a person's identity whilst he is still in police detention if his fingerprints have been taken previously. It will also assist in enabling vulnerable or violent people to be identified more quickly and dealt with more effectively. A speculative search of the fingerprint crime scene database will also reveal if the person may have been involved in other crimes.

Section 10: taking non-intimate samples without consent

This section extends the circumstances in which the police may take without consent a non-intimate sample from a person in police detention to include taking such a sample

Section 10: taking non-intimate samples without consent

This section extends the circumstances in which the police may take without consent a non-intimate sample from a person in police detention to include taking such a sample
from a person arrested for a recordable offence.

Section 63 of PACE 1984 provides powers for taking a non-intimate sample without consent from a person in the following circumstances:

- following charge with a recordable offence or notification that the person will be reported for such an offence;

- if the person is in police detention (or is being held in custody by the police on the authority of a court), on the authority of an inspector which can only be given where the officer has reasonable grounds for believing the suspect is involved in a recordable offence and the sample will tend to confirm or disprove his involvement;

- following conviction for a recordable offence.

In relation to a person in police detention, sub-ss (2) and (3) replace the existing provisions about the taking of a non-intimate sample on the authority of an inspector with a wider power to take a non-intimate sample from any person in police detention in consequence of his arrest for a recordable offence. This is conditional on him not having had a sample of the same type and from the same part of the body taken already in the course of the investigation or, if one has been taken, that it proved insufficient for the analysis.

The new power is available whether or not the sample is required for the investigation of an offence in which the person is suspected of being involved. However, the police will of course be able to use the new power to obtain samples in cases where, under the present law, an inspector's authorisation would have to be given (for example, in a rape investigation, to obtain a foot impression, a hair sample and a mouth swab).

The existing requirement to give a person from whom a non-intimate sample is taken without consent the reason for doing so and for recording the reason as soon as practicable applies to the new power (see s 10(5)).

The amendments do not affect the existing powers to take samples from persons held in custody by the police on the authority of a court.

DNA profiles extracted from non-intimate samples taken from arrested persons will be added to the samples already held on the National DNA Database and checked for matches with DNA taken from crime scenes.

Section 11: codes of practice

This section makes fundamental changes to the process for establishing and amending codes of practice under PACE 1984. At present, there are codes covering stop and search, searching of premises, detention, identification and the recording of interviews. The amendments provide for a less bureaucratic and more targeted consultation process for new and revised codes and for a simpler process of seeking parliamentary approval for minor or straightforward changes to existing codes. The amendment to s 67 of PACE 1984 will maintain the requirement for an order bringing a new code into operation to be laid before Parliament and approved by each House.

Sub-section (1) establishes a new procedure whereby orders bringing revisions into operation to the codes may be either laid before Parliament or subject to the draft affirmative procedure. The government has undertaken (see *Hansard*, 7 July 2003, col 45) to be bound by the advice of the Home Affairs Select Committee on the appropriate procedure to be followed for proposed changes.

Sub-sections (2)–(4) amend the procedure for making and revising codes of practice applicable to the military police to require codes and revisions simply to be laid before Parliament.

SUMMARY OF CHAPTER 13

THE CRIMINAL PROCESS: (1) THE INVESTIGATION OF CRIME

Legal advisers and their clients are bound to be relatively powerless in a situation in which it is police officers who decide when an interview takes place, how it is to be conducted and for how long. Interviews take place on police territory and on police terms. Police officers can even determine who sits where in the interview room and they may deliberately prevent eye contact between legal representatives and their clients by physically bolting the chairs to the floor. Their power to eject troublesome advisers from the interview room (Code of Practice C, para 6.9), though very infrequently exercised, underlines still further who is in charge.

At the beginning of the 21st century, we can see the first governmental recognition of something called a 'criminal justice system'. The police, the probation service, the prison service, the magistracy, the Crown Courts and other elements have all been grouped within the system. This means that rules or policy relating to one element can be evaluated in terms of their impact in relation to another part of the system. Conflicting public desires arise in this area. On the one hand, there is a general mistrust of certain sorts of policing, and a desire for more protective civil liberties law, while on the other hand, there is a desire for more offenders to be captured and punished, and the belief that, in order for this to succeed, civil liberties need to be reduced. The Macpherson Report following the stabbing of Stephen Lawrence has given a significant impetus for reform of the law relating to policing.

Remedies

Remedies for unlawful arrest include: (1) an action for habeas corpus, (2) that any subsequent prosecution arising from the arrest should fail – s 78 of the Police and Criminal Evidence Act (PACE) 1984 and (3) a claim for damages for false imprisonment. If the arrest is not lawful, then reasonable force may be used to resist it.

Arrest

Arrest can be: (1) under police warrant, (2) under common law for breach of the peace or (3) under legislation, principally PACE 1984. The details in ss 24 and 25 of PACE 1984 and connected cases are very important.

Detention

Detention short of arrest does not exist. Note this confirmation by s 29 of PACE 1984.

Suspects stopped in the street

Suspects stopped in the street are not legally obliged to help police with enquiries. Note the distinction between *Kenlin v Gardiner* (1967) and *Donnelly v Jackman* (1970). Note also that a person may be arrested for being silent or misleading under s 25 if the officer has reasonable doubts about the suspect's name and address, or whether the summons procedure can be used at the address given. Note the newly enlarged powers of stop and search under s 60.

Procedure on arrest

Procedure on arrest involves the arrestor having to inform the suspect of the grounds for arrest (s 28(3)). Note, though, that an arrest becomes lawful from when the information is given. The extent of the required information to the suspect is important (see *Geldberg v Miller* (1961); *R v Telfer* (1976)).

The use of force

The use of force to effect an arrest must be 'reasonable in all the circumstances' (s 3 of the Criminal Law Act 1967 (citizens); s 117 of PACE 1984 (police officers)).

Stop and search

Stop and search is governed by s 1 and Code A of PACE 1984. The judge can exclude evidence obtained in breach of the Codes (s 67(7) of PACE 1984). There are legal obligations on an officer conducting a search (ss 2 and 3 of PACE 1984). Note that the Code is quite specific about what indices can be grounds for reasonable suspicion and which, individually or combined, may not.

Section 60 of the Criminal Justice and Public Order Act (CJPOA) 1994 has provided a new stop and search power in anticipation of violence. Under it, with authorisation, an officer can stop any pedestrian and search him for offensive weapons or dangerous instruments, or even stop vehicles. The authorising officer must reasonably believe that incidents involving serious violence may take place in the area. Section 81 of the same Act creates a new power of stop and search of people and vehicles where it is expedient to do so to prevent certain acts of terrorism.

Search of arrested persons

Search of arrested persons is governed by s 32 of PACE 1984. The person arrested cannot be required to take off more than outer garments. The place where he was arrested, or where he was immediately before, can also be searched under s 32. Note the differences between this power and those under s 18 regarding premises.

Search on detention

Search on detention is governed by s 54 of PACE 1984 and Code C, para 4.1, which require the custody officer to take charge of the process of searching the detained person.

Premises

Premises can be entered by police: (1) with permission, or (2) to prevent a breach of the peace or (3) pursuant to s 18 or s 32 of PACE 1984. The differences between these provisions are important. They are:

Section 18 (entry and   Section 32 (search of •   search after

arrest)   premises has to be at •time of arrest)

Search of person: for weapons, means to • (only s 32)

escape, evidence relating   to 'an

offence', that is, any •   offence.

Search of premises: the police may enter and to enter and search •   search the arrestee's premises where D was • premises to look for when

arrested or evidence relating to the

immediately before • offence for which the arrest for

evidence • person was arrested or relating to *the offence for* •some other

arrestable *which the person was* • offence connected with *arrested*. They

need not be • that or similar to that his premises but the power •

offence for which he was must be based on • arrested.

reasonable belief that the • officer will find

something • for which a search is •

permitted.

Powers of seizure of articles from searches

Powers of seizure of articles from searches under s 19 and Code B, para 6 are quite wide, including items from any offence. The exemptions, like items under legal professional privilege, are important.

Search warrants and safeguards

Search warrants and safeguards issued under s 8 of PACE 1984 require the magistrate to be satisfied of four things. Note the difficulty of balancing the interests of effective policing with those of civil liberties. Note the ambiguity in s 15 and the way it was resolved in *R v Longman* (1988).

Interrogation, Confession and Admissibility of Evidence

The main problem here is for the law to strike the proper balance between giving the police sufficient power to interrogate and protecting the interests of suspects. Too few rules governing how the police can conduct an interrogation and too few rules restricting the sort of evidence that can be put to a jury might easily lead to oppressive behaviour by the police interviewing suspects. Too many restrictive rules, conversely, will thwart the police in their endeavours to prosecute offenders successfully.

The right to have someone informed

The right to have someone informed after arrest is given (s 56(1), Code C, para 5.1) to all suspects after arrest. It can be delayed, however, under s 116. The case must involve a 'serious arrestable offence' and it must be authorised by a superintendent on certain grounds, for example, the arrested person would alert others involved in a crime.

Access to legal advice

Access to legal advice is provided for under s 58 and Code C. The notification must accord with details set out in Code C. Note the criticisms of the Duty Solicitor Scheme. Is it adequately staffed? Note also the circumstances in which legal advice can be delayed under s 116, Code C, Annex B. In certain circumstances, questioning can begin before the detainee's legal advisor arrives (Code C, para 6.6).

Time limits

Note ss 42 and 38 of PACE 1984 for time limits operational before and after charges. Delayed access to legal advice is possible in cases of serious arrestable offences. A suspect can be held for up to 24 hours without being charged; longer with authorisation from the superintendent and up to 96 hours with magistrates' permission.

The right to silence

The right to silence means that a person cannot be charged with obstructing the police in the execution of their duty simply by failing to answer questions. Note the important difference between *Rice v Connolly* (1966) and *Ricketts v Cox* (1982). There are some circumstances where the suspect does have to answer on pain of penalty (s 2 of the Criminal Justice Act 1987).

What could be said in court before April 1995 about the defendant's silence varied according to whether the questions were put by an officer or someone on equal terms with the questioned person. Generally, no adverse inferences could be invited, although the judge could comment on reticence prior to cautioning. Most defendants did not use the right and of those who did, few seemed, according to research, to benefit from it.

Now, after ss 34–37 of the CJPOA 1994, certain adverse inferences may be drawn from a suspect's failure to answer police questions, or his failure to answer them in court.

CHAPTER 14

THE CRIMINAL PROCESS: (2) THE PROSECUTION

The classification of offences and matters relating to transfers for trial, summary trial and trial on indictment are dealt with in Chapter 4.

Until 1986, England was one of only a few countries which allowed the police to prosecute rather than hand over this task to a State agency like the district attorney in the USA or the prosecutor fiscal in Scotland (an office established in the fifteenth century). The Crown Prosecution Service (CPS) was established by the Prosecution of Offences Act (POA) 1985 and the police now play no part in prosecutions beyond the stage of charging the suspect.

There have been many problems with the new system and some writers like Zander have argued that the change could represent a considerable setback for the criminal justice system (Zander, *Cases and Materials on the English Legal System* (2003)). There used to be five different forms of prosecution, those by:

- the police, who prosecuted most offences;

- the Attorney General/Solicitor General, whose permission was needed to prosecute for many serious crimes and who could enter a *nolle prosequi* to stop certain prosecutions or give a *fiat* to disallow them to begin;

- the Director of Public Prosecutions (DPP), who prosecuted in very serious cases and cases brought to him by the government;

- public bodies like local authorities. These used to amount to about 25% of all prosecutions, most being by the Post Office for television licence offences;

- private prosecutions, which involved having to persuade a magistrate of the propriety in issuing a summons. The Attorney General and the DPP both had the power to take over a private prosecution and then drop it for reasons of public policy. Private bodies like stores and the RSPCA most regularly brought prosecutions. A study in 1980 showed that only 2.4% of prosecutions were private (Lidstone, *Prosecutions by Private Individuals and Non-Police Agencies* (1980). The right to bring private prosecutions was retained by section 6(1) POA 1985.

14.1 The Crown Prosecution Service

The move to establish a CPS was precipitated by a report from JUSTICE, the British section of the International Commission of Jurists, in its 1970 Report, *The Prosecution Process in England and Wales*. It argued that the police were not best suited to be prosecutors because they would often have a commitment to winning a case even where the evidence was weak. They were also not best placed to consider the public policy aspects of the discretion not to prosecute. The police were firmly opposed to such a change. They argued that statistics showed that the police were not given to pursuing cases in a way which led to a high rate of acquittal. They also showed that in cases involving miscarriages of justice, the decision to prosecute had been taken by a lawyer.

The question was referred to the Philips Royal Commission on Criminal Procedure, which judged the then existing system according to its fairness, openness and accountability. It proposed a new system based on several distinct features, including the following:

- that the initial decision to charge a suspect should rest with the police;

- that thereafter all decisions as to whether to proceed, alter or drop the charges should rest with another State prosecuting agency;

- this agency would provide advocates for all cases in the magistrates' courts apart from guilty pleas by post. It should also provide legal advice to the police and instruct counsel in all cases tried on indictment.

The POA 1985 established a national prosecution service under the general direction of the DPP. The 1985 Act gives to the DPP and the CPS as a whole the right to institute and conduct any criminal proceedings where the importance or difficulty of the case make that appropriate (s 3(2)(b)). This applies to cases that could also be started by the police or other bodies like local authorities. It can also, in appropriate circumstances, take over and then discontinue cases. The CPS relies on the police for the resources and machinery of investigation.

In the period following its launch, the CPS experienced severe problems of staff shortage related to the general funding of the service. This improved over the years, and by March 1993, the full lawyer staff establishment had almost been met. It was apparently difficult to recruit staff of an adequate standard for the available pay and there has been considerable use of agents, that is, lawyers in private practice working for the CPS on a fee-for-case basis.

As employed solicitors or barristers, Crown prosecutors were originally unable to conduct cases in the higher courts. Changes to the rules on rights of audience in the higher courts for employed lawyers, introduced by the Access to Justice Act 1999, now permit them to do so. Consequently, any Crown prosecutor who is qualified to appear before the higher courts is able to do so. This involves having rights of audience as a barrister or as a solicitor advocate. The CPS Annual Report for 2003–04 indicates that by the end of March 2004, 524 higher court advocates had been fully trained. Two years earlier there had been 301.

Additionally, changes to the POA 1985 introduced by the Crime and Disorder Act (CDA) 1998 permit some lower court work to be undertaken by designated caseworkers who are not Crown prosecutors. To be able to do so, they must have undergone specified training and have at least three years' experience of casework or have a legal qualification. They are able to review and present straightforward magistrates' court cases which raise no technical issues and which are uncomplicated in terms of fact and law. Essentially, this will involve cases where there is an anticipated guilty plea, or minor road traffic offences where the proof in absence procedure is used. They cannot deal with cases such as indictable only offences, contested trials, where there is election for jury trial, and cases which raise sensitive issues. At the end of March 2001, there were 222 designated caseworkers. Three years later there were 254.

From its inception, the CPS was criticised for a variety of alleged faults, principally that it was inefficient and had a low success rate in prosecutions. Many police officers expressed doubts about the rigour with which cases were handled by the CPS, and dubbed it the 'Criminal Prosecution Society'. The Bar Council passed a motion in 1993 condemning the service for being too ready to abandon cases 'fearing defeat or cost'. The CPS still faces serious criticism. See C. Dyer, 'Judge attacks "scandalous" CPS blunders in fraud case' (2005), *Guardian*, 21 April. The Annual Report for 2003–04 refers (without much discussion or analysis) to the most recent British Crime Survey. This major survey revealed that 40% of the British public believed that the CPS is effective in bringing people to justice. Approximately 60% presumably do not share this view.

The former Director of Public Prosecutions, Barbara Mills QC, who headed the CPS until April 1998, laid much of the responsibility for poor conviction rates at the door of the police. In one public statement, she blamed lack of proper preparation by the police for two-fifths of the 185,824 cases dropped in the magistrates' court in 1992–93. Another 8,046 were dropped at the Crown Court. Mrs Mills claimed that in a quarter of cases that had to be dropped, CPS lawyers had no option because witnesses were missing or refused to give evidence, or because the case was being considered elsewhere in the justice system so the 'double jeopardy' rule applied. Between 1994 and 1997, crime figures fell, but arrest rates remained static, reflecting what police claim was increasing success against offenders. However, the percentage of magistrate level cases discontinued by the CPS crept up. Again, the reasoning for dropping or downgrading cases was found wanting.

To answer criticism, the CPS commissioned an analysis of a sample of 10,000 cases that it had to drop in 1992–93. The results show that 43% were abandoned on the ground of insufficient evidence to provide a realistic prospect of conviction. In 31% of cases, prosecutors abandoned them because it was 'not in the public interest' to proceed, for example, where the defendant had already been convicted and sentenced on another matter (9%) or only a nominal penalty was likely (6%). Much criticism of the CPS has come from police officers who object to the CPS continuing not to pursue cases for these very reasons.

A highly critical report published by a review body headed by Sir Iain Glidewell in June 1998 concluded that the CPS had failed to achieve the expected improvements in the prosecution system since it was set up in 1986 and had become bureaucratic and over-centralised. The report depicted a service where charges were thought to be 'inappropriately downgraded' and a disproportionately large number of serious violent crimes were not prosecuted. Proposals for a complete overhaul of the CPS were strongly backed by many in the criminal justice system ((1998) *The Times*, 2 June).

As a result of the Glidewell Report, the CPS underwent a major structural re-organisation in 1999. Its operation was decentralised so as to realign the CPS areas to match the boundaries of police forces – there were previously 13 CPS areas and now there are 42 to match the 43 police forces of England and Wales (there are two police forces for London, the Metropolitan Police and the City of London police). New Chief Crown Prosecutors (CCPs) for the 42 areas were appointed in 1999. As its case workload is so large, London has three CCPs. The new DPP, David Calvert-Smith QC, stated that:

> The new postholders will, in effect, be local DPPs with the power to act on their own initiative and to take their own decisions. They will be placing a priority on prosecution work which will benefit the local communities they serve [CPS, Official Statement, 109/99, 8 March 1999].

The CCPs will be accountable to their local communities, and the CPS contends that a localised service will enable good working relationships with the other agencies in the criminal justice system, including the police, the courts and the judiciary (CPS, Official Statement, 113/99, 12 April 1999).

In its 2003–04 Annual Report, the CPS states that, in the year under review, it received 1.57 million defendant cases from the police (9.9% more than in 2002–03) and dealt with almost 1.4 million prosecutions. Although the police and the CPS operate independently, it is clear that a person charged with an offence is very likely to be prosecuted (see 14.1.2). Over one million defendants were convicted in magistrates' courts. Another 73,000 were convicted in the Crown Court. The proportion of cases 'discontinued' fell from 15.5% in 2002–03 to 13.8% in 2003–04. The figures for 'ineffective trials' (that is, trials which did not lead to convictions) in magistrates' courts and the Crown Court also fell to 17.8% and 27.1% respectively.

The CPS states that the continuing rise in the number of Crown Court cases which are not proceeded is due, in part, to the implementation of s 51 of the CDA 1998 (in effect since January 2001). As indictable only cases are now sent directly to the Crown Court, it is no longer possible to test witnesses in advance at committal hearings.

The CPS Annual Report 1999 notes that, during the year under review, the CPS dealt with proportionally more serious crime, with indictable only cases – the most serious – rising to 30% of the total Crown Court caseload.

The proportion of indictable only offences in the Crown Court rose from 18.2% in 1991–92 to 26% in 1997–98 and 38.7% in 2001–02. The rise has been influenced by the plea before venue procedure for either way cases, which means that such cases are not unnecessarily committed to the Crown Court.

Pilot schemes aimed at reducing delays in criminal courts have led to more efficient and speedier justice, with more cases dealt with at the first hearing, cases which go to trial being heard more quickly and a reduction in bureaucracy.

The CPS shares key performance targets for the criminal justice system with the Home Office and the Department for Constitutional Affairs. These included halving the time from arrest to sentence for persistent young offenders from 142 to 71 days by 31 March 2002. By September 2001, the time had been reduced to 70 days (see CPS Annual Report 2001–02).

By October 2000, the average time to process such cases was calculated at 94 days, with Youth Court cases taking an average of 81 days and Crown Court cases an average of 230 days. However, averages can conceal some wide variations between individual courts, as a study in 2000 reveals. In an inspection conducted jointly by the Inspectorates of the Constabulary, the CPS and the Magistrates' Courts Service, the comparable figures were 93, 74 and 185 days. Yet the lowest for a Youth Court, for example, was 44 days and the highest 130 days.

14.1.1 The Code for Crown Prosecutors

This Code (CPS, revised 2001) is issued under s 10 of the POA 1985. It explains the principles used by the CPS in its work. It says that 'police officers should take account of the principles of the Code when they are deciding whether to charge a defendant with an offence'.

14.1.2 The discretion to prosecute

The police have a very significant discretion as to what to do when a crime has possibly been committed. They could turn a blind eye, caution the suspect or charge the suspect, in which case, they must decide for what. Environmental health officers and Environment Agency inspectors are in a similar position.

As is very cogently argued by McConville, Sanders and Leng in *The Case for the Prosecution* (1991), prosecution cases are constructed from the evidence and testimony of many people including lay witnesses, victims, the police, CPS lawyers and expert witnesses. Each of these parties is fallible and prone to perceive events in line with their own sorts of experience. The net result of this is that the prosecution case is normally nothing more than an approximation of 'the truth'. The most influential role is that of the police, as it is they who ultimately decide whether to charge anyone, if so, whom and for what. Once these discretions have been exercised, there is a relatively narrow band of data on which the CPS can work.

In 1951, the Attorney General, Lord Shawcross, noted that:

> It has never been the rule in this country – I hope it never will be – that suspected criminal offences must automatically be the subject of prosecution [House of Commons Debates, vol 483, col 681, 29 January 1951].

This *dictum* has been almost universally accepted within the criminal justice system.

There is evidence, however, that the police do (for operational or social reasons) tend to focus their attention on particular types of conduct. Research, for example, by Andrew Sanders has shown a tendency for there to be a bias in favour of prosecuting working class offenders as opposed to middle class offenders. He compared the police response to offences with that of the Factory Inspectorate's response to violation of the Health and Safety laws, and found that the police were much more likely to initiate prosecutions against working class suspects than were the factory inspectors against businesses and business executives. For the police, there was an institutional bias in favour of prosecution reflected in the principle 'let the court decide', whereas with the

Factory Inspectorate, prosecution was only a last resort after an attempt at negotiated compliance had failed. In 1980, there were 22,000 serious cases of tax evasion, but only one in 122 cases was prosecuted. By contrast, there were 107,000 social security frauds, of which one in four was prosecuted. Tax evasion resulted in a loss to the public purse 30 times larger than that caused by social security fraud, yet there was more State money spent on prosecuting people for social security fraud. (See Sanders, 'Class bias in prosecutions' (1985) 24 Howard J 176.) There is also evidence that the Environment Agency has a 'bottom heavy' enforcement policy, that is, it is more concerned to prosecute minor offenders than large companies. Anglers who catch fish without licences are far more likely to appear in court than the directors of companies which pollute the environment. See P. de Prez, 'Biased enforcement or optimal regulation: Reflections on recent Parliamentary scrutiny of the Environment Agency' (2001), 13(3), *Environmental Law and Management*, 145–150.

14.1.3   Police cautioning of offenders

Prior to changes introduced by the Crime and Disorder Act (CDA) 1998, cautioning of both adult and young offenders was a possible alternative to prosecution and was particularly encouraged in the case of the latter. Following implementation of the changes introduced by the 1998 Act, cautions are now available only for adult offenders, with a new system of reprimands and warnings applying to young offenders. The Criminal Justice Act 2003 introduces several changes in this area. These are addressed below.

14.1.3.1   *Cautioning of adults*

The Home Office provided guidance on when to caution in 1990 and 1994 (see Home Office Circulars 1990/59 and 1994/18). A caution is not a conviction, but it remains on an offender's record for a minimum of five years and may be used at the sentencing stage if he is subsequently convicted of another offence. A caution must be administered by an officer of the rank of inspector or above, and attendance at the police station is usually required. Three conditions must be met:

- There must be sufficient evidence to have justified a prosecution.

- The offender must admit guilt.

- The offender must agree to the procedure.

Cautioning may be particularly appropriate where an offender is old or infirm, mentally ill, suffering from severe physical illness, or suffering from severe emotional distress.

14.1.3.2   *Reprimands and warnings for young offenders*

Sections 65–66 of the CDA 1998 introduced a new scheme which includes police reprimands and warnings, accompanied by intervention to reduce the likelihood of re-offending. A first offence can result in a reprimand, final warning or criminal prosecution, depending on its seriousness. A further offence following a reprimand will lead to a warning or a charge. A further offence after a warning will normally lead to a charge, a second warning only being possible in limited circumstances where the latest offence is not serious and more than two years have elapsed since the first warning was given. Reprimands and warnings will be issued at a police station and a police officer may only issue them either where:

- there is sufficient evidence for prosecution;

- guilt is admitted;

- there are no previous convictions; or

- prosecution is not in the public interest.

After a warning has been issued, the young offender will be referred to a youth offending team (as established by s 39 of the CDA 1998), which will assess the offender to determine whether a rehabilitation programme to prevent re-offending is appropriate, and to provide one where it is. Conditional discharge of a young offender who commits an offence within two years of receiving a warning is not possible unless there are exceptional circumstances relating to the offence or the offender. Any reprimand, warning or recorded non-compliance with a rehabilitation programme may be cited in court in the same way as previous convictions.

14.1.3.3   The Criminal Justice Act 2003 and changes to the system

The Criminal Justice Act 2003 has made several changes to this area. The changes are in Part 3 of the Act.

Section 22: conditional cautions

Section 22 defines a conditional caution and provides that it may be given to an adult offender if the five requirements in s 23 are met. The conditions which may be imposed are restricted to those aimed at reparation for the offence, or at the rehabilitation of the offender. A conditional caution may be given by an authorised person as defined in sub-s (4).

Section 23: the five requirements

Section 23 sets out the requirements which need to be met for a conditional caution to be given. The requirements are: that there is evidence against the offender; that a 'relevant prosecutor' (as defined in s 27) considers that the evidence would be sufficient to charge him and that a conditional caution should be given; that the offender admits the offence; that the offender has been made aware of what the caution (and failure to comply with it) would mean; and that he signs a document containing details of the offence, the admission, the offender's consent to the caution and the conditions imposed.

Section 24: failure to comply with the conditions

Section 24 provides that if the offender fails without reasonable excuse to satisfy the conditions attached to the conditional caution, he may be prosecuted for the offence. If proceedings are commenced, the document referred to in s 23 is admissible in evidence, and the conditional caution ceases to have effect.

Section 25: Code of Practice

This section makes provision for the Home Secretary, with the consent of the Attorney General, to publish a Code of Practice setting out the criteria for giving conditional cautions, how they are to be given and who may give them, the conditions which may be imposed and for what period, and arrangements for monitoring compliance.

14.1.4 CPS guidelines

The Code for Crown Prosecutors (promulgated on behalf of the DPP) sets out the official criteria governing the discretion to prosecute.

The revised Code issued in 2001 requires two tests to be satisfied before a prosecution is brought: there must be a 'realistic prospect of conviction' (the evidential test); and the prosecution must be 'in the public interest'.

The evidential test requires prosecutors to predict what a jury or bench, properly directed, would be likely to decide. The guidelines require prosecutors to assess the reliability of evidence, not just its admissibility, hence the questions (para 5.3b): 'Is there evidence which might support or detract from the reliability of a confession? Is the reliability affected by factors such as the defendant's age, intelligence or level of understanding?'

As Glanville Williams ([1985] Crim LR 115)) and Andrew Sanders ((1994) 144 NLJ 946) have argued, this test favours people who are well respected in society – like police officers and businessmen – in whose favour juries and magistrates might be biased. It disfavours the sort of victims who are unlikely to make good witnesses. Sanders proposes a better test: whether, on the evidence, a jury or bench ought (on the balance of probabilities) to convict.

The public interest must be considered in each case where there is enough evidence to provide a realistic prospect of conviction. In cases of any seriousness, a prosecution will usually take place unless there are public interest factors tending against prosecution which clearly outweigh those tending in favour.

The Code lists some 'public interest factors in favour of prosecution' (para 6.4) and some against (para 6.5). The former include cases where:

- a conviction is likely to result in a significant sentence;

- a weapon was used or violence was threatened during the commission of the offence;

- the offence was committed against a person serving the public, like a police officer or a nurse;

- the offence, although not serious in itself, is widespread in the area where it was committed;

- there is evidence that the offence was carried out by a group;

- the offence was motivated by any form of discrimination against the victim's ethnic or national origin, sex, religious beliefs, political views or sexual orientation; or the suspect demonstrated hostility towards the victim based on any of those characteristics.

A prosecution is less likely to proceed, we are told, where:

- the court is likely to impose a very small or nominal penalty;

- the offence was committed as a result of a genuine mistake or misunderstanding (judged against the seriousness of the offence);

- the loss or harm can be described as minor and was the result of a single incident, particularly if it was caused by a misjudgment;

- a prosecution is likely to have a very bad effect on the victim's physical or mental health, always bearing in mind the seriousness of the offence;

- details could be made public that could harm sources of information, international relations or national security.

Crown prosecutors and others must balance factors for and against prosecution carefully and fairly. Deciding on the public interest is, the Code says (para 6.6), 'not simply a matter of adding up the number of factors on each side'.

Barbara Mills has stated that the Attorney General has commended the Code to other prosecutors. This may help to correct inconsistent approaches between the police and CPS on the one hand and, on the other, prosecutors like the Inland Revenue and Health and Safety Executive. As Sanders (see above) has observed, if you illegally gain a fortune or maim someone, you will probably be treated more leniently than ordinary disposals for such offences if the crimes are, technically, tax evasion and operating an unsafe place of work. Local authorities and the Environment Agency seem to be generally reluctant to prosecute environmental offenders. This can lead to a situation in which environmental crime, for example, makes good business sense. See M.Watson, 'Offences against the environment: the economics of crime and punishment' (2004), 16(4), *Environmental Law and Management*, 200–204. For the Health and Safety Executive see D Bergman, 'Boardroom GBH' (1999) 149 NLJ 1656.

14.1.5 CPS independence from the police

The CPS is institutionally separate from the police. The police are no longer in a client–lawyer relationship with the prosecutor, able to give instructions about how to proceed. The police are still, however, in the most influential position as it is only once they have taken the decision to charge a suspect that the CPS will be called on to look at the case. The CPS in practice exercises no supervisory role over the police investigation of cases; it simply acts on the file presented after the investigation by the police. It cannot instruct the police to investigate/further investigate a particular incident.

The power of the CPS to discontinue prosecutions (under s 23 of the POA 1985), or the continuing power to withdraw or offer no evidence, is an important feature of its independence. An argument that 'The system is dominated throughout its stages by the interests and values of the police, with the CPS playing an essentially subordinate and reactive role' is put by McConville in *The Case for the Prosecution* (1991).

The Report of the Runciman Royal Commission on Criminal Justice (1993) recommended that the CPS should play a greater role in the investigative process. It stated (para 93):

> The police should seek the advice of the CPS at the investigation stage in appropriate cases in accordance with guidelines to be agreed between the two services.

The Report also stated (para 95):

> Where a chief officer of police is reluctant to comply with a request from the CPS to investigate further before a decision on discontinuance is taken, HM Chief Inspector of Constabulary in conjunction with the Director of Public Prosecutions should bring about a resolution of the dispute.

Oddly, however, the rationale underlying the establishment of the CPS (independence from the police) appears to have been undermined since 1998, when many police stations have had CPS liaison officers working in the stations themselves.

Further evidence of encouragement of the relationship between the CPS and the police appears in the response to recommendations made by the Glidewell Committee in 1998. The Committee recommended that the CPS should take responsibility for the prosecution process immediately following charge. There should be a single integrated unit to assemble and manage case files, combining the current police Administrative Support Units and those parts of the CPS branch which deal with file preparation and review. The Committee proposed as a model a 'Criminal Justice Unit' in the charge of a CPS lawyer with mainly CPS staff, although many of these might be the civilian police staff currently employed in Administrative Support Units. The Committee suggested that such a unit would need to be able to call on the police to take action in obtaining more evidence and so a senior police officer would need to be part of the unit, which would be housed in or near the relevant police station. The unit would deal with fast track cases in their entirety and with simple summary cases, that is, with both the file preparation and the necessary advocacy. The CPS should primarily be responsible, in the magistrates' courts, for the timely disposal of all cases prosecuted by its lawyers, and share with the court one or more performance indicators related to timeliness. The Committee recommended the formation of Trial Units to deal with advocacy in some trials in the magistrates' courts and the management and preparation of all cases in the Crown Court, the hope being to lead to a shift in the centre of gravity of the CPS towards the Crown Court.

These recommendations were put into effect in six pilot areas and a report by the Glidewell Working Group in February 2001 found that, following a study carried out in September and October 2000, they: eliminated unnecessary work through improved communications; speeded up notification of proposed discontinuance; improved notification of case results to victims and witnesses; freed up staff to take on additional functions; and established a single contact point for the public on the prosecution of magistrates' court cases.

The following letter to *The Times* (6 August 1999) raises several noteworthy points on the other side of the argument:

> From His Honour Judge Barrington Black
>
> Sir, You report (3 August) that staff from the Crown Prosecution Service are to work with police officers in police stations to speed justice, and save £20 million a year.
>
> Twenty years, and many millions of pounds ago, prior to the creation of the CPS, in the city where I practised, and throughout the country, the county prosecutor and his staff occupied an office above police headquarters.
>
> They were available for consultations with police officers at any time, and they knew about the details of a case as it progressed. The police officer was responsible for the main papers and ensuing witness attendance. Defence solicitors also had direct contact with someone who could make decisions.
>
> The words 'plea bargaining' are now forbidden but, in those days, a calculated assessment of the evidence and an indictment appropriate to that evidence were often determined to the benefit of the victim, the defendant, the public purse and justice.
>
> I am delighted to hear that a system which was tried, tested and worked is to be revived.
>
> Yours truly,
>
> BARRINGTON BLACK
>
> Harrow Crown Court

There may, however, be serious problems in developing too cosy a relationship between the police and the prosecuting authorities, as sometimes the former have to come under the professional consideration of the latter. In August 1999, the CPS came under severe criticism in an official report into decisions not to prosecute police officers in circumstances where people had died in police custody. The report, *Inquiry into Crown Prosecution Service Decision Making in Relation to Deaths in Custody and Related Matters*, by His Honour Judge Gerald Butler QC (HMSO) states that the way the CPS responded to such cases was 'inefficient and fundamentally unsound'. It led to a 'thoroughly unsatisfactory situation' which needed to be urgently rectified. Following the criticisms in the Butler Report and further analysis by the CPS Inspectorate, the relevant decision making processes were revised.

14.1.6 Judicial control of prosecution policy

There is a very limited way in which the courts can control the exercise of prosecutorial discretion by the police. Lord Denning MR gave the example in one case of a chief constable issuing a directive to his men that no person should be prosecuted for stealing goods worth less than £100 (around £2,000 in 2005 prices), and said 'I should have thought the court could countermand it. He would be failing in his duty to enforce the law'. More generally, the courts had no control (*per* Lord Denning MR, *R v Metropolitan Police Commissioner ex p Blackburn* (1968)):

> For instance, it is for the Commissioner of Police of the Metropolis, or the Chief Constable, as the case may be, to decide in any particular case whether inquiries should be pursued, or whether an arrest should be made or a prosecution brought. It must be for him to decide on the disposition of his force and the concentration of his resources on any particular crime or area. No court can or should give him directions on such a matter.

Apart from this, there is the doctrine of constabulary independence (see *Fisher v Oldham Corp* (1930)), which regards the constable as an independent office-holder under the Crown who cannot be instructed by organisational superiors or by governmental agency about how to exercise his powers. The constable is accountable only to law.

An interesting instance of the courts being used to attack a use of police discretion is *R v Coxhead* (1986). The appellant was a police sergeant in charge of a police station. A young man was brought into the station to be breathalysed and the sergeant recognised him as the son of a police inspector at that station. The sergeant knew the inspector to be suffering from a bad heart condition. In order not to exacerbate this condition, the sergeant did not administer the test and allowed the motorist to go free. The sergeant was prosecuted and convicted for conduct tending and intended to pervert the course of justice. The sergeant's defence was that his decision came within the legitimate scope of discretion exercised by a police officer. The trial judge said the matter should be left for the jury to determine; they must decide the extent of any police discretion in accordance with the facts. The jury convicted the sergeant and this was upheld by the Court of Appeal. In minor cases, the police had a very wide discretion whether to prosecute, but in major cases they had no discretion or virtually none. Thus, in a serious case like drink-driving, there was no discretion which the sergeant could have been exercising legitimately. It is odd, however, that this is left for the jury to decide after the event rather than being subject to clear rules.

14.1.7 State prosecutors in the Crown Courts

Reference has already been made to the fact that Crown prosecutors are now able to appear in the higher courts if they are suitably qualified. This has caused a great deal of concern in some quarters. The basis of the worry is that, as full time salaried lawyers working for an organisation, CPS lawyers will sometimes be tempted to get convictions using dubious tactics or ethics because their own status as employees and prospects of promotion will depend on conviction success rates. Where, as now, barristers from the independent Bar are used by the CPS to prosecute, there is (it is argued) a greater likelihood of the courtroom lawyer dropping a morally unsustainable case.

Section 42 of the Access to Justice Act 1999 tries to overcome the possible difficulties with a provision (amending s 27 of the Courts and Legal Services Act (CLSA) 1990) that every advocate 'has a duty to the court to act with independence in the interests of justice', in other words, a duty which overrides any inconsistent duty, for example, one to an employer. Professor Michael Zander QC has contended, however, that these are 'mere words'. He has said (letter to *The Times*, 29 December 1998) that they are unlikely to exercise much sway over CPS lawyer employees concerned with performance targets set by their line managers, and that:

> The CPS as an organisation is constantly under pressure in regard to the proportion of discontinuances, acquittal and conviction rates. These are factors in the day-to-day work of any CPS lawyer. It is disingenuous to imagine they will not have a powerful effect on decision making.

The Bar is also very wary of this change, an editorial in Counsel (the journal of the Bar of England and Wales) saying:

> ... we are gravely concerned about the extent to which prosecutions will be done in-house by the CPS when the need for independent prosecutors is so well established in our democracy [(1999) Counsel 3, February].

It is important to set the arguments in a wider context. What are the social, economic or political debates surrounding this issue of how best to run a system of courtroom prosecutors? The change to having Crown Court prosecutions carried out by salaried CPS lawyers will be more efficient (as the whole prosecution can be handled in-house without engaging the external service of an independent barrister), and will, ultimately, cost the State less than is currently spent on prosecutions. Some will argue that justice is being sacrificed to the deity of cost cutting. On the other hand, it could be argued that justice and efficiency are not mutually exclusive phenomena.

14.2 Bail

Bail is the release from custody, pending a criminal trial, of an accused on the promise that money will be paid if he absconds. All decisions on whether to grant bail therefore involve delicate questions of balancing interests. A person is presumed innocent of a criminal charge unless he is proved guilty of it; this implies that no one should ever be detained unless he has been found guilty. For several reasons, however, it can be regarded as undesirable to allow some accused people to go back to society before the case against them is tried in a criminal court. Indeed, about 12% of offenders who are bailed to appear in court fail to appear for their trials. In January 2005 the Attorney General called for a crackdown on defendants who skip bail. At the time in question, 60,000 failed to appear (FTA) warrants were outstanding. Lord Goldsmith said: 'They will see that they can't thumb their nose at the criminal justice system. Turning up at court is not optional. It is a serious obligation and we will enforce it' (C. Dyer, 'Bail bandits blitz begins today' (2005), *Guardian*, 14 January.

To refuse bail to an accused might involve depriving someone of liberty who is subsequently found not guilty or convicted but given a non-custodial sentence. Such a person will probably have been kept in a police cell or in a prison cell for 23 hours a day. Unlike the jurisdictions in the Netherlands, Germany and France, no compensation is payable in these circumstances. On the other hand, to allow liberty to the accused pending trial might be to allow him to abscond, commit further offences, interfere with witnesses and obstruct the course of justice. A suspected terrorist might commit further outrages (a controversial issue following the explosions in London on 7 July 2005).

The difficulties involved in finding the proper balance have been highlighted by several cases of serious assault and rape being committed by persons who were on bail, and by the fleeing of Asil Nadir to Northern Cyprus in May 1993. Mr Nadir skipped his £3.5 million bail to travel to a jurisdiction which would not extradite him to England. He claimed that he would not be given a fair trial for the offences of theft and false accounting with which he was charged, and went on the public record as saying that his sureties would not suffer hardship as he would repay those who had put up bail for him.

The basic way in which the law currently seeks to find the right balance in such matters is by operating a general presumption in favour of bail, a presumption which can be overturned if one or more of a number of indices of suspicion exist in respect of a particular defendant. Even where bail is granted, it may be subject to certain conditions to promote public safety and the interests of justice. The Criminal Justice Act 2003, which received Royal Assent on 20 November 2003, will be implemented during the period 2004–06. The Act makes several changes to the law of bail, although these will be phased in at various times. All the changes are addressed in 14.2.3 below.

14.2.1   The Criminal Justice and Public Order Act 1994

Over the recent years, the government took the view that bail was too easily granted and that too many crimes were being committed by those on bail who deserved to be in custody while awaiting trial. The Bail (Amendment) Act 1993 and the Criminal Justice and Public Order Act (CJPOA) 1994 (ss 25–30) emanate from that philosophy, their aim being to restrict the granting of bail. A case which caught public sympathy for this view involved a young man who had many convictions for car crime and joyriding. Whilst on bail, he was joyriding in a vehicle when he smashed into a schoolgirl. She clung to the bonnet but he shook her off and thus killed her. The Home Secretary commented publicly that the new legislative measures would prevent such terrible events.

Each year (prior to the Acts), about 50,000 offences were committed by people on bail. A study by the Metropolitan Police in 1988 indicated that 16% of those charged by that force were already on bail for another offence. Another study in 1993, from the same force, showed that, of 537 suspects arrested in one week during a clampdown on burglary, 40% were on bail. Some had been bailed 10 or 15 times during the preceding year (figures from Robert Maclennan MP, HC Committee, col 295, 1994). A recent survey revealed that males in prison for motor vehicle theft who had previous experience of bail claimed on average to have committed a similar offence *each month* while on bail (*Justice for All*, Cm 5563, 2002, The Stationery Office).

In the criminal process, the first stage at which bail is usually raised as an issue is at the police station. If a person is arrested on a warrant, this will indicate whether he is to be held in custody or released on bail. If the suspect is arrested without a warrant, then the police will have to decide whether to release the suspect after he has been charged. After a person has been charged, s 38(1)(a) of the Police and Criminal Evidence Act (PACE) 1984 states that a person must be released unless: (a) his name and address are not known; or (b) the custody officer reasonably thinks that his detention is necessary for his own protection or (c) to prevent him from injuring someone or damaging property or because he might abscond or interfere with the course of justice. Most arrested people are bailed by the police. In 1990, 83% of those arrested in connection with indictable offences and 88% of those arrested for summary offences (other than motoring offences) were released. This area has been amended by s 28 of the CJPOA 1994. A custody officer can now, in the case of an imprisonable offence, refuse to release an arrested person after charge if the officer has reasonable grounds for believing that the detention of that person is necessary to prevent him from committing any offence. Previously, many cases were caught by (b) (above), but some likely conduct, for example, drink-driving, was not.

Section 27 of the CJPOA 1994 amends PACE 1984 (ss 38 and 47) so as to allow the police to grant conditional bail to persons charged. The conditions can be whatever is required to ensure that the person surrenders to custody, does not commit an offence while on bail, or does not interfere with witnesses or otherwise obstruct the course of justice. The new powers of the custody officer, however, do not include a power to impose a requirement to reside in a bail hostel. By amending Part IV of PACE 1984, s 29 of the CJPOA 1994 gives the police power to arrest without warrant a person who, having been granted conditional police bail, has failed to attend at a police station at the appointed time.

The Bail Act (BA) 1976 created a statutory presumption of bail. It states (s 4) that, subject to Sched 1, bail shall be granted to a person accused of an offence and brought before a magistrates' court or a Crown Court and to people convicted of an offence who are being remanded for reports to be made. The court must therefore grant bail (unless one of the exceptions applies) even if the defendant does not make an application. Schedule 1 provides that a court need not grant bail to a person charged with an offence punishable with imprisonment if it is satisfied that there are substantial grounds for believing that, if released on bail, the defendant would:

- fail to surrender to custody;

- commit an offence while on bail; or

- interfere with witnesses or otherwise obstruct the course of justice.

The court can also refuse bail if it believes that the defendant ought to stay in custody for his or her own protection, or if it has not been practicable, for want of time, to obtain sufficient information to enable the court to make its decision on bail, or if he or she has previously failed to answer to bail (Sched 1, Part I, paras 2–6).

When the court is considering the grounds stated above, all relevant factors must be taken into account, including the nature and seriousness of the offence, the character, antecedents, associations and community ties of the defendant, and his record for satisfying his obligations under previous grants of bail.

If the defendant is charged with an offence not punishable with imprisonment, Sched 1 provides that bail may only be withheld if he has previously failed to surrender on bail and if the court believes that, in view of that failure, he will fail again to surrender if released on bail.

Section 25 of the CJPOA 1994 provided that in some circumstances, a person who had been charged with or convicted of murder, attempted murder, manslaughter, rape or attempted rape must not be granted bail. The circumstances were simply that the conviction must have been within the UK, and that, in the case of a manslaughter conviction, it must have been dealt with by way of a custodial sentence. The word 'conviction' is given a wide meaning and includes anyone found 'not guilty by way of insanity'.

There was debate about whether the changes wrought by s 25 were justifiable. A Home Office Minister, defending the section, stated that it would be worth the risk if it prevented just one murder or rape, even though there might be a few 'hard cases', that is, people eventually acquitted of crime, who were remanded in custody pending trial. (David Maclean MP, Minister of State, Home Office, HC Committee, col 282, 1994.) As Card and Ward remarked in a commentary on the CJPOA 1994, the government when pushed was unable to cite a single case where a person released on bail in the circumstances covered by s 25 re-offended in a similar way. There is no time limit on the previous conviction and there is no requirement of any connection between the previous offence and the one in question. Card and Ward suggest that there is a world of difference between a person who was convicted of manslaughter 30 years ago on the grounds of complicity in a suicide pact and who is now charged with attempted rape (of which he must be presumed innocent), and the person who was convicted of rape eight years ago and now faces another rape charge. The first person is not an obvious risk to society and it is, they argue, regrettable that bail will be denied to him. There is also argument to be had with the contents of the s 25 list. Why should some clearly dangerous and prevalent crimes like robbery be omitted from it? In any case, it might have been better had the offences in the list raised a strong presumption against bail as opposed to an absolute ban, as the former could be rebutted in cases where there was, on the facts, no risk.

A further significant difficulty with this approach was that it appeared to be incompatible with the requirements of Art 5(3) of the European Convention on Human Rights (ECHR), decisions of the court on which make it clear that the decision to remand a defendant in custody before trial must be a decision of the court based on the merits after a review of the facts. By precluding bail in the specified circumstances, s 25 denied the court the opportunity to take a decision based on the merits. Thus, in *CC v UK* (1999) (subsequently confirmed by the European Court of Human Rights (ECtHR) in *Caballero v UK* (2000)), the European Court found that s 25 violated rights under Art 5(3) where the claimant had been denied bail on a rape charge in 1996 because of a conviction for manslaughter in 1987.

Anticipating this decision, s 25 was amended by the CDA 1998 to provide that bail should only be granted in homicide and rape cases if the court is 'satisfied that there are exceptional circumstances which justify it'. However, doubts have been expressed by the Law Commission and others about whether this change achieves compliance with obligations under the ECHR (all the more important now that the Human Rights Act (HRA) 1998 is fully in force). The argument is that the presumption required by the ECHR is innocence and therefore that the defendant should be released, whilst that required by the amended s 25 is that the defendant should not be released.

Bail can be granted as conditional or unconditional. Where it is unconditional, the accused must simply surrender to the court at the appointed date. Failure to appear without reasonable cause is an offence under the Bail Act (BA) 1976 (s 6) and can result, if tried in a Crown Court, in a sentence of up to 12 months' imprisonment or a fine. Conditions can be attached to the granting of bail where the court thinks that it is necessary to ensure that the accused surrenders at the right time and does not interfere with witnesses or commit further offences. There is no statutory limit to the conditions the court may impose, and the most common include requirements that the accused reports daily or weekly to a police station, resides at a particular address, surrenders his passport or does not go to particular places or associate with particular people.

Section 7 of the BA 1976 gives the police power to arrest anyone on conditional bail whom they reasonably suspect is likely to break the conditions or has already done so. Anyone arrested in these circumstances must be brought before a magistrate within 24 hours. The magistrate may then reconsider the question of bail.

Personal recognisances, by which the suspect agreed to pay a sum if he failed to surrender to the court, were abolished by the BA 1976 (s 3(2)) except in cases where it is believed that he might try to flee abroad. The Act did retain the court's right to ask for sureties as a condition of bail. By putting sureties in a position where they can have large sums of money 'estreated' if the suspect does not surrender to the court, significant pressure (not using the resources of the criminal justice system) is put on the accused. The proportion of those who do not answer to bail is very small – consistently about 4% of those given bail. Section 9 of the BA 1976 strengthens the surety principle by making it a criminal offence to agree to indemnify a surety. This sort of thing could happen, for example, if the accused agreed to reimburse the surety in the event that the accused skipped bail and the surety was requested to pay.

The CDA 1998 makes further changes to the law relating to bail. Section 54, which amended ss 3 and 3A of the BA 1976, provides for increased powers to require security or impose conditions (by taking away the requirement that the defendant must appear unlikely to remain in Great Britain). The amendment also allows courts to be able to require defendants to attend interviews with a legal representative as a condition of bail.

14.2.2   Appeals and re-applications

The rules which govern how someone who has been refused bail might re-apply and appeal have also been framed with a view to balancing the interests of the accused with those of the public and justice. The original refusal should not be absolute and final but, on the other hand, it is seen as necessary that the refusals are not reversed too easily.

If the court decides not to grant the defendant bail, then Sched 1, Part IIA (inserted by s 154 of the Criminal Justice Act (CJA) 1988) provides that it is the court's duty to consider whether the defendant ought to be granted bail at each subsequent hearing. At the first hearing after the one at which bail was first refused, he may support an application for bail with any arguments, but at subsequent hearings, the court need not hear arguments as to fact or law which it has heard before. The CJA 1988 enables a court to remand an accused, in his absence, for up to three successive one week remand hearings provided that he consents and is legally represented. Such repeated visits are costly to the State and can be unsettling for the accused, especially if he has to spend most of the day in a police cell only to be told the case has been adjourned again without bail. If someone does not consent, they are prevented from applying for bail on each successive visit if the only supporting arguments are those that have been heard by the court before (*R v Nottingham JJ ex p Davies* (1980)).

To avoid unproductive hearings, that is, to promote courts being able to adjourn a case for a period within which reasonable progress can be made on it, s 155 of the CJA 1988 allows for adjournments for up to 28 days provided the court sets the date for when the next stage of the proceedings should take place. What began as an experiment under this section has now by statutory order (SI 1991/2667) been extended to all courts.

The interests of the accused are also served by the variety of appeals he may make if bail has been refused. If bail has been refused by magistrates then, in limited circumstances, an application may be made to another bench of magistrates. Applications for reconsideration can also be made to a judge in chambers (through a legal representative) or to the Official Solicitor (in writing). Appeal can also be made to a Crown Court in respect of bail for both pre-committal remands and where a defendant has been committed for trial or sentence at the Crown Court.

Section 3 of the BA 1976 allows for an application to vary the conditions of court bail to be made by the person bailed, the prosecutor or a police officer. Application may also be made for the imposition of conditions on unconditional court bail. As amended by the CJPOA 1994, s 3 of the BA 1976 now allows for the same thing in relation to police bail, although the new provisions do not allow the prosecutor to seek reconsideration of the decision to grant bail itself. Under the Bail (Amendment) Act 1993, however, the prosecution does now have a right to appeal against the grant of bail by a court. This right applies to offences which carry a maximum sentence of imprisonment of five years or more, and to offences of taking a vehicle without consent (joyriding). When this right of appeal is exercised, the defendant will remain in custody until the appeal is heard by a Crown Court judge who will decide whether to grant bail or remand the defendant in custody within 48 hours of the magistrate's decision.

Parliament was concerned that this power could be abused and has stated that it should be reserved 'for cases of greatest concern, when there is a serious risk of harm to the public' or where there are 'other significant public interest grounds' for an appeal. Section 18 of the Criminal Justice Act 2003 has changed the law so as to allow the prosecution to appeal against bail in all cases of imprisonable offences (see 14.2.3 below).

Section 67(1) of the CJA 1967 states that time spent in custody pre-trial or pre-sentence can generally be deducted from the ultimate sentence (if the relevant provisions of ss 87 and 88 of the Powers of Criminal Courts (Sentencing) Act 2000 are brought into force, s 67 will be repealed). No compensation, however, is paid to people who have been remanded in custody but are subsequently found not guilty. Several European countries, like France and Germany, will sometimes offer compensation in similar circumstances.

Although this area of law was subject to a comprehensive revision after a Home Office special working party reported in 1974, and has been legislatively debated and modified twice since the BA 1976, it is still a matter of serious concern both to those civil libertarians, who consider the law too tilted against the accused, and to the police and commentators, who believe it too lenient in many respects. This criticism of the law from both sides to the debate might indicate a desirable state of balance reached by the current regulatory framework:

- *Opposition to the current arrangements – civil libertarian perspective*

  It is a cause for concern that, in the 1990s, of those dealt with summarily after being remanded in custody, about 50% received non-custodial sentences and a further 25% were acquitted.

  There are wide variations in the local policies of different courts; one study has shown, for instance, that the number of indictable custodial remands per 1,000 indictable proceedings was 111 in Brighton as against 313 in Bournemouth (B Gibson, 'Why Bournemouth?' (1987) 151 JP 520, 15 August).

  The last decade has seen a disturbing rise in the remand prison population. In 1980, it accounted for 15% of the average prison population. By 1990, it had risen to over 10,000 prisoners, 22% of the average prison population.

- *Opposition to the current arrangements – a police/public perspective*

  There are arguments which point to the numbers of people who commit offences whilst out on bail. A study conducted in Bristol, for example, showed that over one-third of all defendants charged with burglary were on bail for another offence at the time of their arrest. Following some dreadful cases of serious offences being committed whilst the perpetrator was on bail, s 153 of the CJA 1988 required magistrates to give reasons if they decided to grant bail against police objections in cases of murder, manslaughter or rape.

The percentage of people who skip bail is too high, especially for the more minor offences. Note: the annual figure, however, of those who do not answer to bail is consistently under 4%.

Positive developments in recent years have been the use of Bail Information Schemes (BIS) for courts (about 100 courts now operate such schemes) and government concern to increase the number of bail hostels. The BIS resulted from pilot schemes organised by the Vera Institute of Justice of New York. They give courts verified information from the probation service about defendants' accommodation or community ties. The evidence suggests that the courts using such schemes make greater use of bail than those which do not have the schemes.

14.2.3   Bail and the Criminal Justice Act 2003

The Criminal Justice Act 2003 makes many changes to the law of bail. First we need to discuss those concerned with police bail at the point at which someone is arrested.

Section 4: bail elsewhere than at a police station

This section amends s 30 of PACE to enable police officers to grant bail to persons following their arrest without the need to take them to a police station. It provides the police with additional flexibility following arrest and the scope to remain on patrol where there is no immediate need to deal with the person concerned at the station. It is intended to allow the police to plan their work more effectively by giving them new discretion to decide exactly when and where an arrested person should attend a police station for interview. See A. Hucklesby, 'Not necessarily a trip to the police station: the introduction of police bail' (2004), CrimLR, 803–813.

Sub-sections (2)–(6) amend s 30 to take account of the new power to grant bail. The basic principle remains that a person arrested by a constable or taken into custody by a constable after being arrested by someone else must be taken by a constable to a police station as soon as practicable. However, this is subject to the provisions dealing with release either on bail or without bail.

Sub-section (4) expands existing s 30(7) of PACE 1984 to provide that a constable must release the person concerned without bail if, before reaching the police station, he is satisfied that there are no grounds for keeping him under arrest or releasing him on bail under the new provisions.

Sub-section (5) replaces existing s 30(10) and (11) of PACE 1984 to make it clear that a constable may delay taking an arrested person to a police station or releasing him on bail if that person's presence elsewhere is necessary for immediate investigative purposes. The reason for such delay must be recorded either on arrival at the police station or when the person is released on bail.

Sub-section (7) inserts a series of new sections into PACE 1984 which provide police officers with the framework of powers to grant bail following arrest. Section 30A provides that a constable has power to release a person on bail at any time prior to arrival at a police station. It specifies that the person released on bail must be required to attend a police station and that any police station may be specified for that purpose. No other requirement may be imposed on the person as a condition of bail.

Section 30B requires that the constable must give the person bailed a written notice, prior to release, setting out the offence for which he was arrested and the ground on which that arrest was made. It must tell him that he is required to attend a police station and may specify the relevant station and time. If these details are not specified in that initial notice, they must be set out in a further notice provided to the person at a later stage. Police have the capacity to change the specified station or time if necessary and the person concerned must be given written notice of any such change.

Section 30C contains various supplemental provisions. Section 30C(1) allows for the police to remove a requirement to attend a police station to answer bail, provided they give the person a written notice to that effect.

Section 30C(2) makes it clear that where someone attends a non-designated police station to answer bail following arrest, he must be released or taken to a designated police station within six hours of his arrival. Designated stations are those nominated by chief officers as suitable for detention purposes and are generally stations with appropriate facilities to cater for extended periods of custody.

Section 30C(3) specifies that nothing in the BA 1976 applies in relation to bail under these new arrangements. The law which applies to this form of bail is set out in PACE 1984 as amended by the Criminal Justice Act 2003.

Section 30C(4) clarifies that a person who has been released under the new bail provisions may be re-arrested if new evidence justifying that has come to light since their release.

Section 30D deals with failure to answer to bail under the new arrangements. Section 30D(1) allows a constable to arrest without a warrant a person who fails to attend the police station at the specified time. Section 30D(2) states that a person arrested in such circumstances must be taken to a police station as soon as practicable after the arrest. Section 30D(3) defines the station relevant for the purposes of sub-s (1) as whichever station is defined in the latest notice provided to the person concerned. Section 30D(4) clarifies that such an arrest for failure to answer to bail is to be treated as an arrest for an offence for certain PACE purposes.

The Act also addresses bail other than at the immediate point someone is arrested, such as in court, where it has to be decided whether the defendant should be kept in custody or let free before the next court appearance.

Section 13: grant and conditions of bail

Sub-section (1) makes a number of changes to s 3(6) of the BA 1976 to enable bail conditions to be imposed for a defendant's own protection or welfare, in the same circumstances that he might have been remanded in custody for that purpose.

Sub-section (4) amends para 5 of Part 2 of Sched 1 to the Bail Act 1976 so that, where a defendant charged with a non-imprisonable offence is arrested under s 7, bail may be refused only if the court is satisfied that there are substantial grounds for believing that if released on bail (whether subject to conditions or not) he would fail to surrender to custody, commit an offence whilst on bail, or interfere with witnesses or otherwise obstruct the course of justice.

Section 14: offences committed on bail

Sub-section (1) requires the court to refuse bail to an adult defendant who was on bail in criminal proceedings at the date of the offence, unless the court is satisfied that there is no significant risk that he would commit an offence if released on bail. This replaces para 2A of Part I of Sched 1 to the BA 1976 (which provides that a defendant need not be granted bail if he was on bail at the time of the alleged offence).

Section 15: absconding by persons released on bail

Sub-section (1) requires the court to refuse bail to an adult defendant who failed without reasonable cause to surrender to custody in answer to bail in the same proceedings, unless the court is satisfied that there is no significant risk that he would so fail if released.

Sub-section (2) requires the court, in the case of defendants under 18, to give particular weight to the fact that they have failed to surrender to bail, in assessing the risk of future absconding.

Sub-section (3) disapplies s 127 of the Magistrates' Court Act 1980 (which prevents summary proceedings from being instituted more than six months after the commission of an offence) in respect of offences under s 6 of the Bail Act, and instead provides that such an offence may not be tried unless an information is laid either within six months of the commission of the offence, or within three months of the defendant's surrender to custody, arrest or court appearance in respect of that offence. This will ensure that a defendant cannot escape being prosecuted for the Bail Act offence merely by succeeding in absconding for more than six months.

Section 16: appeal to the Crown Court

Section 16 creates a new right of appeal to the Crown Court against the imposition by magistrates of certain conditions of bail. The conditions which may be challenged in this way are requirements relating to residence, provision of a surety or giving a security, curfew, electronic monitoring or contact. This complements the removal by s 17 of the existing High Court power to entertain such appeals.

Section 18: appeal by the prosecution

Section 18 amends s 1 of the Bail (Amendment) Act 1993 so that the prosecution's right of appeal to the Crown Court against a decision by magistrates to grant bail is extended to cover all imprisonable offences.

Section 19: drug users: restriction on bail

Evidence accepted by the Home Office suggests that there is a link between drug addiction and offending. In addition, it is widely accepted that many abusers of drugs fund their misuse through acquisitive crime. There is thus a real concern that, if such offenders who have been charged with an imprisonable offence are placed on bail, they will merely re-offend in order to fund their drug use.

Under this section, an alleged offender aged 18 or over, who has been charged with an imprisonable offence, will not be granted bail (unless the court is satisfied that there is no significant risk of his or her committing an offence while on bail), where the three conditions below exist:

- there is drug test evidence that the person has a specified Class A drug in his or her body (by way of a lawful test obtained under s 63B of PACE or s 161 of this Act); and

- either the offence is a drugs offence associated with a specified Class A drug or the court is satisfied that there are substantial grounds for believing that the misuse of a specified Class A drug caused or contributed to that offence or provided its motivation; and

- the person does not agree to undergo an assessment as to his dependency upon or propensity to misuse specified Class A drugs, or has undergone such an assessment but does not agree to participate in any relevant follow-up action offered.

The assessment will be carried out by a suitably qualified person, who will have received training in the assessment of drug problems. If an assessment or follow-up is proposed and agreed to, it will be a condition of bail that they be undertaken. The provision can only apply in areas where appropriate assessment and treatment facilities are in place.

14.3　Plea Bargaining

'Plea bargaining' has been defined as 'the practice whereby the accused enters a plea of guilty in return for which he will be given some consideration that results in a sentence concession' (Baldwin and McConville, *Negotiated Justice: Pressures on Defendants to Plead Guilty* (1977)). In practice, this can refer to:

- a situation either where there has been a plea arrangement for the accused to plead guilty to a lesser charge than the one with which he or she is charged (for example, charged with murder, agrees to plead guilty to manslaughter). This is sometimes called 'charge bargaining'; or

- where there is simply a sentencing discount available on a plea of guilty by the accused. This is sometimes called a 'sentence bargain'.

Plea bargaining is widespread in some common law countries, for example the USA.

14.3.1 *R v Turner* (1970)

A plea of guilty by the accused must be made freely. The accused must only be advised to plead guilty if he has committed the crime in question. In *R v Turner* (1970), Lord Parker CJ set out guidelines on plea bargaining. He stated that:

(1) it may sometimes be the duty of counsel to give strong advice to the accused that a plea of guilty with remorse is a mitigating factor which might enable the court to give a lesser sentence (displays of remorse following a not guilty plea tend to be unconvincing);

(2) the accused must ultimately make up his or her own mind as to how to plead;

(3) there should be open access to the trial judge and counsel for both sides should attend each meeting, preferably in open court; and

(4) the judge should never indicate the sentence which he is minded to impose, nor should he ever indicate that on a plea of guilty he would impose one sentence, but that on a conviction following a plea of not guilty he would impose a severer sentence.

The judge could say what sentence he would impose on a plea of guilty (where, for example, he has read the depositions and antecedents) but without mentioning what he would do if the accused were convicted after pleading not guilty. Even this would be wrong, however, as the accused might take the judge to be intimating that a severer sentence would follow upon conviction after a guilty plea. The only exception to this rule is where a judge says that the sentence will take a particular form, following conviction, whether there has been a plea of guilty or not guilty.

14.3.2 Court of Appeal *Practice Direction*

These guidelines were subsequently embodied in a Court of Appeal *Practice Direction* [1976] Crim LR 561, which are now included in *Practice Direction (Criminal: Consolidated)* [2002] 1 WLR 2870, para 45. A number of difficulties have been experienced in applying these principles. Perhaps the greatest problem has resulted from the fact that, although the principles state (No 45.4) that a judge should never say that a sentence passed after a conviction would be more severe than one passed after a guilty plea, it is a generally known rule that guilty pleas lead to lesser sentences. In *R v Cain* (1976), it was stressed that, in general, defendants should realise that guilty pleas attract lesser sentences. Lord Widgery said, 'Any accused person who does not know about it should know about it'. The difficulty is that the trial judge must not mention it, otherwise he could be construed as exerting pressure on the accused to plead guilty.

In *R v Turner*, the defendant pleaded not guilty on a charge of theft. He had previous convictions and during an adjournment he was advised by counsel in strong terms to change his plea. After having spoken with the judge, whom the defendant knew, counsel advised that in his opinion a plea of guilty would result in a non-custodial sentence, whereas if he persisted with a not guilty plea and thereby attacked police witnesses, there was a real possibility of receiving a custodial sentence. The defendant changed his plea to guilty and then appealed on the ground that he did not have a free choice in changing his plea. His appeal was allowed on the basis that he might have formed the impression that the views being expressed to him by his counsel were those of the judge, particularly as it was known by the accused that counsel had just returned from seeing the judge when he gave his advice to the accused.

The advantages for the prosecution in gaining a guilty plea are obvious, but justice demands that the court should be able to pass a proper sentence consistent with the gravity of the accused's actions, and if a plea is accepted, then the defendant can only be sentenced on the basis of the crime that he has admitted. The Farquharson Committee on the Role of Prosecuting Counsel thought that there is a general right for the prosecution to offer no evidence in respect of any particular charge, but that where the judge's opinion is sought on whether it is desirable to reassure the public at large that the right course is being taken, counsel must abide by the judge's decision. Where the judge thinks that counsel's view to proceed is wrong, the trial can be halted until the DPP has been consulted and given the judge's comments. In the notorious case of *R v Sutcliffe* (1981), the 'Yorkshire Ripper' case, the prosecution and defence had agreed that Sutcliffe would plead guilty to manslaughter on the grounds of diminished responsibility, but the trial judge rejected that agreement and, after consultations with the DPP, Sutcliffe was eventually found guilty of murder.

14.3.3 *R v Pitman* (1991)

The extent of the difficulties in framing rules on plea bargaining which achieve clarity and fairness can be judged by the remark of Lord Lane CJ in the case of *R v Pitman* (1991):

> There seems to be a steady flow of appeals to this court arising from visits by counsel to the judge in his private room. No amount of criticism and no amount of warnings and no amount of exhortation seems to be able to prevent this from happening.

In this case, on counsel's advice, the appellant pleaded not guilty to causing death by reckless driving. On Cup Final day in 1989, he had driven, having been drinking all afternoon, in a car without a rear view mirror. He had crashed into another car, killing one of its passengers, whilst having double the permitted level of alcohol in his blood.

During the trial, the judge called both counsel to his room and stated that he did not think there was a defence to the charge. Counsel for the appellant explained that although the appellant had admitted that his carelessness caused the accident, the advice to plead not guilty was based on the fact that the prosecution might not be able to prove the necessary recklessness. The trial judge replied that the appellant's plea was a matter for the appellant himself and not counsel, and that if the appellant accepted responsibility for the accident, he ought to plead guilty and if he did so, he would receive 'substantial credit' when it came to sentencing.

Counsel for the appellant then discussed this with the appellant who changed his plea to guilty and was sentenced to nine months' imprisonment and disqualified from driving for four years. His appeal was allowed as the judge had put undue pressure on the appellant and his counsel to change his plea to guilty, as the remarks suggested that his chances of acquittal were slight if he pleaded not guilty and that if he was found guilty, he would certainly be sentenced to imprisonment. Lord Lane CJ emphasised that a judge should not initiate discussions in private and that where, at the behest of counsel, they are absolutely necessary, they should be recorded by shorthand or on a recording device.

Another problem here concerns framing the guidelines so that they are sufficiently permissive to allow counsel access to the judge in his private room in deserving instances, but avoiding the problems of confidentiality. As Mustill LJ said in *R v Harper-Taylor and Barker* (1988): 'The need to solve an immediate practical problem may combine with the more relaxed atmosphere of the private room to blur the formal outlines of the trial.' There is a risk that counsel and solicitors may hear something said to the judge which they would rather not hear, putting them into a state of conflict between their duties to their clients and their obligations to maintain the confidentiality of the private room. Reviewing the current state of the law, Curran has written that the effect of cases like *R v Bird* (1977) and *R v Agar* (1990) (the latter not a plea bargaining case but one which hinged on a judge's ruling in his private room as complied with by counsel to the appellant's detriment) is that defence counsel has a duty to disclose to his client any observations made by the judge in his room which significantly affect the client's case, whether or not the judge expresses them to be made confidentially.

The difficulties in this area of law stem largely not from deficient rules, but rather from the wish that the rules should achieve diverse aims. As Zander has observed, the fundamental problem is that the Court of Appeal wants to have it both ways: 'On the one hand, it wants defendants to appreciate that, if they plead guilty, they will receive a lesser sentence. On the other hand, it does not want judges to provide defendants with solid information as to how great the discount will be.'

14.3.4   Runciman Royal Commission recommendations

A more open system of plea bargaining was advocated by the Runciman Royal Commission on Criminal Justice (para 156). The Report argued that this would do much to alleviate the problem of 'cracked trials' in which defendants do not plead guilty until the last moment, wasting the time of witnesses, the police, the CPS and the court. In a system where the vast majority of cases in the Crown Court and magistrates' courts result in guilty pleas (79% and 81.5%, respectively), the operation of the plea bargain becomes very important.

The Commission research indicated that 'cracked trials' accounted for more than one-quarter of all cases. The Commission also noted that sentence discounts of between 25% and 30% for guilty pleas have been long-established practice in the Crown Court. The Commission suggested that higher discounts should be available for those who plead guilty earlier in the process. The Report stated:

> The most common reason for defendants delaying a plea of guilty until the last minute is a reluctance to face the facts until they are at the door of the court. It is often said too that a defendant has a considerable incentive to behave in this way. The longer the delay, the

more the likelihood of witnesses becoming intimidated or forgetting to turn up or disappearing.

It recommended (para 157):

> At the request of defence counsel on instructions from the defendant, judges should be able to indicate the highest sentence that they would impose at that point on the basis of the facts as put to them.

On the issue of charges, it recommended (para 161):

> Discussions on the level of charge (charge bargaining) should take place as early as possible in order to minimise the need for cases to be listed as contested trials.

Requests made to the judge could be made at a preparatory hearing, at a hearing called especially for the purpose or at the trial itself. The Report denied that such a system was at all near the American scheme, which is widely regarded as promoting injustice as it acts as a wholesale plea bargaining system in which the prosecution can suggest the appropriate sentence. Lord Runciman stated that: 'We agree that to face defendants with a choice between what they might get on an immediate plea of guilty and what they might get if found guilty by the jury does amount to unacceptable pressure.'

Research conducted by Professor Zander for the Royal Commission on Criminal Justice (Zander and Henderson, *The Crown Court Study*, Royal Commission on Criminal Justice Study 19, 1993, p 145) found that, in a study of 900 Crown Court cases, 90% of barristers and two-thirds of judges were in favour of formalising plea bargaining based on sentence discounts. The study suggested that 11% of those who pleaded guilty in fact maintained their innocence but wanted to secure a reduction in sentence.

The Court of Appeal has consistently indicated that the information should not be given to defendants because that might put undue pressure on them to plead guilty, but sentence discounts are legally recognised. In DA Thomas (ed), *Current Sentencing Practice*, para A8 2(b) states that: 'a guilty plea attracts a lighter sentence, the extent of the reduction is usually between one-quarter and one-third of what would have otherwise been the sentence.' Moreover, Lord Widgery has stated (see 14.3.2 above) that defendants should know about them. The pressure could scarcely be increased by providing a defendant with details rather than leaving it to his general knowledge. If anything, Zander has argued, it would diminish the pressure by making it clear that the defendant's fears about the penalty for pleading not guilty are exaggerated.

In a detailed research report on this issue, the reform group JUSTICE has cast serious doubt on many aspects of the system, which could soon be adopted if the Runciman Royal Commission proposals are enacted. In *Negotiated Justice: A Closer Look at the Implications of Plea Bargaining* (1993), it is argued that, although favoured in some form by 90% of barristers and 60% of judges, plea bargaining can not only lead to unjust convictions, but also to inaccurate and unfair sentences. The latter occur because when the trial judge is making an offer of a reduced penalty, the defendant is still at that stage formally protesting his innocence, so it is extremely difficult for his lawyer to present a plea in mitigation of sentence. The reform body JUSTICE argues that the earlier withdrawal of weak prosecution cases, better liaison between defence and prosecution, and earlier contact between defendant and barrister would result in greater efficiency and fairness.

There is, though, reason for anxiety with such a call for more openness. Sanders and Young ((1994) 144 NLJ 1200) regard it as 'an idealistic notion' that one can improve the effectiveness of the system in convicting the guilty without also increasing its effectiveness in convicting the innocent. They say that one simply has to make a 'value choice' about the weight to be given to protecting the innocent relative to other important values, such as repressing crime and economy in the use of scarce resources. In one Home Office study (*Magistrates' Court or Crown Court? Mode of Trial Decisions and Sentencing*, Home Office Study No 125, 1992), Hedderman and Moxon found that 65% of those pleading guilty in Crown Court cases said that their decision had been influenced by the prospect of receiving a discount in sentence, and nearly one-third claimed to have pleaded guilty as a direct result of a charge bargain. Even the Runciman Royal Commission recognised that not all those pleading guilty are in fact guilty; some may have just capitulated to the pressure of taking the reduced sentence rather than run the risk of the full sentence. As Sanders and Young contend, this issue goes to the heart of constitutional principles. Only if the State acts properly in collecting and presenting evidence can punishment be justified according to commonly accepted principles. Even the guilty are entitled to due process of law. A system of plea bargaining may undermine such principles, as it allows the State to secure convictions based on unproven allegations.

Informal plea bargaining is obviously open to abuse: P Darbyshire, 'The mischief of plea bargaining' [2000] Crim LR 895; C Dyer, 'Making a pact with the Devil' (2000) *The Guardian*, 30 October. The recent White Paper, *Justice for All*, states (4.42–4.43):

> We ... intend to introduce a clearer tariff of sentence discount, backed up by arrangements whereby defendants could seek advance indication of the sentence they would get if they pleaded guilty ... We do not take lightly the danger of putting innocent defendants under pressure to plead guilty ... The defendant, through their legal advisers ... should initiate the request. It should be made formally in court sitting in private ... It should be fully recorded. All relevant information about the offence and defendant should be put to the judge, who would indicate the maximum sentence on a guilty plea made at that stage (but not what the sentence might be were a contested trial to result in a guilty verdict).

14.3.5 *R v Goodyear* [2005] EWCA Crim 888

The ban on plea-bargaining (which tended to inhibit realistic discussions between judges and barristers) has recently been abandoned; *R v Goodyear* [2005]. The Court of Appeal has expressed support for the approach recommended by the Runciman Royal Commission on Criminal Justice in 1993. This may encourage more defendants to plead guilty – assuming that they are guilty. See M. Zander, 'Please m'lud, how long will I get?' (2005), 155, NLJ, 677.

14.4 The Jury

It is generally accepted that the jury of '12 good men and true' lies at the heart of the British legal system. The implicit assumption is that the presence of 12 ordinary lay persons, randomly introduced into the trial procedure to be the arbiters of the facts of the case, strengthens the legitimacy of the legal system. It supposedly achieves this end by introducing a democratic humanising element into the abstract impersonal trial process, thereby reducing the exclusive power of the legal professionals who would otherwise command the legal stage and control the legal procedure without reference to the opinion of the lay majority.

According to Thompson, EP:

> The English common law rests upon a bargain between the law and the people. The jury box is where the people come into the court; the judge watches them and the jury watches back. A jury is the place where the bargain is struck. A jury attends in judgement not only upon the accused but also upon the justice and humanity of the law [*Writing by Candlelight*].

Few people have taken this traditional view to task but, in a thought-provoking article in the Criminal Law Review ([1991] Crim LR 740), Penny Darbyshire did just that. In her view, the jury system has attracted the most praise and the least theoretical analysis of any component of the criminal justice system. As she correctly pointed out, and as will be shown below, juries are far from being either a random or a representative section of the general population. In fact, Darbyshire goes so far as to characterise the jury as 'an anti-democratic, irrational and haphazard legislator, whose erratic and secret decisions run counter to the rule of law'. She concedes that while the 20th century lay justices are not representative of the community as a whole, neither is the jury. She points out that jury equity, by which is meant the way in which the jury ignores the law in pursuit of justice, is a double-edged sword which may also convict the innocent; and counters examples such as the *Clive Ponting* case with the series of miscarriages of justice relating to suspected terrorists in which juries were also involved.

Darbyshire is certainly correct in taking to task those who would simply endorse the jury system in an unthinking, purely emotional manner. With equal justification, she criticises those academic writers who focus attention on the mystery of the jury to the exclusion of the hard reality of the magistrates' court. It is arguable, however, that she goes to the other extreme. Underlying her analysis and conclusions is the idea that 'the jury trial is primarily ideological' and that 'its symbolic significance is magnified beyond its practical significance by the media, as well as academics, thus unwittingly misleading the public'. Whilst one might not wish to contradict the suggestion that the jury system operates as a very powerful ideological symbol, supposedly grounding the criminal legal system within a framework of participative democracy and justifying it on that basis, it is simply inadequate to reject the practical operation of the procedure on that basis alone. Ideologies do not exist purely in the realm of ideas, they have real, concrete manifestations and effects; in relation to the jury system, those manifestations operate in such a way as to offer at least a vestige of protection to defendants. In regard to the comparison between juries and the summary procedure of the magistrates' courts, Darbyshire puts two related questions. First, she asks whether the jury system is more likely to do justice and get the verdict right than the magistrates' courts; then she goes on to ask why the majority of defendants are processed through the magistrates' courts. These questions are highly pertinent; it is doubtful, however, whether her response to them is equally pertinent. Her answers would likely be that the jury does not perform any better than the magistrates and, therefore, it is immaterial that the magistrates deal with the bulk of cases. Her whole approach would seem to be concentrated on denigrating the performance of the jury system. A not untypical passage from her article admits that, in relation to the suspect terrorist miscarriages of justice, juries 'were not to blame for these wrongful convictions'. However, she then goes on in the same sentence to accuse the juries of failing 'to remedy the lack of due process at the pre-trial stage', and thus blames them for not providing 'the brake on oppressive State activity claimed for the jury by its defenders'.

Although there is most certainly scope for a less romantic view of how the jury system actually operates in practice, Darbyshire's argument seems to be that the magistrates are not very good but then neither are the juries; and as they only operate in a small minority of cases anyway, the implication would seem to be that their loss would be no great disadvantage. Others, however, would maintain that the jury system does achieve concrete benefits in particular circumstances and would argue further that these benefits should not be readily given up. Amongst the latter is Michael Mansfield QC who, in an article in response to the Runciman Report, claimed that the jury 'is the most democratic element of our judicial system' and the one which 'poses the biggest threat to the authorities'. (These questions will be considered further in relation to the Report of the Runciman Commission and the Criminal Justice (Mode of Trial) Bills, at 14.8.1 below.)

It should be noted that the jury system influences court procedure and the admissibility of evidence. Character evidence is an obvious example (see McEwan, J, 'Previous conduct at the crossroads: which "way ahead"?' [2002] Crim LR 180–91). The alleged ability of defence lawyers to manipulate the system has been criticised by the Association of Chief Police Officers: see Francis, I, 'Letting the frogs out of the kitchen' (2002) 152 NLJ 83. The recent White Paper, *Justice for All*, states (4.57):

> ... where a defendant's previous convictions, or other misconduct, are relevant to an issue in the case, then unless the court considers that the information will have a disproportionate effect, they should be allowed to know about it. It will be for the judge to decide whether the probative value of introducing this information is outweighed by its prejudicial effects.

New rules were introduced in December 2004. See P. Plowden, 'Making sense of character evidence' (2005), 155, NLJ, 47–49.

Having defended the institution of the jury generally, it has to be recognised that there are particular instances which tend to bring the jury system into disrepute. For example, in October 1994, the Court of Appeal ordered the re-trial of a man convicted of double murder on the grounds that four of the jurors had attempted to contact the alleged victims using a Ouija board in what was described as a 'drunken experiment' (*R v Young* (1995). A second convicted murderer appealed against his conviction on the grounds of irregularities in the manner in which the jury performed its functions. Amongst the allegations levelled at the jury was the claim that they clubbed together and spent £150 on drink when they were sent to a hotel after failing to reach a verdict. It was alleged that some of the jurors discussed the case against the express instructions of the judge and that on the following day, the jury foreman had to be replaced because she was too hung-over to act. One female juror was alleged to have ended up in bed with another hotel guest.

A truly remarkable case came to light in December 2000 when a trial, which had been going on for 10 weeks, was stopped on the grounds that a female juror was conducting what were referred to as 'improper relations' with a male member of the jury protection force that had been allocated to look after the jury during the trial. The relationship had become apparent after the other members of the jury had found out that they were using their mobile phones to send text messages to one another during breaks in the trial. That aborted trial was estimated to have cost £1.5 million, but it emerged that this was the second time the case had to be stopped on account of inappropriate behaviour on the part of jury members. The first trial had been abandoned after some of the jury were found playing cards when they should have been deliberating on the case.

Another example of the possible criticisms to be levelled against the misuse of juries occurred in Stoke-on-Trent, where the son of a court usher and another six individuals were found to have served on a number of criminal trial juries. Whilst one could praise the public spirited nature of this dedication to the justice process, especially given the difficulty in getting members of jury panels (see 14.6 and 14.7 below), it might be more appropriate to condemn the possibility of the emergence of a professional juror system connected to court officials. Certainly, the Court of Appeal was less than happy with the situation, and overturned a conviction when the Stoke practice was revealed to it.

Over the past 10 years, the operation of the jury system has been subject to one Royal Commission (Runciman), one review (Auld) and several statutory attempts to alter it. An examination of these various endeavours will be postponed until the end of this chapter; for the moment, attention will be focused on the jury system as it currently functions.

14.5 The Role of the Jury

It is generally accepted that the function of the jury is to decide on matters of fact, and that matters of law are the province of the judge. Such may be the ideal case, but most of the time, the jury's decision is based on a consideration of a mixture of fact and law. The jurors determine whether a person is guilty on the basis of their understanding of the law as explained to them by the judge.

The oath taken by each juror states that they 'will faithfully try the defendant and give a true verdict according to the evidence', and it is contempt of court for a juror subsequent to being sworn in to refuse to come to a decision. In 1997, Judge Anura Cooray sentenced two women jurors to 30 days in prison for contempt of court for their failure to deliver a verdict. One of the women, who had been the jury foreman, claimed that the case, involving an allegation of fraud, had been too complicated to understand, and the other had claimed that she could not ethically judge anyone. Judge Cooray was quoted as justifying his decision to imprison them on the grounds that:

> I had to order a re-trial at very great expense. Jurors must recognise that they have a responsibility to fulfil their duties in accordance with their oath.

The women only spent one night in jail before the uproar caused by Cooray's action led to their release and the subsequent overturning of his sentence on them.

It should be appreciated that serving on a jury can be an extremely harrowing experience. Jurors are the arbiters of fact, but the facts they have to contend with can be horrific. Criticisms have been levelled at the way in which the jury system can subject people to what in other contexts would be pornography, of either a sexual or violent kind, and yet offer them no counselling when their jury service comes to an end. Many jurors fear reprisals from defendants and their associates. In April 2003, two illegal immigrants, Baghdad Meziane and Brahim Benmerzouga, were convicted of various offences under the Terrorism Act 2000. It appears that they had raised hundreds of thousands of pounds for Al Qa'ida and other radical Islamic organisations. The trial at Leicester Crown Court became a 'drama unprecedented in legal history' (S Bird, 'Jurors too scared to take on case' (2003) *The Times*, 2 April):

> The case began in February, amid extraordinary security arrangements. A jury was sworn in and retired overnight ... The next morning one frightened female juror had worked herself up into such a state that she vomited in the jury room. Two others burst into tears ... The jury was dismissed – as was a second after a male juror expressed fears for his family's safety.

The third jury was down to nine when it was time to deliver a verdict. Jurors receive inadequate protection and support. The only recognition currently available is that the judge can exempt them from further jury service for a particular period. Many would argue that such limited recognition of the damage that jurors might sustain in performing their civic duty is simply inadequate.

Jury service can make excessive (many would say unreasonable) demands on jurors. In May 2005 a fraud trial collapsed after jurors had spent almost two years at the Old Bailey in London. One juror said that the case had been 'a nightmare and a total waste of taxpayers' money'; J. Robins, 'Rough justice for jurors when the call up comes', *Observer*, 12 June 2005. For disgruntled jurors see P. Ferguson, 'Whistleblowing jurors' (2004), 154, NLJ, 370–371. See generally T. Grove (2000), *The Juryman's Tale*.

14.5.1   The jury's function in trials

Judges have the power to direct juries to acquit the accused where there is insufficient evidence to convict them, and this is the main safeguard against juries finding defendants guilty in spite of either the absence, or the insufficiency, of the evidence. There is, however, no corresponding judicial power to instruct juries to convict (*DPP v Stonehouse* (1978); *R v Wang* (2005)). That being said, there is nothing to prevent the judge summing up in such a way as to make it evident to the jury that there is only one decision that can reasonably be made, and that it would be perverse to reach any other verdict but guilty.

What judges must not do is overtly put pressure on juries to reach guilty verdicts. Finding of any such pressure will result in the overturning of any conviction so obtained. The classic example of such a case is *R v McKenna* (1960), in which the judge told the jurors, after they had spent all of two and a quarter hours deliberating on the issue, that if they did not come up with a verdict in the following 10 minutes, they would be locked up for the night. Not surprisingly, the jury returned a verdict; unfortunately for the defendant, it was a guilty verdict; even more unfortunately for the judicial process, the conviction had to be quashed on appeal for clear interference with the jury.

In the words of Cassels J:

> It is a cardinal principle of our criminal law that in considering their verdict, concerning, as it does, the liberty of the subject, a jury shall deliberate in complete freedom, uninfluenced by any promise, unintimidated by any threat. They stand between the Crown and the subject, and they are still one of the main defences of personal liberty. To say to such a tribunal in the course of its deliberations that it must reach a conclusion ... is a disservice to the cause of justice ... [*R v McKenna* (1960)].

Judges do have the right, and indeed the duty, to advise the jury as to the proper understanding and application of the law that it is considering. Even when the jury is considering its verdict, it may seek the advice of the judge. The essential point, however, is that any such response on the part of the judge must be given in open court, so as to obviate any allegation of misconduct (*R v Townsend* (1982)).

In criminal cases, even perversity of decision does not provide grounds for appeal against acquittal. There have been occasions where juries have been subjected to the invective of a judge when they have delivered a verdict with which he disagreed. Nonetheless, the fact is that juries collectively, and individual jurors, do not have to justify, explain or even give reasons for their decisions. Indeed, under s 8 of the Contempt of Court Act 1981, it would be a contempt of court to try to elicit such information from a jury member in either a criminal or a civil law case.

In *Attorney General v Associated Newspapers* (1994), the House of Lords held that it was contempt of court for a newspaper to publish disclosures by jurors of what took place in the jury room while they were considering their verdict, unless the publication amounted to no more than a re-publication of facts already known. It was decided that the word 'disclose' in s 8(1) applied not just to jurors, but to any others who published their revelations.

In an interview for *The Times* in January 2001, the Lord Chief Justice, Lord Woolf, expressed himself very strongly in favour of lifting the ban on jury research, though he emphasised that great care was needed in the conduct of any such research. Fresh impetus may be given to this proposal by the concerns about juries engendered by the decision of the Court of Appeal in *Grobbelaar v News Group Newspapers* (see 14.7.1 below).

There is evidence that the courts are ignoring inappropriate behaviour in order to maintain the principle of jury secrecy; D. Corker and N. Johnson, 'Jury malpractice' (2005), 155, NLJ, 946–947. A strong case can be made for permitting researchers to investigate the effectiveness of the jury system. This seems to be recognised by Lord Chancellor Falconer. See J. Holroyd, 'Judging the jury' (2005), 155, NLJ, 398–399.

These factors place juries in a very strong position to take decisions that are 'unjustifiable' in accordance with the law, for the simple reason that they do not have to justify the decisions. Thus, juries have been able to deliver what can only be described as perverse decisions. In *R v Clive Ponting* (1985), the judge made clear beyond doubt that the defendant was guilty, under the Official Secrets Act 1911, of the offence with which he was charged: the jury still returned a not guilty verdict. Similarly, in the case of Pat Pottle and Michael Randall, who had openly admitted their part in the escape of the spy George Blake, the jury reached a not guilty verdict in open defiance of the law.

In *R v Kronlid* (1996), three protestors were charged with committing criminal damage, and another was charged with conspiracy to cause criminal damage, in relation to an attack on Hawk Jet aeroplanes that were about to be sent to Indonesia. The damage to the planes allegedly amounted to £1.5 million and they did not deny their responsibility for it. They rested their defence on the fact that the planes were to be delivered to the Indonesian State, to be used in its allegedly genocidal campaign against the people of East Timor. On those grounds, they claimed that they were in fact acting to prevent the crime of genocide. The prosecution cited assurances, given by the Indonesian government, that the planes would not be used against the East Timorese, and pointed out that the UK government had granted an export licence for the planes. As the protestors did not deny what they had done, it was apparently a mere matter of course that they would be convicted as charged. The jury, however, decided that all four of the accused were innocent of the charges laid against them. A government Treasury minister, Michael Jack, subsequently stated his disbelief at the verdict of the jury. As he stated:

> I, and I am sure many others, find this jury's decision difficult to understand. It would appear there is little question about who did this damage. For whatever reason that damage was done, it was just plain wrong [(1996) *The Independent*, 1 August].

As stated above, jurors swear to return 'a true verdict according to the evidence'. Such verdicts may be politically inconvenient.

It is perhaps just such a lack of understanding, together with the desire to save money on the operation of the legal system, that has motivated the government's expressed wish to replace jury trials in relation to either way offences (see 14.8 below). In any event, juries continue to reach perverse decisions where they are sympathetic to the causes pursued by the defendants. Thus, in September 2000, 28 Greenpeace volunteers, including its executive director Lord Melchett, were found not guilty of criminal damage after they had destroyed a field containing genetically modified maize. They had been found not guilty of theft in their original trial in April of that year. Judge David Mellor told the jury:

It is not about whether GM crops are a good thing for the environment or a bad thing. It is for you to listen to the evidence and reach honest conclusions as to the facts.

However, the jury seemed to have adopted a different approach.

Fear of not achieving a successful conviction also appears to be the reason behind the CPS's belated decision, in February 2004, not to pursue the prosecution of Katherine Gun. Gun was the former GCHQ translator who revealed that the UK and the USA were involved in spying on members of the United Nations before a crucial vote on whether the 2003 war on Iraq would be sanctioned by the UN. Although she admitted she was the source of the leak and was consequently, at least *prima facie*, in breach of the Official Secrets Act, her prosecution was dropped after she had put forward the defence of necessity. The decision was apparently taken on the guidance of the Attorney General who was involved in the Iraq question from the beginning, being the source of the government's advice that the war was legal without the need for a specific resolution to that effect by the United Nations.

A non-political example of this type of case can be seen in the jury's refusal to find Stephen Owen guilty of any offence after he had discharged a shotgun at the driver of a lorry that had killed his child. And, in September 2000, a jury in Carlisle found Lezley Gibson not guilty on a charge of possession of cannabis after she told the court that she needed it to relieve the symptoms of the multiple sclerosis from which she suffered. The tendency of the jury occasionally to ignore legal formality in favour of substantive justice is one of the major points in favour of its retention, according to its proponents.

14.5.2 Appeals from decisions of the jury

In criminal law, it is an absolute rule that there can be no appeal against a jury's decision to acquit a person of the charges laid against him.

Although there is no appeal as such against acquittal, there does exist the possibility of the Attorney General referring the case to the Court of Appeal, to seek its advice on points of law raised in criminal cases in which the defendant has been acquitted. This procedure was provided for under s 36 of the CJA 1972, although it is not commonly resorted to. It must be stressed that there is no possibility of the actual case being reheard or the acquittal decision being reversed, but the procedure can highlight mistakes in law made in the course of Crown Court trial and permits the Court of Appeal to remedy the defect for the future. (See *Attorney General's Reference (No 1)* (1988) for an example of this procedure, in the area of insider dealing in relation to shares on the Stock Exchange. This case is also interesting in relation to statutory interpretation. See also *Attorney General's Reference (No 3 of 1999)*, considered at 6.5.12 above.)

In civil law cases, the possibility of the jury's verdict being overturned on appeal does exist, but only in circumstances where the original verdict was perverse, that is, no reasonable jury properly directed could have made such a decision.

14.5.3 Majority verdicts

The possibility of a jury deciding a case on the basis of a majority decision was introduced by the CJA 1967. Prior to this, the requirement was that jury decisions had to be unanimous. Such decisions are acceptable where there are:

- not less than 11 jurors and 10 of them agree; or

- there are 10 jurors and nine of them agree.

Where a jury has reached a guilty verdict on the basis of a majority decision, s 17(3) of the Juries Act (JA) 1974 requires the foreman of the jury to state in open court the number of jurors who agreed and the number who disagreed with the verdict. See *R v Barry* (1975), where failure to declare the details of the voting split resulted in the conviction of the defendant being overturned. In *R v Pigg* (1983), the House of Lords held that it was unnecessary to state the number who voted against where the foreman stated the number in favour of the verdict, and thus the determination of the minority was a matter of simple arithmetic.

However, in *R v Mendy* (1992), when the clerk of the court asked the foreman of the jury how a guilty decision had been reached, he replied that it was 'by the majority of us all'. The ambiguity of the reply is obvious when it is taken out of context and this was relied on in a successful appeal. It was simply not clear whether it referred to a unanimous verdict, as the court at first instance had understood it, or whether it referred to a real majority vote, in which case it failed to comply with the requirement of s 17(3) as applied in *R v Barry*. The Court of Appeal held that in such a situation, the defendant had to be given the benefit of any doubt and he was discharged.

The Court of Appeal adopted a different approach in *R v Millward* (1999). The appellant had been convicted, at Stoke-on-Trent Crown Court, of causing grievous bodily harm. Although the jury actually had reached a majority decision, the foreman in response to the questioning of the clerk of the court mistakenly stated that it was the verdict of them all. The following day, the foreman informed the judge that the verdict had in fact been a majority verdict of 10 for guilty and two against.

The Court of Appeal met the subsequent challenge with the following exercise in sophisticated reasoning. The court at first instance had apparently accepted a unanimous verdict. Therefore, s 17 had not been brought into play at all. And, bearing in mind s 8 of the Contempt of Court Act 1981, discouraging the disclosure of votes cast by jurors in the course of their deliberations, the issue had to be viewed under the policy of the law. It would set a very dangerous precedent if an apparently unanimous verdict of a jury delivered in open court, and not then challenged by any juror, was re-opened and subjected to scrutiny. It would be difficult to see how the court could properly investigate a disagreement as to whether jurors had dissented or not.

In the instant case, there was a proper majority direction and proper questions asked of the jury and apparently proper and unambiguous answers given without challenge. Therefore, there should be no further inquiry.

There is no requirement for the details of the voting to be declared in a majority decision of not guilty.

14.5.4 Discharge of jurors or the jury

The trial judge may discharge the whole jury if certain irregularities occur. These would include the situation where the defendant's previous convictions are revealed inadvertently during the trial. Such a disclosure would be prejudicial to the defendant. In such a case, the trial would be ordered to commence again with a different jury. Individual jurors may be discharged by the judge if they are incapable of continuing to act through illness 'or for any other reason' (s 16(1) of the Juries Act (JA) 1974). Where this happens, the jury must not fall below nine members.

14.6 The Selection of the Jury

In theory, jury service is a public duty that citizens should readily undertake. In practice, it is made compulsory, and failure to perform one's civic responsibility is subject to the sanction of a £1,000 fine.

14.6.1 Liability to serve

In 2004, 409,807 people were summoned to sit on juries. Of these, 186,024 actually did so. The JA 1974, as amended by the CJA 1988 and the CJA 2003, sets out the law relating to juries. Prior to the JA 1974, there was a property qualification in respect to jury service which skewed jury membership towards middle class men. Now, the legislation provides that any person between the ages of 18 and 70, who is on the electoral register and who has lived in the UK for at least five years, is qualified to serve as a juror.

The procedure for establishing a jury is a threefold process:

- An officer of the court summons a randomly selected number of qualified individuals from the electoral register.

- From that group, panels of potential jurors for various cases are drawn up.

- The actual jurors are then randomly selected by means of a ballot in open court.

As has been pointed out, however, even if the selection procedure were truly random, randomness does not equal representation. Random juries, by definition, could be: all male, all female, all white, all black, all Conservative or all members of the Raving Loony Party. Such is the nature of the random process; the question that arises from the process is whether such randomness is necessarily a good thing in itself, and whether the summoning officer should take steps to avoid the potential disadvantages that can result from random selection.

As regards the actual random nature of the selection process, a number of problems arise from the use of electoral registers to determine and locate jurors:

- Electoral registers tend to be inaccurate. Generally, they misreport the number of younger people who are in an area simply because younger people tend to move about more than older people and therefore tend not to appear on the electoral role of the place in which they currently live.

- Electoral registers tend to under-report the number of members of ethnic minorities in a community. The problem is that some members of the ethnic communities, for a variety of reasons, simply do not notify the authorities of their existence.

- The problem of non-registration mentioned above was compounded by the disappearance of a great many people from electoral registers in order to try to avoid payment of the former poll tax. It is a matter of some doubt whether such people have registered with the passing of that particular tax or whether they will simply cease to exist for the purpose of jury service. The Runciman Commission, not surprisingly, suggested that every endeavour should be made to ensure that electoral registers are accurate.

14.6.2 Ineligibility exceptions, disqualification and excusal

Prior to the CJA 2003, the general qualification for serving as a juror was subject to a number of exceptions.

A number of people were deemed to be ineligible to serve on juries on the basis of their employment or vocation. Amongst this category are: judges; Justices of the Peace; members of the legal profession; police and probation officers; and members of the clergy or religious orders. Those suffering from a mental disorder were also deemed to be ineligible. Paragraph 2 of Sched 33 to the CJA 2003 removes the first three groups of persons ineligible, the judiciary, others concerned with the administration of justice, and the clergy, leaving only mentally disordered persons with that status. This reform came into effect in April 2005. The extent to which 'ordinary' jurors will be influenced by contact with solicitors, barristers and judges remains to be seen (assuming that research into such matters is eventually permitted).

In an endeavour to maintain the unquestioned probity of the jury system, certain categories of persons are disqualified from serving as jurors. Amongst these are anyone who has been sentenced to a term of imprisonment, or youth custody, of five years or more. In addition, anyone who, in the past 10 years, has served a sentence, or has had a suspended sentence imposed on them, or has had a community punishment order made against them, is also disqualified. The CJA 2003 makes a number of amendments to reflect recent and forthcoming developments in sentencing legislation. Thus, juveniles sentenced under s 91 of the Powers of Criminal Courts (Sentencing) Act 2000 to detention for life, or for a term of five years or more, will be disqualified for life from jury service. People sentenced to imprisonment or detention for public protection, or to an extended sentence under s 227 or 228 of the Act are also to be disqualified for life from jury service. Anyone who has received a community order (as defined in s 177 of the Act) will be disqualified from jury service for 10 years.

Those on bail in criminal proceedings are disqualified from serving as a juror in the Crown Court.

Certain people were excused as of right from serving as jurors on account of their jobs, age or religious views. Amongst these were members of the medical professions, Members of Parliament and members of the armed forces, together with anyone over 65 years of age. Paragraph 3 of Sched 33 to the CJA 2003 repeals s 9(1) of the JA 1974 and consequently no one will in future be entitled to excusal as of right from jury service.

It has always been the case that if a person who has been summoned to do jury service could show that there was a 'good reason' why their summons should be deferred or excused, s 9 of the JA 1974 provided discretion to defer or excuse service. With the abolition of most of the categories of ineligibility and of the availability of excusal as of right, it is expected that there will be a corresponding increase in applications for excusal or deferral under s 9 being submitted to the Jury Central Summoning Bureau (see below).

Grounds for such excusal or deferral are supposed to be made only on the basis of good reason, but there is at least a measure of doubt as to the rigour with which such rules are applied.

A Practice Note issued in 1988 (now *Practice Direction (Criminal: Consolidated)* [2002] 1 WLR 2870, para 42) stated that applications for excusal should be treated sympathetically and listed the following as good grounds for excusal:

(a) personal involvement in the case;

(b) close connection with a party or a witness in the case;

(c) personal hardship;

(d) conscientious objection to jury service.

However, a new s 9AA, introduced by the CJA 2003, places a statutory duty on the Lord Chancellor, in whom current responsibility for jury summoning is vested, to publish and lay before Parliament guidelines relating to the exercise by the Jury Central Summoning Bureau of its functions in relation to discretionary deferral and excusal. Although the historic office of Lord Chancellor seems to have been preserved, the future rôle of Lord Chancellors is unclear.

The aim of the guidelines should be to ensure that all jurors are treated equally and fairly and that the rules are enforced consistently, especially in regard to requests to be excused from service, and thus to reduce at least some of the potential difficulties mentioned above.

The previous, somewhat antiquated procedure for selecting potential jury members, with its accompanying disparity of treatment, is in the process of being modernised by the introduction of a Central Summoning Bureau based at Blackfriars Crown Court Centre in London. Progressively from October 2000, the new Bureau is using a computer system to select jurors at random from the electoral registers and issue the summonses, as well as dealing with jurors' questions and requests. It is intended to link the jury summoning system to the national police records system to allow checks to be made against potentially disqualified individuals. However, severe doubts have been expressed as to the accuracy of the police national computer (PNC), which might not only render the checks on juries inaccurate, but might actually contravene the Data Protection Act 1998. When the Metropolitan Police conducted an audit of the PNC in 1999, it was found to have 'wholly unacceptable' levels of inaccuracy, with an overall error rate of 86%. In one case in 2000 at Highbury Corner magistrates' court in north London, a man charged with theft of £2,700 was granted bail on the grounds that the PNC showed that he had no previous convictions. In fact, he was a convicted murderer released from prison on licence.

14.6.3 Physical disability and jury service

It is to be hoped that the situation of people with disabilities has been altered for the better by the CJPOA 1994, which introduced a new s 9B into the JA 1974. Previously, it was all too common for judges to discharge jurors with disabilities, including deafness, on the assumption that they would not be capable of undertaking the duties of a juror.

Under this provision, where it appears doubtful that a person summoned for jury service is capable of serving on account of some physical disability, that person, as previously, may be brought before the judge. The new s 9B, however, introduces a presumption that people should serve and provides that the judge shall affirm the jury summons unless he is of the opinion that the person will not be able to act effectively.

It would appear, however, that the CJPOA 1994 does not improve the situation of profoundly deaf people who could only function as jurors with the aid of a sign language interpreter. That was the outcome of a case decided in November 1999, that profoundly deaf Jeff McWhinney, chief executive of the British Deaf Association, could not serve as a juror. For him to do so would have required that he had the assistance of an interpreter in the jury room and that could not be allowed as, at present, only jury members are allowed into the jury room.

14.6.4 Challenges to jury membership

That juries can be 'self-selecting' provides grounds for concern as to the random nature of the jury, but the traditional view of the jury is further and perhaps even more fundamentally undermined by the way in which both prosecution and defence seek to influence its constitution.

Under s 12(6) of the JA 1974, both prosecution and defence have a right to challenge the array where the summonsing officer has acted improperly in bringing the whole panel together. Such challenges are rare, although an unsuccessful action was raised in *R v Danvers* (1982), where the defendant tried to challenge the racial composition of the group of potential jurors.

14.6.5   Challenge by the defence

Until the CJA 1988, there were two ways in which the defence could challenge potential jurors:

- *Peremptory challenge*

  The defence could object to any potential jury members, up to a maximum number of three, without having to show any reason or justification for the challenge. Defence counsel used this procedure in an attempt to shape the composition of the jury in a way they thought might best suit their client, although it has to be said that it was an extremely inexact process, and one that could upset or antagonise rejected jurors. In spite of arguments for its retention on a civil liberties basis, the majority of the Roskill Committee on Fraud Trials (January 1986, HMSO) recommended that the right be abolished, and abolition was provided for in the CJA 1988.

- *Challenge for cause*

  The defence retains the power to challenge any number of potential jurors for cause, that is to say that there is a substantial reason why a particular person should not serve on the jury to decide a particular defendant's case. A simple example would be where the potential juror has had previous dealings with the defendant or has been involved in the case in some way. There may be less obvious grounds for objection, however, which may be based on the particular juror's attitudes, or indeed political beliefs. The question arises whether such factors provide grounds for challenge. In what is known as *The Angry Brigade* case in 1972 (see (1971) *The Times*, 10–11 December (1972) *The Times*, 12–15 December), a group of people was charged with carrying out a bombing campaign against prominent members of the Conservative government. In the process of empanelling a jury, the judge asked potential jurors to exclude themselves on a variety of socio-political grounds, including active membership of the Conservative Party. As a consequence of the procedure adopted in that case, the Lord Chief Justice issued a practice direction in which he made it clear that potential jurors were not to be excluded on account of race, religion, politics or occupation. Since that practice direction, it is clear that the challenge for cause can only be used within a restricted sphere, and this makes it less useful to the defence than it might otherwise be if it were to operate in a more general way.

It has been argued that the desire of civil libertarians to retain the right of the defence to select a jury that might be more sympathetic to its case is contradictory, because although in theory they usually rely on the random nature of the jury to ensure the appearance of justice, in practice they seek to influence its composition. When, however, the shortcomings in the establishment of panels for juries is recalled, it might be countered that the defence is attempting to do no more than counter the inbuilt bias that ensues from the use of unbalanced electoral registers.

14.6.6 Challenge by the prosecution

If the defence attempts to ensure that any jury will not be prejudiced against its case, if not predisposed towards it, the same is true of the prosecution. However, the prosecution has a greater scope to achieve such an aim. Whilst the prosecution has the same right as the defence to challenge for cause, it has the additional option of excluding potential jury members by simply asking them to stand by until a jury has been empanelled. The request for the potential juror to stand by is only a provisional challenge and, in theory, the person stood by can at a later time take their place on the jury if there are no other suitable candidates. In practice, of course, it is unlikely in the extreme for there not to be sufficient alternative candidates to whom the prosecution do not object and prefer to the person stood by.

When the Roskill Committee recommended the removal of the defence's right to pre-emptive challenge, it recognised that, in order to retain an equitable situation, the right of the Crown to ask potential jurors to stand by should also be withdrawn. Unfortunately, although the government of the day saw fit to follow the Committee's recommendation in relation to the curtailment of the defence rights, it did not feel under the same obligation to follow its corresponding recommendation to curtail the rights of the prosecution. Thus, the CJA 1988 made no reference to the procedure and, in failing to do so, established a distinct advantage in favour of the prosecution in regard to selecting what it considered to be suitable juries.

The manifest unreasonableness of this procedure led to the Attorney General issuing a practice note (1988) to the effect that the Crown should only exercise its power to stand by potential jurors in the following two circumstances:

- To prevent the empanelment of a 'manifestly unsuitable' juror, with the agreement of the defence. The example given of 'manifest unsuitability' is an illiterate person asked to sit in a highly complex case. It is reasonable to doubt the ability of such a person to follow the process of the case involving a number of documents, and on that basis they should be stood by.

- In circumstances where the Attorney General has approved the vetting of the potential jury members and that process has revealed that the particular juror in question might be a security risk. In this situation, the Attorney General is also required to approve the use of the 'stand by' procedure.

14.6.7 Jury vetting

Jury vetting is the process by which the Crown checks the background of potential jurors to assess their suitability to decide particular cases. The procedure is clearly contrary to the ideal of the jury being based on a random selection of people, but it is justified on the basis that it is necessary to ensure that jury members are not likely to divulge any secrets made open to them in the course of a sensitive trial or, alternatively, on the ground that jurors with extreme political views should not be permitted the opportunity to express those views in a situation where they might influence the outcome of a case.

The practice of vetting potential jurors developed after the *Angry Brigade* trial in 1972, but it did not become public until 1978. In that year, as a result of an Official Secrets Act case, known by the initials of the three defendants as the ABC trial, it became apparent that the list of potential jurors had been checked to establish their 'soundness'. As a consequence of that case, the Attorney General published the current guidelines for vetting jury panels. Since that date, the guidelines have been updated and the most recent guidelines were published in 1988. These guidelines maintain the general propositions that jury members should normally be selected at random from the panel and should be disqualified only on the grounds set out in the JA 1974. The guidelines do, however, make reference to exceptional cases of public importance where potential jury members might properly be vetted. Such cases are broadly identified as those involving national security, where part of the evidence may be heard on camera, and terrorist cases.

Vetting is a twofold process. An initial check into police criminal records and police Special Branch records should be sufficient to reveal whether a further investigation by the security services is required. Any further investigation requires the prior approval of the Attorney General.

In addition to vetting properly so-called, the Court of Appeal in *R v Mason* (1980) approved the checking of criminal records to establish whether potential jurors had been convicted of criminal offences in the past and therefore were not eligible to serve as jurors. The Runciman Commission recommended that this process of checking on those who should be disqualified on the basis of previous criminal conviction should be regularised when the collection and storage of criminal records is centralised. This was achieved when the Criminal Records Bureau was established as a result of Part V of the Police Act 1997.

14.6.8   The racial mix of the jury

In *R v Danvers* (1982), the defence had sought to challenge the array on the basis that a black defendant could not have complete confidence in the impartiality of an all white jury. The question of the racial mix of a jury has exercised the courts on a number of occasions. In *R v Ford* (1989), the trial judge's refusal to accept the defendant's application for a racially mixed jury was supported by the Court of Appeal on the grounds that, 'fairness is achieved by the principle of random selection' as regards the make up of a jury, and that to insist on a racially balanced jury would be contrary to that principle, and would be to imply that particular jurors were incapable of impartiality. A similar point was made in *R v Tarrant* (1997), in which a person accused of drug-related offences was convicted by a jury that had had been selected from outside the normal catchment area for the court. The aim of the judge had been to minimise potential jury intimidation, but nonetheless, the Court of Appeal overturned the conviction on the grounds that the judge had deprived the defendant of a randomly selected jury.

To deny people the right to have their cases heard by representatives of their own race, on the basis of a refusal to recognise the existence of racial discriminatory attitudes, cannot but give the appearance of a society where such racist attitudes are institutionalised. This has particular resonance given the findings of the Macpherson Inquiry that the police force were 'institutionally racist'. Without suggesting that juries as presently constituted are biased, it remains arguable that if, in order to achieve the undoubted appearance of fairness, jury selection has to be manipulated to ensure a racial mix, then it should at least be considered.

An interesting case study in this respect is the trial in 1994 of Lakhbir Deol, an Asian who was accused of the murder of a white youth in Stoke-on-Trent in 1993. Mr Deol's lawyers sought to have the case moved from Stafford to Birmingham Crown Court on the grounds that Stafford has an almost completely white population, whereas Birmingham has an approximately 25% ethnic minority population. Mr Justice McKinnon repeatedly refused the request and the trial was heard in Stafford as scheduled. Mr Deol was acquitted, so his fears were proved groundless, but surely the worrying fact is that he had those fears in the first place.

It is heartening to note that the Runciman Commission fully endorsed the views expressed above and recommended that either the prosecution or the defence should be able to insist that up to three jury members be from ethnic minorities, and that at least one of those should be from the same ethnic minority as the accused or the victim. Sir Robin Auld, in his review of the criminal courts, also recommended that provision should be made to enable ethnic minority representation on juries where race is likely to be relevant to an important issue in the case.

It is of interest, if not concern, to note that the former Lord Chief Justice, Lord Taylor, whilst recognising that the criminal justice system was:

> ... failing blacks and Asians, by tolerating racist attitudes and allowing ethnic minorities to believe that they were beyond the protection of the law ...,

was equally sure that proposals for ethnically balanced juries, and indeed, the new offence of racially motivated attacks, were:

> Attractive sounding, but deeply flawed proposals.

He went on to criticise the Runciman proposals as:

> ... the thin edge of a particularly insidious wedge ...

And, somewhat ironically, given subsequent proposals by the recent Home Secretaries, he asserted that:

> We must on no account introduce measures which allow the State to start nibbling away at the principle of random selection of juries [speech to NACRO reported in *The Guardian*, 1999].

In *R v Smith* (2003), the Court of Appeal re-affirmed the traditional view in holding that it had not been unfair for Smith to be tried by a randomly selected all-white jury. In addition, however, the court held that the selection process had not infringed Smith's rights under Art 6 of the ECHR.

Another case which raised a human rights issue was *R v Mushtaq* (2002), in which the defendant appealed against his conviction for conspiracy to defraud. He had admitted to police that he had played a minor part in the conspiracy, but later claimed that his confession had been obtained by oppression. The judge ruled during the trial that Mushtaq's confession had not been obtained by oppression and was therefore admissible, and in his summing up to the jury, he emphasised that the confession was central and crucial to the case. Mushtaq claimed that the judge's direction to the jury was in breach of Art 6 of the ECHR and that the jury, *as a separate and distinct public authority*, had a duty to protect his rights. The Court of Appeal dismissed the appeal, holding that the separate functions allocated to the judge and the jury in relation to disputed confessions had significant advantages for ensuring that justice was done. The admissibility of a confession was a matter for the judge and if the prosecution failed to satisfy the judge that a confession was not obtained by oppression, the jury would not hear it. This division of function between judge and jury complied with the requirement to provide an adequate safeguard for a defendant's Art 6 rights, and it could not be said that the jury was a separate public authority having a distinct and separate duty from the judge to protect Mushtaq's rights. In a criminal trial, it was the court acting collectively that had the shared responsibility of ensuring a fair trial.

14.6.9 Racial bias in juries

If the law does not allow for the artificial creation of ethnic balance in juries, then it must ensure that ethnically unbalanced juries do not become ethnically biased ones.

In May 2000, the ECtHR held by a majority of 4:3 that the right of a British Asian to be tried by an impartial tribunal had been violated on the basis of alleged racism within the jury that had convicted him. Kuldip Sander had been charged with conspiracy to commit fraud and was tried at Birmingham Crown Court in March 1995. During the trial, one of the jurors sent a note to the judge stating:

> I have decided I cannot remain silent any longer. For some time during the trial I have been concerned that fellow jurors are not taking their duties seriously. At least two have been making openly racist remarks and jokes and I fear are going to convict the defendants not on the evidence but because they are Asian. My concern is the defendants will not therefore receive a fair verdict. Please could you advise me what I can do in this situation.

The judge adjourned the case, but kept the juror who had written the letter apart from the other jurors whilst he listened to submission from counsel in open court. The defence asked the judge to dismiss the jury on the ground that there was a real danger of bias. The judge, however, decided to call the jury back into court, at which stage the juror who had written the complaint joined the others. The judge read out the complaint to them and told them the following:

> I am not able to conduct an inquiry into the validity of those contentions and I do not propose to do so. This case has cost an enormous amount of money and I am not anxious to halt it at the moment, but I shall have no compunction in doing so if the situation demands ... I am going to ask you all to search your conscience overnight and if you feel that you are not able to try this case solely on the evidence and find that you

cannot put aside any prejudices you may have will you please indicate that fact by writing a personal note to that effect and giving it to the jury bailiff on your arrival at court tomorrow morning. I will then review the position.

The next morning, the judge received two letters from the jury. The first letter, which was signed by all the jurors including the juror who had sent the complaint, refuted any allegation of racial bias. The second letter was written by a juror who appeared to have thought himself to have been the one who had been making the jokes. The juror in question stated that he was sorry if he had given any offence, that he had many connections with people from ethnic minorities and that he was in no way racially biased.

The judge decided not to discharge the jury and it went on to find the applicant guilty, although it acquitted another Asian defendant. The applicant's appeal, partly on the grounds of bias on the part of the jury, was dismissed by the Court of Appeal.

The majority of the ECtHR, however, held that the trial was conducted contrary to Art 6(1) of the ECHR. The Court considered that the allegations contained in the note were capable of causing the applicant and any objective observer to have legitimate doubts as to the impartiality of the court, which neither the collective letter nor the redirection of the jury by the judge could have dispelled.

In reaching its decision, the Court distinguished the decision in the similar case of *Gregory v UK* (1998). In the *Gregory* judgment, there was no admission by a juror that he had made racist comments, in the form of a joke or otherwise; there was no indication as to who had made the complaint and the complaint was vague and imprecise. Moreover, in the present case, the applicant's counsel had insisted throughout the proceedings that dismissing the jury was the only viable course of action.

The Court accepted that, although discharging the jury might not always be the only means to achieve a fair trial, there were certain circumstances where this was required by Art 6(1) of the ECHR. As the Court stated:

> Given the importance attached by all Contracting States to the need to combat racism, the Court considers that the judge should have reacted in a more robust manner than merely seeking vague assurances that the jurors could set aside their prejudices and try the case solely on the evidence. By failing to do so, the judge did not provide sufficient guarantees to exclude any objectively justified or legitimate doubts as to the impartiality of the court. It follows that the court that condemned the applicant was not impartial from an objective point of view.

The Court, however, refused his claim for compensation of some £458,000, which suggests that it was not convinced that a substitute jury would not have convicted him as well.

It has already been seen that s 8 of the Contempt of Court Act 1981 prevents investigation into what occurs in the privacy of the jury room and such prohibition applies equally to judges. In *R v Qureshi* (2001), the defendant had been convicted of arson and of attempting to attain property by deception. Three days after the verdict, a juror in the trial informed the court that some members of the jury had been racially prejudiced against Qureshi and had decided he was guilty from the outset of the trial.

Qureshi's application for permission to appeal against his conviction was rejected by the Court of Appeal on the grounds that the complaint did not arise during the trial, but only after an apparently regular verdict had been delivered. In order to pursue the allegation, the court would have had to investigate what had happened in the jury room and that was precluded by s 8 of the Contempt of Court Act 1981. In reaching this decision, the Court of Appeal distinguished *Sander*, where the complaint arose during the trial, and followed *R v Miah* (1997), where the complaint arose after the event. In the latter case, it was stated that the rule against breaching jury secrecy applied to 'anything said by one juror to another about the case from the moment the jury is empanelled, at least provided what is said is not overheard by anyone who is not a juror'. It has to be asked whether such a rule is acceptable, especially when it conceals possible injustice. For a detailed analysis of these cases, see P Robertshaw, 'Responding to bias amongst jurors' (2002) 66(1) Journal of Criminal Law 84–95.

14.7 The Decline of the Jury Trial

Many direct attempts have been made in the recent past to reduce the operation of the jury system within the English legal system. These particular endeavours, however, have to be understood in the context of the general historical decline in the use of the jury as the mechanism for determining issues in court cases. Perhaps the heat engendered in the current debate is a consequence of the fact that the continued existence of the jury as it is presently constituted cannot be taken for granted.

14.7.1 The jury trial in civil procedure

There can be no doubt as to the antiquity of the institution of trial by jury, nor can there be much doubt as to its supposed democratising effect on the operation of the legal system. Neither, unfortunately, can there be any grounds for denying the diminishment that has occurred in the fairly recent past in the role of the jury as the means of determining the outcome of trials, nor can the continued existence of the jury as it is presently constituted be taken for granted.

In respect of civil law, the use of juries has diminished considerably and automatic recourse to trial by jury is restricted to a small number of areas and, even in those areas, the continued use of the jury is threatened. Prior to 1854, all cases that came before the common law courts were decided by a judge and jury. The Common Law Procedure Act of that year provided that cases could be settled without a jury where the parties agreed, and since then, the role of the jury has been gradually curtailed until, at present, under s 69 of the Supreme Court Act 1981, the right to a jury trial is limited to only four specific areas: fraud, defamation, malicious prosecution and false imprisonment. (Similar provisions are contained in the County Courts Act 1984.)

Even in these areas, the right is not absolute and can be denied by a judge under s 69(i) where the case involves 'any prolonged examination of documents or accounts or any scientific or local investigation which cannot conveniently be made with a jury'.

(See *Beta Construction Ltd v Channel Four TV Co Ltd* (1990) for an indication of the factors that the judge will take into consideration in deciding whether a case should be decided by a jury or not.)

The question of whether or not juries should be used in libel cases gained wider consideration in the case involving McDonald's, the fast food empire, and two environmentalists, Dave Morris and Helen Steel. McDonald's claimed that their reputation was damaged by an allegedly libellous leaflet issued by members of an organisation called London Greenpeace including Morris and Steel, which linked McDonald's' products to heart disease and cancer as well as the despoilation of the environment and the exploitation of the Third World. In a preliminary hearing, later confirmed by the Court of Appeal, it was decided that the evidence to be presented would be of such scientific complexity that it would be beyond the understanding of a jury (see (1997) *The Times*, 10 June).

The right to jury trial in defamation cases has been the object of particular criticism. In 1975, the Faulks Committee on the Law of Defamation recommended that the availability of jury trial in that area should be subject to the same judicial discretion as all other civil cases. In its conclusions, the Faulks Report shared the uncertainty of the Court of Appeal in *Ward v James* (1965) as to the suitability of juries to determine the level of damages that should be awarded. Support for these views has been provided by a number of defamation cases decided since then, such as *Sutcliffe v Pressdram Ltd* (1990), in which the wife of a convicted serial killer was awarded damages of £600,000. She eventually settled for £60,000 after the Court of Appeal stated that it would reassess the award.

In *Aldington v Watts and Tolstoy* (1990), damages of £1.5 million were awarded. This huge award was subsequently held by the ECtHR to be so disproportionate as to amount to a violation of Tolstoy's right to freedom of expression under Art 10 of the ECHR (*Tolstoy Miloslavsky v UK* (1995)). Domestic law has also sought to deal with what could only be seen as excessive awards of damages in defamation cases, even prior to the HRA, which makes the ECtHR *Tolstoy* decision and Art 10 of the ECHR binding in UK law.

Section 8 of the CLSA 1990 gave appeal courts the power to alter damages awards made by juries to a level that they felt to be 'proper'. Nonetheless, the question of what actually constitutes a proper level of damages continued to present problems for juries, which continued to award very large sums. The problem arose from the limited guidance that judges could give juries in making their awards. In *Rantzen v Mirror Group Newspapers* (1993), the Court of Appeal stated that judges should advise juries, in making their awards, to consider the purchasing power of the award and its proportionality to the damage suffered to the reputation of the plaintiff, and should refer to awards made by the courts under s 8 of the CLSA (Rantzen's original award of £250,000 was reduced to £110,000). Still, extremely large awards continued to be made, and in *John v MGN Ltd* (1996), the Court of Appeal stated that past practice should be altered to allow juries to refer to personal injury cases to decide the level of award, and that the judge could indicate what sort of level would be appropriate (John's awards of £350,000 for the libel and £275,000 in exemplary damages were reduced to £75,000 and £50,000 respectively).

In 1996, statute law intervened in the form of the Defamation Act, which was designed to simplify the procedure of defamation cases. The main provisions of the Act are:

(a) a new one year limitation period for defamation claims;

(b) a new statutory defence based on responsibility for publication. This replaces the common law defence of innocent dissemination;

(c) an updating of defences in relation to privilege, that is, reporting on the proceedings and publications of, for example, the courts and government;

(d) a new streamlined procedure for dealing with a defendant who has offered to make amends. This would involve paying compensation, assessed by a judge, and publishing an appropriate correction and apology;

(e) new powers for judges to deal with cases without a jury. Under this provision, the judge can dismiss a claim if he considers it has no realistic prospect of success. Alternatively, if he considers there to be no realistic defence to the claim, he can award summary relief. Such relief can take the form of a declaration of the falsity of the statement; an order to print an apology; an order to refrain from repeating the statement; and damages of up to £10,000.

It is a matter of constitutional interest that s 13 of the Defamation Act 1996, altering the operation of s 9 of the Bill of Rights 1689, was specially introduced to allow the former Conservative MP, Neil Hamilton, to bring a defamation action against *The Guardian* newspaper which had accused him of accepting money for asking questions in the House of Commons. The Bill of Rights had granted qualified privilege to MPs, but *The Guardian* had successfully argued that, as they could not sue Hamilton in regard to parliamentary matters, he in turn could not sue them. Unusually, as Law Lords are not supposed to involve themselves in party political matters, s 13 of the Defamation Act, which allowed MPs to waive their privilege, was moved by Lord Hoffmann, apparently at the behest of the then Lord Chancellor, Lord Mackay. Hamilton's action against *The Guardian* subsequently collapsed and he lost his parliamentary seat in the 1997 election. Lord Hoffmann went on to demonstrate his lack of political grasp in the infamous *Pinochet* case (see Chapter 6).

The most significant elements of the Defamation Act came into effect at the end of February 2000, but in January 2001, the Court of Appeal used its common law powers to completely overturn the award of damages in the case of *Grobbelaar v News Group Newspapers Ltd* (2001). Grobbelaar, an ex-football player, had been accused of accepting money to fix football matches. He had been found not guilty in a criminal case and had been awarded £85,000 damages for defamation in a related civil case against *The Sun* newspaper. On appeal, the Court of Appeal held that the newspaper could not rely on the defence of limited qualified privilege, as recently recognised in *Reynolds v Times Newspapers Ltd and Others* (1999), and could be held to account for such defamatory statements as could not be proved true. However, although the court stated that it would be most reluctant to find perversity in a jury's verdict, it had such jurisdiction and, therefore, duty to consider that ground of appeal. The court then went on to conclude that no reasonable jury could have failed to be satisfied on the balance of probabilities, and to a relatively high degree of probability, that Grobbelaar had been party to corrupt conspiracies. The court considered that the evidence led inexorably to the view that Grobbelaar's story was 'quite simply incredible. All logic, common sense and reason compelled one to that conclusion'.

As regards overturning the decision of the jury, in the words of Thorpe LJ:

> I recognise and respect the unique function of a jury that heard all of the evidence over some 16 days of trial, nevertheless it would be an injustice to the defendants to allow the outcome to stand.

On further appeal, the House of Lords held that the Court of Appeal was correct in holding that the jury's decision was open to review on the grounds of perversity. However, it found that the Court of Appeal had been wrong to overturn the jury's verdict on the grounds of perversity in this instance, as the verdict could have been explained in such a way that did not necessarily require the imputation of adversity. Grobbelaar's victory, however, was pyrrhic in the extreme; due to his breach of his legal and moral obligations, the damages awarded by the jury were quashed and substituted by the award of nominal damages of £1, with no costs awarded.

The extent of damages and, in particular, exemplary damages awarded against the police in a number of civil actions has also been problematic (see 6.4.3 above for a consideration of types of damages). These actions have arisen from wrongful arrest, false imprisonment, assault and malicious prosecution and usually have involved connotations of racist behaviour on the part of the police. In setting the level of damages, juries have wished signally to demonstrate their disapproval of such police behaviour, but as the courts have correctly pointed out, any payments made come from the public purse, not from the individuals involved. The issue came to a head in *Thompson and Another v Commissioner of Police for the Metropolis* (1997), in which the Court of Appeal considered awards made to two plaintiffs. The first had been assaulted in custody and false evidence was used against her in a criminal trial during which she was held in prison. In a civil action, she was awarded £51,500 damages, of which £50,000 were exemplary damages. The second plaintiff was physically and racially abused by police when they broke into his house and arrested him. In a consequential civil action, he was awarded £220,000 for wrongful arrest, false imprisonment and assault, of which £200,000 were exemplary damages. On appeal, the Court of Appeal stated that in such cases, the judge should direct the jury that:

(i) damages, save in exceptional circumstances, should be awarded only as compensation and in line with a scale which keeps the damages proportionate with those payable in personal injury cases;

(ii) where aggravated damages are appropriate, they are unlikely to be less than £1,000, or to be more than twice the basic damages except where those basic damages are modest;

(iii) in relation to the award of exemplary damages the jury should be told of the exceptional nature of the remedy, and told that the basic and aggravated damages together must be insufficient to punish the defendant before any exemplary damages can be considered. Where exemplary damages are appropriate they are unlikely to be less than £5,000. Conduct must be particularly deserving of condemnation to warrant an award of £25,000 and the absolute maximum should be £50,000. It would be unusual for such damages to be more than three times the basic damages being awarded unless those basic damages are modest.

In the two cases in question, the first exemplary award was reduced from £50,000 to £25,000; and in the second, the exemplary component was reduced from £200,000 to £15,000.

The reasoning in the *Thompson* case was followed in *Hill v Commissioner of Police for the Metropolis* (1998), where the plaintiff was awarded £45,600 for wrongful arrest, false imprisonment, assault and malicious prosecution. The most contentious award was that of exemplary damages, the bracket having been set by the judge as between £5,000–15,000, but the jury awarded the plaintiff £20,000. The Court of Appeal held that the jury had only gone beyond the guidelines to a limited extent and it was clear that they had taken a poor view of the police officers' conduct. In those circumstances, although the total award was high and might be seen to be out of proportion to awards made in personal injury cases, it was not seen as manifestly excessive in relation to Thompson's case.

If the extent of damages has been a particular problem in relation to defamation claims, especially when they are compared to the much smaller awards made in relation to personal injury, it should also be noted that public funding is not normally available in defamation cases, although it is available in relation to malicious falsehood. This effectively has made defamation a rich person's claim. As a consequence, people without the necessary wealth to finance legal proceedings find it extremely difficult to gain redress when they have suffered from what subsequently turns out to be false and damaging press coverage of their affairs. It is to be hoped that the new summary procedure, under the Defamation Act 1996, will redress this situation. But of equal concern is the way some wealthy people were able and allowed to abuse the system. One example was the late and notorious publisher, Robert Maxwell, who often used libel proceedings or the threat of them to silence critics. As it turned out, much of what Mr Maxwell sought to prevent from becoming public knowledge was in fact illegal and harmful business conduct.

In all other civil cases, there is a presumption against trial by jury although, under s 69(3), the judge has the discretion to order a trial by jury. (See *Ward v James* (1965), where the court decided that a jury should be used in civil cases only in 'exceptional circumstances', although no exhaustive list as to what amounted to exceptional circumstances was provided.)

14.7.2 Juries in criminal trials

It has to be borne in mind that the criminal jury trial is essentially the creature of the Crown Court, and that the magistrates' courts deal with at least 95% of criminal cases. In practice, juries determine the outcome of less than 1% of the total of criminal cases for the reason that, of all the cases that are decided in the Crown Court, 60% of defendants plead guilty on all counts and therefore have no need of jury trial. It can be seen, therefore, that in absolute and proportional terms, the jury does not play a significant part in the determination of criminal cases.

If trial by jury is not statistically significant, it cannot be denied that it is of major significance in the determination of the most serious cases. Even this role, however, has not gone without scrutiny, as will be seen below.

It should not be forgotten that the right to jury trial has been abolished in Northern Ireland since 1973. In response to the problem of the intimidation of jury members, the *Report of the Commission to Consider Legal Procedures to Deal with Terrorist Activities in Northern Ireland*, headed by Lord Diplock, recommended that cases be decided without juries in particular situations. The so-called 'Diplock courts' operate in relation to certain 'scheduled offences', particularly, but not exclusively, associated with terrorism.

14.7.3 Jury tampering

The term 'jury tampering' covers a range of circumstances in which the jury's independence is or may appear to be compromised. Such a situation could come about because of actual harm or threats of harm to jury members. It might equally involve intimidation or bribery of jury members. Alternatively, it could also include similar improper approaches to a juror's family or friends.

Sections 44 and 46 of the CJA 2003 provide for a trial on indictment in the Crown Court to be conducted without a jury where there is a danger of jury tampering, or continued without a jury where the jury has been discharged because of jury tampering. For an application under s 44 to be granted, the court must be satisfied that there is evidence of a real and present danger that jury tampering would take place. In addition, the court must also be satisfied that the danger of jury tampering is so substantial, notwithstanding any steps that could reasonably be taken to prevent it, as to make it necessary in the interests of justice for the trial to be conducted without a jury. Sub-section (6) sets out examples of what might constitute evidence of a real and present danger of jury tampering, which include:

- a case where the trial is a retrial and the jury in the previous trial was discharged because jury tampering had taken place;

- a case where jury tampering has taken place in previous criminal proceedings involving the defendant or any of the defendants;

- a case where there has been intimidation, or attempted intimidation, of any person who is likely to be a witness in the trial.

Section 46 deals with trials already underway, where jury tampering has or appears to have taken place. In these circumstances, if the judge decides to discharge the jury, as he has a right to do in common law, and is satisfied that tampering has occurred, he may order that the trial should continue without a jury if he is satisfied that this would be fair to the defendant. On the other hand, if the judge considers it necessary in the interests of justice to terminate the trial due to tampering, he may order that the re-trial should take place without a jury.

14.7.4 Complex fraud trials

In 1986, the Roskill Committee on Fraud Trials critically examined the operation of the jury in complex criminal fraud cases. Its report recommended the abolition of trial by jury in such cases. The Roskill Committee did not go as far as to recommend that all fraud cases should be taken away from juries, only the most complex, of which it was estimated that there were about two dozen or so every year. It was suggested that these cases would be better decided by a judge assisted by two lay persons drawn from a panel with specialist expertise. The government declined to implement the recommendations of the Roskill Committee, and instead introduced procedures designed to make it easier to follow the proceedings in complex fraud cases.

After being found not guilty of a £19 million fraud charge, George Walker, the former chief executive of Brent Walker, said: 'Thank God for the jury. It would be madness to lose the jury system.' This enthusiastic endorsement of the jury system is in no little way undercut, however, by the fact that Walker is reported as going on to state that he was sure the jury had not properly understood much of the highly detailed material in the trial, as he admitted: 'I didn't understand a lot of it, so I can't see how they could.'

Mr Walker's enthusiasm perhaps was not shared by his co-accused, Wilfred Aquilina, who was found guilty, on a majority verdict, of false accounting.

The Royal Commission on the Criminal Justice System of 1993 (the Runciman Commission) recognised the particular difficulties faced by jurors in fraud trials but, somewhat surprisingly in the light of its recommendations in relation to offences triable either way, it did not suggest the removal of the jury from such cases. It merely recommended that s 10(3) of the CJA 1988 should be amended to permit judges to put the issues before the jury at the outset of the trial.

In February 1998, the Home Office issued a Green Paper entitled *Juries in Serious Fraud Trials*. The Consultation Paper suggested the need for a new procedure in relation to complex fraud trials, due to the fact that 'the detection, investigation and trial of serious criminal fraud offences have presented certain difficulties not commonly found amongst other types of offences'. A variety of possible alternatives were put forward:

- *Special juries*: these would be made up of qualified people and might be drawn from a special pool of potential jurors. Alternatively, ordinary jurors would have to be assessed as to their competency to sit on the case.

- *Judge run trials*: specially trained judges, either singly or in a panel, and possibly with the help of lay experts.

- *Fraud tribunals*: following Roskill, these would be made up of a judge and qualified lay members with the power to question witnesses.

- *Verdict only juries*: in this situation, the judge would hear the evidence and sum up the facts, leaving the jury simply to vote on guilt or innocence.

- *A special juror*: here, 11 of the jury would be selected as normal, but the 12th would be specially qualified in order to be able to assist the others on complex points.

With respect to these alternatives, the government stated that it had no particular preference.

Subsequently, in April 1998, the Home Secretary requested the Law Commission to carry out a review of fraud trials, focusing particularly on whether the existing law was:

- readily comprehensible to juries;

- adequate for effective prosecution;

- fair to defendants; and

- able to cope with changes in technology.

However, in its response in Consultation Paper No 155, *Fraud and Deception* (1999), the Law Commission addressed only the issues of possible criminal offences and did not deal with any procedural issues.

In his extensive *Review of the Criminal Courts* (2001), Sir Robin Auld LJ recommended that in serious and complex frauds, the nominated trial judge should have the power to direct trial by himself and two lay members drawn from a panel established by the Lord Chancellor for the purpose or, if the defendant requested, by himself alone. However, in the White Paper preceding the CJA 2003, it was claimed that each year 15–20 complex fraud trials emerged that would be better dealt with by a judge sitting alone: Part 7 of the CJA 2003 provides for exactly that possibility. Section 43 allows the prosecution to apply for a serious or complex fraud trial on indictment in the Crown Court to proceed in the absence of a jury. Before granting the application, the court has to be satisfied that the length or complexity of the trial is likely to make it so burdensome upon the jury that, in the interests of justice, serious consideration should be given to conducting the trial without a jury. Any order to that effect requires the approval of the Lord Chief Justice.

The CJA 2003 has thus introduced measures much more restrictive than any previous body had recommended, but, at least for supporters of juries, the situation could have been worse, as the initial Criminal Justice Bill proposed a similar potential curtailment in all complex or lengthy trials, not just fraud cases. It is likely that juries will soon be denied the (dubious) pleasure of dealing with such cases; C. Dyer and T. Branigan, 'Juries to be scrapped in complex fraud cases', *Guardian*, 22 June 2005. Proposals for non-jury trials in terrorism cases were abandoned in May 2005. They may be revived following terrorist outrages in July. R. Ford and F. Gibb, 'Jury trials saved after U-turn on terror laws' (2005), *The Times*, 16 May.

14.8   Jury Reform

The foregoing has considered the historical decline of the jury trial; it remains to consider its prospects for the future and the related matter of how and whether research can be conducted into the way in which juries operate in practice.

14.8.1   Either way offences: the role of the jury

In order to understand the full implications of the recommendation, it is necessary to reconsider points that have been discussed previously in Chapter 4.

It is essential to appreciate the distinction between offences to be tried only by summary procedure, offences to be tried only on indictment and offences triable 'either way'. Summary offences are those which are triable only in the magistrates' courts and cases which, as has been noted previously, magistrates decide on their own without the assistance of a jury. There are literally hundreds of summary offences; given the limitations on the sentencing powers of magistrates, they are by necessity the least serious of criminal acts, such as road traffic offences and minor assault. The most serious offences, such as major theft, serious assault, rape, manslaughter and murder, have to be tried on indictment before a jury in the Crown Court. There is, however, a third category, offences triable 'either way' which, as the name suggests, may be tried either summarily or on indictment.

The current way of determining how an offence triable 'either way' is actually heard is set out in the Magistrates' Courts Act (MCA) 1980. Under s 19 of that Act, the magistrates' court has to decide whether the offence is more suitable for summary trial or trial on indictment. In reaching that decision, the magistrates must take into account the nature of the case, its seriousness, whether the penalty they could impose would be adequate, and any other circumstances which appear to the court to make it more suitable for the offence to be tried one way rather than the other. If the accused agrees to a summary hearing, the trial goes ahead in the magistrates' court. If, however, the defendant objects to the summary procedure, the case goes on indictment to the Crown Court and the magistrates merely act as examining justices. It should be noted that the CJA 2003 alters the procedure in relation to the allocation of offences triable either way (see 4.3.2 above).

14.8.1.1   The Royal Commission on Criminal Justice

The Runciman Commission's Report stated that defendants should not 'be able to choose their court of trial solely on the basis that they think that they will get a fairer hearing at one level than another' (see para 6.18 of the Report). The conclusion of the Commission seemed to be that, because defendants do not trust the magistrates' court, and there is some justification for this in respect of the rates of acquittal, and do have more faith in the Crown Court than is warranted in terms of sentencing, then they should be forced to use the magistrates' court. As the Report stated: 'Magistrates' courts conduct over 93% of all criminal cases and should be trusted to try cases fairly' (see para 6.18 of the Report). It is at least arguable that in this conclusion, the Commission missed the point. Put starkly, the evidence supports the conclusion that defendants do not trust magistrates' courts. Indeed, the evidence as to the number of people changing their plea to guilty in the Crown Court would seem to support the conclusion, not so much that defendants trust juries, but more that they do not trust magistrates. This lack of trust in the magistracy is further highlighted by the fact that those who do not plead guilty would rather have their guilt or innocence determined by a jury.

Simply forcing such people to use the magistrates' courts does not address the underlying problem, let alone solve it.

It would have been possible for the Commission to have achieved its end by simply recommending that particular offences that are defined as triable 'either way' at present should be re-categorised as offences only open to summary procedure. That it did not do so further indicates the weakness of the underlying logic of its case for removing the right to insist on trial on indictment. The Commission rejected the reclassification of offences partly because of the difficulty and uncertainty inherent in the task. Additionally, and more importantly, however, it rejected this approach because it wished to leave available the possibility of the defendant successfully insisting on trial on indictment in the case of first offenders, where the consequences of loss of reputation would be significant. In the words of the Commission: 'Loss of reputation is a different matter, since jury trial has long been regarded as appropriate for cases involving that issue. But, it should only be one of the factors to be taken into account and will often be relevant only to first offenders' (see para 6.18 of the Report).

There are two assumptions in this proposal. First, there is the surely objectionable assumption that the reputation of anyone with a previous conviction is not important. But of even more concern is the fact that it is recognised that in the cases of first offenders, they should be permitted access to the jury. The question has to be asked: why should this be the case if juries do no more than magistrates do? It appears that in the instance of first offenders, it is recognised that juries do offer more protection than magistrates. Again, this demands the question: why should the extra protection not be open to all?

14.8.1.2 *Criminal Justice (Mode of Trial) Bills*

The Runciman Commission Report was produced under the auspices of a Conservative government operating under an economic imperative to reduce costs. If those who were opposed to its findings found comfort in the election of a New Labour government in 1997, they were soon to be disabused when the new (now former) Home Secretary, Jack Straw, announced his intention to reduce the rights to jury trials, essentially to the same end as the Runciman proposals. Thus, the first Criminal Justice (Mode of Trial) Bill was introduced in the parliamentary session of 1999–2000. This Bill sought to amend the MCA 1980 by introducing sections which gave the magistrates, rather than the accused, the power to decide whether a case should be tried summarily or on indictment. As Runciman's Report had been, so the new Bill was solicitous of the protection of those accused whose reputation 'would be seriously damaged as a result of conviction'. The Bill was generally criticised as an illiberal measure by civil liberties organisations and the legal professions, but was particularly attacked for the manner in which it sought to protect the rights of individuals with reputations to protect. Such solicitude for those with reputations to protect, apparently as opposed to the common majority of people, was seen as inherently unjust and dangerously class-based. The opposition to the Bill outside Parliament was matched, and more importantly so in relation to its legislative progress, by equal opposition within the House of Lords, which voted against its passage.

Undaunted by the rejection of his Bill, the Home Secretary re-introduced a reformed version of it in the Criminal Justice (Mode of Trial) (No 2) Bill. In acknowledgement of criticisms of the earlier Bill, the (No 2) Bill made it clear that the reputation, or any other personal characteristic, of the accused was not something to be taken into account by the magistrates in deciding on the mode of trial. Nonetheless, the Bill was once again defeated in the House of Lords in 2001.

Although the newly re-elected government insisted that it retained the power to use the Parliament Acts to force a mode of trial Bill through the House of Lords, its approach altered following the publishing of the report on the criminal courts conducted by Sir Robin Auld.

14.8.1.3   *The Auld Review*

In his extensive *Review of the Criminal Courts* (2001) Sir Robin Auld LJ included recommendations which were aimed specifically at the current operation of the jury within the criminal justice system. In summary, he recommended the following points:

- Jurors should be more widely representative than they are of the national and local communities from which they are drawn.

- No one in future should be ineligible for, or excusable as of right from, jury service. While those with criminal convictions and mental disorder should continue to be disqualified, any claimed inability to serve should be a matter for discretionary deferral or excusal.

- Provision should be made to enable ethnic minority representation on juries where race is likely to be relevant to an important issue in the case.

- The law should not be amended to permit more intrusive research than is already possible into the workings of juries, though in appropriate cases, trial judges and/or the Court of Appeal should be entitled to examine alleged improprieties in the jury room.

- The law should be declared, by statute if need be, that juries have no right to acquit defendants in defiance of the law or in disregard of the evidence.

- If the jury's verdict appears to be perverse, the prosecution should be entitled to appeal on the grounds that the perversity is indicative that the verdict is likely to be unfair or untrue.

- The defendant should no longer have an elective right to trial by judge and jury in 'either way' cases.

- Trial by judge and jury should remain the main form of trial of the more serious offences triable on indictment, that is, those that would go to the Crown Division, subject to four exceptions:

  (i) defendants should be entitled, with the court's consent, to opt for trial by judge alone;

  (ii) in serious and complex frauds, the nominated trial judge should have the power to direct trial by himself and two lay members drawn from a panel established by the Lord Chancellor for the purpose (or, if the defendant requests, by himself alone);

  (iii) a Youth Court, constituted by a judge of an appropriate level and at least two experienced youth panel magistrates, should be given jurisdiction to hear all grave cases against young defendants;

  (iv) legislation should be introduced to require a judge, not a jury, to determine the issue of fitness to plead.

14.8.1.4 The Criminal Justice Act 2003

As has been seen, the CJA 2003 introduced significant changes in the role and place of juries in the criminal system, but it did so without addressing the contentious issue of either way offences. Perhaps this course of action was adopted in the belief that the increase in the sentencing power of the magistrates' courts to 12 months would reduce the pressure on the Crown Courts by cutting down the number of cases sent for sentencing. It is unlikely, however, that the issue will have gone away forever.

14.8.2 Investigation of jury behaviour

The very first recommendation made by the Royal Commission on Criminal Justice was that s 8 of the Contempt of Court Act 1981 should be repealed to enable research to be conducted into juries' reasons for their verdicts. At present, s 8 makes it an offence to obtain, disclose or solicit any particulars of statements made, opinion expressed, arguments advanced or votes cast by members of a jury in the course of their deliberations in any legal proceedings.

In *Attorney General v Associated Newspapers* (1994), the House of Lords held that it was contempt of court for a newspaper to publish disclosures by jurors of what took place in the jury room while they were considering their verdict, unless the publication amounted to no more than a restatement of facts already known. It was decided that the word 'disclose' in s 8(1) applied not just to jurors, but to any others who published their revelations.

The continued legality of s 8 in the light of Art 6 of the ECHR was considered in *R v Mirza* in January 2004.

The appellant Mirza had been convicted on six counts of indecent assault by a majority verdict of 10:2. He had arrived in the UK from Pakistan in 1988 and, during the trial, he had made use of an interpreter. During the course of the trial, the jury sent a note asking the interpreter whether it was typical of a man with Mirza's background to require an interpreter, despite having lived in the UK for so long. It was explained to the jury that it was usual for people who were not fluent to have an interpreter in complicated and serious cases and, in his summing up, the judge directed the jury not to draw an adverse inference from Mirza's use of an interpreter.

Six days after the case finished, the defence counsel received a letter from one of the jurors claiming that some jurors had, from the beginning of the trial, believed that the use of the interpreter had been a devious ploy. The question of the interpreter was raised early during the jury's deliberations, and the letter writer was 'shouted down' when she objected and sought to remind the other members of the jury of the judge's directions. Members of the jury specifically refused to accept the judge's direction, and some regarded defence counsel's warnings against prejudice in her final speech as 'playing the race card'. The writer concluded that the decision of the jury was that of bigots who considered Mirza guilty because he used an interpreter in court after declining one for his police interviews.

When the case came on appeal to the House of Lords, it was confirmed by a majority of 4:1 that s 8 of the Contempt of Court Act 1981 prevented any investigation into what had taken place within the confines of the jury room. The majority also relied on a passage in *Gregory v UK* (1998), in which the ECtHR had previously approved the protection of jury secrecy under UK law in deciding that s 8 was not in conflict with Art 6 of the ECHR. In reaching its conclusion, the majority focused on the difficulties involved in assessing and investigating such matters of jury misbehaviour but, as Lord Steyn stated in his minority judgment:

> In my view it would be an astonishing thing for the ECtHR to hold, when the point directly arises before it, that a miscarriage of justice may be ignored in the interest of the general efficiency of the jury system. The terms of Art 6(1) of the ECHR, the rights revolution, and 50 years of development of human rights law and practice, would suggest that such a view would be utterly indefensible.

Following the decision in *Mirza*, the Department for Constitutional Affairs announced its intention to conduct a wide-ranging consultation exercise into the operation of the jury system. The consultation would canvas opinion on whether or not research should be allowed into jury deliberation and jury impropriety.

14.8.3 Conclusion

It has been repeatedly suggested by those in favour of abolishing, or at least severely curtailing, the role of the jury in the criminal justice system that the general perception of the jury is romanticised and has little foundation in reality. Runciman did not actually make this point explicitly, but it is implicit in his assessment of the jury system as against the magistrates' courts. Others have been more explicit; thus, the Roskill Committee expressed the view that:

> Society appears to have an attachment to jury trial which is emotional or sentimental rather than logical [para 8.21].

A similar point had been made previously by the Faulks Committee, but that report also recognised the source of the public's opinion and was careful not to dismiss it as unimportant:

> Much of the support for jury trials is emotional and derives from the undoubted value of juries in serious criminal cases where they stand between the prosecuting authority and the citizen [para 496].

The jury system certainly commands considerable public support. A survey published in January 2004, involving interviews with 361 jurors, found that, for the vast majority of respondents, juries were seen as an essential component of providing a fair and just trial process, and the diversity of the jury was seen as the best way of avoiding bias and arriving at a sound verdict. The major conclusion of the survey were as follows:

- The majority of respondents had a more positive view of the jury trial system after completing their service than they did before. Furthermore, despite the considerable personal inconvenience they may have suffered, virtually all jurors interviewed considered jury trials to be an important part of the criminal justice system.

- Confidence in the jury system was closely associated with the process, fairness, respect for the rights of defendants and ability of all the members of the jury to consider evidence from different perspectives. A jury's representation of a broad spectrum of views was a key factor in jurors' confidence in the Crown Court trial.

- Jurors were very impressed with the professionalism and helpfulness of the court personnel. In particular, they praised the judge's performance, commitment and competence.

- The main impediment to understanding proceedings was the use of legal terminology, although jurors also felt that evidence could sometimes be presented more clearly.

- Over half of the respondents said that they would be happy to do jury service again, while 19% said that they 'would not mind' doing it again. The most positive aspects of engaging in jury service were reported to be having a greater understanding of the criminal court trial, a feeling of having performed an important civic duty and finding the experience personally fulfilling.

The ideological power of the jury system should not be under-estimated. It represents the ordinary person's input into the legal system and it is at least arguable that in that way, it provides the whole legal system with a sense of legitimacy. It is argued by some civil libertarians that the existence of the non-jury Diplock courts in Northern Ireland brings the whole of the legal system in that province into disrepute.

As Lord Devlin noted (*Trial By Jury*, 1966):

> The first object of any tyrant in Whitehall would be to make Parliament utterly subservient to his will; and the next to overthrow or diminish trial by jury, for no tyrant could afford to leave a subject's freedom in the hands of 12 of his countrymen.

It should also be noted that most jurors seem to be reasonably happy with the system despite the stress and inconvenience it can impose on them. In 2000, the Court Service carried out a 'Jury Satisfaction Survey' (unpublished). This revealed that 95% of those questioned were satisfied or very satisfied with their treatment by the criminal justice system.

THE CRIMINAL PROCESS: (2) THE PROSECUTION

The Crown Prosecution Service

The Crown Prosecution Service (CPS) was introduced in 1986, and it is important to understand the five types of prosecution which existed before this time and how the CPS was supposed to resolve the criticisms of the old system. What sort of biases can occur in the use of prosecutorial discretion and why? Why were the police regarded as not the most suitable agency to exercise the prosecutorial discretion? What were the police defences to those criticisms? The police argued that conviction rates vindicated the way they exercised their discretion. The Code for Crown Prosecutors (2000) specifies factors which should weigh for and against a prosecution.

Cautioning offenders

Cautioning offenders is now applicable only to adults, with a new system of reprimands and warnings applying to young offenders. The CPS guidelines on prosecution require a 'realistic prospect of conviction' and that the 'public interest' is served by any prosecution. What difficulties are caused by such formulae?

Judicial control

Judicial control of prosecution policy is very limited and amounts to being able to correct only flagrantly irrational decisions by senior officers (*R v Metropolitan Police Commissioner ex p Blackburn* (1968)).

Bail

Bail is the release from custody, pending a criminal trial, of an accused on the promise that money will be paid if he absconds. The important issue raised here is how best the regulations should be framed so as to balance the conflicting interests of public safety and civil liberty. Public safety would perhaps be best served by keeping in custody everyone accused of a crime until their trial; this, though, would clearly be unnecessarily draconian. Conversely, civil liberty might be best served by allowing every suspect to remain free, however heinous the crime of which they have been accused and whatever their past record. The important statutory provisions are s 38 of the Police and Criminal Evidence Act 1984 and ss 3, 4 and 6 of and Sched 1 to the Bail Act 1976. Changes made by the Bail (Amendment) Act 1993 and the Criminal Justice and Public Order Act 1994 allow prosecutors to appeal against the granting of bail, restrict some aspects of it being granted, and afford greater opportunities for police bail.

Plea Bargaining

Plea bargaining is the practice where the accused enters a plea of guilty in return for which he will be given a sentence concession. It can also refer to 'plea arrangements' where the accused agrees to plead guilty to a lesser charge than the one with which he is, or is to be, charged. Note the recommendation of the Runciman Commission to introduce sentence discounting as a means to avoid 'cracked trials'. Dangers arising from such procedures include innocent persons being pressurised to 'take a plea' and serious offenders being processed for minor offences. In a system where the vast majority of cases in the Crown Court and magistrates' courts result in guilty pleas (79% and 81.5%, respectively), the operation of the plea bargain becomes very important.

The Jury

The jury has come under close public scrutiny since the Runciman Commission's recommendation to curtail the right to jury trial. It is important to know the standard arguments in favour of the jury and also the arguments showing it to be not truly random and representative. The detail of the jury's function in a trial and the extent to which its verdict can be appealed against are important. In what ways can the membership of the jury be challenged? What arguments were adopted by the Runciman Commission when recommending fewer jury trials? Juries lie at the heart of the English criminal justice system. There is debate about whether juries provide any better justice than magistrates' courts or whether the role is purely symbolic. The recommendations in Auld LJ's report on the criminal courts are important; they include the proposal to make juries more widely representative of national and local communities.

The Role of the Jury

To decide matters of fact – judges decide matters of law. Judges can instruct juries to acquit but not to convict. Juries do not have to give reasons for their decision. There is no appeal against an acquittal verdict, although points of law may be clarified by an Attorney General's reference. Civil cases can be overturned if perverse – but not criminal cases. Verdicts can be delivered on the basis of majority decisions. The use of juries has declined in relation to criminal and civil law.

CHAPTER 15

LEGAL SERVICES

15.1 Introduction

We are concerned here with a number of issues related to the provision and organisation of legal services, and issues of public access to legal services. The delivery of legal services at the outset of the 21st century looks very different from the way things were as recently as 1970. The legal profession has undergone a series of major changes as a result of the Courts and Legal Services Act (CLSA) 1990; the provision of public funding, advice and assistance has been drastically altered as a result of changes introduced in 1999. The introduction of the 'conditional fee arrangement' (no win, no fee) in 1995 was another contentious issue in this area. In the 1950s, only a minute proportion of the population used lawyers to solve problems. Now, in the 2000s, a great many individuals, small businesses and organisations are using lawyers often as a matter of course.

In several respects, the delivery of legal services is working effectively and is set on a path of improvement in respect of both the nature and extent of what is being offered. In 2003, for example, the Chairman of the Bar of England and Wales noted:

> We have a strong Bar. In 1980, there were 4,589 barristers in practice. By 1986 that number had risen to 5,489. By 1990 there were 6,579 in practice. Today there are 10,207 in private practice plus 3,300 in employed practice [that is, working for companies or organisations not from chambers]. That growth in numbers shows a steadily increasing demand for the services which the Bar has to offer [Matthias Kelly QC, *Counsel*, February 2003].

The Law Society, whose membership has also risen steadily over the same period (from about 58,000 members in 1986 to 101,000 in 2006), presented the following among its 'Key Objectives' for the period 2002–04:

> ... to provide prompt redress for consumers and effective enforcement and disciplinary mechanisms; to reinforce the Law Society's role as a promoter of equal opportunities and diversity within the profession; to establish the Law Society as an authoritative voice on law reform in the public interest; to promote effective justice for all; to champion the unique role of the solicitor in society ... to help solicitors break into new markets and new areas of employment ... [The Law Society, *The Corporate Plan, Annual Report*, 2002].

According to The Law Society's annual statistical report for 2001, the law firms of England and Wales generate £10.5 billion a year, and if the rate of growth in the profession continues at the rate at which it has been expanding since the 1970s (Neil Rose, 'The way we are' (2002) *The Gazette*, 19 September, p 22) then by 2055, we shall have one million lawyers. Whether such a development is an index of a healthy, rights-conscious society or an unhealthy, disputatious society is an interesting question. The global lawyer–population ratio is 1:2,370, whereas in England and Wales it is 1:600.

There are, however, many aspects of the provision of legal services that are problematic. In a consultative document published by the Lord Chancellor's Department, *Legal Advice Services: A Pathway Out of Social Exclusion* (Lord Chancellor's Department, 16 November 2001), the result of a collaboration between the Lord Chancellor's Department and the Law Centres Federation, the problem of providing legal services to poor, marginal or insecure people is addressed. Case studies in the report show how legal and advice services can help in a variety of situations and can link with the objectives of other government departments. The case studies cover homelessness, mental health problems, debt and money problems, welfare benefit issues, family and relationship difficulties, education problems and diversity issues. In all of them legal and advice services can play an important role alongside other agencies in helping to bring social justice to the socially excluded. It is clear that early and appropriate legal help can save much worry and hardship for a large group of people, and legal and advice services are an effective partner for other agencies helping the socially excluded. Social exclusion is what happens when people or areas suffer from a combination of linked problems such as lack of access to services, unemployment, poor skills, low incomes, poor housing, crime, poor health and family breakdowns. These problems are bad enough on their own, but, as the report notes, the problems are made worse through the way they are often interlinked, which compounds the deprivation which many people face in their everyday lives. Social exclusion can affect anyone. But certain groups, such as those growing up in low income households or with family conflict, those who do not attend school and some minority ethnic communities, are particularly at risk. These groups tend to get their services from any of the wide range of providers of legal and advice services, and while solicitors' firms make up the largest number of legal service providers, there are a growing number of other sources of help, such as Law Centres, Citizens Advice Bureaux, independent advice centres and local authority services.

In 2001, the Office of Fair Trading (OFT) published a report by the Director General of Fair Trading entitled *Competition in Professions*. That report was accompanied by a detailed report from the OFT consultants, Law and Economics Consulting Group (LECG). The paper touches on matters like conveyancing, multi-disciplinary partnerships and the QC system.

It is to be noted that restrictions on competition may be justified if, for example, they are in the public interest. The OFT report highlighted some of the potential anti-competitive restrictions found in the legal professions, like the requirement for a consumer to use a solicitor and a barrister in some cases where the work could, apparently, be adequately executed by a single expert. The OFT did not, however, examine justifications of restrictions (for example, countervailing consumer benefits). As was noted by another committee investigating legal services:

> In examining restrictive practices, a balance has to be struck between de-regulation on the one hand and the need to safeguard consumers on the other [*A Time for Change* – the Marre Committee report on the future of the legal professions, 1988].

The government's aim is to ensure that the professions are properly subject to competition. In most cases, the theory of modern capitalism is that open and competitive markets are the best way to ensure that consumers get the best possible service. On all the issues raised in this consultation, the government's position was that the market should be opened up to competition unless there existed strong reasons why that should not be the case, such as evidence that real consumer detriment might result from such a change. At the beginning of 2004, the Secretary of State for Constitutional Affairs asked Sir David Clementi, a businessman, to review the regulation of the legal profession and to report to him with recommendations. The main recommendations of the review, which can be found at www.legal services.gov.uk, include:

- The creation of a Legal Services Board, a new legal regulator which would supervise the Law Society, the Bar Council and all regulators of legal services.

- The creation of an Office of Legal Complaints, a single independent body which would handle consumer complaints against all providers of regulated legal services. Any discipline and conduct issues about solicitors would continue to be dealt with by the Law Society.

- The creation of Legal Disciplinary Practices. These would be law practices which would enable lawyers from different professional backgrounds, for example solicitors and barristers, to work together, and which would permit non-lawyers to become involved in the management and ownership of legal practices.

It is important when considering all the elements of this chapter to ask yourself questions about the aims of all the systems and proposed changes to them. What is their immediate aim? Is such an immediate aim part of a wider legal or social objective? How does the funding of any given component operate and what do its critics say is wrong or undesirable about it or the way it works?

15.2 The Legal Profession

The English legal system is one of only three in the world to have a divided legal profession where a lawyer is either a solicitor or a barrister. Each branch has its own separate traditions, training requirements and customs of practice. It is important to remember that not only lawyers regularly perform legal work. As one text notes (Bailey and Gunn, *Smith & Bailey on the Modern English Legal System* (1991), p 105):

> ... many non-lawyers perform legal tasks, some of them full time. For example, accountants may specialise in revenue law, trade union officials may appear regularly before industrial tribunals on behalf of their members, and solicitors may delegate work to legal executives. Conversely, many of the tasks performed by lawyers are not strictly 'legal'.

15.3 Solicitors

The solicitor can be characterised as a general practitioner: a lawyer who deals with clients direct and, when a particular specialism or litigation is required, will engage the services of counsel, that is, a barrister. Looking at the solicitor as a legal GP and the barrister as a specialist, however, can be misleading. Most solicitors, especially those in large practices, are experts in particular areas of law. They may restrict their regular work to litigation or commercial conveyancing or revenue work. Many barristers on the other hand might have a quite wide range of work including criminal, family matters and a variety of common law areas like tort and contract cases. The origins of the solicitor go back to the attornatus, or later the 'attorney', a medieval officer of the court whose main function was to assist the client in the initial stages of the case. One group of people practising in the Court of Chancery came to be known as 'solicitors'. Originally, they performed a variety of miscellaneous clerical tasks for employers such as landowners and attorneys. Their name was derived from their function of 'soliciting' or prosecuting actions in courts of which they were not officers or attorneys. Eventually, neither of these groups was admitted to the Inns of Court (where barristers worked); they merged and organised themselves as a distinct profession.

It was not, however, until 1831 that 'The Society of Attorneys Solicitors Proctors and Others not being Barristers Practising in the Courts of Law and Equity in the UK' was given its Royal Charter. This body emerged as the governing body of solicitors, the term 'attorney' falling from general use.

According to the latest Law Society figures available in July 2004 (*Key Facts 2004: The Solicitors' Profession*), there are 121,165 solicitors 'on the Roll', that is, people qualified to work as solicitors, of whom 96,757 have a current practising certificate (PC). This represents a growth of about 50% during the last 10 years. The number of women solicitors with pcs has increased over the same period by 120% to 39,199. The percentage of pc holders drawn from minority ethnic groups has increased from 2.2% to 9% (8,031). Just over half of all solicitors with a PC are aged 40 or under. The geographical distribution of solicitors leaves much room for improvement. Of the 9,211 law firms in England and Wales, 27.1% are in London, and approaching one-half of all firms are in a single region: the south east. Firms in London employ 41.6% of the 75,079 solicitors in private practice.

One very significant area of development and concern for solicitors at the beginning of the 21st century is the extent to which their monopolies of certain sorts of practice have been eroded. They have already lost their monopoly on conveyancing (although only a solicitor is authorised to give final endorsement to such work if carried out by a licensed conveyancer). Then, in 1999, the Access to Justice Act (see Chapter 12) introduced the provision that the Lord Chancellor would in future be able to authorise bodies other than The Law Society to approve of their members carrying out litigation. This, however, should be seen in the wider context of the policy to break down the historical monopolies of both branches of the legal profession. Thus, we can note the growth, since the CLSA 1990, of solicitors' rights of audience in court, and a corresponding anxiety at the Bar when these rights were granted.

The 1999 Act provides that every barrister and every solicitor has a right of audience before every court in relation to all proceedings. The right, however, is not unconditional. In order to exercise it, solicitors and barristers must obey the rules of conduct of the professional bodies and must have met any training requirements that have been prescribed, like the requirement to have completed pupillage in the case of the Bar, or to have obtained a higher courts advocacy qualification in the case of solicitors who wish to appear in the higher courts.

15.3.1 Training

The standard route to qualification is a law degree followed by a one year Legal Practice Course (LPC) and then a term as a trainee solicitor which, like the barrister's pupillage, is essentially an apprenticeship. Non-law graduates can complete the Postgraduate Diploma in Law in one year and then proceed as a law graduate. All newly admitted solicitors must now undergo regular continuing education, which means attendance at non-examined legal courses designed to update knowledge and improve expertise. After completion of the LPC and traineeship, a trainee solicitor may apply to The Law Society to be 'admitted' to the profession. The Master of the Rolls will add the names of the newly qualified to the roll of officers of the Supreme Court. To practise, a solicitor will also require a practising certificate (£830 in 2004/5) issued by The Law Society, and will be required to make a contribution to the compensation fund run by The Law Society to pay clients who have suffered loss through the misconduct of a solicitor. Additionally, solicitors have to pay an annual premium for indemnity insurance.

15.3.2 The Law Society

This is the profession's governing body controlled by a council of elected members and an annually elected President. Its powers and duties are derived from the Solicitors Act 1974. Complaints against solicitors used to be dealt with by the Solicitors' Complaints Bureau and the Solicitors' Disciplinary Tribunal, the latter having power to strike from the roll the name of an offending solicitor. It had been sometimes seen as worrying that the Society combined two roles with a possible conflict of interests: maintenance of professional standards for the protection of the public, and as the main professional association to promote the interests of solicitors. Consider a rather basic example. Acting for its members, The Law Society should perhaps try to ensure that insurance policies against claims for negligence are always available for solicitors even if they have been sued for this several times. For such insurance to be granted to someone with such a questionable professional record is, however, clearly not in the best interests of the public who use solicitors.

15.3.2.1 Consumer Complaints Service

From 1 September 1996, the Solicitors' Disciplinary Tribunal continued to work as before, but the Office for the Supervision of Solicitors (OSS) took over the work of the Solicitors' Complaints Bureau, and the old organisation was abolished. The OSS was subsequently renamed in April 2004 as the Consumer Complaints Service (CCS). The CCS, based in Leamington Spa, has more than 200 staff and employs solicitors, accountants, qualified mediators and administrative support staff. The CCS is divided into two parts, one of which deals with client-related matters and the other with regulation. All new cases are examined upon arrival and directed to one or other of them. Staff work in small teams, and one member of staff will follow a complaint through from start to finish.

A Remuneration Certificate Department carries out free reviews of solicitors' bills to ensure that they are fair and reasonable. The Office for Professional Regulation (a part of the CCS) ensures that solicitors comply with the regulations that govern them, like the Solicitors' Investment Business Rules.

The Compensation Fund was set up in 1941 by The Law Society to protect the clients of dishonest solicitors. The fund is supervised by the CCS. In matters of professional misconduct, the CCS can either impose an internal disciplinary sanction or prosecute the most serious cases before the Solicitors' Disciplinary Tribunal. In cases of inadequate professional services, the CCS can order a solicitor to forgo all or part of his fees and can award compensation of up to £5,000. The mission statement of the CCS states that, 'our aim is to work for excellence and fairness in guarding the standards of the solicitors' profession'. How far that aim is achieved must be judged in the light of developments over the next couple of years.

Members of the public with criticisms about solicitors' work will receive an initial response within 24 hours under the new practice of the CCS. Staff have been asked to be more open with the public, make greater use of telephones in contacting complainants and to write letters in plain English rather than in legalistic language. Advertisements were placed in the media for 10 lay people to join a committee dealing with the supervision of the profession.

The CCS is, however, funded by The Law Society, so a serious question arises as to whether this body will be seen as sufficiently independent by the public. Its efficiency has also come into question. Asked about the effectiveness of the CCS during Lord Chancellor's Department questions in the House of Commons, minister Rosie Winterton said, 'We are not satisfied that the OSS (now CCS) is currently working as effectively as it should' ((2003) *The Gazette*, 13 February, p 3). The Society's independent commissioner, Sir Stephen Lander, has said that the problem with the CCS is that it takes 'an approach which looks at the consumer through the prism of the Society's own regulations and jurisdiction', something he termed 'an insider view' ((2003) *The Gazette*, 6 February, p 1). He explained that he thought the CCS 'should not, of course, favour the client over the solicitor, or stop approaching each case strictly on its merits. Those remain the most important requirements', but rather the CCS should explicitly respond to the layman when things have gone wrong with a solicitor, regardless in the first instance of the cause or context. In a survey conducted by The Law Society's regulation directorate in 2002, of 209 firms chosen at random, only 35% had a satisfactory complaints procedure ((2002) *The Gazette*, 7 November, p 39). In an effort to improve the standards of firms, The Law Society's practice standards unit (PSU) will inspect all of the 1,100 firms that have three or more outstanding complaints against them ((2002) *The Gazette*, 17 October).

In *Wood v Law Society* (1995), the plaintiff (W) alleged that she was the victim of continuing misconduct by a firm of solicitors. She complained that H, a partner in a law firm, wrongly acted for both sides when arranging a series of loans for W on the security of W's home, and that H failed to disclose that H's husband was a director of one of the lenders. H's firm acted for the lenders in issuing court proceedings and obtained possession of the cottage for them. After many complaints to them by W, The Law Society conceded, after much delay, that it had been 'unwise' for H's firm to act for the lenders and that this was 'conduct unbefitting a solicitor'. The Society issued a formal rebuke. W sought damages from The Law Society, arguing that, as a result of the Society's incompetence and delay, she lost the chance of avoiding repossession of her home and suffered anxiety and distress.

The Court of Appeal held that if there was a duty owed to W by the Society, *it did not include a duty to provide peace of mind or freedom from distress.* Even though the Society appeared not to have lived up to the standards reasonably to be expected of it, there was no prospect of establishing that its failure to properly or timely investigate her complaints could have any sounding in damages. The loss suffered by W was not directly caused by The Law Society's incompetence and delay.

Another case dealing with the liability of solicitors is *White v Jones* (1995). This decision arguably widened the liability of solicitors. The House of Lords decided that a solicitor owes a duty of care to the intended beneficiary of a will when instructed by the testator to draw up that will. A firm of solicitors had been instructed by a client to change his will so that his daughters (whom he had previously cut out of an inheritance) should each receive £9,000. The firm did not act promptly on these instructions and the father eventually died before the will had been changed. Thus, the daughters received nothing. The person actually acting in the matter was a legal executive, not a solicitor, but it was the liability of the firm which was in issue. The Court of Appeal allowed an appeal by the plaintiffs, and granted that they should be awarded damages from the firm of solicitors to cover the loss, that is, the amounts they would have inherited had the firm acted professionally. The House of Lords upheld this decision.

The case is an interesting illustration of the judicial development of the common law. There was no obvious way in which the claimants had an action. They could not sue the firm in contract because they had made no contract with the firm; only their father had done so. The daughters were outside of the arrangements between their father and his solicitors; they were third parties and the law did not at that time recognise a *ius quaesitum tertio* (a contractual right for the benefit of a third party). The precedents in the tort of negligence did not provide much assistance because, unlike the facts of those cases, the daughters here were not people who had relied upon the firm (as in a case like *Ross v Caunters* (1979)).

The leading opinion was given by Lord Goff who decided that there was a need to give people like the claimants a remedy in this sort of situation, a remedy which was not available according to technical rules of law. He thus favoured 'practical justice', recognising that:

> ... cases such as these call for an appropriate remedy and that the common law is not so sterile as to be incapable of supplying that remedy when it is required [at p 777].

By a majority of 3:2, the Lords extended the duty of care owed by professionals as it had been expressed in *Hedley Byrne v Heller* (1963). They said that, where the loss suffered by the victim was purely economic, it would be possible to bring an action where the professional had given negligent advice or made negligent statements, but also extended this to the general principle that the provider of professional services could be liable for pure economic loss where his skills were being relied upon.

The 96,000 solicitors of England and Wales play a very important part in modern life. Their clients are nearly always very concerned about the quality of work done because something important is at stake. People go to a solicitor often in circumstances where there is understandable intense concern – they might be facing a serious charge a conviction for which would entail a long prison sentence, or lose their driving licence, or be in the throes of a divorce, or a neighbour dispute, or struggling with a commercial business problem. Even where the outcome of a legal event or transaction is good for the client – where he is buying a house or a flat, or a business – there is often heightened anxiety that everything goes as smoothly as possible. Solicitors need to make sure that, like other professions, if there are any bad practitioners among them, the consequential problems are dealt with as quickly and effectively as possible for the good of the legal profession at large. There is some evidence that this is not happening. The Law Society, the professional body of solicitors, has increased spending on complaints handling and redress from £6.4 million in 2000 to £9 million in 2003. However, the 2003 annual report of the Legal Services Ombudsman, Zahida Manzoor, is critical of the Consumer Complaints Service (CCS), the body responsible for examining complaints against solicitors.

Ms Manzoor says, commenting on her report, 'There is a real problem. We are half-way through The Law Society's financial year and there is no appreciable improvement on meeting the agreed targets' ((2003) *The Gazette*, 10 July, p 3). The Ombudsman's office dealt with 1,731 allegations about the handling of complaints by the CCS in 2004, a fall of 20% compared with the previous year, though this has been attributed to an equivalent fall in referrals from the CCS. In 2001, the Lord Chancellor was very critical about the large backlog of complaint cases being dealt with by the CCS and the backlog was then reduced to about 5,400, but the number of cases has since risen again, sharply, and is now about 9,000.

15.3.3 The Institute of Legal Executives

The Institute of Legal Executives (ILEX) represents over 22,000 legal executives employed in solicitors' offices. They are legally trained (the Institute runs its own examinations) and carry out much of the routine legal work which is a feature of most practices. The Institute was established in 1963 with the support of The Law Society. The Managing Clerks' Association, from which ILEX developed, recognised that many non-solicitor staff employed in fee earning work, and in the management of firms, needed and wanted a training route which would improve standards and award recognition for knowledge and skills. The education and training facilities ILEX offers have developed in number and diversity so that ILEX is able to provide a route to a career in law which is open to all.

Legal executives are, in the phrase of the ILEX website (www.ilex.org.uk), qualified lawyers specialising in a particular area of law. They will have passed the ILEX Professional Qualification in Law in an area of legal practice to the same level as that required of solicitors. They will have at least five years' experience of working under the supervision of a solicitor in legal practice or the legal department of a private company or local or national government. Fellows are issued with an annual practising certificate, and only Fellows of ILEX may describe themselves as 'Legal Executives'. Specialising in a particular area of law, their day to day work is similar to that of a solicitor.

Legal executives might handle the legal aspects of a property transfer; assist in the formation of a company; be involved in actions in the High Court or county courts; draft wills; advise clients accused of serious or petty crime, or families with matrimonial problems; and many other matters affecting people in their domestic and business affairs. Legal executives are fee earners – in private practice their work is charged directly to clients – making a direct contribution to the income of a law firm. This is an important difference between legal executives and other types of legal support staff who tend to handle work of a more routine nature. In March 2000, six legal executives qualified to become the first legal executive advocates under the CLSA 1990. The advocacy certificates were approved by the ILEX Rights of Audience Committee. The advocates now have extended rights of audience in civil and matrimonial proceedings in the county courts and magistrates' courts. In some circumstances, Fellows of ILEX can instruct barristers directly. BarDIRECT (the Bar Council's scheme by which barristers can be directly instructed by some professional and voluntary organisations, rather than by solicitors) enables legal executives to access a wide choice of legal advice and representation for their clients and their employers.

15.4 Barristers

The barrister is often thought of as primarily a court advocate, although many spend more time on drafting, pleadings (now called statements of case) and writing advices for solicitors. Professional barristers are technically competent to perform all advocacy for the prosecution or defence in criminal cases, and for a claimant or defendant in a civil claim. More generally, however, established barristers tend to specialise in particular areas of work. Over 60% of practising barristers work in London.

In 2004, there were 11,564 barristers in independent practice in England and Wales, of whom 8,153 were men and 3,411 were women. There were 1,078 Queen's Counsel, of whom 991 were men and 87 were women (Bar Council, 2004).

The Bar had been organised as an association of the members of the Inns of Court by the 14th century. Today, there are four Inns of Court (Inner and Middle Temples, Lincoln's Inn and Gray's Inn), although there were originally more, including Inns of Chancery and Sergeants' Inns, the latter being an association of the king's most senior lawyers. Until the CLSA 1990, the barrister had a virtual monopoly on advocacy in all the superior courts (in some cases solicitors could act as advocates in the Crown Court). In most situations, they cannot deal directly with clients but must be engaged by solicitors (but see 15.8 below).

15.4.1 Training

Entry to the Bar is now restricted to graduates and mature students. An aspirant barrister must register with one of the four Inns of Court in London. Commonly, a barrister will have a law degree and then undertake professional training for one year leading to the Bar Examinations. Alternatively, a non-law graduate can study for the Common Professional Examination for one year and, if successful in the examinations, proceed to the Bar Examinations. The successful student is then called to the Bar by his or her Inn of Court. It is also a requirement of being called that, during study for the vocational course, the student attends his or her Inn to become familiar with the customs of the Bar. The student then undertakes a pupillage, essentially, an apprenticeship to a junior counsel. Note that all barristers, however senior in years and experience, are still 'junior counsel' unless they have 'taken silk' and become Queen's Counsel (QCs). Barristers who do not intend to practise do not have to complete the pupillage.

15.4.2 The Inns of Court

The Inns of Court are administered by their senior members (QCs and judges) who are called Benchers. The Inns administer the dining system and are responsible for calling the students to the Bar.

15.4.3 The General Council of the Bar

The General Council of the Bar of England and Wales and of the Inns of Court (the Bar Council) is the profession's governing body. It is run by elected officials. It is responsible for the Bar's Code of Conduct, disciplinary matters and representing the interests of the Bar to external bodies like the Lord Chancellor's Department, the government and The Law Society. According to its own literature, this Council:

> ... fulfils the function of what might be called a 'trade union', pursuing the interests of the Bar and expanding the market for the Bar's services and is also a watchdog regulating its practices and activities.

15.4.4 Education

The Bar Council Education and Training Department regulates education and training for the profession.

15.4.5 Queen's Counsel

Queen's Counsel (QCs) are senior barristers of special merit. In 2004, the Bar had 1,078 QCs in practice, the status being conferred on about 45 barristers each year. They are given this status (known as 'taking silk' because a part of the robe they are entitled to wear is silk) by the Queen on the advice of the Lord Chancellor. There were, until the suspension of the system in 2003, annual invitations from the Lord Chancellor for barristers to apply for this title. Applicants needed to show at least 10 years of successful practice at the Bar. However, under arrangements announced recently a new independent selection procedure has replaced the widely criticised, former system which relied on secret soundings among senior legal figures. Candidates will be chosen by the Lord Chancellor on the recommendation of an independent panel set up by the Law Society and the Bar Council. If appointed, the barrister will become known as a 'Leader' and he or she will often appear in cases with a junior. The old 'Two Counsel Rule' under which a QC always had to appear with a junior counsel, whether one was really required or not, was abolished in 1977. He or she will be restricted to high level work (of which there is less available in some types of practice) so appointment can be financially difficult but, in most cases, it has good results for the QC as he or she will be able to considerably increase fee levels. The first report by Sir Colin Campbell, First Commissioner of the Commission for Judicial Appointments, published at the end of 2002, revealed serious deficiencies in the previous system of appointment. The report upheld four complaints against the Lord Chancellor's Department and invited the Lord Chancellor (who is a member of the Cabinet, and thus could be seen as 'political') to reconsider his role in the appointments system. However, only 10 individuals made formal complaints from well over 3,000 unsuccessful applicants for judicial posts or for 'silk' (QC). Complaints were upheld on behalf of four people and rejected for two others. The four complaints were upheld on the basis of procedural and administrative failings, but did not go to the merits of any particular substantive decision. The number of solicitor-advocate QCs is expected to be more than double by the end of 2005 after the Lord Chancellor, Lord Falconer of Thoroton, announced that he was handing the task of candidate selection to The Law Society and Bar Counsel ((2004) *The Gazette*, 4 June, p 1), a system of selection which has now been implemented. The guidance of the new competition requires the comments of consultees on candidates to be supported by detailed reasons and to be based on recent experience. In addition, the 'sift panel' will include an independent assessor. In 2002, for the first time, the names of 55 commercial law firms who were consulted by the LCD about the suitability of applicants for silk were released. This sort of consultation has been used since 1999. There are, though, calls for even wider consultation of law firms, and even calls for all solicitors to be consulted (see (2002) *The Gazette*, 10 October, p 29).

15.4.6   The barrister's chambers

Barristers are not permitted to form partnerships (except with lawyers from other countries); they work in sets of offices called chambers. Most chambers are run by barristers' clerks who act as business managers, allocating work to the various barristers and negotiating their fees. Imagine the situation where a solicitor wishes to engage a particular barrister for a case on a certain date and that barrister is already booked to be in another court three days before that date. The clerk cannot be sure whether the first case will have ended in time for the barrister to be free to appear in the second case. The first case might be adjourned after a day or, through unexpected evidential arguments in the early stages in the trial, it might last for four days. If the barrister is detained, then his brief for the second case will have to be passed to another barrister in his chambers very close to the actual trial. This is known as a late brief. Who will be asked to take the brief and at what point is a matter for the clerk. The role of the barrister's clerk is thus a most influential one. Since 2003, lay clients have been able to enjoy direct access to barristers: see www.barcouncil.org.uk, under 'BarDIRECT'. It is currently possible for barristers to accept instructions from some licensed organisations (as opposed to the normal practice of being briefed by solicitors), but the new plans will permit ordinary people to instruct barristers in some situations (see 15.8 below).

15.5   Professional Etiquette

The CLSA 1990 introduced a statutory committee, the Lord Chancellor's Advisory Committee on Legal Education and Conduct (ACLEC), which, until recently, had responsibilities in the regulation of both branches of the profession.

As part of the government's reforms of legal services, generally and publicly funded legal advice specifically, the Access to Justice Act 1999 (s 35) has replaced the ACLEC (considered by some as slow and ponderous) with the Legal Services Consultative Panel, launched at the beginning of 2000. The Consultative Panel has: (a) the duty of assisting in the maintenance and development of standards in the education, training and conduct of persons offering legal services and, where appropriate, making recommendations to the Lord Chancellor; and (b) the duty of providing to the Lord Chancellor, at his request, advice about particular matters relating to any aspect of the provision of legal services (including the education, training and conduct of persons offering legal services).

The Law Society and the Bar Council exercise tight control over the professional conduct of their members. Barristers can only meet the client when the solicitor or his or her representative is present. This is supposed to promote the barrister's detachment from the client and his or her case, and thus lend greater objectivity to counsel's judgment. Barristers and solicitors must dress formally for court appearances, although solicitors, when appearing in the Crown, county or High Court, are required to wear robes but not wigs. A barrister not wearing a wig and robe cannot be 'seen' or 'heard' by the judge.

Traditionally, lawyers were not permitted to advertise their services, although this area has been subject to some deregulation in the light of recent trends to expose the provision of legal services to ordinary market forces. Solicitors can, subject to some regulations, advertise their services in print and on broadcast media.

15.5.1 Immunity from negligence claims

Until recently barristers could not be sued by their clients for negligent performance in court or for work which was preparatory to court work (*Rondel v Worsley* (1969)); this immunity had also been extended to solicitors who act as advocates (*Saif Ali v Sidney Mitchell* (1980)). The client of the other side, however, may sue for breach of duty (*Kelly v London Transport Executive* (1982)). This was changed in a major case in 2000.

Advocates' liability

Arthur JS Hall and Co v Simons and Other Appeals (2000)

15.5.1.1 Background

Lawyers are, for the general public, the most central and prominent part of the English legal system. They are, arguably, to the legal system what doctors are to the health system. For many decades, a debate had grown about why a patient injured by the negligence of a surgeon in the operating theatre could sue for damages, whereas a litigant whose case was lost because of the negligence of his advocate could not sue. It all seemed very unfair. Even the most glaringly obvious courtroom negligence was protected against legal action by a special advocates' immunity. The claim that this protection was made by lawyers (and judges who were lawyers) for lawyers was difficult to refute. In this House of Lords' decision, the historic immunity was abolished in respect of both barristers and solicitor-advocates (of whom there are now over 1,787 with higher courts rights of audience), and for both civil and criminal proceedings.

15.5.1.2 Facts

In three cases, all conjoined on appeal, a claimant raised a claim of negligence against a firm of solicitors, and in each case, the firms relied on the immunity attaching to barristers and other advocates from claims in negligence. At first instance, all the claims were struck out. Then, on appeal, the Court of Appeal said that the claims could have proceeded. The solicitors appealed to the Lords and two key questions were raised: should the old immunity rule be maintained and, in a criminal case, what was the proper scope of the principle against 'collateral attack'? A 'collateral attack' is when someone convicted in a criminal court tries to invalidate that conviction outside the criminal appeals process by suing his trial defence lawyer in a civil court. The purpose of such a 'collateral attack' is to win in the civil case, proving negligence against the criminal trial lawyer, and thus by implication showing that the conviction in the criminal case was unfair.

15.5.1.3 Held

The House of Lords held (Lords Hope, Hutton and Hobhouse dissenting in part) that, in the light of modern conditions, it was now clear that it was no longer in the public interest in the administration of justice that advocates should have immunity from suit for negligence for acts concerned with the conduct of either civil or criminal litigation.

Lord Hoffmann (with Lords Steyn, Browne-Wilkinson and Millett delivering concurring opinions) said that over 30 years had passed since the House had last considered the rationale for the immunity of the advocate from suit in *Rondel v Worsley*. Public policy was not immutable and there had been great changes in the law of negligence, the functioning of the legal profession, the administration of justice and public perceptions. It was once again time to re-examine the whole matter. Interestingly, Lord Hoffmann chose to formulate his opinion in a creative mode to reflect public policy, rather than in the tradition of what can be seen as slavish obedience to the details of precedent:

> I hope that I will not be thought ungrateful if I do not encumber this speech with citations. The question of what the public interest now requires depends upon the strength of the arguments rather than the weight of authority.

The point of departure was that, in general, English law provided a remedy in damages for a person who had suffered injury as a result of professional negligence. It followed that any exception which denied such a remedy required a sound justification. The arguments relied on by the court in *Rondel v Worsley* as justifying the immunity had to be considered. One by one, these arguments are evaluated and rejected.

15.5.1.4   *Advocate's divided loyalty*

There were two distinct versions of the divided loyalty argument. The first was that the possibility of being sued for negligence would actually inhibit the lawyer, consciously or unconsciously, from giving his duty to the court priority over his duty to his client. The second was that the divided loyalty was a special factor that made the conduct of litigation a very difficult art and could lead to the advocate being exposed to vexatious claims by difficult clients. The argument was pressed most strongly in connection with advocacy in criminal proceedings, where the clients were said to be more than usually likely to be vexatious.

There had been recent developments in the civil justice system designed to reduce the incidence of vexatious litigation. The first was r 24.2 of the Civil Procedure Rules, which provided that a court could give summary judgment in favour of a defendant if it considered that 'the claimant had no real prospect of succeeding on the claim'. The second was the changes to the funding of civil litigation introduced by the Access to Justice Act 1999, which would make it much more difficult than it had been in the past to obtain legal help for negligence claims which had little prospect of success.

There was no doubt that the advocate's duty to the court was extremely important in the English justice system. The question was whether removing the immunity would have a significantly adverse effect. If the possibility of being held liable in negligence was calculated to have an adverse effect on the behaviour of advocates in court, one might have expected that to have followed, at least to some degree, from the introduction of wasted costs orders (where a court disallows a lawyer from being able to claim part of a fee for work which is regarded as unnecessary and wasteful). Although the liability of a negligent advocate to a wasted costs order was not the same as a liability to pay general damages, the experience of the wasted costs jurisdiction was the only empirical evidence available in England to test the proposition that such liability would have an adverse effect upon the way advocates performed their duty to the court, and there was no suggestion that it had changed standards of advocacy for the worse.

15.5.1.5   The 'cab rank'

The 'cab rank' rule provided that a barrister could not refuse to act for a client on the ground that he disapproved of him or his case. The argument was that a barrister who was obliged to accept any client would be unfairly exposed to vexatious claims by clients for whom any sensible lawyer with freedom of action would have refused to act. Such a claim was, however, in the nature of things intuitive, incapable of empirical verification and did not have any real substance.

15.5.1.6   The witness analogy

The argument started from the well established rule that a witness was absolutely immune from liability for anything that he said in court. So were the judge, counsel and the parties. They could not be sued for libel, malicious falsehood or conspiring to give false evidence. The policy of the rule was to encourage persons who took part in court proceedings to express themselves freely. However, a witness owed no duty of care to anyone in respect of the evidence he gave to the court. His only duty was to tell the truth. There was no analogy with the position of a lawyer who owed a duty of care to his client. The fact that the advocate was the only person involved in the trial process who was liable to be sued for negligence was because he was the only person who had undertaken such a duty of care to his client.

15.5.1.7   Collateral attack

The most substantial argument was that it might be contrary to the public interest for a court to re-try a case which had been decided by another court. However, claims for negligence against lawyers were not the only cases that gave rise to a possibility of the same issue being tried twice. The law had to deal with the problem in numerous other contexts. So, before examining the strength of the collateral challenge argument as a reason for maintaining the immunity of lawyers, it was necessary to consider how the law dealt with collateral challenge in general.

The law discouraged re-litigation of the same issues except by means of an appeal. The Latin maxims often quoted were *nemo debet bis vexari pro una et eadem causa* and *interest rei publicae ut finis sit litium*. The first was concerned with the interests of the defendant: a person should not be troubled twice for the same reason. That policy had generated the rules which prevented re-litigation when the parties were the same: *autrefois acquit* (someone acquitted of a crime cannot be tried again for that crime); *res judicata* (a particular dispute decided by a civil court cannot be re-tried); and issue estoppel (a person cannot deny the fact of a judgment previously decided against him).

The second policy was wider: it was concerned with the interests of the State. There was a general public interest in the same issue not being litigated over again. The second policy could be used to justify the extension of the rules of issue estoppel to cases in which the parties were not the same, but the circumstances were such as to bring the case within the spirit of the rules. Criminal proceedings were in a special category, because although they were technically litigation between the Crown and the defendant, the Crown prosecuted on behalf of society as a whole. So, a conviction had some of the quality of a judgment *in rem*, which should be binding in favour of everyone.

Not all re-litigation of the same issue, however, would be manifestly unfair to a party or bring the administration of justice into disrepute. Sometimes there were valid reasons for re-hearing a dispute. It was therefore unnecessary to try to stop any re-litigation by forbidding anyone from suing their lawyer. It was 'burning down the house to roast the pig; using a broad-spectrum remedy without side effects could handle the problem equally well'.

The scope for re-examination of issues in criminal proceedings was much wider than in civil cases. Fresh evidence was more readily admitted. A conviction could be set aside as unsafe and unsatisfactory when the accused appeared to have been prejudiced by 'flagrantly incompetent advocacy': see *R v Clinton* (1993). After conviction, the case could be referred to the Court of Appeal if the conviction was on indictment, or to the Crown Court, if the trial was summary, by the Criminal Cases Review Commission.

It followed that it would ordinarily be an abuse of process for a civil court to be asked to decide that a subsisting conviction was wrong. That applied to a conviction on a plea of guilty as well as after a trial. The resulting conflict of judgments was likely to bring the administration of justice into disrepute. The proper procedure was to appeal, or if the right of appeal had been exhausted, to apply to the Criminal Cases Review Commission. It would ordinarily be an abuse, because there were bound to be exceptional cases in which the issue could be tried without a risk that the conflict of judgments would bring the administration of justice into disrepute.

Once the conviction has been set aside, there could be no public policy objection to a claim for negligence against the legal advisers. There could be no conflict of judgments. On the other hand, in civil, including matrimonial, cases, it would seldom be possible to say that a claim for negligence against a legal adviser or representative would bring the administration of justice into dispute. Whether the original decision was right or wrong was usually a matter of concern only to the parties and had no wider implications. There was no public interest objection to a subsequent finding that, but for the negligence of his lawyers, the losing party would have won.

But again, there might be exceptions. The claim for negligence might be an abuse of process on the ground that it was manifestly unfair to someone else. Take, for example, the case of a defendant who published a serious defamation which he attempted unsuccessfully to justify. Should he be able to sue his lawyers and claim that if the case had been conducted differently, the allegation would have been proved to be true? It seemed unfair to the claimant in the defamation claim that any court should be allowed to come to such a conclusion in proceedings to which he was not a party. On the other hand, it was equally unfair that he should have to join as a party and rebut the allegation for a second time. A man's reputation was not only a matter between him and the other party; it represented his relationship with the world. So, it might be that in such circumstances, a claim for negligence would be an abuse of the process of the court.

Having regard to the power of the court to strike out claims which had no real prospect of success, the doctrine was unlikely in that context to be invoked very often. The first step in any application to strike out a claim alleging negligence in the conduct of a previous action had to be to ask whether it had a real prospect of success.

Lords Hope, Hutton and Hobhouse delivered judgments in which they agreed that the immunity from suit was no longer required in relation to civil proceedings, but dissented to the extent of saying that the immunity was still required in the public interest in the administration of justice in relation to criminal proceedings.

15.5.1.8 Comment

This decision is of major and historic importance in the English legal system for several reasons. It can be seen as a bold attempt by the senior judiciary to drag the legal profession (often a metonymy for the whole legal system) into the 21st century world of accountability and fair business practice. In his judgment, Lord Steyn makes this dramatic observation:

> ... public confidence in the legal system is not enhanced by the existence of the immunity. The appearance is created that the law singles out its own for protection no matter how flagrant the breach of the barrister. The world has changed since 1967. The practice of law has become more commercialised: barristers may now advertise. They may now enter into contracts for legal services with their professional clients. They are now obliged to carry insurance. On the other hand, today we live in a consumerist society in which people have a much greater awareness of their rights. If they have suffered a wrong as the result of the provision of negligent professional services, they expect to have the right to claim redress. It tends to erode confidence in the legal system if advocates, alone among professional men, are immune from liability for negligence.

The case raises and explores many key issues of the legal system, including: the proper relationship between lawyers and the courts; the proper relationship between lawyers and clients; the differences between criminal and civil actions; professional ethics; the nature of dispute resolution and the circumstances under which the courts should make new law. Above all, however, the case has one simple significance: 'it will', in the words of Jonathan Hirst QC, a former Chairman of the Bar Council, 'mean that a claimant who can prove loss, as the result of an advocate's negligence, will no longer be prevented from making a claim. We cannot really say that is wrong' ((2000) *Bar News*, August, p 3).

15.6   Fusion

The division of the legal profession into two branches can be seen as problematic in some respects. Even before the changes wrought by the CLSA 1990, solicitors did a reasonable amount of advocacy in the lower courts and in tribunals. On the other hand, barristers quite often give advice to clients, albeit through solicitors. Both barristers and solicitors do pleadings and drafting work. For many years, there was a strong movement for fusion of the two branches. Submissions made to the Benson Royal Commission on Legal Services argued that the necessity of a member of the public employing a barrister as well as a solicitor for certain work (for example, litigation) was like insisting on a taxi traveller hiring two taxis at once when one would be sufficient to get him to his destination. The legal need to hire two lawyers when one will do causes inefficiency (failures in communication, delay, return of briefs by barristers who are fully booked), damages the client's confidence in the legal process (as barristers are regarded as too remote and often insufficiently prepared), and is more expensive than simply engaging a single lawyer.

Fusion was strongly opposed by The Law Society and the Bar Council in their submissions to the Benson Commission (1979). It was argued that fusion would lead to a fall in the quality of advocacy. The leading barristers in a single-profession environment would simply join the major law firms and thus be unavailable for general engagement. Smaller firms would be unlikely to generate enough litigation to keep a barrister as a partner, and then would find it increasingly challenging to brief counsel of equal standing with that of an opponent. This would create an overall pattern of larger firms expanding and smaller ones – those serving small towns, etc – going out of business.

There would be a reduced number of specialist advocates because, whereas with the divided profession a specialist barrister could 'sell' his specialism to a queue of solicitors from different firms, under the fused profession, he would be pressured into working at one firm. Another opposition hinged on two features of the English court process: orality and single, continuous hearings designed to make the best use of judicial time but at the expense of practitioners. It has been argued that barristers are better placed organisationally to meet both such requirements.

Additionally, unlike the American system, judges do not have researchers or much time to prepare themselves for cases. The judge relies on the parties to present the case thoroughly. In such circumstances, it was argued, there is a critical need for the judge to have confidence in the competency of the advocates appearing in the case. This can only be properly achieved in the system which cultivates the barrister as a separate professional branch.

The Benson Royal Commission on Legal Services unanimously rejected the idea of fusion. The Commission conceded that fusion might lead to some saving, but only in the smaller cases, and in larger cases, the expense could be even greater. Using two lawyers did not necessarily entail duplicated work.

It is arguable now that fusion has effectively been organised covertly and gradually. Solicitors' monopolies over conveyancing and the right to conduct litigation have been technically removed (by the CLSA 1990 and the Access to Justice Act 1999, respectively), and the Bar's monopoly over rights of audience, even in the higher courts, has also been removed (by the same legislation). Specialism thus becomes a *de facto* matter more than an automatic function of one branch of the profession. We begin the new century with specialist criminal law solicitor-advocates operating from dedicated offices in some cities (a sort of solicitors 'chambers'), and barristers who are effectively working as in-house lawyers in companies doing work which seems very like the traditional work of solicitors. There are still, however, some suggestions for further mergers between the branches of the profession. In January 2003, the chairman of the Bar Council, Matthias Kelly QC, called for all advocates, including solicitor-advocates, to be regulated by the Bar Council. He said, 'That is a logical position. The present position is that the Bar Council regulates all barristers, even those employed in solicitors offices, in the same way as The Law Society regulates sole practitioner solicitor-advocates' ((2003) *The Gazette*, 9 January, p 5).

15.7 The Courts and Legal Services Act 1990

Both branches of the legal profession have traditionally enjoyed monopolies in the provision of certain legal services (for example, advocacy was reserved almost exclusively to barristers, while conveyancing was reserved to solicitors). In the 1980s, Lord Mackay, the then Lord Chancellor, argued that these monopolies did not best serve the users of legal services as they entailed unnecessarily limited choice and artificially high prices. The CLSA 1990 was introduced to reform the provision of legal services along such lines. Today, many of the old monopolies have been broken. Thus, we have solicitor-advocates and non-solicitor licensed conveyancers.

In 1990 in the CLSA, the government broke the solicitors' conveyancing monopoly by allowing licensed conveyancers to practise. There was initially evidence that this increased competition resulted in benefits to the consumer. From 1985, The Law Society had permitted solicitors to sell property, like estate agents, so as to promote 'one-stop' conveyancing. The Consumers' Association estimated that solicitors' conveyancing prices fell by a margin of 25–33% before licensed conveyancers actually began to practise.

Under the CLSA 1990, apart from allowing the Bar Council and The Law Society to grant members rights of audience as before, The Law Society is able to seek to widen the category of those who have such rights. Applications are made to the Lord Chancellor, who refers the matter to his Advisory Committee. If the Committee favours the application, it must also be approved by four senior judges (including the Master of the Rolls and the Lord Chief Justice), each of whom can exercise a veto. The Director General of the Office of Fair Trading must also be consulted by the Lord Chancellor. All those who consider applications for extended rights of audience or the right to conduct litigation must act in accordance with the 'general principle' in s 17.

15.7.1 Section 17

The principle in s 17 states that the question whether a person should be granted a right of audience or to conduct litigation is to be determined only by reference to the following four questions:

- Is the applicant properly qualified in accordance with the educational and training requirements appropriate to the court or proceedings?

- Are applicants members of a professional or other body with proper and enforced rules of conduct?

- Do such rules have the necessary equivalent of the Bar's 'cab rank rule', that is, satisfactory provision requiring its members not to withhold their services: on the ground that the nature of the case is objectionable to them or any section of the public; on the ground that the conduct, opinions or beliefs of the prospective client are unacceptable to them or to any section of the public; on any ground relating to the prospective client's source of financial support (for example, public funding)?

- Are the body's rules of conduct 'appropriate in the interests of the proper and efficient administration of justice'?

Subject to the above, those who consider applications must also abide by s 17's 'statutory objective' of 'new and better ways of providing such services and a wider choice of persons providing them, while maintaining the proper and efficient administration of justice'.

Successful applications were made by The Law Society, the Head of the Government Legal Service and the Director of Public Prosecutions (DPP). The Advisory Committee, whilst rejecting the idea of an automatic extension of solicitors' rights of audience upon qualification (for example, guilty plea cases in Crown Courts), accepted the principle that they should qualify for enlarged rights after a course of advocacy training. Non-lawyers can also apply for rights of audience in the courts: the Chartered Institute of Patent Agents successfully applied for rights to conduct litigation in the High Court. Under s 11 of the CLSA 1990, the Lord Chancellor will use his power to enable lay representatives to be used in cases involving debt and housing matters in small claims procedures. Similarly, under ss 28 and 29 of the CLSA 1990, the right to conduct litigation is thrown open to members of any body which can persuade the Advisory Committee, the Lord Chancellor and the four senior judges that its application should be granted as the criteria set out in s 17 (above) are satisfied.

The historic monopoly of barristers to appear for clients in the higher courts was formally ended in 1994 when the Lord Chancellor approved The Law Society's proposals on how to certify its members in private practice as competent advocates. The innovation is likely to generate significant change in the delivery of legal services, especially in the fields of commercial and criminal cases. The prospective battle between solicitors and barristers for advocacy work can be simply characterised.

15.7.2 Solicitors' rights of audience

In February 1997, the Lord Chancellor, Lord Mackay, and the four designated judges (Lord Bingham, Lord Woolf, Sir Stephen Brown and Sir Richard Scott; see s 17 of the CLSA 1990) approved The Law Society's application for rights of audience in the higher courts for employed solicitors, but subject to certain restrictions.

Under The Law Society's 1998 regulations approved by the Lord Chancellor's Department, some solicitors (those who are also barristers or part time judges) are granted exemption from the new tests of qualification for advocacy. Others need to apply for the grant of higher courts qualifications, either in civil proceedings, criminal proceedings or in both. A holder of the higher courts (criminal proceedings) qualification has rights of audience in the Crown Court in all proceedings (including its civil jurisdiction) and in other courts in all criminal proceedings. A holder of the higher courts (civil proceedings) qualification may appear in the High Court in all proceedings and in other courts in all civil proceedings. Applicants for these qualifications must have practised as a solicitor for at least three years. The qualifying scheme is designed only for solicitors who are already lower court advocates. The three elements which must be demonstrated by an applicant are:

- two years' experience of advocacy in the lower courts and experience of the procedures of the relevant higher court;

- competency in a written test on evidence and procedure; and

- satisfactory completion of an advocacy training course.

Large city firms of solicitors already have their litigation lawyers trained to qualify for advocacy in the High Court. One problem, however, for these large firms is that they have found it very difficult for their applicants (for audience rights) to meet The Law Society's requirement for county court advocacy experience. Although the expansion of this court's jurisdiction under the CLSA 1990 (in particular commercial litigation involving sums up to £50,000) has given more county court work to large firms, they generally do very little of this. Large firms have had to take on perhaps hundreds of county court cases just to get the ones that will go to trial, and even then, these would only be a means to an end, namely the qualification to appear in the High Court.

One benefit for law firms is that those which offer advocacy training are likely to attract the best graduates. This is a worry for the commercial Bar, as some graduates will see a training contract with an advocacy element as a better option than the less secure Bar pupillage. The Bar is determined that it will not lose any significant ground in the face of this new competition. Its representatives claim that solicitors will not be able to compete with barristers because of their much higher overheads.

From 2000, there have been three routes to qualification: the 'development' route leading to the all proceedings qualification; the 'accreditation' route appropriate for solicitors who have significant experience of the higher civil and/or higher criminal courts; and the 'exemption' route which has existed under both the 1992 and 1998 regulations. The accreditation and exemption routes will be phased out by 31 October

2005 leaving only the development route. The development route has three stages: training and assessment in procedure, evidence and ethics in the higher civil and higher criminal courts; training and assessment in advocacy skills; and experience of either civil or criminal proceedings, some of which may take place pre-admission. Trainee solicitors, therefore, can get training and assessment and up to six months' experience behind them during their training contract. However, this new fast track for novice lawyers has left The Law Society open to criticism of lowering standards and allowing inexperienced advocates into the higher courts without the necessary competence. The Law Society, however, recognises the need to maintain standards and believes that its proposals not only maintain standards, but have the capacity to enhance standards through the provision of advocacy services.

The figures show there has been a steady increase in the number of solicitor-advocates, which in 2003 amounted to a total of 1,787. This is made up of 384 qualified for all proceedings, 430 with the civil qualification and 973 with the criminal qualification, including 400 Crown Prosecution lawyers. With commercial firms increasingly bringing low end work in-house, and a streamlined qualification procedure, these figures, especially on the civil side, are now likely to increase. A solicitor-advocate chambers in Birmingham called Midlands Solicitor Chambers is already a model for such developments elsewhere. The larger firms are finding it propitious to create general or specialist advocacy units, a point the significance of which is best seen when the influence of the large firms is appreciated. It is clear that the face of advocacy is changing. When the relevant part of the Access to Justice Act 1999 (see 15.7.3 below) came into force, even employed solicitors gained the right to present cases in the higher courts.

Many barristers are very worried about the threat to their traditional work. A potentially significant development is BarDIRECT, a pilot scheme set up in 1999 that enables certain professions and organisations to have direct access to barristers without referral through a solicitor. While this initiative could be one of the keys to the continuing success of the Bar, it is argued that it makes barristers no different from solicitors and could even encroach on the solicitors' market. However, Bruce Holder QC, chairman of the Bar Public Affairs Committee, does not see it as an attempt to deprive solicitors of work, but merely as trying to reduce unnecessary restrictive practices. He argues ((2000) *The Gazette*, 10 January) that BarDIRECT will benefit a few specific organisations such as police forces, trades unions, professional organisations and doctors' defence bodies, who would not traditionally be using solicitors anyway and who require a specialised opinion from a barrister, but are currently forced to go through a solicitor to get one.

15.7.3 The Access to Justice Act 1999 and rights of audience

Lawyers' rights of audience before the courts were further addressed in Part III of the Access to Justice Act 1999. It replaces the Lord Chancellor's Advisory Committee on Legal Education and Conduct with a new Legal Services Consultative Panel:

- It provides that, in principle, all lawyers should have full rights of audience before any court, subject only to meeting reasonable training requirements.

- It reforms the procedures for authorising further professional bodies to grant rights of audience or rights to conduct litigation to their members; and for approving changes to professional rules of conduct relating to the exercise of these rights.

The Act also contains sections which:

- simplify procedures for approving changes to rules and the designation of new authorised bodies;

- give the Lord Chancellor power, with the approval of Parliament, to change rules which do not meet the statutory criteria set out in the CLSA 1990 as amended by these sections;

- establish the principle that all barristers and solicitors should enjoy full rights of audience; and

- establish the primacy of an advocate's ethical duties over any other civil law obligations.

The legislation enables employed advocates, including Crown Prosecutors, to appear as advocates in the higher courts if otherwise qualified to do so, regardless of any professional rules designed to prevent their doing so because of their status as employed advocates.

15.7.3.1 Background

The background to these proposals is set out in a Consultation Paper issued by the Lord Chancellor's Department in June 1998 – *Rights of Audience and Rights to Conduct Litigation in England and Wales: The Way Ahead.*

Rights to appear as an advocate in court (rights of audience) and rights to do the work involved in preparing cases for court (rights to conduct litigation) are governed by the CLSA 1990. The 1990 Act left it to 'authorised bodies' (currently the Bar Council, The Law Society and the Institute of Legal Executives) to set the rules which govern the rights of their members, subject to a statutory approval process in which new or altered rules were submitted for the approval of the Lord Chancellor and the four 'designated judges' (the Lord Chief Justice, Master of the Rolls, President of the Family Division and Vice Chancellor). Before making their decisions, the Lord Chancellor and the designated judges were to receive and consider the advice of the Lord Chancellor's Advisory Committee on Legal Education and Conduct (ACLEC) and of the Director General of the Office of Fair Trading. Applications for the designation of new authorised bodies were subject to a similar procedure, but the designation of the new body was made by Order in Council subject to approval by both Houses.

The government argued that the old approval procedures were convoluted and slow, and that rights of audience were too restrictive. Some applications for approvals took several years to be processed, in part due to the need for applications to meet the approval of several parties. Rights of audience in the higher courts (the House of Lords, Court of Appeal, High Court and Crown Court) remain restricted to barristers and a small number of solicitors in private practice.

The 1999 Act simplified and expedited the approval procedure. The ACLEC was replaced by a smaller and less expensive committee, the Legal Services Consultative Panel. The functions of the Panel were not prescribed in detail in the statute, and its composition was left to the Lord Chancellor to determine, although in appointing members, he was required to have regard to specified criteria setting out appropriate knowledge and experience.

The 1999 Act provides that every barrister and every solicitor has a right of audience before every court in relation to all proceedings. These general rights were not present for solicitors in the 1990 Act. The Act also restates the current position that all solicitors have rights to conduct litigation before all courts. These rights are not unconditional; in order to exercise them, solicitors and barristers must obey the rules of conduct of the professional bodies and must have met any training requirements that may be prescribed (such as the requirement to complete pupillage in the case of the Bar, or to have obtained a higher courts advocacy qualification in the case of solicitors who wish to appear in the higher courts).

Section 38 of the Access to Justice Act 1999 provides that advocates and litigators employed by the Legal Services Commission can provide their services to members of the public. Without this clause, they might be prevented from doing so by professional rules.

Section 40 of the 1999 Act gives the General Council of the Bar and ILEX the power to grant their members rights to conduct litigation.

Section 42 of the 1999 Act gives statutory force to the existing professional rules, which make it clear that the overriding duties of advocates and litigators are their duty to the court to act with independence in the interests of justice, and their duty to comply with their professional bodies' rules of conduct. Those duties override any other civil law obligation which a person may be under, including the duty to the client or a contractual obligation to an employer or to anyone else. A barrister, solicitor or other authorised advocate or authorised litigator must refuse to do anything required, either by a client or by an employer, that is not in the interests of justice (for example, suppress evidence). The purpose of this clause is to protect the independence of all advocates and litigators.

15.7.4   Partnerships and transnational firms

By virtue of s 66 of the CLSA 1990, solicitors are enabled to form partnerships with non-solicitors (multi-disciplinary partnerships or MDPs), and the section confirms that barristers are not prevented by the common law from forming such relationships. They are, however, prohibited from doing so (unless with a foreign lawyer) by the Bar. Solicitors are able, under s 89 of the CLSA 1990 (Sched 14), to form multi-national partnerships (MNPs). The arrival of MNPs over the coming years will raise particular problems concerning the maintenance of ethical standards by The Law Society over foreign lawyers. MDPs also raise potentially serious problems, as even in arrangements between solicitors and others, it will be likely that certain work (for example, the conduct of litigation) would have to be performed by solicitors.

In a move to pave the way towards allowing MDPs, The Law Society has devised a scheme, 'legal practice plus', which would allow non-solicitor partners (NSPs) to join firms and enter into a contract with The Law Society agreeing to be bound by its professional rules. There are, however, concerns over the scheme's viability, particularly over the preservation of legal professional privilege.

Accountants are doing more legal work and solicitors are doing more accountancy work than ever before, but the two professional bodies do not allow their members to join a single practice. The main obstacle is r 7 of the Solicitors Practice Rules, which prohibits solicitors from sharing fees with non-solicitor professionals. There is a build up of pressure for this obstacle to be removed; see, for example, Nigel S Cobb (2002) 152 NLJ 1341. Indeed, there has been a recent relaxation of the rule on fee-sharing by the introduction of r 7(1A), which gives practitioners greater freedom as to the methods available to fund their practices or to pay for services provided to their practices.

The business organisation called the limited liability partnership (LLP) was introduced by the Limited Liability Partnership Act 2000. The new business form seeks to amalgamate the advantages of the company's corporate form with the flexibility of the partnership form. Although called a 'partnership', the new form is, in fact, a distinct legal entity that enjoys an existence apart from that of its members. The LLP can enter into agreements in its own name, it can own property, sue and be sued. Traditional partnerships by contrast entail liability for the partners as individuals. Although the LLP enjoys corporate status, it is not taxed as a separate entity from its members. Solicitors do not seem to have been keen to adopt these as their preferred form of firm. Of those formed so far (and there were, in 2002, fewer than 100 from the existing 8,300 law firms at that time), most were formed because of international constraints in mergers, that is, the foreign firm could not merge with the British one unless the British one became an LLP. One perceived risk that seems to be important to many lawyers is that an LLP can be sued itself rather than proceedings being launched against only one or two partners (Mark Smulian, 'Doing the dirty deed' (2002) *The Gazette*, 31 October, p 23).

15.7.4.1 Law firms

There is, however, a widening gap between the work and remuneration of the top few hundred commercial firms and the 10,000 smaller High Street firms.

A recent series of mergers has created a few relatively huge law firms, and the merger of an English firm with an American one has produced the world's first billion dollar practice. Partners at Clifford Chance voted to merge with the USA's Rogers & Wells to form a firm employing 5,800 people in 30 offices worldwide. The new firm generates over one billion dollars in turnover in a year. The firm specialises in corporate finance, commercial property, anti-trust law and litigation. Keith Clark, senior partner at Clifford Chance, has explained that the aim of the merger was to create a truly international firm capable of offering an integrated legal service to an increasingly global business community. He has said, 'Clients don't want all the time delays and inefficiencies of dealing with half a dozen legal firms around the world. What they want is one firm which has the capacity to be a one-stop shop for all their corporate needs' ((1999) *The Times*, 12 July). In the context of legal and social theory, it is of interest to some that these events can be seen as illustrative of the theory of dialectical materialism – the interaction between ideas, action and the material world. During the 1980s, law firms, by doing all the legal work on mergers for commercial companies (for example, telecommunications, energy and manufacturing) helped to create a new environment of transnationals operating on a world basis. Now, that new material environment has affected the very law firms who helped to create it. These law firms are now themselves changing into global firms in order to do the ordinary legal work for the new commercial giants. By contrast, law firms that gave a public funding service to under-privileged groups are progressively reducing such activity. As Paula Rohan has noted, 'After almost 60 years of giving the most disadvantaged members of society access to legal advice, the system is on its last legs – at least according to a major *Gazette* survey' (see (2003) *The Gazette*, 23 January, p 1, and 30 January, 'A Dying Breed', p 20). As a consequence of very low rates of remuneration making even a break-even policy virtually impossible, and political attacks on public funding lawyers, 78% of the 291 firms who responded to the survey were considering cutting down on their public funding work, and 91% stated they were dissatisfied with the current system.

15.7.5 Employed solicitors

This is the fastest growing area of practice with more than a fifth of those holding a practising certificate working outside private practice. Employed solicitors are professionals who work for salaries as part of a commercial firm, private or public enterprise, charity or organisation, as opposed to solicitors in private practice who take instructions from various clients. As Janet Paraskeva, The Law Society chief executive, notes: 'In-house lawyers can provide cost-effective legal advice, and have an increasingly important role in corporate governance. [They] often act as co-ordinators for the outsourcing of legal work and become involved with public affairs, risk management and general business analysis' ((2003) *The Gazette*, 20 February). In the decade 1994–2004, the numbers of employed solicitors grew from 10,910 to 21,678 – a 99% increase. In fact, the number of solicitors working in the employed sector is likely to be much higher because the figures come from The Law Society list of those with practising certificates but, because of their employed status, many lawyers are not required to have such a certificate. In-house solicitors often enjoy more flexible working terms than their private practice counterparts, so it is probably no accident that 48.9% of solicitors holding PCs in commerce and industry are women, while only 38.1% of PC holders in private practice are women (*Key Facts 2004: The Solicitors' Profession*).

15.7.6 Monopoly conveyancing rights

Historically, barristers, solicitors, certified notaries and licensed conveyancers enjoyed statutory monopolies, making it an offence for any other persons to draw up or prepare documents connected with the transfer of title to property for payment. The CLSA 1990 broke this monopoly by allowing any person or body not currently authorised to provide conveyancing services to make an application to the Authorised Conveyancing Practitioners Board (established by s 34) for authorisation under s 37. The Board must be satisfied, before granting authorisation, that the applicant's business is, and will be, carried on by fit and proper persons, and must believe that the applicant will establish or participate in the systems for the protection of the client specified in s 37(7) including, for example, adequate professional indemnity cover and regulations made under s 40 concerning competence and conduct. Banks and building societies were in a privileged position (s 37(8)) since they were already regulated by statute. These institutions did not initially appear enthusiastic to compete with solicitors by establishing in-house lawyers. They have preferred instead to use panels of local practitioners.

The solicitors' monopoly on the grant of probate has also been abolished. Under ss 54–55 of the CLSA 1990, probate services were opened up to be available from approved bodies of non-lawyers. Grant of probate is the legal proof that a will is valid, which is needed for a person to put the will into effect. New probate practitioners directly compete with solicitors for probate work. The grant of probate is only a small part of the probate process, but when it was restricted as business which only a solicitor could perform, it effectively prevented others, except some banks, from being involved in probate. The banks seem best placed to take up work in this area as they already have trustee and executor departments. Like the slow take-up to do conveyancing work (there are still only relatively few commercial licensed conveyancers handling among them about 5% of all conveyancing), enthusiasm to break into the probate business has been hard to detect.

In its Green Papers published in 1989, the government stated that the means it favoured to produce the most efficient and effective provision of legal services would be 'the discipline of the market'. This technique, however, has not been without its problems. There was not a rush to use the conveyancing services of solicitors who had made their prices very competitive in the wake of competition from licensed conveyancers. In one survey, The Law Society found that only 8% of clients had opted for cheaper services ((1993) *The Lawyer*, 12 October). More worrying is the allegation that a significant number of those offering 'cut-price' conveyancing are not producing a respectable quality of service. Tony Holland, a former president of The Law Society, argued that this is a result of a rush of inadequately trained persons to make money from that part of solicitors' erstwhile monopoly which has been thrown open to non-lawyers ((1994) 144 NLJ 192). He noted, however, that at the time of writing the article he was engaged in giving expert testimony in no fewer than 19 actions for negligence arising from incompetent conveyancing.

Nevertheless, research published by the Department of the Environment, Transport and the Regions showed that conveyancing in England and Wales was the cheapest of the 10 European countries surveyed, even though it was the slowest. It takes an average of six to eight weeks for a contract to be exchanged in England and Wales, while in the USA and South Africa the average is a week. Even so, while the legal fee for conveyancing on a £60,000 house in England and Wales is about £1,500, the same service in France costs about £3,600 and in Portugal, it is about £6,000 (see News in Brief, 'Cheap conveyancing' (1998) 148 NLJ 8). The Lord Chancellor's Department's 2002 Consultation Paper on legal services, *In the Public Interest*, suggested that the introduction of the licensed conveyancer system has not worked well because licensed conveyancers are handling only 5% of conveyancing services. The system has not, therefore, succeeded in providing real competition. There is a growing concentration of conveyancing into a small number of polarised firms (see, for example, Nigel S Cobb (2002) 152 NLJ 1340) according to some observers of conveyancing.

15.7.7   The Legal Services Ombudsman

An Ombudsman (a name taken from Sweden where the post has existed for over 170 years) is a person independent of the government or a given field of activity who investigates complaints of maladministration. The post of Legal Services Ombudsman (LSO) was created in 1990 by s 21 of the CLSA 1990 and covers England and Wales. The Act provides that the LSO must not be a lawyer. The Access to Justice Act 1999 gave the LSO powers to make orders rather than recommendations requiring the legal professional bodies and individual practitioners to pay appropriate compensation to complainants. Zahida Manzoor, the LSO for England and Wales, said when she was appointed in March 2003 that she would take a robust stance to ensure that the legal professions had fair, open and efficient complaints handling systems that met public needs. In the period March 2002–March 2003, she observed that the Office of the Legal Services Ombudsman had received 1,750 new cases from members of the public who remained dissatisfied with the way their complaint had been handled by the lawyers' own professional bodies. She said that there was a lot to be done regarding the professional bodies' complaints handling systems, especially in relation to the Office for the Supervision of Solicitors (now CCS), part of The Law Society. She observed that the number of cases being referred to her Office was continuing to rise:

> Not only is this unacceptable but it may only be the tip of the iceberg. It is highly likely that these cases only reflect those people who are aware of their rights and have the perseverance to pursue their complaints. There may be many more people who are unhappy at the level of service they have received from the legal profession but are unaware of their rights to get redress.

The number of complaints should always be seen in the context of the number of practising lawyers and the number of transactions during the period under review. There are, altogether, over 96,000 solicitors and barristers in England and Wales, who between them work on over two million contentious and non-contentious cases each year.

This Ombudsman is empowered by s 22 of the 1990 Act to 'investigate any allegation which is properly made to him and relates to the manner in which a complaint made to a professional body with respect to an authorised advocate, authorised litigator, licensed conveyancer, recognised body or notary who is a member of that professional body; or any employee of such a person, has been dealt with by that professional body'. The LSO cannot normally investigate any complaint whilst it is being investigated by a professional body, nor if it has been dealt with by a court or the Solicitors' Disciplinary Tribunal or the disciplinary tribunal of the Council of the Inns of Court, since the procedures in such tribunals satisfy the need for public accountability.

Upon completing an investigation, the LSO must send a copy of her reasoned conclusions to the complainant and the person or body under investigation. The report can make any of the following recommendations:

- that the complaint be reconsidered by the professional body;

- that the professional body should consider its powers in relation to the person who was the subject of complaint;

- that the person complained about, or any person connected to him or her, should pay compensation to the complainant for loss suffered or inconvenience or distress caused;

- that the professional body concerned should pay such compensation;

- that a separate payment be made to the complainant in respect of costs related to the making of the allegation.

The person or body to whom these recommendations are sent must reply within three months explaining what action has been, or is proposed to be, taken to comply with the recommendation(s) made.

15.8   Lawyers and Fair Trading

If you want your car's electrical wiring repaired, you can approach an auto-electrician and ask for the work to be done. You do not have to first ask a car mechanic to engage the services of the auto-electrician on your behalf and then pay them both. Yet in law there is often a situation in which a client has to pay for both a solicitor and a barrister when it is only the barrister who does the job the client wants done. The Office of Fair Trading (OFT) has asked the government to put an end to the restrictive practice whereby the public has to pay for both a solicitor and barrister, in some circumstances, when in fact it is the services of only one person that are required. Clients' bills are thus increased unnecessarily (*Competition in Professions*, 2002, OFT, www.oft.gov.uk).

OFT investigators were particularly concerned that under the Bar's code of conduct, barristers can only be approached directly by a member of the public after first 'instructing' a solicitor. The report concludes that this rule is an unnecessary and costly obstacle to access to legal services. Ministers are now expected to implement the OFT's recommendation.

In response, the Bar Council stated that it welcomed any proposal which improved choice for the consumer. The Council, however, has cautioned that a wholesale change would not work to the client's advantage in all cases. Its stance has been that there is no benefit, for example, to a person who has been arrested in going to a chamber for help when a solicitor is in a much better position to advise them at the police station.

The government is now considering whether it is best to remove the 'double lawyer' obligation in the Bar's rules or to develop the BarDIRECT scheme which currently licenses specified organisations and public bodies, such as police forces and trade unions, to leapfrog the solicitor and go directly to a barrister. In 2002, the Bar Council published an agreed response to the OFT report (www.barcouncil.org.uk). The key proposals put to the OFT were as follows:

- From 2003, a relaxation of the Bar's rules limiting direct access by lay clients, subject to safeguards to protect the client.

- A further liberalisation of the Bar's rules to allow comparative advertising on fees, but not on so-called 'success rates'.

- A robust defence of the Bar's ban on partnerships, on the grounds that this promotes competition between 10,000 barristers in private practice, and preserves their fundamental independence, which is at the core of the justice system.

- A firm rejection of the suggestion that private practice barristers should be able to conduct litigation, on the basis that the rules preventing this have no adverse effects on competition and promote specialisation by the Bar in advocacy and advice.

- An acceptance that the system for appointing Queen's Counsel should be kept under review, but a strong assertion of the value of QCs to purchasers in the legal services market.

- Strong support for upholding legal professional privilege (under which communications between lawyer and client are secret and cannot be accessed by others or used against them), on the grounds that the protection this provides is a fundamental human right for the client.

As it stands, the Bar is a professional grouping with a common system of education, training, professional rules and standards, and discipline. There are those who think that allowing experts from various professions to combine to form single businesses is desirable, as these would produce helpful one-stop shops for clients (especially corporate clients). By contrast, others take the view that the standards of the Bar would be compromised by such changes.

When solicitors acquired rights of audience in the higher courts, the Bar responded with the BarDIRECT scheme, but that was limited to barristers accepting work directly from licensed organisations that had satisfied the Bar that they could provide the same service to barristers that solicitors usually performed. There is some opposition among barristers to the scheme being extended so as to allow barristers to accept instructions directly from lay people – a scheme that was introduced in late 2003. David Mason, a barrister from Newcastle Upon Tyne, puts the case against such change very clearly ('Will direct access work?' (2003) 153 NLJ 332). The public, Mason argues, are likely to be very positive about the possibility of having direct access to a barrister, but in practice, there will be much disappointment:

> Barristers cannot conduct litigation in the way that solicitors do. The rules will not allow them to correspond with the other side, instruct expert witnesses, take witness statements other than from their lay client, handle clients' money, or undertake many of the activities that the public expects from solicitors. The cost may be less because only one professional person is engaged, but the product the client will be buying will be very different, and will undoubtedly disappoint.

Mason argues that, in fact, large areas of practice, like crime and family work, will be excluded because the Legal Services Commission has indicated that it will not fund such direct access work. The cases where it might have some uptake are criminal appeals where no new evidence is likely to be involved. In family cases, clients are often stressed and anxious and want immediate and constant contact with solicitors, and the same is often true of commercial and corporate clients, but barristers might be caught up in court for days or weeks without being able to get back to the client. The clerks to chambers are there to serve the barristers and deal with solicitors' requests, not to assuage the anxieties of clients. Mason concludes that 'many direct access arrangements will flounder and end in tears over this sort of issue'.

CHAPTER 16

THE FUNDING OF LEGAL SERVICES

16.1   Introduction

Legal aid (now called public funding) was introduced after World War II to enable people who could not otherwise afford the services of lawyers to be provided with those services by the State. The system grew and extended its reach and range of services enormously over the decades. Costs to the government were gigantic. The system underwent various restrictions and cut-backs during the late 1990s and was replaced by other systems like the Community Legal Service (2000) and the Criminal Defence Service (2001). The term 'legal aid' is still used as a descriptive, non-technical term to refer to State-funded services.

In 2004, the public debate about access to justice through publicly funded legal services was very animated. Much concern, for example, was felt when it was reported (Frances Gibb (2004) *The Times*, 26 January) that there existed a proposal to end public funding for thousands of middle-class defendants accused of motoring offences. The proposal was part of a plan to curb the £2 billion annual public funding expenditure. The proposal would affect those coming through the courts on drink-driving or other motoring offences. Defendants would be means-tested to see whether they were entitled to criminal legal aid in the magistrates' courts, a procedure that does not presently exist in magistrates' courts. The rationale for the change is that the saving would be significant (593,000 people went through the courts in 2002 charged with motoring offences, at least 20,000 of whom would have made use of legal aid), and would largely affect people seen as being able to afford their own lawyers.

Additionally, the Department for Constitutional Affairs announced in February 2004 that it would be making various changes to the system in order to release funds of £15–19 million a year. The changes would involve tightening up procedures covering the Recovery of Defence Costs Orders, which are currently determined by judges in the Crown Courts. The plan is to reduce the courts' discretion over their imposition, so that it would not be so easy for defendants' lawyers to recover their costs from the State. Another measure will abolish advocacy assistance for early hearings in the magistrates' courts. This will enable help to be focused on more serious cases where representation is necessary according to the interests of justice test. If implemented, the newly proposed scheme would mean that the court duty solicitor scheme will be restricted to those in custody or to those charged with an imprisonable offence. Post-charge advice and assistance (that is, advice to citizens after that provided following arrest and charge) would be abolished. Another measure would limit the provision of legal advice in the police station to telephone advice in certain cases where a solicitor cannot advance the client's case by attending the police station. In more serious cases, solicitors would still be able, as now, to offer advice at the police station.

Two factors combined in the early 1990s to cause great change in the way that legal services are funded. The first factor was the spiralling cost of legal aid to the State during a period of recession. The money available to the government was insufficient to meet the rising cost of maintaining the level and extent of legal services previously available. The second factor was the professed aim of the government in general and Lord Mackay, the then Lord Chancellor, in particular to reduce the State's role in the provision of legal services. There is some evidence that, given the aim of the reforms, the project has not been entirely successful. In 2003, the legal aid budget went into the red by £100 million (Paula Rohan, 'LCD reveals £100 million legal aid overspend' (2003) *The Gazette*, 13 February).

Over 10 million people were taken out of the bracket of legal aid eligibility as a result of governmental changes to the eligibility criteria (see Smith, *Shaping the Future: New Directions in Legal Services* (1995), Legal Action Group). To try to compensate for this exclusion of millions of people from the effective right to use the law, other schemes have been promoted and developed. These include the use of 'no win, no fee' arrangements, the use of non-lawyer legal services, and legal services private insurance.

The legal aid budget for 1996–97 was £1.48 billion. It was in that context that the White Paper *Striking the Balance: The Future of Legal Aid in England and Wales* (HMSO) was published in 1996. The Paper proposed the most radical changes to the legal aid system since its launch in 1951. The main aims of the White Paper in relation to funding legal services were: (a) to impose cash limits on the legal aid scheme (instead of allowing it to have a demand-led budget); (b) to require some form of payment from all users and (c) to operate a separate budget for major, expensive cases.

There are several State-funded schemes to facilitate the provision of aid and advice. Each scheme has different rules relating to its scope, procedures for application and eligibility. Because of the importance of justice and access to the legal machinery, the idea behind legal aid is to give people who could otherwise not afford professional legal help the same services as more wealthy citizens. This raises important social, political and economic questions. Do poorer people deserve the same quality of legal advice as that which can be afforded by wealthy people? If so, how should such schemes be funded?

16.2   A Brief Historical Overview

The legal aid system was introduced under the Legal Aid and Advice Act 1949 by the Labour government after World War II to allow poor people to have access to the justice system. Before this time, such people had to rely on charity if they went to court. The system was seen by the government as the 'second arm of the Welfare State' (the first one being the National Health Service). The system expanded throughout the 1950s and 1960s. It moved from just covering the higher courts to covering the lower courts, and from just civil courts to criminal courts. The present scheme was introduced by the Access to Justice Act 1999 following the government White Paper, *Modernising Justice*, published on 2 December 1998. The old scheme was contained in the Legal Aid Act 1988. Under the 1988 Act, the term 'legal aid' strictly referred to only representation in court. In fact, it covered a wide range of subsidised or free services. There were three main types of legal aid, which were Legal Advice and Assistance, Civil Legal Aid and Criminal Legal Aid.

Legal Advice and Assistance, also known as the Green Form scheme, enabled a solicitor to undertake ordinary legal work (excluding court work) up to a limit, initially, of three hours' worth of work for a client who passed the relevant means test administered by the solicitor. The amount of work could be extended with the permission of the local Legal Aid Area Committee. Assistance by way of representation (ABWOR), also means tested, was an extension of the Legal Advice and Assistance scheme which covered court appearances where advice or letter writing had not solved a problem. It was available for domestic proceedings in magistrates' courts proceedings, before mental health review tribunals, representations under the Police and Criminal Evidence Act (PACE) 1984 for warrants of further detention and representation in certain child care proceedings. The scheme covered the cost of a solicitor preparing a case and representing a client in most civil cases in magistrates' courts, now known as Family Proceedings Courts. These cases included separation, maintenance (except child maintenance where the Child Support Agency has jurisdiction), residence/contact, paternity and defended adoption proceedings.

The Green Form scheme and ABWOR were the most widely used of the legal aid schemes prior to the Access to Justice Act. At the beginning of the 1990s, the take-up was stable at around one million acts of assistance per year, but then the scheme began to grow, reaching a peak of 1.6 million acts of assistance in 1993–94. This growth was principally fuelled by increased demand for advice on social and economic matters, such as housing, debt and welfare benefits, although advice on personal injuries, employment and immigration matters also grew during that period (Legal Aid Board, *Annual Report*, 1998–99, section 3, p 117). From 1996, the volume of Green Form cases paid for by the Legal Aid Board started to rise again, due largely to the introduction of standard fees for Criminal Legal Aid in the magistrates' courts in 1993, but a renewed demand for advice on civil, non-matrimonial matters, especially immigration and nationality and welfare benefits, led to the peak of 1994 being reached again in 1998 (*Annual Report*, 1998–99, p 120).

Civil Legal Aid was available for many types of action but not, notably, for proceedings in coroners' courts or tribunals (except the Lands Tribunal and the Employment Appeal Tribunal), nor for proceedings involving libel or slander. From 1989, Civil Legal Aid was run by the Legal Aid Board. An applicant had to satisfy two tests: a means test and a merits test. The means test used the concepts of 'disposable capital' and 'disposable income', which are still applied. The former includes savings, jewellery and the value of the house you live in (although any equity of up to a specified sum was excluded); the latter involved actual income less income tax, national savings, money for dependants, necessaries, travel to work, etc. Disability Living Allowance, Attendance Allowance, Constant Attendance Allowance, Council Tax Benefit, Housing Benefit payments made under the Earnings Top-up scheme or the Community Care Direct Payment scheme are not counted as income. If an applicant's income and/or capital was below a certain amount, representation was free; if it was above that amount, then a contribution would be payable on a sliding scale, but with a ceiling figure above which the applicant would not be eligible for financial assistance. Under the merits test, the applicant had to show the Board that he had reasonable grounds for taking, defending or being party to an action, but the applicant could be refused aid if it appeared to the Board unreasonable to grant representation.

Criminal Legal Aid covered the cost of case preparation and representation in criminal cases. The decision as to whether to grant legal aid was made by the court clerk according to criteria in the Legal Aid Act 1988. In the event of a refusal, there was a statutory right of appeal to Criminal Legal Aid committees run by The Law Society. As with Civil Legal Aid, the applicant had to pass a merits and a means test. The merits test was simply whether it was in the 'interests of justice', with the following factors being taken into account:

(a) Whether the offence was such that if proved it would be likely that the court would impose a sentence that would deprive the defendant of his liberty or lead to his loss of livelihood or serious damage to his reputation.

(b) If the determination of the case might involve consideration of a substantial question of law.

(c) If the defendant had linguistic difficulties or other disability.

(d) If the defence required expertise like cross-examination.

(e) Whether it was in the interests of another party that the accused be represented. This was usually satisfied by defendants in the Crown Court – the success rate was about 98%.

The means test was normally carried out by court clerks and was similar to the test for Civil Legal Aid, although the threshold amounts differed.

In addition to these schemes, some solicitors were prepared to give a free or fixed-fee interview without carrying out any means test related to the interviewee's income or capital. Duty Solicitor Schemes are available at most magistrates' courts and police stations. Solicitors can give *free* legal advice to someone who is being questioned by the police whether or not such a suspect has been arrested; advice and free representation can also be given for someone's first appearance for a particular offence at a magistrates' court. A number of historical and economic factors combined to reduce the scope of the system from the mid-1970s. By the 1990s, the system applied to a much smaller section of the community than it had done in previous decades. In the 1950s, about 80% of the population were covered by the legal aid system, whereas by 1998, less than 40% of the population were covered.

The scope of eligibility had expanded quickly in the 1970s. As a result, more lawyers were setting up practices catering for legal aid clients. Divorces were becoming much more common (as the result of social factors and legislation which made divorce easier), and divorce accounted for a very large part of Civil Legal Aid. Alongside all this, the economy was going into recession, and this had two effects: (a) it resulted in there being less money in government funds from which to finance legal aid; and (b) it generated waves of economically related problems (unemployment, family break-ups, welfare problems) which needed legal services for people who could not afford to pay for them.

From the mid-1980s, successive Lord Chancellors were engaged in a series of measures to try to reduce public expenditure on the legal system. A common feature of the Civil and Criminal Legal Aid schemes was that expenditure on them was demand-led. Any lawyer could do legal aid work for a client who passed the relevant means test (if any) and whose case passed the statutory merits test (in the case of Civil Legal Aid) or the 'interests of justice' test (in the case of Criminal Legal Aid). Lawyers were paid on a case by case basis for each individual case or other act of assistance, usually at rates or fees set in regulations, but in some cases on the same basis as a privately funded lawyer.

This, in the government's view, meant that there were few mechanisms or incentives for promoting value for money or assuring the quality of the services provided, and that neither the government nor the Legal Aid Board was able to exert adequate control over expenditure or determine the priorities for that expenditure.

From August 1994, the Legal Aid Board operated a voluntary quality assurance scheme, known as franchising. Solicitors who met certain management criteria were devolved certain administrative powers, enabling them to undertake cases in one or more of the 10 subject categories in which they are awarded (criminal, family, personal injury, housing, etc) a contract, without obtaining prior approval from what was the Legal Aid Board. These practices received certain fiscal benefits such as a lump sum payment from the Legal Aid Board on account, immediately upon the approval of a case. In relation to these firms, the Legal Aid Board moved from being an approving body to a quality control organisation. This has become the main method of delivery of legal aid under the Access to Justice Act 1999, in spite of fears amongst many lawyers and commentators that this trend will lead to seriously reduced access to legal services. The fear was based on the notion that, because the smaller firms would find it too difficult to satisfy the management criteria, and would become uncompetitive, a number would go out of business.

16.3   The New Legal Aid Scheme

The Access to Justice Act 1999 set up a new legal aid system and made provisions about rights to supply legal services (see Chapter 11), court procedure (see Chapter 7), magistrates and magistrates' courts (see Chapter 3). The provisions in the Act form part of the wide-ranging programme of reforms to legal services and the courts, described in the government's White Paper, *Modernising Justice*, published on 2 December 1998. Except where noted, the Act only affects England and Wales.

Part I of the 1999 Act established a Legal Services Commission (LSC) to maintain and develop the Community Legal Service (CLS) and the Criminal Defence Service (CDS) which replaced the Civil and Criminal Legal Aid schemes respectively. The Act also enabled the Lord Chancellor to give the Commission orders, directions and guidance about how it should exercise its functions. The Community Legal Service Fund replaced the legal aid fund in civil and family cases. The Commission uses the resources of the Fund in a way that reflects priorities set by the Lord Chancellor, and its duty to secure the best possible value for money, to procure or provide a range of legal services. The Commission also has a duty to liaise with other funders of legal services to facilitate the development of co-ordinated plans for making the best use of all available resources. The strategy is to develop a network of legal service providers of assured quality, offering the widest possible access to information and advice about the law, and assistance with legal problems. The CDS is intended to ensure that people suspected or accused of a crime are properly represented, while securing better value for money than was possible under the legal aid scheme.

16.3.1   Controlled and licensed work

As noted at 16.2 above, legal aid funding was granted on a case by case basis until the system of franchising was introduced in August 1994, where firms of solicitors meeting certain requirements were able to contract to undertake certain cases without prior approval, and claim funding on a more advantageous basis than previously. This franchise or 'contract' system has formed the basis of the new legal aid scheme. Under this new scheme, funded services fall under the headings of 'controlled work' and 'licensed work'. Controlled work comes under the contract system and consists of all legal help and legal representation. The decision about whether to provide services in a particular case is made by the supplier, who is either a solicitor or a not-for-profit organisation, such as a law centre or Citizens Advice Bureau (discussed at 16.8 below). They bid for a contract to provide legal services funded by the LSC to the Regional Legal Services Committees. Under the contract, the number of cases that may be undertaken by the suppliers is limited. Licensed work is the equivalent of the case by case approval granted for all State-funded legal work prior to 1994 and all non-franchised work prior to the establishment of the LSC. Licensed work is administered through a certification process requiring the Commission's initial approval of the cost, timing and scope of each case. Once the licence is granted, it covers all legal representation before the courts, except for very expensive cases referred to as 'very high cost cases' (VHCC) which are managed under individual case contracts with the Commission. The VHCC are those in which a solicitor is instructed with a criminal case that is likely to last 25 days or more at trial, or is likely to accrue more than £150,000 defence costs, where he then notifies the Criminal High Cost Case (CHCC) Unit of the Commission and special arrangements are made in respect of the funding of the case.

16.3.2   Contracting

The work that may be undertaken by a supplier, whether a solicitor or a not-for-profit organisation, has been divided into the following categories: crime, family, personal injury, clinical negligence, housing, immigration, welfare benefit, employment, mental health, debt, consumer and general contract, education, community care, actions against police, public law. A General Civil Contract under the CLS or a General

Criminal Contract under the CDS may be awarded to allow a supplier to undertake work within one or more categories. The contract will state the categories and terms under which the supplier may provide legal advice and representation. The purpose of specifying categories in respect of civil contracts is to ensure an appropriate distribution of legal and advice services to meet demand in each region. In order to assess demand and ensure that the right kind of services are available to meet the needs of a region, Community Legal Service Partnerships (CLSPs) have been set up. The service provided may be at different levels depending on the case. The different levels of service are:

- *Legal Help*: this is the provision of initial advice and assistance.

- *Help at Court*: this enables a solicitor or adviser to speak on behalf of a person at certain court hearings without formally acting for that person in the whole proceedings.

- *Approved Family Help*: this is the provision of help in relation to family disputes including the resolution of the matter by negotiation or otherwise. This covers initial advice and assistance, issuing proceedings and representation where necessary in order to obtain disclosure of information from another party or to obtain a consent order when matters in dispute have been agreed. It is available in two forms: Help with Mediation where a person is attending mediation sessions and General Family Help.

- *Family Mediation*: this covers mediation for a family dispute, including finding out whether mediation is suitable or not.

- *Legal Representation*: under this, a person can be represented in court. It is available in two forms:

    (i) *Investigative Help*: funding is limited to investigation of the strength of a claim.

    (ii) *Full Representation*: funding is provided to represent people in legal proceedings.

- *Support Funding*: this provides partial funding for very expensive cases which are otherwise funded privately. It is available in two forms:

    (i) *Investigative Support*: funding is limited to investigation of the strength of a claim with a view to a conditional fee agreement.

    (ii) *Litigation Support*: this provides partial funding of high cost proceedings under a conditional fee agreement.

16.3.3 Quality Mark

In order to be a supplier under either the CLS or the CDS, the solicitor or not-for-profit organisation must achieve the minimum standards under the respective Quality Marks. There are three kinds of Quality Mark: information, general help and specialist help, with a supplier displaying an appropriately endorsed logo on its premises. A supplier of information will typically be a library and provide leaflets, reference material and access to the CLS or CDS *Directory of Services*. A supplier of general help will provide information and advice and will be a Citizens Advice Bureau or other advice agency. A supplier of specialist information will be a solicitor, a law centre, or some Citizens Advice Bureaux, and it will be able to give information and advice on a complex problem in a specialist legal area which will be shown next to the supplier's entry in the CLS or CDS *Directory*.

16.4   The Legal Services Commission

As from 1 April 2000, the Legal Services Commission replaced the Legal Aid Board. It was considered necessary to establish a new body to reflect the fundamentally different nature of the CLS when compared to Civil Legal Aid. Within the broad framework of priorities set by the Lord Chancellor, the Commission is responsible for taking detailed decisions about the allocation of resources. It is also required to liaise with other funders to develop the CLS more widely. The Commission has a wider role in respect of the CDS than the Legal Aid Board did in respect of Criminal Legal Aid. The Board had very limited responsibilities for legal aid in the higher criminal courts. Membership of the Commission differs from that of the old Legal Aid Board, to reflect a shift in focus from the needs of providers to the needs of users of legal services. Also, the Commission is smaller than the Board: 7–12 members rather than 11–17. This is intended to facilitate 'focused decision making'.

16.5   The Community Legal Service

The LSC has two main duties in respect of the CLS:

- First, it manages a CLS Fund (ss 4–11 of the 1999 Act), which has replaced legal aid in civil and family cases. The CLS Fund is used to secure the provision of appropriate legal services within the resources made available to it, and according to priorities set by the Lord Chancellor and by regional and local assessments of need. A Funding Code, drawn up by the Commission and approved by the Lord Chancellor, sets out the criteria and procedures for granting contracts and deciding whether to fund individual cases. As spending has been brought under better control, it has been possible to expand the scope of the fund into areas that were not covered by legal aid, in particular to alternatives to lawyers and courts, like mediation and advice agencies. Mediation is already a requirement in family matters (see Part III of the Family Law Act 1996).

- Second, as part of a wider CLS, the Commission has, in co-operation with local funders and interested bodies, developed local, regional and national plans to match the delivery of legal services to identified needs and priorities.

16.5.1 Community Legal Service contract

In carrying out the first duty of managing the CLS, the LSC developed the General Civil Contract to introduce contracting within the statutory framework created by the Access to Justice Act 1999, in effect since 1 January 2000. There are two versions of the General Civil Contract, one for solicitors and one for not-for-profit agencies, because of the differences in the terminology and methods of delivery used by these types of suppliers. An important aspect of the new scheme is that the right kind of services should be available to meet the needs of a region. In furtherance of this aim, the Commission published a Consultation Paper in 2002, setting out its proposals for establishing regional priorities for civil contracting through the production of Regional Legal Services Committees' reports, Regional Directors' contracting strategies and CLSPs. Following this consultation, the Commission has put in place a new process for the regional prioritisation of needs. As a result, new bid rules for the award of General Civil Contracts for Controlled Work apply as from 1 January 2003, although these were further revised on 1 April 2004 to reflect regional priorities and to hold a wider bidding process.

The new term for litigants who obtain LSC funding is 'LSC funded clients', and the fund out of which litigants who obtain LSC funding is referred to as the CLS Fund. Section 7 of the 1999 Act allows the Lord Chancellor, using regulations, to set financial eligibility limits. Therefore, an applicant must be able to show that his capital *and* income are within the current financial limits.

16.5.2 Financial eligibility test

The Community Legal Service (Financial) Regulations 2005 sets out the thresholds for financial eligibility for all applications for funding made on or after 11 April 2005. The test uses the basic concepts of 'disposable income', that is, income available to a person after deducting essential living expenses; and 'disposable capital', that is, the assets owned by a person after essential items like a home. If a person could sell her home, pay off the mortgage and still have more than £100,000 left (called 'equity'), then she will not qualify for aid.

Certain services are free regardless of financial resources, such as services consisting exclusively of the provision of general information about the law, legal system and availability of legal services, legal representation in some cases involving the Children Act 1989 and related proceedings, and representation at a mental health review tribunal. Some services are non-contributory and a client is either eligible or not, whereas others are contributory in accordance with a sliding scale dependent on how much a client's income or capital exceeds a given threshold. There is a cap amount over which a person is ineligible for legal aid. In summary, the financial eligibility amounts for applications are as follows:

- For all levels of service, there is (as of April 2005) a gross income cap of £2,288 per month. This cap may be increased by £145 per month for each child in excess of four.

A client who is directly or indirectly in receipt of Income Support or income-based Job Seeker's Allowance automatically satisfies the gross income test for all levels of service.

- For the service of Legal Help, Help at Court and Legal Representation before Immigration Adjudicators and the Immigration Appeal Tribunal, the disposable income must not exceed £632 per month and there is a capital limit of £3,000.

- For the service of Family Mediation, Help with Mediation and other Legal Representation (which may be subject to a contribution from income and capital), the disposable income must not exceed £632 per month and there is a capital limit of £8,000.

When assessing gross income and disposable income, State benefits under the Social Security Contributions and Benefits Act 1992 (Disability Living Allowance, Attendance Allowance, Constant Attendance Allowance, Invalid Care Allowance, Severe Disablement Allowance, Council Tax Benefit, Housing Benefit and any payment out of the social fund), back to work bonuses under the Job Seekers Act 1995, war and war widows' pensions and fostering allowances are disregarded.

Band	Monthly disposable income	Monthly contribution
A	£273–400	One quarter of income in excess of £268
B	£401–531	£33 plus one third of income in excess of £400
C	£532–632	£76.70 plus half of income in excess of £531

The only level of service assessed by the supplier for which contributions can be sought is Legal Representation in Specified Family Proceedings. However, provided that the client's gross income is below the prescribed limit, clients with a disposable income of £272 or below per month will not need to pay any contributions from income, but may still have to pay a contribution from capital. A client with disposable income in excess of £272 and up to £632 per month will be liable to pay a monthly contribution of a proportion of the excess over £268, assessed in accordance with the following bands:

A client whose disposable capital exceeds £3,000 is required to pay a contribution of either the capital exceeding that sum or the likely maximum costs of the funded service, whichever is the lesser.

For example, if disposable income is £415 per month, the contribution will be in Band B, the excess income is £15 (£415–£400), the monthly contribution would therefore be £38 (£33 + £5).

Provided it is not disregarded as subject matter of the dispute, a client's main or only dwelling in which he resides must be taken into account as capital, subject to the following rules:

(a) The dwelling should be valued at the amount for which it could be sold on the open market.

(b) The amount of any mortgage or charge registered on the property must be deducted, but the maximum amount that can be deducted for such a mortgage or charge is £100,000.

(c) The first £100,000 of the value of the client's interest after making the above mortgage deduction must be disregarded.

The original proposal was that homeowners with £3,000 equity in their homes would be liable to make contributions to the cost of their legal aid. This was dropped following outrage by practitioners and legal interest groups, as it was said that such a move would effectively abolish legal aid for virtually all homeowners.

16.5.3   The Funding Code

In addition to financial eligibility, an applicant's case must also satisfy a new merits test. The Commission has prepared a Code which will replace, and is intended to be more flexible than, the merits test that was used for Civil Legal Aid. The Code sets out the criteria for determining whether services funded by the CLS Fund should be provided in a particular case and, if so, what services it is appropriate to provide. The Code also sets out the procedures for making applications. In drafting the Code, the Commission was required to consider the extent to which the criteria for assessment should reflect the following factors (s 8 of the Access to Justice Act 1999):

(a) The likely cost of funding the services and the benefit which may be obtained by their being provided.

(b) The availability of sums in the CLS Fund for funding the services and, having regard to the present and likely future demands on that Fund, the appropriateness of applying them to fund the services.

(c) The importance of the matters in relation to which the services would be provided for the individual.

(d) The availability to the individual of services not funded by the Commission and the likelihood of his being able to avail himself of them.

(e) If the services are sought by the individual in relation to a dispute, the prospects of his success in the dispute.

(f) The conduct of the individual in connection with services funded as part of the CLS (or an application for funding) or in, or in connection with, any legal proceedings.

(g) The public interest.

(h) Such other factors as the Lord Chancellor may by order require the Commission to consider.

The Code is required to reflect the principle that in many family disputes, mediation is more appropriate than court proceedings. This is intended to reinforce the development, under the Family Law Act 1996, of mediation as a means of resolving private law family disputes in a way that promotes as good a continuing relationship between the parties concerned as is possible in the circumstances. The government has argued that mediation is more constructive than adversarial court proceedings, and that litigation in these cases usually serves only to reinforce already entrenched positions and further damage the relationship between the parties. In addition, the cost of court proceedings is higher than that of mediation, and additional costs have to be borne by the property of the family, reducing the amount available to the parties and their children in future. The credibility of mediation as an appropriate forum for family matters in general took a blow in 1999, when the government abandoned plans to introduce the scheme related to divorce after pilot studies failed to produce good results.

The Commission revised the merits test for Controlled Legal Representation and issued guidance which came into force on 16 December 2002. The reform of the merits test, which regulates the demand that qualifies for help, is said by the government to complement the reforms of the supply of services – with the intention of creating a flexible system for deploying resources to meet a range of priorities within a controlled budget.

The Funding Code sets out general criteria in relation to services for all categories except very expensive cases, judicial review, claims against public authorities, clinical negligence, housing, family, mental health and immigration, for which there are criteria specific to the particular category. The Code defines which factors are relevant in a given category, how they should be taken into account, and what weight should be given to them. For example, standard criteria for the service of legal representation include: whether there is alternative funding available; whether there are alternatives to litigation; or whether the case could be allocated to the small claims track. For services in most categories, consideration must be given to whether there is sufficient benefit to the client in receiving a particular service and what the prospect of success is. Where this is a consideration, cases are put into one of six categories according to their chances of success as follows: very good (80% or better chance of success); good (60–80%); moderate (50–60%); borderline (50%); poor (less than 50%) or unclear. The considerations are not the same for all services, categories or types of case within those categories: for example, prospects of success will not be a relevant factor in cases about whether a child should be taken into local authority care.

16.5.4 Legal services provided

Section 4 of the 1999 Act describes the services that may be provided under the CLS. These range from the provision of basic information about the law and legal services to providing help towards preventing or resolving disputes and enforcing decisions which have been reached. The scheme encompasses advice, assistance and representation by lawyers (which have long been available under the legal aid scheme), and also the services of non-lawyers. It will extend to other types of service including, for example, mediation in family or civil cases where appropriate.

Under Sched 2, restrictions are specified in respect of other services for certain categories. Only basic information and advice will be available for:

- disputes involving allegations of negligent damage to property or the person ('personal injury'), apart from those about clinical negligence. These cases are generally considered suitable for conditional fees;

- allegations of defamation or malicious falsehood. Generally, legal aid was not available for representation in defamation, but it was sometimes possible to get legal aid by categorising the case as one of malicious falsehood. The government's view is that these cases do not command sufficient priority to justify public funding; in any event, they may often be suitable for a conditional fee;

- disputes arising in the course of business. Legal aid was not available for firms and companies, but a sole trader could get legal aid to pursue a business dispute. Businessmen have the option of insuring against the possibility of having to take or defend legal action. The government does not believe that the taxpayer should meet the legal costs of sole traders who fail to do so;

- matters concerned with the law relating to companies or partnerships;

- matters concerned with the law of trusts or trustees; boundary disputes. The government does not consider that these command sufficient priority to justify public funding. In addition, funding for representation at proceedings before the Lands Tribunal or Commons Commissioners is no longer available. Other services, including assistance with preparing a case, continue to be available.

For some categories, subject to local priorities, a full range of services will be available, whereas for others, all services except representation at court by a lawyer may be obtained.

The Lord Chancellor can make directions bringing cases that would be excluded within the provisions of the Act in exceptional circumstances. For example, the Lord Chancellor may direct that personal injury cases (which are generally excluded by Sched 2, because most such cases are suitable for conditional fees) be funded by the CLS fund where exceptionally high investigative or overall costs are likely to be necessary, or where issues of wider public interest are involved. The Consultation Paper, *Access to Justice with Conditional Fees* (Lord Chancellor's Department (LCD), 1998), notes that it will be necessary to decide what should constitute public interest (para 3.31). For example, a test case about a novel point of law might have no more than a 50% chance of success, but the decision could impact on numerous future cases (in the way that recent cases involving sporting injuries have extended the duty of care owed by officials wider than was previously accepted: see *Vowles v Evans and Welsh Rugby Union* (2003)), or a claim for a relatively small sum in damages might benefit a large number of other people with a similar claim. Examples might be claims arising out of the use of pharmaceutical products and pollution of water supplies or the atmosphere. Very expensive cases often include this type of public interest aspect: they are expensive because they are novel and complex, or because their wide potential impact means that they are hard fought.

16.5.5   The CLS Fund

The CLS Fund, as established under s 5 of the 1999 Act, is not uncapped, as was the old Legal Aid Fund. In the pre-1999 system, if more money was needed after the initial budgeting by the government, supplementary funding could be found. Today, the amount of the Fund is to be fixed each year by the Lord Chancellor, who takes account of the receipts from contributions (for example, from local authorities) with the balance from money voted by Parliament. The Lord Chancellor is able to direct the Commission to use specified amounts within the Fund to provide services of particular types (s 5(6)). The Lord Chancellor divides the Fund into two main budgets, for providing services in: (i) family; and (ii) other civil cases, while allowing the Commission limited flexibility to switch money between the two areas. The Lord Chancellor may set further requirements within these two budgets, by specifying the amount, or the maximum or minimum amount, that should be spent on, say, services from the voluntary advice sector, mediation or cases involving a wider public interest. The idea here is that in this way, it will be possible to ensure that resources are allocated in accordance with the government's priorities.

The Commission may use the CLS Fund to provide services (s 6(3)). These include making contracts with, or grants to, service providers, or employing staff to provide services directly to the public. These flexible powers are intended to give effect to one of the principal objectives of the reform of publicly funded legal services: that is, the ability to tailor the provision of services, and the means by which services are delivered, to the needs of local populations and particular circumstances. The Commission is allowed to test new forms of service provision through pilot projects such as the Family Advice and Information Networks Pilot Project (FAINS) and telephone advice service. The Commission is under a duty to obtain the best value for money – a combination of price and quality – when using the resources of the Fund to provide services; and as part of the government's Best Value initiative, local authorities that are able to demonstrate success in developing community legal services are awarded a CLS Beacon Award. To date, eight local authorities have been given this status.

In line with the principle of flexibility, it may be possible to exclude further categories which can generally be funded privately, as conditional fees, legal expenses insurance and other forms of funding develop more widely. Equally well, as resources become available through the greater control of spending and value for money provided by the new scheme and the development of private alternatives, it may be possible to extend the scheme's scope to cover services that are excluded now because, although they would command some priority, they are unaffordable.

16.5.6 Extension of financial conditions on an assisted party

The 1999 Act extends the potential scope of financial conditions imposed on an assisted party in two ways, although there are no immediate plans to use either of these powers:

- It will be possible to make the provision of services in some types of cases subject to the assisted person agreeing to repay an amount in excess of the cost of the services provided, in the event that their case is successful (s 10(2)). This might make it possible to fund certain types of case on a self-financing basis, with the additional payments from successful litigants applied to meet the cost of unsuccessful cases. It would also be possible to mix public funding with a private conditional fee arrangement, subject to the same conditions about the uplift to the costs in the event of a successful outcome. The government has suggested that this might be appropriate, for example, where a case could not be taken under a wholly private arrangement, because the solicitors firm was not large enough to bear the risk of the very high costs likely to be involved.

- It will be possible (s 10(3), (4)) to require the assisted person to repay, over time and with interest, the full cost of the service provided (for example, through continuing contributions from income). This will make it possible to provide services in some categories of case in the form of a loan scheme.

Section 11 of the 1999 Act establishes limits on the liability of the person receiving funded services to pay costs to the unassisted party. The costs he must pay cannot go above what is 'reasonable' (s 11(1)), taking into account the financial resources of all parties. It also provides that regulations may specify the principles that are to be applied in determining the amount of any costs awarded against the party receiving funded services, and the circumstances in which a costs order may be enforced against the person receiving funded services.

Today, the regulations that limit the circumstances in which the costs order may be enforced against the person receiving funded services (or the liability of the Commission to meet any costs order on behalf of the person receiving funded services) are made on a more flexible basis. Previously, protection from costs was seen by governments to create too great an advantage in litigation for the person receiving legal aid.

16.5.7 Matching delivery with needs and priorities

The fulfilment of the second duty of the Commission, to match the delivery of legal services to identified needs and priorities at a local level, is dependent in practice on the formation of CLSPs in each local authority area. The CLSPs are intended to provide a forum, in each local authority area, for the local authority and the LSC, and if possible other significant funders, to come together to co-ordinate funding and planning of local legal and advice services, to ensure that delivery of services better matches local needs. The Commission and the CLSPs are intended to encourage innovation by the voluntary sector in the delivery of advice, through increased use of information technology and mobile 'outreach' services providing help to people in remote communities.

Overall, the intention is to:

- make best use of all the resources available for funding legal services, by facilitating a co-ordinated approach to planning;

- improve value for money through contracting and the development of quality assurance systems;

- establish a flexible system for allocating central government funding, in a rational and transparent way within a controlled budget, so as to provide legal services where they are judged to be most needed; and

- ensure that the scheme is capable of adapting to meet changing priorities and opportunities.

The establishment of CLSPs is ahead of schedule. Partnerships now cover in excess of 99% of the population of England and Wales. There were 206 partnerships in operation by March 2004.

16.5.8 Relative success of the scheme

When the scheme was proposed, government plans appeared so vague that some lawyers questioned the credibility of the service and warned that it ran the risk of being a 'leafleting service' (News, 'The legal profession and the Community Legal Service' (1999) 149 NLJ 1195). However, a report from the National Audit Office (NAO), *Community Legal Service: The Introduction of Contracting* (HC 89 2002–2003), identifies significant improvements that have taken place in the administration of Civil Legal Aid, with better control, targeting and scrutiny of suppliers by the LSC since the CLS was created in April 2000 (see www.nao.gov.uk). In 2001–02, net expenditure borne by the CLS Fund totalled £734 million, with expenditure on licensed work totalling £476 million and expenditure on controlled work totalling £258 million. These positive points, though, should be read in the context of the general overspend on legal services cited at the outset of this chapter (16.1).

The report also identifies some problems in the new system. There is cause for concern about the volume of suppliers opting out of contracting in family work and the need for additional supply in high priority categories of law, such as community care, housing and mental health. Since the introduction of new contracting arrangements, there has been a decline in the number of solicitors firms providing legal aid services from 4,866 in January 2000 to 4,427 by July 2002. However, the number of not-for-profit firms providing services rose from 344 to 402 over the same period. The reduction in the supplier base is partly a deliberate move away from reliance on a large number of generalist support firms towards a smaller number of specialist quality-assured providers. However, the reduction also reflects concern amongst some firms about the level of remuneration offered on Civil Legal Aid work. The Commission has identified gaps in provision in some parts of the country, particularly in rural areas, and in some areas of law, for example, family law, but has had some success in attracting suppliers to immigration work.

The government says that while there is no immediate threat to the supply of services in most areas, there is a need for action to relieve pressure in the medium to long-term. Initiatives such as the 'Developing Legal Aid Solicitors' scheme might help address this. Under this scheme, the LSC provides grants to meet the tuition fees of students on the Legal Practice Course (LPC) and grants to support the provision of training contracts for successful LPC students. This has led to better scrutiny of suppliers by the LSC and to a greater degree of control over the Civil Legal Aid budget. The report to Parliament notes that the Commission has, in some cases, disallowed a significant proportion of the costs claimed on help and advice work, although in some cases, these amounts have been reinstated after mediation with the supplier. Audits conducted by the Commission of case files kept by suppliers suggest that 35% of suppliers were over-claiming in excess of 20%, although some suppliers have complained about the basis of some of these decisions. The 2001–02 audit results suggest that there has been some improvement in suppliers' performance over the previous year. However, a significant minority of suppliers have not improved. The Commission has stated its intention to remove suppliers who persistently over-claim on controlled work. The removal process currently takes a minimum of around 18 months and could be reduced, although there are risks in what are relatively new procedures.

16.6   The Criminal Defence Service

The CDS Commission is under a duty to secure the provision of advice, assistance and representation, according to the interests of justice, to people suspected of a criminal offence who are arrested and held in custody or facing criminal proceedings (s 12(2) of the Access to Justice Act 1999). Criminal proceedings are defined in the Act as including criminal trials, appeals and sentencing hearings, extradition hearings, binding over proceedings, appeals on behalf of a convicted person who has died, and proceedings for contempt in the face of any court (s 13(1)). The Act allows the Lord Chancellor to add further categories by regulation. This power will be used, for example, to prescribe Parole Board reviews of discretionary life sentences. Advice and assistance is provided to people subject to criminal investigations or proceedings by duty solicitors at a magistrates' court, at a solicitor's office and to a 'volunteer' at a police station.

Section 13(2) enabled the Commission to comply with this duty by securing advice and assistance through entering into contracts; by paying non-contracted lawyers on a case by case basis; by making payments to persons or bodies; by making grants or loans to persons or bodies; by establishing and maintaining bodies; by making grants to individuals; by providing them through salaried defenders employed by non-profit-making organisations; or by doing anything else which the Commission considers appropriate for funding advice and assistance except providing it itself. It also enabled the Commission to secure the provision of advice and assistance by different means in different areas in England and Wales and in relation to different descriptions of cases. All contractors are expected to meet quality assurance standards and contracts will, where possible, cover the full range of services from arrest until the case is completed. (The old arrangements for Criminal Legal Aid were widely seen as fragmented: a person could receive assistance in respect of the same alleged offence under several separate schemes, each resulting in a separate payment for the lawyers involved.)

Applications for publicly funded representation are made by way of a form supplied by the court (Form A for magistrates' court proceedings and Form B for the Crown Court). The appropriate officer, usually the court clerk, will grant or refuse the application. If the application is refused, the court must give reasons and a renewed application may be made. If an application is granted, a Representation Order will be issued. Failure to complete details of a defendant's means on the form could lead to a Recovery of Defence Costs Order (RDCO) (see further below) being made in relation to Crown Court proceedings.

The legislation provides that defendants granted a Representation Order can choose their representative. However, s 15 enables this right to be restricted by regulations. The Criminal Defence Service (General) (No 2) Regulations 2001, which took effect from 2 April 2001, limited the choice of representative to those holding contracts with the Commission. In serious fraud cases, the defendant's choice is further limited to representatives from a panel of firms or individual advocates who specialise in a particular type of case. Membership of a panel depends on meeting pre-determined criteria. In this way, the Commission can ensure that defendants facing charges in these exceptional cases are represented by those with the necessary expertise, experience and resources. In addition, s 15(2)(a) of the 1999 Act enables the Lord Chancellor to make regulations defining circumstances where defendants will not have a right to a choice of representative, but will instead have a representative assigned to them.

As under the old system, the courts will grant representation under the scheme to defendants according to 'the interests of justice'. However, the courts will no longer have to conduct a means test as well before granting representation, although a financial eligibility test is applied for advice and assistance. Under the old Criminal Legal Aid scheme, most defendants (about 95%) were not required to make a contribution to their defence costs. Those who did contribute and were acquitted usually had their contributions returned. The cost of means testing and enforcing contribution orders was high in relation to the contributions recovered. In 1997–98, Criminal Legal Aid contributions totalled £6.2 million, while the direct cost of administering the system was about £5 million. Means testing also led to delays in cases being brought to court, because cases had to be adjourned when the evidence required to conduct the test was not produced.

Instead of means testing, s 17 of the 1999 Act and the Criminal Defence Service (Recovery of Defence Costs Orders) Regulations 2001 give the trial judge at the end of a case in the Crown Court power to make an RDCO. The scheme is an arrangement to collect costs incurred where an individual has been granted publicly funded representation in criminal proceedings before any court except the magistrates' court. It applies to all other proceedings other than committals for sentence and appeals against sentence. The judge has a duty to consider making an RDCO at the end of the case after all other financial orders or penalties have been made. In exercising the duty, the judge must consider whether it is reasonable in all the circumstances to make such an RDCO, including the means of the defendant and his or her partner. Generally, an order will not be made against the first £3,000 of any capital, and although the defendant's house may be considered as capital, the property will be assessed at market value less any mortgage and the first £100,000 of any equity will be disregarded. RDCOs will be usually made on the basis of capital and income will not be considered unless gross annual income is in excess of £24,000. The Order is not dependent on the defendant being convicted and does not form part of the sentence, although an Order against an acquitted defendant will be exceptional. The Order can be for any amount up to the full costs incurred not only in the court making the RDCO, but also in other courts. The court may refer a case to the Special Investigations Unit of the Commission to investigate the defendant's means where the defendant is considered to have complex financial affairs. The judge may require the solicitor acting for the defendant to provide an estimate of the costs likely to be incurred in the proceedings. If, after the making of the RDCO, it is an over-estimate, the balance must be repaid. The RDCO will specify the amount of the costs to be paid and the terms of payment. In addition, the court has powers to make an order freezing the defendant's assets where appropriate to ensure payment of an RDCO. Payment is made to the Commission who may enforce the Order as a civil debt.

As mentioned above, advice and assistance (including advocacy assistance), other than by way of legal representation, is subject to a financial eligibility test. The Criminal Defence Service (General) Regulations 2001 provide that advice and assistance may be granted without reference to the financial resources of an individual for the following:

- advocacy assistance before a magistrates' court or Crown Court; or

- for advice and assistance (including advocacy assistance) provided by a court duty solicitor; or

- for police station advice and assistance to a client who is arrested and held in custody or who is a volunteer or who is in military custody; or

- advocacy assistance on an application for a warrant for further detention or an extension of that warrant.

In all other cases, the client's disposable income and disposable capital must be below certain limits. The limits (as at July 2005) are: Clients automatically qualify if they are in receipt of Income Support, income-based Job Seeker's Allowance, or Working Tax Credit, unless their disposable capital exceeds £1,000. Unlike the CLS, the CDS is a demand-led scheme and s 18 of the Access to Justice Act requires the Lord Chancellor to provide the necessary funding, but may seek to secure the best possible value for money.

16.7   Public Defender Service

The Commission is piloting its own Public Defender Service (PDS). Section 13(2)(f) of the 1999 Act contains powers to enable the Commission to provide services through lawyers in its own employment. These powers are intended to provide flexibility if, for example, there is limited coverage by private lawyers in rural areas. Using employed lawyers should also, the government has argued, provide the Commission with better information about the real costs of providing these services. The Commission in its Annual Report for 2001–02 states that the PDS has been established to:

- provide independent, high quality value for money criminal defence services to the public;

- provide examples of excellence in the provision of criminal defence services nationally and locally;

- provide benchmarking information to be used to improve the performance of the contracting regime for private practice suppliers;

- raise the level of understanding within government and all levels and areas of the Commission of the issues facing criminal defence lawyers in providing high quality services to the public;

- provide an additional option for ensuring the provision of quality criminal defence services in geographical areas where existing provision is low or of a poor standard;

- recruit, train and develop people to provide high quality criminal defence services, in accordance with the PDS's own business needs which will add to the body of such people available to provide criminal defence services generally; and

- share with private practice suppliers best practice in terms of forms, systems, etc, developed within the PDS to assist in the overall improvement of CDS provision locally.

Under the four year pilot, which began in 2002, eight offices have been established, comprising staff directly employed by the Commission. The pilot will form the basis of research into the merits of a mixed (private practice and employed) CDS.

The offices are situated in Birmingham, Liverpool, Middlesbrough, Swansea, Cheltenham, Pontypridd, Chester and Darlington. The individual offices will operate and run crime files as they would if they were in the private sector, and will take their turn on the duty solicitor rotas and compete with private suppliers in that area. The Public Defender offices offer a full range of services, from police station advice to representation in court, and instruct agents in the same way as private suppliers. It is believed that clients will be attracted and retained by word of mouth recommendation arising from the quality of service provided. It is anticipated that as the pilot progresses, individual offices may develop specialisms such as youth work. This is likely to be a natural development based on the location of the particular office and, at least initially, the skills of the people recruited. After some time in operation the service received mixed responses from the public and lawyers (see *The Times*, 25 January 2005).

Independence of lawyers in the PDS is a major concern. The government aims to achieve independence for the PDS lawyers by the appointment of a professional head of service and the effective implementation of a Code of Conduct. Section 16 of the 1999 Act requires salaried defenders employed by the LSC to be subject to a Code guaranteeing minimum standards of professional behaviour. A Code has been approved by Parliament following consultation and includes the following duties: to avoid discrimination; to protect the interests of the individuals for whom services are provided; to avoid conflicts of interest and of confidentiality. In particular, the Code of Conduct contains a clause specifically designed to ensure that public defenders are not 'too ready to plea bargain'. It says: 'A professional employee shall not put a client under pressure to plead guilty and, in particular, shall not advise a client that it is in his interests to plead guilty unless satisfied that the prosecution is able to discharge the burden of proof.'

16.8 The Voluntary Sector

There are over 1,500 not-for-profit advice agencies in England and Wales. They receive their funding – over £150 million a year in total – from many different sources, mainly local authorities, but also charities including the National Lottery Charities Board, central government and the LSC. The provision of advice services is not spread consistently across the country. Some areas appear to have relatively high levels of both legal practitioners and voluntary outlets, while others have few or none. For example, the LSC's South East Area has one Citizens Advice Bureau per 46,000 people, but, in the East Midlands, 138,000 people share a Citizens Advice Bureau. The government believes that the fragmented nature of the advice sector obstructs effective planning and prevents local needs for legal advice and help from being met as rationally and fully as possible.

16.8.1 Law Centres

There are 51 Law Centres in England and Wales staffed by salaried solicitors, trainee solicitors and non-lawyer experts in other areas like debt management. They are funded by local and central government and charity. They have 'shop front' access and aim to be user-friendly and unintimidating. They are managed by committees and represented by the Law Centres Federation. The report of the Rushcliffe Committee on Legal Aid and Advice (1945) had recommended a nationwide network of State salaried lawyers providing advice for a low, fixed fee. There was provision in the Legal Aid and Advice Act 1949 for this, but it was never implemented. The first centre was established in England in North Kensington in July 1970 in the face of great opposition from The Law Society. Since then, the Society has developed a more tolerant stance to the centres as it acknowledges that they can confer benefits to local law firms through the referrals of clients.

Law Centres take on individual cases, providing, for example, advice on landlord and tenant matters and representing people at tribunals. Some centres also take on group work since quite often the problems of one client are part of a wider problem. This sort of work is controversial.

How far is it correct for lawyers to become involved in socio-legal problems in an effort to combat the disadvantages of the poor? In 1974, in a collective statement of purpose, the Law Centres supported American statements such as one which claimed that the effective solution of the problems of the poor may require the lawyer 'to direct his attention away from the particular claim or grievance to the broader interests and policies at stake'. Such campaigns could deal, for example, with slum clearance or matters concerning roads and pavements. The Benson Commission rejected this sort of work for its proposed Citizens' Law Centres (CLCs), taking the view that community action tends to involve only one section of the community and that the independence of a centre can be compromised if it becomes a base for campaigns.

The Commission's proposed CLCs seemed to be an attempt to win back for private practitioners the large number of clients who were being assisted by Law Centres, as the CLCs would have been operated under the control of The Law Society and Bar Council and users would pay on the same basis as publicly funded clients of private practitioners. This would have increased the burden on the Legal Aid Fund, though, when the government was keen to make retrenchments, so the proposal was rejected.

16.8.2 Other voluntary advice

There are now 496 Citizens Advice Bureaux in England and Wales providing free, independent and impartial information and advice from over 3,200 locations. They deal with a high number of cases (over six million a year) and a very wide range of problems of which between one-third and one-half are legal problems. There are, however, very few trained lawyers working for the Bureaux.

The Bar Council supports a Free Representation Unit for clients at a variety of tribunals for which legal aid is not available. Most of the representation is carried out by Bar students supported and advised by full time caseworkers. A special Bar unit based in London was formed in 1996 through which more senior barristers provide representation. Some colleges and universities also offer advice. For example, the College of Law in London operates a free advice service in which vocational students give advice on such matters as personal injury cases and employment law.

Both barristers and solicitors operate 'pro bono' (from the Latin phrase pro bono publico, meaning for the public good) schemes under which legal work is done without charge or at reduced cost for members of the public ineligible for legal aid from the LSC but with limited means, or charitable and other non-profit-making organisations. Examples of pro bono activities include: solicitors attending advice sessions at Citizens Advice Bureaux or other free services, free advice to members of organisations, for example, trade union general advice schemes, secondment to Law Centres and free advice to charitable organisations.

16.9 Conditional Fee Arrangements

As part of the scheme to expose the provision of legal services to the full rigour of market forces, the then Lord Chancellor chose to devote an entire Green Paper in 1989 to *Contingency Fees*. Following a recommendation from the Civil Justice Review, the Paper had sought opinion on the funding of litigation on a contingent fee basis. This provides that litigation is funded by the claimant only if he wins, in which event, the lawyer claims fees as a portion of the damages payable to the claimant. The response to this idea was largely hostile.

The traditional opposition to contingency fees in the English legal system was that they were 'maintenance' (the financial support of another's litigation) and 'champerty' (taking a financial interest in another's litigation). Champerty occurs when the person maintaining another takes as his reward a portion of the property in dispute. It taints an agreement with illegality and renders it void (for a discussion of the principle, see *Grovewood Holding plc v James Capel & Co Ltd* (1995)). Section 14 of the Criminal Justice Act 1967 abolished maintenance and champerty as crimes and torts, but kept the rules making such arrangements improper for solicitors.

English litigation uses the Indemnity Rule, by which the loser pays the costs of the winner and thus puts him, more or less, in the position he enjoyed before the damage was done. Objectors to contingency fee agreements pointed out that such things were incompatible with the Indemnity Rule because, although the winner's costs would be paid for him by the other side, he would still have to pay for his lawyer from his damages (calculated to put him in the position he would have enjoyed if no wrong had been done to him) so he would not really be 'made whole' by his award. The position is different in the USA, where contingency agreements are common in personal injury cases, because there each side bears its own costs.

It was further contended by objectors to the contingency fee that the legal aid system adequately catered for those who were too poor to afford an ordinary private action. Even if there were people who were just above the legal aid financial thresholds but still too poor to pay for an action, this should be dealt with simply by changing the threshold.

Section 58 of the Courts and Legal Services Act (CLSA) 1990 permitted the Lord Chancellor to introduce conditional fee arrangements, although these cannot apply to criminal cases, family cases or those involving children (s 58(10)). However, there are a number of different arrangements for conditional fees, so one issue to be addressed was the type of conditional fee system that should be applied in England and Wales. The Scottish model, for which initially there was reasonable support, is that of the 'speculative fee', whereby the solicitor can agree with his client that he would be paid his ordinary taxed costs only if he won the case. Two other forms of contingency fee were rejected during the consultation period as being unsuitable. The first was a restricted contingency fee system in which the fee payable in the event of a successful action would be a *percentage of the damages*, but where the actual levels of recovery would be governed by rules. The second was an unrestricted contingency arrangement, similarly based on a percentage of damages, but at uncontrolled levels. These plans were rejected because it was thought that to give the lawyer a stake in the claimant's damages would be likely to create unacceptable temptations for the lawyer to behave unprofessionally in order to secure his fee.

The system eventually adopted is that where conditional fees are based on an 'uplift' from the level of fee the lawyer would normally charge for the sort of work in question. Originally, the maximum uplift was to be 20% in order to induce lawyers to take on potentially difficult cases and to help finance lawyers' unsuccessful conditional fee cases. This would have meant they could charge the fee that they would normally charge for a given type of case, plus an additional fifth.

In August 1993, after a long process of negotiation with the profession, Lord Mackay, the then Lord Chancellor, finally announced that he would allow the conditional fee to operate on a 100% uplift. Thus, solicitors receive no fee if they lose a case, but double what they would normally charge if they win the case. The Law Society had campaigned vigorously against the proposed 20% uplift, arguing that such risks as the no win, no fee arrangement entailed would not be regarded as worth taking by many solicitors simply on the incentive that their fee for winning the case would be 20% more than they would normally charge for such a case. The LCD originally decided to restrict the scheme to cases involving personal injury, insolvency and the European Court of Human Rights.

The system came into effect in June 1995. Such agreements are now legal, provided that they comply with any requirements imposed by the Lord Chancellor and are not 'contentious business agreements'. These are defined under s 59 of the Solicitors Act 1974 as agreements between a solicitor and his client made in writing by which the solicitor is to be remunerated by a gross sum, or a salary, at agreed hourly rates or otherwise, and whether higher or lower than that at which he would normally be remunerated.

In 1998, the Lord Chancellor produced another Consultation Paper, *Access to Justice with Conditional Fees*, where he proposed that insurance premiums supporting conditional fee arrangements should be recoverable between the parties. The Legal Aid Board was in favour of this change. It said in its response document (para 2.7) that 'this would make conditional fee agreements more viable and more attractive for clients and lawyers without unduly penalising opponents'.

The Law Society was less enthusiastic, pointing out that there is still a risk of a 'perverse incentive' operating – defendants with meritorious defences might end up paying higher premiums than those with no real defence. This is because an insurance company backing a defendant with a good defence will realise that the case will last longer than one where the defendant only has a mediocre defence. If the defendant then loses after a long case, he will have a bigger bill to pay for the other side's costs than in a shorter case. This leads to the paradox that the stronger the case you have as a defendant, the higher the premium you will have to pay, as your case will last longer. Weak defendants get defeated early on in proceedings. If a losing defendant has to pay not only the other side's lawyer's fee, but also the other side's insurance premium, the paradox above is worsened because a strong defendant will mean that a claimant's premium will be high, and if the claimant's premium is high, and the defendant might end up having to cover that cost if he loses, then the defendant's premium will also be raised!

'Pursuit' is the name of a legal expenses insurance policy offered by Royal Sun Alliance. Under the policy, the premium is only paid if the case is won, although there is a £200 non-refundable assessment fee. The government has endorsed this policy, although The Law Society and the Bar have been more reserved. The Law Society Vice President, Robert Sayer, said: 'No insurance product, this included, will provide a solution to the removal of legal aid' ((1999) Law Soc Gazette, 24 March).

The right to use 'no win, no fee' agreements to pursue civil law claims was extended by the Conditional Fee Agreements Order 1998. The Order allowed lawyers to offer conditional fee agreements to their clients in all civil cases excluding family cases. Speaking in the House of Lords on 23 July, the then Lord Chancellor, Lord Irvine, said:

> These agreements will result in a huge expansion of access to justice. Today, only the very rich or the very poor can afford to litigate. In future, everyone with a really strong case will be able to secure his rights free of the fear of ruin if he loses. They will bring the majority of our people into access to justice.

Conditional fees have been the means by which at least 60,000 personal injury cases have been brought, and many, in all likelihood, would not have been brought but for the existence of conditional fees. The Order retains the old rule that the maximum uplift on the fees lawyers can charge is 100%. Thus, a lawyer may take on a claim against an allegedly negligent employer whose carelessness has resulted in the client being injured. The lawyer, who might normally charge £2,000 for such a case, can say 'I shall do this work for nothing if we lose, but £3,000 if we win'. In fact, as the price uplift can be up to 100% of the normal fee, he can stipulate for up to £4,000 in this example. The Law Society has recommended an additional voluntary cap of 25% of damages, and this has been widely accepted in practice.

The real problems continued to be:

(a) that the new system, designed really to help the millions who have been regulated out of the legal aid system, does not help people whose cases stand only a limited chance of success, as lawyers will not take their cases; and

(b) the difficulties of a claimant getting insurance to cover the costs that he will have to pay, if he loses the claim, for the other side's lawyers. Where a personal injury claim arises from a road traffic incident, it is almost always clear to a solicitor where blame and legal liability probably lie. Risks are therefore calculable by insurance companies, so one can presently insure against having to pay the other side's costs in the event of losing an action on a personal injury case for about £100 in a 'no win, no fee' arrangement. There are, however, many areas, and medical negligence cases are good examples, where the chances of success are notoriously difficult to predict. Thus, insurance against having to pay the other side's costs is prohibitively high, running into many thousands of pounds in some cases. It is quite unrealistic to assume that all such cases, arising often from highly distressing circumstances, will be dealt with in future on a 'no win, no fee' basis. Lawyers will generally not want to take on such cases on such a basis, and even where they do, clients will often not be able to afford the necessary insurance. As insurance to cover client costs in medical 'no win, no fee' cases has proven so expensive, legal aid continues to cover clinical negligence cases.

One possible development with the conditional fee system is the use of the arrangement by a litigant in order to improve his bargaining power when trying to negotiate a settlement with an opponent. This is based on the idea that because no win, no fee arrangements are only taken on by solicitors if they believe that they have a good chance of winning, a no win, no fee client should be able to face his opponent with some confidence. However, as one very experienced litigator has observed, the no win, no fee arrangement is 'not a piece of advice to the client which the client can then use for his own negotiating purposes. Rather it is the solicitor's own approach to the commercial transaction with the client and it can be changed on re-consideration and reflection' (Richard Harrison, 'Conditional fees and conflicts of interest' (2002) 152 NLJ 1505).

16.9.1 The Access to Justice Act 1999

The Access to Justice Act 1999 (ss 27–31), together with the Conditional Fee Arrangements Regulations 2000 and the Collective Conditional Fee Arrangements Regulations 2000, reformed the law relating to conditional fees to enable the court to order a losing party to pay, in addition to the other party's normal legal costs, the uplift on the successful party's lawyers' fees and, in any case where a litigant has insured against facing an order for the other side's costs, any premium paid by the successful party for that insurance. The intention was to:

- ensure that the compensation awarded to a successful party is not eroded by any uplift or premium. The party in the wrong will bear the full burden of costs;

- make conditional fees more attractive, in particular to defendants and to claimants seeking non-monetary redress (these litigants can rarely use conditional fees now, because they cannot rely on the prospect of recovering damages to meet the cost of the uplift and premium);

- discourage weak cases and encourage settlements;

- provide a mechanism for regulating the uplifts that solicitors charge. In future, unsuccessful litigants will be able to challenge unreasonably high uplifts when the court comes to assess costs.

In the first version of conditional fee arrangements, only people who expected to win money from their case could benefit from conditional fees. This was the only way that most people could afford to pay the success fee. There were also available insurance policies which could be taken out by someone contemplating litigation to cover the costs of the other party and the client's own costs (including, if not a conditional fee case, a client's solicitor's fees) if the case was lost. However, it meant that a successful litigant would not receive all the money he was awarded, so the government made provision in the Access to Justice Act 1999 to make it possible for the winning party to recover the success fee and any insurance premium from the losing party. This came into effect on 1 April 2000 and ensures that it is the person or organisation that has committed the legal wrong who pays, and it allows defendants and claimants (other than in family law cases) whose case is not about money to use conditional fee arrangements. However, these measures were primarily designed for the High Street solicitor. The Conditional Fee Agreements Regulations 2000 require that before an agreement is made, the legal representative must inform the client of the circumstances in which the client may be liable for the legal representative's costs, and advise the client as to whether and how the costs might be covered by insurance or by other methods of finance. In addition, the conditional fee agreement must specify the particular proceedings to which the arrangement relates and the circumstances in which the legal representative's fees and expenses are payable. If the agreement provides for a success fee, then it must briefly specify the reasons for setting the percentage increase at the level stated in the agreement.

16.9.1.1   Collective conditional fee arrangements

A further development is a set of regulations (www.dca.gov.uk) enabling the bulk purchase and provision of legal services through collective conditional fee agreements, which came into effect on 30 November 2000. The collective conditional fee agreements are designed specifically for mass providers and purchasers of legal services, such as trade unions, insurers or commercial organisations. A collective conditional fee agreement will enable a trade union to enter into a single agreement with solicitors to govern the way in which cases for its members will be run and paid for; by simplifying the process, it will reduce the cost of pursuing separate individual cases. The scheme will also benefit commercial organisations which will be able to enter collective conditional fee agreements to pursue or defend claims arising in the course of business.

16.9.2   The advantages of conditional fee arrangements

For claimants, the advantages can be summarised as being:

- that lawyers acting in any case will be confident (they will have had to weigh carefully the chances of success before taking the case as their fee depends on winning) and determined;

- there will be freedom from the anxiety of having to pay huge fees;

- there will be no need to pay fees in advance; and

- there will be no delays or worries with legal aid applications.

For defendants there will be advantages too, as the contingency fee system will probably reduce the number of spurious claims. In a period where legal aid is being cut back so drastically, preventing so many people from going to law, this system can be seen as a way of preserving at least some limited access to the legal process. Losing parties will still be liable to pay the other side's costs, so it will be unlikely that people will take action unless they consider they have a good chance of success.

The taxpayer can also be given the advantage in the form of a significant reduction in the funding of the legal aid system. Furthermore, practitioners who are competent to assess and willing to take the risks of litigation will arguably enjoy a better fee paying basis, increased fee income and overall business, fewer reasons for delay and more satisfied clients with fewer complaints.

Consider two examples. First, a middle class couple consult their solicitor about injuries received in a road accident. Their joint income and savings put them outside the legal aid scheme. The proposed litigation is beset with uncertainties as the other driver's insurers have denied liability. The couple have to worry about their own expenses and the possibility under the Indemnity Rule of paying for the defendant's costs. Second, a young man who has been injured at work wants to sue his employer. The case will turn on some difficult health and safety law on which there are currently conflicting decisions. He is eligible for legal aid, but he will have to make substantial contributions because of his level of income, and if his claim fails, he will have to pay the same sum again towards the expenses of his employers. In both cases, the prospective litigants might well drop any plan to litigate. Both cases, however, might proceed expeditiously if they found a lawyer to act on a no win, no fee basis.

16.9.3 The disadvantages of conditional fee arrangements

Critics of the system argue that it encourages the sort of speculative actions that occur frequently in the USA, taken up by the so called 'ambulance chasing' lawyers. It can be argued that the system of contingency fees creates a conflict of interest between the lay client and the lawyer, with a consequential risk of exploitation of the client. Where a lawyer's fee depends on the outcome of a case, there is a greater temptation for him to act unethically. When the Royal Commission on Legal Services (1979) rejected the idea of contingent fees, it stated that such a scheme might lead to undesirable practices by lawyers including, 'the construction of evidence, the improper coaching of witnesses, the use of professionally partisan expert witnesses, especially medical witnesses, improper examination and cross-examination, groundless legal arguments designed to lead the courts into error and competitive touting'. If the case was won, the lawyer claimed a significant part of the damages, but there was also a real danger that lawyers would be pressured to settle too readily to avoid the costs of preparing for a trial that could be lost and therewith the fee. An example would be where an insurance company admits liability but contests the level of damages. The claimant might stand to get substantially higher compensation by contesting the case. Under the new system, however, his solicitor will have a strong interest in advising him to settle. A settlement would guarantee the solicitor's costs and the agreed 'mark up' (up to 100% more than a normal fee for such work), both of which would be completely lost if the case was fought and lost. This would not occur outside of a conditional fee arrangement. Although the conventional system of payment was not without problems, as Walter Merricks, then of The Law Society, has stated:

... when a lawyer is being paid by the hour, he may have a financial interest in encouraging his client to go on with an open-and-shut case, increasing his own fees.

The Law Society has argued that the system, if not properly regulated, could promote the sort of 'ambulance chasing' practised by American lawyers in the wake of the 1984 Bhopal disaster, in which over 2,500 people were killed by escaping gas from a US company (Union Carbide Corporation) plant in India. American lawyers flew out to act for victims and their relatives and some were reported to be taking fees of 50% of the claimants' damages.

It was argued by some that by allowing lawyers to *double* their normal fee for certain cases, the Lord Chancellor risked eliminating any benefit speculative fees might bring. If the successful client was not to be able to recover the *uplift* from the other side, he would have to fund it himself out of the damages he had been awarded. In effect, this often resulted in his damages being halved. The uplift can now be recovered, subject to taxation (that is, court official approval), following changes made by the Access to Justice Act 1999.

It is not even clear that the main claim made for the system – that it increases access to the courts – is correct. The Scottish experience is that speculative cases do not exceed 1% of the cases in the caseload of the Faculty of Advocates. One firm opponent of the system is Lord Justice Auld. He has argued that the system will eventually endanger the esteem in which lawyers are held by the public. He has doubted whether the scheme will produce greater commitment by lawyers to their cases: 'There is a distinction to be drawn between the lawyer's commitment to the case and his anxiety to recover his fees. The two do not always correspond.'

16.9.4 The operation of conditional fee arrangements

The workings of conditional fee agreements in England and Wales have been of particular concern to those looking at how the English legal system is managing to provide access to legal services to those (perhaps 60% of the adult population) who are too poor to pay full legal fees but too rich to get State-funded services from the CLS. A major study of the conditional fee system (Yarrow (1997)) commissioned by the Lord Chancellor's Advisory Committee on Legal Education and Conduct, assessed how widely and in what ways conditional fees were being used. The research was based on a survey of 120 firms of solicitors and an analysis of 197 conditional fee cases begun in the personal injury field. The research found evidence of considerable inconsistency in the size of the 'success fee' calculated for cases with similar chances of success. Moreover, the fee appeared to be too high in up to 6 cases in 10 which had 'very good' chances of winning.

Yarrow found that a surprisingly high proportion of cases were regarded as having relatively low chances of success given that personal injury cases usually have an extremely high success rate. This could indicate that some solicitors could be over-estimating the chances of failure and therefore charging a higher 'success fee'. Yarrow concludes that such concerns could cast doubt over the entire system. Overall, the average 'success fee' charged by solicitors was 43% but, for 1 in 10 cases, it was close to the maximum of 100%. However, the voluntary 25% cap on the proportion of damages that can be swallowed up by the 'success fee' recommended by The Law Society is used by almost all solicitors.

Further research in 1999 by Yarrow and Abrams into the client's experience of conditional fee agreements reported widespread confusion and a general lack of understanding of the arrangements, which were so complex that solicitors found it difficult to explain to their clients how they worked. The University of Westminster Report, *Nothing to Lose?*, said that the recoverability proposals of the success fee and the insurance premium under the Access to Justice Act, while benefiting clients, would add another layer of complication to the arrangements. Of the 40 clients interviewed in the study, only 1 understood the conditional fee agreement scheme in its entirety, but he had 'considerable' experience of law. The majority, however, said they were satisfied with the outcome of their case, which they would otherwise have been unable to pursue.

Since the introduction of conditional fees, the common law has been developed in two decisions by the courts (*Thai Trading Co (A Firm) v Taylor* (1998) and *Bevan Ashford v Geoff Yeandle (Contractors) Ltd* (1998)). In the first of these cases, the Court of Appeal held that there were no longer public policy grounds to prevent lawyers agreeing to work for less than their normal fees in the event that they were unsuccessful, provided that they did not seek to recover more than their normal fees if they were successful (the latter was only permissible in those proceedings in which conditional fee agreements were allowed). In *Bevan Ashford*, the Vice Chancellor held that it was also lawful for a conditional fee agreement to apply in a case which was to be resolved by arbitration (under the Arbitration Act 1996), even though these were not court proceedings, provided all the requirements specified by regulations as to the form and content of the agreement were complied with.

Following the decision in *Thai Trading Co (A Firm) v Taylor*, r 8 of the Solicitors' Practice Rules was amended in January 1999 to allow any arrangement already permitted under statute or common law. At the time, this appeared to permit solicitors to enter into *Thai Trading* types of agreements referred to as 'conditional normal fee arrangements' (that is, a normal fee if successful, a reduced fee if not successful).

However, the case law was not settled. The decision of the Court of Appeal in *Geraghty v Awwad* (2000) created confusion over the enforceability of *Thai Trading* types of arrangements. In *Geraghty v Awwad*, it was argued that at the time the agreement was entered into in 1993, the Solicitors' Practice Rules did not allow such agreements. The Court of Appeal considered itself bound by the House of Lords' decision in *Swain v The Law Society* (1983), which had not been considered in *Thai Trading Co (A Firm) v Taylor*, and held that the Practice Rules had the effect of statute. The argument that by 1993 the common law allowed for such agreements was also rejected. Accordingly, in *Geraghty v Awwad*, the agreement was held to be unenforceable as being both contrary to legislation and the common law. (In *Thai Trading Co (A Firm) v Taylor*, it was argued that just because the Solicitors' Practice Rules prohibited a certain practice, this did not in itself render that practice illegal.)

On 1 April 2000, the new Conditional Fee Agreements Regulations 2000 came into effect under s 27 of the Access to Justice Act 1999, permitting a number of different arrangements as conditional fee agreements, including acting speculatively without a success fee or at a discounted rate in a losing case. Thus, *Thai Trading* type of agreements entered into after 1 April 2000 are now enforceable provided they comply with the new Regulations, dispelling any confusion created by the case law.

Recently, there have been a number of difficulties arising from conditional fee agreements. First, the House of Lords in *Callery v Gray* (2002) expressed concern that conditional fee agreements are open to abuse, with excessive claims being pursued for base costs, insurance premiums and success fees (uplift), as claimants are acting without risk and, because there is no market restriction on costs, lawyers are able to set off the cases they lose against those they win. Second, differing views are taken by the courts as to what is considered to be a 'reasonable success fee' for particular types of work. In *Callery v Gray*, 20% was thought permissible in a modest and straightforward road traffic accident claim. However, in *Halloran v Delaney* (2002), 5% was thought an appropriate figure.

Third, the courts have been required to consider the extent to which a conditional fee agreement must comply with reg 4 of the Conditional Fee Agreements Regulations 2000 in order to be enforceable. The regulation requires the solicitor to explain the agreement. However, in *English v Clipson* (Peterborough county court, unreported, 5 August 2002), the explanation was given by the representative of an organisation called The Accident Group (a scheme of claimant representatives). He was not a solicitor, so therefore the Regulations had not been complied with and the conditional fee agreement was not enforceable. By contrast, it was held in *Sharratt v London Central Bus Co* (Supreme Court Cost Office, 27 November 2002) that it was possible for a solicitor to delegate the explanation to such a person.

Fourth, the terms of the conditional fee agreement and its validity are of critical importance to the defendant, as it is he who will have to pay the costs if the claimant is successful. In *Worth v McKenna* (Liverpool County Court, unreported, 2002), it was claimed that the agreement was privileged and therefore the defendant was not entitled to see it. The circuit judge held that it was a privileged document although it could be disclosed if put in issue, for example, by questioning the claimant solicitor's bill of costs. However, there is an argument that disclosure should be permitted earlier in proceedings, as the contents of the agreement could affect the manner in which the case is conducted. As already noted, the conditional fee arrangement does not sit comfortably with the indemnity principle in the English system, under which the unsuccessful party pays the costs of the successful party, and it may be appropriate that limitation should be put on what might be included in the indemnity. For example, the unsuccessful party might be obliged to pay the base fee which is the usual fee for such work, but any 'uplift' or insurance premiums could be paid out of the damages awarded.

An alternative to the conditional fee arrangement is the fixed fee. These are being considered by the Civil Justice Council (which monitors the civil justice system) as a means of keeping costs down in certain cases. The rationale behind fixed fees is that costs should be more certain and affordable in order to increase access to justice. The cases in which they are considered to be appropriate are road traffic accident claims which are settled without negotiation between the claimant's solicitors and the insurers and without the need for court proceedings, and which are limited in value to £10,000. For a scheme to operate effectively, the fees must be certain and in proportion to the work required. There must also be an opportunity for claimants to opt out of the scheme and pursue their claims in court if justice requires. The fees must be reasonable and regularly reviewed or solicitors will not be prepared to undertake the work, and there must be sanction for those parties who do not pay promptly as such payment is an advantage of the system. In December 2002, at the second Costs Forum, comprising representatives of the legal profession, insurance industry, judiciary and academics, the following was agreed for claims of £10,000 or less:

- the basic cost, being the minimum that could be charged for such work, was £800;

- a percentage of the damages awarded, which should be 20% for amounts up to £5,000 and 15% for those between £5,000 and £10,000;

- a success fee (uplift) of 5% (if payable);

- plus VAT and disbursements.

The matter now has to be considered by the Civil Justice Council with a view to its inclusion in the Civil Procedure Rules. The question that then follows is to what extent can fixed fees be applied to other areas of work?

16.10 Unmet Legal Need

Since the early 1970s, there have been many published research papers and texts which cast doubt on how effectively the legal profession provides for the needs of the whole community. It has been argued that whilst presenting itself as available to give service to everyone on the full range of matters which are capable of being effectively resolved by law, the truth is that lawyers are generally only used by a narrow social group for a narrow range of services. Many problems people suffer which are susceptible to legal resolution are not taken to lawyers for their advice and assistance. The reasons for this appear to be multifarious, but are broadly to do with:

(a) the inaccessibility of lawyers;

(b) the failure of sufferers to perceive their problem as something a lawyer could help to solve;

(c) the failure of lawyers to market themselves as being able to help with as wide a range of problems as the law could help solve; and

(d) financial barriers (real or apparent).

Early American research by Mayhew and Reiss ('The social organisation of legal contacts' (1969) 34 American Sociological Rev 311) surveyed American residents and found that while 7 out of 10 had seen a lawyer at least once, and 1 in 4 had visited 1 in the last 5 years, only 39% had ever sought advice on a matter other than property. They concluded:

> The association between income and legal contacts is in part an organisational effect. The legal profession is organised to serve business and property interests. The social organisation of business and property is highly legalised. Out of this convergence emerges a pattern of citizen contact with attorneys that is heavily orientated to property ...

The results of a mass observation study in England, in which the legal experiences of 2,004 people were examined, showed similar results to the Detroit study. Of the respondents, 81% said they had never come into contact with a solicitor. Of those who did consult solicitors, 45% went about a property matter (see Zander, 'Who goes to solicitors?' (1969) 16 Law Soc Gazette 174, March).

It is appropriate first to consider the nature of a 'legal' problem. The basic premise of pioneering research on this subject is that it is wrong to define as 'legal problems' simply those predicaments which are usually taken to lawyers to solve. Such a definition excludes problems which could be solved by legal means but are not dealt with by lawyers. Solicitors have been criticised for the restricted view they have of their work, but there is evidence to suggest that the public has an even narrower perception of the sort of thing a solicitor could help them with than do solicitors themselves (Morris, White and Lewis (1973)). As far as the solicitors themselves are concerned, some of their narrow-minded approaches might be attributable to their legal education. Subjects like welfare law, for example, are only optional and are not widely available to undergraduates. In any event, the subjects which offer more lucrative career paths, like revenue law or company law, have always been more popular than welfare subjects. The Marre Report on the future of the legal profession (*A Time for Change*, 1988) made a specific call for a better response from lawyers to problems involving housing and immigration law.

The largest survey of what lawyers do and for whom was conducted for the Benson Royal Commission on Legal Services (*Survey of Users and Non-users of Legal Services in England and Wales*, RCLS, Vol 2). The sample was based on 2,026 consultations in 1977, which involved 1,770 people out of 7,941 households interviewed. It found that some 15% of adults used a lawyer's service in 1977. It also found that of 27 categories of work used by the survey, just 7 accounted for over 80% of all the work taken to solicitors: domestic conveyancing, probate, wills, divorce and matrimonial, motoring and other offences, personal injury cases and property matters. A survey conducted for The Law Society in 1989 confirmed this general pattern.

There has been much debate as to the true significance of these research findings. Do they reflect a restricted public perception of what solicitors deal with, or simply a failure to approach solicitors for other reasons like, for example, perceived costs? The Commission found that, during 1977, a solicitor was used by 25% of the professional class, 21% of employers and managers, but only 10% of unskilled workers. Michael Zander has argued that the results of the survey demonstrate that the use of lawyers is 'problem connected' even more than it is 'type-of-person connected': that is, that although people from different socio-economic backgrounds use solicitors to a different extent, it is not simply their background that provides the best explanation. In fields of work involving property (for example, conveyancing, probate), those with property use lawyers much more than those who have none. As this is the largest single source of work for the solicitors' profession, it explains why lawyer use appears to reflect the differences between classes. Zander has argued that this impression is misleading: 'If one looks at non-property types of work, the use of lawyers is relatively even as between members of different socio-economic backgrounds.'

One main reason for people not using solicitors is ignorance that the lawyer could be useful. Genn ('Who claims compensation', in Harris *et al*, *Compensation and Support for Illness and Injury* (1984)) has shown how many people fail to pursue proper claims because their first line of inquiry to another body (for example, employers, police, trade union) results in misleading advice. Apathy in prospective litigants is also a significant factor. The rules permitting solicitors to advertise, made in 1983, and their further relaxation in 1987, will perhaps bring more people into solicitors' offices. This will only help, however, to the extent that the apathy is not as a result of fear of costs. All research on the matter, including that of Genn (1984) and the Marre Committee (1988), has demonstrated that costs have a deterrent effect on seeking legal advice. Widespread ignorance of the legal aid schemes must also be relevant to this point.

The image of lawyers has sometimes been identified as a barrier to a greater range of customers. The Marre Committee (1988) focused on the facts that most solicitors' offices are inaccessible and unwelcoming and that they do not cater for many needs like those of linguistic minorities. The results of the most recent population census of 2001 show that 7.9% of the population is from ethnic minorities, and whilst that figure does not represent those who are not conversant in English, it suggests that there might be a real problem for many people who are perhaps likely to have problems that lawyers could help to solve. The Law Society survey (1989) found that the image of solicitors amongst the general public is 'good but not outstanding'. Compared with bank managers, accountants, NHS doctors and estate agents, although they were found to be easier to talk to than all the others bar doctors, solicitors were regarded as 'after your money' only less than estate agents. In 1999, it found its image was poor enough in the public eye to warrant spending £60,000 on a public relations exercise to improve the way lawyers are perceived.

In *Rethinking Legal Need: The Case of Criminal Justice* (1991), Paul Robertshaw rejects normative definitions of need, arguing that these rely too heavily on the assumptions of whoever is doing the defining, tend to be lawyer orientated and result in other people's problems being redefined by experts. He also rejects self-defined notions of 'legal need', as they are too uncertain and subject to methodological difficulties. Instead, he uses a concept of comparative need and tries to establish a negative definition of need by comparing outcomes: '... if those in receipt of the [legal] service are not significantly better off than those without them, there can be no need.' He analyses existing research data on the outcomes of legally aided representation and non-legally aided cases and concludes that the general assumption that people assisted by representation need it because they get a better outcome by using it is not proven. There are several problems with such reasoning, as Ed Cape has demonstrated (1994). Basically, Robertshaw equates the provision of legal services with 'representation', whereas in fact representation is only a part of any legal service. If one just measures the outcome of representation as opposed to the whole legal service, the result is likely to be very misleading. A suspect may well need legal advice at a police station, and such advice may well result in the police deciding not to charge the suspect.

16.10.1   Does it matter if such needs remain unmet?

In the Dimbleby Lecture 1992, the late Lord Chief Justice Taylor observed that there might be very serious social problems, even resulting in 'unrest', if the law did not become more accessible.

The true extent of unmet need might be less than is apparent simply by asking questionnaire respondents whether they have consulted solicitors about certain matters. This is because people might be making use of other sources of advice, for example, Citizens Advice Bureaux, accountants, building societies and licensed conveyancers, in circumstances where they might otherwise have consulted lawyers.

The greater the level of unmet need, the worse the social implications. It is, though, notoriously difficult to ascertain the extent of the unmet need. Similar problems affect different people to different degrees. When does a person *need* legal advice? The pioneering research by Abel-Smith, Zander and Brooke adopted a partly subjective test of 'need'. They used a test of what would constitute 'a risk of substantial loss or disadvantage which would be important for the individual concerned'. This standard differed for each category of problem. Zander, writing five years later, acknowledged that these tests for need were highly artificial.

On the whole, poor people use lawyers much less than do rich people. Although, as Zander has argued, the current picture of unmet need has come from researchers who have concentrated on the poor, not the whole population, and Genn has found that people from the higher socio-economic groups are less likely to make a claim consequent upon personal injury (Genn (1984)), it is not difficult to see that the poor are legally disadvantaged by their lack of legal awareness, influence and resources like energy and time.

THE FUNDING OF LEGAL SERVICES

Legal Aid

The scheme prior to the Access to Justice Act 1999 was contained in the Legal Aid Act 1988. A common feature of the Civil and Criminal Legal Aid schemes was that expenditure on them was demand-led. Any lawyer could do legal aid work for a client who passed the relevant means test (if any), and whose case passed the statutory merits test (in the case of Civil Legal Aid) or the interests of justice test (in the case of Criminal Legal Aid). Lawyers were (and will continue to be under the transitional arrangements) paid on a case-by-case basis for each individual case or other act of assistance, usually at rates or fees set in regulations, but in some cases on the same basis as a privately funded lawyer.

This, in the government's view, meant that there were few mechanisms or incentives for promoting value for money or assuring the quality of the services provided.

The New Legal Aid Scheme

The Access to Justice Act 1999 replaces the legal aid system with two new schemes, and makes provisions about rights to supply legal services, appeals, and court procedure, magistrates and magistrates' courts.

The provisions in the Act form part of the wide-ranging programme of reforms to legal services and the courts, described in the government's White Paper, *Modernising Justice*, published in 1998.

The 1999 Act established a Legal Services Commission (LSC) to run the Community Legal Service (CLS), which replaces the legal aid fund in civil and family cases, and the Criminal Defence Service (CDS), which replaces the legal aid scheme in criminal cases, to secure the provision of publicly funded legal services for people who need them. It also enabled the Lord Chancellor to give the Commission orders, directions and guidance about how it should exercise its functions.

The Commission must use the resources of the CLS Fund in a way that reflects priorities set by the Lord Chancellor and its duty to secure the best possible value for money, to procure or provide a range of legal services. The Commission also has a duty to liaise with other funders of legal services to facilitate the development of co-ordinated plans for making the best use of all available resources. The intention is to develop a network of legal service providers of assured quality, offering the widest possible access to information and advice about the law, and assistance with legal problems.

The CDS is intended to ensure that people suspected or accused of a crime are properly represented, while securing better value for money than was possible under the legal aid scheme.

The Legal Services Commission

The 1999 Act established the new LSC and makes provision for appointments to it. The Commission replaces the Legal Aid Board. It was considered necessary to establish a new body to reflect the fundamentally different nature of the CLS compared to Civil Legal Aid. Within the broad framework of priorities set by the Lord Chancellor, the Commission will be responsible for taking detailed decisions about the allocation of resources.

The Community Legal Service

The LSC has two main duties in respect of the CLS.

First, it manages a CLS Fund, which replaces legal aid in civil and family cases. The CLS Fund is used to secure the provision of appropriate legal services, within the resources made available to it, and according to priorities set by the Lord Chancellor and by regional and local assessments of need through Community Legal Service Partnerships. A Funding Code has been drawn up by the Commission and approved by the Lord Chancellor, and sets out the criteria and procedures for deciding whether to fund individual cases.

Second, as part of a wider CLS, the Commission, in co-operation with local funders and interested bodies, develops local, regional and national plans to match the delivery of legal services to identified needs and priorities.

Overall, the intention is to:

- make best use of all the resources available for funding legal services, by facilitating a co-ordinated approach to planning;

- improve value for money through contracting and the development of quality assurance systems.

The Access to Justice Act 1999 describes the services which may be provided under the CLS. These range from the provision of basic information about the law and legal services, to providing help towards preventing or resolving disputes and enforcing decisions which have been reached. The scheme encompasses advice, assistance and representation by lawyers (which had long been available under the legal aid scheme), and also the services of non-lawyers. It extends to other types of service, including, for example, mediation in family or civil cases where appropriate.

The Commission uses the CLS Fund to provide services by contracting with service providers, employing staff or making grants to provide services directly to the public. These flexible powers are intended to give effect to one of the principal objectives of the reform of publicly funded legal services, that is, the ability to tailor the provision of services, and the means by which services are to be delivered, to the needs of local populations and particular circumstances. The Commission also tests new forms of service provision through pilot projects.

Subject to exceptions that the Lord Chancellor makes by direction, only basic information and advice will be available for:

- disputes involving allegations of negligent damage to property or the person ('personal injury'), apart from those about clinical negligence. These cases are generally considered suitable for conditional fees;

- allegations of defamation or malicious falsehood. Generally, legal aid is not currently available for representation in defamation, but it is sometimes possible to get legal aid by categorising the case as one of malicious falsehood. The government's view is that these cases do not command sufficient priority to justify public funding and, in any event, they may often be suitable for a conditional fee.

The Lord Chancellor, using regulations, has set financial eligibility limits for people to receive services funded by the CLS Fund. Different conditions, or no conditions, are set for different circumstances or types of case or service.

The funding assessment under the Code replaces the merits test for Civil Legal Aid with a more flexible assessment, applying different criteria in different categories according to their priority.

The Code reflects the principle that, in many family disputes, mediation is more appropriate than court proceedings. This is intended to reinforce the development, under the Family Law Act 1996, of mediation as a means of resolving private law family disputes in a way that promotes as good a continuing relationship between the parties concerned as is possible in the circumstances.

The 1999 Act extends the potential scope of financial conditions in two ways, although there are no immediate plans to use either of these powers:

- it will be possible to make the provision of services in some types of cases subject to the assisted person agreeing to repay an amount in excess of the cost of the services provided, in the event that their case is successful. This might make it possible to fund certain types of case on a self-financing basis, with the additional payments from successful litigants applied to meet the cost of unsuccessful cases;

- it will be possible to require the assisted person to repay, over time and with interest, the full cost of the service provided (for example, through continuing contributions from income). This will make it possible to provide services in some categories of case in the form of a loan scheme.

The Act establishes limits on the liability of the person receiving funded services to pay costs to the unassisted party.

The Criminal Defence Service

The purpose of the CDS is to secure the provision of advice, assistance and representation, according to the interests of justice, to people suspected of a criminal offence or facing criminal proceedings.

The Commission is empowered to secure these services through contracts with lawyers in private practice, or by providing them through salaried defenders employed by non-profit making organisations. This will necessarily mean that suspects' and defendants' choice of representative is limited to contracted or salaried defenders, although the intention is to maintain an element of choice in all but exceptional cases.

The Access to Justice Act 1999 places a duty on the Commission to fund representation for individuals granted a right to representation. It enables the Commission to comply with this duty in the same ways as for advice and assistance. The courts will grant representation under the scheme to defendants according to 'the interests of justice', but will no longer have to conduct a means test before granting representation, although a financial eligibility test is applied for advice and assistance and assisted advocacy. Instead of means testing, the trial judge at the end of a case in the Crown Court has a duty to consider whether it is reasonable in all the circumstances, taking into account the means of the defendant, to make a Recovery of Defence Costs Order. The Order can be for any amount up to the full costs incurred.

Public Defender Service

The Commission is piloting its own Public Defender Service to provide services through lawyers in its own employment. The Public Defender offices offer a full range of services from police station to representation in court. It is believed that clients will be attracted and retained by recommendation arising from the quality of service provided.

Conditional Fees

The 1999 Act reforms the law relating to conditional fees to enable the court to order a losing party to pay, in addition to the other party's normal legal costs, the uplift on the successful party's lawyers' fees and, in any case where a litigant has insured against facing an order for the other side's costs, any premium paid by the successful party for that insurance. The intention is to ensure that the compensation awarded to a successful party is not eroded by any uplift or premium. The party in the wrong will bear the full burden of costs. It is also the intention to make conditional fees more attractive, in particular to defendants and to claimants seeking non-monetary redress.

INDEX